MULTIVARIATE
STATISTICAL METHODS IN
BEHAVIORAL RESEARCH

McGraw-Hill Series in Psychology
Consulting Editors: NORMAN GARMEZY and LYLE V. JONES

ADAMS: Human Memory
BERKOWITZ: Aggression: A Social Psychological Analysis
BERLYNE: Conflict, Arousal, and Curiosity
BLUM: Psychoanalytic Theories of Personality
BOCK: Multivariate Statistical Methods in Behavioral Research
BROWN: The Motivation of Behavior
BROWN AND GHISELLI: Scientific Method in Psychology
BUTCHER: MMPI: Research Developments and Clinical Applications
CAMPBELL, DUNNETTE, LAWLER, AND WEICK: Managerial Behavior, Performance, and Effectiveness
COFER: Verbal Learning and Verbal Behavior
CRAFTS, SCHNEIRLA, ROBINSON, AND GILBERT: Recent Experiments in Psychology
CRITES: Vocational Psychology
D'AMATO: Experimental Psychology: Methodology, Psychophysics, and Learning
DOLLARD AND MILLER: Personality and Psychotherapy
EDGINGTON: Statistical Inference: The Distribution-free Approach
ELLIS: Handbook of Mental Deficiency
FERGUSON: Statistical Analysis in Psychology and Education
FODOR, BEVER, AND GARRETT: The Psychology of Language: An Introduction to Psycholinguistics and Generative Grammar
FORGUS: Perception: The Basic Process in Cognitive Development
FRANKS: Behavior Therapy: Appraisal and Status
GHISELLI: Theory of Psychological Measurement
GHISELLI AND BROWN: Personnel and Industrial Psychology
GILMER: Industrial and Organizational Psychology
GRAY: Psychology Applied to Human Affairs
GUILFORD: Psychometric Methods
GUILFORD: The Nature of Human Intelligence
GUILFORD AND FRUCHTER: Fundamental Statistics in Psychology and Education
GUILFORD AND HOEPFNER: The Analysis of Intelligence
GUION: Personnel Testing
HAIRE: Psychology in Management
HETHERINGTON AND PARKE: Child Psychology: A Contemporary Viewpoint
HIRSCH: Behavior-Genetic Analysis
HIRSH: The Measurement of Hearing
HOROWITZ: Elements of Statistics for Psychology and Education
HULSE, DEESE, AND EGETH: The Psychology of Learning
HURLOCK: Adolescent Development
HURLOCK: Child Development

Hurlock: Developmental Psychology
Jackson and Messick: Problems in Human Assessment
Krech, Crutchfield, and Ballachey: Individual in Society
Lakin: Interpersonal Encounter: Theory and Practice in Sensitivity Training
Lawler: Pay and Organizational Effectiveness: A Psychological View
Lazarus, A.: Behavior Therapy and Beyond
Lazarus, R.: Adjustment and Personality
Lewin: A Dynamic Theory of Personality
Lewin: Principles of Topological Psychology
Maher: Principles of Psychopathology
Marascuilo: Statistical Methods for Behavioral Science Research
Marx and Hillix: Systems and Theories in Psychology
Miller: Language and Communication
Morgan: Physiological Psychology
Mulaik: The Foundations of Factor Analysis
Novick and Jackson: Statistical Methods for Educational and Psychological Research
Nunnally: Introduction to Statistics for Psychology and Education
Nunnally: Psychometric Theory
Overall and Klett: Applied Multivariate Analysis
Porter, Lawler, and Hackman: Behavior in Organizations
Restle: Learning: Animal Behavior and Human Cognition
Robinson and Robinson: The Mentally Retarded Child
Rosenthal: Genetic Theory and Abnormal Behavior
Ross: Psychological Disorders of Children: A Behavioral Approach to Theory, Research, and Therapy
Schwitzgebel and Kolb: Changing Human Behavior: Principles of Planned Intervention
Shaw: Group Dynamics: The Psychology of Small Group Behavior
Shaw and Costanzo: Theories of Social Psychology
Shaw and Wright: Scales for the Measurement of Attitudes
Sidowski: Experimental Methods and Instrumentation in Psychology
Siegel: Nonparametric Statistics for the Behavioral Sciences
Spencer and Kass: Perspectives in Child Psychology
Stagner: Psychology of Personality
Steers and Porter: Motivation and Work Behavior
Townsend: Introduction to Experimental Methods for Psychology and the Social Sciences
Vinacke: The Psychology of Thinking
Wallen: Clinical Psychology: The Study of Persons
Warren and Akert: Frontal Granular Cortex and Behavior
Winer: Statistical Principles in Experimental Design
Zubek and Solberg: Human Development

McGRAW-HILL
BOOK COMPANY
New York
St. Louis
San Francisco
Auckland
Düsseldorf
Johannesburg
Kuala Lumpur
London
Mexico
Montreal
New Delhi
Panama
Paris
São Paulo
Singapore
Sydney
Tokyo
Toronto

R. DARRELL BOCK
The University of Chicago

Multivariate Statistical Methods in Behavioral Research

This book was set in Times New Roman.
The editors were Richard R. Wright and Shelly Levine Langman;
the production supervisor was Dennis J. Conroy.
The drawings were done by Eric G. Hieber Associates Inc.
Kingsport Press, Inc., was printer and binder.

Library of Congress Cataloging in Publication Data

Bock, Richard Darrell, date
Multivariate statistical methods in behavioral research.

(McGraw-Hill series in psychology)
1. Psychometrics. 2. Multivariate analysis.
I. Title. [DNLM: 1. Statistics. QA278 B66m]
BF39.B673 519.5'3 74-8618
ISBN 0-07-006305-2

MULTIVARIATE
STATISTICAL METHODS IN
BEHAVIORAL RESEARCH

234567890KPKP798765

The role of modern statistical theory and practice vis-à-vis the other sciences has been sometimes likened to the role of pure mathematics and sometimes to that of inductive logic, within the general framework of the philosophy of science. The first comparison or analogy would be, in one sense, an enormous overstatement and, in another sense, an understatement. The second one is closer to the mark in the sense that modern statistical theory and practice have added important elements to classical inductive logic, or rather, brought out more clearly and developed very considerably certain elements that were already there in a very latent form in classical inductive logic.—S. N. Roy, from an unfinished manuscript.

In memory of
S. N. ROY

CONTENTS

PREFACE

This book has been prepared as a text for an advanced course in behavioral statistics. It assumes two previous statistics courses, the first covering such topics as probability, descriptive statistics, tests of significance, chi-square, simple correlation, and regression, and the second devoted to least-squares methods, including basic analysis of variance and multiple regression analysis. The treatment of least squares in the second course may be limited to instructing the student in computational procedures and showing him the relevance of least-squares methods to applications in his own field. The student will then have concrete examples in mind when he is exposed to a more theoretical point of view in the present text.

In addition to the statistical prerequisites, this text assumes some mathematical preparation, including at least an elementary knowledge of algebra, coordinate geometry, differential and integral calculus, and matrix algebra. In view of the continuing improvement in mathematical preparation in secondary and undergraduate education, these mathematical prerequisites do not seem unreasonable for students going into a third course in statistics. Those students who need to make up deficiencies may do so by study of the mathematical prerequisites reviewed in Chap. 2 or the texts suggested there.

The content of this book grew out of graduate courses taught at the University of North Carolina and the University of Chicago. Reflecting the needs of students in psychology, education, and human development, it is an attempt to tie together the design of a research study and the statistical analysis and reporting of results. It is not intended primarily as a compendium of results and methods in multivariate analysis. A number of books of that type are available, among which T. W. Anderson's "An Introduction to Multivariate Statistical Analysis" (Wiley, 1958), Donald F. Morrison's "Multivariate Analysis" (McGraw-Hill, 1967), and Maurice Tatsuoka's "Multivariate Analysis" (Wiley, 1971) can be highly recommended.

Multivariate statistical methods are emphasized throughout because they make it possible to encompass all the data from an investigation in one analysis. This approach results in a clearer, better organized account of the investigation than do the piecemeal analyses of portions of data which are often seen in behavioral studies. It also yields more realistic probability statements in hypothesis testing and interval estimation than do separate partial analyses. However, the comprehensive approach makes greater demands on the foresight and organizing ability of the investigator and requires for its success the use of formal statistical models to focus thinking and express hypotheses succinctly. If the investigator can formulate a suitable general model, many aspects of his study—its design, the unknowns to be determined from the data, the assessment of error—all fall into place. Usually the statistical model he employs will have to be multivariate simply because behavioral research typically involves problems in which several, sometimes many, response variables are observed simultaneously. Fortunately, a number of versatile models and allied statistical techniques for multivariate data, well fitted to this role, are now available. They are the culmination of work in multivariate statistics extending over the past 30 to 40 years. Many persons contributed to the development of this field, perhaps most prominantly Harold Hotelling, R. A. Fisher, S. S. Wilks, S. N. Roy, M. S. Bartlett, C. R. Rao, and T. W. Anderson. The present work owes a particular debt to S. N. Roy, who was largely responsible for the development of the methods of multivariate analysis of variance which are emphasized in the text.

Because laborious computations are required in multivariate analysis when the number of variables exceeds two or three, the statistical theory developed in the 1930s and 1940s found little application until electronic computers became available in the 1950s. In spite of the limitations of the early computers and the continual reprogramming required by the appearance of new types of machines, a wide range of multivariate statistical programs have become available in recent years. The trend has been toward the development of large general-purpose programs which give the user options for performing a variety of related statistical analyses on his data. Thus, all the examples in Chaps. 4 to 7 of the present text have been computed using the MULTIVARIANCE program based on Bock [1963] and prepared by Jeremy Finn [1972]. Those of Chap. 8 were computed using the MULTIQUAL program of Bock and Yates [1973].

The existence of these general-purpose multivariate programs considerably simplifies the task of writing a textbook on multivariate statistical methods. The text can concentrate on theory and interpretation and leave the details of practical computation to the machine. The "cookbook" treatment of methods for calculating various descriptive statistics and performing tests of significance can be omitted in favor of more complete discussions of examples and applications.

In the teaching of statistical methods, however, it seems to remain true that many, perhaps most, students need to work numerical problems to consolidate their understanding of theory. If the exercises are limited to special cases and only a few variables, students may be able to do the numerical work on desk calculators. But if more realistic problems are assigned, the computations quickly become too heavy for handwork. A good compromise in this case is to give the students access to a computer with time sharing or fast around time and provide them with a system of matrix-operations subroutines (for example, MATCAL, matrix-operations subroutines for statistical computation, edited by Bock and Repp [1974]). The student is then able to write and operate short programs embodying the logic of the analysis, while the subroutines take care of the arithmetic. Many of the exercises in this text assume accessibility to this type of facility.

This text has benefited immeasurably from interactions with students, both here and at the University of North Carolina. I am indebted to their dissertations and research for a number of the examples which appear in the text. I am also indebted to Dr. Samuel Hung for help in the preparation of Chaps. 2 and 3, to Donald Kolakowski and Graham Douglas for critical reading, and to Eveline Murphy for unfailing excellence in the preparation of the typescript. Michael Waller prepared the table in Appendix A.

R. DARRELL BOCK

MULTIVARIATE
STATISTICAL METHODS IN
BEHAVIORAL RESEARCH

1

THE ROLE OF MULTIVARIATE STATISTICAL METHODS IN BEHAVIORAL RESEARCH

1.1 THE PARADIGM OF STATISTICAL INFERENCE

In scientific work we constantly face the problem of inferring, from the data available to us, the nature of entities or processes that we cannot directly observe. The history of science confirms that such inferences can be successful, often spectacularly so, and that the inferred reality not only accounts fully for given data, but also anticipates correctly the results of subsequent research. In this text we shall be concerned with scientific inference carried out according to the so-called *hypothetico-deductive* paradigm. We consider this paradigm to comprise three steps: (1) hypothesizing a model for something *unobservable*; (2) deducing the *observable* consequences of the model; (3) undertaking an empirical investigation with the aim of showing that the consequences expected in the observations are actually apparent in data.

If the data conform to our expectations, we are encouraged to accept the model as a correct representation of the unobservable reality. Because more than one model may have the same implication for the data we have observed, however, our acceptance is always provisional and subject to modification as other data or ideas for models become available. If the data do *not* conform to expectation, on the other hand, we know that something is wrong—either the model is invalid, or our deduction of its observable consequences is incorrect, or the data are inadequate or defective. Rejection is seldom viewed as provisional; on the contrary, it usually stimulates immediate reconsideration of the problem and renewed research. The difference between success and failure in scientific inference often depends as much on skill in finding the cause of negative results as it does on ingenuity in formulating the model initially, or on the ability to manipulate the model mathematically, or on technical virtuosity in the design and execution of empirical research.

In many cases, some aspect of the hypothesized model is not fully specified in step 1 and must be determined from the data. This part of induction, which occurs in step 3, is referred to as "estimation." An interesting example of estimation figures prominently in the development of modern science. When Newton first formulated his law of gravitation, he was uncertain how the gravitational force varied with distance. His attempts to apply the law to the earth-moon system did not give a plausible result, and for a time he abandoned the problem. Later, however, it was found that the value then accepted for the distance to the moon was incorrect. When the correct figure became available, Newton found that an exponent of the distance equal very nearly to -2 accounted for the lunar orbit. He therefore rounded the exponent exactly to -2 and presented the result in the form we know. Newton's value for the exponent held until recent times, when it was modified slightly on nonempirical grounds by Einstein's theory of relativity (see Gamow [1962]).

It is an obvious but sometimes overlooked fact that estimation *weakens* a hypothetico-deductive inference. This occurs because an aspect of the model that is adjusted to fit the data cannot be tested for goodness of fit in the same data. For this reason, progress in science is usually most rapid in those fields where *strong inference* [Platt, 1964] is possible; that is, where models are almost completely specified and estimation is held to a minimum. Most of physical science, and much of biology, has reached this stage of development. Unfortunately, most of behavioral science has not.

Inaccessibility to strong inference is not the only impediment to progress in behavioral science. Another is the lack of deterministic relationships between models and observations. Almost universally in behavioral science (and to a large extent in biological science as well), the relationships which connect the model with the data are *statistical*. That is, they do not determine each specific datum, but only the probability distribution of the data as a whole. Observed data may be considered a sample from a population whose *probability distribution* is implied by the model (when the model is expanded to include a statistical part). In behavioral studies we face the problem of inferring something about this probability distribution before we can infer anything about the nonstatistical, i.e., deterministic, part of the model. Thus, we require a more elaborate paradigm of inference for behavioral studies than is typical of those areas of science where the relationships between the model and the data are essentially deterministic. We refer to this elaborated paradigm as *statistical inference.*

In statistical texts the essential problem of statistical inference is sometimes introduced in the guise of an "urn" scheme. The reader is asked to imagine an experiment in which balls are drawn, with replacement, from an urn containing red and white balls in some unknown proportion. The problem is to make an inference about the unknown proportion on the basis of the sample of balls drawn. The solution to this problem, as it is presented in statistical texts, contains all the elements of the hypothetico-deductive method. First, the model which describes the sampling process is hypothesized. It is assumed that the physical effect of shaking the balls in the urn, after returning the ball from the previous trial, is to give each ball an equal probability of being drawn on any trial. That is, the sampling may be described as a so-called *Bernoulli* process, characterized by repeated trials in which the probability of observing a specific event is fixed and independent from trial to trial. Second, the observable consequences of the hypothesis in terms of the number of red (or white) balls in the sample is deduced from the laws of probability. In particular, if P represents the proportion of red balls in the urn, their number in a sample of size N is distributed in binomial form with parameters P and N. Third, since the parameter P is unknown, the model is not fully specified, and P must be estimated by fitting the model to the data. Once the value is estimated, the goodness of fit of the model can be checked by comparing the distribution of the number of red balls in a number of samples with those expected for a binomial distribution with parameter set equal to the estimate of P.

It is important to understand that, because the number of red balls observed in the sample is a statistical (random) quantity, both the estimate and the outcome of the goodness-of-fit test can, strictly speaking, be described only in statistical terms. Thus, the estimate can be stated in the form of a confidence interval—i.e., a larger and a smaller value assigned to P, between which the true value will be found with some specified probability. The outcome of the goodness-of-fit test can be stated as a probability (significance level) that the distribution of observed numbers of red balls in a series of samples of size N could have been produced in a Bernoulli process with parameter P. In practical work one often conceals the statistical nature of an estimate by quoting a single "best" value (point estimate). We would discourage this practice unless it is quite clear that a conservative confidence interval is shorter than the smallest difference between estimates which might be interpreted.

In this text we shall examine some of the methodological problems involved in applying the statistical inferential paradigm to behavioral data. Although the many applications of the paradigm that appear in the examples are formally similar to the urn problem, the greater complexity of real research makes more difficult the tasks of model building, estimation, and test of fit. A realistic example of a behavioral experiment for which an urn problem provides the inferential model is the classical psychophysical determination of sensory-difference thresholds. Suppose, for example, we wish to estimate the least difference in pitch in the neighborhood of some specified frequency that can be detected by a given subject. A standard procedure [Bock and Jones, 1968, Chap. 2] consists of repeated presentation of pairs of tones, with the subject instructed to identify the member of each pair which is higher in pitch. If the difference in pitch of the paired tones is sufficiently small, and their order randomized, the subject will sometimes identify the higher tone correctly and sometimes not. The inferential problem is to estimate the proportion of such trials in which the subject can be expected to respond correctly.

The formal connection with the urn problem is obvious: each trial is identified with the drawing of a ball from the urn, the two possible outcomes, "correct" and "incorrect," are identified with the colors of the balls, and the large number of trials potentially obtainable from the subject is identified with the total number of balls in the urn. The quantity to be estimated is the proportion of correct responses in this potential population.

It is clear that statistical considerations are involved in this estimate. Although there are practical limitations to the number of responses obtainable from any one subject, the precise number is at our disposal. Depending on where we decide to terminate the trials, the observed number of correct responses will vary. Yet if the decision to terminate is made independent of the observations, one of these numbers is as valid as any other for computing the estimate. The observed number is clearly a statistical variable, and its relationship to the population proportion is statistical rather than deterministic. For purposes of inference, it is important to know the form of this statistical relationship. If the urn model holds, the form *is* known: the number of correct responses in N trials is a binomial variable whose distribution depends upon N and the unknown population proportion P.

Can we be sure in the practical research setting, however, that the urn model actually holds? It is entirely possible that the probability of a correct response is not constant within the subject, but is changing systematically or even randomly from one time to another. It is also possible that the successive responses of the subject are not independent because the subject's memory of his previous responses may influence his next response. If these are actual complications, we have the option of moving to a more complex model that allows for these effects or of attempting to introduce experimental controls that eliminate them. In fact, in this particular type of psychophysical experiment, if the identity of the stimulus is concealed and the trials are not too closely spaced or continued for too long a time, the assumptions of the urn model are reasonably well met. Thus, the urn problem provides, in this context, a realistic model which makes statistical inference possible.

This model may also be appropriate in practical applications. Suppose, for example, that an employer wishes to assess the spelling ability of a prospective secretary. He might perform the test by randomly sampling N words, say, from a published list of frequently misspelled words (e.g., Krevisky and Linfield [1967]). He would then dictate these words to the applicant and count the number of words spelled correctly.

In this application, the random sampling of words from the list guarantees the constancy of the expected proportion of correct responses and minimizes any possible contingencies between responses. Hence, the data generated by this process should conform well to the urn model. However, in the spelling test the words are sampled *without* replacement from a finite list. Strictly speaking, the statistical model for the number of correct responses is, in this case, the hypergeometric distribution rather than the binomial distribution that we assumed for the psychophysical experiment. If the number of words sampled from the list is small relative to the total number of words in the list, however, the effect of sampling without replacement is negligible, and the binomial distribution will serve for practical purposes.

In a large-scale employee selection program, the result of the spelling test, possibly in conjunction with other information, could be used in an entirely objective and mechanical way to determine whether or not the applicant is hired. If the selection procedure is designed in accordance with the principles of *statistical decision theory*, its operation can be optimized in terms of cost and benefit to the employer (see Chernoff and Moses [1959]).

In many cases, however, the decision to hire or not would be made by the employer or a personnel officer after a subjective appraisal of the spelling score and other information. If so, the province of statistical methodology ends with an estimate or confidence statement, just as it does in most scientific applications. This use of statistical methodology is sometimes called *informative inference*. Scientific inference is in a sense a form of communication from the unobservable reality in nature to the investigator. The purpose of informative inference is to maximize the information rate in this communication channel. Unlike decision theory, it does not encompass the problem of how that information is to be used. Although the present text is devoted primarily to informative inference, certain applications of statistical decision theory to problems of classification are discussed and illustrated in Chap. 6.

1.2 APPLICATIONS OF INFORMATIVE INFERENCE IN BEHAVIORAL RESEARCH

In the preceding examples, the data were generated by sufficiently simple processes so that suitable abstract models for the observations were easily formulated. In more complex settings, however, the choice of the model and the use of the model in inference are difficult to extricate from the concrete details, relevant and irrelevant, in terms of which the problem is initially presented. To see clearly the essential features of the problem, one needs at least some minimal structuring of the inquiry. The following four questions provide a useful rubric for the purpose: (1) What is the material? (2) What are the variables? (3) What is the model? (4) How is the inference to be interpreted? In this chapter we shall discuss these questions in a general way, and in subsequent chapters set up some of the technical machinery necessary to answer them in particular studies. Throughout, we phrase the discussion in the terminology of behavioral research and leave it to the reader to translate the language and examples to those of other fields if he so desires.

1.2.1 The Material

To emphasize the fact that a scientific investigation is necessarily delimited by the physical objects or entities under study, we shall refer to these objects as the *material*. In behavioral research, the material is usually one or more human or animal subjects, although in some cases to be discussed later, a collection of subjects, such as a family or community, serves as the primary object.

A circumstance which makes behavioral research especially difficult is that the material is not always well defined and is neither homogeneous in space nor stable over time. If in behavioral research we were interested in a population of responses within a given subject (as is the psychophysicist estimating the discrimination threshold of a given subject), the problem of identifying the material is relatively simple because the subject may be labeled unambiguously. But in most research the relevant population does not consist of intrasubject responses; it consists rather of subjects identified as members of defined classes. Except in clinical work, we are not usually trying to describe a particular subject, but are attempting to say how a member of a certain population of subjects may be expected to respond to specified conditions. The class with which the subject is identified depends on the application. In animal work we may find it sufficient to identify the species if the animals available can be regarded as representative of the species for purposes of the experiment. In human work we may have to identify the subject as a member of a racial, ethnic, age, sex, socioeconomic status, IQ group, etc.

At whatever level of classification the subject is identified, considerable individual variation among members of the class may be expected and may present difficulties for replication of experiments at different places or different times. Regrettably, these difficulties are often compounded by the tendency of the investigator to think of the members of classes as fixed types which other researchers can identify and study at will. But any defined biological population actually represents a dynamic equilibrium of traits undergoing continual redistribution through evolution, genetic drift, and in-and-out migration. In human populations the problem is especially severe because of the selective effects of in-and-out migration. A human group in any circumscribed location is often the biased result of economic and ecological selection. Thus, any group which lives or works in a particular locality cannot be assumed, without empirical verification, to represent groups in other localities, however similar their superficial characteristics. This truism is well known to workers in survey research, who have demonstrated repeatedly that there is no substitute for rigorous sampling procedures when dealing with human populations, but it is sometimes overlooked by other behavioral scientists.

It is perhaps necessary to emphasize here that the effects of individual differences apply not only to fixed traits but also to the forms of relationship between variables. The practice in physical science of assuming a single universal relationship between variables must not be carried uncritically into biological or behavioral research. In natural populations, no two organisms are the same, nor are the same processes or relationships necessarily involved in producing behavior that appears to be identical in two different individuals. Thus, population concepts, which for the most part have a minor role in physical science, are the very essence of our thinking in biological or behavioral work (see Dobzhansky [1967]).

Another aspect of the problem of identifying the material is that of choosing the unit of material appropriate for the analysis. In experimental studies, the unit is conveniently defined as the smallest division of the material that is independently assigned to the experimental conditions and responds independently. In animal work, the unit may be the individual organism—a litter, a cage of animals, or a larger aggregation according to the experimental design employed. If an aggregation of individuals is the unit, the response of the aggregation as a whole constitutes a single observation for purposes of data analysis. In most cases the mean response of the aggregate will constitute the observation. For example, if the litter is the unit in a study of weight gains, then the average weight gain of the animals in each litter may be used as the observational variable. This choice is based on the assumption that, while the weight gains of different litters will be independent, the weight gains of animals within litters will in general be correlated (intraclass correlation) because they are nursed by the same mother or otherwise share the same food. The same is true of educational experiments carried out on intact classrooms. It is clear that the teacher should be considered the unit assigned to the experimental treatment and that there are only as many experimental units as there are teachers. Certainly this is true if the teacher takes an active part in the instruction of children in her classroom, for the achievement of the children will then be correlated, and separate scores for different pupils on an achievement test will not constitute independent observations. Mean scores for different classrooms will be independent, however, and may serve as data in the analysis.

Similar considerations apply to the estimation of descriptive statistics: the units must enter the sample independently and respond independently. If households are the basic sampling unit, then responses of individuals within households cannot be considered independent observations. At a higher level, if communities are sampled from a state, then from the point of view of describing the variation between communities, the community is the unit, and an average response of the community is the observation. In more sophisticated statistical analysis, the sources of variation from various levels of complex experimental or descriptive studies can be estimated, and information in correlated responses can be used more efficiently, than the above discussion implies. Some aspects of this type of analysis are described in Chap. 6.

1.2.2 The Variables

Having identified the material and unit of the material for the investigation, we can begin to examine the variables that ultimately will appear in the statistical model. We may begin by identifying these variables in general terms and specifying their properties. Variables may be jointly classified as *observable* or *unobservable* and as *random* or *fixed.* Those statistical variables which represent the response of the material are observable and random, whereas the mathematical variables that are set by the investigator or represent given measurements or attributes of the material are observable and fixed. The model may also include mathematical variables that are unobservable but fixed and potentially *estimable.* These variables are usually called *parameters.* Finally, it will usually include components due to individual differences and measurement errors which are unobservable, random, and not estimable.

Observable variables are usually defined operationally as, for example, in the psychophysical experiment, by the steps carried out by the investigator in instructing the subject, generating the stimuli, and recording the responses. In the example above, the count of correct responses is clearly a random variable which takes on different values when different sets of responses are observed. The observable fixed variable is the pitch difference set by the experimenter, presumably, to any degree of accuracy allowed by the physical apparatus. The one *unobservable fixed* variable in this example is the population proportion of correct responses. It is the value of this variable which is being estimated. The *unobservable random* variable in this example is the error due to sampling responses. Although we have no interest in the value of this error in a given experiment and no possibility of estimating it, we are interested in knowing something about its statistical distribution because an estimate of the variance of the distribution is needed for calculating a standard error or confidence interval for the population proportion. Thus, it is important to set up an experiment for estimating the variance of the sampling error if it cannot be derived from the model for the sampling process. In the case of a binomial variable, variance is a function of the unknown population proportion, and its estimate is obtained in the course of estimating the latter.

Notice in the psychophysical experiment that if the subject were drawn from a population, his personal proportion of correct responses could be considered a value of a random variable that has a distribution in the population of subjects. In this case it would be appropriate to employ Bayes' concepts and state the probability with which the subject lies in a given interval of the population distribution. This is another instance in which the population concept enters into the formulation of a behavioral problem—one which takes on considerable importance in the measurement of individual differences [Lord and Novick, 1968].

Among the *observable* variables, further distinctions are useful: The response variable is referred to as the *dependent* variable. Because it is random, some assumption must be made about its statistical distribution. The choice of distribution function depends initially on whether the variable is *discrete* or *continuous*. Measurement is never truly continuous, of course, but if the units of scale are well defined and small relative to the range of the variable, the variable may be considered continuous for practical purposes. Then the statistical model for the variable will be represented by a continuous probability function. If the response variable merely records the occurrence or nonoccurrence of a qualitative attribute, the statistical model will be a discrete probability function. A third possibility is that the response variable orders the material. Ordered variables may appear to be intermediate between continuous and discrete variables, but in fact they are discrete variables that must be represented by special models which take into account the ordered nature of the data. An example of such a model is given in Sec. 8.1.6.

Sometimes the distinction between continuous and discrete random variables is deliberately blurred to make data analysis easier. The distribution for discrete data is approximated by intervals of continuous distribution when, for example, the normal distribution is used to approximate the binomial. Conversely, continuous data may be treated as discrete by grouping in broad categories as, for example, when scores are divided into high, middle, and low groups, and analyzed in the form of a contingency table. Practical work sometimes justifies such approximations, but insofar as possible we shall avoid them in this text.

Among *observable fixed* variables, we find an analogous distinction between the *quantitative* and the *qualitative*. If a fixed variable is a measurement—for example, the level of drug dosage or the age of the subject—we consider it a quantitative variable; if it is the presence or absence of some attribute, we consider it a qualitative variable. In complex experiments, the qualitative variables often represent the assignment of a subject to a subclass of a factorial classification of treatments. In this case the fixed variable may be assigned a value 1 or 0, depending on whether the subject does or does not fall in a particular class. These "all or none" variables, which appear in models for experimental and sampling designs, are sometimes referred to as *design variables*. When models contain both design variables and quantitative variables, the quantitative variables are sometimes referred to as *concomitant* or *ancillary* variables, or *covariables*. These various types of observable fixed variables are generally referred to as the *independent* variables.

A continuing source of confusion in behavioral research is the seemingly endless number of dependent variables that can be invented to characterize some aspect of behavior. The literature is full of examples in which an investigator introduces a behavioral concept and then proceeds to construct a device which he alleges to measure it. He might, for example, believe that human subjects may be characterized by their "need for an aggressive outlet." He may propose to measure this need and attempt to account for individual differences in the measure in terms of other variables in the subject's development. He might, for example, devise a questionnaire in which the subject's agreement or disagreement with certain propositions is supposed to reflect this "need for aggressive outlet." He may, in fact, be successful in finding relationships between the subject's response to this questionnaire and the subject's educational history or familial experience. The difficulty arises when the investigator has to prove that these relationships actually depend upon the "need for aggressive outlet" and not some other content or bias which may also be included in the questionnaire. This difficult and often intractable problem has received much attention in certain areas of psychology, especially psychometrics, where the techniques of factor analysis and analysis of covariance structures have been developed as an aid to resolving variables into more fundamental components (see Bock, Dicken, and Van Pelt [1969]).

1.2.3 The Model

We use the term *model* here in nearly the same sense in which one refers to a scaled-down version of a machine as a "model." The reason for making a mechanical model is to anticipate how the full-scale machine will perform, on the assumption that the working model will simulate the action of the full-sized machine, except for the scale of forces involved. Similarly, the statistical model is supposed to predict the variable response of a system to specified input conditions. The difference between the mechanical and statistical models is that the input and output of the former are physical forces, whereas those of the latter are the numerical values of certain variables and the model itself is merely a mathematical equation relating these variables.

We have stated that, in statistical models, the observation always consists of one or more random variables. The model may also include other random variables, called *components*, which are unobservable. Thus, we refer to a measurement or sampling error as an *error component*. Together with the fixed variables, known constants, and unknown parameters, the components and the response comprise the quantities which are related by the model.

To display the generic form of a class of statistical models that is prominent in this text, we shall let y refer to an observable random variable, x to one or more fixed variables, and ϵ to one or more unobservable random components. Many of the models we shall consider take the form

$$y = f(x) + g(\epsilon) \qquad (1.2\text{-}1)$$

That is, the observation is assumed to be the sum of some function f of the fixed variables and some function g of the random components. Both f and g may involve known or unknown parameters.* Frequently we shall refer to $f(x)$ as the *fixed part* of the model, and $g(\epsilon)$ as the *random part*. The following are some of the specializations of (1.2-1) which appear in the text.

Regression models In Example 4.1-1 the relationship between the size of the Pogendorff illusion y and age of subject x is represented as a second-degree polynomial in x, plus a sampling error ϵ:

$$y = \beta_0 + \beta_1 x + \beta_2 x^2 + \epsilon \tag{1.2-2}$$

In this case $f(x) = \beta_0 + \beta_1 x + \beta_2 x^2$ and $g(\epsilon) = \epsilon$. The β in the fixed part are parameters to be determined. Note that although age has a distribution with respect to the population of subjects, x is a fixed variable in this application because arbitrary numbers of subjects are selected at specified ages. Models of this type, called *regression* models, are considered in Chap. 4.

Another example of a regression model is that of Chap. 6 in which y and x are random variables with a bivariate normal probability distribution. In this application, the equation for y given x is assumed to be of the form

$$y = \beta_0 + \beta_1 x + \epsilon$$

Here x is treated as fixed because it is given prior to the observation. This model could also be called a "prediction" model, since it may be used to predict y from an x already known. For example, y might represent college grade-point average in the freshman year, and x the high-school grade-point average in the senior year. The model predicts the expected value of y corresponding to a given value of x, and hence provides information bearing on the decision whether or not to admit to college a student whose high-school grade-point average is known to be x.

Experimental-design models As mentioned previously, fixed variables are sometimes assigned the value 1 or 0 to represent the presence or absence of a qualitative condition or attribute. Statistical models with this type of fixed variables are usually called *experimental-design* models. A simple example is the model for a 2×2 factorial design given by

$$\begin{aligned}
y_{11} &= \mu + \alpha_1 + \beta_1 + \epsilon_{11} \\
y_{12} &= \mu + \alpha_1 + \beta_2 + \epsilon_{12} \\
y_{21} &= \mu + \alpha_2 + \beta_1 + \epsilon_{21} \\
y_{22} &= \mu + \alpha_2 + \beta_2 + \epsilon_{22}
\end{aligned}$$

* Observable random variables are represented in the text by italic sans serif English letters; unobservable random variables are represented by comparable Greek letters.

The 1s and 0s are the implied coefficients of the μ, α, and β. Thus, the first equation might have been written

$$y_{11} = 1\mu + 1\alpha_1 + 0\alpha_2 + 1\beta_1 + 0\beta_2 + \epsilon_{11}$$

In words, this equation states that the response of an experimental unit to treatment combination 1, 1 is the sum of an effect μ general to all treatment combinations, plus an effect α_1 due to the treatment 1 of the first experimental factor, plus an effect β_1 due to treatment 1 of the second factor, plus a random component ϵ_{11}. As we shall see in Chap. 5, the statistical analysis for experimental-design models is very similar to that for regression models.

Experimental-design models with a concomitant variable Sometimes information about each experimental unit is available in the form of one or more quantitative fixed variables. If these variables help account for the response in a designed experiment, it may be desirable to include them in the model. When two such variables, $x^{(1)}$ and $x^{(2)}$, are included in a model for a 2 × 2 classification of units, we have

$$\begin{aligned}
y_{11} &= \mu + \alpha_1 + \beta_1 + \gamma_1 x_{11}^{(1)} + \gamma_2 x_{11}^{(2)} + \epsilon_{11}^* \\
y_{12} &= \mu + \alpha_1 + \beta_2 + \gamma_1 x_{12}^{(1)} + \gamma_2 x_{12}^{(2)} + \epsilon_{12}^* \\
y_{21} &= \mu + \alpha_2 + \beta_1 + \gamma_1 x_{21}^{(1)} + \gamma_2 x_{21}^{(2)} + \epsilon_{21}^* \\
y_{22} &= \mu + \alpha_2 + \beta_2 + \gamma_1 x_{22}^{(1)} + \gamma_2 x_{22}^{(2)} + \epsilon_{22}^*
\end{aligned}$$

Fixed variables used in this way are called *ancillary* or *concomitant* variables, or sometimes *covariates*. Note that the two qualitatively distinct concomitant variables are designated by superscripts (placed in parenthesis in order to avoid confusion with exponents). Later, when we introduce vector notation for multiple variables, the need for this cumbersome notation will be obviated. The terms involving μ, α, and β will be called the *design* part of the model, those involving $\gamma_1 x^{(1)}$ and $\gamma_2 x^{(2)}$ the *regression* part. The parameters of the design part are called *effects*, whereas those of the regression part (that is, γ_1 and γ_2) are called *regression coefficients* (or sometimes *partial regression coefficients* when two or more are involved). The asterisk attached to the random component is not essential, but merely serves to distinguish error components in the full model from those in a model that includes only the design part. The statistical treatment of experimental designs that include concomitant variables, called *analysis of covariance*, is discussed in Sec. 5.5.

Mixed models An important class of design models incorporating more than one random component consists of the so-called *mixed* models. It includes the randomized block and split-plot designs of Sec. 5.4 and the repeated-measures designs of Chap. 7.

An instance of the latter appears in Sec. 7.2.1, where the analysis is based on the following model for the repeated measurements obtained from subject i:

$$y_{i11} = \mu + a_i + \beta_1 + \gamma_1 + (\beta\gamma)_{11} + \epsilon_{i11}$$

$$y_{i12} = \mu + a_i + \beta_1 + \gamma_2 + (\beta\gamma)_{12} + \epsilon_{i12}$$

$$y_{i21} = \mu + a_i + \beta_2 + \gamma_1 + (\beta\gamma)_{21} + \epsilon_{i21}$$

$$y_{i22} = \mu + a_i + \beta_2 + \gamma_2 + (\beta\gamma)_{22} + \epsilon_{i22}$$

This model includes fixed effects (which do not carry the subscript i) and the value of a random component a which has a sampling distribution with respect to the population subjects. The component a_i is the effect for subject i, and β, γ, and $(\beta\gamma)$ are fixed effects due, respectively, to classes in the treatment design, the time points on the repeated-measures dimension, and interaction of treatments and time points.

Note that, while it may be of interest to estimate the fixed effects or some functions of them, there is no purpose in estimating the random components as such.* It is, however, of interest to estimate parameters which characterize the probability distributions of the random components. In the context of the mixed model, estimation of the variances of these distributions, called *variance components*, is as important as the estimation of the fixed effects themselves. Statistical methods for this purpose are discussed in Sec. 6.4.3.

Models for qualitative data Chapter 8 is devoted to statistical models that are nonlinear and purely random; i.e., the model is not a sum of fixed and random parts as in (1.2-1) but is a so-called *stochastic* model directly describing data in the form of counts or frequencies. Sensory judgments, consumer preferences, classification of subject attributes, questionnaire responses, naturalistic observations, test-item responses, and scores for projective test protocols are examples of such data arising in behavioral studies. Methods discussed in Chap. 8, having the same structure as the methods for continuous variables in earlier chapters, extend the analysis of these types of qualitative data considerably beyond what is possible with the familiar chi-square procedures.

1.2.4 The Interpretation

After the investigator has made a statistical inference in the form of an estimate or test of goodness of fit, he still faces the problem of interpreting the result in the light of the original objectives of his study. Strictly speaking, this problem is outside the

* An exception to this statement is psychological measurement where individual differences are estimated. Because they are estimated for individuals whose identity is retained, they represent fixed quantities.

domain of statistics, but it bears so directly on the success of research that we cannot ignore it in a general discussion of behavioral-research methodology. Many issues of interpretation obviously depend upon the substantive content of particular studies and are too specific to be considered in this text (except incidentally in the examples). Nevertheless, there are certain broad classes of behavioral investigation which have sufficient communality of objectives to allow some general discussion of interpretation. We identify these classes as *experiments*, *comparative studies*, and *surveys*. Other applications such as prediction and classification (see Secs. 6.1 and 6.2) are part of decision theory rather than of inference and are not considered to involve interpretational problems.

Experiments The investigator's objective in a behavioral experiment is to demonstrate that, by manipulating the conditions to which subjects respond, he can alter their behavior in a predictable manner (see Chap. 5). If several types of conditions (stimuli) are involved, and the investigator has the capability of manipulating each independently, he can determine which conditions are or are not necessary for the response to occur. In this way, he can use the experiment to justify a causal interpretation of the relationship between the conditions and the response. This type of interpretation is not supported by nonexperimental studies.

An indispensable requisite of a behavioral experiment is the freedom of the investigator to assign the subjects at will to the experimental conditions. If he has this freedom, he can deal rigorously with the problem of individual differences in the response tendencies of the subjects. This is the same problem that was referred to in Sec. 1.2.1 as lack of homogeneity of the experimental material. It is especially serious in behavioral studies because systematic differences of effects between conditions may be small relative to the magnitude of individual differences within conditions. For this reason it is necessary to establish criteria for the unambiguous detection of the systematic effects against a background of individual-difference variation. A similar situation in agronomical research in the 1920s led to the development of the randomized experiment and significance test by R. A. Fisher [1967]. In the simplest form of randomized experiment, each unit of experimental material is assigned at random to one of the experimental conditions; i.e., the material is randomly partitioned among the experimental groups. The experiment is then conducted in such a way that each subject is constrained to respond independently in his assigned condition, and his response measured and recorded independently.

For purposes of the significance test, it is assumed that a statistic that is sensitive to the effects in question may be computed from the recorded data. Often, the conditions are considered to affect only the level of response, in which case the most defensible choice for this statistic is the mean of the responses under a given condition. Whatever the choice of statistic, it is clear that some differences in its value from one condition to another must be expected merely because of the initial differences in the material. The purpose of the significance test is to provide an objective basis for the investigator's claim that the differences are due to the conditions and not merely to the random effects of such differences. One type of significance test is the so-called *randomization test*, which is carried out by partitioning the observed measurements in all possible ways between experimental groups, subject to the condition that each group shall have the same number of observations as it had in the experiment. Corresponding to each partition, the chosen statistic is calculated. The values of the statistic obtained in this way are then arranged in order of size, and the percentile rank of each value is calculated. Among these values is, of course, the value of the statistic from the actual experiment. If its percentile rank is extreme, tending toward 0 or 100 percent, it is easier to believe that the statistic is reflecting the systematic effects of the conditions than that it is a fortuitous result of the random assignment of the subjects. Although the precise percentile point at which disbelief in the chance nature of the event begins to arise is perhaps a matter of personal opinion, the convention has grown in the scientific community that the 2.5 and 97.5 percent points, leading to an overall 5 percent error rate, should be accepted for this purpose. A statistic which yields a percentile outside these limits is called "significant," and the systematic effect of the conditions is considered to have been demonstrated.

Although randomization tests provide a logical basis for nonparametric significance testing (i.e., tests which do not require a specific statistical model to be assumed), they are not widely used because they are time consuming computationally and do not give a complete description of the data. Parametric tests, such as those introduced by Student and Fisher, are less laborious computationally and articulate better with other statistical methods, especially the method of least squares. In most applications, these tests approximate so closely the result of a randomization test that there is little basis on which to choose between the two approaches from the point of view of accuracy [Fisher, 1966, pages 43–47]. Since the present text is oriented toward model fitting and estimation and introduces statistical tests as adjuncts to these procedures, it is confined entirely to parametric tests. It emphasizes the extension of the familiar fisherian statistical methods to the kinds of multivariate and qualitative data typically encountered in behavioral research.

While considering significance tests, we must take note of the argument of those writers (e.g., Bakan [1966]) who maintain that statistical tests of point hypotheses are irrelevant to behavioral research. From their point of view, precise equality of the effects, say, ξ_1 and ξ_2, of two treatments does not occur in nature; hence, rejection of the typical point hypothesis H_0: $\xi_1 - \xi_2 = 0$ is certain if the sample size is large enough. This argument implies that there are no response thresholds for psychological stimuli, i.e., that no stimulus difference is so feeble as to have absolutely no effect on behavior. Although many psychologists probably would not accept this position in general, it is undoubtedly true that in most behavioral experimentation the treatment effects and differences between effects are above threshold levels.

What then is the purpose of the significance test? In most instances, the significance test is actually used to justify the interpreting of the *direction of difference* between effects. In these studies, the fact that the response to treatment 1 exceeds that of treatment 2 has theoretical implications independent of the magnitude of the effects. What is needed in these cases is an inferential rule directing the investigator to one of three actions: (1) interpret a positive difference, (2) refrain from interpreting the difference, or (3) interpret a negative difference.

As Hodges and Lehmann [1954], Kaiser [1960], and Peizer [1967] have pointed out, simultaneous one-sided tests of the two interval hypotheses

$$H_1: \xi_1 - \xi_2 \leq 0$$

and

$$H_2: \xi_1 - \xi_2 > 0$$

are equivalent to such a three-decision procedure. If the investigator computes a statistic appropriate for testing these hypotheses and cannot reject either H_1 or H_2 at the $\alpha/2$ probability level, then he is not entitled to make a claim about the direction of effect, since the probability that his statistic could have arisen from an effect in the opposite direction is greater than α. On the other hand, if he rejects H_1 at the $\alpha/2$ level, he may interpret an effect difference in favor of treatment 2; or, if he rejects H_2 at this level, he may interpret the difference in favor of treatment 1. The maximum probability that he will erroneously interpret a difference in either direction is α.

The procedure which results from this line of reasoning is, of course, precisely equivalent to the conventional two-tailed test of the point hypothesis $H_0: \xi_1 - \xi_2 = 0$, followed by interpretation of the sign of the statistic [Peizer, 1967]. Thus, the traditional admonition that a difference should not be interpreted unless the null hypothesis is rejected may be justified without appeal to point hypotheses. Similarly, when several contrasts are incorporated in a composite hypothesis, as in the F test for differences among several groups or in multivariate tests, rejection of the point hypothesis is necessary to justify the claim that the direction of *at least one* of the multiple contrasts has been established.

The same reasoning lies behind the use of confidence intervals to establish direction. If the constructed interval does not include zero, the direction is considered to be demonstrated. In this use, significance tests and confidence intervals are merely alternative ways of representing the information about direction in the data. Confidence intervals give additional information about the possible magnitude of the effect, but they are somewhat less convenient to display in written reports than the results of significance tests, especially where composite hypotheses are involved, and are less frequently to be found in the literature.

It must be emphasized that demonstrating the direction of an effect to the satisfaction of the scientific community is not the same as making the best bet about the direction on the basis of the data. If the investigator is forced to take some action regarding direction on the basis of the data, the odds that he is acting correctly will generally be better if the direction of the observed difference is used whether it is significant or not. This has some relevance to research since, in the pilot stages of a study, it may be necessary to make such decisions. For this purpose the logic of decision theory rather than of demonstrating statistical significance is relevant. When the work reaches the stage of reporting, however, there is ordinarily little hope of convincing the scientific community that an effect has been demonstrated unless the odds that the data could have resulted by other causes, such as the effects of the randomization procedure, are small, e.g., 1/20 or less.

Comparative studies The purpose of a comparative study is to describe differences among populations which exist naturally and are not created artificially as in an experiment (see Sec. 6.3). The comparative study is a widely used form of investigation in fields where experimentation is difficult or impossible, such as anthropology, much of social psychology, political science, and developmental psychology. The objective of the comparative study is to obtain, through a description of group differences, some clue to the processes responsible for these differences and to the avenues along which more intensive study might be rewarding. Although the comparative study is sometimes disparaged by experimentally oriented workers, it has been impressively successful in certain areas of research. Especially striking examples may be found in the field of epidemiology. Edward Jenner's discovery of vaccination stemmed from the comparative observation that the incidence of smallpox was lower among milkmaids than in the population generally. From this simple comparison of disease incidence he went on to make the connection that milkmaids were likely to have had cowpox, and that cowpox confers immunity to smallpox, and that people might be protected from smallpox by vaccination with the cowpox virus. The pragmatic success of vaccination convinced everyone of the causal connection long before the mechanism of immunity was understood. To take an example closer to behavioral science, most psychologists would admit that the remarkable constancy of the rate of incidence of schizophrenia in different countries and different socioeconomic classes, as revealed by comparative studies, has an important bearing on our understanding of the disorder; certainly it discourages the theory exclusively based on response to environmental stress which must differ from one population to another; it suggests rather the working of a biogenic mechanism which is more or less in a steady state in these populations. Recent studies in behavior genetics [Heston, 1970; Cavalli-Sforza and Bodmer, 1971, Sec. 9.14] support this view.

The great limitation of the comparative study is that, while demonstrating that certain responses of the subjects are associated with certain characteristics of the populations, it does not establish that the subjects' responses can be changed by changing these characteristics. The comparative study may suggest this possibility, but it takes an experimental study to prove the causal relationship. Unfortunately, when practical action is imperative but causal mechanisms are unknown, it is all too easy to ascribe a cause-and-effect interpretation to mere association. Before the era of public housing, for example, it was widely argued that the crowded, ugly, and insecure living conditions of slum dwellers was the cause of the social disorganization typical of slum neighborhoods. Experience with large-scale public housing in urban centers since that time, however, has shown that mere physical improvement of housing does not have the expected salutary effect on social organization. The sources of the social problems which afflict these areas have had to be sought elsewhere (see Mumford [1968]).

The steps in a comparative study are as follows: First, we identify the populations we wish to compare. Sometimes these populations are actually subclasses that result from a cross-classification of subjects from a larger population according to known characteristics. Since we are interested only in the differences between the responses of subjects in different subclasses, however, we consider each subclass a separate population for purposes of sampling. Next, we select within subclasses a probability sample of subjects; i.e., we select subjects by a method, such as simple random sampling, that gives each member of a subclass an equal chance of entering the sample. Note that, because each subclass constitutes a separate population, only within these subclasses must we maintain random sampling. This may be advantageous since it is usually easier to sample randomly within a narrow class, where all subjects in the population are readily available. Since the number of subjects to be selected for each subclass is completely at our disposal, we may choose it so as to obtain the best precision in making the comparisons in question. In most cases our attention will be focused on the means of these subclasses, and as we shall see in Sec. 6.3, the fitting of a statistical model to account for differences between means will provide an orderly approach to describing differences between the populations.

When the populations are defined in this way, it is not unusual to find that the effects of one of the ways of classification are not constant over classes in another way of classification. We then say that there exists an *interaction* of effects of the ways of classification. Interactions complicate the interpretation of comparative studies because they force the investigator to describe differences between particular subclasses rather than the more comprehensive difference associated with the main classes of each way of classification. The interpretation of interactions has been a source of much confusion because it depends upon whether or not the classes in one or more of the ways of classification are themselves considered to be sampled from some population of classes. If they are so considered, the classes are said to belong to a random way of classification. The interactions involving these classes are then considered to be random variables. This means that the interactive effects have a distribution which the investigator may wish to describe by estimating, say, its mean and variance (see Sec. 6.4). In studies where some ways of classification are random and others are fixed (i.e., not random), an analysis which provides these estimates may be based on the mixed model described in Sec. 7.2.1.

Certain applications of mixed models are common in behavioral research and are discussed in Chap. 7. Studies in which all ways of classification are random are also seen frequently, especially in surveys. Comparative studies and surveys are similar in some respects, but their interpretation can be quite different. Some of these differences are brought out in the next section and in Sec. 6.4.

Surveys The purpose of a survey is to describe the responses of subjects in a single population and, if necessary, to identify sources of variation in the data that are associated with specified classes or subclasses of the population. To carry out a survey, we select a probability sample from the general population, then classify subjects according to the characteristics with which we wish to associate response variability within the population. In a survey, the number of subjects in each subclass of the classification is a random variable and reflects the population proportion for the subclass. Because the subclass numbers in survey data are not arbitrary as they are in a comparative study, it is meaningful to collapse survey data over various ways of classification in order to describe differences between certain main classes while ignoring other ways of classification. However collapsed, the data continue to represent a population, and the distribution of responses in that population has a definite and meaningful interpretation. This is not true of a comparative study, where the number of subjects in the subclasses are arbitrary, because a collapsed way of classification does not represent any real population.

The same reasoning applies to any descriptive statistics which might be calculated for the data as a whole. In survey data, for example, it is permissible to ignore all subclassifications and compute correlations between response variables, or to estimate the multiple correlation between the response variable and various independent variables. In comparative data, it makes no sense to compute these overall statistics, because the choice of populations and the number of subjects sampled within each population are arbitrary. In survey studies, the interest is often found in comparing the expected responses to different variables rather than comparing actual differences among groups. For example, in a study of consumer buying plans, one may be interested in the overall difference in buying plans with respect to durable goods as opposed to consumable goods or services, or the difference between plans for this year and plans for next year. The problem then is to get the best estimate of these differences for the sample as a whole.

If the data are obtained in a stratified sample, for example, by state, county, locality, and household, it may be of interest to estimate the *variance component* that is associated with each of these random ways of classification in order to understand better the sources of variability in the data or how the error of estimation might be reduced by changing the sampling plan (see Sec. 6.4). Of course, survey data can be, and often are, freely used in comparative studies if subpopulations are identified and it is of interest to compare their average response. The converse is true only with qualifications. Data from the comparative study can only be used as survey data if all subgroups of the population are represented, and it is known what proportion of the total population they represent. If this is the case, the means for subpopulations from the comparative study can be weighted by these proportions in order to obtain an estimate of the general population means. The same can be done for other statistics such as correlations.

Because the array of data produced in an experiment, comparative study, or survey may be very similar in appearance, and because the formal statistical procedures applied to such data may be closely related, it is easy to interpret data analyses incorrectly if distinctions between these classes of investigation are overlooked. The methodologies of experiments, comparative studies, and surveys support distinctly different types of inference, and there is no way to substitute one for another. An experiment does not describe a real population, nor does a comparative study or survey reveal the effects that follow an experimental intervention. Of course, as we understand better the actual processes giving rise to observed data, we may see that a single explanation of some phenomenon investigated by each of these methods is possible. But a synthesis at this level goes far beyond the inference supported by any single empirical study.

1.3 SPECIAL PROBLEMS OF MULTIVARIATE RESEARCH

Behavioral research is rarely confined to a single dependent variable. Whether applied to human or animal subjects, it typically employs more than one measure or index to describe the behavior in question and, hence, is in the purview of multivariate statistical methods. The multivariate character of behavioral data has an especially strong bearing on significance testing and interval estimation. It is, for example, quite unsatisfactory in general to compute significance levels separately for each response variable in a multivariate study. To illustrate the difficulties presented by this practice, let us suppose that a psychologist is investigating the differences between the performance of two groups of children on five types of perceptual tasks. Using the ordinary univariate t test, he may calculate the probability of each observed difference on the null hypothesis and find two of those probabilities are slightly less than .05. Does this mean that an event has occurred that is of sufficiently low probability that it must be considered exceptional if the two populations are in fact identical with respect to performance of these tasks? Because the performance measures are undoubtedly correlated in some arbitrary manner (that is, nonindependent), this question cannot be answered in general without resorting to a multivariate test which applies to the five measures jointly. It is quite possible that two p values smaller than .05 could be found among five test statistics when in fact they could be attributed to sampling variability. Conversely, it is possible that each of the probability levels for the separate measures falls short of the .05 level, and yet, because of certain interdependencies in the measures, the multivariate test shows that the observed mean differences are extremely improbable under the null hypothesis. Clearly, what is needed in these cases is a method of calculating a single probability level for all measures taken jointly, and this is precisely what the multivariate test provides.

Similar considerations apply to the construction of interval estimates and confidence bounds in the multiparameter case. The univariate bounds computed for each parameter separately do not give an accurate picture of the range of values included in the confidence region for the several parameters taken jointly. It is possible for the region to be much narrower in some direction of the multivariate space than the confidence interval of any of the separate parameters indicates. A good example of this is presented in Sec. 4.1.12b. (See Bock and Haggard [1968] for a multivariate example.)

Similar deficiencies of a strictly univariate approach to multivariate data appear in descriptive as well as inferential statistics. Because univariate methods ignore the structural relationships among the dependent variables, they do not allow the possibility of describing the data in terms of explanatory variables inferred from these relationships. In behavioral data especially, we often find that several of the observed variables reflect a single underlying variable that cannot be observed directly. In this case, considerable simplification of the data may result if we can find linear combinations of the observed variables that are highly correlated with a few underlying variables. A few such synthetic variables may be able to account for most of the variation in a large number of original variables. This fact is exploited in multiple discriminant analysis and canonical correlation analysis (see Secs. 6.1.6, 6.2.2, and 6.3.1).

Another possibility is that some of the observed variables are derivatives of others. In this case we may simplify the data by seeking a subset of the variables that accounts for all significant effects in the data. For practical purposes the remaining variables may then be discarded. This is the approach taken, in so-called *stepwise* regression analyses, in order to eliminate independent variables. A similar procedure, called *step-down* analysis, aims at eliminating some of the dependent variables from discriminant functions or canonical variates. Both these procedures are more satisfactory when there is an *a priori* ordering of variables that enables the investigator to ask whether some variables can be discarded, given that certain others have been accepted. Usually the investigator has prior expectations about the relative importance of his variables, and he can readily specify an ordering (see Secs. 6.2 and 6.3).

The present text emphasizes the use of multivariate statistical procedures to simplify models and to achieve greater parsimony of description. These procedures can do much to counter the tendency for variables to proliferate in behavioral research as different workers propose new aspects of behavior to be measured or introduce new methods of measurement for old aspects. The burden of proof that a new variable or method of measurement is distinct from, or an improvement on, previous variables or measures should be placed on the investigator who introduces it. Methods for assessing the partial contribution of additional variables to the information provided by given variables are discussed at many points in this text (e.g., Secs. 4.1.9, 4.2.5, and 6.3).

Having advanced the positive aspects of multivariate statistical procedures, we are obligated to include some cautionary remarks. The reader should be forewarned that these procedures are based on very simple models that are designed to be as broadly applicable as possible. This breadth of application is obtained at the expense of minimizing the substantive implication which the models might carry. The models are, in a sense, all-purpose frameworks upon which the investigator can build structures adapted to his own needs. They are well suited to the exploratory phase of research where the investigator is merely trying to detect the presence of certain effects and to determine their direction. Usually in this phase there is such a large component of uncontrolled variation in the data that a more detailed description is not possible, because the fine structure of the relationship is obscured in the background of error.

To progress beyond this point, the investigator must formulate stronger models based on some conception of the actual processes underlying the data. Generally speaking, the stronger models will tend to be specific to particular fields of application and cannot be discussed adequately in a purely methodological text. Nevertheless, the principles of model fitting and estimation presented in this text can be adapted to special models as the need arises. The use of more sophisticated models will, of course, require of the investigator better developed skills in data analysis than is demanded by the simpler all-purpose models. The objective of the present text is to discuss the principles of data analysis on a level that will make it possible for students and researchers to attain these skills and to proceed confidently with more incisive and original model building and data analysis.

2

MATHEMATICAL PREREQUISITES FOR MULTIVARIATE ANALYSIS

A behavioral investigation yields multivariate data whenever the subject's response is represented by more than one score. For present purposes, we are assuming that the several scores for each subject are in the form of measurements which may be qualitatively distinct and have different origins and units of scale. Each such measurement represents a value of a *response variable*, and the set of measurements for each subject constitutes a multivariate observation. Typical multivariate observations are produced by psychological tests that are scored in a number of scales, such as the Minnesota Multiphasic Personality Inventory (MMPI) or the Wechsler Adult Intelligence Scale (WAIS).

2.1 THE PROBLEM OF NOTATION

In this text, we shall denote a multivariate observation by an ordered set of real numbers, e.g.,

$$(y_{ij}^{(1)}, y_{ij}^{(2)}, \ldots, y_{ij}^{(p)}) \qquad (2.1\text{-}1)$$

Each element in (2.1-1) represents the score of one subject on one of p *response variables*. The variables are identified by *superscripts* (in parenthesis). The multiple *subscript* typically identifies the ith subject and the jth experimental condition or population from which the subject was drawn. Following statistical usage, we shall refer to the response variables in (2.1-1) separately as *variates* and collectively as a *p-variate* observation.

It should be apparent even at this point that a notation for multivariate observations that requires an explicit symbol for each variate will be exceedingly tedious if the number of variates is large. We clearly need a more compact notation, preferably one which represents the p-variate observation, or indeed a number of such observations, by a single letter. Fortunately, we have this notation close at hand in the algebras of vectors and matrices. Not only is the notation more concise, but many of the mathematical results of these algebras facilitate the derivation and exposition of the multivariate statistical methods. Matrix algebra has the added advantage of serving as a powerful interpretative language for the computer programming of statistical calculations [Bock and Repp, 1974]. We would therefore prefer to assume in the sequel that the student is already acquainted with vector and matrix algebra. In the event he is not, the following brief review, supplemented by such a text as Aitken [1937], Stoll [1952], Browne [1958], Ayres [1962], Searle [1966], or Noble [1969], should make the remainder of the text intelligible.

2.2 ELEMENTS OF VECTOR ALGEBRA

From a geometric point of view, the multivariate observation may be regarded as a point whose coordinates in n-dimensional space are, say $(x_1, x_2, \ldots, x_n)$. This point may also be viewed as the terminus of a line segment from the origin $(0, 0, \ldots, 0)$ to the point $(x_1, x_2, \ldots, x_n)$. Such a directed line segment is called the *position vector* of the point and may be denoted simply by $\mathbf{x}$. The position vector is an instance of a vector quantity for which an algebra, based on the following postulates, may be elaborated.*

2.2.1 Postulates of Vector Algebra

1 For any vector $\mathbf{x}$ and scalar number c, *scalar multiplication* resulting in another vector $\mathbf{y}$ is defined:

$$\mathbf{y} = c\mathbf{x}$$

The scalar c may be an element of any number field (see Birkoff and MacLane [1965]), but for our purposes it will be understood to be a real number.

2 *Addition* of any two vectors to yield a unique third vector is defined:

$$\mathbf{z} = \mathbf{x} + \mathbf{y}$$

* Vectors are represented in this text by boldface lowercase letters.

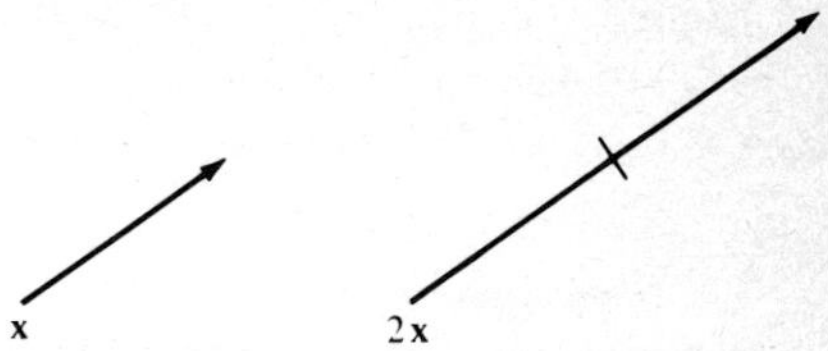

FIGURE 2.2-1
Scalar multiplication of a vector.

3 Vector addition is

Commutative:
$$\mathbf{x} + \mathbf{y} = \mathbf{y} + \mathbf{x}$$

Associative:
$$\mathbf{x} + (\mathbf{y} + \mathbf{z}) = (\mathbf{x} + \mathbf{y}) + \mathbf{z}$$

4 Scalar multiplication is associative

$$(cd)\mathbf{x} = c(d\mathbf{x})$$

and distributes both with respect to scalar addition

$$(c + d)\mathbf{x} = c\mathbf{x} + d\mathbf{x}$$

and vector addition

$$c(\mathbf{x} + \mathbf{y}) = c\mathbf{x} + c\mathbf{y}$$

The scalar unit is the multiplicative identity for scalar multiplication:

$$1\mathbf{x} = \mathbf{x}$$

5 An additive identity element called the *null vector* is defined:

$$\mathbf{x} + \mathbf{0} = \mathbf{x}$$

Scalar multiplication of a vector by zero yields the null vector:

$$0\mathbf{x} = \mathbf{0}$$

The inverse with respect to vector addition is $-\mathbf{x} = (-1)\mathbf{x}$, for

$$\mathbf{x} + (-1)\mathbf{x} = (1)\mathbf{x} + (-1)\mathbf{x} = (1 - 1)\mathbf{x} = (0)\mathbf{x} = \mathbf{0}$$

In the representation of points by position vectors, the preceding postulates are

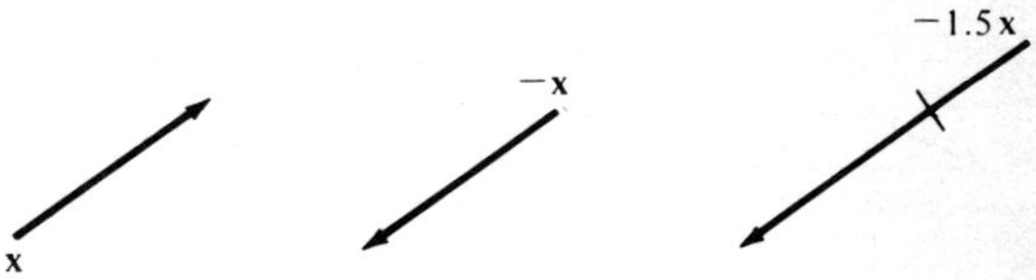

FIGURE 2.2-2
Multiplication of a vector by a negative scalar.

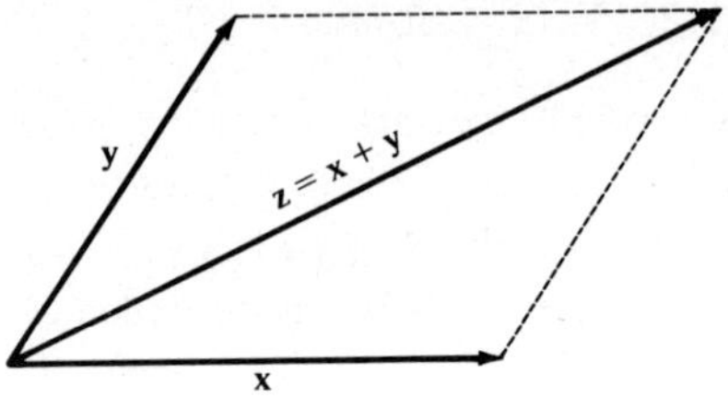

FIGURE 2.2-3
The parallelogram rule for addition of position vectors.

satisfied by (1) multiplication of coordinates by a scalar

$$c\mathbf{x} = c(x_1, x_2, \ldots, x_n) = (cx_1, cx_2, \ldots, cx_n)$$

and (2) elementwise addition of coordinates

$$\mathbf{x} + \mathbf{y} = (x_1, x_2, \ldots, x_n) + (y_1, y_2, \ldots, y_n)$$

$$= (x_1 + y_1, x_2 + y_2, \ldots, x_n + y_n)$$

The interpretation of scalar multiplication in terms of line segments is the changing of the length of a line by a multiple c, without changing its direction (Fig. 2.2-1).

Note that multiplication by a *negative* scalar changes the *sense* of the line, but not the direction (Fig. 2.2-2).

Addition of two position vectors is expressed by the so-called *parallelogram rule*, according to which the vector sum is the diagonal or *resultant* formed by completing the original vectors into a parallelogram (Fig. 2.2-3).

Addition of two or more vectors may also be represented by the completion of a polygon (Fig. 2.2-4). Note that the vectors in Fig. 2.2-4 are geometric vectors and not position vectors.

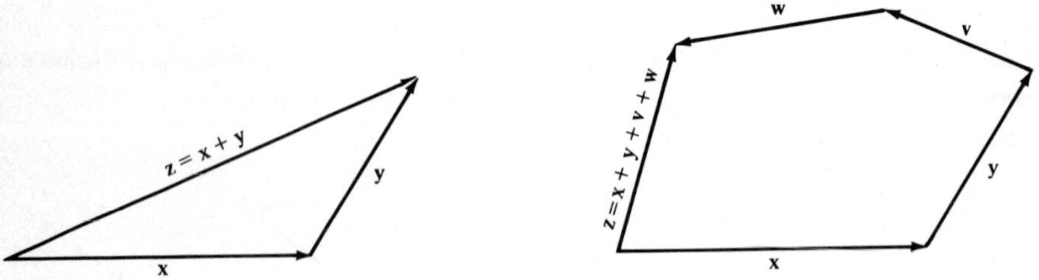

FIGURE 2.2-4
Addition of geometric vectors.

2.2.2 Vector Spaces

By a *vector space* is meant the totality of vectors that can be constructed by scalar multiplication and vector addition from the vectors in a given set. Any set of vectors that is capable of generating the totality of vectors by these operations is said to *span* the space. If this set consists of the least number of vectors that span the space, it is called a *basis* of the space. The number of vectors in the basis is called the *dimensionality* of the space. Thus, n basis vectors generate an n-dimensional space.

Any subset of r basis vectors is the basis of a *subspace* of r dimensions. If $0 < r < n$, the subspace is called *proper*; otherwise, it is *improper*. A subspace is closed under vector operations; that is, the scalar product or vector sum, or any combination of these operations, yields a vector in the subspace. Every subspace contains the null vector.

Let U denote the space spanned by a given set of vectors, and let V denote the space spanned by another set. Then the set of all vectors that belong both to U and to V is a subspace called the *intersection* of U and V and denoted by $U \cap V$. Similarly, the set of all vectors consisting of the sûm of a vector from U and a vector from V is a subspace called the *sum* of U and V and denoted by $U \oplus V$. The dimensionality of $U \oplus V$ is the dimensionality of U plus that of V minus the dimensionality of $U \cap V$.

A necessary and sufficient condition for a set of n vectors to be confined to a proper subspace is that the set is *linearly dependent*. Formally, the requirement for linear dependence is that there exist coefficients c_i, not all zero, such that

$$c_1\mathbf{x}_1 + c_2\mathbf{x}_2 + \cdots + c_n\mathbf{x}_n = \mathbf{0} \qquad (2.2\text{-}1)$$

Otherwise, the set is called *linear independence*.

If the dimensionality of the subspace is r, then every vector in the space can be constructed from any r linearly independent vectors in the subspace. That is, any r linearly independent vectors serve as a basis of the subspace.

2.2.3 Length, Angle, and Distance

The vector space consisting of points specified by rectangular coordinates is an example of a *euclidean* space. For euclidean space there is defined a so-called *inner product* of any two vectors. In terms of coordinates, an inner product is the sum of products of pairs of corresponding coordinates. Thus, the inner product (or "dot" product) of the position vectors **x** and **y** is the scalar quantity

$$\mathbf{x} \cdot \mathbf{y} = \sum_{i=1}^{n} x_i y_i = x_1 y_1 + x_2 y_2 + \cdots + x_n y_n \qquad (2.2\text{-}2)$$

Some properties of the inner product are:

1 Commutativity: $\mathbf{x} \cdot \mathbf{y} = \mathbf{y} \cdot \mathbf{x}$

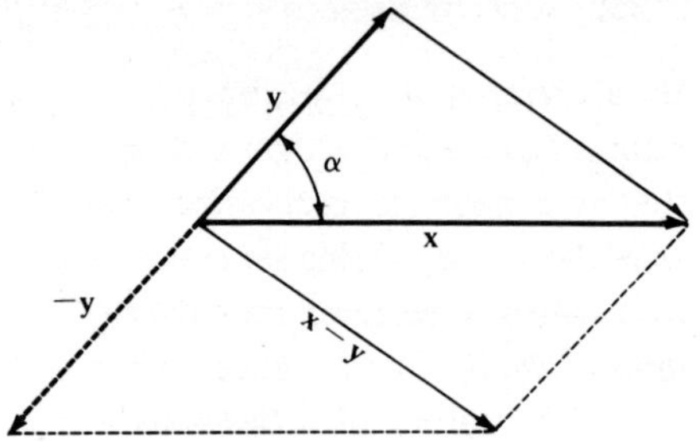

FIGURE 2.2-5
Law of cosines.

2 Associativity of scalar multiplication:

$$(a\mathbf{x}) \cdot (b\mathbf{y}) = ab(\mathbf{x} \cdot \mathbf{y})$$

3 Distribution with respect to vector addition:

$$(\mathbf{x} + \mathbf{y}) \cdot (\mathbf{x} + \mathbf{y}) = \mathbf{x} \cdot \mathbf{x} + 2\mathbf{x} \cdot \mathbf{y} + \mathbf{y} \cdot \mathbf{y}$$

By means of inner products, we may generalize the pythagorean theorem to higher-dimensional euclidean space. In 2- and 3-space, respectively, the pythagorean theorem gives, as the square length of a position vector,

$$r^2 = x_1{}^2 + x_2{}^2$$

and

$$r^2 = x_1{}^2 + x_2{}^2 + x_3{}^2$$

In general, for n-space, the square length is the inner product of a vector with itself:

$$|\mathbf{x}|^2 = \mathbf{x} \cdot \mathbf{x}$$

Thus, if $\mathbf{x}$ is a position vector, its square length is the sum of the squares of its coordinates:

$$|\mathbf{x}|^2 = x_1{}^2 + x_2{}^2 + \cdots + x_n{}^2 = \sum_{i=1}^{n} x_i{}^2$$

Length is defined as the positive square root of the inner product of a vector with itself:

$$|\mathbf{x}| = \sqrt{\mathbf{x} \cdot \mathbf{x}}$$

Angles in euclidean space are also defined in terms of inner products. Given two position vectors $\mathbf{x}$ and $\mathbf{y}$, we may express the square length of the *difference* between them in terms of the cosine of the included angle (law of cosines, Fig. 2.2-5). According to the law of cosines,

$$|(\mathbf{x} - \mathbf{y})|^2 = |\mathbf{x}|^2 + |\mathbf{y}|^2 - 2|\mathbf{x}| \times |\mathbf{y}| \cos \alpha$$

$$(\mathbf{x} - \mathbf{y}) \cdot (\mathbf{x} - \mathbf{y}) = \mathbf{x} \cdot \mathbf{x} + \mathbf{y} \cdot \mathbf{y} - 2\sqrt{(\mathbf{x} \cdot \mathbf{x})(\mathbf{y} \cdot \mathbf{y})} \cos \alpha$$

or

$$-2(\mathbf{x} \cdot \mathbf{y}) = -2\sqrt{(\mathbf{x} \cdot \mathbf{x})(\mathbf{y} \cdot \mathbf{y})} \cos \alpha$$

$$\cos \alpha = \frac{\mathbf{x} \cdot \mathbf{y}}{\sqrt{(\mathbf{x} \cdot \mathbf{x})(\mathbf{y} \cdot \mathbf{y})}} \qquad (2.2\text{-}4)$$

That is, the cosine of the angle between the two vectors is their inner product divided by the square root of the product of their square lengths. It is equivalent to the inner product of two vectors which have been adjusted to unit length. Such vectors are called *unit vectors*. For example, the following are unit vectors:

$$\mathbf{x}^* = \frac{1}{\sqrt{\mathbf{x}\cdot\mathbf{x}}}\,\mathbf{x} \qquad \text{and} \qquad \mathbf{y}^* = \frac{1}{\sqrt{\mathbf{y}\cdot\mathbf{y}}}\,\mathbf{y}$$

Then
$$\mathbf{x}^*\cdot\mathbf{x}^* = \mathbf{y}^*\cdot\mathbf{y}^* = 1 \qquad \text{and} \qquad \cos\alpha = \mathbf{x}^*\cdot\mathbf{y}^*$$

The direction of a position vector may be specified in terms of *direction cosines*, defined as the cosines of the angles between the position vector and each axis of the reference frame. If the position vector is of unit length and the reference axes are orthogonal, the direction cosines are just the coordinates of the vector (see Sec. 2.6).

We may also define a function $d(\mathbf{x},\mathbf{y})$ giving the *distance* between points $\mathbf{x}$ and $\mathbf{y}$:

$$d(\mathbf{x},\mathbf{y}) = |\mathbf{x}-\mathbf{y}| = \sqrt{(\mathbf{x}-\mathbf{y})\cdot(\mathbf{x}-\mathbf{y})} \tag{2.2-5}$$

That is, $d(\mathbf{x},\mathbf{y})$ is the length of the vector $\mathbf{x} - \mathbf{y}$.

The distance function, being nonnegative, is independent of the direction of measurement and satisfies the so-called *triangular inequality*

$$d(\mathbf{x},\mathbf{z}) \le d(\mathbf{x},\mathbf{y}) + d(\mathbf{y},\mathbf{z})$$

The latter follows from the *Cauchy–Schwarz inequality*

$$|\mathbf{a}\cdot\mathbf{b}| \le |\mathbf{a}| \times |\mathbf{b}| \tag{2.2-6}$$

which states, in effect, that the absolute value of the cosine of the angle between $\mathbf{a}$ and $\mathbf{b}$ cannot exceed unity. For in view of (2.2-6), we have

$$\begin{aligned}
d^2(\mathbf{x},\mathbf{z}) &= |\mathbf{x}-\mathbf{z}|^2 \\
&= |(\mathbf{x}-\mathbf{y}) + (\mathbf{y}-\mathbf{z})|^2 \\
&= (\mathbf{x}-\mathbf{y}+\mathbf{y}-\mathbf{z})\cdot(\mathbf{x}-\mathbf{y}+\mathbf{y}-\mathbf{z}) \\
&= (\mathbf{x}-\mathbf{y})\cdot(\mathbf{x}-\mathbf{y}) + (\mathbf{y}-\mathbf{z})\cdot(\mathbf{y}-\mathbf{z}) + 2(\mathbf{x}-\mathbf{y})\cdot(\mathbf{y}-\mathbf{z}) \\
&\le |\mathbf{x}-\mathbf{y}|^2 + |\mathbf{y}-\mathbf{z}|^2 + 2|\mathbf{x}-\mathbf{y}| \times |\mathbf{y}-\mathbf{z}| \\
&\le (|\mathbf{x}-\mathbf{y}| + |\mathbf{y}-\mathbf{z}|)^2
\end{aligned}$$

2.2.4 Orthogonality

Two nonnull vectors are called *orthogonal* if the cosine of the angle between them is zero. This implies, and is implied by, the vanishing of their inner product, that is, $\mathbf{x}\cdot\mathbf{y} = 0$.

It is sometimes desirable (e.g., in the solution of systems of linear equations) to construct an orthonormal basis for an arbitrary set of vectors; that is, each vector in the basis is of unit length ($\mathbf{x}_i \cdot \mathbf{x}_i = 1$), and each pair of basis vectors is made orthogonal ($\mathbf{x}_i \cdot \mathbf{x}_j = 0,\ i \neq j$). To obtain an orthonormal basis for an arbitrary vector set, we may employ the Gram-Schmidt construction. In this construction we assume vectors to be given in some order, e.g.,

$$\mathbf{x}_1, \mathbf{x}_2, \ldots, \mathbf{x}_n$$

The construction proceeds through the set from left to right, making each vector orthogonal to all previous vectors, then adjusting the length of the orthogonalized vector to unity (normalizing). The calculations for the first three stages of the process are as follows:

STAGE 1 Normalize $\mathbf{x}_1$:

$$\mathbf{x}_1^* = \frac{1}{\sqrt{\mathbf{x}_1 \cdot \mathbf{x}_1}} \mathbf{x}_1 \qquad \mathbf{x}_1 \cdot \mathbf{x}_1 \neq 0$$

STAGE 2 Orthogonalize $\mathbf{x}_2$ by first computing the inner product of $\mathbf{x}_1$ and $\mathbf{x}_2^*$, and subtracting from $\mathbf{x}_2$ the component of $\mathbf{x}_1^*$ in $\mathbf{x}_2$:

$$\mathbf{x}_2^{\perp} = \mathbf{x}_2 - (\mathbf{x}_2 \cdot \mathbf{x}_1^*)\mathbf{x}_1^*$$

Then normalize $\mathbf{x}_2^{\perp}$:

$$\mathbf{x}_2^* = \frac{1}{\sqrt{\mathbf{x}_2^{\perp} \cdot \mathbf{x}_2^{\perp}}} \mathbf{x}_2^{\perp} \qquad \mathbf{x}_2^{\perp} \cdot \mathbf{x}_2^{\perp} \neq 0$$

STAGE 3 Compute the inner products of $\mathbf{x}_3$ with $\mathbf{x}_1^*$ and $\mathbf{x}_2^*$, and subtract from $\mathbf{x}_3$ the component of $\mathbf{x}_1^*$ and $\mathbf{x}_2^*$ in $\mathbf{x}_3$:

$$\mathbf{x}_3^{\perp} = \mathbf{x}_3 - (\mathbf{x}_3 \cdot \mathbf{x}_1^*)\mathbf{x}_1^* - (\mathbf{x}_3 \cdot \mathbf{x}_2^*)\mathbf{x}_2^*$$

Normalize $\mathbf{x}_3^{\perp}$:

$$\mathbf{x}_3^* = \frac{1}{\mathbf{x}_3^{\perp} \cdot \mathbf{x}_3^{\perp}} \mathbf{x}_3^{\perp} \qquad \mathbf{x}_3^{\perp} \cdot \mathbf{x}_3^{\perp} \neq 0$$

And so on, until at the nth stage all vectors have entered the construction. If the ith vector in the set is linearly dependent on the previous vectors, $\mathbf{x}_i^{\perp}$ will be the null vector

$$\mathbf{x}_i^{\perp} = \mathbf{0}$$

and the inner product $\mathbf{x}_i^{\perp} \cdot \mathbf{x}_i^{\perp}$ will vanish. In this case, $\mathbf{x}_i$ must be deleted from the set and the process continued with $\mathbf{x}_{i+1}$. The number of nonnull vectors remaining at the end of the construction is the dimensionality of the space spanned by the vectors in the original set.

EXAMPLE 2.2-1 (*The Gram-Schmidt construction*) To illustrate the construction numerically, let us orthonormalize a set of vectors generated as follows:

$$V_n = \begin{bmatrix} 1 & x_1 & x_1^2 & \cdots & x_1^{n-1} \\ 1 & x_2 & x_2^2 & \cdots & x_2^{n-1} \\ \cdots & \cdots & \cdots & \cdots & \cdots \\ 1 & x_n & x_n^2 & \cdots & x_n^{n-1} \end{bmatrix}$$

Vector sets of this type have important applications in polynomial regression (see Sec. 4.1).

It is convenient to allow the value of the exponent to index the vectors in V_n:

$$V_n = [\mathbf{x}_0, \mathbf{x}_1, \ldots, \mathbf{x}_{n-1}]$$

For present purposes, let $n = 4$, and set $x_1 = 1$, $x_2 = 2$, $x_3 = 3$, $x_4 = 4$. Then,

$$V_4 = \begin{bmatrix} 1 & 1 & 1 & 1 \\ 1 & 2 & 4 & 8 \\ 1 & 3 & 9 & 27 \\ 1 & 4 & 16 & 64 \end{bmatrix}$$

Let us carry out the construction from left to right in this set. The calculations proceed in four stages:

STAGE 1 Normalize $\mathbf{x}_0$.

Normalize: $$\mathbf{x}_0^* = \tfrac{1}{2}(1, 1, 1, 1)$$

STAGE 2 Orthonormalize $\mathbf{x}_1$. Compute the inner product:

$$\mathbf{x}_1 \cdot \mathbf{x}_0^* = 5$$

Orthogonalize: $$\mathbf{x}_1^{\perp} = (1, 2, 3, 4) - \tfrac{5}{2}(1, 1, 1, 1) = \tfrac{1}{2}(-3, -1, 1, 3)$$

Normalize: $$\mathbf{x}_1^* = \frac{1}{2\sqrt{5}}(-3, -1, 1, 3)$$

STAGE 3 Orthonormalize $\mathbf{x}_2$. Compute the inner products:

$$\mathbf{x}_2 \cdot \mathbf{x}_0^* = 15 \qquad \mathbf{x}_2 \cdot \mathbf{x}_1^* = 5\sqrt{5}$$

Orthogonalize: $$\mathbf{x}_2^{\perp} = (1, 4, 9, 16) - \tfrac{15}{2}(1, 1, 1, 1) - \tfrac{5}{2}(-3, -1, 1, 3) = (1, -1, -1, 1)$$

Normalize: $$\mathbf{x}_2^* = \tfrac{1}{2}(1, -1, -1, 1)$$

STAGE 4 Orthonormalize $\mathbf{x}_3$. Compute the inner products:

$$\mathbf{x}_3 \cdot \mathbf{x}_0^* = 50 \qquad \mathbf{x}_3 \cdot \mathbf{x}_1^* = \frac{104}{\sqrt{5}} \qquad \mathbf{x}_3 \cdot \mathbf{x}_2^* = 15$$

Orthogonalize:

$$\begin{aligned}\mathbf{x}_3{}^{\perp} &= (1, 8, 27, 64) - 25(1, 1, 1, 1) - \tfrac{52}{5}(-3, -1, 1, 3) \\ &\qquad - \tfrac{15}{2}(1, -1, -1, 1) \\ &= \tfrac{3}{10}(-1, 3, -3, 1)\end{aligned}$$

Normalize: $\qquad \mathbf{x}_3^* = \dfrac{1}{2\sqrt{5}}(-1, 3, -3, 1)$

Bring the orthogonal vectors together as the columns of the orthogonal set

$$P_4 = \begin{bmatrix} \frac{1}{2} & -\frac{3\sqrt{5}}{10} & \frac{1}{2} & -\frac{\sqrt{5}}{10} \\ \frac{1}{2} & -\frac{\sqrt{5}}{10} & -\frac{1}{2} & \frac{3\sqrt{5}}{10} \\ \frac{1}{2} & \frac{\sqrt{5}}{10} & -\frac{1}{2} & -\frac{3\sqrt{5}}{10} \\ \frac{1}{2} & \frac{3\sqrt{5}}{10} & \frac{1}{2} & \frac{\sqrt{5}}{10} \end{bmatrix}$$

The reader may verify that inner products of different vectors in P_4 are zero.

Although the method of calculation illustrated in Example 2.2-1 is convenient for hand calculation, it is not well suited to computer applications. Because the number of significant figures which can be carried economically in the computer is limited, errors of rounding will occur whenever numbers are represented by truncated decimal or binary approximations. These errors may accumulate to such an extent that the orthogonality of the final vectors is grossly disturbed. Better results are obtained if the order in which the calculations are carried out is modified somewhat [Björck, 1967]. In the modified procedure, a component is subtracted from *each* remaining vector at each stage of the process. Vectors at the $(i + 1)$st stage are obtained from those of the ith stage by

$$\mathbf{x}_r{}^{(i+1)} = \mathbf{x}_r{}^{(i)} - \frac{\mathbf{x}_i^{(i)} \cdot \mathbf{x}_r{}^{(i)}}{\mathbf{x}_i^{(i)} \cdot \mathbf{x}_i^{(i)}} \mathbf{x}_i{}^{(i)} \qquad \begin{aligned} i &= 1, 2, \ldots, n-1 \\ r &= i+1, i+2, \ldots, n \end{aligned} \tag{2.2-7}$$

At the completion of the nth stage, the vector set is normalized by scalar multiplication of each orthogonal vector by the reciprocal of its length. (Other aspects of orthonormalization are discussed in Sec. 2.7.2.)

EXAMPLE 2.2-2 (*The modified Gram-Schmidt construction*) We may illustrate the modified procedure, using decimal arithmetic, by again orthogonalizing V_4. At the zeroth stage, $V_4^{(0)} = V_4 = (\mathbf{x}_0^{(0)}, \mathbf{x}_1^{(0)}, \mathbf{x}_2^{(0)}, \mathbf{x}_3^{(0)})$.

STAGE 1 Compute the inner products for $i = 0$, $r = 0, 1, 2$, and 3:

$$\mathbf{x}_0^{(0)} \cdot \mathbf{x}_0^{(0)} = 4 \qquad \mathbf{x}_0^{(0)} \cdot \mathbf{x}_1^{(0)} = 10 \qquad \mathbf{x}_0^{(0)} \cdot \mathbf{x}_2^{(0)} = 30 \qquad \mathbf{x}_0^{(0)} \cdot \mathbf{x}_3^{(0)} = 100$$

Apply (2.2-7):

$$V_4^{(1)} = \begin{bmatrix} 1 & -1.5 & -6.5 & -24 \\ 1 & -.5 & -3.5 & -17 \\ 1 & .5 & 1.5 & 2 \\ 1 & 1.5 & 8.5 & 39 \end{bmatrix} = [\mathbf{x}_0^{(0)}, \mathbf{x}_1^{(1)}, \mathbf{x}_2^{(1)}, \mathbf{x}_3^{(1)}]$$

STAGE 2 Compute the inner products for $i = 1$, $r = 1, 2$, and 3:

$$\mathbf{x}_1^{(1)} \cdot \mathbf{x}_1^{(1)} = 5 \qquad \mathbf{x}_1^{(1)} \cdot \mathbf{x}_2^{(1)} = 25 \qquad \mathbf{x}_1^{(1)} \cdot \mathbf{x}_3^{(1)} = 104$$

Apply (2.2-7):

$$V_4^{(2)} = \begin{bmatrix} 1 & -1.5 & 1 & 7.2 \\ 1 & -.5 & -1 & -6.6 \\ 1 & .5 & -1 & -8.4 \\ 1 & 1.5 & 1 & 7.8 \end{bmatrix} = [\mathbf{x}_0^{(0)}, \mathbf{x}_1^{(1)}, \mathbf{x}_2^{(2)}, \mathbf{x}_3^{(2)}]$$

STAGE 3 Compute the inner products for $i = 2$, $r = 2$ and 3:

$$\mathbf{x}_2^{(2)} \cdot \mathbf{x}_2^{(2)} = 4 \qquad \mathbf{x}_2^{(2)} \cdot \mathbf{x}_3^{(2)} = 30$$

Apply (2.2-7):

$$V_4^{(3)} = \begin{bmatrix} 1 & -1.5 & 1 & -.3 \\ 1 & -.5 & -1 & .9 \\ 1 & .5 & -1 & -.9 \\ 1 & 1.5 & 1 & .3 \end{bmatrix} = [\mathbf{x}_0^{(0)}, \mathbf{x}_1^{(1)}, \mathbf{x}_2^{(2)}, \mathbf{x}_3^{(3)}]$$

STAGE 4 Compute the inner product for $i = 3$, $r = 3$:

$$\mathbf{x}_3^{(3)} \cdot \mathbf{x}_3^{(3)} = 1.8$$

Now normalize the columns of $V_4^{(3)}$. Note that the square lengths from which the normalizing constants are calculated are given by the first inner product at each stage above. That is, the normalizing constants are, respectively, $1/\sqrt{\mathbf{x}_0^{(0)} \cdot \mathbf{x}_0^{(0)}} = .5$, $1/\sqrt{\mathbf{x}_1^{(1)} \cdot \mathbf{x}_1^{(1)}} = 1/\sqrt{5}$, $1/\sqrt{\mathbf{x}_2^{(2)} \cdot \mathbf{x}_2^{(2)}} = .5$, and $1/\sqrt{\mathbf{x}_3^{(3)} \cdot \mathbf{x}_3^{(3)}} = 1/\sqrt{1.8}$. Thus, to six significant figures, the orthonormal set is

$$P_4 = \begin{bmatrix} .5 & -.670807 & .5 & -.223602 \\ .5 & -.223602 & -.5 & .670807 \\ .5 & .223602 & -.5 & -.670807 \\ .5 & .670807 & .5 & .223602 \end{bmatrix}$$

which agrees with the result given above in exact form.

Exercise 2.2-1 Orthonormalize the following matrix using the modified Gram-Schmidt construction:

$$\begin{bmatrix} 2 & 3 & 1 \\ 1 & -3 & 2 \\ 2 & 1 & 3 \end{bmatrix}$$

ANSWER To three significant figures:

$$\begin{bmatrix} .667 & .470 & -.572 \\ .333 & -.885 & -.334 \\ .667 & -.027 & .741 \end{bmatrix}$$

2.3 ELEMENTS OF MATRIX ALGEBRA

In matrix algebra, relations and operations are defined for rectangular arrays of elements called *matrices.** An example of a matrix is

$$\underset{m \times n}{\mathbf{A}} = \begin{bmatrix} a_{11} & a_{12} & \cdots & a_{1n} \\ a_{21} & a_{22} & \cdots & a_{2n} \\ \cdots & \cdots & \cdots & \cdots \\ a_{m1} & a_{m2} & \cdots & a_{mn} \end{bmatrix}$$

Although the elements of a matrix may be any quantities which satisfy the postulates of an abstract field, e.g., rational numbers, complex numbers, and polynomials (see Birkoff and MacLane [1965]; Stoll [1952, page 22 ff]), for our purposes they will be restricted to real numbers.

The number of rows in a matrix is called the *row order*; the number of columns, the *column order*. If the number of rows is m and the number of columns n, we say that the matrix is of order m by n; if there is possible ambiguity as to order, we insert $m \times n$ under the letter which designates the matrix. A matrix may also be designated

* Matrices are represented in this text by boldface uppercase letters.

by exhibiting a typical element in square brackets, possibly with an indication of the range of subscripts; e.g.,

$$\mathbf{A} = [a_{ij}] \qquad i = 1, 2, \ldots, m \qquad j = 1, 2, \ldots, n$$

In multivariate data analysis, we shall often refer to the *data matrix*, any one row of which consists of observations obtained from one subject. Thus, if p responses of each of N subjects have been observed, the data matrix is of order $N \times p$. As we shall see in Chap. 4, the numerical calculations required in data analysis can be expressed as operations on data matrices.

Definitions and postulates of matrix algebra are as follows:

1 Equality. Two matrices, necessarily of the same row and column order, are equal if and only if corresponding elements are equal:

$$\mathbf{A} = \mathbf{B} \text{ implies and is implied by } a_{ij} = b_{ij} \qquad \begin{array}{l} i = 1, 2, \ldots, m \\ j = 1, 2, \ldots, n \end{array}$$

2 Addition. The sum of two matrices of the same order is obtained by summing corresponding elements:

$$\mathbf{A} + \mathbf{B} = [a_{ij}] + [b_{ij}] = [a_{ij} + b_{ij}] \qquad \begin{array}{l} i = 1, 2, \ldots, m \\ j = 1, 2, \ldots, n \end{array}$$

Matrix addition is associative

$$\mathbf{A} + (\mathbf{B} + \mathbf{C}) = (\mathbf{A} + \mathbf{B}) + \mathbf{C}$$

and commutative

$$\mathbf{A} + \mathbf{B} = \mathbf{B} + \mathbf{A}$$

The additive identity is the *null matrix* **O** consisting of zero elements:

$$\underset{m \times n}{\mathbf{A}} + \underset{m \times n}{\mathbf{O}} = \underset{m \times n}{\mathbf{A}}$$

3 Scalar multiplication. The product of a scalar number and a matrix is obtained by multiplying each element of the matrix by the scalar number:

$$c\mathbf{A} = c[a_{ij}] = [ca_{ij}] \qquad \begin{array}{l} i = 1, 2, \ldots, m \\ j = 1, 2, \ldots, n \end{array}$$

Scalar multiplication is associative

$$(cd)\mathbf{A} = c(d\mathbf{A})$$

and distributes with respect to scalar addition

$$(c + d)\mathbf{A} = c\mathbf{A} + d\mathbf{A}$$

and with respect to matrix addition

$$c(\mathbf{A} + \mathbf{B}) = c\mathbf{A} + c\mathbf{B}$$

The additive inverse for matrix addition is the scalar product of -1 and the matrix:

$$\mathbf{A} + (-1)\mathbf{A} = \mathbf{A} - \mathbf{A} = \mathbf{O}$$

4 Matrix multiplication. Matrix multiplication is defined for matrices in which the column order of the left-hand factor equals the row order of the right-hand factor. Such matrices are called *conformable* for multiplication. The (i,k)th element of the product matrix is the sum of products of corresponding elements from the ith row of the left-hand factor and the kth column of the right-hand factor:

$$\mathbf{AB} = \underset{m\times q}{\mathbf{A}} \cdot \underset{q\times n}{\mathbf{B}} = \left[\sum_{j=1}^{q} a_{ij}b_{jk}\right]$$
$$= [a_{i1}b_{1k} + a_{i2}b_{2k} + \cdots + a_{iq}b_{qk}] = [c_{ik}] = \underset{m\times n}{\mathbf{C}}$$

This operation is sometimes referred to as *row-by-column* multiplication. Note that the row and column orders of the matrix product are equal, respectively, to the row order of the first factor and the column order of the second factor. Matrix multiplication is associative

$$(\mathbf{AB})\mathbf{C} = \mathbf{A}(\mathbf{BC})$$

but in general it is not commutative

$$\mathbf{AB} \neq \mathbf{BA}$$

Thus, it is necessary to refer to **AB** as *pre*multiplication of **B** by **A**, or *post*-multiplication of **A** by **B**. Matrix multiplication, pre or post, distributes with respect to matrix addition:

$$\mathbf{A}(\mathbf{B} + \mathbf{C}) = \mathbf{AB} + \mathbf{AC}$$
$$(\mathbf{A} + \mathbf{B})\mathbf{C} = \mathbf{AC} + \mathbf{BC}$$

A square matrix with unities in the diagonal and zeroes elsewhere is called the *unit matrix*:

$$\mathbf{I} = \begin{bmatrix} 1 & 0 & \cdots & 0 \\ 0 & 1 & \cdots & 0 \\ \cdots & \cdots & \cdots & \cdots \\ 0 & 0 & \cdots & 1 \end{bmatrix}$$

Because the unit matrix is the identity for matrix multiplication, it is also called the *identity matrix*:

$$\underset{m\times n}{\mathbf{A}} \cdot \underset{n\times n}{\mathbf{I}} = \underset{m\times n}{\mathbf{A}}$$

$$\underset{m\times m}{\mathbf{I}} \cdot \underset{m\times n}{\mathbf{A}} = \underset{m\times n}{\mathbf{A}}$$

Any square matrix in which the off-diagonal elements are identically equal to zero is called a *diagonal matrix.* Diagonal matrices may be represented as follows:

$$\mathbf{D} = \text{diag}[d_1, d_2, \ldots, d_n] = \begin{bmatrix} d_1 & 0 & \cdots & 0 \\ 0 & d_2 & \cdots & 0 \\ \cdots & \cdots & \cdots & \cdots \\ 0 & 0 & \cdots & d_n \end{bmatrix}$$

Premultiplication by a diagonal matrix merely rescales the rows of the postfactor. Postmultiplication by a diagonal matrix rescales the columns of the prefactor.

5 *The inverse matrix.* If an $n \times n$ square matrix $\mathbf{B}$ exists such that $\underset{n\times n}{\mathbf{A}}\ \underset{n\times n}{\mathbf{B}} = \underset{n\times n}{\mathbf{I}}$ and $\underset{n\times n}{\mathbf{B}}\ \underset{n\times n}{\mathbf{A}} = \underset{n\times n}{\mathbf{I}}$, then $\mathbf{B}$ is called the inverse of $\mathbf{A}$, in which case $\mathbf{B}$ is usually denoted by $\mathbf{A}^{-1}$. If a unique inverse of $\mathbf{A}$ exists, it is an inverse with respect to multiplication both on the left and on the right. For, suppose $\mathbf{B}$ is a right inverse of $\mathbf{A}$, and $\mathbf{C}$ is a left inverse of $\mathbf{A}$. Then

$$\mathbf{CA} = \mathbf{AB} = \mathbf{I}$$

But

$$\mathbf{CAB} = \mathbf{C} = \mathbf{B} = \mathbf{A}^{-1}$$

or

$$\mathbf{A}^{-1}\mathbf{A} = \mathbf{AA}^{-1} = \mathbf{I}$$

That is, multiplication of a matrix and its inverse is commutative. If a matrix has an inverse, the matrix is called *nonsingular*; otherwise, it is called *singular.* The necessary and sufficient condition for nonsingularity will be given in Sec. 2.3.2. Note that the inverse of a matrix product is the product of the inverses in the reverse order:

$$(\mathbf{AB})^{-1} = \mathbf{B}^{-1}\mathbf{A}^{-1}$$

for

$$\mathbf{B}^{-1}\mathbf{A}^{-1}\mathbf{AB} = \mathbf{B}^{-1}\mathbf{B} = \mathbf{I}$$

and

$$\mathbf{ABB}^{-1}\mathbf{A}^{-1} = \mathbf{AA}^{-1} = \mathbf{I}$$

Note that the inverse of a diagonal matrix contains the reciprocals of the diagonal elements; that is, $\mathbf{D}^{-1} = \text{diag}[1/d_1, 1/d_2, \ldots, 1/d_n]$.

6 *The transpose matrix.* A matrix obtained by interchange of the rows and columns of a given matrix is called the *transpose* of the original matrix. It is usually designated by a prime. That is, if $\underset{n\times m}{\mathbf{A}} = [a_{ij}]$, then

$$\underset{m\times n}{\mathbf{A}'} = [a_{ij}]' = [a_{ji}]$$

is the transpose. The transpose of a matrix sum is the sum of the transposes:

$$(\mathbf{A} + \mathbf{B})' = \mathbf{A}' + \mathbf{B}'$$

The transpose of a matrix product is the product of the transposes in the reverse order:

$$(\mathbf{AB})' = \mathbf{B}'\mathbf{A}'$$

That is, the roles of rows and columns in the row-by-column multiplications are exchanged when the product is transposed. Note also that $(\mathbf{A}^{-1})' = (\mathbf{A}')^{-1}$, since $(\mathbf{A}^{-1}\mathbf{A})' = \mathbf{A}'(\mathbf{A}^{-1})' = \mathbf{I}' = \mathbf{I} = \mathbf{A}'(\mathbf{A}')^{-1}$.

7 *Partitioned matrices.* Let the initial r rows of an $m \times n$ matrix $\mathbf{A}$ be partitioned from the remaining $s = m - r$ rows, and the initial p columns partitioned from the remaining $q = n - p$ columns. Then $\mathbf{A}$ may be represented in submatrices as follows:

$$\mathbf{A} = \underset{\begin{matrix} p & \quad q \end{matrix}}{\begin{bmatrix} \mathbf{A}_{11} & \mathbf{A}_{12} \\ \mathbf{A}_{21} & \mathbf{A}_{22} \end{bmatrix}} \begin{matrix} r \\ s \end{matrix}$$

If a matrix $\mathbf{B}$ is similarly partitioned, we refer to $\mathbf{A}$ and $\mathbf{B}$ as *conformably* partitioned for addition, and we readily verify that

$$\mathbf{A} + \mathbf{B} = \begin{bmatrix} \mathbf{A}_{11} + \mathbf{B}_{11} & \mathbf{A}_{12} + \mathbf{B}_{12} \\ \mathbf{A}_{21} + \mathbf{B}_{21} & \mathbf{A}_{22} + \mathbf{B}_{22} \end{bmatrix}$$

Suppose now that $\mathbf{B}$ is partitioned into p and q rows and t and u columns. We then refer to $\mathbf{A}$ and $\mathbf{B}$ as conformably partitioned for premultiplication of $\mathbf{B}$ by $\mathbf{A}$, and we may verify that

$$\mathbf{AB} = \begin{matrix} r \\ s \end{matrix} \underset{\begin{matrix} p & \quad q \end{matrix}}{\begin{bmatrix} \mathbf{A}_{11} & \mathbf{A}_{12} \\ \mathbf{A}_{21} & \mathbf{A}_{22} \end{bmatrix}} \underset{\begin{matrix} t & \quad u \end{matrix}}{\begin{bmatrix} \mathbf{B}_{11} & \mathbf{B}_{12} \\ \mathbf{B}_{21} & \mathbf{B}_{22} \end{bmatrix}} \begin{matrix} p \\ q \end{matrix}$$

$$= \underset{\begin{matrix} t & \qquad\qquad\qquad u \end{matrix}}{\begin{bmatrix} \mathbf{A}_{11}\mathbf{B}_{11} + \mathbf{A}_{12}\mathbf{B}_{21} & \mathbf{A}_{11}\mathbf{B}_{12} + \mathbf{A}_{12}\mathbf{B}_{22} \\ \mathbf{A}_{21}\mathbf{B}_{11} + \mathbf{A}_{22}\mathbf{B}_{21} & \mathbf{A}_{21}\mathbf{B}_{12} + \mathbf{A}_{22}\mathbf{B}_{22} \end{bmatrix}} \begin{matrix} r \\ s \end{matrix}$$

We may similarly verify that

$$\begin{matrix} p \\ q \end{matrix} \underset{\begin{matrix} p & q \end{matrix}}{\begin{bmatrix} \mathbf{A} & \mathbf{B} \\ \mathbf{C} & \mathbf{D} \end{bmatrix}^{-1}}$$

$$= \underset{\begin{matrix} p & \qquad\qquad\qquad\qquad q \end{matrix}}{\begin{bmatrix} \mathbf{A}^{-1} + \mathbf{A}^{-1}\mathbf{B}(\mathbf{D} - \mathbf{C}\mathbf{A}^{-1}\mathbf{B})^{-1}\mathbf{C}\mathbf{A}^{-1} & -\mathbf{A}^{-1}\mathbf{B}(\mathbf{D} - \mathbf{C}\mathbf{A}^{-1}\mathbf{B})^{-1} \\ -(\mathbf{D} - \mathbf{C}\mathbf{A}^{-1}\mathbf{B})^{-1}\mathbf{C}\mathbf{A}^{-1} & (\mathbf{D} - \mathbf{C}\mathbf{A}^{-1}\mathbf{B})^{-1} \end{bmatrix}} \begin{matrix} p \\ q \end{matrix}$$

for $\mathbf{A}$ and $\mathbf{D} - \mathbf{C}\mathbf{A}^{-1}\mathbf{B}$ nonsingular.

2.3.1 Row and Column Matrices

A position vector in its coordinate representation may be considered an $n \times 1$ column matrix, e.g.,

$$\mathbf{x} = \begin{bmatrix} x_1 \\ x_2 \\ \vdots \\ x_n \end{bmatrix}$$

Column matrices are therefore often referred to as vectors, or more specifically as *column vectors,* and are written in vector notation. The transpose of a column matrix is called a row vector ($1 \times n$) and indicated by the transpose sign:

$$\mathbf{x}' = [x_1, x_2, \ldots, x_n]$$

Thus, the $N \times p$ data matrix may be regarded as a set of p column vectors, each comprising the scores of N subjects on a given variable:

$$\mathbf{Y} = \begin{bmatrix} y_1^{(1)} & y_1^{(2)} \cdots y_1^{(p)} \\ y_2^{(1)} & y_2^{(2)} \cdots y_2^{(p)} \\ \cdots & \cdots \\ y_N^{(1)} & y_N^{(2)} \cdots y_N^{(p)} \end{bmatrix} = [\mathbf{y}^{(1)} \quad \mathbf{y}^{(2)} \quad \cdots \quad \mathbf{y}^{(p)}]$$

Each of these $N \times 1$ column vectors will be referred to as an *observational vector.*

Conversely, the data matrix may be considered a set of N row vectors, each comprising the p scores of a given subject; i.e.,

$$\mathbf{Y} = \begin{bmatrix} y_1^{(1)} & y_1^{(2)} & \cdots & y_1^{(p)} \\ y_2^{(1)} & y_2^{(2)} & \cdots & y_2^{(p)} \\ \cdots & \cdots & \cdots & \cdots \\ y_N^{(1)} & y_N^{(2)} & \cdots & y_N^{(p)} \end{bmatrix} = \begin{bmatrix} \mathbf{y}_1' \\ \mathbf{y}_2' \\ \cdots \\ \mathbf{y}_N' \end{bmatrix}$$

where the primes indicate row vectors. Each of these $1 \times p$ row vectors will be termed a *vector observation.* The importance of these two ways of looking at the data matrix will become apparent in Chap. 4.

Rank and nullity The vector space generated by the rows of $\mathbf{A}$ is called the *row space* of $\mathbf{A}$. Similarly, the vector space generated by the columns of $\mathbf{A}$ is called the *column space.* The row rank of $\mathbf{A}$ is the dimensionality of the row space, and the column rank is the dimensionality of the column space. We prove in Sec. 2.3.2 that these two dimensionalities are equal and, therefore, that row and column rank are one and the same number $r = \text{rank}(\mathbf{A})$.

Suppose $\mathbf{A}$ is an $m \times n$ matrix. If $\mathbf{A}$ is the null matrix, then $r = 0$. Otherwise, $0 < r \leq \min(m,n)$, and there are r row vectors in $\mathbf{A}$ which are a basis of the row space, and r columns which are a basis of the column space. If $m \leq n$, the rank of

A cannot exceed m. If $r = m$ we say that **A** is of *full* row rank. If $r < m$, we say that **A** is not of full rank or, equivalently, that the *row nullity* of **A** is $m - r$. Similarly, if $r = n$, **A** is of full column rank. If $r < n$, **A** is not of full column rank, and the column nullity is $n - r$. For an $n \times n$ square matrix, the unique nullity is $n - r$ (*Sylvester's nullity*).

2.3.2 Elementary Row Operations

The practical determination of rank may be accomplished by so-called *elementary row operations*. These are of three types: (1) interchange of rows; (2) multiplication of each element in a row by some scalar constant; and (3) addition of elements in one row, possibly multiplied by a scalar constant, to corresponding elements in another row.

The elementary row operations are equivalent to premultiplying the matrix **A** by certain $m \times m$ matrices called *elementary matrices*, designated in general by **E**.

For example, the operation $\mathbf{E}_\mathrm{I}\mathbf{A}$, with

$$\mathbf{E}_\mathrm{I} = \begin{bmatrix} 0 & 1 & 0 & \cdots & 0 \\ 1 & 0 & 0 & \cdots & 0 \\ 0 & 0 & 1 & \cdots & 0 \\ \cdots & \cdots & \cdots & \cdots & \cdots \\ 0 & 0 & 0 & \cdots & 1 \end{bmatrix}$$

interchanges (permutes) the first and second rows of **A**. The operation $\mathbf{E}_\mathrm{II}\mathbf{A}$, with

$$\mathbf{E}_\mathrm{II} = \begin{bmatrix} 1 & 0 & 0 & \cdots & 0 \\ 0 & a & 0 & \cdots & 0 \\ 0 & 0 & 1 & \cdots & 0 \\ \cdots & \cdots & \cdots & \cdots & \cdots \\ 0 & 0 & 0 & \cdots & 1 \end{bmatrix}$$

multiplies the second row of **A** by the scalar **a**. The operation $\mathbf{E}_\mathrm{III}\mathbf{A}$, with

$$\mathbf{E}_\mathrm{III} = \begin{bmatrix} 1 & 0 & 0 & \cdots & 0 \\ a & 1 & 0 & \cdots & 0 \\ 0 & 0 & 1 & \cdots & 0 \\ \cdots & \cdots & \cdots & \cdots & \cdots \\ 0 & 0 & 0 & \cdots & 1 \end{bmatrix}$$

adds a times each element in the first row of **A** to corresponding elements in the second row of **A**.

Each of these types of elementary matrices has an inverse matrix of the same type which reverses the corresponding row operation. For example, $\mathbf{E}_\mathrm{I}$ is its own inverse; that is, $\mathbf{E}_\mathrm{I}^{-1} = \mathbf{E}_\mathrm{I}$. Also,

$$\mathbf{E}_{\mathrm{II}}^{-1} = \begin{bmatrix} 1 & 0 & 0 & \cdots & 0 \\ 0 & 1/a & 0 & \cdots & 0 \\ 0 & 0 & 1 & \cdots & 0 \\ \cdots & \cdots & \cdots & \cdots & \cdots \\ 0 & 0 & 0 & \cdots & 1 \end{bmatrix}$$

and

$$\mathbf{E}_{\mathrm{III}}^{-1} = \begin{bmatrix} 1 & 0 & 0 & \cdots & 0 \\ -a & 1 & 0 & \cdots & 0 \\ 0 & 0 & 1 & \cdots & 0 \\ \cdots & \cdots & \cdots & \cdots & \cdots \\ 0 & 0 & 0 & \cdots & 1 \end{bmatrix}$$

Note that $\mathbf{E}_\mathrm{I}^{-1}\mathbf{E}_\mathrm{I}$, $\mathbf{E}_{\mathrm{II}}^{-1}\mathbf{E}_{\mathrm{II}}$, and $\mathbf{E}_{\mathrm{III}}^{-1}\mathbf{E}_{\mathrm{III}}$ are each equal to $\mathbf{I}$ as required.

To see that the elementary row operations enable us to determine the rank of some matrix $\mathbf{A}$, we observe first that the rank of $\mathbf{A}$ is invariant under these operations. For if the rank of the $m \times n$ matrix $\mathbf{A}$ is $r < m$, there exist rows of $\mathbf{A}$ from which any of the remaining $m - r$ rows, for example, row h, can be generated by a linear combination of these r rows with coefficients $c_{h1}, c_{h2}, \ldots, c_{hr}$. The rows of $\mathbf{A}$ may be rearranged to bring the r linearly independent rows to leading position without change of rank. Thus, $\mathbf{A}$ may be partitioned as

$$\mathbf{A} = \underset{n}{\begin{bmatrix} \mathbf{A}_1 \\ \mathbf{A}_2 \end{bmatrix}} \begin{matrix} r \\ m - r \end{matrix}$$

and there will exist

$$\mathbf{T} = \begin{bmatrix} \mathbf{I} & \mathbf{O} \\ -\mathbf{C} & \mathbf{I} \end{bmatrix} \begin{matrix} r \\ m - r \end{matrix} \qquad \begin{matrix} r & m - r \end{matrix}$$

for $h = r, r + 1, \ldots, m$, such that

$$\mathbf{TA} = \begin{bmatrix} \mathbf{A}_1 \\ \mathbf{A}_2 - \mathbf{CA}_1 \end{bmatrix} = \underset{n}{\begin{bmatrix} \mathbf{A}_1 \\ \mathbf{O} \end{bmatrix}} \begin{matrix} r \\ m - r \end{matrix} \tag{2.3-1}$$

Now, does there exist a matrix $\mathbf{U}$ such that $\mathbf{U}(\mathbf{EA})$ produces the same result as the right member of (2.3-1)? If we let $\mathbf{U} = \mathbf{TE}^{-1}$, then $\mathbf{UEA} = \mathbf{TE}^{-1}\mathbf{EA} = \mathbf{TA}$. This shows that the number of linearly independent rows and the number of linearly dependent rows of $\mathbf{EA}$, and hence the rank and nullity, are the same as those of $\mathbf{A}$.

To find the linearly independent rows in **A**, and hence to determine its rank, we may apply successive row operations in order to transform **A** into a so-called *echelon* form:

$$\mathbf{E}^{(k)} \cdots \mathbf{E}^{(2)}\mathbf{E}^{(1)} \underset{m\times n}{\mathbf{A}} = \mathbf{PA} = \underset{m\times n}{\mathbf{B}}$$

where

$$\underset{m\times n}{\mathbf{B}} = \begin{bmatrix} 1 & b_{12} & b_{13} & \cdots & b_{1r} & \cdots & b_{1n} \\ 0 & 1 & b_{23} & \cdots & b_{2r} & \cdots & b_{2n} \\ 0 & 0 & 1 & \cdots & b_{3r} & \cdots & b_{3n} \\ \cdots & \cdots & \cdots & \cdots & \cdots & \cdots & \cdots \\ 0 & 0 & 0 & \cdots & 1 & \cdots & b_{rn} \\ 0 & 0 & 0 & \cdots & 0 & \cdots & 0 \\ \cdots & \cdots & \cdots & \cdots & \cdots & \cdots & \cdots \\ 0 & 0 & 0 & \cdots & 0 & \cdots & 0 \end{bmatrix} \tag{2.3-2}$$

That is, the echelon form consists of an $r \times r$ matrix in leading position in which elements below the main diagonal are identically zero and elements in the main diagonal are unity. The remaining elements in the first r rows are in general nonzero, while all elements in the remaining $m - r$ rows are identically zero. *The rank of* **A** *is equal to the number of rows in the echelon form in which there is at least one nonzero element.* The number of *zero* rows equals the row nullity of **A**. It is therefore easy to see that the minimum of the row and column order of **A** fixes its maximum rank, for, if n is less than m, the number of nonzero rows in the echelon form cannot exceed n.

As an example of the practical determination of rank, let us reduce to echelon form the matrix

$$\begin{bmatrix} 1 & 2 & 3 & 2 \\ 2 & 3 & 5 & 1 \\ 1 & 3 & 4 & 5 \end{bmatrix}$$

STEP 1 Row 2 − 2 × row 1, and row 3 − row 1:

$$\begin{bmatrix} 1 & 2 & 3 & 2 \\ 0 & -1 & -1 & -3 \\ 0 & 1 & 1 & 3 \end{bmatrix}$$

STEP 2 Row 3 + row 2, and − (row 2):

$$\begin{bmatrix} 1 & 2 & 3 & 2 \\ 0 & 1 & 1 & 3 \\ 0 & 0 & 0 & 0 \end{bmatrix}$$

The rank is 2.

Postmultiplication of a matrix by the *transpose* of an elementary matrix performs elementary *column* operations. That is, $\mathbf{E}_{\text{I}}'$ interchanges columns, $\mathbf{E}_{\text{II}}'$ rescales a column, and $\mathbf{E}_{\text{III}}'$ adds a scalar multiple of one column to some other column. By means of column operations, the echelon form (2.3-2) may be reduced to an $m \times n$ matrix with unities as the leading r diagonal elements and zeroes elsewhere:

$$\mathbf{BE}^{(k+1)\prime}\mathbf{E}^{(k+2)\prime}\cdots\mathbf{E}^{(k+l)\prime} = \mathbf{BQ} = \mathbf{PAQ} = \underset{\quad r \qquad n-r}{\begin{bmatrix} \mathbf{I} & \mathbf{O} \\ \mathbf{O} & \mathbf{O} \end{bmatrix}}\begin{matrix} r \\ m-r \end{matrix}$$

$$= \mathbf{N}, \text{ say} \tag{2.3-3}$$

N is called a *canonical form* of **A** with respect to transformation by the product of elementary row operations, represented by **P**, and the product of elementary column operations, represented by **Q**.

Because every elementary matrix has an inverse, **A** can be recovered from **N** by premultiplication and postmultiplication by inverse elementary matrices. Let $\mathbf{P}^{-1} = (\mathbf{E}^{(1)})^{-1}(\mathbf{E}^{(2)})^{-1}\cdots(\mathbf{E}^{(k)})^{-1}$ and $\mathbf{Q}^{-1} = (\mathbf{E}^{(k+l)\prime})^{-1}\cdots(\mathbf{E}^{(k+2)\prime})^{-1}(\mathbf{E}^{(k+1)\prime})^{-1}$. Then

$$\mathbf{A} = \mathbf{P}^{-1}\mathbf{N}\mathbf{Q}^{-1} \tag{2.3-4}$$

Since $\mathbf{P}^{-1}\mathbf{P} = \underset{m\times m}{\mathbf{I}}$ and $\mathbf{Q}^{-1}\mathbf{Q} = \underset{n\times n}{\mathbf{I}}$, both **P** and **Q** are of full rank. Thus, the r nonzero rows of $\mathbf{NQ}^{-1}$ comprise a row basis, from which **A** is obtained by the row operations represented in $\mathbf{P}^{-1}$. Similarly, the r nonzero columns of $\mathbf{P}^{-1}\mathbf{N}$ comprise a column basis, from which **A** is obtained by the column operations represented in $\mathbf{Q}^{-1}$. Thus, the dimensionalities of the row and column spaces of **A** are each equal to r, which is the unique rank of **A**.

Using (2.3-4), we can show that *the rank of the product of two matrices cannot exceed the rank of either factor*. For, consider

$$\mathbf{AB} = \mathbf{P}^{-1}(\mathbf{NQ}^{-1}\mathbf{B})$$

The matrix **N**, and therefore the factor $\mathbf{NQ}^{-1}\mathbf{B}$, has $m - r$ rows with elements identically zero. Hence, the dimensionality of the row space of **AB** cannot exceed r = rank(**A**). By the corresponding argument for columns, the dimensionality of the column space cannot exceed rank(**B**). But as we have seen, these dimensionalities are equal; hence, the rank of **AB** is less than or equal to the minimum of rank(**A**) and rank(**B**).

It should be clear that the rank of a product may be *less* than the rank of either factor, for if

$$\mathbf{A} = \begin{bmatrix} 1 & 0 \\ 0 & 0 \end{bmatrix} \quad \text{and} \quad \mathbf{B} = \begin{bmatrix} 0 & 0 \\ 0 & 1 \end{bmatrix}$$

rank(**A**) = rank(**B**) = 1, but rank(**AB**) = 0. However, if **A**, say, is nonsingular, rank(**AB**) = rank(**B**) because, as we shall see, **A** can be expressed as a product of elementary matrices.

Suppose **A** and **B** are both $m \times n$. If rank(**A**) = r_A and rank(**B**) = r_B, then rank(**A** + **B**) cannot exceed $r_A + r_B$. That is, either the row space of **A** has no basis vectors in common with the row space of **B**, in which case rank(**A** + **B**) = $r_A + r_B$, or the two spaces have $1 \leq r_{A,B} \leq \min(r_A, r_B)$ basis vectors in common, in which case rank(**A** + **B**) = $r_A + r_B - r_{A,B}$.

2.3.3 Practical Computation of Matrix Inverses

Consider an $n \times n$ matrix **A**. If and only if rank(**A**) = n, the following are true and equivalent statements: (1) the canonical form of **A** is the $n \times n$ identity matrix; (2) **A** can be reduced to canonical form using *row* operations only; (3) **A** is nonsingular. First, **A** is reduced to echelon form by $g = n(n - 1)/2$ Type III operations followed by n Type II operations. In terms of elementary matrices,

$$\begin{aligned}
\mathbf{U} &= (\mathbf{E}_{\text{II}}{}^{(n)} \cdots \mathbf{E}_{\text{II}}{}^{(2)}\mathbf{E}_{\text{II}}{}^{(1)})(\mathbf{E}_{\text{III}}{}^{(g)} \cdots \mathbf{E}_{\text{III}}{}^{(2)}\mathbf{E}_{\text{III}}{}^{(1)})\mathbf{A} \\
&= (\mathbf{E}_{\text{II}}{}^{(n)} \cdots \mathbf{E}_{\text{II}}{}^{(2)}\mathbf{E}_{\text{II}}{}^{(1)})\mathbf{L}^{-1}\mathbf{A} \\
&= \mathbf{D}^{-1}\mathbf{L}^{-1}\mathbf{A}
\end{aligned}$$

Provided **A** is $n \times n$ of rank n, the echelon matrix **U** is *unit upper triangular*; that is, **U** is a square matrix in which each element in the main diagonal is unity and all elements below the main diagonal are identically zero. Conversely, rank(**A**) $< n$ implies that at least one diagonal element of **U** is zero and, therefore, that **U** is not unit triangular.

As will be seen in Example 2.3-1, an $n \times n$ unit upper-triangular matrix can always be reduced to the $n \times n$ identity matrix by at most g further row operations. Each of these operations may be performed by the transpose of a Type III elementary matrix. Thus, the second step in reducing **A** to canonical form may be expressed as

$$(\mathbf{E}_{\text{III}}{}^{(2g)\prime} \cdots \mathbf{E}_{\text{III}}{}^{(g+2)\prime}\mathbf{E}_{\text{III}}{}^{(g+1)\prime})\mathbf{U} = \mathbf{U}^{-1}\mathbf{U} = \mathbf{I}$$

Combining steps, we have

$$\mathbf{U}^{-1}(\mathbf{D}^{-1}\mathbf{L}^{-1})\mathbf{A} = (\mathbf{U}^{-1}\mathbf{D}^{-1}\mathbf{L}^{-1})\mathbf{A} = \mathbf{A}^{-1}\mathbf{A} = \mathbf{I}$$

That is, **A** has been reduced to the identity by row operations which are equivalent to premultiplication by the $n \times n$ matrix $\mathbf{A}^{-1}$. Thus, $\mathbf{A}^{-1}$ is the unique inverse of **A**, and **A** is nonsingular. It is clear therefore that all nonsingular matrices can be factored as the product of elementary matrices.

The above method is, in fact, a practical procedure for computing the inverse. The calculations are carried out by adjoining to **A** an $n \times n$ identity matrix. The row operations are carried out on each element in the rows of the resulting $n \times 2n$ matrix $[\mathbf{A} \mid \mathbf{I}]$. **A** is first reduced to echelon form in the so-called "forward" part of the solution. At this point, the $n \times 2n$ matrix has become $[\mathbf{U} \mid \mathbf{D}^{-1}\mathbf{L}^{-1}]$. Then further row operations, called the "back" solution, are carried out in order to reduce **U** to the identity and to obtain the inverse matrix:

$$[\mathbf{I} \mid \mathbf{U}^{-1}\mathbf{D}^{-1}\mathbf{L}^{-1}] = [\mathbf{I} \mid \mathbf{A}^{-1}]$$

Since this procedure for computing the inverse is merely an application of Gauss' method of solving simultaneous linear equations by elimination, it is usually referred to as Gauss' method. Details of the calculations are illustrated in the following example.

EXAMPLE 2.3-1 (*Matrix inversion by Gauss' method*) In this example, we invert the matrix whose columns are given by the set of vectors in Example 2.2-1. This matrix, which we shall denote by $\mathbf{V}_4$, is called a *Vandermonde matrix of order 4.* The row operations are carried out on the matrix $[\mathbf{V}_4 \mid \mathbf{I}]$. However, to provide a check on arithmetic, we have also adjoined a column containing the sums of elements in the rows of $\mathbf{V}_4$ and $\mathbf{I}$ and actually carry out the operations on the matrix.

$$[\mathbf{V}_4 \mid \mathbf{I} \mid \mathbf{Sum}] = \left[\begin{array}{cccc|cccc|c} 1 & 1 & 1 & 1 & 1 & 0 & 0 & 0 & 5 \\ 1 & 2 & 4 & 8 & 0 & 1 & 0 & 0 & 16 \\ 1 & 3 & 9 & 27 & 0 & 0 & 1 & 0 & 41 \\ 1 & 4 & 16 & 64 & 0 & 0 & 0 & 1 & 86 \end{array}\right]$$

STAGE 1

$$\begin{array}{l} \text{Row 2} - \text{row 1} \\ \text{Row 3} - \text{row 1} \\ \text{Row 4} - \text{row 1} \end{array} \quad \left[\begin{array}{cccc|cccc|c} 1 & 1 & 1 & 1 & 1 & 0 & 0 & 0 & 5 \\ 0 & 1 & 3 & 7 & -1 & 1 & 0 & 0 & 11 \\ 0 & 2 & 8 & 26 & -1 & 0 & 1 & 0 & 36 \\ 0 & 3 & 15 & 63 & -1 & 0 & 0 & 1 & 81 \end{array}\right]$$

STAGE 2

$$\begin{array}{l} \text{Row 3} - 2 \times \text{row 2} \\ \text{Row 4} - 3 \times \text{row 2} \end{array} \quad \left[\begin{array}{cccc|cccc|c} 1 & 1 & 1 & 1 & 1 & 0 & 0 & 0 & 5 \\ 0 & 1 & 3 & 7 & -1 & 1 & 0 & 0 & 11 \\ 0 & 0 & 2 & 12 & 1 & -2 & 1 & 0 & 14 \\ 0 & 0 & 6 & 42 & 2 & -3 & 0 & 1 & 48 \end{array}\right]$$

STAGE 3

$$\text{Row 4} - 3 \times \text{row 3} \quad \left[\begin{array}{cccc|cccc|c} 1 & 1 & 1 & 1 & 1 & 0 & 0 & 0 & 5 \\ 0 & 1 & 3 & 7 & -1 & 1 & 0 & 0 & 11 \\ 0 & 0 & 2 & 12 & 1 & -2 & 1 & 0 & 14 \\ 0 & 0 & 0 & 6 & -1 & 3 & -3 & 1 & 6 \end{array}\right]$$

STAGE 4

$$\begin{array}{l} \tfrac{1}{2} \text{ row 3} \\ \tfrac{1}{6} \text{ row 4} \end{array} \quad \left[\begin{array}{cccc|cccc|c} 1 & 1 & 1 & 1 & 1 & 0 & 0 & 0 & 5 \\ 0 & 1 & 3 & 7 & -1 & 1 & 0 & 0 & 11 \\ 0 & 0 & 1 & 6 & \tfrac{1}{2} & -1 & \tfrac{1}{2} & 0 & 7 \\ 0 & 0 & 0 & 1 & -\tfrac{1}{6} & \tfrac{1}{2} & -\tfrac{1}{2} & \tfrac{1}{6} & 1 \end{array}\right]$$

The "forward" solution is complete and the "back" solution begins:

STAGE 5

Row 3 − 6 × row 4
Row 2 − 7 × row 4
Row 1 − row 4

$$\left[\begin{array}{cccc|cccc|c} 1 & 1 & 1 & 0 & \frac{7}{6} & -\frac{1}{2} & \frac{1}{2} & -\frac{1}{6} & 4 \\ 0 & 1 & 3 & 0 & \frac{1}{6} & -\frac{5}{2} & \frac{7}{2} & -\frac{7}{6} & 4 \\ 0 & 0 & 1 & 0 & \frac{3}{2} & -4 & \frac{7}{2} & -1 & 1 \\ 0 & 0 & 0 & 1 & -\frac{1}{6} & \frac{1}{2} & -\frac{1}{2} & \frac{1}{6} & 1 \end{array}\right]$$

STAGE 6

Row 2 − 3 × row 3
Row 1 − row 3

$$\left[\begin{array}{cccc|cccc|c} 1 & 1 & 0 & 0 & -\frac{1}{3} & \frac{7}{2} & -3 & \frac{5}{6} & 3 \\ 0 & 1 & 0 & 0 & -\frac{13}{3} & \frac{19}{2} & -7 & \frac{11}{6} & 1 \\ 0 & 0 & 1 & 0 & \frac{3}{2} & -4 & \frac{7}{2} & -1 & 1 \\ 0 & 0 & 0 & 1 & -\frac{1}{6} & \frac{1}{2} & -\frac{1}{2} & \frac{1}{6} & 1 \end{array}\right]$$

STAGE 7

Row 1 − row 2

$$[\mathbf{I} \mid \mathbf{V}_4^{-1} \mid \mathbf{Sum}] = \left[\begin{array}{cccc|cccc|c} 1 & 0 & 0 & 0 & 4 & -6 & 4 & -1 & 2 \\ 0 & 1 & 0 & 0 & -\frac{13}{3} & \frac{19}{2} & -7 & \frac{11}{6} & 1 \\ 0 & 0 & 1 & 0 & \frac{3}{2} & -4 & \frac{7}{2} & -1 & 1 \\ 0 & 0 & 0 & 1 & -\frac{1}{6} & \frac{1}{2} & -\frac{1}{2} & \frac{1}{6} & 1 \end{array}\right]$$

The inversion is complete.

Gauss' method is well suited to hand calculation, although, in larger problems it is usually necessary to employ a desk calculator and to resort to decimal approximations of the rational numbers. The agreement of the row sums and the check-sum column indicates the extent of rounding error as the calculations proceed.

Matrix-inversion routines for electronic computers usually make use of the more compact version of Gauss' method called the *Gauss-Jordan* method [Householder, 1953, 1964]. The calculations are recursive, elements of the matrix at stage $i + 1$ being replaced by the result of a so-called *pivoting* operation on elements at stage i:

$$a_{kl}^{(i+1)} = a_{kl}^{(i)} - \frac{a_{kj}^{(i)} a_{jl}^{(i)}}{a_{jj}^{(i)}} \qquad k \neq l \neq j$$

$$a_{jl}^{(i+1)} = \frac{a_{jl}^{(i)}}{a_{jj}^{(i)}} \qquad l \neq j$$

$$a_{kj}^{(i+1)} = -\frac{a_{kj}^{(i)}}{a_{jj}^{(i)}} \qquad k \neq j$$

$$a_{jj}^{(i+1)} = \frac{1}{a_{jj}^{(i)}}$$

The element $a_{jj}^{(i)}$ is called the *pivot*, and its row and column are called the *pivotal row* and *pivotal column*. After n pivoting operations, the original matrix is replaced by its inverse, provided that each row and column is pivoted only once. (See Sec. 4.1.10b for a statistical application of pivoting.)

When decimal approximations for rational numbers are used in the computations, some increase in accuracy may be obtained by choosing the largest absolute element in the matrix at each stage as the pivot, and by rearranging columns to bring this element to the main diagonal. When the inversion is complete, the columns may be returned to their original order. If rearranging rows and columns is not convenient, a good compromise is to pivot on the largest *diagonal* element at each stage [Noble, 1969].

EXAMPLE 2.3-2 (*Matrix inversion by the Gauss-Jordan method*) Let us illustrate the Gauss-Jordan method by again inverting the order-4 Vandermonde matrix

$$\mathbf{V}_4^{(0)} = \left[\begin{array}{ccc|c} 1 & 1 & 1 & 1 \\ 1 & 2 & 4 & 8 \\ 1 & 3 & 9 & 27 \\ \hline 1 & 4 & 16 & 64 \end{array}\right]$$

STAGE 1 Choosing 64 as the pivot, we have, after the first pivoting operation,

$$\mathbf{V}_4^{(1)} = \left[\begin{array}{cc|c|c} \frac{63}{64} & \frac{15}{16} & \frac{3}{4} & -\frac{1}{64} \\ \frac{7}{8} & \frac{3}{2} & 2 & -\frac{1}{8} \\ \hline \frac{37}{64} & \frac{21}{16} & \frac{9}{4} & -\frac{27}{64} \\ \hline \frac{1}{64} & \frac{1}{16} & \frac{1}{4} & \frac{1}{64} \end{array}\right]$$

STAGE 2 The largest element and next pivot is $\frac{9}{4}$:

$$\mathbf{V}_4^{(2)} = \left[\begin{array}{c|ccc} \frac{19}{24} & \frac{1}{2} & -\frac{1}{3} & \frac{1}{8} \\ \hline \frac{13}{36} & \frac{1}{3} & -\frac{8}{9} & \frac{1}{4} \\ \frac{37}{144} & \frac{7}{12} & \frac{4}{9} & -\frac{3}{16} \\ -\frac{7}{144} & -\frac{1}{12} & -\frac{1}{9} & \frac{1}{16} \end{array}\right]$$

STAGE 3 Now the largest element in a row and column not already pivoted is $\frac{19}{24}$, and that is the next pivot:

$$\mathbf{V}_4^{(3)} = \left[\begin{array}{c|c|cc} \frac{24}{19} & \frac{12}{19} & -\frac{8}{19} & \frac{3}{19} \\ \hline -\frac{26}{57} & \frac{2}{19} & -\frac{14}{19} & \frac{11}{57} \\ \hline -\frac{37}{114} & \frac{8}{19} & \frac{21}{38} & -\frac{13}{57} \\ \frac{7}{114} & -\frac{1}{19} & -\frac{5}{38} & \frac{4}{57} \end{array}\right]$$

STAGE 4 Now $\frac{2}{19}$ is chosen as the last pivot, since it is the element from the only row and the only column not yet pivoted:

$$\mathbf{V}_4^{(4)} = \mathbf{V}_4^{-1} = \begin{bmatrix} 4 & -6 & 4 & -1 \\ -\frac{13}{3} & \frac{19}{2} & -7 & \frac{11}{6} \\ \frac{3}{2} & -4 & \frac{7}{2} & -1 \\ -\frac{1}{6} & \frac{1}{2} & -\frac{1}{2} & \frac{1}{6} \end{bmatrix}$$

2.3.4 Solution of Systems of Linear Equations

In matrix notation, a system of n nonhomogeneous linear equations in n unknowns,

$$\begin{aligned} a_{11}x_1 + a_{12}x_2 + \cdots + a_{1n}x_n &= k_1 \\ a_{21}x_1 + a_{22}x_2 + \cdots + a_{2n}x_n &= k_2 \\ \cdots\cdots\cdots\cdots\cdots\cdots\cdots\cdots \\ a_{n1}x_1 + a_{n2}x_2 + \cdots + a_{nn}x_n &= k_n \end{aligned}$$

may be expressed as

$$\begin{bmatrix} a_{11} & a_{12} & \cdots & a_{1n} \\ a_{21} & a_{22} & \cdots & a_{2n} \\ \cdots & \cdots & \cdots & \cdots \\ a_{n1} & a_{n2} & \cdots & a_{nn} \end{bmatrix} \cdot \begin{bmatrix} x_1 \\ x_2 \\ \cdots \\ x_n \end{bmatrix} = \begin{bmatrix} k_1 \\ k_2 \\ \cdots \\ k_n \end{bmatrix}$$

or

$$\mathbf{Ax} = \mathbf{k} \qquad (2.3\text{-}5)$$

If $\mathbf{A}$ is nonsingular [i.e., if rank($\mathbf{A}$) $= n$], this system of equations has a unique solution in terms of $\mathbf{A}^{-1}$, for

$$\mathbf{A}^{-1}\mathbf{Ax} = \mathbf{Ix} = \mathbf{x} = \mathbf{A}^{-1}\mathbf{k}$$

Thus, rank($\mathbf{A}$) $= n$ is a sufficient condition for the solvability of (2.3-5). This condition is not necessary, however. When the rank of $\mathbf{A}$ is less than n (that is, $\mathbf{A}$ is not of full rank), the system has a solution if the so-called *consistency condition* is met. A system such as (2.3-5), consisting of n nonhomogeneous equations in n unknowns, meets the consistency condition if and only if

$$\text{rank}[\mathbf{A} \mid \mathbf{k}] = \text{rank}[\mathbf{A}] = r \le n \qquad (2.3\text{-}6)$$

That is, the system is consistent if and only if $\mathbf{k}$ is subject to the same linear dependencies as the rows of $\mathbf{A}$. The vector $\mathbf{k}$ is then in the space of $\mathbf{A}$ and does not increase the dimensionality of that space when adjoined to $\mathbf{A}$.

To show that a solution of (2.3-5) exists when (2.3-6) holds, we observe that, if the r linearly independent rows of $\mathbf{A}$ and $\mathbf{k}$ are permuted to leading position, we may express (2.3-5) in the partitioned form

$$\begin{matrix} r \\ n-r \end{matrix} \begin{bmatrix} \mathbf{A}_{11} & \mathbf{A}_{12} \\ \mathbf{A}_{21} & \mathbf{A}_{22} \end{bmatrix} \cdot \begin{bmatrix} \mathbf{x}_1 \\ \mathbf{x}_2 \end{bmatrix} = \begin{bmatrix} \mathbf{k}_1 \\ \mathbf{k}_2 \end{bmatrix}$$
$$\qquad r \quad n-r$$

in which the $r \times r$ submatrix $\mathbf{A}_{11}$ is *nonsingular*. Then, if and only if (2.3-6) holds, there is an $n \times n$ matrix

$$\mathbf{C} = \begin{matrix} r \\ n-r \end{matrix}\begin{bmatrix} \mathbf{C}_{11} & \mathbf{C}_{12} \\ \mathbf{C}_{21} & \mathbf{C}_{22} \end{bmatrix}$$
$$\qquad\qquad r \qquad n-r$$

which reduces the system to the echelon form

$$\begin{bmatrix} \mathbf{C}_{11} & \mathbf{C}_{12} \\ \mathbf{C}_{21} & \mathbf{C}_{22} \end{bmatrix} \cdot \begin{bmatrix} \mathbf{A}_{11} & \mathbf{A}_{12} \\ \mathbf{A}_{21} & \mathbf{A}_{22} \end{bmatrix} \cdot \begin{bmatrix} \mathbf{x}_1 \\ \mathbf{x}_2 \end{bmatrix} = \begin{bmatrix} \mathbf{C}_{11} & \mathbf{C}_{12} \\ \mathbf{C}_{21} & \mathbf{C}_{22} \end{bmatrix} \cdot \begin{bmatrix} \mathbf{k}_1 \\ \mathbf{k}_2 \end{bmatrix}$$

or

$$\begin{bmatrix} \mathbf{I} & \mathbf{C}_{11}\mathbf{A}_{12} + \mathbf{C}_{12}\mathbf{A}_{22} \\ \mathbf{O} & \mathbf{O} \end{bmatrix} \cdot \begin{bmatrix} \mathbf{x}_1 \\ \mathbf{x}_2 \end{bmatrix} = \begin{bmatrix} \mathbf{C}_{11}\mathbf{k}_1 + \mathbf{C}_{12}\mathbf{k}_2 \\ \mathbf{0} \end{bmatrix} \qquad (2.3\text{-}7)$$

That is, the matrix $\mathbf{C}$ incorporates the row operations which set the last $n - r$ rows of $[\mathbf{A} \mid \mathbf{k}]$ to zero. In fact, a unique $\mathbf{C}$ exists:

$$\mathbf{C} = \begin{bmatrix} \mathbf{A}_{11}^{-1} & \mathbf{O} \\ -\mathbf{A}_{21}\mathbf{A}_{11}^{-1} & \mathbf{I} \end{bmatrix}$$

Transposing in (2.3-7), we obtain

$$\mathbf{x}_1 = \mathbf{A}_{11}^{-1}\mathbf{k}_1 - \mathbf{A}_{11}^{-1}\mathbf{A}_{12}\mathbf{x}_2 \qquad (2.3\text{-}8)$$

Thus, if (2.3-5) is consistent, it has a solution in the sense that any values arbitrarily assigned to the elements of $\mathbf{x}_2$ uniquely determine $\mathbf{x}_1$. Because $\mathbf{x}_2$ is arbitrary, however, there is an infinity of solutions, each corresponding to a point in the $(n - r)$-dimensional space of $\mathbf{x}_2$. This space is called the *solution* space of the system.

When $n - r = 1$, the solution space is the real line, and we say that $\mathbf{x}_2$ is determined except for *location*. This kind of indeterminacy is familiar in situations where it is necessary to fix the origin of a measurement scale arbitrarily. For example, geographical elevation is measured relative to mean sea level as the arbitrary zero point.

If $n - r = 2$, the solution space is the real plane, and we say that $\mathbf{x}_1$ is determined except for *location* and *scale*. In this case, we must set two points arbitrarily in order to define a measurement scale. A familiar example is the definition of the Celsius scale of temperature by setting the freezing and boiling points of water to 0° and 100°, respectively.

The availability of practical methods for solving systems of equations not of full rank is essential in data analysis. The statistical estimation theory for commonly used experimental-design models leads to equations of this type (see Chap. 5). In these applications, the solution given by (2.3-8) is perfectly straightforward, but it is not convenient computationally because locating the r linearly independent rows of $\mathbf{A}$ and permuting them to leading position is not easily implemented in a computer program. Other methods of solving the systems of equations in statistical estimation have therefore been proposed and implemented in computer programs. We present here the mathematical background for three of these methods. The first method is conceptually more parsimonious than the other two and leads to more efficient computer programs. We therefore use it in preference to the others in the sequel. But all three methods appear frequently in the statistical literature, and the reader should be familiar with each.

a Reparameterization Consider the solution of a system of equations

$$\underset{m\times n}{\mathbf{B}}\ \underset{n\times 1}{\mathbf{x}} = \underset{m\times 1}{\mathbf{k}} \tag{2.3-9}$$

when the consistency condition

$$\text{rank}[\mathbf{B} \mid \mathbf{k}] = \text{rank}[\mathbf{B}] = r \leq m \leq n$$

is satisfied. Note that we are now allowing the possibility that there are fewer equations than unknowns ($m < n$) and that not all these equations are independent ($r < m$).

Our approach to the solution of (2.3-9) is to introduce a change of unknowns by defining r linear functions of $\mathbf{x}$, namely,

$$\underset{r\times 1}{\mathbf{y}} = \underset{r\times n}{\mathbf{C}}\mathbf{x} \tag{2.3-10}$$

In the context of statistical models, this change of unknowns is called *reparameterization*, and the functions (2.3-10) are called *linear parametric functions* (see Sec. 5.2.2).

We now show that the system (2.3-10) may be solved for $\mathbf{y}$ if and only if the $r \times n$ matrix $\mathbf{C}$ satisfies the following condition:

$$\text{rank}\begin{bmatrix}\mathbf{B}\\ \mathbf{C}\end{bmatrix} = \text{rank}[\mathbf{B}] = \text{rank}[\mathbf{C}] = r \tag{2.3-11}$$

That is, the rows of $\mathbf{C}$ are linearly dependent on (in the space of) the rows of $\mathbf{B}$. If and only if condition (2.3-11) is met, the $m \times n$ matrix $\mathbf{B}$ is factorable into the product of the $r \times n$ matrix $\mathbf{C}$ and a unique $m \times r$ matrix which we denote here by $\mathbf{E}$. That is,

$$\underset{m\times n}{\mathbf{B}} = \underset{m\times r}{\mathbf{E}}\ \underset{r\times n}{\mathbf{C}} \tag{2.3-12}$$

For if $\mathbf{C}$ is in the row space of $\mathbf{B}$, it can serve as a basis from which $\mathbf{B}$ may be constructed by linear operations. In fact, the columns of $\mathbf{E}$ contain the coefficients of the linear functions generating $\mathbf{B}$ from $\mathbf{C}$. Given any $\mathbf{C}$, the corresponding $\mathbf{E}$ may be obtained by

$$\mathbf{E} = \mathbf{EI} = \mathbf{ECC}'(\mathbf{CC}')^{-1} = \mathbf{BC}'(\mathbf{CC}')^{-1} \tag{2.3-13}$$

It should be clear that the $r \times r$ symmetric matrix $\mathbf{CC}'$ is nonsingular, for if its rank were less than r, there would exist some linear combination of rows of $\mathbf{CC}'$, say

$\mathbf{a}'\mathbf{CC}'$, equal to the null vector. This would imply

$$\mathbf{a}'\mathbf{CC}'\mathbf{a} = \mathbf{b}'\mathbf{b} = \sum_{i=1}^{n} b_i^2 = 0$$

But since $\mathbf{b}'\mathbf{b}$ is a sum of squares, it can be zero only if $\mathbf{b} = \mathbf{Ca} = \mathbf{0}$, which is contrary to the assumption that rank($\mathbf{C}$) $= r$.

Thus, $\mathbf{CC}'$ is nonsingular, and a unique factor $\mathbf{E}$ may be calculated by (2.3-13). [And, conversely, if $\mathbf{E}$ is of rank r and is in the column space of $\mathbf{B}$, then $\mathbf{C} = (\mathbf{E}'\mathbf{E})^{-1}\mathbf{E}'\mathbf{B}$.] This means that we can solve for the functions (2.3-10) subject to (2.3-11) as follows:

$$\mathbf{Bx} = \mathbf{ECx} = \mathbf{Ey} = \mathbf{k}$$

$$(\mathbf{E}'\mathbf{E})^{-1}\mathbf{E}'\mathbf{Ey} = \mathbf{Iy} = \mathbf{y} = (\mathbf{E}'\mathbf{E})^{-1}\mathbf{E}'\mathbf{k} \qquad (2.3\text{-}14)$$

This solution has the merit of requiring only a conventional inverse, the order of which is $r \times r$ rather than $n \times n$. Because the number of arithmetic operations required in matrix inversion is proportional to the third power of the matrix order, this reduction in order leads to substantial economies in calculation when n is appreciably larger than r, a condition which is frequently true of statistical models.

In applied work, the rows of $\mathbf{C}$ are chosen so that the new variables $\mathbf{y}$ have some practical interpretation. The following example illustrates a case in which a solution is obtained for *differences* between variables. Since differences serve to *compare* the magnitudes of variables, they may have useful interpretations even though the magnitudes of the separate variables cannot be estimated.

EXAMPLE 2.3-2 (*Solving a system of equations by reparameterization*) Let us solve the system of equations $\mathbf{Bx} = \mathbf{k}$, where

$$\mathbf{B} = \begin{bmatrix} 1 & 1 & 0 & 0 \\ 1 & 0 & 1 & 0 \\ 1 & 0 & 0 & 1 \end{bmatrix} \qquad \mathbf{x} = \begin{bmatrix} x_1 \\ x_2 \\ x_3 \\ x_4 \end{bmatrix} \qquad \mathbf{k} = \begin{bmatrix} 3 \\ 9 \\ 12 \end{bmatrix}$$

The system is of deficient rank because the number of unknowns exceeds the number of equations. By reducing the augmented matrix of coefficients to echelon form, we verify that the system is of rank 3. Thus we may solve for three independent functions of the unknowns; e.g.,

$$\mathbf{y} = \begin{bmatrix} y_1 \\ y_2 \\ y_3 \end{bmatrix} = \begin{bmatrix} 1 & \frac{1}{3} & \frac{1}{3} & \frac{1}{3} \\ 0 & 1 & 0 & -1 \\ 0 & 0 & 1 & -1 \end{bmatrix} \cdot \begin{bmatrix} x_1 \\ x_2 \\ x_3 \\ x_4 \end{bmatrix} = \mathbf{Cx}$$

First we must check that the rows of **C** are linearly dependent on the rows of **B**. This is obviously the case, for row 1 in **C** is the sum of $\frac{1}{3}$ times each row of **B**; row 2 is row 1 − row 2 of **B**, and row 3 is row 1 − row 3 of **B**. Then,

$$\mathbf{CC}' = \begin{bmatrix} \frac{4}{3} & 0 & 0 \\ 0 & 2 & 1 \\ 0 & 1 & 2 \end{bmatrix} \qquad (\mathbf{CC}')^{-1} = \begin{bmatrix} \frac{3}{4} & 0 & 0 \\ 0 & \frac{2}{3} & -\frac{1}{3} \\ 0 & -\frac{1}{3} & \frac{2}{3} \end{bmatrix}$$

$$\mathbf{BC}' = \begin{bmatrix} \frac{4}{3} & 1 & 0 \\ \frac{4}{3} & 0 & 1 \\ \frac{4}{3} & -1 & -1 \end{bmatrix} \qquad \mathbf{E} = \mathbf{BC}'(\mathbf{CC}')^{-1} = \begin{bmatrix} 1 & \frac{2}{3} & -\frac{1}{3} \\ 1 & -\frac{1}{3} & \frac{2}{3} \\ 1 & -\frac{1}{3} & -\frac{1}{3} \end{bmatrix}$$

$$(\mathbf{E}'\mathbf{E}) = \begin{bmatrix} 3 & 0 & 0 \\ 0 & \frac{2}{3} & -\frac{1}{3} \\ 0 & -\frac{1}{3} & \frac{2}{3} \end{bmatrix} \qquad (\mathbf{E}'\mathbf{E})^{-1} = \begin{bmatrix} \frac{1}{3} & 0 & 0 \\ 0 & 2 & 1 \\ 0 & 1 & 2 \end{bmatrix}$$

$$\mathbf{E}'\mathbf{k} = \begin{bmatrix} 24 \\ -5 \\ 1 \end{bmatrix}$$

and the solution is

$$\mathbf{y} = (\mathbf{E}'\mathbf{E})^{-1}\mathbf{E}'\mathbf{k} = \begin{bmatrix} 8 \\ -9 \\ -3 \end{bmatrix}$$

b Restrictions on the unknowns Another approach to solving the system (2.3-9) is frequently seen in connection with simple models for experimental designs. This approach depends upon *restricting the unknowns.* The restrictions take the form of a sufficient number of independent linear equations to bring the system to full rank. These equations may be arbitrarily selected, provided only that they are *not* linearly dependent on the equations already in the system. For example, suppose the consistent system (2.3-9) is to be solved subject to the restriction that the vector of unknowns satisfies the $n - r$ additional equations

$$\underset{(n-r)\times n}{\mathbf{W}} \mathbf{x} = \mathbf{h} \tag{2.3-15}$$

Then, if and only if

$$\text{rank}\begin{bmatrix} \mathbf{B} \\ \mathbf{W} \end{bmatrix} = n \tag{2.3-16}$$

the equations

$$\begin{bmatrix} \mathbf{B} \\ \mathbf{W} \end{bmatrix} \mathbf{x} = \begin{bmatrix} \mathbf{k} \\ \mathbf{h} \end{bmatrix} \tag{2.3-17}$$

are consistent and have a solution which may be obtained by solving any n linearly independent equations selected from the augmented system. This approach is especially convenient in situations such as in the following example, where **W** can be chosen so that the augmented system is easy to solve.

EXAMPLE 2.3-3 (*Solving a system of equations by restricting the unknowns*) In the analysis of a simple 2 × 3 factorial design, a solution is required for a system of equations of the form **Bx** = **k**, namely,

$$\begin{bmatrix} 6 & 3 & 3 & 2 & 2 & 2 \\ 3 & 3 & 0 & 1 & 1 & 1 \\ 3 & 0 & 3 & 1 & 1 & 1 \\ 2 & 1 & 1 & 2 & 0 & 0 \\ 2 & 1 & 1 & 0 & 2 & 0 \\ 2 & 1 & 1 & 0 & 0 & 2 \end{bmatrix} \cdot \begin{bmatrix} m \\ a_1 \\ a_2 \\ b_1 \\ b_2 \\ b_3 \end{bmatrix} = \begin{bmatrix} \sum\sum y_{jk} \\ \sum y_{1k} \\ \sum y_{2k} \\ \sum y_{j1} \\ \sum y_{j2} \\ \sum y_{j3} \end{bmatrix} \tag{2.3-18}$$

It is easily verified that this set is a consistent system with rank equal to 4. Thus, two restrictions on the unknowns are required. A convenient choice which satisfies (2.3-16) is

$$a_1 + a_2 = 0$$

$$b_1 + b_2 + b_3 = 0$$

Then,

$$\mathbf{W} = \begin{bmatrix} 0 & 1 & 1 & 0 & 0 & 0 \\ 0 & 0 & 0 & 1 & 1 & 1 \end{bmatrix}$$

and

$$\mathbf{h} = \begin{bmatrix} 0 \\ 0 \end{bmatrix}$$

With this choice of **W** and **h**, the system is easily simplified by row operations. By subtracting suitable multiples of the rows of **W** from the rows of **B**, we obtain the transformed matrix of coefficients

$$\begin{bmatrix} 6 & 0 & 0 & 0 & 0 & 0 \\ 3 & 3 & 0 & 0 & 0 & 0 \\ 3 & 0 & 3 & 0 & 0 & 0 \\ 2 & 0 & 0 & 2 & 0 & 0 \\ 2 & 0 & 0 & 0 & 2 & 0 \\ 2 & 0 & 0 & 0 & 0 & 2 \\ 0 & 1 & 1 & 0 & 0 & 0 \\ 0 & 0 & 0 & 1 & 1 & 1 \end{bmatrix}$$

while the terms on the right-hand side of the equations are unchanged. Then, eliminating the coefficients remaining below the diagonal in the transformed matrix, we obtain the solution

$$\begin{bmatrix} 1 & 0 & 0 & 0 & 0 & 0 \\ 0 & 1 & 0 & 0 & 0 & 0 \\ 0 & 0 & 1 & 0 & 0 & 0 \\ 0 & 0 & 0 & 1 & 0 & 0 \\ 0 & 0 & 0 & 0 & 1 & 0 \\ 0 & 0 & 0 & 0 & 0 & 1 \end{bmatrix} \begin{bmatrix} m \\ a_1 \\ a_2 \\ b_1 \\ b_2 \\ b_3 \end{bmatrix} = \begin{bmatrix} m \\ a_1 \\ a_2 \\ b_1 \\ b_2 \\ b_3 \end{bmatrix} = \begin{bmatrix} y_{\cdot\cdot} \\ y_{1\cdot} - y_{\cdot\cdot} \\ y_{2\cdot} - y_{\cdot\cdot} \\ y_{\cdot 1} - y_{\cdot\cdot} \\ y_{\cdot 2} - y_{\cdot\cdot} \\ y_{\cdot 3} - y_{\cdot\cdot} \end{bmatrix}$$

where $y_{..} = \sum\sum y_{jk}/6$

$$y_{j\cdot} = \sum_k y_{jk}/3$$

$$y_{\cdot k} = \sum_j y_{jk}/2$$

c A generalized inverse A third approach to the solution of any consistent system of linear equations makes use of the so-called *generalized inverse* matrix. To prepare for its definition, we introduce the *gaussian* factorization of real matrices.

Consider first an $n \times n$ nonsingular matrix $\mathbf{A}$. We have seen in Sec. 2.3.2 that $\mathbf{A}$ may be reduced to echelon form by premultiplication with Type II and Type III elementary matrices. The result of these operations was expressed as

$$\mathbf{D}^{-1}\mathbf{L}^{-1}\mathbf{A} = \mathbf{U} \qquad (2.3\text{-}19)$$

where $\mathbf{U}$ is unit upper triangular. Premultiplying (2.3-19) by the diagonal nonsingular matrix $\mathbf{D}$, we have

$$\mathbf{L}^{-1}\mathbf{A} = \mathbf{DU}$$

The matrix $\mathbf{DU}$ is upper triangular also, but not *unit* upper triangular; its diagonal elements are the same as those of $\mathbf{D}$. The matrix $\mathbf{L}^{-1}$, on the other hand, is *unit lower triangular.* This is true because Type III elementary matrices are unit lower triangular and, as we can readily verify, the product of unit lower-triangular matrices is unit lower triangular (and that of unit upper-triangular matrices is upper triangular). Furthermore, we have already seen that the inverse of a Type III elementary matrix is also unit lower triangular (Sec. 2.3.2); hence,

$$(\mathbf{L}^{-1})^{-1} = [(\mathbf{E}_{\text{III}}^{(1)})^{-1} \cdots (\mathbf{E}_{\text{III}}^{(g-1)})^{-1}(\mathbf{E}_{\text{III}}^{(g)})^{-1}]^{-1} \qquad (2.3\text{-}20)$$

is unit lower triangular, and

$$\mathbf{A} = \mathbf{LDU} \qquad (2.3\text{-}21)$$

That is, *every real nonsingular matrix may be expressed as a unique triple product of a unit lower-triangular matrix, a real diagonal matrix, and a unit upper-triangular matrix.* Since $\text{rank}(\mathbf{A}) = n$, the rank of each factor must be n, which means, in particular, that all diagonal elements of $\mathbf{D}$ are nonzero. The product (2.3-21) is called the *gaussian factorization* of $\mathbf{A}$.

Uniqueness may be proved as follows (after Roy [1957], page 148): Suppose there are two gaussian factorizations $\mathbf{A} = \mathbf{L}_1\mathbf{D}_1\mathbf{U}_1 = \mathbf{L}_2\mathbf{D}_2\mathbf{U}_2$. Then

$$\mathbf{L}_2^{-1}\mathbf{L}_1\mathbf{D}_1 = \mathbf{D}_2\mathbf{U}_2\mathbf{U}_1^{-1}$$

But $\mathbf{L}_2^{-1}\mathbf{L}_1$ and $\mathbf{U}_2\mathbf{U}_1^{-1}$ are unit-triangular matrices of opposite configuration; hence, both members of (2.3-21) are diagonal, and $\mathbf{D}_1 = \mathbf{D}_2 = \mathbf{D}$. Then

$$\mathbf{L}_2^{-1}\mathbf{L}_1 = \mathbf{U}_2\mathbf{U}_1^{-1} = \mathbf{I}$$

or

$$\mathbf{L}_2 = \mathbf{L}_1 = \mathbf{L} \quad \text{and} \quad \mathbf{U}_2 = \mathbf{U}_1 = \mathbf{U}$$

This type of factorization can readily be extended to singular matrices. Suppose $\mathbf{B}$ is an $m \times n$ matrix of rank $r < \min(m,n)$. As in Example 2.3-1, the rows of $\mathbf{B}$ can be reduced to those of an echelon form $\mathbf{G}$, say, by premultiplication by $m \times m$ Type III elementary matrices, the continued product of which is $\mathbf{L}^{-1}$:

$$\underset{m\times m}{\mathbf{L}^{-1}}\ \underset{m\times n}{\mathbf{B}} = \underset{m\times n}{\mathbf{G}}$$

Since rank($\mathbf{B}$) $= r$, certain $n - r$ rows of $\mathbf{G}$ are zero, although not necessarily the last $n - r$ rows. Postmultiplication by $n \times n$ transposed Type III elementary matrices, the continued product of which is $\mathbf{U}^{-1}$, then reduces $\mathbf{G}$ to

$$\underset{m\times n}{\mathbf{D}^*} = \underset{m\times n}{\mathbf{G}}\ \underset{n\times n}{\mathbf{U}^{-1}} = \mathbf{L}^{-1}\mathbf{B}\mathbf{U}^{-1} \tag{2.3-22}$$

where $\mathbf{D}^*$ is a matrix of rank r in which (1) exactly $mn - r$ elements are identically zero; (2) exactly r elements are nonzero; and (3) no row or column contains more than one nonzero element.

As in (2.3-20), both $\mathbf{L}^{-1}$ and $\mathbf{U}^{-1}$ have inverses; hence,

$$\underset{m\times n}{\mathbf{B}} = \underset{m\times m}{\mathbf{L}}\ \underset{m\times n}{\mathbf{D}^*}\ \underset{n\times n}{\mathbf{U}} \tag{2.3-23}$$

That is, every real $m \times n$ matrix of rank r may be expressed as the triple product of an $m \times m$ unit lower-triangular matrix, an $m \times n$ matrix of rank r with exactly r nonzero elements, no two in the same row or column, and a unit upper-triangular matrix. Equation (2.3-23) is the gaussian factorization for a general rectangular matrix. Unlike the gaussian factorization of a nonsingular matrix, this factorization is not unique, because equations of the type

$$\mathbf{L}_1^{-1}\mathbf{L}_2 = \mathbf{D}^* \quad \text{or} \quad \mathbf{U}_2\mathbf{U}_1^{-1} = (\mathbf{D}^*)'$$

do not have unique solutions for $\mathbf{L}_2$ and $\mathbf{U}_2$.

Using (2.3-23), we may define a *generalized inverse* of $\mathbf{B}$ as follows: Let $\mathbf{D}^{-*}$ be an $n \times m$ matrix consisting of the transpose of $\mathbf{D}^*$ with each of the r nonzero elements replaced by its reciprocal. Then the matrix

$$\underset{n\times m}{\mathbf{B}^-} = \mathbf{U}^{-1}\mathbf{D}^{-*}\mathbf{L}^{-1}$$

has the property

$$\underset{m\times n}{\mathbf{B}}\ \underset{n\times m}{\mathbf{B}^-}\ \underset{m\times n}{\mathbf{B}} = \mathbf{LD^*UU^{-1}D^{-*}L^{-1}LD^*U}$$

$$= \mathbf{LD^*D^{-*}D^*U} = \mathbf{LD^*U}$$

$$= \mathbf{B} \tag{2.3-24}$$

This property enables us to express a solution of the system

$$\mathbf{Bx} = \mathbf{k}$$

if and only if the consistency condition

$$\text{rank}[\mathbf{B} \mid \mathbf{k}] = \text{rank}[\mathbf{B}] = r \leq m \leq n \tag{2.3-25}$$

is met. For if the system is consistent, we know that it has at least one solution, say $\mathbf{x}_1$. Then, if $\mathbf{B}^-$ is a generalized inverse of $\mathbf{B}$, $\mathbf{x}_0 = \mathbf{B}^-\mathbf{k}$ satisfies (2.3-9) and is a solution. For if $\mathbf{BB}^-\mathbf{B} = \mathbf{B}$, then

$$\mathbf{Bx}_0 = \mathbf{B}(\mathbf{B}^-\mathbf{k}) = \mathbf{BB}^-\mathbf{Bx}_1 = \mathbf{Bx}_1 = \mathbf{k}$$

Conversely, if $\mathbf{l}$ is any $n \times 1$ vector, the system $\mathbf{Bx} = \mathbf{Bl}$ is consistent, and therefore all vectors of the form $\mathbf{Bl}$ are solutions.

If $\mathbf{x}_0 = \mathbf{B}^-\mathbf{k}$ is a solution of (2.3-9), then

$$\mathbf{Bx}_0 = \mathbf{BB}^-\mathbf{k} = \mathbf{BB}^-\mathbf{Bl} = \mathbf{Bl} = \mathbf{k}$$

But $\mathbf{BB}^-\mathbf{Bl} = \mathbf{Bl}$ can hold for all $\mathbf{l}$ only if $\mathbf{BB}^-\mathbf{B} = \mathbf{B}$; that is, only if $\mathbf{B}^-$ is a generalized inverse. Hence, the converse is proved.

It is clear that $\mathbf{x}_0$ is not unique, for if $\mathbf{Bx}_0 = \mathbf{k}$, then so does

$$\mathbf{B}[\mathbf{x}_0 + \mathbf{z}] = \mathbf{B}[\mathbf{x}_0 + (\underset{n\times n}{\mathbf{I}} - \underset{n\times m}{\mathbf{B}^-}\ \underset{n\times n}{\mathbf{B}})\mathbf{u}] = \mathbf{Bx}_0 + (\mathbf{B} - \mathbf{BB}^-\mathbf{B})\mathbf{u}$$

$$= \mathbf{Bx}_0 + (\mathbf{B} - \mathbf{B})\mathbf{u} = \mathbf{Bx}_0 = \mathbf{k}$$

for any choice of $\mathbf{u}$. Note that, because

$$\mathbf{I} - \mathbf{B}^-\mathbf{B} = \mathbf{I} - (\mathbf{U}^{-1}\mathbf{D}^{-*}\mathbf{L}^{-1})(\mathbf{LD^*U})$$

$$= \mathbf{I} - \mathbf{U}^{-1}\mathbf{D}^{-*}\mathbf{D}^*\mathbf{U}$$

we have

$$\mathbf{U}(\mathbf{I} - \mathbf{B}^-\mathbf{B})\mathbf{U}^{-1} = \mathbf{UU}^{-1} - \mathbf{D}^{-*}\mathbf{D}^*$$

$$= \mathbf{I} - \mathbf{I}^*$$

(where $\mathbf{I}^*$ is a diagonal matrix with r unit and $n - r$ zero elements), and the rank of $\mathbf{I} - \mathbf{B}^-\mathbf{B}$ is $n - r$. This means that the space of solutions $\mathbf{x}_0 + \mathbf{z}$, where $\mathbf{z} =$

(I − B⁻B)u, is $(n - r)$-dimensional, and $\mathbf{z}$ is in the null space of $\mathbf{B}$; that is, $\mathbf{Bz} = \mathbf{B}(\mathbf{I} - \mathbf{B}^{-}\mathbf{B})\mathbf{u} = \mathbf{0}$.

As an example of an application of the generalized inverse, let us solve the system (2.3-18) of Example 2.3-3.

EXAMPLE 2.3-4 (*Solution of a system of equations using a generalized inverse*) To perform the gaussian factorization of the matrix of coefficients in (2.3-18), we border the matrix on the top and on the right by identity matrices:

$$\left[\begin{array}{c|c} \mathbf{I} & \mathbf{O} \\ \hline \mathbf{A} & \mathbf{I} \end{array}\right] = \left[\begin{array}{cccccc|cccccc} 1 &&&&&&&&&&& \\ & 1 &&&&&&&&&& \\ && 1 &&&&&&&&& \\ &&& 1 &&&&&&&& \\ &&&& 1 &&&&&&& \\ &&&&& 1 &&&&&& \\ \hline 6 & 3 & 3 & 2 & 2 & 2 & 1 &&&&& \\ 3 & 3 & 0 & 1 & 1 & 1 && 1 &&&& \\ 3 & 0 & 3 & 1 & 1 & 1 &&& 1 &&& \\ 2 & 1 & 1 & 2 & 0 & 0 &&&& 1 && \\ 2 & 1 & 1 & 0 & 2 & 0 &&&&& 1 & \\ 2 & 1 & 1 & 0 & 0 & 2 &&&&&& 1 \end{array}\right]$$

Using Type III row operations, we reduce the matrix $\mathbf{A}$ to upper-triangular form and replace the identity on the right by $\mathbf{L}^{-1}$:

$$\left[\begin{array}{c|c} \mathbf{I} & \mathbf{O} \\ \hline \mathbf{U} & \mathbf{L}^{-1} \end{array}\right] = \left[\begin{array}{cccccc|cccccc} 1 &&&&&&&&&&& \\ & 1 &&&&&&&&&& \\ && 1 &&&&&&&&& \\ &&& 1 &&&&&&&& \\ &&&& 1 &&&&&&& \\ &&&&& 1 &&&&&& \\ \hline 6 & 3 & 3 & 2 & 2 & 2 & 1 & 0 & 0 & 0 & 0 & 0 \\ 0 & \frac{3}{2} & -\frac{3}{2} & 0 & 0 & 0 & -\frac{1}{2} & 1 & 0 & 0 & 0 & 0 \\ 0 & 0 & 0 & 0 & 0 & 0 & -1 & 1 & 1 & 0 & 0 & 0 \\ 0 & 0 & 0 & \frac{4}{3} & -\frac{2}{3} & -\frac{2}{3} & -\frac{1}{3} & 0 & 0 & 1 & 0 & 0 \\ 0 & 0 & 0 & 0 & 1 & -1 & -\frac{1}{2} & 0 & 0 & \frac{1}{2} & 1 & 0 \\ 0 & 0 & 0 & 0 & 0 & 0 & -1 & 0 & 0 & 1 & 1 & 1 \end{array}\right]$$

Then we perform the Type III column operations to reduce the upper-triangular matrix to diagonal form and obtain $\mathbf{U}^{-1}$. In this instance, the original matrix was symmetric and $\mathbf{U}^{-1} = (\mathbf{L}^{-1})'$. Thus, the completed reduction is

$$
\left[\begin{array}{c|c} \mathbf{U}^{-1} & \mathbf{O} \\ \hline \mathbf{D}^* & \mathbf{L}^{-1} \end{array}\right] =
\left[\begin{array}{cccccc|cccccc}
1 & -\frac{1}{2} & -1 & -\frac{1}{3} & -\frac{1}{2} & -1 & & & & & & \\
0 & 1 & 1 & 0 & 0 & 0 & & & & & & \\
0 & 0 & 1 & 0 & 0 & 0 & & & & & & \\
0 & 0 & 0 & 1 & \frac{1}{2} & 1 & & & & & & \\
0 & 0 & 0 & 0 & 1 & 1 & & & & & & \\
-1 & 0 & 0 & 1 & 1 & 1 & & & & & & \\
\hline
6 & & & & & & 1 & 0 & 0 & 0 & 0 & 0 \\
 & \frac{3}{2} & & & & & -\frac{1}{2} & 1 & 0 & 0 & 0 & 0 \\
 & & 0 & & & & -1 & 1 & 1 & 0 & 0 & 0 \\
 & & & \frac{4}{3} & & & -\frac{1}{3} & 0 & 0 & 1 & 0 & 0 \\
 & & & & 1 & & -\frac{1}{2} & 0 & 0 & \frac{1}{2} & 1 & 0 \\
 & & & & & 0 & -1 & 0 & 0 & 1 & 1 & 1
\end{array}\right]
$$

Now, $\mathbf{D}^{-*} = \operatorname{diag}[\frac{1}{6}, \frac{2}{3}, 0, \frac{3}{4}, 1, 0]$, and we have the generalized inverse

$$\mathbf{A}^{-} = \mathbf{L}^{-1}\mathbf{D}^{-*}\mathbf{U}^{-1}$$

or

$$
\mathbf{A}^{-} = \begin{bmatrix}
\frac{2}{3} & -\frac{1}{3} & 0 & -\frac{1}{2} & -\frac{1}{2} & 0 \\
-\frac{1}{3} & \frac{2}{3} & 0 & 0 & 0 & 0 \\
0 & 0 & 0 & 0 & 0 & 0 \\
-\frac{1}{2} & 0 & 0 & 1 & \frac{1}{2} & 0 \\
-\frac{1}{2} & 0 & 0 & \frac{1}{2} & 1 & 0 \\
0 & 0 & 0 & 0 & 0 & 0
\end{bmatrix}
$$

As a check, we may verify that $\mathbf{A}\mathbf{A}^{-}\mathbf{A} = \mathbf{A}$.

Premultiplying the right member of (2.3-18) by $\mathbf{A}^{-}$, we obtain another solution of the system (in the notation of Example 2.3-3):

$$
\begin{aligned}
m^* &= 4y_{..} - y_{1.} - y_{.1} - y_{.2} \\
a_1^* &= -2y_{..} + 2y_{1.} \\
a_2^* &= 0 \\
b_1^* &= -3y_{..} + 2y_{.1} + y_{.2} \\
b_2^* &= -3y_{..} + y_{.1} + 2y_{.2} \\
b_3^* &= 0
\end{aligned}
$$

But $n - r = 2$, so any vector depending on two arbitrary elements and orthogonal to **A** may be added to this solution to give another solution. In particular,

$$\begin{aligned}
m^* - y_{2\cdot} - y_{\cdot 3} + 2y_{\cdot\cdot} &= y_{\cdot\cdot} \\
a_1^* + y_{2\cdot} - y_{\cdot\cdot} &= y_{1\cdot} - y_{\cdot\cdot} \\
a_2^* + y_{2\cdot} - y_{\cdot\cdot} &= y_{2\cdot} - y_{\cdot\cdot} \\
b_1^* + y_{\cdot 3} - y_{\cdot\cdot} &= y_{\cdot 1} - y_{\cdot\cdot} \\
b_2^* + y_{\cdot 3} - y_{\cdot\cdot} &= y_{\cdot 2} - y_{\cdot\cdot} \\
b_3^* + y_{\cdot 3} - y_{\cdot\cdot} &= y_{\cdot 3} - y_{\cdot\cdot}
\end{aligned}$$

is the same solution obtained in Example 2.3-2.

Various types of "generalized," "conditional," and "pseudo" inverses have been used by many authors, including Bose [undated], Penrose [1955], Rao [1965], and Searle [1966].

Exercise 2.3-1 (From E. T. Browne [1958, page 40]) Invert the following matrix using first the Gauss and then the Gauss-Jordan method:

$$\begin{bmatrix} 1 & 3 & -2 \\ -2 & -5 & 1 \\ 6 & 7 & 23 \end{bmatrix}$$

ANSWER

$$\begin{bmatrix} -61 & -\frac{83}{2} & -\frac{7}{2} \\ 26 & \frac{35}{2} & \frac{3}{2} \\ 8 & \frac{11}{2} & \frac{1}{2} \end{bmatrix}$$

Exercise 2.3-2 Let

$$\mathbf{Bx} = \begin{bmatrix} 1 & 1 & 0 & 0 \\ 1 & 0 & 1 & 0 \\ 1 & 0 & 0 & 1 \end{bmatrix} \cdot \begin{bmatrix} x_1 \\ x_2 \\ x_3 \\ x_4 \end{bmatrix} = \mathbf{k} = \begin{bmatrix} 18 \\ 15 \\ 9 \end{bmatrix}$$

Solve for

$$\mathbf{y} = \mathbf{Cx} = \begin{bmatrix} 1 & \frac{1}{3} & \frac{1}{3} & \frac{1}{3} \\ 0 & 1 & -\frac{1}{2} & -\frac{1}{2} \\ 0 & 0 & 1 & -1 \end{bmatrix} \cdot \begin{bmatrix} x_1 \\ x_2 \\ x_3 \\ x_4 \end{bmatrix}$$

How is the solution of this exercise related to that of Example 2.3-2?

Exercise 2.3-3 For

$$\begin{matrix} p \\ q \end{matrix}\begin{bmatrix} \mathbf{A} & \mathbf{B} \\ \mathbf{C} & \mathbf{D} \end{bmatrix}$$

with **A**, **D**, and $\mathbf{D} - \mathbf{CA}^{-1}\mathbf{B}$ nonsingular, verify that

$$(\mathbf{A} - \mathbf{BD}^{-1}\mathbf{C})^{-1} = \mathbf{A}^{-1} + \mathbf{A}^{-1}\mathbf{B}(\mathbf{D} - \mathbf{CA}^{-1}\mathbf{B})^{-1}\mathbf{CA}^{-1}$$

Specialize this formula to the case $q = 1$ (see Householder [1953, page 79]).

2.4 DETERMINANTS

An important scalar function of an $n \times n$ square matrix **A** is the *determinant* of order n. The determinant is denoted by $|\mathbf{A}|$ and defined as

$$|\mathbf{A}| = \sum^{n!} (-1)^s a_{1\alpha} a_{2\beta} \cdots a_{n\nu} \qquad (2.4\text{-}1)$$

where $\alpha, \beta, \ldots, \nu$ represents one of the permutations of the natural numbers 1 through n. The number of terms in this sum is $n!$, that is, the number of ordered arrangements (permutations) of n distinct things taken n at a time. The exponent s, which determines the sign of each term in (2.4-1), is 1 or 0 according as the *class* of the permutation is *odd* or *even*. A permutation is called *odd* if the number of pairs of numbers which are out of natural order is odd; otherwise, it is called *even*. For example, 1432 is an odd permutation because, of the six possible unordered pairs of the numbers 1 through 4, three are out of natural order, namely, 32, 42, and 43. The permutation 1342, on the other hand, is even because two pairs are out of order, namely, 32 and 42.

Since each of the numbers $1, 2, \ldots, n$ appears once as a row subscript and once as a column subscript in each term of (2.4-1), it is apparent that each term contains as a factor exactly one element from each row and column of **A**. Because each pair of numbers appears in natural order in one of these terms and in reverse order in another, exactly half the terms are positive and half negative (for $n > 1$).

EXAMPLES

$$|a_{11}| = a_{11}$$

$$\begin{vmatrix} a_{11} & a_{12} \\ a_{21} & a_{22} \end{vmatrix} = a_{11}a_{22} - a_{12}a_{21}$$

$$\begin{vmatrix} a_{11} & a_{12} & a_{13} \\ a_{21} & a_{22} & a_{23} \\ a_{31} & a_{32} & a_{33} \end{vmatrix} = a_{11}a_{22}a_{33} - a_{11}a_{23}a_{32} + a_{12}a_{23}a_{31} - a_{12}a_{21}a_{33} + a_{13}a_{21}a_{32} - a_{13}a_{22}a_{31}$$

The definition (2.4-1) is productive of many useful results in linear algebra. In particular, it is motivated by the solution of simultaneous linear equations in terms of "Cramer" determinants. When a system of n simultaneous equations in n unknowns, $\mathbf{Ax} = \mathbf{k}$, is solved by the elimination of variables, it is found that the coordinates of the solution point can be expressed as ratios of determinants in which the denominator is equal to $|\mathbf{A}|$. The numerator in each ratio is called a *Cramer determinant* and is obtained by replacing the column in $\mathbf{A}$ corresponding to the unknown with the column of constant terms in the equations. For example, the solution of

$$a_{11}x_1 + a_{12}x_2 + a_{13}x_3 = k_1$$
$$a_{21}x_1 + a_{22}x_2 + a_{23}x_3 = k_2$$
$$a_{31}x_1 + a_{32}x_2 + a_{33}x_3 = k_3$$

or

$$\mathbf{Ax} = \mathbf{k}$$

is

$$x_1 = \frac{1}{|\mathbf{A}|}\begin{vmatrix} k_1 & a_{12} & a_{13} \\ k_2 & a_{22} & a_{23} \\ k_3 & a_{32} & a_{33} \end{vmatrix} \qquad x_2 = \frac{1}{|\mathbf{A}|}\begin{vmatrix} a_{11} & k_1 & a_{13} \\ a_{21} & k_2 & a_{23} \\ a_{31} & k_3 & a_{33} \end{vmatrix} \qquad x_3 = \frac{1}{|\mathbf{A}|}\begin{vmatrix} a_{11} & a_{12} & k_1 \\ a_{21} & a_{22} & k_2 \\ a_{31} & a_{32} & k_3 \end{vmatrix}$$

provided

$$|\mathbf{A}| = \begin{vmatrix} a_{11} & a_{12} & a_{13} \\ a_{21} & a_{22} & a_{23} \\ a_{31} & a_{32} & a_{33} \end{vmatrix} \neq 0$$

Each numerator in the above ratios is a Cramer determinant.

2.4.1 Properties of Determinants

Certain fundamental theorems for determinants which follow from definition (2.4-1) are presented here without proof:*

1 The determinant of $\mathbf{A}$ transpose equals the determinant of $\mathbf{A}$.

2 If each element in a row or column of $\mathbf{A}$ is multiplied by k, the determinant of $\mathbf{A}$ is multiplied by k.

3 If each element in $\mathbf{A}$ is multiplied by k, the determinant of $\mathbf{A}$ is multiplied by k^n.

4 If any two rows or any two columns of $\mathbf{A}$ are exchanged, the determinant changes sign.

5 If any two rows or any two columns of $\mathbf{A}$ are proportional, the value of the determinant is zero.

* See Aitken [1956] or Browne [1958] for proofs.

6 The determinant obtained by deleting the ith row and jth column of $\mathbf{A}$ is called a *minor* of $|\mathbf{A}|$ and is denoted by $|\mathbf{A}_{ij}|$. A determinant of order n may be expressed in terms of determinants of order $n - 1$ by either of the identities

$$|\mathbf{A}| = \sum_{j=1}^{n} a_{ij}(-1)^{i+j}|\mathbf{A}_{ij}| \qquad (2.4\text{-}2)$$

or

$$|\mathbf{A}| = \sum_{i=1}^{n} a_{ij}(-1)^{i+j}|\mathbf{A}_{ij}| \qquad (2.4\text{-}3)$$

Equation (2.4-2) is called the expansion of $|\mathbf{A}|$ according to elements of row i, and Eq. (2.4-3) the expansion of $|\mathbf{A}|$ according to elements of column j. The quantity $(-1)^{i+j}|\mathbf{A}_{ij}|$ is called the *cofactor* of a_{ij}. A cofactor is a *signed* minor.

7 The expansion of $|\mathbf{A}|$ according to elements of one row or column and the cofactors of a *different* row or column is identically zero. This result is sometimes expressed by the statement that the "expansion by *alien* cofactors vanishes identically."

An important corollary of these theorems is the following: *The addition of a scalar multiple of any row or column of* $\mathbf{A}$ *to any other row or column leaves the value of* $|\mathbf{A}|$ *unchanged.* For if k times elements in row h of $\mathbf{A}$ are added to elements in row i, expansion of $|\mathbf{A}|$ by elements of row i gives

$$\begin{aligned}|\mathbf{A}| &= \sum_{j=1}^{n} (a_{ij} + ka_{hj})(-1)^{i+j}|\mathbf{A}_{ij}| \\ &= \sum_{j=1}^{n} a_{ij}(-1)^{i+j}|\mathbf{A}_{ij}| + k\sum_{j=1}^{n} a_{hj}(-1)^{i+j}|\mathbf{A}_{ij}| \\ &= \sum_{j=1}^{n} a_{ij}(-1)^{i+j}|\mathbf{A}_{ij}|\end{aligned}$$

because $\sum_{j=1}^{n} a_{hj}(-1)^{i+j}|\mathbf{A}_{ij}|$ is an expansion by alien cofactors which vanishes identically. A similar result applies to columns. This means in particular that the determinant is unaffected by premultiplication or postmultiplication of the matrix by Type III elementary matrices.

2.4.2 Numerical Evaluation of Determinants

By applying the above corollary to (2.3-21), we obtain a practical method for the numerical evaluation of determinants. By application of elementary row and column operations, $\mathbf{A}$ is reduced to the diagonal matrix $\mathbf{D}$. Then,

$$|\mathbf{A}| = |\mathbf{L}^{-1}\mathbf{A}\mathbf{U}^{-1}| = |\mathbf{D}| = d_{11}d_{22}\cdots d_{nn}$$

because all terms in the expansion of $|\mathbf{D}|$ have zero as a factor except the term consisting of the diagonal elements. Note that the corollary also implies that $|\mathbf{L}^{-1}\mathbf{A}| = |\mathbf{D}\mathbf{U}| = |\mathbf{D}|$. That is, the determinant of a triangular matrix is just the product of the diagonal elements. This means that in the numerical evaluation of $|\mathbf{A}|$ only the row operations need be performed.

2.4.3 Multiplication Theorem

These results may also be used to prove important partition and multiplication theorems for determinants. Consider a $2n \times 2n$ matrix $\mathbf{A}$ partitioned into $n \times n$ submatrices:

$$\mathbf{A} = \begin{bmatrix} \mathbf{B} & \mathbf{C} \\ \mathbf{D} & \mathbf{E} \end{bmatrix} \begin{matrix} n \\ n \end{matrix}$$
$$\qquad n \quad n$$

We suppose that the determinant of $\mathbf{A}$ is nonzero and that, if necessary, corresponding rows and columns of $\mathbf{A}$ have been interchanged to ensure that $\mathbf{B}$ is nonsingular. Since the number of exchanges of rows *and* columns is necessarily even, the value of $|\mathbf{A}|$ is unchanged. Then, by premultiplication and postmultiplication of $\mathbf{A}$ by elementary matrices, $\mathbf{A}$ may be reduced to *quasi*diagonal form, i.e., diagonal by blocks:

$$\begin{bmatrix} \mathbf{I} & \mathbf{O} \\ -\mathbf{D}\mathbf{B}^{-1} & \mathbf{I} \end{bmatrix} \begin{bmatrix} \mathbf{B} & \mathbf{C} \\ \mathbf{D} & \mathbf{E} \end{bmatrix} \begin{bmatrix} \mathbf{I} & -\mathbf{B}^{-1}\mathbf{C} \\ \mathbf{O} & \mathbf{I} \end{bmatrix} = \begin{bmatrix} \mathbf{B} & \mathbf{O} \\ \mathbf{O} & \mathbf{E} - \mathbf{D}\mathbf{B}^{-1}\mathbf{C} \end{bmatrix}$$

Let $\mathbf{E}^* = \mathbf{E} - \mathbf{D}\mathbf{B}^{-1}\mathbf{C}$. Then, by further elementary row and column operations not involving $\mathbf{E}^*$, $\mathbf{B}$ may be reduced to the diagonal matrix $\mathbf{D}_B$, and, similarly, $\mathbf{E}^*$ may be reduced to the diagonal matrix $\mathbf{D}_{E^*}$. Thus,

$$|\mathbf{A}| = \begin{vmatrix} \mathbf{D}_B & \mathbf{O} \\ \mathbf{O} & \mathbf{D}_{E^*} \end{vmatrix} = |\mathbf{D}_B| \cdot |\mathbf{D}_{E^*}| = |\mathbf{B}| \cdot |\mathbf{E} - \mathbf{D}\mathbf{B}^{-1}\mathbf{C}|$$

This proves that the determinant of a quasidiagonal matrix is the product of the determinants of its principal submatrices,* and that the determinant of a fourfold partitioned matrix may be expressed in terms of the submatrices, provided at least one of the principal submatrices is nonsingular.

Note that if $\mathbf{A}$ is *quasi*triangular, i.e., triangular by blocks, the determinant is the product of the determinants of the principal submatrices:

$$\begin{vmatrix} \mathbf{B} & \mathbf{C} \\ \mathbf{O} & \mathbf{E} \end{vmatrix} = |\mathbf{B}| \cdot |\mathbf{E}| \qquad (2.4\text{-}4)$$

Now we are in a position to prove the simple multiplication theorem: *If* $\mathbf{A}$ *and* $\mathbf{B}$ *are* $n \times n$ *square matrices, then* $|\mathbf{AB}| = |\mathbf{A}| \cdot |\mathbf{B}|$. For, consider the following identity:

$$\begin{bmatrix} \mathbf{I} & \mathbf{A} \\ \mathbf{O} & \mathbf{I} \end{bmatrix} \cdot \begin{bmatrix} \mathbf{A} & \mathbf{O} \\ -\mathbf{I} & \mathbf{B} \end{bmatrix} = \begin{bmatrix} \mathbf{O} & \mathbf{AB} \\ -\mathbf{I} & \mathbf{B} \end{bmatrix}$$

* This also follows from LaPlace's expansion (see Browne [1958, page 21]).

Since the matrix multiplication on the left consists only of Type III elementary row operations, the determinants on the left and right side are

$$\begin{vmatrix} \mathbf{A} & \mathbf{O} \\ -\mathbf{I} & \mathbf{B} \end{vmatrix} = \begin{vmatrix} \mathbf{O} & \mathbf{AB} \\ -\mathbf{I} & \mathbf{B} \end{vmatrix}$$

and n column interchanges are required to put the left-hand side into quasitriangular form:

$$\begin{vmatrix} \mathbf{A} & \mathbf{O} \\ -\mathbf{I} & \mathbf{B} \end{vmatrix} = (-1)^n \begin{bmatrix} \mathbf{AB} & \mathbf{O} \\ \mathbf{O} & -\mathbf{I} \end{bmatrix}$$

Then, from (2.4-4),

$$\begin{aligned} |\mathbf{A}| \cdot |\mathbf{B}| &= (-1)^n |-\mathbf{I}|\,|\mathbf{AB}| = (-1)^n(-1)^n|\mathbf{AB}| \\ &= (-1)^{2n}|\mathbf{AB}| = |\mathbf{AB}| \end{aligned} \tag{2.4-5}$$

Regrettably, there is no similar simple theorem for the determinant of a sum of two matrices.

As a corollary of (2.4-5), we have

$$\begin{aligned} |\mathbf{A}^{-1}\mathbf{A}| &= |\mathbf{I}| \\ |\mathbf{A}^{-1}| \cdot |\mathbf{A}| &= 1 \\ |\mathbf{A}^{-1}| &= \frac{1}{|\mathbf{A}|} = |\mathbf{A}|^{-1} \end{aligned}$$

2.4.4 Determinants and Rank

The determinant of an $r \times r$ submatrix of a larger matrix $\mathbf{A}$, which need not be square, is called a minor of order r. If, possibly after rearrangement of rows and columns, at least one minor of order r is nonzero while all minors of order $r + 1$ vanish, the rank of the matrix $\mathbf{A}$ is r. That all minors of order $r + 1$ in a matrix of rank r vanish is evident in the fact that the reduction of the matrix to echelon form by elementary row operations, which do not alter rank, leaves only r nonzero rows. That a minor of order r is nonzero follows from the fact that the determinant is equal to the product of the leading elements in an echelon form. That is, there must be at least one submatrix whose echelon form contains r rows. This means that if $|\mathbf{A}| \neq 0$, then $\mathbf{A}$ is of full rank or, as we say, $\mathbf{A}$ is nonsingular.

2.4.5 Adjoints, Inverses, and the Solution of Systems of Linear Equations

A matrix in which the element in the ith row and jth column is the cofactor $(-1)^{j+i}|\mathbf{A}_{ji}|$ of the element in the jth row and ith column of $\mathbf{A}$ is called the *adjoint* of $\mathbf{A}$ and denoted by adj($\mathbf{A}$). Note the exchange of subscripts; the adjoint is the *transpose* of the matrix of cofactors of $\mathbf{A}$. It is easy to see that, if $\mathbf{A}$ is nonsingular, the inverse of $\mathbf{A}$ is given by

$$\mathbf{A}^{-1} = \frac{1}{|\mathbf{A}|} \operatorname{adj}(\mathbf{A}) \tag{2.4-6}$$

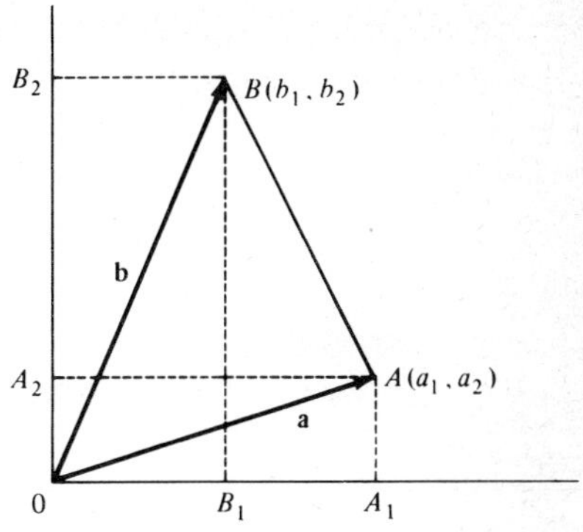

FIGURE 2.4-1
Area of a triangle expressed as a determinant.

For the ith diagonal elements of the product of adj(**A**) and **A** are just the expansion of the determinant of **A** by elements of the ith row, while the off-diagonal elements are expansions by alien cofactors which vanish identically. Hence,

$$\left[\frac{1}{|\mathbf{A}|}\operatorname{adj}(\mathbf{A})\right]\cdot\mathbf{A} = \frac{|\mathbf{A}|}{|\mathbf{A}|}\mathbf{I} = \mathbf{I}$$

Similarly, elements of $\mathbf{A}\cdot\operatorname{adj}(\mathbf{A})$ are expansions of the determinant of **A** by columns; hence $\mathbf{A}\cdot[(1/|\mathbf{A}|)\operatorname{adj}(\mathbf{A})] = \mathbf{I}$ and (2.4-6) is the unique left and right inverse. The condition $|\mathbf{A}| \neq 0$ is clearly necessary and sufficient for the existence of the inverse of **A**, as well as for the solution of a system of nonhomogeneous linear equations whose matrix of coefficients is **A**. In fact, the solution using the adjoint matrix is just the solution by Cramer determinants presented at the beginning of Sec. 2.4.

2.4.6 Area and Volume Expressed as Determinants

The determinant of a matrix **A** has an interpretation in terms of the geometry of the vectors which comprise the columns of **A**. In the two-dimensional case, let the triangle OAB be defined by position vectors **a** and **b** (Fig. 2.4-1). Then the area OAB is the sum of the area of the triangle OB_1B plus the area of the trapezium B_1A_1AB minus the area of the triangle OA_1A; that is,

$$\begin{aligned}\text{Area } OAB &= \tfrac{1}{2}[b_1b_2 + (a_1 - b_1)(a_2 + b_2) - a_1a_2] \\ &= \tfrac{1}{2}(b_1b_2 + a_1a_2 + a_1b_2 - b_1a_2 - b_1b_2 - a_1a_2) \\ &= \tfrac{1}{2}(a_1b_2 - b_1a_2) \\ &= \frac{1}{2}\begin{vmatrix} a_1 & b_1 \\ a_2 & b_2 \end{vmatrix}\end{aligned}$$

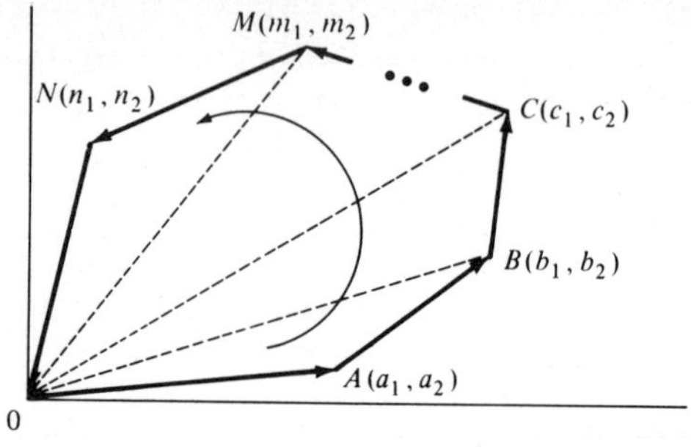

FIGURE 2.4-2
Area of a polygon expressed in determinants.

Since the sign of a determinant is reversed if the columns are interchanged, it is clear the determinant will give a positive area only if some convention is adopted for writing down the columns of $\mathbf{A}$. With respect to the usual (right-handed) co-ordinate system in which the abscissa is positive to the right and the ordinate positive upward, the coordinates of the vertices must be read in a counterclockwise direction from the origin.

Indeed, with this convention, the area of any n-polygon, convex or concave, with one vertex at the origin can be expressed in terms of a half-sum of $n - 1$ determinants of order 2, each representing the area of a triangle (Fig. 2.4-2):

$$\begin{aligned}\text{Area } OABC \cdots MN &= \triangle OAB + \triangle OBC + \cdots + \triangle OMN \\ &= \frac{1}{2}\begin{vmatrix} a_1 & b_1 \\ a_2 & b_2 \end{vmatrix} + \frac{1}{2}\begin{vmatrix} b_1 & c_1 \\ b_2 & c_2 \end{vmatrix} + \cdots + \frac{1}{2}\begin{vmatrix} m_1 & n_1 \\ m_2 & n_2 \end{vmatrix}\end{aligned} \tag{2.4-7}$$

Formula (2.4-7) also generalizes to volume and hypervolume. In particular, the hypervolume of an n-dimensional hypertetrahedron with one vertex at the origin and the coordinates of its remaining n vertices given by the columns of $\mathbf{A}$ is equal to $(1/n!)|\mathbf{A}|$, while the volume of the parallelotope formed by completing this tetrahedron with $n!$ similar tetrahedrons is $|\mathbf{A}|$ [Aitken, 1956]. This result has an important application in multivariate statistics, where the volume of the parallelotope constructed from the p observational vectors of a data matrix is employed as a measure of multi-variate dispersion. The square of this volume is called the *generalized variance* (see Anderson [1958, Sec. 7.5]).

2.5 VECTOR AND MATRIX DERIVATIVES

In the sequel we shall have occasion to express the derivatives of functions involving vectors and matrices. Although we may always rewrite these functions in extended form and apply, element by element, the familiar rules of scalar differentiation, there is considerable advantage in defining rules which retain vector and matrices in the notation [Dwyer, 1967; Dwyer and MacPhail, 1948; Schönemann, 1965; Bargmann, 1967]. The following rules are especially useful in statistical applications.

2.5.1 The Derivative of a Matric Function with Respect to a Scalar Variable

Let the elements of an $m \times n$ matrix **A** be differentiable functions of a scalar variable x. Then the derivative of **A** with respect to x is defined as the $m \times n$ matrix

$$\frac{\partial \mathbf{A}}{\partial x} = \left[\frac{\partial a_{ij}}{\partial x}\right] \qquad \begin{matrix} i = 1, 2, \ldots, m \\ j = 1, 2, \ldots, n \end{matrix} \tag{2.5-1}$$

If the elements of the $m \times n$ matrix **A** and the $p \times q$ matrix **B** are each differentiable in x, then specializing m, n, p, and q as indicated, we have the following rules for elementary functions of **A** and **B** (see Browne [1958, page 255 ff]):

$$\frac{\partial(\mathbf{A} + \mathbf{B})}{\partial x} = \frac{\partial \mathbf{A}}{\partial x} + \frac{\partial \mathbf{B}}{\partial x} \qquad m = p,\ n = q \tag{2.5-2}$$

$$\frac{\partial(\mathbf{AB})}{\partial x} = \mathbf{A}\frac{\partial \mathbf{B}}{\partial x} + \frac{\partial \mathbf{A}}{\partial x}\mathbf{B} \qquad n = p \tag{2.5-3}$$

$$\frac{\partial \mathbf{A}^{-1}}{\partial x} = -\mathbf{A}^{-1}\frac{\partial \mathbf{A}}{\partial x}\mathbf{A}^{-1} \qquad m = n,\ |\mathbf{A}| \neq 0 \tag{2.5-4}$$

If x_{ij} is the element in the ith row and jth column of an $m \times n$ matrix **X**, then

$$\frac{\partial \mathbf{X}}{\partial x_{ij}} = \mathbf{1}_{ij} \tag{2.5-5}$$

where $\mathbf{1}_{ij}$ represents an $m \times n$ matrix in which the element in the ith row and jth column is unity, and all remaining elements are null. If **X** is an $n \times n$ diagonal matrix,

$$\frac{\partial \mathbf{X}}{\partial x_{ii}} = \mathbf{1}_{ii} \tag{2.5-6}$$

2.5.2 Differentiation of a Scalar Function of a Matrix with Respect to a Matric or Vector Variable*

The derivative of the scalar function z of **X** is the matrix

$$\frac{\partial z}{\partial \mathbf{X}} = \left[\frac{\partial z}{\partial x_{ij}}\right]$$

* This section is based on Schönemann [1965].

a The trace A scalar function of a matrix which appears frequently in multivariate statistics is the *trace* of an $n \times n$ square matrix, namely the sum of the elements in the main diagonal:

$$\text{tr}(\mathbf{A}) = \sum_{i=1}^{n} a_{ii} \qquad (2.5\text{-}7)$$

For matrices **A**, **B**, and **C** of order $m \times n$, $p \times q$, and $r \times s$, respectively, the trace has the properties,

$$\text{tr}(\mathbf{A} + \mathbf{B}) = \text{tr}(\mathbf{A}) + \text{tr}(\mathbf{B}) \qquad m = n = p = q \qquad (2.5\text{-}8)$$

$$\text{tr}(c\mathbf{A}) = c\,\text{tr}(\mathbf{A}) \qquad m = n \qquad (2.5\text{-}9)$$

$$\text{tr}(\mathbf{A}') = \text{tr}(\mathbf{A}) \qquad m = n \qquad (2.5\text{-}10)$$

$$\text{tr}(\mathbf{AB}) = \text{tr}(\mathbf{BA}) \qquad m = q,\ n = p \qquad (2.5\text{-}11)$$

Equation (2.5-11) implies that the trace of a matrix product is invariant under cyclic permutation of factors. For example,

$$\text{tr}(\mathbf{ABC}) = \text{tr}[(\mathbf{AB})\mathbf{C}] = \text{tr}(\mathbf{CAB}) \qquad m = s,\ n = p,\ q = r \qquad (2.5\text{-}12)$$

Let **C** be an $r \times s$ matrix of constants, and **X** a $u \times v$ matrix of variables. The following derivatives of trace functions of **C** and **X** with respect to the elements of **X** are matrices of order $u \times v$:

$$\frac{\partial\, \text{tr}(\mathbf{C})}{\partial \mathbf{X}} = \mathbf{O} \qquad r = s \qquad (2.5\text{-}13)$$

$$\frac{\partial\, \text{tr}(\mathbf{X})}{\partial \mathbf{X}} = \mathbf{I} \qquad u = v \qquad (2.5\text{-}14)$$

$$\frac{\partial\, \text{tr}(\mathbf{XC})}{\partial \mathbf{X}} = \mathbf{C}' \qquad r = v,\ s = u \qquad (2.5\text{-}15)$$

$$\frac{\partial\, \text{tr}(\mathbf{X}'\mathbf{CX})}{\partial \mathbf{X}} = (\mathbf{C} + \mathbf{C}')\mathbf{X} \qquad r = s = u = v \qquad (2.5\text{-}16)$$

In view of (2.5-10) through (2.5-12), the preceding derivatives are unchanged by transposition of the matrix in the trace function or by cyclic permutation of factors of that matrix. However, the derivatives with respect to the transpose of **X** are defined to be the $v \times u$ transposes of the above matrices. In particular,

$$\frac{\partial\, \text{tr}(\mathbf{XC})}{\partial \mathbf{X}'} = \mathbf{C} \qquad (2.5\text{-}17)$$

and

$$\frac{\partial\, \text{tr}(\mathbf{X}'\mathbf{CX})}{\partial \mathbf{X}'} = \mathbf{X}'(\mathbf{C}' + \mathbf{C}) \qquad (2.5\text{-}18)$$

Rules for differentiating the traces of elementary functions of matrices may also be defined. Let the elements of **A** and **B** be functions of **X**, and let **C** be a constant matrix. Then

$$\frac{\partial\,\mathrm{tr}(\mathbf{A}+\mathbf{B})}{\partial\mathbf{X}} = \frac{\partial\,\mathrm{tr}(\mathbf{A})}{\partial\mathbf{X}} + \frac{\partial\,\mathrm{tr}(\mathbf{B})}{\partial\mathbf{X}} \qquad m = n = p = q \qquad (2.5\text{-}19)$$

$$\frac{\partial\,\mathrm{tr}(\mathbf{AB})}{\partial\mathbf{X}} = \frac{\partial\,\mathrm{tr}(\mathbf{A}\bar{\mathbf{B}})}{\partial\mathbf{X}} + \frac{\partial(\bar{\mathbf{A}}\mathbf{B})}{\partial\mathbf{X}} \qquad m = q,\ n = p \qquad (2.5\text{-}20)$$

$$\frac{\partial\,\mathrm{tr}(\mathbf{A}^{-1})}{\partial\mathbf{X}} = -\frac{\partial\,\mathrm{tr}(\bar{\mathbf{A}}^{-2}\mathbf{A})}{\partial\mathbf{X}} \qquad m = n,\ |\mathbf{A}| \neq 0 \qquad (2.5\text{-}21)$$

$$\frac{\partial\,\mathrm{tr}(\mathbf{A}^{-1}\mathbf{C})}{\partial\mathbf{X}} = -\frac{\partial\,\mathrm{tr}(\bar{\mathbf{A}}^{-1}\mathbf{C}\bar{\mathbf{A}}^{-1})\mathbf{A}}{\partial\mathbf{X}} \qquad m = n = r = s,\ |\mathbf{A}| = 0 \qquad (2.5\text{-}22)$$

The bar above the matrices **A** and **B** in (2.5-20) through (2.5-22) indicates that the matrix is to be regarded as constant for purposes of differentiation.

b Determinants

$$\frac{\partial|\mathbf{X}|}{\partial\mathbf{X}} = \mathrm{adj}(\mathbf{X}') \qquad u = v \qquad (2.5\text{-}23)$$

$$\frac{\partial\log|\mathbf{X}|}{\partial\mathbf{X}} = \frac{\mathrm{adj}(\mathbf{X}')}{|\mathbf{X}|} = (\mathbf{X}^{-1})' \qquad u = v,\ |\mathbf{X}| \neq 0 \qquad (2.5\text{-}24)$$

These derivative matrices are transposed when taken with respect to **X**′.

2.5.3 Restrictions on the Variables of Differentiation

In the sequel we make use of matric derivatives of scalar functions in the solution of maxima-minima problems. Some of these problems involve maximization or minimization with respect to variables which are subject to subsidiary conditions. Especially important is the case where **X** is required to be symmetric. Then $\mathbf{X} = \mathbf{X}'$, and the off-diagonal elements are subject to the conditions

$$x_{ij} = x_{ji} \qquad i < j \qquad (2.5\text{-}25)$$

The relations (2.5-25) can, of course, be used to express the scalar function in terms of the $n(n+1)/2$ distinct elements of **X**, but it is not then clear what matric form the derivative with respect to distinct elements should take. A better approach is to impose the subsidiary condition by the *method of Lagrange multipliers* [Courant, 1959, vol. II, pages 190–199]. To apply this method in the present instance, we first differentiate with respect to an unconstrained **X** an expression of the form

$$z + \tfrac{1}{2}\,\mathrm{tr}[\mathbf{U}(\mathbf{X} - \mathbf{X}')]$$

where z is a scalar function of **X**, and **U** is an $n \times n$ matrix of Lagrange multipliers. Then at an extremum subject to the subsidiary conditions, **X** must satisfy

$$\frac{\partial z}{\partial \mathbf{X}} + \tfrac{1}{2}(\mathbf{U}' - \mathbf{U}) = \mathbf{O} \tag{2.5-26}$$

as well as

$$\left(\frac{\partial z}{\partial \mathbf{X}}\right)' + \tfrac{1}{2}(\mathbf{U}' - \mathbf{U})' = \left(\frac{\partial z}{\partial \mathbf{X}}\right)' - \tfrac{1}{2}(\mathbf{U}' - \mathbf{U}) = \mathbf{O} \tag{2.5-27}$$

Hence, adding (2.5-26) and (2.5-27), we obtain as a necessary condition for the restricted extremum,

$$\frac{\partial z}{\partial \mathbf{X}} + \left(\frac{\partial z}{\partial \mathbf{X}}\right)' = \mathbf{O} \tag{2.5-28}$$

If $\partial z/\partial \mathbf{X}$ is symmetric, we may divide by 2 and obtain the same necessary condition for an extremum as that for a general matrix **X**. Thus, in applications involving symmetric matrices of derivatives, we need not introduce the Lagrange multipliers explicitly in order to restrict the solution to a symmetric matrix.

Other important cases of restricted **X** are: **X** is an $n \times n$ diagonal matrix, and **Y** is a matric function of **X**,

$$\frac{\partial\, \mathrm{tr}(\mathbf{Y})}{\partial \mathbf{X}} = \mathrm{diag}\left[\frac{\partial\, \mathrm{tr}(\mathbf{Y})}{\partial x_1}, \frac{\partial\, \mathrm{tr}(\mathbf{Y})}{\partial x_2}, \ldots, \frac{\partial\, \mathrm{tr}(\mathbf{Y})}{\partial x_n}\right] \tag{2.5-29}$$

$\mathbf{X} = x\mathbf{I}$ is an $n \times n$ scalar matrix, and **Y** is a matric function of **X**,

$$\frac{\partial\, \mathrm{tr}(\mathbf{Y})}{\partial \mathbf{X}} = \frac{\partial\, \mathrm{tr}(\mathbf{Y})}{\partial x} \tag{2.5-30}$$

2.5.4 The Chain Rule for Scalar Functions of Matrices

Let z be a scalar function of **A** differentiable with respect to the elements of **A**, and let each element of **A** be a differentiable function in x. Then,

$$\frac{\partial z}{\partial x} = \mathrm{tr}\left(\frac{\partial z}{\partial \mathbf{A}} \frac{\partial \mathbf{A}'}{\partial x}\right) \tag{2.5-31}$$

For example, for $|\mathbf{A}| \neq 0$, from (2.5-24),

$$\frac{\partial \log|\mathbf{A}|}{\partial x} = \mathrm{tr}\left(\frac{\partial \log|\mathbf{A}|}{\partial \mathbf{A}} \frac{\partial \mathbf{A}'}{\partial x}\right) = \mathrm{tr}\left[(\mathbf{A}^{-1})' \frac{\partial \mathbf{A}'}{\partial x}\right] \tag{2.5-32}$$

2.5.5 Derivatives of a Vector Function with Respect to a Vector

Let **z** be an $m \times 1$ vector, each element of which is a differentiable function of the elements of the $1 \times n$ vector $\mathbf{x}' = [x_1, x_2, \ldots, x_n]$. Then the derivative of **z** with respect to $\mathbf{x}'$ is the $m \times n$ matrix

$$\frac{\partial \mathbf{z}}{\partial \mathbf{x}'} = \left(\frac{\partial z_i}{\partial x_j}\right)_{ij} \qquad \begin{matrix} i = 1, 2, \ldots, m \\ j = 1, 2, \ldots, n \end{matrix} \tag{2.5-33}$$

For example, from (2.5-16) we have as the first derivative of the form $\mathbf{x}'\mathbf{A}\mathbf{x}$, where $\mathbf{A}$ is symmetric,

$$\frac{\partial(\mathbf{x}'\mathbf{A}\mathbf{x})}{\partial \mathbf{x}} = \frac{\partial \operatorname{tr}(\mathbf{x}'\mathbf{A}\mathbf{x})}{\partial \mathbf{x}} = 2\mathbf{A}\mathbf{x} \qquad (2.5\text{-}34)$$

From (2.5-33), the second derivatives and cross derivatives are represented in matrix form as

$$\frac{\partial^2(\mathbf{x}'\mathbf{A}\mathbf{x})}{\partial \mathbf{x}'\,\partial \mathbf{x}} = \frac{\partial(\partial \mathbf{x}'\mathbf{A}\mathbf{x}/\partial \mathbf{x})}{\partial \mathbf{x}'} = \frac{\partial(2\mathbf{A}\mathbf{x})}{\partial \mathbf{x}'} = 2\mathbf{A} \qquad (2.5\text{-}35)$$

(See Sec. 2.7.3.)

2.6 TRANSFORMATIONS

A set of linear functions represented by

$$\mathbf{v} = \mathbf{B}\mathbf{x} + \mathbf{c} \qquad (2.6\text{-}1)$$

where $\mathbf{B}$ is a matrix of scalar coefficients, and $\mathbf{c}$ is a vector of scalar constants, is called an *affine* transformation of $\mathbf{x}$. If the vector $\mathbf{c}$, which represents merely a translation of origin, is null, the transformation is called *homogeneous*; otherwise, it is called *nonhomogeneous*. For simplicity of expression, it is convenient to redefine $\mathbf{v}$ so as to absorb $\mathbf{c}$; that is, define $\mathbf{y} = \mathbf{v} - \mathbf{c}$. Then it is only necessary to consider homogeneous transformations represented by

$$\mathbf{y} = \mathbf{B}\mathbf{x} \qquad (2.6\text{-}2)$$

The vector $\mathbf{y}$ is called the *image* of $\mathbf{x}$ under the transformation $\mathbf{B}$. That is, we regard the vector (point) $\mathbf{x}$ in a certain space to be mapped into the vector (point) $\mathbf{y}$ in another space.

If $\mathbf{x}$ is itself the image of another vector, say,

$$\mathbf{x} = \mathbf{C}\mathbf{z}$$

then $\mathbf{y}$ is also an affine transformation of $\mathbf{z}$, and the matrix of the transformation is the product of the matrices of the separate transformations; i.e.,

$$\mathbf{y} = \mathbf{B}\mathbf{C}\mathbf{z}$$

If an affine transformation is one-to-one, the matrix of the transformation is nonsingular, and there exists a reciprocal transformation which restores the original vector. Thus, if (2.6-2) is one-to-one, then

$$\mathbf{x} = \mathbf{B}^{-1}\mathbf{y}$$

where $\mathbf{B}^{-1}$ is the inverse of $\mathbf{B}$. Conversely, if an inverse transformation exists, the transformation is one-to-one.

In addition to maintaining the identity of distinct points, a one-to-one affine transformation also maps parallel lines into parallel lines. Thus, the parallelogram formed by the origin and the position vectors $\mathbf{x}_1$, $\mathbf{x}_2$, and their resultant $\mathbf{x}_1 + \mathbf{x}_2$ is mapped by $\mathbf{B}$ into the parallelogram

$$\begin{aligned} \mathbf{B}[\mathbf{x}_1, \mathbf{x}_2, \mathbf{x}_1 + \mathbf{x}_2] &= [\mathbf{Bx}_1, \mathbf{Bx}_2, \mathbf{Bx}_1 + \mathbf{Bx}_2] \\ &= [\mathbf{y}_1, \mathbf{y}_2, \mathbf{y}_1 + \mathbf{y}_2] \end{aligned}$$

However, the lengths and angles in the parallelogram may be altered by the transformation, as can be seen by calculating the square lengths of the sides,

$$\begin{aligned} |\mathbf{y}_1|^2 &= \mathbf{y}_1 \cdot \mathbf{y}_1 = \mathbf{y}_1'\mathbf{y}_1 = \mathbf{x}_1'\mathbf{B}'\mathbf{Bx}_1 \\ |\mathbf{y}_2|^2 &= \mathbf{y}_2 \cdot \mathbf{y}_2 = \mathbf{y}_2'\mathbf{y}_2 = \mathbf{x}_2'\mathbf{B}'\mathbf{Bx}_2 \end{aligned}$$

and by calculating the cosine of the angle between $\mathbf{y}_1$ and $\mathbf{y}_2$:

$$\begin{aligned} \cos(\mathbf{y}_1,\mathbf{y}_2) &= \frac{\mathbf{y}_1 \cdot \mathbf{y}_2}{\sqrt{(\mathbf{y}_1 \cdot \mathbf{y}_1)(\mathbf{y}_2 \cdot \mathbf{y}_2)}} = \frac{\mathbf{y}_1'\mathbf{y}_2}{\sqrt{(\mathbf{y}_1'\mathbf{y}_1)(\mathbf{y}_2'\mathbf{y}_2)}} \\ &= \frac{\mathbf{x}_1'\mathbf{B}'\mathbf{Bx}_2}{\sqrt{(\mathbf{x}_1'\mathbf{B}'\mathbf{Bx}_1)(\mathbf{x}_2'\mathbf{B}'\mathbf{Bx}_2)}} \end{aligned}$$

Similarly, the area of the parallelogram may be altered by the transformation, but the relationship between the new and old areas is easily expressed in determinants. In the plane, for example,

$$\begin{aligned} \begin{vmatrix} y_{11} & y_{12} \\ y_{21} & y_{22} \end{vmatrix} &= |[\mathbf{y}_1, \mathbf{y}_2]| = |\mathbf{B}[\mathbf{x}_1, \mathbf{x}_2]| = |\mathbf{B}| \times |[\mathbf{x}_1, \mathbf{x}_2]| \\ &= |\mathbf{B}| \times \begin{vmatrix} x_{11} & x_{12} \\ x_{21} & x_{22} \end{vmatrix} \end{aligned}$$

That is, the determinant of the matrix of the transformation is the proportion by which the area is changed. The same result holds for higher-dimensional space.

A nonsingular homogeneous linear transformation leaves lengths, angles, and areas invariant if and only if the matrix of the transformation, say $\mathbf{P}$, satisfies

$$\mathbf{P}'\mathbf{P} = \mathbf{I} \tag{2.6-3}$$

For, if $\mathbf{y} = \mathbf{Px}$, then

$$\mathbf{y}_1'\mathbf{y}_2 = \mathbf{x}_1'\mathbf{P}'\mathbf{Px}_2 = \mathbf{x}_1'\mathbf{x}_2$$

and inner products of original and transformed vectors are equal. Similarly,

$$|\mathbf{P}'\mathbf{P}| = |\mathbf{I}| = 1$$

Hence,

$$|\mathbf{P}| = \sqrt{|\mathbf{I}|} = 1$$

and areas before and after transformation are equal. A square matrix that satisfies (2.6-3) is called *orthogonal*. The inverse of an orthogonal matrix is evidently just the transpose of the original matrix. Since a left inverse is a right inverse, we have also $\mathbf{PP}' = \mathbf{I}$. We have seen in Sec. 2.3.2 how any square matrix of full rank may be transformed into an orthogonal matrix via the Gram-Schmidt construction.

2.6.1 Change of Variables in Derivatives and Integrals

Affine (including orthogonal) transformations appear frequently in multivariate statistical theory as changes of variables in functions of multiple variables. In these situations, we often need to know how the derivatives and integrals of functions are changed under the transformation. In general, let some set of n functions, not necessarily linear or one to one, connect $\mathbf{y}$ and $\mathbf{x}$:

$$\begin{aligned}
y_1 &= f_1(x_1, x_2, \ldots, x_m) \\
y_2 &= f_2(x_1, x_2, \ldots, x_m) \\
&\cdots\cdots\cdots\cdots\cdots \\
y_n &= f_n(x_1, x_2, \ldots, x_m)
\end{aligned}$$

Now, suppose we wish to express the x's in terms of p other variables through the relations

$$\begin{aligned}
x_1 &= g_1(z_1, z_2, \ldots, z_p) \\
x_2 &= g_2(z_1, z_2, \ldots, z_p) \\
&\cdots\cdots\cdots\cdots\cdots \\
x_m &= g_m(z_1, z_2, \ldots, z_p)
\end{aligned}$$

Applying the chain rule for the derivatives of functions, we obtain

$$\frac{\partial y_i}{\partial z_j} = \frac{\partial f_i}{\partial x_1}\frac{\partial g_1}{\partial z_j} + \frac{\partial f_i}{\partial x_2}\frac{\partial g_2}{\partial z_j} + \cdots + \frac{\partial f_i}{\partial x_m}\frac{\partial g_m}{\partial z_j}$$

If these functions f and g are linear and homogeneous, for example, $\mathbf{y} = \underset{n \times m}{\mathbf{B}}\,\mathbf{x}$ and $\mathbf{x} = \underset{m \times p}{\mathbf{C}}\,\mathbf{z}$, then the derivatives take on especially simple form. From (2.5-31) we understand by the symbol $\partial\mathbf{y}/\partial\mathbf{x}'$ the partial derivatives of $y_1, y_2, \ldots, y_n$, each with respect to $x_1, x_2, \ldots, x_m$, written in the form of a matrix as follows:

$$\underset{n \times m}{\frac{\partial \mathbf{y}}{\partial \mathbf{x}'}} = \begin{bmatrix}
\frac{\partial y_1}{\partial x_1} & \frac{\partial y_1}{\partial x_2} & \cdots & \frac{\partial y_1}{\partial x_m} \\
\frac{\partial y_2}{\partial x_1} & \frac{\partial y_2}{\partial x_2} & \cdots & \frac{\partial y_2}{\partial x_m} \\
\cdots & \cdots & \cdots & \cdots \\
\frac{\partial y_n}{\partial x_1} & \frac{\partial y_n}{\partial x_2} & \cdots & \frac{\partial y_n}{\partial x_m}
\end{bmatrix}$$

Now,

$$\frac{\partial \mathbf{y}}{\partial \mathbf{x}'} = \frac{\partial \mathbf{Bx}}{\partial \mathbf{x}'} = \mathbf{B}$$

and

$$\frac{\partial \mathbf{x}}{\partial \mathbf{z}'} = \frac{\partial \mathbf{Cz}}{\partial \mathbf{z}'} = \mathbf{C}$$

Therefore the chain rule (2.5-31) gives

$$\frac{\partial \mathbf{y}}{\partial \mathbf{z}'} = \mathbf{BC}$$

as we would expect, since **BC** is the matrix of the transformation from **y** to **z**.

We will also need to know how to introduce a change of variable into a multiple integral. Suppose Q is an integral over some rectangular region specified by the limits $x_1^{(l)}, x_1^{(u)}; x_2^{(l)}, x_2^{(u)}; \ldots; x_n^{(l)}, x_n^{(u)}$,

$$Q = \int_{x_n^{(l)}}^{x_n^{(u)}} \cdots \int_{x_2^{(l)}}^{x_2^{(u)}} \int_{x_1^{(l)}}^{x_1^{(u)}} f(x_1, x_2, \ldots, x_n)\, dx_1\, dx_2 \cdots dx_n \qquad (2.6\text{-}4)$$

and suppose that the x_i are subjected to a one-to-one transformation, not necessarily linear, to obtain the variables $z_1, z_2, \ldots, z_n$; that is, $z_j = g_j(x_1, x_2, \ldots, x_n)$. These functions are assumed to be continuous and to possess continuous first derivatives. Since the transformation is one to one, there will exist inverse functions $x_i = h_i(z_1, z_2, \ldots, z_n)$, also continuous and having continuous first derivatives. Then, under the change of variables from x_i to z_j, (2.6-4) becomes

$$Q = \int_{z_n^{(l)}}^{z_n^{(u)}} \int_{z_2^{(l)}}^{z_2^{(u)}} \int_{z_1^{(l)}}^{z_1^{(u)}} f(h_1, h_2, \ldots, h_n) J\, dz_1, dz_2, \ldots, dz_n \qquad (2.6\text{-}5)$$

where the function $h_i(z_1, z_2, \ldots, z_n)$ is abbreviated h_i, and J is the determinant

$$J = \begin{vmatrix} \dfrac{\partial h_1}{\partial z_1} & \dfrac{\partial h_1}{\partial z_2} & \cdots & \dfrac{\partial h_1}{\partial z_n} \\ \dfrac{\partial h_2}{\partial z_1} & \dfrac{\partial h_2}{\partial z_2} & \cdots & \dfrac{\partial h_2}{\partial z_n} \\ \cdots & \cdots & \cdots & \cdots \\ \dfrac{\partial h_n}{\partial z_1} & \dfrac{\partial h_n}{\partial z_2} & \cdots & \dfrac{\partial h_n}{\partial z_n} \end{vmatrix}$$

J is called the *jacobian* of the transformation. It is assumed to be everywhere nonzero; i.e., the mapping is one to one.

Using the vector notation, we may write (2.6-5) compactly as

$$Q = \int_{\mathbf{z}^{(l)}}^{\mathbf{z}^{(u)}} f[\mathbf{h}(\mathbf{z})] \left| \frac{\partial \mathbf{h}(\mathbf{z})}{\partial \mathbf{z}'} \right| d\mathbf{z} \qquad (2.6\text{-}6)$$

where by $\mathbf{h}(\mathbf{z})$ we denote a vector whose elements are $h_1, h_2, \ldots, h_n$.

In case the transformation is homogeneous linear, say,

$$\mathbf{z} = \mathbf{C}\mathbf{x} \qquad |\mathbf{C}| \neq 0$$

the situation is especially simple. For then

$$\mathbf{x} = \mathbf{C}^{-1}\mathbf{z}$$

is the inverse transformation, and the jacobian of the transformation,

$$J = |\mathbf{C}^{-1}| = \frac{1}{|\mathbf{C}|}$$

does not involve $\mathbf{z}$. It may therefore be removed from the integrand, and (2.6-6) becomes

$$Q = \frac{1}{|\mathbf{C}|} \int_{\mathbf{z}^{(l)}}^{\mathbf{z}^{(u)}} f[\mathbf{h}(\mathbf{z})]\, d\mathbf{z} \qquad (2.6\text{-}7)$$

The derivation of (2.6-7) is given in standard texts such as Courant [1959, vol. II, page 247 ff]. Intuitively, the jacobian can be understood as the proportionate change in the volume of the differential element when it is deformed, by the linear part of the transformation, from a rectangular prism into a parallelotope (see Sec. 2.4.6).

2.6.2 Change of Coordinates

The transformation $\mathbf{y} = \mathbf{A}\mathbf{x}$, which we previously saw as a mapping of a vector from one space to another, we now regard from another point of view. We may consider the transformation to represent a change of coordinate system such that $\mathbf{x}$ is referred to the old axes and $\mathbf{y}$ to the new. From this point of view, $\mathbf{x}$ and $\mathbf{y}$ represent the same vector but with respect to different bases.

In general, an affine transformation translates the origin of the coordinate frame and arbitrarily rotates reference axes, with change of the units of scale. A homogeneous linear transformation rotates axes and changes scale, but leaves the origin fixed. If a homogeneous transformation carries a rectangular coordinate frame into a frame in which the reference axes are inclined to one another, it is called an *oblique* transformation. If the frame is rotated rigidly, so that angles between axes are preserved, the transformation is called *orthogonal*. By the same token, a coordinate frame with inclined axes is called oblique, and a rectangular frame is called orthogonal.

In order to describe the relationship between the new and the old axes when the old axes are orthogonal and the new axes possibly oblique, we exhibit the matrix of *direction cosines*. A direction cosine is the cosine of the angle between a given vector and an orthogonal reference axis, with a sign attached according to the direction of the reference axis. For example, the direction cosines of the vector $\mathbf{p}$ in Fig. 2.6-1*a* are $\delta_1 = \cos\theta_1$ and $\delta_2 = \cos\theta_2$. Those of the vector $\mathbf{q}$ in Fig. 2.6-1*b*, on the other

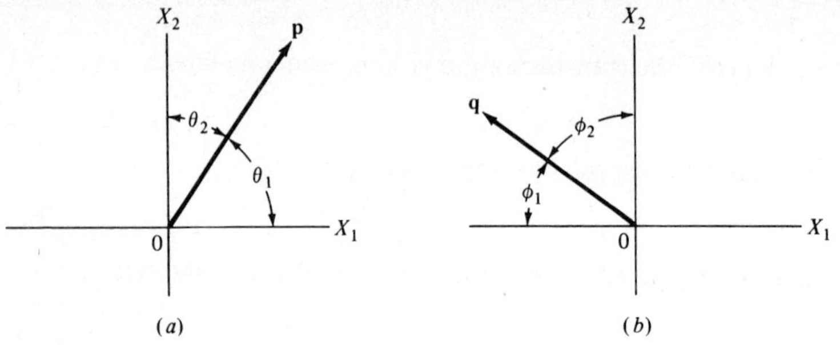

FIGURE 2.6-1
Definition of direction cosines.

hand, are $\delta_1 = -\cos\phi_1$ and $\delta_2 = \cos\phi_2$, because the angle ϕ_1 is defined with respect to the negative direction of axis X_1. Another way of defining direction cosines is to say that they are the orthogonal coordinates of a unit vector colinear with the vector in question.

In the matrix of direction cosines for a transformation of axes, the ith row gives the cosines of angles between the ith new axis and each of the old axes. For example, the transformation in the plane shown in Fig. 2.6-2 is described by

$$\mathbf{M} = \begin{bmatrix} \delta_{11} & \delta_{12} \\ \delta_{21} & \delta_{22} \end{bmatrix} = \begin{bmatrix} \cos\theta_{11} & \cos\theta_{12} \\ -\cos\theta_{21} & \cos\theta_{22} \end{bmatrix} \tag{2.6-8}$$

Because direction cosines are the signed lengths of orthogonal components of a unit vector, the pythagorean theorem for n-space implies that the sum of the squares of the direction cosines in each row of the transformation matrix equals unity; e.g., in (2.6-8),

$$\begin{aligned} \delta_{11}^2 + \delta_{12}^2 &= \cos^2\theta_{11} + \cos^2\theta_{12} = 1 \\ \delta_{21}^2 + \delta_{22}^2 &= \cos^2\theta_{21} + \cos^2\theta_{22} = 1 \end{aligned} \tag{2.6-9}$$

The coordinates of a vector with respect to the new axes are given by the matrix equation

$$\mathbf{y} = \mathbf{M}\mathbf{x} \tag{2.6-10}$$

where $\mathbf{x}$ is the vector of old coordinates, $\mathbf{y}$ the vector of new coordinates, and $\mathbf{M}$ the matrix of direction cosines. Checking (2.6-10) in terms of Fig. (2.6-2), we observe that the vector $\mathbf{p}$ is the sum of vector components of length x_1 and x_2 in the directions OX_1 and OX_2, respectively. But the component of $\mathbf{p}$ in the direction OX_1 may be resolved into components with signed lengths $x_1 \cos\theta_{11}$ and $-x_1 \cos\theta_{21}$ in the directions OY_1 and OY_2, respectively. Similarly, the component of OX in the direction OX_2 may be resolved into components of length $x_2 \cos\theta_{12}$ and $x_2 \cos\theta_{22}$ in

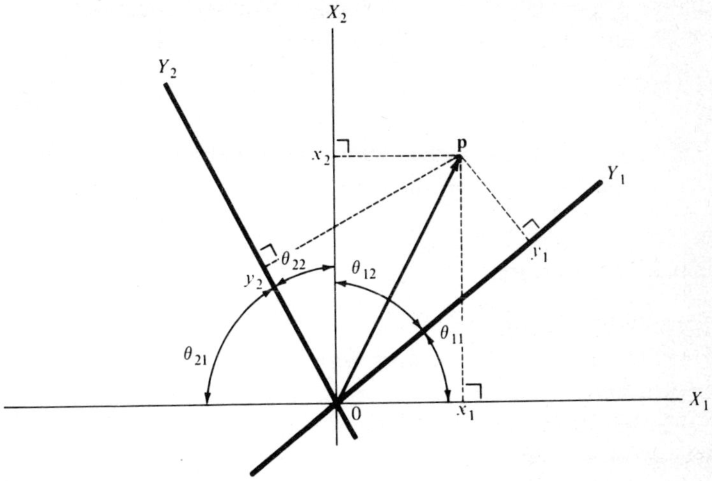

FIGURE 2.6-2
An oblique transformation.

the directions OY_1 and OY_2, respectively. Thus, rearranging terms in these sums, we may express **p** as the sum of components in the directions OY_1 and OY_2, respectively, where the lengths of these components are

$$y_1 = x_1 \cos \theta_{11} + x_2 \cos \theta_{12}$$

and

$$y_2 = -x_1 \cos \theta_{21} + x_2 \cos \theta_{22} \tag{2.6-11}$$

Thus, y_1 and y_2 are the coordinates of **p** relative to the oblique frame Y_1OY_2, expressed in terms of the coordinates relative to the orthogonal frame X_1OX_2 and the direction cosines of the transformation from the orthogonal to the oblique frame.

Because, in the plane, $\cos \theta_{12} = \sin \theta_{11}$, and $\cos \theta_{21} = \sin \theta_{22}$, (2.6-11) may be written

$$y_1 = x_1 \cos \theta_{11} + x_2 \sin \theta_{11}$$

$$y_2 = -x_1 \sin \theta_{22} + x_2 \cos \theta_{22}$$

Then (2.6-9) become the trigonometric identities $\sin^2 \theta_{11} + \cos^2 \theta_{11} = 1$ and $\sin^2 \theta_{22} + \cos^2 \theta_{22} = 1$.

If the transformation is orthogonal rather than oblique, OX_2 must be rotated through the same angle as OX_1. Thus, $\theta_{22} = \theta_{11} = \theta$, say, and (2.6-11) becomes

$$y_1 = x_1 \cos \theta + x_2 \sin \theta$$

$$y_2 = -x_1 \sin \theta + x_2 \cos \theta$$

or

$$\begin{bmatrix} y_1 \\ y_2 \end{bmatrix} = \begin{bmatrix} \cos \theta & \sin \theta \\ -\sin \theta & \cos \theta \end{bmatrix} \begin{bmatrix} x_1 \\ x_2 \end{bmatrix} \tag{2.6-12}$$

In (2.6-12), we observe that in both rows and columns $\sin^2\theta + \cos^2\theta = 1$. Furthermore, the inner product of either rows or columns is

$$\cos\theta\sin\theta - \sin\theta\cos\theta = 0$$

This agrees with our earlier observation that a transformation will preserve lengths and angles if and only if the matrix of the transformation is orthogonal.

2.6.3 Projections

The study of transformations may be extended to include singular (many-to-one) transformations. We consider here an important class of singular transformations which maps vectors into subspaces. Suppose a space of dimension n, with basis $\mathbf{Y}$, is decomposed into complementary subspaces of dimensions r and s with bases $\mathbf{X}$ and $\mathbf{E}$, respectively. Then $n = r + s$. If a linear transformation $\mathbf{G}$ maps any vector in the space into one of these subspaces, it is called a *projection*. By means of projections, a vector $\mathbf{y}$ may be decomposed into a component $\mathbf{x}$ in the r-dimensional subspace, say, and a residual $\mathbf{e}$ in the complementary s-dimensional space:

$$\begin{aligned}\mathbf{y} &= \mathbf{Gy} + (\mathbf{y} - \mathbf{Gy}) = \mathbf{Gy} + (\mathbf{I} - \mathbf{G})\mathbf{y}\\ &= \mathbf{Gy} + \mathbf{Ey} = \mathbf{x} + \mathbf{e}\end{aligned}$$

The vector $\mathbf{x}$ is the projected image of $\mathbf{y}$, and is sometimes referred to as a projection of $\mathbf{y}$ by $\mathbf{G}$. The vector $\mathbf{e}$ is the complementary projection by $\mathbf{E}$. If $\mathbf{G}$ is understood to be the matrix of the transformation, we refer to it as a *projection operator*. Similarly, $\mathbf{E}$ is the operator of the *complementary projection.*

A transformation is a projection if and only if the matrix of the transformation is *idempotent*; i.e., if the matrix is equal to its product with itself:

$$\mathbf{G} = \mathbf{GG} = \mathbf{G}^2 \qquad (2.6\text{-}13)$$

The condition (2.6-13) is necessary because, if $\mathbf{x}$ is a projection of an arbitrary $\mathbf{y}$ by $\mathbf{G}$, then by definition the decomposition of $\mathbf{x}$ is

$$\mathbf{x} = \mathbf{Gx} + \mathbf{0} = \mathbf{G}(\mathbf{Gy}) = \mathbf{G}^2\mathbf{y} = \mathbf{Gy}$$

whence $\mathbf{G}^2\mathbf{y} - \mathbf{Gy} = (\mathbf{G}^2 - \mathbf{G})\mathbf{y} = \mathbf{0}$, and $\mathbf{G}^2 - \mathbf{G}$ must be the null matrix.

It is also sufficient because, if $\mathbf{G}^2 = \mathbf{G}$, then for

$$\mathbf{x} = \mathbf{Gy}$$

we have

$$\mathbf{Gx} = \mathbf{G}^2\mathbf{y} = \mathbf{Gy} = \mathbf{x}$$

Note that (2.6-13) implies that $\mathbf{G}$ is a square matrix.

As the reader may readily verify, the following is an example of an idempotent matrix:

$$\mathbf{G} = \begin{bmatrix} 2 & -2 & -4 \\ -1 & 3 & 4 \\ 1 & -2 & -3 \end{bmatrix}$$

The rank of $\mathbf{G}$ is equal to the dimensionality of the subspace into which it projects. For if the full space is n-dimensional with a basis $\mathbf{Y} = [\underset{n\times r}{\mathbf{X}}, \underset{n\times s}{\mathbf{E}}]$ of rank n, of which the first r columns belong to the subspace and the remainder to its complement, then $\underset{n\times n}{\mathbf{G}}\ \underset{n\times n}{\mathbf{Y}} = [\underset{n\times r}{\mathbf{X}}, \underset{n\times s}{\mathbf{O}}]$, where the rank of $\mathbf{X}$ is r. By the theorem for rank of matrix products (Sec. 2.3.2), the rank of $\mathbf{G}$ must be r since $\mathbf{Y}$ is of full rank. Conversely, if $\mathbf{G}$ is of rank r, the complementary projection operator $\mathbf{I} - \mathbf{G}$ is of rank $n - r$.

Suppose we are given a column basis $\underset{n\times r}{\mathbf{X}}$ for an r-dimensional subspace of $\mathbf{Y}$ and wish to construct a projection operator for the space of $\mathbf{X}$ and its complement. It is clear that the matrix $\mathbf{M} = \mathbf{X}(\mathbf{X}'\mathbf{X})^{-1}\mathbf{X}'$ serves this purpose, for it is clearly a rank-r idempotent,

$$\mathbf{M}^2 = \mathbf{X}(\mathbf{X}'\mathbf{X})^{-1}\mathbf{X}'\mathbf{X}(\mathbf{X}'\mathbf{X})^{-1}\mathbf{X}' = \mathbf{X}(\mathbf{X}'\mathbf{X})^{-1}\mathbf{X}' = \mathbf{M}$$

and any vector $\mathbf{u} = \mathbf{My} = \mathbf{X}[(\mathbf{X}'\mathbf{X})^{-1}\mathbf{X}'\mathbf{y}] = \mathbf{Xb}$, say, is linearly dependent upon the basis $\mathbf{X}$.

Any vector $\mathbf{y}$ in the full space may then be resolved into components

$$\mathbf{y} = \mathbf{X}(\mathbf{X}'\mathbf{X})^{-1}\mathbf{X}'\mathbf{y} + [\mathbf{I} - \mathbf{X}(\mathbf{X}'\mathbf{X})^{-1}\mathbf{X}]\mathbf{y} = \mathbf{My} + (\mathbf{I} - \mathbf{M})\mathbf{y} = \mathbf{u} + \mathbf{v}$$

These components are orthogonal, since $\mathbf{M} = \mathbf{M}'$ and

$$\mathbf{u}'\mathbf{v} = \mathbf{y}'\mathbf{M}(\mathbf{I} - \mathbf{M})\mathbf{y} = \mathbf{y}'(\mathbf{M} - \mathbf{M}^2)\mathbf{y} = \mathbf{y}'\mathbf{O}\mathbf{y} = 0$$

Hence, the square length of $\mathbf{y}$ is partitioned by the projections into the sum of the square lengths of $\mathbf{u}$ and $\mathbf{v}$:

$$\mathbf{y}'\mathbf{y} = \mathbf{u}'\mathbf{u} + \mathbf{v}'\mathbf{v} = \mathbf{y}'\mathbf{X}(\mathbf{X}'\mathbf{X})^{-1}\mathbf{X}'\mathbf{y} + \mathbf{y}'[\mathbf{I} - \mathbf{X}(\mathbf{X}'\mathbf{X})^{-1}\mathbf{X}']\mathbf{y} = \mathbf{y}'\mathbf{My} + \mathbf{y}(\mathbf{I} - \mathbf{M})\mathbf{y}$$

As we shall see in Secs. 4.1.5 and 4.1.7, the technique of analysis of variance may be interpreted geometrically as the projection of the observational vector into orthogonal subspaces. By Pythagoras, the square lengths of these projections sum to the square length of the observational vector. This is the basis of the partition of sums of squares in analysis of variance. The subspaces in any particular analysis are generated from the linear model that is assumed to describe the data. The "degrees of freedom" in the analysis are the dimensionalities of these subspaces.

EXAMPLE 2.6-1 (*Projection*) Suppose the four components of the vector, $[y_1, y_2, z_1, z_2]$ represent two observations of type Y and type Z, respectively. Obtain the projection of this vector on a two-dimensional subspace whose basis vectors represent sums and differences of the two types of observations. These basis vectors are

$$\underset{4\times 2}{\mathbf{X}} = \begin{bmatrix} 1 & 1 \\ 1 & 1 \\ 1 & -1 \\ 1 & -1 \end{bmatrix}$$

To obtain the projection operator for the subspace and the complementary space, we compute first

$$\mathbf{X}'\mathbf{X} = \begin{bmatrix} 4 & 0 \\ 0 & 4 \end{bmatrix} \quad \text{and} \quad (\mathbf{X}'\mathbf{X})^{-1} = \frac{1}{4}\begin{bmatrix} 1 & 0 \\ 0 & 1 \end{bmatrix}$$

Then,
$$\mathbf{M} = \mathbf{X}(\mathbf{X}'\mathbf{X})^{-1}\mathbf{X}' = \begin{bmatrix} \frac{1}{2} & \frac{1}{2} & 0 & 0 \\ \frac{1}{2} & \frac{1}{2} & 0 & 0 \\ 0 & 0 & \frac{1}{2} & \frac{1}{2} \\ 0 & 0 & \frac{1}{2} & \frac{1}{2} \end{bmatrix}$$

and
$$\mathbf{I} - \mathbf{M} = \begin{bmatrix} \frac{1}{2} & -\frac{1}{2} & 0 & 0 \\ -\frac{1}{2} & \frac{1}{2} & 0 & 0 \\ 0 & 0 & \frac{1}{2} & -\frac{1}{2} \\ 0 & 0 & -\frac{1}{2} & \frac{1}{2} \end{bmatrix}$$

Thus, the observational vector may be expressed identically as the sum of the orthogonal components as follows:

$$\begin{bmatrix} y_1 \\ y_2 \\ z_1 \\ z_2 \end{bmatrix} = \frac{1}{2}\begin{bmatrix} y_1 + y_2 \\ y_1 + y_2 \\ z_1 + z_2 \\ z_1 + z_2 \end{bmatrix} + \frac{1}{2}\begin{bmatrix} y_1 - y_2 \\ y_2 - y_1 \\ z_1 - z_2 \\ z_2 - z_1 \end{bmatrix}$$

Because of orthogonality, the square lengths of these vectors satisfy

$$y_1^2 + y_2^2 + z_1^2 + z_2^2 = \tfrac{1}{2}(y_1 + y_2)^2 + \tfrac{1}{2}(z_1 + z_2)^2 + \tfrac{1}{2}(y_1 - y_2)^2 + \tfrac{1}{2}(z_1 - z_2)^2$$

the first two terms on the right being the square lengths of the projection on **X**, and the latter two the square lengths of the projection on the complementary space.

2.7 QUADRATIC FORMS

We have already seen how length and angle may be expressed in terms of rectangular coordinates by invoking the pythagorean theorem and the law of cosines (Sec. 2.2.3). We now consider how these expressions may be generalized to oblique or translated reference axes. In the terminology of vector spaces, we would say that we require definitions of length and angle that are valid for affine space as well as ordinary euclidean space. In terms of bases, this means that the definitions must extend to vectors expressed in components relative to an arbitrary basis and not merely to an orthonormal basis.

2.7.1 Length and Angle in Affine Space

Initially, suppose that an m-component vector $\mathbf{x}$ is expressed in terms of an orthonormal basis. Now rotate the basis vectors by a transformation given by a matrix of direction cosines $\mathbf{M}$; then rescale by a diagonal matrix $\mathbf{D}$, and shift the origin by adding a vector $\mathbf{c}$. According to (2.6-1), the coordinates of the original vector relative to the new basis are

$$\mathbf{v} = \mathbf{DMx} + \mathbf{c} = \mathbf{Bx} + \mathbf{c}, \text{ say} \tag{2.7-1}$$

Let us assume that the transformation is nonsingular and that the inverse transformation is

$$\mathbf{x} = \mathbf{B}^{-1}(\mathbf{v} - \mathbf{c})$$

Then the square length of the vector may be expressed in terms of the new coordinates as

$$Q = \mathbf{x}'\mathbf{x} = (\mathbf{v} - \mathbf{c})'(\mathbf{B}^{-1})'\mathbf{B}^{-1}(\mathbf{v} - \mathbf{c}) = \mathbf{y}'\mathbf{Ay} \tag{2.7-2}$$

The scalar Q represents a so-called *quadratic form*; $\mathbf{A}$ is called the matrix of the form, and $\mathbf{y}$ is the *variable* or *argument* of the form. In scalar quantities, the form may be written

$$Q = \sum_{j=1}^{m} \sum_{k=1}^{m} a_{jk} y_j y_k$$

where $a_{jk} = a_{kj}$.

The *inner product* of $\mathbf{x}$ with itself, when expressed as a matrix product, is a quadratic form in which the matrix is the identity:

$$\mathbf{x}'\mathbf{x} = \mathbf{x}'\mathbf{Ix}$$

By the reverse token, (2.7-2) may be considered a generalized inner product or, as we say, the *inner product of* $\mathbf{y}$ *in the metric* $\mathbf{A}$.

In a similar fashion, we may express the angle between two vectors in terms of transformed coordinates. If the coordinates of vectors $\mathbf{x}_1$ and $\mathbf{x}_2$ become

$$\mathbf{v}_1 = \mathbf{DMx}_1 + \mathbf{c} = \mathbf{Bx}_1 + \mathbf{c}$$

and

$$\mathbf{v}_2 = \mathbf{DMx}_2 + \mathbf{c} = \mathbf{Bx}_2 + \mathbf{c}$$

under the nonsingular affine transformation, the cosine of the angle between the vectors in terms of the new coordinates is

$$\cos(\mathbf{x}_1,\mathbf{x}_2) = \frac{\mathbf{y}_1'\mathbf{Ay}_2}{\sqrt{(\mathbf{y}_1'\mathbf{Ay}_1)(\mathbf{y}_2'\mathbf{Ay}_2)}}$$

That is, angles in affine space may be defined in terms of inner products between vectors in the metric $\mathbf{A}$. The generalized inner products of the type $\mathbf{y}_1'\mathbf{A}\mathbf{y}_2$ are called *bilinear forms.*

Thus, we may define orthogonality in affine space by $\mathbf{y}_1'\mathbf{A}\mathbf{y}_2 = 0$; that is, by the vanishing of the inner product in the metric $\mathbf{A}$. We then say that $\mathbf{y}_1$ and $\mathbf{y}_2$ are *orthogonal in the metric* $\mathbf{A}$. It should now be clear that any geometric construction that employs the concepts of length, angle, and orthogonality may be generalized to vectors represented with respect to other than orthonormal bases. It is only necessary to substitute a general inner product—an inner product with respect to a specified metric—at every point where the calculation of an inner product is required. In particular, the Gram-Schmidt may be generalized in this way in order to construct, from $\mathbf{X}$, a matrix $\mathbf{X}^*$, say, which is orthogonal in the metric $\mathbf{A}$, that is, which satisfies $(\mathbf{X}^*)'\mathbf{A}\mathbf{X}^* = \mathbf{I}$.

Later we shall investigate the conditions under which a given symmetric matrix $\mathbf{A}$ may be a metric matrix, but first let us examine further geometric interpretations for $\mathbf{A}$ when it has arisen from a change of basis as shown in (2.7-1). In that case $\mathbf{A}$ may be expressed as

$$\begin{aligned}\mathbf{A} &= (\mathbf{M}^{-1}\mathbf{D}^{-1})'(\mathbf{M}^{-1}\mathbf{D}^{-1}) = \mathbf{D}^{-1}(\mathbf{M}^{-1})'\mathbf{M}^{-1}\mathbf{D}^{-1} \\ &= \mathbf{D}^{-1}(\mathbf{M}\mathbf{M}')^{-1}\mathbf{D}^{-1} = \mathbf{D}^{-1}\mathbf{R}^{-1}\mathbf{D}^{-1}\end{aligned}$$

so we may write

$$Q = [(\mathbf{v} - \mathbf{c})'\mathbf{D}^{-1}]\mathbf{R}^{-1}[\mathbf{D}^{-1}(\mathbf{v} - \mathbf{c})] = \mathbf{z}'\mathbf{R}^{-1}\mathbf{z} \qquad (2.7\text{-}3)$$

as a standard form for length in an oblique space. The $\mathbf{z}$'s are coordinates with respect to normalized oblique basis vectors. The elements of the matrix $\mathbf{R}$ are the cosines of angles between all pairs of basis vectors. To verify that this interpretation of $\mathbf{R}$ is correct, recall that the direction cosines in the rows of $\mathbf{M}$ are the lengths of orthogonal components of the new basis vectors (Sec. 2.6.2). The diagonal elements of $\mathbf{R}$ are therefore unities, since each is the inner product (square length) of a normalized basis vector with itself. Similarly, the j,k element in $\mathbf{R}$ is the inner product of basis vectors $\mathbf{j}$ and $\mathbf{k}$, which by the law of cosines applied to normalized vectors is just the cosine of the angle between the vectors.

In a statistical context, the matrix $\mathbf{R}$ is interpreted as a matrix of *correlation coefficients* between variables. In situations where the correlations among variables is known, certain statistical results for independent variables may be generalized to the correlated case by using inner products with respect to a metric in place of sums of squares or sums of cross products (Exercise 4.1-5). The metric matrix in these calculations is the inverse of the matrix of correlation coefficients.

2.7.2 Classification of Quadratic Forms

We now consider the question of whether or not a given symmetric matrix is a metric matrix. In order for $\mathbf{A}$ to be a metric matrix it must preserve the positiveness of lengths and the triangular inequality of distance (Sec. 2.2.3). A sufficient condition for a symmetric matrix **A** to be a metric is therefore that the quadratic form $\mathbf{y}'\mathbf{A}\mathbf{y}$ is positive for all nonnull **y**. A matrix that fulfills this condition is called *positive definite* (pd). A necessary and sufficient condition for **A** to be pd is that it is factorable as

$$\underset{m\times m}{\mathbf{A}} = \underset{m\times n}{\mathbf{F}'}\ \underset{n\times m}{\mathbf{F}} \tag{2.7-4}$$

and that rank(**F**) $= m$. For then,

$$\begin{aligned} Q &= \mathbf{y}'\mathbf{A}\mathbf{y} = \mathbf{y}'(\mathbf{F}'\mathbf{F})\mathbf{y} = (\mathbf{y}\mathbf{F})(\mathbf{F}\mathbf{y}) = \mathbf{z}'\mathbf{z} \\ &= z_1^2 + z_2^2 + \cdots + z_n^2 \end{aligned}$$

Because **F** is of full rank, there is no nonnull **y**, such that $\mathbf{z} = \mathbf{F}\mathbf{y} = 0$. Thus, Q is always positive as required.

Conversely, if $\mathbf{y}'\mathbf{A}\mathbf{y}$ is always positive, then a square matrix $\mathbf{Y}^*$, which has the property

$$(\mathbf{Y}^*)'\mathbf{A}\mathbf{Y}^* = \mathbf{I}$$

can be constructed by the Gram-Schmidt construction in the metric **A**, since the lengths of the orthogonalized vectors at each stage are strictly positive. Then

$$(\mathbf{Y}^{*-1})'\mathbf{Y}^{*\prime}\mathbf{A}\mathbf{Y}^*\mathbf{Y}^{*-1} = (\mathbf{Y}^{*-1})'\mathbf{Y}^{*-1} = \mathbf{A}$$

and **A** is expressed in the form of (2.7-4).

That this condition provides a practical test of positive definiteness is implicit in the gaussian factorization of square matrices introduced in Sec. 2.3.4. For, if **A** is symmetric, $\mathbf{A} = \mathbf{A}'$, and the gaussian factorization becomes

$$\underset{m\times m}{\mathbf{A}} = \mathbf{L}\mathbf{D}\mathbf{L}'$$

Then, if the elements of the $m \times m$ diagonal matrix **D** satisfy $d_i > 0$, we may define

$$\mathbf{D}^{1/2} = \operatorname{diag}(d_1^{1/2}, d_2^{1/2}, \ldots, d_m^{1/2})$$

the elements of which are the positive square roots of the elements of **D**. Then we write

$$\underset{m\times m}{\mathbf{A}} = (\mathbf{L}\mathbf{D}^{1/2})(\mathbf{D}^{1/2}\mathbf{L})' = \underset{m\times m}{\mathbf{S}}\ \underset{m\times m}{\mathbf{S}'}$$

The triangular matrix **S** is called the *Cholesky factor* of **A**. In view of the uniqueness of the gaussian factorization (Sec. 2.3.4c), we conclude that every symmetric pd matrix has a unique Cholesky factor, except for possible ambiguity of signs in $\mathbf{D}^{1/2}$. If the signs are taken positive by convention, the factorization is unique. Conversely, if the matrix admits a Cholesky factorization, it is symmetric positive definite. A practical computing method for obtaining the Cholesky factor and its inverse is presented in Example 2.7-1.

If an $m \times m$ matrix **A** is symmetric positive definite, then so is its inverse. For if

$$\mathbf{A} = \mathbf{S}\mathbf{S}'$$

then

$$\mathbf{A}^{-1} = (\mathbf{S}^{-1})'\mathbf{S}^{-1}$$

that is, $\mathbf{A}^{-1}$ is also the product of a rank-m matrix and its transpose.

If **A** arises from (2.7-4), but rank(**F**) $= r \leq m$, then rank(**A**) $= r \leq m$ (Sec. 2.3.4a) and $m - r$ elements of **D** in the gaussian factorization are zero. In this case, the quadratic form in **A** is nonnegative, but it may be zero nontrivially. Such a form and its matrix are called *positive semidefinite* (psd). A symmetric psd matrix cannot serve as a metric, but it is nevertheless factorable into the product of a matrix and its transpose as shown in (2.7-4). Such a matrix (either pd or psd) is called a *grammian* matrix. Its determinant is called the *grammian* of the factor; e.g., the grammian of **F** is $|\mathbf{F}'\mathbf{F}|$. Vanishing of the grammian ($|\mathbf{F}'\mathbf{F}| = |\mathbf{A}| = 0$) implies that **A** is psd. The grammian also provides a test of linear dependency among the columns of **F**, since it vanishes if and only if **F** is of deficient rank.

The gaussian factorization of the matrix of a quadratic form also provides a convenient method of finding a change of basis (transformation of coordinate axes) such that the representation of a quadratic form contains only squared terms. For, if $\mathbf{A} = \mathbf{LDL}'$, and we set

$$\mathbf{y} = (\mathbf{L}^{-1})'\mathbf{u}$$

then

$$Q = \mathbf{u}'\mathbf{L}^{-1}\mathbf{LDL}'(\mathbf{L}^{-1})'\mathbf{u} = \mathbf{u}'\mathbf{D}\mathbf{u}$$
$$= d_1 u_1^2 + d_2 u_2^2 + \cdots + d_m u_m^2$$

That is, the form is reduced to a *diagonal representation* consisting of squared terms only. The coefficients of the squared terms are the elements of the diagonal matrix **D**. This is not the only possible diagonal representation (another is shown in Sec. 2.7.3), but all such representations have the following important property (Sylvester's law of inertia): *The number of terms in a diagonal representation of a quadratic form with positive, negative, or zero coefficients is uniquely determined by the matrix of the form.* The number of terms with nonzero coefficients is called the *rank* of the form; the number of positive coefficients minus the number of negative coefficients is called the *signature* of the form. Sylvester's law of inertia states that the rank and signature of a quadratic form are invariant under change of basis. We have already seen that the rank of a matrix determines the number of nonzero elements in a diagonal matrix obtained by row and column operations on the original matrix. Since these operations include all possible changes of bases, it is clear that the number of nonzero coefficients in the diagonal representation of a quadratic form is determined by the rank of its matrix. The proof that, among these nonzero coefficients, the number of positive coefficients is unique consists of showing that if this number differed in two diagonal representations of the form, then some vectors in the space of the form's variable would yield simultaneously a positive and a negative value of the form, which is impossible (see Stoll [1952, page 120]).

If all coefficients are negative in the diagonal representation, the form is called *negative definite*; if they are nonpositive, the form is called *negative semidefinite*. If the coefficients are both negative and positive, the form is called *indefinite*. The definiteness of quadratic forms is intimately connected with the problem of maximizing quadratic forms which we shall discuss presently.

EXAMPLE 2.7-1 (*The Cholesky factorization*) The Cholesky factorization of a real symmetric positive-definite (spd) matrix is the basis of a computing algorithm which is useful in statistical work. In terms of number of operations, economy of storage, and stability in the presence of rounding error, this algorithm equals or excells all other direct methods of inverting such a matrix or computing its determinant. It also provides an alternative to the Gram-Schmidt construction as a method of orthogonalizing a set of vectors. In the psychological literature, this algorithm is called the *square-root* method, both in reference to matrix inversion [Dickman and Kaiser, 1961] and to orthogonalization in factor analysis [Harman, 1954].

To illustrate the calculation of the Cholesky factor, its inverse, and the inverse of the original matrix, we shall apply the algorithm to the grammian matrix computed from the Vandermonde matrix of order 4 (see Example 2.3-1). The matrix to be factored is

$$\mathbf{A} = \mathbf{V}_4'\mathbf{V}_4 = \begin{bmatrix} 4 & 10 & 30 & 100 \\ 10 & 30 & 100 & 354 \\ 30 & 100 & 354 & 1{,}300 \\ 100 & 354 & 1{,}300 & 4{,}890 \end{bmatrix}$$

The four main steps in the computing algorithm are illustrated in the four sections of Table 2.7-1. The arithmetic operations to be performed in each step are as follows:*

1 Designate the $n \times n$ matrix to be factored and inverted by $\mathbf{A}$, and its elements by a_{ij}. To provide a check on the arithmetic, sum the rows of $\mathbf{A}$, change the signs, and record the result as an additional column to the right of $\mathbf{A}$; carry this column in all subsequent calculations as if it were the $(n + 1)$st column of the original matrix.

2 Transform the matrix $\mathbf{A}$ into $\mathbf{S}'$, the transpose of the Cholesky factor. The elements of $\mathbf{S}'$ not identically zero are computed as follows:

First row:
$$s_{11} = \sqrt{a_{11}} \qquad s_{1j} = \frac{a_{1j}}{s_{11}}$$

ith row:
$$s_{ii} = \left(a_{ii} - \sum_{r=1}^{i-1} s_{ri}^{\,2}\right)^{1/2}$$

$$s_{ij} = \frac{1}{s_{ii}}\left(a_{ij} - \sum_{r=1}^{i-1} s_{ri}s_{rj}\right)$$

Rows of $\mathbf{S}'$ including the "check" column must sum to zero within rounding error.

3 Compute $\mathbf{S}^{-1}$, the inverse of $\mathbf{S}$, with elements s^{ij} as follows:

$$s^{ii} = \frac{1}{s_{ii}} \qquad s^{ij} = -\frac{1}{s_{ii}}\sum_{r=j}^{i-1} s_{ri}s^{rj} \qquad i > j$$

* Adapted from Bock and Jones [1968].

Table 2.7-1 COMPUTATIONS BASED ON THE CHOLESKY FACTORIZATION (DECIMAL ARITHMETIC)

Matrix	i	j: 1	2	3	4	5	Check
A	1	4	10	30	100	−144	0
$[a_{ij}]$	2	10	30	100	354	−494	0
	3	30	100	354	1,300	−1,784	0
	4	100	354	1,300	4,890	−6,644	0
S′	1	2	5	15	50	−72	0
$[s_{ij}]$	2	0	2.23606798	11.18033990	46.51021398	−59.92662186	.00000000
	3	0	0	2.00000000	14.99999994	−16.99999992	.00000002
	4	0	0	0	1.34163979	−1.34163911	.00000068
$\mathbf{S}^{-1}$	1	.50000000	0	0	0		1.00000527
$[s^{ij}]$	2	−1.11803399	.44721359	0	0		.99999157
	3	2.50000001	−2.49999997	.50000000	0		1.00000380
	4	−7.82624364	12.44745404	−5.59017407	.74535655		.99999950
$\mathbf{A}^{-1}$	1	69.00008957	−104.16680696	45.00006427	−5.83334196		1.00093528
$[a^{ij}]$	2	−104.16680696	161.38911192	−70.83343480	9.27779140		.99946464
	3	45.00006427	−70.83343480	31.50004613	−4.16667286		1.00025776
	4	−5.83334196	9.27779140	−4.16667286	.55555639		.99998228

For $i < j$, $s^{ij} = 0$. The elements $s^{j,n+1}$ in the check column of $\mathbf{S}^{-1}$, computed from

$$s^{j,n+1} = -\sum_{r=j}^{n} s_{r,n+1}s^{rj}$$

must equal unity within rounding error.

4 Compute $\mathbf{A}^{-1}$, the inverse of $\mathbf{A}$, from $(\mathbf{S}^{-1})'\mathbf{S}^{-1} = \mathbf{A}^{-1}$. The elements a^{ij} of $\mathbf{A}^{-1}$ (where $a^{ji} = a^{ij}$) are given by

$$a^{ii} = \sum_{r=i}^{n} (s^{ri})^2 \qquad a^{ij} = \sum_{r=i}^{n} s^{ri}s^{rj} \qquad i > j$$

To check $\mathbf{A}^{-1}$, sum the products of elements in the columns of $\mathbf{A}^{-1}$ and the corresponding elements in the sum column of $\mathbf{A}$. These values should satisfy

$$-\sum_{r=1}^{n} a^{ij}a_{i,n+1} = 1$$

within rounding error.

Table 2.7-1 illustrates the difficulties that arise when decimal approximations are used in the inversion of a matrix that is "ill conditioned" for matrix inversion. Although at least nine significant figures have been carried in the intermediate calculations, only five significant figures are accurate in the inverse matrix. In this particular example, the Cholesky factor and inverse can be expressed in integers and represented exactly as shown in Table 2.7-2. Notice in the decimal calculations that

Table 2.7-2 COMPUTATIONS BASED ON THE CHOLESKY FACTORIZATION (INTEGER ARITHMETIC)

Matrix	i	j: 1	2	3	4	5	Check
A $[a_{ij}]$	1	4	10	30	100	−144	0
	2	10	30	100	354	−494	0
	3	30	100	354	1,300	−1,784	0
	4	100	354	1,300	4,890	−6,644	0
S′ $[s_{ij}]$	1	2	5	15	50	−72	0
	2	0	$5/\sqrt{5}$	$25/\sqrt{5}$	$104/\sqrt{5}$	$-134/\sqrt{5}$	0
	3	0	0	2	15	−17	0
	4	0	0	0	$3/\sqrt{5}$	$-3/\sqrt{5}$	0
$\mathbf{S}^{-1}$ $[s^{ij}]$	1	$\frac{1}{2}$	0	0	0		1
	2	$-\sqrt{5}/2$	$\sqrt{5}/5$	0	0		1
	3	$\frac{5}{2}$	$\frac{5}{2}$	$\frac{1}{2}$	0		1
	4	$-7\sqrt{5}/2$	$167\sqrt{5}/3$	$-5\sqrt{5}/2$	$\sqrt{5}/3$		1
$\mathbf{A}^{-1}$ $[a^{ij}]$	1	69	$-104\frac{1}{6}$	45	$-5\frac{5}{6}$		1
	2	$-104\frac{1}{6}$	$161\frac{7}{18}$	$-70\frac{5}{6}$	$9\frac{5}{18}$		1
	3	45	$-70\frac{5}{6}$	$31\frac{1}{2}$	$-4\frac{1}{6}$		1
	4	$-5\frac{5}{6}$	$9\frac{5}{18}$	$-4\frac{1}{6}$	$\frac{5}{9}$		1

the Cholesky factor and the inverse Cholesky factor are considerably more accurate than the inverse matrix.

An analysis of conditioning problems in matrix inversion may be found in Noble [1969, Chap. 8].

The Cholesky factor S and its inverse S^{-1} have the following properties:

Properties	Forms	
$SS' = A$	◺ · ◹ = ☐	(2.7–5)
$S^{-1}S = S'(S^{-1})' = I$	◺ · ◸ = ◹ ◹ – I	
$S^{-1}A = S'$	◺ · ☐ = ◹	(2.7–6)
$A(S^{-1})' = S$	☐ · ◹ = ◺	(2.7–7)
$S^{-1}A(S^{-1})' = I$	◺ · ☐ · ◹ = I	(2.7–8)
$(S^{-1})'S^{-1} = A^{-1}$	◹ · ◺ = ☐	(2.7–9)

Property (2.7-8) is especially interesting because it implies that if A arose as $A = F'F$, then $F^* = F(S^{-1})'$ is orthonormal with respect to columns:

$$S^{-1}F'F(S^{-1})' = I$$

In the present example $F = V_4$ and S^{-1} appears in the second section of Table 2.7-1; hence we may calculate as follows:

$$V_4^* = V_4(S^{-1})'$$

$$= \begin{bmatrix} 1 & 1 & 1 & 1 \\ 1 & 2 & 4 & 8 \\ 1 & 3 & 9 & 27 \\ 1 & 4 & 16 & 64 \end{bmatrix} \begin{bmatrix} .50000000 & -1.11803399 & 2.50000001 & -7.82624364 \\ 0 & .44721359 & -2.49999997 & 12.44745404 \\ 0 & 0 & .50000000 & -5.59017407 \\ 0 & 0 & 0 & .74535655 \end{bmatrix}$$

$$= \begin{bmatrix} .50000000 & -.67082040 & .50000004 & -.22360712 \\ .50000000 & -.22360681 & -.49999993 & .67082056 \\ .50000000 & .22360678 & -.49999990 & -.67082130 \\ .50000000 & .67082037 & .50000013 & .22360660 \end{bmatrix}$$

Notice that V^* is the same matrix within rounding error as we obtained by the Gram-Schmidt method in Example 2.2-2. That this is true in general follows from the uniqueness of the Cholesky factorization. For a proof, observe that the operations in the Gram-Schmidt construction are equivalent to postmultiplication of the original matrix by an upper-triangular matrix, say

$$\underset{n \times m}{F_1^*} = \underset{n \times m}{F} \underset{m \times m}{(S_1^{-1})'} \qquad (2.7\text{-}10)$$

where $\qquad (F_1^*)'F_1^* = S_1^{-1}F'F(S_1^{-1})' = I \qquad$ or $\qquad S_1S_1' = F'F = A$

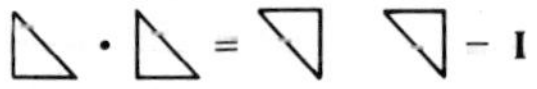

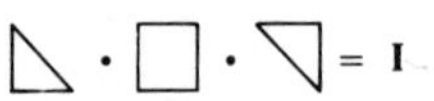

But $\mathbf{S}_1 = \mathbf{S}$ is the unique Cholesky factor of $\mathbf{F}'\mathbf{F}$; whence, the orthogonalization $\mathbf{F}^* = \mathbf{F}(\mathbf{S}^{-1})'$ using the inverse Cholesky factor of $\mathbf{F}'\mathbf{F}$ is identical with the Gram-Schmidt orthogonalization.

Conversely, the inner products between the columns of $\mathbf{F}$ and $\mathbf{F}^*$ that are computed in the Gram-Schmidt construction are just the elements of $\mathbf{S}$:

$$\mathbf{F}'\mathbf{F}^* = \mathbf{F}'\mathbf{F}(\mathbf{S}^{-1})' = \mathbf{A}(\mathbf{S}^{-1})' = \mathbf{S}$$

In Chap. 4, we shall make use of these relationships to perform least-squares calculations by orthogonalization.

2.7.3 Maximizing Quadratic Forms

In statistics and other applied fields, we are often required to maximize a quadratic form relative to variation in the argument of the form. Since $Q = \mathbf{x}'\mathbf{A}\mathbf{x}$ can obviously be made arbitrarily large by taking the elements of $\mathbf{x}$ arbitrarily large, it is necessary to maximize Q conditional on some restriction on the size of $\mathbf{x}$. A convenient condition is to require that $\mathbf{x}$ is normalized by dividing by the square root of its square length. Then the maximization problem may be set as one of maximizing the ratio

$$\lambda = \frac{\mathbf{x}'\mathbf{A}\mathbf{x}}{\mathbf{x}'\mathbf{x}} \qquad (2.7\text{-}11)$$

where $\mathbf{A}$ is any real symmetric matrix.

To solve this problem, we differentiate the right member of (2.7-11) with respect to $x_1, x_2, \ldots, x_n$, set each of these derivatives to zero, and solve the resulting system of equations for the value of $\mathbf{x}$ at the extremal point. These operations may be expressed compactly using the vector and matrix derivatives of Sec. 2.5. In particular, the derivative of a quadratic form with respect to the variable of the form is the vector derivative (2.5-34):

$$\frac{\partial \mathbf{x}'\mathbf{A}\mathbf{x}}{\partial \mathbf{x}} = 2\mathbf{A}\mathbf{x}$$

Thus, using the quotient rule on (2.7-11), we have

$$\frac{\partial \lambda}{\partial \mathbf{x}} = \frac{2\mathbf{A}\mathbf{x}(\mathbf{x}'\mathbf{x}) - 2(\mathbf{x}'\mathbf{A}\mathbf{x})\mathbf{x}}{(\mathbf{x}'\mathbf{x})^2}$$

$$= 2\frac{1}{\mathbf{x}'\mathbf{x}}\left(\mathbf{A} - \frac{\mathbf{x}'\mathbf{A}\mathbf{x}}{\mathbf{x}'\mathbf{x}}\mathbf{I}\right)\mathbf{x} \qquad \mathbf{x}'\mathbf{x} \neq 0$$

Setting the derivatives equal to zero and dividing by $2/\mathbf{x}'\mathbf{x}$, we obtain the system of homogeneous equations

$$(\mathbf{A} - \lambda_i\mathbf{I})\mathbf{x}_i = \mathbf{0} \qquad (2.7\text{-}12)$$

where $\mathbf{x}_i$ is the value of $\mathbf{x}$ at a stationary point, and $\lambda_i = \mathbf{x}_i'\mathbf{A}\mathbf{x}_i/\mathbf{x}_i'\mathbf{x}_i$.

If (2.7-12) is to have a nontrivial solution, it is clear that the matrix $\mathbf{A} - \lambda_i\mathbf{I}$ must be linearly dependent (by columns) and that $\mathbf{x}$ must contain the coefficients which satisfy the condition for linear dependency. This means that $\mathbf{A} - \lambda_i\mathbf{I}$ cannot be of full rank; hence, the determinantal equation

$$|\mathbf{A} - \lambda_i\mathbf{I}| = 0 \qquad (2.7\text{-}13)$$

must be satisfied. The polynomial in λ which results upon expanding the left member of (2.7-13) is called the *characteristic equation* of the matrix $\mathbf{A}$. λ_i is a zero of the function, i.e., a root of (2.7-13), and is called a *characteristic value* of $\mathbf{A}$. $\mathbf{x}_i$ is the *characteristic vector* of $\mathbf{A}$ associated with λ_i. Other terminology employs "eigenvalue, eigenvector," or "proper value, proper vector," or "latent root, latent vector."

The characteristic equation has an important role in the study of transformations and quadratic forms, and appears frequently in multivariate statistics. To investigate its properties we expand (2.7-13) by diagonal elements [Aitken, 1956], thus putting the characteristic equation in the following form:

$$\lambda^n + \text{tr}_1(\mathbf{A})\lambda^{n-1} + \text{tr}_2(\mathbf{A})\lambda^{n-2} + \cdots + \text{tr}_{n-1}(\mathbf{A})\lambda + |\mathbf{A}| = 0 \qquad (2.7\text{-}14)$$

where $\text{tr}_n(\mathbf{A})$ (read "nth-order trace of $\mathbf{A}$") means the sum of all principal minors of order n in the matrix $\mathbf{A}$. Note that $\text{tr}_1(\mathbf{A})$, which is just the sum of diagonal elements of $\mathbf{A}$, is the same as $\text{tr}(\mathbf{A})$ defined by (2.5-7). Suppose $\text{rank}(\mathbf{A}) = r$; since the order of the largest nonzero minor of $\mathbf{A}$ cannot exceed $\text{rank}(\mathbf{A})$, it is clear that the degree of the polynomial (2.7-14) is equal to r. Thus, there are r solutions of (2.7-13) which give nonzero values for λ. In statistical applications where $\mathbf{A}$ is a function of random variables, the roots of (2.7-13) are in general distinct. The largest root, λ_1, corresponds to a proper maximum of the ratio λ, and the remaining r roots correspond to various relative maxima.

The characteristic vectors corresponding to distinct roots are orthogonal, for if

$$(\mathbf{A} - \lambda_j\mathbf{I})\mathbf{x}_j = \mathbf{0}$$

and

$$(\mathbf{A} - \lambda_k\mathbf{I})\mathbf{x}_k = \mathbf{0}$$

then

$$\mathbf{x}_j'\mathbf{A}\mathbf{x}_k = \lambda_j\mathbf{x}_j'\mathbf{x}_k = \lambda_k\mathbf{x}_j'\mathbf{x}_k$$

and

$$(\lambda_j - \lambda_k)\mathbf{x}_j'\mathbf{x}_k = 0$$

if and only if $\mathbf{x}_j'\mathbf{x}_k = 0$.

Thus, if $\mathbf{A}$ is of full rank and the characteristic vectors are normed to unit length, the matrix $\mathbf{X} = [\mathbf{x}_1, \mathbf{x}_2, \ldots, \mathbf{x}_n]$, whose columns are the vectors corresponding to the roots $\lambda_1, \lambda_2, \ldots, \lambda_n$, is an orthogonal matrix. This means that the transform of $\mathbf{A}$ by $\mathbf{X}$ is the diagonal matrix $\Lambda = \text{diag}[\lambda_1, \lambda_2, \ldots, \lambda_n]$:

$$\mathbf{X}'\mathbf{A}\mathbf{X} = \mathbf{X}'\mathbf{X}\Lambda = \mathbf{I}\Lambda = \Lambda$$

By setting $\mathbf{y} = \mathbf{X}\mathbf{z}$, say, the quadratic form $\mathbf{y}'\mathbf{A}\mathbf{y}$ can therefore be reduced to diagonal representation,

$$\mathbf{y}'\mathbf{A}\mathbf{y} = \mathbf{z}'\mathbf{X}'\mathbf{A}\mathbf{X}\mathbf{z} = \mathbf{z}\Lambda\mathbf{z}$$

and by Sylvester's law of inertia the number of positive and negative characteristic values is the same as the number of positive and negative coefficients in other diagonal representations, such as that given by the gaussian factorization. Since the λ_i are solutions of the determinantal equation (2.7-13), these numbers are also given by the number of alterations of signs of coefficients in the polynomial (2.7-14) (Descartes' rule of signs).

If $\text{rank}(\mathbf{A}) = r < n$, then the r characteristic vectors $(\mathbf{x}_1, \mathbf{x}_2, \ldots, \mathbf{x}_r)$ may be completed by any $n - r$ orthogonal vectors which are at the same time orthogonal to the $\mathbf{x}_i$. This is an orthogonal completion and may be carried out by the Gram-Schmidt construction. Call the completed matrix $\mathbf{X}_0$; then

$$\mathbf{X}_0'\mathbf{A}\mathbf{X}_0 = \boldsymbol{\Lambda}_0$$

is a diagonal matrix in which r elements are nonzero and the remaining $n - r$ elements are identically zero.

Note that the characteristic values are invariant under an orthogonal rotation of bases, for if $\mathbf{P}$ is orthogonal, $\mathbf{P}'\mathbf{P} = \mathbf{P}\mathbf{P}' = \mathbf{I}$, and

$$\lambda = \frac{\mathbf{x}'\mathbf{P}'\mathbf{A}\mathbf{P}\mathbf{x}}{\mathbf{x}'\mathbf{x}}$$

Then $\max(\lambda)$ is a root of

$$|\mathbf{P}'\mathbf{A}\mathbf{P} - \lambda\mathbf{I}| = |\mathbf{P}'\mathbf{A}\mathbf{P} - \lambda\mathbf{P}'\mathbf{P}| = |\mathbf{P}'|\,|\mathbf{A} - \lambda\mathbf{I}|\,|\mathbf{P}|$$
$$= |\mathbf{A} - \lambda\mathbf{I}| = 0$$

since $|\mathbf{P}| = 1$. However, the characteristic vectors are transformed by $\mathbf{P}$:

$$(\mathbf{P}'\mathbf{A}\mathbf{P} - \lambda\mathbf{I})\mathbf{x} = \mathbf{P}'(\mathbf{A} - \lambda\mathbf{I})\mathbf{P}\mathbf{x} = (\mathbf{A} - \lambda\mathbf{I})\mathbf{z} = \mathbf{0}$$

2.7.4 Pairs of Quadratic Forms

Of fundamental importance in multivariate analysis is the problem of maximizing a ratio of quadratic forms,

$$\phi = \frac{\mathbf{x}'\mathbf{A}\mathbf{x}}{\mathbf{x}'\mathbf{B}\mathbf{x}} \qquad |\mathbf{B}| \neq 0$$

where $\mathbf{B}$ is a metric matrix (symmetric positive definite).

In this case, the maximum of ϕ with respect to variation in $\mathbf{x}$ is a solution of

$$\frac{\mathbf{x}'\mathbf{B}\mathbf{x}}{2}\frac{\partial\phi}{\partial\mathbf{x}} = \mathbf{A}\mathbf{x} - \frac{\mathbf{x}'\mathbf{A}\mathbf{x}}{\mathbf{x}'\mathbf{B}\mathbf{x}}\mathbf{B}\mathbf{x} = (\mathbf{A} - \phi\mathbf{B})\mathbf{x} = \mathbf{0} \qquad (2.7\text{-}15)$$

As in (2.7-12), this system of homogeneous equations has a nontrivial solution for $\mathbf{x}$ if and only if

$$|\mathbf{A} - \phi\mathbf{B}| = 0 \qquad (2.7\text{-}16)$$

Solution of (2.7-15) and (2.7-16) is sometimes called the *two-matrix eigenproblem*. The values of ϕ which satisfy (2.7-16) are called the *characteristic values* (or *eigenvalues*, *proper values*, *latent roots*) of **A** *in the metric* **B** or *with respect to* **B**. The corresponding **x** are called the characteristic (or eigen, proper, or latent) vectors of **A** in the metric **B**, or with respect to **B**.

Obviously, (2.7-15) can be transformed to a one-matrix characteristic equation by change of basis. For, since **B** is symmetric pd, it has a Cholesky factor, say

$$\mathbf{B} = \mathbf{C}_B\mathbf{C}'_B$$

Thus, we may substitute

$$\mathbf{z} = \mathbf{C}'_B\mathbf{x}$$

or

$$\mathbf{x} = (\mathbf{C}_B^{-1})'\mathbf{z}$$

Then, multiplying (2.7-15) on the left by $\mathbf{C}_B^{-1}$, we have

$$[\mathbf{C}_B^{-1}\mathbf{A}(\mathbf{C}_B^{-1})' - \phi\mathbf{I}]\mathbf{z} = \mathbf{0}$$

since $\mathbf{C}_B^{-1}\mathbf{B}(\mathbf{C}_B^{-1})' = \mathbf{I}$. In this case, the associated determinantal equation is

$$|\mathbf{C}_B^{-1}\mathbf{A}(\mathbf{C}_B^{-1})' - \phi\mathbf{I}| = 0$$

and the solution of the two-matrix problem becomes the same as that of the one-matrix problem, except that $\mathbf{x} = (\mathbf{C}_B^{-1})'\mathbf{z}$ must be recovered once **z** is obtained.

Note that the characteristic values in (2.7-15) are invariant under nonsingular transformation of the variables, for, if

$$\phi = \frac{\mathbf{x}'\mathbf{T}'\mathbf{A}\mathbf{T}\mathbf{x}}{\mathbf{x}'\mathbf{T}'\mathbf{B}\mathbf{T}\mathbf{x}}$$

then max(ϕ) is a root of

$$|\mathbf{T}'\mathbf{A}\mathbf{T} - \phi\mathbf{T}'\mathbf{B}\mathbf{T}| = |\mathbf{T}'|\,|\mathbf{A} - \phi\mathbf{B}|\,|\mathbf{T}| = |\mathbf{T}|^2|\mathbf{A} - \phi\mathbf{B}| = 0$$

so that

$$|\mathbf{A} - \phi\mathbf{B}| = 0$$

if $|\mathbf{T}| \neq 0$. The characteristic vectors are carried into $\mathbf{z} = \mathbf{T}\mathbf{x}$ by this transformation.

2.7.5 Practical Computation of Characteristic Roots and Vectors

As will be apparent in the sequel, computation of characteristic roots and vectors of sample matrices, or functions of sample matrices, is required constantly in multivariate data analysis. The matrices are always symmetric with real elements and, except for certain special applications as in Sec. 6.4.3f, are at least positive semidefinite. Although in principle it is possible to find the roots of the characteristic equation (2.7-13), substitute in (2.7-12), and solve the resulting systems of homogeneous equations to obtain the characteristic vectors, this approach becomes prohibitively laborious when the matrix order exceeds $n = 3$ or 4. Other methods for finding the roots and vectors of real symmetric matrices have therefore been proposed, and three of these are important enough to deserve mention here.

a The power method The power method was introduced in a statistical context by Hotelling [1936]. It is best suited to problems where only the r roots of largest absolute value and their associated vectors are required ($r \ll n$). The method assumes that these roots are distinct and may be strictly ordered by size:

$$|\lambda_1| > |\lambda_2| > \cdots > |\lambda_r| > \max(|\lambda_{r+1}|, \ldots, |\lambda_n|)$$

The roots are obtained one at a time, beginning with the largest, by means of an iterative process involving trial vectors which converge toward a scalar multiple of one of the characteristic vectors. If $\mathbf{v}^{(i)}$ is the trial vector at the ith iteration, the trial vector for the next iteration is

$$\mathbf{v}^{(i+1)} = \mathbf{A}\mathbf{v}^{(i)}$$

The initial trial vector $\mathbf{v}^{(0)}$ may be arbitrary, but fewer iterations will be required if its elements are so chosen that the elements of $\mathbf{v}^{(1)}$ are large in absolute value. Usually a vector with elements ± 1 is used as an initial trial vector.

Provided $\lambda_1 > \lambda_2$, the elements of successive trial vectors will become proportional, to some predetermined accuracy, in a finite number of iterations. At that point the factor of proportionality approximates λ_1, and the iterations are said to have *converged.* If convergence is attained at step s, the iterations are terminated and the approximation to the first characteristic vector is calculated by normalizing $\mathbf{v}^{(s)}$:

$$\mathbf{x}_1 \approx \frac{\mathbf{v}^{(s)}}{\sqrt{(\mathbf{v}^{(s)})'\mathbf{v}^{(s)}}}$$

An improved approximation to the corresponding root is then obtained by evaluating the so-called *Rayleigh quotient,*

$$\lambda_1 = \mathbf{x}_1'\mathbf{A}\mathbf{x}_1 \approx \frac{(\mathbf{v}^{(s)})'\mathbf{A}\mathbf{v}^{(s)}}{(\mathbf{v}^{(s)})'\mathbf{v}^{(s)}}$$

The iterative process is self-correcting; errors are corrected by subsequent iterations at the expense of slowing down convergence.

When accurate approximations of λ_1 and $\mathbf{x}_1$ are available, the second largest root and its vector may be found by a similar process applied to the projection of $\mathbf{A}$ in the space complementary to $\mathbf{x}_1$. The projection operator for this purpose is $\mathbf{P}_1 = \mathbf{I} - \mathbf{x}_1\mathbf{x}_1'$:

$$\begin{aligned}\mathbf{A}_2 &= \mathbf{P}_1\mathbf{A}\mathbf{P}_1' = \mathbf{A} - \mathbf{A}\mathbf{x}_1\mathbf{x}_1' - \mathbf{x}_1\mathbf{x}_1'\mathbf{A} + \mathbf{x}_1\mathbf{x}_1'\mathbf{A}\mathbf{x}_1\mathbf{x}_1' \\ &= \mathbf{A} - \lambda_1\mathbf{x}_1\mathbf{x}_1'\end{aligned}$$

The iterative procedure is then performed with $\mathbf{A}_2$ to obtain approximations to λ_2 and $\mathbf{x}_2$. Then $\mathbf{A}_2$ is projected into the space complementary to $\mathbf{x}_2$ to obtain $\mathbf{A}_3$, the iterative procedure again applied, and so on until approximations have been obtained for the r largest roots and their vectors. Details of the computations are clarified in Example 2.7-2.

This method depends upon the fact that an arbitrary vector such as $\mathbf{v}^{(0)}$ may be expressed in terms of the basis provided by the characteristic vectors of **A**.

$$\mathbf{v}^{(0)} = b_1\mathbf{x}_1 + b_2\mathbf{x}_2 + \cdots + b_n\mathbf{x}_n = \mathbf{Xb}$$

Thus, the iterations amount to

$$\mathbf{v}^{(1)} = \mathbf{Av}^{(0)} = \mathbf{AXb} = (\mathbf{X}\Lambda\mathbf{X}')\mathbf{Xb} = \mathbf{X}\Lambda\mathbf{b}$$

$$\mathbf{v}^{(2)} = (\mathbf{X}\Lambda\mathbf{X}')\mathbf{X}\Lambda\mathbf{b} = \mathbf{X}\Lambda^2\mathbf{b}$$

$$\cdots\cdots\cdots\cdots\cdots\cdots$$

$$\mathbf{v}^{(s)} = \mathbf{X}\Lambda^s\mathbf{b}$$

At iteration s, the vector

$$\left(\frac{1}{\lambda_1}\right)^s \mathbf{v}^{(s)} = b_1\mathbf{x}_1 + \left(\frac{\lambda_2}{\lambda_1}\right)^s b_2\mathbf{x}_2 + \cdots + \left(\frac{\lambda_n}{\lambda_1}\right)^s b_n\mathbf{x}_n$$

approximates $b_1\mathbf{x}_1$ provided λ_1 exceeds the remaining roots in absolute value. The ith components of $\mathbf{v}^{(s)}$ and $\mathbf{v}^{(s-1)}$ are therefore approximately proportional to λ_1:

$$\frac{v_i^{(s)}}{v_i^{(s-1)}} \approx \frac{b_1\lambda_1{}^s x_{i1}}{b_1\lambda_1{}^{s-1}x_{i1}} \approx \lambda_1$$

The same argument applies to the iterative process on $\mathbf{A}_2$ except that, because $\mathbf{A}_2\mathbf{x}_1 = \mathbf{0}$,

$$\mathbf{v}_2{}^{(s)} = \lambda_2{}^s c_2\mathbf{x}_2 + \lambda_3{}^s c_3\mathbf{x}_3 + \cdots + \lambda_n{}^s c_n\mathbf{x}_n$$

and λ_2 takes over the role of largest root. The process is obviously impractical if the two or more nonzero roots are nearly equal, for a very large number of iterations is then required to obtain an acceptable approximation. The power method is therefore not a satisfactory method for obtaining all roots and vectors of large matrices which are functions of random variables, where the probability that at least two of the smaller nonzero roots are nearly equal is appreciable. Fortunately, procedures such as the Jacobi method described below are unaffected by equality or near equality of roots.

EXAMPLE 2.7-2 (*The power method*) We shall apply the power method to obtain the two largest roots and associated vectors of the following real symmetric matrix:*

$$\mathbf{A} = \begin{bmatrix} 5 & 4 & 3 & 2 & 1 \\ 4 & 6 & 0 & 4 & 3 \\ 3 & 0 & 7 & 6 & 5 \\ 2 & 4 & 6 & 8 & 7 \\ 1 & 3 & 5 & 7 & 9 \end{bmatrix} \qquad (2.7\text{-}17)$$

* The roots and vectors of this matrix have been obtained by Businger [1965] and Wilkinson [1962] by other methods.

Because all elements in the matrix are nonnegative, we begin the iterations with a vector of unit elements, $\mathbf{v}' = [1, 1, 1, 1, 1]$. The first five iterations yield

$\mathbf{v}^{(1)}$	$\mathbf{v}^{(2)}$	$\mathbf{v}^{(3)}$	$\mathbf{v}^{(4)}$	$\mathbf{v}^{(5)}$
15.00000	285.0000	6,057.00	133,410.0	2,973,000.0
17.00000	345.0000	7,425.00	163,980.0	3,656,000.0
21.00000	479.0000	10,823.00	243,390.0	5,461,100.0
27.00000	615.0000	13,839.00	310,450.0	6,959,000.0
25.00000	585.0000	13,285.00	298,880.0	6,705,500.0

The approach to proportionality is evident when each vector is divided by its largest element to obtain the rescaled vectors

$\mathbf{w}^{(1)}$	$\mathbf{w}^{(2)}$	$\mathbf{w}^{(3)}$	$\mathbf{w}^{(4)}$	$\mathbf{w}^{(5)}$
.5555555	.4634146	.4376761	.4297310	.4272165
.6296296	.5609756	.5365272	.5282009	.5253628
.7777777	.7788618	.7820651	.7839909	.7847535
1.0000000	1.0000000	1.0000000	1.0000000	1.0000000
.9259259	.9512195	.9599682	.9627315	.9635723

At this point, a greatly improved approximation to $\mathbf{x}_1$ may be obtained by means of *Aitken's δ process* [Aitken, 1956]. The improved approximations to the ith element of $\mathbf{x}_1$ are obtained from each set of three successive vectors, that is, $(\mathbf{w}^{(1)}, \mathbf{w}^{(2)}, \mathbf{w}^{(3)})$, $(\mathbf{w}^{(2)}, \mathbf{w}^{(3)}, \mathbf{w}^{(4)})$, and $(\mathbf{w}^{(3)}, \mathbf{w}^{(4)}, \mathbf{w}^{(5)})$, by means of the formula

$$z_i^{(k)} = \frac{w_i^{(k-1)} w_i^{(k+1)} - (w_i^{(k)})^2}{w_i^{(k-1)} - 2w_i^{(k)} + w_i^{(k+1)}} \tag{2.7-18}$$

Formula (2.7-18) is then applied to the three successive values of z_i and the resulting vector normalized to obtain the final approximation to x_i. The results of these calculations are as follows:

$\mathbf{z}^{(1)}$	$\mathbf{z}^{(2)}$	$\mathbf{z}^{(3)}$
.42769950	.42618336	.42605227
.52300575	.52390076	.52389524
.77722358	.78689347	.78525242
1.00000000	1.00000000	1.00000000
.96459430	.96400722	.96393431

$$\mathbf{x}_1' \approx [.24588700, .30236323, .45334205, .57714531, .55632763]$$

The calculated value of the corresponding root is

$$\lambda_1 = \mathbf{x}_1'\mathbf{A}\mathbf{x}_1 \approx 22.40687489$$

These figures agree to five significant figures with those obtained by Businger [1965], using one of the tridiagonalization methods:

$$\mathbf{x}_1' = [.245877939, .302396040, .453214523, .577172152, .556384584]$$

$$\lambda_1 = [22.40687531]$$

Now we begin the determination of the second root and vector. Projecting **A**, we obtain

$$\mathbf{A}_2 = \mathbf{A} - \lambda_1 \mathbf{x}_1' \mathbf{x}_1$$

$$= \begin{bmatrix} 3.64527101 & 2.33411185 & .50228508 & -1.17981576 & -2.06512007 \\ 2.33411186 & 3.95148452 & -3.07139928 & .08983242 & -.76912815 \\ .50228508 & -3.07139929 & 2.39496104 & .13737117 & -.65116428 \\ -1.17981576 & .08983242 & .13737117 & .53634614 & -.19444047 \\ -2.06512007 & -.76912815 & -.65116428 & -.19444047 & 2.06506240 \end{bmatrix}$$

The sign pattern in $\mathbf{A}_2$ suggests that $\mathbf{v}_2' = [1, 1, 1, -1, -1]$ should be the initial trial vector. Repeating the process used for the first root and vector, we obtain

$$\mathbf{x}_2' = [.55185380, .70945575, -.34046538, -.08970307, -.26108733]$$
$$\lambda_2 = [7.51372347]$$

which agrees with Businger's results to only three decimal places:

$$\mathbf{x}_2' = [.55096195, .70944034, -.34017913, -.08341095, -.265435677]$$
$$\lambda_2 = [7.51372415]$$

If 10 iterations are performed, and the δ process is applied to vectors 6 through 10, the results are more accurate:

$$\mathbf{x}_2' = [.55068067, .70964061, -.34019871, -.08336392, -.26547370]$$
$$\lambda_2 = [7.51372347]$$

Convergence may also be speeded up by performing the multiplications on some power of the original matrix, for example, $\mathbf{A}^2 = \mathbf{AA}$ or $\mathbf{A}^4 = \mathbf{A}^2\mathbf{A}^2$. The roots obtained in this way are the corresponding powers of the roots of **A**. Since the amount of calculation required to square a matrix is equal to that of n iterations, powering the matrix loses its advantage as n increases (see Bodewig [1959, page 284]).

b The Jacobi method Another iterative method for finding the characteristic roots and vectors of real symmetric matrices is implicit in a procedure, proposed by Jacobi in 1846, for improving the numerical conditioning of least-squares equations. Jacobi's procedure was all but forgotten until rediscovered by Kelley [1935] as a method of principal factor analysis and revived independently by Goldstine, Murray, and von Neumann [1959] as an algorithm for machine computation.

The method consists of a sequence of orthogonal transformations on an $n \times n$ real symmetric matrix **A**; that is,

$$\mathbf{D} = \mathbf{Q}_s' \cdots \mathbf{Q}_i' \cdots \mathbf{Q}_1' \mathbf{A} \mathbf{Q}_1 \cdots \mathbf{Q}_i \cdots \mathbf{Q}_s$$

$\mathbf{Q}_i$ is an orthogonal matrix chosen so as to set to zero the largest off-diagonal element at the ith stage in the sequence. As the transformations continue, **D** approaches the diagonal matrix of characteristic roots of **A**,

$$\mathbf{D} \to \mathbf{\Lambda}$$

and the continued product of the transformations approaches a matrix in which the columns are the characteristic vectors associated with the roots in the corresponding columns of **D**,

$$\mathbf{Q}_1\mathbf{Q}_2 \cdots \mathbf{Q}_s \to \mathbf{X}$$

The transformations are performed as follows: Let $a_{jk}^{(i)}$ for $j \neq k$ be the largest off-diagonal element of

$$\mathbf{A}_i = \mathbf{Q}_i' \cdots \mathbf{Q}_2'\mathbf{Q}_1'\mathbf{A}\mathbf{Q}_1\mathbf{Q}_2 \cdots \mathbf{Q}_i$$

Then $\mathbf{Q}_{i+1}$ is constructed by substituting into an $n \times n$ identity matrix the elements

$$q_{jj} = \cos\theta_i \qquad q_{jk} = \sin\theta_i \qquad q_{kj} = -\sin\theta_i \qquad q_{kk} = \cos\theta_i$$

That is, the transformation is a rotation through an angle θ_i in the plane of the j,k coordinate axes. After rotation, the elements of the ith and jth row and column of $\mathbf{A}^{(i+1)}$ are

$$\begin{aligned}
a_{jj}^{(i+1)} &= a_{jj}^{(i)}\cos^2\theta_i - 2a_{jk}^{(i)}\sin\theta_i\cos\theta_i + a_{kk}^{(i)}\sin^2\theta_i \\
a_{kk}^{(i+1)} &= a_{kk}^{(i)}\cos^2\theta_i + 2a_{jk}^{(i)}\sin\theta_i\cos\theta_i + a_{jj}^{(i)}\sin^2\theta_\iota \\
a_{jk}^{(i+1)} &= a_{kj}^{(i+1)} = (a_{jj}^{(i)} - a_{kk}^{(i)})\sin\theta_i\cos\theta_i - a_{jk}^{(i)}(\cos^2\theta_i - \sin^2\theta_i) \\
a_{jh}^{(i+1)} &= a_{hj}^{(i+1)} = a_{jk}^{(i)}\cos\theta_i + a_{kk}^{(i)}\sin\theta_i \\
a_{kh}^{(i+1)} &= a_{hk}^{(i+1)} = -a_{jk}^{(i)}\sin\theta_i + a_{kk}^{(i)}\cos\theta_i
\end{aligned} \qquad h \neq j,k$$

All other elements of $\mathbf{A}^{(i+1)}$ are the same as those of $\mathbf{A}^{(i)}$. The angle θ_i is determined by setting $a_{jk}^{(i+1)} = 0$ and solving for $\tan\theta_i$:

$$1 + a_{jk}^{(i)}\frac{\cot\theta_i - \tan\theta_i}{a_{jj}^{(i)} - a_{kk}^{(i)}} = 0$$

or

$$\tan^2\theta_i + \frac{a_{kk}^{(i)} - a_{jj}^{(i)}}{a_{jk}^{(i)}}\tan\theta_i - 1 = 0 \qquad (2.7\text{-}19)$$

The tangent of θ_i may be taken as the smaller root of the quadratic equation (2.7-19); its sign is set the same as that of $a_{kk}^{(i)} - a_{jj}^{(i)}/a_{jk}^{(i)}$. Then,

$$\cos\theta_i = \frac{1}{\sqrt{1 + \tan^2\theta}}$$

$$\sin\theta_i = \cos\theta_i\tan\theta_i$$

For computer applications, these formulas are manipulated further to improve the conditioning of the arithmetic [Rutishauser, 1966].

After an off-diagonal element has been set to zero, it does not in general remain zero in subsequent rotations. However, it is easy to show that each rotation reduces the sum of squares of the off-diagonal elements of $\mathbf{A}^{(i)}$ by $2(a_{jk}^{(i)})^2$, while increasing the sum of squares of the diagonal elements by a like amount. This is a consequence of the invariance of the so-called *euclidean norm* of a matrix under orthogonal transformation. The euclidean norm $N(\mathbf{A})$ is the total length of all vectors in $\mathbf{A}$. Using results in Sec. 2.5, we may write

$$N^2(\mathbf{A}) = \operatorname{tr}(\mathbf{A}'\mathbf{A})$$

If $\mathbf{Q}$ is orthogonal,

$$\begin{aligned} N^2(\mathbf{Q}'\mathbf{A}\mathbf{Q}) &= \operatorname{tr}(\mathbf{Q}'\mathbf{A}'\mathbf{Q}\mathbf{Q}'\mathbf{A}\mathbf{Q}) = \operatorname{tr}(\mathbf{Q}'\mathbf{A}'\mathbf{A}\mathbf{Q}) = \operatorname{tr}(\mathbf{Q}\mathbf{Q}'\mathbf{A}'\mathbf{A}) \\ &= \operatorname{tr}(\mathbf{A}'\mathbf{A}) = N^2(\mathbf{A}) \end{aligned}$$

Without loss of generality, we may assume that the element a_{12} is to be set to zero and partition $\mathbf{A}$ into

$$\begin{matrix} \begin{bmatrix} \mathbf{A}_{11} & \mathbf{A}_{12} \\ \mathbf{A}_{21} & \mathbf{A}_{22} \end{bmatrix} & \begin{matrix} 2 \\ n-2 \end{matrix} \\ \begin{matrix} \quad 2 & \quad n-2 \end{matrix} & \end{matrix}$$

Then $\mathbf{Q}$ is of the form

$$\begin{matrix} \mathbf{Q} = \begin{bmatrix} \mathbf{Q}_1 & \mathbf{O} \\ \mathbf{O} & \mathbf{I} \end{bmatrix} & \begin{matrix} 2 \\ n-2 \end{matrix} \\ \begin{matrix} \qquad 2 & \quad n-2 \end{matrix} & \end{matrix}$$

Thus, $\mathbf{Q}_1'\mathbf{A}_{11}\mathbf{Q}_1 = \mathbf{D}_1$ is a 2×2 diagonal matrix, and

$$\mathbf{Q}'\mathbf{A}\mathbf{Q} = \begin{bmatrix} \mathbf{D}_1 & \mathbf{Q}_1'\mathbf{A}_{12} \\ \mathbf{A}_{21}\mathbf{Q}_1 & \mathbf{A}_{22} \end{bmatrix}$$

But $N^2(\mathbf{A}_{21}\mathbf{Q}_1) = N^2(\mathbf{Q}_1'\mathbf{A}_{12}) = \operatorname{tr}(\mathbf{Q}_1'\mathbf{A}_{21}\mathbf{A}_{12}\mathbf{Q}_1) = N^2(\mathbf{A}_{21}) = N^2(\mathbf{A}_{12})$, and similarly $N^2(\mathbf{D}_1) = N^2(\mathbf{A}_{11})$, that is, $\operatorname{tr}(\mathbf{D}_1) = a_{11}{}^2 + a_{22}{}^2 + 2a_{12}{}^2$. Thus, the sum of squares of elements in each of the submatrices of $\mathbf{A}$ are unchanged by the transformation. This implies that the sum of squares of elements in the diagonal of $\mathbf{Q}_1'\mathbf{A}_{11}\mathbf{Q}_1$, and hence in the entire diagonal of $\mathbf{Q}'\mathbf{A}\mathbf{Q}$, is increased by $2a_{12}{}^2$ at the expense of the sum of squares of all off-diagonal elements. Since this is true of each transformation, the maximum off-diagonal element may be reduced arbitrarily near zero in a finite number of rotations. The resulting nearly diagonal matrix then contains the required approximations to the characteristic values of $\mathbf{A}$; the product of the orthogonal matrices formed as the rotations proceed contains the approximations to the characteristic vectors in the same order as the roots in $\mathbf{D}$.

Unlike the power method, Jacobi's method gives all roots and vectors simultaneously, and is unaffected by equality or near equality of roots. Although not as fast in general as the tridiagonalization methods to be discussed next, the Jacobi method has the advantage of simplicity of programming and numerical stability and is widely used in computer applications.

c The tridiagonalization methods The most efficient methods presently available for computing roots and vectors of real symmetric matrices stem from the work of Givens [1957]. In Givens' approach the matrix is first subjected to *orthogonal tridiagonalization*, which sets to zero all elements not in the main diagonal or first subdiagonal and superdiagonal. This operation is noniterative and may be performed in a fixed number of steps.

The characteristic roots and vectors of the tridiagonal matrix are then obtained by an iterative method. Because of the invariance of characteristic roots under orthogonal transformation (2.7-19), the roots of the given matrix are the same as those of the tridiagonal matrix. The vectors of the given matrix are obtained from those of the tridiagonal matrix by applying in the reverse order the transformations used in the orthogonal tridiagonalization.

The transformation to tridiagonal form is accomplished by means of an elementary orthogonal matrix of a type introduced by Householder [1952]. These matrices are of the form

$$\mathbf{W} = \mathbf{I} - 2\mathbf{w}\mathbf{w}'$$

where $\mathbf{w}'\mathbf{w} = 1$. They are symmetric and orthogonal:

$$\mathbf{W}\mathbf{W}' = \mathbf{W}'\mathbf{W} = \mathbf{W}\mathbf{W} = \mathbf{I} - 2\mathbf{w}\mathbf{w}' - 2\mathbf{w}\mathbf{w}' + 4\mathbf{w}\mathbf{w}'\mathbf{w}\mathbf{w}' = \mathbf{I}$$

For any two vectors **a** and **b** both of the same length, a **W** matrix may always be constructed which transforms **a** into **b** (because only a rigid rotation of axes is required). That is, if

$$\mathbf{b} = \mathbf{W}\mathbf{a} = \mathbf{a} - 2\mathbf{w}\mathbf{w}'\mathbf{a}$$

then

$$(2\mathbf{w}'\mathbf{a})\mathbf{w} = \mathbf{a} - \mathbf{b} \tag{2.7-20}$$

and the scalar $2\mathbf{w}'\mathbf{a}$ may be obtained by normalizing $\mathbf{a} - \mathbf{b}$; that is,

$$\mathbf{w} = \frac{1}{|\mathbf{a} - \mathbf{b}|}(\mathbf{a} - \mathbf{b})$$

where $|\mathbf{a} - \mathbf{b}| = \sqrt{(\mathbf{a} - \mathbf{b})'(\mathbf{a} - \mathbf{b})}$ is the length of $\mathbf{a} - \mathbf{b}$.

Elementary matrices of this type may be used in the orthogonal triangularization of a general matrix [Householder, 1964], but their use for this purpose has no advantage from a computational point of view over the modified Gram-Schmidt procedure (Sec. 2.2.4). The true merit of the **W** matrices lies in the tridiagonalization of real symmetric matrices. By means of a suitable **W** matrix, we may transform a vector **a** into a vector **b** of the same length in which all elements except b_1 are equal to zero. Because **a** and **b** are the same length, we have immediately

$$b_1 = \pm\sqrt{\mathbf{a}'\mathbf{a}} = \pm\alpha$$

and $\mathbf{b} = \pm\alpha\boldsymbol{\delta}$, where $\boldsymbol{\delta}$ is a vector in which $\delta_1 = 1$ and $\delta_j = 0, j \neq 1$. Then, from (2.7-20),

$$2(\mathbf{w}'\mathbf{a})\mathbf{w} = \mathbf{a} \pm \alpha\boldsymbol{\delta}$$

and

$$2(\mathbf{w}'\mathbf{a})^2 = \alpha^2 \pm \alpha a_1$$

Thus,

$$\mathbf{w} = \frac{1}{\sqrt{2(\alpha^2 \pm \alpha a_1)}}(\mathbf{a} \pm \alpha\boldsymbol{\delta})$$

The sign should be chosen to avoid division by small numbers.

Suppose the real symmetric matrix $\mathbf{A}_1 = \mathbf{A}$ is partitioned as

$$\mathbf{A}_1 = \begin{bmatrix} \mathbf{a}_{11} & \mathbf{a}_1' \\ \mathbf{a}_1 & \mathbf{A}_{22} \end{bmatrix} \begin{matrix} 1 \\ n-1 \end{matrix}$$
$$\qquad\qquad 1 \quad n-1$$

Then we may construct as above an $(n-1) \times (n-1)$ matrix $\mathbf{W}_{11}$, which carries $\mathbf{a}_1$ into the vector $\mathbf{b}_1$, in which the last $n-2$ elements are zero. Then

$$\mathbf{W}_1 = \begin{bmatrix} 1 & 0 \\ 0 & \mathbf{W}_{11} \end{bmatrix}$$

is orthogonal and transforms $\mathbf{A}$ into

$$\mathbf{A}_2 = \mathbf{W}_1'\mathbf{A}\mathbf{W}_1 = \begin{bmatrix} a_{11} & [b_{21} \;\; \mathbf{0}'] \\ \begin{bmatrix} b_{21} \\ \mathbf{0} \end{bmatrix} & \mathbf{B}_{22} \end{bmatrix} \begin{matrix} 1 \\ 1 \\ n-2 \end{matrix}$$
$$\qquad\qquad 1 \quad 1 \quad n-2$$

In the same manner, an orthogonal matrix of the form

$$\mathbf{W}_2 = \begin{bmatrix} 1 & 0 & \mathbf{0}' \\ 0 & 1 & \mathbf{0}' \\ \mathbf{0} & \mathbf{0} & \mathbf{W}_{22} \end{bmatrix} \begin{matrix} 1 \\ 1 \\ n-2 \end{matrix}$$
$$\qquad 1 \quad 1 \quad n-2$$

may be constructed which puts $\mathbf{A}_2$ in the form

$$\mathbf{A}_3 = \mathbf{W}_2'\mathbf{A}_2\mathbf{W}_2 = \begin{bmatrix} \begin{matrix} a_{11} & b_{21} \\ b_{21} & b_{22} \end{matrix} & \begin{bmatrix} 0 & \mathbf{0}' \\ b_{32} & \mathbf{0}' \end{bmatrix} \\ \begin{bmatrix} 0 & b_{32} \\ \mathbf{0} & \mathbf{0} \end{bmatrix} & \mathbf{C}_{33} \end{bmatrix} \begin{matrix} 1 \\ 1 \\ n-2 \end{matrix}$$
$$\qquad 1 \quad 1 \quad n-2$$

and so on down to the tridiagonal matrix,

$$\mathbf{A}_{n-2} = \mathbf{W}_{n-2}' \cdots \mathbf{W}_2'\mathbf{W}_1'\mathbf{A}\mathbf{W}_1\mathbf{W}_2 \cdots \mathbf{W}_{n-2} = \mathbf{W}'\mathbf{A}\mathbf{W} = \mathbf{B}$$

The advantage of this transformation lies in the ease with which the characteristic roots and vectors of a symmetric tridiagonal matrix $\mathbf{B}$ may be calculated.

When only a certain number of the largest or smallest roots are required, the method of *Sturm-sequence bisection* [Ortega, 1960] is especially efficient [Wilkinson, 1965; Barth, Morton, and Wilkinson, 1967]. The principal minors of the determinant $|\mathbf{B} - \lambda\mathbf{I}|$ may be expressed recursively in a *Sturm sequence*.

$$\phi_0(\lambda) = 1$$
$$\phi_1(\lambda) = \lambda - b_{11}$$
$$\cdots\cdots\cdots\cdots$$
$$\phi_i(\lambda) = (\lambda - b_{ii})\phi_{i-1} - b_{i,i-1}{}^2\phi_{i-2}$$

where $\phi_n(\lambda)$ is the characteristic polynomial of **B**.

It can be shown that the number of roots larger than some trial value λ' is equal to the number of alterations in sign of successive terms in the sequence, provided zero terms are given the sign of the preceding term [Ortega, 1960]. Thus, it is relatively easy to find the zeros of the characteristic polynomial in order of size starting either from the largest or smallest root [Wilkinson, 1965]. The associated vectors may be obtained by solving the homogeneous equations

$$(\mathbf{B} - \lambda_i\mathbf{I})\mathbf{z}_i = \mathbf{0}$$

either by elimination, or more accurately, by *inverse iteration* [Wilkinson, 1960, 1965]. Then the corresponding vectors of the given matrix **A** may be recovered by the transformation

$$\mathbf{x}_i = \mathbf{W}\mathbf{z}_i$$

If all the roots and vectors are required, the so-called *QR method* is faster and possibly more accurate [Welsch, 1967]. The QR method is iterative, the *i*th stage of iteration consisting of two steps: (1) a resolution of the tridiagonal matrix into the product of an orthogonal tridiagonal matrix **Q** and an upper triangular matrix **R**

$$\mathbf{Q}_i'\mathbf{B}_i = \mathbf{Q}_i'(\mathbf{Q}_i\mathbf{R}_i) = \mathbf{R}_i$$

and (2) a reforming of the tridiagonal matrix by transformation *on the right*

$$\mathbf{B}_{i+1} = \mathbf{R}_i\mathbf{Q}_i$$

As the iterations continue,

$$\mathbf{B}_i = \mathbf{B}\mathbf{Q}_1\mathbf{Q}_2\cdots\mathbf{Q}_i \rightarrow \Lambda = \operatorname{diag}(\lambda_1, \lambda_2, \ldots, \lambda_n)$$

that is, $\mathbf{B}_i$ approaches a diagonal matrix in which characteristic roots of the given matrix **A** are ordered by absolute size. Similarly, the transformation on the right applied to **W** approaches the matrix of characteristic vectors of **A** in the same order. [Householder, 1964; Francis, 1961.]

Each QR resolution may be made in a sequence of $n - 2$ plane rotations which set the subdiagonal elements of $\mathbf{B}_i$ to zero [Ortega and Kaiser, 1963; Businger, 1965]. Devices which speed up convergence, such as a shift in origin for the smallest root, are also available [Francis, 1961; Businger, 1965; Clyde, Cramer, and Sherin, 1966]. Further improvements in these algorithms may be possible (e.g., Reinsch and Bauer [1968]).

Exercise 2.7-1 Show how to orthogonalize a matrix $\mathbf{X}$ with respect to the spd metric matrix $\mathbf{M}$ using the Gram-Schmidt procedure and the inner product defined by (2.2-2).

3

THE MULTIVARIATE NORMAL DISTRIBUTION

An essential step in the approach to data analysis outlined in Chap. 1 is the choice of a statistical specification for random components in the response variables—especially the error component. Throughout most of this text, we employ a multivariate normal specification for this purpose—i.e., we assume that errors and other random components are distributed in *multivariate normal* form. The only exceptions occur in Chap. 4, where we obtain certain fundamental results in least-square estimation under weaker assumptions, and in Chap. 8, where we consider models for qualitative data.

This all but complete reliance on normal assumptions obviously runs counter to the widely held opinion that statistical methods for behavioral science should be nonparametric and distribution free (e.g., Bradley [1968]). The position of the present text is that nonparametric methods, despite their usefulness in special situations, are too narrowly involved with tests of null hypotheses to provide by themselves a sufficiently comprehensive account of the complex data typical of behavioral studies. Moreover, many of the arguments against parametric methods appear to derive from a misunderstanding of what the analysis actually assumes, or from insufficient cognizance of the theoretical and empirical support for normal assumptions. In the remainder of this section, we review some of this reasoning and evidence and adduce a substantial justification in behavioral research for the use of parametric statistical methods based on the multivariate normal distribution.

3.1 THE ASSUMPTIONS OF MULTIVARIATE NORMAL STATISTICAL ANALYSIS

It is important to understand in connection with normal statistical analysis of models with additive error, that distribution assumptions refer, not to the total variation in the data, but to the residual variation between the observations and the fitted model. The systematic variation in the data is assumed to be accounted for by *fixed* effects in the model; the remaining *random* variation is assumed to arise from small, independent influences which produce normally distributed residuals. An illustration of the importance of the distinction between systematic and random variation is seen in the distribution of any age-dependent trait. In data consisting, for example, of height measurements for samples of boys from successive school grades, the distribution of measurements would certainly tend to be uniform, but deviation scores about the age-trend line could be expected to be normal, or nearly so, because the distribution of stature in males of the same age is essentially normal [Anastasi, 1958, page 29].

Another example is that of a sample of subjects drawn from a mixture of populations. Measurements obtained from such a sample might exhibit an arbitrary, possibly skewed, flattened, or multimodal distribution in the total sample, depending on the size and distributions of the populations. But if the sample is divided in such a way that the ultimate level of classification (by age, sex, SES, etc.) effectively separates the populations, then the distribution within subclasses might be expected to approximate normality. If a model is fitted that accounts for the systematic between-subclass variation, the residuals could reasonably be assumed to belong to the normal within-subclass variation. This is the reasoning on which the analysis of comparative studies in Chap. 6 is based.

A second point often overlooked in the discussion of distribution assumptions is that the probability statements in tests of significance and confidence intervals refer to the distribution of a statistic, such as a sample mean or difference in means, and not to the distribution of individual observations. It is a well-known consequence of the central-limit theorem (see Sec. 3.1.4) that the distributions of statistics typically encountered in practice become essentially normal when data are moderately extensive. This limiting effect has been repeatedly demonstrated in sampling studies of contrived nonnormal populations [Holzinger and Church, 1928; Hey, 1938].

From the point of view of data analysis, there is considerable advantage in working with large samples whenever possible. The assumption that the basic observations are normally distributed is then much less critical in statistical tests and confidence intervals, and the precision of estimation of unknown parameters is better. Furthermore, many statistical methods that have been worked out only in the large-sample case may then be applicable (see Chap. 8). How large the sample must be in order to be considered *large* in the statistical sense depends, of course, upon the limiting properties of the statistic with respect to the given population distribution. For example, the sampling studies of Holzinger and Church [1928] show that the mean is distributed approximately normally, even when the parent is grossly non-normal (U shaped), if the number of independent observations is 50 or more.

In experimental studies limited to small samples, we have the option of resorting to nonparametric-methods analysis, or of planning the experiment so as to justify the assumption of normally distributed error. If we take the nonparametric approach, the randomization test referred to in Sec. 1.2.4a has definite advantages which we can exploit with the aid of high-speed computers. Unlike other nonparametric methods, the randomization test entails no loss of efficiency relative to tests based on the normal distribution when the population is in fact normal (see Mood and Graybill [1963, page 419]).

To use randomization procedures or other nonparametric methods when the sample size is small, and thus lose the possibility of computing descriptive statistics and calculating standard errors may, however, be too conservative in view of the plausibility of normal assumptions for behavioral data. This plausibility derives from our knowledge of the actual processes that give rise to random variation in this type of data.

3.1.1 Error Processes in Behavioral Data; Individual Differences

We shall follow Haggard's [1958] example in discussing variation in behavioral data by distinguishing between (1) *individual differences*, (2) *response error* (trait instability), and (3) *measurement error* (variation contributed by the measuring instrument).

In studies in which individual subjects are the sampling units, each of the above three sources of variation is usually represented in the residual, which is treated as error in the data analysis. Unless steps are taken to control them (see Chaps. 5 and 7), individual differences are typically much more important as a source of error variation than are the two other sources. By *individual differences* we mean any behavioral characteristics varying between individuals but remaining fixed in any given individual over a relatively extended period. Broadly speaking, we may attribute such differences to the joint, and possibly interacting, effects of (1) the genetic makeup of the individual, (2) accidents of development, and (3) learning.

a Genetic differences The mechanism by which genetic differences determine observed (phenotypic) characteristics of organisms, including behavioral traits, is now reasonably well understood (see McKusick [1969]). If a trait is under the control of a single autosomal locus (i.e., a locus on a chromosome other than the sex chromosomes), the expression of the trait depends on the action of the two alleles of the gene which occupy that locus, one contributed to the offspring by the mother, and the other by the father. The joint action of the two alleles may be such that (1) their effects are simply additive, or (2) one allele may be *dominant*, in which case its expression partially or completely masks the expression of the other, or (3) the two alleles may exhibit *overdominance*, in which case the joint expression is greater than can be attributed to the additive effects of either. [In this respect the sex chromosomes in man are exceptional in that, other than in the determination of primary sex differentiation, the male (Y) chromosome contributed to the son by the father appears to be almost completely inactive in males. In females, trait determination on the sex chromosome is more similar to that of the autosomes.]

If a trait is determined by genes at two or more loci, each locus may contribute additively, or there may be some interaction, or *epistacy*, between loci. If many genes at many loci contribute to a trait, with or without dominance and epistacy, the trait is said to be *polygenic* or *multifactorial.* With respect to the population of subjects, the effects of genes contributing to a polygenically determined trait are virtually independent. This is the case because in meiosis the segregation of alleles into the parental egg or sperm is largely random. Such random transmission of genes from parent to child is true not only of loci on different chromosomes, but because of "breaking" and "crossing over" of chromosome segments during meiosis, tends also to hold for loci on the same chromosome (except the Y chromosome). Only loci which are close together on the same chromosomes have any tendency to transmit genes together, and the probability that two or more such loci will determine the same trait is small. The implication of this process of polygenetic trait determination is that the observed trait in different individuals is the cumulative expression of the additive, dominance, or epistatic effects of many *independent* and more or less equally contributing loci. Thus, with respect to samples of unrelated individuals (i.e., with zero coefficients of consanguinity), the conditions of the central-limit theorem (Sec. 3.1.4) are closely approximated, and the trait may be assumed normally distributed. Furthermore, if the trait is not subject to selection, the mean and variance of this distribution will remain stable from one generation to another (Hardy-Weinberg equilibrium).

The assumption that we are dealing with a single random-mating population is crucial here. If a sample of individuals is drawn from two or more exclusive breeding populations, the distributions within each will be normal, but the combined population will be a mixture of normal distributions which in general will not be normal. Of course, if the subpopulations can be identified beforehand, then the sample may be divided into corresponding subclasses within which normality may be assumed. If the trait is under the influence of genes on the sex chromosome, then a similar division of the sample into male and female subjects may be necessary.

Behavioral traits are usually assumed to be polygenically determined and therefore normally distributed [Stern, 1960]. The only presently known exceptions are sensory processes, such as color vision or taste for the specific substance phenylthiocarbamide (PTC), which show clear bimodality [Stern, 1960; Fuller and Thompson, 1960]. Numerous examples of physiological and behavioral measures that have essentially normal distributions may be found in Wright [1968] and Anastasi [1958]. (See however Bock and Kolakowski [1973].)

b Accidents of development If nongenetic sources of variation are also involved, the conditions for assuming normality may need to be further qualified. Developmental accidents, by which is meant any accident or deprivation which permanently alters some characteristic of the individual, fall in this class. Such accidents, whether prenatal or postnatal, tend to produce deviant individuals, usually impaired in some way, such that the frequency at the lower extreme of the population distribution is greater than expected if a normal distribution is assumed. This type of departure from normality has been observed for IQ scores and has been investigated by Roberts [1952]. He finds that severely retarded subjects (IQ less than 60–70) appear to be distinguishable from moderate retardates (IQ 70–80) in that parents and siblings of the former exhibit a full range of normal IQ, whereas those of the latter show mostly below-normal IQ. This suggests that the severe retardate is mostly environmental (accidental) in origin, whereas the moderate retardate tends to be the lower extreme of normal genetic variation.

Because subjects severely affected by developmental accidents seldom appear in samples which have been obtained from the usual convenient sources (schools, businesses, the military, etc.), departures from normality from this source are not ordinarily a problem. Mildly affected subjects probably cannot be identified, however, and will contribute variation to presumedly normal samples. But effects from this source are small by definition and, being independent of genetic variation, would merely alter the mean and variance without affecting the normal form of the distribution. Thus, individual differences due to accidents of development will not ordinarily vitiate normal assumptions.

c Learned behaviors Learning can be a major source of individual differences in traits which are acquired or deliberately cultivated. In human subjects many aspects of language, ability, personality, values, demeanor, and life goals fall into this class. Although the content of what is learned is necessarily acquired, the course and consequences of the learning may not be independent of genetic differences. In fact, the extent or kind of changes which occur in different individuals exposed to the same learning situation probably are strongly dependent on genetically determined individual differences. Twin studies [Block, 1968] show, for example, that performance on vocabulary tests is highly heritable, in spite of the fact that a person's vocabulary is entirely a learned characteristic. This means that among individuals sharing approximately the same linguistic environment (as in the case of fraternal twins), the probability that a given individual will add a new word to his vocabulary and be able to recall it on demand is to a substantial extent under genetic control. Considering the complexity of the trait and the many processes which must be involved in bringing an individual into contact with a new word, consolidating it in long-term memory, and recovering it at a later time, we may reasonably conclude that the genetic contribution is multifactorial.

The implication of this conclusion for data analysis is that, if we are able to assign subjects into sufficiently homogeneous groups with respect to language acquisition, the within-group variation of vocabulary-test scores will be dominated by the multifactorial genetic component and will distribute normally. Thus, the condition of normal residuals required for model fitting is quite plausible for this learned trait. The same conclusion seems warranted for many similar traits, provided that the measuring instrument is sensitive to innate individual differences in the extent or efficiency of learning, and that gross differences in learning experience are eliminated from error variation by homogeneous grouping of subjects.

3.1.2 Response Error

Although it is useful to conceive of individuals as having certain fixed behavioral characteristics, actual responses of subjects almost always show short-term variability. What we regard as a fixed individual difference is actually a longer-term average of variable behavior or the expected course of a systematic time trend in such behavior. Residual variation about a given individual's mean or trend line is called *response error*. (Measurement error may also be involved; see Sec. 3.1.3.) Presumedly, response error is part of the lability of living organisms and is the expression of momentary or circadian variability in states of drive, arousal, fatigue, nutrition, health, etc. This kind of variation could also be called "trait instability," but we prefer to reserve the term "trait" for the long-term average or trend and thus not to regard the variability as part of the trait itself. Almost by definition, the variation between individuals for a given trait must be larger than that due to response errors; otherwise there would be too little behavioral consistency for us to recognize the trait.

For statistical purposes, it is important to establish not only the form of the response error distribution, but also the independence or lack of independence of successive responses. Unfortunately, the psychological literature has little to contribute on this subject, except for early work in the field of psychophysics. Together with a number of other experiments, E. S. Pearson [1922] carried out a long series of bisections and trisections of a line, using himself as subject, consisting of 63 judgments per session in each of 20 sessions, with either one or two sessions per day during the months of May and July. Within a session, successive judgments were about 5 sec apart. The trisections showed definite trends, usually linear, both between and within sessions, while the bisections were largely trend free. Variations about the trend line on average were definitely correlated in adjacent judgments, but the correlations fell to zero for judgments removed by more than six trials. This suggests that independence of response error may be a reasonable assumption if the trials are separated in time or by intervening responses. Pearson did not check the normality of residuals, but indirect evidence from the study of qualitative psychophysical judgments (the constant method) appears to indicate that a normally distributed response process is involved (see Bock and Jones [1968]). Tentatively, we might assume that these findings for psychophysical testing may carry over to other types of psychological tests and thus give some support for the assumption of normally distributed response error. However, the studies of intrasubject variability of response to measures of ability, personality scales, etc., that appear in the literature [Fiske, 1961] do not address themselves to this point.

3.1.3 Measurement Error

In physical science there is a tradition going back to Gauss [1963 reprint] which assumes that errors of observation (i.e., errors contributed by measuring instruments, or instrument × observer interaction) should be assumed normally distributed (see, however, the discussion of outliers in Sec. 3.5). A similar assumption in behavioral studies making use of physical instruments probably would not be challenged and is taken for granted in the present discussion.

However, in many other behavioral investigations, particularly those involving human subjects, the response measures are psychological tests and scales which bear little resemblance to physical instruments. The important point of difference is that the psychological measures have substantial random elements in their construction, while the physical instruments, although possibly including random components (because no manufacturing process can be controlled closely enough to eliminate them entirely), are subject only to minor variation from this source relative to the variation in things measured. Actually, the random component in a psychological instrument may be *deliberately* incorporated during its construction. Consider, for example, the *digit-span test* commonly used to measure auditory short-term memory. This test consists of sets of digits which the test administrator reads to the subject and the subject attempts to repeat. A typical method of constructing multiple forms of the test is to select the sets of digits randomly using a table of random numbers. The effect of this procedure is to introduce random variation between forms that ultimately appear as differences in the response of subjects to these forms. Not only do the forms differ randomly in average difficulty, but between-form differences may, and probably do, interact with individual differences to produce measurement error. That is, some of the digit sequences will be easier for some subjects and not for others, as, for example, if a sequence fortuitously contains part of the telephone number of one of the subjects. It is clear that measurement error of this type cannot be eliminated by the kind of quality control that goes into the making of physical instruments. The best that can be done is to randomize specific features of the item content so that the effect of these features will not bias the total score. This is the basis for the principle of test construction which requires that a test be made up of many independent items obtained by random sampling, possibly stratified random sampling, from an item domain.

It might be thought that the random element in constructing psychological tests could be avoided by creating only one fixed form of the test. Indeed, only one form of tests such as the Rorschach inkblots exists [Beck, 1950; Klopfer, et al., 1954], and other inkblot tests which have been constructed [Zullinger, 1956; Holtzman, et al., 1961], while useful in their own right, are not widely accepted as equivalent. The difficulty with this approach is that it rules out any possibility of detecting and accounting for test-specific, or "methods" factors in response to the instrument. That methods factors are important sources of variation in many widely used psychological tests has become increasingly clear due to the work of Fiske [1971] and Campbell and Fiske [1959]. In most cases, these factors are unrelated to the trait which the test is intended to measure and serve only to confound the interpretation of the test scores or to contribute error variation.

Under certain simplifying assumptions we can specify the exact form of the measurement error distribution of a psychological test score (see Lord and Novick [1968, Chap. 23]). Suppose a test is constructed by randomly sampling n items from a large set of equivalent items. By "equivalent" we mean that all items in the set are equally difficult, i.e., have the same probability P of being responded to correctly by subjects who are at the same level on the trait measured by the test. We suppose that a subject responds independently to each test item, that his responses are scored "right" or "wrong," and that his score on the test is the number of "right" responses.

Under these assumptions, the distribution of scores, with respect to the sampling of items, of subjects who represent the same trait value, is binomial with parameters n and P. It is this distribution which characterizes the measurement error of the test and is the basis for the Kuder-Richardson [1937] Formula 21 for the reliability of a dichotomously scored test. Although the assumption of equal item difficulties may seem rather artificial, it is approximately the condition which modern testing practice attempts to meet. A good objective test consists of a large number of brief, independent items in which the difficulties are homogeneous and are adjusted to a level suitable to the intended population of subjects. When such a test is applied to homogeneous subclasses of subjects from that population, the conditions for a binomial distribution of the measurement error may be approximated rather well. Keats and Lord [1962] have in fact shown that this simple binomial error model predicts quite accurately a number of important properties of score distributions with respect to the population of subjects. A somewhat more realistic model is one in which the probability P may be different for each item. The scores for subjects of the same level on the trait then follow a so-called *compound binomial distribution.* If the variation of the item probabilities is not too large, the form of distribution differs only slightly from a binomial distribution in which the parameters are n and the average value of P. This is the model assumed in the Kuder-Richardson Formula 20 for test reliability.

In the context of data analysis, the importance of the binomial error specification lies in the approach of the binomial distribution to normal form as n increases. If P is not too extreme, the approach is quite rapid; when $P = \frac{1}{2}$ and $n = 10$, for example, the largest discrepancy between cumulative binomial distribution and its normal approximation is only .002. Since a reliable objective test usually must contain in the vicinity of 30 items, mostly of intermediate difficulty, the substitution of a normal component as an approximation to the binomial error is easily justified.

3.1.4 The Central-Limit Theorem

The main thrust of the preceding argument is that errors in behavioral data have their source in numerous small and independent influences which combine additively to determine jointly the characteristics of the subjects, the momentary response state of the subjects, and the characteristics of the measuring instruments which interact with subject characteristics. If this conclusion is correct, we may invoke the central-limit theorem to establish that the distribution of the errors will approach normality as the number of influences increases.

The special case of this theorem for binomial variables, known as De Moivre's theorem, is demonstrated in many elementary texts [Mosteller, Rourke, and Thomas, 1961], and its mathematical proof may be found in Cramér [1951, page 198]. The general case has been the subject of intense study, and proofs may be found in Cramér [1951, page 213] and Gnedenko and Kolmogorov [1954]. The general theorem states that, *subject to conditions which would always be met by bounded behavioral variables, the sum of independent observations having any distributions whatever approaches a normal distribution as the number of observations increases.* The number of observations that must be summed to obtain a "good" approximation to normality depends, of course, upon the forms of distribution of the separate variables. The sampling studies referred to above have shown, however, that even for distributions which depart markedly from normality, sums of 50 or more observations approximate to normality. For more moderately nonnormal distributions, the approximation is good with as few as 10 to 20 observations (see Mood and Graybill [1963, page 152]).

The central-limit theorem may also be generalized to higher-dimensional space to establish that under certain broad conditions, the joint distribution of several distinct sums of independent variables is distributed in *multivariate normal* form

[Rao, 1965, page 108]. It must be emphasized, however, that the central-limit theorem guarantees merely an approximation to normality. Only a sum of normal variables is exactly normally distributed [Cramér, 1951, page 213].

A slightly different conception of the manner in which a number of variables combines leads to another important distribution. If we assume that the amount by which the ith independent variable increases the sum is proportional to the *product* of the variable and the sum at the $i - 1$ stage ($i = 1, 2, \ldots, n$), then the nth-stage sum tends to a *logarithmic-normal* (*log-normal*) distribution as n increases [Cramér, 1951, page 220]. That is, the logarithm of the sum tends to a normal distribution.

The log-normal distribution has interesting behavioral applications in the study of speech and literary style [C. B. Williams, 1940; Yule, 1944; Carroll, 1967]. In these, and similar applications, the log-normal variables may be analyzed by normal methods simply by using logarithms of the observations as variables (see Aitchison and Brown [1966]).

3.2 REVIEW OF ELEMENTARY DISTRIBUTION THEORY

Anticipating the discussion of the multivariate normal distribution in Sec. 3.3, we review here the terminology and concepts used in the study of univariate and bivariate probability distributions generally. The present discussion is limited to continuously distributed variables and is illustrated by applications to the univariate and bivariate normal distributions. Some results for discrete data appear in Chap. 8, where methods for the analysis of qualitative response variables are considered.

3.2.1 Distribution and Density Functions

The *distribution function* (also called the *cumulative distribution function* or *cdf*) of a random variable x expresses the probability that the variable will take on a value less than or equal to some number x:

$$F(x) = P(\mathsf{x} \leq x)$$

We allow x to be any real number in the range minus infinity to plus infinity. In general, any mathematical function F may serve as a distribution function* provided it is nondecreasing with increasing x and satisfies $F(-\infty) = 0$ and $F(\infty) = 1$. For present purposes, however, we shall limit our attention to functions that are absolutely continuous in the interval $-\infty$ to $+\infty$. In other words, we assume that the function has finite derivatives of all orders for all values of x. In particular, the first derivative, represented by

$$f(x) = \frac{dF(x)}{dx} \qquad (3.2\text{-}1)$$

* The function must also be continuous from the right [Cramér, 1951, page 57].

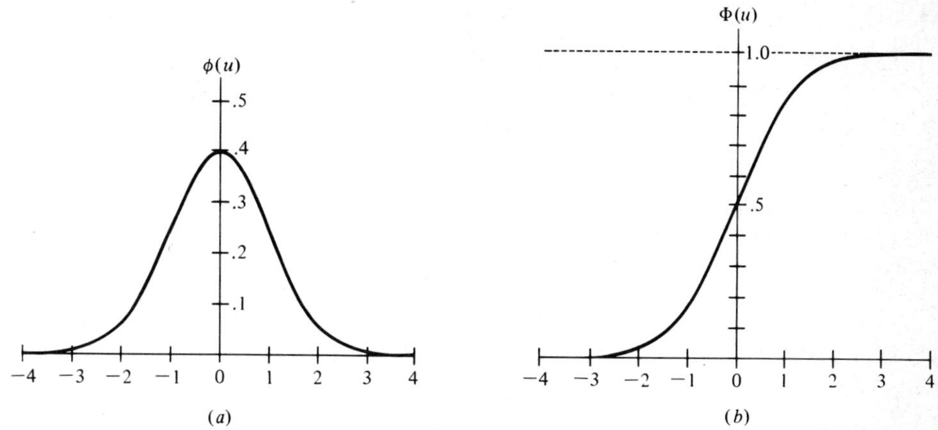

FIGURE 3.2-1
The unit normal (*a*) density function and (*b*) distribution function.

exists and is termed the *probability density function* (or *frequency function*) of the distribution.

As an example of a cdf, we have the *standard normal distribution function*:

$$F(u) = P(u \leq u) = \Phi(u) = \frac{1}{\sqrt{2\pi}} \int_{-\infty}^{u} e^{-t^2/2}\, dt \qquad (3.2\text{-}2)$$

Since $e^{-t^2/2}$ is nonnegative and $\int_{-\infty}^{\infty} e^{-t^2/2} = \sqrt{2\pi}$ [Courant, 1952, vol. I, page 496], (3.2-2) qualifies as a distribution function. It is customary in the statistical literature to use $\Phi(u)$ to denote the value of the standard normal cdf at the point u. A graph of $\Phi(u)$ is shown in Fig. 3.2-1*b*.

Differentiating the right side of (3.2-2) with respect to u, we have the *standard normal density function*,

$$f(u) = \phi(u) = \frac{1}{\sqrt{2\pi}} e^{-u^2/2} \qquad (3.2\text{-}3)$$

The function (3.2-3) describes the familiar bell-shaped curve with maximum at $u = 0$, inflection points at $u = \pm 1$, and zero positive and negative asymptotes. The term *normal ordinate* is often applied to (3.2-3), and the symbol $\phi(u)$ is used to represent its value at the point u. A graph of $\phi(u)$ is shown in Fig. 3.2-1*a*.

Any one-to-one increasing function of a continuous random variable is also a continuous random variable (if the function is decreasing, the sense of one of the variables may be reversed). When the cdf of the original variable is expressed in the form of a definite integral, as in the example (3.2-2), the cdf of the new variable may be obtained by changing the variable of integration. Suppose, for example, that $y = g(x)$ is a continuous function differentiable in x, and $x = h(y)$ is the inverse function, also continuous and differentiable in y. Then $dx = [dh(y)/dy]\,dy = h'(y)\,dy$, and the cdf of the random variable $y = g(x)$ is given by

$$F(y) = P(y \le y) = P[g(x) \le y] = P[x \le h(y)]$$
$$= \int_{-\infty}^{h(y)} f(x)\,dx = \int_{-\infty}^{y} f[h(y)]h'(y)\,dy \qquad (3.2\text{-}4)$$

The density function of the new variable is

$$f(y) = \frac{dF(y)}{dy} = f[h(y)]h'(y) \qquad (3.2\text{-}5)$$

Using (3.2-4) and (3.2-5), we may obtain the cdf and frequency function of a variable y resulting from the measurement of a standard normal variable u on a scale with arbitrary mean b and scale unit a. For then $y = au + b$, $h(y) = n = (y - b)/a$, and $h'(y) = du/dy = 1/a$, for $a \neq 0$. From (3.2-4), the cdf of y is

$$F(y) = \frac{1}{\sqrt{2\pi}\,a} \int_{-\infty}^{y} e^{-(s-b)^2/2a^2}\,ds \qquad (3.2\text{-}6)$$

and the frequency function is

$$f(y) = \frac{1}{\sqrt{2\pi}\,a} e^{-(y-b)^2/2a^2} \qquad (3.2\text{-}7)$$

Functions (3.2-6) and (3.2-7) are the general forms of the normal distribution function and density function, of which (3.2-2) and (3.2-3) are the special cases for $a = 1$, $b = 0$. The constants a and b are *parameters* of the distribution which, as shown in Sec. 3.2.2, serve to index the dispersion and central tendency of the distribution. The intuitive interpretation of these parameters is clarified by the graph of (3.2-7) shown in Fig. 3.2-2. Equating the first derivative of (3.2-7) to zero and solving for y shows that the mode of the distribution is at $y = b$; that is, $df(y)/dy = -(y - b)f(y)/a^2 = 0$ or $y = b$ for $f(y) \neq 0$.

Equating the second derivative of (3.2-7) to zero and solving for y locates the inflection points of the density function at $b \pm a$:

$$\frac{d^2f(y)}{dy^2} = -\frac{f(y)}{a^2} + (y - b)^2\frac{f(y)}{a^4} = 0$$
$$(y - b)^2 = a^2$$
$$y = b \pm a$$

3.2.2 Expectation and Variance

Although numerous indices may be defined in order to characterize probability distribution functions, the *expectation* and *variance* are especially important. The expectation or *expected value*, or *mean*, of a continuously distributed random variable is defined by

$$\mu = \int_{-\infty}^{\infty} xf(x)\,dx \qquad (3.2\text{-}8)$$

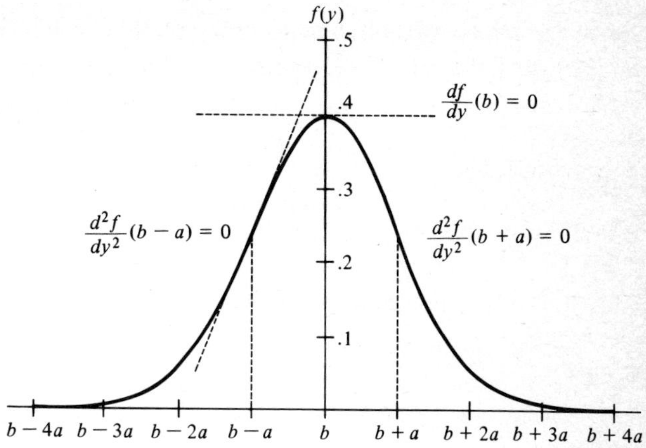

FIGURE 3.2-2
Mode and inflection points of the normal density function.

where $f(x)$ is again the density function of the variable. Provided the density function is such that this integral exists and is finite, the expectation serves to describe the *central tendency* or *location* of the distribution on the continuum of the random variable.

The *variance* is defined by

$$\sigma^2 = \int_{-\infty}^{\infty} (x - \mu)^2 f(x)\, dx \qquad (3.2\text{-}9)$$

This quantity, if it exists, is descriptive of the dispersion of the distribution about μ. For some purposes, the *standard deviation* σ, defined as the positive square root of the variance, is more convenient as an index of dispersion.

When investigating the statistical properties of random variables, we often find it useful to express expected value and variance in *operator* notation. Thus, the operator $\mathscr{E}(x)$ denotes the expectation of x, and the operator $\mathscr{V}(x)$ denotes its variance. The expectation operator has the obvious properties

$$\mathscr{E}(c) = c \qquad (3.2\text{-}10)$$

$$\mathscr{E}(cx) = c\mathscr{E}(x) \qquad (3.2\text{-}11)$$

$$\mathscr{E}(x + y) = \mathscr{E}(x) + \mathscr{E}(y) \qquad (3.2\text{-}12)$$

where c is a constant, and y is a second random variable.

The variance operator has the properties

$$\mathscr{V}(x + c) = \mathscr{V}(x) \qquad (3.2\text{-}13)$$

and

$$\mathscr{V}(cx) = c^2\mathscr{V}(x) \qquad (3.2\text{-}14)$$

If x and y are statistically independent [see Eq. (3.2-42)], then

$$\mathscr{E}(xy) = \mathscr{E}(x)\mathscr{E}(y)$$

and

$$\mathscr{V}(x + y) = \mathscr{V}(x) + \mathscr{V}(y) \tag{3.2-15}$$

Notice that

$$\mathscr{V}(x) = \mathscr{E}[(x - \mu)^2] = \mathscr{E}(x^2) - 2\mu\mathscr{E}(x) + \mu^2$$
$$= \mathscr{E}(x^2) - [\mathscr{E}(x)]^2$$

since $\mu = \mathscr{E}(x)$. For example, the mean of the normal distribution is, from (3.2-7) and (3.2-8),

$$\mu = \mathscr{E}(y) = \frac{1}{\sqrt{2\pi}\, a}\int_{-\infty}^{\infty} ye^{-(y-b)^2/2a^2}\, dy$$

To evaluate this integral, change the variable of integration to $u = (y - b)/a$. Then $y = au + b$, $dy = a\, du$, and

$$\mu = \frac{a}{\sqrt{2\pi}}\int_{-\infty}^{\infty} ue^{-u^2/2}\, du + \frac{b}{\sqrt{2\pi}}\int_{-\infty}^{\infty} e^{-u^2/2}\, du$$
$$= \frac{a}{\sqrt{2\pi}}[-e^{-u^2/2}]_{-\infty}^{\infty} + \frac{b\sqrt{2\pi}}{\sqrt{2\pi}}$$
$$= b$$

Substituting (3.2-7) and setting $\mu = b$ in (3.2-9), we obtain the variance of the normal distribution:

$$\sigma^2 = \mathscr{V}(y) = \mathscr{E}[(y - b)^2] = \frac{1}{\sqrt{2\pi}\, a}\int_{-\infty}^{\infty} (y - b)^2 e^{-(y-b)^2/2a^2}\, dy$$

Again introducing $u = (y - b)/a$, we obtain

$$\sigma^2 = \frac{a^2}{\sqrt{2\pi}}\int_{-\infty}^{\infty} u^2 e^{-u^2/2}\, du$$

and integrating by parts gives

$$\sigma^2 = \frac{a^2}{\sqrt{2\pi}}[-ue^{-u^2/2}]_{-\infty}^{\infty} + \frac{a^2}{\sqrt{2\pi}}\int_{-\infty}^{\infty} e^{-u^2/2}\, du$$
$$= 0 + \frac{a^2\sqrt{2\pi}}{\sqrt{2\pi}} = a^2$$

These results show that the mean of the normal distribution is specified by the parameter b, and the variance by a^2. The parameter a, the positive square root of a^2, is the standard deviation of the distribution. Sometimes we use the symbolism $y \sim N(b, a^2)$ to specify that y is distributed normally with mean b and variance a^2.

If $a = 1$, we say that y has a *unit* normal distribution with mean b. If $a = 1$ and $b = 0$, we say that y has a *standard* normal distribution. Obviously, any normal variable with mean μ and variance σ^2 may be transformed into a standard normal variable by use of the relation $u = (y - \mu)/\sigma$. For this reason, tables of the normal distribution function are ordinarily given only for the standardized variable.

Certain weak statements about the range of a random variable can be made on the basis of the expectation and variance alone. Tchebycheff's inequality states that, for any random variable x distributed with mean μ and variance σ^2, the probability that x will deviate from the mean by magnitude equal to or greater than $k\sigma$ is less than or equal to $1/k^2$, where k is any positive constant. That is,

$$P(|x - \mu| \geq k\sigma) \leq \frac{1}{k^2} \qquad (3.2\text{-}16)$$

If it is known that the density function for x is unimodal and symmetric, this inequality may be sharpened to

$$P(|x - \mu| \geq k\sigma) \leq \frac{4}{9k^2} \qquad (3.2\text{-}17)$$

(See Cramér [1951, page 182].)

These inequalities give a definite meaning to σ as a measure of dispersion in distributions whose functional form cannot be specified in more detail. The probability bounds which they imply may be very broad, however, compared with exact probability points computed from a known distribution function. If x is normally distributed, for example, the probability of $|x - \mu|$ exceeding 1.96σ is approximately .05. But (3.2-16) gives $k = 1/\sqrt{.05} \approx 4.47$ as the multiple of σ which $|x - \mu|$ will exceed with probability less than .05. Similarly, (3.2-17) gives $k = \frac{2}{3}/\sqrt{.05} \approx 2.98$ as this multiple.

3.2.3 Moments and Moment-Generating Functions

When investigating the mathematical properties of distribution functions, it is often useful to compute the moments of the distribution. The concept of moments is borrowed from the science of mechanics, where it is used to characterize the distribution of mass (see Goldstein [1950]).

The *raw* order-r moment of x is defined as the expected value of the rth power of the variable; i.e.,

$$m_r = \int_{-\infty}^{\infty} x^r f(x)\, dx \qquad r = 1, 2, \ldots, n \qquad (3.2\text{-}18)$$

The first moment ($r = 1$), analogous to the centroid in mechanics, is just the expected value or mean:

$$\mu = m_1 = \int_{-\infty}^{\infty} x f(x)\, dx \qquad (3.2\text{-}19)$$

The *central* moments of order $r > 1$ are defined in terms of deviations about the mean; i.e.,

$$\mu_r = \int_{-\infty}^{\infty} (x - \mu)^r f(x)\, dx \qquad r = 2, 3, \ldots, n \tag{3.2-20}$$

The central moment of order 2 (analogous to the moment of inertia of a mass about the point μ) is the *variance*:

$$\sigma^2 = \mu_2 = \int_{-\infty}^{\infty} (x - \mu)^2 f(x)\, dx = m_2 - \mu^2 \tag{3.2-21}$$

The central moment of order 3,

$$\mu_3 = \int_{-\infty}^{\infty} (x - \mu)^3 f(x)\, dx = m_3 - 3\mu m_2 + 2\mu^3 \tag{3.2-22}$$

is a measure of asymmetry of the distribution. An index of asymmetry which is independent of the units of measurement of the random variable is the *coefficient of skewness*,

$$\beta_1 = \frac{{\mu_3}^2}{{\mu_2}^3} \tag{3.2-23}$$

The central moment of order 4,

$$\mu_4 = \int_{-\infty}^{\infty} (x - \mu)^4 f(x)\, dx = m_4 - 4\mu m_3 + 6\mu^2 m_2 - 3\mu^4 \tag{3.2-24}$$

is a measure of the "tendency" of the density function to be peaked in the center and high in the tails. A unitless index of this tendency is the coefficient of *kurtosis*,

$$\beta_2 = \frac{\mu_4}{{\mu_2}^2} \tag{3.2-25}$$

Moments of order higher than 4 are seldom calculated.

The importance of moments for statistical theory lies in the theorem which states that *if two distributions have the same moments of all orders, then except for possible points of discontinuity, they are the same distribution.* The proof of this theorem is beyond the scope of this book (see Cramér [1951, page 176]). In applications of this theorem, the moments of the distributions in question are not usually calculated directly. Instead, a function is sought which generates moments of all orders for these distributions. Then the demonstration that the two distributions are the same consists in showing that they have the same *moment-generating function* (mgf). In addition, the mgf is often useful in the calculation of moments when their direct evaluation is difficult. The moment-generating function is defined as the expected value of e^{tx}; that is,

$$m_x(t) = \mathscr{E}(e^{tx}) = \int_{-\infty}^{\infty} e^{tx} f(x)\, dx \tag{3.2-26}$$

Provided t is absolutely continuous in the neighborhood of zero, the rth moment of x can be obtained by differentiating (3.2-26) r times with respect to t, and setting t equal to zero.

Some obvious properties of the mgf are:

$$m_{x+c}(t) = e^{ct}m_x(t) \qquad \text{where } c \text{ is a constant} \tag{3.2-27}$$

$$m_{cx}(t) = m_x(ct) \qquad \text{for } c > 0 \tag{3.2-28}$$

$$m_{x_1+x_2}(t) = m_{x_1}(t)m_{x_2}(t) \tag{3.2-29}$$

where x_1 and x_2 are two statistically independent random variables.

To illustrate the use of the moment-generating function, let us use it to evaluate the first four moments of the normal distribution. First, we obtain the mgf of a standard normal variable u:

$$\begin{aligned} m_u(t) &= \int_{-\infty}^{\infty} \frac{e^{ut}e^{-u^2/2}}{\sqrt{2\pi}}\,du \\ &= \int_{-\infty}^{\infty} \frac{e^{-(u^2-2ut)/2}}{\sqrt{2\pi}}\,du \end{aligned} \tag{3.2-30}$$

We may evaluate (3.2-30) by completing the square in the exponent and observing that the integrand becomes the normal density with mean t and variance 1.

$$\begin{aligned} m_u(t) &= \int_{-\infty}^{\infty} \frac{e^{-[(u-t)^2-t^2]/2}}{\sqrt{2\pi}}\,du \\ &= e^{t^2/2}\int_{-\infty}^{\infty} \frac{e^{-(u-t)^2/2}}{\sqrt{2\pi}}\,du \\ &= e^{t^2/2} \end{aligned} \tag{3.2-31}$$

Let us now introduce the variable $y = au + b$, for $a > 0$, and use (3.2-27) and (3.2-28) to obtain

$$m_y(t) = e^{bt}m_u(at) = e^{bt+a^2t^2/2} \tag{3.2-32}$$

Thus, (3.2-32) is the moment-generating function of the normal distribution with parameters a and b. Using (3.2-32) to calculate the first moment (mean) of the normal distribution, we obtain

$$\mu = \left[\frac{dm_y(t)}{dt}\right]_{t=0} = [(b + a^2t)e^{bt+a^2t^2/2}]_{t=0} = b$$

which agrees with the result in Sec. 3.2.2.

In calculating the second central moment (variance), we note first that

$$m_{y-\mu}(t) = e^{-\mu t}e^{\mu t + a^2t^2/2} = e^{a^2t^2/2}$$

Then
$$\sigma^2 = \left[\frac{d^2 m_{y-\mu}(t)}{dt^2}\right]_{t=0} = [(a^2 + a^4t^2)e^{a^2t^2/2}]_{t=0} = a^2$$

which agrees with the result in Sec. 3.2.2.

Turning to the third and fourth central moments of the normal distribution, we have, respectively,

$$\mu_3 = \left[\frac{d^3 m_{y-\mu}(t)}{dt^3}\right]_{t=0} = [(3a^4t + a^6t^3)e^{a^2t^2/2}]_{t=0} = 0$$

and

$$\mu_4 = \left[\frac{d^4 m_{y-\mu}(t)}{dt^4}\right]_{t=0} = [(3a^4 + 6a^6t^2)e^{a^2t^2/2} + a^8t^4e^{a^2t^2/2}]_{t=0} = 3a^4$$

Then the coefficient of skewness (3.2-23) for the normal distribution is $\beta_1 = 0$, and the coefficient of kurtosis (3.2-25) is $\beta_2 = 3$. Distributions with β_1 negative are skewed to the left (the long tail is on the left), and those with positive β_1 are skewed to the right. Distributions with $\beta_2 < 3$ are platykurtic (less peaked with lower tails than the normal distribution); those with $\beta_2 > 3$ are leptakurtic (more peaked with higher tails).

We may also calculate moments *for sample data* in order to describe an observed distribution of scores. In these calculations, summation over the sample points $y_1, y_2, \ldots, y_N$ replaces the integrals in (3.2-19), (3.2-21), (3.2-22), and (3.2-24), and $1/N$ serves as the density of each point. Thus, the sample value for the rth raw moment is

$$\tilde{m}_r = \frac{1}{N}\sum_{i=1}^{N} y_i^r \qquad (3.2\text{-}33)$$

Then the sample mean and central second, third, and fourth sample moments are,

Mean: $$\tilde{\mu}_1 = \tilde{m}_1 \qquad (3.2\text{-}34)$$

Variance: $$\tilde{\mu}_2 = \tilde{m}_2 - \tilde{m}_1^{\,2} \qquad (3.2\text{-}35)$$

Skewness: $$\tilde{\mu}_3 = \tilde{m}_3 - 3\tilde{m}_1\tilde{m}_2 + 2\tilde{m}_1^{\,3} \qquad (3.2\text{-}36)$$

Kurtosis: $$\tilde{\mu}_4 = \tilde{m}_4 - 4\tilde{m}_1\tilde{m}_3 + 6\tilde{m}_1^{\,2}\tilde{m}_2 - 3\tilde{m}_1^{\,4} \qquad (3.2\text{-}37)$$

The sample values of the coefficients of skewness and kurtosis are, respectively, $b_1 = \tilde{\mu}_3^{\,2}/\tilde{\mu}_2^{\,3}$ and $b_2 = \tilde{\mu}_4/\tilde{\mu}_2^{\,2}$.

We shall use these quantities in Sec. 3.5 to fit the normal distribution to data and to check distribution assumptions.

EXAMPLE 3.2-1 (*Sample moments*) Compute the mean, variance, skewness, kurtosis, and the coefficients b_1 and b_2 for the sample in the column labeled x below:

x	x^2	x^3	x^4
1	1	1	1
0	0	0	0
2	4	8	16
1	1	1	1
4	16	64	256
6	36	216	1,296
3	9	27	81
2	4	8	16
19	71	325	1,667

We have

$$\tilde{m}_1 = \tfrac{19}{8} = 2.375$$

$$\tilde{m}_2 = \tfrac{71}{8} = 8.875$$

$$\tilde{m}_3 = \tfrac{325}{8} = 40.625$$

$$\tilde{m}_4 = \tfrac{1667}{8} = 208.375$$

$$\tilde{\mu}_1 = 2.375$$

$$\tilde{\mu}_2 = 8.875 - (2.375)^2 = 3.234$$

$$\tilde{\mu}_3 = 40.625 - 3 \times 2.375 \times 8.875 + 2 \times (2.375)^3 = 4.184$$

$$\tilde{\mu}_4 = 208.375 - 4 \times 2.375 \times 40.625 + 6 \times (2.375)^2 \times 8.875 - 3 \times (2.375)^4 = 27.351$$

$$b_1 = (4.184)^2/(3.234)^3 = .517$$

$$b_2 = 27.351/(3.234)^2 = 2.615$$

3.2.4 Bivariate Distributions

Suppose x and y are two continuously distributed random variables—for example, the height and weight of persons in some population. By the *joint probability distribution function* of x and y we mean a mathematical function giving the probability that x and y are simultaneously less than or equal to the values x and y, respectively:

$$F(x,y) = P(\mathsf{x} \le x \text{ and } \mathsf{y} \le y)$$

For example, if $x = 66$ in. and $y = 160$ lb, $F(x,y)$ could represent the probability that a randomly selected subject from the population will be no taller than 66 in. and no heavier than 160 lb. In theory, the range of x and y is potentially the entire real plane. F is required to be an increasing function of x and y bounded by 0 and 1.

Again, we assume that F is absolutely continuous and define its derivative with respect to x and y as the *joint density function*:

$$f(x,y) = \frac{\partial^2 F(x,y)}{\partial x\,\partial y}$$

The distribution of one of the variables, ignoring the other, is called a *marginal distribution.* The marginal distribution function is obtained by integrating the ignored variable out of the joint distribution function. For example, the marginal distribution of x is

$$P(\mathsf{x} \le x) = \int_{-\infty}^{x} \left[\int_{-\infty}^{\infty} f(t,y)\,dy\right] dt \qquad (3.2\text{-}38)$$

Correspondingly, the marginal *density* function of x is

$$f(x) = \int_{-\infty}^{\infty} f(x,y)\,dy \qquad (3.2\text{-}39)$$

Interchanging the roles of x and y in (3.2-38) and (3.2-39) gives the marginal distribution and density functions of y. The distribution of one of the variables when the other variable is held fixed at some given value is called a *conditional* distribution. Thus, if x is fixed at the value x and y remains random, we speak of the conditional distribution of y given x. The distribution function of this conditional distribution is defined by

$$P(\mathsf{y} \le y \mid x) = F(y \mid x) = \int_{-\infty}^{y} \frac{f(x,s)}{f(x)}\,ds \qquad (3.2\text{-}40)$$

for $f(x) > 0$. The corresponding conditional density is

$$f(y \mid x) = \frac{f(x,y)}{f(x)} \qquad (3.2\text{-}41)$$

Similarly, if x is random and y is fixed at the value y, the conditional distribution of x given y is

$$P(\mathsf{x} \le x \mid y) = F(x \mid y) = \int_{-\infty}^{x} \frac{f(t,y)}{f(y)}\,dt$$

for $f(y) > 0$. The conditional density is

$$f(x \mid y) = \frac{f(x,y)}{f(y)}$$

If and only if the joint density function is the product of the marginal density functions, that is,

$$f(x,y) = f(x)f(y) \qquad (3.2\text{-}42)$$

the variables are said to be *statistically* (or *stochastically*) independent. Obviously, the marginal and conditional distributions are identical when the variables are independent. As we shall see in Sec. 6.1.2, this fact is the basis for a practical test of the independence of two sets of variables.

As an example of a joint distribution function, consider the standard bivariate normal distribution:

$$P(\mathsf{u} \le u \text{ and } \mathsf{v} \le v) = \Phi(u, v \mid \rho)$$

$$= \frac{1}{2\pi\sqrt{1-\rho^2}} \int_{-\infty}^{v} \int_{-\infty}^{u} e^{-(t^2 - 2\rho ts + s^2)/2(1-\rho^2)}\, dt\, ds \qquad (3.2\text{-}43)$$

Notice that this function contains ρ as a parameter and is symmetric in u and v (that is, its value is unchanged if u and v are interchanged). The parameter ρ, varying between -1 and $+1$, is called the *correlation* coefficient. The joint density function is

$$f(u,v) = \phi(u, v \mid \rho) = \frac{1}{2\pi\sqrt{1-\rho^2}} e^{-(u^2 - 2\rho uv + v^2)/2(1-\rho^2)} \qquad (3.2\text{-}44)$$

To obtain the marginal distribution of v, say, complete the square in the exponent and write the integrand in (3.2-43) as a product of two terms, one of which does not involve t:

$$\exp\left[-\frac{t^2 - 2\rho ts + s^2}{2(1-\rho^2)}\right] = \exp\left[-\frac{t^2 - 2\rho ts + \rho^2 s^2 + s^2(1-\rho^2)}{2(1-\rho^2)}\right]$$

$$= \exp\left[-\frac{(t-\rho s)^2 + s^2(1-\rho^2)}{2(1-\rho^2)}\right]$$

$$= e^{-(t-\rho s)^2/2(1-\rho^2)} e^{-s^2/2} \qquad (3.2\text{-}45)$$

Now introduce the variable of integration $w = (t - \rho s)/\sqrt{1-\rho^2}$ and differential element $dw = dt/\sqrt{1-\rho^2}$, and express the marginal distribution in the form

$$P(\mathsf{u} \le u) = \frac{1}{\sqrt{2\pi}} \int_{-\infty}^{\infty} e^{-s^2/2} \int_{-\infty}^{\infty} \frac{e^{-w^2/2}}{1/\sqrt{2\pi}}\, dw\, ds$$

But the integral with respect to w is equal to unity; hence

$$P(\mathsf{u} \le u) = \frac{1}{\sqrt{2\pi}} \int_{-\infty}^{u} e^{-s^2/2}\, ds \qquad (3.2\text{-}46)$$

That is, the marginal distribution of u is standard normal. By symmetry, the same is true of v.

It is also evident from (3.2-40) that the conditional distribution of v given u is

$$P(\mathsf{v} \le v \mid u) = \frac{1}{\sqrt{2\pi}\sqrt{1-\rho^2}} \int_{-\infty}^{v} e^{-(t-\rho u)^2/2(1-\rho^2)}\, dt \qquad (3.2\text{-}47)$$

for, if (3.2-45) is used to express the joint density as

$$f(u,v) = \frac{1}{2\pi\sqrt{1-\rho^2}} e^{-(v-\rho u)^2/2(1-\rho^2)} e^{-u^2/2}$$

then

$$f(v \mid u) = \frac{f(u,v)}{f(u)} = \frac{1}{\sqrt{2\pi}\sqrt{1-\rho^2}} e^{-(v-\rho u)^2/2(1-\rho^2)}$$

and (3.2-47) results upon integration from $-\infty$ to v.

From the form of (3.2-47), it is clear that the conditional distribution of v, given u, is normal with mean ρu and variance $1 - \rho^2$ when the joint distribution is standard bivariate normal. Conversely, upon interchanging u and v in (3.2-47), we find that the conditional distribution of u, given v, is normal with mean ρv and variance $1 - \rho^2$.

The bivariate normal cdf may be represented graphically by drawing contours of equal probability. A graph showing contours for five probability levels of a standard bivariate normal cdf appears in Fig. 3.2-3*a*. Contours of the density function appear in Fig. 3.2-3*b*.

The general form of the bivariate normal distribution results if we let $x = b_x + a_x u$ and $y = b_y + a_y v$. Then $u = (x - b_x)/a_x$, $v = (y - b_y)/a_y$, and $du = dx/a_x$, $dv = dy/a_y$. The cdf of x and y is

$$\begin{aligned} F(x,y) &= P(b_x + a_x\mathsf{u} \le x \text{ and } b_y + a_y\mathsf{v} \le y) \\ &= P\left(\mathsf{u} \le \frac{x-b_x}{a_x} \text{ and } \mathsf{v} \le \frac{y-b_y}{a_y}\right) \\ &= \frac{1}{2\pi\sqrt{1-\rho^2}} \int_{-\infty}^{(x-b_x)/a_x} \int_{-\infty}^{(y-b_y)/a_y} e^{-(u^2-2\rho uv+v^2)/2(1-\rho^2)}\, du\, dv \\ &= \frac{1}{2\pi\sqrt{1-\rho^2}\, a_x a_y} \int_{-\infty}^{x} \int_{-\infty}^{y} f(t,s)\, ds\, dt \end{aligned} \tag{3.2-48}$$

where

$$f(t,s) = \exp\left[-\frac{\left(\dfrac{t-b_x}{a_x}\right)^2 - 2\dfrac{t-b_x}{a_x}\dfrac{s-b_y}{a_y}\rho + \left(\dfrac{s-b_y}{a_y}\right)^2}{2(1-\rho^2)}\right]$$

The bivariate normal density function is, therefore,

$$\frac{\partial F(x,y)}{\partial x\,\partial y} = \frac{1}{2\pi\sqrt{1-\rho^2}\, a_x a_y} \times \exp\left[-\frac{\left(\dfrac{x-b_x}{a_x}\right)^2 - 2\dfrac{x-b_x}{a_x}\dfrac{y-b_y}{a_y}\rho + \left(\dfrac{y-b_y}{a_y}\right)^2}{2(1-\rho^2)}\right] \tag{3.2-49}$$

The general bivariate normal distribution thus depends upon five parameters,

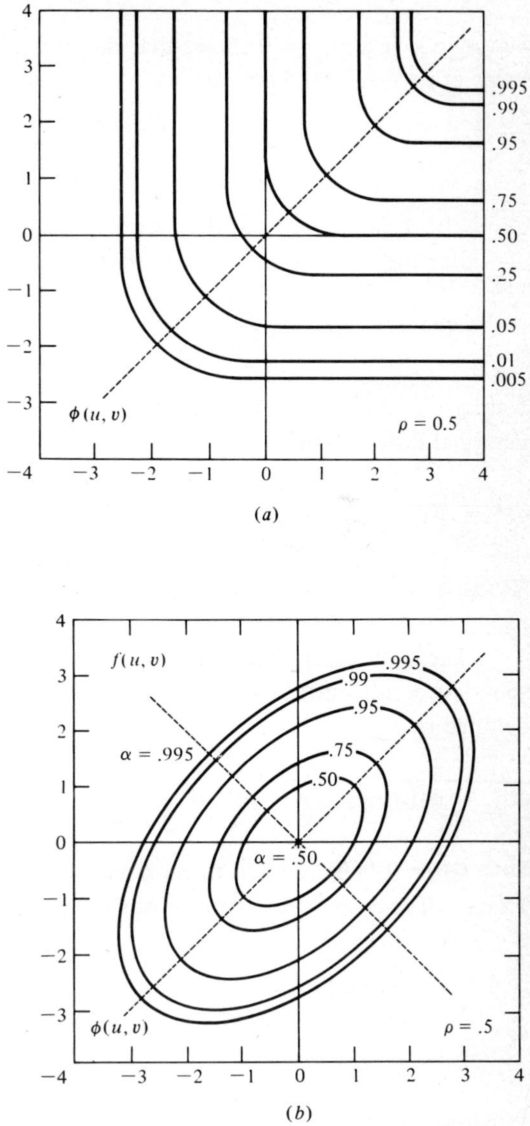

FIGURE 3.2-3
Contours of (*a*) the unit bivariate normal distribution function and (*b*) density function for $\rho = \frac{1}{2}$.

b_x, b_y, a_x, a_y, and ρ, which may be interpreted, as shown below, in terms of moments of the distribution.

The concept of moments and moment-generating functions introduced in Sec. 3.2.3 may be generalized to the bivariate case. Let the $r \times s$ *joint bivariate moment* of random variables x and y be defined by

$$\mathscr{E}(x^r y^s) = \int_{-\infty}^{\infty}\int_{-\infty}^{\infty} x^r y^s f(x, y)\, dy\, dx \qquad \begin{matrix} r = 0, 1, 2, \ldots \\ s = 0, 1, 2, \ldots \end{matrix} \qquad (3.2\text{-}50)$$

Setting $r = 1$ and $s = 0$ shows that the first moment, or mean, of x is the expected value of its marginal distribution:

$$\mu_x = \mathscr{E}(x) = \int_{-\infty}^{\infty} x \int_{-\infty}^{\infty} f(x, y)\, dy\, dx = \int_{-\infty}^{\infty} xf(x)\, dx$$

Similarly, μ_y is the mean of the marginal distribution of y.

For the case $r + s \geq 2$, the *central* joint moment is defined by

$$\mathscr{E}[(x - \mu_x)^r(y - \mu_y)^s] = \int_{-\infty}^{\infty}\int_{-\infty}^{\infty} (x - \mu_x)^r(y - \mu_y)^s f(x, y)\, dy\, dx \qquad (3.2\text{-}51)$$

Setting $r = 2$ and $s = 0$ in the central joint moment gives the variance of x in the marginal distribution:

$$\sigma_x^{\,2} = \mathscr{E}(x - \mu_x)^2 = \int_{-\infty}^{\infty} (x - \mu_x)^2 \int_{-\infty}^{\infty} f(x, y)\, dy\, dx = \int_{-\infty}^{\infty} (x - \mu_x)^2 f(x)\, dx$$

Similarly, setting $r = 0$ and $s = 2$ gives the variance $\sigma_y^{\,2}$ of the marginal distribution of y.

The only other case commonly encountered is $r = 1$ and $s = 1$. The corresponding joint central moment, called the *covariance* of x and y, is conventionally denoted by σ_{xy}:

$$\sigma_{xy} = \mathscr{E}[(x - \mu_x)(y - \mu_y)] = \int_{-\infty}^{\infty}\int_{-\infty}^{\infty} (x - \mu_x)(y - \mu_y) f(x, y)\, dx\, dy \qquad (3.2\text{-}52)$$

Often it is convenient to represent the covariance in operator notation, i.e., as $\mathscr{V}(x,y)$. The covariance operator has the properties

$$\mathscr{V}(x,y) = \mathscr{E}(xy) - \mathscr{E}(x)\mathscr{E}(y) \qquad (3.2\text{-}53)$$

$$\mathscr{V}(cx,dy) = cd\mathscr{V}(x,y) \qquad (3.2\text{-}54)$$

$$\mathscr{V}(x + y, w + z) = \mathscr{V}(x,w) + \mathscr{V}(x,z) + \mathscr{V}(y,w) + \mathscr{V}(y,z) \qquad (3.2\text{-}55)$$

When $w + z = x + y$, (3.2-55) specializes to the *variance of the sum of two random variables*:

$$\mathscr{V}(x + y) = \mathscr{V}(x) + 2\mathscr{V}(x,y) + \mathscr{V}(y) \qquad (3.2\text{-}56)$$

Unlike (3.2-15), the identity (3.2-56) is valid for variables which are not statistically independent. The dependency between the variables is reflected in the covariance term $\mathscr{V}(x,v)$.

Turning now to the moment-generating function, we define, in the bivariate case,

$$m_{x,y}(t_x,t_y) = \mathscr{E}(e^{t_x x + t_y y}) \qquad (3.2\text{-}57)$$

provided this expectation exists in the neighborhood of $t = 0$. The bivariate mgf has the properties

$$m_{x+c_x,y+c_y}(t_x,t_y) = e^{c_x t_x + c_y t_y} m_{x,y}(t_x,t_y) \tag{3.2-58}$$

$$m_{c_x x, c_y y}(t_x,t_y) = m_{x,y}(c_x t_x, c_y t_y) \tag{3.2-59}$$

where c_x and c_y are constants.

Let us use (3.2-57) to evaluate the first- and second-degree moments of the bivariate normal distribution. First, we shall obtain the mgf of the *standard* bivariate normal distribution.

$$\begin{aligned} m_{u,v}(t_u,t_v) &= \int_{-\infty}^{\infty}\int_{-\infty}^{\infty} \frac{e^{t_u u + t_v v} e^{-(u^2-2\rho uv+v^2)/2(1-\rho^2)}}{2\pi\sqrt{1-\rho^2}}\,du\,dv \\ &= \int_{-\infty}^{\infty}\int_{-\infty}^{\infty} \frac{\begin{aligned}\exp\{-[u^2 - 2\rho uv + v^2 - 2(1-\rho^2)t_u u \\ - 2(1-\rho^2)t_v v]/2(1-\rho^2)\}\end{aligned}}{2\pi\sqrt{1-\rho^2}}\,du\,dv \end{aligned} \tag{3.2-60}$$

The quantity in brackets may be expanded into

$$\begin{aligned} -[u^2 - 2t_u u - 2\rho t_v u + (t_u + \rho t_v)^2 + v^2 - 2t_v v - 2\rho t_u v + (t_v + \rho t_u)^2 \\ - 2\rho(uv - t_v u - \rho t_u u - t_u v - \rho t_v v) - 2\rho(t_u + t_v)(t_v + t_u) \\ - (t_u + \rho t_v)^2 - (t_v + \rho t_u)^2 + 2\rho(t_u + \rho t_v)(t_v + \rho t_u)] \end{aligned}$$

and then rewritten as

$$\begin{aligned} -[(u - t_u - \rho t_v)^2 - 2\rho(u - t_u - \rho t_v)(v - t_v - \rho t_u) + (v - t_v - \rho t_u)^2 \\ - (1 - \rho^2)(t_u^2 + 2\rho t_u t_v + t_v^2)] \end{aligned}$$

An exponential term not involving u or v may therefore be factored out of the integrand in (3.2-60), leaving the integral equal to that of a bivariate normal density (with means $t_u + \rho t_v$ and $t_v + \rho t_u$) integrated over the full range of u and v. Since this definite integral is equal to unity, the mgf of the standard bivariate normal distribution is

$$m_{u,v}(t_u,t_v) = e^{(t_u^2 + 2\rho t_u t_v + t_v^2)/2} \tag{3.2-61}$$

Now let $x = a_x u + b_x$ and $y = a_y v + b_y$. According to (3.2-58) and (3.2-59), the mgf of the general bivariate normal distribution is

$$\begin{aligned} m_{x,y}(t_x,t_y) &= e^{b_x t_x + b_y t_y} m_{u,v}(a_x t_x, a_y t_y) \\ &= \exp\left[b_x t_x + b_y t_y + \tfrac{1}{2}(a_x^2 t_x^2 + 2\rho a_x a_y t_x t_y + a_y^2 t_y^2)\right] \end{aligned} \tag{3.2-62}$$

The joint moment corresponding to $r = 1$ and $s = 0$ in (3.2-50) is the mean of the marginal distribution of x. It is obtained from (3.2-62) by taking the derivative with respect to t_x and setting t_x and t_y equal to zero:

$$\mu_x = \left[\frac{\partial m_{x,y}(t_x,t_y)}{\partial t_x}\right]_{\substack{t_x=0\\t_y=0}} = [(b_x + a_x^2 t_x + \rho a_x a_y t_y) m_{x,y}(t_x,t_y)]_{\substack{t_x=0\\t_y=0}} = b_x$$

Similarly, $$\mu_y = b_y$$

The variance of x corresponds to $r = 2$ and $s = 0$ in (3.2-50) and is obtained by using (3.2-62) and taking the second derivative of

$$m_{x-b_x,y}(t_x,t_y) = e^{-b_x t_x} m_{x,y}(t_x,t_y)$$

with respect to t_x. Upon setting $t_x = t_y = 0$, we have

$$\sigma_x^2 = \left[\frac{\partial^2 m_{x-b_x,y}(t_x,t_y)}{\partial t_x^2}\right]_{\substack{t_x=0\\t_y=0}}$$

$$= \{[a_x^2 + (a_x^2 t_x + \rho a_x a_y t_y)^2] m_{x-b_x,y}(t_x,t_y)\}_{\substack{t_x=0\\t_y=0}} = a_x^2$$

Similarly, $\sigma_y^2 = a_y^2$

Finally, the covariance of x and y is obtained by taking $r = 1$, $s = 1$ in (2.2-46) and evaluating, at $t_x = 0$ and $t_y = 0$, the second derivative of $m_{x-b_x,y-b_y}(t_x,t_y) = e^{-b_x t_x - b_y t_y} m_{x,y}(t_x,t_y)$ with respect to t_x and t_y:

$$\sigma_{xy} = \left[\frac{\partial^2 m_{x-b_x,y-b_y}(t_x,t_y)}{\partial t_x\,\partial t_y}\right]_{\substack{t_x=0\\t_y=0}}$$

$$= \{[\rho a_x a_y + (a_x^2 t_x + \rho a_x a_y t_y)^2] m_{x-b_x,y-b_y}(t_x,t_y)\}_{\substack{t_x=0\\t_y=0}} = \rho a_x a_y \tag{3.2-63}$$

$$= \rho\sigma_x\sigma_y$$

Thus, ρ is the covariance of unit normal deviates or, conversely, the covariance of bivariate normal variables is equal to the correlation times the product of their standard deviations. The symbolism $\mathsf{x}, \mathsf{y} \sim N(\mu_x, \mu_y, \sigma_x, \sigma_y, \rho)$ specifies the bivariate normal distribution in terms of its five parameters.

Bivariate moments may also be computed for sample values, but only the first-order moment is met in practice:

$$\tilde{m}_{xy} = \frac{1}{N}\sum_{i=1}^{N} xy \tag{3.2-64}$$

The sample covariance is computed from (3.2-64) as

$$\tilde{\sigma}_{xy} = \tilde{m}_{xy} - \tilde{m}_x \tilde{m}_y$$

where $\tilde{m}_x$ and $\tilde{m}_y$ are the sample means of x and y, respectively.

EXAMPLE 3.2-2 (*Sample covariance and correlation*) Compute the sample covariance and correlation $\tilde{\rho}_{xy}$ for the values of x and y below:

x	y	x^2	y^2	xy
8	2	64	4	16
5	5	25	25	25
2	6	4	36	12
3	6	9	36	18
1	8	1	64	8
4	3	16	9	12
6	1	36	1	6
7	2	49	4	14
36	33	204	179	111

We have

$$\tilde{m}_x = \tfrac{36}{8} = 4.5$$

$$\tilde{m}_y = \tfrac{33}{8} = 4.125$$

$$\tilde{m}_{xy} = \tfrac{111}{8} = 13.875$$

$$\tilde{\sigma}_{xy} = 13.875 - 4.5 \times 4.125 = -4.688$$

$$\tilde{\sigma}_x{}^2 = \tfrac{204}{8} - (4.5)^2 = 5.25$$

$$\tilde{\sigma}_y{}^2 = \tfrac{179}{8} - (4.125)^2 = 5.359$$

$$\tilde{\rho}_{xy} = -\frac{4.688}{\sqrt{4.5 \times 5.359}} = -.955$$

3.3 THE MULTIVARIATE NORMAL DISTRIBUTION

3.3.1 Derivation of the Distribution

In the first section of this chapter, we reviewed reasoning and evidence in support of the assumption that the error variation of a wide class of behavioral variables is normally distributed. Our problem now is to extend this argument to several such variables and to deduce their joint distribution. This problem has a simple solution if we are willing to assume that the observed variables are the result of a number of independent normally distributed latent variables which combine linearly to produce the manifest data. Specifically, let us assume that each of p variates in the vector observation $\mathbf{y}$ is a linear combination of n latent variables $\mathbf{z}$; that is, $\mathbf{y}$ is the affine transformation of $\mathbf{z}$:

$$\mathbf{y} = \mathbf{Tz} + \mathbf{u}$$

We assume that the latent variables are independent, normally distributed, and, without loss of generality, that they are in fact $N(0,1)$.

For the moment, let us assume that $n = p$, so that there are as many observed as latent variables. We will relax this assumption in Sec. 3.3.7 to allow the possibility that $n > p$. Assume also that $\mathbf{T}$ is nonsingular and that the inverse transformation is

$$\underset{p\times 1}{\mathbf{z}} = \underset{p\times p}{\mathbf{T}^{-1}} \underset{p\times 1}{(\mathbf{y} - \boldsymbol{\mu})}$$

Because the z's are independent, the joint density function is the product of their separate density functions (Sec. 3.2.4):

$$f(\mathbf{z}) = \prod_{k=1}^{p} \frac{e^{-(z^{(k)})^2/2}}{\sqrt{2\pi}} = \frac{1}{(2\pi)^{p/2}} \exp\left[-\frac{\sum_{k=1}^{p} (z^{(k)})^2}{2}\right]$$

$$= \frac{1}{(2\pi)^{p/2}} e^{-\mathbf{z}'\mathbf{z}/2}$$

The corresponding distribution function is the integral of the density function over the p-dimensional region $R(\mathbf{z}_0)$, say, extending from $-\infty$ to $z_0^{(k)}$ for the kth latent variable. Then

$$F(\mathbf{z}_0) = P(z^{(1)} \le z_0^{(1)}, z^{(2)} \le z_0^{(2)}, \ldots, z^{(p)} \le z_0^{(p)})$$

is the joint probability distribution function. Expressed in vector notation, this function is the p-fold multiple integral

$$F(\mathbf{z}_0) = \frac{1}{(2\pi)^{p/2}} \int_{R(\mathbf{z}_0)} e^{-\mathbf{z}'\mathbf{z}/2}\, d(\mathbf{z}) \qquad (3.3\text{-}1)$$

Now make the change of variable $\mathbf{z} = \mathbf{T}^{-1}(\mathbf{y} - \mathbf{u})$. Then (3.3-1) becomes

$$F(\mathbf{y}_0) = \frac{1}{(2\pi)^{p/2}} \int_{R(\mathbf{y}_0)} e^{-(\mathbf{y}-\boldsymbol{\mu})'(\mathbf{T}^{-1})'\mathbf{T}^{-1}(\mathbf{y}-\boldsymbol{\mu})/2}\, |\mathbf{T}^{-1}|\, d(\mathbf{y})$$

where $|\mathbf{T}^{-1}| = |\mathbf{T}|^{-1}$ is the jacobian of the transformation. Now let $(\mathbf{T}^{-1})'\mathbf{T}^{-1} = \boldsymbol{\Sigma}^{-1}$; then,

$$F(\mathbf{y}_0) = \frac{|\boldsymbol{\Sigma}|^{-1/2}}{(2\pi)^{p/2}} \int_{R(\mathbf{y}_0)} e^{-(\mathbf{y}-\boldsymbol{\mu})'\boldsymbol{\Sigma}^{-1}(\mathbf{y}-\boldsymbol{\mu})/2}\, d(\mathbf{y}) \qquad (3.3\text{-}2)$$

This is the distribution function of the *multivariate normal distribution*. The corresponding density function is the pth-order derivative with respect to variation in $y_0^{(1)}, y_0^{(2)}, \ldots, y_0^{(p)}$:

$$f(\mathbf{y}) = \frac{|\boldsymbol{\Sigma}|^{-1/2}}{(2\pi)^{p/2}} e^{-(\mathbf{y}-\boldsymbol{\mu})'\boldsymbol{\Sigma}^{-1}(\mathbf{y}-\boldsymbol{\mu})/2} \qquad (3.3\text{-}3)$$

3.3.2 Moments of the Multivariate Normal Distribution

We shall now show that the $p \times p$ symmetric matrix $\boldsymbol{\Sigma}$ and the $p \times 1$ vector $\mathbf{u}$ have an interpretation in terms of moments of the distribution. For this purpose, we define the *multivariate moment-generating function* (mmgf)

$$m_{\mathbf{x}}(\mathbf{t}) = \mathscr{E}(e^{\mathbf{t}'\mathbf{x}}) \qquad (3.3\text{-}4)$$

where $\mathbf{t}$ is a $p \times 1$ fixed vector, and $\mathbf{x}$ is a $p \times 1$ random vector. The mmgf has the properties

$$m_{\mathbf{x}+\mathbf{c}}(\mathbf{t}) = e^{\mathbf{c}'\mathbf{t}} m_{\mathbf{x}}(\mathbf{t}) \qquad (3.3\text{-}5)$$

where $\mathbf{c}$ is a fixed $p \times 1$ vector,

$$m_{c\mathbf{x}}(\mathbf{t}) = m_{\mathbf{x}}(c\mathbf{t}) \qquad (3.3\text{-}6)$$

where c is a fixed scalar, and

$$m_{\mathbf{x}_1+\mathbf{x}_2}(\mathbf{t}) = [m_{\mathbf{x}}(\mathbf{t})]^2 \qquad (3.3\text{-}7)$$

provided $\mathbf{x}_1$ and $\mathbf{x}_2$ are similarly and independently distributed.

Then the mmgf of the multivariate normal distribution is

$$\begin{aligned} m_{\mathbf{y}}(\mathbf{t}) &= (2\pi)^{-p/2}|\boldsymbol{\Sigma}|^{-1/2} \int_{\mathbf{R}(\infty)} \exp\left[\frac{\mathbf{t}'\mathbf{y} - (\mathbf{y}-\boldsymbol{\mu})'\boldsymbol{\Sigma}^{-1}(\mathbf{y}-\boldsymbol{\mu})}{2}\right] d\mathbf{y} \\ &= (2\pi)^{-p/2}|\boldsymbol{\Sigma}|^{-1/2} e^{\mathbf{t}'\boldsymbol{\mu}} \int_{\mathbf{R}(\infty)} \exp\left[\mathbf{t}'(\mathbf{y}-\boldsymbol{\mu}) - \tfrac{1}{2}(\mathbf{y}-\boldsymbol{\mu})'\boldsymbol{\Sigma}^{-1}(\mathbf{y}-\boldsymbol{\mu})\right] d\mathbf{y} \end{aligned}$$

The exponent in the integrand may be written

$$-\frac{-2\mathbf{t}'\boldsymbol{\Sigma}\boldsymbol{\Sigma}^{-1}(\mathbf{y}-\boldsymbol{\mu}) + (\mathbf{y}-\boldsymbol{\mu})'\boldsymbol{\Sigma}^{-1}(\mathbf{y}-\boldsymbol{\mu})}{2}$$

whence, by completing the square, we obtain

$$\begin{aligned} -\tfrac{1}{2}[\mathbf{t}'\boldsymbol{\Sigma}\boldsymbol{\Sigma}^{-1}\boldsymbol{\Sigma}\mathbf{t} - 2\mathbf{t}'\boldsymbol{\Sigma}\boldsymbol{\Sigma}^{-1}(\mathbf{y}-\boldsymbol{\mu}) + (\mathbf{y}-\boldsymbol{\mu})'\boldsymbol{\Sigma}^{-1}(\mathbf{y}-\boldsymbol{\mu}) - \mathbf{t}'\boldsymbol{\Sigma}\mathbf{t}] \\ = -\tfrac{1}{2}\{[(\mathbf{y}-\boldsymbol{\mu})' - \mathbf{t}'\boldsymbol{\Sigma}]\boldsymbol{\Sigma}^{-1}[(\mathbf{y}-\boldsymbol{\mu}) - \boldsymbol{\Sigma}\mathbf{t}] - \mathbf{t}'\boldsymbol{\Sigma}\mathbf{t}\} \end{aligned}$$

Thus,

$$\begin{aligned} m_{\mathbf{y}}(\mathbf{t}) &= e^{\mathbf{t}'\boldsymbol{\mu}} e^{\mathbf{t}'\boldsymbol{\Sigma}\mathbf{t}/2}(2\pi)^{-p/2}|\boldsymbol{\Sigma}|^{-1/2} \\ &\quad \times \int_{\mathbf{R}(\infty)} \exp\left[-\tfrac{1}{2}(\mathbf{y}-\boldsymbol{\mu}-\boldsymbol{\Sigma}\mathbf{t})'\boldsymbol{\Sigma}^{-1}(\mathbf{y}-\boldsymbol{\mu}-\boldsymbol{\Sigma}\mathbf{t})\right] d\mathbf{y} \\ &= e^{\mathbf{t}'\boldsymbol{\mu}+\mathbf{t}'\boldsymbol{\Sigma}\mathbf{t}/2} \end{aligned} \qquad (3.3\text{-}8)$$

since the integral in the above expression equals $(2\pi)^{p/2}|\boldsymbol{\Sigma}|^{1/2}$.

To obtain the multivariate first moment, we differentiate with respect to the vector $\mathbf{t}$ and set $\mathbf{t} = \mathbf{0}$:

$$\mathbf{m}_1 = \left[\frac{\partial m_{\mathbf{y}}(\mathbf{t})}{\partial \mathbf{t}}\right]_{\mathbf{t}=\mathbf{0}} = [(\boldsymbol{\mu} + \boldsymbol{\Sigma}\mathbf{t})e^{\mathbf{t}'\boldsymbol{\mu}+\mathbf{t}'\boldsymbol{\Sigma}\mathbf{t}/2}]_{\mathbf{t}=\mathbf{0}} = \underset{p\times 1}{\boldsymbol{\mu}}$$

That is, $\boldsymbol{\mu}$ is the multivariate expected value or vector mean.

To compute the central second moments, we first use (3.3-5) to set $m_{y-\mu}(\mathbf{t}) = e^{-\mu'\mathbf{t}} m_y(\mathbf{t}) = e^{\mathbf{t}'\Sigma\mathbf{t}/2}$, then differentiate once with respect to $\mathbf{t}$ and once with respect to $\mathbf{t}'$ (see Sec. 2.5) and set $\mathbf{t}$ to zero:

$$\frac{\partial m_{y-\mu}(\mathbf{t})}{\partial \mathbf{t}} = e^{\mathbf{t}'\Sigma\mathbf{t}/2}\Sigma\mathbf{t}$$

$$\left[\frac{\partial^2 m_{y-\mu}(\mathbf{t})}{\partial \mathbf{t}\,\partial \mathbf{t}'}\right]_{\mathbf{t}=\mathbf{0}} = [e^{\mathbf{t}'\Sigma\mathbf{t}/2}(\Sigma + \Sigma\mathbf{t}\mathbf{t}'\Sigma)]_{\mathbf{t}=\mathbf{0}} = \Sigma$$

The second central moments are therefore the elements of the $p \times p$ matrix Σ. The ith diagonal element of this matrix is the variance of the ith variable,

$$\left[\frac{\partial^2 m_{y^{(i)}-\mu^{(i)}}(t_i)}{\partial t_i^2}\right]_{t_i=0} = \mathscr{E}(y^{(i)} - \mu^{(i)})^2 = \sigma_i^2$$

The i,j off-diagonal element of Σ is the central product moment or *covariance* of variables i and j:

$$\left[\frac{\partial^2 m_{y^{(i)}-\mu^{(i)},y^{(j)}-\mu^{(j)}}(t_i t_j)}{\partial t_i\,\partial t_j}\right]_{\substack{t_i=0\\t_j=0}} = \mathscr{E}[(y^{(i)} - \mu^{(i)})(y^{(j)} - \mu^{(j)})] = \sigma_{ij}$$

Since this expression is symmetric in i and j, $\sigma_{ij} = \sigma_{ji}$, and the matrix Σ is symmetric with only $p(p+1)/2$ distinct elements. Σ is referred to as the *covariance matrix* of the distribution. Σ is a one-to-one function of Σ^{-1}; in fact, $\Sigma = (\Sigma^{-1})^{-1}$. The vector mean μ and covariance matrix Σ therefore completely determine the distribution, and we may write $y \sim N(\mu,\Sigma)$ to specify the multivariate normal distribution of y. It also follows that Σ is pd because Σ^{-1} is pd.

Other important properties of the multivariate distribution may be seen in its marginal and conditional distributions. In preparation for obtaining these distributions, we next investigate necessary and sufficient conditions for mutual independence of sets of multivariate normal variables.

3.3.3 Mutual Independence

Suppose that the multivariate normal variables have been assigned to two sets labeled 1 and 2, the first containing p and the second q variables. Then possibly with some rearrangement of the rows of μ and the rows and columns of Σ, the distribution may be specified in partitioned form as follows:

$$\underset{1}{\begin{bmatrix} y_1 \\ y_2 \end{bmatrix}}\begin{matrix} p \\ q \end{matrix} \sim N\left(\underset{1}{\begin{bmatrix} \mu_1 \\ \mu_2 \end{bmatrix}}\begin{matrix} p \\ q \end{matrix},\ \begin{bmatrix} \Sigma_{11} & \Sigma_{12} \\ \Sigma_{21} & \Sigma_{22} \end{bmatrix}\begin{matrix} p \\ q \end{matrix}\right) \tag{3.3-9}$$
$$\qquad\qquad\qquad\qquad\qquad\qquad p \quad q$$

where $\Sigma_{21} = (\Sigma_{12})'$.

If and only if all covariances between the variables in set 1 and those in set 2 are zero, the two sets of variables are mutually independent. For, if $\boldsymbol{\Sigma}_{12} = (\boldsymbol{\Sigma}_{21})' = 0$, the multivariate normal density function may be expressed as the product of two factors as follows:

$$\{(2\pi)^{-p/2}|\boldsymbol{\Sigma}_{11}|^{-1/2} \exp[-\tfrac{1}{2}(\mathbf{y}_1 - \boldsymbol{\mu}_1)'\boldsymbol{\Sigma}_{11}^{-1}(\mathbf{y}_1 - \boldsymbol{\mu}_1)]\}$$
$$\times \{(2\pi)^{-q/2}|\boldsymbol{\Sigma}_{22}|^{-1/2} \exp[-\tfrac{1}{2}(\mathbf{y}_2 - \boldsymbol{\mu}_2)'\boldsymbol{\Sigma}_{22}^{-1}(\mathbf{y}_2 - \boldsymbol{\mu}_2)]\}$$

But continuous variables are by definition statistically independent if the joint density is the product of their separate densities. Thus, set 1 and set 2 are mutually independent.

3.3.4 Marginal and Conditional Distributions

We now show that when the two sets of variables are not independent, i.e., when $\boldsymbol{\Sigma}_{12} = (\boldsymbol{\Sigma}_{21})' \neq 0$, a linear transformation of the variables in one of the sets can be constructed which renders the two sets mutually independent. There will be no loss of generality if we take $\mathbf{y}_1$ as the set of variables to be transformed. Now let

$$\begin{bmatrix} \mathbf{y}_1 - \boldsymbol{\mu}_1^* \\ \mathbf{y}_2 - \boldsymbol{\mu}_2 \end{bmatrix} = \mathbf{T}\begin{bmatrix} \mathbf{y}_1 - \boldsymbol{\mu}_1 \\ \mathbf{y}_2 - \boldsymbol{\mu}_2 \end{bmatrix} = \begin{matrix} p \\ q \end{matrix}\overset{\begin{matrix} \quad p & \qquad\qquad q \end{matrix}}{\begin{bmatrix} \mathbf{I} & -\boldsymbol{\Sigma}_{12}\boldsymbol{\Sigma}_{22}^{-1} \\ \mathbf{O} & \mathbf{I} \end{bmatrix}}\begin{bmatrix} \mathbf{y}_1 - \boldsymbol{\mu}_1 \\ \mathbf{y}_2 - \boldsymbol{\mu}_2 \end{bmatrix}$$

Obviously, $\mathbf{y}_1 - \boldsymbol{\mu}_1^* = \mathbf{y}_1 - [\boldsymbol{\mu}_1 + \boldsymbol{\Sigma}_{12}\boldsymbol{\Sigma}_{22}^{-1}(\mathbf{y}_2 - \boldsymbol{\mu}_2)]$, while $\mathbf{y}_2 - \boldsymbol{\mu}_2$ is unchanged by this transformation. Since the matrix $\mathbf{T}$ is unit triangular, its determinant is unity, and the transformation is nonsingular with jacobian equal to 1. The inverse matrix is of the same form with only a sign change; that is,

$$\mathbf{T}^{-1} = \begin{bmatrix} \mathbf{I} & \boldsymbol{\Sigma}_{12}\boldsymbol{\Sigma}_{22}^{-1} \\ \mathbf{O} & \mathbf{I} \end{bmatrix}$$

Hence, substituting

$$\begin{bmatrix} \mathbf{y}_1 - \boldsymbol{\mu}_1 \\ \mathbf{y}_2 - \boldsymbol{\mu}_2 \end{bmatrix} = \mathbf{T}^{-1}\begin{bmatrix} \mathbf{y}_1 - \boldsymbol{\mu}_1^* \\ \mathbf{y}_2 - \boldsymbol{\mu}_2 \end{bmatrix}$$

we may write the probability element of the distribution as

$$dF = (2\pi)^{-(p+q)/2}|\mathbf{T}\boldsymbol{\Sigma}\mathbf{T}'|^{-1/2} \exp\left\{-\tfrac{1}{2}\begin{bmatrix} \mathbf{y}_1 - \boldsymbol{\mu}_1^* \\ \mathbf{y}_2 - \boldsymbol{\mu}_2 \end{bmatrix}' (\mathbf{T}\boldsymbol{\Sigma}\mathbf{T}')^{-1}\begin{bmatrix} \mathbf{y}_1 - \boldsymbol{\mu}_1^* \\ \mathbf{y}_2 - \boldsymbol{\mu}_2 \end{bmatrix}\right\} d\mathbf{y}_1\, d\mathbf{y}_2$$

Computing the matrix product $\mathbf{T}\boldsymbol{\Sigma}\mathbf{T}'$ and rearranging terms, we obtain

$$dF = \left\{(2\pi)^{-p/2}|\boldsymbol{\Sigma}_{11} - \boldsymbol{\Sigma}_{12}\boldsymbol{\Sigma}_{22}^{-1}\boldsymbol{\Sigma}_{21}|^{-1/2}\right.$$
$$\left.\times \exp\left[-\frac{(\mathbf{y}_1 - \boldsymbol{\mu}_1^*)'(\boldsymbol{\Sigma}_{11} - \boldsymbol{\Sigma}_{12}\boldsymbol{\Sigma}_{22}^{-1}\boldsymbol{\Sigma}_{12})^{-1}(\mathbf{y}_1 - \boldsymbol{\mu}_1^*)}{2}\right]\right\}$$
$$\times \{(2\pi)^{-q/2}|\boldsymbol{\Sigma}_{22}|^{-1/2} \exp[\tfrac{1}{2}(\mathbf{y}_2 - \boldsymbol{\mu}_2)'\boldsymbol{\Sigma}_{22}^{-1}(\mathbf{y}_2 - \boldsymbol{\mu}_2)]\}\, d\mathbf{y}_1\, d\mathbf{y}_2 \qquad (3.3\text{-}10)$$

Several conclusions follow from (3.3-10). First, $\mathbf{y}_1 - \boldsymbol{\mu}_1^*$ and $\mathbf{y}_2 - \boldsymbol{\mu}_2$ are statistically independent.

Second, integration over the range of $\mathbf{y}_1$ leaves the second factor as the density function of the marginal distribution of $\mathbf{y}_2$. The form of this function is obviously that of a q-variate normal distribution with mean $\boldsymbol{\mu}_2$ and covariance matrix $\boldsymbol{\Sigma}_{22}$:

$$\mathbf{y}_2 \sim N(\underset{q\times 1}{\boldsymbol{\mu}_2}, \underset{q\times q}{\boldsymbol{\Sigma}_{22}})$$

In other words, we have only to delete the rows of $\boldsymbol{\mu}$ and rows and columns of $\boldsymbol{\Sigma}$ corresponding to the variables integrated out, in order to obtain the mean and covariance matrix of the marginal distribution, which is itself multivariate normal.

Third, since a conditional density is the joint density divided by the marginal density of the given variables, the conditional density of $\mathbf{y}_1$ given $\mathbf{y}_2$ is obviously that of a p-variate normal distribution with mean $\boldsymbol{\mu}_1^* = \boldsymbol{\mu}_1 + \boldsymbol{\Sigma}_{12}\boldsymbol{\Sigma}_{22}^{-1}(\mathbf{y}_2 - \boldsymbol{\mu}_2)$ and covariance matrix $\boldsymbol{\Sigma}_{11}^* = \boldsymbol{\Sigma}_{11} - \boldsymbol{\Sigma}_{12}\boldsymbol{\Sigma}_{22}^{-1}\boldsymbol{\Sigma}_{21}$:

$$(\mathbf{y}_1 \mid \mathbf{y}_2) \sim N(\underset{p\times 1}{\boldsymbol{\mu}_1^*}, \underset{p\times p}{\boldsymbol{\Sigma}_{11}^*})$$

Note that the conditional mean is a linear function of $\mathbf{y}_2$. This implies that, with respect to variation of the given values of $\mathbf{y}_2$, the mean of the conditional distribution describes a hyperplane in the $\mathbf{y}_1$ space. This plane is called the *regression* plane for the regression of $\mathbf{y}_1$ on $\mathbf{y}_2$. The conditional distribution represents deviation from this plane about the point $\boldsymbol{\mu}_1^* \mid \mathbf{y}_2$. Unlike the mean, the conditional covariance matrix does not depend on $\mathbf{y}_2$. Thus, the dispersion of the conditional distribution is homogeneous (homoscedastic) for all values of the given variables. Linearity of regression planes and homoscedasticity of conditional distributions greatly simplifies many statistical applications of the multivariate normal distribution.

3.3.5 Multivariate Multiple Regression

The role of the conditional distribution in statistical prediction is illustrated by the familiar problem of predicting first-year college grades from high-school grades. Suppose there are p college grades $\mathbf{y}_1$, and q high-school grades $\mathbf{y}_2$. It is assumed that the scores representing these grades are jointly multivariate normal and that the mean $\boldsymbol{\mu}$ and covariance matrix $\boldsymbol{\Sigma}$ are known or have been estimated in a large "calibration" sample. (We discuss in Sec. 6.1 methods of obtaining estimates in prediction problems.)

Once a student's high-school grades, say $\mathbf{y}_{2i}$, are known, the best prediction, in the least-squares sense, of his college grades is given by, say,

$$\underset{p\times 1}{\hat{\mathbf{y}}_{1i}} = \underset{p\times 1}{\boldsymbol{\mu}_1} + \underset{p\times q}{\mathbf{B}}(\mathbf{y}_{2i} - \boldsymbol{\mu}_2) \qquad (3.3\text{-}11)$$

where $\mathbf{B} = \boldsymbol{\Sigma}_{12}\boldsymbol{\Sigma}_{22}^{-1}$, that is, by the mean vector of the conditional distribution of

$\mathbf{y}_1$. Note that (3.3-11) represents p generally distinct linear functions, one for each college grade represented in $\mathbf{y}_1$. These functions are called *multiple-regression* functions. The elements of $\mathbf{B}$ are called *partial-regression* coefficients, or, often, just *regression* coefficients.

As a convenient index of the strength of prediction, we usually compare the conditional variances of the predicted variables with their unconditional variances. The former are the diagonal elements of $\mathbf{\Sigma}_{11}^* = \mathbf{\Sigma}_{11} - \mathbf{\Sigma}_{12}\mathbf{\Sigma}_{22}^{-1}\mathbf{\Sigma}_{21}$, say $\sigma_1^{*2}, \sigma_2^{*2}, \ldots, \sigma_p^{*2}$. The latter are the corresponding diagonal elements of $\mathbf{\Sigma}_{11}$, say $\sigma_1^2, \sigma_2^2, \ldots, \sigma_p^2$. Their ratios are the so-called *coefficients of alienation*. Their complements are the *coefficients of determination*, or *squared multiple correlation coefficients*, $R_1^2 = 1 - \sigma_1^{*2}/\sigma_1^2$, $R_2^2 = 1 - \sigma_2^{*2}/\sigma_2^2, \ldots, R_p^2 = 1 - \sigma_p^{*2}/\sigma_p^2$.

Specializing to the bivariate case, we obtain the familiar results for simple regression. The coefficient of regression of variable i on variable j is $b_{ij} = \sigma_{ij}/\sigma_j^2$. The conditional variance is $\sigma_i^{*2} = \sigma_i^2 - \sigma_{ij}^2/\sigma_j^2$. The coefficient of determination is

$$1 - \frac{\sigma_i^{*2}}{\sigma_i^2} = \frac{\sigma_i^2 - \sigma_i^2 + \sigma_{ij}^2/\sigma_j^2}{\sigma_i^2}$$

$$= \frac{\sigma_{ij}^2}{\sigma_1^2\sigma_j^2} = \rho_{ij}^2$$

That is, the coefficient of determination is the square of the correlation between the two variables.

3.3.6 Standardized Variables and Correlation

It is typical of behavioral data that the origin and unit of measurement of the response variables are not well defined. Usually, the scores produced by the measuring instrument (rating scale, test, etc.) incorporate arbitrary additive and multiplicative constants determined by the conventions adopted when the instrument is developed. A familiar example is the practice of setting the mean and standard deviation of the IQ scale to 100 and 15, respectively, in the general population.

Another common convention is to define standardized scores for each variable by setting the mean at zero and the variance at unity in a defined population. If the variable is normally distributed, the standardized scores have a definite meaning in the sense that they have a one-to-one relationship to a normal probability. Because the probability scale *is* well defined, there is a basis for comparison of the sizes of standard scores, even when they are calculated for qualitatively distinct variables. This is not true of raw (unstandardized) scores; in general, we cannot compare the sizes of raw scores arising from distinct variables because the origin and unit of measurement will generally be different for different variables.

In the multivariate case, the formulas connecting standardized and unstandardized variables may be expressed compactly in matrix notation. Suppose the $p \times 1$ vector variate $\boldsymbol{y}$ is distributed with vector mean and covariance matrix

$$\boldsymbol{\mu} = \begin{bmatrix} \mu^{(1)} \\ \mu^{(2)} \\ \vdots \\ \mu^{(p)} \end{bmatrix} \qquad \boldsymbol{\Sigma} = \begin{bmatrix} \sigma_1^2 & \sigma_{12} & \cdots & \sigma_{1p} \\ \sigma_{12} & \sigma_2^2 & \cdots & \sigma_{2p} \\ \cdots & \cdots & \cdots & \cdots \\ \sigma_{1p} & \sigma_{2p} & \cdots & \sigma_p^2 \end{bmatrix}$$

Let $\mathbf{D}_\sigma = \operatorname{diag}[\sigma_1, \sigma_2, \ldots, \sigma_p]$ be a diagonal matrix of standard deviations (i.e., a diagonal matrix consisting of the positive square roots of the diagonal elements of $\boldsymbol{\Sigma}$). Then the vector of standardized variables is obtained from the raw variables by the transformation

$$\mathbf{z} = \mathbf{D}_\sigma^{-1}(\mathbf{y} - \boldsymbol{\mu}) \qquad (3.3\text{-}12)$$

The transformation is nonsingular, so that $\mathbf{y} = \mathbf{D}_\sigma \mathbf{z} + \boldsymbol{\mu}$.

The covariance matrix of the standardized variables, $\mathbf{z}$, is the *correlation matrix*

$$\mathbf{R} = \mathscr{V}(\mathbf{z}) = \mathscr{V}[\mathbf{D}_\sigma^{-1}(\boldsymbol{y} - \boldsymbol{\mu})] = \mathbf{D}_\sigma^{-1}\mathscr{V}(\mathbf{y})\mathbf{D}_\sigma^{-1} = \mathbf{D}_\sigma^{-1}\boldsymbol{\Sigma}\mathbf{D}_\sigma^{-1} \qquad (3.3\text{-}13)$$

Conversely, the original covariance matrix is related to $\mathbf{R}$ by

$$\boldsymbol{\Sigma} = \mathbf{D}_\sigma \mathbf{R} \mathbf{D}_\sigma \qquad (3.3\text{-}14)$$

$\mathbf{R}$ is a symmetric matrix with unit diagonal elements and correlation coefficients as off-diagonal elements. When $\boldsymbol{y}$ is multivariate normal, $\boldsymbol{z}$ is also distributed in multivariate normal form. This can be seen by using the method of Sec. 3.3.1 to obtain the density function after the change of variable from $\mathbf{y}$ to $\mathbf{z} = \mathbf{D}^{-1}(\mathbf{y} - \boldsymbol{\mu})$. That is, in

$$f(y) = \frac{|\boldsymbol{\Sigma}|^{-1/2}}{(2\pi)^{p/2}} \exp\left[-\frac{(\mathbf{y} - \boldsymbol{\mu})'\boldsymbol{\Sigma}^{-1}(\mathbf{y} - \boldsymbol{\mu})}{2}\right]$$

$$= \frac{|\mathbf{D}_\sigma|^{-1}|\mathbf{R}|^{-1/2}}{(2\pi)^{p/2}} \exp\left[-\frac{(\mathbf{y} - \boldsymbol{\mu})'\mathbf{D}_\sigma^{-1}\mathbf{R}^{-1}\mathbf{D}_\sigma^{-1}(\mathbf{y} - \boldsymbol{\mu})}{2}\right]$$

we substitute $\mathbf{y} = \mathbf{D}_\sigma \mathbf{z} + \boldsymbol{\mu}$ and multiply the density by $|\mathbf{D}_\sigma|$, the jacobian of this transformation. The result is

$$f(\mathbf{z}) = \frac{|\mathbf{R}|^{-1/2}}{(2\pi)^{p/2}} e^{-\mathbf{z}'\mathbf{R}^{-1}\mathbf{z}/2} \qquad (3.3\text{-}15)$$

which is the density function of the standardized variables. Note that (3.3-15) implies that the marginal distribution of each separate variable (each component of $\boldsymbol{z}$) is $N(0,1)$.

Now let $\mathbf{y}$ consist of two sets of variables,

$$\mathbf{y} = \begin{bmatrix} \mathbf{y}_1 \\ \mathbf{y}_2 \end{bmatrix} \begin{matrix} p \\ q \end{matrix}$$
$$\quad 1$$

and let the corresponding mean vector, the covariance matrix, and the diagonal matrix $\mathbf{D}$ be represented in the partitioned matrices

$$\boldsymbol{\mu} = \begin{bmatrix} \boldsymbol{\mu}_1 \\ \boldsymbol{\mu}_2 \end{bmatrix} \begin{matrix} p \\ q \end{matrix} \qquad \boldsymbol{\Sigma} = \begin{bmatrix} \boldsymbol{\Sigma}_{11} & \boldsymbol{\Sigma}_{12} \\ \boldsymbol{\Sigma}_{21} & \boldsymbol{\Sigma}_{22} \end{bmatrix} \begin{matrix} p \\ q \end{matrix} \qquad \mathbf{D}_\sigma = \begin{bmatrix} \mathbf{D}_1 & \mathbf{O} \\ \mathbf{O} & \mathbf{D}_2 \end{bmatrix} \begin{matrix} p \\ q \end{matrix} \tag{3.3-16}$$

$$\quad 1 \qquad\qquad\qquad p \quad q \qquad\qquad\qquad p \quad q$$

The corresponding sets of standardized variables are

$$\mathbf{z}_1 = \mathbf{D}_1^{-1}(\mathbf{y}_1 - \boldsymbol{\mu}_2)$$

$$\mathbf{z}_2 = \mathbf{D}_2^{-1}(\mathbf{y}_2 - \boldsymbol{\mu}_2)$$

Their correlation matrix, also partitioned, is

$$\mathbf{R} = \begin{bmatrix} \mathbf{R}_{11} & \mathbf{R}_{12} \\ \mathbf{R}_{21} & \mathbf{R}_{22} \end{bmatrix} = \begin{bmatrix} \mathbf{D}_1^{-1}\boldsymbol{\Sigma}_{11}\mathbf{D}_1^{-1} & \mathbf{D}_1^{-1}\boldsymbol{\Sigma}_{12}\mathbf{D}_2^{-1} \\ \mathbf{D}_2^{-1}\boldsymbol{\Sigma}_{21}\mathbf{D}_1^{-1} & \mathbf{D}_2^{-1}\boldsymbol{\Sigma}_{22}\mathbf{D}_2^{-1} \end{bmatrix}$$

Thus, the covariance matrix of the original variables, expressed in terms of the partitioned correlation matrix, is

$$\boldsymbol{\Sigma} = \begin{bmatrix} \mathbf{D}_1\mathbf{R}_{11}\mathbf{D}_1 & \mathbf{D}_1\mathbf{R}_{12}\mathbf{D}_2 \\ \mathbf{D}_2\mathbf{R}_{21}\mathbf{D}_1 & \mathbf{D}_2\mathbf{R}_{22}\mathbf{D}_2 \end{bmatrix}$$

Now let us obtain the density function for the conditional distribution of $\mathbf{z}_1$ given $\mathbf{z}_2$. From (3.3.10), recall that the probability element for $\mathbf{y}_1$, given $\mathbf{y}_2$, is

$$d\mathbf{F}(\mathbf{y}_1 \mid \mathbf{y}_2) = \frac{|\boldsymbol{\Sigma}_{11}^*|^{-1/2}}{(2\pi)^{p/2}} \exp\left[-\frac{(\mathbf{y}_1 - \boldsymbol{\mu}_1^*)'(\boldsymbol{\Sigma}_{11}^*)^{-1}(\mathbf{y}_1 - \boldsymbol{\mu}_1^*)}{2}\right] d\mathbf{y}_1 \tag{3.3-17}$$

where $\boldsymbol{\mu}_1^* = \boldsymbol{\mu}_1 + \boldsymbol{\Sigma}_{12}\boldsymbol{\Sigma}_{22}^{-1}(\mathbf{y}_2 - \boldsymbol{\mu}_2)$

$\boldsymbol{\Sigma}_{11}^* = \boldsymbol{\Sigma}_{11} - \boldsymbol{\Sigma}_{12}\boldsymbol{\Sigma}_{22}^{-1}\boldsymbol{\Sigma}_{21}$

In terms of correlations and standardized scores,

$$\boldsymbol{\mu}_1^* = \boldsymbol{\mu}_1 + \boldsymbol{\Sigma}_{12}\boldsymbol{\Sigma}_{22}^{-1}(\mathbf{y}_2 - \boldsymbol{\mu}_2) = \boldsymbol{\mu}_1 + \mathbf{D}_1\mathbf{R}_{12}\mathbf{R}_{22}^{-1}\mathbf{z}_2$$

and

$$\boldsymbol{\Sigma}_{11}^* = \mathbf{D}_1\mathbf{R}_{11}^*\mathbf{D}_1 = \mathbf{D}_1(\mathbf{R}_{11} - \mathbf{R}_{12}\mathbf{R}_{22}^{-1}\mathbf{R}_{21})\mathbf{D}_1$$

Introducing the transformation $\mathbf{y}_1 = \mathbf{D}_1\mathbf{z}_1 + \boldsymbol{\mu}_1$, the jacobian of which is $|\mathbf{D}_1|$, and substituting $\mathbf{y}_2 = \mathbf{D}_2\mathbf{z}_2 + \boldsymbol{\mu}_2$, we obtain the conditional density in terms of standardized variables:

$$f(\mathbf{z}_1 \mid \mathbf{z}_2) = \frac{|\mathbf{D}_1|^{-1}|\mathbf{R}_{11}^*|^{-1/2}}{(2\pi)^{p/2}}$$

$$\times \exp\left[-\frac{(\mathbf{z}_1 - \mathbf{R}_{12}\mathbf{R}_{22}^{-1}\mathbf{z}_2)'(\mathbf{R}_{11}^*)^{-1}(\mathbf{z}_1 - \mathbf{R}_{12}\mathbf{R}_{22}^{-1}\mathbf{z}_2)}{2}\right]|\mathbf{D}_1|$$

$$= \frac{|\mathbf{R}_{11}^*|^{-1/2}}{(2\pi)^{p/2}} \exp\left[-\frac{(\mathbf{z}_1 - \mathbf{B}'\mathbf{z}_2)'(\mathbf{R}_{11}^*)^{-1}(\mathbf{z}_1 - \mathbf{B}'\mathbf{z}_2)}{2}\right]$$

Note that the regression plane, or mean, of the conditional distribution is given by $\mathsf{B}\mathbf{z}_2$. The rows of $p \times q$ matrix $\mathsf{B} = \mathbf{R}_{12}\mathbf{R}_{22}^{-1}$ contain the *standardized regression coefficients*, or *beta weights*, relating each standardized variable in set 1 with the q standardized variables in set 2. Obviously, the beta weights are related to the raw regression coefficients by

$$\mathsf{B}' = \mathbf{D}_1^{-1}\mathbf{B}'\mathbf{D}_2 = \mathbf{D}_1^{-1}\boldsymbol{\Sigma}_{12}\boldsymbol{\Sigma}_{22}^{-1}\mathbf{D}_2 \qquad (3.3\text{-}18)$$

and, conversely,

$$\mathbf{B}' = \mathbf{D}_1\mathsf{B}'\mathbf{D}_2^{-1} \qquad (3.3\text{-}19)$$

Unlike the raw coefficients, which generally contain arbitrary scale parameters, the beta weights are scalefree and may be compared in magnitude for purposes of interpretation. It is to be emphasized that in general beta weights are not correlations and are not limited to the interval -1 to $+1$. Only in the bivariate case is the beta weight a correlation.

EXAMPLE 3.3-1 (*Conditional distribution of the multivariate normal*) The following data are from Cooley and Lohnes [1962, pages 39–40]:

	Variable (test)	Mean	SD	Correlations				
1	STEP* mathematics	14.75	4.38	1.00				(symmetric)
2	STEP science	18.91	3.88	.46	1.00			
3	CTMM† spatial	23.70	4.53	.32	.28	1.00		
4	CTMM numerical	15.47	3.91	.62	.29	.40	1.00	
5	CTMM verbal	20.74	5.65	.47	.35	.15	.43	1.00

* Sequential Tests of Educational Progress (Part I, Form A), Educational Testing Service, Princeton, N.J.

† California Test of Mental Maturity, California Test Bureau, Los Angeles.

Let us treat the above figures as population values and compute the vector mean and covariance matrix of the achievement tests (variables 1 and 2) conditional on the aptitude scores (variables 3, 4, and 5). In this case, $p = 2$ and $q = 3$. Because the correlation matrix is given in the data, we shall carry out the calculations in the standardized metric. Steps in the calculations are as follows:

1 The inverse of the correlation matrix of the fixed variables: Given

$$\mathbf{R}_{22} = \begin{bmatrix} 1.00 & & \\ .40 & 1.00 & \\ .15 & .43 & 1.00 \end{bmatrix}$$

the inverse is easily obtained by the cofactor formula (2.4-6).

$$\mathbf{R}_{22}^{-1} = \frac{1}{|\mathbf{R}_{22}|}\operatorname{adj}(\mathbf{R}_{22}) = \frac{1}{.6842}\begin{bmatrix} .8151 & & \\ -.3355 & .9775 & \\ .0220 & -.3700 & .8400 \end{bmatrix}$$

$$= \begin{bmatrix} 1.19132 & & \\ -.49035 & 1.42868 & \\ .03215 & -.54078 & 1.22771 \end{bmatrix}$$

2 The standardized regression coefficients:

$$\mathbf{B}' = \mathbf{R}_{12}\mathbf{R}_{22}^{-1}$$

$$= \begin{bmatrix} .32 & .62 & .47 \\ .28 & .29 & .35 \end{bmatrix} \cdot \begin{bmatrix} .19132 & & \\ -.49035 & 1.42868 & \\ .03215 & -\ .54078 & 1.22771 \end{bmatrix}$$

$$= \begin{bmatrix} .0923 & .4747 & .2520 \\ .2026 & .0877 & .2819 \end{bmatrix}$$

The corresponding raw regression coefficients are

$$\mathbf{B}' = \mathbf{D}_1\mathbf{B}'\mathbf{D}_2^{-1} = \begin{bmatrix} 4.38 & 0 \\ 0 & 3.88 \end{bmatrix} \cdot \begin{bmatrix} .0923 & .4747 & .2520 \\ .2026 & .0877 & .2819 \end{bmatrix}$$

$$\cdot \begin{bmatrix} 1/4.53 & 0 & 0 \\ 0 & 1/3.91 & 0 \\ 0 & 0 & 1/5.65 \end{bmatrix}$$

$$= \begin{bmatrix} .0893 & .5318 & .1954 \\ .1735 & .0871 & .1936 \end{bmatrix}$$

The conditional vector mean (regression plane) as a function of standardized variables $z_2^{(1)}$, $z_2^{(2)}$, and $z_2^{(3)}$ is, therefore,

$$\hat{z}_1^{(1)} = .0923z_2^{(1)} + .4747z_2^{(2)} + .2520z_2^{(3)}$$

$$\hat{z}_1^{(2)} = .2026z_2^{(1)} + .0877z_2^{(2)} + .2819z_2^{(3)}$$

The corresponding regression planes in terms of the raw variables are

$$y_1^{(1)} - 14.75 = .0893(y_2^{(1)} - 23.70) + .5318(y_2^{(2)} - 15.47) + .1954(y_2^{(3)} - 20.74)$$

or

$$y_1^{(1)} = .3541 + .0893y_2^{(1)} + .5318y_2^{(2)} + .1954y_2^{(3)}$$

$$y_1^{(2)} - 18.91 = .1735(y_2^{(1)} - 23.70) + .0871(y_2^{(2)} - 15.47) + .1936(y_2^{(3)} - 20.74)$$

or

$$y_1^{(2)} = 9.4353 + .1735y_2^{(1)} + .0871y_2^{(2)} + .1936y_2^{(3)}$$

3 The conditional covariance matrix:

$$\mathbf{R}_{11}^* = \mathbf{R}_{11} - \mathbf{R}_{12}\mathbf{R}_{22}^{-1}\mathbf{R}_{21} = \mathbf{R}_{11} - \mathbf{B}'\mathbf{R}_{21}$$

$$= \begin{bmatrix} 1.00 & \\ .46 & 1.00 \end{bmatrix} - \begin{bmatrix} .0923 & .4747 & .2520 \\ .2026 & .0877 & .2819 \end{bmatrix} \cdot \begin{bmatrix} .32 & .28 \\ .62 & .29 \\ .47 & .35 \end{bmatrix}$$

$$= \begin{bmatrix} 1.00 & \\ .46 & 1.00 \end{bmatrix} - \begin{bmatrix} .4423 & \\ .2517 & .1808 \end{bmatrix} = \begin{bmatrix} .5577 & \\ .2083 & .8192 \end{bmatrix}$$

$$\boldsymbol{\Sigma}_{11}^* = \mathbf{D}_1\mathbf{R}_{11}^*\mathbf{D}_1 = \begin{bmatrix} 4.38 & 0 \\ 0 & 3.88 \end{bmatrix} \cdot \begin{bmatrix} .5577 & \\ .2083 & .8192 \end{bmatrix} \cdot \begin{bmatrix} 4.38 & 0 \\ 0 & 4.88 \end{bmatrix}$$

$$= \begin{bmatrix} 10.6989 & \\ 3.5396 & 12.3320 \end{bmatrix}$$

4 The multiple correlation coefficients for the two regressions:

$$R_1^2 = 1 - \frac{10.6989}{19.1844} = .4423 \qquad R_1 = .6651$$

$$R_2^2 = 1 - \frac{12.3320}{15.0544} = .1808 \qquad R_2 = .4252$$

5 The partial correlation matrix (i.e., the correlation matrix of the conditional distribution)

$$\mathbf{R}_{11.2} = \begin{bmatrix} 1/\sqrt{.5577} & 0 \\ 0 & 1/\sqrt{.8192} \end{bmatrix} \cdot \begin{bmatrix} .5577 & \\ .2083 & .8192 \end{bmatrix} \cdot \begin{bmatrix} 1/\sqrt{.5577} & 0 \\ 0 & 1/\sqrt{.8192} \end{bmatrix}$$

$$= \begin{bmatrix} 1.000 & \\ .308 & 1.000 \end{bmatrix}$$

The multiple-regression coefficients for these data show that mathematics achievement ($R_1^2 = .44$) is much better predicted than science achievement ($R_2^2 = .18$). It is also of interest that, in standardized units, the increase of the mathematics achievement score is considerably greater per unit increase in numerical and verbal abilities than per unit of spatial ability. Conversely, it is spatial and verbal ability which contribute the greater per-unit increase for science achievement. This may indicate that good performance on this particular mathematics test depends largely upon formal reasoning rather than geometric intuition, while knowledge of science involves to some extent the visualization of relationships among physical objects.

The fact that adjustment for individual differences in ability leaves the partial correlation between mathematics and science achievement at .31 may indicate the presence of common achievement factors such as motivation, application, and special coaching, which are uncorrelated with the ability measures.

3.3.7 Linear Combinations of Multivariate Normal Variables

Many of the scores and summary statistics which we use in the analysis of behavioral data are linear combinations of multivariate normal variables. If the coefficients, or "weights," in the combinations are known, the distribution of the linear combinations is readily obtained. Suppose n multivariate normal variables $\boldsymbol{x} \sim N(\boldsymbol{\mu},\boldsymbol{\Sigma})$ are transformed by

$$\boldsymbol{y} = \mathbf{A}\boldsymbol{x}$$

where $\mathbf{A}$ is a given $p \times n$ matrix. If $p = n$ and $\mathbf{A}$ is nonsingular ($|\mathbf{A}| \neq 0$), $\boldsymbol{y}$ is multivariate normal with mean $\mathbf{A}\boldsymbol{\mu}$ and covariance matrix $\mathbf{A\Sigma A}'$. This result follows from the substitution of $\mathbf{x} = \mathbf{A}^{-1}\mathbf{y}$ in the density function and multiplication of the density by $|\mathbf{A}|$.

Similarly, if p is less than n, but rank(A) $= p$, the p variables in $\boldsymbol{y}$ are multivariate normal with the above mean and covariance matrix. This can be seen by introducing $n - p$ dummy y variables and completing $\mathbf{A}$ with $n - p$ rows so as to make the transformation nonsingular. That is,

$$\begin{bmatrix} \boldsymbol{y} \\ \boldsymbol{y}^* \end{bmatrix} = \begin{matrix} p \\ n-p \end{matrix} \underset{n}{\begin{bmatrix} \mathbf{A} \\ \mathbf{C} \end{bmatrix}} \boldsymbol{x}$$

where $\left|\frac{\mathbf{A}}{\mathbf{C}}\right| \neq 0$

By means of a Gram-Schmidt construction in the metric Σ, the matrix $\mathbf{C}$ may in fact be chosen so that $\mathbf{A\Sigma C}' = 0$. In that case $\boldsymbol{y}$ and $\boldsymbol{y}^*$ are mutually independent, and the marginal distribution of $\boldsymbol{y}$ is multivariate normal with mean $\mathbf{A}\boldsymbol{\mu}$ and covariance matrix $\mathbf{A\Sigma A}'$.

Finally, if $\mathbf{A}$ is $p \times n$ and rank(A) $< p \leq n$, the matrix $\mathbf{A\Sigma A}'$ is singular, and $\boldsymbol{y}$ is not normally distributed in the usual sense; that is, $|\mathbf{A\Sigma A}'| = 0$, the inverse of $\mathbf{A\Sigma A}'$ does not exist, and a multivariate density at $\mathbf{y}$ cannot be expressed in the form of (3.3-3). However, since rank(A) $= r$, a further $r \times p$ transformation $\mathbf{T}$ may be found such that $\mathbf{Ty}$ has an r-variate multivariate normal distribution with mean $\mathbf{TA}\boldsymbol{\mu}$ and a nonsingular covariance matrix $\mathbf{TA\Sigma A'T}'$. In this case, we would say that $\boldsymbol{y}$ has a *singular* multivariate normal distribution (see Anderson [1958, page 26]). In fact, $\mathbf{T}$ may consist only of 0 and 1 elements chosen so as to select r independent rows of $\mathbf{A}$.

If $p = 1$, the scalar variable $y = \mathbf{a}'\boldsymbol{x}$ is univariate normal with mean $\mathbf{a}'\boldsymbol{\mu}$ and variance $\mathbf{a}'\Sigma\mathbf{a}$, provided $\mathbf{a}$ is not the null vector. Rao [1965, page 437] shows that $\boldsymbol{x}$ has a multivariate normal distribution if and only if $\mathbf{a}'\boldsymbol{x}$ is univariate normal for *all* $\mathbf{a}$. For in this case an $n \times n$ matrix $\mathbf{A}$ can be found such that $\mathbf{A\Sigma A}' = \mathbf{I}$; hence, the argument at the beginning of this section may be used to derive a multivariate normal distribution with mean $\mathbf{A}^{-1}\mathbf{A}\boldsymbol{\mu} = \boldsymbol{\mu}$ and covariance matrix $\mathbf{A}^{-1}\mathbf{A\Sigma A}'(\mathbf{A}^{-1}) = \Sigma$. Conversely, if there are $n - r$ independent vectors $\mathbf{a}$ such that $\mathbf{a}'\Sigma\mathbf{a} = 0$, $\mathbf{x}$ has an r-dimensional *singular* normal distribution.

EXAMPLE 3.3-2 (*Linear transformation of variables*) Suppose the independent variables in Example 3.3-1 are subjected to the transformation

$$\begin{bmatrix} y^{(1)} \\ y^{(2)} \\ y^{(3)} \end{bmatrix} = \begin{bmatrix} \frac{2}{3} & -\frac{1}{3} & -\frac{1}{3} \\ -\frac{1}{3} & \frac{2}{3} & -\frac{1}{3} \\ -\frac{1}{3} & -\frac{1}{3} & \frac{2}{3} \end{bmatrix} \cdot \begin{bmatrix} x^{(1)} \\ x^{(2)} \\ x^{(3)} \end{bmatrix}$$

The vector mean and covariance matrix of the transformed variables are calculated as follows:

MEAN

$$\begin{bmatrix} \frac{2}{3} & -\frac{1}{3} & -\frac{1}{3} \\ -\frac{1}{3} & \frac{2}{3} & -\frac{1}{3} \\ -\frac{1}{3} & -\frac{1}{3} & \frac{2}{3} \end{bmatrix} \cdot \begin{bmatrix} 23.70 \\ 15.47 \\ 20.74 \end{bmatrix} = \begin{bmatrix} 3.73 \\ -4.50 \\ .77 \end{bmatrix}$$

COVARIANCE MATRIX First it is necessary to obtain the covariance matrix for the original variables from the correlations and standard deviations in Example 3.3-1:

$$\begin{bmatrix} 4.53 & & \\ & 3.91 & \\ & & 5.65 \end{bmatrix} \cdot \begin{bmatrix} 1.00 & & \\ .40 & 1.00 & \\ .15 & .43 & 1.00 \end{bmatrix} \cdot \begin{bmatrix} 4.53 & & \\ & 3.91 & \\ & & 5.65 \end{bmatrix} = \begin{bmatrix} 20.520 & & \\ 7.085 & 15.288 & \\ 3.839 & 9.464 & 31.923 \end{bmatrix}$$

The covariance matrix is premultiplied and postmultiplied by the transformation matrix to obtain the transformed covariance matrix:

$$\begin{bmatrix} \frac{2}{3} & -\frac{1}{3} & -\frac{1}{3} \\ -\frac{1}{3} & \frac{2}{3} & -\frac{1}{3} \\ -\frac{1}{3} & -\frac{1}{3} & \frac{2}{3} \end{bmatrix} \cdot \begin{bmatrix} 20.520 & 7.085 & 3.839 \\ 7.085 & 15.288 & 9.464 \\ 3.839 & 9.464 & 31.923 \end{bmatrix} \cdot \begin{bmatrix} \frac{2}{3} & -\frac{1}{3} & -\frac{1}{3} \\ -\frac{1}{3} & \frac{2}{3} & -\frac{1}{3} \\ -\frac{1}{3} & -\frac{1}{3} & \frac{2}{3} \end{bmatrix}$$

$$= \begin{bmatrix} 11.614 & -1.953 & -9.661 \\ -1.953 & 6.121 & -4.168 \\ -9.661 & -4.168 & 13.829 \end{bmatrix}$$

The rank of this transformation is obviously 2; hence, the transformed covariance matrix is singular, and the transformed variables have a singular multivariate normal distribution. The transformation is in fact a symmetric idempotent restricting the variables to sum to zero; that is, it *mean deviates* or *ipsatizes* the variables. As is evident in the calculations, this implies that the elements of the transformed vector mean sum to zero, and that both rows and columns of the transformed covariance matrix sum to zero. We sometimes say in this case that the vector mean is *centered* and the covariance matrix is *double centered.* Multivariate statistical procedures that assume a nonsingular sample covariance matrix will fail if applied to a sample in which the variables have been ipsatized. A transformation to one fewer linearly independent variables is required before these statistical procedures can be applied (see Chap. 7).

The correlation matrix is computed from the above covariance matrix as follows:

$$\begin{bmatrix} 1/\sqrt{11.614} & 0 & 0 \\ 0 & 1/\sqrt{6.121} & 0 \\ 0 & 0 & 1/\sqrt{13.829} \end{bmatrix} \cdot \begin{bmatrix} 11.614 & & \\ -1.953 & 6.121 & \\ -9.661 & -4.168 & 13.829 \end{bmatrix}$$

$$\cdot \begin{bmatrix} 1/\sqrt{11.614} & 0 & 0 \\ 0 & 1/\sqrt{6.121} & 0 \\ 0 & 0 & 1/\sqrt{13.829} \end{bmatrix} = \begin{bmatrix} 1.00 & & \\ -.23 & 1.00 & \\ -.76 & -.45 & 1.00 \end{bmatrix}$$

Note that the rows and columns of the correlation matrix do not sum to zero. The correlation matrix is singular, nevertheless, because a linear transformation cannot increase rank.

Exercise 3.3-1 Suppose a p-variate statistic $\boldsymbol{t}$, based on a sample of size N, is distributed in multivariate normal form with mean $\boldsymbol{\theta}$ and error covariance matrix $(1/N)\boldsymbol{\Sigma}$. Let

$$\underset{n\times 1}{\boldsymbol{z}} = \mathbf{f}(\boldsymbol{t}) = [f_1(\boldsymbol{t}), f_2(\boldsymbol{t}), \ldots, f_n(\boldsymbol{t})]'$$

be an n-variate transformation of $\boldsymbol{t}$, totally differentiable but not necessarily linear.

(*a*) Show that the error covariance matrix of $\boldsymbol{z}$ as N goes to ∞ is

$$\underset{n\times n}{\mathscr{V}(\boldsymbol{z})} = \frac{1}{N}\left[\frac{\partial \mathbf{f}}{\partial \mathbf{t}'}\right]_{\boldsymbol{t}=\boldsymbol{\theta}} \Sigma \left[\frac{\partial \mathbf{f}}{\partial \mathbf{t}'}\right]'_{\boldsymbol{t}=\boldsymbol{\theta}}$$

(See Rao [1965, page 321].)

(*b*) Suppose that $\boldsymbol{y}$ is the result of mean deviating and standardizing $\boldsymbol{t}$ (that is, the elements of $\boldsymbol{y}$ sum to zero, and their squares sum to n). Use results in Sec. 2.5 to show that the error covariance matrix of $\boldsymbol{y}$ as N goes to ∞ is

$$\mathscr{V}(\boldsymbol{y}) = \frac{n}{N\boldsymbol{\theta}'\boldsymbol{\Delta}\boldsymbol{\theta}}\left(\boldsymbol{\Delta} - \frac{\boldsymbol{\Delta}\boldsymbol{\theta}\boldsymbol{\theta}'\boldsymbol{\Delta}}{\boldsymbol{\theta}'\boldsymbol{\Delta}\boldsymbol{\theta}}\right)\Sigma\left(\boldsymbol{\Delta} - \frac{\boldsymbol{\Delta}\boldsymbol{\theta}\boldsymbol{\theta}'\boldsymbol{\Delta}}{\boldsymbol{\theta}'\boldsymbol{\Delta}\boldsymbol{\theta}}\right)$$

where $\boldsymbol{\Delta} = \mathbf{I} - (1/n)\mathbf{1}\mathbf{1}'$, and $\mathbf{1}$ is a vector of n unities (see Example 3.3-2).

(*c*) Show that the rank of $\mathscr{V}(\boldsymbol{y})$ is at most $n - 2$.

3.4 SOME SAMPLING DISTRIBUTIONS DERIVED FROM THE MULTIVARIATE NORMAL DISTRIBUTION

3.4.1 Large-Sample and Exact Sampling Theory

In data analysis, we make frequent use of functions of the observations, called *statistics*, which serve as parameter estimators or as criteria in tests of hypotheses. The sample statistics for tests of multivariate hypotheses, introduced later in this section, are important examples. The interpretation of such statistics often depends upon knowledge of their sampling distributions as deduced from (1) the distribution assumed for the observations, (2) the method of sampling, and (3) the nature of the function of the observations. There are two types of sampling theory available for deriving sampling distributions—so-called *large-sample* theory, which gives the distribution approached as the sample size is increased indefinitely, and small-sample, or *exact*, theory, which is valid for any sample size.

Distributions derived by assuming the sample size indefinitely large are called *asymptotic* or *limiting* distributions. Large-sample theory is especially simple because, as a consequence of the central-limit theorem (Sec. 3.1.4), many univariate statistics can be shown to have normal limiting distributions. For such statistics, we need only determine the mean and variance to specify completely the large-sample distribution. Similarly, where a vector-valued statistic can be shown to have a multivariate normal limiting distribution, the vector mean and covariance matrix specify the large-sample distribution. We shall make extensive use of large-sample theory in connection with the method of maximum likelihood in Chap. 8.

Sampling distributions derived without resort to limiting arguments, on the other hand, generally depend upon the sample size and may be nonnormal in small samples even when the limiting form is normal. If the latter is the case, some indication of how large the sample must be before large-sample theory is sufficiently accurate for practical work can be seen by comparing percentage points computed on large- and small-sample assumptions. For example, the distribution of the variance ratio, or F, statistic (Sec. 3.4.5), for ν_1 degrees of freedom in the numerator and ν_2 degrees of freedom in the denominator, approaches the distribution of chi-square divided by ν_1 as ν_2 increases without limit; that is,

$$\lim_{\nu_2 \to \infty} F(\nu_1,\nu_2) = \frac{\chi^2(\nu_1)}{\nu_1}$$

On comparing tables of F and χ^2/ν_1 [Hald, 1952, page 44], we find that the .05 percentage points agree within 2 units in the second place when ν_2 is greater than 40. Similarly, the .01 percentage points agree to the same order of approximation when ν_2 exceeds 100. As we shall see in Chap. 4, ν_2 is the degrees of freedom for the error estimate and in most cases is of the same order of magnitude as the sample size. This suggests that, relative to the F statistic, the large-sample distribution is adequate for practical work whenever the sample size exceeds, say, 50.

The statistics which apply specifically to the multivariate case (i.e., multiple dependent variables), on the other hand, approach their limiting distribution much more slowly. For example, Hotelling's trace criterion (Sec. 3.4.8) for p variables, ν_1 "numerator" degrees of freedom, and ν_2 "denominator" degrees of freedom, limits to chi-square on $p\nu_1$ degrees of freedom as $\nu_2 \to \infty$. Thus, for $p = 4$ and $\nu_1 = 4$, the limiting 5-percent point is $\chi^2 = 26.3$. The corresponding point for the trace criterion [Pillai, 1960] does not approach this value until ν_2 reaches 100. (When $p = 4$, $\nu_1 = 4$, and $\nu_2 = 105$, the .05 point from Pillai's tables is 28.14.) For $p = 8$ and $\nu_1 = 8$, the .05 points of the two statistics do not attain this order of approximation until ν_2 is nearly 200.

The exact sampling distributions of a number of important statistics have been derived on the assumption that the observations are a simple random sample (or probability sample) from a multivariate normal population. The remainder of this section contains a brief account of these results.*

* For ease of writing, we will drop the typographical distinction between fixed and random variables in this section.

3.4.2 The Mean of N Independent Observations

Suppose N independent observations are drawn from the population $N(\mu,\sigma^2)$. Then the $N \times 1$ observational vector $\mathbf{y}$ is distributed in the multivariate normal form $N(\mu\mathbf{1},\sigma^2\mathbf{I})$, where $\mathbf{1}$ is an $N \times 1$ vector of unities, and $\mathbf{I}$ is the $N \times N$ identity matrix. According to the result in Sec. 3.3.7, any linear form in these observations, for example, $\mathbf{z} = \mathbf{a}'\mathbf{y}$, is distributed normally with mean $\mu\mathbf{a}'\mathbf{1}$ and variance $\sigma^2\mathbf{a}'\mathbf{I}\mathbf{a} = \sigma^2\mathbf{a}'\mathbf{a}$. Because the sample mean $y.$ may be expressed as the linear form

$$y. = \frac{1}{N}(\mathbf{1}'\mathbf{y})$$

we have, for its distribution,

$$y. \sim N\left(\mu\frac{1}{N}\mathbf{1}'\mathbf{1}, \sigma^2\frac{1}{N^2}\mathbf{1}'\mathbf{1}\right) = N\left(\mu, \frac{\sigma^2}{N}\right)$$

If μ and σ are known, percentage points for $y.$ can be obtained from tables of the standard normal distribution function $\Phi(z)$, using

$$z = \frac{y. - \mu}{\sigma/\sqrt{N}}$$

Alternatively, the computing approximation (with maximum error 10^{-6}) due to Hastings [1955, page 169] may be used:

$$\Phi(z) \approx \begin{cases} G & z \leq 0 \\ 1 - G & z > 0 \end{cases} \tag{3.4-1}$$

$$G = (a_1\eta + a_2\eta^2 + a_3\eta^3 + a_4\eta^4 + a_5\eta^5)\phi(z)$$

$$\eta = \frac{1}{1 + .2316418|z|}$$

$$\phi(z) = (2\pi)^{-1/2}e^{-z^2/2}$$

$$a_1 = .319381530$$

$$a_2 = -.356563782$$

$$a_3 = 1.781477937$$

$$a_4 = -1.821255978$$

$$a_5 = 1.330274429$$

3.4.3 The Sum of Squares of N Random Normal Deviates

Let $\mathbf{z}$ be an $N \times 1$ vector of N independent observations from $N(0,1)$. The statistic

$$\chi^2(N) = \mathbf{z}'\mathbf{z} = z_1^2 + z_2^2 + \cdots + z_N^2 \tag{3.4-2}$$

is distributed as a *chi-square variate on N degrees of freedom*. The distribution function for this statistic was obtained by Helmert in 1876 and independently by

Karl Pearson in 1900. A modern derivation may be found in Mood and Graybill [1963, page 226].

Percentage points for the distribution appear in the familiar χ^2 tables (e.g., Hald [1952]). The cdf for χ^2 on ν degrees of freedom, which is usually expressed as the incomplete gamma function

$$P(\chi^2 \leq x \mid \nu) \frac{1}{2^{\nu/2}\Gamma(\frac{\nu}{2})} \int_0^x t^{\nu/2-1} e^{-t/2} \, dt$$

may be approximated in computer applications by the convergent series

$$P(\chi^2 \leq x \mid \nu) = \frac{e^{-x}}{x^{-\nu}} \sum_{n=0}^{\infty} \frac{x^n}{\Gamma(\nu + n + 1)} \tag{3.4-3}$$

when $\frac{1}{2}x < \max(\frac{1}{2}\nu, 13)$, or otherwise by the asymptotic expansion

$$P(\chi^2 \leq x \mid \nu) \approx x^{\nu-1}e^{-x}\left[1 + \frac{\nu - 1}{x} + \frac{(\nu - 1)(\nu - 2)}{x^2} + \cdots\right] \tag{3.4-4}$$

[Abramowitz and Stegun, 1964, page 262]. The value of $\Gamma(a)$ in (3.4-3) may be obtained from Stirling's formula:

$$\begin{aligned} \Gamma(a) &= (a - 1)! \approx e^{-a}a^{a-1/2}(2\pi)^{1/2} \\ &\times \left[1 + \frac{1}{12a} + \frac{1}{288a^2} - \frac{139}{51{,}840a^3} - \frac{571}{2{,}488{,}320a^4} \cdots\right] \end{aligned} \tag{3.4-5}$$

[Abramowitz and Stegun, 1964, page 257]. The recursion relation $\Gamma(a + 1) = a\Gamma(a)$ and $\Gamma(2) = \Gamma(1) = 1$ may be used when a is small. This method for chi-square probabilities has been programmed as a computing routine by Clyde, Cramer, and Sherin [1966].

The mean of the χ^2 distribution is ν, and its variance 2ν. For $\nu > 30$, chi-square probabilities may be closely approximated using $\sqrt{2\chi^2} - \sqrt{2\nu - 1}$ as a unit normal deviate.

3.4.4 The Sum of Squares of N Unit Normal Deviates Subject to r Linear Restrictions

Suppose the $N \times 1$ vector $\mathbf{z}$, consisting of independent observations from $N(0,1)$, is projected orthogonally onto the r-dimensional subspace S_1 and its $(N - r)$-dimensional complement S_2. We have seen in Example 2.6-1 that the singular transformations

$$\mathbf{M} = \mathbf{C}(\mathbf{C}'\mathbf{C})^{-1}\mathbf{C}' \qquad \text{and} \qquad \mathbf{E} = [\mathbf{I} - \mathbf{C}(\mathbf{C}'\mathbf{C})^{-1}\mathbf{C}']$$

are suitable projection operators for this purpose, provided the columns of the $N \times r$ matrix $\mathbf{C}$ constitute a basis for S_1. In that case, $\text{rank}(\mathbf{C}) = r$, the inverse of

$\mathbf{C'C}$ exists, and $\mathbf{M}$ and $\mathbf{E}$ are symmetric idempotents of rank r and $N - r$, respectively. These matrices satisfy $\mathbf{MM} = \mathbf{M}$, $\mathbf{EE} = \mathbf{E}$, and $\mathbf{ME} = \mathbf{EM} = \mathbf{O}$.

Let the projections of $\mathbf{z}$ onto S_1 and S_2 be

$$\mathbf{y}_1 = \mathbf{Mz} \qquad \text{and} \qquad \mathbf{y}_2 = \mathbf{Ez}$$

respectively. Note that $\mathbf{y}_2$ is subject to the r linear restrictions

$$\mathbf{C'y}_2 = \mathbf{C'}[\mathbf{I} - \mathbf{C}(\mathbf{C'C})^{-1}\mathbf{C'}]\mathbf{z} = [\mathbf{C'} - \mathbf{C'}]\mathbf{z} = \mathbf{0}$$

Let us now derive the simultaneous distribution of the square lengths of $\mathbf{y}_1$ and $\mathbf{y}_2$:

$$Q_1 = \mathbf{y}_1'\mathbf{y}_1 = \mathbf{z'MMz} = \mathbf{z'Mz}$$
$$Q_2 = \mathbf{y}_2'\mathbf{y}_2 = \mathbf{z'EEz} = \mathbf{z'Ez}$$

We observe first that $\mathbf{C'C}$ is a rank-r grammian matrix and may be expressed in the form of the Cholesky factor and its transpose (Sec. 2.7.2), $\mathbf{C'C} = \mathbf{S}_c\mathbf{S}_c'$. Accordingly, $(\mathbf{C'C})^{-1} = (\mathbf{S}_c^{-1})'\mathbf{S}_c^{-1}$, and the $N \times r$ matrix $\mathbf{P}_1 = \mathbf{C}(\mathbf{S}_c^{-1})'$ is column orthonormal; that is, $\mathbf{P}_1'\mathbf{P}_1 = \mathbf{S}_c^{-1}\mathbf{C'C}(\mathbf{S}_c^{-1})' = \mathbf{I}$.

Now let the $N \times (N - r)$ matrix $\mathbf{P}_2$ be an orthogonal completion of $\mathbf{P}_1$. It may be obtained, for example, by applying the Gram-Schmidt constructions (Sec. 2.2.4) to the augmented matrix $[\mathbf{P}_1 \mid \mathbf{I}]$. The N nonnull columns of the result then constitute the $N \times N$ matrix $\mathbf{P} = [\mathbf{P}_1 \mid \mathbf{P}_2]$, such that $\mathbf{P'P} = \mathbf{PP'} = \mathbf{I}$.

$\mathbf{M}$ and $\mathbf{E}$ may be expressed in terms of $\mathbf{P}_1$ and $\mathbf{P}_2$ as follows:

$$\mathbf{M} = \mathbf{C}(\mathbf{S}_c^{-1})'\mathbf{S}_c^{-1}\mathbf{C} = \mathbf{P}_1\mathbf{P}_1'$$
$$\mathbf{E} = \mathbf{I} - \mathbf{M} = \mathbf{PP'} - \mathbf{P}_1\mathbf{P}_1' = [\mathbf{P}_1 \mid \mathbf{P}_2]\begin{bmatrix}\mathbf{P}_1' \\ \mathbf{P}_2'\end{bmatrix} - \mathbf{P}_1\mathbf{P}_1'$$
$$= \mathbf{P}_1\mathbf{P}_1' + \mathbf{P}_2\mathbf{P}_2' - \mathbf{P}_1\mathbf{P}_1' = \mathbf{P}_2\mathbf{P}_2'$$

Thus, the transformed variates

$$\begin{matrix} r \\ N - r \end{matrix}\begin{bmatrix}\mathbf{u} \\ \mathbf{w}\end{bmatrix} = \mathbf{P'z} = \begin{bmatrix}\mathbf{P}_1' \\ \mathbf{P}_2'\end{bmatrix}\mathbf{z}$$

are distributed as

$$\begin{bmatrix}\mathbf{u} \\ \mathbf{w}\end{bmatrix} \sim N(\mathbf{P0}, \mathbf{P'P}) = N\left(\begin{matrix} r \\ N - r \end{matrix}\begin{bmatrix}\mathbf{0} \\ \mathbf{0}\end{bmatrix}, \begin{matrix} r \\ N - r \end{matrix}\begin{bmatrix}\mathbf{I} & 0 \\ 0 & \mathbf{I}\end{bmatrix}\right)$$

Hence

$$Q_1 = \mathbf{y}_1'\mathbf{y}_1 = \mathbf{z'Mz} = \mathbf{z'P}_1\mathbf{P}_1'\mathbf{z} = \mathbf{u'u} = u_1^2 + u_2^2 + \cdots + u_r^2$$

is a sum of squares of r independent unit normal deviates and is distributed as $\chi^2(r)$. Similarly,

$$Q_2 = \mathbf{y}_2'\mathbf{y}_2 = \mathbf{z'Ez} = \mathbf{z'P}_2\mathbf{P}_2\mathbf{z} = \mathbf{w'w} = w_1^2 + w_2^2 + \cdots + w_{N-r}^2$$

is a sum of squares of $N - r$ independent unit normal deviates and is distributed as $\chi^2(N - r)$.

Furthermore, **u** and **w** are uncorrelated multinormal variables and are therefore independent; hence, Q_1 and Q_2 are *independently* distributed.

We note also that

$$\mathbf{y}_1 + \mathbf{y}_2 = \mathbf{Mz} + (\mathbf{I} - \mathbf{M})\mathbf{z} = \mathbf{z}$$

and, because $\mathbf{y}_1'\mathbf{y}_2 = \mathbf{z}'\mathbf{MEz} = 0$,

$$\begin{aligned}\mathbf{z}'\mathbf{z} &= (\mathbf{y}_1 + \mathbf{y}_2)'(\mathbf{y}_1 + \mathbf{y}_2) = \mathbf{y}_1'\mathbf{y}_1 + \mathbf{y}_2'\mathbf{y}_2 \\ &= \mathbf{z}'\mathbf{Mz} + \mathbf{z}'\mathbf{Ez}\end{aligned}$$

or

$$Q = Q_1 + Q_2$$

But Q is a sum of squares of N independent unit normal deviates and, hence, is a χ^2 variate on N degrees of freedom, and

$$\chi^2(N) = \chi^2(r) + \chi^2(N - r)$$

Generalized slightly, these results are summarized in Cochran's theorem [Graybill, 1961, page 86]:

Let the $N \times 1$ *observational vector* $\mathbf{z}$ *be distributed* $N(\mathbf{0},\mathbf{I})$, *and let* $\mathbf{z}'\mathbf{z} = \sum_{i=1}^{k} \mathbf{z}'\mathbf{A}_i\mathbf{z}$, *where rank* $\mathbf{A}_i = \nu_i$. *A necessary and sufficient condition for* $\mathbf{z}'\mathbf{A}_1\mathbf{z}, \mathbf{z}'\mathbf{A}_2\mathbf{z}, \ldots, \mathbf{z}'\mathbf{A}_k\mathbf{z}$ *to be distributed independently as* χ^2 *with* $\nu_1, \nu_2, \ldots, \nu_k$ *degrees of freedom, respectively, is that* $\sum_{i=1}^{k} \nu_i = N$. In other words, if the sum of squares of N independent normal deviates is expressed as a sum of quadratic forms in the deviates, the forms are distributed as independent chi-square variates with degrees of freedom equal to the rank of the respective form if and only if the sum of the ranks equals N.

Sufficiency may be proved by induction on k. It is obviously true when $k = 1$. When $k = 2$, we observe that, because $\mathbf{z}'\mathbf{z} = \mathbf{z}'\mathbf{A}_1\mathbf{z} + \mathbf{z}'\mathbf{A}_2\mathbf{z} = \mathbf{z}'(\mathbf{A}_1 + \mathbf{A}_2)\mathbf{z}$ for all $\mathbf{z}$, $\mathbf{A}_1 + \mathbf{A}_2 = \mathbf{I}$. Then, if $\text{rank}(\mathbf{A}_1) = \nu_1$, there exists an orthogonal matrix of characteristic vectors $\mathbf{P} = [\mathbf{P}_1 \mid \mathbf{P}_2]$ such that

$$\mathbf{P}'\mathbf{A}_1\mathbf{P} = \begin{bmatrix}\mathbf{P}_1' \\ \mathbf{P}_2'\end{bmatrix}\mathbf{A}_1[\mathbf{P}_1 \mid \mathbf{P}_2] = \underset{\nu_1 \quad N-\nu_1}{\begin{bmatrix}\Lambda_1 & 0 \\ 0 & 0\end{bmatrix}}\begin{matrix}\nu_1 \\ N - \nu_1\end{matrix}$$

where Λ_1 is the $\nu_1 \times \nu_1$ diagonal matrix of nonzero characteristic values of $\mathbf{A}_1$. Furthermore, if $\text{rank}(\mathbf{A}_2) = \nu_2$ and $\nu_1 + \nu_2 = N$,

$$\begin{aligned}\mathbf{I} = \mathbf{P}'\mathbf{IP} &= \mathbf{P}'\mathbf{A}_1\mathbf{P} + \mathbf{P}'\mathbf{A}_2\mathbf{P} = \mathbf{P}'\mathbf{A}_1\mathbf{P} + \mathbf{P}'(\mathbf{I} - \mathbf{A}_1)\mathbf{P} \\ &= \begin{bmatrix}\Lambda_1 & 0 \\ 0 & 0\end{bmatrix} + \begin{bmatrix}\mathbf{I} - \Lambda_1 & 0 \\ 0 & \mathbf{I}\end{bmatrix} = \begin{bmatrix}\mathbf{I} & 0 \\ 0 & \mathbf{I}\end{bmatrix}\begin{matrix}\nu_1 \\ \nu_2\end{matrix}\end{aligned}$$

where $\Lambda_1 = \mathbf{I}$. That is, the characteristic values of $\mathbf{A}_1$ and $\mathbf{A}_2$ are all 1 or zero, where the characteristic vectors corresponding to nonzero roots in $\mathbf{A}_1$ are those corresponding to the zero roots in $\mathbf{A}_2$, and vice versa. Then $\mathbf{A}_1 = \mathbf{P}_1\mathbf{I}\mathbf{P}_1' = \mathbf{P}_1\mathbf{P}_1'$ and $\mathbf{A}_2 = \mathbf{P}_2\mathbf{I}\mathbf{P}_2' = \mathbf{P}_2\mathbf{P}_2'$; thus, $\mathbf{A}_1$ and $\mathbf{A}_2$ have the same composition as $\mathbf{M}$ and $\mathbf{E}$, and the proof proceeds as above. The proof of necessity, and of the corollative result that $\mathbf{A}_1$ and $\mathbf{A}_2$ are complementary idempotents, is left to the reader.

Cochran's theorem has many important applications in normal data analysis. For example, let $\mathbf{A}_1 = (1/N)\mathbf{1}\mathbf{1}'$ and $\mathbf{A}_2 = \mathbf{I} - (1/N)\mathbf{1}\mathbf{1}'$, where $\mathbf{1}$ is an $N \times 1$ vector of unities. Then,

$$\begin{aligned}\mathbf{y}'\mathbf{y} &= \mathbf{y}'\mathbf{A}_1\mathbf{y} + \mathbf{y}'\mathbf{A}_2\mathbf{y} = Ny._{}^2 + \left(\sum_{i=1}^{N} y_i^2 - Ny._{}^2\right) \\ &= N\tilde{m}_1^2 + N\tilde{\mu}_2 = Q_1 + Q_2\end{aligned}$$

where $\tilde{m}_1$ is the sample first moment (mean), and $\tilde{\mu}_2$ is the sample central second moment (variance). Since the ranks of $\mathbf{A}_1$ and $\mathbf{A}_2$ are evidently 1 and $N - 1$, respectively, Q_1 and Q_2 are independently distributed as $\chi^2(1)$ and $\chi^2(N - 1)$, provided y is independent $N(0,1)$. As we shall see in Chap. 4, if y is independent $N(\mu,\sigma^2)$, the quantity $Q_2 = (N - 1)v^2/\sigma^2$, where v^2 is the *unbiased* estimator of the sample variance,

$$v^2 = \frac{\sum_{i=1}^{N} y_i^2 - Ny._{}^2}{N - 1}$$

and is distributed as $\chi^2(N - 1)$. However, $Q_1 = Ny._{}^2$ is $\chi^2(1)$ only on condition that $\mu = 0$. If $\mu \neq 0$, Q_1 is said to have a *noncentral* chi-square distribution with *noncentrality parameter* $N\mu^2/2\sigma^2$ [Graybill, 1961, page 74].

3.4.5 The Ratio of Independent χ^2 Variates (Fisher's F)

Let χ_1^2 and χ_2^2 be independent χ^2 variates with ν_1 and ν_2 degrees of freedom. Then

$$F = \frac{\chi_1^2/\nu_1}{\chi_2^2/\nu_2}$$

is distributed as an F variate on ν_1 and ν_2 degrees of freedom. The distribution function for F was derived by R. A. Fisher [1924] and is now widely tabulated [Hald, 1952]. In computer applications, the cdf for F may be approximated by the following convergent series for the incomplete beta function:

$$I_x(a,b) = \frac{(x^a1 - x)^b}{aB(a,b)}\left[1 + \sum_{n=0}^{\infty} \frac{B(a + 1, n + 1)}{B(a + b, n + 1)} x^{n+1}\right]$$

where $B(a,b) = \Gamma(a)\Gamma(b)/\Gamma(a + b)$, and the values of the complete Γ function are obtained from Stirling's formula given above [Abramowitz and Stegun, 1964]. Then,

$$P(F,\nu_1,\nu_2) = 1 - I_x\left(\frac{\nu_2}{2}, \frac{\nu_1}{2}\right) \qquad \text{where } x = \frac{\nu_2}{\nu_2 + \nu_1 F}$$

In statistical applications F appears as a variance ratio. Suppose v_1^2 is a variance estimate on ν_1 degrees of freedom for a sample from $N(\mu,\sigma^2)$, and v_2^2 is an independent variance estimate on ν_2 degrees of freedom for a sample from $N(\mu,\sigma^2)$. Then $\nu_1 v_1^2/\sigma^2$ and $\nu_2 v_2^2/\sigma^2$ are distributed independently as $\chi^2(\nu_1)$ and $\chi^2(\nu_2)$, respectively. The ratio

$$F = \frac{v_1^2}{v_2^2} = \frac{\chi^2(\nu_1)/\nu_1}{\chi^2(\nu_2)/\nu_2}$$

is therefore distributed as Fisher's F on ν_1 and ν_2 degrees of freedom, and this distribution does not depend on μ or σ^2.

The ratio of a *noncentral* χ^2, with df $= \nu_1$ and noncentrality parameter γ, and a *central* χ^2 with df $= \nu_2$, is said to be distributed as a noncentral F, with df ν_1 and ν_2 and noncentrality parameter γ [Graybill, 1961, page 78].

When $\nu_1 = 1$, F is the square of student's t statistic on ν_2 degrees of freedom:

$$F(1,\nu_2) = t^2(\nu_2)$$

3.4.6 Sum of Squares and Cross Products of N Independent Observations from $N(0,\Sigma)$: The Wishart Distribution

Let $z = [z^{(1)}, z^{(2)}, \ldots, z^{(p)}]'$ be distributed in multivariate form with vector mean $\mathbf{0}$ and covariance matrix $\boldsymbol{\Sigma}$. Then, the $p(p + 1)/2$ distinct elements in $\mathbf{S} = \sum_{i=1}^{N_0} z_i z_i'$ have a joint Wishart [1928] distribution with parameters N_0, p, and $\boldsymbol{\Sigma}$:

$$f(\mathbf{S}) = \frac{|\mathbf{S}|^{(N_0-p-1)/2} \exp\left[-\frac{1}{2} \operatorname{tr} \boldsymbol{\Sigma}^{-1}\mathbf{S}\right]}{2^{N_0 p/2}\pi^{p(p-1)/4}|\boldsymbol{\Sigma}|^{N_0/2} \prod_{i=1}^{p} \Gamma[(N_0 + 1 - i)/2]}$$

[Anderson, 1958, page 154].

Similarly, if $y = [y^{(1)}, y^{(2)}, \ldots, y^{(p)}]$ is distributed $N(\boldsymbol{\mu},\boldsymbol{\Sigma})$, then the sum of squares and cross products *corrected to the mean*,

$$\mathbf{S} = \sum_{i=1}^{N} (\mathbf{y}_i - \mathbf{y}_.)(\mathbf{y}_i - \mathbf{y}_.)'$$

$$= \sum_{i=1}^{N} \mathbf{y}_i\mathbf{y}_i' - N\mathbf{y}_.\mathbf{y}_.'$$

is distributed in Wishart form with parameters $N_0 = N - 1$, p, and $\boldsymbol{\Sigma}$. Matrices of corrected sums of squares and products of multinormal variates are therefore called

Wishart matrices. These matrices play the role in multivariate analysis of variance that sums of squares play in univariate analysis of variance. The statistics for tests of multivariate hypotheses introduced in Chap. 4 are functions of sample Wishart matrices. Some notes on the distributions of these statistics follow.

3.4.7 Maximum of the Ratio of Quadratic Forms in Two Independent Wishart Matrices (Roy's Largest-Root Criterion)

Let $\mathbf{S}_1$ and $\mathbf{S}_2$ be independent Wishart matrices with parameters ν_1, p, Σ, and ν_2, p, Σ, respectively, for $\nu_2 \geq p$. Then

$$\lambda_1 = \max \frac{\mathbf{x}'\mathbf{S}_1\mathbf{x}}{\mathbf{x}'\mathbf{S}_2\mathbf{x}} \qquad \text{where } |\mathbf{S}_2| \neq 0$$

is the largest root of

$$|\mathbf{S}_1 - \lambda \mathbf{S}_2| = 0 \tag{3.4-6}$$

(See Sec. 2.7.4.)

In general, the equation in λ obtained by expanding (3.4-6) has $s = \min(\nu_1, p)$ nonzero roots. The simultaneous distribution of the roots of (3.4-6) on the hypothesis that $\mathbf{S}_1$ and $\mathbf{S}_2$ arise from the same multivariate normal population was derived independently by Fisher [1939], Roy [1939], and others. Roy [1945] also derived the distribution of the greatest, least, or any individual root. See also Krishnaiah and Chang [1971].

Pillai [1960, 1967] has extensively tabulated the null distribution for the largest-root statistic. He gives the upper .05 and .01 points of the statistic

$$\theta_1 = \frac{\lambda_1}{1 + \lambda_1}$$

in terms of the arguments

$$s = \min(\nu_1, p)$$

$$m = \frac{|\nu_1 - p| - 1}{2}$$

and

$$n = \frac{\nu_2 - p - 1}{2}$$

In Appendix A of the present text, Pillai's percentage points are presented in the form of a generalized F statistic,

$$F_0 = \frac{t}{r} \lambda_1 \tag{3.4-7}$$

in terms of the arguments

$$r = |\nu_1 - p| + 1$$

$$s = \min(\nu_1, p)$$

and

$$t = \nu_2 - p + 1$$

When $p = 1$ or $\nu_1 = 1$, F_0 specializes to the univariate F statistic. In the sequel, we shall make extensive use of F_0 in tests of multivariate hypotheses and construction of multivariate confidence bounds.

3.4.8 The Trace Function of Two Independent Wishart Matrices

Hotelling [1951] proposed the criterion

$$T_0^2 = \nu_2 \operatorname{tr}(\mathbf{S}_1\mathbf{S}_2^{-1}) \tag{3.4-8}$$

for testing multivariate hypotheses, where $\operatorname{tr}(\mathbf{S}_1\mathbf{S}_2^{-1})$, the trace function defined by (2.5-7), is the sum of the diagonal elements of $\mathbf{S}_1\mathbf{S}_2^{-1}$. This criterion may also be expressed in terms of the nonzero roots of $|\mathbf{S}_1 - \lambda\mathbf{S}_2| = 0$:

$$T_0^2 = \nu_2 \sum_{k=1}^{s} \lambda_k$$

where $s = \min(\nu_1,p)$.

Pillai [1956, 1971] has derived the distribution of T_0^2 on the hypothesis that $\mathbf{S}_1$ and $\mathbf{S}_2$ are based on independent samples from the same multivariate normal distribution. He has tabulated $U_s = \sum_{k=1}^{s} \lambda_k$ in terms of the same arguments, m, n, and s, used in tabulating the largest-root statistic.

When $\nu_1 = 1$, (3.4-8) becomes Hotelling's T^2 for p variates and ν_2 degrees of freedom (see Sec. 6.2.1):

$$T^2(p,\nu_2) = T_0^2(p,1,\nu_2)$$

When $\nu_1 = 1$ and $p = 1$, (3.4-8) becomes the square of student's t on ν_2 degrees of freedom:

$$t^2(\nu_2) = T_0^2(1,1,\nu_2)$$

3.4.9 The Ratio of the Determinants of Two Independent Wishart Matrices

Let $\mathbf{S}_1$ and $\mathbf{S}_2$ be independent Wishart matrices estimated on ν_1 and ν_2 degrees of freedom, respectively. In multivariate normal analysis, tests of hypothesis based on the likelihood-ratio principle frequently lead to the determinantal ratio

$$\Lambda = \frac{|\mathbf{S}_2|}{|\mathbf{S}_1 + \mathbf{S}_2|} \tag{3.4-9}$$

called *Wilks' criterion* [Wilks, 1932]. It may be expressed in terms of the roots of $|\mathbf{S}_1 - \lambda\mathbf{S}_2| = 0$, as $\Lambda = \prod_{k=1}^{s} 1/(1 + \lambda_k)$, where $s = \min(\nu_1,p)$. Box [1949] has shown that, on the hypothesis that $\mathbf{S}_1$ and $\mathbf{S}_2$ arise from independent p-variate observations from the same multivariate normal population, percentage points for Λ may be obtained to any specified degree of accuracy by use of approximations based on the χ^2 distribution.

The cdf of the statistic

$$\chi_B^2 = -m \log \Lambda = -\left(\nu_1 + \nu_2 - \frac{p + \nu_1 + 1}{2}\right) \log \Lambda \qquad (3.4\text{-}10)$$

is approximated with error of order ν_2^{-2} by the central chi-square distribution for $p\nu_1$ degrees of freedom; that is,

$$P(\chi_B^2 \le C) \approx P(\chi^2_{p\nu_1} \le C)$$

The error may be reduced to order ν_2^{-4} by use of

$$P(\chi_B^2 \le C) \approx P(\chi^2_{p\nu_1} \le C) + \frac{p\nu_1(p^2 + \nu_1^2 - 5)}{48m^2} [P(\chi^2_{p\nu_1+4} \le C) - P(\chi^2_{p\nu_1} \le C)]$$

[Anderson, 1958, page 208]. χ_B^2 is called *Bartlett's chi-square approximation* [Bartlett, 1947].

An approximation making use of the F distribution has been given by Rao [1951, page 262]. The cdf of the statistic

$$\frac{1 - \Lambda^{1/t}}{\Lambda^{1/t}} \frac{mt - 2k}{p\nu_1} \qquad (3.4\text{-}11)$$

is approximated with error of order ν_2^{-4} by the central F distribution on $p\nu_1$ and $mt - 2k$ degrees of freedom, where m is defined above, and

$$t = \left(\frac{p^2\nu_1^2 - 4}{p^2 + \nu_1^2 - 5}\right)^{1/2} \qquad k = \frac{p\nu_1 - 2}{4}$$

If $mt - 2k$ is not integral, the next larger integer should be used when entering the F table. For $p\nu_1 = 2$, set $t = 1$.

The exact distribution of Λ has been given by Shatzoff [1966] and by Pillai and Gupta [1969]. Tables for correcting (3.4-10) to obtain exact probability levels have been given by Lee [1972].

3.4.10 The Roy-Bargmann Step-down Test

Suppose the likelihood-ratio criterion is computed by pivoting the matrices $\mathbf{S}_2$ and $\mathbf{S}_t = \mathbf{S}_1 + \mathbf{S}_2$ in some predetermined order and forming the continued product of respective pivotal elements, as in

$$\Lambda = \frac{d_2^{(1)} d_2^{(2)} \cdots d_2^{(p)}}{d_t^{(1)} d_t^{(2)} \cdots d_t^{(p)}} \qquad (3.4\text{-}12)$$

It has been shown by Roy and Bargmann [1958] that the so-called *step-down F* statistics,

$$F_i = \frac{n_2(d_t^{(i)} - d_2^{(i)})}{n_1 d_2^{(i)}} \qquad i = 1, 2, \ldots, p \qquad (3.4\text{-}13)$$

are distributed as F on n_1 and n_2 degrees of freedom and are stochastically independent under the null hypothesis. (Roy and Bargmann use beta statistics; J. Roy [1958] uses F.) Applying Roy's union-intersection principle, we have the following test of the null hypothesis that $\mathbf{S}_1$ and $\mathbf{S}_2$ were drawn from Wishart distributions with a common Σ: Reject H_0 if at least one of the p step-down F statistics exceeds the α_i critical level. The probability of rejecting the null hypothesis when it is in fact true is then

$$\alpha = 1 - (1 - \alpha_1)(1 - \alpha_2) \cdots (1 - \alpha_p) \qquad (3.4\text{-}14)$$

Choosing the α_i appropriately, we may set α to any conventional value. Applications of this test in the context of discriminant analysis are discussed in Sec. 6.2.3.

3.4.11 Power of the Alternative Criteria

Because the power of the multivariate test criteria may depend upon departure from the null hypothesis in several dimensions, it is difficult to give a general answer to the question of which criterion is more powerful. Where the multivariate hypothesis spans more than one dimension, there appears to be no "uniformly most powerful" test in the sense of Neyman and Pearson [1933]. However, Pillai and Jayachandran [1968], in a study of the largest root, trace, and likelihood-ratio criteria for the case $p = 2$, found that when the deviation from the null hypothesis was unidimensional (i.e., one nonzero population root) and large, the power of the largest-root criterion generally exceeded that of the others. Otherwise, its power is generally below that of the others. This held both for tests of equality of vector means (see Sec. 5.2.3) and for tests of no association between sets of variables (see Secs. 4.2.4 and 6.1.2).

As the examples in this text suggest, differences between population means, whether in an experiment or a comparative study, in fact often appear to be unidimensional or nearly so (i.e., the vector means tend to collinearity). As a general rule, the effects of experimental treatments or of classificatory variables in behavioral studies are not so complex as to act in a highly independent manner in distinct response variables. To the extent this is true, the largest-root criterion might be expected to have somewhat better power than the other criteria in this class of applications.

In studies of within-group relationships between sets of variables, on the other hand, deviation from the null hypothesis is due to individual-difference variation and is likely to be of higher dimensionality, especially if the data are scores from factored psychological tests. Here, the largest-root criterion would be least advantageous, and we might prefer the likelihood-ratio criterion, which offers the possibility of testing the significance of the smaller roots (see Sec. 6.1). However, if the variables have been deliberately selected to represent a single hypothesized relationship as in Example 6.1-4, the largest-root test would be preferable even in this case.

With respect to the power of multivariate tests, the investigator should be conscious of the fact that power must generally be expected to decline as the number of variates is increased. Das Gupta and Perlman [1973] have shown, for example, that in the case of one-dimensional departure from the null hypothesis, the power of the likelihood-ratio criterion is strictly decreasing as p increases. This is an instance of a more general principle, which we shall encounter in various contexts in the sequel, that statistical inference is weakened when hypotheses are overinclusive with respect to independent or dependent variables.

3.5 CHECKING DISTRIBUTION ASSUMPTIONS

At the present time, no practical method is available for testing the hypothesis that a given sample has arisen from a population which is multivariate normal in form but otherwise unspecified. However, certain necessary conditions for multivariate normality, each of which is assumed at some point in normal data analysis, may readily be checked. One of these conditions, linearity of regression planes, may be investigated by the procedure for polynomial regression analysis described in Chap. 4. Another, homoscedasticity of conditional distributions, may be examined if the data are reasonably extensive by means of tests for homogeneity of variances and covariances presented in Sec. 6.2.4. Finally, the requirement of univariate normality of marginal and conditional distributions may be checked in moderately extensive data by methods discussed in this section.

Elementary texts often recommend that univariate normality be investigated by examining the sample frequency histogram for discrepancies between the observed frequencies and expected frequencies computed from a fitted normal distribution. Usually, it is also suggested that the discrepancies be subjected to a chi-square test of goodness of fit. A significant chi-square is taken as evidence against a normal population. (See Walker and Lev [1953, page 119] for an example of this procedure.)

Although this method of investigating normality has the merit of computational simplicity and freedom from assumptions about the type of departure being tested, it has the disadvantage, when applied to continuous data, of depending upon the arbitrary choice of intervals in terms of which the data are to be grouped. This choice determines the degree of resolution in the histogram and the number of terms to be summed in computing the chi-square statistic. The wrong choice can adversely affect the analysis. If the chosen intervals are too narrow, the histogram may be highly irregular, and the accuracy of the chi-square approximation may suffer because of small expected values. If the intervals are too wide, local departures from normality will be obscured both in the histogram and the chi-square.

To avoid some of these problems, Mann and Wald [1942] have proposed that the intervals be chosen so that the expected frequencies for each class (as computed in the present case from the fitted normal distribution) be set equal, say, to 5 or more. This makes the choice of interval objective and ensures a reasonably good approximation to the chi-square distribution. This rule presents difficulties, however, if the data are not actually continuous, as is often true of behavioral data. Unless the intervals chosen are very broad, the coarse grain of the data is likely to put too much frequency in one interval and too little in the next, with the result that the chi-square is spuriously significant. If this difficulty is corrected by use of very broad intervals, the test becomes insensitive to discrepancies, especially in the tails.

A better approach, avoiding all these difficulties, is to make use of methods for detecting departure from normality which do not require grouping of scores. Fortunately, excellent graphical and computational procedures are available for this purpose.

3.5.1 A Graphical Method

A graphical device for checking normality in ungrouped data is a plot of the sample cumulative distribution versus the corresponding fractiles of a fitted normal distribution. This procedure is readily adapted to computer displays. The steps to be performed in preparing the plot are as follows:

1 Rank the sample observations x_i, and assign rank numbers $r = 1, 2, \ldots, N$ to each, beginning with the smallest observation.

2 Compute percentile rank corresponding to each rank number. The formula for this purpose is

$$p_i = \frac{r_i - \frac{1}{2}}{N} \tag{3.5-1}$$

3 Compute the sample mean

$$x. = \frac{1}{N}\sum_{i=1}^{N} x_i$$

and the biased standard deviation

$$s = \sqrt{\frac{\sum_{i=1}^{N} x_i^2 - Nx.^2}{N}}$$

4 Obtain the normal fractile

$$P_i = \Phi\left(\frac{x_i - x.}{s}\right)$$

by entering the table of the normal integral with argument $(x_i - x.)/s$, or by means of the computing approximation (3.4-1).

5 Plot P_i(abscissa) versus p_i(ordinate). (See Fig. 3.5-1.)

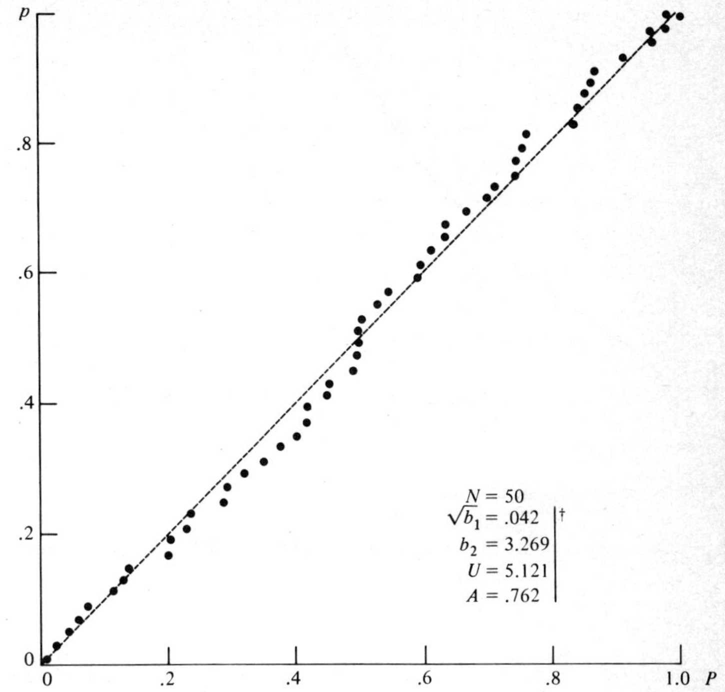

FIGURE 3.5-1
Cumulative normal plot of 50 random normal deviates. †Test statistics for departure from normality. See Sec. 3.5.3.

If the population is normal, the plot will tend to fall on the straight line $P_i = p_i$. Because the plot is cumulative, however, the points are not independent, and successive points will not tend to lie randomly on either side of the line. Rather, a number of points in succession may lie to one side or the other without being indicative of departure from normality. Some familiarity with the shape of these plots is necessary in detecting the departure when it occurs. The following example presents the cases of primary interest in behavioral applications.

EXAMPLE 3.5-1 (*Cumulative normal plots*) Figure 3.5-1 is a cumulative normal plot of 50 unit normal deviates drawn from the Rand table [Rand Corporation, 1955]. In spite of the long runs on either side of the identity line, the plot appears quite straight and gives no evidence of departure from normality.

Part *a* of Figs. 3.5-2 through 3.5-6 show, respectively, the cumulative normal plots of a left skew, right skew, leptokurtic, platykurtic, and bimodal distribution. Each plot includes a random sample of 50 observations from the corresponding

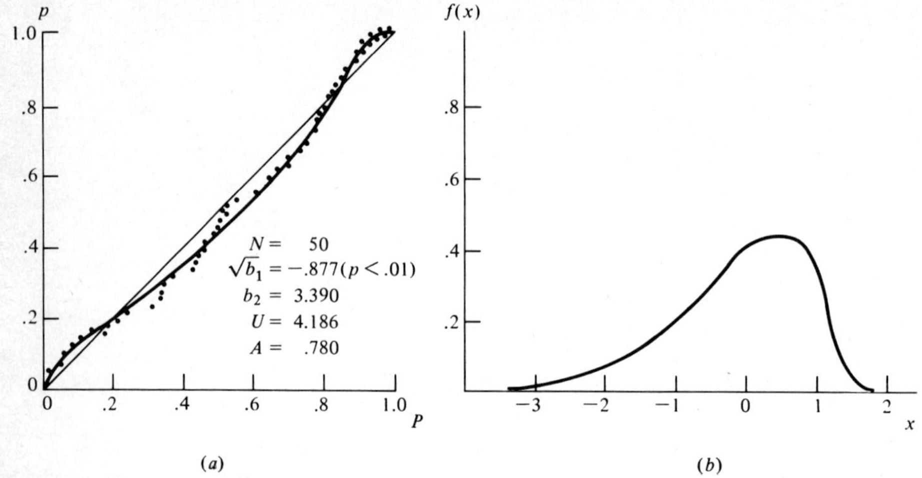

FIGURE 3.5-2
(*a*) Cumulative normal plot of a left-skew population and sample; (*b*) density function.

population. In part *b* of each of these figures is shown the density function of the corresponding population.

The interpretation of the cumulative normal plots is based on the location of the points where the plot crosses the identity line and direction of crossing. When the population density is skewed to the *left* as in Fig. 3.5-2*b*, the population cumulative normal plot begins and ends generally *above* the identity line and crosses it near each

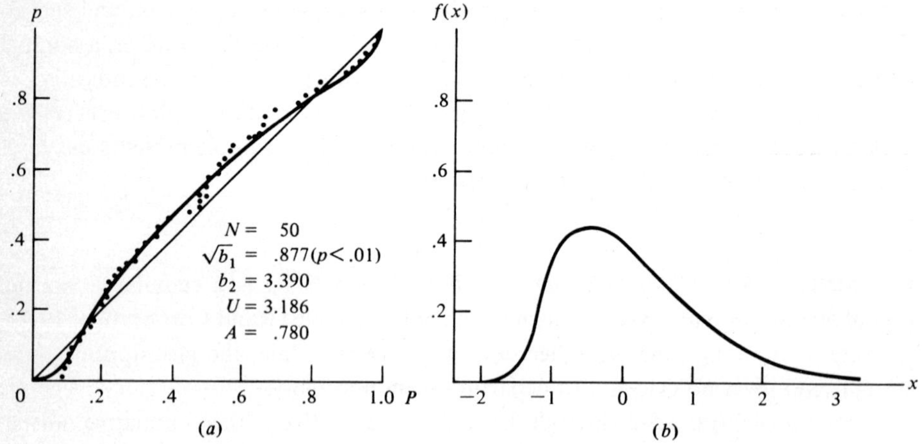

FIGURE 3.5-3
(*a*) Cumulative normal plot of a right-skew population and sample; (*b*) density function.

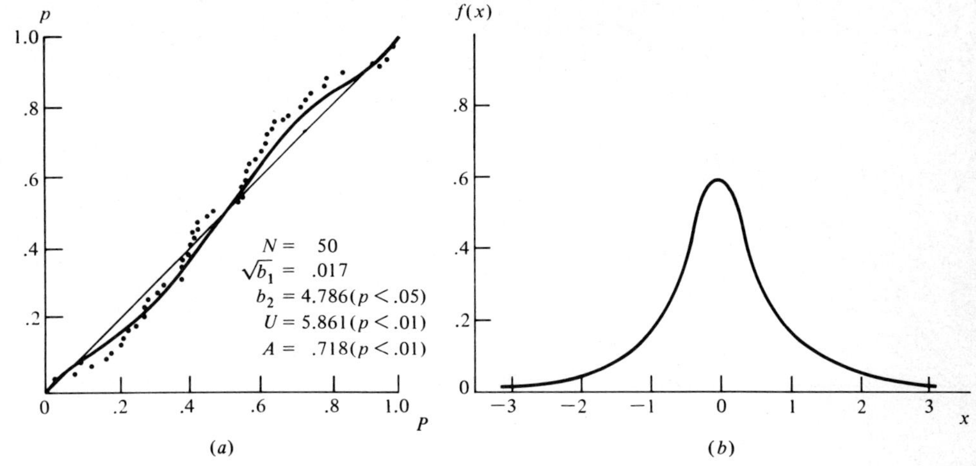

FIGURE 3.5-4
(*a*) Cumulative normal plot of a leptokurtic population and sample; (*b*) density function.

end of the line. Thus, the center part of the plot is *below* the identity line. Conversely, when the plot for a population is skewed to the *right* as in Fig. 3.5-3*b*, the plot begins and ends generally *below* the identity line and has its center *above* the identity line. Thus, the direction of skew is easy to recognize. The observed points on these plots confirm that in samples of at least this size ($N = 50$), the empirical plot reveals the population trend reasonably clearly. With smaller samples, the plot may

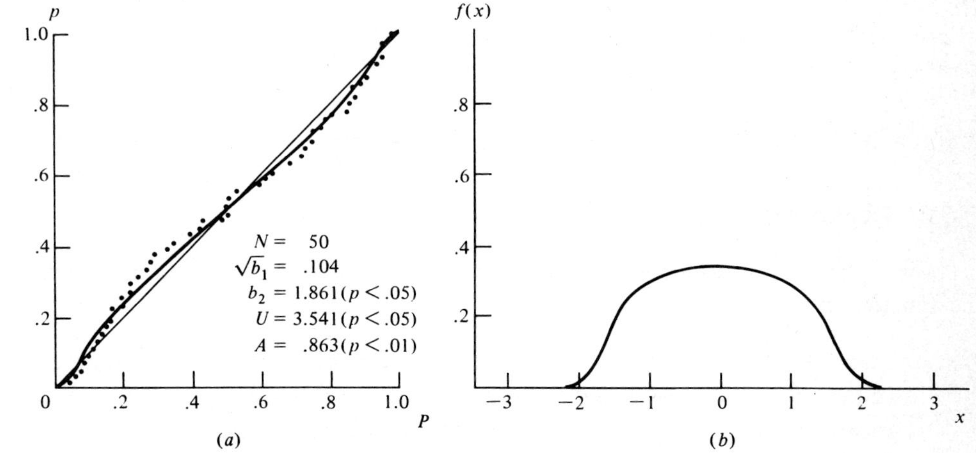

FIGURE 3.5-5
(*a*) Cumulative normal plot of a platykurtic population and sample; (*b*) density function.

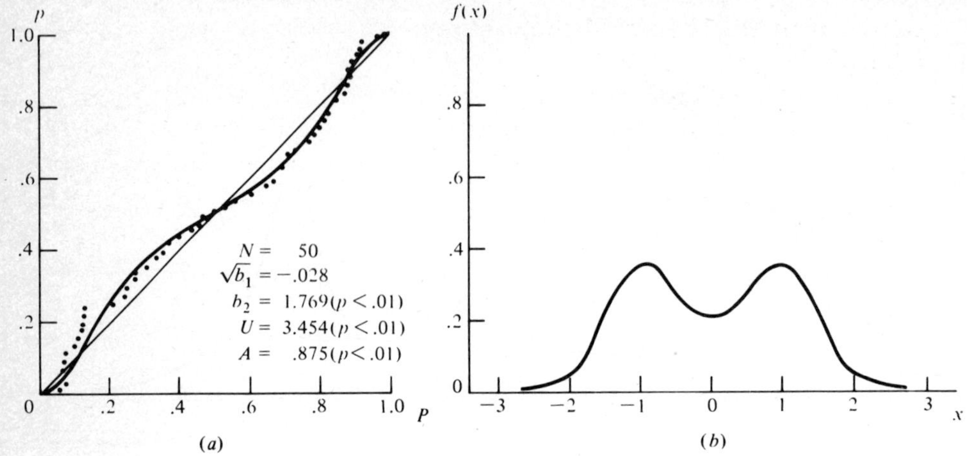

FIGURE 3.5-6
(*a*) Cumulative normal plot of a bimodal population and sample; (*b*) density function.

be less regular and capable of revealing only a very marked skewness of the population.

When the population is symmetric and leptokurtic, as in Fig. 3.5-4*b*, the curve crosses the identity line from the *lower left* to the *upper right* near the center of the plot. Conversely, in a symmetric platykurtic population, as in Fig. 3.5-5, the curve crosses the identity line from *upper left* to *lower right* near the center of the plot. Again the plot for a sample of size 50 conforms closely to the population trend and is easy to interpret.

A symmetric bimodal population, Fig. 3.5-6, appears in the plot as if it were an extreme expression of a platykurtic distribution; i.e., the plot crosses the identity line from *upper left* to *lower right* near the center. However, the departure from the identity line is greater when the population is bimodal.

3.5.2 Departures from Normality

Certain types of departure from normality are common in behavioral data and may be apparent in the cumulative normal plot.

1 Outliers. By far the most frequent and most serious violation of distribution assumptions are due to isolated erroneous data values, usually the result of clerical errors in recording or transcribing. However, in psychological data, such errors may also be due to malingering on the part of the subjects, or failure of subjects to understand instructions. Similarly, instrument malfunction, errors of optical scanning devices, deterioration of magnetic tapes, computer hardware errors, etc., may introduce errors. Usually, errors from these sources produce observed values which are outside the range of the valid data (otherwise they go undetected!). In the cumulative normal plot, they tend to make the sample appear leptokurtic or skew. If the outliers are identified and deleted from the data, the plot of the remaining points may then appear straight and serve to check normality for the valid observations.

2 Truncation. Another serious source of nonnormality is truncation of the observations due to a "floor" or "ceiling" on the range of the measuring instrument. In psychological work, this is often the result of test items or response criteria that are too "hard" or too "easy" for subjects in the population under study. This type of departure appears as a right skew (Fig. 3.5-3) in the cumulative normal plot when the items are too hard, or as a left skew (Fig. 3.5-2) when the items are too easy. If a large fraction of the sample falls beyond the floor or the ceiling, a quantitative treatment of the data may not be possible. However, a qualitative treatment distinguishing subjects above and below the truncation points may salvage some of the information in the data (see Chap. 8).

3 Mixed series. If the investigator has unknowingly defined as a population a mixture of two or more normal populations, the sample distribution may show evidence of departure from normality. The most likely possibility is that the parent populations have different means and possibly different standard deviations. If the populations are the same size and overlap considerably, only a slight tendency toward a platykurtic distribution will be apparent, and the departure will be difficult to detect in samples of moderate size. If one population is larger than the other, the effect will be a skewing of the mixed distribution toward the range of the smaller population.

If two populations are well separated (i.e., the difference between the means is great relative to the standard deviation), the mixed distribution will be bimodal, and the plot will appear as in Fig. 3.5-6. If n separate populations are involved, the density will be multimodal, and the cumulative plot will cross the identity line $n + 1$ times. When only two or three populations are involved and are sufficiently well separated, it is possible, by numerical methods, to resolve the separate distributions from the sample and estimate the separate means, the proportions, and the common standard deviation [Day, 1969].

4 Log normality. In certain types of growth data, it is not unusual to find a logarithmic normal distribution (see Sec. 3.1-4). These distributions are skewed to the right (toward high values) and in the sample yield normal plots of the type shown in Fig. 3.5-3. If the parent population is truly log normal, a plot of $\log x_i$ as the variate will appear as a straight line on the cumulative normal plot. If this is the case, the logarithms of the observations may be treated as normally distributed for the purposes of subsequent data analysis.

3.5.3 Statistical Tests of Departure from Univariate Normality

A number of statistical tests have been proposed that are sensitive to various types of departure from univariate normality. Unlike the chi-square test, certain of these tests do not require grouping of the data. We describe here four tests of this type which are especially valuable in detecting the types of departure from normality discussed in Sec. 3.4.2. References to tables of percentage points required in these tests are given. The values of each of these four statistics are shown for the data of Example 3.5-1 in Figs. 3.5-1*a* to 3.5-6*a*.

The coefficient of skewness The sample coefficient of skewness is defined as the square root of the following ratio of sample second and third central moments, (3.2-35) and (3.2-36):

$$b_1 = \frac{\tilde{\mu}_3{}^2}{\tilde{\mu}_2{}^3}$$

Percentage points for the statistic $\sqrt{b_1}$, when the parent population is normal, may be found in Pearson and Hartley [1966] for $N > 24$, and in D'Agostino and Tietjen [1973] for $N = 5$ to 35. Significance of this statistic is evidence of skew to the left when $\tilde{\mu}_3$ is negative, and skew to the right when $\tilde{\mu}_3$ is positive. In large samples, percentage points for $\sqrt{b_1}$ are well approximated by using as a unit normal deviate the statistic

$$z_1 = \pm\sqrt{\frac{b_1(N+1)(N+3)}{6(N-2)}}$$

where N is the sample size, and the undetermined sign is the same as that of the third moment. The value of $\sqrt{b_1}$ for the sample data in Example 3.5-1 is shown in each figure.

The coefficient of kurtosis The sample coefficient of kurtosis is computed from the sample second and fourth central moments, (3.2-35) and (3.2-37), as follows:

$$b_2 = \frac{\tilde{\mu}_4}{\tilde{\mu}_2{}^2}$$

Percentage points of b_2 when the population is normal may be found in Pearson and Hartley [1966] for $N > 49$, and D'Agostino and Tietjen [1971] for $N = 7$ to 50. In large samples, percentage points may be approximated by using as a unit normal deviate the statistic

$$z_2 = \left(b_2 - 3 + \frac{6}{N+1}\right)\sqrt{\frac{(N+1)^2(N+3)(N+5)}{24N(N-2)(N-3)}}$$

Values of b_2 greater than 3 indicate that the distribution is more peaked with higher tails than the normal distribution; values less than 3 indicate a distribution flatter in the center and with lower tails than the normal distribution.

The *U* statistic (ratio of sample range to sample standard deviation) David, Hartley, and Pearson [1954] propose, as a test which is especially sensitive to outliers, the ratio of the sample range to sample standard deviation:

$$U = \frac{\max(x) - \min(x)}{N\hat{\sigma}}$$

where $\hat{\sigma}$ is obtained from the unbiased estimate of the variance in the same sample; that is,

$$\hat{\sigma} = \sqrt{\frac{\sum_{i=1}^{N} x_i^2 - Nx.^2}{N - 1}}$$

where $x.$ is the sample mean. Percentage points for U are given in Pearson and Hartley [1966].

Geary's *A* statistic (ratio of mean deviation to standard deviation) A test which is sensitive to kurtosis has been proposed by Geary [1947]. The statistic is

$$A = \frac{\sum_{i=1}^{N} |x_i - x.|}{\sqrt{N(\Sigma x_i^2 - Nx.^2)}}$$

Percentage points for A are given in Pearson and Hartley [1966].

4

PRINCIPLES AND METHODS OF MULTIVARIATE LEAST-SQUARES ESTIMATION

4.1 POLYNOMIAL REGRESSION ANALYSIS: UNIVARIATE

A basic problem in data analysis is that of constructing a curve which best represents the relationship between a dependent variable y and an independent variable x. We assume that y is a continuously distributed random variable, but allow the variable x to take on any arbitrary finite values, provided at least two, and preferably more, are distinct.

If a pronounced systematic relationship exists between the dependent and independent variables, their paired values in the data, when plotted in xy coordinates, may clearly determine the line of relationship. For many purposes, it may be satisfactory to draw the best-fitting curve "by eye." In the case of a straight-line relationship, this graphical method can be surprisingly accurate. The equation of the relationship in this case can easily be estimated from the y intercept and slope of the fitted line. (See Bock and Jones [1968, Chaps. 2 and 3] for applications of this method.)

When the relationship is curvilinear, or not well determined by the data, or when the procedure is to be automated, a more accurate and objective method of curve fitting is needed. A quite satisfactory approach is to define a formal goodness-of-fit criterion and to seek a curve which optimizes this criterion in the data. By far the most widely used procedure of this type is the classical *method of least squares*, due to Legendre and Gauss (see Deutsch [1965] for a historical résumé). In this chapter we discuss the method of least squares, and its modern elaborations, in the context of fitting curves which may be represented by univariate and multivariate polynomial models. This application of least squares is called *polynomial regression analysis*. To illustrate its relevance to behavioral research, we begin the discussion with an example from the psychological literature.

EXAMPLE 4.1-1 (*Hypnotic age regression*) It is well known that hypnotized subjects, when under the suggestion of being younger in age, will respond with age-appropriate behavior. It is usually not clear, however, whether the subjects are merely mimicking age-appropriate behavior or are actually regressing to an earlier stage of behavioral development. In order to decide between these two interpretations, Parrish, Lundy, and Leibowitz [1968] tested hypnotic age-regression effects in the Ponzo and Poggendorff illusions (Figs. 4.1-1 and 4.1-2).* The developmental trend in susceptibility to these illusions (Table 4.1-1) established by Leibowitz and Judisch [1967], Leibowitz and Gwozdicki [1967], and others, would not be known to naive subjects.

* In the Ponzo illusion the subject is required to adjust the length of the right-hand vertical line to match that of the line on the left. In the Poggendorff illusion, the subject positions the right-hand bar as a continuation of the bar on the left. The subject's error in these adjustments is measured and recorded.

Table 4.1-1 MAGNITUDE OF THE PONZO AND POGGENDORFF ILLUSIONS AS A FUNCTION OF AGE

Mean age, years	N	Ponzo*		Poggendorff†	
		Mean, in.	SD	Mean, in.	SD
5.0	16	.09	.20	1.83	.36
6.0	16	.28	.23	1.70	.52
7.0	16	.37	.19	1.30	.46
8.5	16	.41	.21	1.29	.36
10.5	16	.48	.28	1.07	.34
12.5	16	.32	.19	1.03	.39
14.5	16	.42	.21	1.03	.41
16.5	16	.49	.18	1.00	.40
19.5	16	.55	.24	1.06	.38

* Adapted from Leibowitz and Judisch [1967].
† Adapted from Leibowitz and Gwozdicki [1967].

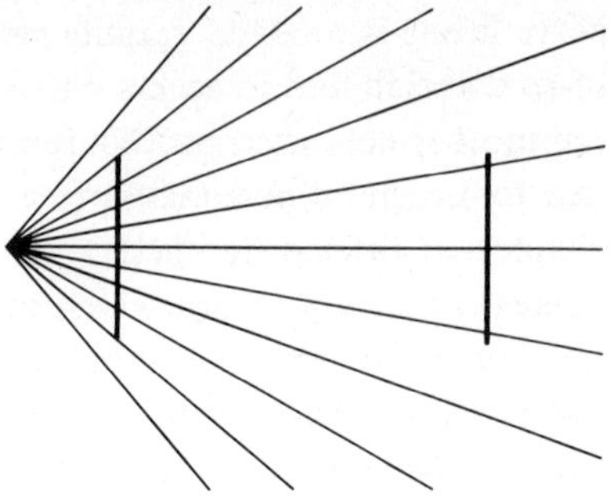

FIGURE 4.1-1
The Ponzo illusion.

The statistical problem in this application is to test the hypothesis that the responses of subjects, hypnotically regressed to a given age, belong to the response distribution typical of nonhypnotized subjects *of that age*. This is a problem in conditional distributions. We wish to know whether the responses of the hypnotized subjects could have arisen from the conditional response distribution for normal subjects of a given age. If the size of illusion y, at age x, is normally distributed for all x, this problem has a unique optimal solution in terms of functions relating the conditional mean and variance to age. Let these functions be designated respectively by

$$\mathscr{E}(y \mid x) = f(x)$$

and

$$\mathscr{V}(y \mid x) = g(x)$$

Suppose we are able to determine these functions empirically from normal developmental data for the illusions such as reproduced in Table 4.1-1. Then we shall be able to express the illusion of an age-regressed subject as a t statistic for deviation from the conditional mean. If this statistic is sufficiently extreme (e.g., beyond the .05 level), we would consider the response of the subject to be evidence against a developmental theory of hypnotic age regression. Otherwise, the response could have arisen from normal subjects of an appropriate age and would not contradict the theory.

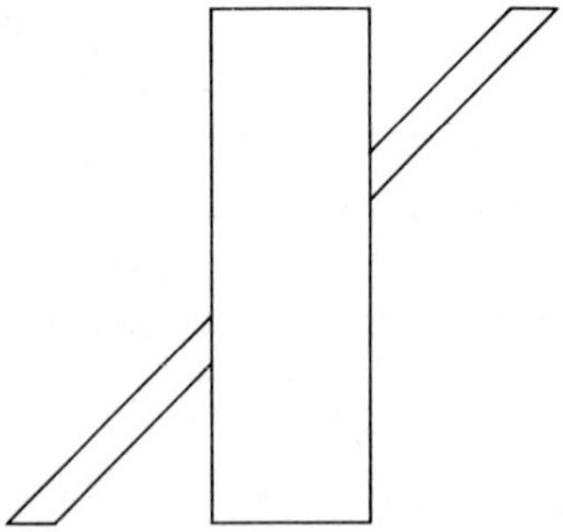

FIGURE 4.1-2
The Poggendorff illusion.

There is ample precedent in the psychological literature for assuming normal distribution of errors in data obtained, as they were in this case, by the method of adjustment [Guilford, 1954]. Indeed, many types of sensory judgments involving small stimulus differences appear to be normally distributed (Culler [1926]; Bock and Jones [1968, page 114]). Thus, we have some empirical justification for assuming normal conditional distributions for the Ponzo and Poggendorff illusions, which in turn justifies our interest in fitting the functions $f(x)$ and $g(x)$ to the data by means of polynomial regression analysis.

As for $g(x)$, we observe first that the standard deviations for the age groups shown in Table 4.1-1 are generally homogeneous for either illusion. This suggests that the conditional variance is homoscedastic, i.e., that we may assume $g(x) = \sigma^2$. Thus, in the regression analysis we only need to obtain some best estimate of this common σ^2. As for $f(x)$, the graphs in Figs. 4.1-6 and 4.1-7, and Sec. 4.1.10a clearly indicate that a quadratic or higher-degree polynomial will be required to fit the illusions. The function for the Ponzo illusion will be increasing and decelerating, while that for the Poggendorff will be decreasing and decelerating. We now take up the problem of fitting these polynomials.

4.1.1 The Polynomial Model

If y is the response variable and x the fixed (nonrandom) variable, the polynomial model of degree g may be expressed as

$$y = \beta_0 + \beta_1 x + \beta_2 x^2 + \cdots + \beta_g x^g + \epsilon \qquad (4.1\text{-}1)$$

The quantity y is the observed response, and x is the corresponding known value of the independent variable. In the example, y is the size of the illusion in inches, and x is the age of the subject in years. The error component ϵ is an unobservable random variable. In the estimation phase of the regression analysis, *we need only assume that ϵ is distributed with zero mean and finite variance*, but in the tests of significance and construction of confidence intervals, we shall require the assumption $\epsilon \sim N(0,\sigma^2)$. The regression coefficients β_k, $k = 0, 1, 2, \ldots, g$, are the unknown parameters of the model which are to be estimated from the data.

4.1.2 The Model for the Group Means

For the sake of generality, let us immediately extend the polynomial model (4.1-1) to the case of replicated observations for each value of x, such as is represented by the data in Table 4.1-1. In this case, we identify subpopulations of subjects for whom $x = x_j$, $j = 1, 2, \ldots, n$. Suppose a random sample of N_j subjects is taken from subpopulation j. Let the mean response for this sample be

$$y_{\cdot j} = \frac{\sum_{i=1}^{N_j} y_{ij}}{N_j} \qquad (4.1\text{-}2)$$

We shall refer to (4.1-2) as the *mean for group j*. If (4.1-1) is the model for each member of this group, the model for the group mean is

$$y_{\cdot j} = \beta_0 + \beta_1 x_j + \beta_2 x_j^2 + \cdots + \beta_g x_j^g + \frac{\sum_{i=1}^{N_j} \epsilon_{ij}}{N_j}$$

$$= \beta_0 + \beta_1 x_j + \beta_2 x_j^2 + \cdots + \beta_g x_j^g + \epsilon_{\cdot j} \tag{4.1-3}$$

Because the observations are independent, the mean error is distributed with mean 0 and variance σ^2/N_j (see Sec. 3.4.2). Also, the group means are independent because each group contains different subjects. In a study consisting of n groups, the number of subjects in the total sample is $N = \sum_{j=1}^{n} N_j$. When all $N_j = 1$, the replicated model specializes to the unreplicated case.

4.1.3 Estimating the Regression Coefficients by Least Squares

For the case of replicated data, the method of least squares may be described as follows: Let

$$e_{\cdot j} = y_{\cdot j} - (\beta_0 + \beta_1 x_j + \beta_2 x_j^2 + \cdots + \beta_g x_j^g)$$

be the difference between the observed mean for group j and the value of the polynomial part of the model for that group. According to the least-squares principle, the model should be fitted by choosing the β's so as to minimize the sum of squares of these differences, weighted by the respective sample sizes—that is, by minimizing

$$Q = \sum_{j=1}^{n} N_j e_{\cdot j}^2 \tag{4.1-4}$$

with respect to variation in $\beta_0, \beta_1, \beta_2, \ldots, \beta_g$.

To carry out this minimization, it is convenient to express Q in matrix notation: Let the $n \times 1$ vector of differences be

$$\mathbf{e}_{\cdot} = \mathbf{y}_{\cdot} - \mathbf{X}\boldsymbol{\beta}$$

where the vector of observed group means is

$$\mathbf{y}'_{\cdot} = [y_{\cdot 1}, y_{\cdot 2}, \ldots, y_{\cdot n}]$$

The matrix of powers of the independent variable is

$$\mathbf{X} = \begin{bmatrix} 1 & x_1 & x_1^2 & \cdots & x_1^g \\ 1 & x_2 & x_2^2 & \cdots & x_2^g \\ \cdots & \cdots & \cdots & \cdots & \cdots \\ 1 & x_n & x_n^2 & \cdots & x_n^g \end{bmatrix} \tag{4.1-5}$$

and the vector of regression coefficients is

$$\boldsymbol{\beta}' = [\beta_0, \beta_1, \beta_2, \ldots, \beta_g]$$

Now let

$$\mathbf{D} = \text{diag}[N_1, N_2, \ldots, N_n]$$

be a diagonal matrix containing the sample sizes. With these quantities, we may express (4.1-4) as

$$Q = \mathbf{e}'_{.}\mathbf{D}\mathbf{e}_{.} = (\mathbf{y}_{.} - \mathbf{X}\boldsymbol{\beta})'\mathbf{D}(\mathbf{y}_{.} - \mathbf{X}\boldsymbol{\beta}) \qquad (4.1\text{-}6)$$

There are several possible approaches to the problem of minimizing Q. One approach is the formal application of calculus using the matrix derivatives of Sec. 2.5. The steps are as follows: First we expand the right member of (4.1-6) to obtain

$$Q = \mathbf{y}'_{.}\mathbf{D}\mathbf{y}_{.} - 2\mathbf{y}'_{.}\mathbf{D}\mathbf{X}\boldsymbol{\beta} + \boldsymbol{\beta}'\mathbf{X}'\mathbf{D}\mathbf{X}\boldsymbol{\beta}$$

Then, by (2.5-13) and (2.5-16),

$$\frac{\partial Q}{\partial \boldsymbol{\beta}} = -2\mathbf{X}'\mathbf{D}\mathbf{y}_{.} + 2\mathbf{X}'\mathbf{D}\mathbf{X}\boldsymbol{\beta}$$

Equating $\partial Q/\partial \boldsymbol{\beta}$ to the null vector as a necessary condition for Q to be a minimum, we obtain the so-called *normal equations*:

$$\mathbf{X}'\mathbf{D}\mathbf{X}\hat{\boldsymbol{\beta}} - \mathbf{X}'\mathbf{D}\mathbf{y}_{.} = \mathbf{0} \qquad (4.1\text{-}7)$$

Transposing the constant vector in (4.1-7), we have a system of $g + 1$ nonhomogeneous linear equations in $g + 1$ unknowns:

$$(\mathbf{X}'\mathbf{D}\mathbf{X})\hat{\boldsymbol{\beta}} = \mathbf{X}'\mathbf{D}\mathbf{y}_{.} \qquad (4.1\text{-}8)$$

According to the results in Sec. 2.3.4, (4.1-8) has a unique solution for $\boldsymbol{\beta}$ if and only if

$$\operatorname{rank}(\mathbf{X}'\mathbf{D}\mathbf{X}) = g + 1 \qquad (4.1\text{-}9)$$

Because the rank of a matrix product cannot exceed the rank of any of its factors, we know that the number of rows in $\mathbf{X}$ must exceed g in order for condition (4.1-9) to hold; that is, the degree of the polynomial model must be less than the number of groups ($g < n$). If we allow the possibility that some of the groups are empty (without subjects), a necessary condition for (4.1-9) is that the number of *nonzero* elements in $\mathbf{D}$ exceeds g.

In the case of the polynomial model, it is easy to show that this is also a sufficient condition. For if we write

$$\mathbf{X}'\mathbf{D}\mathbf{X} = \mathbf{X}'\mathbf{D}^{1/2}\mathbf{D}^{1/2}\mathbf{X} = (\mathbf{D}^{1/2}\mathbf{X})'\mathbf{D}^{1/2}\mathbf{X}$$

we see that $\mathbf{X}'\mathbf{D}\mathbf{X}$ is a grammian matrix whose rank is equal to that of $\mathbf{X}$ (Sec. 2.7.2). The matrix $\mathbf{X}$ consists of the leading $g + 1$ columns of a Vandermonde matrix of order n (see Exercise 2.3-1), and any $g + 1$ rows and leading $g + 1$ columns of $\mathbf{X}$ constitute a Vandermonde matrix of order $g + 1$. But a Vandermonde matrix is well known to be of full rank if the values of x are distinct [Browne, 1958, page 34]; thus, $\mathbf{X}$ is of rank $g + 1$ if any $g + 1$ of the x are distinct. In the case of grouped data, the values of the independent variable corresponding to different groups are necessarily distinct. The existence of $g + 1$ or more nonempty groups is therefore a sufficient condition for (4.1-9) and thus for the existence of a unique solution of the normal equation. The solution is given by

$$\hat{\boldsymbol{\beta}} = (\mathbf{X}'\mathbf{D}\mathbf{X})^{-1}\mathbf{X}'\mathbf{D}\mathbf{y}_{.} \qquad (4.1\text{-}10)$$

The inverse matrix in (4.1-10) may be computed by one of the methods in Sec. 2.3.3 or 2.7.2.

To show that $\hat{\boldsymbol{\beta}}$ corresponds to a *proper minimum* of Q, we obtain the matrix of second derivatives using (2.5-36):

$$\frac{\partial^2 Q}{\partial \boldsymbol{\beta}\, \partial \boldsymbol{\beta}'} = 2(\mathbf{X}'\mathbf{D}\mathbf{X})$$

Because $\mathbf{X}'\mathbf{D}\mathbf{X}$ is a full-rank grammian matrix which does not depend upon the observation or the unknowns, the curvature of the surface described by Q as a function of $\boldsymbol{\beta}$ is constant and is positive everywhere. Hence, one and only one minimum exists in the space of $\boldsymbol{\beta}$, and that minimum is at $\boldsymbol{\beta} = \hat{\boldsymbol{\beta}}$. Of course, the matrix $\mathbf{X}'\mathbf{D}\mathbf{X}$ may be so ill conditioned that a practical solution may be difficult to compute (see Noble [1969, Chap. 8]), but in principle a unique solution always exists.

4.1.4 A Solution Without Calculus

The least-squares estimator may also be obtained algebraically in a solution that is in some ways more instructive than that using calculus. The algebraic solution turns on the fact that the grammian matrix $\mathbf{X}'\mathbf{D}\mathbf{X}$ may be expressed as the product of a matrix factor and its transpose. Let us use the Cholesky factorization

$$\mathbf{X}'\mathbf{D}\mathbf{X} = \mathbf{S}\mathbf{S}'$$

for this purpose (Sec. 2.7.2).

We assume that $\mathbf{X}'\mathbf{D}\mathbf{X}$ is nonsingular so that the inverse of the Cholesky factor, $\mathbf{S}^{-1}$, also exists. Then we may *reparameterize* the model for the group means by setting $\boldsymbol{\beta} = (\mathbf{S}^{-1})'\boldsymbol{\gamma}$. Expanding (4.1-6) and substituting $(\mathbf{S}^{-1})'\boldsymbol{\gamma}$ for $\boldsymbol{\beta}$, we obtain, using (2.7-8),

$$\begin{aligned} Q &= \mathbf{y}_{.}'\mathbf{D}\mathbf{y}_{.} - 2\mathbf{y}_{.}'\mathbf{D}\mathbf{X}(\mathbf{S}^{-1})'\boldsymbol{\gamma} + \boldsymbol{\gamma}'\mathbf{S}^{-1}\mathbf{X}'\mathbf{D}\mathbf{X}(\mathbf{S}^{-1})'\boldsymbol{\gamma} \\ &= \mathbf{y}_{.}'\mathbf{D}\mathbf{y}_{.} - 2\mathbf{y}_{.}'\mathbf{D}\mathbf{X}(\mathbf{S}^{-1})'\boldsymbol{\gamma} + \boldsymbol{\gamma}'\boldsymbol{\gamma} \end{aligned}$$

Now "complete the square" for the part of this expression involving $\boldsymbol{\gamma}$:

$$\begin{aligned} Q &= \mathbf{y}_{.}'\mathbf{D}\mathbf{y}_{.} + [\mathbf{y}_{.}'\mathbf{D}\mathbf{X}(\mathbf{S}^{-1})'\mathbf{S}^{-1}\mathbf{X}'\mathbf{D}\mathbf{y}_{.} - 2\mathbf{y}_{.}'\mathbf{D}\mathbf{X}(\mathbf{S}^{-1})'\boldsymbol{\gamma} + \boldsymbol{\gamma}'\boldsymbol{\gamma}] \\ &\qquad - \mathbf{y}_{.}'\mathbf{D}\mathbf{X}(\mathbf{S}^{-1})'\mathbf{S}^{-1}\mathbf{X}'\mathbf{D}\mathbf{y}_{.} \\ &= \mathbf{y}_{.}'\mathbf{D}\mathbf{y}_{.} + (\mathbf{S}^{-1}\mathbf{X}'\mathbf{D}\mathbf{y}_{.} - \boldsymbol{\gamma})'(\mathbf{S}^{-1}\mathbf{X}'\mathbf{D}\mathbf{y}_{.} - \boldsymbol{\gamma}) - \mathbf{y}_{.}'\mathbf{D}\mathbf{X}(\mathbf{X}'\mathbf{D}\mathbf{X})^{-1}\mathbf{X}'\mathbf{D}\mathbf{y}_{.} \qquad (4.1\text{-}11) \end{aligned}$$

Each term in (4.1-11) may be expressed as a sum of squares and is therefore nonnegative. This implies that Q obtains its minimum with respect to variation in $\boldsymbol{\gamma}$ when the second term equals zero, i.e., when $\boldsymbol{\gamma}$ is set equal to

$$\hat{\boldsymbol{\gamma}} = \mathbf{S}^{-1}\mathbf{X}'\mathbf{D}\mathbf{y}_{.} \qquad (4.1\text{-}12)$$

But if $\hat{\gamma}$ minimizes Q, then so does $\mathbf{S}'\hat{\boldsymbol{\beta}} = \hat{\gamma}$. Since $\mathbf{S}$ is nonsingular,

$$\hat{\boldsymbol{\beta}} = (\mathbf{S}^{-1})'\hat{\gamma} = (\mathbf{S}^{-1})'\mathbf{S}^{-1}\mathbf{X}'\mathbf{D}\mathbf{y}_{.} = (\mathbf{X}'\mathbf{D}\mathbf{X})^{-1}\mathbf{X}'\mathbf{D}\mathbf{y}_{.} \qquad (4.1\text{-}13)$$

which agrees with (4.1-10). It also implies that the value of the residual sum of squares is

$$Q_{\min} = \mathbf{y}'_{.}\mathbf{D}\mathbf{y}_{.} - \mathbf{y}'_{.}\mathbf{D}\mathbf{X}(\mathbf{X}'\mathbf{D}\mathbf{X})^{-1}\mathbf{X}'\mathbf{D}\mathbf{y}_{.}$$

or, equivalently,

$$Q_{\min} = \mathbf{y}'_{.}\mathbf{D}\mathbf{y}_{.} - \hat{\gamma}'\hat{\gamma} = \mathbf{y}'_{.}\mathbf{D}\mathbf{y}_{.} - \hat{\boldsymbol{\beta}}\mathbf{X}'\mathbf{D}\mathbf{X}\hat{\boldsymbol{\beta}}$$

Thus, the weighted sum of squares of the group means, $\mathbf{y}'_{.}\mathbf{D}\mathbf{y}_{.}$, may be expressed identically as a sum of quadratic forms in $\mathbf{y}_{.}$,

$$\mathbf{y}'_{.}\mathbf{D}\mathbf{y}_{.} = \mathbf{y}'_{.}\mathbf{D}\mathbf{X}(\mathbf{X}'\mathbf{D}\mathbf{X})^{-1}\mathbf{X}'\mathbf{D}\mathbf{y}_{.} + \mathbf{y}'_{.}[\mathbf{D} - \mathbf{D}\mathbf{X}(\mathbf{X}'\mathbf{D}\mathbf{X})^{-1}\mathbf{X}'\mathbf{D}]\mathbf{y}_{.} \qquad (4.1\text{-}14)$$

where the first term on the right is the sum of squares due to estimation, and the second term is the residual sum of squares. This partition of sum of squares is the basis of the analysis of variance discussed in Sec. 4.1.7.

An obvious and important corollary of the above result is that, if the parameters of the model are subjected to any nonsingular linear transformation, the least-squares estimate of the transform is the transform of least-squares estimates, and the residual sum of squares is invariant under the transformation. This means that once we have obtained least-squares estimates of certain parameters, we may form any nonsingular linear transformations of them and the resulting transforms will also be least-squares estimates. The fit of the model will not be affected.

4.1.5 A Geometric Solution

Finally and in contrast with the preceding formal solutions, we may obtain the least-squares estimator by purely geometric reasoning. Interpreted geometrically, the model depicts the group mean vector as the resultant of a vector in the space spanned by the columns of $\mathbf{X}$ (the estimation space) and a residual vector in the error space:

$$\begin{aligned}\mathbf{y}_{.} &= \beta_0\mathbf{x}_0 + \beta_1\mathbf{x}_1 + \beta_2\mathbf{x}_2 + \cdots + \beta_g\mathbf{x}_g + \mathbf{e}_{.}\\ &= \mathbf{X}\boldsymbol{\beta} + \mathbf{e}_{.}\end{aligned}$$

For the case $g = 1$ and $n = 3$, the vector representation of the model can be shown concretely in a perspective drawing such as Fig. 4.1-3. The model represented in Fig. 4.1-3 is

$$\underset{3\times 1}{\mathbf{y}_{.}} = \beta_0\underset{3\times 1}{\mathbf{x}_0} + \beta_1\underset{3\times 1}{\mathbf{x}_1} + \underset{3\times 1}{\mathbf{e}_{.}}$$

$$\begin{bmatrix} y_{.1} \\ y_{.2} \\ y_{.3} \end{bmatrix} = \beta_0 \begin{bmatrix} 1 \\ 1 \\ 1 \end{bmatrix} + \beta_1 \begin{bmatrix} x_1 \\ x_2 \\ x_3 \end{bmatrix} + \begin{bmatrix} e_{.1} \\ e_{.2} \\ e_{.3} \end{bmatrix} \qquad (4.1\text{-}15)$$

The termini of the vectors $\mathbf{x}_0, \mathbf{x}_1$, together with the origin, determine the *estimation plane* shown in perspective in Fig. 4.1-3. The observational vector $\mathbf{y}_{.}$ is

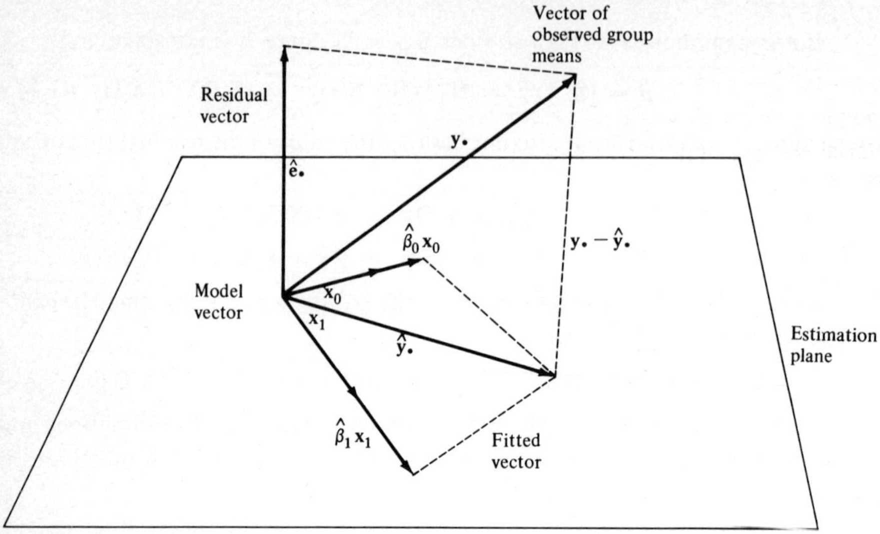

FIGURE 4.1-3
Geometric representation of least-squares estimation.

in general outside the plane as shown. The problem in least-squares estimation is to choose β_0 and β_1 so that the square length of the vector $\mathbf{e}.$ in the metric $\mathbf{D}$ is minimal. This means that the distance, with respect to the metric, between the point $\mathbf{y}.$ and the point $\hat{\mathbf{y}}. = \hat{\beta}_0\mathbf{x}_0 + \hat{\beta}_1\mathbf{x}_1$ in the estimation plane must be as small as possible.

It is well known from Euclid that the shortest distance between a plane and a point outside the plane is along a line normal to the plane. This implies that the least-squares solution is obtained when the vector $\hat{\mathbf{y}}.$ is so placed that the residual vector $\hat{\mathbf{e}}. = \mathbf{y}. - \hat{\mathbf{y}}.$ is normal, in the metric $\mathbf{D}$, to the estimation plane. But to satisfy this condition, $\hat{\mathbf{e}}$ must be orthogonal, with respect to $\mathbf{D}$, to every vector in the estimation plane including, in particular, the vectors $\mathbf{x}_0$ and $\mathbf{x}_1$. Thus, a necessary and sufficient condition for the least-squares solution is that the residual vectors satisfy the *normal* equations

$$\mathbf{x}_0'\mathbf{D}\hat{\mathbf{e}}. = 0$$

$$\mathbf{x}_1'\mathbf{D}\hat{\mathbf{e}}. = 0$$

Writing these equations in a single matrix expression, we have

$$\begin{bmatrix} \mathbf{x}_0' \\ \mathbf{x}_1' \end{bmatrix} \mathbf{D}\hat{\mathbf{e}}. = \mathbf{X}'\mathbf{D}\hat{\mathbf{e}}. = \mathbf{X}'\mathbf{D}(\mathbf{y}. - \mathbf{X}\hat{\boldsymbol{\beta}}) = \mathbf{0}$$

or

$$\mathbf{X}'\mathbf{D}\mathbf{X}\hat{\boldsymbol{\beta}} = \mathbf{X}'\mathbf{D}\mathbf{y}. \tag{4.1-16}$$

which is the same as (4.1-8).

As we shall see in Sec. 4.1.7, the geometric interpretation also clarifies the analysis of variance associated with least squares.

EXAMPLE 4.1-2 (*Computing the least-squares estimates*) To illustrate the calculation of the sample regression coefficients, we attempt to fit a quadratic ($g = 2$) polynomial to the data of Table 4.1-1. The powers x^0, x^1, x^2 of the independent variable, age, appear in the columns of the $\mathbf{X}$ matrix, which is the same for both illusions:

$$\mathbf{X} = \begin{bmatrix} 1 & 5.0 & 25.00 \\ 1 & 6.0 & 36.00 \\ 1 & 7.0 & 49.00 \\ 1 & 8.5 & 72.25 \\ 1 & 10.5 & 110.25 \\ 1 & 12.5 & 156.25 \\ 1 & 14.5 & 210.25 \\ 1 & 16.5 & 272.25 \\ 1 & 19.5 & 380.25 \end{bmatrix}$$

Since all groups have 16 subjects in this example, $\mathbf{D} = 16\mathbf{I}$. Thus,

$$\mathbf{X}'\mathbf{D}\mathbf{X} = 16 \begin{bmatrix} 9 & & (\text{symmetric}) \\ 100 & 1{,}311.5 & \\ 1{,}311.5 & 19{,}364.5 & 309{,}026.375 \end{bmatrix}$$

and the inverse matrix to six decimal places is

$$(\mathbf{X}'\mathbf{D}\mathbf{X})^{-1} = \frac{1}{16} \begin{bmatrix} 5.084278 & & (\text{symmetric}) \\ -.923783 & .178043 & \\ .036309 & -.007236 & .000303 \end{bmatrix}$$

Let us designate the vector of group means for the Ponzo illusion by $\mathbf{y}.^{(1)}$ and for the Poggendorff illusion by $\mathbf{y}.^{(2)}$ (see Table 4.1-1). From these means, we compute the constant terms in the normal equations for the illusions as follows:

$$\mathbf{X}'\mathbf{D}\mathbf{y}.^{(1)} = 16 \begin{bmatrix} 3.4100 \\ 42.1450 \\ 593.8475 \end{bmatrix}$$

and

$$\mathbf{X}'\mathbf{D}\mathbf{y}.^{(2)} = 16 \begin{bmatrix} 11.31 \\ 115.63 \\ 1{,}434.63 \end{bmatrix}$$

Premultiplication of these constant vectors by the inverse matrix gives the corresponding least-squares estimates of the regression coefficients:

$$\hat{\boldsymbol{\beta}}^{(1)} = (\mathbf{X}'\mathbf{D}\mathbf{X})^{-1}\mathbf{X}'\mathbf{D}\mathbf{y}.^{(1)} = \begin{bmatrix} -.0331924 \\ .0563326 \\ -.0014674 \end{bmatrix}$$

and

$$\hat{\boldsymbol{\beta}}^{(2)} = (\mathbf{X}'\mathbf{D}\mathbf{X})^{-1}\mathbf{X}'\mathbf{D}\mathbf{y}.^{(2)} = \begin{bmatrix} 2.776735 \\ -.242116 \\ .008030 \end{bmatrix}$$

for the Ponzo and Poggendorff illusions, respectively.

The corresponding equations of the best-fitting quadratic functions for the means of the conditional distributions are, therefore,

$$\hat{y}._{}^{(1)} = -.0331924 + .0563326x - .0014674x^2 \qquad (4.1\text{-}17)$$

and

$$\hat{y}._{}^{(2)} = 2.776735 - .242116x + .008030x^2 \qquad (4.1\text{-}18)$$

In a continuation of this example in Sec. 4.1.8, we test whether these functions actually fit the data. Less formally, however, it is clear from the residuals in Table 4.1-2 that the function for the Poggendorff illusion is in close accord with the data, whereas that for the Ponzo is not. These residuals are computed as

$$\hat{\mathbf{e}}. = \hat{\mathbf{y}}. - \hat{\mathbf{y}}.$$

Note for the Poggendorff that the largest residual, $-.1753$, is compared to a range of $1.83 - 1.06 = .77$ in the observed means, while the largest for the Ponzo, $-.1218$, is compared to a range of $.55 - .09 = .46$.

4.1.6 Statistical Properties of the Least-Squares Estimator

The least-squares estimator obtained in Secs. 4.1.3 to 4.1.5 is a function of sample quantities and therefore has a sampling distribution. The extent to which we are able to characterize this distribution, and thus determine the statistical properties of the estimate, depends upon the assumptions we make about the error term in the model. If we hold to the minimal assumptions of independent and homoscedastic errors, we cannot obtain the exact form of the distribution, but we may readily derive expressions

Table 4.1-2 RESIDUALS FROM THE GROUP MEANS IN THE FITTING OF A QUADRATIC POLYNOMIAL TO DATA FOR THE PONZO AND POGGENDORFF ILLUSIONS

	Ponzo			Poggendorff		
Age x	Observed $y._{}^{(1)}$	Estimated $\hat{y}._{}^{(1)}$	Residual $\hat{e}._{}^{(1)}$	Observed $y._{}^{(2)}$	Estimated $\hat{y}._{}^{(2)}$	Residual $\hat{e}._{}^{(2)}$
5.0	.09	.2118	−.1218	1.83	1.7688	.0631
6.0	.28	.2520	.0280	1.70	1.6131	.0768
7.0	.37	.2892	.0808	1.30	1.4753	−.1753
8.5	.41	.3396	.0704	1.29	1.2988	.0088
10.5	.48	.3965	.0835	1.07	1.1197	−.0497
12.5	.32	.4417	−.1217	1.03	1.0049	.0250
14.5	.42	.4751	.0551	1.03	.9543	.0756
16.5	.49	.4968	−.0068	1.00	.9678	.0320
19.5	.55	.5073	.0427	1.06	1.1087	−.0487

for its mean and variance. It is convenient in the derivation to write the estimator in the form of a linear transformation of the observed means, i.e., as

$$\boldsymbol{\beta} = \mathbf{M}\boldsymbol{y}. \qquad (4.1\text{-}19)$$

where $\mathbf{M} = (\mathbf{X}'\mathbf{D}\mathbf{X})^{-1}\mathbf{X}'\mathbf{D}$.

We now assume that the statistical model for $\boldsymbol{y}.$ is given by (4.1-3) and that the errors are distributed independently with mean 0 and variance σ^2. It follows that $\boldsymbol{y}.$ is distributed with mean $\mathbf{X}\boldsymbol{\beta}$ and covariance matrix $\sigma^2\mathbf{D}^{-1}$, where

$$\mathbf{D} = \operatorname{diag}(N_1, N_2, \ldots, N_n)$$

(We assume that each group has at least one observation; otherwise it is omitted and the groups renumbered.) Thus, from the rules for the expectation operator (Sec. 3.2.2), we have

$$\mathscr{E}(\boldsymbol{\beta}) = \mathscr{E}(\mathbf{M}\boldsymbol{y}.) = \mathbf{M}\mathscr{E}(\boldsymbol{y}.) = \mathbf{M}\mathbf{X}\boldsymbol{\beta} = (\mathbf{X}'\mathbf{D}\mathbf{X})^{-1}\mathbf{X}'\mathbf{D}\mathbf{X}\boldsymbol{\beta} = \boldsymbol{\beta} \qquad (4.1\text{-}20)$$

That is, the mean of the sampling distribution of the estimator is equal to the parameter being estimated. An estimator with this property is called *unbiased*.

From the rules for the variance operator (Sec. 3.2.2),

$$\begin{aligned}\mathscr{V}(\boldsymbol{\beta}) &= \mathscr{V}(\mathbf{M}\boldsymbol{y}.) = \mathbf{M}\mathscr{V}(\boldsymbol{y}.)\mathbf{M}' = \sigma^2\mathbf{M}\mathbf{D}^{-1}\mathbf{M}' \\ &= \sigma^2(\mathbf{X}'\mathbf{D}\mathbf{X})^{-1}\mathbf{X}'\mathbf{D}\mathbf{D}^{-1}\mathbf{D}\mathbf{X}(\mathbf{X}'\mathbf{D}\mathbf{X})^{-1} = \sigma^2(\mathbf{X}'\mathbf{D}\mathbf{X})^{-1} \qquad (4.1\text{-}21)\end{aligned}$$

That is, the covariance matrix of the estimator is proportional to the inverse of the matrix of cross products which appears in the normal equations. The constant of proportionality is the variance of the error distribution, which is unknown in most applications. We shall see in Sec. 4.1.7 how σ^2 may be estimated from the data. We note also that $\sigma^2(\mathbf{X}'\mathbf{D}\mathbf{X})^{-1}$ is positive definite, so that its diagonal elements, which are variances, are strictly positive. The off-diagonal elements are covariances and not necessarily positive.

The conditions of independent and homoscedastic error assumed in this derivation are also sufficient to establish the important *Gauss-Markoff* theorem, which provides a basic justification for the method of least squares. The theorem states that, *among the class of linear unbiased estimators of $\boldsymbol{\beta}$, the least-squares estimator $\boldsymbol{\beta} = \mathbf{M}\boldsymbol{y}.$ is "best" in the sense that it has smallest variance.*

For suppose there were some other linear estimator, say $\boldsymbol{\beta}^* = \mathbf{A}\boldsymbol{y}.$, where $\mathbf{A}$ is a $(q + 1) \times n$ matrix of the form $[\mathbf{M} + \mathbf{B}]$. If $\boldsymbol{\beta}^*$ is unbiased, we must have

$$\begin{aligned}\mathscr{E}(\boldsymbol{\beta}^*) &= \mathscr{E}(\mathbf{A}\boldsymbol{y}.) = \mathbf{A}\mathscr{E}(\boldsymbol{y}.) = \mathbf{A}\mathbf{X}\boldsymbol{\beta} \\ &= [\mathbf{M} + \mathbf{B}]\mathbf{X}\boldsymbol{\beta} = \boldsymbol{\beta} + \mathbf{B}\mathbf{X}\boldsymbol{\beta}\end{aligned}$$

or

$$\mathbf{B}\mathbf{X} = \mathbf{O}$$

In this case,

$$\begin{aligned}\mathscr{V}(\boldsymbol{\beta}^*) &= \mathbf{A}\mathscr{V}(\boldsymbol{y}.)\mathbf{A}' = \sigma^2[\mathbf{M} + \mathbf{B}]\mathbf{D}^{-1}[\mathbf{M} + \mathbf{B}]' \\ &= \sigma^2[\mathbf{M}\mathbf{D}^{-1}\mathbf{M}' + \mathbf{B}\mathbf{D}^{-1}\mathbf{B}'] = \sigma^2[(\mathbf{X}'\mathbf{D}\mathbf{X})^{-1} + \mathbf{B}\mathbf{D}^{-1}\mathbf{B}']\end{aligned}$$

because the terms containing $\mathbf{BD}^{-1}\mathbf{DX} = \mathbf{BX}$ or $\mathbf{X}'\mathbf{B}'$ are null. The matrix $\mathbf{BD}^{-1}\mathbf{B}'$ is at least positive semidefinite; hence, the minimum of the variance is attained when its diagonal elements are all zero. This implies that $\mathbf{A}\boldsymbol{y}.$ is minimum variance unbiased when $\mathbf{B} = \mathbf{O}$, that is, when $\mathbf{A} = \mathbf{M} = (\mathbf{X}'\mathbf{DX})^{-1}\mathbf{X}'\mathbf{D}$. In other words, (4.1-19) is a *minimum-variance linear unbiased estimator*, the variance being given by (4.1-21).

The method of least squares therefore can be justified without reference to the functional form of the error distribution. When the functional form is left unspecified, however, the method offers little more than a *point estimate* of $\boldsymbol{\beta}$. This point estimate carries no information about the precision of estimation nor any indication of what confidence may be placed in it. For scientific purposes, we may prefer an estimate in the form of a *confidence interval* which has an assigned probability of including the parameter being estimated. Such an interval, being generally smaller when the data are extensive and larger when they are meager, serves to convey the precision of the least-squares estimation.

Strictly speaking, weak forms of interval estimation are possible even in the absence of a specified error distribution. For example, Tchebycheff's inequality (Sec. 3.2.2) may be used to set broad limits on the coefficients of the linear model. Alternatively, when the sample size is large, the central-limit theorem (Sec. 3.1.4) would justify the assumption that the least-squares estimator is approximately normally distributed and that a classical standard error should be reported (see Sec. 4.1.12).

A much more satisfactory solution to the problem of interval estimation is available, however, when the error distribution is specified. In view of the discussion in Sec. 3.1, there is broad justification in the context of behavioral research for assuming a normal error specification. In particular, let us assume that the errors are normally and independently distributed with mean 0 and variance σ^2. It then follows from (4.1-1) that (1) the original observations from each of the n groups are distributed in the multivariate normal form

$$\boldsymbol{y} \sim N(\mathbf{X}\boldsymbol{\beta}, \sigma^2\mathbf{I})$$

where $\mathbf{I}$ is the $n \times n$ identity matrix, (2) the *means* for the n groups are multivariate normal

$$\boldsymbol{y}. \sim N(\mathbf{X}\boldsymbol{\beta}, \sigma^2\mathbf{D}^{-1}) \qquad (4.1\text{-}22)$$

and (3) from the results in Sec. 3.3.7, the estimated regression coefficients are multivariate normal

$$\hat{\boldsymbol{\beta}} \sim N[\boldsymbol{\beta}, \sigma^2(\mathbf{X}'\mathbf{DX})^{-1}] \qquad (4.1\text{-}23)$$

The use of (4.1-23) in the construction of confidence intervals for the elements of $\boldsymbol{\beta}$ is discussed in Sec. 4.1.12. The construction requires, however, an estimate of the error variance σ^2, and it may also be desirable to test the fit of the model before proceeding with other aspects of estimation. These preliminaries are part of the analysis of variance which we now discuss.

4.1.7 Analysis of Variance for the Polynomial Model (Grouped Data)

The technique of analysis of variance was introduced as an adjunct to classical least squares by R. A. Fisher [1967], who also developed the necessary sampling theory [Fisher, 1924]. In the context of polynomial regression analysis in the replicated case, the information required in the analysis of variance may be displayed in the form of Table 4.1-3.

The geometric interpretation of Table 4.1-3 The entries in Table 4.1-3 may be understood in terms of the geometry of least squares presented in Sec. 4.1.5. Each line in the body of the table corresponds to a vector space, the dimensionality of which is the degrees of freedom in that line. The corresponding sum of squares is the square length of a vector in that space. For example, sst, the total sum of squares, is the square length of the vector of observations, and the dimensionality of the total space is the total number of observations $N = \sum_{j=1}^{n} N_j$.

The total space is partitioned into the n-dimensional subspace of group means and a complementary $(N - n)$-dimensional subspace of within-group variation. The N-component observational vector is expressed as the resultant of the n-component vector $\mathbf{y}. = [y._j]$ in the space of means and the N-component vector of deviations $\mathbf{e} = [y_{ij} - y._j]$ in the within-group space. The fact that the square lengths of these components sum to the sst defines this as an orthogonal resolution. It follows that the means and the residuals from the means are uncorrelated—a result which is important in the sampling theory for analysis of variance (see Sec. 4.1.9).

Table 4.1-3 ANALYSIS OF VARIANCE FOR THE POLYNOMIAL MODEL (GROUPED DATA)

Source of variation	Degrees of freedom	Sums of squares	Expected sums of squares
Regression	$g + 1$	ssr $= \mathbf{y}'.\mathbf{DX}(\mathbf{X}'\mathbf{DX})^{-1}\mathbf{X}'\mathbf{Dy}.$ $= \hat{\boldsymbol{\beta}}'\mathbf{X}'\mathbf{Dy}.$	$(g + 1)\sigma^2 + \boldsymbol{\beta}'\mathbf{X}'\mathbf{DX}\boldsymbol{\beta}$
Residual	$n - g - 1$	sse $= \mathbf{y}'.[\mathbf{D} - \mathbf{DX}(\mathbf{X}'\mathbf{DX})^{-1}\mathbf{X}'\mathbf{D}]\mathbf{y}.$ = ssg − ssr	$(n - g - 1)\sigma^2$
Group means	n	ssg $= \sum_{j=1}^{n} N_j y._j^2 = \mathbf{y}'.\mathbf{Dy}.$	$n\sigma^2 + \boldsymbol{\beta}'\mathbf{X}'\mathbf{DX}\boldsymbol{\beta}$
Within groups	$N - n$	ssw $= \sum_{j=1}^{n}\sum_{i=1}^{N_j} (y_{ij} - y._j)^2$ = sst − ssg	$(N - n)\sigma^2$
Total	$N = \sum_{j=1}^{n} N_j$	sst $= \sum_{j=1}^{n}\sum_{i=1}^{N_j} y_{ij}^2$	

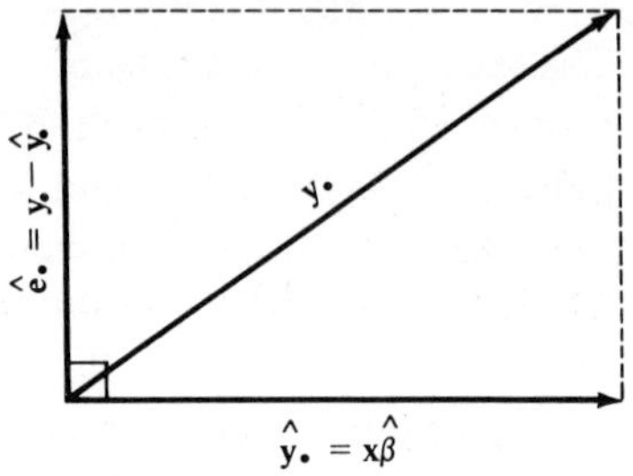

FIGURE 4.1-4
The least-squares resolution of the group-mean vector.

Continuing the geometric interpretation of Table 4.1-3, we observe that the space of group means, or *group-means subspace*, is further partitioned into complementary subspaces for regression and for residual. Note that in the group-means subspace, square length and orthogonality are defined with respect to the metric **D** (see Sec. 2.7.1). Thus, the resolution of the group-mean vector $\mathbf{y}.$ into the fitted vector $\hat{\mathbf{y}}.$ and the residual $\hat{\mathbf{e}}.$, which was shown in perspective in Fig. 4.1-3 may be depicted in the plane as in Fig. 4.1-4, provided it is understood that the right angle in the figure represents orthogonality in the metric **D**.

The square lengths of the vectors $\hat{\mathbf{y}}.$, $\hat{\mathbf{e}}.$, and $\mathbf{y}.$ correspond, respectively, to the sums of squares in the first three lines of Table 4.1-3. The connection is as follows:

$$\begin{aligned}
\text{ssr} &= \hat{\mathbf{y}}'_{.}\mathbf{D}\hat{\mathbf{y}}. = \hat{\boldsymbol{\beta}}'\mathbf{X}'\mathbf{D}\mathbf{X}\hat{\boldsymbol{\beta}} = \mathbf{y}'_{.}\mathbf{D}\mathbf{X}(\mathbf{X}'\mathbf{D}\mathbf{X})^{-1}\mathbf{X}'\mathbf{D}\mathbf{X}(\mathbf{X}'\mathbf{D}\mathbf{X})^{-1}\mathbf{X}'\mathbf{D}\mathbf{y}. \\
&= \mathbf{y}'_{.}\mathbf{D}\mathbf{X}(\mathbf{X}'\mathbf{D}\mathbf{X})^{-1}\mathbf{X}'\mathbf{D}\mathbf{y}. = \hat{\boldsymbol{\beta}}'\mathbf{X}'\mathbf{D}\mathbf{y}. \\
\text{sse} &= \hat{\mathbf{e}}'_{.}\mathbf{D}\hat{\mathbf{e}}. = \mathbf{y}'_{.}\mathbf{D}\hat{\mathbf{e}}. - \hat{\mathbf{y}}'_{.}\mathbf{D}\hat{\mathbf{e}}. \\
&= \mathbf{y}'_{.}\mathbf{D}\mathbf{y}. - \mathbf{y}'_{.}\mathbf{D}\hat{\mathbf{y}}. = \mathbf{y}'_{.}\mathbf{D}\mathbf{y}. - \mathbf{y}'_{.}\mathbf{D}\mathbf{X}\hat{\boldsymbol{\beta}} = \mathbf{y}'_{.}\mathbf{D}\mathbf{y}. - \hat{\boldsymbol{\beta}}'\mathbf{X}'\mathbf{D}\mathbf{y}. \\
&= \text{ssg} - \text{ssr}
\end{aligned}$$

since from (4.1-16), $\hat{\mathbf{y}}'_{.}\mathbf{D}\hat{\mathbf{e}} = \hat{\boldsymbol{\beta}}'\mathbf{X}'\mathbf{D}\hat{\mathbf{e}} = 0$. Finally,

$$\text{ssg} = \mathbf{y}'_{.}\mathbf{D}\mathbf{y}.$$

The statistical interpretation of Table 4.1-3 To understand the statistical implications of Table 4.1-3, we must examine the expected sums of squares shown in the right-hand column. These expectations are evaluated under the hypothesis that all systematic variation in the data is accounted for by the degree-g polynomial. Their derivations are as follows:

$$\begin{aligned}
\mathscr{E}(\text{ssg}) &= \mathscr{E}(\mathbf{y}'_{.}\mathbf{D}\mathbf{y}.) = \mathscr{E}[(\boldsymbol{\beta}'\mathbf{X}' + \boldsymbol{\epsilon}'_{.})\mathbf{D}(\mathbf{X}\boldsymbol{\beta} + \boldsymbol{\epsilon}.)] \\
&= \boldsymbol{\beta}'\mathbf{X}'\mathbf{D}\mathbf{X}\boldsymbol{\beta} + \boldsymbol{\beta}'\mathbf{X}'\mathbf{D}\mathscr{E}(\boldsymbol{\epsilon}.) + \mathscr{E}(\boldsymbol{\epsilon}'_{.})\mathbf{D}\mathbf{X}\boldsymbol{\beta} + \mathscr{E}(\boldsymbol{\epsilon}'_{.}\mathbf{D}\boldsymbol{\epsilon}.) \\
&= \boldsymbol{\beta}'\mathbf{X}'\mathbf{D}\mathbf{X}\boldsymbol{\beta} + n\sigma^2
\end{aligned}$$

since $\mathscr{E}(\boldsymbol{\epsilon}.) = \mathbf{0}$, and

$$\mathscr{E}(\boldsymbol{\epsilon}'_.\mathbf{D}\boldsymbol{\epsilon}.) = \mathscr{E}\left(\sum_{j=1}^{n} N_j \epsilon_{.j}^2\right) = \sum_{j=1}^{n} N_j \mathscr{E}(\epsilon_{.j}^2) = \sigma^2 \sum_{j=1}^{n} \frac{N_j}{N_j} = n\sigma^2$$

To evaluate $\mathscr{E}(\text{ssr})$, we make use of the orthogonal reparameterization $\boldsymbol{\beta} = (\mathbf{S}^{-1})'\boldsymbol{\gamma}$ of Sec. 4.1.4 and the fact that

$$\text{ssr} = \hat{\boldsymbol{\beta}}'\mathbf{X}'\mathbf{D}\mathbf{y}. = \hat{\boldsymbol{\beta}}'\mathbf{X}'\mathbf{D}\mathbf{X}\hat{\boldsymbol{\beta}} = \hat{\boldsymbol{\gamma}}'\hat{\boldsymbol{\gamma}}$$

Then if $\mathbf{\mathsf{y}} = \mathbf{S}^{-1}\mathbf{X}'\mathbf{D}\mathbf{y}.$ is the estimator of $\boldsymbol{\gamma}$,

$$\mathscr{E}(\mathbf{\mathsf{y}}) = \boldsymbol{\gamma} = \mathbf{S}'\boldsymbol{\beta}$$

and

$$\begin{aligned}\mathscr{V}(\mathbf{\mathsf{y}}) &= \mathbf{S}^{-1}\mathbf{X}'\mathbf{D}\mathscr{V}(\mathbf{y}.)\mathbf{D}\mathbf{X}(\mathbf{S}^{-1})' = \sigma^2\mathbf{S}^{-1}\mathbf{X}'\mathbf{D}\mathbf{X}(\mathbf{S}^{-1})' = \sigma^2\mathbf{S}^{-1}\mathbf{S}\mathbf{S}'(\mathbf{S}')^{-1} \\ &= \sigma^2\mathbf{I}\end{aligned}$$

The orthogonal estimates are therefore uncorrelated, and the variance of the kth orthogonal estimate may be expressed as

$$\mathscr{E}(\mathsf{y}_k - \gamma_k)^2 = \mathscr{E}(\mathsf{y}_k^2) - \gamma_k^2 = \sigma^2$$

Thus,

$$\begin{aligned}\mathscr{E}(\text{ssr}) &= \mathscr{E}(\mathbf{\mathsf{y}}'\mathbf{\mathsf{y}}) = \sum_{k=0}^{g} \mathscr{E}(\mathsf{y}_k^2) = (g+1)\sigma^2 + \boldsymbol{\gamma}'\boldsymbol{\gamma} \\ &= (g+1)\sigma^2 + \boldsymbol{\beta}'\mathbf{X}'\mathbf{D}\mathbf{X}\boldsymbol{\beta} \qquad (4.1\text{-}24)\end{aligned}$$

Note that the term $\boldsymbol{\beta}'\mathbf{X}'\mathbf{D}\mathbf{X}\boldsymbol{\beta}$ in (4.1-24) is a quadratic form in the parameters of the model. Since the matrix of the form is the positive-definite matrix $\mathbf{X}'\mathbf{D}\mathbf{X}$, the form is zero if and only if $\boldsymbol{\beta} = \mathbf{0}$. As we shall see in Sec. 4.1.9, this fact has implications for testing hypotheses concerning $\boldsymbol{\beta}$.

The expected sum of squares for the residual may be obtained by subtraction:

$$\begin{aligned}\mathscr{E}(\text{sse}) &= \mathscr{E}(\text{ssg}) - \mathscr{E}(\text{ssr}) \\ &= (n - g - 1)\sigma^2 \qquad (4.1\text{-}25)\end{aligned}$$

Finally, ssw may be expressed in terms of unbiased variance estimates as

$$\text{ssw} = \sum_{j=1}^{n}\left(\sum_{i=1}^{N_j} y_{ij}^2 - N_j y_{.j}^2\right) = \sum_{j=1}^{n}(N_j - 1)\hat{\sigma}_j^2$$

Let σ_j^2 be the unbiased estimator of the variance of group j. Then,

$$\mathscr{E}(\text{ssw}) = \sum_{j=1}^{n}(N_j - 1)\mathscr{E}(\sigma_j^2) = \sum_{j=1}^{n}(N_j - 1)\sigma^2 = (N - n)\sigma^2 \qquad (4.1\text{-}26)$$

4.1.8 Estimating σ^2

It is clear from the expected sums of squares in Table 4.1-3 that the analysis of variance in the replicated case affords two direct estimators of σ^2. The *residual mean square* (the residual sum of squares divided by its degrees of freedom)

$$\text{mse} = \frac{\text{sse}}{n - g - 1} \tag{4.1-27}$$

is an unbiased estimator of σ^2, conditional on the degree-g model fitting the data, while the *within-group mean square*

$$\text{msw} = \frac{\text{ssw}}{N - n} \tag{4.1-28}$$

is an unbiased estimator of σ^2 unconditionally. If there is no doubt as to the validity of the model, a more precise estimator of σ^2 may be obtained by "pooling" these sums of squares and dividing by the pooled degrees of freedom:

$$\text{mse}' = \frac{\text{sse} + \text{ssw}}{N - g - 1} \tag{4.1-29}$$

Frequently in behavioral studies the number of subjects within groups is so large that little is to be gained by pooling the sum of squares. In that case msw may be used routinely as the estimator of σ^2. In either case, we designate as $\hat{\sigma}_{(n_e)}{}^2$ the unbiased estimate of σ^2 obtained from sums of squares corresponding to n_e degrees of freedom. In addition to unbiasedness, its estimator can be shown to be a best, in the sense of minimum variance, among the class of unbiased quadratic estimators [Graybill, 1961, page 347].

In some cases, the decision to pool or not to pool the residual and within-group sum of squares will depend upon the outcome of a test of fit. A basis for such a test is discussed in the following section.

4.1.9 A Test of Fit

Suppose the degree of the polynomial actually is not g, but m, where $g < m < n$. It will then be necessary to add an additional $m - g$ terms to the model as follows:

$$\mathbf{y}_{.} = n\underset{\quad g+1 \quad\; m-g}{[\ \mathbf{X}_1 \mid \mathbf{X}_2\ ]}\begin{bmatrix}\boldsymbol{\beta}_1 \\ \boldsymbol{\beta}_2\end{bmatrix} + \mathbf{e}_{.} \tag{4.1-30}$$

The matrix $\mathbf{X}_1$ in (4.1-30) contains the powers of the independent variable from 0 to

g, and $\mathbf{X}_2$ contains the remaining powers up to m. The vectors $\boldsymbol{\beta}_1$ and $\boldsymbol{\beta}_2$ contain the corresponding regression coefficients. The hypothesis that the polynomial is in fact of degree g is equivalent to the null hypothesis $\boldsymbol{\beta}_2 = \mathbf{0}$. The alternative hypothesis, that the degree is greater than g, is $\boldsymbol{\beta}_2 \neq \mathbf{0}$.

The basis in the analysis of variance for a test of the null hypothesis is seen in the expected sums of squares under the alternative hypothesis. To derive this expectation, we introduce a quasiorthogonal (blockwise orthogonal) reparameterization of the model. Let

$$\begin{bmatrix} \boldsymbol{\beta}_1 \\ \boldsymbol{\beta}_2 \end{bmatrix} = (\mathbf{T}^{-1})' \begin{bmatrix} \boldsymbol{\beta}_1^* \\ \boldsymbol{\beta}_2^* \end{bmatrix}$$

where
$$\begin{bmatrix} \mathbf{I} & \mathbf{O} \\ -\mathbf{X}_2'\mathbf{D}\mathbf{X}_1(\mathbf{X}_1'\mathbf{D}\mathbf{X}_1)^{-1} & \mathbf{I} \end{bmatrix} \begin{matrix} g+1 \\ m-g \end{matrix}$$
$$\qquad g+1 \qquad\qquad m-g$$

See Sec. 3.3.4.

The inverse transformation is

$$\mathbf{T} = \begin{bmatrix} \mathbf{I} & \mathbf{O} \\ \mathbf{X}_2'\mathbf{D}\mathbf{X}_1(\mathbf{X}_1'\mathbf{D}\mathbf{X}_1)^{-1} & \mathbf{I} \end{bmatrix}$$

whence
$$\begin{bmatrix} \boldsymbol{\beta}_1^* \\ \boldsymbol{\beta}_2^* \end{bmatrix} = \begin{bmatrix} \boldsymbol{\beta}_1 + (\mathbf{X}_1'\mathbf{D}\mathbf{X}_1)^{-1}\mathbf{X}_1'\mathbf{D}\mathbf{X}_2\boldsymbol{\beta}_2 \\ \boldsymbol{\beta}_2 \end{bmatrix}$$

Note that $\boldsymbol{\beta}_2$ is unchanged in this reparameterization.

The normal equations for estimating the quasiorthogonal parameters are

$$\mathbf{T}^{-1}[\mathbf{X}_1 \mid \mathbf{X}_2]'\mathbf{D}[\mathbf{X}_1 \mid \mathbf{X}_2](\mathbf{T}^{-1})' \begin{bmatrix} \boldsymbol{\beta}_1^* \\ \boldsymbol{\beta}_2^* \end{bmatrix} = \mathbf{T}^{-1}[\mathbf{X}_1 \mid \mathbf{X}_2]'\mathbf{D}\mathbf{y}.$$

or
$$\begin{bmatrix} \mathbf{X}_1'\mathbf{D}\mathbf{X}_1 & \mathbf{O} \\ \mathbf{O} & \mathbf{X}_2^{*\prime}\mathbf{D}\mathbf{X}_2^* \end{bmatrix} \begin{bmatrix} \boldsymbol{\beta}_1^* \\ \boldsymbol{\beta}_2^* \end{bmatrix} = \begin{bmatrix} \mathbf{X}_1'\mathbf{D}\mathbf{y}. \\ \mathbf{X}_2^{*\prime}\mathbf{D}\mathbf{y}. \end{bmatrix}$$

where $\mathbf{X}_2^* = \mathbf{X}_2 - \mathbf{X}_1(\mathbf{X}_1'\mathbf{D}\mathbf{X}_1)^{-1}\mathbf{X}_1'\mathbf{D}\mathbf{X}_2$.

Because $\mathbf{T}$ is nonsingular, $\mathbf{X}_2^*$ is of full rank if $\mathbf{X}_2$ is of full rank. In the present context, $\mathbf{X}_2$ contains $m - q$ distinct columns of a Vandermonde matrix and is therefore of full rank. Thus, $\mathbf{X}_2^{*\prime}\mathbf{D}\mathbf{X}_2^*$ is nonsingular, and the least-squares estimates of the two sets of parameters are

$$\hat{\boldsymbol{\beta}}_1^* = (\mathbf{X}_1'\mathbf{D}\mathbf{X}_1)^{-1}\mathbf{X}_1'\mathbf{D}\mathbf{y}.$$

and
$$\hat{\boldsymbol{\beta}}_2^* = (\mathbf{X}_2^{*\prime}\mathbf{D}\mathbf{X}_2^*)^{-1}\mathbf{X}_2^{*\prime}\mathbf{D}\mathbf{y}.$$

Because of the quasiorthogonality of the reparameterization, the sum of squares for regression partitions as shown in Table 4.1-4. Note that ssr_1 is equal to ssr in Table 4.1-3. This shows that sse $= \text{ssr}_1 + \text{sse}^*$ and that, under the null and alternative hypotheses, respectively, the residual sum of squares in Table 4.1-3 has the following expected values:

$$H_0: \boldsymbol{\beta}_2 = \mathbf{0} \qquad \mathscr{E}(\text{sse}) = (n - g - 1)\sigma^2$$

$$H_1: \boldsymbol{\beta}_2 \neq \mathbf{0} \qquad \mathscr{E}(\text{sse}) = (n - g - 1)\sigma^2 + \boldsymbol{\beta}_2'\mathbf{X}_2^{*\prime}\mathbf{D}\mathbf{X}_2^*\boldsymbol{\beta}_2$$

Let us now introduce the assumption that the error component in Sec. 4.1.1 is normally distributed. In that case, the results in Sec. 3.4 apply, and sse is distributed under H_0 as a central χ^2 on $n - g - 1$ degrees of freedom; under H_1 it is distributed as a noncentral χ^2 on $n - g - 1$ degrees of freedom and noncentrality parameter $(1/2\sigma^2)\boldsymbol{\beta}_2'\mathbf{X}_2^{*\prime}\mathbf{D}\mathbf{X}_2^*\boldsymbol{\beta}_2$. Because $\mathbf{X}^*$ is of full rank, this noncentrality parameter is zero if and only if $\boldsymbol{\beta}_2 = \mathbf{0}$.

The within-groups sum of squares ssw, on the other hand, is distributed as a central χ^2 on $N - n$ degrees of freedom under either hypothesis. Furthermore, sse and ssw are independent because the group means and the deviations from the group means from which ssw is calculated are uncorrelated, hence independent if the errors are normally distributed (Sec. 3.4.4). Thus, the ratio of mean squares,

$$F = \frac{\text{sse}/(n - g - 1)}{\text{ssw}/(N - n)} \tag{4.1-31}$$

is distributed under H_0 as a *central F statistic* on $n - g - 1$ and $N - n$ degrees of freedom under the null hypothesis, and under H_1 as a noncentral F statistic with these degrees of freedom and noncentrality parameter $\boldsymbol{\beta}_2'\mathbf{X}_2^{*\prime}\mathbf{D}\mathbf{X}_2^*\boldsymbol{\beta}_2/2\sigma^2$.

Table 4.1-4 ANALYSIS OF VARIANCE FOR THE ALTERNATIVE POLYNOMIAL MODEL (GROUPED DATA)

Source of variation	Degrees of freedom	Sums of squares†	Expected sums of squares
Regression 1	$g + 1$	$\text{ssr}_1 = \mathbf{y}_.'\mathbf{D}\mathbf{X}_1(\mathbf{X}_1'\mathbf{D}\mathbf{X}_1)^{-1}\mathbf{X}_1'\mathbf{D}\mathbf{y}_.$	$(g + 1)\sigma^2 + \boldsymbol{\beta}_1^{*\prime}\mathbf{X}_1'\mathbf{D}\mathbf{X}_1\boldsymbol{\beta}_1^*$
Regression 2	$m - g$	$\text{ssr}_2 = \mathbf{y}_.'\mathbf{D}\mathbf{X}_2^*(\mathbf{X}_2^{*\prime}\mathbf{D}\mathbf{X}_2^*)^{-1}\mathbf{X}_2^{*\prime}\mathbf{D}\mathbf{y}_.$	$(m - g)\sigma^2 + \boldsymbol{\beta}_2'\mathbf{X}_2^{*\prime}\mathbf{D}\mathbf{X}_2^*\boldsymbol{\beta}_2$
Reduced residual	$n - m - 1$	$\text{sse}^* = \text{ssg} - \text{ssr}_1 - \text{ssr}_2$	$(n - m - 1)\sigma^2$
Group means	n	$\text{ssg} = \mathbf{y}_.'\mathbf{D}\mathbf{y}_.$	
Within groups	$N - n$	$\text{ssw} = \text{sst} - \text{ssg}$	$(N - n)\sigma^2$
Total	$N = \sum_{j=1}^{n} N_j$	$\text{sst} = \sum_{j=1}^{n}\sum_{i=1}^{N_j} y_{ij}^2$	

† $\mathbf{X}_2^* = \mathbf{X}_2 - \mathbf{X}_1(\mathbf{X}_1'\mathbf{D}\mathbf{X}_1)^{-1}\mathbf{X}_1'\mathbf{D}\mathbf{X}_2$

Using the computing approximation of Sec. 3.4.5, or the table for $s = 1$ in Appendix A, we may determine the probability of a central F statistic equaling or exceeding the value computed from (4.1-31). If this probability is small, say <.05, we reject H_0 in favor of H_1.

To reject H_0 implies $(1/2\sigma^2)\boldsymbol{\beta}_2'\mathbf{X}_2^{*\prime}\mathbf{D}\mathbf{X}_2^*\boldsymbol{\beta}_2 > 0$, and hence that $\boldsymbol{\beta}_2 \neq \mathbf{0}$. But if $\boldsymbol{\beta}_2 \neq \mathbf{0}$, the degree polynomial is greater than g; hence, the test demonstrates significant lack of fit of the degree-g model. Conversely, if this probability is appreciable, say $\geq .05$, we would not consider the obtained F to be evidence of lack of fit of the degree-g model.

It can be shown that (4.1-31) is monotonically increasing in the value of the noncentrality parameter $\boldsymbol{\beta}_2'\mathbf{X}_2^{*\prime}\mathbf{D}\mathbf{X}_2^*\boldsymbol{\beta}_2/2\sigma^2$ [Bose, undated, page 65]. This means that the power of the test (i.e., the probability of rejecting the null hypothesis) increases for a fixed model as the elements in $\mathbf{D}$ and $\boldsymbol{\beta}_2$ increase in magnitude. Thus, as the sample size increases, or the departure from the null hypothesis increases in the sense that the square length of $\boldsymbol{\beta}_2$ in the metric $\mathbf{X}_2^{*\prime}\mathbf{D}\mathbf{X}_2^*$ increases, the power of the test increases. Indeed, for specified $\mathbf{D}$ and $\boldsymbol{\beta}_2$, the power of the test can be determined from tables or computing approximations for the noncentral F [Pearson and Hartley, 1951]. If there is some basis for testing an alternative of some specified size, such calculations can be useful for determining the sample size required to reach an assigned probability that the null hypothesis will be rejected if it is in fact false (see Cohen [1970]).

EXAMPLE 4.1-3 (*Test of fit of the quadratic model for the Ponzo and Poggendorff illusions*) The sums of squares for the analysis of variance are calculated using the formulas in Table 4.1-3:

1 Group means. Because in the data of Table 4.1-1 all $N_j = 16$, the calculation of the group-mean sum of squares simplifies to

$$\text{ssg}^{(1)} = 16(.09^2 + .23^2 + \cdots + .55^2) = 23.0928$$

and

$$\text{ssg}^{(2)} = 16(1.83^2 + 1.70^2 + \cdots + 1.06^2) = 239.7328$$

for the Ponzo and Poggendorff illusions, respectively.

2 Within groups. Ordinarily, ssw is calculated by subtraction as shown in Table 4.1-3. In the present example, however, the data for individual subjects required in the calculation of sst are not given, but it is possible to recover ssw from the group standard deviations in Table 4.1-1. These standard deviations are calculated by the formula

$$(\text{sd})_j = \sqrt{\hat{\sigma}_j^2} = \left[\frac{\sum_{i=1}^{N_j}(y_{ij} - y_{\cdot j})^2}{N_j - 1}\right]^{1/2}$$

Thus, substituting in the expression for ssw in Table 4.1-3, we have

$$\text{ssw} = \sum_{j=1}^{n} \sum_{i=1}^{N_j} (y_{ij} - y_{\cdot j})^2$$
$$= \sum_{j=1}^{n} (N_j - 1)(\text{sd})_j^2$$

Applying this formula to the sd's in Table 4.1-1, we have

$$\text{ssw}^{(1)} = 15(.20 + .23 + \cdots + .23) = 6.3255$$

and

$$\text{ssw}^{(2)} = 15(.36 + .52 + \cdots + .38) = 22.2210$$

3 Regression. As indicated in Table 4.1-3, the regression sum of products may be calculated by summing products of the least-squares estimates and the corresponding constant terms from the normal equations. These quantities appear in the calculation of the estimates in Example 4.1-2.

$$\text{ssr}^{(1)} = 16(-.0331924 \times 3.41 + .0563326 \times 42.145 - .0014674 \times 593.8475)$$
$$= 16 \times 1.38954 = 22.23264$$

$$\text{ssr}^{(2)} = 16(2.776735 \times 11.31 - .242116 \times 115.63 + .008030 \times 1{,}434.63)$$
$$= 16 \times 14.92908 = 238.86528$$

4 Residual. The residual is obtained by subtraction:

$$\text{sse}^{(1)} = 23.0928 - 22.2326 = .8602$$

$$\text{sse}^{(2)} = 239.7328 - 238.8653 = .8675$$

These results are collected in Table 4.1-5.

Table 4.1-5 ANALYSIS OF VARIANCE FOR THE QUADRATIC MODELS OF AGE TREND IN THE PONZO AND POGGENDORFF ILLUSIONS

Source of variation	df	Ponzo (1) Sum of squares	F	p	Poggendorff (2) Sum of squares	F	p
Regression	3	22.2326			238.8653		
Residual	6	.8602	3.06	.007	.8675	.879	.50
Group means	9	23.0928			239.7328		
Within groups	135	6.3255			22.2210		
Total	144	29.4183			261.9538		

F statistics for the test of fit are calculated from the residual and within-group sums of squares as follows:

$$F^{(1)} = \frac{.8602/6}{6.3255/135} = \frac{.1434}{.04686} = 3.058$$

and

$$F^{(2)} = \frac{.8675/6}{22.2210/135} = \frac{.1446}{.16460} = .879$$

The probability values (*p values*) of the calculated F's are then read from the table of the central F distribution for 6 and 135 degrees of freedom or are computed using the approximation in Sec. 3.4.5. In the present instance, these p values lead us to reject the model for the Ponzo illusion, but not that for the Poggendorff. In other words, there is no evidence that the residual mean square for the Poggendorff is not estimating the same variance as the within-group mean square. Thus, we may estimate the error variance from the within-group mean square,

$$\hat{\sigma}_{(2a)}{}^2 = \frac{22.2210}{135} = .16460$$

or from the pooled error sum of squares,

$$\hat{\sigma}_{(2b)}{}^2 = \frac{22.2210 + .8675}{135 + 6} = .16375$$

These variance estimates differ but little in the present example, and either could be used in calculating standard errors for the estimated regression coefficients.

Using, say, $\hat{\sigma}_{(2a)}{}^2$ to estimate σ^2, we calculate from (4.1-23) the sampling variance-covariance matrix pertaining to the estimated regression coefficients for the Poggendorff illusion:

$$\mathbf{S}_{\hat{\boldsymbol{\beta}}^{(2)}} = \frac{.16460}{16}\begin{bmatrix} 5.084278 & & \text{(symmetric)} \\ -.923782 & .178043 & \\ .036309 & -.007236 & .000302 \end{bmatrix}$$

$$= \begin{bmatrix} .062991 & & \text{(symmetric)} \\ -.011445 & .002206 & \\ .000450 & -.000090 & .000004 \end{bmatrix}$$

The standard errors for the respective coefficients are the square roots of the diagonal elements of this matrix:

	$\beta_0^{(2)}$	$\beta_1^{(2)}$	$\beta_2^{(2)}$
Estimate	2.776735	−.242116	.008030
Standard error	.2510	.0470	.0020

Note that, like the estimates, the units of these standard errors are *inches*, *inches/year*, and *inches/year*^{2}, respectively. This accounts for the decreasing magnitude of the standard errors going from the constant term to the squared term of the polynomial. Relative to the magnitude of the coefficient, the standard error is actually larger for the higher-degree terms. This illustrates the fact that it is increasingly difficult to estimate the coefficients of successively higher-degree terms (see Sec. 4.1.12).

Another difficulty in fitting polynomials is the very high correlation between the estimates. If the covariances in the above matrix are converted to correlations by dividing by the row and column standard errors (see Sec. 3.3.6), we obtain

$$\mathbf{R}_{\hat{\beta}(2)} = \begin{bmatrix} 1.0000 & & (\text{symmetric}) \\ -.9709 & 1.0000 & \\ .9266 & -.9868 & 1.0000 \end{bmatrix}$$

These high correlations are another symptom of the poor conditioning of the matrix $\mathbf{X}'\mathbf{D}\mathbf{X}$ for inversion. Fortunately, the elements of this matrix are functions of fixed variables and are known exactly. If enough significant figures are carried in the calculations, the inverse can always be computed with sufficient precision to determine the estimates and their covariance matrix accurately.

From a statistical point of view, the high correlations have implications for tests of significance and confidence bounds on individual coefficients. Because the estimators are far from independent, the joint error rate for tests of individual coefficients is far different than would be the case for the same number of independent tests. It is to avoid this problem that the testing of individual terms in the polynomial is approached by the stepwise regression analysis presented in Sec. 4.1.10. The role of these correlations in determining the joint confidence region for the regression coefficients is discussed in Sec. 4.1.11.

4.1.10 Stepwise Fitting of a Polynomial Model

The analysis of variance presented in Sec. 4.1.9 assumes that prior considerations suggest the degree of the polynomial be tested. In the absence of such considerations, it may be necessary to test a number of models of higher (or lower) degree and to choose the one of least degree which attains acceptable fit. A systematic procedure for carrying out these tests is provided by a so-called *stepwise* regression analysis.

We present here a version of stepwise analysis in which the polynomial is assumed at the onset to be of no greater degree than, say, m. We can then compute and test the significance of the reduction in the regression sum of squares when the model is reduced from degree m to degree $m - 1$. If the reduction is significant, we conclude that a degree-m polynomial is necessary to represent the data and terminate the procedure. Otherwise, we step back and test the reduction of the regression sum of squares due to reducing the $(m - 1)$-degree model to degree $m - 2$. If this reduction is significant, we adopt the $(m - 1)$st degree model, etc., until at some stage a significant reduction is encountered. When the degree of the polynomial is thus determined, we proceed with the estimation of its coefficients as in Example 4.1-2.

The stepwise procedure clearly involves *multiple decisions* based on fallible data, which entail some risk of error at each stage. When performed in the manner described above, however, the successive tests can be shown to be statistically independent [Anderson, 1962; Roy, 1957, page 81], and the exact joint probability of an error at at least one stage can be readily computed. Thus, the Type I error may be set to any assigned level by adjusting the significance levels of the separate tests. The basis for choosing these levels is discussed in the next section.

The calculations of stepwise regression analysis may be set out in the form of a *single-degree-of-freedom analysis of variance* as in Table 4.1-6. In this table, the regression sum of squares is partitioned into as many terms (squares) as there are degrees of freedom for the highest-degree model. Each of these squares provides the numerator of an F statistic for the test of significance at the corresponding stage of the multiple-decision procedure.

There are two widely used methods for calculating numerically the terms in the single-degree-of-freedom partition. The *pivoting method* uses the Gauss-Jordan procedure described in Sec. 2.3.3. The orthogonalization procedure makes use of the Cholesky factorization of Sec. 2.7, or the Gram-Schmidt construction of Sec. 2.2.4. Both pivoting and orthogonalization are highly general procedures which apply to many forms of least-squares analysis in addition to polynomial regression. The orthogonalization method is more transparent conceptually and will be discussed first.

a Stepwise regression analysis by orthogonalization of the model matrix The orthogonalization method is based on the reparameterization of the polynomial model which was introduced in Sec. 4.1.4. Let $\mathbf{X}_m = [\mathbf{x}_0, \mathbf{x}_1, \mathbf{x}_2, \ldots, \mathbf{x}_m]$ be the $n \times (m + 1)$ matrix of the mth-degree model. This matrix is of the same form as (4.1-5) except that the exponents run to m rather than g. The mth-degree model for the means is then

$$\mathbf{y}. = \mathbf{X}_m \boldsymbol{\beta}_m + \mathbf{e}.$$

Now let

$$\boldsymbol{\beta}_m = (\mathbf{S}_m^{-1})' \boldsymbol{\gamma}_m$$

where $\mathbf{S}_m^{-1}$ is the inverse of the Cholesky factor of $\mathbf{X}_m'\mathbf{D}\mathbf{X}_m$. Then the reparameterized model for the means is

$$\mathbf{y}. = \mathbf{X}_m(\mathbf{S}_m^{-1})'\boldsymbol{\gamma}_m + \mathbf{e}. = \mathbf{P}_m\boldsymbol{\gamma}_m + \mathbf{e}.$$

As we have seen in Sec. 4.1.7, $\mathbf{P}_m$ is an $n \times (m + 1)$ matrix orthogonal in the metric $\mathbf{D}$; that is, $\mathbf{P}_m'\mathbf{D}\mathbf{P}_m = \mathbf{I}$. Numerically, $\mathbf{P}_m$ may be obtained as above from inverse Cholesky factor of $\mathbf{X}_m'\mathbf{D}\mathbf{X}_m$, or, alternatively, by orthonormalizing $\mathbf{X}_m$ directly in the metric **D** by the Gram-Schmidt construction (Example 2.2-1). In either case, the least-squares estimates of the orthogonal parameters γ are given by

$$\hat{\gamma} = \mathbf{P}_m'\mathbf{D}\mathbf{y}. = \mathbf{u}, \text{ say} \tag{4.1-32}$$

Alternatively, **u** may be calculated from

$$\underset{m\times 1}{\mathbf{u}} = \underset{m\times m}{\mathbf{S}_m^{-1}} \underset{m\times 1}{(\mathbf{X}_m' \mathbf{D}\mathbf{y}.)} \tag{4.1-33}$$

without obtaining $\mathbf{P}_m$ explicitly. The squares of these estimates are the terms in the single-degree-of-freedom partition in Table 4.1-6. Geometrically, these calculations correspond to a resolution of $\hat{\mathbf{y}}.$ into components which are orthogonal in the metric **D**. The columns of $\mathbf{P}_m$ are the basis vectors in terms of which $\hat{\mathbf{y}}.$ is expressed.

Figure 4.1-5 shows this resolution for the model represented in Fig. 4.1-3. The estimation plane, shown in perspective in Fig. 4.1-3, is in the plane of the paper in Fig. 4.1-5. The vectors of the model are designated as $\mathbf{x}_0$ and $\mathbf{x}_1$ before orthonormalization, and as $\mathbf{x}_0^*$ and $\mathbf{x}_1^*$ after.

From the geometry of Fig. 4.1-5, it is clear that the lengths of the orthogonal components are

$$u_0 = \sqrt{\hat{\mathbf{y}}'.\mathbf{D}\hat{\mathbf{y}}.}\ \cos(\hat{\mathbf{y}}.,\mathbf{x}_0^*)$$

and

$$u_1 = \sqrt{\hat{\mathbf{y}}'.\mathbf{D}\hat{\mathbf{y}}.}\ \cos(\hat{\mathbf{y}}.,\mathbf{x}_1^*)$$

By the law of cosines (Sec. 2.2.3) for a metric **D**,

$$\cos(\hat{\mathbf{y}}.,\mathbf{x}_0^*) = \frac{\hat{\mathbf{y}}'.\mathbf{D}\mathbf{x}_0^*}{\sqrt{\hat{\mathbf{y}}'.\mathbf{D}\hat{\mathbf{y}}.\mathbf{x}_0^{*\prime}\mathbf{D}\mathbf{x}_0^*}}$$

and

$$\cos(\hat{\mathbf{y}}.,\mathbf{x}_1) = \frac{\hat{\mathbf{y}}'.\mathbf{D}\mathbf{x}_1^*}{\sqrt{\hat{\mathbf{y}}'.\mathbf{D}\hat{\mathbf{y}}.\mathbf{x}_1^{*\prime}\mathbf{D}\mathbf{x}_1^*}}$$

Table 4.1-6 SINGLE-DEGREE-OF-FREEDOM ANALYSIS OF VARIANCE FOR THE POLYNOMIAL MODEL

Source of variation	Degrees of freedom	Sums of squares	Expected sums of squares
$\mathbf{x}_0^*$: ($\mathbf{x}_0$, ignoring $\mathbf{x}_1,\mathbf{x}_2,\ldots,\mathbf{x}_m$)	1	$\text{ssr}_0 = u_0^2$	$\sigma^2 + \gamma_0^2$
$\mathbf{x}_1^*$: ($\mathbf{x}_1$, eliminating $\mathbf{x}_0$, and ignoring $\mathbf{x}_2,\ldots,\mathbf{x}_m$)	1	$\text{ssr}_1 = u_1^2$	$\sigma^2 + \gamma_1^2$
....			
$\mathbf{x}_m^*$: ($\mathbf{x}_m$, eliminating $\mathbf{x}_0, \mathbf{x}_1, \mathbf{x}_2, \ldots, \mathbf{x}_{m-1}$)	1	$\text{ssr}_m = u_m^2$	$\sigma^2 + \gamma_m^2$
Residual	$n - m - 1$	$\text{sse} = \text{ssg} - \sum_{k=0}^{m} u_k^2$	$(n - m - 1)\sigma^2$
Group means	n	$\text{ssg} = \mathbf{y}'.\mathbf{D}\mathbf{y}.$	$n\sigma^2 + \boldsymbol{\beta}_m'\mathbf{X}_m'\mathbf{D}\mathbf{X}_m\boldsymbol{\beta}_m$
Within groups	$N - n$	$\text{ssw} = \text{sst} - \text{ssg}$	$(N - n)\sigma^2$
Total	$N = \sum N_j$	$\text{sst} = \sum_{j=1}^{n}\sum_{i=1}^{N_j} y_{ij}^2$	

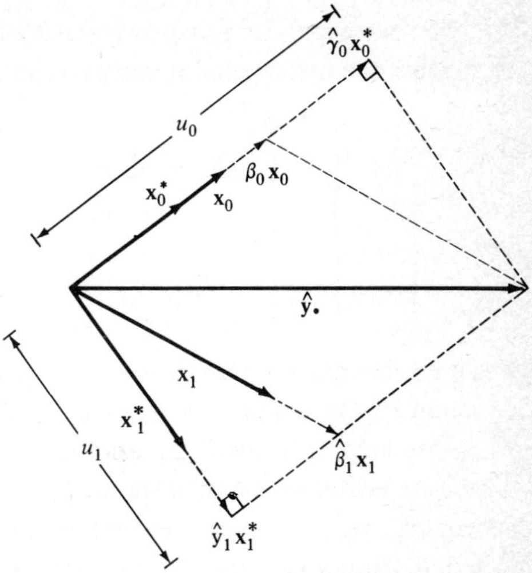

FIGURE 4.1-5
Resolution of the fitted vector $\hat{\mathbf{y}}.$ into orthogonal components.

However, $\mathbf{x}_0^{*\prime}\mathbf{D}\mathbf{x}_0^* = \mathbf{x}_1^{*\prime}\mathbf{D}\mathbf{x}_1 = 1$; hence,

$$u_0 = \hat{\mathbf{y}}'_.\mathbf{D}\mathbf{x}_0^* \qquad u_1 = \hat{\mathbf{y}}'_.\mathbf{D}\mathbf{x}_1^*$$

or, letting

$$\mathbf{X}^* = [\mathbf{x}_0^*, \mathbf{x}_1^*]$$

gives

$$\mathbf{u} = \mathbf{X}^{*\prime}\mathbf{D}\hat{\mathbf{y}}.$$

But, the columns of $\mathbf{X}^*$ are in the estimation plane and are orthogonal to $\hat{\mathbf{e}}.$; hence, $\mathbf{X}^{*\prime}\mathbf{D}\hat{\mathbf{e}}. = \mathbf{0}$ and

$$\mathbf{u} = \mathbf{X}^{*\prime}\mathbf{D}(\mathbf{y}. - \hat{\mathbf{e}}.) = \mathbf{X}^{*\prime}\mathbf{D}\mathbf{y}.$$

which is the same as (4.1-32). (See also Exercise 4.1-1.)

In order to understand the role of the single-degree-of-freedom analysis in testing the polynomial model, we must examine the expected sums of squares in Table 4.1-5. Recall from Sec. 4.1.7 that the orthogonal estimates are distributed with mean γ_k and variance σ^2 and are uncorrelated. Thus, the expected value of u_k^2 is

$$\mathscr{E}(u_k^2) = \mathscr{V}(u_k) + \gamma_k^2 = \sigma^2 + \gamma_k^2$$

If the errors are normally distributed, u_k^2/σ^2 is independently distributed as a central chi-square with one degree of freedom on condition that $\gamma_k = 0$; otherwise it is distributed as a noncentral chi-square with noncentrality parameter $\gamma_k^2/2\sigma^2$. Thus, conditional on $\gamma_k = 0$, the variance ratio

$$F_k = \frac{u_k^2}{\text{SSW}/(N - n)}$$

is distributed as a central F statistic with 1 and $N - n$ degrees of freedom. Otherwise, F_k is a noncentral F statistic with noncentrality parameter $\gamma_k^2/2\sigma^2$. F_k therefore provides a statistical test of the null hypothesis H_k: $\gamma_k = 0$.

To see what accepting or rejecting this hypothesis may imply for the model, let us express the orthogonal parameters in terms of the original parameters as follows:

$$\boldsymbol{\gamma} = \mathbf{S}'\boldsymbol{\beta}$$

or

$$\begin{bmatrix} \gamma_0 \\ \gamma_1 \\ \cdots \\ \gamma_{m-1} \\ \gamma_m \end{bmatrix} = \begin{bmatrix} s_{00}\beta_0 + s_{01}\beta_1 + \cdots + s_{0,m-1}\beta_{m-1} + s_{0m}\beta_m \\ s_{11}\beta_1 + \cdots + s_{1,m-1}\beta_{m-1} + s_{1m}\beta_m \\ \cdots\cdots\cdots\cdots\cdots\cdots \\ s_{m-1,m-1}\beta_{m-1} + s_{m-1,m}\beta_m \\ s_{mm}\beta_m \end{bmatrix}$$

Since all diagonal elements of $\mathbf{S}$ are nonzero, it is clear that rejection of H_m implies rejection of the hypothesis $\beta_m = 0$. On the other hand, accepting H_m implies that γ_{m-1} depends only on β_{m-1} and $s_{m-1,m-1}$, so that subsequent rejection of H_{m-1} implies rejection of the hypothesis $\beta_{m-1} = 0$. This sequence of decisions to reject or accept $H_m, H_{m-1}, \ldots, H_0$ terminates with the first rejection. For if H_g, say, is rejected, β_g cannot be assumed null and appears in the expected value of $u_{g-1}, u_{g-2}, \ldots, u_0$. Thus, u_{g-1} or any lower term in the partition does not provide a valid test of the corresponding coefficient of the polynomial. We then say that all lower terms are *confounded* with β_g and stop the procedure with the test of H_g.

The multiple-decision procedure therefore consists of a series of F tests beginning with the highest-order term in the single-degree-of-freedom analysis and continuing in sequence to the lowest-order term until the first significant F is observed. If this significant F occurs at u_g^2, the polynomial is taken to be of degree g. The least-squares estimates of the $g + 1$ coefficients of this polynomial can then be calculated from

$$\hat{\boldsymbol{\beta}}_g = (\mathbf{X}_g'\mathbf{D}\mathbf{X}_g)^{-1}\mathbf{X}_g'\mathbf{D}\mathbf{y}. = (\mathbf{S}_g^{-1})'\mathbf{S}_g^{-1}\mathbf{X}_g'\mathbf{D}\mathbf{y}. = (\mathbf{S}_g^{-1})'\mathbf{u}_g \qquad (4.1\text{-}34)$$

where $\mathbf{u}_g$ is the vector consisting of the first $g + 1$ orthogonal estimates. The inverse matrix required for calculating the variance-covariance matrix may be obtained from the first $g + 1$ rows and columns of $\mathbf{S}_m^{-1}$ as in (4.1-34).

The Type I error rate of the multiple-decision procedure is calculated as follows: Let α_i be the assigned significance level for the ith test, and suppose $p \leq m$ terms in the partition are to be tested. Because the tests are independent, the probability of accepting the null hypothesis in all m tests when it is in fact true is

$$\prod_{i=1}^{p} (1 - \alpha_i)$$

Then the probability of rejecting at least one of the hypotheses when it is in fact true is the Type I error rate for the procedure, say,

$$\alpha^* = 1 - \prod_{i=1}^{p} (1 - \alpha_i) \qquad (4.1\text{-}35)$$

If all α_i are set to the same value α and p is sufficiently large, α^* may be considerably larger than α. For example, when $\alpha = .01$ and $p = 5$, $\alpha^* = .05$. The difference between α and α^* is the price that the investigator must pay for using a weakly specified model.

EXAMPLE 4.1-4 (*Stepwise regression analysis by orthogonalization*) Having already shown that the Ponzo data depart significantly from the quadratic model, let us attempt to find a suitable polynomial by stepwise regression analysis. We shall assume that the degree of this polynomial does not exceed five, in which case the 9×6 model matrix $\mathbf{X}_6$ is of the form shown in Sec. 4.1.3, extended on the right with columns corresponding to x^3, x^4, and x^5. We may obtain the orthogonal estimates by directly orthonormalizing $\mathbf{X}_6$ in a modified Gram-Schmidt construction in the metric $\mathbf{D}$ (see Example 2.2-2). The result of the orthogonalization is

$$\mathbf{P}_6 = \frac{1}{4}\begin{bmatrix} .33333 & -.43170 & .44225 & -.45329 & .39647 & -.29572 \\ .33333 & -.36105 & .21759 & -.01011 & -.22398 & .39593 \\ .33333 & -.29041 & .02773 & .26321 & -.39409 & .24996 \\ .33333 & -.18445 & -.19182 & .41390 & -.18096 & -.30564 \\ .33333 & -.04317 & -.36281 & .27286 & .29889 & -.38488 \\ .33333 & .09811 & -.39464 & -.06056 & .42483 & .23752 \\ .33333 & .23939 & -.28731 & -.36931 & .03261 & .45345 \\ .33333 & .38068 & -.04082 & -.43871 & -.54506 & -.42852 \\ .33333 & .59260 & .58983 & .38261 & .19129 & .07790 \end{bmatrix}$$

The orthogonal estimates are obtained from

$$\mathbf{u}_6 = \mathbf{P}_6 \mathbf{D} \mathbf{y}\,.^{(1)}$$

and the result is

$$\mathbf{u}_6' = 4[1.136666, .300660, -.084360, .175160, -.115800, -.034000]$$

The corresponding single-degree-of-freedom analysis is shown in Table 4.1-7.

The F statistics in Table 4.1-7 are calculated by dividing each of the squared orthogonal estimates by the within-groups mean square $6.3255/135 = .046855$. Let

Table 4.1-7 STEPWISE REGRESSION ANALYSIS FOR THE PONZO DATA

Source of variation	df	Sums of squares	F	p
$\mathbf{x}_0^*$ (constant)	1	20.67218	441.15	$< .0005$
$\mathbf{x}_1^*$ (linear	1	1.44634	30.87	$< .0005$
$\mathbf{x}_2^*$ (quadratic)	1	.11386	2.43	$.1 < p < .3$
$\mathbf{x}_3^*$ (cubic)	1	.49090	10.48	$.001 < p < .005$
$\mathbf{x}_4^*$ (quartic)	1	.21454	4.58	$.025 < p < .05$
$\mathbf{x}_5^*$ (quintic)	1	.01848	.39	$> .5$
Regression total	6	22.95630		
Residual	3	.13650		
Group means	9	23.09280		
Within groups	135	6.32550		
Total	144	29.41830		

us set the critical levels for these statistics so that a multiple-decision procedure for models of degree 3, 4, and 5 has a joint Type I error of .05; that is, so that

$$.05 = 1 - (1 - \alpha)^3$$

Thus,

$$\alpha = 1 - \sqrt[3]{1 - .05} \approx .025$$

Working from the last F statistic in Table 4.1-7, we find that this criterion is exceeded for the first time at the degree-3 term. The decision rule therefore fixes the degree of the model to be fitted at 3. To obtain the estimated coefficients of the cubic polynomial, we apply (4.1-34) by extracting and inverting the first four rows and columns of the 6 × 6 Cholesky factor of $\mathbf{X}'\mathbf{D}\mathbf{X}$ and postmultiplying by the first four orthogonal estimates. As indicated in Example 2.7-1, this Cholesky factor is produced as a byproduct of the Gram-Schmidt orthogonalization. In this instance,

$$\mathbf{S}_6 = \begin{bmatrix} .30000(1) & & & & & \text{(triangular)} \\ .333333(2) & .14155(2) & & & & \\ .43716(3) & .33853(3) & .57488(2) & & & \\ .64548(4) & .66308(4) & .21174(4) & .22174(3) & & \\ .10300(6) & .12393(6) & .55136(5) & .10786(5) & .77256(3) & \\ .17294(7) & .22970(7) & .12572(7) & .34276(6) & .46303(5) & .23287(4) \end{bmatrix}$$

(Multiply the entries by 10 to the power in parenthesis.)

The inverse of the leading order-4 submatrix is

$$\mathbf{S}_4^{-1} = \begin{bmatrix} .333333 & & & \text{(triangular)} \\ -.784911 & .070642 & & \\ 2.087362 & -.415996 & .017394 & \\ -6.164157 & 1.859952 & -.166104 & .004509 \end{bmatrix}$$

from which the vector $\hat{\boldsymbol{\beta}}_4 = \mathbf{S}_4^{-1}\mathbf{u}_4$ is computed to obtain the coefficients of the fitted regression function

$$\hat{y}^{(1)} = -1.112910 + .382123x - .030562x^2 + .000790x^3 \qquad (4.1\text{-}36)$$

This method of computing the coefficients is more stable numerically than (4.1-10).

A plot of (4.1-36) is shown in Fig. 4.1-6. (A plot of the quadratic function for the Poggendorff illusion appears in Fig. 4.1-7.) The function for the Ponzo illusion is difficult to interpret: The fact that the cubic component is significant indicates that the anomalously low mean for the 12.5-year group cannot be attributed to random sampling variation. Indeed, the pattern of the observed means gives the impression that there is a discontinuity between ages 10.5 and 12.5, and that the upward developmental trend begins anew in this region. If so, a single polynomial could not be expected to fit the data in a smooth curve, nor could the cubic function (4.1-36) be taken at face value.

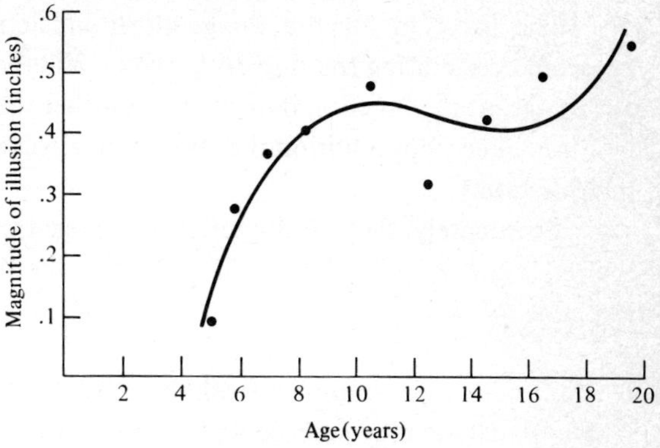

FIGURE 4.1-6
Magnitude of the Ponzo illusion as a function of age.

Although a discontinuity in age trend might be associated with the onset of adolescence, there is no precedent in the literature for the falling back to earlier levels which appears in these data. Perhaps a more likely explanation is that some accidental bias influenced the sampling of the older groups, or some unnoticed change in the experimental conditions affected the measurement procedure. In that case, the cubic function in Fig. 4.1-6 would not warrant any attempt at psychological interpretation.

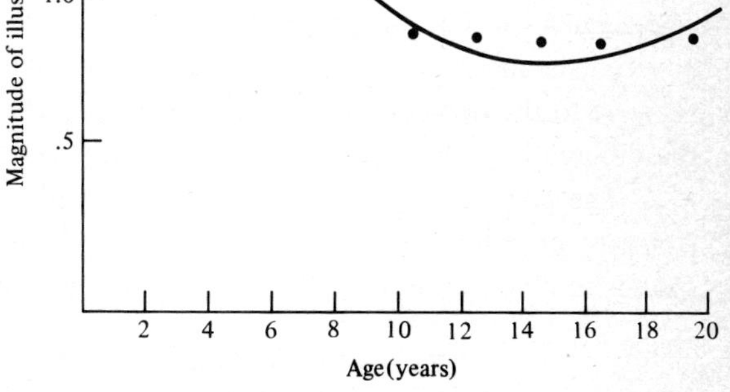

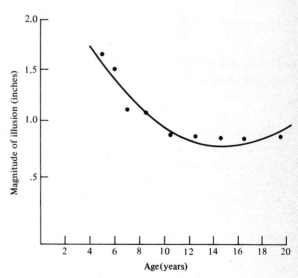

FIGURE 4.1-7
Magnitude of the Poggendorff illusion as a function of age.

The function for the Poggendorff illusion is more plausible and shows the expected decelerating trend to 14.5 years. Whether a turning point is actually reached at this age, as the function indicates, is another matter. A horizontal asymptote would be more likely, but additional data points at older ages would be required to resolve the question.*

Fortunately, these ambiguities in the age trend of the illusions concern primarily the older age groups. They will not affect the testing of hypnotic age regression in Example 4.1-7.

b Stepwise regression analysis by pivoting The calculations of stepwise regression analysis may be executed, by pivoting, in a remarkably compact form called the Wherry-Doolittle method [Wherry, 1940].† The calculations begin with the matrix:

$$\mathbf{M}_m^{(0)} = \begin{bmatrix} \mathbf{X}_m'\mathbf{D}\mathbf{X}_m & \mathbf{X}_m'\mathbf{D}\mathbf{y}. \\ \mathbf{y}_.'\mathbf{D}\mathbf{X}_m & \mathbf{y}_.'\mathbf{D}\mathbf{y}. \end{bmatrix} \begin{matrix} m+1 \\ 1 \end{matrix} \qquad \begin{matrix} m+1 & \quad 1 \end{matrix} \tag{4.1-37}$$

Then, $m + 1$ of the pivoting operations described in Example 2.3-1 are performed with the pivots chosen in order from the leading elements of the main diagonal (see Example 4.1-5).

At the $(k + 1)$st stage of the pivoting procedure, the matrix contains the following quantities:

$$\mathbf{M}_m^{(k)} = \begin{bmatrix} (\mathbf{X}_k'\mathbf{D}\mathbf{X}_k)^{-1} & \cdots & \hat{\boldsymbol{\beta}}_k \\ \cdots & \cdots & \cdots \\ -\hat{\boldsymbol{\beta}}_k' & \cdots & \mathbf{y}_.'[\mathbf{D} - \mathbf{D}\mathbf{X}_k(\mathbf{X}_k'\mathbf{D}\mathbf{X}_k)^{-1}\mathbf{X}_k'\mathbf{D}]\mathbf{y}. \end{bmatrix} \begin{matrix} k+1 \\ m-k \\ 1 \end{matrix} \qquad \begin{matrix} k+1 & m-k & 1 \end{matrix} \tag{4.1-38}$$

That is, the leading $k + 1$ rows and columns contain the inverse of the matrix of coefficients in the normal equations for the degree-k model, the $k + 1$ leading elements of the last column contain the least-squares estimates for the degree-k model, and the $(k + 1)$st leading elements of the last row contain the negative of these estimates. The element in the lower right contains the residual sum of squares for the degree-k model. The increase in the regression sum of squares when stepping from the degree-$(k - 1)$ to the degree-k model, that is, ssr_k in the one-degree-of-freedom analysis, is the difference in the residual sum of squares between the kth and $(k + 1)$st stages.

The pivoting steps thus correspond to adding terms to the polynomial model. Any row or column which is repivoted (or pivoted an even number of times) corresponds to *removing* terms from the polynomial. In a computer, it is most economical

* For developmental data which exhibit an asymptote, a logistic function (see Bock et al. [1973]) may provide a better fit than the polynomial used here. Fitting a logistic function, however, requires nonlinear estimation (see Chap. 8).

† Also called the Efroymson algorithm [Efroymson, 1960].

of storage space to perform the $m + 1$ pivots initially, then to work back, pivoting on the $(m + 1)$st, mth, $(m - 1)$st, etc., diagonal element in turn. At each step the reduction in regression sum of squares may be tested for significance. When a significant reduction is encountered, the last element pivoted is repivoted. The least-squares estimates of the regression coefficients, the residual sum of squares, and the matrix required in computing the variances and covariances of the estimates may then be read directly from the matrix.

The detailed justification of this procedure is given in many texts (e.g., Dempster [1969]) and will not be repeated here. An application of the procedure to the Ponzo data follows.

EXAMPLE 4.1-5 (*Stepwise regression by pivoting*) To save space, the steps in the pivoting procedure are shown only for the degree-3 model. The matrix of squares and cross products to be pivoted, designated $\mathbf{M}_3^{(0)}$, is, to eight significant figures,

$$\mathbf{M}_3^{(0)} = 16 \begin{bmatrix} .90000000(1) & & & & (\text{symmetric}) \\ .10000000(3) & .11311500(4) & & & \\ .13115000(4) & .19364500(5) & .30902638(6) & & \\ .19364500(5) & .30902638(6) & .51883431(7) & .90165545(8) & \\ .34100000(1) & .42145000(2) & .59384750(3) & .91908363(4) & .14433000(1) \end{bmatrix}$$

The results of four successive pivoting steps are as follows:

$$\mathbf{M}_3^{(1)} = 16 \begin{bmatrix} .111111(0) & .111111(2) & .145722(3) & .215161(4) & .378889(1) \\ -.111111(2) & .200389(3) & & & \\ -.145722(3) & .479228(4) & .117912(6) & & (\text{symmetric}) \\ -.215161(4) & .938653(5) & .236651(7) & .485007(8) & \\ -.378889(0) & .425611(1) & .969347(2) & .185384(4) & .151289(0) \end{bmatrix}$$

$$\mathbf{M}_3^{(2)} = 16 \cdot \begin{bmatrix} .727197(0) & -.554477(-1) & -.119999(3) & -.305301(4) & .142897(0) \\ -.554477(-1) & .499030(-2) & .239149(2) & .468416(3) & .212393(-1) \\ .119999(3) & -.239149(2) & .330490(4) & .121728(6) & -.484970(1) \\ .305301(4) & -.468416(3) & .121728(6) & .453273(7) & -.139786(3) \\ -.142897(0) & -.212393(-1) & -.484970(1) & -.139786(3) & .608923(-1) \end{bmatrix}$$

$$\mathbf{M}_3^{(3)} = 16 \cdot \begin{bmatrix} .508428(1) & & (\text{symmetric}) & .136686(4) & -.331924(-1) \\ -.923783(0) & .178043(0) & & -.412432(3) & .563261(-1) \\ .363094(-1) & -.723620(-2) & .302581(-3) & .368326(2) & -.146743(-2) \\ -.136686(4) & .412432(3) & -.368326(2) & .491707(5) & .388408(2) \\ .331924(-1) & -.563326(-1) & .146743(-2) & .388408(2) & .537756(-1) \end{bmatrix}$$

$$\mathbf{M}_3^{(4)} = 16$$

$$\cdot \begin{bmatrix} .430806(2) & & \text{(symmetric)} & & -.111290(1) \\ -.123887(2) & .363742(1) & & & .382120(0) \\ .106019(2) & -.316179(0) & .278930(-1) & & -.305622(-1) \\ -.277983(-1) & .838776(-2) & -.749077(-3) & .203373(-4) & .789918(-3) \\ .112900(1) & -.382120(0) & .305622(-1) & -.789918(-3) & .230946(-1) \end{bmatrix}$$

Differencing the element in the fifth row and column of these matrices gives the squares for the one-degree-of-freedom analysis:

$$\begin{aligned} 16 \times 1.443300 &= 23.092800 \\ 16 \times \ .151289 &= 2.420624 \\ 16 \times \ .060892 &= .974272 \\ 16 \times \ .053776 &= .860416 \\ 16 \times \ .023095 &= .369520 \end{aligned} \qquad \begin{aligned} 20.67218 &= ssr_0 \\ 1.44635 &= ssr_1 \\ .11386 &= ssr_2 \\ .49090 &= ssr_3 \end{aligned}$$

These figures agree closely with those obtained by orthogonalization in Table 4.1-7. In the disagreement in the fifth place, the result from the more accurate orthogonalization procedure is correct. In both cases, the calculations were performed in nine-digit precision.

The regression coefficients which appear in the last column of $\mathbf{M}_3^{(3)}$ and $\mathbf{M}_3^{(4)}$ may be compared with those calculated previously for the degree-2 model (4.1-17) and the degree-3 model (4.1-36). Among the coefficients in $\mathbf{M}_3^{(4)}$, there are a few discrepancies in the sixth place from the more accurate calculations of (4.1-36).

Finally, the inverse matrix for the degree-2 model in the first three rows and columns of $\mathbf{M}_3^{(3)}$ may be compared with that of Example 4.1-2; they agree exactly. The inverse matrix from $\mathbf{M}_3^{(4)}$ will be used in Example 4.1-7 to obtain the sampling covariance matrix for the fitted coefficients of the degree-3 model for the Ponzo data.

c Stepwise regression analysis with ungrouped data In many regression problems the values of the independent variable are scattered irregularly rather than grouped at certain values as in Table 4.1-1. Although it is always possible to group such data *post hoc* in order to apply the preceding methods, it may be more convenient to perform the stepwise regression analysis directly on the ungrouped data. This is possible, provided we are willing to assume that the residual from the highest-degree model represents error variation only. In that case, the error estimate for the denominator of the stepwise F tests may be obtained by subtraction of the regression sum of squares from the total sum of squares. The analysis then takes the form shown in Table 4.1-8.

Again, the F tests based on the values

$$F_j = \frac{u_j^2}{\text{sse}'/(N - m - 1)}$$

are statistically independent, given the error estimate. Thus, the joint Type I error for a number of such tests may be adjusted to an assigned value by (4.1-35).

Anderson [1962] and Das Gupta [1970] have shown that stochastic independence of the F tests also holds when the squares for terms rejected from the model are pooled with the error term and the error degrees of freedom are adjusted accordingly. Except when the number of error degrees of freedom is small, such pooling has little effect on the error estimate and is not essential.

As mentioned in Sec. 4.1.2, the calculations for unreplicated data are a slight specialization of those for grouped data. If there are N ungrouped observations, $\mathbf{D}$ specializes to the $N \times N$ identity matrix $\mathbf{I}$; whence,

$$\mathbf{X}'\mathbf{D}\mathbf{X} = \mathbf{X}'\mathbf{I}\mathbf{X} = \mathbf{X}'\mathbf{X}$$

$$\mathbf{X}'\mathbf{D}\mathbf{y}. = \mathbf{X}'\mathbf{I}\mathbf{y} = \mathbf{X}'\mathbf{y}$$

and

$$\mathbf{y}'.\mathbf{D}\mathbf{y}. = \mathbf{y}'\mathbf{I}\mathbf{y} = \mathbf{y}'\mathbf{y} = \sum_{i=1}^{N} y_i^2$$

where $\mathbf{y}$ is the $N \times 1$ vector of observations. In the absence of replication, there is no within-groups sum of squares, and sst replaces ssg as in Table 4.1-8.

Table 4.1-8 STEPWISE ANALYSIS OF REGRESSION WITH UNGROUPED DATA

Source of variation	df	Sums of squares	Expected sum of squares
$\mathbf{x}_0^*$	1	$\text{ssr}_0 = u_0^2$	$\sigma^2 + \gamma_0^2$
$\mathbf{x}_1^*$	1	$\text{ssr}_1 = u_1^2$	$\sigma^2 + \gamma_1^2$
$\mathbf{x}_2^*$	1	$\text{ssr}_2 = u_2^2$	$\sigma^2 + \gamma_2^2$
...	...	...	...
$\mathbf{x}_m^*$	1	$\text{ssr}_m = u_m^2$	$\sigma^2 + \gamma_m^2$
Residual	$N - m - 1$	$\text{sse}' = \text{sst} - \sum_{k=0}^{m} u_k^2$	$(N - m - 1)\sigma^2$
Total	N	$\text{sst} = \sum_{i=1}^{N} y_i^2$	

In other respects, the calculations for the replicated and unreplicated cases are the same, except that it may not be practical to proceed by direct orthonormalization of $\mathbf{X}$ when N is large. In that case, it is better first to compute $\mathbf{X}'\mathbf{X}$, then its inverse Cholesky factor $\mathbf{S}^{-1}$, and to obtain the orthogonal estimates as

$$\mathbf{u} = \mathbf{S}^{-1}\mathbf{X}'\mathbf{y}\,.$$

Alternatively, the pivoting method may be applied to the matrix

$$\mathbf{M} = \begin{bmatrix} \mathbf{X}'\mathbf{X} & \mathbf{X}'\mathbf{y} \\ \mathbf{y}'\mathbf{X} & \mathbf{y}'\mathbf{y} \end{bmatrix}$$

At the final stage of pivoting, the value which replaces $\mathbf{y}'\mathbf{y}$ is sse$'$.

When the degree of the model has been chosen to be g, say, the least-squares estimates may be calculated from

$$\hat{\boldsymbol{\beta}}_g = (\mathbf{S}_g^{-1})'\mathbf{u}_g \qquad (4.1\text{-}39)$$

[which is just (4.1-34) with $\mathbf{D}$ specialized to $\mathbf{I}$] or extracted at the gth stage of the pivoting procedure.

EXAMPLE 4.1-6 (*Stepwise regression analysis without grouping*) The figures required to perform, on the Ponzo, the stepwise regression in the unreplication case are contained in Table 4.1-7. It is only necessary to subtract the regression total from the total sum of squares to obtain the residual sum of squares on 138 degrees of freedom. The result is shown in Table 4.1-9. The F statistics in this table are almost identical with those in Table 4.1-7. The same choice of polynomial is implied.

Table 4.1-9 STEPWISE REGRESSION ANALYSIS (WITHOUT GROUPING) FOR THE PONZO DATA

Source of variation	df	Sum of squares	F	p
$\mathbf{x}_0^*$	1	20.67218	442.43	$< .0005$
$\mathbf{x}_1^*$	1	1.44634	30.88	$< .0005$
$\mathbf{x}_2^*$	1	.11386	2.43	$.1 < p < .3$
$\mathbf{x}_3^*$	1	.49090	10.48	$.001 < p < .005$
$\mathbf{x}_4^*$	1	.21454	4.58	$.025 < p < .05$
$\mathbf{x}_5^*$	1	.01848	.39	$> .5$
Regression total	6	22.95630		
Residual	138	6.46200		
Total	144	29.41830		

4.1.11 The Dangers of Overfitting

When the regression sum of squares is expressed as the sum of squared orthogonal estimates, as in Table 4.1-6, it is clear that the residual sum of squares is never increased, and in general is reduced, by the addition of terms in the polynomial model. This fact may seem to suggest that, if one is to err in specifying the degree of the polynomial, it is better to err in the direction of overfitting the data by including superfluous higher-degree terms than of underfitting through the omission of essential terms.

This strategy is not well considered, however, for it does not take account of the loss of precision in estimating the regression coefficients that is incurred as additional terms are added. Unless the data are very extensive, the overfitted model will be sensitive to sampling error and will approximate poorly the actual functional relationship between the variables. Thus, the small residuals in the overfitted data are illusionary: They will not be realized when the empirical regression equation is applied to new data.

How the sampling variances of the least-squares estimates increase as terms are added is easily demonstrated. Consider a $k \times k$ symmetric positive-definite matrix $\mathbf{A}_k$, partitioned in the form

$$\mathbf{A}_k = \left[\begin{array}{c|c} \mathbf{A}_{k-1} & \mathbf{a}_k \\ \hline \mathbf{a}_k' & a_{kk} \end{array}\right] \begin{array}{l} k-1 \\ 1 \end{array}$$
$$\qquad\qquad k-1 \quad 1$$

The inverse of $\mathbf{A}_k$ may be expressed in terms of $\mathbf{A}_{k-1}{}^{-1}$ by means of the simple bordering formula as follows:

$$\mathbf{A}_k{}^{-1} = \left[\begin{array}{c|c} \mathbf{A}_{k-1}{}^{-1} & \mathbf{0} \\ \hline \mathbf{0}' & 0 \end{array}\right] + \frac{1}{d_{kk}} \begin{bmatrix} \mathbf{b}_k\mathbf{b}_k' & -\mathbf{b}_k \\ -\mathbf{b}_k' & 1 \end{bmatrix} \tag{4.1-40}$$

where $d_{kk} = a_{kk} - \mathbf{a}_k'\mathbf{A}_{k-1}{}^{-1}\mathbf{a}_k$ and $\mathbf{b}_k = \mathbf{A}_{k-1}{}^{-1}\mathbf{a}_k$ [Feedeva, 1959].

Because $\mathbf{A}_k$ is pd, $\mathbf{A}_k{}^{-1}$ is also pd, and d_{kk} is strictly positive. Thus, the terms added to the diagonal of $\mathbf{A}_{k-1}{}^{-1}$ when forming $\mathbf{A}_k{}^{-1}$ are never negative and are jointly zero only on condition that $\mathbf{a}_k = \mathbf{0}$.

In the present context,

$$\mathbf{A}_{k-1} = \mathbf{X}_{k-1}'\mathbf{D}\mathbf{X}_{k-1}$$
$$a_{kk} = \mathbf{x}_k'\mathbf{D}\mathbf{x}_k$$

and

$$\mathbf{a}_k = \mathbf{X}_{k-1}'\mathbf{D}\mathbf{x}_k$$

Hence, the leading $k - 1$ diagonal elements of $(\mathbf{X}_k'\mathbf{D}\mathbf{X}_k)^{-1}$ are generally larger than those of $(\mathbf{X}_{k-1}'\mathbf{D}\mathbf{X}_{k-1})$, provided $\mathbf{X}_{k-1}'\mathbf{D}\mathbf{x}_k \neq \mathbf{0}$. In fact, they may be much larger, as is evident in the calculations for stepwise regression by pivoting shown in Example 4.1-5. The inverses of $\mathbf{X}_k'\mathbf{D}\mathbf{X}_k$ for $k = 1, 2, 3$, and 4, which appear in the leading k rows and columns of $\mathbf{M}_s{}^{(k)}$, reveal that the diagonal elements already in the inverse increase markedly as columns are added to **X**. In the degree-1 model, for example, the variance of the estimator of the linear coefficient is $.00499\sigma^2/16$; in the degree-3 model, it is $3.63742\sigma^2/16$. The variance has increased, and precision has been lost, by a factor of order 1,000. The estimates for the degree-3 model obviously convey much less information about the true value of the linear coefficient than do the estimates for the degree-1 model.

Note that these differences in precision depend only upon the independent variable, the values of which are at the disposal of the investigator. This fact raises the question of how the values of the independent variable might be chosen to provide optimal precision in estimating the regression coefficients. It is clear from (4.1-40) that we should choose $\mathbf{x}_k$ so that $\mathbf{X}'_{k-1}\mathbf{D}\mathbf{x}_k = \mathbf{0}$, that is, so that column k in the model matrix is orthogonal, in the metric **D**, to all other columns of **X**. In that case, the model is said to be *orthogonal*, and the variance of the kth estimate is proportional to $1/\mathbf{x}_k'\mathbf{D}\mathbf{x}_k$. That is, orthogonal models have the property that the addition of terms has no effect on the precision of estimation for terms already in the model.

In the case of polynomial models, it is obviously impossible to choose values of the independent variable so as to obtain a general orthogonal model. But in the application of least squares to multifactor models discussed in Chap. 5 (see also Exercise 4.1-3), there are opportunities for manipulating the independent variables to obtain partial or complete orthogonality. This is the basis for the subject of experimental design, about which we shall have more to say later.

4.1.12 Confidence Intervals for Regression Coefficients

a Separate confidence intervals Confidence intervals for the regression coefficients may be constructed by a method due to Neyman [1937]. The assumption that the distribution of the group means is multivariate normal, $N(\mathbf{X}\boldsymbol{\beta}, \sigma^2\mathbf{D}^{-1})$, is required. It then follows from (4.1-20) and (4.1-21) that the distribution of $\hat{\boldsymbol{\beta}}$ is multivariate normal, $N[\boldsymbol{\beta}, \sigma^2(\mathbf{X}'\mathbf{D}\mathbf{X})^{-1}]$.

For ease of writing, let $\mathbf{C} = (\mathbf{X}'\mathbf{D}\mathbf{X})^{-1}$; then $\hat{\beta}_k$, the kth element of $\hat{\boldsymbol{\beta}}$, is univariate normal, $N(\beta_k, \sigma^2 c_{kk})$, where c_{kk} is the kth diagonal element of **C**. From the analysis of variance, we obtained an estimator of σ^2 on n_e degrees of freedom, $\hat{\sigma}_{(n_e)}{}^2$, which we showed was distributed as $\chi_{(n_e)}{}^2/\sigma^2$ independent of $\hat{\boldsymbol{\beta}}$. This implies (see Sec. 3.4) that

$$F = \frac{(\hat{\beta}_k - \beta_k)^2}{\hat{\sigma}_{(n_e)}{}^2 c_{kk}}$$

is distributed as a central F statistic on 1 and n_e degrees of freedom. Thus, for an assigned Type I error α, we can write the exact probability statement

$$\text{Prob}\left[\frac{(\hat{\beta}_k - \beta_k)^2}{\hat{\sigma}_{(n_e)}{}^2 c_{kk}} \le F_\alpha^{(1,n_e)}\right] = 1 - \alpha$$

According to the familiar rules for inequalities, this statement is equivalent to

$$\text{Prob}\left(-\sqrt{F_\alpha^{(1,n_e)}} \leq \frac{\beta_k - \beta_k}{\sqrt{\sigma_{(n_e)}{}^2 c_{kk}}} \leq \sqrt{F_\alpha^{(1,n_e)}}\right) = 1 - \alpha$$

and

$$\text{Prob}(\beta_k - \sqrt{F_\alpha^{(1,n_e)}\sigma_{(n_e)}{}^2 c_{kk}} \leq \beta_k \leq \beta_k + \sqrt{F_\alpha^{(1,n_e)}\sigma_{(n_e)}{}^2 c_{kk}}) = 1 - \alpha \qquad (4.1\text{-}41)$$

That is, the probability that the interval $\beta_k \pm \sqrt{F_\alpha^{(1,n_e)}\sigma_{(n_e)}{}^2 c_{kk}}$ includes the true parameter value β_k is $1 - \alpha$. This interval is called the $100(1 - \alpha)$ percent *confidence interval* for β_k.

Since $\sqrt{\sigma_{(n_e)}{}^2 c_{kk}} = \text{SE}(\hat{\beta}_k)$ and $\sqrt{F_\alpha^{(1,n_e)}} = t_{\alpha/2}{}^{(n_e)}$, where $t_\alpha{}^{(n_e)}$ is a Student's t statistic on n_e degrees of freedom, we may also express this interval as

$$\beta_k \pm t_{\alpha/2}{}^{(n_e)}\text{SE}(\hat{\beta}_k) \qquad (4.1\text{-}42)$$

As n_e becomes large (> 30), Student's t approaches z_α, the normal deviate corresponding to the area α in one tail of the normal curve. The confidence coefficient of the interval

$$\beta_k \pm z_{\alpha/2}\,\text{SE}(\hat{\beta}_k) \qquad (4.1\text{-}43)$$

therefore approaches the $100(1 - \alpha)$ percent interval with increasing n_e. Because the .975 point of the normal distribution is very near 2 (actually 1.96), it is common practice to report $\hat{\beta}_k \pm 2\,\text{SE}(\hat{\beta}_k)$ as an approximate 95 percent confidence interval for β_k.

Confidence intervals and standard errors have an important place in the reporting of empirical studies. If the estimated regression coefficient (or indeed any estimate) is accompanied by its confidence interval or standard error, the reader has some idea of the range of hypothetical parameter values which is consistent with the data. He can then judge whether the value implied by some alternative theory is equally acceptable, given the data, as the theory propounded by the investigator.

b Joint confidence regions The confidence intervals derived above do not take into account the correlation among the estimates which was noted in Example 4.1-3. Because of the correlation, it is quite possible for two or more regression coefficients to be consistent with respect to their separate confidence intervals, while being inconsistent jointly. To take account of this possibility, we must construct a *joint confidence region* for two or more parameters simultaneously. In the context of least squares, a confidence region for regression coefficients may be deduced from the orthogonal reparameterization defined in Sec. 4.1.4. In terms of the orthogonal estimator $\boldsymbol{u}$, we can write the exact probability statement

$$\text{Prob}\left[\frac{(\boldsymbol{u} - \gamma)'(\boldsymbol{u} - \gamma)}{(g + 1)\sigma_{(n_e)}{}^2} \leq F_\alpha^{(g+1,n_e)}\right] = 1 - \alpha \qquad (4.1\text{-}44)$$

Substituting

$$(\boldsymbol{u} - \gamma)'(\boldsymbol{u} - \gamma) = (\boldsymbol{\beta} - \boldsymbol{\beta})'\mathbf{SS}'(\boldsymbol{\beta} - \boldsymbol{\beta}) = (\boldsymbol{\beta} - \boldsymbol{\beta})'\mathbf{X}'\mathbf{DX}(\boldsymbol{\beta} - \boldsymbol{\beta})$$

and transforming the inequality, we have

$$\text{Prob}[(\boldsymbol{\beta} - \boldsymbol{\beta})'\mathbf{X}'\mathbf{DX}(\boldsymbol{\beta} - \boldsymbol{\beta}) \leq (g + 1)\sigma_{(n_e)}{}^2 F_\alpha{}^{(g+1,n_e)}] = 1 - \alpha$$

The inequality in this statement defines, with respect to variation in $\boldsymbol{\beta}$, a $(g + 1)$-dimensional ellipsoidal region centered on $\boldsymbol{\beta}$. Points on the boundary of the region are the real solutions of the equation

$$(\boldsymbol{\beta} - \boldsymbol{\beta})\mathbf{X}'\mathbf{DX}(\boldsymbol{\beta} - \boldsymbol{\beta}) = (g + 1)\sigma_{(n_e)}{}^2 F_\alpha{}^{(g+1,n_e)} \qquad (4.1\text{-}45)$$

The probability that this region includes the point $\boldsymbol{\beta}$ is $1 - \alpha$.

As it stands, (4.1-45) includes variation in the estimate of the constant term β_0. In many regression problems, however, β_0 is arbitrary because the origin of measurement of the dependent variable is arbitrary. In that case, we would prefer a confidence region for $\beta_1, \beta_2, \ldots, \beta_g$ conditional on β_0. This region may be constructed from the g orthogonal estimates $\mathbf{u}_0' = [u_1, u_2, \ldots, u_g]$, say.

In terms of the estimator $\boldsymbol{u}_0$, the statistic

$$F^{(g,n_e)} = \frac{(\boldsymbol{u}_0 - \gamma_0)'(\boldsymbol{u}_0 - \gamma_0)}{g\sigma_{(n_e)}{}^2} = \frac{\boldsymbol{\beta}_c'\mathbf{S}_0'\mathbf{S}_0\boldsymbol{\beta}_c}{g\sigma_{(n_e)}{}^2}$$

where $\gamma_0' = [\gamma_1, \gamma_2, \ldots, \gamma_g]$, $\boldsymbol{\beta}_c = [\beta_1, \beta_2, \ldots, \beta_g]$, and $\mathbf{S}_0$ is the last g rows and columns of $\mathbf{S}$, is distributed as a central F on g and n_e degrees of freedom.

The matrix $\mathbf{S}_0'\mathbf{S}_0$ is the matrix of sums of squares and cross products of elements in the columns of $\mathbf{X}$ with the column means eliminated, or, as we say, "corrected" to the column means. In matric terms, the vector of column means can be expressed as

$$\bar{\mathbf{x}}' = \frac{1}{N}\mathbf{1}'\mathbf{DX}$$

where $\mathbf{1}$ is a vector of n unities and $N = \sum N_j$. Then

$$\mathbf{S}_0'\mathbf{S}_0 = \mathbf{X}'\mathbf{DX} - N\bar{\mathbf{x}}\bar{\mathbf{x}}' \qquad (4.1\text{-}46)$$

Thus, the confidence region for the regression coefficients, given β_0, is bounded by the ellipsoid

$$(\boldsymbol{\beta}_c - \boldsymbol{\beta}_c)'(\mathbf{X}'\mathbf{DX} - N\bar{\mathbf{x}}\bar{\mathbf{x}}')(\boldsymbol{\beta}_c - \boldsymbol{\beta}_c) = g\sigma_{(n_e)}{}^2 F_\alpha^{(g,n_e)} \qquad (4.1\text{-}47)$$

Unfortunately, the region defined by (4.1-45) or (4.1-47) is difficult to visualize when the number of parameters exceeds two. Perhaps the best that can be done in this case is to tabulate some typical points on the boundary (see, however, Wallace [1958]). It is unfortunate that confidence regions are too cumbersome to be routinely reported, for, as Example 4.1-7 suggests, the joint confidence region delimits possible values of the parameters much more sharply than the separate intervals when the estimates are highly correlated.

EXAMPLE 4.1-7 (*Interval estimates of the regression coefficient*) The following calculations are for the Poggendorff data only. Ninety-five percent confidence intervals are computed from the standard errors in Example 4.1-3, and the F value for the .05 level on 1 and 135 degrees of freedom from Appendix A:

$$2.7767 - \sqrt{3.91}(.2510) \le \beta_0 \le 2.7767 + \sqrt{3.91}(.2510)$$
$$2.2804 \le \beta_0 \le 3.2730$$

$$-.2421 - \sqrt{3.91}(.0470) \le \beta_1 \le -.2421 + \sqrt{3.91}(.0470)$$
$$-.3350 \le \beta_1 \le -.1492$$

$$.0080 - \sqrt{3.91}(.0020) \le \beta_2 \le .0080 + \sqrt{3.91}(.0020)$$
$$.0040 \le \beta_2 \le .0120$$

To illustrate a joint confidence region, we take β_0 as given and compute the conditional region for β_1 and β_2. The boundary points of the 95 percent region are the real solutions of

$$[(\beta_1 + .2421)(\beta_2 - .0800)]\begin{bmatrix} 200.4 & 4{,}792.3 \\ 4{,}792.3 & 117{,}911.972 \end{bmatrix}\begin{bmatrix} \beta_1 + .2421 \\ \beta_2 - .0800 \end{bmatrix} = \frac{2 \times .16460 \times 3.07}{16}$$

or

$$200.4(\beta_1 + .2421)^2 + 9{,}584.6(\beta_1 + .2421)(\beta_2 - .0080) + 117{,}911.972(\beta_2 - .0800)^2 = .0632 \qquad (4.1\text{-}48)$$

The elements in the matrix of this form were computed by (4.1-46) but could have been obtained (less accurately) from the matrix in the intersection of the second and third rows and columns of the Cholesky factor in Example 4.1-4:

$$\begin{bmatrix} .14155(2) & 0 \\ .33853(3) & .57488(2) \end{bmatrix}\begin{bmatrix} .14155(2) & .33853(3) \\ 0 & .57488(2) \end{bmatrix} = \begin{bmatrix} 200.4 & 4{,}791.9 \\ 4{,}791.9 & 117{,}907. \end{bmatrix}$$

The matrix also appears in the intersection of the second and third rows and columns of $\mathbf{M}_3^{(1)}$ in the pivoting calculations in Example 4.1-5.

The graph of (4.1-48) appears in Fig. 4.1-8. Note that, whereas the margins of the confidence region extend over about the same range of β_1 and β_2 as the intervals above, the region is highly elongated and occupies only a small fraction of the area of the rectangle defined by the separate confidence intervals.

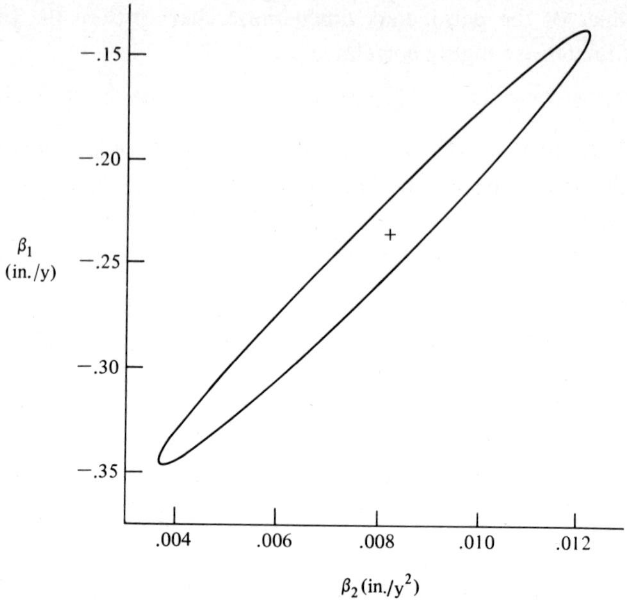

FIGURE 4.1-8
Confidence region for linear and quadratic coefficients of age trend in the Poggendorff illusion.

4.1.13 Tolerance Interval for a New Observation or for the Mean of n New Observations

The regression analysis presented in this chapter enables us to solve a fundamental problem of statistical prediction—namely, for a given value of the independent variable, to construct an interval for the dependent variable which has an assigned probability of including a new, independently sampled observation. Provided the model specified by (4.1-1) is correct and the error component is distributed normally, this problem has a solution in terms of a "tolerance" interval centered on $(\hat{y} \mid x)$, that is, on the predicted value of y for the given x. We begin the construction of this interval by computing the variance of the predictor $(\hat{y} \mid x)$.

Let the $1 \times (g + 1)$ vector $\mathbf{x}'$ be a row of the model matrix $\mathbf{X}$ corresponding to the given value of the independent variable. In polynomial regression this vector is

$$\mathbf{x}' = [1, x, x^2, \ldots, x^g]$$

The value of y predicted from this value of x is then

$$\hat{y} = \mathbf{x}'\hat{\boldsymbol{\beta}}$$

Since $\mathbf{x}$ is fixed, we have

$$\mathscr{V}(\hat{y} \mid x) = \mathbf{x}'[\mathscr{V}(\boldsymbol{\beta})]\mathbf{x} = \sigma^2\mathbf{x}'(\mathbf{X}'\mathbf{D}\mathbf{X})^{-1}\mathbf{x}$$

Because the variance of a new observation is

$$\mathscr{V}(y) = \sigma^2$$

and y and $\hat{y}$ are independent, the variance of the deviation from prediction is

$$\mathscr{V}(y - \hat{y} \mid x) = \sigma^2[1 + \mathbf{x}'(\mathbf{X}'\mathbf{D}\mathbf{X})^{-1}\mathbf{x}]$$

But $\mathscr{E}(y - \hat{y} \mid x) = 0$; hence, the variance ratio

$$F = \frac{(y - \hat{y} \mid x)^2}{\sigma_{(n_e)}{}^2[1 + \mathbf{x}'(\mathbf{X}'\mathbf{D}\mathbf{X})^{-1}\mathbf{x}]} \tag{4.1-49}$$

is distributed as a central F statistic on 1 and n_e degrees of freedom. We may therefore proceed, as in Sec. 4.1.12, to transform the probability statement

$$\text{Prob}\left[\frac{(y - \hat{y} \mid x)^2}{\sigma_{(n_e)}{}^2[1 + \mathbf{x}'(\mathbf{X}'\mathbf{D}\mathbf{X})^{-1}\mathbf{x}]} < F_\alpha^{(1,n_e)}\right] = 1 - \alpha$$

into the tolerance interval

$$(\hat{y} \mid x) - \{F_\alpha^{(1,n_e)}\sigma_{(n_e)}{}^2[1 + \mathbf{x}'(\mathbf{X}'\mathbf{D}\mathbf{X})^{-1}\mathbf{x}]\}^{1/2}$$
$$\leq (y \mid x) \leq (\hat{y} \mid x) + \{F_\alpha^{(1,n_e)}\sigma_{(n_e)}{}^2[1 + \mathbf{x}'(\mathbf{X}'\mathbf{D}\mathbf{X})^{-1}\mathbf{x}]\}^{1/2} \tag{4.1-50}$$

with coefficient $1 - \alpha$.

If there are N independent new observations, a similar but smaller interval may be constructed for their mean,

$$y_{.} = \sum_{i=1}^{N} \frac{y_i}{N}$$

The variance of $y_{.}$ is

$$\mathscr{V}(y_{.}) = \frac{\sigma^2}{N}$$

from which the tolerance interval for $y_{.} \mid x$ is

$$y_{.} \mid x \pm \sqrt{F_\alpha^{(1,n_e)}\sigma_{(n_e)}{}^2\left[\frac{1}{N} + \mathbf{x}'(\mathbf{X}'\mathbf{D}\mathbf{X})^{-1}\mathbf{x}\right]} \tag{4.1-51}$$

This interval also has coefficient $1 - \alpha$.

The tolerance interval on the mean of N new observations makes possible an exact answer to the question posed in the example at the beginning of this chapter—namely, do subjects hypnotically regressed to a given age respond to the Ponzo and Poggendorff illusions in a manner appropriate to that age. This question is examined in the following example.

EXAMPLE 4.1-8 (*Tolerance intervals for new observations of the Ponzo and Poggendorff illusions*) Parrish, Lundy, and Leibowitz [1968] report the following mean illusions for 10 undergraduate students regressed hypnotically to 9 years of age:

Ponzo: .3875 in. Poggendorff: 1.41 in.

According to the functions (4.1-36) and (4.1-18) fitted to the age trend of these illusions, the expected size of illusion at age 9 is, respectively,

$$-1.112915 + .382124 \times 9 - .030563 \times 81 + .000790 \times 729 = .4251$$

and

$$2.776735 - .242116 \times 9 + .008030 \times 81 = 1.2481$$

The corresponding variances of the illusions conditional on age have been estimated (Example 4.1.3) as .04686 and .16460.

In order to obtain from (4.1-51) the tolerance intervals on the mean of 10 new observations, we first compute the terms $\mathbf{x}'(\mathbf{X}'\mathbf{D}\mathbf{X})^{-1}\mathbf{x}$ for the Ponzo and Poggendorff:

$$\tfrac{1}{16}[1, 9, 81, 729] \cdot \begin{bmatrix} .430806(2) & & & (\text{symmetric}) \\ -.123887(2) & .363742(1) & & \\ .106019(1) & -.316179(0) & .278930(-1) & \\ -.277983(-1) & .838776(-2) & -.749077(03) & .203373(-4) \end{bmatrix} \cdot \begin{bmatrix} 1 \\ 9 \\ 81 \\ 729 \end{bmatrix} = .02254$$

$$\tfrac{1}{16}[1, 9, 81] \cdot \begin{bmatrix} .508428(1) & & (\text{symmetric}) \\ -.923783(0) & .178043(0) & \\ .363094(-1) & -.723620(-2) & .302581(-3) \end{bmatrix} \begin{bmatrix} 1 \\ 9 \\ 81 \end{bmatrix} = .01217$$

(The inverses are from Example 4.1-5.)

Using $F_{.05}{}^{(1,135)} = 3.91$, we then obtain

$$\sqrt{3.91 \times .04686(.1 + .02254)} = .1498$$

and

$$\sqrt{3.91 \times .16460(.1 + .01217)} = .2687$$

With respect to the mean of 10 new observations, the .95 tolerance intervals for the illusions are therefore

$$.2753 = .4251 - .1498 \le (y_{\cdot}^{(1)} \mid x = 9) \le .4251 + .1498 = .5749$$

for the Ponzo, and

$$.9794 = 1.2481 - .2687 \le (y_{\cdot}^{(2)} \mid x = 9) \le 1.2481 + .2687 = 1.5168$$

for the Poggendorff. These intervals do in fact include the observed means for the hypnotically regressed group, although the mean for the Poggendorff approaches the margin of the interval. These results are consistent with the view that, under hypnotic suggestion, the subjects can be made to revert to an authentic earlier stage of behavioral development.

This conclusion also could have been reached by using (4.1-49) in an F test or its square root in a t test. The tolerance-interval approach is more convenient, however, because it allows new observations to be checked immediately as they come in.

Exercise 4.1-1 In simple linear regression the data consist of N paired values of the independent variable x and the dependent variable y. Let the $N \times 1$ vector of the former be $\mathbf{x}$, and that of the latter $\mathbf{y}$. Then the matrix of the linear statistical model is $\mathbf{X} = [\mathbf{1},\mathbf{x}]$, where $\mathbf{1}$ is an $N \times 1$ vector of unities.

(*a*) Show that the least-squares estimate of the regression coefficient obtained by (4.1-10) translates into the formula $\hat{\beta} = (\Sigma xy - \Sigma x \Sigma y/N)/[\Sigma x^2 - (\Sigma x)^2/N]$ given in elementary texts. Express algebraically the orthonormalization of $\mathbf{X}$, and use the orthonormal columns to express in the form of Table 4.1-8 the analysis of variance for simple linear regression. Show that

$$\mathrm{ssr}_1 = \frac{(\Sigma xy - \Sigma x \Sigma y/N)^2}{\Sigma x^2 - (\Sigma x)^2/N}$$

which is the formula for the sum of squares for regression as given in elementary texts.

(*b*) Obtain the same results for the case where the observations are weighted by the $N \times N$ diagonal matrix $\mathbf{D}$.

ANSWER See Bock and Jones [1968, Appendix D].

Exercise 4.1-2 Assume that the data point .32 for the Ponzo illusion in Table 4.1-1 is defective. Rework the least-squares analysis, deleting this point by setting $\mathbf{D} = \mathrm{diag}[1, 1, 1, 1, 1, 0, 1, 1, 1]$. Does a quadratic model fit the censored data?

ANSWER $b_0 = -.165996$, $b_1 = .085108$, $b_2 = -.002622$, $\mathrm{sse} = .5330$.

Exercise 4.1-3 Bock and Jones [1968, page 192] give the following preference scores for samples of canned green beans packed in brines with various concentrations of salt and sugar:

Concentration, g/100 cc		
Salt, x	Sugar, y	Preference score, z, arbitrary units
1	1	−.240
1	2	−.159
1	3	−.349
1	4	−.405
2	1	−.039
2	2	.105
2	3	.083
2	4	−.064
3	1	.185
3	2	.271
3	3	.166
3	4	−.020
4	1	.055
4	2	.113
4	3	.136
4	4	.161

An estimate of the error variance is given as .00240 on 224 degrees of freedom.

(*a*) Obtain the least-squares fit to these data of a generalized degree-2 polynomial of the type

$$z = b_{00} + b_{10}x + b_{01}y + b_{20}x^2 + b_{02}y^2 + b_{11}xy$$

(*b*) Is the residual variation significant relative to the given error variance? Is the term with coefficient b_{11} needed in the function?

(*c*) What is the shape of the surface described by the function?

(*d*) Does salt or sugar have a greater effect on preference in this range?

(*e*) According to the fitted function, what concentration of salt and sugar yield the maximum preference value?

Exercise 4.1-4 Carry out the stepwise regression analysis for the Ponzo data assuming the unreplicated case. What alteration of matrix $\mathbf{M}_3^{(0)}$ in Example 4.1-5 is required in this case?

Exercise 4.1-5 Equation 4.1-42 implies that

$$t = \frac{\hat{\beta}_k - \beta_k}{\sqrt{\hat{\sigma}^2(n_e)c_{kk}}} \qquad (4.1\text{-}52)$$

is distributed as a central Student's t, with n_e degrees of freedom, on the hypothesis that $\beta_k = 0$. Show that a test of this hypothesis using (4.1-52) is identical to the step-wise test when β_k is the coefficient of the last term included in the stepwise testing of the polynomial.

[Hint: $(\mathbf{X}'\mathbf{D}\mathbf{X})^{-1} = (\mathbf{S}^{-1})'\mathbf{S}^{-1}$, where $\mathbf{S}$ is the (lower triangular) Cholesky factor of $\mathbf{X}'\mathbf{D}\mathbf{X}$.]

4.2 POLYNOMIAL REGRESSION ANALYSIS: MULTIVARIATE

Having reviewed in Sec. 4.1 the methods of polynomial regression analysis appropriate to a single dependent variable, we now turn to the problem of describing polynomial relationships which involve jointly two or more dependent variables. As pointed out in Chap. 1, this problem arises frequently in behavioral research because the behavior of interest is often impossible to characterize univocally. If such is the case, the only workable strategy may be to begin from a somewhat ambiguous behavioral concept and to attempt to define a number of specific response variables which derive from it. These variables in effect operationalize the concept, and the set of scores they generate for each subject represents the behavior for purposes of the data analysis.

For reasons detailed in Sec. 1.3, it is advisable, at least initially, to enter the multiple response variables jointly and symmetrically into the analysis. In the context of polynomial regression models, this means that the regression coefficients for all response variables should be estimated simultaneously (not separately as in the analysis of the Ponzo and Poggendorff data in Sec. 4.1), and that the joint variation and covariation of the variables, which we call *dispersion*, should be considered when checking the goodness of fit or making confidence statements. Fortunately, there are straightforward multivariate generalizations of univariate least squares which make such an analysis possible. We discuss these generalizations in the remainder of this chapter, continuing as in Sec. 4.1 to restrict our attention for the most part to quantitative response variables which may reasonably be assumed to follow a multivariate normal error distribution.

Numerous interesting and important studies that involve a quantitative behavioral response to an experimentally manipulated variable may be found in the literature of psychopharmacology. An example from this source will be used to illustrate the calculations in this section.

EXAMPLE 4.2-1 (*Screening psychologically active drugs*) For the preliminary assessment of prospective psychopharmaceuticals, Irwin [1968] has developed a method of evaluating the effects of experimental agents on the behavior of laboratory mice. The purpose of the evaluation is to detect and describe possible response relationships between the dosage of the agent and various behavioral indices that reflect psychological state.

Table 4.2-1 is an abstract of data from an evaluation of chloropromozine hydrochloride—a major tranquilizer. Subjects were 15 female Berkeley Swiss white

Table 4.2-1 RESPONSE OF LABORATORY MICE TO VARIOUS DOSES OF CHLOROPROMOZINE HYDROCHLORIDE

			Response variables		
Dose, mg/kg	Log_{10} dose	Animal	1 Visual placing	2 Wire maneuver	3 Palpebral closure
		1	6	0	0
1	0	7	3	1	1
		13	3	0	1
		4	6	0	0
3	.4771	10	4	0	2
		16	3	0	3
		2	2	5	4
10	1	8	3	3	3
		14	2	0	5
		6	0	6	6
30	1.4771	12	.5	4	5
		18	1	3	5.5
		5	0	7	6.5
100	2	11	0	7	5
		17	.5	5	6

mice, each assigned randomly to one of five dosage levels. Of the 49 indices defined by Irwin, only the following are included in the table: (1) visual placing, (2) wire maneuver, and (3) palpebral closure. Visual placing is assessed by lowering the animal by its tail toward a flat surface. The distance (nose to surface) at which the placing response (nose pointed, limbs extended) first occurs is noted. The response is scored as follows:

0 No placing
1 After nose contact
2 After marked contact of vibrissae (6 mm)
4 After slight contact of vibrissae (12 mm)
6 Before contact of vibrissae (18 mm)
8 Early placing (25 mm)

In the wire maneuver, the animal is lifted by the tail, allowed to grasp a horizontal wire with its four limbs, then rotated downward and released. The normal animal is usually able to grasp the wire with its hind legs and support itself, but an impaired animal may be unable to do so. The scoring is:

0 Actively grasps with hind legs
2 Moderate difficulty of grasping with hind legs
4 Unable to grasp with hind legs; slightly raises itself
6 Unable to grasp with hind legs; falls after 6–10 sec
8 Falls immediately

Palpebral closure is observed after the animal is transferred to a receiving jar. The scoring is:

0 Eyes wide open
2 One-quarter closed
4 One-half closed
6 Three-quarters closed
8 Completely closed

Although these scales are not actually continuous, there are sufficient numbers of steps to provide the possibility of a finely graded scale of group means. In the actual use of the procedure, a minimum of six animals per group is recommended, in which case a continuous distribution of the means would be better approximated than it is here (see Exercise 4.2-1).

4.2.1 The Multivariate Model

Because of the necessarily greater complexity of multivariate models, some restriction of generality is required to make them amenable to reasonably simple forms of analysis. Perhaps the most important restriction is that all the dependent variables be described by polynomials of the same degree. Occasionally, this may lead to overfitting of some of the variables: for example, the Ponzo and Poggendorff illusions jointly would require third-degree polynomials, even though the second degree would be sufficient for the Poggendorff alone. In general, however, we would expect that among a related set of dependent variables the degree of the polynomial representations would not vary so widely as to entail really serious overfitting.

One advantage of having polynomials of the same degree is that the model can be written in the form of a matrix equation. For p dependent (response) variables, the model for the p-variate observation written as a row vector may then be expressed as

$$[y^{(1)}, y^{(2)}, \ldots, y^{(p)}] = [1, x, \ldots, x^g] \begin{bmatrix} \beta_0^{(1)} & \beta_0^{(2)} & \cdots & \beta_0^{(p)} \\ \beta_1^{(1)} & \beta_1^{(2)} & \cdots & \beta_1^{(p)} \\ \cdots & \cdots & \cdots & \cdots \\ \beta_g^{(1)} & \beta_g^{(2)} & \cdots & \beta_g^{(p)} \end{bmatrix} + [\epsilon^{(1)}, \epsilon^{(2)}, \ldots, \epsilon^{(p)}]$$

or, more compactly, as

$$\boldsymbol{y}' = \mathbf{x}'\mathbf{B} + \boldsymbol{\epsilon}' \qquad (4.2\text{-}1)$$

Comparison of (4.1-1) and (4.2-1) reveals that the multivariate model is simply p distinct univariate models written simultaneously. Each of the univariate models shares the same values of the independent variables, but each has distinct values of the dependent variables, regression coefficients, and error components.

The minimal error specification for (4.2-1) is that the vector $\boldsymbol{\epsilon}$ has a p-variate distribution with vector mean $\mathbf{0}$ and covariance matrix $\boldsymbol{\Sigma}$. Errors for different observations are assumed independent. Later, the error specification will be narrowed to the multivariate normal distribution:

$$\boldsymbol{\epsilon} \sim N(\mathbf{0},\boldsymbol{\Sigma}) \qquad (4.2\text{-}2)$$

4.2.2 The Multivariate Model for Group Means

Again we anticipate replication at each level of the independent variable and express the model in terms of group means. Let the p-variate vector mean for group j be

$$\mathbf{y}_{\cdot j} = \frac{1}{N_j} \sum_{i=1}^{N_j} \mathbf{y}_{ij} \qquad (4.2\text{-}3)$$

Then the model for the mean is

$$\boldsymbol{y}'_{\cdot j} = \mathbf{x}'_j\mathbf{B} + \boldsymbol{\epsilon}'_{\cdot j} \qquad (4.2\text{-}4)$$

and $\boldsymbol{\epsilon}_{\cdot}$ is distributed with mean $\mathbf{0}$ and covariance matrix $(1/N_j)\boldsymbol{\Sigma}$.

Suppose there are n such groups. Then the model for the $n \times p$ matrix of group means may be written

$$\boldsymbol{Y}_{\cdot} = \mathbf{X}\mathbf{B} + \boldsymbol{E}_{\cdot} \qquad (4.2\text{-}5)$$

where the jth rows of $\boldsymbol{Y}_{\cdot}$, $\mathbf{X}$, and $\boldsymbol{E}_{\cdot}$ are $\boldsymbol{y}'_{\cdot j}$, $\mathbf{x}'_j$, and $\boldsymbol{\epsilon}'_{\cdot j}$, respectively.

To formulate a statistical analysis based on (4.2-5), we need a convention for describing the multivariate distribution of the np elements in the matrix $\boldsymbol{E}_{..}$ Because multivariate distributions are defined only for vectors, it will be necessary to write the elements of $\boldsymbol{E}_{.}$ as an $np \times 1$ vector. Let us do this by picking up elements across successive rows; thus, transposed,

$$[\boldsymbol{\epsilon}'_{.1}, \boldsymbol{\epsilon}'_{.2}, \ldots, \boldsymbol{\epsilon}'_{.n}] = [\epsilon_{.1}{}^{(1)}, \epsilon_{.1}{}^{(2)}, \ldots, \epsilon_{.1}{}^{(p)}, \epsilon_{.2}{}^{(1)}, \epsilon_{.2}{}^{(2)}, \ldots, \epsilon_{.2}{}^{(p)}, \ldots, \ldots, \epsilon_{.n}{}^{(1)}, \epsilon_{.n}{}^{(2)}, \ldots, \epsilon_{.n}{}^{(p)}]$$

Thus, according to our assumptions,

$$\begin{bmatrix} \boldsymbol{\epsilon}_{.1} \\ \boldsymbol{\epsilon}_{.2} \\ \vdots \\ \boldsymbol{\epsilon}_{.n} \end{bmatrix}$$

has a multivariate distribution with mean

$$\begin{bmatrix} \mathbf{0} \\ \mathbf{0} \\ \vdots \\ \mathbf{0} \end{bmatrix}$$

and covariance matrix

$$\begin{bmatrix} \frac{1}{N_1}\Sigma & 0 & \cdots & 0 \\ 0 & \frac{1}{N_2}\Sigma & \cdots & 0 \\ \cdots & \cdots & \cdots & \cdots \\ 0 & 0 & \cdots & \frac{1}{N_n}\Sigma \end{bmatrix}$$

To express the vector mean and covariance matrix more compactly, we need a special type of matrix operation called the *Kronecker product* (also *direct product*), which is defined as

$$\underset{mp \times ng}{\mathbf{C}} = \underset{m \times n}{\mathbf{A}} \times \underset{p \times g}{\mathbf{B}} = [a_{ij}\mathbf{B}] \qquad (4.2\text{-}6)$$

For example,

$$\begin{bmatrix} a_{11} \\ a_{21} \end{bmatrix} \times \begin{bmatrix} b_{11} & b_{12} \\ b_{21} & b_{22} \end{bmatrix} = \begin{bmatrix} a_{11}b_{11} & a_{11}b_{12} \\ a_{11}b_{21} & a_{11}b_{22} \\ a_{21}b_{11} & a_{21}b_{12} \\ a_{21}b_{21} & a_{21}b_{22} \end{bmatrix}$$

That is, the position occupied by each element in $\mathbf{A}$ is replaced by the matrix $\mathbf{B}$ times that element. Thus the row and column order of the product matrix is the product of corresponding orders of the factors.

Properties of Kronecker product that we shall have frequent occasion to use are:

$$(\mathbf{A} \times \mathbf{B}) \times \mathbf{C} = \mathbf{A} \times (\mathbf{B} \times \mathbf{C}) \tag{4.2-7}$$

$$(\mathbf{A} + \mathbf{B}) \times \mathbf{C} = \mathbf{A} \times \mathbf{C} + \mathbf{B} \times \mathbf{C} \tag{4.2-8}$$

$$(\mathbf{A} \times \mathbf{B})' = \mathbf{A}' \times \mathbf{B}' \tag{4.2-9}$$

$$(\mathbf{A} \times \mathbf{C})(\mathbf{B} \times \mathbf{D}) = \mathbf{AB} \times \mathbf{CD} \tag{4.2-10}$$

The Kronecker product enables us to express the vector mean and covariance matrix of the elements in $\boldsymbol{E}.$ as $\mathbf{1} \times \mathbf{0}$ and $\mathbf{D}^{-1} \times \Sigma$, respectively, where $\mathbf{1}$ designates an $n \times 1$ vector of unities, and $\mathbf{D}$ is the diagonal matrix of numbers of subjects. Thus, we may specify a multivariate normal distribution of these elements as

$$\boldsymbol{E}. \sim N(\mathbf{1} \times \mathbf{0}, \mathbf{D}^{-1} \times \Sigma) \tag{4.2-11}$$

4.2.3 Least-Squares Estimation of the Matrix of Regression Coefficients

In multivariate least-squares estimation, the $(g + 1) \times p$ matrix $\mathbf{B}$ is chosen so as to minimize the weighted sum of squares of all elements in the $n \times p$ matrix of residuals

$$\mathbf{E}. = (\mathbf{Y}. - \mathbf{XB}) \tag{4.2-12}$$

The quantity to be minimized may be expressed in terms of the trace function (Sec. 2.5.2):

$$Q = \text{tr}(\mathbf{E}'.)\mathbf{DE}. = \text{tr}(\mathbf{Y}. - \mathbf{XB})'\mathbf{D}(\mathbf{Y}. - \mathbf{XB}) \tag{4.2-13}$$

This quantity, called the *euclidean norm* of $\mathbf{E}.$ with respect to $\mathbf{D}.$, is the sum of the square lengths of the vectors which comprise $\mathbf{E}.$ (see Sec. 2.7.5b). To minimize with respect to variation in $\mathbf{B}$, we expand (4.2-13)

$$Q = \text{tr}(\mathbf{Y}'.\mathbf{DY}. - 2\mathbf{Y}'.\mathbf{DXB} + \mathbf{B}'\mathbf{X}'\mathbf{DXB})$$

apply the matrix derivations (2.5-16) and (2.5-17), and equate to zero to obtain

$$\frac{\partial Q}{\partial \mathbf{B}} = -2\mathbf{X}'\mathbf{DY}. + 2\mathbf{X}'\mathbf{DXB} = \mathbf{O}$$

The least-squares estimate $\hat{\mathbf{B}}$ is then the solution of

$$\mathbf{X}'\mathbf{DX}\hat{\mathbf{B}} = \mathbf{X}'\mathbf{DY}. \tag{4.2-14}$$

As in (4.1-8), $\mathbf{X}'\mathbf{DX}$ is nonsingular, and (4.2-14) has the unique solution

$$\underset{(g+1)\times p}{\hat{\mathbf{B}}} = (\mathbf{X}'\mathbf{DX})^{-1}\mathbf{X}'\mathbf{DY}. \tag{4.2-15}$$

Note that (4.2-15) differs from (4.1-10) only in the substitution of the $N \times p$ matrix $\mathbf{Y}.$ for the vector $\mathbf{y}.$

Investigating the statistical properties of the estimator $\boldsymbol{B}$, we find that it is unbiased:

$$\mathscr{E}(\boldsymbol{B}) = (\mathbf{X}'\mathbf{D}\mathbf{X})^{-1}\mathbf{X}'\mathbf{D}\mathscr{E}(\mathbf{Y}_.) = (\mathbf{X}'\mathbf{D}\mathbf{X})^{-1}\mathbf{X}'\mathbf{D}\mathbf{X}\mathbf{B}$$
$$= \mathbf{B}$$

Using the convention introduced in (4.2-11), we may express the covariance matrix of elements in $\boldsymbol{B}$ as the Kronecker product

$$\underset{(g+1)p\times(g+1)p}{\mathscr{V}(\boldsymbol{B})} = (\mathbf{X}'\mathbf{D}\mathbf{X})^{-1} \times \Sigma \tag{4.2-17}$$

The Kronecker product also enables us to express the $(g + 1) \times p$ matrix of standard errors of the estimates,

$$\mathrm{SE}(\hat{\mathbf{B}}) = [\mathrm{diag}(\mathbf{X}'\mathbf{D}\mathbf{X})^{-1}]^{1/2} \times [\mathrm{diag}(\Sigma)]^{1/2} \tag{4.2-18}$$

The estimate of Σ required to compute sample values of the standard errors from (4.2-18) is obtained in the following multivariate extension of the analysis of variance in Sec. 4.1.

4.2.4 Multivariate Analysis of Variance for the Polynomial Model

As early as 1932, Wilks recognized that the principles of univariate analysis of variance generalize in a remarkably simple way to the multivariate case. The first attempts to apply this generalization appeared in papers by Bartlett [1947] and Tukey [1949]. The generalization to the multivariate case consists of replacing the partition of sum of squares in univariate analysis with a partition of sums of squares and cross products among multiple dependent variates. The latter take the form of real symmetric (grammian) matrices referred to here as *SSP matrices.* Univariate inner products such as $\mathbf{y}'\mathbf{y}$ and $\mathbf{y}'_.\mathbf{D}\mathbf{y}_.$ are replaced by the $p \times p$ SSP matrices $\mathbf{Y}'\mathbf{Y}$ and $\mathbf{Y}'_.\mathbf{D}\mathbf{Y}_.$ in the multivariate case. The parallelism is apparent in the comparison of Table 4.1-3 with Table 4.2-2. The symbol $\mathbf{Y}$ in Table 4.2-2 denotes an $N \times p$

Table 4.2-2 MULTIVARIATE ANALYSIS OF VARIANCE FOR THE POLYNOMIAL MODEL (GROUPED DATA)

Source of dispersion	df	Sums of squares and products ($p \times p$)	Expected sums of squares and products
Regression	$g + 1$	SSR $= \mathbf{Y}'_.\mathbf{D}\mathbf{X}(\mathbf{X}'\mathbf{D}\mathbf{X})^{-1}\mathbf{X}'\mathbf{D}\mathbf{Y}_.$ $= \hat{\mathbf{B}}'\mathbf{X}'\mathbf{D}\mathbf{Y}_.$	$(g + 1)\Sigma + \mathbf{B}'\mathbf{X}'\mathbf{D}\mathbf{X}\mathbf{B}$
Residual	$n - g - 1$	SSE $= \mathbf{Y}'_.[\mathbf{D} - \mathbf{D}\mathbf{X}(\mathbf{X}'\mathbf{D}\mathbf{X})^{-1}\mathbf{X}'\mathbf{D}]\mathbf{Y}_.$ = SSG − SSR	$(n - g - 1)\Sigma$
Group means	n	SSG $= \mathbf{Y}'_.\mathbf{D}\mathbf{Y}_.$	$N\Sigma + \mathbf{B}'\mathbf{X}'\mathbf{D}\mathbf{X}\mathbf{B}$
Within groups	$N - n$	SSW = SST − SSG	$(N - n)\Sigma$
Total	$N = \sum_{j=1}^{n} N_j$	SST $= \mathbf{Y}'\mathbf{Y}$	

matrix of original observations as, for example, in Table 4.2-1. The symbol $\mathbf{Y}_.$ denotes the $n \times p$ matrix of group means.

The setup in Table 4.2-2 may be used in conjunction with the sampling theory of Sec. 3.4 to carry out a joint statistical test of the degree-g polynomial for p dependent variables. The expected sums of squares and products in Table 4.2-2 show that, on the assumption of a multivariate normal error distribution and under the hypothesis of a degree-g polynomial, the elements of SSE follow a central Wishart distribution with parameters $(p, n - g - 1, \Sigma)$, while the elements of SSW are independently and unconditionally distributed in central Wishart form with parameters $(p, N - n, \Sigma)$ (see Sec. 3.4.6).

Under the alternative hypothesis of a degree-m polynomial $(g < m < n)$,

$$\mathscr{E}(\text{SSE}) = (n - m - 1)\Sigma + \mathbf{B}_2'\mathbf{X}^{*\prime}\mathbf{D}\mathbf{X}^*\mathbf{B}_2$$

where the $p \times (m - g)$ matrix $\mathbf{B}_2$ contains the additional coefficients of the degree-m model, and $\mathbf{X}^*$ is defined as in Table 4.1-4. Thus, under the alternative hypothesis, SSE is distributed in Wishart form with parameters

$$p, n - m - 1, \Sigma + \frac{\mathbf{B}_2'\mathbf{X}^{*\prime}\mathbf{D}\mathbf{X}^*\mathbf{B}_2}{n - m - 1}$$

A test of the hypothesis that SSE and SSW are drawn from Wishart distributions with the same parameter Σ is therefore equivalent to a test of the null hypothesis $\mathbf{B}_2 = \mathbf{O}$. Rejection of this hypothesis is taken as evidence that, for at least one of the dependent variables, the degree-g polynomial does not fit the data.

An exact test of the null hypothesis is provided by any one of the statistics discussed from Sec. 3.4.7 on. Each of these statistics is a function of the roots of the determinantal equation in λ of the form

$$|\mathbf{S}_h - \lambda\mathbf{S}_e| = 0 \qquad (4.2\text{-}19)$$

where $\mathbf{S}_h$ is the SSP matrix associated with n_h degrees of freedom for hypotheses in the partition of squares and products, and $\mathbf{S}_e$ is the SSP matrix associated with n_e degrees of freedom for the error estimate. (In the present context, $\mathbf{S}_h$ = SSE and $\mathbf{S}_e$ = SSW.) Since $\mathbf{S}_e$ must be nonsingular in order for (4.2-19) to have a finite solution, $|\mathbf{S}_e| \neq 0$ is a necessary condition for multivariate tests of hypothesis. In general, this condition will be met if n_e is equal to or greater than p. That is, joint tests of significance (and joint confidence bounds) in multivariate analysis require that *the number of variables not exceed the number of degrees of freedom available for the error estimate.*

As indicated in Sec. 3.4, the statistics based on the roots of (4.2-19) are (1) the largest-root criterion, either in the form of the generalized F or Roy's criterion, (2) the trace criterion, and (3) the likelihood-ratio (Wilks') criterion. The null distributions of these criteria are functions of the parameters p, n_h, and n_e. The connection of the present notation with that of Sec. 3.4 is $\mathbf{S}_1 = \mathbf{S}_h$, $\mathbf{S}_2 = \mathbf{S}_e$, $p = p$, $\nu_1 = n_h$, and $\nu_2 = n_e$. Critical points for the null distributions are available from the following sources:

1 Largest-root criterion. Five and one percent points of the generalized F,

$$F_0 = \frac{t}{r}\lambda_1 \qquad (4.2\text{-}20)$$

where λ_1 is the largest root of (4.2-19), are tabulated in Appendix A in terms of the arguments

$$r = |n_h - p| + 1 \qquad (4.2\text{-}21)$$

$$s = \min(n_h, p) \qquad (4.2\text{-}22)$$

$$t = n_e - p + 1 \qquad (4.2\text{-}23)$$

Alternatively, critical points for the largest root can be obtained from

$$\theta = \frac{\lambda_1}{1 - \lambda_1} \qquad (4.2\text{-}24)$$

tabulated by Heck [1960] and Pillai [1960] in the arguments s and

$$m = \tfrac{1}{2}(|n_h - p| - 1) \qquad (4.2\text{-}25)$$

$$n = \tfrac{1}{2}(n_e - p - 1) \qquad (4.2\text{-}26)$$

2 Trace criterion. Critical points for the trace criterion,

$$U_s = \sum_{k=1}^{s} \lambda_k \qquad (4.2\text{-}27)$$

where λ_k are the nonzero roots of (4.2-19), are tabulated by Pillai [1960] in the same arguments s, m, and n.

3 Likelihood-ratio criterion. Probability points for the likelihood-ratio criterion,

$$\Lambda = \sum_{k=1}^{s} \frac{1}{1 + \lambda_k} \qquad (4.2\text{-}28)$$

may be approximated by those of the χ^2 variate

$$\chi_B^2 = -\left(n_e + n_h \frac{n_h + p + 1}{2}\right) \ln \Lambda \qquad (4.2\text{-}29)$$

on $n_h p$ degrees of freedom. An alternative and more accurate approximation due to Rao is the univariate F statistic,

$$F' = \frac{1 - \Lambda^{1/t}}{\Lambda^{1/t}} \frac{mt - 2k}{pn_h} \qquad (4.2\text{-}30)$$

where $m = n_e + n_h - (n_h + p + 1)/2$

$$t = \sqrt{(p^2 n_h^2 - 4)/(p^2 + n_h^2 - 5)}$$

$$k = (pn_h - 2)/4$$

(see Sec. 3.4.9). The degrees of freedom for this statistic are pn_h in the numerator and $mt - 2k$ in the denominator. When $s = 1$ or 2, F' is exactly distributed as F. For $pn_h = 2$, t is set equal to 1.

A typical application of these test criteria is illustrated in Example 4.2-2. This example also illustrates the fact that all figures required for univariate estimation and tests of hypothesis are contained in the multivariate calculations. Thus, the data may be approached from both a univariate and a multivariate point of view in the same analysis.

EXAMPLE 4.2-2 (*Test of a multivariate linear polynomial model for the dosage-response data*) Although the choice of numerical values to be assigned to categories of the behavioral ratings in Example 4.2-1 is largely arbitrary, there are obvious advantages to values which have a simple relationship with dose. If the range of dose is not too wide, a linear relationship to log dose may be attainable. If the range is wide and initial-terminal response thresholds are involved, a sigmoid curve, perhaps roughly representable by a third-degree polynomial, would be expected.

In the data of Table 4.2-1, variable 1 is clearly decreasing with dose, while variables 2 and 3 are increasing; however, it would be difficult to say whether any departure from simple linear decrease or increase is demonstrable with such limited data. To test linearity formally, we may set up the multivariate analysis of variance shown in Table 4.2-3. The calculations for Table 4.2-3 have been simplified by rounding the log dose to 0, .5, 1.0, 1.5, and 2.0 on grounds that the effective dosage in the animal may be somewhat variable.

The matrix of the linear model is then

$$\mathbf{X} = \begin{bmatrix} 1 & 0 \\ 1 & .5 \\ 1 & 1.0 \\ 1 & 1.5 \\ 1 & 2.0 \end{bmatrix}$$

From Table 4.2-1, the means for the three observations at each dosage level comprise the matrix

$$\mathbf{Y}. = \begin{bmatrix} 4.0000 & .3333 & .6667 \\ 4.3333 & 0 & 1.6667 \\ 2.3333 & 2.6667 & 4.0000 \\ .5000 & 4.3333 & 5.5000 \\ .1667 & 6.3333 & 5.8333 \end{bmatrix}$$

The calculations for estimating $\hat{\mathbf{B}}$ run parallel to those of Example 4.1-2:

$$\mathbf{X'DX} = 3\begin{bmatrix} 5 & 5 \\ 5 & 7.5 \end{bmatrix} \qquad (\mathbf{X'DX})^{-1} = \frac{1}{3}\begin{bmatrix} .6 & -.4 \\ -.4 & .4 \end{bmatrix}$$

$$\mathbf{X'DY} = 3\begin{bmatrix} 11.3333 & 13.6667 & 17.6667 \\ 5.5833 & 21.8333 & 24.7500 \end{bmatrix}$$

whence, from (4.2-15),

$$\hat{\mathbf{B}} = \begin{bmatrix} 4.5667 & -.5333 & .7000 \\ -2.3000 & 3.2667 & 2.8333 \end{bmatrix}$$

From these quantities and the total sum of squares and products computed from the data of Table 4.2-1, we obtain the partition of squares and products shown in Table 4.2-3.

We now proceed to check the joint goodness of fit of the linear polynomial model by testing the significance of the residual variation. This involves solving for the $s = \min(3,3) = 3$ nonzero roots of $|\mathbf{S}_h - \lambda \mathbf{S}_e| = 0$, where $\mathbf{S}_h$ and $\mathbf{S}_e$ are the residual and within-group SSP matrices, respectively. We may use the method of Sec. 2.7.4 for this purpose. The calculations involve the computing of (1) the Cholesky

Table 4.2-3 MULTIVARIATE ANALYSIS OF VARIANCE FOR THE LINEAR DOSAGE-RESPONSE RELATIONSHIP

Source of dispersion	df	Sums of squares and products (symmetric)			F_0 / U_s / Λ	p
Regression	2	116.7417				
		36.5833	192.1000			
		71.2583	214.2388	247.4750		
Residual	3	4.7583			4.63	>.05
		−4.2500	6.2333		1.04	>.05
		−2.4250	0.7167	3.0250	4.26	>.05
Group means	5	121.5000				
		32.3333	198.3333			
		68.8333	215.0000	250.5000		
Within groups	10	12.0000				
		−2.8333	20.6667			
		−7.8333	−2.0000	9.0000		
Total	15	133.5000				
		29.5000	219.0000			
		61.0000	213.0000	259.5000		

factor, say $\mathbf{T}_e$, of the positive-definite matrix $\mathbf{S}_e$,

$$\mathbf{T}_e = \begin{bmatrix} 3.46410 & & (\text{triangular}) \\ -\ .81790 & 4.47188 & \\ -2.26126 & -.86076 & 1.77364 \end{bmatrix}$$

(2) the inverse factor

$$\mathbf{T}_e^{-1} = \begin{bmatrix} .28867 & & (\text{triangular}) \\ .05279 & .22361 & \\ .39365 & .10852 & .56381 \end{bmatrix}$$

and (3) the transform of $\mathbf{S}_h$ by $\mathbf{T}_e^{-1}$

$$\mathbf{T}_e^{-1}\mathbf{S}_h(\mathbf{T}_e^{-1})' = \begin{bmatrix} .39652 & & (\text{symmetric}) \\ -.20182 & .22460 & \\ .01290 & -.13014 & .42051 \end{bmatrix}$$

Equation (4.2-19) is thus reduced to the form

$$|\mathbf{T}_e^{-1}\mathbf{S}_h(\mathbf{T}_e^{-1})' - \lambda\mathbf{I}| = 0 \qquad (4.2\text{-}31)$$

which can be solved by one of the numerical methods of Sec. 2.7.5. In this instance, the roots of (4.2-31) obtained by tridiagonalization and Strum-sequence bisections are, in order by size,

$$.5794 \qquad .4009 \qquad .0613$$

The test criteria are computed from these roots.

1 Largest-root criterion (generalized F)

$$r = |3 - 3| + 1 = 1$$

$$s = \min(3,3) = 3$$

$$t = 10 - 3 + 1 = 8$$

$$F_0 = \tfrac{8}{1}(.5794) = 4.6352$$

Unfortunately, the smallest value for the argument t in the table of F_0 ($s = 3$) is 12. However, since for $r = 1$, $s = 3$, and $t = 12$, a value of F_0 must exceed 20.20 to be significant at the .05 level, the value above clearly could not exceed the even larger critical value for $t = 8$. There appears to be no evidence for departure from linearity anywhere in these data.

2 Trace criterion

$$U_3 = .5794 + .4009 + .0613 = 1.0416$$

The critical values of U_s, for $s = 3$, $m = (|3 - 3| - 1)/2 = -\frac{1}{2}$, and $n = \frac{1}{2}(10 - 3 - 1) = 3$, are outside the range of arguments in Pillai's [1960] table. Since the .05 level when $m = 1.5$ and $n = 15$ is 1.172, however, it is clear that the above value is not significant.

3 Likelihood ratio criterion

$$\Lambda = \frac{1}{(1 + .5794)(1 + .4009)(1 + .0613)} = .42586$$

Using (4.2-30), we convert Λ to an approximate F statistic as follows:

$$m = 10 + 3 - \frac{3 + 3 + 1}{2} = 9.5$$

$$t = \sqrt{\frac{9 \times 9 - 4}{9 + 9 - 5}} = \sqrt{\frac{77}{13}} = 2.4337$$

$$k = \frac{3 \times 3 - 2}{4} = 1.75$$

and $$F' = \frac{(1 - .42586)^{1/2.4337}}{.42586^{1/2.4337}} \frac{9.5 \times 2.4337 - 2 \times 1.75}{3 \times 3}$$

$$= .9160$$

The degrees of freedom of this F' are $3 \times 3 = 9$ in the numerator and 19.62 in the denominator. Using the next larger integral value for the denominator degrees of freedom, we obtain, by the computing approximation of Sec. 3.4.5, a p value of .53.

None of the three criteria shows any evidence that the departure from the linear model is greater than would be attributed to the error variation. The univariate F statistics for the separate variables, on 3 and 10 degrees of freedom, are entirely consistent with this conclusion:

Variable	F	p
1 Visual placing	$\frac{4.758/3}{12.0000/10} = 1.32$	.32
2 Wire maneuver	$\frac{6.2333/3}{20.6666/10} = 1.01$	.43
3 Palpebral closure	$\frac{3.0250/3}{9.0000/10} = 1.12$	.39

These univariate statistics are by no means independent, however, as is seen when we inspect the correlation matrix computed from the within-group matrix in Table 4.2-3. The estimated error correlations for the three variables are

$$\begin{array}{c} \\ 1 \\ 2 \\ 3 \end{array} \begin{array}{c} \begin{array}{ccc} 1 & 2 & 3 \end{array} \\ \begin{bmatrix} 1 & & \\ -.180 & 1 & \\ -.753 & -.147 & 1 \end{bmatrix} \end{array}$$

Visual placing and palpebral closure, both of which involve the animal's vision, are highly correlated (negatively, because of the scoring convention). The wire maneuver is much less associated with the other two variables.

Because of a small number of degrees of freedom within groups, we may wish to pool the within-group and residual SSP matrices to obtain an improved estimate of the error covariance matrix, analogous to the suggestion for the univariate case in Sec. 4.1.8:

$$\hat{\Sigma}_{(13)} = \frac{1}{3+10}\left(\begin{bmatrix} 4.7583 & & \\ -4.2500 & 6.2333 & \\ -2.4250 & .7167 & 3.0250 \end{bmatrix} + \begin{bmatrix} 12.0000 & & \\ -2.8333 & 20.6667 & \\ -7.8333 & -2.0000 & 9.0000 \end{bmatrix}\right)$$

$$= \begin{bmatrix} 1.2891 & & \\ -.5449 & 2.0692 & \\ -.7891 & -.0987 & .9250 \end{bmatrix}$$

The diagonal elements of this matrix contain the error-variance estimates for the separate variables, which may be used, together with the diagonal elements of the inverse matrix, to construct confidence intervals for the regression coefficients in the manner of Sec. 4.1.12. In this instance, the 95 percent bounds for the intercept and slope parameters of the three variables are as follows:

Variable	Intercept, β_0	Slope, β_1
1 Visual placing	$4.5667 \pm \sqrt{(4.67)(1.2891)(.1800)}$ 4.5667 ± 1.0410	$-2.3000 \pm \sqrt{(4.67)(1.2891)(.1333)}$ $-2.3000 \pm .8958$
2 Wire maneuver	$-.5333 \pm \sqrt{(4.67)(2.0692)(.1800)}$ $-.5333 \pm 1.3189$	$3.2667 \pm \sqrt{(4.67)(2.0693)(.1333)}$ 3.2667 ± 1.1350
3 Palpebral closure	$.7000 \pm \sqrt{(4.67)(.9250)(.1800)}$ $.7000 \pm .8818$	$2.8333 \pm \sqrt{(4.67)(.9250)(.1333)}$ $2.8333 \pm .7588$

The estimated response functions for these variables are shown graphically in Fig. 4.2-1. Perhaps due to the use of highly inbred animals in these evaluations, the regression lines are quite well determined. The standard deviations of the residuals

$$1 \quad \sqrt{\frac{1.2891}{3}} = .6555$$

$$2 \quad \sqrt{\frac{2.0692}{3}} = .8305$$

$$3 \quad \sqrt{\frac{.9250}{3}} = .5553$$

are small relative to the range of the data, which includes most of the eight units of

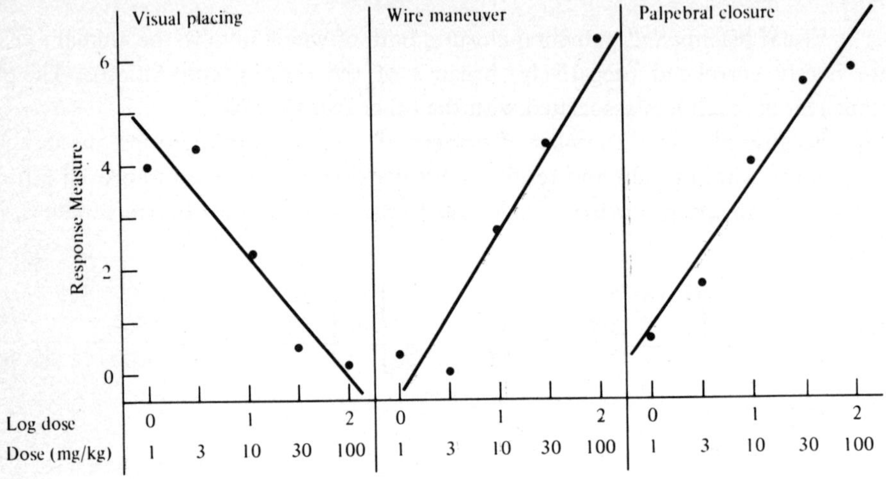

FIGURE 4.2-1
Estimated linear dose-response relations.

scale defined for each measure. The response categories evidently have been judiciously chosen to show regular progression with level of dose. In more extensive data, we might begin to see some consistent nonlinear trend, but there is little in the present data to indicate the direction of departure from linearity.

4.2.5 Multivariate Stepwise Regression Analysis

a Grouped data Both the direct orthogonalization and pivoting methods of stepwise regression analysis have straightforward multivariate generalizations. In the orthogonalization method, we proceed as in the univariate case by first orthogonalizing the degree-m model matrix $\mathbf{X}_m$ in order to obtain the orthonormal matrix $\mathbf{P}_m$. We then compute the matrix of orthogonal estimates from

$$\underset{(m+1)\times p}{\mathbf{U}_m} = \mathbf{P}_m'\mathbf{DY}. \tag{4.2-32}$$

or, alternatively,

$$\mathbf{U}_m = \mathbf{S}_m^{-1}\mathbf{X}_m'\mathbf{DY}. \tag{4.2-33}$$

where $\mathbf{S}_m^{-1}$ is the inverse Cholesky factor of $\mathbf{X}_m'\mathbf{DX}_m$ [see Eq. (4.1-33)].

The estimator $\boldsymbol{U}_m = \mathbf{P}_m'\mathbf{D}\boldsymbol{Y}$. has the properties

$$\mathscr{E}(\boldsymbol{U}_m) = \boldsymbol{\Gamma} = \mathbf{S}_m'\mathbf{B} \tag{4.2-34}$$

where $\boldsymbol{\Gamma}' = [\gamma_0, \gamma_1, \ldots, \gamma_m]$, and

$$\mathscr{V}(\boldsymbol{U}_m) = \underset{(m+1)\times(m+1)}{\mathbf{I}} \times \underset{p\times p}{\Sigma} \tag{4.2-35}$$

The single-degree-of-freedom partition of squares and cross products is then computed from the rows of $\mathbf{U}$ as shown in Table 4.2-4, where $\mathbf{U}' = [\mathbf{u}_0, \mathbf{u}_1, \ldots, \mathbf{u}_m]$.

Beginning at line m of Table 4.2-4, we may test the null hypothesis $H_m: \boldsymbol{\gamma}_m = \mathbf{0}$ by setting $\mathbf{S}_h = \text{SSR}_m$ and $\mathbf{S}_e = \text{SSW}$ in (4.2-19), and assigning the critical level for the test statistic by (4.1-35). If H_m is rejected, we terminate the procedure and accept the degree-m model; otherwise we test $H_{m-1}: \boldsymbol{\gamma}_{m-1} = \mathbf{0}$ and terminate or continue according as H_{m-1} is rejected or not. Continuing in this way until the first rejection occurs, say at line g, we estimate the matrix of coefficients $\mathbf{B}_g$ by (4.2-15) or by

$$\hat{\mathbf{B}}_g = (\mathbf{S}_g^{-1})'\mathbf{U}_g \qquad (4.2\text{-}36)$$

where $\mathbf{U}_g$ contains the first $g + 1$ rows of $\mathbf{U}_m$, and $\mathbf{S}_g^{-1}$ is the leading $(g + 1)$-order submatrix of $\mathbf{S}_m^{-1}$.

When the degrees of freedom for hypothesis is less than the number of variables, as will be the case in the stepwise analysis, the computations for the multivariate test can be simplified from those of Sec. 4.2.4. The alternative method depends on the fact that the squares and products for a given hypothesis can be expressed in the form

$$\mathbf{S}_h = \mathbf{U}_h'\mathbf{U}_h \qquad (4.2\text{-}37)$$

where the $n_h \times p$ matrix $\mathbf{U}_h$ contains the orthogonal estimates corresponding to the n_h degrees of freedom for that hypothesis. This shows that $\mathbf{S}_h$ is grammian and that $\text{rank}(\mathbf{S}_h) = \min(n_h, p)$, because there is no probability that the $n_h \times p$ matrix $\mathbf{U}_h$ is of less than full rank.

We have seen in Sec. 2.7, however, that the number of nonzero roots of (4.2-19) equals $\text{rank}(\mathbf{S}_h)$. This implies that, if n_h is less than p, there exists a $p \times n_h$ matrix of characteristic vectors $\mathbf{Z}_{n_h}$ with the property

$$\mathbf{S}_h\mathbf{Z}_{n_h} = \mathbf{S}_e\mathbf{Z}_{n_h}\boldsymbol{\Lambda}_{n_h} \qquad (4.2\text{-}38)$$

where $\boldsymbol{\Lambda}_{n_h}$ is the diagonal matrix of the n_h nonzero roots of (4.2-19). We then have

$$\mathbf{U}_h\mathbf{S}_e^{-1}\mathbf{U}_h'\mathbf{U}_h\mathbf{Z}_{n_h} = \mathbf{U}_h\mathbf{Z}_{n_h}\boldsymbol{\Lambda}_{n_h} \qquad (4.2\text{-}39)$$

since we assume $|\mathbf{S}_e| \neq 0$. This shows that $\mathbf{U}_h\mathbf{Z}_{n_h}$ are characteristic vectors of

Table 4.2-4 SINGLE-DEGREE-OF-FREEDOM MULTIVARIATE ANALYSIS OF VARIANCE FOR THE POLYNOMIAL MODEL

Source of dispersion	df	Sums of squares and products ($p \times p$)	Expected sums of squares and products
$\mathbf{x}_0^*$	1	$\text{SSR}_0 = \mathbf{u}_0\mathbf{u}_0'$	$\boldsymbol{\Sigma} + \boldsymbol{\gamma}_0\boldsymbol{\gamma}_0'$
$\mathbf{x}_1^*$	1	$\text{SSR}_1 = \mathbf{u}_1\mathbf{u}_1'$	$\boldsymbol{\Sigma} + \boldsymbol{\gamma}_1\boldsymbol{\gamma}_1'$
.....	.....	.....	.....
$\mathbf{x}_m^*$	1	$\text{SSR}_m = \mathbf{u}_m\mathbf{u}_m'$	$\boldsymbol{\Sigma} + \boldsymbol{\gamma}_m\boldsymbol{\gamma}_m'$
Residual	$n - m - 1$	$\text{SSE} = \text{SSB} - \mathbf{U}_m'\mathbf{U}_m$	$(n - m - 1)\boldsymbol{\Sigma}$
Group means	n	$\text{SSG} = \mathbf{Y}_.'\mathbf{D}\mathbf{Y}_.$	$n\boldsymbol{\Sigma} + \mathbf{B}_m'\mathbf{X}_m'\mathbf{D}\mathbf{X}_m\mathbf{B}_m$
Within groups	$N - n$	$\text{SSW} = \text{SST} - \text{SSB}$	$(N - n)\boldsymbol{\Sigma}$
Total	$N = \sum_{j=1}^{n} N_j$	$\text{SST} = \mathbf{Y}'\mathbf{Y}$	

$\mathbf{U}_h\mathbf{S}_e^{-1}\mathbf{U}_h'$, having the same roots as (4.2-19). The computational advantage of (4.2-39) when $n_h < p$ is that the matrix in

$$|\mathbf{U}_h\mathbf{S}_e^{-1}\mathbf{U}_h' - \lambda\mathbf{I}| = 0 \qquad (4.2\text{-}40)$$

is of smaller order than that in (4.2-19) and the calculations required to solve (4.2-40) are correspondingly lighter. In particular, when $n_h = 1$, no further computation is required, for

$$\lambda_1 = \mathbf{u}_h'\mathbf{S}_e^{-1}\mathbf{u}_h \qquad (4.2\text{-}41)$$

In this case λ is, in fact, proportional to *Hotelling's* T^2,

$$T^2 = n_e\lambda_1$$

It can be shown [Anderson, 1958, page 101] that $F_0 = [(n_e - p + 1)/(n_e p)]\, T^2$ is distributed as a univariate F with p and $n_e - p + 1$ degrees of freedom. This is also apparent from the fact that the generalized F is referred to the univariate F table when $s = 1$, and that Rao's approximation (4.2-30) reduces to the same value of F. Thus, there is a duality between hypothesis degrees of freedom and variates such that, when either is equal to 1, the sampling problem becomes univariate and these three multivariate test criteria become identical when expressed as F. The use of (4.2-41) in the single-degree-of-freedom analysis is illustrated in Example 4.2-3.

The partition of the sum of squares and products in Table 4.2-4 may also be obtained by pivoting. The procedure begins with the matrix

$$\mathbf{M}_m^{(0)} = \begin{bmatrix} \mathbf{X}_m'\mathbf{D}\mathbf{X}_m & \mathbf{X}_m'\mathbf{D}\mathbf{Y}_. \\ \mathbf{Y}_.'\mathbf{D}\mathbf{X}_m & \mathbf{Y}_.\mathbf{D}\mathbf{Y}_. \end{bmatrix} \begin{matrix} m+1 \\ p \end{matrix} \qquad (4.2\text{-}42)$$
$$\qquad\qquad m+1 \qquad\quad p$$

At the $(k + 1)$st stage of the pivoting procedure described in Sec. 4.1.10b, the matrix contains the quantities

$$\mathbf{M}_m^{(k)} = \left[\begin{array}{ccc} (\mathbf{X}_k'\mathbf{D}\mathbf{X}_k)^{-1} & \cdots & \hat{\mathbf{B}}_k \\ \cdots\cdots & \cdots\cdots & \cdots\cdots \\ -\hat{\mathbf{B}}_k' & \cdots & \mathbf{Y}_.'[\mathbf{D} - \mathbf{D}\mathbf{X}_k(\mathbf{X}_k'\mathbf{D}\mathbf{X}_k)^{-1}\mathbf{X}_k'\mathbf{D}]\mathbf{Y}_. \end{array}\right] \begin{matrix} k+1 \\ m-k \\ p \end{matrix} \qquad (4.2\text{-}43)$$
$$\qquad\qquad k+1 \qquad m-k \qquad\qquad p$$

As in the analogous univariate procedure, the matrix at the $(k + 1)$st stage contains the inverse matrix $(\mathbf{X}_k'\mathbf{D}\mathbf{X}_k)^{-1}$, the matrix of estimates $\hat{\mathbf{B}}_k$, and the residual SSP matrix $\mathbf{Y}_.'[\mathbf{D} - \mathbf{D}\mathbf{X}_k(\mathbf{X}_k'\mathbf{D}\mathbf{X}_k)^{-1}\mathbf{X}_k'\mathbf{D}]\mathbf{Y}_.'$. The difference between residual matrices at each stage of pivoting equals the SSP matrix for the corresponding degree of freedom in the partition of Table 4.2-4.

Regrettably, much of the programming advantage of the pivoting algorithm in the multivariate case is lost because of the inaccessibility of the orthogonal estimates required for the short method of computing the test criteria when $n_h < p$.

Ungrouped data In ungrouped data the multivariate stepwise analysis parallels exactly the univariate treatment in Sec. 4.1.10c. The residual SSP matrix must be assumed as the error matrix. It is obtained by subtracting the sum of the regression SSP matrices directly from SST. The number of residual degrees of freedom must, of course, equal or exceed p.

If the pivoting method is used for ungrouped data, (4.2-42) becomes

$$\mathbf{M}_m^{(0)} = \begin{bmatrix} \mathbf{X}_m'\mathbf{X}_m & \mathbf{X}_m'\mathbf{Y} \\ \mathbf{Y}'\mathbf{X}_m & \mathbf{Y}'\mathbf{Y} \end{bmatrix} \qquad (4.2\text{-}44)$$

The computations thereafter are identical with those for grouped data, except that the residual SSP matrix is used as $\mathbf{S}_e$ in the multivariate tests.

EXAMPLE 4.2-3 (*Stepwise analysis of a multivariate polynomial model for the dosage-response data*) To illustrate the multivariate stepwise analysis, let us assume that at most a cubic polynomial in the log dose describes the dose-response relationship. If we proceed by orthogonalization, we find that, because the log-dose levels are equally spaced and the number of replicates equal at all levels, the orthogonalized model matrix is proportional to the matrix of orthogonal polynomials for $n = 5$ (see Sec. 5.2.5c). Specifically,

$$\mathbf{X}_3 = \begin{bmatrix} 1 & 0 & 0 & 0 \\ 1 & .5 & .25 & .125 \\ 1 & 1.0 & 1.00 & 1.00 \\ 1 & 1.5 & 2.25 & 3.375 \\ 1 & 2.0 & 4.00 & 8.00 \end{bmatrix}$$

$$\mathbf{P}_3 = \frac{1}{\sqrt{3}} \left[\frac{1}{\sqrt{5}} \begin{pmatrix} 1 \\ 1 \\ 1 \\ 1 \\ 1 \end{pmatrix}, \frac{1}{\sqrt{10}} \begin{pmatrix} -2 \\ -1 \\ 0 \\ 1 \\ 2 \end{pmatrix}, \frac{1}{\sqrt{14}} \begin{pmatrix} 2 \\ -1 \\ -2 \\ -1 \\ 2 \end{pmatrix}, \frac{1}{\sqrt{10}} \begin{pmatrix} 1 \\ -2 \\ 0 \\ -2 \\ 1 \end{pmatrix} \right]$$

Then the orthogonal estimates are

$$\mathbf{U}_3 = \mathbf{P}_3'\mathbf{D}\mathbf{Y}. = \sqrt{3} \begin{bmatrix} 5.1378 & 6.1119 & 7.9008 \\ -3.6366 & 5.1650 & 4.4799 \\ -\ .3118 & .9800 & -.5791 \\ 1.2122 & -.8433 & -.7906 \end{bmatrix}$$

These estimates, together with the between- and within-group SSP matrices in Table 4.2-3, are used in the partition in Table 4.2-4. The result is shown in Table 4.2-5.

As discussed above, the statistic (4.2-41) for testing the one-degree-of-freedom hypothesis reduces to a univariate F on 3 and 8 degrees of freedom. Not until the linear term is reached is there any indication of statistical significance. In these data, the significance of the linear term is beyond question, but with some other drug there might be no dosage effect whatsoever, in which case even the linear term would be nonsignificant. Rejection of at least one of the stepwise multivariate tests at a suitable joint α level would be required before evidence for a dosage effect could be claimed.

As an example of the pivoting method for the multivariate single-degree-of-freedom partition, we assume that no higher-degree model than a quadratic will be required and construct the matrix $\mathbf{M}_2^{(0)}$ out of the submatrices $\mathbf{X}_2'\mathbf{D}\mathbf{X}_2$, $\mathbf{Y}.\mathbf{D}\mathbf{X}_2$, and $\mathbf{Y}'.\mathbf{D}\mathbf{Y}..$ The latter is taken from Table 4.2-3.

$$\mathbf{M}_2^{(0)} = \begin{bmatrix} 15 & & & & & \text{(symmetric)} \\ 15 & 22.5 & & & & \\ 22.5 & 37.5 & 66.375 & & & \\ 34 & 16.75 & 15.625 & 121.5 & & \\ 41 & 65.5 & 113.25 & 32.3333 & 198.333 & \\ 53 & 74.25 & 120.375 & 68.8333 & 215 & 250.5 \end{bmatrix}$$

Table 4.2-5 STEPWISE MULTIVARIATE REGRESSION ANALYSIS OF THE DOSAGE-RESPONSE DATA

Source of variation	df	Sums of squares and products (symmetric)	λ_1	F_0	p
$\mathbf{x}_0^*$ (constant)	1	$\begin{bmatrix} 77.0667 & & \\ 92.9333 & 112.0667 & \\ 120.1333 & 144.8667 & 187.2667 \end{bmatrix}$	166.2203	443.25	<.0001
$\mathbf{x}_1^*$ (linear)	1	$\begin{bmatrix} 39.6750 & & \\ -56.3500 & 80.0333 & \\ -48.8750 & 69.4167 & 60.2083 \end{bmatrix}$	14.3027	38.14	<.0001
$\mathbf{x}_2^*$ (quadratic)	1	$\begin{bmatrix} .2917 & & \\ -.9167 & 2.8809 & \\ .5417 & -1.7023 & 1.0060 \end{bmatrix}$	.5002	1.33	.33
$\mathbf{x}_3^*$ (cubic)	1	$\begin{bmatrix} 4.4083 & & \\ -3.0667 & 2.1333 & \\ -2.8750 & 2.0000 & 1.8750 \end{bmatrix}$	.4247	1.13	.39
Residual	1	$\begin{bmatrix} .0583 & & \\ -.2667 & 1.2190 & \\ -.0917 & .4190 & .1440 \end{bmatrix}$			
Between groups	5				
Within groups	10	(See Table 4.2–3.)			
Total	15				

The results of three stages of pivoting are as follows:

$$\mathbf{M}_2^{(1)} = \begin{bmatrix} .0667 & 1.0000 & 1.5000 & 2.2667 & 2.7333 & 3.5333 \\ -1.0000 & 7.5000 & & & & \\ -1.5000 & 15.0000 & 32.6250 & & & (\text{symmetric}) \\ -2.2667 & -17.2500 & -35.3750 & 44.4333 & & \\ -2.7333 & 24.5000 & 51.7500 & -60.0000 & 86.2663 & \\ -3.5333 & 21.2500 & 40.8750 & -51.3000 & 70.1333 & 63.2333 \end{bmatrix}$$

$$\mathbf{M}_2^{(2)} = \begin{bmatrix} .2000 & -.1333 & -.5000 & 4.5667 & -.5333 & .7000 \\ -.1333 & .1333 & 2.0000 & -2.3000 & 3.2667 & 2.8333 \\ .5000 & -2.0000 & 2.6250 & & & \\ -4.5667 & 2.3000 & -.8750 & 4.7583 & & (\text{symmetric}) \\ .5333 & -3.2667 & 2.750 & -4.2500 & 6.2333 & \\ -.7000 & -2.8333 & -1.6250 & -2.4250 & .71667 & 3.0250 \end{bmatrix}$$

$$\mathbf{M}_2^{(3)} = \begin{bmatrix} .2952 & & (\text{symmetric}) & 4.4000 & -.0095 & .3905 \\ -.5143 & 1.6571 & & -1.6333 & 1.1714 & 4.0714 \\ .1905 & -.7619 & .3810 & -.3333 & 1.0476 & -.6190 \\ -4.4000 & 1.6333 & .3333 & 4.4667 & & (\text{symmetric}) \\ .0095 & -1.1714 & -1.0476 & -3.3333 & 3.3520 & \\ -.3905 & -4.0714 & .6190 & -2.9667 & 2.4190 & 2.0190 \end{bmatrix}$$

The reader should compare the first three terms of the partition in Table 4.2-5 with the difference between successive residual matrices in the lower right corner of the matrix. Discrepancies in the last place are due to rounding.

4.2.6 Confidence Bounds for Multivariate Regression Coefficients

We have seen in Sec. 4.1.12 how the correlation among elements of $\hat{\boldsymbol{\beta}}$ complicate the problem of representing the Neyman confidence region for the elements of $\boldsymbol{\beta}$. This problem is doubly difficult in the multivariate case because, according to (4.2-17), the matrix estimator $\boldsymbol{B}$ is not only correlated between rows owing to the effect of the term $(\mathbf{X}'\mathbf{D}\mathbf{X})^{-1}$, but there is superimposed a correlation between columns owing to the effect of $\boldsymbol{\Sigma}$. Together with the high dimensionality of $\mathbf{B}$ in all but the most trivial cases, the complexity of this correlational structure makes any exact representation of the simultaneous confidence region virtually impossible.

In an effort to obtain a practical method of interval estimation for multivariate parameters, S. N. Roy [1957, Chap. 14] introduced a system of confidence bounds based on the largest-root statistic. This system includes the so-called *Scheffé bound* for all possible contrasts among regression coefficients in the univariate case [Scheffé, 1953; Roy and Bose, 1953].

Like the confidence region in Sec. 4.1.12, the Scheffé bound may be derived from the probability statement (4.1-41). This statement is exactly equivalent to

$$\text{Prob}\left[-\sqrt{F_\alpha^{(g+1,n_e)}} \le \sqrt{\frac{(\boldsymbol{u}-\boldsymbol{\gamma})'(\boldsymbol{u}-\boldsymbol{\gamma})}{(g+1)\sigma_{(n_e)}{}^2}} \le \sqrt{F_\alpha^{(g+1,n_e)}}\right] = 1-\alpha \qquad (4.2\text{-}45)$$

We know from the Cauchy inequality (Sec. 2.2.3) that for any vector $\mathbf{b}$ such that $\mathbf{b}'\mathbf{b} = 1$,

$$(\boldsymbol{u}-\boldsymbol{\gamma})'\mathbf{b} \le \sqrt{(\boldsymbol{u}-\boldsymbol{\gamma})'(\boldsymbol{u}-\boldsymbol{\gamma})} \qquad (4.2\text{-}46)$$

Hence, we may set

$$\mathbf{b} = \frac{1}{\sqrt{\mathbf{c}'(\mathbf{S}^{-1})'\mathbf{S}^{-1}\mathbf{c}}}\mathbf{S}^{-1}\mathbf{c} \qquad (4.2\text{-}47)$$

and write

$$\text{Prob}\left[-\sqrt{F_\alpha^{(g+1,n_e)}} \le \frac{(\boldsymbol{u}-\boldsymbol{\gamma})'\mathbf{S}^{-1}\mathbf{c}}{\sqrt{(g+1)\sigma_{(n_e)}{}^2\mathbf{c}'(\mathbf{X}'\mathbf{D}\mathbf{X})^{-1}\mathbf{c}}} \le \sqrt{F_\alpha^{(g+1,n_e)}}\right] \ge 1-\alpha \qquad (4.2\text{-}48)$$

But $(\boldsymbol{u}-\boldsymbol{\gamma})'\mathbf{S}^{-1}\mathbf{c} = (\boldsymbol{\beta}-\boldsymbol{\beta})'\mathbf{c}$; whence the interval

$$\mathbf{c}'\boldsymbol{\beta} \pm \sqrt{(g+1)F_\alpha^{(g+1,n_e)}\sigma_{(n_e)}{}^2\mathbf{c}'\mathbf{X}'\mathbf{D}\mathbf{X}\mathbf{c}} \qquad (4.2\text{-}49)$$

has $1-\alpha$ as the *lower bound* of its probability of including the linear combination of parameters $\boldsymbol{\beta}'\mathbf{c}$. Thus, for any contrast or other linear function of the regression coefficients, we can say that (4.2-49) includes the same combination of parameters with confidence coefficient *at least*, and possibly much higher than, $1-\alpha$.

Roy generalized this result to the multivariate case beginning from a probability statement equivalent to

$$\text{Prob}\left[\max_{\mathbf{a}}\left(\frac{\mathbf{a}'(\boldsymbol{U}-\boldsymbol{\Gamma})'(\boldsymbol{U}-\boldsymbol{\Gamma})\mathbf{a}}{n_e\mathbf{a}'\boldsymbol{\Sigma}_{(n_e)}\mathbf{a}}\right) \le \frac{r}{t}F_{0,\alpha}^{(r,s,t)}\right] = 1-\alpha \qquad (4.2\text{-}50)$$

(see Sec. 2.7.4), where $\boldsymbol{\Sigma}_{(n_e)}$ is the estimator of Σ, on n_e degrees of freedom, and $F_{0,\alpha}^{(r,s,t)}$ is the upper α point of the distribution of the largest root in the form of a generalized F (Sec. 3.4.7). [In this instance, $r = |p-(g+1)|+1$, $s = \min(p, g+1)$, $t = n_e - p + 1$.] Thus, for *any* vector $\mathbf{a}$,

$$\text{Prob}\left[-\sqrt{\frac{r}{t}F_{0,\alpha}^{(r,s,t)}} \le \sqrt{\frac{\mathbf{a}'(\boldsymbol{U}-\boldsymbol{\Gamma})'(\boldsymbol{U}-\boldsymbol{\Gamma})\mathbf{a}}{n_e\mathbf{a}'\boldsymbol{\Sigma}_{(n_e)}\mathbf{a}}} \le \sqrt{\frac{r}{t}F_{0,\alpha}^{(r,s,t)}}\right] \ge 1-\alpha \qquad (24.\text{-}51)$$

Again, we may employ the Cauchy inequality and set

$$(\mathbf{U}-\boldsymbol{\Gamma})\mathbf{a} = \frac{1}{\sqrt{\mathbf{c}'(\mathbf{S}^{-1})'\mathbf{S}^{-1}\mathbf{c}}}\mathbf{S}^{-1}\mathbf{c}$$

to obtain the interval

$$\mathbf{c}'\boldsymbol{\beta}\mathbf{a} \pm \sqrt{\frac{n_e r}{t} F_{0,\alpha}^{(r,s,t)} \mathbf{a}'\boldsymbol{\Sigma}_{(n_e)}\mathbf{a}\mathbf{c}'(\mathbf{X}'\mathbf{D}\mathbf{X})^{-1}\mathbf{c}} \qquad (4.2\text{-}52)$$

The lower bound to the probability that (4.2-52) includes the bilinear form $\mathbf{a}'\mathbf{B}'\mathbf{c}$ is $1 - \alpha$. In this form, $\mathbf{a}$ performs the linear combination of the regression coefficients with respect to variables, and $\mathbf{c}$ performs the combinations with respect to terms of the polynomial.

In particular, $\mathbf{a}$ and $\mathbf{c}$ may be specialized to vectors in which the kth element of $\mathbf{a}$ and lth element of $\mathbf{c}$ are unity, while all remaining elements are zero. Then (4.2-49) specializes to

$$\beta_{kl} \pm \sqrt{(g+1)F_{\alpha}^{(g+1,n_e)}\sigma_{k(n_e)}^{2}c_{ll}} \qquad (4.2\text{-}53)$$

where c_{ll} is the lth diagonal element of $(\mathbf{X}'\mathbf{D}\mathbf{X})^{-1}$, and (4.2-52) specializes to

$$\beta_{kl} \pm \sqrt{\frac{n_e r}{t} F_{0,\alpha}^{(r,s,t)}\sigma_{k(n_e)}^{2}c_{ll}} \qquad (4.2\text{-}54)$$

where β_{kl} is the element in the kth row and lth column of $\boldsymbol{B}'$, and $\sigma_{k(n_e)}^{2}$ is the error variance estimator for variable k.

If in a multivariate problem we choose to look at variable k separately (ignoring the remaining $p - 1$ variables), the interval (4.2-53) on β_{kl} would apply. But if we choose to look at the p variables jointly, (4.2-54) would apply, and, as is apparent from inspection of entries in the table of the generalized F, (4.2-54) may be considerably larger than (4.2-53), especially when p is large and n_e is moderate. Thus, a multivariate confidence bound, when many variables are involved, may be much larger than the corresponding univariate interval. This is the price we pay for a weak specification of the model with respect to variables. We pay a similar, but generally smaller, price in terms of length when we use the Scheffé bound to look at one among $g + 1$ multiple parameters rather than at one parameter separately. This may be seen by comparing (4.2-53) with the exact interval (4.1-42). The relative sizes of these intervals are illustrated in Example 4.2-4.

It is sometimes suggested that the Scheffé bound be used to locate, *post hoc*, coefficients in a regression function that are "significantly" different from zero (in which case the bound does not include zero). A similar use of Roy's bound has been suggested when estimated multivariate regression coefficients are to be inspected *post hoc*. Because these bounds are extremely conservative, however, these procedures are likely to yield excessive numbers of false negatives, especially when the sample size is moderate, and cannot be recommended in general. These considerations are discussed in more detail in Sec. 6.3, where alternative procedures for locating salient terms or variables are proposed. In spite of these limitations, the Scheffé and Roy bounds are valuable in scientific reporting for conveying to the reader a conservative assessment of the precision of multiparameter and/or multivariable estimates. Other aspects of the Roy system of confidence bounds are discussed in Sec. 5.2.5.

EXAMPLE 4.2-4 (*Multivariate confidence bounds*) Presented below are 95 percent simultaneous confidence bounds for the intercept and slope parameters for Example 4.2-2. Both the Scheffé bounds for each response variable separately and the Roy bounds for all variables jointly are shown. The Scheffé bounds differ from the confidence intervals in Example 4.2-2 only in the substitution of $(g + 1)F_{\alpha}^{(g+1,n_e)} = 2F_{.05}^{(2,13)} = 7.62$ for $F^{(1,n_e)} = F_{.05}^{(1,13)} = 4.67$ as a factor under the square root. In the Roy bounds, this factor becomes $(n_e r/t)F_{0,\alpha}^{(r,s,t)} = [(13 \times 2)/11]F_{0,.05}^{(1,2,11)} = 18.67$.* Thus, the Scheffé and Roy bounds are, in this instance, $\sqrt{7.62/4.67} = 1.2273$ and $\sqrt{18.67/4.67} = 1.9995$ times larger than the univariate confidence interval.

Bounds	Variable	Intercept, β_0	Slope, β_1
Scheffé	*1* Visual placing	4.5667 ± 1.2776	-2.3000 ± 1.0994
	2 Wire maneuver	$-.5333 \pm 1.6187$	3.2667 ± 1.3930
	3 Palpebral closure	$.7000 \pm .7185$	$2.8333 \pm .9313$
Roy	*1* Visual placing	4.5667 ± 2.0815	-2.3000 ± 1.7912
	2 Wire maneuver	$-.5333 \pm 2.6371$	3.2667 ± 2.2694
	3 Palpebral closure	$.7000 \pm 1.7632$	2.8333 ± 1.5172

4.2.7 Testing whether a New Multivariate Observation is Drawn from a Given Multivariate Normal Distribution

In the multivariate setting we can pose a problem similar to that of Sec. 4.1.14: Could a new p-variate observation $\mathbf{y}$, associated with a given value of x, be regarded as having been drawn from a population distributed as $N(\mathbf{B}'\mathbf{x},\Sigma)$, assuming that $\mathbf{B}$ and Σ are known only through estimates from an independent sample? To solve this problem we need the distribution of the vector deviation from the predicted mean $\hat{\mathbf{y}} \mid x = \hat{\mathbf{B}}'\mathbf{x}$. Along the lines of Sec. 4.1.13, we have

$$\mathscr{E}(\mathbf{y} - \hat{\mathbf{y}} \mid x) = \mathbf{Bx} - \mathbf{Bx} = 0$$

$$\mathscr{V}(\mathbf{y} - \hat{\mathbf{y}} \mid x) = d\Sigma$$

where $d = 1 + \mathbf{x}'(\mathbf{X}'\mathbf{D}\mathbf{X})^{-1}\mathbf{x}$ (4.2-55)

Since only linear functions of observations are involved, the distribution of $(\mathbf{y} - \hat{\mathbf{y}} \mid \mathbf{x})$ is multivariate normal if the observations are multivariate normal.

* Linear extrapolation to $t = 11$ in the table of F_0, Appendix A.

Assuming that Σ has been estimated by $\Sigma_{(n_e)}$ on n_e degrees of freedom independent of $\hat{\mathbf{B}}$, the largest root of

$$|(\mathbf{y} - \hat{\mathbf{y}} \mid x)(\mathbf{y} - \hat{\mathbf{y}} \mid x)' - \lambda n_e\, d\boldsymbol{\Sigma}_{(n_e)}| = 0 \qquad (4.2\text{-}56)$$

multiplied by t/r, is distributed as F_0 with parameters $r = p$, $s = 1$, and $t = n_e - p + 1$. As we have seen in Sec. 4.2.5, (4.2-56) has one nonzero root equal to $(\mathbf{y} - \hat{\mathbf{y}} \mid x)'\boldsymbol{\Sigma}_{(n_e)}^{-1}(\mathbf{y} - \hat{\mathbf{y}} \mid x)$, and F_0 is the univariate F statistic with r and t degrees of freedom. Thus,

$$F = \frac{n_e - p + 1}{pn_e d}(\mathbf{y} - \hat{\mathbf{y}} \mid x)'\boldsymbol{\Sigma}_{(n_e)}^{-1}(\mathbf{y} - \hat{\mathbf{y}} \mid x) \qquad (4.2\text{-}57)$$

is distributed as F with p and $n_e - p + 1$ degrees of freedom and may be used in a statistical test of the hypothesis that $\mathbf{y}$ was drawn from the given population.

If $\mathbf{y}_.$ is the mean of N independent new observations, a similar result holds for $(\mathbf{y}_. - \hat{\mathbf{y}} \mid x)$ but with $d = 1/N + \mathbf{x}'(\mathbf{X}'\mathbf{D}\mathbf{X})^{-1}\mathbf{x}$.

EXAMPLE 4.2-5 (*Testing a new observation from a p-variate population*) Suppose replication of the drug trials described in Example 4.2-1 was contuined with a new lot of the drug beginning with animal number 16. If this animal responded to a dose of 3 mg/kg with scores of 6, 0, 0 on the three variables, would there be reason to suspect that the new lot was defective?

In order to test this possibility, we could compute a value of the F statistic (4.2-57), first evaluating d, using $\log_{10} 3 \approx .5$ as the value of x:

$$d = 1 + \tfrac{1}{3}[1, .5]\begin{bmatrix} .6 & -.4 \\ -.4 & .4 \end{bmatrix}\begin{bmatrix} 1 \\ .5 \end{bmatrix}$$

$$= 1 + \frac{.3}{3} = 1.1$$

Then, the deviations from the fitted regression lines are

$$y^{(1)} - \hat{y}^{(1)} \mid x = 6 - (4.5667 - 2.3000 \times .5) = 2.5833$$

$$y^{(2)} - \hat{y}^{(2)} \mid x = 0 - (-.5333 + 3.2667 \times .5) = -1.1001$$

$$y^{(3)} - \hat{y}^{(3)} \mid x = 0 - (.700 + 2.8333 \times .5) = -2.1167$$

and, finally,

$$F = \frac{13 - 3 + 1}{3 \times 13 \times 1.1}[2.5883, -1.1001, -2.1167]$$

$$\times \begin{bmatrix} 1.2891 & & \text{(symmetric)} \\ -.5449 & 2.0692 & \\ -.7891 & -.0987 & .9250 \end{bmatrix}\begin{bmatrix} 2.5883 \\ -1.1001 \\ -2.1167 \end{bmatrix}$$

$$= \frac{11}{42.9} 26.5183 = 6.80$$

Since the .05 point of F on $p = 3$ and $n_e - 3 + 1 = 11$ degrees of freedom is 3.59, there would be presumptive evidence that the new lot of the drug is defective. Some effort to check the drug, or otherwise account for the lack of response in this animal, would certainly be indicated.

Exercise 4.2-1 The following data from Irwin [1968, page 246] give the mean response of groups of six mice (female Berkeley Swiss) to five levels of oral chloropromozine hydrochloride at three time periods post dose:

		Measure		
Time post dose, min	Dose, mg/kg	*1* Visual placing	*2* Wire maneuver	*3* Palpebral closure
	1	4.6	.2	.9
	3	3.6	0	1.3
30	10	2.5	1.3	3.5
	30	1.2	5.3	5.7
	100	.7	6.3	5.4
	1	4.6	.2	1.2
	3	4.1	0	1.7
60	10	1.6	2.8	4.5
	30	.2	5.5	5.8
	100	.1	6.7	6.1
	1	4	0	.7
	3	4	0	1.4
90	10	2.4	3.2	3.9
	30	.6	4.8	5.8
	100	0	6.9	6.4

Assuming errors are independent between time points, find the simplest polynomial in log dose and time which fits these data. Use the covariance matrix on p as the error estimate. Is it possible to determine from these data at what post-dose time the peak effect of the drug occurs?

Exercise 4.2-2 Prove that the estimated error-covariance matrix in multivariate analysis is positive definite with probability 1 if $n_e \geq p$.

Exercise 4.2-3 For what linear combination of parameters is the lower bound of the confidence coefficient for the Scheffé interval attained?

Exercise 4.2-4 Generalize multivariate least squares to the case where the error matrix in (4.2-5) has a known correlation $\underset{n \times n}{\mathbf{R}}$ *between rows.*

5

LINEAR MODELS FOR DESIGNED EXPERIMENTS

The prerequisites of scientific experimentation have traditionally included controlled conditions, standardized materials, and reproducibility of measurement. Much of scientific progress in the eighteenth and nineteenth centuries was undoubtedly due to the seriousness with which experimentalists accepted these requirements and the ingenuity they displayed in meeting them. With the development of statistical theory in the present century, however, there began a close examination of the possibility of conducting successful experiments when the traditional prerequisites could not be met. The first steps in this direction were little more than direct applications of the Gauss-Legendre error analysis to duplicated experiments. But as the subject developed, an essentially new conception of experimentation, able to cope with uncontrolled variation, was formulated in the statistical discipline now called *design of experiments*.

The origin of this field can perhaps be traced to W. S. Gosset's [Student, 1908] use of a linear statistical model to represent the outcome of an experiment. Gosset was concerned with the problem of distinguishing between natural variation in the material and the actual effect of the experimental conditions. The familiar t test represents his solution to this problem (Sec. 3.4.5). As he began to explore the problem of designing experiments to maximize the power of this discrimination, he arrived at the principle of *blocking*, i.e., of stratifying the experimental material in homogeneous blocks and comparing the effects of the conditions within these blocks [Student, 1923].

The subsequent development and formalization of Gosset's ideas were largely the work of R. A. Fisher [1966, 1967]. In collaboration with Frank Yates and the agronomists at Rothamstead Experimental Station, Fisher elaborated a statistical methodology for field trials of agricultural techniques. This methodology was presented in quite general terms, however, and its usefulness wherever experiments had to be carried out in the presence of substantial uncontrolled variation was readily apparent. Industrial, medical, biological, and ultimately behavioral research rapidly adopted the fisherian methods for conducting experiments and analyzing the results.

The present chapter of this text represents the multivariate extensions of these methods as they apply to behavioral research. Fisher [1939] contributed to this extension, as did Hotelling [1931], Wilks [1932], Bartlett [1947b], Rao [1952], Roy [1957], Anderson [1958], and others.

The terminology of experimental design, regardless of the area of application, tends to be that of agricultural field trials. Thus, experimental units are referred to as *plots*, the conditions as *treatments*, the types of units as *varieties*, and the response as *yield*. We shall continue this practice to the extent of using "treatment" to denote the experimental stimulus, agent, or manipulation, and shall occasionally use "variety" to refer to a subpopulation of subjects. But we shall uniformly use "unit" in place of "plot" and "response" or "outcome" in place of "yield."

In many respects, the dosage-response study in Example 4.2-1 is typical of a designed experiment. The experimental units (animals) are assigned randomly to the treatments (levels of dose), the treatment applied, and the responses of the units observed and recorded. The special feature of this particular example, which places it within the purview of the polynomial regression model of Chap. 4, is its *quantitative* treatment variable. In the more general form of experiment, the treatments represent merely nominal or at most ordered classes, and the analysis of their effects requires the more inclusive approach based on the *experimental-design model* introduced in this chapter.

Experiments which have only one classification of treatments are called *one-way designs*. Experiments in which several types of treatment are applied jointly to the experimental material, or in which the material is subdivided or classified according to variety, are called *crossed designs*. Formally, these designs correspond to cartesian products of the sets of treatments and/or the sets of varieties. As we shall see in Sec. 5.3, an algebra which is isomorphic with that of cartesian set products may be exploited in the construction of models for crossed designs.

Another class of experimental designs is generated by *hierarchical* arrangements of the material. These designs, called *nested*, occur frequently in survey research, where the ways of classification correspond to geographical divisions (states, counties within states, municipalities within counties, etc.). Formal operations that generate models for these designs will be discussed in Sec. 6.4.

Finally, designs from the foregoing classes may be combined to generate crossed-*and*-nested designs. Of these, the so-called *split-plot* designs are by far the most important in behavioral research, for they include the *repeated-measures* designs widely used in psychological investigations. The whole of Chap. 7 is devoted to the analysis and interpretation of the latter designs.

Throughout the present chapter we shall assume that the arithmetic of the data analysis will be performed by computing machinery. Although special cases of the designs can be analyzed by hand if the data are univariate, the general case and most multivariate problems are too laborious computationally for hand work. Moreover, the hand methods for univariate analysis are well explicated in texts such as Cochran and Cox [1957] and Winer [1971] and need not be detailed here.

5.1 RANDOMIZATION AND GAUSS-MARKOV THEORY IN THE ANALYSIS OF EXPERIMENTS

The least-squares analysis of designed experiments may be justified on two lines of argument, both crucially dependent upon randomization of treatment assignments. The first argument is based on the assumption that the experimental material is a sample from a population. Random assignment of units to treatments then guarantees that the parent distribution is identical within treatments at the onset of the experiment. In particular, the population mean and covariance matrix are initially the same in all treatment groups. The critical assumption in the Gauss-Markov analysis is that the treatment alters only the mean of the distribution. The variance and other moments are assumed unaffected or, if affected, to change uniformly in all treatments and so remain homogeneous at outcome.

With respect to variance, this strong assumption can be relaxed somewhat if it is assumed that the effect of the treatment on variance is functionally related to the effect on the mean. If this is the case, a transformation of the dependent variable can usually be found which restores homogeneity of variance [Bartlett, 1947a; Rao, 1965, page 319]. Gauss-Markov analysis of the transformed variable is then justified. If the transformation has a similar effect on covariance, a comparable multivariate analysis may be justified.

Although the literature has little direct evidence on this point, the instances in which significant changes in variance are reported are few. The limitations on treatments appear to be such that only relatively small changes can occur in most behavioral experiments. The systematic effects of these changes may be large enough to be seen in treatment differences, but differential effects on variation about these means are often too small to be detectable. (There are, of course, experiments in which treatments have virtually an all-or-none response, but they generate qualitative data suitable for the methods of Chap. 8 rather than for linear least squares.) Taken with the evidence from sampling studies demonstrating the robustness of least-squares analysis in the presence of moderate nonhomogeneity of variance and covariance when the numbers of units per treatment are substantially equal, these considerations generally support an approach to behavioral data analysis based on Gauss-Markov assumptions [Ito and Schull, 1964]. The methods presented in this chapter, like those of Chap. 4, are developed from this point of view.

The second argument assumes merely that the material in the experiment is an arbitrary collection of units rather than a sample. The statistical tests in the least-squares analysis are then justified as approximations to randomization tests such as described in Sec. 1.2.4. The caveat at the end of Sec. 1.2.4 then applies—the randomization experiment supports only the inference that a treatment effect has occurred; it gives no information about the expected size of treatment effects with respect to a naturally occurring population, since no such population is defined. This is not as serious a limitation as it might at first seem, for in the early stages of research an investigator may be quite satisfied to have demonstrated the existence of an effect, and to work out details concerning magnitude later.

5.2 ONE-WAY DESIGNS

The simplest class of designed experiments is the *completely randomized* design with one way of classification. The experimental setup consists of n treatment conditions, possibly including a control, to which the experimental units, usually animals or subjects (or groups of subjects if a group response is involved), are assigned randomly. If possible, equal numbers of units should be assigned to each treatment. Although analysis and interpretation of the experiment are not irreparably complicated by unequal numbers, *grossly* unequal numbers affect adversely the robustness of the least-squares analysis to nonnormality or heterogeneity of variance, and should be avoided. For the sake of generality, both the equal- and unequal-number cases will be discussed in this section. A display of real data from a simple multivariate experiment in the case of unequal numbers is presented in the following example.

EXAMPLE 5.2-1 (*An educational evaluation*) Data for this example are drawn from a large-scale educational experiment reported by Milton Mair [1962] (see also Bock [1966]). The purpose of the study was to compare mathematics achievement in a traditional ninth-grade algebra course with that in an alternative course developed by the School Mathematics Study Group (SMSG). Forty-three teachers from schools throughout the United States agreed to participate in the study; 22 were selected at random to teach the traditional course, and 21 to teach the SMSG course. At the end of the experimental year, achievement of students in all 43 classrooms was evaluated using both a traditional algebra test published by the Cooperative Test

Division of Educational Testing Service, and a new test based on the objectives of the School Mathematics Study Group.

Since the teacher was the unit of randomization in this study, the average score of students taught by each teacher should be considered the basic observation (see Sec. 1.2.1). Means for the two groups on each test appear in Table 5.2-1. These data are used in Example 5.2-2 to illustrate the multivariate analysis for the one-way design.

5.2.1 The Model for the One-Way Design

In elementary texts, the analysis of one-way designs is usually presented as a problem in testing the significance of group differences and of estimating group means. In keeping with the point of view of the present text, however, we shall approach the analysis as a problem in model fitting and parameter estimation. We begin by considering alternative models for the treatment effect.

Table 5.2-1 AVERAGE SCORES IN MATHEMATICS ACHIEVEMENT OF NINTH-GRADE ALGEBRA CLASSES RANDOMLY ASSIGNED TO TRADITIONAL AND SMSG COURSES OF INSTRUCTION

Traditional course			SMSG course		
Class	Traditional test	SMSG test	Class	Traditional test	SMSG test
1	24.32	15.06	1	20.10	24.71
2	17.91	9.10	2	8.69	15.72
3	25.70	15.35	3	8.93	15.11
4	19.93	12.27	4	12.47	17.50
5	13.92	10.29	5	11.37	16.84
6	18.45	12.35	6	25.09	24.14
7	11.17	9.70	7	17.62	22.12
8	17.36	12.43	8	5.88	13.46
9	22.54	14.92	9	10.69	15.86
10	15.92	11.29	10	7.40	14.25
11	22.57	11.77	11	12.29	16.76
12	12.92	10.96	12	9.73	18.46
13	18.14	12.18	13	10.44	15.89
14	22.50	11.79	14	26.18	25.59
15	13.75	10.00	15	2.75	9.75
16	7.00	9.31	16	10.70	19.39
17	19.12	12.92	17	4.28	13.00
18	19.33	10.78	18	11.56	14.20
19	23.75	13.39	19	10.18	16.11
20	20.50	13.33	20	12.86	17.21
21	15.88	11.92	21	10.70	16.17
22	8.82	8.14			

Let the outcome for unit i in group j be the p-variate observation $\mathbf{y}_{ij}$. There are two possible models to be considered:

$$\boldsymbol{y}_{ij} = \boldsymbol{\mu} + \boldsymbol{\epsilon}_{ij} \qquad (5.2\text{-}1)$$

and

$$\boldsymbol{y}_{ij} = \boldsymbol{\mu} + \boldsymbol{\alpha}_j + \boldsymbol{\epsilon}_{ij} \qquad (5.2\text{-}2)$$

The vector $\boldsymbol{\mu}$ may be interpreted as the common mean of the groups before treatment (i.e., the mean of the multivariate population from which the experimental units were drawn), $\boldsymbol{\alpha}_j$ is the effect of applying the jth treatment, and $\boldsymbol{\epsilon}_{ij}$ is the random error. Assuming a normal error specification and no alteration of variances and covariances by the treatments, $\boldsymbol{\epsilon}_{ij}$ is distributed $N(\mathbf{0},\Sigma)$.

If the treatments have no effect, (5.2-1) is the model to be fitted; otherwise, (5.2-2) is fitted. If, as is usually the case, $\boldsymbol{\mu}$ is unknown, (5.2-2) cannot be distinguished from (5.2-1) when the treatment effects are equal, i.e., when $\boldsymbol{\alpha}_1 = \boldsymbol{\alpha}_2 = \cdots = \boldsymbol{\alpha}_n$. Thus, any test which might discriminate between the models when $\boldsymbol{\mu}$ is unknown is sensitive only to *differences* among treatment effects. In particular, a test of the goodness of fit of (5.2-1) is equivalent to a test of the hypothesis of equality of treatment-group means,

$$H_0\colon (\boldsymbol{\mu}_1 = \boldsymbol{\mu}_2 = \cdots = \boldsymbol{\mu}_n) \qquad \text{where } \boldsymbol{\mu}_1 = \boldsymbol{\mu} + \boldsymbol{\alpha}_1,\ \boldsymbol{\mu}_2 = \boldsymbol{\mu} + \boldsymbol{\alpha}_2, \ldots$$

From the point of view of model fitting, however, we retain the distinction between $\boldsymbol{\mu}$ and $\boldsymbol{\alpha}_j$ and write the model for the group means as

$$\boldsymbol{y}_{\cdot j} = \boldsymbol{\mu} + \boldsymbol{\alpha}_j + \boldsymbol{\epsilon}_{\cdot j} \qquad (5.2\text{-}3)$$

If the normal errors are similarly distributed and the N_j units in group j respond independently, the mean error is distributed

$$\boldsymbol{\epsilon}_{\cdot j} \sim N\left(\mathbf{0}, \frac{1}{N_j}\Sigma\right) \qquad (5.2\text{-}4)$$

From (5.2-3), the model for all n treatment groups may be expressed in the matrix equation

$$\underset{n\times p}{\boldsymbol{Y}_{\cdot}} = \underset{n\times m}{\mathbf{A}}\ \underset{m\times p}{\Xi} + \underset{n\times p}{\boldsymbol{E}_{\cdot}} \qquad (5.2\text{-}5)$$

where

$$\boldsymbol{Y}_{\cdot} = \begin{bmatrix} \boldsymbol{y}'_{\cdot 1} \\ \boldsymbol{y}'_{\cdot 2} \\ \cdots \\ \boldsymbol{y}'_{\cdot n} \end{bmatrix} \qquad \mathbf{A} = \begin{bmatrix} 1 & 1 & 0 & \cdots & 0 \\ 1 & 0 & 1 & \cdots & 0 \\ \cdots & \cdots & \cdots & \cdots & \cdots \\ 1 & 0 & 0 & \cdots & 1 \end{bmatrix}$$

and

$$\Xi' = [\boldsymbol{\mu}, \boldsymbol{\alpha}_1, \boldsymbol{\alpha}_2, \ldots, \boldsymbol{\alpha}_n] \qquad \boldsymbol{E}'_{\cdot} = [\boldsymbol{\epsilon}_{\cdot 1}, \boldsymbol{\epsilon}_{\cdot 2}, \ldots, \boldsymbol{\epsilon}_{\cdot n}]$$

(transposed).

The joint distribution of elements in $\boldsymbol{E}_{\cdot}$ is then the same as in (4.2-11). The reader should understand that, in contrast to the nested and mixed models to be presented later, the above is a so-called *fixed-effects* model; i.e., the treatments are individually identified and their effects are fixed, nonstochastic variables.

It is of interest to compare the design model (5.2-5) with the polynomial model (4.2-5). Note that the only real difference between the models is in the structure of the $\mathbf{X}$ and $\mathbf{A}$ matrices. [The use of Ξ in (5.2-5) rather than $\mathbf{B}$ is merely a notational convention.] Whereas quantitative values of the independent variable (e.g., dose) appear in the $\mathbf{X}$ matrix, the elements of $\mathbf{A}$ are restricted to 1s and 0s indicating the presence or absence of effects represented in the Ξ matrix. Nevertheless, the elements of $\mathbf{A}$, like those of $\mathbf{X}$, are known coefficients of linear forms in the unknown parameters which comprise Ξ. Thus, the statistical problem of estimating Ξ is formally identical to that of estimating the regression coefficients $\mathbf{B}$. In particular, routine application of the least-squares principle of Chap. 4 gives the normal equations

$$\mathbf{A'DA}\hat{\Xi} = \mathbf{A'DY}. \qquad (5.2\text{-}6)$$

Difficulties arise at this point, however, because the condition $|\mathbf{A'DA}| \neq 0$ necessary for a unique solution of (5.2-6) fails. The rank of the $n \times m$ matrix $\mathbf{A}$ cannot exceed n, and $m = n + 1$; hence the $m \times m$ matrix $\mathbf{A'DA}$ is at most rank n, and its determinant is zero.

Actually, the rank of $\mathbf{A}$ is exactly n, for by column operations (subtracting each of the n rightmost columns from the left columns), $\mathbf{A}$ may be reduced to the canonical form (Sec. 2.3.2) consisting of the $n \times n$ identity matrix. Thus, if $\mathbf{D}$ contains no zero diagonal elements, $\mathbf{A'DA}$ is of rank n. Note, however, that if rank($\mathbf{A'DA}$) $= n$, so does rank($\mathbf{A'DA} \mid \mathbf{A'DY}.$), for the linear dependency by rows induced by $\mathbf{A}'$ in $\mathbf{A'DA}$ obtains in every column of $\mathbf{A'DY}.$ as well. Thus, the condition (2.3-6) required for a consistent solution of (5.2-6) is met in the system of equations corresponding to each of the p variates. The difficulty presented by the vanishing determinant is therefore easily circumvented by one of the methods described in Sec. 2.3 for the solution of consistent nonhomogeneous systems not of full rank. Of these methods, reparameterization is perhaps the most transparent from the point of view of interpretation and is in general the most economical computationally (see Bock [1963]).

5.2.2 Reparameterization

According to (2.3-11) and (2.3-12), the model matrix may be expressed as the matrix product

$$\underset{n\times m}{\mathbf{A}} = \underset{n\times l}{\mathbf{K}}\ \underset{l\times m}{\mathbf{L}} \qquad (5.2\text{-}7)$$

if and only if

$$\text{rank}\begin{bmatrix}\mathbf{A}\\ \mathbf{L}\end{bmatrix} = \text{rank}[\mathbf{A} \mid \mathbf{K}] = \text{rank}(\mathbf{A}) = \text{rank}(\mathbf{K}) = \text{rank}(\mathbf{L}) = l \qquad (5.2\text{-}8)$$

The factorization (5.2-7) is not unique, but given an $\mathbf{L}$ which satisfies (5.2-8), we may compute $\mathbf{K}$ from

$$\mathbf{K} = \mathbf{AL}'(\mathbf{LL}')^{-1} \qquad (5.2\text{-}9)$$

Conversely, given a **K** satisfying (5.2-8), we may compute **L** from

$$\mathbf{L} = (\mathbf{K}'\mathbf{K})^{-1}\mathbf{K}'\mathbf{A} \qquad (5.2\text{-}10)$$

The matrix **K** may be described as a *column basis* of **A**, and **L** as a *row basis* of **A**.

In terms of (5.2-7), (5.2-5) becomes

$$\boldsymbol{Y}_{.} = \mathbf{K}\mathbf{L}\boldsymbol{\Xi} + \boldsymbol{E}_{.}$$

or

$$\boldsymbol{Y}_{.} = \mathbf{K}\boldsymbol{\Theta} + \boldsymbol{E}_{.} \qquad (5.2\text{-}11)$$

That is, the deficient-rank model in terms of the mp parameters in $\boldsymbol{\Xi}$ is replaced by the full-rank model in terms of the *lp linear parametric functions* in $\boldsymbol{\Theta}$.

Then, estimating $\boldsymbol{\Theta}$ by least squares, we obtain the normal equations

$$\underset{l\times l}{\mathbf{K}'\mathbf{D}\mathbf{K}}\,\underset{l\times p}{\hat{\boldsymbol{\Theta}}} = \underset{l\times p}{\mathbf{K}'\mathbf{D}\mathbf{Y}_{.}} \qquad (5.2\text{-}12)$$

These equations are easily solved, because rank($\mathbf{K}'\mathbf{D}\mathbf{K}$) $= l$ if **D** is of full rank; hence, $|\mathbf{K}'\mathbf{D}\mathbf{K}| \neq 0$, and (5.2-12) has the unique solution

$$\hat{\boldsymbol{\Theta}} = (\mathbf{K}'\mathbf{D}\mathbf{K})^{-1}\mathbf{K}'\mathbf{D}\mathbf{Y}_{.} \qquad (5.2\text{-}13)$$

Thus the deficiency of rank in the design model is overcome, and the only problem remaining is to choose **L**. Within the restriction imposed by (5.2-8), **L** is arbitrary, but its choice is constrained by the need to retain separability of the models (5.2-1) and (5.2-2). An example of a matrix which retains this separability is

$$\underset{n\times(n+1)}{\mathbf{L}_C^{(n)}} = \begin{bmatrix} 1 & \frac{1}{n} & \frac{1}{n} & \cdots & \frac{1}{n} & \frac{1}{n} \\ 0 & 1 & 0 & \cdots & 0 & -1 \\ 0 & 0 & 1 & \cdots & 0 & -1 \\ \cdots & \cdots & \cdots & \cdots & \cdots & \cdots \\ 0 & 0 & 0 & \cdots & 1 & -1 \end{bmatrix} \qquad (5.2\text{-}14)$$

This matrix clearly satisfies (5.2-8), for the rows of (5.2-14) are obviously dependent on **A** [that is, row 1 of (5.2-14) is $1/n$ times the sum of the rows in **A**, and the remaining rows are differences between the first $n - 1$ rows of **A** and the last row]. Also, $l = n$, and since (5.2-14) is an n-rowed echelon matrix (Sec. 2.3.2), it is of rank n as required. With this choice of **L**, the parametric functions in the rows of $\boldsymbol{\Theta}$ are

$$\begin{aligned} \boldsymbol{\theta}_0' &= \boldsymbol{\mu}' + \frac{1}{n}(\boldsymbol{\alpha}_1' + \boldsymbol{\alpha}_2' + \cdots + \boldsymbol{\alpha}_n') \\ \boldsymbol{\theta}_1' &= \boldsymbol{\alpha}_1' - \boldsymbol{\alpha}_n' \\ \boldsymbol{\theta}_2' &= \boldsymbol{\alpha}_2' - \boldsymbol{\alpha}_n' \\ &\cdots\cdots \\ \boldsymbol{\theta}_{n-1}' &= \boldsymbol{\alpha}_{n-1}' - \boldsymbol{\alpha}_n' \end{aligned} \qquad (5.2\text{-}15)$$

The last $n - 1$ functions are contrasts of the first $n - 1$ treatment effects with that of the last treatment. Alternatively, these functions may be interpreted as the values of the first $n - 1$ treatment effects as measured from the arbitrary origin $\boldsymbol{\alpha}_n = \mathbf{0}$.

Note that if the set of treatments is arbitrary, the function $\boldsymbol{\theta}_0$ has no useful interpretation in the presence of nonzero treatment effects (i.e., the mean of an arbitrary collection of classes is arbitrary). If there are no treatment effects, however, its value becomes that of the original population mean:

$$\boldsymbol{\theta}_0 = \boldsymbol{\mu}$$

Thus, a choice of $\mathbf{L}$ with a structure such as (5.2-14) provides an interpretable reparameterization both for the rank-n model (5.2-2) and the rank-1 model (5.2-1). If the rank-n model holds, the contrasts in $\mathbf{L}$ represent treatment differences which presumably will be interpretable. If the rank-1 model holds, the contrasts have zero expectation (hence belong to the error space), and $\boldsymbol{\theta}_0$ becomes potentially interpretable.

Clearly, any $n \times (n + 1)$ matrix in which the first row is the same as in (5.2-14), and the remaining rows are contrasts of the last n columns, is suitable as a reparameterization of (5.2-5). Indeed, we shall see that the partition of sums of squares in the analysis of variance for the one-way model is invariant with respect to choice of these contrasts. Nevertheless, certain types of contrasts are convenient for special purposes and are discussed in Sec. 5.2.5.

The column basis corresponding to the parameterization (5.2-15) is obtained as follows: Express (5.2-14) as

$$\mathbf{L}_C^{(n)} = \underset{\begin{matrix} 1 \quad\quad n \end{matrix}}{\begin{bmatrix} 1 & \frac{1}{n}\mathbf{1}_n' \\ \mathbf{0} & \mathbf{C}_n' \end{bmatrix}} \begin{matrix} 1 \\ n-1 \end{matrix} \tag{5.2-16}$$

where

$$\underset{(n-1)\times n}{\mathbf{C}_n'} = [\mathbf{I}_{n-1}, -\mathbf{1}_{n-1}]$$

Then, from (5.2-9), compute

$$\mathbf{K}_C^{(n)} = \mathbf{A}\mathbf{L}_C^{(n)\prime}(\mathbf{L}_C^{(n)}\mathbf{L}_C^{(n)\prime})^{-1} = [\mathbf{1}_n, \mathbf{I}_n] \begin{bmatrix} 1 & \mathbf{0}' \\ \frac{1}{n}\mathbf{1}_n & \mathbf{C}_n \end{bmatrix} \begin{bmatrix} \frac{n+1}{n} & \mathbf{0}' \\ \mathbf{0} & \mathbf{C}_n'\mathbf{C}_n \end{bmatrix}^{-1} \tag{5.2-17}$$

The matrix $\mathbf{C}_n'\mathbf{C}_n = \mathbf{I}_{n-1} + \mathbf{1}_{n-1}\mathbf{1}_{n-1}'$ is one of a general class $\mathbf{A} \pm \mathbf{u}\mathbf{v}'$ which has the explicit inverse

$$(\mathbf{A} \pm \mathbf{u}\mathbf{v}')^{-1} = \mathbf{A}^{-1} \mp \frac{1}{1 \pm \mathbf{v}'\mathbf{A}^{-1}\mathbf{u}}(\mathbf{A}^{-1}\mathbf{u})(\mathbf{v}'\mathbf{A}^{-1}) \tag{5.2-18}$$

[Householder, 1953, page 79] (see also Exercise 2.3-2).

Thus, (5.2-17) becomes

$$\underset{n\times n}{\mathbf{K}_C^{(n)}} = \begin{bmatrix} \dfrac{n+1}{n}\mathbf{1}_n & \begin{matrix}\mathbf{I}_{n-1} \\ -\mathbf{1}'_{n-1}\end{matrix} \end{bmatrix} \begin{bmatrix} \dfrac{n}{n+1} & \mathbf{0}' \\ \mathbf{0} & \mathbf{I}_{n-1} - \dfrac{1}{n}\mathbf{1}_{n-1}\mathbf{1}'_{n-1} \end{bmatrix} \tag{5.2-19}$$

$$= \underset{1 \quad n-1}{[\mathbf{1}_n, \mathbf{C}_D^{(n)}]}\, n$$

where $$\underset{n\times(n-1)}{\mathbf{C}_D^{(n)}} = \begin{bmatrix} \mathbf{I}_{n-1} - \dfrac{1}{n}\mathbf{1}_{n-1}\mathbf{1}'_{n-1} \\ -\dfrac{1}{n}\mathbf{1}'_{n-1} \end{bmatrix}$$

For example, when $n = 3$,

$$\underset{3\times 4}{\mathbf{L}_C^{(3)}} = \begin{bmatrix} 1 & \frac{1}{3}\mathbf{1}'_3 \\ 0 & \mathbf{C}'_3 \end{bmatrix} = \begin{bmatrix} 1 & \frac{1}{3} & \frac{1}{3} & \frac{1}{3} \\ 0 & 1 & 0 & -1 \\ 0 & 0 & 1 & -1 \end{bmatrix} \tag{5.2-20}$$

and

$$\underset{3\times 3}{\mathbf{K}_C^{(3)}} = [\mathbf{1}_3, \mathbf{C}_D^{(3)}] = \begin{bmatrix} 1 & \frac{2}{3} & -\frac{1}{3} \\ 1 & -\frac{1}{3} & \frac{2}{3} \\ 1 & -\frac{1}{3} & -\frac{1}{3} \end{bmatrix} \tag{5.2-21}$$

Interestingly, $\mathbf{C}_n$ and $\mathbf{C}_D^{(n)}$ are duals of one another. That is, if

$$\mathbf{L}_D^{(n)} = \begin{bmatrix} 1 & \dfrac{1}{n}\mathbf{1}'_n \\ \mathbf{0} & \mathbf{C}_D^{(n)\prime} \end{bmatrix} \tag{5.2-22}$$

then

$$\mathbf{K}_D^{(n)} = [\mathbf{1}_n, \mathbf{C}_n] \tag{5.2-23}$$

For example,

$$\mathbf{L}_D^{(3)} = \begin{bmatrix} 1 & \frac{1}{3} & \frac{1}{3} & \frac{1}{3} \\ 0 & \frac{2}{3} & -\frac{1}{3} & -\frac{1}{3} \\ 0 & -\frac{1}{3} & \frac{2}{3} & -\frac{1}{3} \end{bmatrix} \tag{5.2-24}$$

and

$$\mathbf{K}_D^{(3)} = \begin{bmatrix} 1 & 1 & 0 \\ 1 & 0 & 1 \\ 1 & -1 & -1 \end{bmatrix} \tag{5.2-25}$$

The contrasts in $\mathbf{C}_D^{(n)}$ are called *deviation contrasts*. They represent differences between the effect of given classes and the mean of the effects of all classes.

As for the actual arithmetic of least squares, we see from (5.2-13) that it is **K** rather than **L** which is needed in the calculations. This is fortunate because **K** can always be generated directly from formulas such as (5.2-19) and (5.2-23) without explicitly constructing **L**. In order to interpret the reparameterization implied in a given **K** matrix, however, it is necessary to know at least the form of the corresponding **L** matrix. Relationships between particular **K** and **L** matrices are discussed in Secs. 5.2.5 and 5.3.6b. Other treatments of analysis of variance employing reparameterization refer to **K** as a matrix of "dummy" variables, but they do not explicitly identify the **L** matrix [Mendenhall, 1968]. We shall refer to **K** as the *basis* matrix for the design, and to **L** as the *parameterization* matrix.

5.2.3 Multivariate Analysis of Variance for the One-Way Design

In the geometric interpretation, the estimation space of the one-way design is the sum (see Sec. 2.2.2) of two subspaces—namely, the space of the constant term and the space of treatment effects. The vectors which generate these spaces are denoted explicitly when the model matrix is written in the partitioned form

$$\underset{n\times(n+1)}{\mathbf{A}} = [\mathbf{1}_n, \mathbf{I}_n]$$

The n-component *equiangular* vector $\mathbf{1}_n$ spans the one-dimensional space of the constant term (or *general mean*), and the $n \times n$ identity matrix $\mathbf{I}_n$ spans the n-dimensional space of treatment effects. Clearly, the model is not of full rank because $\mathbf{1}_n$ is in the space spanned by $\mathbf{I}_n$. To obtain a full-rank model, we employ the results in the previous section to reparameterize (5.2-2) so that the model matrix **A** is replaced by a basis matrix of the form

$$\mathbf{K}_C{}^{(n)} = [\mathbf{1}_n, \mathbf{C}_D{}^{(n)}] \qquad (5.2\text{-}26)$$

where $\mathbf{C}_D{}^{(n)}$ is an $n \times (n - 1)$ matrix orthogonal to $\mathbf{1}_n$. In the reparameterized model, $\mathbf{C}_D{}^{(n)}$ spans the $(n - 1)$-dimensional space of treatment-effect *contrasts*.

Our purpose in the analysis of variance for the one-way model is to determine whether the presence of the effect contrasts in the model significantly reduces the residual variation. If so, we adopt model (5.2-2) and proceed with the estimation of treatment differences. This analysis is essentially the same as testing the significance of an additional term in the polynomial model, except that in the case of the one-way model we test the $n - 1$ treatment contrasts jointly. Because this type of testing, which is typical of design models, involves joint tests on blocks of parameters, it is called a *blockwise* analysis, in distinction to the stepwise analysis of Chap. 4. In formulating the blockwise analysis for one-way designs, we have two cases to consider—the *orthogonal case*, in which the number of units per treatment are equal, and the *nonorthogonal case*, in which the numbers are unequal.

a Orthogonal case Suppose the rank-n model is reparameterized by setting

$$\underset{n\times(n+1)}{\mathbf{L}_H^{(n)}} = \begin{bmatrix} 1 & \frac{1}{n} & \frac{1}{n} & \cdots & \frac{1}{n} & \frac{1}{n} \\ 0 & 1 & \frac{-1}{n-1} & \cdots & \frac{-1}{n-1} & \frac{-1}{n-1} \\ 0 & 0 & 1 & \cdots & \frac{-1}{n-2} & \frac{-1}{n-2} \\ \cdots & \cdots & \cdots & \cdots & \cdots & \cdots \\ 0 & 0 & 0 & \cdots & 1 & -1 \end{bmatrix} \tag{5.2-27}$$

$$= \begin{bmatrix} 1 & \frac{1}{n}\mathbf{1}_n' \\ \mathbf{0} & \mathbf{H}_n' \end{bmatrix} \begin{matrix} 1 \\ n-1 \end{matrix}, \text{ say}$$
$$\quad\;\; \begin{matrix} 1 & n \end{matrix}$$

The rows of $\mathbf{H}_n'$ are called *Helmert contrasts* (see Sec. 5.2.5b). The first row in $\mathbf{H}_n'$ is the difference between the effect of the first treatment and the mean of those of the remaining $n - 1$ treatments; the second is the difference between the effect of the second treatment and the mean of the remaining $n - 2$ treatments, and so on to row $n - 1$ which is the difference between treatment $n - 1$ and treatment n. (A practical application of these contrasts appears in Example 5.2-5.)

Because the Helmert contrasts are mutually orthogonal, (5.2-27) is orthogonal (but not orthonormal) with respect to rows. Moreover, the columns of the corresponding basis matrix are orthogonal, for, from (5.2-9),

$$\mathbf{K}_H^{(n)} = [\mathbf{1}_n, \mathbf{I}_n] \begin{bmatrix} 1 & \mathbf{0}' \\ \frac{1}{n}\mathbf{1}_n & \mathbf{H}_n \end{bmatrix} \begin{bmatrix} \frac{n+1}{n} & \mathbf{0}' \\ \mathbf{0} & \mathbf{D}_{H_n} \end{bmatrix}^{-1}$$

where
$$\underset{(n-1)\times(n-1)}{\mathbf{D}_{H_n}} = \mathbf{H}_n'\mathbf{H}_n = \operatorname{diag}\left[\frac{n}{n-1}, \frac{n-1}{n-2}, \ldots, 2\right]$$

Whence,
$$\underset{n\times n}{\mathbf{K}_H^{(n)}} = [\mathbf{1}_n, \mathbf{H}_n\mathbf{D}_{H_n}^{-1}] = [\underset{1}{\mathbf{1}_n}, \underset{n-1}{\mathbf{C}_H^{(n)}}]\, n$$

$$= \begin{bmatrix} 1 & \frac{n-1}{n} & 0 & \cdots & 0 \\ 1 & \frac{-1}{n} & \frac{n-2}{n-1} & \cdots & 0 \\ \cdots & \cdots & \cdots & \cdots & \cdots \\ 1 & \frac{-1}{n} & \frac{-1}{n-1} & \cdots & \frac{1}{2} \\ 1 & \frac{-1}{n} & \frac{-1}{n-1} & \cdots & -\frac{1}{2} \end{bmatrix} \tag{5.2-28}$$

is orthogonal with respect to columns.

If the number of units per treatment are equal (to r, say), the least-squares estimates of the parametric functions $\boldsymbol{\Theta}_H{}^{(n)} = \mathbf{L}_H{}^{(n)}\boldsymbol{\Xi}$ satisfy the normal equations (5.2-12). (For convenience of writing, we omit the superscript n in the remainder of Sec. 5.2.)

$$r\mathbf{K}'_H\mathbf{K}_H\hat{\boldsymbol{\Theta}}_H = r\mathbf{K}'_H\mathbf{Y}.$$

whence,

$$\hat{\boldsymbol{\Theta}}_H = \mathbf{D}^{-1}_{K_H'K_H}\mathbf{K}'_H\mathbf{Y}. \qquad (5.2\text{-}29)$$

where $\mathbf{D}^{-1}_{K_H'K_H}$ is the inverse of the diagonal matrix

$$\mathbf{K}'_H\mathbf{K}_H = \mathbf{D}_{K_H'K_H} = \operatorname{diag}\left[n, \frac{n-1}{n}, \frac{n-2}{n-1}, \ldots, \frac{1}{2}\right]$$

Because the Cholesky factor of $\mathbf{K}'_H\mathbf{K}_H$ is in this instance the diagonal matrix $\mathbf{D}^{1/2}_{K_H'K_H}$ (5.2-29) may be transformed to orthogonal estimates merely by rescaling rows:

$$\underset{n \times p}{\mathbf{U}_H} = r^{1/2}\mathbf{D}^{-1/2}_{K_H'K_H}\mathbf{K}'_H\mathbf{Y}. = r(r^{-1/2}\mathbf{Q}'_H)\mathbf{Y}. \qquad (5.2\text{-}30)$$

where

$$\mathbf{U}'_H = [\underset{p\times 1}{\mathbf{u}_{H(0)}}, \underset{p\times 1}{\mathbf{u}_{H(1)}}, \underset{p\times 1}{\mathbf{u}_{H(2)}}, \ldots, \underset{p\times 1}{\mathbf{u}_{H(n-1)}}]$$

The reader may verify that $\mathbf{P}_H = r^{-1/2}\mathbf{Q}_H$ is orthogonal in the metric $r\mathbf{I}$, as required.

The $n \times n$ orthogonal matrix $\mathbf{P}_H$ is known as the *Helmert matrix of order n.* The first column of this matrix is the normalized *equiangular* vector $(1/\sqrt{n})\mathbf{1}$. The square of the orthogonal estimate in (5.2-30) corresponding to this vector is the *constant* term, or "correction to the mean" in a conventional one-way univariate analysis of variance. The sum of squares of the orthogonal estimates computed from the remaining $n - 1$ columns is the *between-treatment* term in the univariate analysis. In the *multivariate* case, there is a corresponding partition of the sum of squares and products as shown in Table 5.2-2.

Table 5.2-2 MULTIVARIATE ANALYSIS OF VARIANCE FOR THE ORTHOGONAL ONE-WAY DESIGN

Source of dispersion	df	Sums of squares and products ($p \times p$)	Expected sums of squares and products
Constant term	1	$\text{SSM} = \mathbf{u}_{H(0)}\mathbf{u}'_{H(0)} = \frac{r}{n}\mathbf{Y}'.\mathbf{1}\mathbf{1}'\mathbf{Y}.$	$\boldsymbol{\Sigma} + \boldsymbol{\gamma}_{H(0)}\boldsymbol{\gamma}'_{H(0)}$
Between treatments	$n - 1$	$\text{SSB} = \sum_{k=1}^{n-1}\mathbf{u}_{H(k)}\mathbf{u}'_{H(k)}$	$(n-1)\boldsymbol{\Sigma} + \sum_{k=1}^{n-1}\boldsymbol{\gamma}_{H(k)}\boldsymbol{\gamma}'_{H(k)}$
		$= r\mathbf{Y}'.(\mathbf{I} - \frac{1}{n}\mathbf{1}\mathbf{1}')\mathbf{Y}.$	
		$= \text{SSG} - \text{SSM}$	
Group means	n	$\text{SSG} = r\mathbf{Y}'.\mathbf{Y}.$	$n\boldsymbol{\Sigma} + \boldsymbol{\Theta}'\mathbf{D}_{K_H'K_H}\boldsymbol{\Theta}$
Within groups	$n(r-1)$	$\text{SSW} = \text{SST} - \text{SSG}$	$n(r-1)\boldsymbol{\Sigma}$
Total	nr	$\text{SST} = \mathbf{Y}'\mathbf{Y}$	

Because of the role of $\mathbf{P}_H$ in the one-way univariate or multivariate analysis of variance, we shall refer to it as a *solution* matrix for the one-way design. As we shall see in Sec. 5.2.5, other parameterizations give rise to other solution matrices. All such matrices are orthogonal, having $(1/\sqrt{n})\mathbf{1}$ as their first column and an orthogonal completion as their remaining columns. It is easy to show that if the solution matrix has this form, the partition of squares and products into a constant and a between-treatment term is invariant with respect to the choice of solution matrices.

Relative to a multivariate normal error distribution, the orthogonal estimator (5.2-30) is multivariate normal with mean

$$\mathscr{E}(\boldsymbol{U}_H) = r\mathbf{P}'_H\mathscr{E}(\boldsymbol{Y}.) = r\mathbf{D}_{K_HK_H}^{-1/2}\mathbf{K}'_H\mathbf{K}_H\mathbf{L}_H\boldsymbol{\Xi} = r\mathbf{D}_{K_HK_H}^{1/2}\mathbf{L}_H\boldsymbol{\Xi} = \boldsymbol{\Gamma}$$

where $$\boldsymbol{\Gamma}' = [\boldsymbol{\gamma}_{H(0)}, \boldsymbol{\gamma}_{H(1)}, \ldots, \boldsymbol{\gamma}_{H(n-1)}]$$

and covariance matrix $\mathscr{V}(\boldsymbol{U}_H) = \mathbf{I}_n \times \boldsymbol{\Sigma}$.

In terms of the parameters of the rank-n one-way model, the composition of the expected orthogonal estimates is proportional to

$$\begin{aligned}
\boldsymbol{\gamma}_{H(0)} &\doteq \boldsymbol{\mu} + \frac{\boldsymbol{\alpha}_1 + \boldsymbol{\alpha}_2 + \cdots + \boldsymbol{\alpha}_n}{n} \\
\boldsymbol{\gamma}_{H(1)} &\doteq \boldsymbol{\alpha}_1 - \frac{\boldsymbol{\alpha}_2 + \boldsymbol{\alpha}_3 + \cdots + \boldsymbol{\alpha}_n}{n-1} \\
\boldsymbol{\gamma}_{H(2)} &\doteq \boldsymbol{\alpha}_2 - \frac{\boldsymbol{\alpha}_3 + \boldsymbol{\alpha}_4 + \cdots + \boldsymbol{\alpha}_n}{n-2} \qquad (5.2\text{-}31) \\
&\cdots\cdots\cdots\cdots\cdots\cdots \\
\boldsymbol{\gamma}_{H(n-1)} &\doteq \boldsymbol{\alpha}_{n-1} - \boldsymbol{\alpha}_n
\end{aligned}$$

It is clear from (5.2-31) that a necessary condition for the between-treatments SSP matrix to arise from the same Wishart distribution as the within-groups matrix is that the treatment effects be equal. Thus, a statistical test of the hypothesis H_0: $\boldsymbol{\alpha}_1 = \boldsymbol{\alpha}_2 = \cdots = \boldsymbol{\alpha}_n$ is provided by setting $\mathbf{S}_h$ = SSB and $\mathbf{S}_e$ = SSW and computing a criterion (such as F_0) for a multivariate test based on $n - 1$ and $n(r - 1)$ degrees of freedom. If we reject this hypothesis, we adopt the rank-n model and proceed to estimate the treatment effects as in Sec. 5.2.4.

If we accept the hypothesis, we may wish to proceed as if the treatment effects are in fact absent and take the rank-1 model as appropriate for describing the data. Provided the origins of variate measurements are meaningful, a test of the hypothesis H_0: $\boldsymbol{\mu} = \mathbf{0}$ may then be of interest. If so, SSM, with one degree of freedom, may serve as $\mathbf{S}_h$ in computing the multivariate test criteria.

b Nonorthogonal case If the numbers of observations in the cells of the one-way design are unequal, the Helmert matrix does not provide a solution matrix for the design, for $\mathbf{P}_H$ is not orthogonal in the metric $\mathbf{D} = \text{diag}[N_1, N_2, \ldots, N_n]$. Numerically, this is no great problem because $\mathbf{P}_H$ can be orthogonalized with respect to this metric by one of the methods of Sec. 2.2. For best accuracy, the preferred method is to apply the modified Gram-Schmidt procedure with respect to the metric $\mathbf{D}$. This produces a matrix $\mathbf{P}_H^*$, say, in which the first column is the equiangular vector normed to unity in the metric $\mathbf{D}$. The remaining $n - 1$ columns constitute an orthonormal completion of the equiangular vector in the same metric. Owing to the *triangularity* of $\mathbf{P}_H$, the elements of the orthogonalized matrix $\mathbf{P}_H^*$ are reasonably straightforward functions of the elements of $\mathbf{D}$:

$$\underset{n\times n}{\mathbf{P}_H^*} = \underset{n\times n}{\mathbf{P}_H^{\perp}}\ \underset{n\times n}{\mathbf{G}^{-1/2}} \tag{5.2-32}$$

where

$$\underset{n\times n}{\mathbf{P}_H^{\perp}} = \begin{bmatrix} 1 & \Sigma_2^n N_j & 0 & \cdots & 0 \\ 1 & -N_1 & \Sigma_3^n N_j & \cdots & 0 \\ \cdots & \cdots & \cdots & \cdots & \cdots \\ 1 & -N_1 & -N_2 & \cdots & N_n \\ 1 & -N_1 & -N_2 & \cdots & -N_{n-1} \end{bmatrix} \tag{5.2-33}$$

and $\mathbf{G} = \operatorname{diag}(\mathbf{P}_H^{\perp\prime}\mathbf{D}\mathbf{P}_H^{\perp})$ (that is, $\mathbf{G}^{-1/2}$ is the diagonal matrix of normalizing constants). Then $\mathbf{P}_H^{*\prime}\mathbf{D}\mathbf{P}_H^* = \mathbf{I}_n$ as required, and the orthogonal estimates are

$$\mathbf{U}_H^* = \mathbf{P}_H^{*\prime}\mathbf{D}\mathbf{Y}_{.} = [\mathbf{u}_{H(0)}^*, \mathbf{u}_{H(1)}^*, \ldots, \mathbf{u}_{H(n-1)}^*]' \tag{5.2-34}$$

The partition of squares and products computed from these estimates is represented in Table 5.2-3.

As we saw in Sec. 4.1.9, the orthogonalization of the model is accomplished by factoring the model matrix into the product of a column-orthogonal matrix and an upper-triangular matrix, the latter being absorbed in the parameters. That is,

$$\boldsymbol{Y}_{.} = \mathbf{P}_H\boldsymbol{\Gamma}_H + \boldsymbol{E}_{.} = \mathbf{P}_H^*\mathbf{T}_H^{*\prime}\boldsymbol{\Gamma}_H + \boldsymbol{E}_{.} = \mathbf{P}_H^*\boldsymbol{\Gamma}_H^* + \boldsymbol{E}_{.}$$

Table 5.2-3 MULTIVARIATE ANALYSIS OF VARIANCE FOR THE GENERAL ONE-WAY DESIGN

Source of dispersion	df	Sums of squares and products ($p \times p$)	Expected sums of squares and products
Constant term	1	$SSM = \mathbf{u}_{H(0)}^*\mathbf{u}_{H(0)}^{*\prime}$	$\Sigma + \gamma_{H(0)}^*\gamma_{H(0)}^{*\prime}$
Between treatments	$n - 1$	$SSB = \sum_{k=1}^{n-1} \mathbf{u}_{H(k)}^*\mathbf{u}_{H(k)}^{*\prime}$ $= \mathbf{Y}_{.}'(\mathbf{D} - \frac{1}{N}\mathbf{D}\mathbf{1}\mathbf{1}'\mathbf{D})\mathbf{Y}_{.}$ $= SSG - SSM$	$(n-1)\Sigma + \sum_{k=1}^{n-1} \gamma_{H(k)}^*\gamma_{H(k)}^{*\prime}$
Group means	n	$SSG = \mathbf{Y}_{.}'\mathbf{D}\mathbf{Y}_{.}$	$n\Sigma + \boldsymbol{\Theta}'K_H'\mathbf{D}K_H\boldsymbol{\Theta}$
Within groups	$N - n$	$SSW = SST - SSG$	$(N-n)\Sigma$
Total	$N = \Sigma N_j$	$SST = \mathbf{Y}'\mathbf{Y}$	

In this particular case, it is not difficult to express $\mathbf{T}_H^*$ explicitly.

$$\mathbf{P}_H^{*\prime}\mathbf{D}\mathbf{P}_H^*\mathbf{T}_H^{*\prime} = \mathbf{P}_H^{*\prime}\mathbf{D}\mathbf{P}_H = \mathbf{T}_H^{*\prime} \tag{5.2-35}$$

Using (5.2-28) and (5.2-33), we obtain from (5.2-35)

$$\mathbf{T}_H^{*\prime} = \mathbf{G}^{-1/2}(\mathbf{P}_H^{\perp})'\mathbf{D}\mathbf{K}_H\mathbf{D}_{K_H'K_H}^{-1/2} = \mathbf{G}^{-1/2}\mathbf{T}_H'\mathbf{D}_{K_H'K_H}^{-1/2} \tag{5.2-36}$$

where

$$\mathbf{T}_H' = \begin{bmatrix} N & N_1 - \dfrac{\Sigma_1^n N_j}{n} & N_2 - \dfrac{\Sigma_2^n N_j}{n-1} & \cdots & N_{n-1} - \dfrac{N_{n-1}+N_n}{2} \\ 0 & N_1\Sigma_2^n N_j & \dfrac{N_1}{n-1}(\Sigma_2^n N_j - 1) & \cdots & \dfrac{N_1}{2}(N_{n-1}+N_n-1) \\ 0 & 0 & N_2\Sigma_3^n N_j & \cdots & \dfrac{N_2}{2}(N_{n-1}+N_n-1) \\ \cdots & \cdots & \cdots & \cdots & \cdots \\ 0 & 0 & 0 & \cdots & N_{n-1}N_n \end{bmatrix}$$

Because $\boldsymbol{\Gamma}_H^*$ is related to $\boldsymbol{\Gamma}_H$ by the triangular transformation $\mathbf{T}_H^{*\prime}$, the reorthogonalization in the metric $\mathbf{D}$ in no way alters the inference that can be drawn from the analysis of variance. Nullity of the reorthogonalized parameters still implies equal treatment effects, and the constant term continues to be interpretable only in the absence of treatment effects. The multivariate tests of significance in connection with Table 5.2-2 also apply to Table 5.2-3.

The calculations for Table 5.2-3 may also be performed by pivoting as in Sec. 4.1.9. In this case, the matrix to be pivoted is

$$\mathbf{M}_H = \begin{bmatrix} \mathbf{K}_H'\mathbf{D}\mathbf{K}_H & \mathbf{K}_H'\mathbf{D}\mathbf{Y}_{.} \\ \mathbf{Y}_{.}'\mathbf{D}\mathbf{K}_H & \mathbf{Y}_{.}'\mathbf{D}\mathbf{Y}_{.} \end{bmatrix}$$

In practice, neither orthogonalization nor pivoting need be carried out explicitly in a simple one-way analysis. The between-treatment SSP matrix may always be obtained by subtracting SSM from SSG, with these matrices computed by the formulas in Table 5.2-3. However, in the special types of one-way analysis discussed in Sec. 5.2.5, further partition of the treatment SSP matrix is necessary, and the sums of squares and products must be computed by orthogonalization or pivoting.

EXAMPLE 5.2-2 (*Multivariate analysis of variance for the one-way design*) The data of Table 5.2-1 were obtained in a simple randomized experiment with two treatment groups and two response variables. Although the table entries are means for classrooms with varying numbers of pupils and should, strictly speaking, be subjected to weighted least-squares analysis for full efficiency, the variation in classroom size is too small in the present case (range 20–35) to cause appreciable loss of efficiency if the weighting is omitted. We shall therefore ignore differences in precision and treat the classroom means as the primary observations. As discussed in Sec. 5.1, we also assume that the treatments do not alter the dispersion between classrooms. This is not strictly true, for there is evidence that SMSG instruction increases somewhat the variability on the SMSG test [Bock, 1966]. For present purposes, however, we shall ignore this effect and proceed with the one-way multivariate analysis of variance.

The matrices required in the computations are:

1 The 43×2 data matrix $\mathbf{Y}$ consisting of the 22 traditional-course scores and the 21 SMSG-course scores from Table 5.1-1
2 The order-2 diagonal matrix of subclass numbers $\mathbf{D} = \text{diag}[22, 21]$
3 The 2×2 matrix of treatment means $\mathbf{Y}.$ shown in the body of Table 5.2-4

From the $\mathbf{Y}$, $\mathbf{D}$, and $\mathbf{Y}.$ matrices, the SSP matrices shown in Table 5.2-5 are computed by the formulas given in Table 5.2-3. The results, accurate to two decimal places, are shown in Table 5.2-5.

The multivariate test of significance of the treatment effect is based on the largest root of $|\text{SSB} - \lambda\text{SSW}| = 0$ as computed by one of the methods of Sec. 2.7. In this case, $\lambda_1 = 8.918$ and the corresponding $F_0 = (t/r)\lambda_1$ is

$$\frac{41 - 2 + 1}{|1 - 2| + 1} 8.918 = 178.4$$

Since there is one degree of freedom for hypothesis, $s = \min(2, 1) = 1$, and F_0 is distributed exactly as F on $|1 - 2| + 1 = 2$ and $41 - 2 + 1 = 40$ degrees of freedom. The treatment differences are obviously highly significant ($p < .0001$).

Table 5.2-4 MEAN ALGEBRA ACHIEVEMENT OF CLASSES RANDOMLY ASSIGNED TO DIFFERENT COURSES OF INSTRUCTION

	Algebra achievement	
Course of instruction	Traditional test	SMSG test
Traditional course	17.7954	11.8209
SMSG course	11.9005	17.2495

Judging by the following univariate F's, both the traditional and SMSG tests contribute to the significant bivariate effect:

Test	F	df	p
Traditional	$\dfrac{41 \times 373.36}{1{,}239.20}$	$\dfrac{1}{41}$	<.0011
SMSG	$\dfrac{41 \times 316.63}{398.33}$	$\dfrac{1}{41}$	<.0001

The type of algebra instruction to which these classes were exposed has obviously had substantial differential effects on mathematics achievement. The direction and magnitude of these effects will be apparent when the treatment contrasts are estimated in Example 5.2-3.

An estimate of the error covariance matrix is obtained from Table 5.2-3 by dividing SSW by its degrees of freedom. The result is

$$\hat{\Sigma} = \begin{bmatrix} 30.2244 & \text{(symmetric)} \\ 15.1353 & 9.7153 \end{bmatrix} \tag{5.2-37}$$

Although the profile of test means (Table 5.2-4) for the two groups is quite different, the correlation of individual differences in traditional and SMSG achievement within groups is high. Computing standard deviations for the two measures and converting (5.2-38) to a correlation matrix gives

Test	Standard deviation	Correlations
Traditional SMSG	5.4977 3.1169	$\begin{bmatrix} 1.0 & \text{(symmetric)} \\ .8832 & 1.0 \end{bmatrix}$

Table 5.2-5 MULTIVARIATE ANALYSIS OF VARIANCE OF MATHEMATICS ACHIEVEMENT SCORES

Source	df	SSP (symmetric)	Generalized F	p
Constant term	1	$\text{SSM} = \begin{bmatrix} 9{,}567.56 & \\ 9{,}282.50 & 9{,}005.94 \end{bmatrix}$		
Between treatments	1	$\text{SSB} = \begin{bmatrix} 373.36 & \\ -343.83 & 316.63 \end{bmatrix}$	$F_0 = 178.4$	<.0001
Group means	2	$\text{SSG} = \begin{bmatrix} 9{,}940.92 & \\ 8{,}938.67 & 9{,}322.57 \end{bmatrix}$		
Within groups	41	$\text{SSW} = \begin{bmatrix} 1{,}239.20 & \\ 620.55 & 398.33 \end{bmatrix}$		
Total	43	$\text{SST} = \begin{bmatrix} 11{,}180.12 & \\ 9{,}559.22 & 9{,}720.90 \end{bmatrix}$		

This result is a clear illustration of the fact that the direction of differences of group means cannot necessarily be inferred from the within-groups correlations. It would be all too easy to suppose that a correlation of the order of .9 between two variables would imply that if one of the treatment groups exceeded the other on one of the variables, it would exceed on the other variable also. The estimated means in Table 5.2-4 and contrasts in Table 5.2-6 show that this is definitely not the case in the present data.

5.2.4 Estimation of Treatment Contrasts

If the rank-n model is assumed for the one-way design, the number of unknowns (after reparameterization) equals the number of observed means. The observations do not then overdetermine the unknowns, and there is no need to invoke the least-squares principle to obtain unique estimates. It is sufficient merely to substitute observations for expected values in the equations of expectation and solve:

$$\mathscr{E}(Y.) = \mathbf{K}\boldsymbol{\Theta}$$

$$\underset{n \times p}{\mathbf{Y}.} = \underset{n \times n}{\mathbf{K}} \underset{n \times p}{\hat{\boldsymbol{\Theta}}}$$

$$\hat{\boldsymbol{\Theta}} = \mathbf{K}^{-1}\mathbf{Y}.$$

Note, however, that routine application of least squares gives the same result:

$$\boldsymbol{\Theta} = (\mathbf{K}'\mathbf{D}\mathbf{K})^{-1}\mathbf{K}'\mathbf{D}\mathbf{Y}. = \mathbf{K}^{-1}\mathbf{D}^{-1}(\mathbf{K}')^{-1}\mathbf{K}'\mathbf{D}\mathbf{Y}. = \mathbf{K}^{-1}\mathbf{Y}.$$

We see in this special case that the estimates do not depend upon the subclass numbers in the matrix $\mathbf{D}$; they are computed directly from the subclass means. However, the variance-covariance matrix of the estimator depends on $\mathbf{D}$:

$$\mathscr{V}(\Theta) = \mathscr{V}(\mathbf{K}^{-1}Y.) = \mathbf{K}^{-1}\mathbf{D}^{-1}(\mathbf{K}^{-1})' \times \Sigma = (\mathbf{K}'\mathbf{D}\mathbf{K})^{-1} \times \Sigma$$

[See Eq. (4.2-18).]

As we might expect intuitively in the rank-n case, the treatment-effect contrasts are estimated by a similar contrast of treatment-group means. To prove this, let the rows of the $(n - 1) \times n$ matrix $\mathbf{C}'$ be $n - 1$ independent contrasts; that is, $\mathbf{C}'\mathbf{1}_n = \mathbf{0}$ and rank $\mathbf{C} = n - 1$. Then the $\mathbf{L}$ matrix incorporating these contrasts has the structure

$$\underset{n \times (n+1)}{\mathbf{L}_C} = \begin{bmatrix} 1 & \frac{1}{n}\mathbf{1}'_n \\ \mathbf{0} & \mathbf{C}' \end{bmatrix}$$

and the corresponding basis is

$$\mathbf{K}_C = \mathbf{A}\mathbf{L}'_C(\mathbf{L}_C\mathbf{L}'_C)^{-1} = [\mathbf{1}_n, \mathbf{I}_n] \begin{bmatrix} 1 & \mathbf{0}' \\ \frac{1}{n}\mathbf{1}_n & \mathbf{C} \end{bmatrix} \begin{bmatrix} \frac{n+1}{n} & \mathbf{0}' \\ \mathbf{0} & \mathbf{C}'\mathbf{C} \end{bmatrix}^{-1}$$

$$= \begin{bmatrix} \frac{n+1}{n}\mathbf{1}_n, & \mathbf{C} \end{bmatrix} \begin{bmatrix} \frac{n}{n+1} & \mathbf{0}' \\ \mathbf{0} & (\mathbf{C}'\mathbf{C})^{-1} \end{bmatrix} = [\mathbf{1}_n, \mathbf{C}(\mathbf{C}'\mathbf{C})^{-1}]$$

Thus, if we let

$$\mathbf{K}_C^{-1} = \begin{bmatrix} \frac{1}{n}\mathbf{1}'_n \\ \mathbf{C}' \end{bmatrix}$$

$\mathbf{K}_C^{-1}\mathbf{K}_C = \mathbf{I}_n$, and we have the unique inverse of $\mathbf{K}_C$. We conclude, therefore, that in the rank-n case the treatment contrasts $\boldsymbol{\theta}_C$, say, are estimated by

$$\hat{\boldsymbol{\Theta}}_C = \mathbf{C}'\mathbf{Y}. \tag{5.2-38}$$

The variance-covariance matrix of the estimator is

$$\mathscr{V}(\boldsymbol{\Theta}_C) = \mathbf{C}'\mathbf{D}^{-1}\mathbf{C} \times \Sigma \tag{5.2-39}$$

(See Example 5.2-3.)

The reader is warned that these simple results do not hold for a nonorthogonal design when a model of rank less than n is fitted. In that case, the contrast estimates will be functions of the means and subclass numbers as determined in the solution of the normal equations (see Sec. 5.3.6).

EXAMPLE 5.2-3 (*Estimating treatment contrasts in the one-way design*) When there are two treatments, the effect difference $\boldsymbol{\theta}_1 = \boldsymbol{\alpha}_1 - \boldsymbol{\alpha}_2$ is a convenient and easily interpreted contrast. The contrast matrix in (5.2-38) is then $\mathbf{C} = [1, -1]$, and the estimate is

$$\hat{\boldsymbol{\theta}} = \mathbf{y}_{\cdot 1} - \mathbf{y}_{\cdot 2}$$

Thus, for the data of Table 5.2-1, the estimated contrasts are merely the difference of group means computed for each of the two variables. These estimates are shown in Table 5.2-4.

The sampling variance-covariance matrix for these estimates is given by substituting the estimated error covariance matrix (5.2-37) in (5.2-39):

$$\begin{aligned}
\boldsymbol{\Sigma}_{\hat{\theta}} &= [1 \quad -1] \begin{bmatrix} \frac{1}{22} & 0 \\ 0 & \frac{1}{21} \end{bmatrix} \begin{bmatrix} 1 \\ -1 \end{bmatrix} \times \begin{bmatrix} 30.2244 & \text{(symmetric)} \\ 15.1353 & 9.7153 \end{bmatrix} \\
&= \frac{21 + 22}{21 \times 22} \begin{bmatrix} 30.2244 & \text{(symmetric)} \\ 15.1353 & 9.7153 \end{bmatrix} \qquad (5.2\text{-}40) \\
&= \begin{bmatrix} 2.8023 & \text{(symmetric)} \\ 1.4087 & .9144 \end{bmatrix}
\end{aligned}$$

Taking the square roots of the diagonal elements in (5.2-40), we obtain the standard errors shown in Table 5.2-6. The small magnitude of these standard errors relative to that of the contrasts indicates that the treatment differences have been estimated with good precision.

It must be remembered that the magnitudes of the contrasts in Table 5.2-4 may not be comparable owing to possibly different scaling conventions in the two tests. To make between-variable comparisons possible, we may compute *standardized contrasts* by dividing each contrast by the error standard deviation of the respective variable. The standardized contrasts are interpreted as the number of error standard deviations separating the group means.

In the present case, we may estimate standardized contrasts for the traditional and SMSG tests, respectively, using the sample standard deviations in Example 5.2-2:

Standardized contrast (Traditional-SMSG): $\frac{5.8949}{5.4977} = 1.0722 \qquad \frac{-5.4286}{3.1169} = -1.7417$

These values show that the traditionally instructed classes are superior to SMSG classes in achievement on traditional material, while SMSG classes are superior to an even greater extent in achievement on SMSG material. Any hope that the SMSG course might convey traditional material at least as well as the traditional course was not realized in this study. Somewhat similar results have been found in more extensive studies of curricula based on traditional and modern mathematics texts [Begel and Wilson, 1970]. These studies demonstrate convincingly that, unlike the verbal skills [Coleman, et al., 1966], mathematics achievement is strongly influenced by course of instruction and textbook. The quality of instruction and instructional materials appears to be especially critical in the teaching of mathematics.

5.2.5 Special Contrasts

Up to this point, we have assumed that the classes in the one-way design are nominal and arbitrarily arranged. The choice of contrasts for reparameterizing the model is arbitrary in this case because the treatment sum of squares and products is invariant with respect to nonsingular linear transformation of the effect contrasts. If obtained by subtraction, the treatment SSP does not even require the explicit use of contrasts in the calculations. Similarly, direct use of contrasts in the estimation of treatment effects can be sidestepped by reporting treatment means.

If the classes stand in some logical relation to one another, however, there may be definite advantages in constructing certain special types of contrasts and using

Table 5.2-6 ESTIMATED TREATMENT CONTRASTS AND STANDARD ERRORS

	Traditional test	SMSG test
Contrast (Traditional-SMSG)	5.895	−5.429
Standard error	1.677	.951

them explicitly in the analysis. A way of classification made up of such classes is termed *structured.* Generally speaking, an analysis will be more powerful and readily interpretable if contrasts are so chosen as to exploit whatever structure is present in the design. In this section, we discuss three common types of structured ways of classifications and the special contrasts appropriate to each.

a Several treatments and a control When one of the groups in a one-way design is a control and the remaining $n - 1$ groups are treatments, it is natural to set up simple contrasts between the control and each of the remaining groups. With this choice of contrasts, the estimates are interpreted directly as differences between the respective treatments and the control. Since the contrast of a group with itself is by definition zero, this choice of contrasts implicitly sets the effect of the control group equal to zero. Thus, the simple contrasts may be plotted on a continuum with the control group defining the zero point (see Example 5.3-4). Also, other contrasts may be obtained from the simple contrasts by assigning to the control the value zero in the calculations (see Example 5.3-4).

Although in the one-way case the simple contrasts can be estimated by taking contrasts of the group means as in (5.2-38), they may be obtained directly from the reparameterized model by constructing an appropriate **K** matrix. As we saw in (5.2-19), simple contrasts between the first $n - 1$ groups and the last group are estimated when the **K** matrix contains deviation contrasts of the type

$$\mathbf{C}_D{}^{(n)} = \begin{bmatrix} \mathbf{I}_{n-1} - \dfrac{1}{n}\mathbf{1}_{n-1}\mathbf{1}'_{n-1} \\ \\ -\dfrac{1}{n}\mathbf{1}'_{n-1} \end{bmatrix}$$

For example,

$$\mathbf{C}_D{}^{(3)} = \begin{bmatrix} \frac{2}{3} & -\frac{1}{3} \\ -\frac{1}{3} & \frac{2}{3} \\ -\frac{1}{3} & -\frac{1}{3} \end{bmatrix}$$

A similar result applies if some group other than the last is the control: The $-(1/n)\mathbf{1}'_{n-1}$ row of **K** is then shifted to the row corresponding to that of the control. For example, if group 2 is the control,

$$\mathbf{K}_C = \begin{bmatrix} 1 & \frac{2}{3} & -\frac{1}{3} \\ 1 & -\frac{1}{3} & -\frac{1}{3} \\ 1 & -\frac{1}{3} & \frac{2}{3} \end{bmatrix}$$

Thus, the **K** matrix required to estimate contrasts between treatment groups and any group chosen as a control is easily generated. An example of the estimation of simple contrasts with a control group follows.

EXAMPLE 5.2-4 (*Contrasts of treatments with a control*) An experiment on the effects of word association in verbal learning has been reported by Postman and Stark [1969]. Subjects in the study performed a paired-associates learning task in which English words were the stimuli and letters were the responses. The material to be learned consisted of two lists of eight word-letter pairs. The experimental conditions represented differing degrees of association between the words in the first and second lists, as follows:

1 *Identical.* The same stimulus words (but unrelated responses) appear in the two lists.
2 *High association.* Each stimulus word on the second list is a strong associate of a stimulus word on the first list as judged by the Palermo and Jenkins [1964] norms (average frequency of association, 26.3/1,000).
3 *Low association.* Each stimulus word on the second list is a weak associate of a stimulus word on the first list (average frequency of association, 2.3/1,000).
4 *No association.* The words in the second list do not appear in the Palermo and Jenkins norms as an associate of a word in the first list.
5 *Control.* Only the first list is presented.

Sixteen subjects were assigned randomly to each condition. All subjects learned the first list to a $\frac{7}{8}$ correct response criterion; the subjects in conditions 1 through 4 then learned the second list in 1 study trial and 15 anticipation trials. The same first lists were used in all conditions.

Two of the dependent variables in this experiment were scores on recall tests for the first-list pairs. The first of these tests was administered immediately after the learning trials; the second test was administered after subjects in all groups except the control reviewed their first test responses. The controls performed a comparable amount of unrelated activity. Results for the two tests are shown in Table 5.2-7.

The authors do not report subclass standard deviations for the data, but an estimated error variance can be recovered for the first test from a reported F statistic.

Table 5.2-7 MEAN SCORES (NUMBER RIGHT) ON TESTS OF FIRST-LIST RECALL

		Test	
Conditions	N	1	2
1 Identical	16	4.7	5.3
2 High association	16	6.7	7.2
3 Low association	16	6.1	6.6
4 No association	16	6.5	6.7
5 Control	16	7.0	7.0

For the sake of discussion, let us assume that this estimate also applies to the second test. Neither do the authors report the within-group correlation of the two tests, but presumedly it would be high; let us assume .6. The estimated error covariance matrix would then be

$$\hat{\Sigma} = \begin{bmatrix} 1.55 & \text{(symmetric)} \\ .93 & 1.55 \end{bmatrix} \tag{5.2-41}$$

From (5.2-28) and the figures in Table 5.2-7, the multivariate analysis of variance in Table 5.2-8 can be computed. The treatment effects are significant and warrant interpretation. For present purposes, we are interested only in the contrasts between the control and the other conditions. The estimates are:

	Estimate	
Condition contrast	Test 1	Test 2
1 1-5	−2.3	−1.7
2 2-5	−.3	.2
3 3-5	−.9	−.4
4 4-5	−.5	−.3

Since each group has 16 subjects, and the error variance is the same for all of these contrasts,

$$\text{SE} = \sqrt{2\,\frac{1.55}{16}} = .44$$

Only the difference between the control and the identity condition is large relative to

Table 5.2-8 MULTIVARIATE ANALYSIS OF VARIANCE OF FIRST-LIST RECALL SCORES

Source	df	SSP	(symmetric)	F_0	p
Constant	1	3,075.20			
		3,253.76	3,442.68		
Treatments	4	51.84		11.75	<.01
		41.60	35.37		
Group means	5	3,127.04			
		3,295.36	3,478.05		
Within groups	75	116.25			
		65.75	116.25		
Total	80	3,243.29			
		3,365.11	3,594.30		

this standard error, and it presumably accounts for most of the significant between-treatment effects. Apparently the task of learning a new set of responses to the *same* words interferes much more with memory for the original set than learning new responses to associated or unrelated words. However, contrasts 2, 3, and 4 are with one exception negative, suggesting that learning the second set of responses did interfere somewhat under the latter conditions. This possibility will be examined statistically in Example 5.2-5.

b Ordered treatments If there is a prior logical ordering of the treatments, the Helmert contrasts defined by (5.2-27) provide a useful reparameterization of the design model. Unlike simple contrasts or deviation contrasts, the Helmert contrasts permit a meaningful stepwise, single-degree-of-freedom analysis even in the one-way case. An example will make this clear: Suppose psychiatric patients are assigned randomly to treatments consisting of (1) a control, (2) psychotherapy, (3) drug therapy A, and (4) drug therapy B. If the treatment effects are reparameterized as shown in (5.2-31), the orthogonal estimates $H(1)$ through $H(3)$ have the following interpretations:

$\gamma_{H(1)}$ contrasts the control with the mean of the therapy groups.
$\gamma_{H(2)}$ contrasts psychotherapy with the mean of the drug therapies.
$\gamma_{H(3)}$ contrasts drug therapies A and B.

The logic of the stepwise analysis depends upon the ordered nature of these contrasts. The hypothesis $H_3\colon \gamma_{H(3)} = 0$ is tested first. If H_3 is rejected, the drug therapies are presumed to differ in effectiveness; hence, at least one of them must differ from psychotherapy and from the control. In this case, the stepwise analysis would terminate, and the rank-n model would be fitted to provide estimates of the drug effects relative to each other and to the other treatments.

On the other hand, if H_3 is accepted, there is no evidence that the drugs differ in effectiveness; hence, it would be meaningful, at least provisionally, to compare the best estimate of the common drug effect with psychotherapy. This is the import of $H_2\colon \gamma_{H(2)} = 0$. If H_2 is rejected, the analysis would terminate, and a rank-2 model would be fitted to estimate the relative effectiveness of control, psychotherapy, and drug therapy. If H_2 is accepted, however, there is no evidence for differences in the effectiveness of the therapies, and a comparison of the control with the common effect of all the therapies would be in order; that is, $H_1\colon \gamma_{H(1)} = 0$ would be tested. Presumably, $H_0\colon \gamma_{H(0)} = 0$ would not be a meaningful hypothesis, and the analysis would terminate with H_1. In a multivariate problem, this stepwise analysis takes essentially the same form as that of the polynomial analysis in Table 4.2-4; however, not all the degrees of freedom need be tested separately. This is illustrated in the following example.

EXAMPLE 5.2-5 (*Estimating Helmert contrasts*) In the study described in Example 5.2-4, the investigators were interested not only in comparing the control with experimental conditions, but also in comparing the identity condition 1 with the nonidentity conditions 2, 3, and 4, and in comparing the effects of differing association strengths among the nonidentity conditions. This is an example of ordered relationships among classes that is amenable to analysis with Helmert contrasts. In setting up the contrasts, it is convenient to relabel the conditions so that the control is the first group. Then the coefficients of the linear parametric functions that define the contrasts take the following form:

	Contrast coefficients			
Condition	**1**	**2**	**3**	**4**
1 Control	1	0	0	0
2 Identical	$-\frac{1}{4}$	1	0	0
3 High association	$-\frac{1}{4}$	$-\frac{1}{3}$	1	0
4 Low association	$-\frac{1}{4}$	$-\frac{1}{3}$	$-\frac{1}{2}$	1
5 No association	$-\frac{1}{4}$	$-\frac{1}{3}$	$-\frac{1}{2}$	-1

These contrasts serve to operationalize, in a form suitable for linear least-squares analysis, the comparisons required in such a study. They are also the basis for an analysis of variance carried out by the method of Sec. 5.2.3. Because the subclass numbers are equal, reorthogonalization is not required, and the calculations proceed as follows.

The Helmert matrix of order 5 is constructed by adjoining a column of 1s to the above contrast coefficients and normalizing (i.e., dividing the elements of each column by the reciprocal square root of the column sum of squares). The result is

$$\mathbf{H}_5 = \begin{bmatrix} .44721 & .89443 & 0 & 0 & 0 \\ .44721 & -.22361 & .86603 & 0 & 0 \\ .44721 & -.22361 & -.28867 & .81650 & 0 \\ .44721 & -.22361 & -.28867 & -.40825 & .70711 \\ .44721 & -.22361 & -.28867 & -.40825 & -.70711 \end{bmatrix} \tag{5.2-42}$$

From (5.2-30), the orthogonal estimates are computed as

$$\mathbf{U}_5 = r^{1/2}\mathbf{H}_5'\mathbf{Y}.$$

In this case $r = 16$, and the elements of $\mathbf{Y}.$ appear in Table 5.2-7. The orthogonal estimates are

$$\mathbf{U}_5 = \begin{bmatrix} \mathbf{u}_0' \\ \mathbf{u}_1' \\ \mathbf{u}_2' \\ \mathbf{u}_3' \\ \mathbf{u}_4' \end{bmatrix} = \begin{bmatrix} 55.4545 & 58.6744 \\ 3.5777 & 1.9672 \\ -6.0042 & -5.3104 \\ 1.3044 & 1.7963 \\ -1.1314 & -\ .2828 \end{bmatrix}$$

The successive SSP matrices in Table 5.2-9 are formed as matrix products of these vectors, namely, $\mathbf{u}_0\mathbf{u}_0'$, $\mathbf{u}_1\mathbf{u}_1'$, $\mathbf{u}_2\mathbf{u}_2'$, and $\mathbf{u}_3\mathbf{u}_3' + \mathbf{u}_4\mathbf{u}_4'$. Note that the degrees of freedom and the sum of squares and products corresponding to $H(3)$ and $H(4)$ are pooled.

Using the generalized F as the multivariate test statistic, we find no evidence that differences in the level of association between words in the first list and those in the second had any effect on immediate or delayed recall ($p > .05$). The effect of identical versus nonidentical words is quite clear, however: the generalized F is ($p < .01$) and the corresponding univariate F's (df $= 1, 75$) are 23.2 and 18.2 ($p < .0001$) for test 1 and test 2, respectively.

Since the inequality of effects of the identical and nonidentical conditions implies that one or both differ from the control, a formal test of $H(1)$ is not needed. A rank-3 model should be fitted, but because the design is orthogonal, each contrast can be estimated separately without explicit consideration of rank. In this instance, $H(2)$ is the only contrast of interest, and it is estimated by forming the corresponding contrast of the group means

$$\hat{\theta}_{H(2)}{}^{(1)} = 4.7 - \tfrac{1}{3}(6.7 + 6.1 + 6.5) = -1.73$$

$$\hat{\theta}_{H(2)}{}^{(2)} = 5.3 - \tfrac{1}{3}(7.2 + 6.6 + 7.0) = -1.63$$

The standard error of these estimates is the square root of $1/r$, times the sum of squares of coefficients in the contrast, times the error variance, which in this case is the same for both variables; that is,

$$\text{SE} = \sqrt{\tfrac{1}{16} \times \tfrac{4}{3} \times 1.55} = .359$$

Table 5.2-9 MULTIVARIATE ANALYSIS OF VARIANCE OF ORDERED ORTHOGONAL CONTRASTS

	Source	df	SSP	(symmetric)	F_0	p
$H(0)$	Constant	1	3,075.20			
			3,253.76	3,442.68		
$H(1)$	Control vs.	1	12.80		4.09	<.01
	experimental		7.04	3.87		
$H(2)$	Identical vs.	1	36.05		12.93	<.01
	nonidentical		31.89	28.20		
$H(3)$, $H(4)$	Between asso-	2	2.99		2.35	>.05
	ciation levels		2.67	3.30		
	Group means	5	3,127.04			
			3,295.36	3,478.04		
	Within groups	75	116.25			
			69.75	116.25		
	Total	80	3,243.29			
			3,365.11	3,594.30		

The data give a reasonably accurate estimate of 1.73 fewer words recalled when the stimulus words are identical on both lists than are recalled when the words are merely associated or unrelated. The conclusions to be drawn from this study are discussed further in Example 5.2-6.

c Equally spaced quantitative treatments When the experimental treatments consist of levels of a quantitative variable, the design model may be specialized to a polynomial regression model and analyzed by the methods of Chap. 4. The dosage-response study discussed in Sec. 4.2 is, in fact, an example of a designed experiment analyzed in this way.

If the quantitative levels are equally spaced, however, it is often more convenient to retain the design-model setup and reparameterize in *orthogonal polynomial* contrasts. These contrasts, which have been tabled by Fisher and Yates [1963] and others [DeLury, 1950], transform the design-model analysis into stepwise polynomial regression analysis. Details are as follows.

To simplify computations, let us code the treatment levels $x_1, x_2, \ldots, x_n$, into integral values by setting

$$x_j^{(0)} = \frac{2(x_j - \bar{x})}{d} \tag{5.2-43}$$

where

$$\bar{x} = \sum_{j=1}^{n} \frac{x_j}{n}$$

is the mean level, and

$$d = x_j - x_{j-1}$$

is the signed constant difference between levels. The Vandermonde matrix in the polynomial model (4.2-5) then has the standard form $\mathbf{V}_n^{(0)}$, say, generated from the coded x values $n - 1, \ldots, -4, -2, 0, 2, 4, \ldots, n - 1$ when n is odd (divided by 2 in Appendix B), or $n - 1, \ldots, -3, -1, 1, 3, \ldots, n - 1$ when n is even. Columnwise orthogonalization of $\mathbf{V}_n^{(0)}$ yields the Fisher-Tchebycheff orthogonal polynomials presented in integral form in Appendix B.

According to Sec. 4.1.10a, we require for the polynomial regression analysis the factorization

$$\mathbf{V}_n^{(0)} = \mathbf{P}_n\mathbf{S}_n' \tag{5.2-44}$$

where $\mathbf{P}_n$ is an orthogonal matrix ($\mathbf{P}_n'\mathbf{P}_n = \mathbf{I}_n$), and $\mathbf{T}_n'$ is upper triangular. Appendix B actually contains terms of the related integer-valued factorization

$$\mathbf{V}_n^{(0)} = \mathbf{P}_n^{\perp}\mathbf{D}_n^{-1}\mathbf{T}_n'$$

where $\mathbf{P}_n^{\perp}$ is the unnormalized orthogonal polynomial matrix, $\mathbf{D}_n = (\mathbf{P}_n^{\perp})'\mathbf{P}_n^{\perp}$ is a diagonal matrix, and $\mathbf{T}_n$ is triangular. $\mathbf{P}_n$ and $\mathbf{S}_n$ are obtained from the quantities in Appendix B by the column rescalings

$$\mathbf{P}_n = \mathbf{P}_n^{\perp}\mathbf{D}_n^{-1/2} \qquad \mathbf{S}_n = \mathbf{T}_n\mathbf{D}_n^{-1/2} \tag{5.2-45}$$

The values presented for $\mathbf{T}_n$ assume a quantitative treatment variable coded by (5.2-43). The stepwise analysis making use of Appendix B is set up as follows.

ORTHOGONAL CASE Let the polynomial model for the means in terms of the coded x be

$$Y. = \mathbf{V}_n^{(0)}\mathbf{B}^{(0)} + E.$$

The orthogonal polynomial reparameterization gives

$$Y. = \mathbf{P}_n\mathbf{S}_n'\mathbf{B}^{(0)} + E. = \mathbf{P}_n\Gamma_n^{(0)} + E., \text{ say}$$

If the subclass numbers are equal, the matrix of subclass numbers specialized to $\mathbf{D} = r\mathbf{I}$, where r is the number of experimental units per level. The normal equations for estimating $\Gamma_n^{(0)}$ are then

$$r\mathbf{P}_n'\mathbf{P}_n\hat{\Gamma}_n^{(0)} = r\mathbf{P}_n'\mathbf{Y}.$$

or

$$\hat{\Gamma}_n^{(0)} = \mathbf{P}_n'\mathbf{Y}. \qquad (5.2\text{-}46)$$

That is, the estimates are obtained merely by premultiplying the matrix of means by the transposed matrix of orthogonal polynomials. The estimator has mean and covariance matrix

$$\mathscr{E}(\hat{\Gamma}_n^{(0)}) = \Gamma_n^{(0)} \qquad (5.2\text{-}47)$$

$$\mathscr{V}(\hat{\Gamma}_n^{(0)}) = \frac{1}{r}\mathbf{I}_n \times \Sigma \qquad (5.2\text{-}48)$$

Furthermore, these estimates are proportional to the orthogonal estimates required in the stepwise analysis shown in Tables 4.1-5 and 4.2-4. That is,

$$\mathbf{U}_n = r^{1/2}\hat{\Gamma}_n^{(0)} = r^{1/2}\mathbf{P}_n'\mathbf{Y}. \qquad (5.2\text{-}49)$$

Each row of $\mathbf{U}_n$ generates the SSP matrix for one degree of freedom in the stepwise multivariate analysis of variance. Thus, $\text{SSP}_0 = \mathbf{u}_0\mathbf{u}_0'$, $\text{SSP}_1 = \mathbf{u}_1\mathbf{u}_1'$, $\text{SSP}_2 = \mathbf{u}_2\mathbf{u}_2'$, etc., are the square and product matrices for the constant, linear, quadratic, etc., terms in the analysis. These matrices are compared with an appropriate SSP matrix for error in the tests of significance of the polynomial effects. These computations are illustrated in Example 5.2-6.

Once the degree of a suitable polynomial model has been established, say as $g < n$, the coefficients of the polynomial in $x^{(0)}$ may be computed from

$$\hat{\mathbf{B}}_g^{(0)} = (\mathbf{S}_{n(g)}^{-1})'\hat{\Gamma}_g^{(0)} \qquad (5.2\text{-}50)$$

where $\mathbf{S}_{n(g)}$ is the leading $g + 1$ rows and columns of $\mathbf{S}_n$ obtained from Appendix B, and $\Gamma_g^{(0)}$ is the leading $g + 1$ rows of $\Gamma_n^{(0)}$. The estimated coefficients may then be returned to the scale of the original x values by multiplying by $2/d$ raised to the power of the term in the polynomial. (See Example 5.2-6.)

NONORTHOGONAL CASE If the subclass numbers are unequal, some of the computational convenience of the orthogonal polynomial analysis is lost. This occurs because **D** is then a general diagonal matrix, and the matrix of coefficients in the normal equations,

$$\mathbf{P}_n'\mathbf{D}\mathbf{P}_n\hat{\Gamma}_n^{(0)} = \mathbf{P}_n'\mathbf{D}\mathbf{Y}. \qquad (5.2\text{-}51)$$

is a general symmetric pd matrix.

The preferred method of analysis in this case is to *reorthogonalize* $\mathbf{P}_n$ *in the metric* **D** to obtain the solution matrix $\mathbf{P}_n^*$ (see Sec. 5.2.3b). This requires essentially the same computations as orthogonalizing the matrix **X** of the original polynomial model as described in Sec. 4.1.10, but, in general, the calculations based on (5.2-51) are better conditioned numerically. The improvement is especially noticeable when the polynomial is of high degree [Wampler, 1970].

Except for replacing of the matrix **X** with the corresponding **P** matrix, the stepwise orthogonal polynomial analysis in the nonorthogonal case is the same as that in Sec. 4.1.10 and need not be repeated here. Orthogonal polynomials may also be defined for unequally spaced levels [Robson, 1959; Emerson, 1968]; they offer some improvement in computing accuracy when used in place of conventional polynomial regression analysis.

When carried out in connection with an experimental-design analysis, orthogonal polynomial regression is sometimes called *trend analysis*. The following example is typical.

EXAMPLE 5.2-6 (*Trend analysis*) In Example 5.2-5, we tested the hypothesis of no difference in the effects of the three levels of association between words in the first and second lists. Actually, Postman and Stark had in mind the more specific hypothesis of increasing levels of association showing increasingly disruptive effect on first-list recall. If this hypothesis is in fact true, a specific test of increasing trend will be more powerful than a general test of differences between levels.

We show in Sec. 5.2.6 that, if the effects of n treatments are $\alpha_1, \alpha_2, \ldots, \alpha_n$, say, the linear parametric function which provides the most powerful test of the hypothesis $\alpha_1 = \alpha_2 = \cdots = \alpha_n = 0$ is

$$\theta_{\max} = \alpha_1\alpha_1 + \alpha_2\alpha_2 + \cdots + \alpha_n\alpha_n$$

That is, the most powerful test is provided by an lpf in which the coefficients are equal to the effects. Since location and scale of the effects are usually arbitrary, it is in practice sufficient for the coefficients to have the same spacing as the effects. Hence, if the effects are expected to be equally spaced (i.e., the trend is linear), the coefficients defined by the first-degree orthogonal polynomial will provide the most powerful test. We may, of course, wish to check the hypothesis of linearity by including the higher-degree polynomials in the analysis, but the degrees of freedom for these terms should not be pooled with the linear term in the tests of significance.

In the Postman and Stark experiment, the degree of association represented in the treatments is expressed quantitatively by the association frequencies from Palermo and Jenkins [1964], namely, 26.3/1,000, 2.3/1,000, and 0. We have very little idea of the quantitative relationship, if any, between these association strengths and the first-list recall, but we may wish to assume the spacing $-1, 0, 1$ rather than ignore the treatment structure entirely. This assumption would lead us to perform an orthogonal polynomial trend analysis, including a specific test of the linear trend.

To perform this analysis on the data of Table 5.2-7, we omit the control and identical groups and rearrange the data as in Table 5.2-10.

Any trend apparent in Table 5.2-10 is, in fact, counter to the hypothesis of Postman and Stark: the highest levels of recall are under the strong-association condition. The trend is weak, however, and, in view of the size of the error variance in Example 5.2-4, probably not significant. This impression may be tested by means of the orthogonal polynomials for $n = 3$.

In the unnormalized form in Appendix B, the order-3 orthogonal polynomial matrix, with its column sums of squares, is

$$\begin{bmatrix} 1 & -1 & 1 \\ 1 & 0 & -2 \\ 1 & 1 & 1 \end{bmatrix}$$
$$\begin{matrix} 3 & 2 & 6 \end{matrix}$$

Normalizing columns, we obtain

$$\mathbf{P}_3 = \begin{bmatrix} .57735 & -.70711 & .40825 \\ .57735 & 0 & -.81650 \\ .57735 & .70711 & .40825 \end{bmatrix}$$

Premultiplying the matrix of means in Table 5.2-10 by $\mathbf{P}_3'$ produces the estimated orthogonal polynomial coefficients shown in Table 5.2-11.

In this instance, $r = 16$, and the orthogonal estimates (5.2-49) are four times the values in Table 5.2-11. The SSP matrices computed from the orthogonal estimates are as shown in Table 5.2-12. The tests of significance in Table 5.2-12 are made with respect to the same error matrix as in Example 5.2-4. Since the .05 level of $F_0(2,2,76)$ is 5.7, neither the linear nor quadratic trend is significant. There is no evidence that recall of the first list of paired associates was impaired by the relationships between

Table 5.2-10 FIRST-LIST RECALL VERSUS ASSOCIATION STRENGTH

		Mean first-list recall	
Association	N_j	Test 1	Test 2
1 None	16	6.5	6.7
2 Weak	16	6.1	6.6
3 Strong	16	6.7	7.2

lists which the word-association norms represent. Postman and Stark suggest that these relationships are mobilized by the subject only when they facilitate recall, and are avoided or abandoned when they do not.

Purely for the sake of illustrating the recovery of estimated coefficients for the original polynomial, let us assume that the recall scores are related quadratically to the following transformation of the association frequencies:

$$w_1 = \log \frac{25.1}{1{,}000} = .4 - 2 = -1.6$$

$$w_2 = \log \frac{2.51}{1{,}000} = .4 - 3 = -2.6$$

$$w_3 = \log \frac{.251}{1{,}000} = .4 - 4 = -3.6$$

Since the mean w is -2.6, the coding by (5.2-43) gives $w_1^{(0)} = 2$, $w_2^{(0)} = 0$, and $w_3^{(0)} = -2$.

From Appendix B, we obtain for $n = 3$

$$\mathbf{S}_3 = \begin{bmatrix} 3 & 0 & 0 \\ 0 & 4 & 0 \\ 8 & 0 & 8 \end{bmatrix} \cdot \begin{bmatrix} 3^{-1/2} & & \\ & 2^{-1/2} & \\ & & 6^{-1/2} \end{bmatrix}$$

of which the inverse is

$$\mathbf{S}_3^{-1} = \begin{bmatrix} 3^{1/2} & & \\ & 2^{1/2} & \\ & & 6^{1/2} \end{bmatrix} \cdot \begin{bmatrix} \frac{1}{3} & 0 & 0 \\ 0 & \frac{1}{4} & 0 \\ -\frac{1}{3} & 0 & \frac{1}{8} \end{bmatrix}$$

whence, from (5.2-50) and Table 5.2-11, we have

$$\hat{\mathbf{B}}_3^{(0)} = \begin{bmatrix} .57735 & 0 & -.81650 \\ 0 & .35355 & \\ 0 & 0 & .30619 \end{bmatrix} \cdot \begin{bmatrix} 11.14286 & 11.83568 \\ -.14142 & -.35356 \\ .40825 & .28578 \end{bmatrix}$$

$$= \begin{bmatrix} 6.1 & 6.6 \\ -.05 & -.125 \\ .125 & .0875 \end{bmatrix}$$

Table 5.2-11 ESTIMATED COEFFICIENTS OF TREND

Trend	Test 1	Test 2
Constant	11.14286	11.83568
Linear	−.14142	−.35356
Quadratic	.40825	.28578

To return these estimates to the scale of the original w variable, we multiply the linear coefficients by $2/d = 2/(-1) = -2$, and the quadratic coefficients by 4:

$$\mathbf{B}_3 = \begin{bmatrix} 6.1 & 6.6 \\ .1 & .25 \\ .5 & .35 \end{bmatrix}$$

Transposing the constant term gives the fitted linear equations in the form

$$y = b_0 + b_1(w - \bar{w}) + b_2(w - \bar{w})^2$$

or

$$y^{(1)} = 6.1 + .1(w + 2.6) + .5(w + 2.6)^2$$

$$y^{(2)} = 6.6 + .25(w + 2.6) + .35(w + 2.6)^2$$

Since there are only three points fitted, these equations reproduce the observed means exactly. For example,

$$y_1^{(1)} = 6.1 + .1 \times 1 + .5 \times 1 = 6.7$$

$$y_2^{(1)} = 6.1 + .1 \times 0 + .5 \times 0 = 6.1$$

$$y_3^{(1)} = 6.1 + .1 \times (-1) + .5 \times 1 = 6.5$$

Because both the orthogonal polynomial matrix and the triangular factor are exact, and the triangular matrix can easily be inverted in integer arithmetic (see Example 2.7-1), this method of computing the coefficients makes it possible to fit a high-degree polynomial without instability due to rounding error.

Table 5.2-12 ORTHOGONAL POLYNOMIAL TREND ANALYSIS OF FIRST-LIST RECALL

Source	df	SSP Test 1	SSP Test 2	F_0	p
Constant	1	1,986.6133			
		2,110.1333	2,241.3333		
Linear	1	.3200			
		.8000	2.0000	1.93	$>.05$
Quadratic	1	2.6667			
		1.8667	1.3067	2.38	$>.05$
Group means	3	1,989.60			
		2,112.80	2,244.64		
Within groups	75	116.25			
		69.75	116.25		
Total	78	2,105.85			
		2,182.55	2,360.89		

5.2.6 Confidence Bounds and Multiple Comparisons

The Roy system of confidence bounds described in Sec. 4.2.6 in connection with regression coefficients may also be applied to the effect contrasts. Because of the formal identity of the regression model and the reparameterized design model, the Roy bound on linear functions of effects may be obtained merely by changing the notation in (4.2-52):

$$\mathbf{c}'\mathbf{\Theta}\mathbf{a} \pm \sqrt{\frac{n_e r}{t} F_{0,\alpha}{}^{(r,s,t)}\mathbf{a}'\mathbf{\Sigma}_{(n_e)}\mathbf{a}\mathbf{c}'(\mathbf{K}'\mathbf{D}\mathbf{K})^{-1}\mathbf{c}} \tag{5.2-52}$$

where

$\mathbf{c}$ = $l \times 1$ vector of coefficients of a linear function of the effect contrasts

$\mathbf{\Theta}$ = $l \times p$ matrix estimator of parameters for the fitted model

$\mathbf{a}$ = $p \times 1$ vector of coefficients of a linear function of variables

n_e = number of degrees of freedom of the error estimates

r = $|n_h - p| + 1$, where $n_h < l$ is the number of effect contrasts in the reference set for the bound, and p is the number of variables in the reference set (see below)

$F_{0,\alpha}{}^{(r,s,t)}$ = the α critical value for the generalized F with arguments $r = |n_h - p| + 1$, $s = \min(n_h, p)$, and $t = n_e - p + 1$

$\mathbf{\Sigma}_{(n_e)}$ = error covariance matrix estimator independent of $\mathbf{\Theta}$ on n_e degrees of freedom

$(\mathbf{K}'\mathbf{D}\mathbf{K})^{-1}$ = $(\mathbf{T}^{-1})'\mathbf{T}^{-1}$ is the inverse of the $l \times l$ matrix of coefficients in the normal equations for estimating $\boldsymbol{\Theta}$

The interval (5.2-52) has probability not less than $1 - \alpha$ of including the population value $\mathbf{c}'\boldsymbol{\Theta}\mathbf{a}$.

In most applications to experimental-design models, the reference set of the bound includes the $n - 1$ contrasts between treatments and the full number of variables p. In that case, $n_h = n - 1$, and $\mathbf{c}$ is specialized to an $n_h \times 1$ vector $\mathbf{c}_B$ containing coefficients of any linear combination of the contrasts in the $n_h \times p$ matrix $\boldsymbol{\Theta}_B$, say. With this specialization, (5.2-52) becomes

$$\mathbf{c}_B'\mathbf{\Theta}_B\mathbf{a} \pm \sqrt{\frac{n_e r_B}{t} F_{0,\alpha}{}^{(r_B,s_B,t)}\mathbf{a}'\mathbf{\Sigma}_{(n_e)}\mathbf{a}\mathbf{c}_B'[(\mathbf{K}'\mathbf{D}\mathbf{K})^{-1}]_B\mathbf{c}_B} \tag{5.2-53}$$

where $r_B = |n - 1 - p| + 1$, $s_B = \min(n - 1, p)$, and $[(\mathbf{K}'\mathbf{D}\mathbf{K})^{-1}]_B = (\mathbf{T}_B{}^{-1})'\mathbf{T}_B$ is the $n_h \times n_h$ submatrix of $(\mathbf{K}'\mathbf{D}\mathbf{K})^{-1}$ which corresponds to the effect contrasts. It may be obtained as indicated from $\mathbf{T}_B$, say, which is the corresponding $n_h \times l$ submatrix of triangular matrix $\mathbf{T}$ generated in the orthonormalization of $\mathbf{K}$ with respect to $\mathbf{D}$. The use of (5.2-53) is illustrated in Example 5.3-5.

As pointed out in Sec. 4.2-6, the bound given by (5.2-53) is conservative because it holds for all $\mathbf{c}_B$ and $\mathbf{a}$. In particular, it holds when these vectors have been chosen to maximize in the sample the absolute value of a linear combination of contrasts and/or variables. For example, in a univariate problem with multiple treatment groups, the vector which maximizes $|c_B'\hat{\theta}_B|$, subject to a restriction on the scale of $\mathbf{c}_B$, is proportional to $\hat{\theta}_B$. This may be demonstrated by maximizing $(c_B'\hat{\theta}_B)^2 = c_B'\hat{\theta}_B\hat{\theta}_B'c_B$ subject to $\mathbf{c}_B'c_B = 1$ using the method of Lagrange multipliers and the vector derivatives of Sec. 2.5. The maximum is obtained when $\mathbf{c}_B$ is the characteristic vector corresponding to the one nonzero root of $\hat{\theta}_B\hat{\theta}_B'$. This characteristic vector is, of course, $(1/\sqrt{\hat{\theta}_B'\hat{\theta}_B})\hat{\theta}_B$. A similar result holds for **a** with respect to one contrast and multiple variables.

Note that in the orthogonal case, the noncentrality term in the expected sum of squares for n_h degrees of freedom, as in Table 5.2-2, is proportional to $\theta_B'\theta_B$. Since the power of the F test is a monotonic function of this noncentrality parameter, the above result shows that a linear function of contrasts with coefficients proportional to θ_B gives the most powerful one-degree-of-freedom test of the treatment effect. This is the reason for attempting to detect treatment effects, as we did with the orthogonal polynomials, by regressing on an independent variable with the same spacing as the expected treatment effect.

In the present context, the implication of these results is that (5.2-52) is conservative because it must allow for the capitalizing on change which occurs when sample quantities are maximized. It is therefore considerably larger than a bound at the same confidence level on a narrower class of *a priori* contrasts or variate functions.

With respect to treatment effects, the simple contrasts between each of several treatments and a control is a useful restricted class for which narrower bounds than (5.2-53) can be obtained. In the univariate case, these bounds have been derived by Dunnet [1964]. Another useful class of contrasts consists of differences between each of the $n(n - 1)/2$ possible pairs of n treatments. Tukey (see Kurtz et al. [1965]) has proposed univariate bounds for these contrasts based on the Studentized range statistic. Unfortunately, neither of these types of bounds has been generalized to the multivariate case.

It can be argued [Duncan, 1965] that even these more restricted bounds are too conservative, and that a simple *protected t-test* rule gives a more sensitive discrimination among treatments while maintaining the error rate per experiment at about the nominal values for the test. In this rule, due to Fisher [1951], the differences between treatment groups are examined further only when the F statistic for treatments is significant (say, at the .05 level). If this condition is met, each treatment contrast is divided by its sample standard error and treated as a conventional t statistic. Where any of these statistics is significant, the corresponding contrast is assumed to warrant interpretation.

This procedure has the merit of generalizing directly to the multivariate case [Duncan, 1965]. In connection with the multivariate analysis of variance, it requires that we compute the univariate F statistics for each variable if the overall multivariate test statistic is significant. We then examine the F statistic for significance to locate the individual variables which are contributing to the multivariate effect. In the multiple-treatment case, these variables are then inspected further for significant treatment contrasts as indicated by the univariate t statistics. Since, in the estimation phase of the analysis, we routinely compute the standard error of each estimated contrast, it is a simple matter to obtain these t statistics. The degrees of freedom to be used in referring them to the t table are, of course, those of the error estimate n_e. Alternatively, the square of the t statistic may be referred to the table in Appendix B with $s = 1$, $r = 1$, and $t = n_e$. These protected F and t tests are employed frequently in the examples in this text and are discussed further in Sec. 6.3.

Exercise 5.2-1 The model matrix for a one-way design with four groups is

$$\begin{bmatrix} 1 & 1 & 0 & 0 & 0 \\ 1 & 0 & 1 & 0 & 0 \\ 1 & 0 & 0 & 1 & 0 \\ 1 & 0 & 0 & 0 & 1 \end{bmatrix}$$

Numerically perform the factorization of this matrix according to (5.2-9) and (5.2-14), and check that the results agree with (5.2-16) and (5.2-19). In performing the computations, use the adjoint method of Sec. 2.4 to obtain an exact inverse.

Exercise 5.2-2 Verify that the partitions of squares and products in Tables 5.2-2 and 5.2-3 represent projections of the matrix of means into complementary subspaces as discussed in Sec. 2.6.3. That is, show that the $n \times n$ matrices in the expressions for SSM and SSB are idempotent (in the metric $\mathbf{D}$ in the case of Table 5.2-3), and that their products (with respect to $\mathbf{D}$) are null. State the main results of analysis of variance developed in terms of idempotent matrices (see Graybill [1963, page 82 ff]).

Exercise 5.2-3 The F statistic from Postman and Stark [1969] alluded to in Example 5.2-4 was for the difference, for the test-1 variable, between the control group and the mean of the other conditions. The reported value was 8.25, and the reported degrees of freedom were 1 and 75. Using the data in Table 5.2-7, recover the error estimate (5.2-34) used in the example.

Exercise 5.2-4 Use orthogonal polynomials in Appendix B to analyze the data of Example 4.2-1. Assume that log dose is equally spaced. Convert the estimated orthogonal polynomial coefficients into linear polynomials in log dose, and check that they agree with the results of Example 4.2-2.

Exercise 5.2-5 Use Robson's [1959] method to compute orthogonal polynomials for the unequally spaced points log(26.3 + .5), log(2.3 + .5), log .5. Reanalyze the data in Example 5.2-6 using these polynomials. Use Emerson's [1968] method for the same purpose.

5.3 CROSSED DESIGNS

In crossed designs, the experimental material is classified jointly according to two or more ways of classification. The ways may represent types of treatment, varieties of material, or both. A typical example of a crossed design is D. G. Freedman's [1958] study of the effects of rearing practices on different breeds of dogs. In his study, four littermates from each of four breeds (Shetland, basenji, fox terrier, and beagle) were assigned at three weeks of age to "indulgent" and "disciplined" rearing conditions. At eight and twelve weeks of age the dogs were rated for behavioral signs of timidity and fear of human beings. The data revealed that the different breeds responded differentially to the treatment conditions.

This experiment represents a two-way treatments-by-varieties design. The two classes of the treatment way of classification consist of the indulgent and disciplined rearing regimens. The varieties correspond to the established breeding populations of the dogs. Since the inference in this study is directed toward the breeds, it must be assumed that the breeding populations are in genetic equilibrium and that the dogs are drawn randomly from these populations. This means, in particular, that the males and females which produce the puppies for the respective breeds must be randomly selected and randomly mated.

In a more elaborate experiment, the treatments and material could have been further cross-classified, for example, by adding isolated and nonisolated conditions to the rearing practices and by separating breeds into male and female animals. The design would then have been a four-way $2 \times 2 \times 4 \times 2$ crossed design in which the differential effects of the treatment combinations in specific sex and breed classes could have been investigated. Many of the problems in analyzing these more complex designs are adequately illustrated in the two-way case, however, and in the interests of simplicity, we shall limit the discussion in Sec. 5.3 to this case.

The two-way crossed design may be represented schematically as a twofold array (Fig. 5.3-1) with a classes in the A way and b classes in the B way. The rows and columns of such an array are called *main classes*, and the cells *subclasses*.

Subclasses of the two-way design may be identified by row and column indices as shown in Fig. 5.3-1. These indices serve as the subscripts which identify observations and numbers of observations within subclasses. For example, y_{ijk} designates the score of the ith subject in the jk subclass, and N_{jk} designates the number of subjects in this subclass.

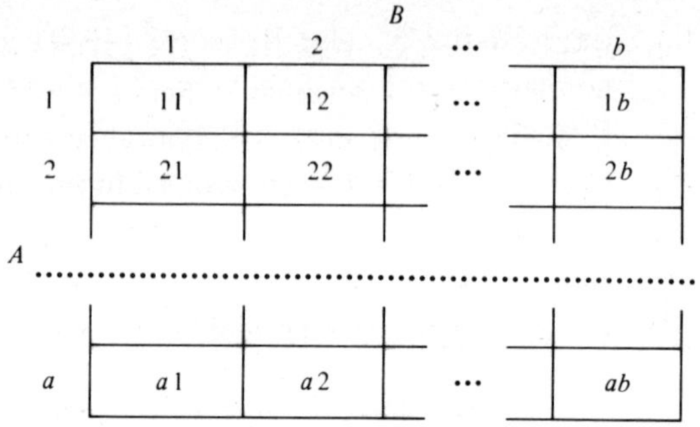

FIGURE 5.3-1
Schematic two-way crossed design.

The N_{jk} for all j and k are called the *subclass numbers.* In case $N_{jk} = r$, say, the design is said to have *equal* subclass numbers; otherwise, it is said to have *unequal* subclass numbers. If $N_{jk} > 0$ for all j and k, the design is called *complete*; otherwise, it is called *incomplete.* (The analysis of incomplete designs is discussed in Sec. 5.4.)

The display of univariate data for a two-way design is typically presented in a row-and-column table similar to the design scheme in Fig. 5.3-1. For multivariate data, however, this type of table may be too crowded when there are more than two or three variables per observation. In that case, a better format is a subjects × variables array such as shown in Table 5.3-2. The rows of this table correspond to subjects in their respective subclasses, while columns correspond to variables.

As a convention for ordering the subclass in the subjects × variables table, let us adopt the practice of enumerating subclasses in ascending order of subclass indices when read as natural numbers, for example, $11, 12, \ldots, 1b, 21, 22, \ldots, 2b, \ldots, a1, a2, \ldots, ab$. We shall refer to this as the *natural order* of the subclasses. Because the units *within* subclasses are selected randomly, the order enumeration of the $i = 1, 2, \ldots, N_{jk}$ observations within subclass j, k may be arbitrary. With this convention, the body of the table of multivariate observations unambiguously represents the $N \times p$ data matrix $\mathbf{Y}$, where N is the sum of the subclass numbers, and p is the number of response variables.

The multivariate *means* of the subclasses may be similarly represented by the $n \times p$ matrix $\mathbf{Y}_{\cdot}$, where n is the number of subclasses. Matrices of subclass means appear, for example, in Tables 5.3-3 and 5.3-7. All the foregoing conventions generalize in obvious ways to 3-, 4-, . . . , f-fold cross-classifications.

5.3.1 Linear Models for the Analysis of Crossed Designs

As in the one-way case, the Gauss-Markoff analysis of data arising from a crossed experiment requires the assumption that the error covariance matrix is homogeneous across all subclasses of the design. This means not only that the treatments leave the covariance matrix homogeneous (possibly after a nonlinear transformation of the response variables), but also that the varietal populations have a common covariance matrix. We have discussed in Secs. 3.1 and 5.1 the circumstances that broadly justify these assumptions in behavioral research.

The first problem to be resolved in the analysis is the choice of the model for the observations. In the case of a two-way design in Fig. 5.3-1, there are five competing models to be considered. Listed in order of increasing complexity (as indicated by the rank of the model matrix), they are as follows:

Model	Rank	
Constant $\mathbf{y}_{jk} = \boldsymbol{\mu} + \boldsymbol{\epsilon}_{jk}$	1	(5.3-1)
A-way $\mathbf{y}_{jk} = \boldsymbol{\mu} + \boldsymbol{\alpha}_j + \boldsymbol{\epsilon}_{jk}$	$1 + (a-1) = a$	(5.3-2)
B-way $\mathbf{y}_{jk} = \boldsymbol{\mu} + \boldsymbol{\beta}_k + \boldsymbol{\epsilon}_{jk}$	$1 + (b-1) = b$	(5.3-3)
Main class $\mathbf{y}_{jk} = \boldsymbol{\mu} + \boldsymbol{\alpha}_j + \boldsymbol{\beta}_k + \boldsymbol{\epsilon}_{jk}$	$1 + (a-1) + (b-1) = a + b - 1$	(5.3-4)
Rank n $\mathbf{y}_{jk} = \boldsymbol{\mu} + \boldsymbol{\alpha}_j + \boldsymbol{\beta}_k + (\boldsymbol{\alpha\beta})_{jk} + \boldsymbol{\epsilon}_{jk}$	$1 + (a-1) + (b-1) + (a-1)(b-1) = ab = n$	(5.3-5)

Since we allow the possibility of a multivariate response, each term in these models is a p-component vector. A typical observation $\mathbf{y}_{ijk}$, the transpose of which represents a row in the data matrix, is the response of unit i in subclass j, k; $\boldsymbol{\mu}$ is a constant which in most applications is determined by the arbitrary origins of the response measures; $\boldsymbol{\alpha}_j$ is the main effect of class j in A, $\boldsymbol{\beta}_k$ is the main effect of class k in B, $(\boldsymbol{\alpha\beta})_{jk}$ is an effect specific to subclass j, k; and $\boldsymbol{\epsilon}_{jk}$ is a random error which in most cases we assume to arise from the distribution $N(\mathbf{0},\Sigma)$.

As in Sec. 4.1.2, it is convenient to derive the analysis from the models for the subclass means, in which case $y_{\cdot jk} = \sum_{i=1}^{N_{jk}} \mathbf{y}_{ijk}/N_{jk}$. The rank-$n$ model for the means contains the others and serves to illustrate the complete set. For example, the model for $a = 2$ and $b = 3$, when expressed *in extenso*, is

$$\begin{bmatrix} \mathbf{y}'_{\cdot 11} \\ \mathbf{y}'_{\cdot 12} \\ \mathbf{y}'_{\cdot 13} \\ \mathbf{y}'_{\cdot 21} \\ \mathbf{y}'_{\cdot 22} \\ \mathbf{y}'_{\cdot 23} \end{bmatrix} = \begin{bmatrix} 1 & 1 & 0 & 1 & 0 & 0 & 1 & 0 & 0 & 0 & 0 & 0 \\ 1 & 1 & 0 & 0 & 1 & 0 & 0 & 1 & 0 & 0 & 0 & 0 \\ 1 & 1 & 0 & 0 & 0 & 1 & 0 & 0 & 1 & 0 & 0 & 0 \\ 1 & 0 & 1 & 1 & 0 & 0 & 0 & 0 & 0 & 1 & 0 & 0 \\ 1 & 0 & 1 & 0 & 1 & 0 & 0 & 0 & 0 & 0 & 1 & 0 \\ 1 & 0 & 1 & 0 & 0 & 1 & 0 & 0 & 0 & 0 & 0 & 1 \end{bmatrix} \begin{bmatrix} \boldsymbol{\mu}' \\ \boldsymbol{\alpha}'_1 \\ \boldsymbol{\alpha}'_2 \\ \boldsymbol{\beta}'_1 \\ \boldsymbol{\beta}'_2 \\ \boldsymbol{\beta}'_3 \\ (\boldsymbol{\alpha\beta})'_{11} \\ (\boldsymbol{\alpha\beta})'_{12} \\ (\boldsymbol{\alpha\beta})'_{13} \\ (\boldsymbol{\alpha\beta})'_{21} \\ (\boldsymbol{\alpha\beta})'_{22} \\ (\boldsymbol{\alpha\beta})'_{23} \end{bmatrix} + \begin{bmatrix} \boldsymbol{\epsilon}'_{\cdot 11} \\ \boldsymbol{\epsilon}'_{\cdot 12} \\ \boldsymbol{\epsilon}'_{\cdot 13} \\ \boldsymbol{\epsilon}'_{\cdot 21} \\ \boldsymbol{\epsilon}'_{\cdot 22} \\ \boldsymbol{\epsilon}'_{\cdot 23} \end{bmatrix}$$

or, more compactly,

$$\underset{6\times p}{\boldsymbol{Y}.} = \underset{6\times 12}{\mathbf{A}} \; \underset{12\times p}{\boldsymbol{\Xi}} + \underset{6\times p}{\boldsymbol{E}.} \tag{5.3-6}$$

The system (5.3-6) is obviously deficient in rank, for there are 12 parameters and only 6 equations. That the rank is exactly $n = ab = 6$ is evident from the identity matrix comprising the last six columns of the model matrix. Thus, the model including all possible interactive effects is mathematically equivalent to a one-way model with six classes. The row-by-column classification cannot then be exploited, for there are not enough equations to estimate simultaneously specific subclass effects and the main-class effects. (The situation is somewhat different in a survey study; see Sec. 6.4.)

In the absence of interactions, however, the main-class model (5.3-3) comprising the first six columns in (5.3-6) may be assumed. We see by inspection that the main-class model matrix has only four linearly independent columns (e.g., those corresponding to the constant term, one of the A effects, and two of the B effects). The main-class model is therefore overdetermined by the data, and least-squares fitting of the model is nontrivial. Reparameterization will again be necessary and is discussed in Sec. 5.3.3.

In the absence of either the A or the B effect, the model reduces to a one-way model (5.3.3) or (5.3.2) in the B or the A way of classification, respectively. The A-way model consists of columns 1, 2, and 3 in (5.3-6), and the B-way model consists of columns 1, 4, 5, and 6. Routine application of least squares in these cases is equivalent to combining subclasses with the same expectation and applying the one-way analysis described in Sec. 5.2. The combining of subclasses is often referred to as *collapsing* rows or columns.

In the absence of both main effects and interactions, the model reduces to (5.3-1) consisting of column 1 of (5.3-6), corresponding to the (usually arbitrary) constant term. If for some reason an estimate of the constant term is required, routine application of least squares is equivalent to collapsing all subclasses and computing the mean for the total data.

In discussing models such as (5.3-6), it is customary and natural to use the terminology of vector spaces. Thus, the columns of the model matrix are said to span various subspaces of the *estimation space*. For example, column 1 spans the space of the constant term; columns 2 and 3, the space of A effects; columns 4 to 6, the space of B effects; and columns 7 through 12, the interaction space. These spaces are obviously not disjoint, for each intersects with the space of the constant term, and the interaction space intersects the main-effect space as well. An essential step in formulating a general least-squares analysis for the crossed-design model is therefore the construction of a basis for the estimation space. The tests of fit of the alternative models then consist in examining the reduction of the residual sum of squares as bases of subspaces are added or deleted. In algebraic terms, this is the same as saying that the analysis provides for estimation and testing of subsets of interpretable linear functions of the original parameters.

An elegant solution to the problem of constructing models and bases for crossed designs is contained in the remarkable result that *models and bases for designs of any complexity can be generated from the models and bases of one-way designs.* As discussed in the next section, this result leads to the completely straightforward multiway generalization of the one-way analysis. Various facets of this discussion are based on Corsten [1958], Kurkjian and Zelen [1962], and Bock [1963]. However, the essential ideas were foreshadowed in Yates [1937].

5.3.2 Generating Models for Crossed Designs

As the notation of (5.3-5) suggests, the observational equation for a given subclass of a crossed design is generated by operations upon the subclass index. To describe these operations in complete generality, let us assume an f-way crossed design with $n_1, n_2, \ldots, n_f$ levels in ways of classification, $1, 2, \ldots, f$. Subclasses of this design may then be denoted by an index consisting of ordered elements $j_1, j_2, \ldots, j_f$, which run from 1 to $n_1, n_2, \ldots, n_f$, respectively.

In this notation, the model for an observation in subclass $(j_1 j_2 \cdots j_f)$ is

$$y_{j_1 j_2 \cdots j_f} = \xi(j_1, j_2, \ldots, j_f) + \epsilon_{j_1 j_2 \cdots j_f} \qquad (5.3\text{-}7)$$

where $\epsilon_{j_1 j_2 \cdots j_f}$ is a random error, and $\xi(j_1, j_2, \ldots, j_f)$ is the expected value (i.e., the fixed part of the model) for observations in this subclass.

For the f-way crossed design, $\xi(j_1, j_2, \ldots, j_f)$ *is sum of* 2^f *terms whose subscripts are generated from the elements in the subclass index taken* $0, 1, 2, \ldots, f$ *at a time without respect to order.* Of these terms, the one having no subscript is called the *constant* or *general mean*; those having one-element subscripts are called *main effects*; those having two-element subscripts are called *two-factor interactions*; those having three-element subscripts are called *three-factor interactions*; etc.; up to the terms with f-element subscripts which are called the *f-factor interactions.*

As in (5.3-5), it is convenient to identify the interaction terms by "symbolic products" of the main-effect parameters that correspond to the respective main classes represented in the subscript. These symbolic products are shown enclosed in parentheses to indicate that they are merely names of parameters and not actual arithmetic products. As an example of the generating rule and the symbolic product notation, we let $j_1 = j$, $j_2 = k$, $j_3 = l$ and write as follows the model for the ith observation from the j, k, l subclass of a three-way design:

$$y_{jkl} = \mu + \alpha_j + \beta_k + \gamma_l + (\alpha\beta)_{jk} + (\alpha\gamma)_{jl} + (\beta\gamma)_{kl} + (\alpha\beta\gamma)_{jkl} + \epsilon_{jkl} \qquad (5.3\text{-}8)$$

To employ the approach of Sec. 5.2 to the least-squares analysis of models such as (5.3-8), it is helpful to express the generating rule in terms of matrix operations. To this end, we follow Kurkjian and Zelen [1962] in defining a symbolic Kronecker product, the elements of which are symbolic products:

$$\mathbf{A} \otimes \mathbf{B} = [(a_{ij} b_{kl})] \qquad (5.3\text{-}9)$$

The symbolic Kronecker product has the same associative and distributive properties as the Kronecker product (see Sec. 4.2.2).

With this notational device, we may state the following fundamental theorem for crossed-design models:

Let an f-way crossed design consist of ways of classification 1, 2, . . . , *f, and let the ways contain* $n_1, n_2, \ldots, n_f$ *classes, respectively. Let* $\mathbf{A}_1\xi_1, \mathbf{A}_2\xi_2, \ldots, \mathbf{A}_f\xi_f$ *be the expected value (fixed part) of the rank-n one-way design models for the respective ways. Then the expected value of the rank* $n = n_1 n_2 \cdots n_f$ *model for the f-way crossed design is generated by the operation* $*$, *such that*

$$\mathbf{A}_1\xi_1 * \mathbf{A}_2\xi_2 * \cdots * \mathbf{A}_f\xi_f = (\mathbf{A}_1 \times \mathbf{A}_2 \times \cdots \times \mathbf{A}_f)(\xi_1 \otimes \xi_2 \otimes \cdots \otimes \xi_f)$$
$$= \mathbf{A}_{12\cdots f}\xi_{12\cdots f} \tag{5.3-10}$$

In other words, the rank-n model matrix implied by the generating rule is precisely the f-fold Kronecker product $\mathbf{A}_{12\cdots f}$ of the model matrices for the one-way designs. Similarly, the parameter vector $\xi_{12\cdots f}$ for the f-way design is the f-fold *symbolic* Kronecker product of the parameter vectors of the one-way design.

To prove this theorem, let the model matrix for the one-way design with, say, n_h levels, be

$$\mathbf{A}_h = [\mathbf{1}_{n_h}, \mathbf{I}_{n_h}]$$

and let the corresponding parameter vector be $\xi_h' = [\mu, \alpha_h'] = [\mu, \alpha_{h_1}, \alpha_{h_2}, \ldots, \alpha_{hn_h}]$. The n_h rows of $\mathbf{A}_h$ are identified with classes of the one-way design and may be indexed by the subclass subscript $j_h = 1, 2, \ldots, n_h$. The $n_h + 1$ columns of $\mathbf{A}_h$ are identified with the components in ξ_h and are conveniently indexed by $k_h = 0, 1, 2, \ldots, n_h$. Thus, row j_h of $\mathbf{A}_h$ contains two elements equal to 1, which occur in columns $k_h = 0$ and j, say, and it contains zeroes elsewhere. Since these 1s correspond to the elements μ and α_{jk} in ξ_h, the j component of $\mathbf{A}_h\xi_h$ is, say,

$$\xi(j) = \mu + \alpha_j$$

Now recall from (4.2-6) that the elements of the Kronecker product $\mathbf{A}_{12} = \mathbf{A}_1 \times \mathbf{A}_2$ are products of all combinations of one element from $\mathbf{A}_1$ and one element from $\mathbf{A}_2$ without repetitions. If the rows of $\mathbf{A}_{12}$ are indexed by $(j_1 j_2)$ and the columns by $(k_1 k_2)$, the general element of the Kronecker product may be expressed as

$$[a_{12(j_1j_2)(k_1k_2)}] = [a_{1(j_1k_1)}a_{2(j_2k_2)}]$$

Similarly, the general element of the symbolic Kronecker product $\xi_{12} = \xi_1 \otimes \xi_2$ may be expressed as

$$[\xi_{12(k_1k_2)}] = [(\xi_{1(k_1)}\xi_{2(k_2)})]$$

Thus, row $(j_1 j_2)$ of $\mathbf{A}_{12}$ contains exactly $2 \times 2 = 2^2$ elements equal to 1, which occur in columns 00, $0k_2$, $k_1 0$, and $k_1 k_2$, and it contains zeroes elsewhere. The 1s in this row correspond to the elements $\mu\mu$, $\mu\alpha_{2j_2}$, $\alpha_{1j_1}\mu$, and $\alpha_{1j_1}\alpha_{2j_2}$ in ξ_{12}. Thus, by suppressing the redundant μ's in the symbolic products, and rearranging terms and subscripts, we may express the $j_1 j_2$ component of $\mathbf{A}_{12}\xi_{12}$ as

$$\xi(j_1, j_2) = \mu + \alpha_{1j_1} + \alpha_{2j_2} + (\alpha_1\alpha_2)_{j_1j_2}$$

which agrees with the generating rule.

Because of the associativity of Kronecker multiplication, these results generalize immediately to the f-way case. That is, the general element of the f-fold Kronecker product $\mathbf{A}_{12\cdots f} = \mathbf{A}_1 \times \mathbf{A}_2 \times \cdots \times \mathbf{A}_f$ is

$$[a_{12\cdots f(j_1j_2\cdots j_f)(k_1k_2\cdots k_f)}] = [a_{1(j_1k_1)}a_{2(j_2k_2)}\cdots a_{f(j_fk_f)}]$$

and the corresponding element of $\xi_{12\cdots f} = \xi_1 \otimes \xi_2 \otimes \cdots \otimes \xi_f$ is

$$[\xi_{12\cdots f(k_1k_2\cdots k_f)}] = [(\xi_{(k_1)}\xi_{2(k_2)}\cdots \xi_{f(k_f)})]$$

The $j_1 j_2 \cdots j_f$ row of $\mathbf{A}_{12\cdots f}$ therefore contains exactly 2^f elements equal to 1, and all remaining elements 0, such that the 1s occur in columns

$$\begin{aligned}
&(00\cdots 0), (j_1 0\cdots 0), (0\, j_2\cdots 0)\cdots(00\cdots j_f)\\
&(j_1j_20\cdots 0)(j_10\, j_3\cdots 0)\cdots(0\cdots 0\, j_{f-1}j_f)\\
&(j_1j_2j_30\cdots 0)(j_1j_20\, j_4\cdots 0)\cdots(0\cdots 0\, j_{f-2}j_{f-1}j_f)\\
&\qquad\qquad\cdots\ \cdots(j_1j_2\cdots j_f)
\end{aligned}$$

In the $j_1 j_2 \cdots j_f$ component of the matrix product $\mathbf{A}_{12\cdots f}\xi_{12\cdots f}$, these unit elements multiply elements of $\xi_{12\cdots f}$ which, after simplification of notation, sum to

$$\begin{aligned}
\xi(j_1, j_2, \ldots, j_f)&\\
= \mu &+ \alpha_{1j_1} + \alpha_{2j_2} + \cdots + \alpha_{fj_f} + (\alpha_1\alpha_2)_{j_1j_2} + (\alpha_1\alpha_3)_{j_1j_3} + \cdots\\
&+ (\alpha_{f-1}\alpha_f)_{j_{f-1}j_f} + (\alpha_1\alpha_2\alpha_3)_{j_1j_2j_3} + (\alpha_1\alpha_2\alpha_4)_{j_1j_2j_4} + \cdots\\
&+ (\alpha_{f-2}\alpha_{f-1}\alpha_f)_{j_{f-2}j_{f-1}j_f} + \cdots\cdots + (\alpha_1\alpha_2\cdots\alpha_f)_{j_1j_2\cdots j_f}
\end{aligned}$$

The terms in this sum agree with the generating rule for the expected value for the $j_1 j_2 \cdots j_f$ subclass and thus establish the theorem.

To apply this theorem, however, we must generate not only the model matrix, but also the basis matrix and corresponding linear parametric functions of the full-rank factorization. The matrix operations for generating these objects are contained in the following important corollary of the above theorem:

The rank $r = r_1 r_2 \cdots r_f$ factorization of the f-way model matrix is the f-fold Kronecker product of rank $r_1, r_2, \ldots, r_f$ factorizations of the respective one-way matrices from which the f-way matrix is generated.

The proof depends upon (4.2-10):

$$\begin{aligned}
\mathbf{A}_{12\cdots f} &= \mathbf{A}_1 \times \mathbf{A}_2 \times \cdots \times \mathbf{A}_f\\
&= \mathbf{K}_1\mathbf{L}_1 \times \mathbf{K}_2\mathbf{L}_2 \times \cdots \times \mathbf{K}_f\mathbf{L}_f\\
&= (\mathbf{K}_1 \times \mathbf{K}_2 \times \cdots \times \mathbf{K}_f)(\mathbf{L}_1 \times \mathbf{L}_2 \times \cdots \times \mathbf{L}_f)\\
&= \mathbf{K}_{12\cdots f}\mathbf{L}_{12\cdots f} \qquad (5.3\text{-}11)
\end{aligned}$$

In most cases, it will be necessary to express $\mathbf{K}_{12\ldots f}$ and $\mathbf{L}_{12\ldots f}$ in partitioned form by subspaces to retain the conventional order of terms in the reparameterized model. When $f = 2$, for example, the factorization corresponding to the simple contrast reparameterization of the one-way designs with n_1 and n_2 classes is (see Sec. 5.2.2)

$$\underset{n_1 \times (n_1+1)}{\mathbf{A}_1} = \mathbf{K}_1\mathbf{L}_1 = [\mathbf{1}_{n_1}, \mathbf{C}_D^{(n_1)}]\begin{bmatrix} 1 & \dfrac{1}{n_1}\mathbf{1}'_{n_1} \\ \mathbf{0} & \mathbf{C}'_{n_1} \end{bmatrix} \tag{5.3-12}$$

and

$$\underset{n_2 \times (n_2+1)}{\mathbf{A}_2} = \mathbf{K}_2\mathbf{L}_2 = [\mathbf{1}_{n_2}, \mathbf{C}_D^{(n_2)}]\begin{bmatrix} 1 & \dfrac{1}{n_2}\mathbf{1}'_{n_2} \\ \mathbf{0} & \mathbf{C}'_{n_2} \end{bmatrix} \tag{5.3-13}$$

Then a factorization of the $n_1 \times n_2$ model matrix for the two-way crossed design (expressed in conventional order) is $\underset{n_1 n_2 \times (n_1+1)(n_2+2)}{\mathbf{A}_{12}} = \mathbf{K}_{12}\mathbf{L}_{12}$, where

$$\mathbf{K}_{12} = [\underset{1}{\mathbf{1}_{n_1} \times \mathbf{1}_{n_2}}, \underset{n_1-1}{\mathbf{C}_D^{(n_1)} \times \mathbf{1}_{n_2}}, \underset{n_2-1}{\mathbf{1}_{n_1} \times \mathbf{C}_D^{(n_2)}}, \underset{(n_1-1)(n_2-1)}{\mathbf{C}_D^{(n_1)} \times \mathbf{C}_D^{(n_2)}}]\; n_1 n_2 \tag{5.3-14}$$

and

$$\mathbf{L}_{12} = \begin{bmatrix} 1 & \dfrac{1}{n_1}\mathbf{1}'_{n_1} & \dfrac{1}{n_2}\mathbf{1}'_{n_2} & \dfrac{1}{n_1 n_2}\mathbf{1}'_{n_1} \times \mathbf{1}'_{n_2} \\ \mathbf{0} & \mathbf{C}'_{n_1} & \mathbf{O} & \dfrac{1}{n_2}\mathbf{C}'_{n_1} \times \mathbf{1}'_{n_2} \\ \mathbf{0} & \mathbf{O} & \mathbf{C}'_{n_2} & \dfrac{1}{n_1}\mathbf{1}'_{n_1} \times \mathbf{C}'_{n_2} \\ \mathbf{0} & \mathbf{O} & \mathbf{O} & \mathbf{C}'_{n_1} \times \mathbf{C}'_{n_2} \end{bmatrix} \begin{matrix} 1 \\ n_1 - 1 \\ n_2 - 1 \\ (n_1-1)(n_2-1) \end{matrix} \tag{5.3-15}$$

$$\qquad\quad 1 \qquad n_1 \qquad n_2 \qquad\quad n_1 n_2$$

It is easy to show that the rank of a Kronecker product is the product of the ranks of the factors [express the factor matrices in gaussian factorizations and use (4.2-10)]. Hence, the ranks of the respective subspaces (submatrices) in $\mathbf{K}_{12}$ are 1, $(n_1 - 1)$, $(n_2 - 1)$, $(n_1 - 1)(n_2 - 1)$. Since the sum of these ranks equals $n_1 n_2$, the columns of $\mathbf{K}_{12}$ are mutually independent, and the reparameterized model with matrix equal to $\mathbf{K}_{12}$, or any subset of columns from $\mathbf{K}_{12}$, is of full rank. That is, $\mathbf{K}_{12}$ is a basis for the rank-n model and is suitable for ordinary least-squares analysis. This result generalizes to the f-way case.

For a numerical example of these results, consider a two-way design with two A classes and three B classes. If each of the one-way models is reparameterized in simple contrasts with the last group, the basis matrices are, respectively,

$$\mathbf{K}_A = [\mathbf{1}_2, \mathbf{C}_D{}^{(2)}] = \begin{bmatrix} 1 & \frac{1}{2} \\ 1 & -\frac{1}{2} \end{bmatrix}$$

and

$$\mathbf{K}_B = [\mathbf{1}_3, \mathbf{C}_D{}^{(3)}] = \begin{bmatrix} 1 & \frac{2}{3} & -\frac{1}{3} \\ 1 & -\frac{1}{3} & \frac{2}{3} \\ 1 & -\frac{1}{3} & -\frac{1}{3} \end{bmatrix}$$

Then, in conventional order,

$$\mathbf{K}_{AB} = [\mathbf{1}_2 \times \mathbf{1}_3, \mathbf{C}_D{}^{(2)} \times \mathbf{1}_3, \mathbf{1}_2 \times \mathbf{C}_D{}^{(3)}, \mathbf{C}_D{}^{(2)} \times \mathbf{C}_D{}^{(3)}] \tag{5.3-16}$$

$$= \begin{bmatrix} 1 & \frac{1}{2} & \frac{2}{3} & -\frac{1}{3} & \frac{1}{3} & -\frac{1}{6} \\ 1 & \frac{1}{2} & -\frac{1}{3} & \frac{2}{3} & -\frac{1}{6} & \frac{1}{3} \\ 1 & \frac{1}{2} & -\frac{1}{3} & -\frac{1}{3} & -\frac{1}{6} & -\frac{1}{6} \\ 1 & -\frac{1}{2} & \frac{2}{3} & -\frac{1}{3} & -\frac{1}{3} & \frac{1}{6} \\ 1 & -\frac{1}{2} & -\frac{1}{3} & \frac{2}{3} & \frac{1}{6} & -\frac{1}{3} \\ 1 & -\frac{1}{2} & -\frac{1}{3} & -\frac{1}{3} & \frac{1}{6} & \frac{1}{6} \end{bmatrix}$$

The coefficients of the linear parametric functions (lpf) which correspond to this basis are generated from the respective **L** matrices of the one-way designs:

$$\mathbf{L}_A = \begin{bmatrix} 1 & \frac{1}{2}\mathbf{1}'_2 \\ 0 & \mathbf{C}'_2 \end{bmatrix} = \begin{bmatrix} 1 & \frac{1}{2} & \frac{1}{2} \\ 0 & 1 & -1 \end{bmatrix}$$

and

$$\mathbf{L}_B = \begin{bmatrix} 1 & \frac{1}{3}\mathbf{1}'_3 \\ \mathbf{0} & \mathbf{C}'_3 \end{bmatrix} = \begin{bmatrix} 1 & \frac{1}{3} & \frac{1}{3} & \frac{1}{3} \\ 0 & 1 & 0 & -1 \\ 0 & 0 & 1 & -1 \end{bmatrix}$$

Whence, in the order corresponding to (5.3-14),

$$\mathbf{L}_{AB} = \begin{bmatrix} 1 \times 1 & \frac{1}{2}\mathbf{1}'_2 \times 1 & 1 \times \frac{1}{3}\mathbf{1}'_3 & \frac{1}{2}\mathbf{1}'_2 \times \frac{1}{3}\mathbf{1}'_3 \\ 0 \times 1 & \mathbf{C}'_2 \times 1 & 0 \times \frac{1}{3}\mathbf{1}'_3 & \mathbf{C}'_2 \times \frac{1}{3}\mathbf{1}'_3 \\ 1 \times \mathbf{0} & \frac{1}{2}\mathbf{1}'_2 \times \mathbf{0} & 1 \times \mathbf{C}'_3 & \frac{1}{2}\mathbf{1}'_2 \times \mathbf{C}'_3 \\ 0 \times \mathbf{0} & \mathbf{C}'_2 \times \mathbf{0} & 0 \times \mathbf{C}'_3 & \mathbf{C}'_2 \times \mathbf{C}'_3 \end{bmatrix}$$

$$= \begin{bmatrix} 1 & \frac{1}{2} & \frac{1}{2} & \frac{1}{3} & \frac{1}{3} & \frac{1}{3} & \frac{1}{6} & \frac{1}{6} & \frac{1}{6} & \frac{1}{6} & \frac{1}{6} & \frac{1}{6} \\ 0 & 1 & -1 & 0 & 0 & 0 & \frac{1}{3} & \frac{1}{3} & \frac{1}{3} & -\frac{1}{3} & -\frac{1}{3} & -\frac{1}{3} \\ 0 & 0 & 0 & 1 & 0 & -1 & \frac{1}{2} & 0 & -\frac{1}{2} & \frac{1}{2} & 0 & -\frac{1}{2} \\ 0 & 0 & 0 & 0 & 1 & -1 & 0 & \frac{1}{2} & -\frac{1}{2} & 0 & \frac{1}{2} & -\frac{1}{2} \\ 0 & 0 & 0 & 0 & 0 & 0 & 1 & 0 & -1 & -1 & 0 & 1 \\ 0 & 0 & 0 & 0 & 0 & 0 & 0 & 1 & -1 & 0 & -1 & 1 \end{bmatrix}$$

Only the basis matrix $\mathbf{K}_{AB}$ would actually be generated for the least-squares analysis for this model. This is fortunate because the structure of the basis matrix (**K** matrix) is considerably simpler than that of the lpf matrix (**L** matrix). We shall discuss the role of the basis matrix in the computation and that of the lpf matrix in the interpretation after introducing some shorthand notation intended to economize the description of designs and bases.

5.3.3 Symbolic Representation of Designs and Bases

The theorems of the preceding section lead to simple algorithms for constructing bases for crossed-design models. These algorithms play an important role in general computer programs for least-squares analysis of design models [Bock, 1963]. Nelder [1965] has supplied a convenient notation for communicating the structure of crossed, nested, and crossed-and-nested designs to the computer. For crossed designs (see Sec. 6.4.1 for the nested case), the notation is

$$A_1(n_1) \times A_2(n_2) \times \cdots \times A_f(n_f) \qquad (5.3\text{-}17)$$

for an f-way design with ways $A_1, A_2, \ldots, A_f$ consisting of $n_1, n_2, \ldots, n_f$ classes, respectively. If left-right order is understood to identify the ways, the notation can be simplified to

$$n_1 \times n_2 \times \cdots \times n_f \qquad (5.3\text{-}18)$$

Thus, a three-way design with two classes in A_1, three classes in A_2, and four classes in A_3 could be expressed as

$$A_1(2) \times A_2(3) \times A_3(4)$$

or

$$2 \times 3 \times 4$$

We shall refer to (5.3-17) or (5.3-18) as a *design formula*. The design formula implies that the complete design consists of

$$n = n_1 n_2 \cdots n_f$$

subclasses and that subspaces and degrees of freedom are ordered conventionally as shown in Table 5.3-1.

From the design formula and an ordering of subspaces, it is but a short step to a notational device which prescribes precisely the construction of the basis matrices for the least-squares computations. The design formula specifies that the basis matrices for the full-rank one-way models for ways $A_1, A_2, \ldots, A_f$ shall be of orders $n_1, n_2, \ldots, n_f$, respectively. Suppose these matrices are $K_{n_1}, K_{n_2}, \ldots, K_{n_f}$, respectively, and let their columns be indexed

$$\begin{array}{c} 0, 1, 2, \ldots, h_1, \ldots, n_1 - 1 \\ 0, 1, 2, \ldots, h_2, \ldots, n_2 - 1 \\ \cdots\cdots\cdots\cdots\cdots\cdots \\ 0, 1, 2, \ldots, h_f, \ldots, n_f - 1 \end{array}$$

Then, according to the theorem in Sec. 5.3.3, the basis vectors of the f-way crossed design are the f-fold Kronecker products of columns $h_1, h_2, \ldots, h_f$ from the respective one-way bases. An example appears in Table 5.3-1, under the heading "Symbolic Basis Vectors" (SBV). Note that, as required, the number of symbolic basis vectors in each subspace is equal to the number of degrees of freedom for the space.

From a basis constructed in this way the analysis can proceed to statistical tests of the contributions of successive subspaces in the model to the reduction of residual variation. These tests are part of the blockwise analysis of variance for crossed designs, which we now discuss.

5.3.4 Blockwise Multivariate Analysis of Variance for Crossed Designs

The basis matrix generated for the crossed design by the method of Sec. 5.3.3 is of full column rank; hence, the condition $|\mathbf{K}'\mathbf{K}| \neq 0$ is satisfied, and the fit of the reparameterized model may be investigated by an analysis of variance similar to that derived in Chap. 4 for testing polynomial regression models. Peculiar to the design analysis, however, is the blockwise testing of effects and pooling of degrees of freedom within successive subspaces of the model. The design analysis is also more difficult to interpret, partly because the parametric structure of the model is more complex initially, and partly because of the complication of reparameterization to full rank and, in the nonorthogonal case, by the orthogonal reparameterization required for the analysis of variance. We consider these interpretational problems in this section while continuing to limit the discussion to the two-way design. Problems of interpreting three- and higher-way crossed designs are postponed until Sec. 5.4. As in Sec. 5.2, we treat the orthogonal and nonorthogonal cases separately.

a Orthogonal case When the subclass numbers are equal (to r), an orthogonal basis for the $a \times b$ design can be generated directly from orthogonal bases for one-way designs with a and b levels, respectively. This follows from the result, easily established from (4.2-10), that *the Kronecker product of orthogonal matrices is orthogonal.* This also applies to orthogonality of subspaces. As a result, the column $\times$ column orthogonalization of $\mathbf{K}^{(ab)}$ may be effected merely by replacing the deviation bases in (5.3-19) with Helmert bases given by (5.2-28). The result is

$$\mathbf{K}_H{}^{(ab)} = [\mathbf{1}_a \times \mathbf{1}_b, \mathbf{C}_H{}^{(a)} \times \mathbf{1}_b, \mathbf{1}_a \times \mathbf{C}_H{}^{(b)}, \mathbf{C}_H{}^{(a)} \times \mathbf{C}_H{}^{(b)}] \qquad (5.3\text{-}20)$$

That is, $\mathbf{K}_H{}^{(ab)}$ is formed by first generating, according to (5.2-28), the Helmert bases of size a and b, respectively,

$$\mathbf{K}_H{}^{(a)} = \begin{bmatrix} 1 & \frac{a-1}{a} & 0 & \cdots & 0 \\ 1 & -\frac{1}{a} & \frac{a-2}{a-1} & \cdots & 0 \\ \cdots & \cdots & \cdots & \cdots & \cdots \\ 1 & -\frac{1}{a} & -\frac{1}{a-1} & \cdots & \frac{1}{2} \\ 1 & -\frac{1}{a} & -\frac{1}{a-1} & \cdots & -\frac{1}{2} \end{bmatrix}$$
$$\quad (0) \qquad (1) \qquad (2) \qquad\qquad (a-1)$$

$$\mathbf{K}_H{}^{(b)} = \begin{bmatrix} 1 & \dfrac{b-1}{b} & 0 & \cdots & 0 \\ 1 & -\dfrac{1}{b} & \dfrac{b-2}{b-1} & \cdots & 0 \\ \cdots & \cdots & \cdots & \cdots & \cdots \\ 1 & -\dfrac{1}{b} & -\dfrac{1}{b} & \cdots & \dfrac{1}{2} \\ 1 & -\dfrac{1}{b} & -\dfrac{1}{b} & \cdots & -\dfrac{1}{2} \end{bmatrix}$$
$$\quad (0) \qquad (1) \qquad (2) \qquad \cdots \qquad (b-1)$$

and then generating the basis $\mathbf{K}_H{}^{(ab)}$ for the crossed design by computing the Kronecker products of columns of $\mathbf{K}_H{}^{(a)}$ and $\mathbf{K}_H{}^{(b)}$ as designated by the symbolic basis vectors in Table 5.3-1 (see Example 5.3-1).

For ease of writing from this point on, let us denote the Helmert basis for the crossed design by $\mathbf{K}_H$. Then the model for the means in this parameterization is

$$\boldsymbol{Y}. = \mathbf{K}_H \mathbf{L}_H \boldsymbol{\Xi} + \boldsymbol{E}. = \mathbf{K}_H \hat{\boldsymbol{\Theta}}_H + \boldsymbol{E}.$$

In the orthogonal case, the normal equations for estimating $\boldsymbol{\Theta}_H$ are

$$r\mathbf{K}_H'\mathbf{K}_H\boldsymbol{\Theta}_H = r\mathbf{K}_H'\mathbf{Y}. \tag{5.3-21}$$

But since $\mathbf{K}_H$ is orthogonal column by column,

$$\mathbf{K}_H'\mathbf{K}_H = \mathbf{D}_{K_H'K_H}$$

is a diagonal matrix, and (5.3-21) is solved as in (5.2-29) merely by rescaling rows of (5.3-21) by $(1/r)\mathbf{D}_{K_H'K_H}^{-1}$. Similarly, the orthogonal estimates $\mathbf{U}_H$ required in the analysis of variance are obtained by rescaling rows of (5.3-21) by $r^{-1/2}\mathbf{D}_{K_H'K_H}^{-1/2}$. Partitioned by subspaces, the orthogonal estimates are

$$\mathbf{U}_H = r^{1/2}\mathbf{D}_{K_H'K_H}^{-1/2}\mathbf{K}_H'\mathbf{Y}. = \begin{bmatrix} \mathbf{U}_0 \\ \mathbf{U}_A \\ \mathbf{U}_B \\ \mathbf{U}_{AB} \end{bmatrix} \begin{matrix} 1 \\ a-1 \\ b-1 \\ (a-1)(b-1) \end{matrix} \tag{5.3-22}$$
$$p$$

The expected value of the estimator, similarly partitioned, is (transposed)

$$\mathscr{E}(\boldsymbol{U}_H') = \boldsymbol{\Gamma}_H' = [\boldsymbol{\Gamma}_0', \boldsymbol{\Gamma}_A', \boldsymbol{\Gamma}_B', \boldsymbol{\Gamma}_{AB}']$$

and its covariance matrix is

$$\mathscr{V}(\boldsymbol{U}_H) = \mathbf{I}_{ab} \times \boldsymbol{\Sigma}$$

The expected sums of squares and products in Table 5.3-1 show that the partition may be used to test the null hypotheses, $H_{AB}\colon \boldsymbol{\Gamma}_{AB} = \mathbf{O}$; $H_B\colon \boldsymbol{\Gamma}_B = \mathbf{O}$; $H_A\colon \boldsymbol{\Gamma}_A = \mathbf{O}$; and $H_m\colon \boldsymbol{\Gamma}_0 = \mathbf{O}$. To see the implications of these hypotheses, we

Table 5.3-1 MULTIVARIATE ANALYSIS OF VARIANCE FOR THE $a \times b$ DESIGN WITH r UNITS PER SUBCLASS

Source	SBV	df	SSP($p \times p$)	$\mathscr{E}$(SSP)
Constant	0, 0	1	$\text{SSM} = \mathbf{U}_0'\mathbf{U}_0$	$\boldsymbol{\Sigma} + \boldsymbol{\Gamma}_0'\boldsymbol{\Gamma}_0$
A effects	1, 0 2, 0 . . . $(a-1)$, 0	$a - 1$	$\text{SSA} = \mathbf{U}_A'\mathbf{U}_A$	$(a-1)\boldsymbol{\Sigma} + \boldsymbol{\Gamma}_A'\boldsymbol{\Gamma}_A$
B effects	0, 1 0, 2 . . . 0, $(b-1)$	$b - 1$	$\text{SSB} = \mathbf{U}_B'\mathbf{U}_B$	$(b-1)\boldsymbol{\Sigma} + \boldsymbol{\Gamma}_B'\boldsymbol{\Gamma}_B$
$A \times B$ interaction	1, 1 1, 2 . . . $(a-1)$, $(b-1)$	$(a-1)(b-1)$	$\text{SSAB} = \mathbf{U}_{AB}'\mathbf{U}_{AB}$	$(a-1)(b-1)\boldsymbol{\Sigma} + \boldsymbol{\Gamma}_{AB}'\boldsymbol{\Gamma}_{AB}$
Group means		ab	$\text{SSG} = r\mathbf{Y}_{\cdot}'\mathbf{Y}_{\cdot}$	$ab\boldsymbol{\Sigma} + \boldsymbol{\Gamma}'\boldsymbol{\Gamma}$
Within groups		$N - ab$	$\text{SSW} = \mathbf{Y}'\mathbf{Y} - r\mathbf{Y}_{\cdot}'\mathbf{Y}_{\cdot}$	$(N - ab)\boldsymbol{\Sigma}$
Total		$N = nr$	$\text{SST} = \mathbf{Y}'\mathbf{Y}$	

express the orthogonal parameters in terms of the original parameters:

$$\boldsymbol{\Gamma}_H = r^{1/2}\mathbf{D}^{1/2}_{K'_H K_H}\boldsymbol{\Theta}_H \qquad (5.3\text{-}23)$$

where

$$\boldsymbol{\Theta}_H = \mathbf{L}_H\boldsymbol{\Xi}$$

For the $a \times b$ design, and in terms of the one-way $\mathbf{L}$ matrices (5.2-27) with $n = a$ and $n = b$,

$$\mathbf{L}_H = \begin{bmatrix} 1 & \frac{1}{a}\mathbf{1}'_a & \frac{1}{b}\mathbf{1}'_b & \frac{1}{ab}\mathbf{1}'_a \times \mathbf{1}'_b \\ \mathbf{0} & \mathbf{H}_a & \mathbf{O} & \frac{1}{b}\mathbf{H}_a \times \mathbf{1}'_b \\ \mathbf{0} & \mathbf{O} & \mathbf{H}_b & \frac{1}{a}\mathbf{1}'_a \times \mathbf{H}_b \\ \mathbf{0} & \mathbf{O} & \mathbf{O} & \mathbf{H}_a \times \mathbf{H}_b \end{bmatrix} \begin{matrix} 1 \\ a-1 \\ b-1 \\ (a-1)(b-1) \end{matrix} \qquad (5.3\text{-}24)$$
$$\qquad\qquad 1 \qquad a \qquad b \qquad ab$$

The original parameters, transposed and similarly partitioned, are

$$\boldsymbol{\Xi}' = [\boldsymbol{\Xi}'_0, \boldsymbol{\Xi}'_A, \boldsymbol{\Xi}'_B, \boldsymbol{\Xi}'_{AB}]\ p$$
$$\quad 1 \quad a \quad b \quad ab$$
$$= \{[\mu], [\alpha_1, \alpha_2, \ldots, \alpha_a], [\beta_1, \beta_2, \ldots, \beta_b], [(\alpha\beta)_{11}, (\alpha\beta)_{12}, \ldots, (\alpha\beta)_{ab}]\}$$

Since $\boldsymbol{\Gamma}_H$ represents only a rescaling of rows of $\boldsymbol{\Theta}_H$ by strictly positive quantities, we can interpret the hypotheses in terms of the parametric functions in $\boldsymbol{\Theta}_H$. Because $\mathbf{L}_H$ is upper triangular by blocks, $\boldsymbol{\Gamma}_{AB}$ vanishes independent of other parameters in the model if $\boldsymbol{\Xi}_{AB} = \mathbf{O}$. Thus, the null hypothesis H_{AB}: $\boldsymbol{\Gamma}_{AB} = \mathbf{O}$ corresponds to a necessary condition for the interaction parameters to be null. Since $\boldsymbol{\Gamma}_{AB} = \mathbf{O}$ if and only if $\boldsymbol{\Gamma}'_{AB}\boldsymbol{\Gamma}_{AB} = \mathbf{O}$, a statistical test of the hypothesis that SSP_{AB} and SSP_W arise from the same population is equivalent to testing H_{AB}. This is the justification for performing the multivariate tests of Sec. 4.2.4 with $\mathbf{S}_h = \text{SSP}_{AB}$, $\mathbf{S}_e = \text{SSP}_W$, $n_h = (a-1)(b-1)$, and $n_e = N - ab$.

If H_{AB} is rejected, the blockwise testing terminates, and a rank $n = ab$ model is assumed. H_B: $\boldsymbol{\Gamma}_B = \mathbf{O}$ and H_A: $\boldsymbol{\Gamma}_A = \mathbf{O}$ are not then meaningful because, as is apparent from the form of (5.3-24), $\boldsymbol{\Gamma}_B$ and $\boldsymbol{\Gamma}_A$ are functions of both the main effects and the interactions. This fact is summarized in the statement "main effects are not testable in the presence of interaction."*

On the other hand, if H_{AB} is accepted, tests of H_A and H_B are possible. The orthogonal parameters in $\boldsymbol{\Gamma}_A$ then involve only the A main-effect contrasts, and $\boldsymbol{\Gamma}_B$ involves only the B main-effect contrasts; that is, H_A and H_B are separately and independently testable. Moreover, their interpretation is independent of the order in which the A and B spaces appear in the model.

As in (5.2.1), the main-effect contrasts vanish if and only if the effects are equal.

* This statement applies only to the fixed-effects model.

Thus, H_A and H_B are equivalent, respectively, to the hypotheses

$$\boldsymbol{\alpha}_1 = \boldsymbol{\alpha}_2 = \cdots = \boldsymbol{\alpha}_a$$

and

$$\boldsymbol{\beta}_1 = \boldsymbol{\beta}_2 = \cdots = \boldsymbol{\beta}_b$$

If either or both of these hypotheses is rejected, the rank of the model is taken as a, b, or $a + b - 1$, as the case may be.

Finally, if H_{AB}, H_A, and H_B are each accepted, $H_0: \boldsymbol{\Gamma}_0 = \mathbf{0}$ provides a test of the hypothesis $\boldsymbol{\mu} = \mathbf{0}$. In situations where the origin of measurement of the dependent variables is not arbitrary, this is a meaningful hypothesis and may be tested with $\mathbf{S}_a = \text{SSM}$.

This method of performing the blockwise two-way analysis of variance is illustrated in the following artificial example adapted from Winer [1971].

EXAMPLE 5.3-1 (*An orthogonal* 2×3 *design with replication*) Winer supposes that samples of nine psychiatric patients have been randomly selected from each of two clinical populations, $A(1)$ and $A(2)$. Subjects in each sample are assumed to be randomly assigned in equal numbers ($r = 3$) to three drug-therapy groups, $B(1)$, $B(2)$, and $B(3)$. Behavioral responses $y^{(1)}$ and $y^{(2)}$, measured after therapy, are given in Table 5.3-2, and subclass means in Table 5.3-3.*

* Winer's example includes $y^{(1)}$ only.

Table 5.3-2 RESPONSES OF SUBJECTS CLASSIFIED BY CLINICAL POPULATION AND DRUG

Population	Drug	Subject	Response scores $y^{(1)}$	Response scores $y^{(2)}$
		1	8	10
	$B(1)$	2	4	10
		3	0	7
		4	10	13
$A(1)$	$B(2)$	5	8	9
		6	6	11
		7	8	9
	$B(3)$	8	6	6
		9	4	12
		12	14	12
	$B(1)$	11	10	11
		12	6	13
		13	4	16
$A(2)$	$B(2)$	14	2	17
		15	0	12
		16	15	12
	$B(3)$	17	12	9
		18	9	9

Orthogonal bases for the constituent one-way designs, with SBVs shown below each matrix, are as follows:

$$\mathbf{K}_H^{(2)} = \underset{\quad (0) \quad (1)}{\begin{bmatrix} 1 & \frac{1}{2} \\ 1 & -\frac{1}{2} \end{bmatrix}} \qquad \mathbf{K}_H^{(3)} = \underset{\quad (0) \quad (1) \quad (2)}{\begin{bmatrix} 1 & \frac{2}{3} & 0 \\ 1 & -\frac{1}{3} & \frac{1}{2} \\ 1 & -\frac{1}{3} & -\frac{1}{2} \end{bmatrix}}$$

The 2 × 3 basis is generated by forming Kronecker products of columns from $\mathbf{K}_H^{(2)}$ and $\mathbf{K}_H^{(3)}$ as specified by the symbolic basis vectors shown below each column:

$$\mathbf{K}_H^{(2,3)} = \underset{(00) \quad (10) \quad (01) \quad (02) \quad (11) \quad (12)}{\begin{bmatrix} 1 & \frac{1}{2} & \frac{2}{3} & 0 & \frac{1}{3} & 0 \\ 1 & \frac{1}{2} & -\frac{1}{3} & \frac{1}{2} & -\frac{1}{6} & \frac{1}{4} \\ 1 & -\frac{1}{2} & -\frac{1}{3} & -\frac{1}{2} & -\frac{1}{6} & -\frac{1}{4} \\ 1 & -\frac{1}{2} & \frac{2}{3} & 0 & -\frac{1}{3} & 0 \\ 1 & -\frac{1}{2} & -\frac{1}{3} & \frac{1}{2} & \frac{1}{6} & -\frac{1}{4} \\ 1 & -\frac{1}{2} & -\frac{1}{3} & -\frac{1}{2} & \frac{1}{6} & \frac{1}{4} \end{bmatrix}}$$

Summing squares in each column of $\mathbf{K}_H^{(2,3)}$, we obtain the diagonal matrix

$$[6, \tfrac{3}{2}, 3, 1, \tfrac{1}{3}, \tfrac{1}{4}]$$

of which the reciprocal square root is

$$[.40825, .81650, 1, 1.73205, 2]$$

Thus, we obtain from (5.3-22) the orthogonal estimates for $r = 3$.

$$\mathbf{U}_H^{(2,3)} = \begin{bmatrix} 29.69847 & 46.66902 & (00) \\ -4.24264 & -5.65685 & (10) \\ 0 & -1.5 & (01) \\ -6.92820 & 6.06218 & (02) \\ -6.0 & -\ .5 & (11) \\ 10.39227 & -2.59806 & (12) \end{bmatrix}$$

Table 5.3-3 MEAN RESPONSES OF SUBJECTS CLASSIFIED BY POPULATION AND DRUG

Population	Drug	Subclass	Mean response score $y_{\cdot}^{(1)}$	$y_{\cdot}^{(2)}$
	$B(1)$	11	4	9
$A(1)$	$B(2)$	12	8	11
	$B(3)$	13	6	9
	$B(1)$	21	10	12
$A(2)$	$B(2)$	22	2	15
	$B(3)$	23	12	10

Each row of **U** is indexed by the SBV from which it arises, as shown in Table 5.3-4. These indices determine the pooling of squares and products for the blockwise analysis. As previously shown, the within-groups sum of squares and products is obtained by subtraction.

The largest-root statistic and the quantities r, s, and t needed for the multivariate tests with F_0 in Table 5.3-4 are as follows:

Effect	λ_1	r	s	t
A	.6273	2	1	11
B	1.6540	1	2	11
AB	1.8061	1	2	11

The interpretation of Table 5.3-4 is straightforward. The multivariate test gives clear evidence of interaction, shown by the univariate tests to be confined entirely to variable 1. Thus, the tests of main-class effects in this variable are confounded and are not interpretable. Variable 2, which shows no evidence of interaction, has significant effects both with respect to clinical populations (A) and drugs (B). The nature of the interactive effect in variable 1 and the main-class effects in variable 2 are discussed in connection with estimation in Example 5.3-3.

b Proportional subclass numbers The condition for an orthogonal analysis of variance of a crossed design can be generalized to include the case of *proportional subclass numbers*. By proportional is meant that the subclass numbers are functions

Table 5.3-4 UNIVARIATE AND MULTIVARIATE ANALYSIS OF VARIANCE OF THE CLINICAL POPULATION × DRUG DATA

			SSP (symmetric)		Univariate		Multivariate	
Source	SBV	df	$y^{(1)}$	$y^{(2)}$	F	p	F_0	p
Constant	0,0	1	882					
			1,386	2,178				
A effects	1,0	1	18		2.04	.18	3.45	.07
			24	32	7.11	.02		
B effects	0,1	2	48		2.72	.11	18.19	<.05
	0,2		−42	39	4.33	.04		
AB interaction	1,1	2	144		8.15	.006	19.87	<.05
	1,2		−24	7	.78	.48		
Group means		6	1,092					
			1,344	2,256				
Within groups		12	106					
			23	54				
Total		18	1,108					
			1,367	2,310				

of the main-class numbers and total N as follows:

		B				
		1	2	$\cdots$	b	
	1	$N_1.N._1/N$	$N_1.N._2/N$	$\cdots$	$N_1.N._b/N$	$N_1.$
	2	$N_2.N._1/N$	$N_2.N._2/N$	$\cdots$	$N_2.N._b/N$	$N_2.$
A	$\cdots$	$\cdots$	$\cdots$	$\cdots$	$\cdots$	$\cdots$
	a	$N_a.N._1/N$	$N_a.N._2/N$	$\cdots$	$N_a.N._b/N$	$N_a.$
		$N._1$	$N._2$	$\cdots$	$N._b$	N

Observe in this case that the diagonal matrix of subclass numbers, say $\mathbf{D}_{ab}$, is $1/N$ times the Kronecker product of the matrices of main-class numbers; i.e.,

$$\mathbf{D}_{ab} = \frac{1}{N}\mathbf{D}_a \times \mathbf{D}_b$$

Now suppose basis matrices for the A and B one-way designs are constructed by the method of Sec. 5.2.3b to be orthogonal in the metric $\mathbf{D}_A$ and $\mathbf{D}_B$, respectively; that is, $\mathbf{P}_H^{(a)\prime}\mathbf{D}_a\mathbf{P}_H^{(a)}$ and $\mathbf{P}_H^{(b)\prime}\mathbf{D}_b\mathbf{P}_H^{(b)}$ are diagonal matrices of size a and b, respectively. Then, according to the theorem of Sec. 5.3.3,

$$\mathbf{P}_H^{(ab)} = \mathbf{P}_H^{(a)} \times \mathbf{P}_H^{(b)}$$

is a basis for the $a \times b$ design. This basis is orthonormal with respect to $\mathbf{D}_{ab}$, for

$$\begin{aligned}\mathbf{P}_H^{(ab)\prime}\mathbf{D}_{ab}\mathbf{P}_H^{(ab)} &= \frac{1}{N}(\mathbf{P}_H^{(a)} \times \mathbf{P}_H^{(b)})'(\mathbf{D}_a \times \mathbf{D}_b)(\mathbf{P}_H^{(a)} \times \mathbf{P}_H^{(b)}) \\ &= \frac{1}{N}\mathbf{P}_H^{(a)\prime}\mathbf{D}_a\mathbf{P}_H^{(a)} \times \mathbf{P}_H^{(b)\prime}\mathbf{D}_b\mathbf{P}_H^{(b)}\end{aligned}$$

is an ab-diagonal matrix.

Thus, the parametric functions can be estimated and the orthogonal estimates calculated merely by rescaling the right member of the normal equations as in (5.3-21) with $\mathbf{D}_{ab}^{1/2}$ replacing $r^{1/2}$. Furthermore, the independence of the tests of main-class effects which is true of the orthogonal case also holds. Thus, the proportional subclass-number designs are blockwise orthogonal. This is of considerable importance because the common practice of dividing of subjects into naturally occurring strata before assigning them in equal numbers to treatments necessarily produces proportional subclass numbers. All the foregoing results generalize to higher-way designs.

c Nonorthogonal case If the subclass numbers of the crossed design are disproportionate, the general least-squares analysis in Chap. 4 must be applied without benefit of any computational shortcut. Either the pivoting or the orthogonalization method may be used. In the orthogonalization method, the basis $\mathbf{K}_{ab}$ is orthonormalized with respect to the matrix of subclass numbers **D**, preferably by the modified Gram-Schmidt procedure (Sec. 2.2.4). This procedure yields the orthonormal basis $\mathbf{K}^*_{ab}$, orthonormal with respect to **D**. At the same time the triangular matrix $\mathbf{T}_{ab}$ is formed from the inner products at each stage in the orthonormalization. The inverse of this matrix is needed in the estimation phase of the analysis (Sec. 5.3.6).

Once the basis is orthonormalized, the computations for the analysis of variance are the same as in the orthogonal case; i.e., the orthogonal estimates are computed, partitioned by subspace, and the SSP matrices computed as in Table 5.3-1. Because of the nonorthogonality in the design, however, the interpretation of the analysis-of-variance table is altered considerably. The independent interpretation of the main-class hypothesis no longer holds, and the order in which the corresponding subspaces enter the orthonormalization is not arbitrary. These complications become apparent when we examine the reparameterization implied in the orthonormalization. Recall that the rank-*ab* model for the subclass means is reparameterized as follows:

$$\begin{aligned} \boldsymbol{Y}. &= \mathbf{A}_{ab}\boldsymbol{\Xi}_{ab} + \boldsymbol{E}. = \mathbf{K}_{ab}\mathbf{L}_{ab}\boldsymbol{\Xi}_{ab} + \boldsymbol{E}. \\ &= \mathbf{K}_{ab}\boldsymbol{\Theta}_{ab} + \boldsymbol{E}. \end{aligned} \tag{5.3-25}$$

(As previously, we assume $\boldsymbol{E}.$ to be distributed multinormally with mean **O** and covariance matrix $\mathbf{D}^{-1} \times \boldsymbol{\Sigma}$.)

The effect of the orthonormalization is to introduce the identity factor

$$(\mathbf{T}_{ab}{}^{-1})'\mathbf{T}'_{ab} = \mathbf{I}_{ab}$$

in (5.3-25):

$$\begin{aligned} \boldsymbol{Y}. &= \mathbf{K}_{ab}(\mathbf{T}_{ab}{}^{-1})'\mathbf{T}'_{ab}\boldsymbol{\Theta}_{ab} + \boldsymbol{E}. = \mathbf{K}^*_{ab}\mathbf{T}'_{ab}\boldsymbol{\Theta}_{ab} + \boldsymbol{E}. \\ &= \mathbf{K}^*_{ab}\boldsymbol{\Gamma}^*_{ab} + \boldsymbol{E}. \end{aligned} \tag{5.3-26}$$

Since $\mathbf{K}^*_{ab}$ is orthonormal with respect to **D**, the least-squares estimates of the orthogonal parameters are the elements of

$$\hat{\boldsymbol{\Gamma}}^*_{ab} = \mathbf{K}^{*\prime}_{ab}\mathbf{D}\mathbf{Y}. = \mathbf{U}_{ab} \tag{5.3-27}$$

whence $\mathscr{E}(\boldsymbol{U}_{ab}) = \boldsymbol{\Gamma}^*_{ab}$ and $\mathscr{V}(\boldsymbol{U}_{ab}) = \mathbf{I}_{ab} \times \boldsymbol{\Sigma}$.

Note that, because of the triangularity of $\mathbf{T}_{ab}$, the leading columns of $\mathbf{K}^*_{ab}$ are unchanged as additional columns are brought into the orthonormalization. This implies that (5.3-25) and (5.3-26) hold for the rank $l \leq ab$ model of which the leading l columns of $\mathbf{K}_{ab}$ comprise the basis. Thus, only that part of the crossed-design model that is of interest in the analysis need be included in the orthonormalization.

The form of the orthonormal parameters in (5.3-27) differs from that of (5.3-23) in the orthogonal case, however, because $\mathbf{T}_{ab}$ is a general full-rank triangular matrix. Partitioned by subspaces, the form is, say,

$$\boldsymbol{\Gamma}^*_{ab} = \begin{bmatrix} \boldsymbol{\Gamma}^*_0 \\ \boldsymbol{\Gamma}^*_A \\ \boldsymbol{\Gamma}^*_B \\ \boldsymbol{\Gamma}^*_{AB} \end{bmatrix} = \begin{bmatrix} \mathbf{T}_{0,0} & \mathbf{T}_{0,a} & \mathbf{T}_{0,b} & \mathbf{T}_{0,ab} \\ \mathbf{O} & \mathbf{T}_{a,a} & \mathbf{T}_{a,b} & \mathbf{T}_{a,ab} \\ \mathbf{O} & \mathbf{O} & \mathbf{T}_{b,b} & \mathbf{T}_{b,ab} \\ \mathbf{O} & \mathbf{O} & \mathbf{O} & \mathbf{T}_{b,ab} \end{bmatrix} \begin{bmatrix} \boldsymbol{\Theta}_0 \\ \boldsymbol{\Theta}_A \\ \boldsymbol{\Theta}_B \\ \boldsymbol{\Theta}_{AB} \end{bmatrix} \tag{5.3-28}$$

[Diagonal submatrices in (5.3-28) are triangular. All others are general rectangular matrices.]

The blockwise structure of the parameterization in $\boldsymbol{\Theta}$ is therefore replaced by an upper-triangular structure in $\boldsymbol{\Gamma}^*$. Thus, it is apparent that the hypotheses $H_{AB}^*: \boldsymbol{\Gamma}_{AB}^* = \mathbf{O}$ and $H_B^*: \boldsymbol{\Gamma}_B^* = \mathbf{O}$ have the same implication as in the orthogonal case. Because $\mathbf{T}_{a,b}$ is in general nonnull, however, the hypothesis $H_A^*: \boldsymbol{\Gamma}_A^* = \mathbf{O}$ is interpretable as a test of equality of A effects only if $\boldsymbol{\Xi}_B = \mathbf{O}$, that is, only if the B effects are null. This is the import of the statement "main effects are not independently testable in the nonorthogonal design." Any one orthonormalization enables us to eliminate effects in one order only. To eliminate in the other order, we would have to rearrange vectors in the basis so that the B main-effect space preceded the A main-effect space. This is sometimes done (e.g., Rao [1952]), and the analysis of variance is displayed in the form shown in Table 5.3-5. The results of the two orders of elimination are not independent, and no exact probability statement can be made for the joint procedure. Thus, if it is important to hold the Type I error probability for the nonorthogonal blockwise analysis to an assigned figure, a single order for eliminating effects should be specified beforehand. The statistical tests for successive blocks are then independent, given the error estimate, and the joint probability of a Type I error can be calculated by (4.1-35). Fortunately, there is usually sufficient asymmetry of interest in the main-class effects to dictate the order of elimination. Effects that are known *a priori* to be significant are always eliminated from doubtful effects, which require a critical test. Similarly, effects that are well understood and accepted as explanatory variables should in general be eliminated from new and unfamiliar

Table 5.3-5 ALTERNATIVE ORDERS OF ELIMINATING EFFECTS IN AN $a \times b$ NONORTHOGONAL DESIGN

Constant*	
A, ignoring B	B, ignoring A
B, eliminating A	A, eliminating B
AB interaction eliminating A and B	
Group means	
Within groups	
Total	

* The constant term ("correction to the mean") is eliminated from all others and is usually omitted from the display.

sources of variation. This places on the investigator the burden of demonstrating that the new source explains variation in the dependent variable that is not already accounted for by the established variable. These principles of ordering effects in a nonorthogonal analysis are illustrated in Example 5.3-2.

The partition of squares and products in the nonorthogonal analysis may also be carried out by the pivoting method of Sec. 4.1.10b. The matrix to be pivoted is

$$\mathbf{M}_{ab} = \begin{bmatrix} \mathbf{K}'_{ab}\mathbf{D}\mathbf{K}_{ab} & \mathbf{K}'_{ab}\mathbf{D}\mathbf{Y}_{.} \\ \mathbf{Y}'_{.}\mathbf{D}\mathbf{K}_{ab} & \mathbf{Y}'_{.}\mathbf{D}\mathbf{Y}_{.} \end{bmatrix}$$

The order in which the diagonal elements of $\mathbf{K}'_{ab}\mathbf{D}\mathbf{K}_{ab}$ are chosen as pivots then determines the order of elimination. The SSP matrices for the analysis of variance are equal to the difference between residual matrices in the lower right-hand corner before and after pivoting the respective spaces of $\mathbf{K}_{ab}$.

In both the orthogonalization and pivoting methods, the computations can be shortened considerably by omitting the interaction space from the basis and obtaining the interaction sum of squares and products by subtraction. An illustration of this shortcut in connection with orthogonalization appears in Example 5.3-2.

Finally, estimation of effect contrasts presents somewhat different problems in the orthogonal and nonorthogonal cases. These problems are discussed in Sec. 5.3.5.

EXAMPLE 5.3-2 (*Analysis of a two-way design with disproportionate subclass numbers*) Data for this example have been reconstructed approximately from results of an experiment reported by E. Kahana [1968]. The purpose of the study was to test the effects of age segregation on the behavioral status of elderly psychiatric patients. With the cooperation of the staff of a large state psychiatric hospital, Kahana randomly assigned 75 suitable consecutive admissions aged 60 and older to one of three types of ward: (1) age-segregated custodial ward—composed of patients over 60 who were not infirm or incapable of self-care; (2) therapy ward—for subjects over 60, but structured with a "homelike" atmosphere designed to minimize the institutional attributes of hospitalization; (3) age-integrated custodial ward—composed of adults of all ages. After admission these subjects were classified into three broad diagnostic categories: (1) confused, (2) psychotic, and (3) alcoholic.

The behavioral status of each subject was assessed at admission and after 3 weeks in the ward. Due to death, medical transfer, accidental discharge, or unauthorized leave, 20 of the patients were lost to the study. This left the disproportionate diagnosis by ward classification shown in Table 5.3-6.

Subjects in the study were measured and rated on a number of behavioral indices before and after a 3-week period in the hospital. For present purposes, we shall limit the discussion to final scores on two objective measures of mental status adapted for geriatric research by Kahn [1960]. These measures are the Mental Status Questionnaire (MSQ) and the Face-Hand (F-H) test, scored in terms of the number of errors in 10 and 20 items, respectively. Mean error scores of the experimental groups at the end of 3 weeks are shown in Table 5.3-7.

If we assume that the loss of subjects from the study is unrelated to the effect of ward on behavioral status, we can consider Table 5.3-7 to be the outcome of a valid experimental test of ward effects. We can then test the ward effects statistically by analyzing the data as a nonorthogonal diagnosis × ward design. There is no ambiguity as to order of eliminating effects: Diagnosis is well known to reflect behavioral status, and its effect must be eliminated for a critical test of ward effects. Thus, the ordered subspaces of the model should be *constant*, *diagnosis*, *ward*, and *diagnosis* × *ward*. The corresponding degrees of freedom are 1, 2, 2, and 4, respectively, and the SBVs are (00), (10), (20), (01), (02), (11), (21), (12), and (22).

To economize computation, let us follow an earlier suggestion and obtain the interaction SSP by subtraction. We may then generate the basis for the first five symbolic basis vectors only, using, say, (5.2-21) as the one-way basis. The result, labeled by columns, is

$$\mathbf{K}_{C(5)}{}^{(3,3)} = \begin{bmatrix} 1 & \frac{2}{3} & -\frac{1}{3} & \frac{2}{3} & -\frac{1}{3} \\ 1 & \frac{2}{3} & -\frac{1}{3} & -\frac{1}{3} & \frac{2}{3} \\ 1 & \frac{2}{3} & -\frac{1}{3} & -\frac{1}{3} & -\frac{1}{3} \\ 1 & -\frac{1}{3} & \frac{2}{3} & \frac{2}{3} & -\frac{1}{3} \\ 1 & -\frac{1}{3} & \frac{2}{3} & -\frac{1}{3} & \frac{2}{3} \\ 1 & -\frac{1}{3} & \frac{2}{3} & -\frac{1}{3} & -\frac{1}{3} \\ 1 & -\frac{1}{3} & -\frac{1}{3} & \frac{2}{3} & -\frac{1}{3} \\ 1 & -\frac{1}{3} & -\frac{1}{3} & -\frac{1}{3} & \frac{2}{3} \\ 1 & -\frac{1}{3} & -\frac{1}{3} & -\frac{1}{3} & -\frac{1}{3} \end{bmatrix} \tag{5.3-29}$$

$$\begin{matrix} (00) & (10) & (20) & (01) & (02) \end{matrix}$$

Proceeding with the analysis of variance, we orthogonalize (5.3-29) in the

Table 5.3-6 NUMBER OF PATIENTS BY DIAGNOSIS AND WARD

	Ward		
Diagnosis	Age-segregated	Therapy	Age-integrated
Confused	6	8	8
Psychotic	6	6	5
Alcoholic	6	4	6

metric of the subclass numbers, [6, 8, 8, 6, 6, 5, 6, 4, 6]. The result is

$$
\mathbf{K}_{C(5)}{}^{(3,3)} = \begin{bmatrix} .13484 & .16515 & 0 & .20998 & -.00398 \\ .13484 & .16515 & 0 & -.07874 & .16661 \\ .13484 & .16515 & 0 & -.07874 & -.16363 \\ .13484 & -.11010 & .16888 & .18682 & -.01325 \\ .13484 & -.11010 & .16888 & -.10190 & .15734 \\ .13484 & -.11010 & .16888 & -.10190 & -.17290 \\ .13484 & -.11010 & .17944 & .18045 & .01722 \\ .13484 & -.11010 & .17944 & -.10827 & .18781 \\ .13484 & -.11010 & .17944 & -.10827 & -.14243 \end{bmatrix} \qquad (5.3\text{-}30)
$$
$$
\begin{matrix} (00) & (10) & (20) & (01) & (02) \end{matrix}
$$

The matrix of inner products generated in the orthogonalization, which we will require later for estimation, is

$$
\mathbf{T}_5{}^{(3,3)} = \begin{bmatrix} 7.41620 & & & & \text{(triangular)} \\ .49441 & 3.63318 & & & \\ -.17979 & -1.87164 & 2.87096 & & \\ -.04495 & -.33029 & -.06333 & 3.46352 & \\ -.04495 & .22019 & .29554 & -1.67444 & 3.02816 \end{bmatrix} \qquad (5.3\text{-}31)
$$

Premultiplying the matrix of subclass means in the body of Table 5.3-7 by $\mathbf{K}_{C(5)}{}^{(3,3)}\mathbf{D}$, we obtain the orthogonal estimates, labeled by rows:

$$
\mathbf{U}_C{}^{(3,3)} = \begin{bmatrix} 31.48511 & 36.15056 \\ 20.45589 & 31.55360 \\ -1.22839 & .19144 \\ 2.17708 & .30377 \\ 2.82222 & 7.41132 \end{bmatrix} \begin{matrix} (00) \\ (10) \\ (20) \\ (01) \\ (02) \end{matrix} \qquad (5.3\text{-}32)
$$

Table 5.3-7 MEAN ERROR SCORES BY DIAGNOSIS AND WARD AT THE END OF 3 WEEKS

Diagnosis	Ward	Mental-status questionnaire	Face-Hand test
Confused	Age-segregated	7.38	10.50
	Therapy	8.16	11.59
	Age-integrated	7.27	8.27
Psychotic	Age-segregated	2.19	1.41
	Therapy	1.97	2.50
	Age-integrated	1.08	.18
Alcoholic	Age-segregated	3.31	1.15
	Therapy	2.09	2.24
	Age-integrated	1.20	1.00

Computing the SSP matrices space by space from (5.3-32) gives the partition of squares and products for constant and main-class effects shown in Table 5.3-8. Summing these matrices and subtracting from $\mathbf{Y}'_{.}\mathbf{D}\mathbf{Y}_{.}$, we obtain the interaction SSP shown in the table.

The within-groups SSP is obtained by recovering from Kahana [1968] the error covariance matrix

$$\hat{\boldsymbol{\Sigma}} = \begin{bmatrix} 6.40 & \text{(symmetric)} \\ 3.20 & 6.32 \end{bmatrix} \tag{5.3-33}$$

and multiplying by the degrees of freedom, $55 - 9 = 46$, to obtain the error sums of squares and products.

In preparation for computing F_0 for the multivariate tests, we calculate the following quantities:

	λ_1	r	s	t
Diagnosis	3.5160	1	2	45
Ward	.1929	1	2	45
Ward × diagnosis	.0920	3	2	45

Referring to Appendix A, we find that the value of F_0 for interaction is well below the .05 level. There is no apparent differential effect of the wards on the diagnosis groups. A test for a general ward effect is therefore warranted. The .05 critical value of $F_0^{(1,2,45)}$ is 9.48. Although the value for ward effect does not reach this figure, it is close enough to suggest that we inspect the univariate tests. While there is no evidence of ward effect in the MSQ scores ($p = .38$), the univariate F for the face-hand test is at the .02 level. This result is certainly strong enough to warrant further study, particularly in view of the relatively small sample size and the short time interval spanned by the experiment. Estimation of the ward effect is carried out in Example 5.3-3.

5.3.5 Estimating Effect Contrasts and Interpreting Interactions

a Orthogonal case If the main-class model holds, estimation and interpretation of the main-class effects is justified and may be productive. If the design is orthogonal, including the case of proportional subclass numbers, these estimates are especially simple to obtain. For in this case, the result (5.2-38) generalizes to the main classes of the crossed design. That is, the estimate of any main-effect contrast is a similar contrast of the corresponding main-class means. Thus, estimation in the orthogonal case is conveniently carried out by tabulating the subclass means by the respective ways of classification and computing the marginal means. For the $a \times b$ design, the

Table 5.3-8 MULTIVARIATE ANALYSIS OF VARIANCE FOR THE 3 × 3 NONORTHOGONAL DESIGN

			SSP (symmetric)		Univariate		Multivariate	
Source	SBV	df	MSQ	F-H	F	p	F_0	p
Constant	0, 0	1	991.312					
			1,138.205	1,306.864				
Diagnosis	1, 0	2	419.952		32.81	< .01	158.22	< .01
	2, 0		645.222	995.666	78.77	< .01		
Ward	0, 1	2	13.704		.99	.38	8.68	≈ .05
	0, 2		21.578	55.020	4.35	.02		
Diagnosis	By	4	8.068		.31	.87	1.38	> .05
× ward	subtraction		−4.672	9.312	.37	.83		
Group means		9	1,433.036					
			1,800.333	2,366.862				
Within groups		46	294.400					
			147.200	290.720				
Total		55	1,727.436					
			1,947.533	2,657.582				

data take the form

$$
\begin{array}{cc|cccc|c}
 & & & & B & & \\
 & & 1 & 2 & & b & \\
\hline
 & 1 & \mathbf{y}_{\cdot 11} & \mathbf{y}_{\cdot 12} & \cdots & \mathbf{y}_{\cdot 1b} & \mathbf{y}_{\cdot 1 \cdot} \\
 & 2 & \mathbf{y}_{\cdot 21} & \mathbf{y}_{\cdot 22} & \cdots & \mathbf{y}_{\cdot 2b} & \mathbf{y}_{\cdot 2 \cdot} \\
A & \cdots & \cdots & \cdots & \cdots & \cdots & \cdots \\
 & a & \mathbf{y}_{\cdot a1} & \mathbf{y}_{\cdot a2} & \cdots & \mathbf{y}_{\cdot ab} & \mathbf{y}_{\cdot a \cdot} \\
\hline
 & & \mathbf{y}_{\cdot \cdot 1} & \mathbf{y}_{\cdot \cdot 2} & \cdots & \mathbf{y}_{\cdot \cdot b} &
\end{array}
\qquad (5.3\text{-}34)
$$

where $\mathbf{y}_{\cdot jk} = \sum_{i=1}^{N_{jk}} \mathbf{y}_{ijk}/N_{jk}$

$$\mathbf{y}_{\cdot j \cdot} = \sum_{k=1}^{b} N_{jk}\mathbf{y}_{\cdot jk}/(N_{j\cdot})$$

$$N_{j\cdot} = \sum_{k=1}^{b} N_{jk}$$

$$\mathbf{y}_{\cdot\cdot k} = \sum_{j=1}^{a} N_{jk}\mathbf{y}_{\cdot jk}/(N_{\cdot k})$$

$$N_{\cdot k} = \sum_{j=1}^{a} N_{jk}$$

Writing the marginal mean vectors as $p \times a$ and $p \times b$ matrices $\mathbf{Y}_{A\cdot}$ and $\mathbf{Y}_{B\cdot}$, respectively, we may compute the main-effect contrasts as

$$\hat{\boldsymbol{\Theta}}_A = \mathbf{C}_a'\mathbf{Y}_{A\cdot} \qquad (5.3\text{-}35)$$

and

$$\hat{\boldsymbol{\Theta}}_B = \mathbf{C}_b'\mathbf{Y}_{B\cdot} \qquad (5.3\text{-}36)$$

whence

$$\mathscr{E}(\boldsymbol{\Theta}_A) = \mathbf{C}_a'\boldsymbol{\Xi}_A \qquad (5.3\text{-}37)$$

$$\mathscr{E}(\boldsymbol{\Theta}_B) = \mathbf{C}_b'\boldsymbol{\Xi}_B \qquad (5.3\text{-}38)$$

and

$$\mathscr{V}(\boldsymbol{\Theta}_A) = \mathbf{C}_a'\mathbf{D}_A^{-1}\mathbf{C}_a \times \boldsymbol{\Sigma} \qquad (5.3\text{-}39)$$

$$\mathscr{V}(\boldsymbol{\Theta}_B) = \mathbf{C}_b'\mathbf{D}_B^{-1}\mathbf{C}_b \times \boldsymbol{\Sigma} \qquad (5.3\text{-}40)$$

In this case,

$$\mathbf{D}_A = \text{diag}[N_{1\cdot}, N_{\cdot 2}, \ldots, N_{a\cdot}]$$

and

$$\mathbf{D}_B = \text{diag}[N_{\cdot 1}, N_{\cdot 2}, \ldots, N_{\cdot b}]$$

contain the number of observations in the A and B main classes, respectively. In the case of equal subclass numbers r, these variances simplify to $(1/br)\mathbf{C}_a'\mathbf{C}_a \times \boldsymbol{\Sigma}$ and $(1/ar)\mathbf{C}_b'\mathbf{C}_b \times \boldsymbol{\Sigma}$, respectively.

For many purposes, it is sufficient merely to report the marginal means and allow the reader to compute contrasts as he chooses.

The problems of simultaneous confidence bounds and multiple comparisons

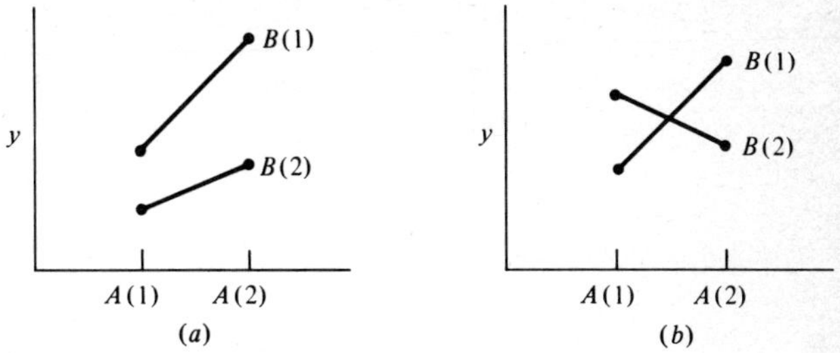

FIGURE 5.3-2
(*a*) Ordinal and (*b*) disordinal interactions.

that were discussed in Sec. 5.2.6 also apply here. Marginal means for given ways of classification are treated in the same manner as if they had arisen from one-way designs. The error estimate, however, is based on the within-groups sum of squares from the crossed design.

If the main-class model does not hold, main-class effects and interactive effects in the fixed-effect model are inextricably confounded and cannot be estimated separately. Presumably, the interaction term in the analysis of variance will then be significant and rule out estimation of main-class effects. In that case, the marginal means of the two-way design are not informative, and we must go directly to the subclass means to interpret the interactive effect. Our object is to explain the responses in particular rows or columns of the design. It is helpful in this connection to prepare a graph of the type shown in Figs. 5.3-2 and 5.3-4, which depict the "profile" of subclass means in each row or column. Interpretation of such graphs must bring to bear substantive knowledge of the phenomena to explain why certain classes in one way of classification produce different profiles than others. An example is the age × sex interaction shown in Fig. 7.2-1, which probably would be attributed to the different timing of maturation in adolescent boys and girls.

Some authors distinguish between "ordinal" interactions (Fig. 5.3-2*a*) and "disordinal" interactions (Fig. 5.3-2*b*). These terms obviously have no meaning when the treatment levels are arbitrary, for if another level is included, an ordinal interaction might become disordinal. Nevertheless, if the treatments in the experiment are the only ones in question, and if a subject population is specified, it may be meaningful to conclude from Fig. 5.3-2, for example, that treatment $B(1)$ is uniformly superior to $B(2)$, even though the degree of superiority is greater in the $A(2)$ class.

EXAMPLE 5.3-3 (*Estimation and interpretation: orthogonal case*) According to the analysis in Example 5.3-1, the outcome for variable 2 is adequately explained as an additive effect of population and drug. The comparative size of effect for population and for drug is seen by inspecting the least-squares estimates of contrasts of these

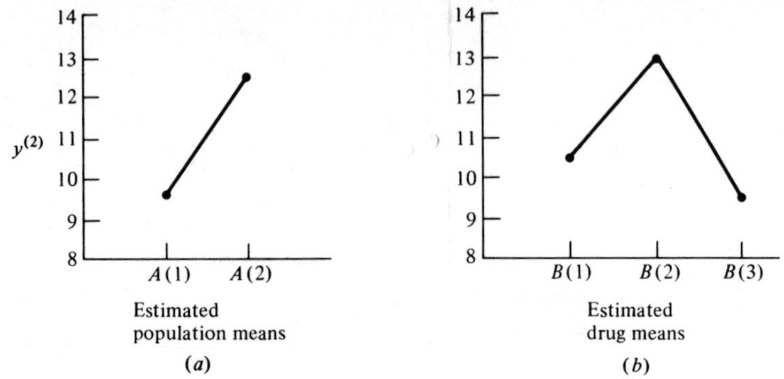

FIGURE 5.3-3
(*a*) Population and (*b*) drug effects for variable 2.

effects. Since the design is orthogonal, the contrast estimates may be obtained from the marginal means shown in Table 5.3-9. The effect of belonging to population 2 is to increase response by an estimated $2\frac{2}{3}$ units over that of population 1. Differences of similar magnitude result from the drug effects. These relationships are shown graphically in Fig. 5.3-3. With respect to variable 2, the figure shows that population 2 experiences the greater response to the drug therapies. In the drug effect, drug 2 is more effective in both populations than are drugs 1 and 3. The standard errors in Table 5.3-9 are so large in relation to differences in the marginal means, however, that the true magnitudes of the effects cannot be considered well established by these data. These standard errors have been computed from the error variance estimate based on the within-groups SSP matrix in Table 5.3-4.

With respect to variable 1, it is the interaction in Table 5.3-4 which requires interpretation. The graph of the subclass means for this variable appears in Fig. 5.3-4.

The figure shows that the interaction is due entirely to a failure of population 2 to respond to drug 2. If these were real data, results of this type would be of con-

Table 5.3-9 SUBCLASS AND MARGINAL MEANS FOR VARIABLE 2 IN TABLE 5.3-2

A classes	*B* classes 1	2	3	Mean	SE
1	9	11	9	9.6667	(.7071)
2	12	15	10	12.3333	(.7071)
Mean	10.5	13.0	9.5		
SE	(.8660)	(.8660)	(.8660)		

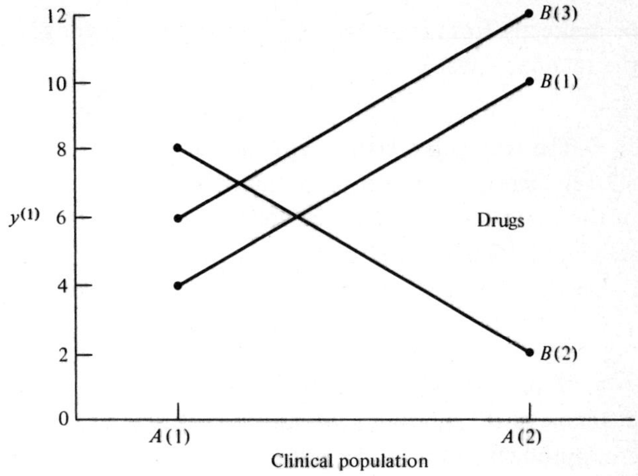

FIGURE 5.3-4
Population × drug interaction for variable 1.

siderable interest both in guiding the therapeutic use of the drugs in the two populations and, perhaps equally important, as a diagnostic aid in assigning patients to the clinical populations. Other problems of interpreting interactions are discussed in Sec. 5.4.4 in connection with factorial designs.

b Nonorthogonal case With respect to estimation, the nonorthogonal case differs from the orthogonal case in that models of different rank will give numerically different estimates of effect contrasts already in the model. It is therefore essential that we determine the rank of the model before proceeding with the least-squares solution. The nonorthogonal analysis of variance will presumably give some indication of what the rank should be. That is, the rank is the sum of the degrees of freedom of the subspaces that are retained in the model because they show evidence of accounting for significant variation in the response. For example, if a main-class model is assumed for an $a \times b$ design, the rank will be $l = 1 + (a - 1) + (b - 1) = a + b - 1$.

The least-squares solution (which will involve a matrix inversion or equivalent operations) is then essentially the same as that in Chap. 4 for a degree $g = l - 1$ polynomial model, except that the basis $\mathbf{K}_l$ corresponding to the retained subspace will take the place of the matrix $\mathbf{X}$. The least-squares estimate of the parameter matrix $\boldsymbol{\Theta}_l$ is then the solution of the normal equations

$$\mathbf{K}_l'\mathbf{D}\mathbf{K}_l\hat{\boldsymbol{\Theta}}_l = \mathbf{K}_l'\mathbf{D}\mathbf{Y}. \qquad (5.3\text{-}41)$$

where $\mathbf{K}_l$ is of order $n \times l$. Since $|\mathbf{K}_l'\mathbf{D}\mathbf{K}_l| \neq 0$, the normal equations may be solved directly by

$$\hat{\boldsymbol{\Theta}}_l = (\mathbf{K}_l'\mathbf{D}\mathbf{K}_l)^{-1}\mathbf{K}_l'\mathbf{D}\mathbf{Y}. \qquad (5.3\text{-}42)$$

or indirectly from the l rows of the matrix of orthogonal estimates corresponding to the retained subspaces:

$$\hat{\boldsymbol{\Theta}}_l = (\mathbf{T}_l^{-1})'\mathbf{U}_l = (\mathbf{T}_l^{-1})'\mathbf{K}_l^*\mathbf{D}\mathbf{Y}_. \qquad (5.3\text{-}43)$$

The triangular matrix $\mathbf{T}_l$ consists of those rows and columns of $\mathbf{T}_{ab}$ (see Sec. 5.3.5c) corresponding to the retained subspaces. The indirect method is preferable to the direct because it articulates better with the analysis of variance and is more accurate [Wampler, 1970]. A numerical example of the indirect method appears in Example 5.3-4. The covariance matrix for the estimator obtained by either method is

$$\mathscr{V}(\boldsymbol{\Theta}_l) = (\mathbf{K}_l'\mathbf{D}\mathbf{K}_l)^{-1} \times \Sigma = [(\mathbf{T}_l^{-1})'\mathbf{T}_l^{-1}] \times \Sigma \qquad (5.3\text{-}44)$$

If pivoting (Sec. 4.1.10b) is used in analysis of variance, the estimates are available in the matrix at the lth stage of pivoting where they appear in place of the cross-product terms in the upper right and lower left submatrices. That is, if $\mathbf{K}_l$ is the first $l \leq m$ columns of $\mathbf{K}_m$, the matrix before pivoting is

$$\mathbf{M}_m^{(0)} = \begin{bmatrix} \mathbf{K}_m'\mathbf{D}\mathbf{K}_m & \mathbf{K}_m'\mathbf{D}\mathbf{Y}_. \\ \mathbf{Y}_.'\mathbf{D}\mathbf{K}_m & \mathbf{Y}_.'\mathbf{D}\mathbf{Y}_. \end{bmatrix} \begin{matrix} m \\ p \end{matrix} \qquad (5.3\text{-}45)$$
$$\qquad\qquad m \qquad\quad p$$

At the lth stage, the matrix contains the quantities

$$\mathbf{M}_m^{(l)} = \begin{bmatrix} (\mathbf{K}_l'\mathbf{D}\mathbf{K}_l)^{-1} & \cdots & \hat{\boldsymbol{\Theta}}_l \\ \cdots & \cdots & \cdots \\ -\hat{\boldsymbol{\Theta}}_l' & \cdots & \mathbf{Y}_.'[\mathbf{D} - \mathbf{D}\mathbf{K}_l(\mathbf{K}_l'\mathbf{D}\mathbf{K}_l)^{-1}\mathbf{K}_l'\mathbf{D}]\mathbf{Y}_. \end{bmatrix} \begin{matrix} l \\ m-l \\ p \end{matrix} \qquad (5.3\text{-}46)$$
$$\qquad l \qquad m-l \qquad\qquad p$$

Note that, if l is the rank of the main-class model, the residual matrix in the lower right corner of $M_m^{(l)}$ is the SSP for interaction. This is the shortcut method for computing interactions in connection with pivoting mentioned in Sec. 5.3.4c.

Whichever method is used to compute the estimates, it is important to understand that the type of contrast estimated depends upon the type of one-way basis matrices from which the basis for the crossed design was generated. The relationships between bases and contrasts obtained in Sec. 5.2 are summarized for the convenience of the reader in Table 5.3-10. The quantity n in Table 5.3-10 refers to the number of classes in a given way of classification.

Estimation based on the different types of contrasts is, of course, equivalent in the sense that one type of estimate can be obtained from another by linear operations. In much of the analysis-of-variance literature, deviation contrasts are used exclusively. But, as we have seen, orthogonal contrasts are convenient when the design is orthogonal. When it is nonorthogonal, simple contrasts are perhaps the most convenient. Simple contrasts may be represented graphically as points on a line (see Fig. 5.3-5), with the contrast of the nth class with itself (zero by definition) as the origin. Also, estimated differences between any two other classes can be obtained simply as the difference of the corresponding simple contrasts.

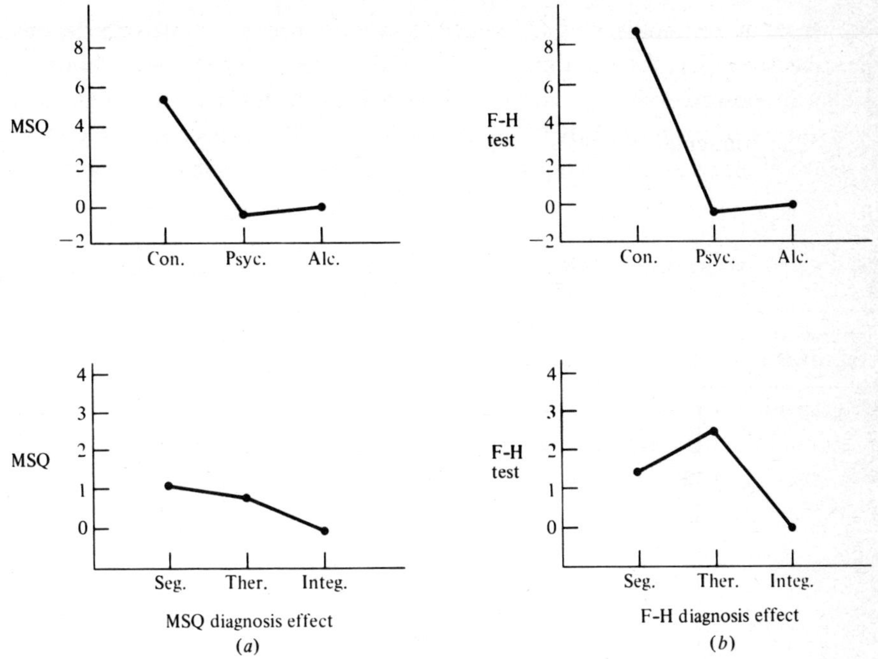

FIGURE 5.3-5
Effect of diagnosis (Confused, Psychotic, Alcoholic) and ward (Age segregated, Therapy, Age integrated) on errors in the Mental Status Questionnaire and the Face-Hand test.

Persons who are accustomed to interpreting results from orthogonal designs, however, may find the arbitrary origin of the simple contrasts disturbing and may prefer to think of the marginal means as the effect estimates. Their needs can be met in the nonorthogonal case by computing from the model the least-squares estimates of the subclass means, and averaging these estimates by rows and columns to obtain best estimates of the marginal means. That is, if $\hat{\boldsymbol{\Theta}}_l$ is the matrix of least-squares estimates obtained under the rank-l model, the best estimate of the matrix of subclass means is

$$\hat{\mathbf{Y}}. = \mathbf{K}_l\hat{\boldsymbol{\Theta}}_l \qquad (5.3\text{-}47)$$

The covariance matrix for this estimator is

$$\mathscr{V}(\hat{\mathbf{Y}}.) = \mathbf{K}_l(\mathbf{K}_l'\mathbf{D}\mathbf{K}_l)^{-1}\mathbf{K}_l' \times \boldsymbol{\Sigma} \qquad (5.3\text{-}48)$$

The estimated marginal means may be calculated from the elements of $\hat{\mathbf{Y}}.$ in a two-way array such as (5.3-34) by obtaining the unweighted arithmetic average for rows and columns. With respect to the treatment way of classification, these averages are called the *adjusted treatment means* [Anderson and Bancroft, 1952, page 298].

If the model holds, (5.3-47) is actually a more precise estimate of the means of the subclass population than are the observed subclass means. Note, however, that unlike the observed subclass means, the estimated means are correlated because of the presence of the term $\mathbf{K}_l(\mathbf{K}_l'\mathbf{D}\mathbf{K}_l)^{-1}\mathbf{K}_l'$ in (5.3-48). If it is necessary to compute the variance of marginal means reproduced from the estimated subclass means, the effect

Table 5.3-10 SOME BASES AND CORRESPONDING CONTRASTS USED TO REPARAMETERIZE DESIGN MODELS

Type of contrast	Basis (columns)	Contrasts (rows)
1 Simple*	$\begin{bmatrix} \frac{n-1}{n} & -\frac{1}{n} & \cdots & -\frac{1}{n} \\ -\frac{1}{n} & \frac{n-1}{n} & \cdots & -\frac{1}{n} \\ \cdots & \cdots & \cdots & \cdots \\ -\frac{1}{n} & -\frac{1}{n} & \cdots & \frac{n-1}{n} \\ -\frac{1}{n} & -\frac{1}{n} & \cdots & -\frac{1}{n} \end{bmatrix}$	$\begin{bmatrix} 1 & 0 & \cdots & 0 & -1 \\ 0 & 1 & \cdots & 0 & -1 \\ \cdots & \cdots & \cdots & \cdots & \cdots \\ 0 & 0 & \cdots & 1 & -1 \end{bmatrix}$
2 Deviation†	$\begin{bmatrix} 1 & 0 & \cdots & 0 \\ 0 & 1 & \cdots & 0 \\ \cdots & \cdots & \cdots & \cdots \\ 0 & 0 & \cdots & 1 \\ -1 & -1 & \cdots & -1 \end{bmatrix}$	$\begin{bmatrix} \frac{n-1}{n} & -\frac{1}{n} & \cdots & -\frac{1}{n} & -\frac{1}{n} \\ -\frac{1}{n} & \frac{n-1}{n} & \cdots & -\frac{1}{n} & -\frac{1}{n} \\ \cdots & \cdots & \cdots & \cdots & \cdots \\ -\frac{1}{n} & -\frac{1}{n} & \cdots & \frac{n-1}{n} & -\frac{1}{n} \end{bmatrix}$
3 Helmert	$\begin{bmatrix} \frac{n-1}{n} & 0 & \cdots & 0 \\ -\frac{1}{n} & \frac{n-2}{n-1} & \cdots & 0 \\ \cdots & \cdots & \cdots & \cdots \\ -\frac{1}{n} & -\frac{1}{n-1} & \cdots & \frac{1}{2} \\ -\frac{1}{n} & -\frac{1}{n-1} & \cdots & -\frac{1}{2} \end{bmatrix}$	$\begin{bmatrix} 1 & -\frac{1}{n-1} & \cdots & -\frac{1}{n-1} & -\frac{1}{n-1} \\ 0 & 1 & \cdots & -\frac{1}{n-2} & -\frac{1}{n-2} \\ \cdots & \cdots & \cdots & \cdots & \cdots \\ 0 & 0 & \cdots & 1 & -1 \end{bmatrix}$
4 Orthogonal polynomial	See Appendix B	Same as basis

* Contrasts with nth class. For contrast with any other class, exchange last row in basis with row of given class.

† Deviation contrasts for the first $n - 1$ classes; the deviation contrast for the last class is equal to the negative of the sum of the other contrasts.

of this term must be taken into account. Example 5.3-4 illustrates the calculation of estimated means.

Provided the design is not grossly nonorthogonal, quick and reasonably accurate unbiased estimates of the main-class means can be obtained merely by computing unweighted marginal means from the *observed* subclass means. An approximate analysis of variance for nonorthogonal designs based on these estimates is available in the so-called *method of unweighted means* [Anderson and Bancroft, 1952, page 279]. When computing equipment is not available, this method provides, for the nonorthogonal case, a practical analysis which can be carried out by hand methods, at least in the univariate data.

EXAMPLE 5.3-4 (*Estimation and interpretation: nonorthogonal case*) Assuming a rank-5 main-class model for the data of Example 5.3-2, we may compute the estimated effects from the orthogonal estimates (5.3-32) using (5.3-43). The result is presented in Table 5.3-11. Standard errors in this table were obtained from

$$\mathrm{SE} = \mathrm{diag}^{1/2}\{[(\mathbf{T}_l^{-1})'\mathbf{T}_l^{-1}] \times \hat{\Sigma}\}$$

where $\mathbf{T}_l$ is (5.3-31) and $\hat{\Sigma}$ is (5.3-33). In these calculations,

$$\mathbf{T}_l^{-1} = \begin{bmatrix} .134840 & & & & \text{(triangular)} \\ -.018349 & .275241 & & & \\ -.020406 & .179435 & .348316 & & \\ -.003873 & .029528 & .006369 & .288724 & \\ .003466 & -.021199 & -.030473 & .159654 & .330238 \end{bmatrix} \tag{5.3-49}$$

The diagonal elements of $(\mathbf{K}_l'\mathbf{D}\mathbf{K}_l)^{-1} = (\mathbf{T}^{-1})'\mathbf{T}^{-1}$ are just the sums of squares of elements in the respective columns of (5.3-49). In this case,

$$\mathrm{diag}[(\mathbf{K}_l'\mathbf{D}\mathbf{K}_l)^{-1}] = [.018544, .109276, .122293, .108850, .109057] \tag{5.3-50}$$

Table 5.3-11 ESTIMATED EFFECTS FOR THE DESIGN IN EXAMPLE 5.3-4

Effect	Estimate (SE) MSQ	Estimate (SE) F-H test
Constant	3.8846 (.3445)	4.3219 (.3423)
Diagnosis contrast		
Confused-alcoholic	5.4143 (.8363)	8.5711 (.8310)
Psychotic-alcoholic	−.5000 (.8847)	−.1572 (.8791)
Ward contrast		
Age segregated-age integrated	1.0792 (.8347)	1.2710 (.8294)
Therapy-age integrated	.9320 (.8354)	2.4475 (.8302)

Multiplying elements in (5.3-50) by each diagonal element in (5.3-33) and taking the square root, we obtain the SE in Table 5.3-11 [discrepancies are due to rounding in (5.3-49)].

It is apparent in Table 5.3-11 that the diagnosis effect in both variables is due almost entirely to the difference between the confused group and the others. The much smaller ward effect, on the other hand, is confined primarily to the face-hand test and is largest between the therapy and age-integrated wards.

The same information is conveyed by the estimated marginal means shown in Table 5.3-12. The subclass means in this table were obtained by applying (5.3-47) to the estimates in Table 5.3-11. The reader may verify that the marginal means yield the same plots as those in Fig. 5.3-5, except for a translation of the origin. Although the ward effect is small relative to the diagnosis effect, it appears to be significant and clearly favors the age-integrated treatment. Apparently the greater social and cognitive stimulation of the integrated ward leads to some improvement in mental status [Kahana, 1968].

EXAMPLE 5.3-5 (*Confidence bounds on effect contrasts*) Confidence bounds for the two diagnosis contrasts in Example 5.3-4 will serve to illustrate the Roy bounds for multivariate contrasts. For this purpose, we specialize **c** and **a** in (5.2-52), or $\mathbf{C}_B$ and **a** in (5.2-53), to vectors containing one unit element and the remaining elements zero. The unit element is positioned to pick up one contrast and one variable. In this way we obtain bounds on the four diagnosis contrasts in Table 5.3-11. Applying (5.2-53) then consists simply of multiplying the SE in Table 5.3-11 by the quantity $\sqrt{n_e r F_{0,\alpha}{}^{(r,s,t)}/t} = \sqrt{46 \times 9.48/45} = 3.11$. The values of r, s, and t in this quantity are given in Example 5.3-2 in connection with the analysis of variance, and $F_{0,.05}{}^{(1,2,45)} = 9.48$ is read from Appendix A. The simultaneous bounds for the

Table 5.3-12 SUBCLASS AND MARGINAL MEANS ESTIMATED BY THE RANK-5 MAIN-CLASS MODEL

	Ward							
	Age segregated		Therapy		Age integrated		Mean	
Diagnosis	MSQ	F-H	MSQ	F-H	MSQ	F-H	MSQ	F-H
Confused	8.07	10.12	7.92	11.30	6.99	8.85	7.66	10.09
Psychotic	2.16	1.39	2.01	2.57	1.08	.12	1.75	1.36
Alcoholic	2.66	1.55	2.51	2.73	1.58	.28	2.25	1.52
Mean	4.29	4.35	4.15	5.53	3.21	3.08		

two contrasts and two variables are therefore

$$\pm 3.11(.8363) = \pm 2.60 \qquad \pm 3.11(.8310) = 2.58$$

$$\pm 3.11(.8847) = \pm 2.75 \qquad \pm 3.11(.8791) = 2.73$$

Only the large effect due to the confused subjects is detected by this criterion.

Exercise 5.3-1 Table 5.3-13 contains mean semantic differential ratings of filmed psychotherapy sessions as reported by Jones [1961]. Student therapists were classified in three levels of authoritarianism as measured by the California *F* scale. They were then randomly assigned to one of four groups to view a film of a patient in therapy. After the viewing, the students rated the patient in the film on each of six semantic-differential scales. Subclass means for four of these scales are shown in Table 5.3-13. The within-group covariance matrix appears in Table 5.3-14. Analyze and discuss these data (see Jones [1966]).

Table 5.3-13 GROUP MEANS FOR THE SEMANTIC DIFFERENTIAL RATINGS

Experimental groups			Semantic-differential mean ratings			
Rater authoritarianism	Patient	N_j	Friendly-hostile	Strong-weak	Active-passive	Sincere-deceitful
High	*A*	5	1.8	2.4	−2.4	3.6
	B	5	1.8	4.2	1.2	0
	C	5	1.2	6.6	5.4	2.4
	D	5	6.6	5.4	.6	1.8
Medium	*A*	5	1.8	−.6	−7.2	−5.4
	B	5	−4.8	4.2	1.2	−3.6
	C	5	−3.6	7.2	4.8	−3.6
	D	5	5.4	4.2	2.4	−.6
Low	*A*	5	1.8	0	−4.2	−2.4
	B	5	−5.4	3.6	1.2	−2.4
	C	5	−1.2	6.0	6.0	−4.2
	D	5	7.2	6.6	4.2	−2.4

Table 5.3-14 WITHIN-GROUP COVARIANCE MATRIX FOR SEMANTIC-DIFFERENTIAL RATINGS ($n_e = 48$)

Rating	1	2	3	4
1 Friendly-hostile	23.02			
2 Strong-weak	5.85	11.92		
3 Active-passive	.60	3.93	17.92	
4 Sincere-deceitful	4.23	5.24	3.52	13.80

Exercise 5.3-2 Analyze the data of Example 5.3-2 by the pivoting method.

Exercise 5.3-3 Use a design model to analyze the data of Exercise 4.1-3. Construct the basis for the 4 × 4 design from the order-4 orthogonal polynomials in Appendix B. Check that the analysis of variance and the fitted coefficients agree with those obtained previously by the polynomial regression model.

Exercise 5.3-4 Data in Tables 5.3-15 and 5.3-16 are taken from a study by Hudson [1971] of outcomes of reading instruction by means of the Edison Responsive Environment Typewriter ("talking typewriter"), developed by Moore and Kobler [Moore, 1963], versus a comparable amount of conventional

Table 5.3-15 MEAN SCORES FOR SUBJECTS RANDOMLY ASSIGNED TO READING INSTRUCTIONAL METHODS AND CROSS-CLASSIFIED BY TYPE OF SOCIAL SERVICE AND BY SEX

Experimental groups				Outcome measures		
Instructional method	Social service	Sex	*N*	Binet IQ	MRRT	FFI
Talking typewriter	Intensive	M	20	89.60	24.10	4.77
		F	14	90.36	30.21	4.62
	Regular	M	20	89.00	19.65	4.63
		F	14	94.14	25.57	4.36
Conventional	Intensive	M	14	87.63	20.57	4.31
		F	20	83.50	21.25	4.41
	Regular	M	13	85.00	19.00	4.15
		F	21	89.10	20.76	4.36

Table 5.3-16 WITHIN-GROUP STANDARD DEVIATIONS AND CORRELATIONS FOR READING-METHODS STUDY

		Correlations		
Outcome measure	Standard deviation	Binet IQ	MRRT	FFI
Binet IQ	10.431	1.0	(symmetric)	
MRRT	7.353	.3171	1.0	
FFI	.7152	.0480	.1148	1.0

reading instruction. Subjects were preschool children from families who were receiving public assistance in Cook County, Illinois. Subjects were randomly assigned to the talking typewriter and conventional instructional groups. The families of the subjects had also been assigned nonrandomly to intensive or regular casework service, and this classification as well as sex of subject is included in the design. Outcome measures included, among others, the Stanford Binet IQ, Metropolitan Reading Readiness Test (MMRT), and the Family Functioning Instrument (FFI), a rating of the quality of the family environment.

Analyze the data of Table 5.3-15 and discuss the effects of instructional methods and the other ways of classification in the design. (These data are also used in Example 5.5-1.)

5.4 APPLICATIONS OF CROSSED DESIGNS

Many of the experimental designs developed for agricultural and biological research are directly applicable to behavioral investigation. In addition to the simple randomized design discussed in Sec. 5.2, these include (1) randomized block designs, (2) latin squares and crossover designs, (3) incomplete block designs, (4) factorial designs, (5) fractional and block confounded factorials, and (6) repeated-measures designs. All these are basically crossed designs. Excellent texts discussing their behavioral applications are now available and should be consulted for a detailed treatment of the standard univariate analysis appropriate to each [Winer, 1970; Kirk, 1968]. For more general applications, Cochran and Cox [1957] remains perhaps the best source. The present treatment will concentrate on methods of analysis based on the scheme introduced in Sec. 5.3 for generating bases for crossed-design models. The treatment will include the standard methods, but also cover the irregular and nonstandard cases likely to occur in behavioral studies outside the laboratory setting.

The six classes of crossed designs listed above may be further classified according to the purpose they serve in empirical investigations. Designs of types 1, 2, and 3 are employed to control error due to individual differences by the stratagem of "blocking"—that is, by making the treatment comparisons within groups or "blocks" of the material that have been selected to be as homogeneous as possible with respect to some criterion. (When the criterion is a measured quantity, the technique of analysis of covariance, discussed in Sec. 5.5, may serve as an alternative to blocking.) Randomized block designs are called *complete* if all treatments occur in each block. If not, they are called *incomplete*. Balanced and partially balanced incomplete blocks are examples of incomplete randomized block designs in which the pattern of assigning treatments to blocks is so chosen that the designs are efficient and easy to analyze.

Designs 4 and 5 facilitate the investigation of the simultaneous and possibly interacting effects of many independent variables. In the factorial designs, combinations of treatments and treatment levels are constructed in such a way that the estimated effects of the treatments and their interactions are mutually uncorrelated under Gauss-Markov assumptions. This keeps the standard errors of the estimated effects from becoming excessive and makes possible independent tests of the effects in the analysis of variance. Factorial designs may also be complete or incomplete. Under conditions where high-order interactions can be assumed null, incomplete fractional factorial designs make possible the testing and estimation of main effects and low-order interactions without performing the experiment on all possible combinations of treatment conditions as required in the complete factorial designs. Block confounded factorials relieve the experimenter of the necessity of presenting all treatment combinations in the same block. These designs are especially useful in behavioral research because high-order interactions (3-factor and higher) are seldom encountered and reasonably may be assumed null in many cases.

Finally, the repeated-measures designs in class 6 focus on the estimation of change and of the effects of treatments on change. These designs are especially important in behavioral research and are discussed in some detail in Chap. 7.

Before beginning the discussion of designs 1 through 5, we note that if one has to choose between alternative designs, one needs a measure of their relative efficiency in attaining the objective of the investigation. Since the primary objective is estimation of the treatment differences, the ratio of the average variance of the estimated differences for the two designs is a reasonable measure of the relative efficiency of alternative designs. We therefore include comparisons of the efficiencies of randomized blocks relative to the simple randomized design, and of incomplete relative to complete designs in the following sections.

5.4.1 Randomized Block Designs

If there is a relevant criterion for partitioning the experimental material into homogeneous subsets or "blocks" before the treatments are assigned, it may be possible with very little additional effort to improve upon the efficiency of the simple randomized design. The experimental setup consists simply of independently and randomly partitioning the units within blocks to the treatment conditions. The identity of the blocks is retained so that, if there are a treatments and b blocks, the arrangement gives rise to an $a \times b$ randomized block design. To have the advantages of an orthogonal analysis, the investigator should assign equal numbers of units to each block and to each treatment within blocks. If he cannot keep the number of units the same in all blocks, he should at least keep the number per treatment within blocks equal so as to retain proportionality of subclass numbers. If even this is not possible, he should make every effort to keep the subclass numbers roughly of the same order of magnitude in order to preserve the robustness of the F tests.*

As an illustration of the relevance of randomized block designs in behavioral research, consider the following example from the field of education: Suppose that three alternative instructional methods are to be evaluated, and that 12 schools in a large urban system have been made available for this purpose. If the investigator chooses to proceed with a simple randomized design, he would partition the schools randomly into three groups of four schools and assign randomly one of the methods to each group. This would clearly provide an unbiased comparison of the three methods. But schools within urban systems differ greatly in levels of scholastic aptitude associated with differences in socioeconomic status among neighborhoods. As a result, variation among the four schools within the three groups might be large relative to differences in the effectiveness of the instruction methods, and the experiment would not be sensitive to these differences. A better design is one in which the schools are classified into four "blocks" of three schools corresponding, insofar as possible, to homogeneous levels of socioeconomic status. The instructional methods are then randomly assigned within these blocks, giving rise to a 3×4 orthogonal randomized block design. Provided roughly the same number of children are participating in the experiment in each school, it is quite satisfactory to analyze the outcome of the experiment using mean score of the pupils in the experiment in each school as the observation. If, as is usually the case, the achievement measure is multivariate, the statistical model for a multivariate outcome measure (consisting of, say, p achievement mean scores) for the school assigned to the jth method in the kth block is

$$\underset{p\times 1}{\mathbf{y}_{jk}} = \boldsymbol{\mu} + \boldsymbol{\alpha}_j + \boldsymbol{\beta}_k + \boldsymbol{\epsilon}_{jk}$$

where $\boldsymbol{\alpha}$ is the method effect, $\boldsymbol{\beta}$ is the block effect, and $\boldsymbol{\epsilon}$ is a random error assumed distributed $N(\mathbf{0},\boldsymbol{\Sigma})$. Method $\times$ block interaction is assumed null in this model. Given this model for the simplest possible two-way crossed design without replication, the reader may readily verify that a general solution for an orthogonal crossed design applied to an unreplicated randomized block design with, say, a treatments and b blocks, gives the following estimates and analysis of variance.

* This allocation of the material is appropriate when the experimenter's interest in the alternative treatments is symmetric. If one of the treatments is a control (e.g., the existing program), however, the number of units in each group might be chosen to minimize the average variance of estimated differences between the control and the remaining $n - 1$ treatments. Since the variances of these differences are

$$\mathscr{V}(y_{\cdot c} - y_{\cdot j}) = \left(\frac{1}{N_c} + \frac{1}{N_j}\right)\sigma^2$$

the average variance is minimized by setting

$$N_c = N_j(n - 1)^{1/2}$$

(See Finney [1960, page 12].)

The estimated *deviation* contrasts among methods and blocks are

$$\hat{\boldsymbol{\alpha}}_j^{(0)} = \mathbf{y}_{j\cdot} - \mathbf{y}_{\cdot\cdot} \qquad (5.4\text{-}1)$$

$$\hat{\boldsymbol{\beta}}_k^{(0)} = \mathbf{y}_{\cdot k} - \mathbf{y}_{\cdot\cdot} \qquad (5.4\text{-}2)$$

where $\mathbf{y}_{j\cdot}$ and $\mathbf{y}_{\cdot k}$ are the row and column vector means, respectively, and $\mathbf{y}_{\cdot\cdot}$ is the vector grand mean. The expected value of the mean treatment difference is, say,

$$\mathscr{E}(\mathbf{y}_{j\cdot} - \mathbf{y}_{j'\cdot}) = \boldsymbol{\alpha}_j^{(0)} - \boldsymbol{\alpha}_{j'}^{(0)} = (\boldsymbol{\alpha}_j - \boldsymbol{\alpha}_\cdot) - (\boldsymbol{\alpha}_{j'} - \boldsymbol{\alpha}_\cdot) = \boldsymbol{\alpha}_j - \boldsymbol{\alpha}_{j'}$$

and the variance-covariance matrix of the difference is

$$\mathscr{V}(\mathbf{y}_{j\cdot} - \mathbf{y}_{j'\cdot}) = \frac{2}{b}\boldsymbol{\Sigma} \qquad (5.4\text{-}3)$$

Diagonal elements of this matrix are, of course, the variances of mean differences for the respective outcome measures.

The multivariate analysis of variance associated with this design is shown in Table 5.4-1. Of primary interest in this analysis are the tests of significance of treatment differences. As in Sec. 4.2.4, these tests include the largest-root, trace, and likelihood-ratio tests based on the roots of $|\text{SSA} - \lambda\text{SSE}| = 0$, for $p \leq (a-1)(b-1)$. In particular, the largest-root statistic in the form of the generalized F is $F_0 = (t/r)\lambda_1$, with $r = |a - p - 1| + 1$, $s = \min(a - 1, p)$, and $t = (a-1)(b-1) - p + 1$. Similarly, the hth diagonal elements of SSA and SSE provide the univariate F statistics, $F(h) = [\text{ssa}(h)/(a-1)]/[\text{sse}(h)/(a-1)(b-1)]$, on $a - 1$ and $(a-1)(b-1)$ degrees of freedom, for response variable h. If required, the block differences can be tested in an analogous manner using SSB and SSE, although in most applications the significance of block differences would be assumed *a priori* and not tested.

If the hypothesis of no treatment differences is rejected, estimation of treatment contrasts using (5.4-1) may be productive. Univariate and multivariate confidence bounds can then be constructed using (5.2-52) with $\boldsymbol{\Sigma}$ estimated by

$$\hat{\boldsymbol{\Sigma}} = \text{SSE}/(a-1)(b-1)$$

Diagonal elements of $\hat{\boldsymbol{\Sigma}}$ provide estimates of the error variance of the separate variables (see Example 5.4-1).

Further gains in efficiency of the evaluation study might be achieved through a still more rigorous blocking strategy. Suppose, for example, that three classrooms suitable for the study are available in each of the 12 schools. For present purposes, let us assume that the classrooms within schools are not "tracked"; that is, they do not correspond to a sorting of the children into high, middle, and low reading-readiness levels (this case will be considered in Sec. 5.4.2). The assignment of children to classrooms does not have to be strictly random, although random assignment will increase within-block homogeneity; it is only necessary that the three alternative reading programs be randomly assigned within schools. Then the randomized block

Table 5.4-1 MULTIVARIATE ANALYSIS OF VARIANCE FOR THE RANDOMIZED BLOCK DESIGN

Source	df	SSP ($p \times p$)	$\mathscr{E}$(SSP)
Constant	1	$\text{SSM} = n\mathbf{y}_{..}\mathbf{y}'_{..}$	$\boldsymbol{\Sigma} + n(\boldsymbol{\mu} + \boldsymbol{\alpha}_{.} + \boldsymbol{\beta}_{.})(\boldsymbol{\mu} + \boldsymbol{\alpha}_{.} + \boldsymbol{\beta}_{.})'$
Blocks	$b - 1$	$\text{SSB} = a \sum_{k=1}^{b} \mathbf{y}_{.k}\mathbf{y}'_{.k} - \text{SSM}$	$(b - 1)\boldsymbol{\Sigma} + a \sum_{k=1}^{b} (\boldsymbol{\beta}_k - \boldsymbol{\beta}_{.})(\boldsymbol{\beta}_k - \boldsymbol{\beta}_{.})'$
Treatments	$a - 1$	$\text{SSA} = b \sum_{j=1}^{a} \mathbf{y}_{j.}\mathbf{y}'_{j.} - \text{SSM}$	$(a - 1)\boldsymbol{\Sigma} + b \sum_{j=1}^{a} (\boldsymbol{\alpha}_j - \boldsymbol{\alpha}_{.})(\boldsymbol{\alpha}_j - \boldsymbol{\alpha}_{.})'$
Residual	$(a - 1)(b - 1)$	$\text{SSE} = \text{SST} - \text{SSA} - \text{SSB} - \text{SSM}$	$(a - 1)(b - 1)\boldsymbol{\Sigma}$
Total	$n = ab$	$\text{SST} = \sum_{j=1}^{a} \sum_{k=1}^{b} \mathbf{y}_{jk}\mathbf{y}'_{jk}$	

design will consist of 12 blocks (schools) crossed by three treatments (reading methods). This design would exclude all between-school variation from the error term.

With respect to the statistical model, this design differs slightly from the preceding because the schools should be considered a sample from a population of schools rather than the fixed categories represented by the occupational and ethnic groups. The model will therefore have two random components, $\boldsymbol{\beta}$ and $\boldsymbol{\epsilon}$, and thus constitute a so-called *mixed model.* In the more complex situation described in Chap. 7, the mixed model requires a specialized statistical treatment, but in the case of the randomized block design without replication, the analysis is formally identical to the case of fixed blocks. When the blocks are random, there is the possibility of estimating the variance-covariance matrix for block effects. This matrix is not directly involved in the test of treatment effects, but it may be of interest in a survey of sources of variation influencing achievement. Estimation procedures for this purpose are discussed in Sec. 6.4.

A further refinement in the blocking scheme would be available if the same teacher could teach different instructional methods in different classrooms on the same or alternate days. The teacher may then serve as the block in the design, thus removing differences in teaching experience and skill from the error term (see Page [1958]; also Wiley and Bock [1967]). A design of this type is illustrated in Example 5.4-1.

Efficiency The efficiency of the simple randomized design relative to the randomized block design is the ratio of the error variance estimate, $\hat{\sigma}_{ab}^2 = \mathrm{SSAB}/(a-1) \times (b-1)$, computed from Table 5.4-1, to the corresponding estimate for a simple randomized design with the same number of observations and treatments and the same total sum of squares. Cochran and Cox [1957, page 112] show that the latter estimate is

$$\hat{\sigma}_w^2 = \frac{\mathrm{SSB} + (n_e + n_a)\mathrm{SSE}/n_e}{n_b + n_a + n_e}$$

Thus, the relative efficiency is

$$E = \frac{\hat{\sigma}_{ab}^2}{\hat{\sigma}_w^2}$$

Since the critical values of the F statistic are slightly different for the two designs, however, we may wish to express the relative efficiencies of the statistical test as

$$E' = \frac{F^{(\alpha)}_{a-1,n_e+n_b}}{F^{(\alpha)}_{a-1,n_e}} E$$

As we would expect, the efficiency of the simple randomized design relative to the randomized block design declines as the between-block mean square increases relative to the error mean square. A calculation of this efficiency appears in Example 5.4-1.

Replicated and nonorthogonal randomized block designs Up to this point we have considered only the unreplicated randomized block design (i.e., one score per subclass). If the design is replicated, a within-subclass error estimate becomes available with which to test the block × treatment interaction. It is quite possible that this test will contradict the assumption of no interaction which is implicit in the model as, for example, when a school × method interaction is introduced because a particular school is better equipped to implement one of the methods. This does not necessarily vitiate the analysis, however, for if we consider the blocks to be random, the interaction sum of squares provides an appropriate error term for the test of the treatment differences. This means that we are restricting our attention to the average performance of the methods and regarding the deviation of particular schools from that average merely as error variation which may be estimated by the interaction mean square.

On the other hand, if there is no interaction, the within-subclass and interaction sum of squares may be pooled in obtaining the error estimate. The test of treatment effect does not then depend on the fixed or random status of the blocks.

Finally, note that, if the replication is irregular or incomplete and the subclass numbers are disproportionate, it will be necessary to employ a nonorthogonal analysis of variance to analyze the data. Because block effects are always presumed to exist, they will appear first in the model and will be eliminated when testing the treatment effect. The problems of analysis in this case are essentially the same as those already discussed in connection with the nonorthogonal analysis of crossed designs in Sec. 5.3. Note that this includes the case of a single replicate of the design with missing observations for some cells. The general solution then involves a matrix of subclass numbers **D** consisting of 1 where an observation is present in the subclass and 0 where it is not. Provided the 1s and 0s are so positioned that **K′DK** remains nonsingular, the solution exists. Certain patterns of missing cells, such as occur in latin squares, balanced and partially balanced incomplete block designs, and fractional factorial designs are of special interest because they lead to structured **K′DK** matrices that have simple inverses. These designs may be solved without resort to the general solution (see Secs. 5.4.2, 5.4.3, and 5.4.5).

EXAMPLE 5.4-1 (*Randomized block comparison of a programmed and a conventional textbook*) An experimental evaluation of the programmed textbook *Analysis of Behavior* [Holland and Skinner, 1961] and a conventional textbook covering the same content [Skinner, 1953] was reported by Daniels and Murdoch [1968] (see also Bock [1966]). Students in an undergraduate general psychology course were randomly assigned to one of 24 discussion sections, each comprising from 21 to 26 students. Each of 12 graduate teaching assistants served as instructors for two of these sections. The programmed text was assigned at random to one section of each instructor, and the conventional text to the other. All students used their respective texts throughout the semester and were then tested in an objective and essay examination. Table 5.4-2 shows the section means for the objective tests measuring knowledge of specific content and understanding of concepts. The multivariate analysis of variance for these data is shown in Table 5.4-3.

The interpretation of these data is entirely straightforward. As is obvious on inspection of the table of means, the programmed text is superior to the conventional text in all blocks save one, and this superiority is confirmed in the analysis of variance. The effect contrasts (programmed-conventional) are 1.628 for content and 1.699 for concepts. The respective standard errors are .350 and .207. In practical terms the difference in favor of the programmed text is not overwhelming, amounting to only about 10 percent of the mean score for the two measures, but the experiment is so well controlled that this difference is highly significant. The design appears to have

Table 5.4-2 SECTION MEANS FOR PROGRAMMED TEXT (1) AND CONVENTIONAL TEXT (2)

		Section mean	
Instructor	Text	Content	Concepts
1	1	15.902	15.565
	2	15.938	13.550
2	1	15.793	16.304
	2	13.837	14.077
3	1	16.208	16.667
	2	14.833	14.792
4	1	18.406	17.250
	2	15.250	15.038
5	1	17.490	16.500
	2	13.931	15.056
6	1	15.738	15.143
	2	14.240	13.708
7	1	15.310	15.190
	2	14.693	14.727
8	1	16.240	16.080
	2	16.167	15.208
9	1	17.272	16.130
	2	14.775	14.100
10	1	15.943	15.636
	2	14.337	13.731
11	1	15.396	15.708
	2	15.000	14.840
12	1	16.130	17.000
	2	13.295	13.955

benefited from the random assignment of students to sections and the fact that the instructors were about equally experienced. As a result the within-treatment variation is small, and there are no apparent block effects. The efficiency for the concept measure relative to an equivalent simple randomized design, as computed from (5.4-4) through (5.4-6), favors the randomized block design,

$$\hat{\sigma}_w{}^2 = \frac{6.2033 + 12(2.8269/11)}{23} = .4221$$

$$E = \frac{.4221}{.2570} = 1.6424$$

$$E' = \frac{4.30}{4.84}\,1.6424 = 1.49$$

but the adjusted efficiency for the *content* measure is $E' = .944$, which represents a slight loss of efficiency due to blocking. Note, however, that if the subjects had not been assigned to sections at random (which would in no way invalidate the randomized block experiment) the between-instructor variation would have been greater, and blocking would undoubtedly increase efficiency with respect to both variables.

5.4.2 Latin Squares

Suppose now that the experimental material is heterogeneous in two dimensions for which there exist relevant independent blocking criteria. If the material is partitioned into *b* classes per the first criterion and *c* classes per the second, cross-classification with respect to both criteria generates *bc* blocks within which the *a* treatments might

Table 5.4-3 MULTIVARIATE ANALYSIS OF VARIANCE OF CONTENT AND CONCEPTS MEASURES FROM THE TEXTBOOK EVALUATION

		SSP (symmetric)		Univariate		Multivariate	
Source	df	Content	Concepts	F	p	F_0	p
Constant	1	2,644.5064					
		2,600.6785	2,557.5770				
Instructors	11	9.1459		1.13	.42	1.55	.16
		3.6999	6.2033	2.19	.10		
Texts	1	15.9007		21.63	.0008	30.64	.0001
		16.5989	17.3277	67.42	.0001		
Error	11	8.0859					
		2.6879	2.8269				
Total	24	2,703.2147					
		2,623.6652	2,583.9349				

be tested. The result is an $a \times b \times c$ randomized block design, possibly with b and c greater than a, which could be analyzed by the method of Sec. 5.4.1.

If it is reasonable to assume no interaction between the treatments and the blocking dimensions, however, a test of treatment effects with block effects eliminated from error may be possible with many fewer than abc treatment trials. Designs for this purpose requiring only a^2 trials when $a = b = c$ are available in the so-called *latin squares*.

Blocking dimensions in the latin-square designs are conventionally referred to as *rows* and *columns*. The design consists of assignment treatments to rows and columns under the restriction that each treatment shall appear exactly once in each row and column. With the treatments denoted by uppercase italic letters, the design can be written in the form of a *latin square*, e.g.,

		Columns 1	2	3	4
Rows	1	*A*	*B*	*C*	*D*
	2	*B*	*C*	*D*	*A*
	3	*C*	*D*	*A*	*B*
	4	*D*	*A*	*B*	*C*

(5.4-7)

Letters in the square can be rearranged in $a!\,(a-1)!$ distinct ways. In practice, one of these squares is chosen at random, and the row, column, and treatment assignments are made randomly. If a is too large to permit examination of all squares, the randomization procedure described by Fisher and Yates [1963] may be applied.

Squares in the range $a = 5$ to 8 are most commonly used. Those with $a \leq 4$ provide too few error degrees of freedom, and the changeover designs described below are preferable in these cases. Opportunities to employ squares larger than 8×8 are rare.

An industrial application of a 5×5 latin square is described in Example 5.4-2. The effect of music on production of workers in a rug-manufacturing plant was tested in a latin-square design involving five types of musical programming on five days of the week for five successive weeks. The treatment comparison was thus free of variation in productivity due to days of the week and to trend over the five-week period. The experiment could have been done in randomized blocks only if the five treatments could have been tested simultaneously in five different production units or if the experiment were extended to 25 weeks.

Analysis, orthogonal case Because rows and columns are crossed completely and each treatment occurs once in each row and column, the row, column, and treatment effects are orthogonal and their least squares estimates of effect contrasts are given by contrasts of the corresponding marginal means. The statistical model for a p-variate response to the jth treatment in the kth row and lth column is

$$\mathbf{y}_{jkl} = \boldsymbol{\mu} + \boldsymbol{\alpha}_j + \boldsymbol{\beta}_k + \boldsymbol{\gamma}_l + \boldsymbol{\epsilon}_{jkl}$$

where $\boldsymbol{\epsilon} \sim N(\mathbf{0},\boldsymbol{\Sigma})$. Note that no interactions are assumed. The estimated treatment, row, and column effects in the form of deviation contrasts are, respectively,

$$\hat{\boldsymbol{\alpha}}_j^{(0)} = \mathbf{y}_{j\cdot\cdot} - \mathbf{y}_{\cdot\cdot\cdot}$$
$$\hat{\boldsymbol{\beta}}_k^{(0)} = \mathbf{y}_{\cdot k \cdot} - \mathbf{y}_{\cdot\cdot\cdot}$$
$$\hat{\boldsymbol{\gamma}}_l^{(0)} = \mathbf{y}_{\cdot\cdot l} - \mathbf{y}_{\cdot\cdot\cdot}$$

Treatment, row, and column differences all have the same variance; e.g.,

$$\mathscr{V}(\mathbf{y}_{j\cdot\cdot} - \mathbf{y}_{j'\cdot\cdot}) = \frac{2}{a}\boldsymbol{\Sigma} \tag{5.4-8}$$

The associated p-variate analysis of variance is shown in Table 5.4-4. The quantity n_{jkl} in this table equals 1 if treatment j appears in row k and column l, and 0 otherwise. We shall refer to the n_{jkl} as *incidence* numbers.

With SSE as the error term, significance of the treatment, row, and column effects may be tested separately using any of the multivariate or univariate test criteria. Since p must be less than or equal to $(a-1)(a-2)$ for the multivariate test, the number of response variables is sharply restricted in the smaller squares.

Nonorthogonal analysis If there are unequal numbers of observations in the cells of the latin-square design, the general least-squares analysis of Secs. 5.2 and 5.3 will be required. For purposes of this analysis, the square (5.4-7), for example, would be regarded as an incomplete treatments × rows × columns design described by the formula

$$4 \times 4 \times 4$$

and the matrix of subclass numbers would take the form

$$\begin{aligned}
\mathbf{D} = \text{diag}[&N_{111}, & 0, && 0, && 0,\\
&0, & 0, && 0, && N_{124},\\
&0, & 0, && N_{133}, && 0,\\
&0, & N_{142}, && 0, && 0,\\[4pt]
&0, & N_{212}, && 0, && 0,\\
&N_{221}, & 0, && 0, && 0,\\
&0, & 0, && 0, && N_{234},\\
&0, & 0, && N_{243}, && 0,\\[4pt]
&0, & 0, && N_{313}, && 0,\\
&0, & N_{322}, && 0, && 0,\\
&N_{331}, & 0, && 0, && 0,\\
&0, & 0, && 0, && N_{344},\\[4pt]
&0, & 0, && 0, && N_{414},\\
&0, & 0, && N_{423}, && 0,\\
&0, & N_{432}, && 0, && 0,\\
&N_{441}, & 0, && 0, && 0\;]
\end{aligned}$$

Table 5.4-4 MULTIVARIATE ANALYSIS OF VARIANCE FOR AN $a \times a$ LATIN SQUARE (ONE OBSERVATION PER CELL)

Source of dispersion	df	Sums of squares and products ($p \times p$)	Expected sums of squares and products
Constant	1	$\text{SSM} = a^2\mathbf{y}_{\cdots}\mathbf{y}'_{\cdots}$	$\boldsymbol{\Sigma} + a^2(\boldsymbol{\mu} + \boldsymbol{\alpha}_. + \boldsymbol{\beta}_. + \boldsymbol{\gamma}_.)(\boldsymbol{\mu} + \boldsymbol{\alpha}_. + \boldsymbol{\beta}_. + \boldsymbol{\gamma}_.)'$
Rows	$a - 1$	$\text{SSB} = a \sum_{k=1}^{a} \mathbf{y}_{.k.}\mathbf{y}'_{.k.} - \text{SSM}$	$(a - 1)\boldsymbol{\Sigma} + a \sum_{k=1}^{a} (\boldsymbol{\beta}_k - \boldsymbol{\beta}_.)(\boldsymbol{\beta}_k - \boldsymbol{\beta}_.)'$
Columns	$a - 1$	$\text{SSC} = a \sum_{l=1}^{a} \mathbf{y}_{..l}\mathbf{y}'_{..l} - \text{SSM}$	$(a - 1)\boldsymbol{\Sigma} + a \sum_{l=1}^{a} (\boldsymbol{\gamma}_l - \boldsymbol{\gamma}_.)(\boldsymbol{\gamma}_l - \boldsymbol{\gamma}_.)'$
Treatments	$a - 1$	$\text{SSA} = a \sum_{j=1}^{a} \mathbf{y}_{j..}\mathbf{y}'_{j..} - \text{SSM}$	$(a - 1)\boldsymbol{\Sigma} + a \sum_{j=1}^{a} (\boldsymbol{\alpha}_j - \boldsymbol{\alpha}_.)(\boldsymbol{\alpha}_j - \boldsymbol{\alpha}_.)'$
Residual	$(a - 1)(a - 2)$	$\text{SSE} = \text{SST} - \text{SSA} - \text{SSB} - \text{SSC} - \text{SSM}$	$(a - 1)(a - 2)\boldsymbol{\Sigma}$
Total	$a^2 = \sum\sum\sum n_{jkl}$	$\text{SST} = \sum_{l=1}^{a} \sum_{k=1}^{a} \sum_{j=1}^{a} n_{jkl}\mathbf{y}_{jkl}\mathbf{y}'_{jkl}$	

That is, the subclasses represented in the latin square would contain possibly unequal numbers of observations N_{jkl}, and the subclasses not in the square would contain no observations.

A 64×10 basis matrix **K** for this design is then given by 10 columns of the fourfold Kronecker product of a basis matrix for the four-level one-way design. The symbolic basis vectors corresponding to these columns are shown for the general $a \times a$ square in Table 5.4-5.

At first sight, this method of calculation appears wasteful both of storage and computing time because of the large number of missing rows of the data matrix and the excessive size of the basis. However, given only the 64 elements in the diagonal matrix **D**, the computer can be instructed to bypass rows of **K** corresponding to zero elements in **D**. Thus, only a 16×10 basis matrix $\mathbf{K}_0$ need be generated explicitly. All subsequent computations then involve the nonzero elements in **D**, say $\mathbf{D}_0$. In terms of these "edited" matrices, the least-squares estimates of reparameterized effects are

$$\underset{10 \times p}{\hat{\boldsymbol{\Theta}}} = \underset{10 \times 10}{(\mathbf{K}_0'\mathbf{D}_0\mathbf{K}_0)^{-1}}\underset{10 \times 16}{\mathbf{K}_0'\mathbf{D}_0}\ \underset{16 \times p}{\mathbf{Y}.}$$

where $\mathbf{Y}.$ is the matrix of means arranged in the natural order of the j, k, l subscripts. As before,

$$\mathscr{E}(\boldsymbol{\Theta}) = \boldsymbol{\Theta} \qquad \text{and} \qquad \mathscr{V}(\boldsymbol{\Theta}) = (\mathbf{K}_0'\mathbf{D}_0\mathbf{K}_0)^{-1} \times \boldsymbol{\Sigma}$$

Similarly, the orthogonal estimates are

$$\mathbf{U} = \mathbf{S}_0{}^{-1}\mathbf{K}'\mathbf{D}\mathbf{Y}.$$

where $\mathbf{S}^{-1}$ is the inverse of the Cholesky factor of $\mathbf{K}_0'\mathbf{D}_0\mathbf{K}_0$. For purposes of the analysis of variance, the orthogonal estimates (transposed) are partitioned corresponding to the partition of degrees of freedom:

$$\mathbf{U}' = [\mathbf{U}_0', \mathbf{U}_B', \mathbf{U}_C', \mathbf{U}_A']$$

Then

$$\mathscr{E}(\boldsymbol{U}) = \mathbf{S}'\boldsymbol{\Theta}$$

where $\mathbf{S}'$ is upper triangular, and $\mathbf{S} = [\mathbf{S}_0', \mathbf{S}_B', \mathbf{S}_C', \mathbf{S}_A']$.

The nonorthogonal analysis of variance computed from the orthogonal estimates is shown in Table 5.4-5.

EXAMPLE 5.4-2 (*Music in industry*) McGeehee and Gardner [1949] studied the effect of background music on production of workers performing a complex operation in rug manufacture. Four music programs (A, B, C, and D) and one no-music program (E) were presented to the first and second shifts in the latin-square design shown in Table 5.4-6. Average hourly units of production for the first shift are shown in Table 5.4-6 beneath the letters representing the treatments. The analysis of variance

Table 5.4-5 MULTIVARIATE ANALYSIS OF VARIANCE FOR THE $a \times a$ LATIN SQUARE (NONORTHOGONAL CASE)

Source	SBV	df	SSP ($p \times p$)	$\mathscr{E}$(SSP)
Constant	0, 0, 0	1	$\text{SSM} = \mathbf{U}_0'\mathbf{U}_0$	$\boldsymbol{\Sigma} + \boldsymbol{\Theta}'\mathbf{S}_0\mathbf{S}_0'\boldsymbol{\Theta}$
Rows, eliminating constant and ignoring columns and treatments	1, 0, 0 2, 0, 0 . . . $(a-1)$, 0, 0	$a-1$	$\text{SSB} = \mathbf{U}_B'\mathbf{U}_B$	$(a-1)\boldsymbol{\Sigma} + \boldsymbol{\Theta}'\mathbf{S}_B\mathbf{S}_B'\boldsymbol{\Theta}$
Columns, eliminating constant and rows and ignoring treatments	0, 1, 0 0, 2, 0 . . . 0, $(a-1)$, 0	$a-1$	$\text{SSC} = \mathbf{U}_C'\mathbf{U}_C$	$(a-1)\boldsymbol{\Sigma} + \boldsymbol{\Theta}'\mathbf{S}_C\mathbf{S}_C'\boldsymbol{\Theta}$
Treatments, eliminating constant, rows, and columns	0, 0, 1 0, 0, 2 . . . 0, 0, $(a-1)$	$a-1$	$\text{SSA} = \mathbf{U}_A'\mathbf{U}_A$	$(a-1)\boldsymbol{\Sigma} + \boldsymbol{\Theta}'\mathbf{S}_A\mathbf{S}_A'\boldsymbol{\Theta}$
Residual		$(a-1)(a-2)$	$\text{SSR} = \text{SSG} - \text{SSA} - \text{SSB} - \text{SSC} - \text{SSM}$	$(a-1)(a-2)\boldsymbol{\Sigma}$
Between subclasses		a^2	$\text{SSG} = \sum_{j=1}^{a}\sum_{k=1}^{a}\sum_{l=1}^{a} N_{jkl}\mathbf{y}_{.jkl}\mathbf{y}_{.jkl}'$	
Within subclasses		$N - a^2$	$\text{SSW} = \text{SST} - \text{SSG}$	$(N - a^2)\boldsymbol{\Sigma}$
Total		$N = \sum\sum\sum N_{jkl}$	$\text{SST} = \sum_{l=1}^{a}\sum_{k=1}^{a}\sum_{j=1}^{a}\sum_{i=1}^{N_{jkl}} n_{jkl}\mathbf{y}_{ijkl}\mathbf{y}_{ijkl}'$	

of these data is shown in Table 5.4-7. The figures in Table 5.4-7 differ from those of McGeehee and Gardner, which appear to be in error.

There is no indication in Table 5.4-7 that the musical programming has had any effect on production. The investigators attribute this to the fact that the workers are experienced and highly stable in work expectations and in the pacing of the operation. There is, however, a significant day-of-the-week effect and a marginally significant weekly effect. The marginal means for days and weeks in Table 5.4-8 show that production is off on Mondays and that fourth-week production was unusually low.

It is perhaps of interest that in spite of the absence of program effects, a majority of workers stated in response to a questionnaire that they thought the music increased their production.

Crossover designs When comparing two, three, or four treatments, it will generally be necessary to replicate the latin square a number of times in order to obtain sufficient degrees of freedom for the error estimate. For example, if two methods of reading

Table 5.4-6 AVERAGE HOURLY PRODUCTION WITH RESPECT TO DAY, WEEK, AND TYPE OF MUSICAL PROGRAM

	Days				
Weeks	M	T	W	T	F
1	*A* 133	*B* 139	*C* 140	*D* 140	*E* 145
2	*B* 136	*C* 141	*D* 143	*E* 146	*A* 139
3	*C* 140	*A* 138	*E* 142	*B* 139	*D* 139
4	*D* 129	*E* 132	*A* 137	*C* 136	*B* 140
5	*E* 132	*D* 144	*B* 143	*A* 142	*C* 142

Table 5.4-7 ANALYSIS OF VARIANCE OF AVERAGE HOURLY PRODUCTION

Source	df	SS	F	p
Constant	1	483,581.00		
Weeks	4	30.86	3.06	.059
Days	4	44.46	4.41	.020
Programs	4	2.96	.29	.876
Residual	12	120.86		
Total	25	483,780.14	$\hat{\sigma}^2 = 10.07$	

instruction, *A* and *B*, are to be tested in four schools where the reading classes are divided into low- and high-aptitude groups, the design shown in Table 5.4-9 would serve to assess the method effect. The design requires two classrooms per school assigned at random to the columns of a 2×2 latin square. Rows of the squares correspond to the aptitude groups. Aptitude $\times$ treatment interaction is assumed null.

If variation due to school is negligible, the classification of classrooms into squares may be ignored. In this case Cochran and Cox [1957] refer to the arrangement in Table 5.4-9 as a *crossover* design (other authors use the term *changeover* [John, 1971]). A simple form of analysis results if we regard a crossover design with, say, a treatments and m squares, as an incomplete three-way design with the formula

$$a \times a \times ma$$

We then let $n_{jkl} = 1$ if the jkl subclass is occupied and 0 otherwise, and obtain the multivariate analysis of variance shown in Table 5.4-10.

Deviation contrasts of treatment effects for this design are estimated by

$$\hat{\boldsymbol{\alpha}}_j^{(0)} = \mathbf{y}_{j\cdot\cdot} - \mathbf{y}_{\cdot\cdot\cdot}$$

Differences of these estimates are unbiased estimates of the treatment-effect difference; i.e.,

$$\mathscr{E}(\mathbf{y}_{j\cdot\cdot} - \mathbf{y}_{j'\cdot\cdot}) = \boldsymbol{\alpha}_j - \boldsymbol{\alpha}_{j'}$$

and

$$\mathscr{V}(\mathbf{y}_{j\cdot\cdot} - \mathbf{y}_{j'\cdot\cdot}) = \frac{2}{ma}\boldsymbol{\Sigma}$$

$\boldsymbol{\Sigma}$ is estimated by SSE/$(ma - 2)(a - 1)$.

Table 5.4-8 MEAN HOURLY PRODUCTION FOR DAYS AND WEEKS (SE = 1.42)

Day	M	T	W	T	F
Production	134	138.8	141	140.6	141
Week	1	2	3	4	5
Production	139.4	150	139.6	134.8	140.6

Table 5.4-9 FOUR REPLICATES OF A 2×2 LATIN SQUARE

	Schools (squares) 1		2		3		4	
Aptitude group	Classrooms (columns) 1	2	3	4	5	6	7	8
High	*A*	*B*	*A*	*B*	*A*	*B*	*A*	*B*
Low	*B*	*A*	*B*	*A*	*B*	*A*	*B*	*A*

The preceding analysis assumes no row × square interaction and includes variation from this source in the error estimate. This assumption may not be justified in cases such as the above example where differences in the rigor of the aptitude grouping could introduce row × school variation. Cochran and Cox suggest eliminating this variation from the error estimate by treating the design as m replicate latin squares. That is, they regard the design as, say, squares × treatments × rows × columns, with the formula

$$m \times a \times a \times a \times a$$

Then the ma^2 degrees of freedom corresponding to nonvacant subclasses may be partitioned as follows:

Constant	1
Squares	$m - 1$
Rows	$a - 1$
Rows × squares	$(m - 1)(a - 1)$
Columns	$a - 1$
Columns × squares	$(m - 1)(a - 1)$
Treatments	$a - 1$
Residual	$m(a - 1)^2 - (a - 1)$
Total	ma^2

The estimates of treatment contrasts are unaffected by this change in the analysis, but the error estimate will be reduced if sufficient row × square variation is eliminated from the residual. An illustration of this form of analysis appears in Example 5.4-3.

Table 5.4-10 MULTIVARIATE ANALYSIS OF VARIANCE FOR THE CROSSOVER DESIGN

Source	df	SSP ($p \times p$)
Constant	1	$\text{SSM} = ma^2\mathbf{y}_{...}\mathbf{y}'_{...}$
Rows	$a - 1$	$\text{SSB} = ma \sum_{k=1}^{a} \mathbf{y}_{.k.}\mathbf{y}'_{.k.} - \text{SSM}$
Columns	$ma - 1$	$\text{SSC} = a \sum_{l=1}^{ma} \mathbf{y}_{..l}\mathbf{y}'_{..l} - \text{SSM}$
Treatments	$a - 1$	$\text{SSA} = ma \sum_{j=1}^{a} \mathbf{y}_{j..}\mathbf{y}'_{j..} - \text{SSM}$
Residual	$(ma - 2)(a - 1)$	$\text{SSE} = \text{SST} - \text{SSA} - \text{SSB} - \text{SSC} - \text{SSM}$
Total	$ma^2 = \sum\sum\sum n_{jkl}$	$\text{SST} = \sum_{i=1}^{ma} \sum_{k=1}^{a} \sum_{j=1}^{a} n_{jkl}\mathbf{y}_{jkl}\mathbf{y}'_{jkl}$

Repeated measures and residual effects It is important to understand that the latin-square and crossover designs provide no possibility of assessing row (or column) $\times$ treatment interaction. This can be a serious shortcoming in educational research if, as is often the case, the interaction between treatment effects and subject characteristics is of interest. In the above example, interaction between aptitude level and reading method is certainly a possibility which should be investigated. A suitable design for this purpose is one in which aptitude groups within schools are randomly partitioned and assigned to methods A and B, respectively. An example of this design is shown in Table 5.4-11. Formally, the design is equivalent to the one-sample repeated-measures design discussed in Sec. 7.1, and the analysis presented there applies.

If the investigator is constrained to apply the treatments in a temporal sequence, complications not considered in Chap. 7 may arise. Suppose, for example, that within each school the same teacher is instructing the four treatment groups serially in successive class periods. Because there are likely to be systematic effects due to period, it would be desirable to make use of four teachers per school in a $4 \times 4 \times 4$ crossover design. The repeated-measures analysis of Chap. 7 can be readily generalized to cover this case. But there may also be a persistent influence of a given method on the methods that follow in the sequence. This could occur if the teacher has difficulty shifting from one method to another. Designs which provide for the detection and estimation of these so-called *residual* effects have been proposed by Williams [1949]. The analysis is discussed in Cochran and Cox [1957] and John [1971]. Behavioral applications of designs balanced for residual effects have been reviewed by Namboodiri [1972]. Extension of the analysis for these designs to the multivariate case is straightforward.

EXAMPLE 5.4-3 (*Test of calculating speed*) Cochran and Cox [1957] report the results of a test of the speed of calculating the sum of squares of 27 numbers on two brands of desk calculator designated A and B. Each of 10 subjects performed the

Table 5.4-11 DESIGN FOR TESTING APTITUDE $\times$ TREATMENT (A AND B) INTERACTION

Aptitude group	School 1	2	3	4
High	A B	A B	A B	A B
Low	A B	A B	A B	A B

calculation first on one and then on the other machine. The order of the machines in these trials was balanced and assigned randomly to the subjects. The resulting data, arranged in the form of five replicate 2 × 2 latin squares, are shown in Table 5.4-12.

Regarded as a squares × treatments × rows × columns design, the index numbers of the observations in Table 5.4-12 are as follows:

1111	1212	2111	2212	3111	3212	4111	4212	5111	5212
1221	1122	2221	2122	3221	3122	4221	4122	5221	5122

Incidence numbers with these subscripts are 1; all others are 0.

We compute the sums of squares for the analysis by constructing a basis for a 5 × 2 × 2 × 2 crossed design and applying the general solution of Sec. 5.3 with the elements of **D** specified by the incidence numbers. The resulting analysis of variance is shown in Table 5.4-13.

The treatment contrast, which is estimated by the difference of row means

Table 5.4-12 TIME (SECONDS MINUS 2 MINUTES) REQUIRED TO CALCULATE A SUM OF SQUARES ON MACHINES *A* AND *B*

	Squares 1		2		3		4		5	
Calculation	Subjects 1	2	3	4	6	5	8	7	9	10
1	*A* 30	*B* 21	*A* 22	*B* 13	*A* 29	*B* 13	*A* 12	*B* 7	*A* 23	*B* 24
2	*B* 14	*A* 21	*B* 5	*A* 22	*B* 17	*A* 18	*B* 14	*A* 16	*B* 8	*A* 23

Table 5.4-13 ANALYSIS OF VARIANCE FOR THE TEST OF CALCULATING SPEED IN FIVE REPLICATE 2 × 2 LATIN SQUARES (SQUARES × TREATMENTS × ROWS × COLUMNS)

Source	df	SS	F	p
Constant	1	6,195.2		
Squares	4	218.3	4.69	.082
Rows	1	64.8	5.57	.078
Rows × squares	4	120.9	2.69	.187
Columns	1	.8	.07	.806
Columns × squares	4	138.7	3.0	.158
Treatments	1	320.0	27.5	.006
Residual	4	46.5		
Total	20	910.8		

$A - B$, equals 8 sec in favor of machine A. The contrast is highly significant, and its standard error is

$$\text{SE} = \sqrt{(2 \times 46.5)/(4 \times 10)} = 1.525$$

Note that if these data were analyzed as a crossover design, the sum of squares for squares and rows × squares would amalgamate with the residual leading to a reduction in the F for treatments. Columns would also be combined with columns × squares, but this would have no effect on the test of treatments.

5.4.3 Incomplete Block Designs

The experimental designs of Secs. 5.4.1 and 5.4.2 obviously cannot be applied when there are more treatments to be compared than can be accommodated within the blocks of the material. This limitation is particularly troublesome in behavioral-research applications where the subject is the block. In sensory testing, for example, receptor fatigue may sharply curtail the number of stimuli (treatments) that can be presented to a subject (block) at one sitting. Design strategies which circumvent this limitation have received considerable attention [David, 1963; Bock and Jones, 1968].

An obvious strategy is to assign different subsets of treatments to different blocks in such a way that the treatment comparisons are connected by treatments that occur together in the same block, thus making all treatment contrasts estimable. The problem then is one of constructing plans for assigning treatments which have good properties in least-squares analysis and cover a practical range of numbers of treatments and blocks. This problem has been largely solved, and there is now available a large catalog of *incomplete block designs* (e.g., in Cochran and Cox [1957]) which provide (1) computationally simple estimates of the treatment contrasts, (2) uniform or nearly uniform standard errors of these estimates, and (3) high efficiency relative to a complete randomized block design with the same number of observations. In the present section we discuss the analysis of two classes of these designs—the balanced incomplete block designs (BIB) introduced by Yates [1936], and the partially balanced incomplete block designs (PBIB) due to Bose and Nair [1939].

Balanced incomplete blocks (BIB) An incomplete block design is called "balanced" if:

1 Each of b blocks contains exactly k from among t treatments ($k < t$).
2 Each treatment appears in exactly r blocks.
3 Each treatment appears with every other treatment in the same block an equal number of times λ.

The BIB designs may be indexed by the parameters t, b, k, r, and λ, and described by the $t \times b$ matrix of incidence numbers

$$n_{ij} = \begin{cases} 1 & \text{if treatment } i \text{ appears in block } j \\ 0 & \text{otherwise} \end{cases}$$

An example of a plan for a BIB design is presented in Table 5.4-14. The treatments are numbered from 1 to t, and the blocks from 1 to b. The plan specifies the numbers of the treatments that appear in the numbered blocks. (These block and treatment numbers correspond to the subscript values of the nonzero incidence numbers.) Note that the complement of a BIB design obtained by setting $n'_{ij} = 1 - n_{ij}$ is also a BIB design.

Plans for BIB designs with $k \leq 10$ and $r \leq 10$ appear in Fisher and Yates [1963] and Cochran and Cox [1957]. The theory of constructing these designs has been discussed by Bose [1939].

BIB designs have simple least-squares solutions when analyzed under the (multivariate) model

$$\mathbf{y}_{ij} = \boldsymbol{\mu} + \boldsymbol{\beta}_i + \boldsymbol{\tau}_j + \boldsymbol{\epsilon}_{ij} \qquad (5.4\text{-}9)$$

$$\boldsymbol{\epsilon} \sim N(\mathbf{0}, \Sigma)$$

(assuming a p-variate response).

Since the block parameters are of no intrinsic interest and serve only to eliminate unwanted variation, we may simplify matters in deriving the analysis by setting $\boldsymbol{\beta}_i^* = \boldsymbol{\mu} + \boldsymbol{\beta}_i$ and rewriting (5.4-9) as

$$\mathbf{y}_{ij} = \boldsymbol{\beta}_i^* + \boldsymbol{\tau}_j + \boldsymbol{\epsilon}_{ij} \qquad (5.4\text{-}10)$$

Then the normal equations for estimating $\boldsymbol{\beta}_i^*$ and $\boldsymbol{\tau}_j$ take the form

$$\begin{bmatrix} k\mathbf{I} & \mathbf{N} \\ \mathbf{N}' & r\mathbf{I} \end{bmatrix} \begin{bmatrix} \hat{\mathbf{B}}^* \\ \hat{\mathbf{T}} \end{bmatrix} = \begin{bmatrix} \sum_{j=1}^{t} n_{ij}\mathbf{y}'_{ij} \\ \sum_{i=1}^{b} n_{ij}\mathbf{y}'_{ij} \end{bmatrix} = \begin{bmatrix} \mathbf{Y}_B \\ \mathbf{Y}_T \end{bmatrix} \qquad (5.4\text{-}11)$$

Table 5.4-14 A BALANCED INCOMPLETE BLOCK DESIGN

		Treatments (j)		Complement
	1	2 4 6		
Blocks (k)	*2*	1 4 5	$t = 7$	$t' = 7$
	3	3 4 7	$b = 7$	$b' = 7$
	4	1 2 3	$k = 3$	$k' = 4$
	5	2 5 7	$r = 3$	$r' = 4$
	6	1 6 7	$\lambda = 1$	$\lambda' = 2$
	7	3 5 6		

where $\mathbf{N} = [n_{ij}]$ is called the *incidence* matrix of the design

$\mathbf{Y}_B$ = the $b \times p$ matrix of block sums

$\mathbf{Y}_T$ = the $t \times p$ matrix of treatment sums

We may orthogonalize (5.4-11) by means of the transformation

$$\begin{bmatrix} \mathbf{I} & \mathbf{0} \\ -\frac{1}{k}\mathbf{N}' & \mathbf{I} \end{bmatrix}$$

and its inverse

$$\begin{bmatrix} \mathbf{I} & \mathbf{0} \\ \frac{1}{k}\mathbf{N}' & \mathbf{I} \end{bmatrix}$$

as follows:

$$\begin{bmatrix} \mathbf{I} & \mathbf{0} \\ -\frac{1}{k}\mathbf{N}' & \mathbf{I} \end{bmatrix} \begin{bmatrix} k\mathbf{I} & \mathbf{N} \\ \mathbf{N}' & r\mathbf{I} \end{bmatrix} \begin{bmatrix} \mathbf{I} & -\frac{1}{k}\mathbf{N} \\ \mathbf{0} & \mathbf{I} \end{bmatrix} \begin{bmatrix} \mathbf{I} & \frac{1}{k}\mathbf{N} \\ \mathbf{0} & \mathbf{I} \end{bmatrix} \begin{bmatrix} \hat{\mathbf{B}}^* \\ \hat{\mathbf{T}} \end{bmatrix}$$

$$= \begin{bmatrix} \mathbf{I} & \mathbf{0} \\ -\frac{1}{k}\mathbf{N}' & \mathbf{I} \end{bmatrix} \begin{bmatrix} \mathbf{Y}_B \\ \mathbf{Y}_T \end{bmatrix}$$

or

$$\begin{bmatrix} k\mathbf{I} & 0 \\ 0 & r\mathbf{I} - \frac{1}{k}\mathbf{N}'\mathbf{N} \end{bmatrix} \begin{bmatrix} \hat{\mathbf{B}}^* + \frac{1}{k}\mathbf{N}'\hat{\mathbf{T}} \\ \hat{\mathbf{T}} \end{bmatrix} = \begin{bmatrix} \mathbf{Y}_b \\ \mathbf{Y}_T - \frac{1}{k}\mathbf{N}'\mathbf{Y}_B \end{bmatrix} \tag{5.4-12}$$

The elements of the matrix $\mathbf{Q} = \mathbf{Y}_T - (1/k)\mathbf{N}'\mathbf{Y}_B$, say, in the right member of (5.4-12), are called the *adjusted treatment sums.* The jth row of $\mathbf{N}'\mathbf{Y}_B$ in this expression contains the *total of all blocks that contain treatment j.* To estimate $\mathbf{T}$ we solve the system

$$\left[r\mathbf{I} - \frac{1}{k}\mathbf{N}'\mathbf{N}\right]\hat{\mathbf{T}} = \mathbf{Q} \tag{5.4-13}$$

The solution is straightforward because the conditions for a balanced design imply that

$$\mathbf{N}'\mathbf{N} = (r - \lambda)\mathbf{I} + \lambda\mathbf{1}\mathbf{1}' \tag{5.4-14}$$

and that the parameters of the design satisfy

$$\text{trace}(\mathbf{N}\mathbf{N}') = \text{trace}(\mathbf{N}'\mathbf{N}) = rt = bk \tag{5.4-15}$$

$$(\mathbf{1}'\mathbf{N})(\mathbf{N}'\mathbf{1}) = \mathbf{1}'\mathbf{N}\mathbf{N}'\mathbf{1} = bk^2 = t(r - \lambda) + t^2\lambda \tag{5.4-16}$$

and, setting $bk^2 = rtk$ in (5.4-16),

$$r(k - 1) = \lambda(t - 1) \tag{5.4-17}$$

Thus, we may substitute (5.4-14) in (5.4-13) to obtain

$$\left[\frac{r(k-1)+\lambda}{k}\mathbf{I} - \frac{\lambda}{k}\mathbf{11}'\right]\hat{\mathbf{T}} = \mathbf{Q}$$

which, from (5.4-17), becomes

$$\left[\mathbf{I} - \frac{1}{t}\mathbf{11}'\right]\hat{\mathbf{T}} = \frac{k}{\lambda t}\mathbf{Q} \tag{5.4-18}$$

We recognize $[\mathbf{I} - (1/t)\mathbf{11}'] = \Delta$, say, as the symmetric idempotent matrix (i.e., projection operator) described in Example 3.3-2 (see also Sec. 2.6.3) which mean deviates any vector upon which it operates. Thus,

$$\Delta\hat{\mathbf{T}} = \hat{\mathbf{T}}^0 = \frac{k}{\lambda t}\mathbf{Q} = \frac{1}{rE_f}\mathbf{Q} \tag{5.4-19}$$

(where $E_f = \lambda t/rk$ is called the *efficiency factor* of the design) gives directly the estimated treatment effects in the form of deviation contrasts. The estimator is unbiased,

$$\mathscr{E}(\boldsymbol{T}^0) = \Delta\mathbf{T}$$

and its variance-covariance matrix is

$$\mathscr{V}(\boldsymbol{T}^0) = \Delta \times \frac{1}{rE_f}\Sigma \tag{5.4-20}$$

Any contrast $\mathbf{c}'\mathbf{T}$ of treatment effects ($\mathbf{c}'\mathbf{1} = 0$) is therefore estimated by

$$\mathbf{c}'\hat{\mathbf{T}} = \frac{1}{rE_f}\mathbf{c}'\mathbf{Q} \tag{5.4-21}$$

with

$$\mathscr{V}(\mathbf{c}'\boldsymbol{T}) = \frac{1}{rE_f}\mathbf{c}'\mathbf{c}\Sigma \tag{5.4-22}$$

For example, the estimate of the difference between treatments j and j' is

$$\widehat{\boldsymbol{\tau}_j - \boldsymbol{\tau}_{j'}} = \frac{\mathbf{q}_j - \mathbf{q}_{j'}}{rE_f} \tag{5.4-23}$$

with

$$\mathscr{V}(\boldsymbol{\tau}_j - \boldsymbol{\tau}_{j'}) = \frac{2}{rE_f}\Sigma \tag{5.4-24}$$

The analysis of dispersion associated with this solution follows from (5.4-12) and is presented in Table 5.4-15.

The foregoing solution applies, of course, to the case of one observation per subclass. If there are multiple and possibly disproportionate numbers of observations N_{jk} per subclass, the general solution of Sec. 5.3.5c with $\mathbf{D} = [N_{jk}]$ must be used.

The efficiency factor of the BIB design gives the effective proportion of the same number of replicates in a complete randomized block design and hence expresses

Table 5.4-15 MULTIVARIATE ANALYSIS OF VARIANCE FOR THE BALANCED INCOMPLETE BLOCK DESIGN

Source	df	SSP ($p \times p$)	$\mathscr{E}$(SSP)
Constant and blocks, ignoring treatments	b	$\text{SSB} = \frac{1}{k}\mathbf{Y}_b'\mathbf{Y}_b$	$b\boldsymbol{\Sigma} + k[\mathbf{B}^* + \frac{1}{k}\mathbf{N}'\mathbf{T}]'[\mathbf{B}^* + \frac{1}{k}\mathbf{N}'\mathbf{T}]$
Treatments, eliminating blocks	$t - 1$	$\text{SSA} = \frac{k}{t}\mathbf{Q}'\mathbf{Q}$	$(t-1)\boldsymbol{\Sigma} + \frac{\lambda t}{k}\mathbf{T}'\boldsymbol{\Delta}\mathbf{T}$
Residual	$b(k-1) - t + 1$	$\text{SSE} = \text{SST} - \text{SSA} - \text{SSB}$	$[b(k-1) - t + 1]\boldsymbol{\Sigma}$
Total	$tr = bk$	$\text{SST} = \sum_{i=1}^{b}\sum_{j=1}^{t} n_{ij}\mathbf{y}_{ij}\mathbf{y}_{ij}'$	

the relative efficiency of the incomplete design. It is only a lower bound to efficiency, however, because the smaller block size in the incomplete design would probably result in more effective blocking.

Partially balanced incomplete blocks (PBIB) Because balanced incomplete block designs exist only for certain restricted combinations of parameter values, it may not be possible to find a design which fits the size of a given experiment. In this case, the much wider class of incomplete block designs developed by Bose and his associates may be useful. These designs, called *partially balanced*, do not enjoy the uniform variances for treatment contrasts which characterize BIB designs, but they have simple solutions and relatively high efficiencies.

Of the several types of PBIB designs with two associate classes cataloged by Bose, Clatworthy, and Sirkhande [1954], we discuss here only the so-called *group-divisible* and *triangular* designs. In presenting the analysis, however, we give the general solution for PBIB designs with two associate classes. These designs satisfy the following conditions:

1 For t treatments and b blocks, each treatment appears exactly once in each of r blocks ($r < b$), and each block contains exactly k treatments ($k < t$).
2 Any two treatments are either first associates or second associates, but not both.
3 Each treatment has exactly n_1 first associates and n_2 second associates.
4 Any two treatments which are first associates appear together in the same block exactly λ_1 times, and any two which are second associates appear together in the same block exactly λ_2 times.
5 Any two treatments which are first associates have exactly $p_{jk}{}^1$ treatments that are jth associates of the first treatment and kth associates of the second treatment. Similarly, any two treatments that are second associates have exactly $p_{jk}{}^2$ such associates. For any given design the quantities

$$P_1 = \begin{bmatrix} p_{11}{}^1 & p_{12}{}^1 \\ p_{21}{}^1 & p_{22}{}^1 \end{bmatrix} \quad \text{and} \quad P_2 = \begin{bmatrix} p_{11}{}^2 & p_{12}{}^2 \\ p_{21}{}^2 & p_{22}{}^2 \end{bmatrix}$$

are the same for all treatment pairs.

These conditions imply the following relationships among the design parameters:

$$\begin{aligned} n_1 + n_2 &= b - 1 & n_1 p_{12}{}^1 &= n_2 p_{11}{}^2 \\ n_1\lambda_1 + n_2\lambda_2 &= r(k-1) & n_1 p_{22}{}^1 &= n_2 p_{12}{}^2 \\ p_{11}{}^1 + p_{12}{}^1 &= n_1 - 1 & p_{22}{}^2 + p_{21}{}^2 &= n_2 - 1 \\ p_{11}{}^2 + p_{12}{}^2 &= n_1 & p_{22}{}^1 + p_{21}{}^1 &= n_2 \\ p_{12}{}^1 &= p_{21}{}^1 & p_{12}{}^2 &= p_{21}{}^2 \end{aligned}$$

Group-divisible designs Group-divisible PBIB designs exist for any nonprime number of treatments $t = mn$. The *association scheme* for the design is specified by writing the treatment designations in an $m \times n$ rectangular array. Treatments in the same row are first associates, and those in different rows are second associates. For example, an association scheme for $t = 6$ with $m = 3$ and $n = 2$ is

$$\begin{matrix} 1 & 2 \\ 3 & 4 \\ 5 & 6 \end{matrix}$$

Guided by this scheme, we can easily write down a design which satisfies the condition for partial balance:

		Treatments		
Blocks	*1*	1	2	3
	2	3	4	5
	3	5	6	1
	4	1	2	4
	5	3	4	6
	6	5	6	2

Since each block has two treatments from the same row of the association scheme and one from another row, $\lambda_1 = 2$ and $\lambda_2 = 1$. Also, we see that $k = 3$, $r = 3$, $n_1 = 1$, and $n_2 = 4$. From the association scheme, it is apparent that treatments in the same row each have just one first associate and four second associates; hence, $p_{11}{}^1 = 1$ and $p_{22}{}^1 = 4$. Further, $p_{12}{}^1 = p_{21}{}^1 = 0$ since the same treatment cannot be both a first and second associate of treatments which are first associates. Similar inspection of the association scheme reveals that $p_{11}{}^2 = 0$, $p_{22}{}^2 = 2$, and $p_{12}{}^2 = p_{21}{}^2 = 1$. These values agree with the general conditions for a group-divisible design, namely,

$$n_1 = n - 1 \qquad\qquad n_2 = n(m - 1)$$

$$P_1 = \begin{bmatrix} n-2 & 0 \\ 0 & n(m-1) \end{bmatrix} \qquad P_2 = \begin{bmatrix} 0 & n-1 \\ n-1 & n(m-2) \end{bmatrix}$$

Triangular designs Triangular designs exist for numbers of treatments $t = n(n - 1)/2$. The association scheme is obtained by writing the treatment designations in a symmetric array illustrated for $n = 5$ by

$$\begin{matrix} * & 1 & 2 & 3 & 4 \\ 1 & * & 5 & 6 & 7 \\ 2 & 5 & * & 8 & 9 \\ 3 & 6 & 8 & * & 10 \\ 4 & 7 & 9 & 10 & * \end{matrix} \qquad (5.4\text{-}26)$$

Treatments appearing in the same row or column are first associates; those not in the same row or column are second associates. The triangular association scheme satisfies

$$n_1 = 2(n-2) \qquad n_2 = \tfrac{1}{2}(n-2)(n-3)$$

$$P_1 = \begin{bmatrix} n-2 & n-3 \\ n-3 & \tfrac{1}{2}(n-3)(n-4) \end{bmatrix} \qquad P_2 = \begin{bmatrix} 4 & 2(n-4) \\ 2(n-4) & \tfrac{1}{2}(n-4)(n-5) \end{bmatrix} \qquad (5.4\text{-}27)$$

For example, a PBIB design with $b = 5$, $k = 4$, $r = 2$, $\lambda_1 = 1$, and $\lambda_2 = 0$ is obtained by assigning treatments in each row of the association scheme to a block:

		Treatments			
	1	1	2	3	4
	2	1	5	6	7
Blocks	*3*	2	5	8	9
	4	3	6	8	10
	5	4	7	9	10

By inspecting the association scheme, we can verify that $n_1 = 6$, $n_2 = 3$,

$$P_1 = \begin{bmatrix} 3 & 2 \\ 2 & 1 \end{bmatrix} \qquad P_2 = \begin{bmatrix} 4 & 2 \\ 2 & 0 \end{bmatrix}$$

Analysis of PBIB designs with two associate classes As in the analysis of BIB designs, we let $\mathbf{N} = [n_{ij}]$ be the $b \times t$ incidence matrix, such that $n_{ij} = 1$ if treatment j appears in block i, and 0 otherwise. Eliminating the constant and between-block effects, we again come to

$$\left[r\mathbf{I} - \frac{1}{k}\mathbf{N}'\mathbf{N}\right]\hat{\mathbf{T}} = \mathbf{Y}_T - \frac{1}{k}\mathbf{N}'\mathbf{Y}_B = \mathbf{Q} \qquad (5.4\text{-}28)$$

as the normal equations for the treatment effects. The system (5.4-28) has a simple solution because of the special structure of $\mathbf{N}'\mathbf{N}$. To describe this structure, let us define the $t \times t$ symmetric matrices $\mathbf{A}_1 = [a_{jk}]$, where

$$a_{jj} = 0$$

$$\underset{j \neq k}{a_{jk}} = \begin{cases} 1 & \text{if treatment } k \text{ is a first associate of treatment } j \\ 0 & \text{otherwise} \end{cases}$$

Then,

$$\mathbf{N}'\mathbf{N} = r\mathbf{I} + \lambda_1\mathbf{A}_1 + \lambda_2(\mathbf{1}\mathbf{1}' - \mathbf{A}_1 - \mathbf{I})$$
$$= (r - \lambda_2)\mathbf{I} + (\lambda_1 - \lambda_2)\mathbf{A}_1 + \lambda_2\mathbf{1}\mathbf{1}'$$

The solution depends upon the fact that the structure of $\mathbf{A}_1\mathbf{A}_1$, in turn, may be described in terms of the parameters n_1 and $p_{11}{}^1$ and $p_{11}{}^2$:

$$\mathbf{A}_1\mathbf{A}_1 = n_1\mathbf{I} + p_{11}{}^1\mathbf{A}_1 + p_{11}{}^2(\mathbf{1}\mathbf{1}' - \mathbf{A}_1 - \mathbf{I})$$

These relationships make it possible for us to find, after considerable calculation, scalar quantities B_{22} and B_{12}, which enable us to simplify the normal equations (5.4-28) as follows:

$$[B_{22}\mathbf{I} - B_{12}\mathbf{A}_1]\left[r\mathbf{I} + \frac{1}{k}\mathbf{N}'\mathbf{N}\right]\hat{\mathbf{T}} = [B_{22}\mathbf{I} - B_{12}\mathbf{A}_1]\mathbf{Q}$$

$$\frac{d}{k}\Delta\hat{\mathbf{T}} = B_{22}\mathbf{Q} - B_{12}\mathbf{A}_1\mathbf{Q} \qquad (5.4\text{-}29)$$

$$\hat{\mathbf{T}}^0 = \frac{k}{d}[B_{22}\mathbf{Q} - B_{12}\mathbf{A}_1\mathbf{Q}]$$

where $B_{22} = r(k-1) + \lambda_2 + (\lambda_2 - \lambda_1)(p_{11}{}^1 - p_{11}{}^2)$

$B_{12} = \lambda_2 - \lambda_1$

$d = (rk - r + \lambda_2)B_{22} - (n_1 - p_{11}{}^2)(\lambda_2 - \lambda_1)^2$

Row h, say, of the matrix product $\mathbf{A}_1\mathbf{Q}$ in (5.4-29) is the sum of the adjusted treatment sums of those treatments which are first associates of treatment h. Thus, we obtain the estimated treatment deviation contrasts $\hat{\mathbf{T}}^0$ by subtracting B_{12} times this product from B_{22} times the adjusted treatment sums, and multiplying the result by k/d.

The estimator is unbiased, and its variance-covariance matrix is

$$\mathscr{V}(\boldsymbol{T}^0) = \frac{k}{d}[B_{22}\mathbf{I} - B_{12}\mathbf{A}_1] \times \boldsymbol{\Sigma} \qquad (5.4\text{-}30)$$

Thus, for example,

$$\mathscr{V}(\boldsymbol{\tau}_j - \boldsymbol{\tau}_{j'}) = \begin{cases} 2\frac{k}{d}(B_{22} + B_{12})\boldsymbol{\Sigma} & \text{if } j \text{ and } j' \text{ are first associates} \\ 2\frac{k}{d}B_{22}\boldsymbol{\Sigma} & \text{if } j \text{ and } j' \text{ are second associates} \end{cases} \qquad (5.4\text{-}31)$$

This form of the solution is due to Rao [1947]. Bose, Clatworthy, and Sirkhande [1954] give an equivalent solution in somewhat different notation (see also John [1971, Chap. 12]).

The analysis of variance for the present solution is shown in Table 5.4-16.

PBIB designs have two efficiencies, one for the comparison of first associates, and the other for comparison of second associates. In general, these efficiencies are lower than that of a BIB design with the same parameters b, t, k, and r. The smaller $\lambda_2 - \lambda_1$, the more similar are the variances of comparisons of first associates and comparisons of second associates, and the more closely the PBIB efficiency approaches the BIB efficiency. In choosing PBIB designs, it is therefore advantageous to seek designs with small values of $\lambda_2 - \lambda_1$.

Table 5.4-16 PARTITION OF SQUARES AND PRODUCTS FOR THE PARTIALLY BALANCED INCOMPLETE BLOCK DESIGN

Source	df	SSP ($p \times p$)	$\mathscr{E}$(SSP)
Blocks, ignoring treatments	b	$\mathrm{SSB} = \frac{1}{k}\mathbf{Y}_B'\mathbf{Y}_B$	$(b-1)\boldsymbol{\Sigma} + [\mathbf{B}^* + \frac{1}{k}\mathbf{N}'\mathbf{T}]'[\mathbf{B}^* + \frac{1}{k}\mathbf{N}'\mathbf{T}]$
Treatments, eliminating blocks	$t-1$	$\mathrm{SSA} = \frac{k}{d}\mathbf{Q}'[B_{22}\mathbf{I} - B_{12}\mathbf{A}_1]\mathbf{Q}$	$(t-1)\boldsymbol{\Sigma} + \mathbf{T}^{0\prime}[r\mathbf{I} + \frac{1}{k}\mathbf{N}'\mathbf{N}]\mathbf{T}^0$
Residual	$kt - b - t + 1$	SSE = SST − SSA − SSB − SSM	$(kt - b - t + 1)\boldsymbol{\Sigma}$
Total	$kt = \sum\sum n_{ij}$	$\mathrm{SST} = \sum_{i=1}^{b}\sum_{j=1}^{t} n_{ij}\mathbf{y}_{ij}\mathbf{y}_{ij}'$	

The analysis of PBIB designs presented in this section is called the *intrablock* solution because it makes use only of information in the within-block contrasts for estimating treatment effects. It is possible to improve the precision of these estimates by recovery of *interblock* information relevant to treatment contrasts. An analysis of PBIB designs for this purpose has been introduced by Yates and is discussed, for example, in John [1971, page 235 ff]. Gains in precision by recovering interblock information become appreciable only in large designs and only when the between-block variation is large. For many applications, the intrablock solution is quite satisfactory.

EXAMPLE 5.4-4 (*Preference measurement*) For a study of the rational origin of a preference-measurement scale (see Bock and Jones [1968, page 264]), McKeon [1961] required estimates of preference scores for 55 objects consisting of birthday gifts and combinations of birthday gifts. He wished to obtain the preference judgments by a ranking method but felt that the subjects would have difficulty placing this number of objects in a single rank order. He therefore assigned sets of 10 objects to each of the 11 blocks of the triangular partially balanced incomplete block design for $t = 11(11 - 1)/2 = 55$. The subjects ($N = 178$) were then required to make 11 rankings of 10 objects rather than one ranking of 55 objects. Not only was the ranking task simplified by this method, but the accuracy of ranking was improved because each object was ranked in two distinct blocks.

The association scheme for the design, expressed in terms of arbitrarily assigned object numbers, was as follows:

*	1	2	3	4	5	6	7	8	9	10
1	*	55	11	20	28	41	35	46	50	53
2	55	*	47	51	21	54	12	18	36	42
3	11	47	*	52	22	13	33	27	37	43
4	20	51	52	*	38	49	49	44	17	23
5	28	21	22	38	*	31	48	25	34	15
6	41	54	13	14	31	*	32	19	26	39
7	35	12	33	49	48	32	*	16	45	40
8	46	18	27	44	25	19	16	*	29	30
9	50	36	37	17	34	26	45	29	*	24
10	53	42	43	23	15	39	40	30	24	*

Objects in each row of the association scheme comprised the blocks of the design.

According to (5.4-27), the parameters of this design are

$$n = 11 \qquad t = 55 \qquad k = 10 \qquad r = 2$$

$$\lambda_1 = 1 \qquad \lambda_2 = 0 \qquad n_1 = 18 \qquad n_2 = 36$$

$$P_1 = \begin{bmatrix} 9 & 8 \\ 8 & 28 \end{bmatrix} \qquad\qquad P_2 = \begin{bmatrix} 4 & 14 \\ 14 & 21 \end{bmatrix}$$

As a preliminary to estimating the preference scores, McKeon scaled the rankings within each block to obtain the rank scores within each block shown in Table 5.4-17. Because of a scaling convention, the rank scores in each block sum exactly to zero. This simplifies the solution somewhat because the adjusted treatment sums are equal to the raw treatment sums.

As an illustration of the solution for this design, let us estimate the preference score for object 1. The adjusted treatment sum for this object is

$$q_1 = 0.821 + 0.098 = 0.919$$

and the adjusted treatment sums of the first associates of object 1 are:

$$\begin{array}{lll} q_2 = 1.813 & q_8 = -2.795 & q_{28} = 2.775 \\ q_3 = 1.165 & q_9 = -.412 & q_{41} = -1.821 \\ q_4 = .719 & q_{10} = -1.614 & q_{35} = .772 \\ q_5 = -1.735 & q_{55} = -.357 & q_{46} = -3.050 \\ q_6 = -2.428 & q_{11} = 3.255 & q_{50} = -2.772 \\ q_7 = -3.281 & q_{20} = 3.970 & q_{53} = -1.770 \end{array}$$

The sum of the latter values is -7.566, and, from (5.4-29),

$$\begin{aligned} B_{22} &= 2 \times 9 - (9 - 4) = 13 \\ B_{12} &= 0 - 1 = -1 \\ d &= (20 - 2)13 - (18 - 4) = 220 \end{aligned}$$

Then,

$$\hat{\tau}_1^{\,0} = \tfrac{10}{220}[13(0.919) - 7.566] = .1991$$

Corresponding estimates for the remaining objects are shown in Table 5.4-18.

The analysis of variance is hardly needed here to test the statistical significance of preference differences between objects, which is a foregone conclusion, but it is required in estimating the error variance. The partition of the sum of squares for this purpose is shown in Table 5.4-19. Using this estimate, we obtain from Sec. 5.4 the variance of a contrast of first associates,

$$2 \times 10(13 - 1)\frac{.3919}{220} = .4275$$

and for a contrast of second associates,

$$2 \times 10 \times 13\,\frac{.3919}{220} = .4631$$

As is the case for many PBIB designs, these two variances differ only slightly.

McKeon [1961] was able to locate a rational origin for the preference values estimated with this design.

Table 5.4-17 SCALED PREFERENCE RANKINGS OF OBJECTS WITHIN BLOCKS

Blocks	Objects (scaled preference scores)									
1	1	2	3	4	5	6	7	8	9	10
	.821	1.170	1.016	.615	−.331	−.528	−1.400	−1.027	.039	−.374
2	1	55	11	20	28	41	35	46	50	53
	.098	−.148	1.734	1.884	1.543	−.767	.288	−1.563	−2.036	−1.034
3	2	55	47	51	21	54	12	18	36	42
	.643	−.209	−1.388	−1.232	1.764	−1.206	1.851	.825	.332	−1.379
4	3	11	47	52	22	13	33	27	37	43
	.149	1.521	−1.634	−1.682	.529	1.454	.744	.614	−.349	−1.346
5	4	20	51	52	38	14	49	44	17	23
	.104	2.086	−1.193	−1.669	.295	.653	−.933	−.416	.283	.790
6	5	28	21	22	38	31	48	25	34	15
	−1.404	1.232	1.334	.318	−.262	−.520	−1.147	.002	.296	.152
7	6	41	54	13	14	31	32	19	26	39
	−1.900	−1.054	−1.398	1.601	.358	−.105	.188	.482	1.095	.733
8	7	35	12	33	49	48	32	16	45	40
	−1.881	.484	1.774	1.068	−1.074	−.569	.418	−.008	−.779	.566
9	8	46	18	27	44	25	19	16	29	30
	−1.768	−1.487	.808	.954	−.474	.350	.661	−.178	.641	.495
10	9	50	36	37	17	34	26	45	29	24
	−.451	−.736	.241	−.131	.183	.690	1.198	−.735	.639	−.897
11	10	53	42	43	23	15	39	40	30	24
	−1.240	−.736	−1.194	−1.004	1.004	.760	.875	.403	.696	.395

5.4.4 Factorial Designs

In an early stage of an empirical study, we may be justified in attempting to explore the effects of a considerable number of potentially interesting independent variables. Our objective at this stage would be to gain quickly and economically a broad view of the role of these variables in determining the response of the material and, on this basis, to focus future work on the more critical variables. As we have seen in Sec. 4.1.11, however, the prospects for accurately estimating effects of many variables with fallible data will be poor unless steps are taken to prevent loss of precision as additional variables are included in the model. In linear least-squares estimation, the most productive step is to manipulate the values of the independent variables so that the basis matrix for the linear model is orthogonal.

An experimental arrangement which has this property relative to the linear model represented, for example, by (5.3-8), is the so-called *factorial design* [Yates, 1937]. The experimental rubric is as follows: First, a limited number of values, or *levels*, are selected for each independent variable, or *factor*. If only linear effects are expected two levels per factor are sufficient; if curvilinear effects of degree q_k are expected for factor k, then at least $q_k + 1$ levels should be chosen for that factor. In general, it is advisable to space the levels equally (on an arithmetic or logarithmic scale, as appropriate) and to span the relevant range of variation of each factor.

Table 5.4-18 PREFERENCE SCORES OF 55 OBJECTS

1	.199	*12*	1.760	*23*	.784	*34*	.713	*45*	−.803
2	.548	*13*	1.743	*24*	−.360	*35*	.432	*46*	−1.427
3	.348	*14*	.578	*25*	.411	*36*	.272	*47*	−1.408
4	−.017	*15*	.575	*26*	1.245	*37*	−.130	*48*	−.676
5	−.991	*16*	−.124	*27*	.908	*38*	.211	*49*	−1.076
6	−1.460	*17*	.200	*28*	1.699	*39*	.802	*50*	−1.302
7	−2.030	*18*	.817	*29*	.648	*40*	.339	*51*	−1.254
8	−1.734	*19*	.685	*30*	.503	*41*	−.721	*52*	−1.592
9	−.557	*20*	2.044	*31*	.013	*42*	−1.401	*53*	−.902
10	−1.259	*21*	1.762	*32*	.363	*43*	−1.164	*54*	−1.211
11	1.829	*22*	.761	*33*	.978	*44*	−.463	*55*	−.102

Table 5.4-19 ANALYSIS OF VARIANCE FOR THE TRIANGULAR PBIB DESIGN

Source	df	SS	
Blocks	10	(Identically zero)	
Objects	54	ssa = 110.7540	
Residual	45	sse = 1.7637	$\hat{\sigma}^2 = .03919$
Total	110	sst = 112.5377	

The units of experimental material are then assigned randomly to all possible combinations of one level from each factor. Thus, if there are three factors with levels a, b, and c, the number of factorial combinations is $n = abc$. In the terminology of Sec. 5.3, the resulting arrangement may be described as a three-way crossed design with the formula

$$a \times b \times c$$

A factorial experiment containing exactly one experimental unit per subclass, or a total of n units, constitutes one *replicate* of the design. The design may be replicated r times, say, with independent units in each replicate, thus requiring a total of rn units. If each unit is identified with a particular replicate (as when the replicates correspond to blocks), the design is in effect crossed by another way of classification, and its formula becomes

$$a \times b \times c \times r$$

If the replicate units within subclasses have no individual identity, the formula remains $a \times b \times c$, and the variation between replicate units within subclasses necessarily is assigned to error. It may happen in the latter case that the numbers of units per subclass are unequal and disproportionate. The design is then said to be *unbalanced* or *nonorthogonal*. In general, nonorthogonal factorial designs should be avoided because they do not make optimal use of the material and are more difficult to analyze. This should not be taken to imply, however, that data already in hand should be discarded in order to make an unbalanced design orthogonal. If the design is unbalanced, the general nonorthogonal analysis presented in Secs. 5.3.5c and 5.3.6b may be applied. Issues peculiar to the analysis of nonorthogonal factorial designs are discussed in Sec. 5.4.4b.

An example of an educational application where, in fact, strict orthogonality could not be maintained appears in a study of programmed instruction reported by Krumboltz and Yabroff [1965]. The purpose of the study was to compare the effectiveness of alternative sets of programmed instructional material generated from two factors in writing the instructional frames. One factor consisted of an inductive versus a deductive approach to the subject matter; the other involved high versus low frequency of alternation of rules and examples in the sequences of frames. Programmed booklets representing the four combinations of levels of these factors were randomly distributed to a large college class. At this point, the design was orthogonal; for purposes of analysis, however, the class was partitioned into a high and low "intelligence" population according to scores on the Miller Analogies Test. The design within these populations then deviated somewhat from equality or proportionality of subclass numbers. A suitable treatment of these data would therefore be a nonorthogonal analysis of a $2 \times 2 \times 2$ design which includes the blocking of subjects with respect to intelligence (see Exercise 5.4-1).

Another situation which in general will require a nonorthogonal analysis is the absence of data for one or more subclasses of the design. When this happens by accident (because data are lost or one of the combinations of factor levels cannot be carried out), the balance of the design may be so disrupted that only a nonorthogonal analysis will salvage the study. It is possible, however, to omit factor combinations deliberately in such a way that the orthogonality of the design is retained. Designs of this type, called *fractional factorials*, have proved extremely useful in studies involving many (5 to 10) factors. The construction and analysis of fractional factorial designs is discussed in Sec. 5.4.5.

a Equal subclass numbers An important advantage of the factorial design with the same numbers of observations in all subclasses is the numerical simplicity of the least-squares analysis. For example, the first step in the analysis of an $a \times b$ factorial design with r observations per subclass would be to test whether the data should be represented by the main-class model (5.3-4) or the rank-n model including interactions (5.4-5).

If the subclass numbers are equal, the multivariate analysis of variance for this test takes the form shown in Table 5.4-20, which is just a specialization of the general two-way analysis shown in Table 5.3-1. The interpretation of Table 5.4-20 follows from the expected sums of squares and products in the right-hand column. We observe that the noncentrality term of the expected SSAB depends only upon the deviations of the interaction effects from their row and column means. A necessary condition for SSAB and SSW to be distributed as independent Wishart variates with $(a - 1)(b - 1)$ and $ab(r - 1)$ degrees of freedom is that these deviations be null. Thus, a statistical test which rejects the hypothesis that SSAB and SSW arise from the same Wishart population rejects a necessary condition for the main-class model (5.3-4).

Rejecting the nullity of the interactions also precludes the interpretation of the A and B terms in the analysis, for the noncentrality of the expected SSA and SSB are functions of both main effects and interactions. This point deserves emphasis because many texts speak of imposing the constraints $\boldsymbol{\alpha}. = \boldsymbol{\beta}. = (\boldsymbol{\alpha\beta})_{j\cdot} = (\boldsymbol{\alpha\beta})_{\cdot k} = (\boldsymbol{\alpha\beta}).. = \mathbf{0}$ in order to bring the system of normal equations to full rank. This leaves the reader with the impression that the main-effect sums of squares are free of interaction terms even when the hypothesis of no interaction is rejected. Actually, all that is implied by the constraints is that the effects in the model will be estimated in the form of deviations about these means. Because of the deficiency of rank in the initial model, no information about the mean of the interaction terms is available in the data, so that it is impossible to say empirically whether they are or are not null.

Nevertheless, if there is no evidence of deviation of the interaction terms from their row and column means, this is usually taken to imply that the interactions are in fact nonexistent, and that the noncentrality terms in the expected SSA and SSB involve only the main-effect parameters. Thus, the null hypotheses on the A and B

Table 5.4-20 MULTIVARIATE ANALYSIS OF VARIANCE FOR A REPLICATED TWO-FACTOR DESIGN

Source	df	SSP ($p \times p$)	$\mathscr{E}$(SSP)*
Constant	1	$\text{SSM} = abr\mathbf{y}_{...}\mathbf{y}'_{...}$	$\boldsymbol{\Sigma} + abr\boldsymbol{\mu}^0\boldsymbol{\mu}^{0\prime}$
A	$a-1$	$\text{SSA} = rb\sum_{j=1}^{a}\mathbf{y}_{.j.}\mathbf{y}'_{.j.} - \text{SSM}$	$(a-1)\boldsymbol{\Sigma} + rb\sum_{j=1}^{a}\boldsymbol{\alpha}_j^0\boldsymbol{\alpha}_j^{0\prime}$
B	$b-1$	$\text{SSB} = ra\sum_{k=1}^{b}\mathbf{y}_{..k}\mathbf{y}'_{..k} - \text{SSM}$	$(b-1)\boldsymbol{\Sigma} + ra\sum_{k=1}^{b}\boldsymbol{\beta}_j^0\boldsymbol{\beta}_j^{0\prime}$
AB	$(a-1)(b-1)$	$\text{SSAB} = \text{SSG} - \text{SSA} - \text{SSB} - \text{SSM}$	$(a-1)(b-1)\boldsymbol{\Sigma} + r\sum_{k=1}^{b}\sum_{j=1}^{a}(\boldsymbol{\alpha\beta})_{jk}^0(\boldsymbol{\alpha\beta})_{jk}^{0\prime}$
Subclass means	ab	$\text{SSG} = r\sum_{k=1}^{b}\sum_{j=1}^{a}\mathbf{y}_{\cdot jk}\mathbf{y}'_{\cdot jk}$	
Within subclasses	$ab(r-1)$	$\text{SSW} = \text{SST} - \text{SSG}$	$ab(r-1)\boldsymbol{\Sigma}$
Total	abr	$\text{SST} = \sum_{k=1}^{b}\sum_{j=1}^{a}\sum_{i=1}^{r}\mathbf{y}_{ijk}\mathbf{y}'_{ijk}$	

* $\boldsymbol{\mu}^0 = \boldsymbol{\mu} + \boldsymbol{\alpha}_. + \boldsymbol{\beta}_. + (\boldsymbol{\alpha\beta})_{..}$ $\quad \boldsymbol{\alpha}_. = \sum_{j=1}^{a}\boldsymbol{\alpha}_j/a \quad (\boldsymbol{\alpha\beta})_{.k} = \sum_{j=1}^{a}(\boldsymbol{\alpha\beta})_{jk}/a$

$\boldsymbol{\alpha}_j^0 = \boldsymbol{\alpha}_j - \boldsymbol{\alpha}_. + (\boldsymbol{\alpha\beta})_{j.} - (\boldsymbol{\alpha\beta})_{..}$ $\quad \boldsymbol{\beta}_. = \sum_{k=1}^{b}\boldsymbol{\beta}_j/b \quad (\boldsymbol{\alpha\beta})_{..} = \sum_{k=1}^{b}\sum_{j=1}^{a}(\boldsymbol{\alpha\beta})_{jk}/ab$

$\boldsymbol{\beta}_k^0 = \boldsymbol{\beta}_k - \boldsymbol{\beta}_. + (\boldsymbol{\alpha\beta})_{.k} - (\boldsymbol{\alpha\beta})_{..}$ $\quad (\boldsymbol{\alpha\beta})_{j.} = \sum_{k=1}^{b}(\boldsymbol{\alpha\beta})_{jk}/b$

$(\boldsymbol{\alpha\beta})_{jk}^0 = (\boldsymbol{\alpha\beta})_{jk} - (\boldsymbol{\alpha\beta})_{j.} - (\boldsymbol{\alpha\beta})_{.k} + (\boldsymbol{\alpha\beta})_{..}$

effects are assumed testable if there is no positive evidence that the interactions are nonnull.

Estimation of the main-class effects under model (5.3-3) is also greatly simplified in the orthogonal case. As shown in Sec. 5.3.6a, the marginal means minus the grand mean give the deviation contrasts of the corresponding main-class effects:

$$\mathscr{E}(\boldsymbol{\alpha}_j{}^0) = \mathscr{E}(\mathbf{y}_{\cdot j \cdot} - \mathbf{y}_{\cdots}) = \boldsymbol{\alpha}_j{}^0$$

$$\mathscr{E}(\boldsymbol{\beta}_k{}^0) = \mathscr{E}(\mathbf{y}_{\cdot\cdot k} - \mathbf{y}_{\cdots}) = \boldsymbol{\beta}_k{}^0$$

The variances of these estimators are

$$\mathscr{V}(\boldsymbol{\alpha}_j{}^0) = \frac{1}{rb}\boldsymbol{\Sigma} \qquad \mathscr{V}(\boldsymbol{\beta}_k{}^0) = \frac{1}{ra}\boldsymbol{\Sigma} \tag{5.4-32}$$

Any contrast of parameters is estimated by the corresponding contrast of deviation estimates or main-class means; for example,

$$\mathscr{E}(\boldsymbol{\alpha}_j{}^{(0)} - \boldsymbol{\alpha}_{j'}{}^{(0)}) = \mathscr{E}(\mathbf{y}_{\cdot j \cdot} - \mathbf{y}_{\cdot j' \cdot}) = \boldsymbol{\alpha}_j - \boldsymbol{\alpha}_{j'}$$

and

$$\mathscr{V}(\boldsymbol{\alpha}_j{}^{(0)} - \boldsymbol{\alpha}_{j'}{}^{(0)}) = \frac{2}{rb}\boldsymbol{\Sigma}$$

These results generalize directly to higher-order factorial designs. For a design with f factors, the between-subclass partition in the multivariate analysis of variance has a separate term for each combination, without respect to order, of factors taken $0, 1, 2, \ldots, f$ at a time. The term involving no factors is the constant or one degree of freedom. Those involving one factor are the main-effect terms, each with degrees of freedom one less than the number of levels of the corresponding factor. Those terms involving $2, 3, \ldots, f$ factors are the 2-, 3-, . . . , f-factor interactions with degrees of freedom equal to the product of the main-effect degrees of freedom of the respective factors.

To compute sums of squares and products in the manner of Table 5.4-20, all possible marginal means are first computed. Next, the constant or "correction" term is computed as the total number of observations times the matrix product of the vector grand mean. The main-effect terms are obtained by multiplying the sum of matrix products of the corresponding vector marginal means by the number of observations which make up these means and subtracting the correction term.

The terms for the two-factor interactions are computed as the sums of matrix products of the vector means in the two-way marginal table for the factors involved. This sum is multiplied by the number of observations which make up these means, and the correction term and the main-effect terms for the two factors are subtracted.

The terms for the three-factor interactions are obtained in a similar way from the subclass means in the corresponding three-way marginal table. In this case, the correction term and main-effect and two-factor interaction terms of the factors involved are subtracted. For example, the SSP for the ABD interaction of an $a \times b \times c \times d$ design is given by

$$\text{SSABD} = rc \sum_{m=1}^{d} \sum_{k=1}^{b} \sum_{j=1}^{a} \mathbf{y}_{\cdot jk \cdot m} \mathbf{y}'_{\cdot jk \cdot m}$$

$$- \text{SSA} - \text{SSB} - \text{SSD} - \text{SSAB} - \text{SSAD} - \text{SSBD} - \text{SSM}$$

where

$$\mathbf{y}_{\cdot jk \cdot m} = \frac{1}{rc} \sum_{l=1}^{c} \sum_{i=1}^{r} \mathbf{y}_{ijklm}$$

is a vector mean in the marginal table obtained when the data are averaged over the C factor.

Computationally, the preceding technique is well suited to hand calculation in the univariate case. For computer applications it is not as convenient as the method presented in Sec. 5.3.5a, which has the advantage of directly generalizing to the nonorthogonal case and of allowing single-degree-of-freedom analyses. In the following discussion of nonorthogonal factorial designs, we shall assume that the general method described in Sec. 5.3.5c is used in the multivariate analysis of variance, and the method of Sec. 5.3.6b is used in the estimation of effect contrasts.

b Nonorthogonal factorial designs If the replication of a factorial experiment is unavoidably irregular or incomplete, the investigator may be left with disproportionate numbers of observations in the subclasses of the design. To make best use of the data in this case, he should apply the exact least-squares analysis described in Sec. 5.3.5 in connection with general crossed designs. As pointed out in that section, there are several aspects of the nonorthogonal analysis that prove more complex than the orthogonal solution and raise special problems of procedure and interpretation. A brief outline of these problems follows.

1 ORDER OF EFFECTS IN THE STEPWISE ANALYSIS For reasons given in Sec. 5.3.5c, a nonorthogonal analysis of variance is necessarily "stepwise" or "blockwise" in the manner of a regression analysis. That is, parameters in the model that might serve to explain or account for the effects of a given factor or interaction must appear prior to and be eliminated from the latter in the partition of the sum of squares and products. When bases for the factorial model are generated by the method of Sec. 5.3.3, it is obligatory in the order of elimination that higher-order interactions must not be placed before main effects or lower-order interactions of the same factors. In this method of constructing the basis, the vectors in the space of the higher-order interaction span only that part of the original interaction space that is complementary to the space of the main effects and lower-order interactions. For example, the

dimensionality of the AB space in an $a \times b$ design is originally ab, but the dimensionality of the subspace for AB in the basis is $(a - 1)(b - 1)$. Thus, the orderings

$$A$$
$$A, B$$
$$A, B, AB$$

of subspaces in the basis corresponds to a reasonable succession of models for stepwise testing, but

$$AB$$
$$AB, A$$
$$AB, A, B$$

does not because the subspace AB alone is not a complete model.

In other situations, the choice of orderings may involve questions of parsimony. If, for example, the AB term proved to be the only insignificant effect in a nonorthogonal ordering

$$A, B, C, AB$$

while C was the only insignificant term in an analysis of the same data in the ordering

$$A, B, AB, C$$

we would have to choose between a three-factor additive model and a two-factor interactive model. Since the trend in science has been to reduce qualitative distinctions while increasing quantitative complexity, we would presumably prefer the latter.

2 MULTIPLE ORDERS OF ELIMINATION In the nonorthogonal analysis illustrated in Example 5.3-2, the order of elimination of effects in the two-way design was determined by substantive considerations. Regrettably, this will less often be the case in factorial experiments where the causal role of the factors tends to be symmetric. If the purpose of the experiment is to assess the unique contribution of each factor, we shall have no other alternative than performing the nonorthogonal analysis for several orderings of the factors. The results of the several analyses will not be independent, but they represent the closest equivalent to the analysis of the corresponding orthogonal design and serve a useful purpose in this role. An application of this procedure appears in Example 5.4-4.

3 ESTIMATING EFFECTS IN NONORTHOGONAL DESIGNS One of the convenient properties of orthogonal factorial designs is that the least-squares estimates of effects are invariant with respect to the addition or deletion of terms in the model. This property is lost in the nonorthogonal analysis, and a decision about the number of effects to be included in the model must be made before the effect contrasts can be estimated

(see Sec. 5.3.6b). This implies, in particular, that in the nonorthogonal case the least-squares estimates are not given by the *observed* marginal means. Workers accustomed to orthogonal designs find this fact difficult to assimilate for they tend not to make any distinction between the marginal means and the estimated effects. Furthermore, they are in the habit of representing interactions graphically by plotting means from the marginal tables of the factors involved.

For purposes of communicating the results of an unbalanced factorial experiment, it is therefore advisable to recover the estimated subclass means using formula (5.3-47) and from these obtain the *estimated* marginal means by unweighted averaging of the estimated subclass means. These estimated means can be used for all purposes served by the observed marginal means in the orthogonal case. From the variance-covariance matrix of the estimated subclass means given by (5.3-48), the variances (and thence the standard errors) of the estimated marginal means may also be calculated.

4 VACANT SUBCLASSES For each vacant subclass (i.e., without observations) in the design, one degree of freedom is lost from the partition squares and cross products, and one of the effects in the general model is confounded with the remaining effects. If the number of vacant subclasses is less than the least number of degrees of freedom for any subspace in the partition, the lost degrees of freedom may be taken from the highest-order interaction on the assumption that the corresponding interactive effects are null. In that case the highest-order interaction should be obtained by subtraction and assigned the reduced number of degrees of freedom.

If a greater number of cells are vacant, it will be necessary to determine what confounding relations are implied in order to know which degrees of freedom must be excluded from the partition. In simple cases, the confounding relations may be deduced by the methods described in Sec. 5.4.5 in connection with fractional factorial designs. In complex cases, it may be necessary to find the relationships numerically in the course of pivoting or Gram-Schmidt orthogonalization of the basis of the rank-n model in the metric of the subclass numbers.

EXAMPLE 5.4-5 (*A three-factor nonorthogonal design*) This example is based on artificial univariate data shown in summary form in Table 5.4-21. The within-group variance estimate, reconstructed from the subclass standard deviations, is

$$\hat{\sigma}^2 = 9.3569$$

The analysis of variance of these data is presented in Table 5.4-22 with the

Table 5.4-21 OBSERVED SUBCLASS MEANS AND STANDARD DEVIATIONS

	Subclass					
	A	*B*	*C*	*N*	Mean	SD
1	1	1	1	10	2.1	3.125
2	1	1	2	9	3.5	2.986
3	1	1	3	8	9.8	3.271
4	1	2	1	7	0	3.111
5	1	2	2	10	1.5	2.895
6	1	2	3	10	2.9	3.175
7	2	1	1	6	4.7	3.250
8	2	1	2	9	5.4	3.011
9	2	1	3	10	9.9	2.943
10	2	2	1	9	2.2	2.751
11	2	2	2	8	3.4	3.167
12	2	2	3	10	4.7	3.112

Table 5.4-22 ANALYSIS OF VARIANCE OF A NONORTHOGONAL $2 \times 2 \times 3$ FACTORIAL DESIGN

Source	df	SS	*F*	*p*
Constant	1	1,865.6530		
A	1	100.6869	10.76	.0015
B	1	302.7512	32.35	<.0001
C	2	385.0050	20.57	<.0001
AB	1	.4493	.05	.83
AC	2	9.6102	.51	.60
BC	2	91.6400	4.89	.009
B	1	295.9646	31.63	<.0001
C	2	405.3582	21.66	<.0001
BC	2	101.3810	5.42	.006
A	1	77.1443	8.24	.005
AB	1	1.4657	.16	.69
AC	2	8.8288	.47	.63
ABC	2	5.5035	.29	.75
Group means	12	2,417.4387		
Within groups	94	879.5486		
Total	106	3,296.9873		

first partition of the sum of squares, shown in the solid rectangle, arbitrarily carried out in lexical order. It is apparent that there is a significant *BC* interaction, indicating that the *B* and *C* factors should be included in the model. The questions remain, however, as to the need for factor *A* and the other interactions. These questions are answered by the partition, shown in the dashed rectangle, in which the *BC* model is ordered before the *A* main effect and the remaining interactions. Since the *A* effect continues clearly significant, but no remaining interaction is significant, it appears that a model of rank 7, consisting of the constant, the *A*, *B*, and *C* main effects, and the *BC* interaction, provides a good representation of these data.

The estimated effects for the rank-7 model generated from the simple contrasts *A*1-*A*2, *B*1-*B*2, *C*1-*C*3, *C*2-*C*3, are shown with their standard errors in Table 5.4-23. While the *A* contrast in Table 5.4-23 is easily interpreted (i.e., the contribution of the *A*2 factor exceeds that of *A*1 by 1.72 units), the nature of *BC* interaction represented by these contrasts is not readily apparent to the unpracticed eye. The situation is clarified, however, if the *estimated* subclass means are computed by premultiplying the vector of contrasts estimated by the basis matrix of the model under which they were estimated [Formula (5.3-47)]. From these estimates, which are shown in Table 5.4-24, the $B \times C$ marginal means displayed in the table are obtained by unweighted averaging of the *A* levels. For completeness, the *A* main-class means are also shown in this table.

It is quite apparent in Table 5.4-24 that the effect of level 3 of factor *C* is much greater when it occurs in combination with level 2 of factor *B*. This interpretation of the *BC* interaction is also conveyed in Fig. 5.4-1 by a plot of the $B \times C$ estimated means.

It is of interest to compute the loss in efficiency which attends the lack of balance in the design. If the 106 observations were spread equally over the subclasses, the number of replicates would have been $r = 8.8333$. According to (5.4-32), the

Table 5.4-23 ESTIMATED CONTRASTS AND STANDARD ERRORS

Effect	Estimate	SE
Constant	4.1450	.2981
A	−1.7200	.5990
B	3.3767	.5962
*C*1	−4.5700	.7353
*C*2	−3.3350	.7127
*BC*1	−3.8000	1.4760
*BC*2	−3.9500	1.4239

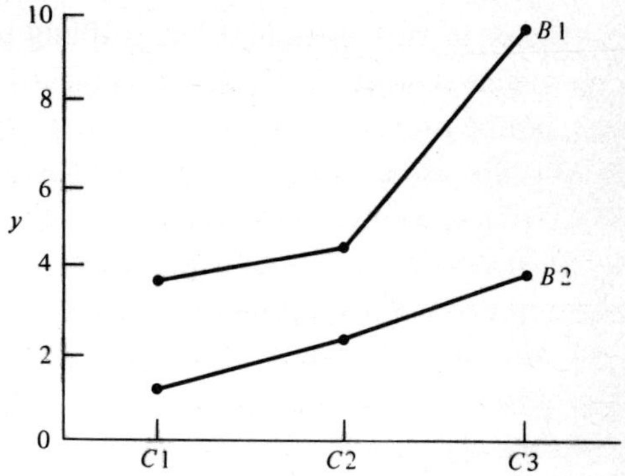

FIGURE 5.4-1
The *BC* interaction.

standard error for the *A* contrast, for example, would then have been

$$\sqrt{\frac{2 \times 9.3569}{6 \times 8.8333}} = .5943$$

This compares with .5990 from Table 5.4-23, indicating an efficiency of 99.2 percent for estimating the *A* contrast by means of the nonorthogonal design. There is no appreciable loss in efficiency in this case.

5.4.5 Fractional Factorial Designs

When investigating the joint effects of many independent variables, we may find that the labor of preparing and administering the treatment combinations may be so great as to rule out a complete factorial experiment. Even restricting the number of levels

Table 5.4-24 ESTIMATED SUBCLASS AND MARGINAL MEANS

1	2.43
2	3.59
3	8.90
4	.27
5	1.58
6	2.94
7	4.15
8	5.31
9	10.62
10	1.99
11	3.30
12	4.66

	*B*1	*B*2
*C*1	3.78	1.13
*C*2	4.45	2.44
*C*3	9.76	3.80

*A*1	3.28
*A*2	5.00

per factor to two, we might be unwilling to undertake, for example, an eight-factor experiment with its $2^8 = 256$ treatment combinations. All combinations may, in fact, not be necessary for an informative experiment. In applications where there is a within-subclass estimate of error and high-order interactions are unlikely to exist, it is quite possible to evaluate main effects and many of the low-order interactions in an incomplete factorial experiment with fewer than the full 2^n combinations. If the retained combinations are properly chosen, the resulting designs are efficient, easy to analyze, and sacrifice only the estimability of high-order interactions.

Experimental arrangements of this type are called *fractional factorial* designs. With respect to the 2^n designs, they typically require only one-fourth, one-half, three-fourths or a similar fraction of the full number of treatment combinations. In this section we shall present briefly the main results for this class of designs and refer the reader to Finney [1960, page 57] or John [1971, pages 143 and 165] for more general fractional designs.

a Half replicates of 2^n designs Recall from Sec. 5.3.3 that the basis matrix of the linear model for a 2^n crossed design may be constructed from the n-fold Kronecker product of columns of the basis matrix for a one-way design with two levels. For example, the basis matrix corresponding to a 2^3 design may be generated from the columns of

$$\begin{bmatrix} 1 & 1 \\ 1 & -1 \end{bmatrix}$$
$$\begin{matrix} (0) & (1) \end{matrix}$$

as specified by the symbolic basis vectors which appear below the following basis matrix:

Subclass				Effects							
A	*B*	*C*	Combinations	*I*	*A*	*B*	*C*	*AB*	*AC*	*BC*	*ABC*
1	1	1	(1)	1	1	1	1	1	1	1	1
1	1	2	*c*	1	1	1	−1	1	−1	−1	−1
1	2	1	*b*	1	1	−1	1	−1	1	−1	−1
1	2	2	*bc*	1	1	−1	−1	−1	−1	1	1
2	1	1	*a*	1	−1	1	1	−1	−1	1	−1
2	1	2	*ac*	1	−1	1	−1	−1	1	−1	1
2	2	1	*ab*	1	−1	−1	1	1	−1	−1	1
2	2	2	*abc*	1	−1	−1	−1	1	1	1	−1
			Symbolic basis vectors	(000)	(100)	(010)	(001)	(110)	(101)	(011)	(111)

Rows of the basis correspond to subclasses enumerated in the natural order of the factorial arrangement as shown at the left of the matrix. Also shown is Yates' [1937] notation for the corresponding treatment combinations: The combination is designated by letters representing level 2 of each treatment, together with the symbol (1) representing treatments all at level 1.

Columns correspond to effects in the design, which may be represented abstractly by the letters designating subspaces shown at the top of the matrix or by the symbolic basis vectors at the bottom. For reasons which will become apparent, the constant effect is denoted by the identity symbol *I*.

To partition the treatment combinations into half replicates, we first choose one of the effects (other than *I*) as the *defining contrast*. Those treatment combinations for which the elements in the basis vector of the defining contrast are positive are then assigned to the first half replicate, and those for which the elements are negative are assigned to the second half replicate. For example, if *ABC* is the defining contrast, the first and second half replicates are the treatment combinations (1), *bc*, *ac*, *ab*, and *c*, *b*, *a*, *abc*, respectively.

The assignment of treatment combinations to half replicates of any 2^n design can be obtained without explicitly constructing the basis by the following rule: The first half replicate consists of those treatment combinations which have an even (or no) letters in common with the defining contrast. The second half replicate has an odd number of letters in common with the defining contrast. Thus, (1), *bc*, *ac*, *ab* have two or no letters in common with *ABC*, and *a*, *b*, *c*, *abc* have one or three letters in common with *ABC*.

Let us now examine the bases for the half replicates by extracting the rows corresponding to the treatment combinations:

Half replicates	Subclasses *A*	*B*	*C*	Treatment combinations	Effects *I*	*A*	*B*	*C*	*AB*	*AC*	*BC*	*ABC*
1	1	1	1	(1)	1	1	1	1	1	1	1	1
	1	2	2	*bc*	1	1	−1	−1	−1	−1	1	1
	2	1	2	*ac*	1	−1	1	−1	−1	1	−1	1
	2	2	1	*ab*	1	−1	−1	1	1	−1	−1	1
2	1	1	2	*c*	1	1	1	−1	1	−1	−1	−1
	1	2	1	*b*	1	1	−1	1	−1	1	−1	−1
	2	1	1	*a*	1	−1	1	1	−1	−1	1	−1
	2	2	2	*abc*	1	−1	−1	−1	1	1	1	−1

We observe that in the bases of the half replicates, certain of the columns are equal and the corresponding effects are thus not separately estimable. We say that such effects are *confounded* and express the *confounding relations* as follows:

Half replicates	
1	*2*
$I = ABC$	$I = -ABC$
$A = BC$	$A = -BC$
$B = AC$	$B = -AC$
$C = AB$	$C = -AB$

The first of these relations (that is, $I = ABC$ and $I = -ABC$) are called the *defining relations* of half replicates. It can be shown that these confounding relations form an abstract (abelian) group with the identity element I under the operations

$$AA = A^2 = I$$

$$BB = B^2 = I$$

$$CC = C^2 = I$$

Operating on both sides of the defining relation with A, B, and C, respectively, we thus generate the confounding relations shown above.

The implication of the defining relations for these half replicates is that the main effects are confounded with the two-factor interactions. The usefulness of these particular designs for testing or estimating main effects is therefore limited to applications where the two-factor as well as the three-factor interactions can be assumed null (cf, the latin-square designs). On this assumption, a conventional 2^2 factorial analysis of the half replicates provides sums of squares and estimates for the main effects of the 2^3 design. That is, the analysis of the half replicates is the same as that for a 2^2 design, but the interpretation is in terms of the main effects of the 2^3 design. In the absence of two-factor interaction, the correspondence of sums of squares, for example, is as follows:

Complete 2^2	Fractional 2^3
M	M
A	A
B	B
AB	C

Similarly, the estimate of the AB contrast in the first half replicate estimates the C contrast, while this estimate in the second half replicate estimates the negative of the C contrast. These correspondences are implied in the confounding relations.

The smallest designs of this class with any general utility are the half replicates of the 2^4 factorial defined by the contrast $ABCD$. Written in lexical order, the treatment combinations for these designs are obviously (1), *ab*, *ac*, *ad*, *bc*, *bd*, *cd*, *abcd* and *a*, *b*, *c*, *d*, *abc*, *abd*, *acd*, *bcd*, and the confounding relations are:

$$\begin{array}{rlrl} I = & ABCD & I = & -ABCD \\ A = & BCD & A = & -BCD \\ B = & ACD & B = & -ACD \\ C = & ABD & C = & -ABD \\ D = & ABC & D = & -ABC \\ AB = & CD & AB = & -CD \\ AC = & BD & AC = & -BD \\ BC = & AD & BC = & -AD \end{array}$$

With these designs, the main-effect analysis requires only the assumption that three- and four-factor interactions are null. The two-factor interactions are confounded with each other but could be tested jointly. With no three- or four-factor interaction, the interpretation of sums of squares in the 2^3 analysis of these half replicates of the 2^4 design is as follows:

Complete 2^3	Fractional 2^4
M	M
A	A
B	B
C	C
AB	$CD + AB$
AC	$BD + AC$
BC	$AD + BC$
ABC	D

b Quarter replicates Quarter replicates of 2^n designs are the intersections of two defining contrasts; i.e., they are half replicates of half replicates. Suppose the defining contrasts are in general P and Q. Then the treatment combinations in the replicates are specified by the four combinations of an even number (or no) letters in common with P and/or Q, and an odd number of letters in common with P and/or Q. The defining relations are $I = \pm P = \pm Q = \pm PQ$, where PQ, called the *general interaction*, is the result of the group operation upon P and Q and is also part of the confounding relation.

Suppose, for example, that two defining contrasts for a 2^4 design are $P = AB$ and $Q = ACD$. Then the quarter replicates and their defining relations are

Fraction	P	Q	Treatment combinations	Defining relations
11	Even	Even	*ab,c,d,abd*	$I = AB = ACD = BCD$
12	Even	Odd	*a,bc,bd,acd*	$I = -AB = ACD = -BCD$
21	Odd	Even	*(1),cd,abc,abd*	$I = AB = -ACD = -BCD$
22	Odd	Odd	*b,ac,ad,bcd*	$I = -AB = -ACD = BCD$

This design is not very useful because main effects are confounded. In fraction *11*, for example:

$$A = B = CD = ABCD$$
$$B = A = ABCD = CD$$
$$C = ABC = AD = BD$$
$$D = ABD = AC = BC$$

Furthermore, the 2^2 analysis of this fraction is not informative because AB is confounded with I. Quarter replicates of larger designs may be valuable, however, and even the above quarter replicates are useful for generating *three-quarter* replicates without prohibitive confounding.

c Three-quarter replicates Suppose one of the above quarter replicates, say *11*, is omitted from the complete 2^4 design. From the remaining quarters, we may construct the three distinct half replicates *12* + *21*, *12* + *22*, and *21* + *22*. Since the union of the treatment combinations defined by $I = P$ and $I = -P$ is the complete design, we have for these half replicates the following specifications:

Fraction	Treatment combinations	Defining relations
12 + *21*	(1),*a*,*bc*,*cd*,*abc*,*abd*,*acd*	$I = -BCD$
12 + *22*	*a*,*b*,*ac*,*ad*,*bc*,*bd*,*acd*,*bcd*	$I = -AB$
21 + *22*	(1),*ac*,*ad*,*cd*,*abc*,*abd*,*bcd*	$I = -ACD$

Thus, in *12* + *21*, A is confounded only with the four-factor interaction; in *21* + *22*, B is confounded with $-ABCD$; and in *12* + *23*, C and D are confounded only with three-factor interactions. Furthermore, AB is confounded only with three-factor interactions in both *12* + *21* and *21* + *22*; AC and AD are similarly estimable from *12* + *21*; BC and BD are estimable from *21* + *22*; and CD is estimable from *12* + *22*.

The analysis of variance and estimation for the three-quarter replicates follow from the general least-squares solution and will not be discussed here. The results are straightforward, however, and hand solution is quite feasible (see John [1971, page 161]). An application of a three-quarter replication of a 2^4 factorial design appears in Example 5.4-4.

d Block confounded factorials Confounding is also useful in situations where the block size is too small to accept all treatment combinations. If the blocks are each large enough to accommodate a half replicate of a 2^n design, the experiment can be carried out by confounding one of the treatment effects (usually the highest-order interaction) with the block effects. This is done by assigning the treatment combinations specified by $I = P$ to one or more blocks and those specified by $I = -P$

to an equal number of other blocks. All effects other than P can then be estimated without bias due to block effects. Furthermore, if the blocks are arranged in replicates containing a pair of blocks, different effects may be confounded in different replicates. It may then be possible to estimate all effects, although the confounded effects will be estimated with less precision than the unconfounded effects. Block confounding is valuable in educational studies in which schools are blocks and classrooms within schools are the experimental units. Because few schools have even as many as eight classes per grade, block-confounded designs may be needed whenever joint effects of three or more factors are in question (see Kirk [1968]).

EXAMPLE 5.4-6 (*A three-quarter-replicate study of aptitude × treatment interaction*) In dissertation research, Whang [1971] investigated the interaction of individual differences in short-term memory span with conditions of paired-associate learning. The experimental task, which was presented to sixth-grade school children, was to learn the English meanings of 16 French words. None of the subjects had any previous exposure to French. The paired English and French words were presented by means of tape recording under the following conditions:

- A With versus without overt rehearsal
- B With versus without visual aids
- C With versus without semantic organization

An additional factor (D) was introduced by classifying subjects in each treatment group as high or low on the auditory memory span subtest of the WAIS.

Of the 2^3 possible treatment combinations, the two involving semantic organization of the stimuli with no rehearsal were difficult to realize and were omitted. Thus, the design included only 12 of the 16 possible subclasses of the 2^4 design with factor D. The subclasses retained in the design are identified in Table 5.4-25.

The subjects in each treatment group were exposed to paired presentations of the stimulus words. At the end of each trial and in a posttest on a day following the experiment, the number of associates known to each subject was evaluated in a paper-and-pencil test. For each subclass of the four-factor design, Table 5.4-25 shows the mean and standard deviation of the posttest scores transformed as

$$y = \sin^{-1}\sqrt{\frac{r + \frac{1}{2}}{n + \frac{1}{2}}}$$

(where r is the number right, and $n = 16$ is the number of pairs) in order to remove dependency of the subclass variance on the mean.

In order to analyze the data in Table 5.4-25, we must deduce the confounding relations among the effects in the 2^4 design of which the present design is a three-quarter replicate. Inspecting the treatment combinations, we see that the four which have been omitted are *c*, *bc*, *cd*, and *bcd*. The defining relations of this quarter replicate are obviously $I = A$ and $I = -C$, for *a* appears no times and *c* appears an odd number of times in each. Thus, the defining relations and treatment combinations of the other three-quarter replicates are

$I = A = C = AC$	$I = -A = C = -AC$	$I = -A = -C = AC$
22 (1)	*21* *a*	*11* *ac*
b	*ab*	*abc*
d	*ad*	*acd*
bd	*abd*	*abcd*

From these quarter replicates, the following three half replicates and their confounding relations can be constructed:

22 + 21		*22 + 11*		*21 + 11*	
	$I = C$		$I = AC$		$I = A$
	$A = AC$		$B = ABC$		$C = AC$
	$AB = ABC$		$D = ACD$		$BC = ABC$
	$AD = ACD$		$BD = ABCD$		$CD = ACD$
	$ABD = ABCD$				$BCD = ABCD$

Thus, if *AC* is assumed null, all main effects are estimable; if *ABC* and *ACD* are assumed null, all two-factor interactions except *AC* are estimable; if *ABCD* is assumed null, *ABD* and *ACD* are estimable. An interpretable general solution can therefore be carried out on these data if the basis is generated according to the follow-

Table 5.4-25 TRANSFORMED SCORES FOR THE POSTTEST OF PAIRED ASSOCIATE LEARNING

Factors *A*	*B*	*C*	*D*	Treatment combinations	*N*	Mean	SD
1	1	1	1	(1)	19	.8478	.2211
1	1	1	2	*d*	15	1.0888	.2045
1	2	1	1	*b*	18	.9476	.2918
1	2	1	2	*bd*	17	1.1103	.2946
2	1	1	1	*a*	20	1.1313	.2546
2	1	1	2	*ad*	12	1.1145	.2044
2	1	2	1	*ac*	17	1.1544	.2963
2	1	2	2	*acd*	11	1.2943	.1862
2	2	1	1	*ab*	18	1.1509	.1862
2	2	1	2	*abd*	10	1.2589	.2767
2	2	2	1	*abc*	16	1.3852	.2089
2	2	2	2	*abcd*	12	1.4028	.2213

ing symbolic basis vectors:

Effect	SBV	Effect	SBV
M	0 0 0 0	*AD*	1 0 0 1
A	1 0 0 0	*BC*	0 1 1 0
B	0 1 0 0	*BD*	0 1 0 1
C	0 0 1 0	*CD*	0 0 1 1
D	0 0 0 1	*ABD*	1 1 0 1
AB	1 1 0 0	*BCD*	0 1 1 1

The analysis and interpretation of the data in Table 5.4-25 are left to the reader as Exercise 5.4-2.

Exercise 5.4-1 Table 5.4-26 presents summary data taken from the programmed-instruction study by Yabroff and described in Sec. 5.4.4. Although the authors reported results for a variety of outcome measures, only the counts of errors during instruction, classified according to their occurrence on rule frames or problem frames, are reproduced in the table. The authors do not report an error covariance matrix for these measures, but they give the total standard deviations and correlations, presented in Table 5.4-27, from which the within-groups covariance matrix can be recovered for purposes of this exercise.

Perform a bivariate analysis of variance on these data for evidence of treatment effects and possible interactions with IQ level. More than one order of elimination may be necessary. Make use of the within-groups SSP matrix for the error estimate.

Exercise 5.4-2 The main hypothesis of Whang's [1971] study discussed in Example 5.4-6 was that subjects with poor auditory short-term memory would benefit more from overt rehearsal than subjects who were proficient in this respect. Perform an analysis of variance to test this hypothesis, bearing in mind that the hypothesis is directional. Use the within-groups variance estimate of .059052 on 173 degrees of freedom as the error term.

Discuss all significant effects in the data and depict significant interactions graphically, using the appropriate estimated marginal means.

5.5 ERROR REDUCTION BY ANALYSIS OF COVARIANCE

It is not uncommon in behavioral experimentation for the investigator to have available one or more quantitative measures related to the initial state of the material. An example might be a rating of the clinical status of mental patients prior to their assignment to experimental therapeutic programs. This information could, of course, be used to increase the efficiency of the experiment by blocking the material with respect to the rating levels, and employing a randomized block design, but this would not necessarily be the best use to which the information could be put. In general, a greater gain in efficiency could be achieved by retaining the simple randomized design and using the rating measure as a *covariable* in an *analysis of covariance* of the outcome measures.

Analysis of covariance typically delivers a greater gain in efficiency than blocking because, first, some heterogeneity of the material remains within the blocks after blocking and, second, the regression of error on the covariable may be linear or low-degree polynomial, and thus its estimation in the analysis of covariance will consume fewer degrees of freedom than estimation of block effects. Exploitation of one or more covariables does not, however, preclude blocking on other variables. Any purely qualitative (nominal) indicators of heterogeneity should obviously be retained as blocking criteria and the analysis of covariance carried out in the context of the

Table 5.4-26 ERRORS DURING INSTRUCTION WITH FOUR TYPES OF PROGRAMS IN TWO IQ GROUPS

Experimental groups				Mean errors	
IQ	Instructional method	Sequence of rule and problem frames	N	Rule frames	Problem frames
High	Inductive	Mixed	33	4.36	11.30
		Blocked	33	5.12	12.45
	Deductive	Mixed	38	2.05	10.07
		Blocked	32	2.25	7.34
Low	Inductive	Mixed	37	5.05	14.70
		Blocked	31	4.09	14.64
	Deductive	Mixed	31	3.54	13.54
		Blocked	37	3.48	11.48

Table 5.4-27 TOTAL STANDARD DEVIATIONS AND CORRELATIONS (CORRECTED TO THE GRAND MEAN) OF ERRORS DURING INSTRUCTION ($N = 272$)

	1	*2*
Correlations		
1 Errors on rule frames	1.00	
2 Errors on problem frames	.61	1.00
SD	3.0	7.6

randomized block analysis. Indeed, if covariables are available, analysis of covariance can be applied to experimental designs of any complexity. The major caution which should be observed, however, is that the measurements for the covariables are obtained *prior to* the assignment of experimental units to treatments. This ensures that the treatment effect will not be correlated with the covariables and helps ensure that the regression of errors on the covariables will be homogeneous from one treatment group to another.

In large samples, the analysis of covariance can be carried out by first calculating residuals from the common within-subclass regression, and then performing on these residuals the analysis of variance appropriate to the experimental design. In small samples, however, this method is inexact because it neglects the sampling errors incurred in the estimation of the regression coefficients. A better procedure for routine use is the exact least-squares solution given by Fisher [1967, page 272ff]. In this section we discuss the multivariate generalization of this solution.

5.5.1 The Combined Design and Regression Model

Consider a randomized experiment in which there are p response variables and q covariables (for example, the response variables and covariables might be, respectively, the "posttest" and "pretest" scores of an educational experiment). Let there be a total of n subclasses in the design with possibly unequal numbers $N_1, N_2, \ldots, N_n$ of experimental units in subclasses $1, 2, \ldots, n$. Let the $(p + q) \times 1$ vector observation of the ith subject in the jth subclass be represented by

$$[\mathbf{y}'_{ij}, \mathbf{x}'_{ij}] = [y_{ij}{}^{(1)} \quad y_{ij}{}^{(2)} \quad \cdots \quad y_{ij}{}^{(p)} \quad x_{ij}{}^{(1)} \quad x_{ij}{}^{(2)} \quad \cdots \quad x_{ij}{}^{(q)}]$$

where the y's designate response variables, and the x's covariables. (In the case of a crossed design, j may actually be a multiple subscript.) Then the vector mean for the jth subclass is

$$[\mathbf{y}'_{\cdot j}, \mathbf{x}'_{\cdot j}] = \left[\frac{1}{N_j}\sum_{i=1}^{N_j} \mathbf{y}'_{ij}, \frac{1}{N_j}\sum_{i=1}^{N_j} \mathbf{x}'_{ij}\right]$$

and, according to our conventions, the total data matrix and matrix of subclass means may be represented as

$$\underset{N \times (p+q)}{[\mathbf{Y}, \mathbf{X}]} \qquad \text{and} \qquad \underset{n \times (p+q)}{[\mathbf{Y}_{\cdot}, \mathbf{X}_{\cdot}]}$$

where $N = \sum_{j=1}^{n} N_j$.

Assume now a model for the design effects which, reparameterized, may be expressed for the subclass means as

$$\underset{n \times p}{\boldsymbol{Y}_{\cdot}} = \underset{n \times l}{\mathbf{K}} \underset{l \times p}{\boldsymbol{\Theta}} + \underset{n \times p}{\boldsymbol{E}_{\cdot}} \qquad (5.5\text{-}1)$$

Assume further that the regression of the errors on the covariables is

$$\underset{N\times p}{\boldsymbol{E}} = \underset{N\times q}{\mathbf{X}}\underset{q\times p}{\mathbf{B}} + \underset{N\times p}{\boldsymbol{E}^*}$$

where $\boldsymbol{E}^*$ are the reduced errors distributed as $\boldsymbol{E}^* \sim N(\underset{N\times 1}{\mathbf{1}} \times \underset{p\times 1}{\mathbf{0}}, \underset{N\times N}{\mathbf{I}} \times \underset{p\times p}{\Sigma})$.

Then the regression of the mean errors is

$$\underset{n\times p}{\boldsymbol{E}.} = \underset{n\times q}{\mathbf{X}.}\underset{q\times p}{\mathbf{B}} + \underset{n\times p}{\boldsymbol{E}^*_.} \tag{5.5-2}$$

with

$$\boldsymbol{E}^*_. \sim N(\underset{n\times 1}{\mathbf{1}} \times \underset{p\times 1}{\mathbf{0}}, \underset{n\times n}{\mathbf{D}^{-1}} \times \underset{p\times p}{\Sigma})$$

where $\mathbf{D} = \text{diag}[N_1, N_2, \ldots, N_n]$.

Substituting (5.5-2) in (5.5-1), we have a linear model incorporating both the design effects and the regression effects:

$$\boldsymbol{Y}. = \mathbf{K}\boldsymbol{\Theta} + \mathbf{X}.\mathbf{B} + \boldsymbol{E}^*_. \tag{5.5-3}$$

There is, however, an additional complication to be considered. In most cases, some of the design effects are hypothesized and must be tested critically, while others are known or assumed to exist and need not be tested. (Treatment effects are examples of the former, and block effects examples of the latter.) Let there be n_h degrees of freedom for the hypothesized effects, and n_o degrees of freedom for the other effects ($n_o + n_h = l$). Then we may set

$$\mathbf{K} = \underset{\quad n_o \quad n_h}{[\mathbf{K}_o, \mathbf{K}_h]}\ n \qquad \text{and} \qquad \boldsymbol{\Theta} = \underset{p}{\begin{bmatrix} \boldsymbol{\Theta}_o \\ \boldsymbol{\Theta}_h \end{bmatrix}} \begin{matrix} n_o \\ n_h \end{matrix}$$

and write (5.5-3) as

$$\mathbf{Y}. = \mathbf{K}_o\boldsymbol{\Theta}_o + \mathbf{K}_h\boldsymbol{\Theta}_h + \mathbf{X}.\mathbf{B} + \boldsymbol{E}^*_. \tag{5.5-4}$$

In fitting (5.5-4) to the data, there are two main questions to be considered: (1) Is the regression term required? That is, can we reject

$$H_0(1)\colon \mathbf{B} = \mathbf{O}$$

(2) Given that $\mathbf{B} \neq \mathbf{O}$, are the hypothesized design effects required? That is, can we reject

$$H_0(2)\colon \boldsymbol{\Theta}_h = \mathbf{O}$$

The first question may be answered by a stepwise or blockwise least-squares analysis proceeding through the terms in (5.5-3) in the order shown. We shall refer to this procedure as the *analysis of regression.* The second question is answered by a similar analysis after reordering (5.5-4) and adding terms from left to right in

$$\boldsymbol{Y}. = \mathbf{K}_o\boldsymbol{\Theta}_o + \mathbf{X}.\mathbf{B} + \mathbf{K}_h\boldsymbol{\Theta}_h + \boldsymbol{E}^*_. \tag{5.5-5}$$

The test of $H_0(2)$ by means of the latter procedure is the *analysis of covariance* as such. In general, these two tests of hypotheses will not be independent, but there is no way to avoid this difficulty, and both tests are usually performed.

The calculations for both the analysis of regression and analysis of covariance can be carried out by direct application of the orthogonalization or pivoting algorithms to (5.5-1) and (5.5-5). But when there are several sets of hypothesized effects to be tested in one analysis, the following indirect method, based on a preliminary analysis of variance of the response variables and covariables jointly, is much more convenient.

5.5.2 The Joint Multivariate Analysis of Variance

All the sample statistics required for the analysis of regression and the analysis of covariance may be obtained from a partition of sums of squares and products (as appropriate for the design part of the model) in which the response variables and covariables are entered as one $p + q$ set of variables. This partition will take essentially the form presented in Table 5.5-1. Each of the SSP matrices in this table may be partitioned into submatrices as shown, but only the submatrices of SSH and SSE enter into the subsequent computations.

At the same time that the calculations of Table 5.5-1 are performed, it is convenient to compute estimates of design effects for the two sets of variables jointly. In an obvious notation, the estimates are given by

$$[\hat{\Theta}^{(y)}, \hat{\Theta}^{(x)}] = \begin{bmatrix} \hat{\Theta}_o^{(y)} & \hat{\Theta}_o^{(x)} \\ \hat{\Theta}_h^{(y)} & \hat{\Theta}_h^{(x)} \end{bmatrix} = (\mathbf{K}'\mathbf{D}\mathbf{K})^{-1}\mathbf{K}'\mathbf{D}[\mathbf{Y}_{.}, \mathbf{X}_{.}] \qquad (5.5\text{-}6)$$

Table 5.5-1 PARTITION OF THE SUM OF SQUARES AND PRODUCTS OF THE RESPONSE VARIABLES AND THE COVARIABLES JOINTLY

Source	df	SSP $(p + q) \times (p + q)$
Other effects, ignoring hypothesized effects	n_o	$\text{SSO} = \begin{bmatrix} \mathbf{S}_o^{(y)} & \mathbf{S}_o^{(yx)} \\ \mathbf{S}_o^{(xy)} & \mathbf{S}_o^{(x)} \end{bmatrix} \begin{matrix} p \\ q \end{matrix}$ with columns p, q
Hypothesized effects, eliminating other effects	n_h	$\text{SSH} = \begin{bmatrix} \mathbf{S}_h^{(y)} & \mathbf{S}_h^{(yx)} \\ \mathbf{S}_h^{(xy)} & \mathbf{S}_h^{(x)} \end{bmatrix} \begin{matrix} p \\ q \end{matrix}$ with columns p, q
Error	n_e	$\text{SSE} = \begin{bmatrix} \mathbf{S}_e^{(y)} & \mathbf{S}_e^{(yx)} \\ \mathbf{S}_e^{(xy)} & \mathbf{S}_e^{(x)} \end{bmatrix} \begin{matrix} p \\ q \end{matrix}$ with columns p, q
Total	N	$\text{SST} = \begin{bmatrix} \mathbf{S}_t^{(y)} & \mathbf{S}_t^{(yx)} \\ \mathbf{S}_t^{(xy)} & \mathbf{S}_t^{(x)} \end{bmatrix} \begin{matrix} p \\ q \end{matrix}$ with columns p, q

These estimates will be required later when the time comes to estimate $\boldsymbol{\Theta}_h$ under model (5.5-5).

The role of SSH and SSE in the analysis of regression and the analysis of covariance will perhaps be most easily understood if the results are presented first and their derivation deferred until after an example has been exhibited.

5.5.3 Analysis of Regression

The test of $H_0(1)$ is based on a further partition of $\mathbf{S}_e^{(y)}$ from Table 5.5-1 as shown in Table 5.5-2.

For a multivariate test of $H_0(1)$, we may compute and order by size the $\min(p,q)$ nonzero roots of

$$|\mathbf{S}_r^{(y)} - \lambda \mathbf{S}_e^*| = 0$$

required for one of the test criteria of Sec. 3.4. In particular, the largest-root statistic in the form of a generalized F with $\nu_1 = q$ and $\nu_2 = n_e$ is

$$F_0 = \frac{t}{r} \lambda_1 \qquad (5.5\text{-}7)$$

where $r = |p - q| + 1$

$s = \min(p,q)$

$t = n_e - q - p + 1$

The trace criterion and likelihood-ratio criterion are the same as in Sec. 3.4, with ν_1 and ν_2 defined as in (5.5-7).

Finally, the ratio of the kth diagonal elements of $\mathbf{S}_r^{(y)}$ and $\mathbf{S}_e^{(y)}$ divided by their degrees of freedom is a univariate F for the kth response variable:

$$F_k = \frac{[\mathbf{S}_r^{(y)}]_{kk}/q}{[\mathbf{S}_e^*]_{kk}/(n_e - q)} \qquad (5.5\text{-}8)$$

on q and $n_e - q$ degrees of freedom. These tests will be illustrated in Example 5.5-1.

If $H_0(1)$ is rejected and the covariates incorporated in the model, then the

Table 5.5-2 MULTIVARIATE ANALYSIS OF REGRESSION

Source	df	SSP ($p \times p$)	$\mathscr{E}$(SSP)
Regression effects, eliminating design effects	q	$\mathbf{S}_r^{(y)} = \mathbf{S}_e^{(yx)}(\mathbf{S}_e^{(x)})^{-1}\mathbf{S}_e^{(xy)}$	$q\boldsymbol{\Sigma} + \mathbf{B}'\mathbf{S}_e^{(y)}\mathbf{B}$
Reduced residual	$n_e - q$	$\mathbf{S}_e^* = \mathbf{S}_e^{(y)} - \mathbf{S}_r^{(y)}$	$(n_e - q)\boldsymbol{\Sigma}$
Error	n_e	$\mathbf{S}_e^{(y)} = \mathbf{S}_t^{(y)} - \mathbf{S}_o^{(y)} - \mathbf{S}_h^{(y)}$	

least-squares estimate of **B** jointly with the design effects is

$$\hat{\mathbf{B}} = (\mathbf{S}_e^{(x)})^{-1}\mathbf{S}_e^{(xy)} \qquad (5.5\text{-}9)$$

The estimator is unbiased,

$$\mathscr{E}(\boldsymbol{B}) = \mathbf{B}$$

and its variance-covariance matrix is

$$\mathscr{V}(\boldsymbol{B}) = (\mathbf{S}_e^{(x)})^{-1} \times \Sigma \qquad (5.5\text{-}10)$$

The elements of $\hat{\mathbf{B}}$ are the estimated raw regression coefficients which are used in (5.5-13) to compute the estimate of $\boldsymbol{\Theta}_h$ in the full model specified by (5.5-4). For interpretational purposes, we may wish to standardize the regression coefficients by dividing columns of $\hat{\mathbf{B}}$ by the reduced error standard deviation of the response variables and multiplying rows by the corresponding standard deviations of the covariables, as in (3.3-18).

5.5.4 Analysis of Covariance

For the test of $H_0(2)$, we extract from Table 5.5-1 the error and hypothesis SSP matrix and form the provisional "total" matrix

$$\mathbf{S}_{t'} = \begin{bmatrix} \mathbf{S}_{t'}^{(y)} & \mathbf{S}_{t'}^{(yx)} \\ \mathbf{S}_{t'}^{(xy)} & \mathbf{S}_{t'}^{(x)} \end{bmatrix} = \begin{bmatrix} \mathbf{S}_h^{(y)} & \mathbf{S}_h^{(yx)} \\ \mathbf{S}_h^{(xy)} & \mathbf{S}_h^{(x)} \end{bmatrix} + \begin{bmatrix} \mathbf{S}_e^{(y)} & \mathbf{S}_e^{(yx)} \\ \mathbf{S}_e^{(xy)} & \mathbf{S}_e^{(x)} \end{bmatrix}$$

Using the submatrices of $\mathbf{S}_{t'}$, we compute, as shown in Table 5.5-3, the matrix $\mathbf{S}_h^*$ of sums of squares and products for the hypothesized effects, eliminating effects

Table 5.5-3 MULTIVARIATE ANALYSIS OF COVARIANCE

Source	df	SSP ($p \times p$)	$\mathscr{E}$(SSP)*
Other effects, ignoring regression and hypothesized effects	n_o	$\mathbf{S}_o^{(y)} = \mathbf{Y}_{.}\mathbf{D}\mathbf{K}_o(\mathbf{K}_o'\mathbf{D}\mathbf{K}_o)^{-1}\mathbf{K}_o'\mathbf{D}\mathbf{Y}_{.}$	
Regression, ignoring hypothesized effects and eliminating other effects	q	$\mathbf{S}_{r'}^{(y)} = \mathbf{S}_{t'}^{(yx)}(\mathbf{S}_{t'}^{(x)})^{-1}\mathbf{S}_{t'}^{(xy)}$	$q\Sigma + [\mathbf{B} + (\mathbf{X}'\mathbf{X})^{-1}\mathbf{X}_{.}\mathbf{D}\mathbf{K}_h^{*\prime}\boldsymbol{\Theta}_h]' \cdot \mathbf{S}_t^{(x)}[\mathbf{B} + (\mathbf{X}'\mathbf{X})^{-1}\mathbf{X}_{.}\mathbf{D}\mathbf{K}_h^{*\prime}\boldsymbol{\Theta}_h]$
Hypothesized effects, eliminating other effects and regression	n_h	$\mathbf{S}_h^* = \mathbf{S}_{t'}^{(y)} - \mathbf{S}_{r'}^{(y)}$	$n_h\Sigma + \boldsymbol{\Theta}_h'\mathbf{K}_h^{*\prime}[\mathbf{D} - \mathbf{D}\mathbf{X}_{.}(\mathbf{X}'\mathbf{X})^{-1} \cdot \mathbf{X}_{.}'\mathbf{D}]\mathbf{K}_h^*\boldsymbol{\Theta}_h$
Reduced residual	$n_e - q$	(from Table 5.5-2)	$(n_e - q)\Sigma$
Total	N	$\mathbf{S}_t^{(y)} = \mathbf{Y}\mathbf{Y}$	

* See Sec. 5.5.5.

due to other terms in the design model and to regression on the covariates. This matrix is referred to as the *adjusted* sum of squares and products for the hypothesis. From this matrix and the reduced error matrix of Table 5.5-2, the criteria for the test of $H_0(2)$ are computed in terms of the roots of

$$|\mathbf{S}_h^* - \lambda \mathbf{S}_e^*| = 0$$

In particular, the generalized F with $\nu_1 = n_h$ and $\nu_2 = n_e - q$ is computed from the largest root as

$$F_0 = \frac{t}{r}\lambda_1 \qquad (5.5\text{-}11)$$

with $r = |n_h - p| + 1$

$s = \min(p,n_h)$

$t = n_e - q - p + 1$

For the kth separate response variable, the univariate F statistic is computed from the kth diagonal elements of $\mathbf{S}_h^*$ and $\mathbf{S}_e^*$; that is,

$$F_k = \frac{[\mathbf{S}_h^*]_{kk}/n_h}{[\mathbf{S}_e^*]_{kk}/(n_e - q)} \qquad (5.5\text{-}12)$$

on n_h and $n_e - q$ degrees of freedom.

If both $H_0(1)$ and $H_0(2)$ are rejected, we shall wish to estimate Θ_h with the covariables included in the model. These estimates are most easily obtained by "adjusting" the estimates in (5.5-6) as follows:

$$\hat{\Theta}_h^* = \hat{\Theta}_h^{(y)} - \hat{\Theta}_h^{(x)}\hat{\mathbf{B}} \qquad (5.5\text{-}13)$$

The adjusted estimator is unbiased,

$$\mathscr{E}(\mathbf{\Theta}_h^*) = \Theta_h$$

and its variance-covariance matrix is

$$\mathscr{V}(\mathbf{\Theta}_h^*) = \{[(\mathbf{K}'\mathbf{D}\mathbf{K})^{-1}]_h + \hat{\Theta}_h^{(x)}(\mathbf{S}_e^{(x)})^{-1}\hat{\Theta}_h^{(x)\prime}\} \times \Sigma \qquad (5.5\text{-}14)$$

where $[(\mathbf{K}'\mathbf{D}\mathbf{K})^{-1}]_h$ is the $n_h \times n_h$ lower-right submatrix of $(\mathbf{K}'\mathbf{D}\mathbf{K})^{-1}$. For purposes of obtaining standard errors and constructing confidence bounds for elements of Θ_h, Σ is estimated from the reduced error matrix by dividing by the reduced error degrees of freedom:

$$\hat{\Sigma} = \frac{1}{n_e - q}\mathbf{S}_e^* \qquad (5.5\text{-}15)$$

It should be understood, of course, that (5.5-14) is the *conditional* covariance matrix of $\mathbf{\Theta}_h^*$. That is, it gives the variances and covariances of the estimates in samples in which the covariables are set at the given values $\mathbf{X}$ so that $\Theta_h^{(x)}$ is a fixed and not a random quantity. Actually, to realize these variances and covariances and the associated standard errors and confidence bounds, it would be necessary to select experimental units in future samples so as to reproduce the covariable values exactly.

If $H_0(1)$ is rejected but $H_0(2)$ is not, the model to be fitted is, say,

$$\boldsymbol{Y}. = \mathbf{K}_o\boldsymbol{\Theta}_o + \mathbf{X.B} + \boldsymbol{E}^{**} \qquad (5.5\text{-}16)$$

In this model, the regression coefficients are estimated by

$$\hat{\mathbf{B}}_{t'} = \mathbf{S}_{t'}^{(yx)}(S_{t'}^{(x)})^{-1} \qquad (5.5\text{-}17)$$

with $\qquad \mathscr{E}(\boldsymbol{B}_{t'}) = \mathbf{B} \qquad \mathscr{V}(\boldsymbol{B}_{t'}) = (\mathbf{S}_{t'}^{(x)})^{-1} \times \Sigma$

The adjusted design effects are then

$$\underset{n_o \times p}{\hat{\boldsymbol{\Theta}}_o} = \underset{n_o \times p}{\hat{\boldsymbol{\Theta}}_o^{(y)}} - \underset{n_o \times q}{\hat{\boldsymbol{\Theta}}_o^{(x)}} \underset{q \times p}{\hat{\mathbf{B}}_{t'}} \qquad (5.5\text{-}18)$$

where $\qquad [\hat{\boldsymbol{\Theta}}_o^{(y)}, \hat{\boldsymbol{\Theta}}_o^{(x)}] = (\mathbf{K}_o'\mathbf{D}\mathbf{K}_o)^{-1}\mathbf{K}_o'\mathbf{D}[\mathbf{Y}., \mathbf{X}.]$

and $\quad \mathscr{E}(\boldsymbol{\Theta}_o) = \boldsymbol{\Theta}_o \qquad \mathscr{V}(\boldsymbol{\Theta}_o) = [(\mathbf{K}_o'\mathbf{K}\mathbf{D}_o)^{-1} + \hat{\boldsymbol{\Theta}}_o^{(x)}(\mathbf{S}_t^{(x)})^{-1}\hat{\boldsymbol{\Theta}}_o^{(x)'}] \times \Sigma \qquad (5.5\text{-}19)$

Again, the variances of these estimators are conditional on the observed values of the covariables.

EXAMPLE 5.5-1 (*Machine-assisted versus conventional reading instruction*) The study of reading methods described in Exercise 5.3-4 [Hudson, 1971] also included pretest scores for Binet IQ and the Family Functioning Instrument. We may use these pretest scores as covariables to exemplify the calculations of analysis of covariance and to demonstrate the gain in experimental efficiency that can be obtained by its use.

The group means and the within-group standard deviations and correlations for the three posttests and two pretests are shown in Table 5.5-4. For purposes of the

Table 5.5-4 MEANS, STANDARD DEVIATIONS AND CORRELATIONS (WITHIN GROUP) FOR PRETEST AND POSTTEST SCORES FROM A STUDY OF MACHINE-ASSISTED READING INSTRUCTION IN TWO SOCIAL-SERVICE POPULATIONS

Group means			Posttests			Pretests	
Instructional method	Casework	*N*	Binet(2)	MRRT	FFI(2)	Binet(1)	FFI(1)
Talking typewriter	Intensive	34	89.9118	26.1760	4.7088	89.1176	4.2000
	Regular	34	91.1176	22.0882	4.5176	89.7647	4.2059
Conventional	Intensive	34	85.2059	20.9706	4.4368	88.6176	3.9441
	Regular	34	87.4090	20.0364	4.2664	89.7722	4.1352
Within-group standard deviations			10.43117	7.35293	.71517	10.58159	.77730
Correlations			1.00000				(symmetric)
			.31716	1.00000			
			.10931	.10119	1.00000		
			.52966	.28801	.19597	1.00000	
			.04806	.11479	.60225	.16328	1.00000

present example, the data have been simplified by combining scores for the two sexes (sex effects were not significant in this study). The within-group statistics are, however, the same as those of the original analysis and exclude the degree of freedom due to sex. Slightly different values would have been obtained if the within-group statistics had been computed from the original data, ignoring sex.

The first step in the analysis of covariance is the partition of the sum of squares and products for the five variables jointly. SSP matrices of this partition are shown in Table 5.5-5. Note that because the design is orthogonal, the order of elimination of effects is immaterial and the formulas of Table 5.4-1 apply. Note also that the error SSP matrix of Table 5.5-5 has been obtained by reproducing the within-group covariance matrix from the standard deviations and correlations in Table 5.5-4, then multiplying by the within-group degree of freedom for the present analysis (df = 132).

The second step in the computations is the regression analysis performed on the error SSP matrix according to the formulas of Table 5.5-2. The result is the partition of $\mathbf{S}_e^{(y)}$ shown in Table 5.5-6. In preparation for the statistical test of regression, the characteristic roots of the regression SSP in the metric of the reduced error SSP

Table 5.5-5 SSP MATRICES COMPUTED FROM THE DATA OF TABLE 5.5-4 (CONSTANT AND TOTAL OMITTED)

		SSP (symmetric)				
Source	df	Binet(2)	MRRT	FFI(2)	Binet(1)	FFI(1)
		98.7762				
		−158.3125	253.7335			
Casework	1	− 10.4776	16.7929	1.114		
		52.2051	−83.6711	−5.5376	27.5914	
		5.7082	− 9.1488	− .6055	3.0169	.3299
		601.8330				
		550.6433	503.8076			
Instructional method	1	37.4209	34.2381	2.3268		
		35.2259	32.2298	2.1903	2.0618	
		23.3595	21.3726	1.4525	1.3673	.9067
		8.4542				
		30.4767	109.8664			
Interaction	1	.1763	.6356	.0037		
		4.3020	15.5085	.0897	2.1891	
		1.5700	5.6596	.0327	.7989	.2915
		14,363.5904				
		3,211.0104	7,136.6064			
Within-group error	132	107.6346	70.2404	67.5144		
		7,717.6291	2,958.0153	208.9582	14,779.9475	
		51.4354	86.5981	44.1931	177.2678	79.7537

(that is, the roots of $|\mathbf{S}_r - \lambda \mathbf{S}_e^*| = 0$) are computed, giving $\lambda_1 = 1.7093$ as the largest root. The generalized F is

$$F_0 = \frac{128}{2} 1.7093 = 109.40$$

which greatly exceeds the .01 critical value for $r = 2$, $s = 2$, and $t = 128$. Thus, the inclusion of the covariables in the model clearly results in a significant reduction of the error dispersion; moreover, the univariate F statistic shows that the reduction is significant for each of the response variables separately.

The estimated coefficients of the multivariate regression are shown with the corresponding multiple correlation of coefficients (see Secs. 3.3.5 and 6.1.4) in Table 5.5-7. Both the raw regression coefficients to be used in computing the adjusted treatment contrasts and the standardized coefficients which are preferable for interpretation are shown in this table.

Table 5.5-6 ANALYSIS OF REGRESSION (WITHIN GROUPS) OF POSTTESTS ON THE PRETESTS

		SSP (symmetric)						
Source	df	Binet(2)	MRRT	FFI(2)	F_0	p	F	p
Regression $[\mathbf{S}_r^{(y)}]$	2	4,051.9300			109.40	<.01	25.53	<.0001
		1,517.3332	625.6090				6.25	.0026
		104.5363	66.7326	25.1491			38.59	<.0001
Reduced error $[\mathbf{S}_e^*]$	130	10,311.6604						
		1,693.6772	6,510.9974					
		3.0983	3.5078	42.3653				
Within-group error $[\mathbf{S}_e^{(y)}]$	132	14,363.5904						
		3,211.0104	7,136.6064					
		107.6346	70.2404	67.5144				

Table 5.5-7 REGRESSION COEFFICIENTS, (SE), AND MULTIPLE R

		Posttests		
	Pretests	Binet(2)	MRRT	FFI(2)
Raw regression coefficient and (SE)	Binet(1)	.52848 (.0743)	.19224 (.0590)	.00678 (.0048)
	FFI(1)	−.52973 (1.0108)	.65851 (.8032)	.53905 (.0648)
Standardized regression coefficient	Binet(1)	.5361	.2766	.1003
	FFI(1)	−.0395	.0696	.5859
Multiple R		.531	.296	.610

The latter coefficients reveal that Binet(2) is predicted almost exclusively by Binet(1). In fact, the standard error shown for the raw coefficient FFI(1) in the regression equation for Binet(2) indicates that this coefficient is not significantly different from zero. Conversely, FFI(2) is predicted primarily by FFI(1), and the coefficient for Binet(1) is not significantly different from zero. As we might have anticipated, MRRT, which is not represented directly among the pretests, is predicted less well, predominantly by Binet(1). Thus, if the response variables had been limited to the Binet and the MRRT, only Binet(1) would be required as a covariate. Because FFI is included in the response variables and a joint covariance analysis is to be performed, however, both Binet(1) and FFI(1) must be retained as covariates.

The SSP matrices for design effects adjusted for both covariates are shown in Table 5.5-8. These adjusted matrices have been computed by applying the formulas of Table 5.5-3 to SSP matrices for the effects shown in Table 5.5-5. For example, the adjusted SSP for instructional method is computed by adding the SSP for instructional method in Table 5.5-5 to that for error to obtain the provisional total

$$\mathbf{S}_{t'} = \left[\begin{array}{ccc|cc} 14{,}965.4234 & & & & \text{(symmetric)} \\ 3{,}761.6537 & 7{,}640.4140 & & & \\ 145.0555 & 104.4785 & 69.8412 & & \\ \hline 7{,}752.8550 & 3{,}990.2451 & 221.1485 & 24{,}782.0093 & \\ 74.7949 & 107.9707 & 45.6456 & 178.6351 & 80.6604 \end{array}\right]$$

The matrix $\mathbf{S}_h^*$ is computed from the submatrices of $\mathbf{S}_{t'}$ as follows:

$$\mathbf{S}_h^* = \begin{bmatrix} 14{,}965.4234 & \text{(symmetric)} & \\ 3{,}761.6537 & 7{,}640.4140 & \\ 145.6555 & 104.4785 & 69.8412 \end{bmatrix} - \begin{bmatrix} 7{,}752.8550 & 74.7949 \\ 3{,}990.2451 & 107.9707 \\ 211.1485 & 45.6456 \end{bmatrix}$$

$$\cdot \begin{bmatrix} 2{,}478.0093 & \text{(symmetric)} \\ 178.6351 & 80.6604 \end{bmatrix}^{-1} \cdot \begin{bmatrix} 7{,}752.8550 & 3{,}990.2451 & 211.1485 \\ 74.7949 & 107.9707 & 45.6456 \end{bmatrix}$$

$$= \begin{bmatrix} 582.7695 & \text{(symmetric)} & \\ 517.1111 & 458.8516 & \\ 24.0609 & 21.3501 & .9934 \end{bmatrix}$$

The roots of $|\mathbf{S}_h^* - \lambda \mathbf{S}_e^*| = 0$ are then computed. In this instance $\lambda_1 = .1261$ and the corresponding generalized F is

$$F_0 = \frac{128}{3}\,.1261 = 5.38$$

Since $s = 1$, F_0 is distributed exactly as F on $r = 3$ and $t = 128$ degrees of freedom, and the corresponding probability level is .002. The difference between the instructional methods is therefore significant.

As is shown in Table 5.5-8, similar calculations reveal no significant effect of interaction, while for the casework populations, the generalized F has probability .004, and the difference between the groups is clearly significant.

In order to interpret the results more specifically, let us examine the univariate F statistics in Table 5.5-8 and the corresponding estimated effects, adjusted for the two covariates. The latter may be computed by applying Formula (5.5-6) to all design effects retained in the model. In the present example, we retain the constant and the two main effects and omit the nonsignificant interaction. The estimates of these effects, unadjusted, are shown with their standard errors in Table 5.5-9. Estimates for both the response variable and covariables obtained in the initial joint analysis are shown. From these values and the raw regression coefficients in Table 5.5-7, the

Table 5.5-8 ANALYSIS OF COVARIANCE OF CASEWORK, INSTRUCTIONAL-METHOD, AND INTERACTIVE EFFECTS

Source of dispersion	df	SSP (symmetric, adjusted for two covariates) Binet(2)	MRRT	FFI(2)	F_0	p	F	p
Casework	1	55.4648			4.60	.004	.70	.404
		−128.6304	298.3164				5.96	.016
		−10.3951	24.1080	1.9483			5.98	.016
Instructional methods	1	582.7695			5.38	.002	7.35	.008
		517.1111	458.8516				9.16	.003
		24.0609	21.3501	.9934			3.05	.083
Interaction	1	5.7930			.69	.55	.07	.79
		23.6482	96.5039				1.92	.16
		−.5779	−2.3578	.0576			.18	.67

Table 5.5-9 ESTIMATED EFFECTS FOR RESPONSE VARIABLES AND COVARIABLES JOINTLY

Effect	Estimates and (SE) Binet(2)	MRRT	FFI(2)	Binet(1)	FFI(1)
Constant	88.4110	22.4282	4.4824	89.3180	4.1213
Intensive-regular casework	−1.7045	2.7318	.1808	−.9008	−.0985
	(1.7889)	(1.2610)	(.1227)	(1.8147)	(.1333)
Experimental-conventional instruction	4.2073	3.8494	.2616	.2463	.1633
	(1.7889)	(1.2610)	(.1227)	(1.8147)	(.1333)

adjusted effects shown in Table 5.5-10 are then computed as follows:

$$\hat{\Theta}^* = \begin{bmatrix} 88.4110 & 22.4282 & 4.4824 \\ -1.7045 & 2.7318 & .1808 \\ 4,2073 & 3.8494 & .2616 \end{bmatrix} - \begin{bmatrix} 89.3180 & 4.1213 \\ -.9008 & -.0985 \\ .2463 & .1633 \end{bmatrix}$$

$$\cdot \begin{bmatrix} .52849 & .19224 & .00678 \\ -.52973 & .65851 & .53905 \end{bmatrix}$$

$$= \begin{bmatrix} 43.3908 & 2.5440 & 1.6553 \\ -1.2806 & 2.9698 & .2400 \\ 4.1636 & 3.6945 & .1719 \end{bmatrix}$$

Note that the conditional standard errors of the adjusted main-effect contrasts are the positive square roots of the variances computed by means of Formula (5.5-14). In this particular case, the estimators of the two unadjusted contrasts are uncorrelated with variance $\frac{1}{34}\sigma^2$, while those of the adjusted contrasts are correlated with covariance matrix

$$\sigma^2 \begin{bmatrix} \frac{1}{34} & 0 \\ 0 & \frac{1}{34} \end{bmatrix} + \begin{bmatrix} -.9008 & -.0985 \\ .2463 & .1633 \end{bmatrix}$$

$$\cdot \begin{bmatrix} 14,779.9475 & \text{(symmetric)} \\ 177.2678 & 79.7537 \end{bmatrix}^{-1} \begin{bmatrix} -.9008 & .2463 \\ -.0985 & .1663 \end{bmatrix}$$

$$= \sigma^2 \begin{bmatrix} .029412 & \text{(symmetric)} \\ 0 & .029412 \end{bmatrix} + \begin{bmatrix} .000155 & \text{(symmetric)} \\ -.000196 & .000335 \end{bmatrix}$$

Substituting for σ^2 the reduced error mean square, we have, for the Binet(2), for example,

$$\frac{10,311.6604}{130} \begin{bmatrix} .029567 & \text{(symmetric)} \\ -.000196 & .029747 \end{bmatrix} = \begin{bmatrix} 2.3453 & \text{(symmetric)} \\ -.0155 & 2.3595 \end{bmatrix}$$

Table 5.5-10 ADJUSTED ESTIMATED EFFECTS FOR THE DESIGN MODEL

	Estimates and (SE)		
Effect	Binet(2)	MRRT	FFI(2)
Constant	43.3908	2.5440	1.6553
Intensive-regular casework	−1.2806 (1.5314)	2.9698 (1.2169)	.2400 (.09816)
Experimental-conventional instruction	4.1636 (1.5361)	3.6945 (1.2206)	.1719 (.0985)

The square roots of the diagonal elements of this matrix are the standard errors for Binet(2) which appear in Table 5.5-10.

It is clear from the univariate F statistics in Table 5.5-8 that instructional method has a highly significant effect on both Binet(2) and FFI(2). The estimates of these effects presented in Table 5.5-10 show that the talking typewriter was superior to conventional instruction by approximately 4 scale points on each of these variables. The effect on FFI(2), on the other hand, is in the same direction but is only marginally significant. Returning to the group means in Table 5.5-4, we see that the positive Binet(2) contrast is due not to a gain in the talking-typewriter group, but to a loss in the conventional-instruction group. It appears that the latter group is not keeping pace with the mental age norms, while the experimental group is holding its position (see Hudson [1971]).

As for the differences between the two casework populations, they are confined to MRRT and FFI(2) with the intensive-casework group favored in each. Because the families were not assigned randomly to the casework conditions, we cannot be certain that these gains were actually due to the additional social services received by the intensive group. However, the fact that the two populations showed no evidence of difference on the pretests suggests that this may have been the case. If so, it is of some interest, because the gain in MRRT from this source is comparable in magnitude to that due to the talking typewriter.

The increased efficiency of the analysis of covariance is indicated by the ratio of the squared standard errors of the unadjusted and adjusted estimates. For Binet(2), MRRT, and FFI(2), respectively, these ratios are

$$\frac{1.7889^2}{1.5361^2} = 1.36 \qquad \frac{1.2610^2}{1.2206^2} = 1.06 \qquad \frac{.1227^2}{.0985^2} = 1.56$$

Note that the gain in efficiency is greater for the Binet and the FFI, which are represented in the covariates, than for the MRRT, which gains only through variance shared with the Binet.

5.5.5 Derivation

Let us first derive the least-squares estimates of $\boldsymbol{\Theta}$ and $\mathbf{B}$ when the model (5.5-3) is assumed. In terms of this model, we may express the response measures for subject i in group j as the row vector

$$\underset{1\times p}{\mathbf{y}'_{ij}} = \underset{1\times l}{\mathbf{k}'_j}\ \underset{l\times p}{\boldsymbol{\Theta}} + \underset{1\times q}{\mathbf{x}'_{ij}}\ \underset{q\times p}{\mathbf{B}} + \underset{1\times p}{\boldsymbol{\epsilon}^{*\prime}_{ij}}$$

where $\mathbf{k}'_j$ is the jth row of $\mathbf{K}$, $\mathbf{x}'_{ij}$ contains the covariate values for subject i in group j, and $\boldsymbol{\epsilon}^*$ is an error distributed $N(\mathbf{0},\boldsymbol{\Sigma})$. In this notation, the normal equations may be expressed as

$$\begin{bmatrix} \sum_j N_j \mathbf{k}_j \mathbf{k}'_j & \sum_{ij} \mathbf{k}_j \mathbf{x}'_{ij} \\ \sum_{ij} \mathbf{x}_{ij} \mathbf{k}'_j & \sum_{ij} \mathbf{x}_{ij} \mathbf{x}'_{ij} \end{bmatrix} \begin{bmatrix} \hat{\boldsymbol{\Theta}} \\ \hat{\mathbf{B}} \end{bmatrix} = \begin{bmatrix} \sum_{ij} \mathbf{k}_j \mathbf{y}'_{ij} \\ \sum_{ij} \mathbf{x}_{ij} \mathbf{y}'_{ij} \end{bmatrix}$$

or

$$\begin{bmatrix} \mathbf{K'DK} & \mathbf{K'DX.} \\ \mathbf{X'.DK} & \mathbf{X'X} \end{bmatrix} \begin{bmatrix} \hat{\boldsymbol{\Theta}} \\ \hat{\mathbf{B}} \end{bmatrix} = \begin{bmatrix} \mathbf{K'DY.} \\ \mathbf{X'Y} \end{bmatrix} \tag{5.5-20}$$

where **X**, **Y**, **X.**, **Y.**, and **D** are defined as in Sec. 5.5.1.

In the manner of Sec. 4.1.9, let us orthogonalize (5.5-20) blockwise by introducing the transformation

$$\mathbf{T}_1^{-1} \begin{bmatrix} \mathbf{K'DK} & \mathbf{K'DX.} \\ \mathbf{X'.DK} & \mathbf{X'X} \end{bmatrix} (\mathbf{T}_1^{-1})'\mathbf{T}_1' \begin{bmatrix} \hat{\boldsymbol{\Theta}} \\ \hat{\mathbf{B}} \end{bmatrix} = \mathbf{T}_1^{-1} \begin{bmatrix} \mathbf{K'DY.} \\ \mathbf{X'Y} \end{bmatrix}$$

where

$$\mathbf{T}_1^{-1} = \begin{bmatrix} \mathbf{I} & \mathbf{O} \\ -\mathbf{X'.DK}(\mathbf{K'DK})^{-1} & \mathbf{I} \end{bmatrix} \qquad \mathbf{T}_1 = \begin{bmatrix} \mathbf{I} & \mathbf{O} \\ \mathbf{X'.DK}(\mathbf{K'DK})^{-1} & \mathbf{I} \end{bmatrix}$$

Then

$$\begin{bmatrix} \mathbf{K'DK} & \mathbf{O} \\ \mathbf{O} & \mathbf{X'X} - \mathbf{X'.DK}(\mathbf{K'DK})^{-1}\mathbf{K'DX.} \end{bmatrix} \begin{bmatrix} \hat{\boldsymbol{\Theta}} + (\mathbf{K'DK})^{-1}\mathbf{K'DX.}\hat{\mathbf{B}} \\ \mathbf{B} \end{bmatrix}$$

$$= \begin{bmatrix} \mathbf{K'DY.} \\ \mathbf{X'Y} - \mathbf{X'.DK}(\mathbf{K'DK})^{-1}\mathbf{K'DY.} \end{bmatrix}$$

or

$$\begin{bmatrix} \mathbf{K'DK} & \mathbf{O} \\ \mathbf{O} & \mathbf{S}_e^{(x)} \end{bmatrix} \begin{bmatrix} \hat{\boldsymbol{\Theta}} + \hat{\boldsymbol{\Theta}}^{(x)}\hat{\mathbf{B}} \\ \hat{\mathbf{B}} \end{bmatrix} = \begin{bmatrix} \mathbf{K'DY.} \\ \mathbf{S}_e^{(xy)} \end{bmatrix}$$

where

$$\hat{\boldsymbol{\Theta}} = (\mathbf{K'DK})^{-1}\mathbf{K'DY.} - \hat{\boldsymbol{\Theta}}^{(x)}\hat{\mathbf{B}} = \hat{\boldsymbol{\Theta}}^{(y)} - \hat{\boldsymbol{\Theta}}^{(x)}\hat{\mathbf{B}}$$

which agrees with (5.5-13), and

$$\hat{\mathbf{B}} = (\mathbf{S}_e^{(x)})^{-1}\mathbf{S}_e^{(xy)}$$

which agrees with (5.5-9).

The corresponding multivariate analysis of variance is shown in Table 5.5-11. The formulas for $\mathbf{S}_r^{(y)}$ and $\mathbf{S}_e^*$ in Table 5.5-2 are taken from this table.

To express the sum of squares and products for hypothesized effects, eliminating other design effects and regression, let us assume that $\mathbf{K}_h$ in (5.5-4) is orthogonalized

Table 5.5-11 MULTIVARIATE ANALYSIS OF VARIANCE ELIMINATING DESIGN EFFECTS FROM REGRESSION EFFECTS

Source	df	SSP ($p \times p$)	$\mathscr{E}$(SSP)
Design effects, ignoring regression	l	$\mathbf{S}_o^{(y)} + \mathbf{S}_h^{(y)} = \mathbf{Y'.DK}(\mathbf{K'DK})^{-1}\mathbf{K'DY.}$	$l\Sigma + (\boldsymbol{\Theta} + \boldsymbol{\Theta}^{(x)}\mathbf{B})' \times \mathbf{K'DK}(\boldsymbol{\Theta} + \boldsymbol{\Theta}^{(x)}\mathbf{B})$
Regression, eliminating design effects	q	$\mathbf{S}_r^{(y)} = \mathbf{S}_e^{(yx)}(\mathbf{S}_e^{(x)})^{-1}\mathbf{S}_e^{(xy)}$	$q\Sigma + \mathbf{B}'\mathbf{S}_e^{(x)}\mathbf{B}$
Reduced residual	$n_e - q$	$\mathbf{S}_e^* = \mathbf{S}_t^{(y)} - \mathbf{S}_o^{(y)} - \mathbf{S}_h^{(y)} - \mathbf{S}_r^{(y)} = \mathbf{S}_e^{(y)} - \mathbf{S}_r^{(y)}$	$(n_e - q)\Sigma$
Total	N	$\mathbf{S}_t^{(y)} = \mathbf{Y'Y}$	

relative to $\mathbf{K}_o$ in the metric $\mathbf{D}$; that is, $\mathbf{K}_o'\mathbf{D}\mathbf{K}_h = \mathbf{O}$. No generality is lost, for, if necessary, (5.5-4) may be orthogonally reparameterized by substituting $\mathbf{K}_h - \mathbf{K}_o(\mathbf{K}_o'\mathbf{D}\mathbf{K}_o)^{-1}\mathbf{K}_o'\mathbf{D}\mathbf{K}_h$ for $\mathbf{K}_h$ and $\boldsymbol{\Theta}_o + (\mathbf{K}_o'\mathbf{D}\mathbf{K}_o)^{-1}\mathbf{K}_o'\mathbf{D}\boldsymbol{\Theta}_h$ for $\boldsymbol{\Theta}_o$.

In this case, the normal equations corresponding to (5.5-4) are

$$\begin{bmatrix} \mathbf{K}_o'\mathbf{D}\mathbf{K}_o & \mathbf{K}_o'\mathbf{D}\mathbf{X}_. & \mathbf{O} \\ \mathbf{X}_.'\mathbf{D}\mathbf{K}_o & \mathbf{X}'\mathbf{X} & \mathbf{X}_.'\mathbf{D}\mathbf{K}_h \\ \mathbf{O} & \mathbf{K}_h'\mathbf{D}\mathbf{X}_. & \mathbf{K}_h'\mathbf{D}\mathbf{K}_h \end{bmatrix} \begin{bmatrix} \hat{\boldsymbol{\Theta}}_o \\ \hat{\mathbf{B}} \\ \hat{\boldsymbol{\Theta}}_h \end{bmatrix} = \begin{bmatrix} \mathbf{K}_o'\mathbf{D}\mathbf{Y}_. \\ \mathbf{X}'\mathbf{Y} \\ \mathbf{K}_h'\mathbf{D}\mathbf{Y}_. \end{bmatrix} \tag{5.5-21}$$

Now, put (5.5-21) in blockwise diagonal form by introducing the transformations

$$\mathbf{T}_2^{-1} = \begin{bmatrix} \mathbf{I} & \mathbf{O} & \mathbf{O} \\ -\mathbf{X}_.'\mathbf{D}\mathbf{K}_o(\mathbf{K}_o'\mathbf{D}\mathbf{K}_o)^{-1} & \mathbf{I} & \mathbf{O} \\ \mathbf{O} & -\mathbf{K}_h'\mathbf{D}\mathbf{X}_.(\mathbf{X}'\mathbf{X})^{-1} & \mathbf{I} \end{bmatrix}$$

and

$$\mathbf{T}_2 = \begin{bmatrix} \mathbf{I} & \mathbf{O} & \mathbf{O} \\ \mathbf{X}_.'\mathbf{D}\mathbf{K}_o(\mathbf{K}_o'\mathbf{D}\mathbf{K}_o)^{-1} & \mathbf{I} & \mathbf{O} \\ \mathbf{O} & \mathbf{K}_h'\mathbf{D}\mathbf{X}_.(\mathbf{X}'\mathbf{X})^{-1} & \mathbf{I} \end{bmatrix}$$

The result is

$$\begin{bmatrix} \mathbf{K}_o'\mathbf{D}\mathbf{K}_o & \mathbf{O} & \mathbf{O} \\ \mathbf{O} & \mathbf{S}_{t'}^{(x)} & \mathbf{O} \\ \mathbf{O} & \mathbf{O} & \mathbf{K}_h'[\mathbf{D} - \mathbf{D}\mathbf{X}_.(\mathbf{X}'\mathbf{X})^{-1}\mathbf{X}_.'\mathbf{D}]\mathbf{K}_h \end{bmatrix} \begin{bmatrix} \hat{\boldsymbol{\Theta}}_o + \hat{\boldsymbol{\Theta}}_o^{(x)}\hat{\mathbf{B}} \\ \hat{\mathbf{B}} + (\mathbf{X}'\mathbf{X})^{-1}\mathbf{X}_.\mathbf{D}\mathbf{K}_h'\hat{\boldsymbol{\Theta}}_h \\ \boldsymbol{\Theta}_h \end{bmatrix}$$

$$= \begin{bmatrix} \mathbf{K}_o'\mathbf{D}\mathbf{Y}_. \\ \mathbf{S}_{t'}^{(xy)} \\ \mathbf{K}_h'\mathbf{D}\mathbf{Y}_. - \mathbf{K}_h'\mathbf{D}\mathbf{X}_.(\mathbf{X}'\mathbf{X})^{-1}\mathbf{X}'\mathbf{Y} \end{bmatrix}$$

or, say,

$$\begin{bmatrix} \mathbf{K}_o'\mathbf{D}\mathbf{K}_o & \mathbf{O} & \mathbf{O} \\ \mathbf{O} & \mathbf{S}_{t'}^{(x)} & \mathbf{O} \\ \mathbf{O} & \mathbf{O} & \mathbf{K}_h'\mathbf{M}\mathbf{K}_h \end{bmatrix} \begin{bmatrix} \hat{\boldsymbol{\Theta}}_o + \hat{\boldsymbol{\Theta}}_o^{(x)}\hat{\mathbf{B}} \\ \hat{\mathbf{B}}^* \\ \hat{\boldsymbol{\Theta}}_h \end{bmatrix} = \begin{bmatrix} \mathbf{K}_o'\mathbf{D}\mathbf{Y}_. \\ \mathbf{S}_{t'}^{(xy)} \\ \mathbf{K}_h'\mathbf{D}[\mathbf{Y}_. - \mathbf{X}_.(\mathbf{X}'\mathbf{X})^{-1}\mathbf{X}'\mathbf{Y}] \end{bmatrix} \tag{5.5-22}$$

The partition of $\mathbf{S}_t^{(y)}$ corresponding to this order of elimination has already been presented in Table 5.5-3. It is apparent from (5.5-22) that

$$\mathbf{S}_h^* = [\mathbf{Y}_. - \mathbf{X}_.(\mathbf{X}'\mathbf{X})^{-1}\mathbf{X}'\mathbf{Y}]'\mathbf{D}\mathbf{K}_h(\mathbf{K}_h'\mathbf{M}\mathbf{K}_h)^{-1}\mathbf{K}_h'\mathbf{D}[\mathbf{Y}_. - \mathbf{X}_.(\mathbf{X}'\mathbf{X})^{-1}\mathbf{X}'\mathbf{Y}]$$

but in computation it is more easily obtained by subtraction as in Table 5.5-3.

Exercise 5.5-1 The evaluation study which is presented in Example 5.2-1 also included pretesting with the STEP mathematics computation test and a test of knowledge of number systems. The class means for these tests are given in Table 5.5-12. Using the data of Table 5.2-1 as response variables and those of Table 5.5-12 as covariables, analyze the effect of the SMSG course versus the traditional course in ninth-grade algebra.

Table 5.5-12 AVERAGE SCORES ON PRETESTS OF MATHEMATICAL ABILITY FOR ALGEBRA CLASSES REPRESENTED IN TABLE 5.2-1

Classes in traditional course	Pretest 1*	Pretest 2†	Classes in SMSG course	Pretest 1*	Pretest 2†
1	41.26	11.03	1	39.24	14.05
2	34.73	5.45	2	31.90	5.38
3	36.75	12.05	3	34.39	4.61
4	36.43	7.80	4	32.33	7.53
5	32.17	5.88	5	33.05	6.00
6	35.95	8.85	6	41.73	15.23
7	32.04	3.91	7	39.92	9.54
8	35.57	6.86	8	29.38	4.42
9	38.13	11.79	9	32.92	5.44
10	31.67	5.38	10	27.10	3.95
11	39.10	10.33	11	33.31	7.53
12	31.04	5.43	12	32.31	5.54
13	33.45	11.32	13	36.59	7.22
14	36.53	6.94	14	43.82	11.65
15	33.87	4.04	15	20.56	1.63
16	24.00	3.46	16	37.67	6.79
17	36.28	5.36	17	28.52	4.20
18	36.00	9.96	18	31.20	5.80
19	40.04	11.04	19	28.50	6.07
20	36.79	7.50	20	34.03	6.52
21	39.73	11.42	21	30.90	8.00
22	29.14	3.77			

* STEP mathematics computation.
† Number systems.

6

LINEAR MODELS IN NONEXPERIMENTAL STUDIES

There exists a large class of behavioral studies in which the investigator is not at liberty, as he is in an experiment, to select samples from an artificial population created by randomization and to expose these samples to prearranged treatments. In these *nonexperimental* studies, the investigator is confined to the role of a passive observer of conditions, attributes, and responses of subjects in naturally occurring populations. Nevertheless, the methods of linear least-squares analysis of Chaps. 4 and 5 are potentially applicable to this class of studies, provided one important requirement is satisfied: The investigator must be able to select or identify for observation a probability sample of subjects from each of the populations under study. The choice of subjects to be observed cannot be left to administrative discretion, or to the subjects themselves, because in behavioral studies the traits under investigation may influence these decisions. When conducting a normative study of school achievement, for example, the investigator cannot allow the teachers to select pupils or the pupils to volunteer to be tested. Such procedures would almost certainly produce norms biased toward high achievers.

We consider in this chapter the application of least-squares analysis to four broad classes of nonexperimental study—namely, (1) prediction, (2) classification, (3) comparative studies, and (4) surveys. The caveat for comparative studies stated in Sec. 1.2.4 applies to all these classes: The data obtained in such studies do not directly support an inference concerning a cause-and-effect relationship between variables. The aim of prediction and classification is the purely practical one of profiting from experience, while that of a comparative study and survey is to describe appearances rather than to reveal causes. This is not to say that a successful prediction or classification, or a coherent description of population differences, implies nothing about the *plausibility* of alternative causal models. But because the logic of these studies does not rest upon physical or randomized control of extraneous variables, the results never rule out the possibility that the observations actually reflect an unknown causal influence which is responsible for the statistical association seen in the data. Thus, what might appear to be a relationship that could be broadly exploited to control behavior may only be a contingency of the particular setting where the unknown cause is operative. Manipulation of the gratuitously assumed independent variable may merely create a new situation where the association will not be apparent. A case in point is Example 6.1, where a substantial correlation is demonstrated between highest grade completed and soldier performance at the conclusion of basic training. This correlation does not necessarily imply that performance could be improved by reducing school dropout. More likely, highest grade completed is merely an indirect measure, rather than a cause, of those personal qualities which make for good soldier performance among inductees. If so, it could be used to *select* but not to create good soldiers (see Cochran [1972]).

Throughout the present chapter, we shall continue to assume that the values taken on by each of the response variables are measurements, possibly with arbitrary origin and unit, to be regarded as continuous for purposes of analysis. Discussion of qualitative response variables in both experimental and nonexperimental settings is relegated to Chap. 8.

6.1 PREDICTION

The subject of statistical prediction was broached in Chap. 3 in the discussion of the multivariate normal distribution. That discussion served only to illustrate the connection between prediction and the concept of a conditional distribution and was therefore phrased entirely in terms of population parameters. The problem of estimating these parameters was deferred until this section.

We assume here that there are two sets of variables measured on each unit of the material (usually a subject): the set X consisting of q *predictors*, and a set Y of p *criteria*. The practical problem is, for some defined population of units, to use knowledge of X to predict jointly the variables in set Y with least loss due to error.

In the absence of any prior knowledge of how Y depends upon X, we must proceed empirically and arrange to observe both X and Y in a probability sample of units from the specified population. These units are called the *calibration sample*, and the usual situation is that the X variables are observed at some earlier time and the Y variables are observed at some later time. An industrial psychologist, for example, might endeavor to assess the efficiency of a battery of personnel tests by first hiring, without selection, a randomly chosen group of applicants. Then during the job interviews, he would obtain scores on the battery of tests and, after the workers had been on the job for some period of time, would measure their productivity. In this case, X would represent the scores of the selection tests, and Y the measures of productivity (number of pieces, number of rejects, quality of work, etc.). Given data of this kind, the investigator would be in a position to develop a prediction equation by the routine application of least squares as described in this section.

6.1.1 Multivariate Multiple-Regression Analysis

The statistical methods applied to multivariate experiments in Chap. 4 may be extended to prediction studies under the following assumptions:

1 For any given values of the X variables, the conditional distribution of the Y variables has a finite $(p \times 1)$ vector mean $\boldsymbol{\mu}^*$, and a $(p \times p)$ common covariance matrix $\boldsymbol{\Sigma}^*$.

2 The conditional vector mean may be expressed by the multivariate linear-regression model

$$\boldsymbol{\mu}^* = \mathbf{B}'\mathbf{x}$$

where $\mathbf{x}$ is the $q \times 1$ vector of given values of the X variables and possibly their powers and cross products in cases where the regression is curvilinear or interactive.

3 The loss due to errors of prediction is proportional to the sum of squared errors.

On these assumptions the prediction problem is formally identical to the multivariate curve-fitting problem of Chap. 4 in the case of unreplicated data. Except for minor differences in the computing conventions, the estimation procedures of Chap. 4 apply and need not be derived anew. It is customary, however, to express the prediction equations in terms of scores standardized in the sample and to perform the calculations on correlations rather than on sums of cross products as in Chap. 4. Thus, if the data matrix for a sample of size N is the $N \times (p + q)$ array

$$\underset{\quad p \quad q}{[\mathbf{Y} \mid \mathbf{X}]N}$$

the sample means may be expressed as the row vector

$$[\mathbf{y}'_{\cdot} \mid \mathbf{x}'_{\cdot}] = \frac{1}{N}\mathbf{1}'[\mathbf{Y} \mid \mathbf{X}]$$

where $\mathbf{1}$ is an $N \times 1$ vector of unities. The sample correlation matrix,

$$\begin{array}{c} \begin{bmatrix} \mathbf{R}_{yy} & \mathbf{R}_{yx} \\ \mathbf{R}_{xy} & \mathbf{R}_{xx} \end{bmatrix} \begin{matrix} p \\ q \end{matrix} \\ \quad p \qquad q \end{array}$$

is then comprised of the submatrices

$$\mathbf{R}_{yy} = \mathbf{D}_y^{-1/2} (\mathbf{Y}'\mathbf{Y} - N\mathbf{y}_{.}\mathbf{y}'_{.}) \mathbf{D}_y^{-1/2}$$

$$\mathbf{R}_{yx} = \mathbf{R}'_{xy} = \mathbf{D}_y^{-1/2} (\mathbf{Y}'\mathbf{X} - N\mathbf{y}_{.}\mathbf{x}'_{.}) \mathbf{D}_x^{-1/2}$$

and

$$\mathbf{R}_{xx} = \mathbf{D}_x^{-1/2} (\mathbf{X}'\mathbf{X} - N\mathbf{x}_{.}\mathbf{x}'_{.}) \mathbf{D}_x^{-1/2}$$

where $\mathbf{D}_y = \operatorname{diag}(\mathbf{Y}'\mathbf{Y} - N\mathbf{y}_{.}\mathbf{y}'_{.})$

$\mathbf{D}_x = \operatorname{diag}(\mathbf{X}'\mathbf{X} - N\mathbf{x}_{.}\mathbf{x}'_{.})$

The sample standard deviations are the elements of

$$\mathbf{D}_{\sigma_y} = \left(\frac{1}{N-1}\mathbf{D}_y\right)^{1/2}$$

and

$$\mathbf{D}_{\sigma_x} = \left(\frac{1}{N-1}\mathbf{D}_x\right)^{1/2}$$

If the data matrix standardized in the sample is represented by $[\mathbf{Z}_y|\mathbf{Z}_x]$, where $\mathbf{Z}_y = (\mathbf{Y} - \mathbf{1}\mathbf{y}'_{.})\mathbf{D}_{\sigma_y}^{-1}$, and $\mathbf{Z}_x = (\mathbf{X} - \mathbf{1}\mathbf{x}'_{.})\mathbf{D}_{\sigma_x}^{-1}$, the assumed statistical model for the standard scores in a row of this matrix is

$$\underset{1\times p}{\mathbf{z}'_y} = \underset{1\times q}{\mathbf{z}'_x}\ \underset{q\times p}{\boldsymbol{\beta}} + \underset{1\times p}{\boldsymbol{\zeta}}$$

where

$$\mathscr{E}(\mathbf{z}'_y) = \mathbf{z}'_x\boldsymbol{\beta}$$

is the mean of the conditional distribution of the standardized variables, and the standardized conditional error component has

$$\mathscr{E}(\boldsymbol{\zeta}) = \mathbf{0} \qquad \mathscr{V}(\boldsymbol{\zeta}) = \mathbf{D}_{\sigma_y}^{-1}\boldsymbol{\Sigma}^*\mathbf{D}_{\sigma_y}^{-1}$$

The elements in the columns of $\boldsymbol{\beta}$ are the so-called "β weights" for the corresponding dependent variable. Obviously, the raw regression coefficients are related to $\boldsymbol{\beta}$ by

$$\mathbf{B} = \mathbf{D}_{\sigma_x}^{-1}\boldsymbol{\beta}\mathbf{D}_{\sigma_y} \qquad (6.1\text{-}1)$$

According to the results in Sec. 4.2, the least-squares estimate of $\boldsymbol{\beta}$ is

$$\hat{\boldsymbol{\beta}} = (\mathbf{Z}'_x\mathbf{Z}_x)^{-1}\mathbf{Z}'_x\mathbf{Z}_y = \mathbf{R}_{xx}^{-1}\mathbf{R}_{xy} \qquad (6.1\text{-}2)$$

for $|\mathbf{R}_{xx}| \neq 0$. The estimator is unbiased, and its variance-covariance matrix is

$$\mathscr{V}(\boldsymbol{\beta}) = \mathbf{R}_{xx}^{-1} \times \mathbf{D}_{\sigma_y}^{-1}\boldsymbol{\Sigma}^*\mathbf{D}_{\sigma_y}^{-1} \qquad (6.1\text{-}3)$$

The conditional covariance matrix Σ^* may be estimated by rescaling the residual sum of products of the analysis of regression shown in Table 6.1-1:

$$\hat{\Sigma}^* = \mathbf{D}_{\sigma_y}[\mathbf{R}_{yy} - \mathbf{R}_{yx}\mathbf{R}_{xx}^{-1}\mathbf{R}_{xy}]\mathbf{D}_{\sigma_y} \qquad (6.1\text{-}4)$$

Thus, the standard errors of the estimated β weights may be computed as the Kronecker product of the positive square roots of the diagonal elements of $\mathbf{R}_{xx}^{-1}$ and $\mathbf{D}_{\sigma_y}^{-1}\hat{\Sigma}^*\mathbf{D}_{\sigma_y}^{-1}$ expressed as a column and a row vector, respectively:

$$\underset{q \times p}{\mathrm{SE}(\hat{\boldsymbol{\beta}})} = \underset{q \times 1}{[\mathrm{diag}^{1/2}(\mathbf{R}_{xx}^{-1})]} \times \underset{1 \times p}{[\mathrm{diag}^{1/2}(\mathbf{D}_{\sigma_y}^{-1}\hat{\Sigma}^*\mathbf{D}_{\sigma_y}^{-1})]'} \qquad (6.1\text{-}5)$$

Like (5.5-14), this formula is conditional on the values of the predictors observed in the calibration sample.

6.1.2 A Composite Test of No Association

Up to this point we have made no assumption about the joint distribution of the X and Y variables or about the specific form of the conditional distribution of Y given X. If we assume the latter is multivariate normal,

$$Y \mid X \sim N(\mu^*, \Sigma^*)$$

then the statistical tests and confidence bounds described in Sec. 4.2 may be applied to the prediction problem. Thus, we may test the null hypothesis

$$\boldsymbol{\beta} = \mathbf{O} \qquad (6.1\text{-}6)$$

by means of the multivariate analysis of variance shown in Table 6.1-1. The test statistic is computed from the s nonzero roots of

$$|\mathbf{R}_{yx}\mathbf{R}_{xx}^{-1}\mathbf{R}_{xy} - \lambda(\mathbf{R}_{yy} - \mathbf{R}_{yx}\mathbf{R}_{xx}^{-1}\mathbf{R}_{xy})| = 0 \qquad (6.1\text{-}7)$$

For example, the largest-root criterion in the form of the generalized F is

$$F_0 = \frac{t}{r}\lambda_1 \qquad (6.1\text{-}8)$$

Table 6.1-1 MULTIVARIATE ANALYSIS OF REGRESSION (IN STANDARD SCORE UNITS)

Source of dispersion	df	Sum of squares and products ($p \times p$)
Regression	q	$\mathbf{S}_h = \mathbf{R}_{yx}\mathbf{R}_{xx}^{-1}\mathbf{R}_{xy}$
Residual	$N - q - 1$	$\mathbf{S}_e = \mathbf{R}_{yy} - \mathbf{R}_{yx}\mathbf{R}_{xx}^{-1}\mathbf{R}_{xy}$
Corrected total	$N - 1$	$\mathbf{S}_t = \mathbf{R}_{yy}$

where $r = |q - p| + 1$

$s = \min(p,q)$

$t = N - p - q$

Pillai's trace statistic is

$$U_s = \sum_{k=1}^{s} \lambda_k = \mathrm{tr}[\mathbf{R}_{yx}\mathbf{R}_{xx}^{-1}\mathbf{R}_{xy}(\mathbf{R}_{yy} - \mathbf{R}_{yx}\mathbf{R}_{xx}^{-1}\mathbf{R}_{xy})^{-1}] \qquad (6.1\text{-}9)$$

with the arguments, $s = \min(p,q)$

$$m = \frac{|p - q| - 1}{2}$$

$$n = \frac{N - p - q - 2}{2}$$

and Wilks' criterion is

$$\Lambda = \prod_{k=1}^{s} \frac{1}{1 + \lambda_k} = \frac{|\mathbf{R}_{yy} - \mathbf{R}_{yx}\mathbf{R}_{xx}^{-1}\mathbf{R}_{xy}|}{|\mathbf{R}_{yy}|} \qquad (6.1\text{-}10)$$

Alternatively, we may compute these statistics from the canonical correlations between X and Y as discussed in Sec. 6.1.6.

6.1.3 Stepwise Test of the Partial Contribution of an Additional Predictor

Rejection of hypothesis (6.1-6) is evidence that at least one of the X variables is useful in predicting at least one of the Y variables. In most applications, however, more specific tests of the contribution of individual predictors are required. If a prior ordering of the predictors is specified in which the more dubious predictors are ordered last, stepwise tests such as were applied to the polynomial model in Chap. 4 are suitable for assessing the gain in information supplied by additional predictors. The calculations for these tests may be performed by pivoting the sample correlation matrix (Sec. 4.1.10b), or more accurately by the following factorization method:

1 Compute the Cholesky factor of $\mathbf{R}_{xx}$, designated here $\mathbf{R}_{xx}^{1/2}$ (Sec. 2.7.2).

2 Compute the inverse Cholesky factor $\mathbf{R}_{xx}^{-1/2}$ and obtain the orthogonal estimates

$$\underset{q \times p}{\mathbf{U}} = \mathbf{R}_{xx}^{1/2}\mathbf{R}_{xy}$$

3 The hypothesis product matrix, on one degree of freedom, for the ith test is then

$$\mathbf{S}_h^{(i)} = \mathbf{u}_i\mathbf{u}_i'$$

where $\mathbf{u}_i'$ is the ith row of $\mathbf{U}$, and the error product matrix is

$$\mathbf{S}_e^{(i)} = \mathbf{R}_{yy} - \sum_{j=1}^{i} \mathbf{u}_j\mathbf{u}_j'$$

Then

$$|\mathbf{S}_h^{(i)} - \lambda\mathbf{S}_e^{(i)}| = 0$$

has precisely one nonzero root given by

$$\lambda_i = \mathbf{u}_i'(\mathbf{S}_e^{(i)})^{-1}\mathbf{u}_i$$

and

$$F_i = \frac{t}{r}\lambda_i$$

with $r = p$ and $t = N - i - p$ may be referred to the F distribution on p and $N - i - p$ degrees of freedom. If $N - q$ is large, an essentially equivalent test is obtained by using $\mathbf{S}_e$ in place of $\mathbf{S}_e^{(i)}$, thus avoiding the labor of computing $(\mathbf{S}_e^{(i)})^{-1}$ at each stage.

It will also be useful at each stage to compute the univariate F statistics for each Y variate, as well as the step-down tests described in Sec. 3.4.10. (Further discussion of the step-down tests appears below in connection with discriminant analysis.)

6.1.4 Measures of Multiple Determination

The conventional measure for expressing the degree to which the X variables predict a given Y variable is the sample value of the *coefficient of determination* R^2 defined in Sec. 3.3.5. The sample value is obtained from the analysis of regression in Table 6.1-1 as the ratio of the regression sum of squares to the total sum of squares for that variable. These sums of squares are given by the respective diagonal elements of the $\mathbf{S}_h$ and $\mathbf{S}_t$ product matrices. Thus, for criterion k,

$$R_k^2 = \frac{[\mathbf{S}_h]_{kk}}{[\mathbf{S}_t]_{kk}}$$

If the calculations are performed in standard score units in the manner of Table 6.1-1, (6.1-8) simplifies to

$$R_k^2 = \mathbf{r}_{kx}'\mathbf{R}_{xx}^{-1}\mathbf{r}_{kx} = \hat{\boldsymbol{\beta}}_k'\mathbf{r}_{kx} = \hat{\boldsymbol{\beta}}_k'\mathbf{R}_{xx}\hat{\boldsymbol{\beta}}_k$$

where $\mathbf{r}_{kx}'$ is the kth row of $\mathbf{R}_{yx}$, and $\hat{\boldsymbol{\beta}}_k$ is the kth column of $\boldsymbol{\beta}$.

The univariate F statistic, on q and $N - q - 1$ degrees of freedom, for testing the respective subhypothesis of (6.1-6) may be expressed in terms of R_k^2 as

$$F_k = \frac{R_k^2/q}{(1 - R_k^2)/(N - q - 1)}$$

The positive square root of the coefficient of determination, called the *multiple correlation coefficient* R_k, is the sample value of the correlation between the kth criterion variable and the linear combination of predictors with coefficients $\hat{\boldsymbol{\beta}}_k$. R_k

is not an unbiased estimate of the corresponding population correlation, however, and is not a very satisfactory statistic for comparing the goodness of prediction in small and moderate-sized samples when different numbers of predictors are involved. If the number of predictors q is appreciable relative to the number of subjects N, the sample value of R_k is biased upward considerably. A better measure is the complement of the ratio of the unbiased estimates of the conditional variance and the unconditional variance:

$$R_k^{*2} = 1 - \frac{\hat{\sigma}_k^{*2}}{\hat{\sigma}_k^{\,2}} \qquad (6.1\text{-}11)$$

This *adjusted* coefficient of determination may be computed from $R_k^{\,2}$ by the formula

$$R_k^{*2} = 1 - (1 - R_k^{\,2})\frac{N-1}{N-q} \qquad (6.1\text{-}12)$$

[If (6.1-12) should happen to be negative, R_k^{*2} is set to zero.]

Ezekiel and Fox [1959] report a Monte Carlo study of the bias of the adjusted and unadjusted multiple correlation coefficient in samples from a population with coefficient .62. For $q = 10$, their results were:

N	R	R^*
30	.77	.64
50	.71	.63
100	.68	.65

The bias of R^* is much less than that of R. The exact expression for the expected value of R^2 as a function of N and q has been given by Olkin and Pratt [1958], but (6.1-12) is sufficiently accurate for practical work. Exact confidence bounds for R^2, taking into account the number of independent variables, may be constructed from tables given by Kramer [1963] and Lee [1972]. See also Pearson and Hartley [1972].

Regrettably, there are many erroneous interpretations of R^2 in the literature. Perhaps the worst is the identification of the jth term in the sum

$$R^2 = \hat{\boldsymbol{\beta}}'\mathbf{r}_x = \sum_{j=1}^{q} \beta_j r_{x_j y}$$

as the proportion of variance attributable to the jth predictor. In general, some of these terms may be negative and could not be interpreted as proportions. Only when the X variables are uncorrelated in the sample or have been orthogonalized are these terms nonnegative and do they represent proportions of predictable variation.

A correct, but less straightforward, interpretation is contained in the "path" diagram, due to Wright [1934], illustrating the formula $R_k^{\,2} = \hat{\boldsymbol{\beta}}_k'\mathbf{R}_{xx}\boldsymbol{\beta}_k$. For the case

of two predictors, this diagram is

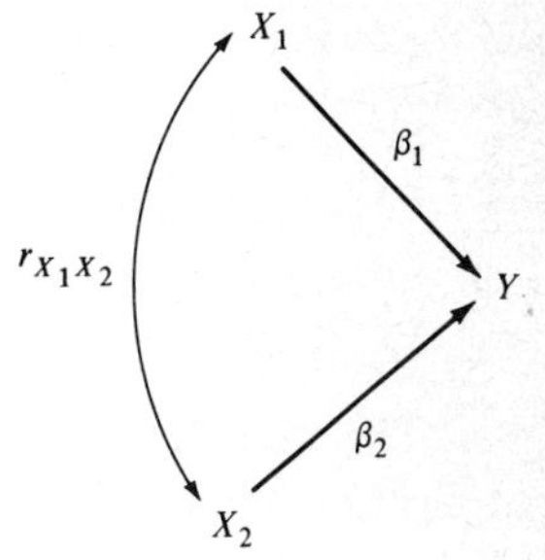

The expression for R^2 is obtained by tracing all possible paths going from and returning to Y, and multiplying the coefficients shown along the paths above. According to the rules of path diagrams, one may trace a path going backward over an arrow and then frontward, but not vice versa. The two-headed path representing correlation may be traced in both directions. The sums of these products for the four possible paths is R^2:

$$R^2 = \hat{\beta}_1{}^2 + \hat{\beta}_2{}^2 + 2\hat{\beta}_1\hat{\beta}_2 r_{x_1x_2}$$

The terms $\hat{\beta}_1{}^2$ and $\hat{\beta}_2{}^2$ in this sum are called the *direct* contribution of X_1 and X_2, and $2\hat{\beta}_1\hat{\beta}_2 r_{x_1x_2}$ is called the *indirect* contribution. Wright shows how these diagrams may be elaborated to describe causal relationships among the variables in complex systems (see Li [1955]).

EXAMPLE 6.1-1 (*Soldier selection*) An important application of statistical prediction is in the selection of recruits for military service. Table 6.1-2 shows statistics from a study, conducted during the Korean conflict, to validate a screening test for the Puerto Rican Selective Service [Schenkel, et al., 1957].* For purposes of the study, a probability sample of 528 men in the pool supplied by the Puerto Rican draft boards were inducted and assigned to designated platoons in the basic-training camp at Tortugero. During induction, scores were obtained on the following measures:

ECFA, Examen Calification de Fuerzas Armadas (a Spanish-language version of the Armed Forces Qualification Test)
HGC, Highest Grade Completed
NLT, Non-Language Test (of reasoning ability)
EFB(pre), English Fluency Battery pretest

* Field study directed by Col. Stanley E. Jacobs.

At the conclusion of basic training, which included English-language instruction, the following scores were obtained:

SP, Soldier Performance Test
EFB(Post), English Fluency Battery posttest
SP RANK, Platoon rank in soldier performance
EF RANK, Platoon rank in English fluency

The rankings of soldier performance and English fluency were made by the sergeant in command of each of the platoons in the study. To allow for the different numbers of men in the platoons, the ranks were converted to percentiles by the formula

$$p = \frac{n - r + \frac{1}{2}}{n}$$

where r is the rank position and n is the number of men ranked. To better approximate a normal distribution, the percentiles were transformed to

$$y = \sin^{-1} \sqrt{p}$$

The means, standard deviations and correlations based on a one-third random sample of the 528 cases are given in Table 6.1-2.

The overall result of the multivariate regression analysis is shown in Table 6.1-3 in terms of the multiple R^2, R, the adjusted R, the univariate F and its p value under the hypothesis of no association. A multivariate test of no association between criteria and predictors is hardly needed in this case, but as an illustration of the use

Table 6.1-2 SAMPLE MEANS, STANDARD DEVIATIONS, AND CORRELATIONS FROM THE SOLDIER SELECTION STUDY ($N = 165$)

			Correlations							
Variables	Mean	SD	1	2	3	4	5	6	7	8
Criteria										
1 SP	608.65	114.95	1.0000							
2 EFB(post)	59.09	38.64	.8383	1.0000						
3 SP rank	.8075	.3776	.6149	.5739	1.0000					
4 EF rank	.8553	.3554	.6837	.7181	.6899	1.0000				
Predictors										
5 ECFA	40.75	24.87	.7106	.7893	.5478	.7120	1.0000			
6 HGC	7.679	2.710	.6891	.7597	.5055	.7109	.8105	1.0000		
7 NLT	94.55	44.48	.6722	.6851	.4975	.6172	.7704	.7318	1.0000	
8 EFB(pre)	42.56	34.09	.7046	.9299	.5639	.6934	.7546	.7413	.6736	1.0000

of the generalized F for this test, we obtain, from (6.1-7) and (6.1-8),

$$\lambda_1 = 8.452 \qquad \lambda_2 = .190 \qquad \lambda_3 = .027 \qquad \lambda_4 = .002$$

$$r = |2 - 2| + 1 = 1 \qquad s = \min(4,4) = 4 \qquad t = 165 - 4 - 4 = 157$$

$$F_0 = (\tfrac{157}{1})8.452 = 1{,}327 \qquad p < .01$$

and the hypothesis of no association is rejected. (The significance of the remaining three roots is assessed in the continuation of this analysis in Sec. 6.1.6.)

We see also in Table 6.1-3 that the univariate tests indicate significant association for each of the criteria and, perhaps not surprisingly, considerably better determination of the objective tests of soldier performance and English fluency than of the platoon sergeants' subjective rankings. The latter are probably both less reliable and more influenced by personality variables unrelated to soldier performance than are the objective tests. Note also that the English-fluency test, which is also represented in the pretests, is better predicted than the Soldier Performance test. It is nevertheless remarkable to find the purely cognitive pretests predicting a performance measure with a correlation of .767. The explanation undoubtedly is that the basic-training program puts heavy demands on the ability of the trainees to assimilate new information in a relatively short time—an ability that is well known to be accurately predicted by tests of general intellectual attainment.

The partial contribution of the separate predictors is assessed in one selected ordering in Table 6.1-4. Residual degrees of freedom for the successive tests are 163, 162, 161, and 160. The additional determination of EFB and EF rank afforded by Highest Grade Completed, after eliminating the Spanish-language ECFA, probably reflects the fact that the trainees who leave school at eighth grade have very little English knowledge. ECFA would not pick up this source of variation. The Non-Language Test, on the other hand, contributes little additional information over that supplied by ECFA and is only marginally significant in the stepwise test. The English-fluency pretest makes a partial contribution to all criteria because it is the most direct measure of English competence, a skill helpful to the trainees because a substantial amount of the soldier training was presented in English.

Table 6.1-3 REGRESSION ANALYSIS COMPUTED FROM THE CORRELATIONS IN TABLE 6.1-2

Criterion	R^2	R	R adjusted	F	p
1 SP	.598	.773	.767	59.4	<.0001
2 EFB(post)	.884	.940	.938	304.0	<.0001
3 SP rank	.358	.598	.585	22.3	<.0001
4 EF rank	.589	.767	.761	57.3	<.0001

The standardized coefficients of the regression of each criterion on the predictors are shown with their standard errors in the columns of Table 6.1-5. The significant partial contribution of each predictor to regression, given that the $q - 1$ remaining predictors are already included in the model, is readily assessed from this table because the ratio of each estimate to its standard error is distributed as t on $N - q - 1$ degrees of freedom. As a rough guide, one may take the estimated coefficient to be significantly different from zero if it exceeds twice the magnitude of its standard error. On this basis it is apparent that NLT makes an additional contribution to prediction only for the soldier-performance variables.

The values of the other coefficients are entirely plausible; general ability, education, and English competence all figure in the prediction of soldier performance, while posttraining English fluency is predicted predominantly by the English-fluency pretest.

6.1.5 Testing Homogeneity of Regressions

In prediction studies and in analysis of covariance (see Secs. 5.5 and 7.3), we may wish to compare regressions in two or more populations. As a preliminary to such

Table 6.1-4 PARTIAL CONTRIBUTION TO REGRESSION OF SEPARATE PREDICTORS IN THE ORDER ECFA, NGC, NLT, EFB(pre)

		Generalized and univariate partial F statistics and p values							
Criteria		ECFA		HGC | ECFA		NLT | ECFA, HGC		EFB(pre) | ECFA, HGC, NLT	
	F_0	86.2	<.0001	8.6	<.0001	2.1	.089	73.2	<.0001
SP	F	166.3	.0001	13.2	.0004	7.9	.005	13.6	.0004
EFB(post)		269.3	.0001	20.2	.0001	2.0	.156	295.3	.0001
SP rank		69.9	.0001	2.6	.109	2.0	.159	9.5	.003
EF rank		167.6	.0001	19.2	.0001	.7	.402	10.8	.001

Table 6.1-5 ESTIMATED STANDARDIZED REGRESSION COEFFICIENTS (STANDARD ERRORS)

	Criteria			
Predictor	*1* SP	*2* EFB(post)	*3* SP rank	*4* EF rank
5 ECFA	.206 (.100)	.166 (.054)	.204 (.127)	.256 (.102)
6 HGC	.154 (.093)	.063 (.050)	.025 (.118)	.277 (.094)
7 NLT	.198 (.083)	.001 (.045)	.107 (.105)	.034 (.084)
8 EFB(pre)	.303 (.082)	.757 (.044)	.319 (.104)	.292 (.083)

comparisons, it is advisable to test the null hypothesis that the population regressions are in fact identical; i.e.,

$$H_0: \mathbf{B}_1 = \mathbf{B}_2 = \cdots = \mathbf{B}_n = \mathbf{B} \qquad (6.1\text{-}13)$$

Note that this hypothesis specifies homogeneous slopes of the regression surface but not necessarily equal intercepts. It is therefore referred to as the hypothesis of *parallel* regression planes (lines). If parallel planes are assumed, the test of differences between intercepts is provided by the analysis of covariance.

A multivariate test of (6.1-13) may be carried out by comparing the residual sum of products after estimating **B** in the total sample with the pooled residual after estimating $\mathbf{B}_j$ in the samples from each of the n populations. If the former indicates significantly greater dispersion than the latter, the hypothesis is rejected. (This test assumes homogeneity of the conditional covariance matrices of the n populations. A statistical test for checking the latter assumption is given in Sec. 6.2.)

The calculations for the test of parallelism are most conveniently carried out in raw scores rather than standardized scores: the data matrix takes the form

$$\begin{array}{c}\left[\begin{array}{c|c} \mathbf{Y}_1 & \mathbf{X}_1 \\ \mathbf{Y}_2 & \mathbf{X}_2 \\ \cdots & \cdots \\ \mathbf{Y}_n & \mathbf{X}_n \end{array}\right] \begin{array}{c} N_1 \\ N_2 \\ \cdots \\ N_n \end{array} \\ \quad p \qquad q \end{array}$$

As in Sec. 5.5, a row of this matrix is $[\mathbf{y}'_{ij},\mathbf{x}'_{ij}]$, representing the $(p + q)$-vector observation of subject i in group j of the sample, and $[\mathbf{y}'_{\cdot j},\mathbf{x}'_{\cdot j}]$ is the vector mean of group j. The total sample size is $N = \sum_{j=1}^{n} N_j$.

To estimate the separate regressions, we compute the group sums of products,

$$\mathbf{S}_j^{(y)} = \mathbf{Y}_j'\mathbf{Y}_j - N_j\mathbf{y}_{\cdot j}\mathbf{y}'_{\cdot j}$$

$$\mathbf{S}_j^{(x)} = \mathbf{X}_j'\mathbf{X}_j - N_j\mathbf{x}_{\cdot j}\mathbf{x}'_{\cdot j}$$

$$\mathbf{S}_j^{(xy)} = (\mathbf{S}_j^{(yx)})' = \mathbf{X}_j'\mathbf{Y}_j - N_j\mathbf{x}_{\cdot j}\mathbf{y}'_{\cdot j}$$

and estimate $\mathbf{B}_j$ as

$$\hat{\mathbf{B}}_j = (\mathbf{S}_j^{(x)})^{-1}\mathbf{S}_j^{(xy)} \qquad (6.1\text{-}14)$$

for $|\mathbf{S}_j^{(x)}| \neq 0$.

Similarly, we estimate the common regression from the within-group sums of products,

$$\mathbf{S}_w^{(y)} = \sum_{j=1}^{n} \mathbf{S}_j^{(y)}$$

$$\mathbf{S}_w^{(x)} = \sum_{j=1}^{n} \mathbf{S}_j^{(x)}$$

$$\mathbf{S}_w^{(xy)} = (\mathbf{S}_w^{(yx)})' = \sum_{j=1}^{n} \mathbf{S}_j^{(xy)}$$

Then
$$\hat{\mathbf{B}} = (\mathbf{S}_w^{(x)})^{-1}\mathbf{S}_w^{(xy)} \qquad (6.1\text{-}15)$$

The associated partition of the total sum of products is shown in Table 6.1-6.

A multivariate test of the hypothesis of parallel regression planes may be carried out in the manner of Sec. 3.4.7 from the roots of
$$|\mathbf{S}_h + \lambda\mathbf{S}_e| = 0 \qquad (6.1\text{-}16)$$

where $\mathbf{S}_h$ and $\mathbf{S}_e$ and their respective degrees of freedom are defined in Table 6.1-6.

Similarly, univariate F ratios may be formed from corresponding elements in the diagonals of $\mathbf{S}_h$ and $\mathbf{S}_e$.

If the hypothesis is rejected, estimation and interpretation of the separate regressions computed by (6.1-14) is justified. The variance-covariance matrix of the estimator of $\mathbf{B}_j$ is given by
$$\mathscr{V}(\mathbf{B}_j) = (\mathbf{S}_j^{(x)})^{-1} \times \boldsymbol{\Sigma}^* \qquad (6.1\text{-}17)$$

with $\boldsymbol{\Sigma}^*$ estimated from the multivariate analysis of variance as
$$\hat{\boldsymbol{\Sigma}}^* = \frac{1}{N - n - nq}\mathbf{S}_e$$

The raw regression coefficients may be converted to β weights by
$$\hat{\boldsymbol{\beta}}_j = \mathbf{D}_{\sigma_x}^{(j)}\hat{\mathbf{B}}(\mathbf{D}_{\sigma_y}^{(j)})^{-1}$$

where $\mathbf{D}_{\sigma_x}^{(j)}$ and $\mathbf{D}_{\sigma_y}^{(j)}$ are diagonal matrices of sample standard deviations for group j.

EXAMPLE 6.1-2 (*Soldier selection, continued*) Because the trainees described in Example 6.1-1 would be more likely to have some degree of English-language competence if they had attended high school, we might suppose that the English-fluency pretest would have a different weight in that part of the sample with nine or more

Table 6.1-6 PARTITION OF SUM OF PRODUCTS FOR COMMON AND SEPARATE REGRESSIONS

Source	df	Sum of products ($p \times p$)
Common regression	q	$\mathbf{S}_r = \mathbf{S}_w^{(yx)}(\mathbf{S}_w^{(x)})^{-1}\mathbf{S}_w^{(xy)}$
Between regressions	$n_h = (n-1)q$	$\mathbf{S}_h = \mathbf{S}_w^{(y)} - \mathbf{S}_r - \mathbf{S}_e$
Residual	$n_e = N - n - nq$	$\mathbf{S}_e = \sum_{j=1}^{n} [\mathbf{S}_j^{(y)} - \mathbf{S}_j^{(yx)}(\mathbf{S}_j^{(x)})^{-1}\mathbf{S}_j^{(xy)}]$
Within groups	$N - n$	$\mathbf{S}_w^{(y)} = \sum_{j=1}^{n} \mathbf{S}_j^{(y)}$

grades completed than in the part with eight or fewer grades completed. We can test this supposition by means of the analysis outlined in Sec. 6.1.5. The sample statistics for this purpose, $\mathbf{S}_1$ and $\mathbf{S}_2$, may be recovered from the correlations and standard deviations in Table 6.1-7 by the formula

$$\mathbf{S}_j = (N_j - 1)\mathbf{D}_\sigma^{(j)}\mathbf{R}_j\mathbf{D}_\sigma^{(j)}$$

where $\mathbf{D}_\sigma^{(j)}$ is the diagonal matrix of sample standard deviations for criteria and predictors jointly. For these data, Table 6.1-6 takes on the values shown in Table 6.1-8, for which the three nonzero roots of (6.1-16) are found to be

$$\lambda_1 = .1107 \qquad \lambda_2 = .0172 \qquad \lambda_3 = .0074$$

Thus
$$F_0 = (157 - 4 + 1)\frac{.1107}{|3 - 4| + 1} = 154\,\frac{.1107}{2} = 8.53$$

exceeds the .05 point for F_0 with $r = 2$, $s = 3$, and $t = 154$. The univariate F statistics on 3 and 157 degrees of freedom indicate that the departure from parallelism is concentrating the English-fluency measures:

Criterion		F	p
1	SP	1.57	.199
2	EFB(post)	3.40	.019
3	SP rank	.25	.864
4	EF rank	2.69	.048

Table 6.1-7 SAMPLE CORRELATIONS AND STANDARD DEVIATIONS FOR TRAINEES CLASSIFIED BY HIGHEST GRADE COMPLETED

Tests	SD	Correlations 1	2	3	4	5	6	7
Group 1: HGC < 9(N = 100)								
1 SP	85.65	1.0000						
2 EFB(post)	20.42	.5625	1.0000					
3 SP rank	.3106	.4729	.2862	1.0000				
4 EF rank	.2999	.5374	.4087	.6452	1.0000			
5 ECFA	18.69	.5131	.4916	.3683	.4770	1.0000		
6 NLT	33.70	.5202	.4424	.2922	.4096	.6091	1.0000	
7 EFB(pre)	13.03	.5199	.7526	.7526	.3243	.4095	.3260	1.0000
Group 2: HGC ≥ 9(N = 65)								
1 SP	108.98	1.0000						
2 EFB(post)	34.50	.6070	1.0000					
3 SP rank	.3823	.5197	.5164	1.0000				
4 EF rank	.2329	.5127	.6591	.5479	1.0000			
5 ECFA	16.40	.5956	.7264	.4001	.5073	1.0000		
6 NLT	38.91	.4978	.4869	.3670	.3627	.6411	1.0000	
7 EFB(pre)	35.48	.5803	.9201	.4772	.6484	.7260	.5629	1.0000

As we might expect, the estimated β weights shown in Table 6.1-9 reveal that EFB(post) and EF rank depend more heavily on EFB(pre) among subjects with a higher level of education.

Table 6.1-8 PARTITION OF SUM OF PRODUCTS FOR TEST OF HOMOGENEITY OF REGRESSION IN SOLDIER-SELECTION DATA

Source of dispersion	df	Sums of products			
		SP	EFB(post)	SP rank $\times 10^2$	EF rank $\times 10^2$
Common regression	3	601,211			
		209,830	89,427		
		151,603	55,869	38,834	
		146,241	52,242	37,328	36,487
Between regressions	3	25,787			
		5,481	1,714		
		1,094	182	704	
		9,232	1,984	1,234	4,271
Residual	157	859,403			
		28,161	26,327		
		110,372	5,500	149,455	
		64,477	4,452	52,148	83,012
Within groups	163	1,486,401			
		243,472	117,468		
		263,069	61,551	188,993	
		219,950	58,678	90,710	123,770

Table 6.1-9 ESTIMATED REGRESSION COEFFICIENTS (β WEIGHTS) COMPUTED FROM THE DATA IN TABLE 6.1-7

Predictors	Criteria			
	1 SP	*2* EFB(post)	*3* SP rank	*4* EF rank
Group 1: HGC < 9				
1 ECFA	.1960	.1356	.2352	.2856
2 NLT	.2882	.1484	.0834	.1617
3 EFB(pre)	.3457	.6487	.2008	.2268
Group 2: HGC ≥ 9				
1 ECFA	.2947	.1747	.0511	.0949
2 NLT	.1502	−.1048	.1266	−.0357
3 EFB(pre)	.2818	.8523	.3688	.5996

6.1.6 The Most Predictable Criterion: Canonical Correlation

Responding to a query from Truman Kelley, Harold Hotelling in 1936 investigated the problem of finding the linear combination of criteria that has the greatest multiple correlation with the predictors. The solution to this problem that Hotelling published in the 1935 volume of the *Journal of Educational Psychology* was the basis for his formulation of canonical correlation as a general method for analyzing linear relations between two sets of variables [Hotelling, 1936a]. The problem may be stated as follows:

Let the sample correlation matrix of the p criteria and q predictors be

$$\begin{bmatrix} \mathbf{R}_{yy} & \mathbf{R}_{yx} \\ \mathbf{R}_{xy} & \mathbf{R}_{xx} \end{bmatrix} \begin{matrix} p \\ q \end{matrix}$$
$$\quad p \qquad q$$

Assume the data are expressed in standard score units, and let $v_y = \boldsymbol{\alpha}'\mathbf{z}_y$ be a linear combination of criterion scores, and $v_x = \boldsymbol{\beta}'\mathbf{z}_x$ be a linear combination of predictor scores. Then the correlation between these linear combinations is given by

$$\rho = \frac{\boldsymbol{\alpha}'\mathbf{R}_{yx}\boldsymbol{\beta}}{\sqrt{\boldsymbol{\alpha}'\mathbf{R}_{yy}\boldsymbol{\alpha}\boldsymbol{\beta}'\mathbf{R}_{xx}\boldsymbol{\beta}}}$$

(See Sec. 3.3.6.)

We wish to choose $\boldsymbol{\alpha}$ and $\boldsymbol{\beta}$ so as to maximize the absolute value of ρ. Accordingly, we apply the matrix derivatives of Sec. 2.5 to obtain necessary conditions on the maximum of

$$\rho^2 = \frac{(\boldsymbol{\alpha}'\mathbf{R}_{yx}\boldsymbol{\beta})^2}{\boldsymbol{\alpha}'\mathbf{R}_{yy}\boldsymbol{\alpha}\boldsymbol{\beta}'\mathbf{R}_{xx}\boldsymbol{\beta}}$$

with respect to variation in $\boldsymbol{\alpha}$ and $\boldsymbol{\beta}$, for $\boldsymbol{\alpha}'\mathbf{R}_{yy}\boldsymbol{\alpha} = \boldsymbol{\beta}'\mathbf{R}_{xx}\boldsymbol{\beta} \neq 0$.

The extremal equations are

$$\boldsymbol{\alpha}: \quad \mathbf{R}_{yx}\hat{\boldsymbol{\beta}} - \hat{\rho}\mathbf{R}_{yy}\hat{\boldsymbol{\alpha}} = \mathbf{0} \qquad (6.1\text{-}18)$$

$$\boldsymbol{\beta}: \quad -\hat{\rho}\mathbf{R}_{xx}\hat{\boldsymbol{\beta}} + \mathbf{R}_{xy}\hat{\boldsymbol{\alpha}} = \mathbf{0} \qquad (6.1\text{-}19)$$

Solving for $\boldsymbol{\alpha}$ and $\boldsymbol{\beta}$, we obtain

$$(\mathbf{R}_{yx}\mathbf{R}_{xx}{}^{-1}\mathbf{R}_{xy} - \hat{\rho}^2\mathbf{R}_{yy})\hat{\boldsymbol{\alpha}} = \mathbf{0} \qquad (6.1\text{-}20)$$

and

$$(\mathbf{R}_{xy}\mathbf{R}_{yy}{}^{-1}\mathbf{R}_{yx} - \hat{\rho}^2\mathbf{R}_{xx})\hat{\boldsymbol{\beta}} = \mathbf{0} \qquad (6.1\text{-}21)$$

We recognize each of these equations as the two-matrix eigenproblem discussed in Sec. 2.7.3. The nontrivial solutions of (6.1-20) and (6.1-21) are characteristic vectors associated with those values of ρ^2 that satisfy

$$|\mathbf{R}_{yx}\mathbf{R}_{xx}{}^{-1}\mathbf{R}_{xy} - \hat{\rho}^2\mathbf{R}_{yy}| = 0 \qquad (6.1\text{-}22)$$

and

$$|\mathbf{R}_{xy}\mathbf{R}_{yy}{}^{-1}\mathbf{R}_{yx} - \hat{\rho}^2\mathbf{R}_{xx}| = 0 \qquad (6.1\text{-}23)$$

As we have seen in Sec. 2.7.3, the number of nonzero roots of (6.1-22) and (6.1-23) is determined by $\text{rank}(\mathbf{R}_{yy}\mathbf{R}_{xx}^{-1}\mathbf{R}_{xy}) = \text{rank}(\mathbf{R}_{yx}\mathbf{R}_{xx}^{-1}\mathbf{R}_{xy}) = \text{rank}(\mathbf{R}_{xy}) = \text{rank}(\mathbf{R}_{yx})$. Assuming no linear dependencies between the two sets of variables, the number of nonzero roots is therefore

$$s = \min(p,q)$$

The solution of (6.1-22) and (6.1-23) corresponding to the largest root provides the most predictable criterion. Actually, only the eigenproblem of smaller order need be solved, for if $\boldsymbol{\alpha}$ is determined, then from (6.1-19),

$$\hat{\boldsymbol{\beta}} = \frac{1}{\hat{\rho}} \mathbf{R}_{xx}^{-1}\mathbf{R}_{xy}\hat{\boldsymbol{\alpha}}$$

or, conversely, from (6.1-18),

$$\hat{\boldsymbol{\alpha}} = \frac{1}{\hat{\rho}} \mathbf{R}_{yy}^{-1}\mathbf{R}_{yx}\hat{\boldsymbol{\beta}}$$

The s nonzero roots of (6.1-22) and (6.1-23) are the squared *canonical correlations* between the two sets of variables. Corresponding to root $\hat{\rho}_j^2$, say, are the canonical variates

$$\hat{v}_y^{(j)} = \hat{\boldsymbol{\alpha}}_j'\mathbf{z}_y \qquad (6.1\text{-}24)$$

and

$$\hat{v}_x^{(j)} = \hat{\boldsymbol{\beta}}_j'\mathbf{z}_x \qquad (6.1\text{-}25)$$

whose correlation is given by $\hat{\rho}_j$ with a positive sign. The canonical variates are set to unit standard deviation in the sample,

$$\hat{\boldsymbol{\alpha}}_j'\mathbf{R}_{yy}\hat{\boldsymbol{\alpha}}_j = 1$$

$$\hat{\boldsymbol{\beta}}_j'\mathbf{R}_{xx}\hat{\boldsymbol{\beta}}_j = 1$$

and variates corresponding to different roots ($j \neq k$) are uncorrelated

$$\hat{\boldsymbol{\alpha}}_j'\mathbf{R}_{yy}\hat{\boldsymbol{\alpha}}_k = 0$$

$$\hat{\boldsymbol{\beta}}_j'\mathbf{R}_{xx}\hat{\boldsymbol{\beta}}_k = 0$$

These results follow from properties of characteristic roots and vectors discussed in Sec. 2.7.3. Similarly, from (6.1-18) or (6.1-19), $v_y^{(j)}$ and $v_x^{(k)}, j \neq k$, are uncorrelated; that is,

$$\hat{\boldsymbol{\alpha}}_j'\mathbf{R}_{yx}\hat{\boldsymbol{\beta}}_k = 0$$

The canonical correlations are so-called *invariant* statistics because they are invariant with respect to affine transformation of the variables. Invariance with respect to change of origin and scale is implied in their definition in terms of product-moment correlation. Invariance with respect to nonsingular homogeneous linear transformation is demonstrated as follows. Let

$$\mathbf{z}_y = \mathbf{T}_y\mathbf{u} \qquad \text{and} \qquad \mathbf{z}_x = \mathbf{T}_x\mathbf{w}$$

where $|\mathbf{T}_y| \neq 0$ and $|\mathbf{T}_x| \neq 0$. Then

$$\mathbf{R}_{yy} = \mathbf{T}_y\mathbf{R}_{uu}\mathbf{T}_y' \qquad \mathbf{R}_{xy} = \mathbf{T}_x\mathbf{R}_{wu}\mathbf{T}_y' \qquad \mathbf{R}_{xx} = \mathbf{T}_x\mathbf{R}_{ww}\mathbf{T}_x'$$

whence, (6.1-20) and (6.1-21) become

$$[\mathbf{T}_y\mathbf{R}_{uw}\mathbf{T}'_x(\mathbf{T}'_x)^{-1}\mathbf{R}_{ww}^{-1}(\mathbf{T}_x)^{-1}\mathbf{T}_x\mathbf{R}_{wu}\mathbf{T}'_y - \hat{\rho}^2\mathbf{T}_y\mathbf{R}_{uu}\mathbf{T}'_y]\hat{\boldsymbol{\alpha}} = 0$$

$$[\mathbf{T}_x\mathbf{R}_{wu}\mathbf{T}'_y(\mathbf{T}'_y)^{-1}\mathbf{R}_{uu}^{-1}(\mathbf{T}_y)^{-1}\mathbf{T}_y\mathbf{R}_{uw}\mathbf{T}'_x - \hat{\rho}^2\mathbf{T}_x\mathbf{R}_{ww}\mathbf{T}'_x]\hat{\boldsymbol{\beta}} = 0$$

or

$$(\mathbf{R}_{uw}\mathbf{R}_{ww}^{-1}\mathbf{R}_{wu} - \hat{\rho}^2\mathbf{R}_{uu})\mathbf{T}'_y\hat{\boldsymbol{\alpha}} = 0$$

$$(\mathbf{R}_{wu}\mathbf{R}_{uu}^{-1}\mathbf{R}_{uw} - \hat{\rho}^2\mathbf{R}_{ww})\mathbf{T}'_x\hat{\boldsymbol{\beta}} = 0$$

Setting $\hat{\boldsymbol{\gamma}} = \mathbf{T}'_y\hat{\boldsymbol{\alpha}}$ and $\hat{\boldsymbol{\delta}} = \mathbf{T}'_x\hat{\boldsymbol{\beta}}$, we see that, in addition to leaving $\hat{\rho}_j$ unchanged, the transformation has no effect on the canonical variates (6.1-24) and (6.1-25):

$$\hat{v}_y^{(j)} = \hat{\boldsymbol{\gamma}}'_j\mathbf{u} = \hat{\boldsymbol{\alpha}}'\mathbf{T}_y\mathbf{T}_y^{-1}\mathbf{z}_y = \hat{\boldsymbol{\alpha}}'\mathbf{z}_y$$

$$\hat{v}_x^{(j)} = \hat{\boldsymbol{\delta}}'_j\mathbf{w} = \hat{\boldsymbol{\beta}}'\mathbf{T}_x\mathbf{T}_x^{-1}\mathbf{z}_x = \hat{\boldsymbol{\beta}}\mathbf{z}_x$$

We observe also that the roots of (6.1-7) and those of (6.1-22) or (6.1-23) are related. For

$$|\mathbf{S}_h - \lambda\mathbf{S}_e| = |\mathbf{R}_{yx}\mathbf{R}_{xx}^{-1}\mathbf{R}_{xy} - \lambda(\mathbf{R}_{yy} - \mathbf{R}_{yx}\mathbf{R}_{xx}^{-1}\mathbf{R}_{xy})| = 0$$

$$= \left|\mathbf{R}_{yx}\mathbf{R}_{xx}^{-1}\mathbf{R}_{xy} - \frac{\lambda}{1+\lambda}\mathbf{R}_{yy}\right| = 0$$

whence

$$\rho^2 = \frac{\lambda}{1+\lambda} \qquad (6.1\text{-}26)$$

Conversely,

$$\lambda = \frac{\rho^2}{1-\rho^2} \qquad (6.1\text{-}27)$$

Thus, the test of the multivariate hypothesis (6.1-27) is equivalent to a test of the hypothesis that the canonical correlations are jointly null:

$$\rho_1 = \rho_2 = \cdots = \rho_s = 0 \qquad (6.1\text{-}28)$$

In particular, the generalized F testing this hypothesis is

$$F_0 = \frac{t}{r}\frac{\rho_1^2}{1-\rho_1^2}$$

with r, s, and t defined as in (6.1-8).

Using (6.1-27), the trace and likelihood ratio statistic (6.1-9) and (6.1-10) may also be expressed in terms of the squared canonical correlations.

The composite test of no association may be of less interest than a test of the *dimensionality* of significant relationships between the two sets of variables. If the $s - s_0$ smallest canonical correlations are not significantly different from zero, we say that the data contain evidence of association in only s_0 dimensions. An approximate test of the hypothesis that the $s - s_0$ smallest roots are jointly null is provided by Bartlett's chi-square,

$$\chi_B^2 = [n_e - \tfrac{1}{2}(p + q + 1)] \sum_{j=s_0+1}^{s} \log_e(1 - \hat{\rho}_j^2) \qquad (6.1\text{-}29)$$

which under the null hypothesis is distributed asymptotically as a central chi-square on $(p - s_0)(q - s_0)$ degrees of freedom [Bartlett, 1947; Williams, 1967].

EXAMPLE 6.1-3 (*Soldier selection, continued*) To estimate the canonical correlation between predictors and criteria for the data described in Example 6.1-1, we first compute, from the correlations in Table 6.1-10, the matrix $\mathbf{R}_{yx}\mathbf{R}_{xx}^{-1}\mathbf{R}_{xy}$.

From this matrix and $\mathbf{R}_{yy}$ of Table 6.1-2, we solve eigenproblem (6.1-22) and obtain the canonical correlation coefficients and weights for the canonical variates as shown in Table 6.1-10. Before interpreting Table 6.1-10, let us investigate the dimensionality of the relationship between the two sets of variables by computing Bartlett's chi-square approximations (6.1-29). The results are as follows:

Roots	Chi-square	df	p
1, 2, 3, 4	390.64	16	<.0001
2, 3, 4	32.31	9	.0002
3, 4	4.52	4	.34

Thus, no significant association between the two groups remains after the first two canonical variates are eliminated. From the standardized coefficients for the first canonical variate (weights) in Table 6.1-10, it is clear that the "most predict-

Table 6.1-10 CANONICAL CORRELATION ANALYSIS OF THE SOLDIER-SELECTION DATA IN TABLE 6.1-7

	Canonical correlation (squared)			
	1	2	*3*	*4*
	.9456	.4000	.1612	.0450
	.8942	.1600	.0260	.0020
	Standardized weights			
1 SP	.0882	.9579	−.9906	.8300
2 EFB(post)	.8395	−1.3709	.2280	.2694
3 SP rank	.0084	−.3078	−.7560	−1.1809
4 EK rank	.1163	1.0111	1.3122	−.2404
5 ECFA	.2000	.4135	.0973	−1.9466
6 HGC	.1045	.8310	1.2770	1.0693
7 NLT	.0244	.4744	−1.4338	.6719
8 EFB(pre)	.7367	−1.4290	−.0685	.2853

able criterion" is a measure of posttraining English fluency, with having essentially zero weight.

For the second variate, the English-fluency factor is suppres ment of a negative weight to EFB(post) and a positive weight to EF variate appears to measure that component of soldier performanc ich is uncorrelated with English fluency. The positive correlation between soldier performance and English fluency (r = .7383) makes this component difficult to predict, and the estimate of the corresponding canonical correlation is only .4000.

6.1.7 Interpretation of Canonical Correlation

The weights for the canonical variates represent a sort of compromise, under the constraint of orthogonality, between maximizing the interset covariance and minimizing the intraset variance. In many cases, the result of this compromise is difficult to interpret substantively, and it is sometimes suggested that the interpretation should be based, not on the weights, but on the correlation between the canonical variate for a given set and each of the original variates which make up that set. This is a questionable practice, however, because these correlations may reflect the variation unique to the set rather than the covariation between sets. Since only the latter is germane to interpretation, a better strategy is to correlate the canonical variates for one set with the original variates of the *other* set. These correlations may characterize the between-set relationships much more simply than the standardized weights. The following example is a case in point.

EXAMPLE 6.1-4 (*Cognitive and somatic variables*) As part of a dissertation study, Petersen [1973] sought to replicate results of Broverman and Klaiber [1969] showing an association between certain cognitive measures and somatic indicators of androgenicity. Using test data and ratings of whole-body photographs of 35 eighteen-year-old male subjects in the Fels Longitudinal Study, Petersen obtained the correlation shown below the diagonal in Table 6.1-11. (For purposes of Exercise 6.1-1, the correlations for female subjects are shown above the diagonal in this table.) A canonical correlation analysis, reproduced in part in Table 6.1-12, showed a significant largest root and, as expected from previous results, weights for the cognitive variables in the form of a contrast between the two cognitive measures. The weights for the somatic variables were peculiar, however, in that the overall androgenicity rating had a negative weight even though it was measured in the same direction as the other indicators. That this is some form of suppressor effect is apparent in the correlations between the cognitive contrast and the separate somatic variables. All the correlations are positive and suggest the action of a single factor of androgencity.

Exercise 6.1-1

(*a*) Perform a canonical correlation analysis of the data for female subjects in Table 6.1-11, and interpret the results.

(*b*) Test the hypothesis that the regression of the cognitive contrast on the somatic variables is the same, except for sign, in males and females.

Table 6.1-11 CORRELATIONS OF COGNITIVE AND SOMATIC VARIABLES FOR 35 EIGHTEEN-YEAR-OLD MALE SUBJECTS (BELOW DIAGONAL) AND 44 EIGHTEEN-YEAR-OLD FEMALE SUBJECTS (ABOVE DIAGONAL)

Variables:	*1*	*2*	*3*	*4*	*5*	*6*	*7*
Cognitive							
1 Spatial visualization		.1683	−.0082	.0355	.2211	.0006	.3059
2 Fluent production	−.1027		−.2693	−.1869	−.1605	−.2165	.0303
Somatic							
3 Age at peak height velocity	−.2190	.0731		−.2099	−.1732	−.0895	−.0774
4 Muscles	−.4721	.2739	−.0074		.8155	.5184	−.1509
5 Overall rating	−.3103	.1873	.1945	.8444		.5237	−.1835
6 Genital/breast size	−.2054	.2999	.0038	.6270	.5662		−.2506
7 Pubic hair	.1462	.3083	−.3545	−.1117	−.3638	−.0724	

Table 6.1-12 CANONICAL WEIGHTS AND CORRELATION OF THE COGNITIVE CONTRAST WITH THE SOMATIC VARIABLES

Variables	Standardized weights	Correlation of the cognitive contrast with the somatic variables
Cognitive		
1 Spatial visualization	−.76	
2 Fluent production	.58	
Somatic		
3 Age at peak height velocity	.34	.20
4 Muscles	1.33	.50
5 Overall rating	−.61	.33
6 Genital/breast size	.06	.34
7 Pubic hair	.30	.11
Canonical correlation: $r = .58$ ($F_0 = 4.78, p < .05$)		

6.2 CLASSIFICATION

Classification procedures based on behavioral data are routinely used by large organizations to assign or counsel persons with respect to jobs, instructional programs, therapeutic regimens, military specialties, etc. The economic importance of these applications is so great as to have stimulated intensive study, notably by Wald [1950], of the statistical properties of various classification strategies (see also Rao [1970] and Anderson [1958]). These studies provide the foundations of *statistical decision theory*, a topic which has implications not only for classification but also for the theory of hypothesis testing (see Blackwell and Girshick [1954], Das Gupta [1973]).

In the context of personnel classification, we consider a statistical decision problem with the following given elements: (1) a subject is known to belong to one of n populations; (2) the relative sizes of the populations are known or can be estimated; (3) there is information about the subject in the form of a p-component score vector $\mathbf{y}$; (4) the density function of each population is known or can be estimated.

The problem is to formulate from these elements a decision function that assigns the subject to one of the populations with, in some sense, minimum loss due to errors of misclassification. In the following discussion, we shall define "minimum loss" as minimum expected loss.* This loss criterion is satisfied by the following so-called *Bayes* classification procedure:

Let $f_k(\mathbf{y})$ be the probability density of population k at the point $\mathbf{y}$. Let π_k be the relative size of population k, where $\sum_{k=1}^{n} \pi_k = 1$; that is, π_k is the *prior probability* that the subject is from population k. The conditional probability that a subject with score vector $\mathbf{y}$ comes from population k is

$$P(k \mid \mathbf{y}) = \frac{\pi_k f_k(\mathbf{y})}{\sum_{h=1}^{n} \pi_h f_h(\mathbf{y})}$$

The expected loss due to classifying the subject in population j is therefore

$$C_j = \sum_{\substack{k=1 \\ k \neq j}}^{n} P(k \mid \mathbf{y}) c_{jk}$$

where c_{jk} is the cost associated with classifying the subject in population j when he in fact belongs to k. The expected loss is minimized if the subject with score vector $\mathbf{y}$ is assigned to the population j for which

$$\sum_{\substack{k=1 \\ k \neq j}}^{n} \pi_k f_k(\mathbf{y}) c_{jk} \qquad (6.2\text{-}1)$$

* Other criteria such as the *minimax* principle (minimizing the maximum expected loss) are also reasonable (see Blackwell and Girshick [1954]).

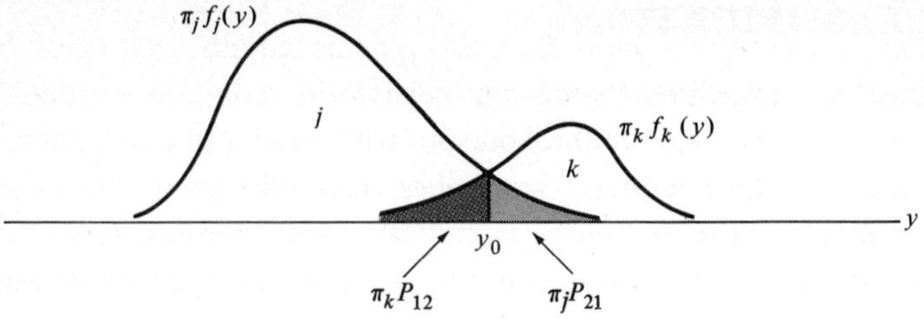

FIGURE 6.2-1
The Bayes classification rule when costs of misclassification are equal. The cutting point is at y_0.

is a minimum. Assuming that the prior probabilities, densities, and costs are known, (6.2-1) can be computed for each population, and the minimum value located. If the densities are continuous, there is no probability of (6.2-1) being exactly equal for any two populations; hence, the procedure will almost always assign the subject uniquely.

In effect, any classification rule based on the vector **y** partitions the p-dimensional space into classification regions $R_1, R_2, \ldots, R_n$. The expected loss due to classifying the subject in population j is obtained by integrating (6.2-1) over this region:

$$\int_{R_j} \sum_{\substack{k=1 \\ k \neq j}}^{n} \pi_k f_k(\mathbf{y}) c_{jk} \, d\mathbf{y} \qquad (6.2\text{-}2)$$

For the Bayes procedure, the integral (6.2-2) is necessarily minimal with respect to the assignment since j is chosen to minimize the integrand at every point **y** in R_j. It can be shown [Anderson, 1958] that the Bayes procedure has the desirable properties of (1) *admissibility*, i.e., there is no better procedure under the minimum-expected-loss criterion, and (2) *completeness*, i.e., every admissible procedure is a Bayes procedure.

When the costs of misclassification are equal and only two populations are involved, the Bayes rule simplifies as follows: assign subject i to population j if

$$\frac{f_j(\mathbf{y}_i)}{f_k(\mathbf{y}_i)} > \frac{\pi_k}{\pi_j} \qquad (6.2\text{-}3)$$

In the univariate case, (6.2-3) divides the real line at a "cutting point" y_0, where the densities stand in inverse proportion to the prior probabilities, that is, where $\pi_j f_j(y) = \pi_k f_k(y)$, as in Fig. 6.2-1. The probability that a subject belongs to population j and is classified in population k is $\pi_j P_{kj}$, the area indicated by the shaded region to the right of y_0 in the figure. Conversely, the probability that a subject belongs to population k and is classified in population j is $\pi_k P_{jk}$, indicated by the shaded region to the left of y_0. P_{kj} is the conditional probability that a subject is misclassified, given that he belongs to population j. P_{jk} is the conditional probability that a subject is misclassified given that he belongs to population k.

Similar results hold in the multivariate case if the score vector is projected on a line connecting the points in the p-space corresponding to the vector means of the two population distributions. The two-group discriminant function defined in the following section is an example of such a projection. (Multiple-group discriminant functions are discussed in Secs. 6.2.3 and 6.3.1.)

6.2.1 Classification into One of Two Multivariate Normal Populations*

Suppose it is known that the subjects belong exclusively to population 1 or 2, in which their score vectors are distributed $N(\boldsymbol{\mu}_1,\boldsymbol{\Sigma}_1)$ and $N(\boldsymbol{\mu}_2,\boldsymbol{\Sigma}_2)$, respectively. Then we may apply the Bayes rule by examining the log difference

$$v_{12} = \ln \frac{\pi_1 c_{12}}{\pi_2 c_{21}} - \tfrac{1}{2} \ln \frac{|\boldsymbol{\Sigma}_1|}{|\boldsymbol{\Sigma}_2|} - \tfrac{1}{2}[(\mathbf{y} - \boldsymbol{\mu}_1)'\boldsymbol{\Sigma}_1^{-1}(\mathbf{y} - \boldsymbol{\mu}_1) - (\mathbf{y} - \boldsymbol{\mu}_2)'\boldsymbol{\Sigma}_2^{-1}(\mathbf{y} - \boldsymbol{\mu}_2)] \tag{6.2-4}$$

and assigning the subject (whose score vector is $\mathbf{y}$) to population 1 if $v_{12} \geq 0$, and to population 2 otherwise.

For the moment, let us simplify matters further by assuming that the costs of misclassification are equal and that the populations have a common covariance matrix, We shall relax the latter assumption in Sec. 6.2.4 after introducing a test for homogeneity of covariance matrices. Setting $c_{12}/c_{21} = 1$ and $\boldsymbol{\Sigma}_1 = \boldsymbol{\Sigma}_2 = \boldsymbol{\Sigma}$ in (6.2-4), we obtain

$$v_{12} = \ln \frac{\pi_1}{\pi_2} + \mathbf{y}'\boldsymbol{\Sigma}^{-1}(\boldsymbol{\mu}_1 - \boldsymbol{\mu}_2) - \tfrac{1}{2}(\boldsymbol{\mu}_1 + \boldsymbol{\mu}_2)'\boldsymbol{\Sigma}^{-1}(\boldsymbol{\mu}_1 - \boldsymbol{\mu}_2) \tag{6.2-5}$$

For subjects from population 1, (6.2-5) is distributed as

$$v_{12} \sim N(l_{12} + \tfrac{1}{2}\Delta_{12}^2, \Delta_{12}^2)$$

where $l_{12} = \ln (\pi_1/\pi_2)$

$$\Delta_{12}^2 = (\boldsymbol{\mu}_1 - \boldsymbol{\mu}_2)'\boldsymbol{\Sigma}^{-1}(\boldsymbol{\mu}_1 - \boldsymbol{\mu}_2)$$

that is, Δ_{12}^2 is the generalized distance between populations 1 and 2. For subjects from population 2, on the other hand, the distribution of (6.2-5) is

$$v_{12} \sim N(l_{12} - \tfrac{1}{2}\Delta_{12}^2, \Delta_{12}^2)$$

* For ease of writing in the remainder of Sec. 6.2, we drop the typographical distinction between fixed and random variables.

Thus, the probability of misclassifying a subject who belongs to population 1 is

$$P_{21} = P(\upsilon_{12} < 0) = \Phi\left(-\frac{l_{12} + \frac{1}{2}\Delta_{12}^2}{\Delta_{12}}\right) \tag{6.2-6}$$

and the probability of the converse misclassification is

$$P_{12} = P(\upsilon_{12} \geq 0) = \Phi\left(\frac{l_{12} - \frac{1}{2}\Delta_{12}^2}{\Delta_{12}}\right) \tag{6.2-7}$$

where $\Phi(z)$ represents the unit normal integral from $-\infty$ to the deviate z.

To depict this classification rule graphically, we express (6.2-5) as

$$\upsilon_{12} = l_{12} + \mathbf{y}'\boldsymbol{\beta} - \tfrac{1}{2}(\boldsymbol{\mu}_1 + \boldsymbol{\mu}_2)'\boldsymbol{\beta} \tag{6.2-8}$$

where

$$\boldsymbol{\beta} = \Sigma^{-1}(\boldsymbol{\mu}_1 - \boldsymbol{\mu}_2)$$

The term $\mathbf{y}'\boldsymbol{\beta}$ in (6.2-8) is the *discriminant function* of R. A. Fisher. This function projects the multivariate distribution into one dimension as shown in Fig. 6.2-2. For ease of interpretation, the scale of the discriminant function has been altered so that the common within-population variance is unity. That is, the graph depicts the distribution of the standardized discriminant score

$$v = \mathbf{y}'\boldsymbol{\alpha} \tag{6.2-9}$$

where

$$\boldsymbol{\alpha} = \Delta_{12}^{-1}\boldsymbol{\beta}$$

On the discriminant-score continuum, the population means are separated by $(\mathbf{y}_{\cdot 1} - \mathbf{y}_{\cdot 2})'\boldsymbol{\alpha} = \Delta_{12}$ standard-deviation units. The cutting score which divides the continuum into regions R_1 and R_2 is

$$v_0 = \tfrac{1}{2}(\boldsymbol{\mu}_1 + \boldsymbol{\mu}_2)'\boldsymbol{\alpha} - \Delta_{12}^{-1}l_{12} \tag{6.2-10}$$

If the prior probabilities are equal, $l_{12} = 0$ and v_0 is midway between the mean discriminant scores; i.e., at a distance $\frac{1}{2}\Delta_{12}$ from $\boldsymbol{\mu}_1'\boldsymbol{\alpha}$ and $-\frac{1}{2}\Delta_{12}$ from $\boldsymbol{\mu}_2'\boldsymbol{\alpha}$. Unequal prior probabilities move this point by an amount $-l_{12}/\Delta_{12}$ (see Fig. 6.2-2).

In typical applications of this method of classification, a calibration study is required to obtain estimates of the population proportions, means, and common covariance matrix. Ideally, this should be a prospective study in which the subjects are measured at the time when classification would ordinarily occur and at some later time identified as to population membership. The study of high-school dropout and delinquency described in Example 6.2-2 illustrates this approach.

For the classification procedure to be an improvement on random assignment in the case of equal covariance matrices, there must be an observable difference between the population means. In doubtful cases, a preliminary two-group multivariate analysis of variance should be performed, aimed at rejecting the hypothesis of equal means.

Suppose that the calibration study shows a significant difference between

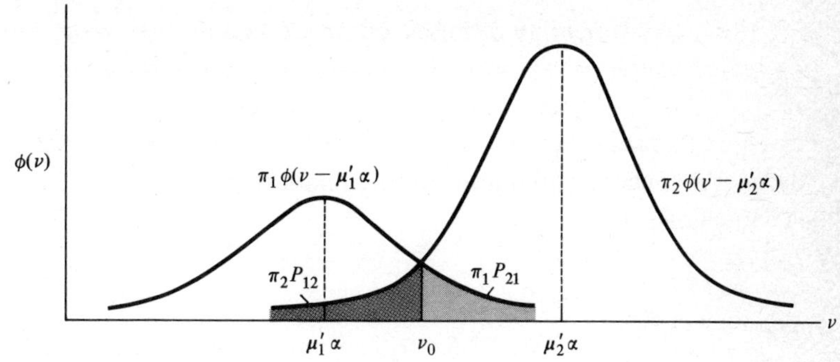

FIGURE 6.2-2
Error rates of the two-group discrimination.

populations, so that it would be productive to compute the discriminant function. Then if N_h $(h = 1,2)$ is the number of subjects ultimately identified with population h, and $\mathbf{y}_{ih}$ is the observed score vector of sample subject i from population h, the estimates of π_h, $\boldsymbol{\mu}_h$, and Σ required in the calculations are given, respectively, by,

$$p_h = \frac{N_h}{N_1 + N_2}$$

$$\mathbf{y}_{\cdot h} = \frac{1}{N_h}\sum_{i=1}^{N_h} \mathbf{y}_{ih}$$

$$\hat{\Sigma} = \frac{1}{N_1 + N_2 - 2}\left(\sum_{h=1}^{2}\sum_{i=1}^{N_h} \mathbf{y}_{ih}\mathbf{y}'_{ih} - \sum_{h=1}^{2} N_h \mathbf{y}_{\cdot h}\mathbf{y}'_{\cdot h}\right)$$

The unscaled discriminant-function coefficients are components of the vector

$$\mathbf{b} = \hat{\Sigma}^{-1}(\mathbf{y}_{\cdot 1} - \mathbf{y}_{\cdot 2})$$

and the scaled coefficients are those of

$$\mathbf{a} = D_{12}{}^{-1}\mathbf{b} \qquad (6.2\text{-}11)$$

where $D_{12}{}^2 = \mathbf{b}'\hat{\Sigma}\mathbf{b} = (\mathbf{y}_{\cdot 1} - \mathbf{y}_{\cdot 2})'\Sigma^{-1}(\mathbf{y}_{\cdot 1} - \mathbf{y}_{\cdot 2}) = (\mathbf{y}_{\cdot 1} - \mathbf{y}_{\cdot 2})'\mathbf{b}$ is the sample generalized distance (Mahalanobis D^2).

A new subject with score vector $\mathbf{y}$ is classified by computing his discriminant score

$$v = \mathbf{y}'\mathbf{a} \qquad (6.2\text{-}12)$$

and assigning him to population 1 if $v < v_0$, and to population 2 otherwise, where

$$v_0 = \tfrac{1}{2}(\mathbf{y}_{\cdot 1} + \mathbf{y}_{\cdot 2})'\mathbf{a} - D_{12}{}^{-1}L_{12}$$

and

$$L_{12} = \ln \frac{p_1}{p_2}$$

From (6.2-6) and (6.2-7), the estimated conditional error rates p_{21} and p_{12} are, respectively, the normal probabilities corresponding to the deviates $-\frac{1}{2}D_{12} - D_{12}{}^{-1}L_{12}$ and $D_{12}{}^{-1}L_{12} - \frac{1}{2}D_{12}$.

A multivariate test of significance of the differences between the two groups may be obtained by making use of the relationship between the generalized distance and Hotelling's T^2:

$$T^2 = \frac{N_1 N_2}{N_1 + N_2} D_{12}{}^2 \qquad (6.2\text{-}13)$$

As indicated in Sec. 4.2.5a critical points for T^2, when there are p variables, may be obtained by referring

$$F = \frac{N_1 + N_2 - p - 1}{p(N_1 + N_2 - 2)} T^2 \qquad (6.2\text{-}14)$$

to the F distribution with p and $N_1 - N_2 - p - 1$ degrees of freedom.

Unless the calibration sample is large relative to the number of variables, however, the rates computed in this way will be biased downward because the discriminant function *maximizes* the relative distance between the mean discriminant scores *in the sample*. (See Exercise 6.2-1.) This is evident when we observe that the discriminant function is just the regression, on the observed scores, of dummy variables,

$$\frac{N_2}{N_1 + N_2} \qquad \text{and} \qquad -\frac{N_1}{N_1 + N_2}$$

for membership in populations 1 and 2, respectively. The bias in the error rates thus arises from the same source as the bias in the sample multiple correlation coefficient (see Sec. 6.1.4). Lachenbruch [1968] shows that this bias can be largely eliminated by adapting formula (6.1-12) for adjusting R^2. To obtain the adjusted rates we "shrink" the distance between the sample distributions to D_{12}^*, where

$$(D_{12}^*)^2 = D_{12}{}^2 \frac{N_1 + N_2 - p}{N_1 + N_2 - 1} - \frac{(p-1)(N_1 + N_2)(N_1 + N_2 - 2)}{(N_1 + N_2 - 1)N_1 N_2} \qquad (6.2\text{-}15)$$

If (6.2-15) is negative, the adjustment fails, but this will happen only if the distance between the means is small and p is large relative to N_1 and N_2. If the deviates in (6.2-6) and (6.2-7) are computed from the adjusted distance, the bias in the error rates will be much reduced. This correction is illustrated in the following example.

EXAMPLE 6.2-1 (*An endocrine correlate of male homosexuality*) The hypothesis that diminished androgen/estrogen ratios predispose males to homosexuality was investigated by Margolese [1970], who measured the 24-hour output of metabolites of testosterone and estrogen in normal and homosexual subjects. Table 6.2-1 shows his data for 24-hour androsterone (A) and etiocholanolone (E) in 11 healthy heterosexual males and 15 healthy homosexual males. The age of each subject is also shown.

For purposes of the discriminant analysis, we compute from these data the differences [1.01818, − 1.1400] (hetero-homo) for A and E, respectively, and the common covariance matrix and its inverse,

$$\begin{bmatrix} .71319 & \\ .61667 & 1.10150 \end{bmatrix}^{-1} = \begin{bmatrix} 2.71778 & \\ -1.52154 & 1.75968 \end{bmatrix}$$

Then, from (6.2-12), the unscaled discriminant-function coefficients are

$$\begin{bmatrix} 4.50175 \\ -3.55524 \end{bmatrix} = \begin{bmatrix} 2.71778 \times 1.01818 + 1.52154 \times 1.14000 \\ -1.52154 \times 1.01818 - 1.75968 \times 1.14000 \end{bmatrix}$$

The generalized distance is computed as indicated following (6.2-11):

$$8.63653 = 4.50175 \times 1.01818 + 3.55524 \times 1.14000$$

It is convenient at this point to compute Hotelling's T^2 from (6.2-13):

$$54.8087 = \frac{11 \times 15}{11 + 15} 8.63653$$

From (6.2-14), this value corresponds to an F of

$$26.26 = \frac{(11 + 15 - 2 - 1)}{2(11 + 15 - 2)} 54.8087$$

Table 6.2-1 VALUES OF URINARY ANDROSTERONE (A) AND ETIOCHOLANOLONE (E) IN HEALTHY HETEROSEXUAL AND HOMOSEXUAL MALES (mg 24 HOURS)

Group 1: Heterosexual				Group 2: Homosexual			
Subject No.	Age	A	E	Subject No.	Age	A	E
1	20	3.9	1.8	1	41	2.5	2.1
2	25	4.0	2.3	2	28	1.6	1.1
3	29	3.8	2.3	3	37	3.9	3.9
4	24	3.9	2.5	4	31	3.4	3.6
5	21	2.9	1.3	5	33	2.3	2.5
6	37	3.2	1.7	6	29	1.6	1.7
7	21	4.6	3.4	7	25	2.5	2.9
8	33	4.3	3.1	8	32	3.4	4.0
9	28	3.1	1.8	9	40	1.6	1.9
10	42	2.7	1.5	10	25	4.3	5.3
11	37	2.3	1.4	11	24	2.0	2.7
				12	29	1.8	3.6
				13	43	2.2	4.1
				14	34	3.1	5.2
				15	42	1.3	4.0

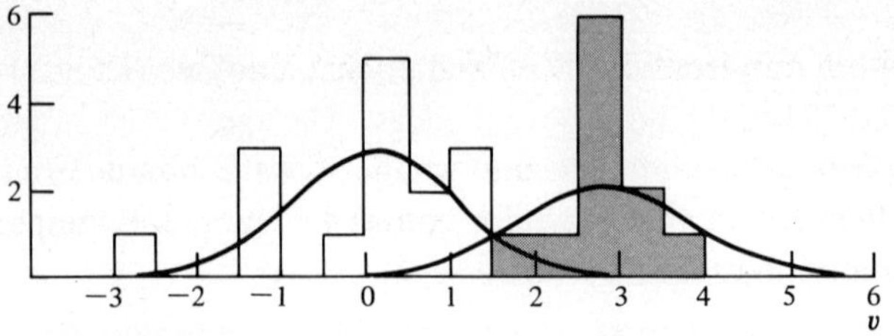

FIGURE 6.2-3
Distributions of discriminant scores of homosexual and heterosexual (shaded) subjects.

on 2 and 23 degrees of freedom. The difference between the groups is highly significant ($p < .0001$) and suggests that the discriminant function might be useful for identifying males predisposed to homosexuality. (Controlling the difference in the mean age of the groups does not alter this conclusion.)

The scaled discriminant-function coefficients (6.2-12) are

$$\begin{bmatrix} 1.53183 \\ -1.20976 \end{bmatrix} = \frac{1}{\sqrt{8.63653}} \begin{bmatrix} 4.50175 \\ -3.55524 \end{bmatrix}$$

and the mean discriminant scores of the heterosexual and homosexual groups are, respectively,

$$2.84877 = 1.53183 \times 3.521818 - 1.20976 \times 2.1$$

$$-0.09013 = 1.53183 \times 2.5 - 1.20976 \times 3.24$$

Note that the difference between these means is $2.93880 = \sqrt{8.63653}$ as required. A histogram of the discriminant scores of the sample subjects is shown in Fig. 6.2-3.

In the sample, a cutting point at $1.37932 = (2.84877 - .09013)/2$, midway between the means, correctly classifies all the subjects. This cutting point does not take into account the relative size of the two populations, however. These sizes are unknown, but for purposes of discussion might reasonably be set at .95 for hetero and .05 for homo. If so, the cutting point (6.2-10) is

$$.3770 = 1.37932 - \frac{\ln .95/.05}{2.93880} = 1.37932 - 1.00192$$

With this cutting point, the probabilities of misclassifying a subject as homosexual or heterosexual is obtained by substituting sample values in (6.2-6) and (6.2-7), respectively.

$$\pi_1 P_{21} = .95\Phi(-1.00192 - 1.46940) = .95 \times .0060 = .0057$$

$$\pi_2 P_{12} = .05\Phi(1.00192 - 1.46940) = .05 \times .32 = .016$$

These figures indicate very little unconditional risk of misclassification, but the .32

conditional risk of misclassifying a subject, given that he is homosexual, is rather high.

The preceding calculations do not account for the bias due to maximizing the generalized distance in the sample. To correct for bias, we compute the adjusted generalized distance given by (6.2-15):

$$8.13980 = 8.63653 \frac{11 + 15 - 2}{11 + 15 - 1} - \frac{(11 + 15)(11 + 15 - 2)}{(11 + 15 - 1)(11 \times 15)}$$

Then $D_{12}^* = 2.85303 = \sqrt{8.13980}$, $(D_{12}^*)^{-1}L_{12} = .971$, and the corrected probabilities of misclassification are

$$\pi_1 P_{21}^* = .95\Phi(-.971 - 1.42651) = .95 \times .008 = .0076$$

$$\pi_2 P_{12}^* = .05\Phi(.971 - 1.42651) = .05 \times .325 = .01625$$

The effect of the correction is rather small. These rates are based on very limited data and are perhaps not to be taken too seriously. The existence of an endocrine correlate of male homosexuality has, however, been confirmed in other studies [Kolodny and Masters, et al., 1971].

6.2.2 Classification into n Multivariate Normal Populations: Multiple Discriminant Analysis

To apply the Bayes rule in the case of n populations, we compute (6.2-4) for all distinct pairs of populations and assign the subject to that population for which all values are positive. Thus, if $v_{12} > 0, v_{13} > 0, \ldots,$ and $v_{1n} \geq 0$, we assign the subject to population 1. In the multivariate case with equal costs of misclassification and equal covariance matrices, this rule has the effect of assigning the subject to the population k in which the mean vector $\boldsymbol{\mu}_k$ is closest in generalized distance to the score vector $\mathbf{y}$, after the distance is adjusted by $-2 \ln \pi_k$ to allow for unequal prior probabilities (see Tatsuoka [1971]).

In the practical implementation of this procedure, there is considerable advantage in seeking a reduction in the dimensionality of the problem by a preliminary *multiple discriminant* analysis of the sample data [Rao, 1970] (also called *multiple-group* discriminant analysis [Tatsuoka, 1971]). As will be apparent in the following discussion, this analysis is a special case of canonical correlation in which one of the sets of variables consists of $n - 1$ linearly independent contrasts among the n groups. It may also be formulated as a special case of analysis of variance in which the variate is a linear combination

$$v = \mathbf{y}'\mathbf{a} \qquad (6.2\text{-}16)$$

of the observed score components. As we shall see, multiple discriminant analysis reduces to simple discriminant analysis in the case of two groups, thus justifying the identical notation of this and the preceding section.

The one-way analysis of variance of (6.2-16) in the case of n groups and N_j subjects per group is shown in Table 6.2-2. Notice that this table is obtained from the one-way multivariate analysis in Table 5.2-3 by substituting scalar quadratic forms in $\mathbf{a}$ for the respective $p \times p$ sums-of-products matrices.

In multiple discriminant analysis, we choose the elements of $\mathbf{a}$ to maximize differences between groups in the sense that the ratio of the between-group sum of squares to the within-group sum of squares is maximal. The function to be maximized with respect to variation in $\mathbf{a}$ is

$$\psi = \frac{\text{ssb}}{\text{ssw}} = \frac{\mathbf{a}'\mathbf{SSBa}}{\mathbf{a}'\mathbf{SSWa}}$$

This is precisely the problem discussed in Sec. 2.7.4 of maximizing a ratio of quadratic forms with respect to the variable of the forms. We saw there that the matrix SSW must be positive definite, which implies here that $N - n \geq p$. Then $\mathbf{a}$, at the maximum, satisfies

$$(\mathbf{SSB} - \psi\mathbf{SSW})\mathbf{a} = \mathbf{0} \qquad (6.2\text{-}17)$$

where ψ is the largest root of

$$|\mathbf{SSB} - \psi\mathbf{SSW}| = 0 \qquad (6.2\text{-}18)$$

In general, the

$$\text{rank}(\mathbf{SSB}) = \min(n - 1, p) = s$$

positive roots of (6.2-18) are distinct and may almost always be uniquely ordered as

$$\psi_1 > \psi_2 > \cdots > \psi_s$$

The function

$$v^{(k)} = \mathbf{y}'\mathbf{a}_k \qquad (6.2\text{-}19)$$

where $\mathbf{a}_k$ is the solution of (6.2-17) when $\psi = \psi_k$, is called the kth *canonical variate*

Table 6.2-2 MULTIPLE DISCRIMINANT ANALYSIS: ANALYSIS OF VARIANCE OF A LINEAR FUNCTION OF p-VARIATES

Source of variation	df	Sums of squares
Constant	1	$\text{ssm} = Nv_{..}^2 = \mathbf{a}'\left(\frac{1}{N}\mathbf{Y}'_{.}\mathbf{D11}'\mathbf{DY}_{.}\right)\mathbf{a} = \mathbf{a}'\mathbf{SSMa}$
Between groups	$n - 1$	$\text{ssb} = \text{ssg} - \text{ssm} = \mathbf{a}'(\mathbf{SSG} - \mathbf{SSM})\mathbf{a} = \mathbf{a}'\mathbf{SSBa}$
Group means	n	$\text{ssg} = \sum_{j=1}^{n} N_j v_{.j}^2 = \mathbf{a}'\mathbf{Y}'_{.}\mathbf{DY}_{.}\mathbf{a} = \mathbf{a}'\mathbf{SSGa}$
Within groups	$N - n$	$\text{ssw} = \text{sst} - \text{ssg} = \mathbf{a}'(\mathbf{SST} - \mathbf{SSG})\mathbf{a} = \mathbf{a}'\mathbf{SSWa}$
Total	$N = \sum N_j$	$\text{sst} = \sum_{j=1}^{n}\sum_{i=1}^{N_j} v_{ij}^2 = \mathbf{a}'\mathbf{Y}'\mathbf{Ya} = \mathbf{a}'\mathbf{SSTa}$

for the n-group discrimination. It is customary to choose the scale of $\mathbf{a}_k$ so that the common within-group variance of (6.2-16) is unity:

$$\frac{\text{ssw}}{N-n} = \frac{\mathbf{a}'\text{SSW}\mathbf{a}}{N-n} = \mathbf{a}'\hat{\Sigma}\mathbf{a} = 1 \qquad (6.2\text{-}20)$$

In this scale, the between-group mean square is

$$\lambda_k = \frac{\psi_k}{n-1} = \frac{\mathbf{a}_k'\text{SSB}\mathbf{a}_k}{n-1}$$

and is referred to as the *canonical variance* of the kth variate.

Consider now the $r \leq s$ leading canonical variates, and express their values, when the observed score vector is $\mathbf{y}$, as the $1 \times r$ vector

$$\mathbf{v}' = [v^{(1)}, v^{(2)}, \ldots, v^{(r)}] = \mathbf{y}'[\mathbf{a}_1, \mathbf{a}_2, \ldots, \mathbf{a}_r] = \mathbf{y}'\mathbf{A}$$

The $p \times r$ matrix $\mathbf{A}$ represents a transformation which simultaneously diagonalizes SSB and SSW (see Sec. 2.7):

$$\mathbf{A}'\text{SSB}\mathbf{A} = (n-1)\Lambda = (n-1)\,\text{diag}[\lambda_1, \lambda_2, \ldots, \lambda_r] \qquad (6.2\text{-}21)$$

$$\mathbf{A}'\text{SSW}\mathbf{A} = (N-n)\mathbf{A}'\hat{\Sigma}\mathbf{A} = (N-n)\mathbf{I} \qquad (6.2\text{-}22)$$

Thus, the between-group sums of squares of the canonical variates are proportional to the roots of (6.2-18), and the variates are uncorrelated in the sample. Variate $v^{(1)}$ maximizes the between-group sum of squares and is the single best discriminant function. Variate $v^{(2)}$ maximizes the between-group sum of squares under the restriction that $v^{(1)}$ and $v^{(2)}$ have zero correlation in the sample. Similarly, $v^{(3)}$ maximizes the between-group sum of squares under the restriction that its correlations with $v^{(1)}$ and $v^{(2)}$ are both zero. And so on, down to $v^{(r)}$ which has the smallest between-group sum of squares and has zero correlation with all the preceding variates.

We now show that when $n = 2$, $v^{(1)}$ is just (6.2-12): In the case of two groups, the between-group product matrix in Table 6.2-2 may be expressed as

$$\begin{aligned}\text{SSB} &= \mathbf{Y}'\left(\mathbf{D} - \frac{1}{N}\mathbf{D}\mathbf{1}\mathbf{1}'\mathbf{D}\right)\mathbf{Y}. \\ &= N_1\mathbf{y}_{\cdot 1}\mathbf{y}_{\cdot 1}' + N_2\mathbf{y}_{\cdot 2}\mathbf{y}_{\cdot 2}' \\ &\quad - \frac{1}{N_1+N_2}(N_1\mathbf{y}_{\cdot 1} + N_2\mathbf{y}_{\cdot 2})(N_1\mathbf{y}_{\cdot 1} + N_2\mathbf{y}_{\cdot 2})' \\ &= \frac{N_1N_2}{N_1+N_2}(\mathbf{y}_{\cdot 1} - \mathbf{y}_{\cdot 2})(\mathbf{y}_{\cdot 1} - \mathbf{y}_{\cdot 2})'\end{aligned}$$

and (6.2-17) may be expressed as

$$\left[\frac{N_1N_2}{(N_1+N_2)(N_1+N_2-2)}(\mathbf{y}_{\cdot 1} - \mathbf{y}_{\cdot 2})(\mathbf{y}_{\cdot 1} - \mathbf{y}_{\cdot 2})' - \psi\hat{\Sigma}\right]\mathbf{a} = \mathbf{0} \qquad (6.2\text{-}23)$$

Thus, $\mathbf{a} = D_{12}^{-1}\mathbf{b}$ satisfies (6.2-23) with $\psi = [N_1N_2/(N_1 + N_2)(N_1 + N_2 - 2)]D_{12}^2$. Note that $(N_1 + N_2 - 2)\psi$ is Hotelling's T^2 for the two-group case given by (6.2-13).

The advantage in the transformation to canonical variates is the reduction in dimensionality when the number of groups is less than the number of observed variates. The classification rule and its graphical representation (see Example 6.2-2) can then be expressed in terms of at most $n - 1$ canonical variates. Indeed, it may be possible to reduce dimensionality further with little adverse effect on the error rates by choosing r so as to exclude the $s - r$ canonical variates that show no significant between-group variation. A statistical test of significance of the $s - r$ smallest canonical variances is therefore a useful preliminary to the n-group classification procedure. Bartlett's approximate chi-square test for canonical correlations (6.1-29) may be adapted for this purpose:

$$\chi_B^2 = [(N - n) - \tfrac{1}{2}(n + p)] \sum_{k=r+1}^{s} \log_e(1 + \psi_k) \qquad (6.2\text{-}24)$$

On the hypothesis that the $s - r$ smallest canonical variances are zero in the population, (6.2-24) is distributed asymptotically as chi-square on $(p - r)(n - r - 1)$ degrees of freedom.

In terms of the r canonical variates retained subsequent to this test, the n-group Bayes classification rule assuming multivariate normal populations and equal costs of misclassification is as follows: Let $\mathbf{v}' = \mathbf{y}'\mathbf{A}$ be the canonical variates computed from the subjects' observed scores, and let $\mathbf{v}_{\cdot k} = \mathbf{y}'_{\cdot k}\mathbf{A}$ be the mean canonical variate for group k. Assign the subject to population k if

$$u_{kh} = \ln \frac{p_k}{p_h} + \mathbf{v}'(\mathbf{v}_{\cdot k} - \mathbf{v}_{\cdot h}) + \tfrac{1}{2}(\mathbf{v}_{\cdot k} + \mathbf{v}_{\cdot h})'(\mathbf{v}_{\cdot k} - \mathbf{v}_{\cdot h}) \geq 0 \qquad (6.2\text{-}25)$$

for all $h \neq k$.

To compute the misclassification rates for this rule when the subject in fact belongs to population j, we need the multivariate distribution of the vector of discriminant scores $\mathbf{u}' = [u_{j1}, u_{j2}, \ldots, u_{j,n-1}]$ on the hypothesis of membership in population j. The distribution of the u_{jh}, $h \neq j$, on this hypothesis is multivariate normal with means and variances estimated respectively by $L_{jh} + \frac{1}{2}D_{jh}^2$ and D_{jh}^2, where $L_{jh} = \ln(p_h/p_j)$ and $D_{jh}^2 = (\mathbf{v}_{\cdot j} - \mathbf{v}_{\cdot h})'(\mathbf{v}_{\cdot j} - \mathbf{v}_{\cdot h})$. The covariance of u_{jh} and $u_{jh'}$ is estimated by

$$D_{jhh'} = (\mathbf{v}_{\cdot j} - \mathbf{v}_{\cdot h})'(\mathbf{v}_{\cdot j} - \mathbf{v}_{\cdot h'})$$

Since misclassification results if any $u_{jh} < 0$, the probability of misclassification is given by the complement of the positive orthant of a multivariate distribution with the corresponding parameters. Because of the difficulty of evaluating general high-dimensional multivariate normal integrals, the practical computation of these error rates is difficult except in the case $n = 3$, where tables of the bivariate normal distribution apply [U.S. National Bureau of Standards, 1956].

From these tables, the conditional error rates for subjects belonging to populations 1, 2, and 3, respectively, can be obtained as follows:

$$P_{23,1} = P[(u_{12} < 0) \cup (u_{13} < 0)]$$
$$P_{13,2} = P[(u_{21} < 0) \cup (u_{23} < 0)]$$
$$P_{12,3} = P[(u_{31} < 0) \cup (u_{32} < 0)]$$

For $n = 4$ or 5, similar error rates may be computed by the method of integral transforms [Dutt, 1973]. For $n > 5$, the only feasible alternative at present is to approximate the rate of misclassification by Monte Carlo simulation. Computation of the error rate in the three-population case is illustrated in the following example.

EXAMPLE 6.2-2 (*Delinquency and dropout in high school*) In a prospective study of delinquency and dropout of high-school students, Kelly, Veldman, and McGuire [1964] obtained a variety of psychomotor, personality, sociometric, sociological, and cognitive measures on all seventh-grade children in four nonurban Texas communities (634 subjects). Four years later, the investigators assessed the school status of 402 of the subjects who could then be located. Of these, 322 were attending school in the original communities, 50 had dropped out of school, and 30 had records of delinquency.

The measures employed in the initial phase of the study were four psychomotor tests [Dotting, Discrimination Reaction Time (DRT), Copying, Writing X's], a personality self report (the surgency scale of the Junior Personality Quiz), two sociometric nomination items (Wild Ones and Left Out), an index of socioeconomic status (ISS, a measure based on reported income, occupation, and education of parent), the California Test of Mental Maturity (CTMM), and STEP Listening Test.

From the authors' published report of this study the group means and common within-group standard deviations have been reconstructed in Table 6.2-3. Regrettably, the correlations among the variables were not reported, but for purposes of the present example, they have been assigned plausible values in the table.

A preliminary multivariate analysis of variance, summarized in Table 6.2-4, reveals clearly significant between-population differences involving the 10 variables jointly and each of the separate variables, except Left Out. These results justify further examination of the data to assess the value of the measures for identifying potential delinquents and dropouts. As a first step, we compute by (6.2-17) the discriminant functions associated with the two degrees of freedom between groups. These are shown in Table 6.2-4, together with the canonical variances and Bartlett's chi-square. Both functions are significant and are retained in the calculation of the canonical variate group contrasts. For purposes of computing discriminant scores, we require the three distinct pairwise canonical contrasts shown at the top of Table 6.2-5. These are the result of the calculation

$$V_C = \mathbf{A}'[\mathbf{y}_{\cdot 1} - \mathbf{y}_{\cdot 3}, \mathbf{y}_{\cdot 2} - \mathbf{y}_{\cdot 3}, \mathbf{y}_{\cdot 1} - \mathbf{y}_{\cdot 2}] \qquad (6.2\text{-}26)$$

Table 6.2-3 GROUP MEANS AND COMMON STANDARD DEVIATIONS AND CORRELATIONS OF DELINQUENT, DROPOUT, AND NORMAL HIGH-SCHOOL STUDENTS

		Variables									
Group means	*N*	*1*	*2*	*3*	*4*	*5*	*6*	*7*	*8*	*9*	*10*
1 Delinquent	30	4.10	4.40	4.65	4.85	6.50	3.25	1.30	59.30	30.05	266.90
2 Dropout	50	4.40	5.50	4.35	4.50	5.85	1.75	1.85	62.15	26.85	265.70
3 Normal	322	4.85	4.95	5.30	5.30	5.35	1.20	1.20	52.90	32.90	275.65
Common SD		1.44	1.14	1.47	1.38	2.11	2.73	1.95	13.77	9.50	12.58
Correlations*											
1 Dotting		1.00									
2 Writing X's		.24	1.00								
3 Copying		−.21	−.17	1.00							
4 DRT		−.21	−.17	.22	1.00						
5 Surgency		.24	.19	−.24	−.24	1.00					
6 Wild Ones		.24	.19	−.24	−.24	.43	1.00				
7 Left Out		−.24	−.19	.24	.24	−.34	−.43	1.00			
8 ISS		.21	.17	−.21	−.21	.29	.29	−.29	1.00		
9 CTMM		.21	−.17	.21	.21	−.29	−.29	.29	−.73	1.00	
10 STEP LSN		.21	−.17	.21	.21	−.29	−.29	.29	−.73	.73	1.00

* Actual sample correlations are not available. These values have been assigned for purposes of this example.

Table 6.2-4 MULTIVARIATE ANALYSIS OF VARIANCE AND CANONICAL ANALYSIS OF DATA FROM TABLE 6.2-3

			Discriminant functions*	
Variates	Univariate *F* (2/399)	*p*	1	2
1 Dotting	5.30	.005	.5187	−.3842
2 Writing X's	3.35	.036	.1459	−.3109
3 Copying	10.79	<.0001	.3039	.1377
4 DRT	8.13	.0004	.2621	.1738
5 Surgency	4.87	.008	−.0993	.1479
6 Wild Ones	8.15	.004	−.1359	.2171
7 Left Out	2.41	.092	−.2340	−.2111
8 ISS	11.71	<.0001	−.0579	.0281
9 CTMM	9.41	.0002	−.0650	.0880
10 STEP LSN	18.36	<.0001	.0081	.0169
F_0	12.07			
p	<.01			
λ			.2786	.0643
Bartlett's χ^2			121.5	24.6
df			20	9
p			.0001	.004

* Standardized coefficients of these functions appear in Table 6.2-2.

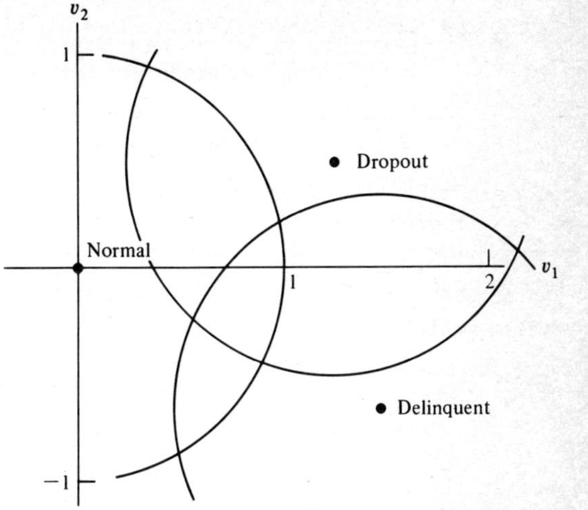

FIGURE 6.2-4
Canonical representation of group centroids. The arcs of circles represent one standard deviation of the canonical variation.

Using the contrast of the normal group with itself (i.e., the null contrast) as origin, the canonical representation may be plotted as in Fig. 6.2-4. The circles about the centroids represent the one-standard-deviation contour of the bivariate normal distribution of the canonical variates. The considerable overlap of the three distributions suggests that the discriminant functions would not be very useful for identifying potential dropouts and delinquents. This impression is confirmed by the following calculation of misclassification rates.*

To obtain the generalized distances and the covariances of the discriminant scores, we compute $V_C'V_C$, the matrix of inner products of the canonical contrasts also shown in Table 6.2-5. The diagonal elements are the variances of the discriminant

* The behavioral interpretation of Fig. 6.2-4 is deferred to Sec. 6.3.

Table 6.2-5 CANONICAL VARIATE CONTRASTS, VARIANCES, COVARIANCES, AND CORRELATIONS FOR DELINQUENT, DROPOUT, AND NORMAL GROUPS

	Contrasts		
	(1,3) Del-Norm	(2,3) DO-Norm	(1,2) Del-DO
Canonical variates			
1	1.456901	1.223448	.233453
2	−.666812	.497123	−1.163937
Contrast variances and covariances			
(1, 3)	2.567199		
(2, 3)	1.450955	1.743956	
(1, 2)	1.116245	−.293002	1.409249
Contrast correlations			
(1, 3)	1.0000		
(2, 3)	.6857	1.0000	
(1, 2)	.5869	−.1869	1.0000

scores u_{13}, u_{23}, and u_{12} and are equal to the generalized distances D_{13}^2, D_{23}^2, and D_{12}^2. The off-diagonal elements are the covariances of the pairs of discriminant scores which, when divided by the respective standard deviations, become the correlations in the bottom section of the table.

From the quantities in Table 6.2-5, the means $L_{jk} + \frac{1}{2}D_{jk}^2$, standard deviations D_{jk}, standard deviates $L_{jk}D_{jk}^{-1} + \frac{1}{2}D_{jk}$, and correlations $\rho_{jkk'}$ of the bivariate distributions of the discriminant scores involved in the classification of subjects into subpopulations 1, 2, and 3 (Delinquent, Dropout, Normal) are calculated with the result shown in Table 6.2-6. The conditional error rates are then obtained from the unit bivariate normal distribution as indicated on page 407 and multiplied by the prior probabilities to give the unconditional error rates:

$$\begin{aligned}
\pi_1 P_{23,1} &= .075\Phi(-.163, .680, .587) \\
&= .0745[\Phi(.680) + \Phi(.163, .680, -.587)] \\
&= .075 \times .753 = .056 \\
\pi_2 P_{13,2} &= .124\Phi(-1.024, .750, -.187) \\
&= .124[\Phi(.750) + \Phi(1.024, 750, .187)] \\
&= .124 \times .820 = .102 \\
\pi_3 P_{12,3} &= .801(-2.282, -2.071, .686) \\
&= .801[\Phi(-2.282) + \Phi(-2.071) - \Phi(2.282, 2.071, .686)] \\
&= .801 \times .031 = .025
\end{aligned}$$

Note that because the table of the bivariate normal distribution [U.S. National Bureau of Standards, 1959] gives probabilities only for positive deviates, the volumes of the error regions must be obtained with the combined use of the bivariate and univariate normal distributions as indicated.

The error rates estimated in these calculations are little better than the rate

Table 6.2-6 DISCRIMINANT-SCORE MEANS, STANDARD DEVIATIONS, DEVIATES, AND CORRELATIONS

Subpopulation	Prior probability	Discriminant score	Mean	SD	Deviate (mean SD)	Correlation
1	.0746	u_{12}	.1938	1.1871	.1633	.5869
		u_{13}	−1.0897	1.6022	−.6801	
2	.1244	u_{21}	1.2154	1.1871	1.0239	−.1869
		u_{23}	− .9905	1.3206	−.7501	
3	.8010	u_{31}	3.6570	1.6022	2.2824	.6857
		u_{32}	2.7345	1.3206	2.0707	

which would be incurred if all subjects were classified as normal. The routine use of these instruments to identify seventh-grade children with a disposition to delinquency or dropout could not be justified.

6.2.3 Testing the Contribution of Additional Variables to Discrimination

Because of the connection between two-group discriminant analysis and multiple correlation (see Sec. 6.2.1), it is clear that the contribution of additional variables to two-group discrimination can be tested in a manner analogous to stepwise regression. In the multiple-group case, the same purpose is served by the Roy-Bargmann step-down test in Sec. 3.4.10. On the same assumptions as discriminant analysis [namely, that the observations are distributed $N(\boldsymbol{\mu}_j, \Sigma)$, $j = 1, 2, \ldots, n$], the kth step-down F statistic tests the null hypothesis

$$H_0: \mu_1^{(k)} = \mu_2^{(k)} = \cdots = \mu_n^{(k)}$$

with variation due to variables $1, 2, \ldots, k - 1$ eliminated. Rejection of this hypothesis implies that the kth variable is reflecting differences between groups which cannot be accounted for by a linear combination of the preceding $k - 1$ variables. These differences increase the average generalized distance between the groups and thus contribute to improved discrimination. Acceptance of the null hypothesis implies that the variable makes no partial contribution to discrimination and can be dropped without significantly decreasing the generalized distance.

As in stepwise regression analysis, the order in which the contribution of the variables is tested affects the decision to retain or delete a given variable. In general, the variables that are assumed *a priori* to differ in their population means should appear earlier in the step-down ordering, and those of more uncertain status later.

The calculations for the step-down test may be carried out as described in Sec. 3.4.10 with $\mathbf{S}_1 = \text{SSB}$, $\mathbf{S}_2 = \text{SSW}$, $n_1 = n - 1$, and $n_2 = N - n$. Alternatively, the step-down F for the kth variable may be obtained by using the preceding $k - 1$ variables as covariates in an analysis of covariance of the between-group effect [Williams, 1967]. In either case, the kth step-down F is distributed under the null hypothesis as a central F statistic on $n - 1$ and $N - n - k + 1$ degrees of freedom.

EXAMPLE 6.2-3 (*Delinquency and dropout, continued*) The ordering of variables in Example 6.2-2 is taken directly from Kelly, Veldman, and McGuire [1964] and appears to have been arranged by these authors to represent increasing prior expectation of significance between group differences. Thus, the cognitive and SES measures, which certainly would be deviant in delinquents and dropouts, are ordered last; the peer nominations which directly rate asocial behavior are next to last; the personality report is next; and the psychomotor measures which are much less obviously connected with behavioral problems are first in the ordering. It seems plausible, therefore, to reverse the ordering for purposes of the step-down test, and this has been done in the step-down analysis shown in Table 6.2-7.

The reader is reminded that the results in Table 6.2-7 depend critically on the pattern of the common within-group correlation that was assigned artificially for purposes of this example. Nevertheless, it is typical of what might be expected in a study of this kind. Thus, the cognitive and SES measures are assumed highly correlated, as we have come to expect, and neither CTMM nor ISS contributes to discrimination beyond STEP LSN. The peer nominations bring in new information, each representing a distinct dimension of social deviance. The self report appears to be sufficiently consistent with the peer judgments as to supply no additional information. The psychomotor measures, on the other hand, are assumed not highly correlated, either among themselves or with the other measures, and each contributes to improved discrimination. This does not necessarily imply, however, that each represents a new *dimension* of variation. If their low intercorrelations reflect the instability typical of motor performance, the contribution of each to discrimination is like the effect of "test lengthening" on validity. That is, each additional variable increases the reliability with which some discriminating underlying dimension can be measured, and it is the effect of increasing reliability of measurement in this dimension, rather than inclusion of a new dimension, that accounts for the significant partial contribution of each of the psychomotor variables.

6.2.4 Unequal Covariance Matrices

If the population covariance matrices are unequal, the minimum rates of misclassification of multivariate normal observations can be obtained only by use of the general form of the Bayes rule given by (6.2-4) or its multigroup extension (see Melton [1963],

Table 6.2-7 STEP-DOWN ANALYSIS OF DATA FROM TABLE 6.2-4

Variable		Step-down F	p
1	STEP LSN	18.35	<.0001
2	CTMM	1.54	.22
3	ISS	.29	.75
4	Left Out	7.75	.0005
5	Wild Ones	7.47	.0007
6	Surgency	.95	.38
7	DRT	4.84	.008
8	Copying	5.16	.006
9	Writing X's	6.09	.003
10	Dotting	9.89	<.0001

Tatsuoka [1971]). Since the error rates are then difficult to evaluate, the general form should perhaps be avoided unless there is clear evidence that the population covariance matrices are unequal. The likelihood-ratio test of equality of covariance matrices from Wishart populations has been given by Bartlett [1947]. He shows that, on the hypothesis

$$\boldsymbol{\Sigma}_1 = \boldsymbol{\Sigma}_2 = \cdots = \boldsymbol{\Sigma}_n = \boldsymbol{\Sigma}$$

the statistic

$$\chi_C^2 = -\left[1 - \left(\sum_{j=1}^{n} \frac{1}{N_j - 1} - \frac{1}{N-n}\right)\left(\frac{2p^2 + 3p - 1}{6(p+1)(n-1)}\right)\right] \times \left[\sum_{j=1}^{n} (N_j - 1) \ln |\hat{\boldsymbol{\Sigma}}_j| - (N - n) \ln |\hat{\boldsymbol{\Sigma}}|\right] \qquad (6.2\text{-}27)$$

is distributed asymptotically as a central chi-square on $(n - 1)p(p + 1)/2$ degrees of freedom. In this formula, $\boldsymbol{\Sigma}_j$ denotes the unbiased estimate of the population covariance matrix based on the N_j observation in group j, and $\hat{\boldsymbol{\Sigma}} = \mathrm{SSE}/(N - n)$ is the pooled within-group unbiased estimate of the common covariance matrix.

When (6.2-27) rejects the null hypothesis and (6.2-4) is used to classify the subjects, the only presently available method of evaluating the error rates is a Monte Carlo simulation. In the two-group case, for example, random observations are drawn from $N(\boldsymbol{\mu}_1,\boldsymbol{\Sigma}_1)$ and classified using (6.2-4). The proportion of observations assigned to population 2 estimates P_{21}. Conversely, the proportion of observations drawn from $N(\boldsymbol{\mu}_2,\boldsymbol{\Sigma}_2)$ as classified in population 1 estimates P_{12}. Random variate values for this purpose may be obtained as follows: Independent unit normal deviates may be read from the Rand [1955] tables or generated by a suitable computer subroutine. The vector variate consisting of deviates is distributed $\mathbf{z} \sim N(0,\mathbf{I})$. Then,

$$\mathbf{y} = \mathbf{T}(\mathbf{z} + \boldsymbol{\mu}) \qquad (6.2\text{-}28)$$

where $\mathbf{T}$ is the Cholesky factor of $\boldsymbol{\Sigma}$ such that $\mathbf{TT}' = \boldsymbol{\Sigma}$ (Sec. 2.7) is distributed $N(\boldsymbol{\mu},\boldsymbol{\Sigma})$. Provided sufficiently good estimates of the population means and covariance matrices are available to replace $\boldsymbol{\mu}$ and $\boldsymbol{\Sigma}$ in (6.2-28), observations from any specified multivariate normal distribution can be simulated by this method. If the calibration data are not extensive enough to accurately determine $\boldsymbol{\Sigma}_1$ and $\boldsymbol{\Sigma}_2$, however, the error rates based on simulation may not be any great improvement over rates computed on the assumption $\boldsymbol{\Sigma}_1 = \boldsymbol{\Sigma}_2$ even when it is false.

EXAMPLE 6.2-4 (*Test of equality of covariance matrices*) The distribution of sample discriminate scores shown in Fig. 6.2-3 suggests that the dispersion of endocrine metabolite output is greater in the homosexual population than in the heterosexual. To investigate this possibility, we compute the covariance matrices for the separate groups (where $N_1 = 11$ and $N_2 = 15$) as follows:

$$\hat{\Sigma}_1 = \begin{bmatrix} .51964 & \\ .44700 & .47600 \end{bmatrix} \qquad \hat{\Sigma}_2 = \begin{bmatrix} .85143 & \\ .73786 & 1.54828 \end{bmatrix}$$

Then $\ln|\hat{\Sigma}_1| = -3.0692181$, $\ln|\hat{\Sigma}_2| = -.2564228$, and $\ln|\Sigma| = -.9031351$ (the latter covariance matrix is taken from Example 6.2-1). The value of the test statistic computed from these values is

$$\chi_c^2 = -\left[1 - \left(\frac{1}{10} + \frac{1}{14} - \frac{1}{24}\right)\frac{2(4) + 3(2) - 1}{6(3)1}\right]$$
$$\times [-10(3.0692181) - 14(.256428) + 24(.9031351)] = 11.43$$

on $2 \times \frac{3}{2} = 3$ degrees of freedom. Since this value exceeds the .01 central point of the chi-square distribution, there would appear to be evidence that the covariance matrices of the two populations are not equal. The use of (6.2-3) would presumably improve classification, but might not be warranted in this case because of the small sample sizes.

Exercise 6.2-1 (*WPPSI scores and reading ability*) Table 6.2-8 represents data on the subscales of the Wechsler Preschool and Primary Scale of Intelligence

Table 6.2-8 WPPSI SCORES OF FIVE-YEAR-OLDS CLASSIFIED AT AGE SEVEN AS HIGH OR LOW IN READING ABILITY

		Subscales									
	N	1	2	3	4	5	6	7	8	9	10
Group means											
High	75	11.77	12.41	1.95	10.76	10.80	12.01	11.17	12.12	12.59	12.39
Low	75	9.84	9.81	9.96	9.52	9.43	9.99	9.52	10.23	11.33	10.39
Group SD's											
High		2.63	2.56	2.55	2.28	1.93	2.20	2.65	2.45	2.96	2.25
Low		3.01	3.17	2.39	2.37	2.82	2.64	2.33	2.95	3.09	2.44
Correlations*											
1 Information			.409	.332	.270	.483	−.048	.091	−.100	.137	.106
2 Vocabulary		.641		.285	.266	.453	.138	.201	−.055	.026	.169
3 Arithmetic		.662	.585		.323	.360	.221	.183	.094	.221	.411
4 Similarities		.547	.547	.428		.262	.262	.164	.068	.222	.383
5 Comprehension		.631	.682	.575	.458		.201	.208	.165	.234	.252
6 Animal House		.384	.240	.336	.391	.171		.389	.315	.036	.266
7 Picture Completion		.581	.523	.589	.435	.484	.412		.371	.127	.472
8 Mazes		.460	.351	.500	.228	.423	.207	.562		.352	.432
9 Geometric Design		.381	.251	.401	.231	.354	.100	.228	.405		.330
10 Block Design		.467	.544	.536	.355	.411	.475	.557	.653	.394	

* High group above diagonal; low, below diagonal.

(WPPSI) administered at average age five years, five months, to subjects who were subsequently classified at age seven according to high and low attainment in a test of reading [Maxwell, 1972]. Cases were randomly discarded to balance the groups for sex (38 boys and 37 girls in each group).

(*a*) Test the hypothesis of equal covariance matrices in these populations.

(*b*) Compute the means and covariance matrices for the customary Verbal and Performance scales defined by the sum of subscales 1 through 5 and 5 through 10, respectively. Test for equality of these covariance matrices.

(*c*) Assume a common covariance matrix for the Verbal and Performance scales, and compute a discriminant function to classify future good or poor readers. Compute the rates of misclassification. Does the variance of this function differ in the two groups

6.3 COMPARATIVE STUDIES

The purpose of a comparative study is to describe differences between naturally occurring populations. If we assume, as elsewhere in this text, that the comparison is made in terms of variables that are multivariate normal within populations, a complete description is contained in the vector means and covariance matrices of the respective population. Thus, there are three cases to be considered: (1) the population vector means are unequal but there is a common within-population covariance matrix; (2) both vector means and covariance matrices are unequal; (3) the vector means are equal but the covariance matrices are unequal.

Present multivariate methods have little to contribute to the analysis of cases 2 and 3, except the test of equality of covariance matrices presented in Sec. 6.2.4. If the population covariance matrices are in fact unequal, then no general exact test of equality of vector means is available. This is not as serious a limitation as it might seem, however, because the test of this hypothesis based on multivariate analysis of variance is valid in large samples even in this case. Since in comparative studies the subject is typically the unit of observation, the behavioral investigator usually has the possibility of obtaining large samples if the need arises. In consideration of this, the discussion in the present section will be confined to statistical methods based on case-1 assumptions.

As pointed out in the discussion of comparative studies in Chap. 1, it is necessary to assume that the subjects constitute a probability sample from each population. However, there is no requirement that the numbers of subjects in the samples reflect the sizes of the respective populations. Indeed, if all contrasts between populations are of equal interest, the sample numbers should be equal. On the other hand, if one population represents a norm to which the others are compared, the sample numbers should stand in the proportions specified in the footnote on page 307.

It was also pointed out in Chap. 1 that the comparative study is in most instances exploratory rather than confirmatory and is intended to suggest hypotheses rather than to test them. As a consequence, comparative studies are typically inclusive, sometimes overinclusive, with respect to the numbers of response variables and populations being studied. For this reason, it is essential that the statistical methods for these studies provide rules for distinguishing between informative and non-informative variables, for amalgamating redundant variables, and for determining which population contrasts are worth describing and which are not.

In multivariate analysis there are two basic approaches to these tasks. One is an "inclusive" approach, exemplified by the form of canonical analysis described in Sec. 6.2.2; it has the objective of reducing dimensionality through the use of optimal artificial variates. All the original variates are retained, but only a limited number of linear combinations of them (the canonical variates) are interpreted and discussed. The second, "exclusive," approach is represented by the step-down tests in Sec. 6.2.3; it aims at discarding noninformative and redundant variables and limiting the discussion to some subset of the original measures. Some, perhaps many, of the original measures may be excluded at an early stage in the step-down analysis.

Each of these approaches has its advantages and disadvantages. The resort to canonical variates is advantageous when the response variables are measured unreliably. Working with linear combinations of these variables tends to reduce variation due to measurement error and to enhance the effect of latent sources of variation common to two or more variables. In this respect, the role of the canonical variates is similar to that of factor scores (see Harman [1960]), except that canonical variates are so defined as to be maximally sensitive to between-group effects, which are the center of interest in a comparative study. Factor scores are defined with respect to individual-difference variation (which typically is part of the within-group error) and may actually tend to minimize between-group differences.

The disadvantage of the canonical approach is that the original variables, which in many cases are already familiar to other workers, are replaced for purposes of discussion by artificial variates that depend to a considerable extent upon the particular sample and the set of variables in the study at hand. Thus, the true meaning of a canonical variate may not become apparent until the results of a number of independent studies utilizing the same set of variables become available.

The approach based on excluding noninformative and redundant variables avoids this interpretational problem, but it necessarily assumes the actual existence of a few reliable variables which carry most of the information in the data. This assumption will be increasingly justified as an area of research moves out of the exploratory stage and into strong inference based on well-identified variables and precise measurement, but may not be realistic at early stages of investigation.

When there are multiple populations in a comparative study, analogous approaches apply to the between-population contrasts. The axes of the canonical representation may be interpreted as synthetic contrasts with which to search for clustering or structuring of the sample centroids. Again, the definition of these axes has the disadvantage of depending to a considerable extent upon the particular study, and we may prefer the approach of judging all possible contrasts or of examining specified contrasts among populations. Ideally, we would prefer to examine ordered orthogonal contrasts in terms of which powerful single-degree-of-freedom tests of the structure of differences between populations could be carried out. But such a specification may be impossible in an exploratory study, and all pairwise contrasts would have to be examined.

In Sec. 6.3.1 we discuss the inclusive approach based on canonical analysis, and in Sec. 6.3.2 the exclusive approach based on judging all variates and all contrasts.

6.3.1 Canonical Representation

We have seen in connection with multiple-group classification problems (Sec. 6.2.2) how the canonical variates may be used to represent the centroids of n groups in an at most $(n - 1)$-dimensional subspace of the original $p \geq n - 1$ variates. When plotted as in Fig. 6.2-4, the configuration of the group centroids in the space of the first two or three canonical variates may directly suggest an interpretation of differences between the populations.* More often, however, the interpretation is not entirely clear until some substantive meaning is assigned to each of the canonical variates through an interpretation of the coefficients of the corresponding discriminant function (6.2-8). Because the interpretation of these coefficients is not always straightforward, it will be helpful to study a number of artificial examples designed to reveal how the functions achieve maximum separation between groups by maximizing the ratio of between-group variation to within-group variation.

Before turning to these examples, we must take account of the fact that the magnitudes of the raw coefficients defined by (6.2-17) cannot in general be compared with one another while they incorporate the unit of measurement of the original variables. For purposes of interpretation, we must compute the sample standardized coefficients

$$\hat{\mathbf{A}} = \mathbf{D}_\sigma \hat{\mathbf{A}} \qquad (6.3\text{-}1)$$

where $\mathbf{D}_\sigma$ is the diagonal matrix of common within-group standard deviations. It is these standardized discriminant-function coefficients which we shall examine in the artificial data shown in Table 6.3-1. (Actually, all variables in these samples have the same standard deviation, and the raw and standardized coefficients are proportional.)

Example 1 in Table 6.3-1 represents three groups which differ only in respect to the levels of the four variates. Because the direction of the differences is the same

* An example of this in a taxonomic study, where the populations are species of primates and the configuration has an obvious evolutionary interpretation, is seen in Oxnard [1969].

for all variables and the within-group correlations are uniform, the discriminant-function coefficients all have the same sign and are proportional to the between-group variance for each variate, as indicated by the corresponding univariate F statistic. Furthermore, the group means are essentially collinear, and virtually all the canonical variance λ is incorporated in the first function. The second function is essentially an arbitrary orthogonal completion of the first and should not be interpreted. The

Table 6.3-1 HYPOTHETICAL DISCRIMINANT FUNCTIONS

Example 1

		Variates			
	N	I	II	III	IV
Group means					
1	16	95.0	95.0	100.0	100.0
2	16	99.5	99.5	105.0	105.0
3	16	104.5	104.5	110.0	110.0
SD		4	4	4	4
Within-group	I	1.0			
correlation	II	.7	1.0		
	III	.7	.7	1.0	
	IV	.7	.7	.7	1.0
Univariate F		22.6	22.6	25.0	25.0
	λ				
Discriminant	1.372	.209	.209	.358	.358
functions	.003	−.933	−.933	.887	.887
(standardized)					

Example 2

		Variates			
	N	I	II	III	IV
Group means					
1	16	95	95	100	100
2	16	100	100	95	95
3	16	95	100	95	100
SD		4	4	4	4
Within-group	I	1.0			
correlation	II	.7	1.0		
	III	.7	.7	1.0	
	IV	.7	.7	.7	1.0
Univariate F		8.3	8.3	8.3	8.3
	λ				
Discriminant	3.704	.913	.913	−.913	−.913
functions	1.24	.913	−.913	.913	−.913
(standardized)					

interpretation of the first function would be the general construct implied in whatever is common to the four variates when they are measured in a direction which leads to all positive correlations in the within-group (individual-difference) variation.

In Example 2, we see a pattern of between-group differences which is contrary to the common direction of measurement of the variates as indicated by the within-group correlations. That is, the difference reverses direction from one variable to

Table 6.3-1 *continued*

Example 3

		Variates			
	N	I	II	III	IV
Group means					
1	16	95	95	100	100
2	16	100	100	95	95
3	16	95	100	95	100
SD		4	4	4	4
Within-group correlation	I	1.0			
	II	0	1.0		
	III	0	0	1.0	
	IV	0	0	.7	1.0
Univariate *F*		8.3	8.3	8.3	8.3
	λ				
Discriminant functions (standardized)	.882	−.561	−.561	.330	.330
	.803	−.304	.340	−1.132	1.132

Example 4

		Variates			
	N	I	II	III	IV
Group means					
1	16	100	100	100	100
2	16	100	100	95	95
3	16	100	100	95	100
SD		4	4	4	4
Within-group correlation	I	1.0			
	II	.7	1.0		
	III	.7	.7	1.0	
	IV	.7	.7	.7	1.0
Univariate *F*		0	0	8.3	8.3
	λ				
Discriminant functions (standardized)	1.015	.787	.787	−.956	−.956
	.617	0	0	−1.291	1.291

another relative to the given direction of measurement. We say in this case that the group means differ in "profile." The discriminant functions then take the form of contrasts between variables and may be interpreted as "bipolar." Both canonical variates in Example 2 are bipolar and reflect the orthogonal structure of the between-group differences. Because the covariance term subtracts in the computation of the within-group variance, profile differences are especially favorable to discrimination when the variates manifest substantial positive correlations. This is evident in the fact that the canonical variances are much larger in Example 2 than in Example 1, in spite of the larger univariate F's in the latter. In this circumstance, multivariate analysis can be much more powerful than separate univariate analyses.

Example 3 shows the effect of two positively correlated variables appearing in the same discriminant function with uncorrelated variables. Note that, whereas the univariate F's are the same for all variables, the coefficients of the correlated variables are smaller in the first function where these variables are working in the same direction. This is because the variables act in the function essentially as one variable, and the weight is divided between them. When they act in the opposite direction, as in the second function, their coefficients are large because in this role they can reduce the within-group variance, whereas the uncorrelated variables cannot.

Finally, in Example 4, we have an instance of variables (I and II) contributing to a discriminant function in spite of their group means being exactly equal. We say that these are *suppressor* variables; they operate purely by suppressing within-group variation through their positive correlation with the variables which show differences. Their action is, of course, precisely the same as that of covariates in a randomized experiment (see Sec. 5.5). The interpretation of the discriminant function in this case is determined by the variates that show the between-group effect and not by the suppressor variables. Note the first function measures the general level of the group means for variates III and IV, with the suppressor variables entering with the opposite sign as required to reduce the within-group variance when all the variables are positively correlated. The second function picks up the profile difference between groups by means of the contrast of variates III and IV. Because this contrast is uncorrelated with variates I and II, no error suppression is possible, and the latter variates have zero weight in this function.

Guided by these artificial examples, let us attempt to interpret the discriminant functions and the associated canonical representations in the following example.

EXAMPLE 6.3-1 (*Delinquency and dropout in high school, continued*) Using (6.3-1) in standardizing the discriminant-function coefficients in Table 6.2-4, we obtain the values shown in Table 6.3-2. The group means, SD's, and correlations required in the interpretation of these coefficients were given earlier in Table 6.2-3.

As the first step in interpreting Table 6.3-2, we examine the canonical representation in Fig. 6.2-4 and observe that the first function separates the Delinquents *and* Dropouts from the Normals, while the second separates the Delinquents from the Dropouts. The standardized coefficients of the first function show the four psychomotor variables working in the same direction, the three personality-sociometric measures working in the opposite direction, and the cognitive variables, including ISS, entering as suppressor variables. Notice that the ISS scale is scored "backward," and the correlation between socioeconomic level and performance on the cognitive variables is negative. Thus, ISS and CTMM enter the function in converse directions and have the effect of suppressing variation due to level of cognitive functioning (general verbal-scholastic ability). The first canonical variate can therefore be identified with the dimension of impulse control which consistently appears in comparative studies of normal and delinquent children [Ostrov, et al., 1972]. The group means in Table 6.2-3 show the more impulsive delinquents to score poorly on the repetitive, control-demanding psychomotor tasks and to have shorter reaction times. They score higher on the personality and sociometric measures associated with impulsiveness (Surgency and Wild Ones), and differ only slightly from Normals on the insignificant Left Out measure.

In the second discriminant function, the psychomotor measures enter with positive and negative coefficients and act to suppress impulse-control variation. The remaining variables then appear to define a school-participation-and-success dimension. The CTMM measure is heavily represented, Wild Ones and Surgency enter in the same direction as CTMM, and Left Out enters in the converse direction. Drop-

Table 6.3-2 STANDARDIZED DISCRIMINANT-FUNCTION COEFFICIENTS AND DEVIATION CONTRASTS FOR THE DATA IN TABLE 6.2-3

	Discriminant functions		Deviation contrasts*		
Variable	1	2	Del	DO	Norm
1 Dotting	.747	−.553	−.243	−.034	.278
2 Writing X's	.166	−.355	−.336	.190	.146
3 Copying	.447	.202	−.079	−.283	.363
4 DRT	.362	.240	−.025	−.278	.302
5 Surgency	−.210	.312	.284	−.024	−.261
6 Wild Ones	−.371	.593	.437	−.116	−.317
7 Left Out	−.456	−.412	−.077	.205	−.129
8 ISS	−.797	.387	.086	.292	−.379
9 CTMM	−.618	.836	.012	−.325	.312
10 STEP LSN	.102	.212	−.200	−.295	.496
λ	.279	.064			

* As an aid in interpreting the differences between groups, the means from Table 6.2-3 are shown in this table in the form of standardized deviation contrasts. (The contrasts are obtained by subtracting the mean of the means for each variable and dividing by the standard deviation of the corresponding variable.)

outs receive a low score on this dimension because of their poor performance on the cognitive measures, lack of Surgency and Wild Ones relative to Delinquents, and tendency to exceed both Normals and Delinquents in the Left Out nominations. Although ISS might have been expected to enter this function in the same direction as CTMM, it appears that the gain due to suppressing some of the within-group variation in the cognitive dimension and the consequent enhancement of the personality-sociometric effects outweighs the direct contribution of this variable.

Given this interpretation of the canonical variates, we can explain Fig. 6.2-4 as (1) a separation of Delinquents and Dropouts from Normals on the basis of the greater impulse control of the latter, and (2) a separation of the scholastically unsuccessful and noninvolved Dropouts from the more participating and somewhat higher achieving Delinquents. These distinctions are examined further in the continuation of this analysis in Example 6.3-2.

6.3.2 Judging All Variables and All Contrasts

According to the view advanced in Sec. 1.2.4, we should refrain from interpreting the direction of a difference between sample means (or other sample quantity) when we cannot reject in a two-tailed test the hypothesis that the difference is zero. In a multivariate multipopulation comparative study, this view naturally raises the question, "for which variables and population comparisons should the sign of a sample contrast be interpreted?"

In one sense, an answer to this question is given by Roy's [1957] system of confidence bounds described in Secs. 4.2 and 5.2.6. This system, based on the generalized F statistics and including the Scheffé univariate bound as a special case, enables us to identify with confidence equal to or greater than some specified value those variables and comparisons which merit interpretation. As indicated in Sec. 5.2.6, however, these bounds are extremely conservative when the numbers of variables and comparisons are moderate or large. Their use at the conventional 90-percent confidence level will lead the investigator to overlook many differences that should be interpreted and thus defeat the purposes of an exploratory comparative study. More focused methods of judging all variables and contrasts are needed in this context; several rules for this purpose are discussed and evaluated in this section.

a Protected *F* tests *If the generalized F is not significant at the α_0 level, none of the variables or comparisons in the sample will be interpreted. If F_0 is significant at this level, those variables for which univariate F is significant at the α_1 level will be interpreted.**

* A somewhat more conservative procedure, based on the so-called Bonferroni inequality, viz., $1 - P(X \cup Y) \geq 1 - P(X) - P(Y)$, is to set the error rates for the p separate F tests at α/p. This gives reasonably accurate per-comparison error rates if α is small (.01) and p is not too large (say, ≤ 10). (See Miller [1966], Dunn [1961], Perlmutter and Meyers [1973], Petrinovich and Hardyck [1969].)

This rule results in an experimentwise rate of Type I error equal to α_0, and a variablewise Type I error approximately at α_1. Simulation studies [Hummel and Sligo, 1971] have shown that this procedure yields error rates considerably closer to their nominal values than does the Roy procedure.

A disadvantage of the protected F test is that it may fail to detect an interpretable difference which is confined to one or two variables in the midst of many noninformative variables. In some such cases, the Roy bound might be satisfactory, but in general a less conservative procedure is needed. The Roy-Bargmann step-down test (Secs. 3.4.10 and 6.2.3) can serve this purpose. In applications where the investigator has some reason to believe that certain variables are more likely than others to differ between populations, the critical values of the step-down F's can be chosen so that the test of the joint null hypothesis is more sensitive in the former and less sensitive in the latter. The Type I error rate for the overall step-down test is given in (3.4-14) as a function of the Type I error rates of the separate step-down F's. By setting increasingly stringent error rates for variables as we proceed through the step-down ordering, we increase the sensitivity of the test to earlier variables while keeping the error rate of the overall test constant. For example, if there are four variables and we set $\alpha_1 = .02$, $\alpha_2 = .02$, $\alpha_3 = .005$, $\alpha_4 = .005$, then the Type I error rate of the test is

$$\alpha = 1 - (1 - .02)(1 - .02)(1 - .005)(1 - .005) = .0492$$

If we are correct in our belief that the power of the univariate F tests is greater for the earlier variables, this choice of α levels would yield a more powerful multivariate test than assignment of equal levels. In fact, if we knew the Type II error rates as a function of the Type I rates, we could assign the levels to maximize the power of the joint test. Regrettably, these functions depend upon differences between population means, which are unknown in most applications.

b Protected T^2 and t tests *If the generalized F is not significant at the α_0 level, the Hotelling T^2 for multivariate pairwise comparisons of groups will not be interpreted. If F_0 is significant at this level, those comparisons for which T^2 is significant at the α_2 level will be interpreted.*

If F_0 is significant at the α_0 level, while the univariate F for a given variable is significant at the α_1 level and the T^2 for a given comparison is significant at the α_2 level, then the univariate t for that variable and that comparison will be interpreted if significant at the α_3 level.

This procedure gives an experimentwise Type I error rate of α_0, and approximate per-variable rate of α_1, a per-comparison rate of α_2, and an approximate per-variable per-comparison rate of α_3.*

* Again, the Bonferroni inequality might be employed here if the number of variates and comparisons is not too large.

If the computation of the T^2 for each contrast and t for each variable are obtained as a by-product of a one-degree-of-freedom test in a multivariate analysis of variance, it is *mandatory* that the contrast in question be last in the order of elimination of between-group effects. Thus, if the sample sizes are unequal, there must be as many reorderings of the basis vectors for the between-group effects as there are contrasts. On the other hand, if the T^2 is computed directly from the estimated vector contrast and its error variance-covariance matrix, as t is computed from each estimated univariate contrast and its standard error, the order in which the basis vectors appear in the linear model is irrelevant. The direct method is, of course, much more economical computationally.

The interpretation of all contrasts and all variables is simpler than the interpretation of the canonical analysis because relationships between variables are ignored. For the same reason, it is also less informative. A clear idea of the distinctions between the two types of interpretation of a multivariate multigroup comparison may be gained by comparing the following example with Example 6.3-1.

EXAMPLE 6.3-2 (*Delinquency and dropout in high school, continued*) Table 6.3-3 gives the T^2 and t statistics for the contrasts Delinquent-Normal (DEL-NORM), Dropout-Normal (DO-NORM), and Delinquent-Dropout (DEL-DO), We have already seen in Table 6.2-4 that the generalized F for these data is significant ($p < .01$). The T^2 for each of the pairwise contrasts is also significant, thus justifying the interpretation of the t statistics for the separate variables.

All the variables show significant differences between Delinquents and Normals, with the exception of Left Out. The same is true of differences between Dropouts and Normals, with the exceptions being Writing X's, Wild Ones, and Surgency. The Dropouts are especially deviant from the Normals in the cognitive-related variables ISS, CTMM, and STEP LSN.

Dropouts and Delinquents are much less differentiated, with only Writing X's and Wild Ones significant at the .05 level. Thus, we might view Dropouts and Delin-

Table 6.3-3 T^2 AND t STATISTICS FOR PAIRWISE CONTRASTS OF DELINQUENTS, DROPOUTS AND NORMALS (df = 399, $t_{.05}$ = 1.96, $t_{.01}$ = 2.57)

			Variables									
Contrast	T^{2*}	p	*1*	*2*	*3*	*4*	*5*	*6*	*7*	*8*	*9*	*10*
Del-Norm	.177	.0001	−2.74	−2.53	−2.32	−1.72	2.87	3.95	.27	2.44	−1.58	−3.66
DO-Norm	.189	.0001	−2.06	.28	−4.26	−3.81	1.56	1.32	2.20	4.43	−4.20	−5.21
Del-DO	.066	.005	.90	2.28	.90	1.10	1.34	2.38	−1.23	−.89	1.46	.41

* The corresponding F statistics are 6.89, 7.37, and 2.58 on 10/390 df.

Table 6.3-4 MEAN PMA STANDARD SCORES AND AGE OF MALE AND FEMALE DIZYGOTIC AND MONOZYGOTIC COTWINS; WITHIN-GROUP CORRELATIONS AND STANDARD DEVIATIONS

			Variable					
			1	*2*	*3*	*4*	*5*	*6*
Sex	Zygosity	*N*	Number	Verbal meaning	Space	Word fluency	Reasoning	Age
Male	Di	34	.0867	.0114	.3405	−.2537	−.3058	15.85
	Mono	38	−.1467	.0382	.4706	−.0464	−.2031	15.58
Female	Di	53	−.0556	−.0073	−.2184	.1628	.1962	15.74
	Mono	47	−.0428	−.2313	−.2595	.2278	.0342	15.55
SD			.9340	.9578	.8889	.8577	.8808	1.5763
Correlations								
Variable		*1*	1.0000					
		2	.5283	1.0000				
		3	.2846	.3130	1.0000			
		4	.4492	.6309	.3470	1.0000		
		5	.5630	.6793	.5063	.5913	1.0000	
		6	.3047	.2334	.1226	.1996	.2258	1.0000

quents as having much the same characteristics of impulsiveness and poor achievement, but with Dropouts being less obvious social misfits as indicated by nominations as Wild Ones.

Exercise 6.3-1 (*Twin data*) Table 6.3-4 gives means and within-group correlations and standard deviations of scores on the Primary Mental Abilities Tests [Thurstone and Thurstone, 1947] for male and female monozygotic and dizygotic twin pairs. Age is also included. Each score in the analysis is the mean of the scores of cotwins. Examine the data for effects of sex, zygosity, and their interaction. Is there any evidence in these data to support the conclusion that identical twins are disadvantaged relative to fraternal twins?

Repeat the analysis using age as a covariate.

6.4 SURVEYS

In this section we use the term *survey* to mean specifically a study of characteristics of a single population based on a probability sample in which each unit of the population has an equal chance of appearing.* The unit may be a community, institution, respondent, subject, etc., and the population may be finite or effectively infinite in size. In most applications, the population has a structure, consisting of crossed

* We use the term "probability sample" in this restricted sense in this section.

and/or nested classes, which the survey is intended to characterize in greater or lesser detail. The use of the probability sample ensures that the subclasses at every level will be self-weighting; i.e., that the expected number of sample units in each subclass will be proportional to the relative size of the subclass in the population. This is in sharp distinction to experiments and comparative studies, in which the subclass numbers are arbitrarily fixed by the investigator.

Many survey studies are based on an enumeration of purely qualitative characteristics of the units and thus give rise to qualitative data such as discussed in Chap. 8. Census surveys, consumer-preference studies, public-opinion polling, epidemiological studies, etc., are often of this type. More behaviorally oriented surveys, on the other hand, tend to employ multiple-item rating scales measuring one or more continuous latent traits. This type of survey yields data that, for purposes of analysis, must be considered metric rather than qualitative. The same is true of surveys of educational attainment based on achievement-test scores.

This section of the text is devoted exclusively to surveys that yield metric data. (Qualitative survey data are covered in Chap. 8.) It is assumed in general that the data are multivariate, and that the population distribution can be characterized by its vector mean and covariance matrix. Multivariate normality is, however, not strictly assumed until Sec. 6.4.3d.

From a statistical point of view, a survey of such a population is an exercise in the estimation of the mean and covariance matrix of the population or each of the subpopulations. The vector means of subpopulations characterize effects associated with fixed ways of classification of the units while the covariance matrices characterize variation associated with random ways of classification (in which the classes represent sampled units rather than specified attributes). Thus, for example, a study of achievement in newly integrated schools would examine not only the fixed effects of age, race, sex, and their interactions, but also the sources of variation due to classrooms within school and grade, schools within districts, districts within counties, counties within states, and possibly also the fixed effects of states and national regions (see Example 6.4-1).

Survey studies of fixed effects pose no problems for data analysis beyond those already considered in connection with experiments and comparative studies. Surveys do, however, offer a logical basis for interpretation that is not available in the other types of study. This logic depends upon the self-weighting feature and the fact that marginal samples (when one or more ways of classification are ignored) always represent well-defined populations. As a consequence, the stricture against interpreting main effects in the presence of interaction does not apply in survey studies. Any statement about a main effect between any of the marginal populations is descriptively meaningful independently of effects summed over when the other ways of classification are ignored. From some points of view, these "on-average" statements about marginal distributions may seem oversimplifications, but in practical work they may be necessary and even desirable. The well-known sex × race × age interaction in school achievement [Baughman and Dahlstrom, 1968] does not preclude the practical interpretation of sex differences ignoring race, of race differences ignoring sex, or of age differences ignoring race and sex. Most primary and secondary schools, for example, are equipped to adapt their programs to differences in age, but not to sex and race. Average levels of achievement of children of both sexes and races at a given age are therefore important indices for administrative decisions and are, in fact, routinely assessed.

Because the existence of a random way of classification implies a population, it implies also that interactions between a random and fixed way of classification may be ignored when estimating and interpreting the fixed effects. As we shall see in Chap. 7, where the so-called *mixed model* is discussed, such interactions are random components tending to inflate the error of estimating the fixed effects, but not introducing any bias into the estimator. Quite the contrary is true of the pure fixed-effects model for experiments and comparative studies, where in general the interactions bias any estimator of the main-class effects. The unconditional estimability of main and subclass effects in survey studies offers many opportunities for the investigator to discuss the data as broadly or narrowly as suits his purposes.

A typical feature of surveys is the *nested* (or *hierarchical*) sampling design. The levels of nesting are called *strata*. In sociological surveys, for example, the strata usually correspond to successively more inclusive political or geographic units. Because nested classes are always random, a purely nested design requires a so-called "random" or "model II" analysis of variance (see Searle [1971] for a discussion of the univariate model II analysis). The purpose of the model II analysis is to estimate variances (called *variance components*) of the random variation due to each stratum of the nested design. In the remainder of this section, we shall discuss the model II analysis assuming, of course, that the data are multivariate and that component variance-covariance matrices will be estimated in place of the variance components of univariate model II analysis.

6.4.1 Nested Sampling Designs

Abstractly, these designs may be described in Nelder's [1965] notation for the block structure of randomized experiments. The nesting of classes of the B stratum within those of the A stratum is represented by

$$A \rightarrow B$$

This formula describes a two-stage nesting such as

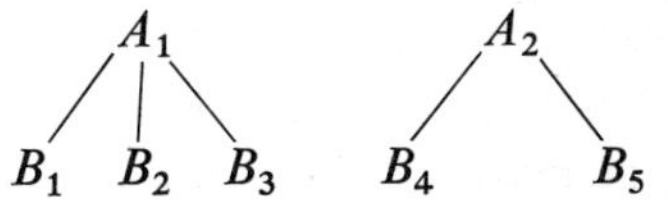

(6.4-1)

If the identification of the strata is understood to be in the left-to-right order, the design may be completely specified by inserting lists in the formula which give the number of classes contained in each superordinate class. Thus,

$$a \rightarrow (b_1, b_2, \ldots, b_a)$$

states that stratum A comprises a classes, of which A_1 contains b_1 classes of B, A_2 contains b_2 classes of B, and so on to A_a, which contains b_a classes of B. Expressed in this way, the design formula for (6.4-1) is

$$2 \rightarrow (3,2)$$

The nesting operation may be repeated (for example, $A \rightarrow B \rightarrow C$) to any depth of nesting. Thus,

$$2 \rightarrow (3,2) \rightarrow (2,1,2,2,2) \qquad (6.4\text{-}2)$$

specifies the design

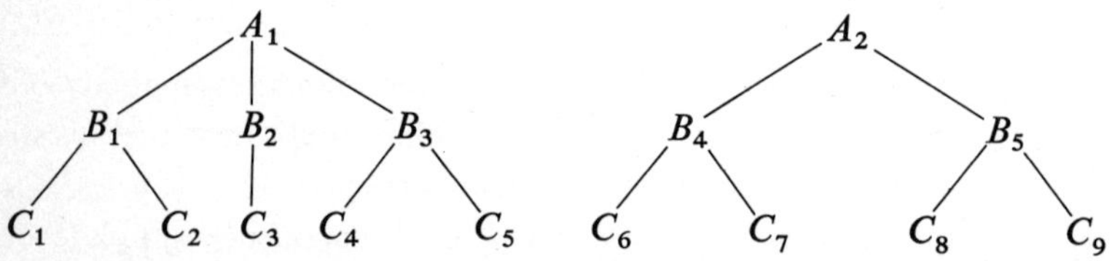

Notice also that the crossing operator ($\times$) defined in Sec. 5.3.3 can operate on nested classes to describe a crossed-and-nested design, although parentheses may be necessary to indicate the order in which the operations are carried out. Thus,

$$(A \rightarrow B) \times C$$

describes a cross-classification by C of the units in each of the nested subclasses of B (split-plot design; see Sec. 7.2). Conversely,

$$A \times (B \rightarrow C)$$

describes a one-way design in which the replicates have the same nested structure in each A class. By repeated applications of the crossing and nesting operations, designs of any complexity can be described. For example,

$$(A \rightarrow B) \times C \times D \qquad (6.4\text{-}3)$$

describes a twofold cross-classification of the B classes which are nested in A (see page 453). In a survey application, (6.4-3) might describe children classified by sex (C) and SES (D) within schools (B) within school districts (A).

Like the crossed designs of Chap. 5, nested designs may be *balanced* or *unbalanced*. A balanced nested design has equal numbers of subclasses in each superordinate class. The formula for a balanced design,

$$A \rightarrow B$$

may therefore be abbreviated as

$$a \rightarrow b$$

indicating that each of the a classes of the A stratum contains b classes of the B stratum. Both the statistical theory (see Sec. 6.4.3a) and the computational algorithms for balanced nested designs are simpler than for the unbalanced designs. There is, in fact, some conceptual advantage to regarding an unbalanced design as a balanced design with missing observations. For example, (6.4.2) could be described as

$$2 \rightarrow 3 \rightarrow 2$$

in which all subclasses of B_6 and one subclass of B_2 are missing. We use this device in a method for constructing model and basis matrices for unbalanced nested designs, which we now describe.

6.4.2 Construction of Models for Nested Designs

Without committing ourselves at this point on the fixed or random status of each term, we may write the model for a p-variate observation in a balanced g-strata nested design, specified by

$$n_1 \rightarrow n_2 \rightarrow \cdots \rightarrow n_g \tag{6.4-4}$$

as

$$\mathbf{y}_{j_1 j_2 \cdots j_g} = \boldsymbol{\zeta}_0 + \boldsymbol{\zeta}_{j_1} + \boldsymbol{\zeta}_{j_1 j_2} + \cdots + \boldsymbol{\zeta}_{j_1 j_2 \cdots j_g} \tag{6.4-5}$$

with $j_k = 1, 2, \ldots, n_k$ and $k = 1, 2, \ldots, g$. The total number of observations is $n = n_1 n_2 \cdots n_g$; the model includes one term $\boldsymbol{\zeta}_0$ for the constant, or general mean, n_1 terms $\boldsymbol{\zeta}_{j_1}$ due to stratum-1 variation, $n_1 n_2$ terms $\boldsymbol{\zeta}_{j_1 j_2}$ due to stratum-2 variation, and so on up to n terms $\boldsymbol{\zeta}_{j_1 j_2 \cdots j_g}$ due to stratum-g variation. Representing the observations by rows of an $n \times p$ observational matrix, we may express (6.4-5) as

$$\underset{n \times p}{\mathbf{Y}} = \mathbf{BZ} = \mathbf{B}_0\mathbf{Z}_0 + \mathbf{B}_1\mathbf{Z}_1 + \mathbf{B}_2\mathbf{Z}_2 + \cdots + \mathbf{B}_g\mathbf{Z}_g \tag{6.4-6}$$

Again making use of Kronecker products of matrices (see Sec. 5.3.3), we may represent the submatrices of $\mathbf{B}$ in vectors of n_k unities $\mathbf{1}_{n_k}$ and n_k identity matrices $\mathbf{I}_{n_k}$; thus,

$$\begin{aligned}
\underset{n \times 1}{\mathbf{B}_0} &= \mathbf{1}_{n_1} \times \mathbf{1}_{n_2} \times \cdots \times \mathbf{1}_{n_g} \\
\underset{n \times n_1}{\mathbf{B}_1} &= \mathbf{I}_{n_1} \times \mathbf{1}_{n_2} \times \cdots \times \mathbf{1}_{n_g} \\
\underset{n \times n_1 n_2}{\mathbf{B}_2} &= \mathbf{I}_{n_1} \times \mathbf{I}_{n_2} \times \mathbf{1}_{n_3} \times \cdots \times \mathbf{1}_{n_g} \\
&\cdots\cdots\cdots\cdots\cdots\cdots \\
\underset{n \times n_1 n_2 \cdots n_g}{\mathbf{B}_g} &= \mathbf{I}_{n_1} \times \mathbf{I}_{n_2} \times \cdots \times \mathbf{I}_{n_g}
\end{aligned} \tag{6.4-7}$$

For example, the model for the design

$$2 \rightarrow 2 \rightarrow 2$$

is

$$\underset{8 \times p}{\mathbf{Y}} = [\mathbf{1}_2 \times \mathbf{1}_2 \times \mathbf{1}_2, \quad \mathbf{I}_2 \times \mathbf{1}_2 \times \mathbf{1}_2, \quad \mathbf{I}_2 \times \mathbf{I}_2 \times \mathbf{1}_2, \quad \mathbf{I}_2 \times \mathbf{I}_2 \times \mathbf{I}_2]\mathbf{Z}$$

or, *in extenso*,

$$
\begin{bmatrix} \mathbf{y}'_{111} \\ \mathbf{y}'_{112} \\ \mathbf{y}'_{121} \\ \mathbf{y}'_{122} \\ \mathbf{y}'_{211} \\ \mathbf{y}'_{212} \\ \mathbf{y}'_{221} \\ \mathbf{y}'_{222} \end{bmatrix}
=
\begin{bmatrix}
1 & 1 & 0 & 1 & 0 & 0 & 0 & 1 & 0 & 0 & 0 & 0 & 0 & 0 & 0 \\
1 & 1 & 0 & 1 & 0 & 0 & 0 & 0 & 1 & 0 & 0 & 0 & 0 & 0 & 0 \\
1 & 1 & 0 & 0 & 1 & 0 & 0 & 0 & 0 & 1 & 0 & 0 & 0 & 0 & 0 \\
1 & 1 & 0 & 0 & 1 & 0 & 0 & 0 & 0 & 0 & 1 & 0 & 0 & 0 & 0 \\
1 & 0 & 1 & 0 & 0 & 1 & 0 & 0 & 0 & 0 & 0 & 1 & 0 & 0 & 0 \\
1 & 0 & 1 & 0 & 0 & 1 & 0 & 0 & 0 & 0 & 0 & 0 & 1 & 0 & 0 \\
1 & 0 & 1 & 0 & 0 & 0 & 1 & 0 & 0 & 0 & 0 & 0 & 0 & 1 & 0 \\
1 & 0 & 1 & 0 & 0 & 0 & 1 & 0 & 0 & 0 & 0 & 0 & 0 & 0 & 1
\end{bmatrix}
\begin{bmatrix} \zeta'_0 \\ \zeta'_1 \\ \zeta'_2 \\ \zeta'_{11} \\ \zeta'_{12} \\ \zeta'_{21} \\ \zeta'_{22} \\ \zeta'_{111} \\ \zeta'_{112} \\ \cdots \\ \zeta'_{222} \end{bmatrix}
$$

Because the model (6.4-5) is not of full rank, we shall need the following theorem for nested designs, comparable to that for crossed designs (Sec. 5.3.2), which specifies a column basis for **B**.

Let (6.4-7) be the submatrices of the model matrix **B** of the balanced nested design (6.4-4). Then a basis for **B** is the $n \times n$ matrix

$$\mathbf{K} = [\mathbf{K}_0, \mathbf{K}_1, \mathbf{K}_2, \ldots, \mathbf{K}_g] \tag{6.4-8}$$

in which

$$
\begin{aligned}
\underset{n\times 1}{\mathbf{K}_0} &= \mathbf{1}_{n_1} \times \mathbf{1}_{n_2} \times \cdots \times \mathbf{1}_{n_g} \\
\underset{n\times(n_1-1)}{\mathbf{K}_1} &= \mathbf{C}_{n_1} \times \mathbf{1}_{n_2} \times \cdots \times \mathbf{1}_{n_g} \\
\underset{n\times n_1(n_2-1)}{\mathbf{K}_2} &= \mathbf{I}_{n_1} \times \mathbf{C}_{n_2} \times \mathbf{1}_{n_3} \times \cdots \times \mathbf{1}_{n_g} \qquad (6.4\text{-}9) \\
&\cdots\cdots\cdots\cdots\cdots\cdots\cdots\cdots\cdots \\
\underset{n\times n_1 n_2\cdots n_{g-1}(n_g-1)}{\mathbf{K}_g} &= \mathbf{I}_{n_1} \times \mathbf{I}_{n_2} \times \cdots \times \mathbf{I}_{n_{g-1}} \times \mathbf{C}_{n_g}
\end{aligned}
$$

where $\mathbf{C}_{n_k}$ is an $n_k \times (n_k - 1)$ contrast matrix such that $\mathbf{C}_{n_k}\mathbf{1}_{n_k} = \mathbf{0}$ and $\mathbf{C}'_{n_k}\mathbf{C}_{n_k} = \mathbf{I}$.

To prove this theorem, we define the two mutually orthogonal matrices

$$\mathbf{Q}_{n_h}\mathbf{S}_{n_k} = [\mathbf{1}_{n_k}, \mathbf{C}_{n_k}]\begin{bmatrix} \dfrac{1}{n_k}\mathbf{1}_{n_k}, \mathbf{C}_{n_k} \end{bmatrix} = \mathbf{I}_{n_k}$$

Then, $\mathbf{Q}_1 = \mathbf{S}_1 = 1$, and, using (4.2-10), we may reparameterize successive terms in (6.4-6) as follows:

$$\mathbf{B}_0\mathbf{Z}_0 = [\mathbf{1}_{n_1} \times \mathbf{1}_{n_2} \times \cdots \times \mathbf{1}_{n_g}]\mathbf{Q}_1\mathbf{S}_1\mathbf{Z}_0 = \mathbf{K}_0\boldsymbol{\Omega}_{00}$$

$$
\begin{aligned}
\mathbf{B}_1\mathbf{Z}_1 &= [\mathbf{I}_{n_1} \times \mathbf{1}_{n_2} \times \cdots \times \mathbf{1}_{n_g}]\mathbf{Q}_{n_1}\mathbf{S}_{n_1}\mathbf{Z}_1 \\
&= [\mathbf{Q}_{n_1} \times \mathbf{1}_{n_2} \times \cdots \times \mathbf{1}_{n_g}]\mathbf{S}_{n_1}\mathbf{Z}_1 \\
&= [\mathbf{1}_{n_1} \times \mathbf{1}_{n_2} \times \cdots \times \mathbf{1}_{n_g}, \mathbf{C}_{n_1} \times \mathbf{1}_{n_2} \times \cdots \times \mathbf{1}_{n_g}] \\
&\qquad \cdot \begin{bmatrix} \dfrac{1}{n_1}\mathbf{Z}_1\mathbf{1}_{n_1}, \mathbf{Z}_1\mathbf{C}_{n_1} \end{bmatrix}' \\
&= [\mathbf{B}_0, \mathbf{K}_1][\boldsymbol{\Omega}_{01}, \boldsymbol{\Omega}_{11}]'
\end{aligned}
$$

$$\begin{aligned}
\mathbf{B}_2\mathbf{Z}_2 &= [\mathbf{I}_{n_1} \times \mathbf{I}_{n_2} \times \mathbf{1}_{n_3} \times \cdots \times \mathbf{1}_{n_g}][\mathbf{I}_{n_1} \times \mathbf{Q}_{n_2}\mathbf{S}_{n_2}]\mathbf{Z}_2 \\
&= [\mathbf{I}_{n_1} \times \mathbf{Q}_{n_2} \times \mathbf{1}_{n_3} \times \cdots \times \mathbf{1}_{n_g}][\mathbf{I}_{n_1} \times \mathbf{S}_{n_2}]\mathbf{Z}_2 \\
&= [\mathbf{I}_{n_1} \times \mathbf{1}_{n_2} \times \cdots \times \mathbf{1}_{n_g}, \mathbf{I}_{n_1} \times \mathbf{C}_{n_2} \times \mathbf{1}_{n_3} \times \cdots \times \mathbf{1}_{n_g}] \\
&\qquad \cdot \left[\frac{1}{n_2}\mathbf{Z}_2(\mathbf{I}_{n_1} \times \mathbf{1}_{n_2}), \mathbf{Z}_2(\mathbf{I}_{n_1} \times \mathbf{C}_{n_2})\right]' \\
&= [\mathbf{B}_1, \mathbf{K}_2][\boldsymbol{\Omega}_{02}, \boldsymbol{\Omega}_{12}]'
\end{aligned}$$

and so on down to

$$\begin{aligned}
\mathbf{B}_g\mathbf{Z}_g &= [\mathbf{I}_{n_1} \times \mathbf{I}_{n_2} \times \cdots \times \mathbf{I}_{n_g}][\mathbf{I}_{n_1} \times \mathbf{I}_{n_2} \times \cdots \times \mathbf{Q}_{n_g}\mathbf{S}_{n_g}]\mathbf{Z}_g \\
&= [\mathbf{I}_{n_1} \times \mathbf{I}_{n_2} \times \cdots \times \mathbf{Q}_{n_g}][\mathbf{I}_{n_1} \times \mathbf{I}_{n_2} \times \cdots \times \mathbf{S}_{n_g}]\mathbf{Z}_g \\
&= [\mathbf{I}_{n_1} \times \mathbf{I}_{n_2} \times \cdots \times \mathbf{1}_{n_g}, \mathbf{I}_{n_1} \times \mathbf{I}_{n_2} \times \cdots \times \mathbf{C}_{n_g}] \\
&\quad \cdot \left[\frac{1}{n_g}\mathbf{Z}_g(\mathbf{I}_{n_1} \times \mathbf{I}_{n_2} \times \cdots \times \mathbf{1}_{n_g}), \mathbf{Z}_g(\mathbf{I}_{n_1} \times \mathbf{I}_{n_2} \times \cdots \times \mathbf{C}_{n_g})\right]' \\
&= [\mathbf{B}_{n_{g-1}}, \mathbf{K}_g][\boldsymbol{\Omega}_{0g}, \boldsymbol{\Omega}_{1g}]'
\end{aligned}$$

But

$$\begin{aligned}
\mathbf{B}_0'\mathbf{K}_1 &= \mathbf{0}' \\
\mathbf{B}_1'\mathbf{K}_2 &= \mathbf{O} \\
&\cdots\cdots\cdots \\
\mathbf{B}_{g-1}'\mathbf{K}_g &= \mathbf{O}
\end{aligned}$$

Thus, $\mathbf{K}_0 = \mathbf{B}_0$, and the columns of $\mathbf{K}_1$ form a basis of $\mathbf{B}_1$ orthogonal to $\mathbf{K}_0$; similarly, the columns of $\mathbf{K}_2$ from a basis of $\mathbf{B}_2$ orthogonal to $\mathbf{B}_1$, and so on to $\mathbf{K}_g$, the columns of which form a basis of $\mathbf{B}_g$ orthogonal to $\mathbf{B}_{g-1}$. $\mathbf{K}$ is therefore a full-rank orthonormal basis of $\mathbf{B}$, and the contrasts $\boldsymbol{\Omega}_{1k}$ are estimable linear functions of the parameters in (6.4-6). The parametric function $\boldsymbol{\Omega}_{0k}$ (which is the mean for the kth stratum) is, however, nonestimable and is by convention set to zero.

Vectors of this basis may be described symbolically in a notation similar to that employed for crossed designs in Sec. 5.3.3. Let $I(i_k)$, $i_k = 1, 2, \ldots, n_k$, represent the ith column of $\mathbf{I}_{n_k}$; let $C(h_k)$, $h_k = 1, 2, \ldots, n_k - 1$, represent the hth column of $\mathbf{C}_{n_k}$; and let 0 represent the vector $\mathbf{1}_{n_k}$. Then, the ordered g-tuples

$$\begin{aligned}
&0, 0, \ldots, 0 \\
&C(h_1), 0, \ldots, 0 \\
&I(i_1), C(h_2), 0, \ldots, 0 \qquad\qquad (6.4\text{-}10) \\
&\cdots\cdots\cdots\cdots\cdots\cdots \\
&I(i_1), I(i_2), \ldots, I(i_{g-1}), C(h_g)
\end{aligned}$$

specify the g-fold Kronecker products that constitute each of the n columns of $\mathbf{K}$.

This symbolism explicitly identifies orthogonal subspaces of the basis for purposes of the analysis of variance in the balanced case as discussed in Sec. 6.4.3. Notice that if the design is balanced down to the next-to-last stratum, the observations in the last stratum may be treated as unequal numbers of replicates within subclasses. The analysis of variance then requires that **K** be orthogonalized in the metric of subclass numbers **D**. Indeed, if provision is made for the loss of degrees of freedom owing to vacant subclasses, this method of analysis can be applied to any unbalanced nested design beginning from the smallest balanced design that includes the actual design. This approach to the analysis of general nested designs is also discussed in Sec. 6.4.3.

The symbolism (6.4-10) is in fact sufficiently general to describe the bases of crossed-and-nested designs. Consider, for example, the design discussed by Millman and Glass [1967], which combines features of an educational survey and an educational experiment:

Type of school	Classes within type of school	Treatments 1	2	...	c
1	1 2 ... b				
2	1 2 ... b				
...	...	...	...	...	...
a	1 2 ... b				

The design formula is

$$(a \rightarrow b) \times c$$

and the subspaces of the basis are

Subspace	df	Description
$0, 0, 0$	1	General mean
$C(h_a), 0, 0$	$a - 1$	Between types of school
$I(i_a), C(h_b), 0$	$a(b - 1)$	Between classes within types
$0, 0, C(h_c)$	$c - 1$	Between treatments
$C(h_a), 0, C(h_c)$	$(a - 1)(c - 1)$	Types × treatment interaction
$I(i_a), C(h_b), C(h_c)$	$a(b - 1)(c - 1)$	Class × treatment interaction within types
	abc	

There may also be, say, r replications within classes, in which case there exists a space of within-group variation, on $abc(r - 1)$ degrees of freedom, orthogonal to the above between-group space.

6.4.3 Estimation of Variance and Covariance Components

A way of classification in the survey design is called *random* if the classes are units of a sample rather than fixed treatments or attributes. The population from which the classes are sampled may be finite or infinite; if finite and sampling is without replacement, correction for finite population size must be incorporated in the analysis as shown below.

A characteristic of a random way of classification is that the interpretation of the analysis is unaltered by random permutation of the class labels. This means that the classes have no fixed identity and are of interest only as nameless representatives of the population. There is then no purpose in estimating effects of specific classes, but only in assessing the contribution of the way of classification to random variation in the data. Methods for the latter purpose are discussed in this section.

a Balanced nested designs The fact that a nested way of classification is always random implies that all terms in (6.4-5) except the general mean and possibly ζ_{j_1} are random components. For present purposes, let us assume that ζ_{j_1} is also random. Then, since the means of the components are not estimable, let us assume that the components $\zeta_{j_1}, \zeta_{j_1 j_2}, \ldots, \zeta_{j_1 j_2 \cdots j_g}$ are distributed with zero vector means and variance-covariance matrices $\Sigma_1, \Sigma_2, \ldots, \Sigma_g$. Except where tests of hypothesis or confidence intervals are involved, we need not assume that these components are normally distributed.

If the nested design is balanced, best* estimators of the variance-covariance components may be obtained from the partition of sums of squares and products in the multivariate analysis-of-variance table for the design. The form of the table can be deduced from the design formula. Suppose, for example, that the design consists of b classes B nested within a classes A, with c replicates within each B class. Then the design formula is

$$a \rightarrow b \rightarrow c$$

and the analysis of variance has three lines, plus one for the general mean as shown in Table 6.4-1. We assume in Table 6.4-1 that a, b, and c classes have been sampled without replacement from populations of sizes $\mathscr{A}$, $\mathscr{B}$, and $\mathscr{C}$ in strata A, B, and C, respectively. This assumption introduces finite population corrections such as $(\mathscr{C} - c)/\mathscr{C}$ into the expected mean products. Note that these corrections become 1 when the corresponding population is infinite, and zero when the sample includes all population classes (in which case there is no sampling variation from that source). (See also Sec. 6.4.3e.)

The variance-covariance components Σ_a, Σ_b, and Σ_c are estimated by solving the

* Unbiased minimum-variance quadratic estimators (see Graybill [1961]). They are also maximum-likelihood estimators in the balanced case.

equations of expectation of the mean products MSA = SSA/$(a - 1)$, MSB = SSB/$a(b - 1)$, and MSC = SSC/$ab(c - 1)$. Thus,

$$\hat{\Sigma}_c = \text{MSC}$$

$$\hat{\Sigma}_b = \frac{\text{MSB} - [(\mathscr{C} - c)/\mathscr{C}]\,\text{MSC}}{c}$$

and

$$\hat{\Sigma}_a = \frac{\text{MSA} - [(\mathscr{B} - b)/\mathscr{B}]\text{MSB} - [(\mathscr{C} - c)/\mathscr{C}](b/\mathscr{B})\text{MSC}}{cb}$$

A shortcoming of these estimates is that they are not restricted to be at least positive semidefinite (i.e., all characteristic roots nonnegative), and hence may not represent the covariance matrices of real variables. We show in Sec. 6.4.3f, however, how to subject the estimation of the components to the restriction of positive semidefiniteness.

In principle, the hypotheses $\mathbf{\Sigma}_a = \mathbf{O}$ and $\mathbf{\Sigma}_b = \mathbf{O}$ may be tested by means of the partition of sums of products in Table 6.4-1, the error term in each case being obtained from the sum of products of the lower strata (see Wilk and Kempthorne [1955]). Any of the multivariate test criteria of Sec. 3.4.10 may be used for this purpose. Such tests are rarely employed, however, because the sampling of classes is assumed always to introduce some variation into the data. The interest in these analyses is comparing the relative importances of the variation, both between sources and between variables. The following example illustrates this use of components-of-variance analysis.

EXAMPLE 6.4-1 (*Sources of variation in school achievement*) Wiley and Bock [1967] report a components-of-variance analysis of data obtained by Anthony [1967] in a study of factors of achievement among fifth-grade children. The data consist

Table 6.4-1 THE p-VARIATE ANALYSIS OF VARIANCE FOR AN ALL-RANDOM NESTED DESIGN

Source	df	SSP ($p \times p$)	$\mathscr{E}$(SSP/df)
Mean	1	SSM = $n\mathbf{y}_{\cdot\cdot\cdot}\mathbf{y}'_{\cdot\cdot\cdot}$	
A	$a - 1$	SSA = $bc \sum_{i=1}^{a} \mathbf{y}_{i\cdot\cdot}\mathbf{y}'_{i\cdot\cdot}$ − SSM	$\left(\frac{\mathscr{C} - c}{\mathscr{C}}\right)\mathbf{\Sigma}_c + c\left(\frac{\mathscr{B} - b}{\mathscr{B}}\right)\mathbf{\Sigma}_b + cb\mathbf{\Sigma}_a$
B in A	$a(b - 1)$	SSB = $c \sum_{i=1}^{a}\sum_{j=1}^{b} \mathbf{y}_{ij\cdot}\mathbf{y}'_{ij\cdot}$ − SSA	$\left(\frac{\mathscr{C} - c}{\mathscr{C}}\right)\mathbf{\Sigma}_c + c\mathbf{\Sigma}_b$
C in B	$ab(c - 1)$	SSC = SST − SSB	$\mathbf{\Sigma}_c$
Total	$n = abc$	SST = $\sum_{i=1}^{a}\sum_{j=1}^{b}\sum_{k=1}^{c} \mathbf{y}_{ijk}\mathbf{y}'_{ijk}$	

of scores on nine tests of the Stanford Intermediate Achievement Test, Form W, from nine schools in an Illinois community (population 50,000). Each school was represented by two classrooms, each with a different teacher. The classrooms were not tracked and will be regarded for present purposes as random samples of fifth-grade pupils within schools.

To save space, we omit the covariance components between tests and discuss here only the variance components. The data constitute a nested design of classrooms within schools and pupils within classrooms. The data may be analyzed in the manner of Table 6.4-1 by randomly deleting subjects to obtain a balanced design, or as an unbalanced design by the method of Sec. 6.4.3c. In either case, the results will approximate those of Table 6.4-2 (which actually were obtained in an unbalanced analysis).

Because the tests were scored in grade equivalents, the estimated variance components in Table 6.4-2 are squared grade equivalents. It is clear that the most important source of variation is due to individual differences (between pupils) within classrooms. The between-classroom and between-school sources are significant, however, and the comparison of the contributions of these sources to scores on the various tests is instructive. To facilitate these comparisons, the components are expressed as a percent of their total in the right-hand section of the table.

All schools in the study were using the same textbooks and were ostensibly following the same plan of study. This homogeneity of content and method is apparent in the relatively small between-school component of tests such as *Arithmetic Computation* and *Arithmetic Concepts*. Because the item content of these tests is tied closely to the material presented in the classroom, the percent of between-classroom variance is large, reflecting the differing thoroughness and quality of instruction in

Table 6.4-2 ESTIMATED VARIANCE COMPONENTS FOR STANFORD-ACHIEVEMENT-TEST SCORES

	Variance components (grade equivalents)^2			Variance components (percent)		
Test	Between schools	Between classrooms	Between pupils	Between schools	Between classrooms	Between pupils
1 Word Meaning	.160	.046	1.573	9.0	2.5	88.5
2 Paragraph Meaning	.243	.069	2.243	9.4	2.5	88.1
3 Spelling	.129	.032	2.592	4.7	1.2	94.1
4 Language	.159	.258	2.928	4.8	7.7	87.5
5 Arithmetic						
Computation	.023	.108	0.848	2.3	11.0	86.7
6 Arithmetic Concepts						
7 Arithmetic	.061	.081	1.227	4.5	6.0	89.5
Applications	.094	.111	2.622	3.3	3.9	92.8
8 Social Studies	.133	.151	1.814	6.3	7.2	86.5
9 Science	.371	.033	3.172	10.4	.9	88.7

different classrooms. The same is true of *Language*, which in these tests is mechanics of punctuation and grammar. It is less true of the *Arithmetic Applications*, which are more affected by the pupil's experience with money, weights and measures, time and distance, etc., with the result that the school and classroom components are almost equal.

The percent of between-school variance for *Word Meaning* and *Paragraph Meaning* are relatively greater, undoubtedly because the universe of possible item content of these tests is far broader than the material that can be taught in the classroom. In addition, these tests depend on vocabulary and general knowledge which is certainly obtained as much out of school as in school.

Finally, the large between-school component for *Science* is an artifact of course scheduling in these schools. In some of the schools, fifth-grade science was taught in the first term and health in the second. In others the schedule was reversed. Because the tests were given at midyear, large between-school differences resulted.

The interesting aspect of this study is the substantial differences in school, classroom, and pupil variation in different subject-matter areas. This suggests that studies of the institutional determinants of achievement must be multivariate, and not limited to a single test of general achievement, which would tend to be dominated by verbal ability and general knowledge.

b Balanced crossed designs: fixed and random ways of classification Crossed ways of classification in a sample survey may be either fixed or random. Fixed cross-classifications correspond to the identification of subjects in terms of multiple attributes (sex, age, socioeconomic status, etc.). Random cross-classifications arise when the sampling of units is carried out in two or more dimensions (for example, assessing stability of attitudes by obtaining responses of a random sample of subjects on each of several randomly selected occasions). Sampling from a finite population generates a way of classification that is, in effect, intermediate between fixed and random. An infinite population corresponds to a completely random classification, and a population that consists only of the sample classes corresponds to a fixed dimension. By considering all ways of classification as samples from finite populations, we may set up the analysis in terms that can be readily specialized to *fixed* (all terms fixed except one random error term), *mixed* (some terms fixed and two or more random), or *random* (all terms random except the mean) models.

A two-way crossed design illustrates the main points of this formulation. Suppose the A and B ways consist of a and b classes from finite populations of size $\mathscr{A}$ and $\mathscr{B}$, respectively; let r be the number of replicates in each subclass (group). The (p-variate) model for the analysis is

$$\mathbf{y}_{ijk} = \boldsymbol{\mu} + \boldsymbol{\alpha}_j + \boldsymbol{\beta}_k + (\boldsymbol{\alpha\beta})_{jk} + \boldsymbol{\epsilon}_{ijk} \qquad \begin{aligned} i &= 1, 2, \ldots, r \\ j &= 1, 2, \ldots, a \\ k &= 1, 2, \ldots, b \end{aligned}$$

where $\boldsymbol{\mu}$ is the general vector mean; $\boldsymbol{\alpha}$, $\boldsymbol{\beta}$, and $\boldsymbol{\alpha\beta}$ are either fixed or random; and $\boldsymbol{\epsilon}$ is strictly random with mean $\mathbf{0}$ and covariance matrix $\boldsymbol{\Sigma}$. If random, $\boldsymbol{\alpha}$, $\boldsymbol{\beta}$, and $\boldsymbol{\alpha\beta}$ are distributed with means $\mathbf{0}$ and covariance matrices $\boldsymbol{\Sigma}_a$, $\boldsymbol{\Sigma}_b$, and $\boldsymbol{\Sigma}_{ab}$, respectively. If these terms are fixed, the $\boldsymbol{\Sigma}_a$, $\boldsymbol{\Sigma}_b$, $\boldsymbol{\Sigma}_{ab}$ will represent factors of noncentrality terms in the distribution of the corresponding sums of squares. The partition of the sum of products under this model is precisely that of Table 5.4-20, but the expected mean products differ as follows:

$$\mathscr{E}(\mathsf{MSA}) = \mathscr{E}\left(\frac{\mathsf{SSA}}{a-1}\right) = \boldsymbol{\Sigma} + r\,\frac{\mathscr{A}-a}{\mathscr{A}}\,\boldsymbol{\Sigma}_{ab} + rb\boldsymbol{\Sigma}_a$$

$$\mathscr{E}(\mathsf{MSB}) = \mathscr{E}\left(\frac{\mathsf{SSB}}{b-1}\right) = \boldsymbol{\Sigma} + r\,\frac{\mathscr{B}-b}{\mathscr{B}}\,\boldsymbol{\Sigma}_{ab} + ra\boldsymbol{\Sigma}_b$$

$$\mathscr{E}(\mathsf{MSAB}) = \mathscr{E}\left[\frac{\mathsf{SSAB}}{(a-1)(b-1)}\right] = \boldsymbol{\Sigma} + r\boldsymbol{\Sigma}_{ab}$$

"Rules of thumb" for terms in the expected mean squares (or products) of more complex models, including both crossed and nested factors, have been outlined by Henderson [1969] and Millman and Glass [1967]. Briefly, the rules state that when letters identifying factors are used both as coefficients and subscripts, as above, each term except that of the replication error contains all the letters either as coefficients or as subscripts of the variance-covariance component. The letter identifying the mean square in question appears only as a subscript. The other letters appear one, two, etc., at a time in the components corresponding to first-order, second-order, etc., interactions. Finally, the finite population factors correspond to each subscripted letter, except that identifying the mean square in question.

As an example, the expected mean square for the A way of classification in an $a \times b \times c$ balanced all-random design is

$$\begin{aligned}\mathscr{E}(\mathsf{MSA}) &= \mathscr{E}\left(\frac{\mathsf{SSA}}{a-1}\right)\\ &= \boldsymbol{\Sigma} + r\,\frac{\mathscr{B}-b}{\mathscr{B}}\,\frac{\mathscr{C}-c}{\mathscr{C}}\,\boldsymbol{\Sigma}_{abc} + rb\,\frac{\mathscr{C}-c}{\mathscr{C}}\,\boldsymbol{\Sigma}_{ac} + rc\,\frac{\mathscr{B}-b}{\mathscr{B}}\,\boldsymbol{\Sigma}_{ab}\\ &\qquad + rbc\boldsymbol{\Sigma}_a\end{aligned}$$

These formulas specialize to the fixed effects when the number of sample classes for a given way of classification equals the number of population classes.

c Unbalanced nested designs In most large-scale surveys it would be unlikely that a balanced nested design could be used without compromising the probability sample. It is therefore important that we generalize the model II analyses to the unbalanced case—a not too difficult task if we follow the widely used heuristic approach of estimating the mean products in a nonorthogonal analysis of variance and equating the estimates to their expected values [Henderson, 1953; Searle, 1971]. This method of estimation in the unbalanced case has no established good property other than unbiasedness, although presumably the minimum-variance property will not be too seriously affected if the design is only somewhat out of balance.

The first step is the computation of mean-product matrices for each stratum of the design. This requires a nonorthogonal multivariate analysis of variance that in principle may be carried out by the method of Chap. 5. That is, the basis for a balanced design that includes the actual design is constructed by the method of Sec. 6.4.3, down to the $g - 1$ stratum. The basis is then orthogonalized in the metric of the stratum-g subclass numbers, some of which will be zero. The number of basis vectors generated for the space of each stratum is, of course, equal to the number of degrees of freedom for the within-stratum variation. Thus, the number of degrees of freedom for stratum K is

$$\text{df}_K = \sum_{j_1 j_2 \cdots j_k} n_{j_1 j_2 \cdots j_k} - \sum_{j_1 j_2 \cdots j_{k-1}} n_{j_1 j_2 \cdots j_{k-1}}$$

After the orthogonalization (proceeding from the highest to the lowest stratum), the orthogonal estimates, sums of products, and mean products are computed. Although the mean products for successive spaces are invariant with respect to the choice of contrasts for the basis, Helmert contrasts of the type

$$\begin{bmatrix} 2^{-1/2} & (1 & -1 & 0 & \cdots & 0) \\ 6^{-1/2} & (1 & 1 & -2 & \cdots & 0) \\ \cdots & \cdots & \cdots & \cdots & \cdots & \cdots \\ (n^2+n)^{-1/2} & (1 & 1 & 1 & \cdots & -n) \end{bmatrix}$$

have the advantage of remaining orthogonal (by rows) and interpretable when applied within classes containing different numbers of subclasses.

Actually, the orthogonalization method is of more theoretical interest than practical, because the partition of the sum of products can be obtained much more economically by performing successive one-way analyses of adjacent strata (see Graybill [1963, page 354] for a univariate sample).

The next step in the heuristic method is that of deriving expressions for the expected mean products. The general result applicable to any design is as follows:

Note first that if $\boldsymbol{x}$ and $\boldsymbol{y}$ are two m-component random vectors such that $\mathscr{E}(\boldsymbol{xy}') = \mathscr{E}(\boldsymbol{yx}') = \sigma_{xy}\mathbf{I}_m$, then $\mathscr{E}(\boldsymbol{x}'\mathbf{A}\boldsymbol{y}) = \text{tr}[\mathscr{E}(\boldsymbol{x}'\mathbf{A}\boldsymbol{y})] = \text{tr}(\mathbf{A})\mathscr{E}(\boldsymbol{yx}') = \sigma_{xy}\text{tr}(\mathbf{A})$ (see Sec. 2.5.2). Thus, if $\mathscr{E}(\boldsymbol{X}'\boldsymbol{X}) = \boldsymbol{\Sigma}$, then $\mathscr{E}(\boldsymbol{X}\mathbf{A}\boldsymbol{X}') = [\text{tr}(A)]\boldsymbol{\Sigma}$.

Now consider a multivariate linear model for the means of the stratum-$(g - 1)$ subclasses:

$$\underset{n \times p}{\boldsymbol{Y}_{.}} = [\underset{m_0}{\mathbf{A}}, \underset{m_1}{\mathbf{B}_1}, \underset{m_2}{\mathbf{B}_2}] \underset{p}{\begin{bmatrix} \boldsymbol{\Xi} \\ \mathbf{Z}_1 \\ \mathbf{Z}_2 \end{bmatrix}} + \underset{n \times p}{\boldsymbol{E}_{.}}$$

From (6.4-9), the submatrices of the model matrix satisfy rank(**A**) $= L_0$, rank[**A**,**B**] $= L_0 + L_1$, and rank[**A**,$\mathbf{B}_1$,$\mathbf{B}_2$] $= L_0 + L_1 + L_2 = L$. There are m_0 p-variate fixed effects Ξ, m_1 and m_2 independent random p-variate components $\mathbf{Z}_1$ and $\mathbf{Z}_2$, with

$$\mathscr{E}(\mathbf{Z}_1) = \mathbf{O} \qquad \mathscr{E}(\mathbf{Z}_2) = \mathbf{O} \qquad \mathscr{V}(\mathbf{Z}_1,\mathbf{Z}_2) = \mathbf{I}_{m_1+m_2} \times \begin{bmatrix} \Sigma_1 & \mathbf{O} \\ \mathbf{O} & \Sigma_2 \end{bmatrix} \tag{6.4-11}$$

and an $n \times p$ error matrix independent of $\mathbf{Z}_1$ and $\mathbf{Z}_2$, with $\mathscr{E}(\boldsymbol{E}.) = \mathbf{O}$, $\mathscr{V}(\boldsymbol{E}.) = \mathbf{D}^{-1} \times \Sigma$ (zero elements in the diagonal of **D** are set to zero in $\mathbf{D}^{-1}$).

As we have seen in Chap. 5, a partition of the sum of products corresponding to elimination of effects from left to right in (6.4-6) may be obtained by expressing an $n \times L$ basis as $\mathbf{K} = \mathbf{PT}'$ where $\mathbf{P}'\mathbf{DP} = \mathbf{I}_L$ and **T** is the (lower-triangular) Cholesky factor of **K′DK**.

Then, if **P** is partitioned $\underset{L_0 \;\; L_1 \;\; L_2}{[\mathbf{P}_0,\mathbf{P}_1,\mathbf{P}_2]}n$, (where $\mathbf{P}_1'\mathbf{A} = \mathbf{O}$, $\mathbf{P}_2'[\mathbf{A},\mathbf{B}_1] = [\mathbf{O},\mathbf{O}]$) the orthogonal estimates are

$$\mathbf{U}_0 = \mathbf{P}_0'\mathbf{DY}. \qquad \mathbf{U}_1 = \mathbf{P}_1'\mathbf{DY}. \qquad \mathbf{U}_2 = \mathbf{P}_2'\mathbf{DY}.$$

and the corresponding sums of products are

$$\text{SSA} = \mathbf{U}_0'\mathbf{U}_0 \qquad \text{SSB}_1 = \mathbf{U}_1'\mathbf{U}_1 \qquad \text{SSB}_2 = \mathbf{U}_2'\mathbf{U}_2$$

In addition, there is the within-subclass sum of products

$$\text{SSW} = \text{SST} - \text{SSA} - \text{SSB}_1 - \text{SSB}_2$$

The expected sums of products are therefore

$$\begin{aligned}\mathscr{E}(\text{SSA}) &= \mathscr{E}(\boldsymbol{Y}'.\mathbf{DP}_0\mathbf{P}_0'\mathbf{D}\boldsymbol{Y}.) \\ &= \Xi'\mathbf{A}'\mathbf{DP}_0\mathbf{P}_0'\mathbf{DA}\Xi + \operatorname{tr}(\mathbf{B}_1'\mathbf{DP}_0\mathbf{P}_0'\mathbf{DB})\Sigma_1 + \operatorname{tr}(\mathbf{B}_2'\mathbf{DP}_0\mathbf{P}_0'\mathbf{DB}_2)\Sigma_2 \\ &\qquad + L_0\Sigma \\ \mathscr{E}(\text{SSB}_1) &= \mathscr{E}(\boldsymbol{Y}'.\mathbf{DP}_1\mathbf{P}_1'\mathbf{D}\boldsymbol{Y}.) \\ &= \operatorname{tr}(\mathbf{B}_1'\mathbf{DP}_1\mathbf{P}_1'\mathbf{DB}_1)\Sigma_1 + \operatorname{tr}(\mathbf{B}_2'\mathbf{DP}_1\mathbf{P}_1'\mathbf{DB}_2)\Sigma_2 + L_1\Sigma \\ \mathscr{E}(\text{SSB}_2) &= \mathscr{E}(\boldsymbol{Y}'.\mathbf{DP}_2\mathbf{P}_2'\mathbf{D}\boldsymbol{Y}.) = \operatorname{tr}(\mathbf{B}_2'\mathbf{DP}_2\mathbf{P}_2'\mathbf{DB}_2)\Sigma_2 + L_2\Sigma\end{aligned}$$

Thus, the expected *mean products* are, say

$$\begin{aligned}\mathscr{E}(\text{MSA}) &= \frac{1}{L_0}\mathscr{E}(\text{SSA}) = \Sigma + k_{02}\Sigma_2 + k_{01}\Sigma_1 + \Xi'\mathbf{A}'\mathbf{DP}_0\mathbf{P}_0'\mathbf{DA}\Xi \\ \mathscr{E}(\text{MSB}_1) &= \frac{1}{L_1}\mathscr{E}(\text{SSB}_1) = \Sigma + k_{12}\Sigma_2 + k_{11}\Sigma_1 \\ \mathscr{E}(\text{MSB}_2) &= \frac{1}{L_2}\mathscr{E}(\text{SSB}_2) = \Sigma + k_{22}\Sigma_2 \\ \mathscr{E}(\text{MSW}) &= \frac{1}{N-n}\mathscr{E}(\text{SSW}) = \Sigma\end{aligned} \tag{6.4-12}$$

In simple cases, the coefficients k_{ij} can be expressed in a form suitable for hand calculation (see Graybill [1963, Chap. 16]). In more complex cases, numerical evaluation by computer may be necessary. Hartley [1967] has made the inspired observation that these coefficients are just the sums of (univariate) mean squares in an analysis of variance with respect to subclass numbers **D** in which **A**, $\mathbf{B}_1$, and $\mathbf{B}_2$ are used as data in place of **Y**. (see also Rao [1968]). Thus, the same computer program that performs the nonorthogonal analysis of variance can be used to obtain the coefficients in the expected mean products. In addition, similar calculations can be employed to obtain the sampling variances and covariances of the estimates based on equating sample mean products to their expectation. (See Sec. 6.4-3g and Speed and Hocking [1974].)

According to Henderson's "Method III" [Henderson, 1953], the variance-covariance components are estimated by equating the mean products for the random effects to their expected values and solving the resulting systems of linear equations. The mean products for fixed effects are not used in these estimates.

The above treatment may be generalized by further partitioning of the subspaces. It also applies to crossed and crossed-and-nested designs if certain complications, which we discuss in Sec. 6.4.3e, are dealt with.

EXAMPLE 6.4-2 (*Analysis of an unbalanced nested design*) Graybill presents the artificial data shown in Table 6.4-3 to illustrate the variance-component analysis for an unbalanced nested design. The data are supposed to represent measures of yield in a breeding experiment in which each of four sires is mated with varying numbers of dams to produce varying numbers of offspring.

For purposes of the analysis of variance, the design is regarded as $4 \rightarrow 4$ with subclass numbers given by

$$\mathbf{D} = \text{diag}[4, 5, 7, 0, 3, 4, 5, 3, 3, 4, 0, 0, 4, 5, 5, 0]$$

Table 6.4-3 RESULTS OF A BREEDING EXPERIMENT (ARTIFICIAL DATA) $N = 52$

Sires	1			2				3		4		
Dams	1	2	3	4	5	6	7	8	9	10	11	12
Scores of offspring	32	30	34	26	22	23	21	16	14	31	42	26
	31	26	30	20	31	21	21	20	18	34	43	25
	23	29	26	18	20	24	30	32	16	41	40	29
	26	28	34		21	26			17	40	35	40
		18	32			18					29	37
			31									
			26									

The spaces in the basis are then represented by

Space (SBV)	df	Description
0, 0	1	General mean
$C(h_1)$, 0, $h_1 = 1, 2, 3$	3	Between sires
$I1$, $C(h_2)$, $h_2 = 1, 2$	2	
$I2$, $C(h_2)$, $h_2 = 1, 2, 3$	3	Between dams
$I3$, $C(h_2)$, $h_2 = 1$	1	
$I4$, $C(h_2)$, $h_2 = 1, 2$	2	
Total	12	

The analysis of variance, which results upon orthogonalizing the basis with respect to the metric **D** (and in top-to-bottom order in the above list), is shown in Table 6.4-4.

In this simple design, the coefficients of the expected mean squares are easily calculated from the subclass numbers (see below), but to illustrate the general case, we shall obtain them numerically by Hartley's [1967] method. The procedure is to carry out the above analysis using as data the columns of the model matrix **B** which corresponds to the effects of sires (to obtain the coefficients k_{11} and k_{12}) and to the effects of dams (to obtain the coefficients k_{21}). These sets of columns are, respectively, the 16 × 4 and 16 × 16 matrices $\mathbf{I}_4 \times \mathbf{1}_4$ and $\mathbf{I}_4 \times \mathbf{I}_4$. The results of these analyses are the following mean squares:

Sires "variates"	Between-sires mean squares	Between-dams mean squares
1	3.6923	0
2	3.5577	0
3	2.0192	0
4	3.4103	0
	k_{11} = 12.6795	

Table 6.4-4 ANALYSIS OF VARIANCE FOR THE DATA IN TABLE 6.4-3

Source of variation	df	Sums of squares	Mean squares	Expected mean squares
General mean	1	38,940.94		
Between sires	3	1,669.94	556.650	$\sigma_c^2 + k_{12}\sigma_b^2 + k_{11}\sigma_a^2$
Between dams	8	258.32	31.290	$\sigma_c^2 + k_{22}\sigma_b^2$
Between offspring	40	949.80	23.745	σ_c^2
Total	52	41,819.00		

Dams "variates"	Between-sires mean squares	Between-dams mean squares
1	.2308	.3750
2	.3606	.4297
3	.7067	.4922
4	.0	.0
5	.1423	.3000
6	.2530	.3667
7	.3953	.4167
8	.1425	.3000
9	.3709	.2143
10	.6593	.2143
11	.0	.0
12	.0	.0
13	.2787	.3571
14	.4350	.4018
15	.4350	.4018
16	.0	.0
	$k_{12} = 4.4101$	$k_{22} = 4.2696$

The results agree with the standard formulas for the unbalanced nested design (Graybill [1961, page 355]):

$$k_{11} = \frac{1}{a-1}\sum_{i=1}^{a} n_i^2\left(\frac{1}{n_i} - \frac{1}{n}\right) = 12.679$$

$$k_{12} = \frac{1}{a-1}\sum_{i=1}^{a}\sum_{j=1}^{b} n_{ij}^2\left(\frac{1}{n_i} - \frac{1}{n}\right) = 4.410$$

$$k_{22} = \frac{1}{\sum_{i=1}^{a} n_i - a}\sum_{i=1}^{a}\sum_{j=1}^{b} n_{ij}^2\left(\frac{1}{n_{ij}} - \frac{1}{n_i}\right) = 4.270$$

In these formulas, the n_{ij} are the subclass numbers in **D** above, and $n_i = \sum_{j=1}^{b} n_{ij}$.

Solving the equations of expectation, we obtain the variance-component estimates

$$\hat{\sigma}_c^2 = 23.745$$

$$\hat{\sigma}_b^2 = \frac{31.290 - 23.745}{4.2696} = 1.767$$

$$\hat{\sigma}_a^2 = \frac{556.650 - 4.4101(1.767)}{12.6795} = 43.330$$

Hartley's method is quite general and applies to any random crossed and/or nested design and to mixed designs if fixed effects are eliminated from the sums of products for random effects. It may also be used to obtain the variances of these estimators (see Sec. 6.4.3g).

d Unbalanced random cross-classifications A difficulty with the analysis-of-variance method of estimating variance-covariance components in unbalanced crossed designs is the possibility of more than one way in which random effects can be eliminated. Each ordering for a given effect would result in a somewhat different mean-product matrix and a different estimate of the corresponding component. One of the solutions to this problem which has been suggested by Henderson [1953] is always to eliminate all fixed effects from the random effect in question, but to estimate the mean product for the given random effects ignoring all other random effects. This will not correspond to an additive partition of the sum of products, but at least it is an objective rule which leads to unique estimates.

Another difficulty with the random crossed design (and this also is true of the balanced case) is that there is no sum of products that provides an appropriate error term for testing main effects in designs with three or more ways of classification. This is not a serious problem because, as mentioned in Sec. 6.4.3, there is seldom any value in testing the hypothesis that a variance-covariance component is null. If such a test is required, however, approximate tests based on linear combinations of mean squares are available [Satterthwaite, 1946; Gaylor and Hopper, 1969].

e Finite populations Corrections for finite populations may be included in the variance-covariance component estimators for any design, crossed and/or nested, balanced or unbalanced. The formulas for cases not covered by Table 6.4-1 or in Sec. 6.4.3b are given in Searle and Fawcett [1970].

f Estimation of component covariance matrices under the restriction of positive semidefiniteness Bock and Petersen [1974] have shown that, if $\boldsymbol{S}_A$ and $\boldsymbol{S}_B$ are independent Wishart matrices of order p (i.e., independent sum-of-product matrices from p-variate normal populations), and

$$\mathscr{E}(\boldsymbol{S}_A) = n_a\boldsymbol{\Sigma}_B + k\boldsymbol{\Sigma}_A$$

$$\mathscr{E}(\boldsymbol{S}_B) = n_b\boldsymbol{\Sigma}_B$$

where $\boldsymbol{S}_B$ is pd, then the maximum-likelihood estimate of $\boldsymbol{\Sigma}_A$ subject to the restriction that $\hat{\boldsymbol{\Sigma}}_A$ be positive semidefinite may be obtained as follows:

Let $\mathbf{M}_A = (1/n_a)\mathbf{S}_A$ and $\mathbf{M}_B = (1/n_b)\mathbf{S}_B$ be the sample mean-product matrices, and compute the characteristic roots and vectors of $\mathbf{M}_A$ in the metric $\mathbf{M}_B$; that is, solve

$$(\mathbf{M}_A - \lambda_i\mathbf{M}_B)\mathbf{x}_i = \mathbf{0} \qquad i = 1, 2, \ldots, p \qquad (6.4\text{-}13)$$

for $\mathbf{M}_B$ pd and $\mathbf{x}_i \neq \mathbf{0}$.

Let $\boldsymbol{\Lambda} = \text{diag}[\lambda_1, \lambda_2, \ldots, \lambda_p]$ be the diagonal matrix of characteristic roots, and $\mathbf{X} = [\mathbf{x}_1, \mathbf{x}_2, \ldots, \mathbf{x}_p]$ be the corresponding characteristic vectors. Now let $\boldsymbol{\Lambda}^*$ be the diagonal matrix in which the ith element is $\max(\lambda_i,1)$. Under the restriction $\hat{\boldsymbol{\Sigma}}_A$ psd,

$$\hat{\boldsymbol{\Sigma}}_A = \frac{1}{k}\mathbf{X}'(\boldsymbol{\Lambda}^* - \mathbf{I})\mathbf{X} \qquad (6.4\text{-}14)$$

is the maximum-likelihood estimate of $\boldsymbol{\Sigma}_A$, and

$$\hat{\boldsymbol{\Sigma}}_B = \mathbf{X}'\boldsymbol{K}\mathbf{X} \tag{6.4-15}$$

where $\boldsymbol{K}$ is a diagonal matrix in which the ith element is $[n_b + n_a \min(\lambda_i,1)]/(n_a + n_b)$, is the maximum-likelihood estimate of $\boldsymbol{\Sigma}_B$. The rank of $\hat{\boldsymbol{\Sigma}}_A$ is equal to the number of nonzero elements in $\boldsymbol{\Lambda}^* - \mathbf{I}$.

When the rank of $\hat{\boldsymbol{\Sigma}}_A = p$, (6.4-14) and (6.4-15) become, respectively,

$$\hat{\boldsymbol{\Sigma}}_A = \frac{1}{k}(\mathbf{M}_A - \mathbf{M}_B) \qquad \text{and} \qquad \boldsymbol{\Sigma}_B = \mathbf{M}_B$$

Applications of this result to multivariate behavior genetic analysis may be found in Bock and Vandenberg [1968] and Bock [1974].

g Standard errors of estimated components of variance and covariance General results for the sampling variances and covariances of the component estimators discussed in Sec. 6.4.3c and d have been given by Rohde and Tallis [1969]. In reference to Sec. 6.4.3d, let $q_{ij}^{(1)}$, $q_{ij}^{(2)}$, and q_{ij} be the i,j elements of MSB_1, MSB_2, and MSW, respectively. Let $\sigma_{ij}^{(1)}$, $\sigma_{ij}^{(2)}$, and σ_{ij} be corresponding elements of $\boldsymbol{\Sigma}_1$, $\boldsymbol{\Sigma}_2$, and $\boldsymbol{\Sigma}$. Then, from (6.4-12), the unbiased estimates of the variance and covariance components are

$$\begin{aligned}
\hat{\sigma}_{ij} &= q_{ij} \\
\hat{\sigma}_{ij}^{(2)} &= \frac{q_{ij}^{(2)} - q_{ij}}{k_{22}} \\
\hat{\sigma}_{ij}^{(1)} &= \frac{q_{ij}^{(1)} - k_{12}q_{ij}^{(2)} - (1 - k_{12}/k_{22})q_{ij}}{k_{11}}
\end{aligned} \tag{6.4-16}$$

Since the forms in (6.4-16) are linear in the mean products, we may readily compute their variances if we know the covariances among corresponding elements in the mean products. On the assumption that the components are normally and independently distributed with means and covariances given by (6.4-11), the following covariances, given by Rohde and Tallis [1969], may be obtained by lengthy application of the rules for expectations and variances of linear functions of random variables (L_1 and L_2 are the ranks of $\mathbf{B}_1$ and $\mathbf{B}_2$, respectively):

$$\operatorname{cov}(q_{ij}^{(1)},q_{kl}^{(2)}) = \frac{\operatorname{tr}[(\mathbf{B}_2'\mathbf{D}\mathbf{P}_1\mathbf{P}_1'\mathbf{D}\mathbf{B}_2)(\mathbf{B}_2'\mathbf{D}\mathbf{P}_2\mathbf{P}_2'\mathbf{D}\mathbf{B}_2)](\sigma_{jl}^{(2)}\sigma_{ik}^{(2)} + \sigma_{il}^{(2)}\sigma_{jk}^{(2)})}{L_1L_2}$$

$$\operatorname{cov}(q_{ij}^{(1)},q_{kl}) = \operatorname{cov}(q_{ij}^{(2)},q_{kl}) = 0$$

$$\operatorname{cov}(q_{ij}^{(1)},q_{kl}^{(1)}) = \frac{1}{L_2^2}\{\operatorname{tr}(\mathbf{B}_1'\mathbf{D}\mathbf{P}_1\mathbf{P}_1'\mathbf{D}\mathbf{B}_1)^2(\sigma_{jl}^{(1)}\sigma_{ik}^{(1)} + \sigma_{jk}^{(1)}\sigma_{il}^{(1)})$$

$$+ \operatorname{tr}[(\mathbf{B}_1'\mathbf{D}\mathbf{P}_1\mathbf{P}_1'\mathbf{D}\mathbf{B}_2)(\mathbf{B}_2'\mathbf{D}\mathbf{P}_1\mathbf{P}_1'\mathbf{D}\mathbf{B}_1)]$$

$$\times (\sigma_{ik}^{(2)}\sigma_{jl}^{(1)} + \sigma_{jl}^{(2)}\sigma_{ik}^{(1)} + \sigma_{il}^{(2)}\sigma_{jk}^{(1)} + \sigma_{jk}^{(2)}\sigma_{il}^{(1)})$$

$$+ L_1k_{11}(\sigma_{jl}^{(1)}\sigma_{ik} + \sigma_{ik}^{(1)}\sigma_{jl} + \sigma_{jk}^{(1)}\sigma_{il} + \sigma_{il}^{(1)}\sigma_{jk}) \qquad (6.4\text{-}17)$$

$$+ \operatorname{tr}(\mathbf{B}_2'\mathbf{D}\mathbf{P}_1\mathbf{P}_1'\mathbf{D}\mathbf{B}_2)^2(\sigma_{jl}^{(2)}\sigma_{ik}^{(2)} + \sigma_{jk}^{(2)}\sigma_{il}^{(2)})$$

$$+ L_1k_{12}(\sigma_{jl}^{(2)}\sigma_{ik} + \sigma_{ik}^{(2)}\sigma_{jl} + \sigma_{jk}^{(2)}\sigma_{il} + \sigma_{il}^{(2)}\sigma_{jk})$$

$$+ L_1(\sigma_{jl}\sigma_{ik} + \sigma_{jk}\sigma_{il})\}$$

$$\operatorname{cov}(q_{ij}^{(2)},q_{kl}^{(2)}) = \frac{1}{L_2^2}[\operatorname{tr}(\mathbf{B}_2'\mathbf{D}\mathbf{P}_2\mathbf{P}_2'\mathbf{D}\mathbf{B}_2)^2(\sigma_{ik}^{(2)}\sigma_{jl}^{(2)} + \sigma_{il}^{(2)}\sigma_{jk}^{(2)})$$

$$+ L_2k_{22}(\sigma_{il}^{(2)}\sigma_{jk} + \sigma_{jk}^{(2)}\sigma_{il} + \sigma_{jl}^{(2)}\sigma_{ik} + \sigma_{ik}^{(2)}\sigma_{jl})$$

$$+ L_2(\sigma_{ik}\sigma_{jl} + \sigma_{il}\sigma_{jk})]$$

$$\operatorname{cov}(q_{ij},q_{kl}) = \sigma_{ik}\sigma_{jl} + \sigma_{il}\sigma_{jk}$$

Terms for the variance components are obtained by setting $i = k$ and $j = l$ in the above expressions. The traces in the coefficients can also be calculated by Hartley's method from the mean product of a multivariate analysis of variance for the design in question, using $[\mathbf{B}_1,\mathbf{B}_2]$ as the data matrix (see Rao [1968]). This analysis will give rise to the $(m_1 + m_2) \times (m_1 + m_2)$ mean product matrices

$$\text{MSB}_1 = \begin{bmatrix} \mathbf{B}_1'\mathbf{D}\mathbf{P}_1\mathbf{P}_1'\mathbf{D}\mathbf{B}_1 & \mathbf{B}_1'\mathbf{D}\mathbf{P}_1\mathbf{P}_1'\mathbf{D}\mathbf{B}_2 \\ \mathbf{B}_2'\mathbf{D}\mathbf{P}_1\mathbf{P}_1'\mathbf{D}\mathbf{B}_1 & \mathbf{B}_2'\mathbf{D}\mathbf{P}_1\mathbf{P}_1'\mathbf{D}\mathbf{B}_2 \end{bmatrix}$$

$$\text{MSB}_2 = \begin{bmatrix} \mathbf{B}_1'\mathbf{D}\mathbf{P}_2\mathbf{P}_2'\mathbf{D}\mathbf{B}_1 & \mathbf{B}_1'\mathbf{D}\mathbf{P}_2\mathbf{P}_2'\mathbf{D}\mathbf{B}_2 \\ \mathbf{B}_2'\mathbf{D}\mathbf{P}_2\mathbf{P}_2'\mathbf{D}\mathbf{B}_1 & \mathbf{B}_2'\mathbf{D}\mathbf{P}_2\mathbf{P}_2'\mathbf{D}\mathbf{B}_2 \end{bmatrix}$$

The traces in the above expressions are sums of products of elements in each of the three distinct submatrices of MSB_1, and in the lower-right submatrix of MSB_2.

Using the covariances in (6.4-17), we may construct the covariance matrix of the elements in the mean-square matrices and premultiply and postmultiply by the coefficients of (6.4-16) to obtain the sampling variances of the variance-covariance estimators. The standard errors corresponding to these variates may then be used to construct large-sample-interval estimates of the variance by inverting the critical-ratio test. These intervals should be adequate in practical work to give a useful idea of the precision with which the variance-covariance components can be estimated.

Exercise 6.4-1 (*School-achievement survey*) Table 6.4-5 gives the classroom means and pooled within-classroom covariance matrix of four of the nine tests in Anthony's data (Example 6.4-1). Estimate the variance-covariance components between schools, between classrooms within schools, and between pupils within classrooms. Use Hartley's method to obtain the coefficients of the expected mean squares. Calculate the sampling variance for the estimated between-classroom variance component for the Language test using Hartley's method.

Convert each of the estimated component covariance matrices to correlation matrices, and discuss any differences between them.

Table 6.4-5 CLASSROOM MEANS AND WITHIN-GROUP COVARIANCE MATRIX FOR FOUR STANFORD ACHIEVEMENT TESTS (GRADE EQUIVALENTS)

			Tests			
School	Classroom	N	*1* Word meaning	*2* Language	*3* Arithmetic computation	*4* Arithmetic concepts
1	1	29	5.3586	5.7897	5.1138	5.1655
	2	29	5.2827	5.5862	4.6551	5.3241
2	1	35	5.6000	6.4429	4.8371	5.8114
	2	35	5.2486	5.4314	5.0571	5.5257
3	1	22	4.7182	5.7773	4.0545	5.3091
	2	20	4.0950	4.3850	4.7500	5.2350
4	1	20	4.9000	5.0250	4.2950	4.7050
	2	23	5.6565	6.5261	5.3260	5.6696
5	1	26	5.0923	5.0615	4.4923	5.3192
	2	28	5.2071	5.2357	4.4679	5.6643
6	1	22	4.7591	4.7636	4.5909	5.0091
	2	26	5.0462	5.0808	4.3462	5.4462
7	1	21	5.7905	6.4619	4.6572	5.4000
	2	21	5.6238	6.6619	5.4285	6.0905
8	1	27	6.5926	7.1593	5.4296	6.2852
9	1	27	4.8889	5.0667	4.2148	4.9889
	2	26	5.6615	5.9500	4.5154	5.6231
10	1	23	5.3956	5.5086	4.9435	5.5739
	2	24	5.3625	6.1083	4.7542	5.7083
Covariance matrix df = 465						
	Tests	1	1.5479			
		2	1.4729	2.9375		
		3	.4201	.7954	.8353	
		4	.6994	1.0138	.5355	1.1886

7

ANALYSIS OF REPEATED MEASUREMENTS

In this chapter we consider a class of behavioral experiments having the following general form: (1) each of a number of subjects is measured with respect to the behavior under investigation, (2) an experimental intervention is carried out, and (3) each subject is measured again with respect to the same behavior. The question to be answered is, "Does the intervention change the behavior?" This experimental setup is sometimes described as one in which "each subject serves as his own control." In the statistical literature, it would be regarded as a randomized block design when one sample of subjects is involved, and a split-plot design when there is more than one sample. In this text, however, we shall follow Winer [1962, page 298] in referring to this form of experiment as a *repeated-measures* design.

An early example of a repeated-measures design is seen in the study [Cushny and Peebles, 1905] used by Student to illustrate the statistical procedure later known as the t test [Student, 1908]. The objective of the study was to assess gains in the hours of sleep of subjects who had been administered various derivatives of the hypnotic drug scopolamine (see Example 7.1-3). Although hours of sleep of each subject were carefully observed before and after administration of the drug, there was sufficient normal variation from day to day to present statistical problems in detecting the effect of the drug and in estimating the (possible) average gain of sleep.

Student proposed the one-sample t test as a solution to the first of these problems. The procedures presented in this chapter may be viewed as the generalization of Student's method to repeated-measures designs of any complexity.

Since the measurements and the experimental intervention cannot ordinarily be carried out simultaneously in the same subject, we may identify the repeated measure with the *occasion* on which it is taken and express the design as subjects $\times$ occasions.* For N subjects and p occasions, the design formula is therefore $N \times p$.

In the simplest design the measures are repeated on two occasions, corresponding to a pretest and a posttest, and there is one intervening experimental treatment. In more complex designs, there may be multiple measures and multiple treatments or treatment combinations structuring the temporal sequence of occasions. We speak of this part of the experimental setup as the *design on the occasions.*

In general, there will also be a *sampling design* on the subjects. The simplest case is that of a single sample, as in Student's example, but in more complex cases there will be n samples of subjects, and these samples may arise from populations arranged in any of the treatment and/or variety designs in Chap. 5. We speak of this part of the experiment as the *design on the sample.* Thus, the repeated-measures designs are generated in their full generality by the crossing of the design on the occasions by the design on the sample. Although the methods of the present chapter are completely general for all such designs, there is some didactic value in discussing first the designs with only one sample of subjects. This is done in Sec. 7.1, while the n-sample case is left to Sec. 7.2. Discussion of repeated-measures designs that also include covariables is postponed until Sec. 7.3.

In keeping with the general approach in this text, we exploit the fact that repeated measures, by generating multiple scores for each subject, yield a class of multivariate data. It is, however, a special class in which the scores are assumed to have the same metric properties throughout. That is, the scores on each occasion are assumed to be measurements on the same scale with the some origin and unit (e.g., amount of sleep measured in hours).

Thus, repeated measures are to be distinguished from general multivariate data in which each score in the response vector is qualitatively distinct, usually with a different origin and unit. Of course, a repeated-measures study may also be multivariate in the latter sense if each of a number of qualitatively distinct responses is measured on each of a number of occasions. Such *doubly multivariate* data occur frequently in behavioral research, and their analysis is discussed in Sec. 7.3.4.

When psychological tests are used in repeated-measures designs, it may not be practical to readminister the same form of a test to the same subject. Parallel forms of the test are then required and must, for this purpose, be strongly parallel; that is,

* An exception is a type of experiment in which different anatomical parts or psychological processes are measured more or less simultaneously in the same subject; e.g., left and right palmar galvanic skin response.

they must measure the same factor, have the same population distribution (e.g., same mean and variance), and have the same reliability. In extenuating circumstances, scores on what are assumed to be the same components in distinct test batteries might be standardized and considered metrically commensurate for the purposes of repeated-measures analysis. That is essentially what we do when we make longitudinal comparisons among IQ scores obtained with different instruments such as the Stanford-Binet and the WAIS or WISC. A better practice would be, of course, to use parallel forms of the same instrument. Alternatively, item-invariant scoring procedures based on psychometric models may be employed to obtain metrically commensurate scores for items sampled from a defined domain. The scores presented in Example 7.1-1 were obtained in this way. Models for estimating scaled scores have been proposed by Lawley [1943], Lord [1952], Rasch [1960], Birnbaum [1968], Samejima [1969], and Bock [1972]. Practical procedures for their implementation have been developed by Kolakowski and Bock [1971, 1972].

7.1 ANALYSIS OF REPEATED MEASUREMENTS IN THE ONE-SAMPLE CASE

7.1.1 Mixed-Model Analysis

On certain assumptions, which may be plausible for behavioral data, the mixed-model analysis for the unreplicated randomized block design in Sec. 5.3 is applicable to the one-sample repeated-measures design. The assumption most critical for the analysis is that of independence of response errors within subjects. Independence of response errors is the basis of the following statistical model for the score of the ith subject on the kth occasion:

$$y_{ik} = \mu + a_i + \gamma_k + \epsilon_{ik} \qquad (7.1\text{-}1)$$

where μ = a possibly arbitrary location constant
a_i = an individual difference component specific to subject i and constant over occasions
γ_k = an effect of occasion k general to all subjects; if a treatment intervenes between occasions, γ_k may include treatment effect
ϵ_{ik} = an error component specific to subject i and occasion k; it may include temporal instability of the subject as well as measurement error

The subjects are assumed sampled from a population in which the a component is distributed independently as

$$a \sim N(0,\sigma_\alpha^2) \qquad (7.1\text{-}2)$$

The error component is assumed sampled both with respect to subjects and occasions and distributed independently as

$$\epsilon \sim N(0,\sigma^2) \qquad (7.1\text{-}3)$$

This model implies that the covariance matrix of the repeated measures in the population of subjects has the special structure

$$\mathscr{V}(\mathbf{y}) = \sigma_\alpha^2 \mathbf{11}' + \sigma^2\mathbf{I} \qquad (7.1\text{-}4)$$

The conformity of the data to this structure may be examined in the sample covariance matrix

$$\hat{\mathbf{\Sigma}} = \frac{1}{N-1}\left(\sum_{i=1}^{N} \mathbf{y}_i\mathbf{y}_i' - N\mathbf{y}.\mathbf{y}'.\right) \qquad (7.1\text{-}5)$$

where $\mathbf{y}_i$ is a vector consisting of the p repeated measures for the ith subject in a sample of size N, and $\mathbf{y}.$ is the vector of occasion means (see Example 7.1-2).

If the model holds, each diagonal element in (7.1-5) estimates $\sigma_\alpha^2 + \sigma^2$, and each off-diagonal element estimates σ_α^2. A statistical test of the homogeneity of the elements thus provides a check on the condition (7.1-4), which is necessary for the mixed-model analysis. A heuristic test for this purpose is discussed in Sec. 7.1-2; a likelihood-ratio test is given by Bock and Bargmann [1966] and Jöreskog [1970].

For the present, let us assume that the structure (7.1-4) holds and that the one-sample mixed-model analysis can proceed. The purpose of the analysis is to assess the evidence for an occasion effect and to characterize the effect if it is present. On mixed-model assumptions, a test of the overall occasion effect is provided by a subjects × occasions analysis of variance of data in the format of Table 7.1-1. This analysis may be carried out in the manner of Sec. 5.3.4 by generating an orthogonal solution matrix as the Kronecker product of an $N \times N$ and a $p \times p$ Helmert matrix. If the number of blocks (subjects) is large, however, this method of performing the analysis is cumbersome, and a computationally more efficient method is provided by the multivariate treatment of the data discussed in Sec. 7.2 or the conventional hand method, which we now discuss (see also Winer [1971]).

Table 7.1-1 REPEATED-MEASURES DATA AND MARGINAL MEANS IN THE ONE-SAMPLE CASE

	Occasions				
Subjects	1	2	⋯	p	Mean
1	y_{11}	y_{12}	⋯	y_{1p}	$y_{1.}$
2	y_{21}	y_{22}	⋯	y_{2p}	$y_{2.}$
⋯	⋯	⋯	⋯	⋯	⋯
N	y_{N1}	y_{N2}	⋯	y_{Np}	$y_{N.}$
Mean	$y_{.1}$	$y_{.2}$	⋯	$y_{.p}$	$y_{..}$

In the hand method, the row, column, and grand means of the subjects × occasions array are calculated and recorded. The partition of the total sum of squares is then calculated with these means according to the formulas in Table 7.1-2. The expected sums of squares in Table 7.1-2 have the same forms as in the analysis for the randomized block design (see Table 5.4-1): Note first that, in addition to the error variance, the expectation of the subject sums of squares contains the individual-difference component σ_α^2. This variance would in general be assumed positive and would not be tested. However, its unbiased estimate may be of interest and can be obtained from

$$\hat{\sigma}_\alpha^2 = \frac{\text{ssa} - \text{sse}/(p-1)}{p(N-1)}$$

Now note that the expectation of the occasion sum of squares includes the sum of squared deviations of the occasion effects about the occasion mean. Since equality of the occasion effects implies that this term vanishes, a test of the null hypothesis

$$H_{0(C)}: \gamma_1 = \gamma_2 = \cdots = \gamma_p$$

is provided by the variance ratio

$$F_C = \frac{\text{ssc}/(p-1)}{\text{sse}/(N-1)(p-1)}$$

Under the null hypothesis, F_C may be referred to the central F distribution on $p - 1$ and $(N - 1)(p - 1)$ degrees of freedom. Rejection of the null hypothesis implies that there is some additive effect in the response between occasions, possibly due to the treatment intervention.

Table 7.1-2 MIXED-MODEL ANALYSIS OF VARIANCE OF THE SUBJECTS × OCCASIONS REPEATED-MEASURES DESIGN (ONE-SAMPLE CASE)

Source of variation	df	Sums of squares	Expected sums of squares*
Constant	1	$\text{ssm} = Npy_{..}^2$	$\sigma^2 + p\sigma_\alpha^2 + \omega_\mu^2$
Subjects	$N - 1$	$\text{ssa} = p\sum_{i=1}^{N} y_{i.}^2 - \text{ssm}$	$(N-1)(\sigma^2 + p\sigma_\alpha^2)$
Occasions	$p - 1$	$\text{ssc} = N\sum_{k=1}^{p} y_{.k}^2 - \text{ssm}$	$(p-1)\sigma^2 + \omega_\gamma^2$
Subjects × occasions	$(N-1)(p-1)$	$\text{sse} = \text{sst} - \text{ssm} - \text{ssa} - \text{ssc}$	$(N-1)(p-1)\sigma^2$
Total	Np	$\text{sst} = \sum_{k=1}^{p}\sum_{i=1}^{N} y_{ik}^2$	

* $\omega_\mu^2 = Np(\mu + \gamma_.)^2$; $\omega_\gamma^2 = N\sum(\gamma_k - \gamma_.)^2$; $\gamma_. = \sum \gamma_k/p$.

In many applications, however, the existence of a general occasion effect is a foregone conclusion (as in Example 7.1-1), and the overall test is not of interest. What is required in that case is a more specific assessment of the trend over occasions. A widely used analysis for this purpose is a single-degree-of-freedom orthogonal polynomial decomposition of the occasion sum of squares. The procedure is identical to that of Sec. 5.2-5c, but is applied to the repeated measures rather than to experimental groups.

If the occasions are considered equally spaced, the orthogonal polynomials of Appendix B may be used.* The calculations consist simply of the matrix multiplication

$$\mathbf{u}_p = [u_0, u_1, \ldots, u_{p-1}]' = \mathbf{P}_p'\mathbf{y}. \qquad (7.1\text{-}3)$$

where $\mathbf{P}_p$ is the matrix of orthogonal polynomials of order p, and $\mathbf{y}.$ is the $p \times 1$ vector of occasion means from Table 7.1-1. The squares of the estimated orthogonal polynomial coefficients, exclusive of the constant, are then multiplied by N to obtain the single-degree-of-freedom partition of the occasion sum of squares shown in Table 7.1-3. These squares serve as the numerator of the F statistics

$$F_{C_1} = \frac{\text{ssc}_1}{\text{sse}/(N-1)(p-1)}$$

$$F_{C_2} = \frac{\text{ssc}_2}{\text{sse}/(N-1)(p-1)}$$

$$\cdots\cdots\cdots\cdots\cdots\cdots$$

$$F_{C_{(p-1)}} = \frac{\text{ssc}_{p-1}}{\text{sse}/(N-1)(p-1)}$$

each with 1 and $(N-1)(p-1)$ degrees of freedom. Starting with the last of these statistics and working back, we determine the degree of the polynomial trend by the

* Orthogonal polynomials for unequally spaced levels may be obtained by the method of Robson [1959] or Emerson [1968].

Table 7.1-3 ORTHOGONAL POLYNOMIAL RESOLUTION OF THE OCCASION SUM OF SQUARES FROM TABLE 7.1-2

Source	df	ss
Occasions		
Linear	1	$\text{ssc}_1 = Nu_1^2 = N\mathbf{p}_1'\mathbf{y}.\mathbf{y}'.\mathbf{p}_1$
Quadratic	1	$\text{ssc}_2 = Nu_2^2 = N\mathbf{p}_2'\mathbf{y}.\mathbf{y}'.\mathbf{p}_2$
⋯	⋯	⋯
$(p-1)$ic	1	$\text{ssc}_{p-1} = Nu_{p-1}^2 = N\mathbf{p}_{p-1}'\mathbf{y}.\mathbf{y}'.\mathbf{p}_{p-1}$
	$p-1$	

term where significance is first observed. These tests are stochastically independent, given the error variance estimate, and their joint Type I error may be set using (3.4-14) or (4.1-35). Once the degree of the polynomial is determined, the estimated coefficients may be recovered from $\mathbf{u}_p$ by the method of Sec. 5.2-5c. If the trend is curvilinear, a graph of the occasion means will aid in interpreting the occasion effects.

Other structuring of the repeated-measures dimension is possible. The measures may represent, for example, a factorial arrangement of treatment combinations applied to each subject. In the n-sample case, such designs are called *split-split plots*. Although they are amenable to conventional mixed-model analysis, there is some conceptual and computational advantage in formulating the analysis in multivariate terms. The discussion of these designs is therefore postponed until Sec. 7.2, where an example is presented. The present case of temporally ordered repeated measures is illustrated in the following example.

EXAMPLE 7.1-1 (*Mixed-model analysis of vocabulary growth*) Data for this example are drawn from test results on file in the Records Office of the Laboratory School of the University of Chicago. They consist of scores, obtained from a cohort of pupils at the eighth through eleventh grade level, on alternative forms of the vocabulary section of the Cooperative Reading Tests [Davis, 1950]. Since these data cover an age range in which physical growth is beginning to decelerate, it is of interest to inquire whether a similar deceleration can be observed in the acquisition of new vocabulary.

The Cooperative tests do not, of course, yield an estimate of actual vocabulary size, but they do provide a basis for estimating a vocabulary score on a scale with a common origin and unit. The method of computing these scaled scores, including calibration of the vocabulary items with an independent cross-sectional sample and application of a psychometric model, is described in Keesling, Bock, et al. [1974]. The resulting scaled scores, with origin and unit fixed arbitrarily, are shown for the longitudinal sample of 64 subjects in Table 7.1-4 (table entries are rounded from four decimal places).

Although individual growth curves of the latent scores can be examined in these data, attention will be confined in this example to the average vocabulary growth. Such an analysis effectively ignores the longitudinal aspect of the data, although it does benefit from its protection against secular changes in the composition of the sample. The plot of average scores versus grade shown in Fig. 7.1-1 suggests that the rate of increase is indeed decelerating in this population. Certainly, it would not be possible to construct a straight line which falls within one standard error (67 percent confidence interval) of the four means.

The impression of curvilinearity is confirmed in the trend analysis of these data. As the first step in this analysis, we compute the total and marginal sums of squares in Table 7.1-4 and apply the formulas in Table 7.1-2 to obtain the analysis of variance shown in Table 7.1-5. Table 7.1-5 is not primarily of interest for its test of occasion effects, which are not in doubt, but for the estimate of error variance

$$\hat{\sigma}^2 = \frac{\text{sse}}{(N-1)(p-1)} = \frac{154.97}{189} = .8199 \qquad (7.1\text{-}4)$$

which is required in the orthogonal polynomial trend analysis.

Table 7.1-4 SCALED VOCABULARY SCORES (LONGITUDINAL)

	Grade						Grade				
Subject	8	9	10	11	Mean	Subject	8	9	10	11	Mean
1	1.75	2.60	3.76	3.68	2.95	33	−.47	.93	1.30	.76	.63
2	.90	2.47	2.44	3.43	2.31	34	2.18	6.42	4.64	4.82	4.51
3	.80	.93	.40	2.27	1.10	35	4.21	7.08	6.00	5.65	5.73
4	2.42	4.15	4.56	4.21	3.83	36	8.26	9.55	10.24	10.58	9.66
5	−1.31	−1.31	−.66	−2.22	−1.38	37	1.24	4.90	2.42	2.54	2.78
6	−1.56	1.67	.18	2.33	.66	38	5.94	6.56	9.36	7.72	7.40
7	1.09	1.50	.52	2.33	1.36	39	.87	3.36	2.58	1.73	2.14
8	−1.92	1.03	.50	3.04	.66	40	−.09	2.29	3.08	3.35	2.15
9	−1.61	.29	.73	3.24	.66	41	3.24	4.78	3.52	4.84	4.10
10	2.47	3.64	2.87	5.38	3.59	42	1.03	2.10	3.88	2.81	2.45
11	−.95	.41	.21	1.82	.37	43	3.58	4.67	3.83	5.19	4.32
12	1.66	2.74	2.40	2.17	2.24	44	1.41	1.75	3.70	3.77	2.66
13	2.07	4.92	4.46	4.71	4.04	45	−.65	−.11	2.40	3.53	1.29
14	3.30	6.10	7.19	7.46	6.02	46	1.52	3.04	2.74	2.63	2.48
15	2.75	2.53	4.28	5.93	3.87	47	.57	2.71	1.90	2.41	1.90
16	2.25	3.38	5.79	4.40	3.96	48	2.18	2.96	4.78	3.34	3.32
17	2.08	1.74	4.12	3.62	2.89	49	1.10	2.65	1.72	2.96	2.11
18	.14	.01	1.48	2.78	1.10	50	.15	2.69	2.69	3.50	2.26
19	.13	3.19	.60	3.14	1.77	51	−1.27	1.26	.71	2.68	.85
20	2.19	2.65	3.27	2.73	2.71	52	2.81	5.19	6.33	5.93	5.06
21	−.64	−1.31	−.37	4.09	.44	53	2.62	3.54	4.86	5.80	4.21
22	2.02	3.45	5.32	6.01	4.20	54	.11	2.25	1.56	3.92	1.96
23	2.05	1.80	3.91	2.49	2.56	55	.61	1.14	1.35	.53	.91
24	1.48	.47	3.63	3.88	2.37	56	−2.19	−.42	1.54	1.16	.02
25	1.97	2.54	3.26	5.62	3.35	57	1.55	2.42	1.11	2.18	1.82
26	1.35	4.63	3.54	5.24	3.69	58	−.04	.50	2.60	2.61	1.42
27	−.56	−.36	1.14	1.34	.39	59	3.10	2.00	3.92	3.91	3.24
28	.26	.08	1.17	2.15	.92	60	−.29	2.62	1.60	1.86	1.45
29	1.22	1.41	4.66	2.62	2.47	61	2.28	3.39	4.91	3.89	3.62
30	−1.43	.80	−.03	1.04	.09	62	2.57	5.78	5.12	4.98	4.61
31	−1.17	1.66	2.11	1.42	1.00	63	−2.19	.71	1.56	2.31	.60
32	1.68	1.71	4.07	3.30	2.69	64	−.04	2.44	1.79	2.64	1.71
						Mean	1.14	2.54	2.99	3.47	2.53

Table 7.1-5 ONE-SAMPLE MIXED-MODEL ANALYSIS OF VARIANCE OF THE VOCABULARY SCALED SCORES

Source	df	ss	F	p
Constant term	1	ssm = 1,644.90		
Subjects	63	ssa = 873.85		
Occasions	3	ssc = 194.18	5.73	.0001
Subjects × occasions	189	sse = 154.97		
Total	256	sst = 2,867.90		

For purposes of the trend analysis, we normalize columns of the order-4 orthogonal polynomial matrix in Appendix B to obtain

$$\mathbf{P}_4 = \begin{bmatrix} .5 & -.67082 & .5 & -.22361 \\ .5 & -.22361 & -.5 & .67082 \\ .5 & .22361 & -.5 & -.67082 \\ .5 & .67082 & .5 & .22361 \end{bmatrix}$$

Premultiplying the 4×1 vector of column means from Table 7.1-4 by the transpose of this matrix, we obtain the orthogonal estimates shown in Table 7.1-6. The squares of these estimates $\times$ 64, exclusive of the constant term, are the numerators of the F ratios for linear, quadratic, and cubic trends shown in Table 7.1-7. The denominator in each case is the error estimate (7.1-4). The significant quadratic term, together with the negative sign of the corresponding estimated coefficient, shows that a deceleration is clearly in evidence in these data. In fact, the cubic term also reaches significance and suggests that the tendency for the deceleration to increase with age, which is apparent in Fig. 7.1-1, is also real. To the extent that the scaled scores reflect vocabulary size (see Keesling, Bock, et al. [1974]), the data support

Table 7.1-6 ESTIMATED ORTHOGONAL POLYNOMIAL COEFFICIENTS

Constant	5.0696
Linear	1.6652
Quadratic	−.4599
Cubic	.2230

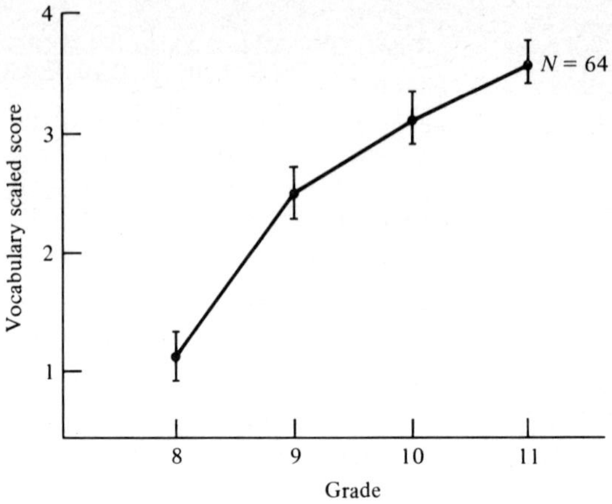

FIGURE 7.1-1
Average vocabulary scores of 64 pupils of the University of Chicago Laboratory School (longitudinal data).

the conclusion that vocabulary acquisition is slowing down as the subjects approach maturity. Further analysis of these data appears in Example 7.2-1.

7.1.2 Multivariate Analysis of Variance of Repeated Measurements: One-Sample Case*

From a multivariate point of view, we regard the p repeated measures for the ith subject as a p-component vector observation, for which the assumed model is

$$\mathbf{y}_i = \boldsymbol{\tau} + \boldsymbol{\epsilon}_i \qquad (7.1\text{-}5)$$

where $\boldsymbol{\tau}$ = the $p \times 1$ vector mean for occasions

$\boldsymbol{\epsilon}$ = a $p \times 1$ vector of sampling errors distributed $N(\mathbf{0},\boldsymbol{\Sigma})$ in the population of subjects

If the mixed-model assumptions hold, the vector mean has the composition

$$\boldsymbol{\tau} = \mu\mathbf{1} + \boldsymbol{\gamma}$$

* This section is based on the treatment in Bock [1963a] specialized to the one-sample case.

Table 7.1-7 ORTHOGONAL POLYNOMIAL DECOMPOSITION OF THE OCCASION SUM OF SQUARES

Source	df	ss	F	p
Occasions				
Linear	1	$ssc_1 = 177.47$	216.42	$<.0001$
Quadratic	1	$ssc_2 = 13.53$	16.50	$<.0005$
Cubic	1	$ssc_3 = 3.18$	3.88	.05

where $\gamma = [\gamma_1, \gamma_2, \ldots, \gamma_p]'$; otherwise, $\boldsymbol{\tau}$ is general. (If μ is arbitrary, these two interpretations of $\boldsymbol{\tau}$ cannot be distinguished.) Similarly, under the mixed model, $\boldsymbol{\epsilon}_i$ has the composition

$$\boldsymbol{\epsilon}_i = \alpha_i \mathbf{1} + [\epsilon_{ik}]$$

and is distributed $N(\mathbf{0},\boldsymbol{\Sigma}) = \sigma_\alpha^2 \mathbf{11}' + \sigma^2 \mathbf{I}$; otherwise, it is general.

The chief merit of the multivariate treatment of repeated measures, aside from computational convenience, is the validity of the analysis under both mixed-model and general assumptions. When the mixed model obtains, the univariate analysis of Sec. 7.1.1 is readily extracted from the multivariate computations. Where general assumptions are required and the mixed model fails, the multivariate analysis will give valid probability statements.

In the one-sample case the objective of both the mixed-model and the multivariate analysis is to characterize the occasion vector mean $\boldsymbol{\tau}$. The appropriate characterization depends upon the structure of the repeated-measures dimension. If the occasions correspond to points on a continuum (preferably equally spaced), a polynomial representation may be useful. If they correspond to a crossed and/or nested classification of treatments, a characterization in terms of treatment contrasts and interactions is indicated.

Let us consider first the polynomial representation, assuming the vector mean to have the composition

$$\begin{bmatrix} \tau_1 \\ \tau_2 \\ \vdots \\ \tau_p \end{bmatrix} = \beta_0 \begin{bmatrix} 1 \\ 1 \\ \vdots \\ 1 \end{bmatrix} + \beta_1 \begin{bmatrix} x_1 \\ x_2 \\ \vdots \\ x_p \end{bmatrix} + \beta_2 \begin{bmatrix} x_1^2 \\ x_2^2 \\ \vdots \\ x_p^2 \end{bmatrix} + \cdots + \beta_q \begin{bmatrix} x_1^q \\ x_2^q \\ \vdots \\ x_p^q \end{bmatrix} \qquad (7.1\text{-}6)$$

or
$$\underset{p\times 1}{\boldsymbol{\tau}} = \underset{p\times q}{\mathbf{X}}\ \underset{q\times 1}{\boldsymbol{\beta}}$$

where $x_1, x_2, \ldots, x_p$ are the p points on the continuum, and $q \leq p - 1$.

As we have seen in Sec. 5.2.5c, equally spaced points (possibly recoded) permit the polynomial reparameterization

$$\boldsymbol{\tau} = \mathbf{X}(\mathbf{T}^{-1})'\mathbf{T}'\boldsymbol{\beta} = \mathbf{PT}'\boldsymbol{\beta} = \mathbf{P}\boldsymbol{\gamma}^*$$

where $\mathbf{P}$ is the matrix of orthogonal polynomials, and the components of $\boldsymbol{\gamma}^*$ are the orthogonal polynomial coefficients. Thus, if the vector observations are transformed by $\mathbf{P}'$, (7.1-5) becomes

$$\mathbf{P}'\mathbf{y}_i = \mathbf{P}'\boldsymbol{\tau} + \mathbf{P}'\boldsymbol{\epsilon}_i = \boldsymbol{\gamma}^* + \boldsymbol{\epsilon}_i^*$$

and $\boldsymbol{\epsilon}^*$ is distributed $N(\mathbf{0},\boldsymbol{\Sigma}^* = \mathbf{P}'\boldsymbol{\Sigma}\mathbf{P})$.

The $p \times 1$ vector $\boldsymbol{\gamma}^*$ is then the population mean under the transformation, and its least-squares estimate is the transformed sample mean

$$\hat{\boldsymbol{\gamma}}^* = \frac{1}{N}\sum_{i=1}^{N} \mathbf{P}'\mathbf{y}_i = \mathbf{P}'\mathbf{y}.$$

The least-squares estimates of the coefficients of (7.1-6) can then be computed as

$$\hat{\boldsymbol{\beta}} = (\mathbf{T}^{-1})'\hat{\boldsymbol{\gamma}}^* \qquad (7.1\text{-}7)$$

Similarly, $\boldsymbol{\Sigma}^*$, the population covariance matrix under the transformation, is estimated from the corresponding transformation of the SSP matrix for subjects as shown in Table 7.1-8; that is,

$$\hat{\boldsymbol{\Sigma}}^* = \frac{\mathbf{P}'(\text{SSE})\mathbf{P}}{\mathbf{N} - 1} \qquad (7.1\text{-}8)$$

(The $N \times p$ matrix $\mathbf{Y}$ in Table 7.1-8 comprises the original observations in the form shown in the body of Table 7.1-1.)

The multivariate analysis under the orthogonal polynomial transformation, shown in Table 7.1-8, contains as a subset all the figures in Tables 7.1-2 and 7.1-3.

The first diagonal element in SSM*, namely,

$$N\mathbf{p}_0'\mathbf{y}_{.}\mathbf{y}_{.}'\mathbf{p}_0 = \frac{N\mathbf{1}'\mathbf{y}_{.}\mathbf{y}_{.}'\mathbf{1}}{p} = Npy_{..}^2$$

is just the constant term in Table 7.1-2. The remaining $p - 1$ diagonal elements in SSM*, namely, $\mathbf{p}_1'\mathbf{y}_{.}\mathbf{y}_{.}'\mathbf{p}_1, \mathbf{p}_2'\mathbf{y}_{.}\mathbf{y}_{.}'\mathbf{p}_2, \ldots, \mathbf{p}_{p-1}'\mathbf{y}_{.}\mathbf{y}_{.}'\mathbf{p}_{p-1}$ times N, are the terms of the orthogonal polynomial decomposition of the occasion sum of squares in Table 7.1-3.

Similarly, the first diagonal element of SSE* is the subject sum of squares from Table 7.1-2,

$$\mathbf{p}_0'(\mathbf{Y}'\mathbf{Y} - N\mathbf{y}_{.}\mathbf{y}_{.}')\mathbf{p}_0 = \frac{1}{p}(\mathbf{1}'\mathbf{Y}'\mathbf{Y}\mathbf{1} - N\mathbf{1}'\mathbf{y}_{.}\mathbf{y}_{.}'\mathbf{1}) = p\sum_{i=1}^{N} y_{i.}^2 - Npy_{..}^2 = \text{ssa}$$

while the sum of the remaining $p - 1$ elements in SSE* is the subject $\times$ occasions sum of squares. The latter assertion may be proved by writing

$$\text{ssa} + \text{sse} = \mathbf{p}_0'(\text{SSE})\mathbf{p}_0 + \text{tr}\,\mathbf{P}_1'(\text{SSE})\mathbf{P}_1 = \mathbf{P}'(\text{SSE})\mathbf{P}$$

Table 7.1-8 MULTIVARIATE ANALYSIS OF VARIANCE OF TRANSFORMED REPEATED MEASUREMENTS (ONE-SAMPLE CASE)

Source of dispersion	df	SSP ($p \times p$)	$\mathscr{E}$(SSP)
Constant	1	$\text{SSM}^* = \mathbf{P}'(\text{SSM})\mathbf{P}$ $= N\mathbf{P}'\mathbf{y}_{.}\mathbf{y}_{.}'\mathbf{P}$	$\mathbf{P}'[\boldsymbol{\Sigma} + N\boldsymbol{\tau}\boldsymbol{\tau}']\mathbf{P}$
Subjects within group	$N - 1$	$\text{SSE}^* = \mathbf{P}'(\text{SSE})\mathbf{P}$ $= \mathbf{P}'(\mathbf{Y}'\mathbf{Y} - N\mathbf{y}_{.}\mathbf{y}_{.}')\mathbf{P}$	$(N - 1)\mathbf{P}'\boldsymbol{\Sigma}\mathbf{P}$
Total	N	$\text{SST}^* = \mathbf{P}'\mathbf{Y}'\mathbf{Y}\mathbf{P}$	

where $\mathbf{P}_1$ consists of the last $p - 1$ columns of $\mathbf{P}$. Then, from (2.5-11),

$$\text{tr } \mathbf{P}'(\text{SSE})\mathbf{P} = \text{tr}(\text{SSE})\mathbf{PP}' = \text{tr}(\text{SSE})$$

(since $\mathbf{P}$ is orthonormal by columns), and

$$\text{tr}(\text{SSE}) = \text{tr}\,(\mathbf{Y}'\mathbf{Y} - N\mathbf{y}.\mathbf{y}'.) = \sum_{k=1}^{p} \sum_{i=1}^{N} y_{ik}{}^2 - N \sum_{k=1}^{p} y_{\cdot k}{}^2 = \text{ssa} + \text{sse}$$

Note that each of the components of the subjects $\times$ occasion sum of squares accounts for $N - 1$ degrees of freedom, thus verifying $(N - 1)(p - 1)$ as the df for error.

Table 7.1-9 contains all of the information required for a stepwise analysis to determine the polynomial of least degree capable of representing $\boldsymbol{\tau}$. The manner in which we use this information depends upon our assumptions about $\boldsymbol{\Sigma}$:

a Assumption I (mixed model)

$$\boldsymbol{\Sigma} = \sigma_\alpha{}^2\mathbf{11}' + \sigma^2\mathbf{I} \qquad (7.1\text{-}9)$$

If the sampling covariance matrix has the structure (7.1-9), the expected error sum of products after the orthogonal polynomial transformation is the diagonal matrix

$$(N - 1)\mathbf{P}'\boldsymbol{\Sigma}\mathbf{P} = (N - 1)\text{ diag}[p\sigma_\alpha{}^2 + \sigma^2, \sigma^2, \sigma^2, \ldots, \sigma^2]$$

In the sample, SSE* will, of course, show some departure from diagonality even when (7.1-9) holds for the population. To test the hypothesis that SSE* has arisen from a diagonal population matrix, we may test for no association in the correlation matrix computed from SSE*. The likelihood-ratio criterion for testing the hypothesis that $\mathbf{P}'\boldsymbol{\Sigma}\mathbf{P}$ is diagonal against a general alternative is the determinant of this correlation matrix:

$$\Lambda = |\text{corr}(\text{SSE*})| \qquad (7.1\text{-}10)$$

Table 7.1-9 COMPOSITION OF THE SSP MATRICES IN TABLE 7.1-8

Constant	df = 1					Squares in diagonal
	ssm				(symmetric)	Constant term
	ssmc_1^*	ssc_1^*				Linear occasion
SSM* =	ssmc_2^*	ssc_1c_2^*	ssc_2^*			Quadratic occasion
	⋯	⋯	⋯	⋯	⋯	⋯
	ssmc_{p-1}^*	$\text{ssc}_1\text{c}_{p-1}^*$	$\text{ssc}_2\text{c}_{p-1}^*$	⋯	ssc_{p-1}^*	$(p - 1)$ic occasion
Subjects within group	df = $N - 1$					
	ssa				(symmetric)	Subjects within group
	ssae_1^*	sse_1^*				Linear occasion $\times$ subjects within group
SSE* =	ssae_2^*	sse_1e_2^*	sse_2^*			Quadratic occasion $\times$ subjects within group
	⋯	⋯	⋯	⋯	⋯	⋯
	ssae_{p-1}^*	$\text{sse}_1\text{e}_{p-1}^*$	$\text{sse}_2\text{e}_{p-1}^*$	⋯	sse_{p-1}^*	$(p - 1)$ic occasion $\times$ subjects within group

Percentage points of the null distribution of (7.1-10) are well approximated by referring

$$\chi_A{}^2 = -\left(N - 1 - \frac{2p + 5}{6}\right) \ln \Lambda \qquad (7.1\text{-}11)$$

to the central χ^2 distribution on $p(p - 1)/2$ degrees of freedom. Significance of this χ^2 rejects the hypothesis that $\boldsymbol{\Sigma}$ has the structure specified in assumption I.

A further condition on (7.1-9) is that $\mathscr{E}(\mathsf{sse}_1^*) = \mathscr{E}(\mathsf{sse}_2^*) = \cdots = \mathscr{E}(\mathsf{sse}_{p-1}^*) = (N - 1)\sigma^2$. A statistical test of the hypothesis of a common population variance σ^2 may be carried out by applying one of the tests, for example, that of Pearson and Hartley [1958], for homogeneity of variance. A numerical example of this test and the preceding test of no association appears in Example 7.1-2. (Beckman and Tietjen, 1973).

If the orthogonal polynomial transformation does in fact yield the independent and similarly distributed error components implied by the mixed model, then the pooling of the corresponding error sums of squares to obtain the error estimate is justified by the fact that $\mathsf{sse}/\sigma^2 = (\mathsf{sse}_1^* + \mathsf{sse}_2^* + \cdots + \mathsf{sse}_{p-1}^*)/\sigma^2$ is distributed unconditionally as a central χ^2 on $(N - 1)(p - 1)$ degrees of freedom.

Furthermore, each diagonal element of $(1/\sigma^2)\mathsf{SSM}^*$ is also distributed under the null hypothesis as a central χ^2 on one degree of freedom; otherwise, it is a noncentral χ^2 with typical noncentrality parameter $N\gamma_h^{*2}/2\sigma^2$.

Thus, assumption I justifies the use of F statistics with sse as the denominator in a stepwise testing of the polynomial terms, beginning with the highest-degree term and working backward until a significant F is encountered. These single-degree-of-freedom tests are statistically independent, and the overall error rate may be calculated by (4.1-35). Except for the computational format, this is precisely the same analysis as the univariate mixed-model analysis.

b Assumption II

$$\mathbf{P}'\boldsymbol{\Sigma}\mathbf{P} = \operatorname{diag}[\mathbf{p}_0'\boldsymbol{\Sigma}\mathbf{p}_0, \mathbf{p}_1'\boldsymbol{\Sigma}\mathbf{p}_1, \ldots, \mathbf{p}_{p-1}'\boldsymbol{\Sigma}\mathbf{p}_{p-1}]$$

A slightly less restrictive assumption is that $\mathbf{P}'\boldsymbol{\Sigma}\mathbf{P}$ is diagonal [as may be verified with the likelihood-ratio test (7.1-11)], but not necessarily homogeneous in its last $p - 1$ diagonal elements. On this assumption, $\mathsf{sse}_1^*/\sigma_1{}^2, \mathsf{sse}_2^*/\sigma_2{}^2, \ldots,$ and $\mathsf{sse}_{p-1}^*/\sigma_{p-1}^2$ are each independently distributed as central χ^2's on $N - 1$ degrees of freedom. This means that variance ratios formed from corresponding diagonal elements in SSM^* and SSE^*, namely,

$$F_0 = \frac{\mathsf{ssm}}{\mathsf{ssa}/(N - 1)} \qquad \text{constant}$$

$$F_1 = \frac{\mathsf{ssc}_1^*}{\mathsf{sse}_1^*/(N - 1)} \qquad \text{linear}$$

$$F_2 = \frac{\mathsf{ssc}_2^*}{\mathsf{sse}_2^*/(N - 1)} \qquad \text{quadratic}$$

and $$F_{p-1} = \frac{\mathrm{ssc}^*_{p-1}}{\mathrm{sse}^*_{p-1}/(N-1)} \qquad (p-1)\text{ic}$$

are independently distributed as F on 1 and $N - 1$ degrees of freedom.

Thus, assumption II justifies a univariate treatment of terms in the polynomial analysis, provided the component error sums of squares are *not* pooled. When $p > 2$, the statistical tests under this assumption are necessarily less powerful than those of the mixed-model analysis because there are fewer denominator degrees of freedom, but, as is apparent in the F table (Appendix A), the loss of power becomes proportionally smaller as the number of subjects is increased.

Admittedly, assumption II may not be plausible for behavioral data, since any influence that might make the polynomial component error variances heterogeneous might also be expected to introduce correlation between components. The presence of a general correlation pattern among the measures would require an analysis based on an unrestricted assumption as follows:

c Assumption III

$$\mathbf{P}'\boldsymbol{\Sigma}\mathbf{P} \text{ general}$$

If the polynomial error components are correlated as well as heteroscedastic, the term-by-term F statistics under assumption II remain valid separately but are not independent. Formula (4.1-35) does not then apply, and the joint Type I error level of the several tests cannot readily be evaluated. Nevertheless, any subset of components can be tested jointly and exactly by one of the multivariate criteria discussed in previous chapters. Thus, for example, the hypothesis that the occasion effect is linear in time could be investigated by means of a joint test of the quadratic, cubic, etc., effects. This test would be performed by extracting the $(p - q - 1) \times (p - q - 1)$ submatrices SSM^*_{p-q} and SSE^*_{p-q}, say, from the lower right corner of SSM* and SSE*, respectively (where q is the degree of the hypothesized polynomial). Then the determinantal equation

$$|\mathrm{SSM}^*_{p-q} - \lambda \mathrm{SSE}^*_{p-q}| = 0$$

has one nonzero root λ_1, and $F_0 = t\lambda_1/r$, with

$$r = p - q - 1$$
$$s = 1$$
$$t = N - (p - q) + 1$$

may be referred to the F distribution on r and t degrees of freedom. Statistical significance in this test would be evidence that a polynomial of degree higher than q is needed to describe the trend over occasions. Calculations for this test are illustrated in the following example.

EXAMPLE 7.1-2 (*Multivariate analysis of the vocabulary-growth data: one-sample case*) Summary statistics for the one-sample multivariate analysis of the vocabulary-growth data are contained in the $p \times 1$ vector of sample means and the $p \times p$ sample covariance matrix, or, equivalently, the sample means, standard deviations, and correlations. Computed from the data of Table 7.1-4, these statistics are shown in the latter form in Table 7.1-10.

The transformation of the vector mean in Table 7.1-10 by the order-4 matrix of orthogonal polynomials (page 455) yields the coefficients already shown in Table 7.1-6. The polynomial occasion SSP matrix SSM*, which appears in Table 7.1-11, is obtained by multiplying the squares and cross products of these coefficients by $N = 64$.

Similarly, SSE*, the matrix for subjects within group in Table 7.1-11, may be computed from the statistics in Table 7.1-10 by first applying (3.3-14) to recover the sample covariance matrix $\hat{\Sigma}$, and then performing the calculation

$$\text{SSE}^* = (N - 1)\mathbf{P}'\mathbf{\Sigma}\mathbf{P}$$

In the present data, the SSE* matrix shows close conformity to mixed-model assumptions. The off-diagonal elements are small relative to the diagonal, and the last three diagonal elements are of the same magnitude. We may formally test the hypothesis of no association by applying (3.3-13) to convert SSE* into the correlation matrix

$$\text{corr}(\text{SSE}^*) = \begin{bmatrix} 1.00000 & & & (\text{symmetric}) \\ .01844 & 1.00000 & & \\ -.25480 & .25668 & 1.00000 & \\ -.10338 & -.06141 & -.08264 & 1.00000 \end{bmatrix} \tag{7.1-12}$$

and then computing the determinant of the matrix by one of the methods of Sec. 2.4 to evaluate (7.1-11). In this instance, the determinant of (7.1-12) is .845386, and

$$\chi^2 = -\left[63 - \frac{2(4) + 5}{6}\right] \ln .845386 = -(60.833333)(-.167962) = 10.22$$

Table 7.1-10 MEANS, STANDARD DEVIATIONS, AND CORRELATIONS OF THE VOCABULARY-GROWTH DATA IN TABLE 7.1-1 ($N = 64$)

Grade	Mean	SD	Correlation (symmetric)			
8	1.1379	1.8888	1.0000			
9	2.5420	2.0853	.8102	1.0000		
10	2.9876	2.1694	.8668	.7846	1.0000	
11	3.4718	1.9257	.7846	.7570	.8115	1.0000

Since the .05 critical value for χ^2 on $p(p - 1)/2 = 6$ degrees of freedom is 12.6, the hypothesis of no association is not rejected.

We may also test, by means of the F_{max} statistic of Pearson and Hartley [1966], the homogeneity-of-variance assumption for the three diagonal elements 50.43, 43.95, and 60.59. In this case, $F_{max} = 1.4$. Since the .05 critical value for three variances and 63 degrees of freedom is 1.85, there is no indication of heterogeneity. The vocabulary scaled scores are therefore entirely consistent with the assumption I error structure required for the mixed-model analysis.

The reader may verify that the univariate sums of squares in Tables 7.1-5 and 7.1-7 may be obtained from Table 7.1-11 as follows: The constant term is the first diagonal element of SSM*; the polynomial occasion squares in Table 7.1-7 are the remaining diagonal elements of SSM*. Similarly, the subjects sum of squares is the first diagonal element of SSE*; the subjects × occasions sum of squares is the sum of the remaining three elements of SSE*.

As an illustration of the analysis under assumption II, Table 7.1-11 also contains the F statistics computed from corresponding diagonal elements of SSM* and SSE*. The results for the linear and quadratic terms are essentially the same as in the mixed-model analysis in Table 7.1-7, but the result for the cubic term drops below the .05 level under the less restrictive assumption.

To illustrate the analysis under assumption III, let us perform a joint test of the quadratic and cubic departure from linear growth. For this purpose, we extract

Table 7.1-11 MULTIVARIATE ANALYSIS OF VARIANCE OF THE ORTHOGONAL POLYNOMIAL TRANSFORMED VOCABULARY-GROWTH DATA

Source	df	SSP (symmetric)				F	p
Constant	1						
Constant term		1,644.90					
Linear occasion		540.30	177.47			221.72	<.0001
Quadratic occasion		−149.22	−49.02	13.54		19.40	<.0001
Cubic occasion		72.34	23.76	−6.56	3.18	3.30	.074
Subjects within group	63						
Between subjects		873.85					
Linear error		3.87	50.43				
Quadratic error		−49.94	12.08	43.95			
Cubic error		−23.79	−3.39	−4.26	60.59		
Total	64						
Constant		2,518.75					
Linear		544.17	227.90				
Quadratic		−199.16	−36.94	57.49			
Cubic		48.55	20.37	−10.82	63.77		

the 2 × 2 submatrices in the lower right corners of SSM* and SSE* and solve the eigenproblem:

$$\left| \begin{pmatrix} 13.54 & -6.56 \\ -6.56 & 3.18 \end{pmatrix} - \lambda \begin{pmatrix} 43.95 & -4.26 \\ -4.26 & 60.59 \end{pmatrix} \right| = 0$$

The nonzero root proves to be $\lambda_1 = .3418$.

For $r = 4 - 1 - 1 = 2$, $s = 1$, and $t = 64 - 3 + 1 = 62$,

$$F_0 = \tfrac{1}{2}(62 \times .3418) = 10.59$$

Since the probability of obtaining this value of a central F on 2 and 62 degrees of freedom is less than .0002, the hypothesis of linearity is clearly rejected.

Other multivariate criteria, particularly the step-down F statistics, may also be employed for the joint test. In the present instance, the step-down F's and their p values are:

	F	p
Quadratic	19.40	.0001
Cubic	1.60	.2102

For a Type I error rate of .01 for the union to two independent F tests, the rate for the separate tests must be set at

$$\alpha = 1 - \sqrt{1 - .01} = .005$$

Since the probability of the F for the quadratic term is far below this value, the null hypothesis is definitively rejected. There is strong evidence for curvature of the time trend in vocabulary average growth.

7.1.3 Other Design Structures for the Repeated Measures

The polynomial analysis in Secs. 7.1.1 and 7.1.2 is prototypical of the treatment of any of the design structures that might be imposed on the repeated-measures dimension. The only modifications required in the analysis are (1) the substitution of the solution matrix for the particular design (computed by the methods of Sec. 5.3) for the orthogonal polynomial matrix used in the trend analysis, and (2) the appropriate pooling or joint testing of effects within subspaces of the model for the design on the repeated measures. Typical examples of other design structures are hierarchically ordered treatments and 2^n factorial combinations of treatments. For the former, the Helmert matrix provides a suitable transformation for the multivariate analysis: for the latter, the order-2^n Hadamard matrix serves this purpose. The following example illustrates the use of the Helmert transformation in the one-sample case. An application of a Hadamard transformation in connection with a 2-factorial design on the repeated measures appears in Example 7.2-3.

EXAMPLE 7.1-3 (*Soporific effects of scopolamine derivatives*) In his 1908 paper, Student illustrated the t test with data reported earlier by Cushny and Peebles [1905]. The data showed the effect of the hydrobromides of L-hyoscyamine, L-hyoscine, and DL-hyoscine (scopolamine) on the duration of sleep of 10 mental patients.* The drugs were given orally on alternate evenings, and the hours of sleep were compared with the intervening control night. Each of the drugs was tested in this manner a number of times in each subject. The results are shown in Table 7.1-12.

The questions which Cushny and Peebles raised concerning this data were: (1) Do the hypnotic drugs have any effect on duration of sleep? (2) Is the amine different from the alkaloid in effectiveness? (3) Is there any difference between the effectiveness of levo-hyosçine HBr and that of the racemic mixture (scopolamine)? The questions correspond to a set of hierarchical hypotheses of the type discussed in Sec. 5.2.5b. They can be answered by an analysis based on the orthogonal contrasts

* Student identified the first two drugs incorrectly as D-hyoscyamine HBr and L-hydroscyamine HBr. He did not make use of the data for scopolamine in his example.

Table 7.1-12 EFFECTS OF CERTAIN HYPNOTIC DRUGS ON DURATION OF SLEEP*

	Control (no hypnotic)		L-hyoscyamine HBr		L-hyoscine HBr		DL-hyoscine HBr	
Subject	No. of obs.	Ave. hours of sleep	No. of obs.	Ave. hours of sleep	No. of obs.	Ave. hours of sleep	No. of obs.	Ave. hours of sleep
1	9	.6	6	1.3	6	2.5	6	2.1
2	9	3.0	6	1.4	6	3.8	6	4.4
3	8	4.7	6	4.5	6	5.8	6	4.7
4	9	5.5	3	4.3	3	5.6	3	4.8
5	9	6.2	3	6.1	3	6.1	3	6.7
6	8	3.2	4	6.6	3	7.6	3	8.3
7	8	2.5	3	6.2	3	8.0	5	8.2
8	7	2.8	6	3.6	6	4.4	5	4.3
9	8	1.1	5	1.1	6	5.7	6	5.8
10	9	2.9	5	4.9	5	6.3	2	6.4

* Adapted from Cushny and Peebles [1905].

contained in the order-4 Helmert matrix

$$\mathbf{H}_4 = \begin{bmatrix} .5 & .86603 & 0 & 0 \\ .5 & -.28868 & .81650 & 0 \\ .5 & -.28868 & -.40825 & .70711 \\ .5 & -.28868 & -.40825 & -.70711 \end{bmatrix} \qquad (7.1\text{-}13)$$

When (7.1-13) is applied to the vector mean and covariance matrix of Table 7.1-13, the partition of squares and products shown in Table 7.1-14 is obtained.

The off-diagonal elements of the error (subjects within group) matrix in Table 7.1-14 are moderately large relative to the diagonal and might arouse suspicion of deviation from mixed-model assumptions. However, the sample size is small, and the chi-square statistic (7.1-11) on 6 degrees of freedom is not significant:

$$\chi^2 = 6.833333(.780899) = 5.34$$

Thus, independence of the Helmert transformed components is not rejected.

Table 7.1-13 MEANS, STANDARD DEVIATIONS AND CORRELATIONS OF THE DURATION-OF-SLEEP DATA IN TABLE 7.1-12 ($N = 10$)

Treatment	Mean	SD	Correlation (symmetric)			
1 Control	3.25	1.77843	1.00000			
2 L-hyoscyamine HBr	4.00	2.10239	.58604	1.00000		
3 L-hyoscine HBr	5.58	1.66120	.32384	.81128	1.00000	
4 D- hyoscine HBr	5.57	1.90791	.24578	.76427	.95194	1.00000

Table 7.1-14 MULTIVARIATE ANALYSIS OF VARIANCE OF THE HELMERT TRANSFORMED DURATION-OF-SLEEP DATA

Source		df	SSP (symmetric)				F	p
Constant		1						
Constant term	$H(0)$		846.3972					
Contrast	$H(1)$		−143.4135	24.3000			8.78	.016
Contrast	$H(2)$		−118.3101	20.0464	16.5375		15.23	.004
Contrast	$H(3)$		.6506	−.1102	−.0909	.0005	≈0	.960
Subjects within group		9						
Between subjects	$H(0)$		89.5016					
Error contrast	$H(1)$		−14.5493	24.9199				
Error contrast	$H(2)$		8.9957	5.8018	9.7774			
Error contrast	$H(3)$		−3.1503	2.7211	1.0811	1.6448		

There is, however, definite evidence that the error variances for the contrasts $H(1)$, $H(2)$, and $H(3)$ are not homogeneous:

$$F_{\max} = \frac{24.9199}{1.6448} = 15.3$$

The .01 critical value of $F_{\max}$ for three variances on 9 degrees of freedom is 8.5. Thus, we appear to be dealing with a situation where assumption II is appropriate, and the F statistics in Table 7.1-14 have been computed on that basis. It is clear from these statistics that, while the two forms of hyoscine HBr show no difference in activity, they are significantly ($p = .004$) different from L-hyoscyamine HBr in their effect on sleep. From the means in Table 7.1-13, we see that the hyoscines average 1.575 additional hours of sleep over the hyoscyamine and 2.325 over the control. On the basis of the data, there is no reason to prefer either L-hyoscyamine or L-hyoscine to scopolamine as a hypnotic drug.

As an estimate of the gain in hours of sleep due to scopolamine, we improve precision by using the figure 2.325 based on the average for the two forms of hyoscine. The standard error of this contrast may be estimated from the figures in Table 7.1-13 by the calculation

$$\mathrm{SE}(\mathbf{c}'\mathbf{y}.) = \frac{\sqrt{\mathbf{c}'\mathbf{DRDc}}}{N}$$

where $\mathbf{c}' = [-1, 0, \frac{1}{2}, \frac{1}{2}]$, $\mathbf{D}$ is the diagonal matrix of standard deviations, and $\mathbf{R}$ is the correlation matrix. The result is .669; hence, the 90 percent confidence interval on the hours gained is

$$\mathbf{c}'\mathbf{y}. \pm t_{.05}^{(9)}\,\mathrm{SE}(\mathbf{c}'\mathbf{y}.) = 2.22 \pm 1.51 \text{ hr}$$

This calculation emphasizes the fact that the normalized Helmert contrasts are in general useful only in the model-fitting (hypothesis-testing) phase of the analysis. For purposes of estimation and interpretation, some nonnormalized form of contrast such as the above is preferable.

Exercise 7.1-1 Derive the least-squares analysis for the data of Table 7.1-12, incorporating weights proportional to the number of observations represented in each data point. Perform the weighted analysis numerically, and compare the size of confidence intervals for treatment differences with those of the unweighted solution.

Exercise 7.1-2 Suppose the repeated measures are structured in a $C \times D$ cross-classification with two levels of C and two levels of D. Let the statistical model include independent random components attributable to the interaction of subjects with the C, D, and $C \times D$ repeated-measures effects. Show that this implies a population covariance matrix of the form

$$\boldsymbol{\Sigma} = \begin{bmatrix} v & a & b & c \\ a & v & c & b \\ b & c & v & a \\ c & b & a & v \end{bmatrix} \qquad (7.1\text{-}14)$$

Show that this matrix is reduced to diagonal form if the repeated measures are transformed by the Hadamard matrix of order 4.

Bargmann [1957] calls (7.1-14) the "equipredictability pattern." Why?

ANSWER See Bock [1960a].

Exercise 7.1-3 Suppose p repeated measures are generated by the Markov process

$$\begin{aligned} y_1 &= \rho y_0 + \varepsilon_1 \\ y_2 &= \rho y_1 + \varepsilon_2 \\ &\cdots\cdots\cdots\cdots \\ y_p &= \rho y_{p-1} + \varepsilon_p \end{aligned}$$

where the y_k are independent unit normal variates. Show that the covariance matrix of the measures has the form

$$\boldsymbol{\Sigma}\ \frac{1}{1-\rho^2}\begin{bmatrix} 1 & \rho & \rho^2 & \cdots & \rho^{p-1} \\ \rho & 1 & \rho & \cdots & \rho^{p-2} \\ \rho^2 & \rho & 1 & \cdots & \rho^{p-3} \\ \cdots & \cdots & \cdots & \cdots & \cdots \\ \rho^{p-1} & \rho^{p-2} & \rho^{p-3} & \cdots & 1 \end{bmatrix} \qquad (7.1\text{-}15)$$

Compare the above with the covariance matrix for a Winer process as described by Anderson [1960]. Compare the covariance patterns with those observed by Bilodeau [1961] for successive trials in a complex coordination task. (See Mukherjee [1966], Bock and Bargmann [1966].)

ANSWER See Kendall and Stuart [1961, Vol. II, page 472 ff].

7.2 ANALYSIS OF REPEATED MEASUREMENTS IN THE *n*-SAMPLE CASE

We now turn to the analysis of repeated-measures designs in which the subject way of classification is partitioned into a number of mutually exclusive groups. In a randomized experiment, the groups correspond to the treatments or treatment combinations. In a comparative study, they represent the subpopulations or varieties of subjects. In more elaborate designs, the groups arise from the crossing of treatment factors and varieties.

Whatever the details of the sampling structure, the important consideration is that there are n mutually exclusive groups of subjects, and that the subjects within groups are crossed by occasions. Thus, from the univariate point of view, the design formula is groups × subjects within groups × occasions. Specifically, if the numbers of subjects, which need not be equal, are $N_1, N_2, \ldots, N_n$ in the respective groups, the design formula becomes

$$n \rightarrow (N_1, N_2, \ldots, N_n) \times p \qquad (7.2\text{-}1)$$

When the details of the sampling structure are considered, the term n in (7.2-1) is replaced by the design formula for that structure. For example, if the subject groups correspond to the $n = ab$ treatment combinations generated by a levels in factor A and b levels in factor B, the formula becomes $a \times b \rightarrow (N_1, N_2, \ldots, N_{ab}) \times p$.

Similarly, if there is a design on the repeated measures, the term p may be elaborated in a crossed or nested structure.

The general form of the data for n-sample repeated measures is shown in Table 7.2-1. If a univariate analysis is contemplated, the marginal means are usually in-

Table 7.2-1 REPEATED-MEASURES DATA AND MARGINAL MEANS FOR THE GROUPS × SUBJECTS WITHIN GROUPS × OCCASIONS DESIGN

Groups	Subjects within groups	Occasions 1	2	⋯	p	Mean
1	1	y_{111}	y_{112}	⋯	y_{11p}	$y_{11\cdot}$
	2	y_{211}	y_{212}	⋯	y_{21p}	$y_{21\cdot}$
	⋯	⋯	⋯	⋯	⋯	⋯
	N_1	$y_{N_1 11}$	$y_{N_1 12}$	⋯	$y_{N_1 1p}$	$y_{N_1 1\cdot}$
Mean		$y_{\cdot 11}$	$y_{\cdot 12}$	⋯	$y_{\cdot 1p}$	$y_{\cdot 1\cdot}$
2	1	y_{121}	y_{122}	⋯	y_{12p}	$y_{12\cdot}$
	2	y_{221}	y_{222}	⋯	y_{22p}	$y_{22\cdot}$
	⋯	⋯	⋯	⋯	⋯	⋯
	N_2	$y_{N_2 21}$	$y_{N_2 22}$	⋯	$y_{N_2 2p}$	$y_{N_2 2\cdot}$
Mean		$y_{\cdot 21}$	$y_{\cdot 22}$	⋯	$y_{\cdot 2p}$	$y_{\cdot 2\cdot}$
⋯	⋯	⋯	⋯	⋯	⋯	⋯
n	1	y_{1n1}	y_{1n2}	⋯	y_{1np}	$y_{1n\cdot}$
	2	y_{2n1}	y_{2n2}	⋯	y_{2np}	$y_{2n\cdot}$
	⋯	⋯	⋯	⋯	⋯	⋯
	N_n	$y_{N_n n1}$	$y_{N_n n2}$	⋯	$y_{N_n np}$	$y_{N_n n\cdot}$
Mean		$y_{\cdot n1}$	$y_{\cdot n2}$	⋯	$y_{\cdot np}$	$y_{\cdot n\cdot}$
Grand mean		$y_{\cdot\cdot 1}$	$y_{\cdot\cdot 2}$	⋯	$y_{\cdot\cdot p}$	$y_{\cdot\cdot\cdot}$

cluded as shown. Data occur in this form when, for example, group differences in development or learning are studied or when "the subject is his own control." In developmental data, the rows in Table 7.2-1 represent measures obtained on each subject at successive points in time. In learning data, the rows represent scores on successive blocks of response trials. In experiments where the subject is his own control, the scores in each row correspond to the responses of the subject to the several treatments and may or may not be recorded in the actual time order of treatment administration. Notwithstanding these diverse interpretations of the repeated-measures dimension, we shall continue to identify the columns of Table 7.2-1 as *occasions*, although in particular applications *trials* or *treatments* might be more appropriate.

The statistical analysis of n-sample data is concerned with comparisons among the mean curves or profiles of the groups. The questions to be answered are: (1) Can the curves or profiles of the several groups be considered to be *parallel*? (2) If *parallel*, are they also *coincident*? (3) If *coincident*, are they also *constant*; i.e., do they show no change over occasions?

If the curves or profiles are *not* parallel, the problem becomes one of describing and interpreting differences in shape between groups. If they *are* parallel, only the occasion main effects and differences in overall level between groups need be discussed. If they are *coincident*, only the occasion main effects require interpretation.

As in the one-sample case, these questions can be investigated in a univariate analysis if the data conform to the mixed-model assumptions. If more general assumptions are required, the investigation can proceed in a multivariate analysis of the repeated measures. In fact, the multivariate treatment simplifies the problems of partitioning the sum of squares and choosing the correct error term to such an extent that it is advantageous to use the multivariate method routinely, and to extract the univariate analysis from it when mixed-model assumptions are warranted. For purposes of clarifying the relationships between the univariate and the multivariate analysis in the n-sample case, however, we shall present in Sec. 7.2.1 a conventional mixed-model analysis before turning to the multivariate treatment in Sec. 7.2.2. The mixed-model treatment presented here is identical to the analysis of "Type I" designs discussed by Lindquist. For more advanced mixed-model treatments, see Winer [1971].

7.2.1 Mixed-Model Analysis

In the n-sample case, the linear statistical model (7.1-1) generalizes to

$$y_{ijk} = \mu + a_{ij} + \beta_j + \gamma_k + (\beta\gamma)_{jk} + \epsilon_{ijk} \qquad (7.2\text{-}2)$$

where, in addition to the terms defined in (7.1-1), a_{ij} is the individual-difference component for subject i in group j; β_j is the overall effect of group j; $(\beta\gamma)_{jk}$ is the interactive effect of group j and occasion k; and ϵ_{ijk} is an error component specific to subject i in group j on occasion k.

The random components are assumed similarly and independently distributed in all groups. In particular, it is assumed that

$$\alpha \sim N(0,\sigma_\alpha^2) \qquad \text{and} \qquad \epsilon \sim N(0,\sigma^2)$$

Model (7.2-2) corresponds to a simple one-way design on the sample and yields the straightforward additive partition of sum of squares shown in Table 7.2-2. The expected sums of squares in Table 7.2-2, which we shall derive in connection with the multivariate treatment in Sec. 7.2.2, make quite clear the logic of the n-sample mixed-model analysis:

Note that the expected values corresponding to ssm, ssb, ssc, and ssbc contain sums of squares of linear functions of the original parameters. These functions arise in the orthogonal reparameterization of the model and have the usual blockwise triangular structure (see Sec. 5.3.5c). In particular, the term $\omega_{\beta\gamma}^2$ depends only upon the effects of the groups × occasions interaction. This term can be positive only if some of the interactive effects are nonzero. Thus, rejection of the null hypothesis,

$$H_{BC}\colon \omega_{\beta\gamma}^2 = 0$$

would be taken as evidence of differences between group mean curves or profiles that may be profitably examined in the data.

Table 7.2-2 GROUPS × SUBJECTS WITHIN GROUPS × OCCASIONS REPEATED-MEASURES DESIGN

Source	df	ss	$\mathscr{E}$(ss)*
Constant term	1	$\text{ssm} = Npy_{...}^2$	$\sigma^2 + p\sigma_\alpha^2 + \omega_\mu^2$
Groups	$n-1$	$\text{ssb} = p\sum N_j y_{.j.}^2 - \text{ssm}$	$(n-1)(\sigma^2 + p\sigma_\alpha^2) + \omega_\beta^2$
Occasions	$p-1$	$\text{ssc} = N\sum y_{..k}^2 - \text{ssm}$	$(p-1)\sigma^2 + \omega_\gamma^2$
Groups × occasions	$(n-1)(p-1)$	$\text{ssbc} = \sum\sum N_j y_{.jk}^2 - \text{ssb} - \text{ssc} - \text{ssm}$	$(n-1)(p-1)\sigma^2 + \omega_{\beta\gamma}^2$
Subjects within groups	$N-n$	$\text{ssa} = p\sum\sum y_{ij.}^2 - \text{ssb} - \text{ssm}$	$(N-n)(\sigma^2 + p\sigma_\alpha^2)$
Error (subjects within groups × occasions)	$(N-n)(p-1)$	$\text{sse} = \text{sst} - \text{ssm} - \text{ssb} - \text{ssc} - \text{ssbc} - \text{ssa}$	$(N-n)(p-1)\sigma^2$
Total	$pN = p\sum N_j$	$\text{sst} = \sum\sum\sum y_{ijk}^2$	

*
$$\omega_\mu^2 = Np[\mu + \gamma. + \beta. + (\beta\gamma)..]^2$$
$$\omega_\beta^2 = p\sum N_j[\beta_j - \beta. + (\beta\gamma)_j. - (\beta\gamma)..]^2$$
$$\omega_\gamma^2 = N\sum [\gamma_k - \gamma. + (\beta\gamma)._k - (\beta\gamma)..]^2$$
$$\omega_{\beta\gamma}^2 = \sum\sum N_j[(\beta\gamma)_{jk} - (\beta\gamma)_j. - (\beta\gamma)._k + (\beta\gamma)..]^2$$

$$\gamma. = \sum \gamma_k/p$$
$$\beta. = \sum N_j\beta_j/N$$
$$(\beta\gamma)_j. = \sum_k (\beta\gamma)_{jk}/p$$
$$(\beta\gamma)._k = \sum_j N_j(\beta\gamma)_{jk}/N$$
$$(\beta\gamma).. = \sum (\beta\gamma)._k/p = \sum N_j(\beta\gamma)_j./N$$

Furthermore, the composition of ω_β^2 and $\omega_{\beta\gamma}^2$ in Table 7.2-2 shows that, if $\omega_{\beta\gamma}^2$ is nonzero, the group and occasion main effects are confounded with the group-occasion interaction and cannot be separately tested or estimated. The presence of groups × occasions interaction implies that the population mean curves or profiles are not parallel. Their shape can therefore be described only with reference to specific groups, and their levels can be described only with reference to specific occasions.

Conversely, if $\omega_{\beta\gamma}^2$ is *null*, we may assume

$$\omega_\gamma^2 = N \sum (\gamma_k - \gamma.)^2 \qquad \text{and} \qquad \omega_\beta^2 = p \sum (\beta_j - \beta.)^2$$

Thus, in the absence of interaction, the hypotheses

$$H_C: \gamma_1 = \gamma_2 = \cdots = \gamma_p = \gamma.$$

$$H_B: \beta_1 = \beta_2 = \cdots = \beta_n = \beta.$$

are separately and independently testable. Rejection of H_C implies that the mean trend over occasions cannot be described by a horizontal line. Rejection of H_B implies that the groups have distinct, but possibly parallel, mean curves or profiles.

Finally, if occasion and group effects are assumed not only equal but *null*, then

$$\omega_\mu^2 = Np\mu^2$$

and the hypothesis

$$H_M: \mu = 0$$

is testable, provided the scale of measurement has a meaningful origin.

Turning now to ssa and sse, we see that the corresponding expectations depend, apart from known constants, only on the variances of the random components in (7.2-2). Equating expectations to observations, we obtain the unbiased estimates

$$\hat{\sigma}^2 + p\hat{\sigma}_\alpha^2 = \frac{\text{ssa}}{N - n} \qquad (7.2\text{-}3)$$

$$\hat{\sigma}^2 = \frac{\text{sse}}{(N - n)(p - 1)} \qquad (7.2\text{-}4)$$

On normal-distribution assumptions, the corresponding estimators are independent. On somewhat more general assumptions, they can be shown to be best unbiased quadratic estimators [Graybill, 1961].

From (7.2-3) and (7.2-4), we may obtain the unbiased estimate of the individual-difference variance:

$$\hat{\sigma}_\alpha^2 = \frac{\text{ssa} - \text{sse}/(p - 1)}{p(N - n)} \qquad (7.2\text{-}5)$$

This estimate is not necessarily constrained to be nonnegative. In certain applications, (7.2-5) can be interpreted as an estimate of a covariance, which can be negative [McHugh and Mielke, 1968].

The hypothesis

$$H_A: \sigma_\alpha^2 = 0$$

may be tested under normal assumptions by referring

$$F_A = \frac{\text{ssa}/(N - n)}{\text{sse}/(N - n)(p - 1)} \tag{7.2-6}$$

to the central F distribution on $N - n$ and $(N - n)(p - 1)$ degrees of freedom. In principle, a test of H_A is of interest as a preliminary to assuming σ_α^2 null and combining ssa and sse to obtain the best estimate of the common variance σ^2. However, in behavioral data it is unlikely that there will be no general individual-difference component, and we would ordinarily assume $\sigma_\alpha^2 > 0$ without testing. We may, however, be interested in estimating the variance components, using (7.2-4) and (7.2-5), and in expressing the relative magnitude of $\hat{\sigma}_\alpha^2$ in the form of the intraclass correlation coefficient $r = \hat{\sigma}_\alpha^2/(\hat{\sigma}_\alpha^2 + \hat{\sigma}^2)$.

The roles of ssa and sse in the error terms for the tests of H_{BC}, H_C, H_B, and H_M are also readily apparent from the expected sums of squares. Since the expectations of the numerator and denominator in the F statistic may differ only in the fixed term, the test statistics take the following form:

Hypothesis	F	df	
H_{BC}	$F_{BC} = \dfrac{\text{ssbc}/(n-1)(p-1)}{\text{sse}/(N-n)(p-1)}$	$(n-1)(p-1)/(N-n)(p-1)$	
H_B	$F_B = \dfrac{\text{ssb}/(n-1)}{\text{ssa}/(N-n)}$	$(n-1)/(N-n)$	(7.2-7)
H_C	$F_C = \dfrac{\text{ssc}/(p-1)}{\text{sse}/(N-n)(p-1)}$	$(p-1)/(N-n)(p-1)$	
H_M	$F_M = \dfrac{\text{ssm}}{\text{ssa}/(N-n)}$	$1/(N-n)$	

As in the one-sample case, there will be many applications in which more specific hypotheses may be entertained. In particular, where occasions represent equally spaced points on a continuum, the orthogonal polynomial resolution of the groups × occasions interaction and the occasion effect may lead to more powerful tests and more informative estimates. For this purpose, a polynomial single-degree-of-freedom partition of ssbc and ssc is required. The first step in the calculations is to compute the orthogonal estimates by means of the order-p matrix of orthogonal polynomials as follows:

Occasions: $\quad \mathbf{u}. = [u_{\cdot 0}, u_{\cdot 1}, \ldots, u_{\cdot p-1}]' = \mathbf{P}_p'\mathbf{y}_{\cdot\cdot}$

Groups × occasions: $\quad \mathbf{u}_j = [u_{j0}, u_{j1}, \ldots, u_{jp-1}]' = \mathbf{P}_p'\mathbf{y}_j - \mathbf{P}'\mathbf{y}_{\cdot\cdot}$

From these estimates, the partitioned sums of squares are computed as shown in Table 7.2-3.

The terms in the groups × occasions sum of squares provide the statistics

$$F_{BC_1} = \frac{\text{ssbc}_1/(n-1)}{\text{sse}/(N-n)(p-1)}$$

$$F_{BC_2} = \frac{\text{ssbc}_2/(n-1)}{\text{sse}/(N-n)(p-1)}$$

$$\cdots\cdots\cdots\cdots\cdots\cdots$$

$$F_{BC_{p-1}} = \frac{\text{ssbc}_{p-1}/(n-1)}{\text{sse}/(N-n)(p-1)}$$

each distributed in the null case as a central F with $n - 1$ and $(N - n)(p - 1)$ degrees of freedom. As usual, we determine the polynomial of least degree for the data by working back from the test of the $(p - 1)$ic term until a significant F is encountered. These stepwise tests are approximately independent in the null case, and (4.1-35) may be used to set the joint error rate.

If these tests indicate that a polynomial of degree q is required to describe the groups × occasions interactions, then any contrasts among the groups can presumably be described by a polynomial of this degree. For example, a degree-2 interaction would imply that the differences between groups, in addition to possible linear trend, are accelerating or decelerating with respect to occasions. In most cases, these relationships will be apparent in a plot of the group means versus occasions (see Example 7.2-1). The actual polynomial describing the contrast as a function of the time points can be recovered from contrasts of the orthogonal estimates by applying (7.1-7).

Table 7.2-3 ORTHOGONAL POLYNOMIAL PARTITION OF THE OCCASION AND GROUP × OCCASION SUM OF SQUARES FROM TABLE 7.2-2

Source	df	SS
Occasions		
Linear	1	$\text{ssc}_1 = Nu_{.1}^2 = N\mathbf{p}_1'\mathbf{y}_{..}\mathbf{y}_{..}'\mathbf{p}_1$
Quadratic	1	$\text{ssc}_2 = Nu_{.2}^2 = N\mathbf{p}_2'\mathbf{y}_{..}\mathbf{y}_{..}'\mathbf{p}_2$
⋯	⋯	⋯
$(p-1)$ic	$\frac{1}{p-1}$	$\text{ssc}_{p-1} = Nu_{.p-1}^2 = N\mathbf{p}_{p-1}'\mathbf{y}_{..}\mathbf{y}_{..}'\mathbf{p}_{p-1}$
Groups × occasions		
Linear	$n-1$	$\text{ssbc}_1 = \sum N_j u_{j1}^2 = \sum N_j \mathbf{p}_1'\mathbf{y}_{.j}\mathbf{y}_{.j}'\mathbf{p}_1 - \text{ssc}_1$
Quadratic	$n-1$	$\text{ssbc}_2 = \sum N_j u_{j2}^2 = \sum N_j \mathbf{p}_2'\mathbf{y}_{.j}\mathbf{y}_{.j}'\mathbf{p}_2 - \text{ssc}_2$
⋯	⋯	⋯
$(p-1)$ic	$\frac{n-1}{(n-1)(p-1)}$	$\text{ssbc}_{p-1} = \sum N_j u_{jp-1}^2 = \sum N_j \mathbf{p}_{p-1}'\mathbf{y}_{.j}\mathbf{y}_{.j}'\mathbf{p}_{p-1} - \text{ssc}_{p-1}$

Where the group × occasion effects can be assumed null, a similar polynomial resolution of ssc may be useful in characterizing the overall occasion effect. The calculations are the same as in the one-sample case except that the transformation is applied to the grand means for occasions and the subjects within groups × occasions sum of squares provides the error term. The F statistics on $n - 1$ and $(N - n)(p - 1)$ degrees of freedom are

$$F_{C_1} = \frac{\text{ssc}_1}{\text{sse}/(N - n)(p - 1)}$$

$$F_{C_2} = \frac{\text{ssc}_2}{\text{sse}/(N - n)(p - 1)}$$

$$\cdots\cdots\cdots\cdots\cdots\cdots$$

$$F_{C_{p-1}} = \frac{\text{ssc}_{p-1}}{\text{sse}/(N - n)(p - 1)}$$

The coefficients of the polynomial are estimated by applying (7.1-7) to the occasion orthogonal estimates.

EXAMPLE 7.2-1 (*Sex differences in vocabulary growth*) The common observation that girls complete their physical growth earlier than boys raises the question of whether the same is true of the development of abilities as, for example, verbal ability measured by vocabulary scores. The data in Table 7.2-4 provide an opportunity for answering this question: the 36 first-listed subjects are boys, and the remainder are girls. The mean vocabulary-scaled scores for the two sexes are listed in Table 7.2-4 and plotted in Fig. 7.2-1. The two curves appear rather similar in shape, but there is some suggestion of greater deceleration in the curve for girls.

Table 7.2-4 VOCABULARY-SCALED SCORE GROUP MEANS AND WITHIN-GROUP CORRELATIONS AND STANDARD DEVIATIONS

		Grade			
	N	8	9	10	11
Boys	36	1.1410	2.3749	2.8797	3.5408
Girls	28	1.1340	2.7568	3.1263	3.3831
Correlations df = 62					
		1.0000			
		.8138	1.0000		
		.8684	.7839	1.0000	
		.7852	.7646	.8158	1.0000
Standard deviations		1.9040	2.0933	2.1832	1.9395

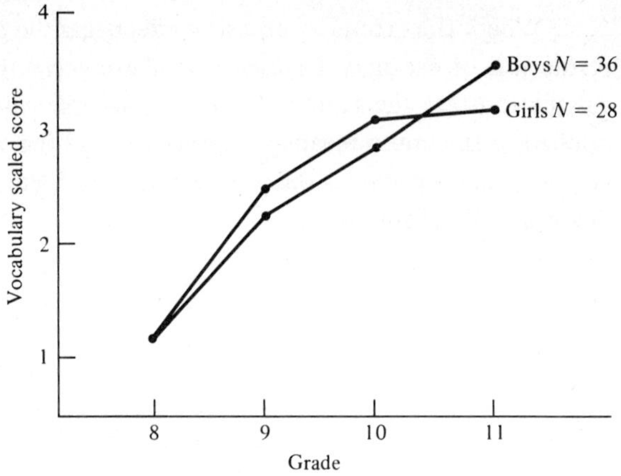

FIGURE 7.2-1
Average vocabulary scores of boys and girls in a cohort from the University of Chicago Laboratory School (longitudinal data).

To check on the significance of this effect, we may adopt mixed-model assumptions and test the hypothesis that the curves for the two sexes are parallel. The relevant format for the analysis of variance appears in Table 7.2-2. The corresponding numerical results are shown in Table 7.2-5.

Computing the F statistic for sex × occasions from (7.2-7), we find no evidence rejecting the hypothesis that the growth curves are parallel in the population. A test that the curves are coincident is therefore justified. Computing the between-group F statistic, we find no evidence of any real difference between the curves for boys and girls.

Our hypothesis that vocabulary growth in girls is decelerating faster than in

Table 7.2-5 MIXED-MODEL ANALYSIS OF VARIANCE OF SEX EFFECTS IN THE VOCABULARY-SCALED SCORES

Source	df	ss	F	p
Constant	1	ssm = 1,644.90		
Sex	1	ssb = .85	.06	>.5
Occasions	3	ssc = 194.18		
Sex × occasions	3	ssbc = 2.79	1.12	>.1
Subjects within groups	62	ssa = 873.00		
Occasions × subjects within groups	186	sse = 152.17		
Total	256	sst = 2,867.90		

boys is not tested specifically in this analysis, however. For a specific and, hence, more powerful test, let us partition sex × occasion sum of squares into orthogonal polynomial components and test the quadratic term. Performing this resolution as in Table 7.2-3, we obtain the squares shown in Table 7.2-6 and compute corresponding F statistics with occasions × subjects within groups as the error term. The statistic for quadratic effect now shows some slight evidence ($p < .1$) that sex influences deceleration. In fact, if we were to make the directional hypothesis that girls decelerate faster than boys, the observed F would be significant ($p < .05$). The result is certainly strong enough to suggest further investigation.

7.2.2 Multivariate Analysis of Variance of Repeated Measurements in the *n*-Sample Case

We now regard each row in the body of Table 7.2-1 as a p-variate observation that, for the ith subject in the jth group, we represent by

$$\mathbf{y}_{ij} = \boldsymbol{\tau} + \boldsymbol{\theta}_j + \boldsymbol{\epsilon}_{ij} \qquad (7.2\text{-}8)$$

where $\boldsymbol{\tau}$ = the vector defined as in (7.1-5)

$\boldsymbol{\theta}_j$ = the $p \times 1$ vector effect for the population from which the jth group of subjects was drawn

$\boldsymbol{\epsilon}_j$ = a $p \times 1$ vector of sampling errors assumed to be distributed as $N(\mathbf{0},\boldsymbol{\Sigma})$ in each of the populations

It is important to understand that the subscript i in (7.2-8) refers to a subject *within* the jth group. Thus, subscripts 11 and 12, for example, identify distinct subjects.

The multivariate analysis of variance of repeated measures under (7.2-8) differs from the one-sample case only in the interpolation of the between-groups source of

Table 7.2-6 REPEATED-MEASURES POLYNOMIAL TREND ANALYSIS OF SEX DIFFERENCES IN VOCABULARY GROWTH

Source	df	ss	F	p
Sex × occasions				
Linear	1	$ssbc_1$ = .27	.33	
Quadratic	1	$ssbc_2$ = 2.47	3.02	$<.1$
Cubic	1	$ssbc_3$ = .05	.06	
		2.79		
Occasions × subjects within sex	186	ssc = 152.17		

dispersion. The partition of the sum of squares and products for this analysis appears in Table 7.2-7. In the discussion concerning Table 7.2-7, the matrix **P** will be regarded as the order-p matrix of orthogonal polynomials, but it could be any $p \times p$ solution matrix (see Example 7.2-2).

The derivation of the expected sums of squares and products in Table 7.2-7 is straightforward:

$$\begin{aligned}
\mathscr{E}(\mathsf{SST}^*) &= \mathbf{P}'\mathscr{E}(\mathsf{SST})\mathbf{P} = \mathbf{P}' \sum\sum \mathscr{E}[(\boldsymbol{\tau} + \boldsymbol{\theta}_j + \boldsymbol{\epsilon}_{ij})(\boldsymbol{\tau} + \boldsymbol{\theta}_j + \boldsymbol{\epsilon}_{ij})']\mathbf{P} \\
&= \mathbf{P}'[\textstyle\sum N_j(\boldsymbol{\tau} + \boldsymbol{\theta}_j)(\boldsymbol{\tau} + \boldsymbol{\theta}_j)' + N\boldsymbol{\Sigma}]\mathbf{P} \\
\mathscr{E}(\mathsf{SSM}^*) &= \mathbf{P}'\mathscr{E}(\mathsf{SSM})\mathbf{P} = N\mathbf{P}'\mathscr{E}[(\boldsymbol{\tau} + \boldsymbol{\theta}. + \boldsymbol{\epsilon}..)(\boldsymbol{\tau} + \boldsymbol{\theta}. + \boldsymbol{\epsilon}..)']\mathbf{P} \\
&= N\mathbf{P}'\left[(\boldsymbol{\tau} + \boldsymbol{\theta}.)(\boldsymbol{\tau} + \boldsymbol{\theta}.)' + \frac{1}{N^2}\sum\sum \mathscr{E}(\boldsymbol{\epsilon}_{ij}\boldsymbol{\epsilon}'_{ij})\right]\mathbf{P} \\
&= \mathbf{P}'[N(\boldsymbol{\tau} + \boldsymbol{\theta}.)(\boldsymbol{\tau} + \boldsymbol{\theta}.)' + \boldsymbol{\Sigma}]\mathbf{P} \\
\mathscr{E}(\mathsf{SSB}^*) &= \mathbf{P}'\mathscr{E}(\mathsf{SSB})\mathbf{P} = \mathbf{P}'\{\textstyle\sum N_j\mathscr{E}[(\boldsymbol{\tau} + \boldsymbol{\theta}_j + \boldsymbol{\epsilon}._j)(\boldsymbol{\tau} + \boldsymbol{\theta}_j + \boldsymbol{\epsilon}._j)'] \\
&\qquad\qquad - \mathscr{E}(\mathrm{SSM})\}\mathbf{P} \\
&= \mathbf{P}'\Bigg[N\boldsymbol{\tau\tau}' + \boldsymbol{\tau}\textstyle\sum N_j\boldsymbol{\theta}'_j + \sum N_j\boldsymbol{\theta}_j\boldsymbol{\tau}' + \Sigma N_j\boldsymbol{\theta}_j\boldsymbol{\theta}'_j - N\boldsymbol{\tau\tau}' \\
&\qquad - N\boldsymbol{\tau\theta}'. - N\boldsymbol{\theta}.\boldsymbol{\tau}' - N\boldsymbol{\theta}.\boldsymbol{\theta}'. + \sum N_j \sum \frac{1}{N_j^2}\mathscr{E}(\boldsymbol{\epsilon}_{ij}\boldsymbol{\epsilon}'_{ij}) - \boldsymbol{\Sigma}\Bigg]\mathbf{P} \\
&= \mathbf{P}'(\textstyle\sum N_j\boldsymbol{\theta}_j\boldsymbol{\theta}'_j - N\boldsymbol{\theta}.\boldsymbol{\theta}'. + n\boldsymbol{\Sigma} - \boldsymbol{\Sigma})\mathbf{P} \\
&= \mathbf{P}'[\textstyle\sum N_j(\boldsymbol{\theta}_j - \boldsymbol{\theta}.)(\boldsymbol{\theta}_j - \boldsymbol{\theta}.)' + (n-1)\boldsymbol{\Sigma}]\mathbf{P}
\end{aligned}$$

Table 7.2-7 MULTIVARIATE ANALYSIS OF VARIANCE OF TRANSFORMED REPEATED MEASUREMENTS (n-SAMPLE CASE)

Source	df	SSP ($p \times p$)	$\mathscr{E}$(SSP)*
Constant	1	$\mathrm{SSM}^* = \mathbf{P}'(\mathrm{SSM})\mathbf{P}$ $= N\mathbf{P}'\mathbf{y}..\mathbf{y}'..\mathbf{P}$	$\mathbf{P}'[\boldsymbol{\Sigma} + N(\boldsymbol{\tau} + \boldsymbol{\theta}.)(\boldsymbol{\tau} + \boldsymbol{\theta}.)']\mathbf{P}$
Between groups	$n - 1$	$\mathrm{SSB}^* = \mathbf{P}'(\mathrm{SSB})\mathbf{P}$ $= \mathbf{P}'\left(\sum_{j=1}^{n} N_j\mathbf{y}._j\mathbf{y}'._j - \mathrm{SSM}\right)\mathbf{P}$	$\mathbf{P}'\left[(n-1)\boldsymbol{\Sigma} + \sum_{j=1}^{n} N_j(\boldsymbol{\theta}_j - \boldsymbol{\theta}.) \cdot (\boldsymbol{\theta}_j - \boldsymbol{\theta}.)'\right]\mathbf{P}$
Subjects within groups	$(N - n)$	$\mathrm{SSW}^* = \mathbf{P}'(\mathrm{SSW})\mathbf{P}$ $= \mathbf{P}'(\mathrm{SST} - \mathrm{SSB} - \mathrm{SSM})\mathbf{P}$	$(N - n)\mathbf{P}'\boldsymbol{\Sigma}\mathbf{P}$
Total	$N = \sum_{j=1}^{n} N_j$	$\mathrm{SST}^* = \mathbf{P}'(\mathrm{SST})\mathbf{P}$ $= \mathbf{P}'\sum_{j=1}^{n}\sum_{i=1}^{N_j} \mathbf{y}_{ij}\mathbf{y}'_{ij}\mathbf{P}$	

* $\boldsymbol{\theta}. = \sum_{j=1}^{n} N_j\boldsymbol{\theta}_j/N$

$$\begin{aligned}\mathscr{E}(\mathsf{SSW}^*) &= \mathbf{P}'\mathscr{E}(\mathsf{SST} - \mathsf{SSB} - \mathsf{SSM})\mathbf{P}' \\ &= \mathbf{P}'[N\boldsymbol{\tau}\boldsymbol{\tau}' + N\boldsymbol{\tau}\boldsymbol{\theta}'_. + N\boldsymbol{\theta}_.\boldsymbol{\tau}' + \sum N_j\boldsymbol{\theta}_j\boldsymbol{\theta}'_j - \sum N_j\boldsymbol{\theta}_j\boldsymbol{\theta}'_j \\ &\qquad + N\boldsymbol{\theta}_.\boldsymbol{\theta}'_. - N\boldsymbol{\tau}\boldsymbol{\tau}' - N\boldsymbol{\tau}\boldsymbol{\theta}'_. \\ &\qquad - N\boldsymbol{\theta}_.\boldsymbol{\tau}' - N\boldsymbol{\theta}_.\boldsymbol{\theta}'_. + N\boldsymbol{\Sigma} - (n-1)\boldsymbol{\Sigma} - \boldsymbol{\Sigma}]\mathbf{P} \\ &= (N - n)\mathbf{P}'\boldsymbol{\Sigma}\mathbf{P}\end{aligned}$$

As we have seen in Sec. 7.1, the effect of the transformation **P** is to decompose the SSP matrices into sums of squares and products for the constant, between groups, and subjects within groups as shown in Table 7.2-8. Since the sums of squares in the mixed-model analysis arise from the diagonal elements in Table 7.2-7, the expected sums of squares in Table 7.2-2 are easily derived by introducing the mixed-model specifications for $\boldsymbol{\tau}$, $\boldsymbol{\theta}_j$, and $\boldsymbol{\Sigma}$.

Returning to the interpretation of Table 7.2-7, we note that, as in the one-sample case, the statistical tests applied to Table 7.2-7 depend upon the assumed error structure. If the mixed-model structure is assumed, the univariate tests described in 7.2-1 may be performed by extracting the diagonal elements from the respective SSP matrices (Table 7.2-8) and computing sums of squares as follows:

$$\begin{aligned}\text{ssm} &= \text{ssm} \\ \text{ssc} &= \text{ssc}_1 + \text{ssc}_2 + \cdots + \text{ssc}_{p-1} \\ \text{ssb} &= \text{ssb} \\ \text{ssbc} &= \text{ssbc}_1 + \text{ssbc}_2 + \cdots + \text{ssbc}_{p-1} \\ \text{ssa} &= \text{ssa} \\ \text{ssa} &= \text{ssac}_1 + \text{ssac}_2 + \cdots + \text{ssac}_{p-1}\end{aligned}$$

The univariate tests of significance, either for overall occasion and group × occasion effects, or for each polynomial term in these effects separately, are then carried out with sse as the denominator. The test of overall group effect is, of course, carried out with ssa as the denominator. If we move to the less restrictive assumption of $\mathbf{P}'\boldsymbol{\Sigma}\mathbf{P}$ diagonal, we then test each polynomial effect separately with respect to its own error estimate. For the overall group effect corresponding to the zeroth-degree polynomial, the F statistic is the same as in the mixed-model analysis. For groups × occasion interaction corresponding to polynomials of degree 1 through $p - 1$, the F statistics are

$$\begin{aligned}F_{BC_1} &= \frac{\text{ssbc}_1/(n-1)}{\text{ssac}_1/(N-n)} \\ F_{BC_2} &= \frac{\text{ssbc}_2/(n-1)}{\text{ssac}_2/(N-n)} \\ &\cdots\cdots\cdots \\ F_{BC_{p-1}} &= \frac{\text{ssbc}_{p-1}/(n-1)}{\text{ssac}_{p-1}/(N-n)}\end{aligned} \qquad (7.2\text{-}9)$$

each on $n - 1$ and $N - n$ degrees of freedom.

In the absence of any group × occasion interaction, the polynomial trend for all the data can be tested in the same manner as in the one-sample case. The power of these tests will, of course, be increased if the group × occasion interaction and error sums of squares are pooled, but in cases where the interaction degrees of freedom are small relative to the error degrees of freedom, the loss of power if pooling is omitted will not be appreciable.

Finally, the assumption of a general error structure will necessitate multivariate tests of the polynomial effects. These tests may encompass all $p - 1$ degrees of freedom for trend, or may be confined to the $p - q - 1$ terms remaining if a $q < p$ degree trend is considered given. For the sake of generality, let us assume the latter, since it includes the former when $q = 0$. For the test of the group × occasion interaction, we extract the $(p - q - 1) \times (p - q - 1)$ submatrices SSB^*_{p-q} and SSE^*_{p-q} from the lower right corners of SSB* and SSE*, respectively. We then find the $\min(n - 1, p - q - 1)$ nonzero roots of

$$|\mathrm{SSB}^*_{p-q} - \lambda \mathrm{SSE}^*_{p-q}| = 0 \qquad (7.2\text{-}10)$$

and compute one of the multivariate test statistics of Sec. 3.4. In the case of the generalized F, the tabular arguments required are

$$r = |n - p + q| + 1$$
$$s = \min(n - 1, p - q - 1)$$
$$t = N - n - p + q + 2$$

Table 7.2-8 ORTHOGONAL POLYNOMIAL PARTITION OF SUM OF SQUARES AND PRODUCTS (n-SAMPLE CASE)

						Diagonal elements
Constant df = 1						
	ssm				(symmetric)	Constant (general mean)
	spmc_1	ssc_1				Linear occasions
SSM* =	spmc_1	$\mathrm{spc}_1\mathrm{c}_2$	ssc_2			Quadratic occasions
	....	....	....	....	....	....
	spmc_{p-1}	$\mathrm{spc}_1\mathrm{c}_{p-1}$	$\mathrm{spc}_2\mathrm{c}_{p-1}$	⋯	ssc_{p-1}	$(p - 1)$ic occasions
Between groups df = $n - 1$						
	ssb				(symmetric)	Between groups
	spbc_1	ssbc_1				Groups × linear occasions
SSB* =	spbc_2	$\mathrm{spc}_1\mathrm{c}_2$	ssbc_2			Groups × quadratic occasions
	....	....	....	....	....	....
	spbc_{p-1}	$\mathrm{spc}_1\mathrm{c}_{p-1}$	$\mathrm{spc}_2\mathrm{c}_{p-1}$	⋯	ssbc_{p-1}	Groups × $(p - 1)$ic occasions
Subjects within groups df = $N - n$						
	ssa				(symmetric)	Between subjects
	spaac_1	ssac_1				Subjects within groups × linear occasions
SSW* =	spaac_2	$\mathrm{spac}_1\mathrm{ac}_2$	ssac_2			Subjects within groups × quadratic occasions
	....	....	....	....	....	....
	spaac_{p-1}	$\mathrm{spac}_1\mathrm{ac}_{p-1}$	$\mathrm{sspac}_2\mathrm{ac}_{p-1}$	⋯	ssac_{p-1}	Subjects within groups × $(p - 1)$ic occasions

In the absence of group × occasion interaction, similar multivariate tests of overall trend in the data may be carried out as described for the one-sample case. If desired, the error and interaction SSP matrices may be pooled.

EXAMPLE 7.2-2 (*Multivariate analysis of sex differences in vocabulary growth*) The multivariate analysis of variance for the occasion and sex × occasion effects in the vocabulary-growth data is shown in Table 7.2-9. For the multivariate test of profile differences between sexes, we compute the one nonzero root λ_1 of

$$\left|\begin{pmatrix} .27 & \text{(symmetric)} & \\ .82 & 2.48 & \\ -.11 & -.36 & .05 \end{pmatrix} - \lambda \begin{pmatrix} 50.16 & & \text{(symmetric)} \\ 11.26 & 41.48 & \\ -3.29 & -3.81 & 60.54 \end{pmatrix}\right| = 0$$

We then have, as the quantities for computing the generalized F,

$$\lambda_1 = .0600$$
$$r = |1 - 3| + 1 = 3$$
$$s = \min(1,3) = 1$$
$$t = 62 - 4 + 2 = 60$$

The value $F_0 = 1.20$ which result is not significant, shows that the univariate and the general multivariate tests agree.

The test of differences in level between sexes is the same as in the univariate analysis and is also nonsignificant.

However, the specific test of the quadratic term for sex × occasions with respect to the quadratic term within groups gives

$$F = \frac{2.48}{41.48/62} = 3.71$$

The p value for a central F, on 1 and 62 degrees of freedom, equal to or greater than 3.70 is .06. Thus, the test under assumption II gives approximately the same p value as the mixed-model test of this term—a result which reflects the close conformity of the vocabulary data to mixed-model assumptions.

The multivariate test of quadratic and cubic trend over occasions may be carried out in these data in the same way as the one-sample analysis in Example 7.1-2. However, if subjects within sex × occasions is used as the error term, the generalized F will differ somewhat, owing to the exclusion of the between-sex variation from the error estimate.

Table 7.2-9 MULTIVARIATE ANALYSIS OF VARIANCE OF SEX EFFECTS IN THE ORTHOGONAL POLYNOMIAL TRANSFORMED VOCABULARY-GROWTH DATA

						Multivariate		Univariate	
Source	df	SSP (symmetric)				F_0	p	F	p
Constant	1								
Constant term		1,644.90							
Linear occasions		540.30	177.47					219.38	<.0001
Quadratic occasions		−149.22	−49.01	13.53		96.10	≪.01	20.24	<.0001
Cubic occasions		72.34	23.76	−6.56	3.18			3.26	.0760
Sex	1								
Between sexes		.85							
Sex × linear occasions		−.48	.27					.33	.56
Sex × quadratic occasions		−1.45	.82	2.48		1.20	>.05	3.71	.06
Sex × cubic occasions		.21	−.11	−.35	.05			.05	.81
Subjects within sex	62								
Between subjects		873.00							
Linear error		4.35	50.16						
Quadratic error		−48.49	11.26	41.48					
Cubic error		−24.00	−3.28	−3.91	60.54				
Total	64	(Same as Table 7.1-11)							

7.2.3 Multivariate Analysis of Repeated Measurements When There Is a Factorial Design on the Measures

In areas of behavioral research such as learning, perception, psycholinguistics, and related studies, wide use is made of repeated-measures designs in which factorial combinations of treatment conditions are presented to each subject. Because the number of treatment combinations a subject can tolerate is limited, the design on the repeated measures is usually confined to low-order factorials such as 2^2, 2×3, 2^3, or 3^2. It is essential in many applications to include alternative sequences of the within-subject treatment combinations as a main class of the sampling design. This will provide the possibility of assessing and controlling carryover effects from one treatment to another. Subjects are assigned at random to the alternative sequences. The main effects of the sequences, and the interaction with the repeated-measures factors, can then be investigated and, in favorable cases, the treatment effects unconfounded by sequence can be estimated. Sequence designs which balance position and order of the treatments are available [Wagenaar, 1969].

The multivariate analysis of variance for a factorial design on the measures is closely parallel to that of Sec. 7.2.2. If the repeated-measures dimension is, for example, 2^2, the four scores for each subject are transformed in the analysis by a solution matrix generated from the design formula

$$2 \times 2$$

The several contrasts represented in this transformation may then be tested individually or jointly in the manner of Example 7.2-1. The steps of the procedure are illustrated in Example 7.2-3. When alternative orders of treatments within subjects are used to assess sequence effects, it is essential that the order of treatment combinations represented in the subject's score vector agree with the natural order of the factorial arrangement implied in the design formula for the repeated-measures dimension. That is, the scores must be permuted from presentation order into the natural order before the analysis is begun.

The range of application of these types of repeated-measures designs may be expanded if, where many repeated-measures factors are to be investigated, the number of treatment combinations presented to a given subject is reduced by using one of the fractional factorial designs of Sec. 5.4.5. The orthogonal estimator for the incomplete design computed by the method of Sec. 5.3.5c provides the transformation matrix for the analysis of this type of repeated-measures data. The analysis of fractional factorial repeated measures has also been discussed under mixed-model assumptions by Wiley [1964].

EXAMPLE 7.2-3 (*A 2^2 factorial design on the repeated measures and on the subjects: a study of the Holzman inkblot technique*) The data in Table 7.2-10 are drawn from a study by Morter [1963] of the effects of requiring two responses per card when administering the Holtzman inkblot technique. Standard instructions for the Holtzman technique call for one response to each of 45 cards, but two responses are considered permissible if more productivity is desired. Morter was concerned about the comparability of first and second responses and undertook to investigate systematic differences between them, using a preadolescent population as a source of subjects.

Of the 10 Holtzman variables included in Morter's study, only Form Definiteness, corrected for rejections, and Form Appropriateness, also corrected, will be used

Table 7.2-10 SCALED SCORES FOR CORRECTED FORM DEFINITENESS (FD_c) AND FORM APPROPRIATENESS (FA_c) ON FIRST AND SECOND RESPONSES TO THE HOLTZMAN INKBLOT PLATES

		FD_c		FA_c	
Group	Subject	1	2	1	2
Grade 4					
High IQ	1	2	1	0	2
	2	−7	−2	−2	−5
	3	−3	−1	−3	−1
	4	1	1	0	−3
	5	1	−1	−4	−2
	6	−7	1	−4	−3
Low IQ	7	0	−4	−9	−7
	8	−1	−9	−9	−4
	9	−6	−6	3	−4
	10	−2	−4	−4	−5
	11	−2	−1	−3	−3
	12	−9	−9	−3	1
Grade 7					
High IQ	13	3	4	2	−3
	14	−1	−1	−3	−3
	15	2	2	2	0
	16	2	0	−2	0
	17	0	−1	2	2
	18	3	3	−4	−2
	19	−1	2	2	−1
	20	−3	−2	3	−2
Low IQ	21	−3	−2	5	2
	22	2	3	−2	−3
	23	2	4	1	3
	24	3	2	−5	−5
	25	−4	−3	−3	−3
	26	6	4	−9	−9
	27	2	1	−3	0
	28	−1	−4	−2	0
	29	−2	−1	2	−2
	30	−2	−4	−1	0

in this example. The results for these variables are reproduced in Table 7.2-10. Scores in Table 7.2-10 are in a scaled form obtained by normalizing each variable in the total sample and coding in one-digit scores. Subjects are classified by grade and IQ. (A further classification by sex which was included in the original study has been omitted here.)

These data may reasonably be considered to arise from a repeated-measures design in which there is a 2^2 factorial arrangement on the repeated measures and a 2^2 classification of subjects. The four measures on each subject characterize the quality of form in the percept. The first two measures represent the definiteness of form of the first and second responses. The second two measures represent the appropriateness of form of the first and second responses. The subjects, in turn, are cross-classified in two grades and two IQ levels.

The solution matrix for these 2^2 designs, constructed by the method of Sec. 5.3, is the Hadamard matrix of order 4:

$$\mathbf{Hd}_4 = \frac{1}{2}\begin{bmatrix} 1 & 1 & 1 & 1 \\ 1 & 1 & -1 & -1 \\ 1 & -1 & 1 & -1 \\ 1 & -1 & -1 & 1 \end{bmatrix} \tag{7.2-11}$$

This matrix is orthogonal as required. With respect to the *repeated measures* in the order shown in Table 7.2-10, column 1 of (7.2-11) characterizes general form quality (constant), column 2 contrasts definiteness and appropriateness (D-A), column 3 contrasts first response with second response (1-2), and column 4 is the interactive contrast (D-A) × (1-2).

With respect to the *sample subclasses* in the order shown in Table 7.2-11, column 1 of (7.2-11) characterizes the general mean, column 2 the grade effect (4-7), column 3 the IQ effect (H-L), and column 4, the grade by IQ interaction (4-7) × (H-L).

Table 7.2-11 GROUP MEANS AND WITHIN-GROUP CORRELATIONS AND STANDARD DEVIATIONS FOR HOLTZMAN FORM DEFINITENESS AND FORM APPROPRIATENESS

		FD_c		FA_c	
	N_J	1	2	1	2
Group means					
1 Fourth grade, high IQ	6	−2.1667	−.1667	−2.1667	−2.0000
2 Fourth grade, low IQ	6	−3.3333	−5.5000	−4.1667	−3.6667
3 Seventh grade, high IQ	8	.6250	.8750	.2500	−1.1250
4 Seventh grade, low IQ	10	.3000	0	−1.7000	−1.7000
Within-group (df = 26) correlations		1.0000			
		.6292	1.0000		
		−.4287	−.1371	1.0000	
		−.2598	−.2907	.5665	1.0000
Standard deviations		3.2114	2.6545	3.4265	2.7478

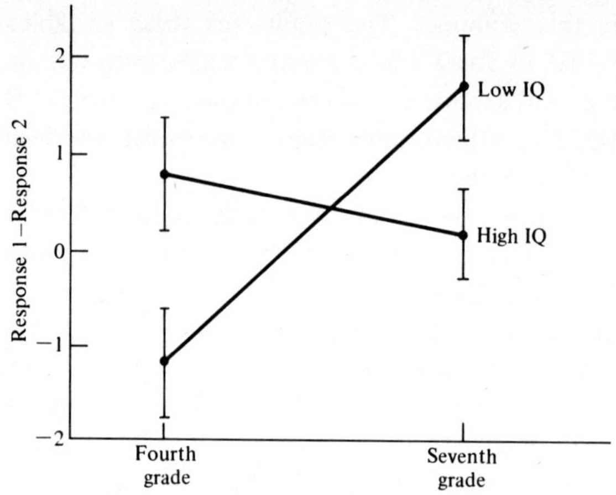

FIGURE 7.2-2
Difference in average Form Definiteness and Form Appropriateness for each grade and IQ level.

The within-group correlations and standard deviations shown in Table 7.2-11 are somewhat unusual in that the correlations between Form Appropriateness and Form Definiteness are negative. Nevertheless, the covariance structure is reduced to diagonal form under transformation by the Hadamard matrix. This is evident in the error sum of products in Table 7.2-12. The test of no association given by (7.1-11) does not reject the null hypothesis:

$$\chi^2 = -\left(26 - \frac{2 \times 4 + 5}{6}\right) \ln .85916 = -23.83333(-.15180) = 3.62$$

This value of χ^2 on $4 \times \frac{3}{2} = 6$ degrees of freedom is less than expectation and not significant.

The analysis might therefore proceed on the mixed-model assumptions. (Note that there is no need to pool degrees of freedom for the error estimates; hence, no test of homogeneity of variance is required.) In Table 7.2-12 we have, nevertheless, shown both the univariate and multivariate test statistics to illustrate the possibility of performing overall tests of profile differences. The analysis in Table 7.2-12 is nonorthogonal, the order of eliminating effects being determined by prior knowledge that older children show better form quality.

Examining first the Grade × IQ interaction with respect to the three repeated-measures contrasts jointly, we obtain a generalized F of 2.10, on 3 and 24 degrees of freedom, and corresponding p value of .13. Although not significant, this result is perhaps suggestive in view of its obvious origin in the (1-2) contrast. The cell means for this contrast, plotted in Fig. 7.2-2, show that the interaction, if real, results from

Table 7.2-12 NONORTHOGONAL MULTIVARIATE ANALYSIS OF VARIANCE OF TRANSFORMED HOLTZMAN FORM DEFINITENESS AND FORM APPROPRIATENESS*

Source	df	SSP (symmetric)				Multivariate		Univariate	
						F_0	p	F_0	p
Constant	1								
Constant term		226.87						1.57	.22
(D-A)		−83.87	31.01					.31	.58
(1-2)		−12.38	4.58	.68		.64	.59	.04	.57
(D-A) × (1-2)		6.87	−2.54	−.37	.21				
Grade	1								
Between grades		185.03						19.85	.002
Grade × (D-A)		49.17	13.07					.66	.42
Grade × (1-2)		16.73	4.44	1.51		.56	.64	.70	.41
Grade × (D-A) × (1-2)		−17.74	−4.72	−1.60	1.70			.31	.58
IQ	1								
Between IQ groups		74.35						7.98	.009
IQ (D-A)		4.13	.23					.01	.92
IQ (1-2)		−12.38	−.68	2.06		1.58	.22	.95	.34
IQ (D-A) × (1-2)		−34.85	−1.93	5.80	16.34			2.99	.10
Grade × IQ	1								
Grade × IQ interaction		18.58						1.99	.17
Grade × IQ × (D-A)		11.99	7.74					.39	.54
Grade × IQ × (1-2)		−13.44	−8.67	9.72		2.10	.13	4.49	.04
Grade × IQ × (D-A) × (1-2)		−7.43	−4.79	5.37	2.97			.54	.47
Within group	26								
Between subjects		242.40							
(D-A) error		−12.17	512.20						
(1-2) error		14.71	7.59	56.28					
(D-A) × (1-2) error		−19.60	82.24	−12.94	142.04				

* Total omitted.

the form quality for the Low-IQ group scoring higher on the second response in the fourth grade and higher on the first response in the seventh grade. A possible explanation is that the children with the least cognitive development are benefiting from practice in formulating the percept, whereas older and more intelligent children are able to attain a well-formed percept on the first try.

There is no other evidence in these data of differential effects of Grade or IQ on Definiteness versus Appropriateness (D-A), or on the interaction of (D-A) with first versus second response. The effect of IQ on overall Form Quality ($p = .009$) is quite apparent, however, and indicates an unmistakable cognitive component in the Form variable. Retaining the distinction between Definiteness and Appropriateness is apparently not essential when describing the relationship of Form with IQ.

Because the analysis in Table 7.2-12 is nonorthogonal, the test of Grade on overall Form Quality is confounded by the significant IQ effect and is not interpretable. However, the improvement in form of percept with age, which is readily apparent in the group means of Table 7.2-11, is too well known to require testing.

If the small interactive effect of Grade and IQ is ignored, the best estimates of the overall Grade and IQ effects may be obtained by fitting a rank-3 model. With respect to the function of the repeated measures defined by the first column of (7.2-11), the estimate of contrasts for Grade (4-7) and for IQ (High-Low) are -5.2450 ± 1.1396 and 3.1604 ± 1.1191, respectively. If estimates of mean effects over the repeated measures are preferred, the above values may be divided by 2 to obtain $-2.6225 \pm .5698$ and $1.5802 \pm .5596$, respectively.

Exercise 7.2-1 (*Learning trials*) The data in Table 7.2-13, taken from Lindquist [1953], represent scores of animals in a learning experiment. Examine the data for conformity to mixed-model assumptions. Perform an orthogonal polynomial analysis of differences between the mean learning curves for the two experimental conditions. Use both univariate and multivariate tests.

ANSWER Estimated orthogonal polynomial regression coefficients: Constant, 5.35, .313, −.800, −.156; Deprived-Satiated, 2.000, −.313, −.700, .268.

Exercise 7.2-2 The following are group means and within-group covariance matrices for repeated-measures data after transformation by the Hadamard matrix of order 4. Recover the original means and within-group correlations and standard deviations.

Means:

3.4615	−1.1731	3.9615	1.2115
4.4559	− .7353	3.9853	1.1177

Covariance matrix:

$$\begin{bmatrix} 9.1023 & & & \text{(symmetric)} \\ -.8928 & 4.9970 & & \\ -.8285 & .0595 & 5.2002 & \\ .10634 & .84167 & .2461 & 1.7812 \end{bmatrix}$$

ANSWER See Table 7.3-1.

Table 7.2-13 LINDQUIST'S DATA

Group	Subject	Successes in five trials 1	2	3	4	Mean
1 Deprived	1	3	3	3	3	3.0
	2	2	2	4	4	3.0
	3	4	2	5	5	4.0
	4	3	5	5	5	4.5
	5	2	5	5	4	4.0
	6	3	5	4	0	3.0
	7	1	3	4	1	2.25
	8	4	5	3	3	3.75
	9	3	5	4	2	3.50
	10	0	2	1	0	.75
Mean		2.5	3.7	3.8	2.7	3.175
2 Satiated	1	0	1	2	2	1.25
	2	3	0	2	2	1.75
	3	2	3	4	4	3.25
	4	0	1	2	1	1.0
	5	1	3	5	4	3.25
	6	1	2	3	2	2.0
	7	2	5	1	1	2.25
	8	2	3	4	2	2.75
	9	3	1	2	1	1.75
	10	3	2	2	3	2.50
Mean		1.7	2.1	2.7	2.2	2.175
Grand mean		2.1	2.9	3.25	2.45	2.675

7.3 ANALYSIS OF COVARIANCE OF REPEATED MEASUREMENTS

Correctly applied and interpreted, analysis of covariance and step-down tests are valuable adjuncts to the multivariate analysis of repeated measures presented in Sec. 7.2. The attendant interpretational problems, which are far from trivial, appear even in relation to the simplest pretest-intervention-posttest designs. In the interest of clarity, we begin the discussion of these procedures in this limited context.

Let the pretest score of individual i in group j be y_{ij1}, and the posttest score y_{ij2}. In these terms, the analysis of Sec. 7.2 may be viewed as a univariate analysis of variance of the *simple gain score* $y_{ij2} - y_{ij1}$. Strictly speaking, it is the normalized gain $(1/\sqrt{2})(y_{ij2} - y_{ij1})$ that appears in the analysis, but this has no effect other than to change the scale of the estimates; the test statistics, which are scalefree, are unaffected. Note also that the univariate analysis of gain scores is equivalent to the familiar t test for group differences in paired data (see Kurtz [1963]).

The analysis of gains is not, however, the only means of handling pretest-posttest data. From the discussion in Sec. 5.5, it is clear that we also have the possibility of performing an analysis of covariance of the posttest, using the pretest as the covariate. Provided the covariance structure of the measures is homogeneous among groups (which is always assumed in multivariate analysis of variance), the assumptions of analysis of variance are necessarily met and the analysis can proceed. In general, however, the result will differ numerically from that obtained in the analysis of gains. The gains analysis may yield a significant between-groups effect, while the analysis of covariance does not, and vice versa. The question of which technique to apply to given data is therefore a matter of consequence that must be resolved before the analysis begins. The issue has been presented forcibly by Lord [1967], who poses the following paradox in the interpretation of group comparisons.

7.3.1 Lord's Paradox

Suppose a large university obtains measurements, at the beginning and end of the school year, of the weight of each student who takes his meals in the university dining halls. When the resulting data are classified by sex of student, their scatter plot takes the form shown schematically in Fig. 7.3-1. The 45° line represents equality of weights in September and June. The ellipses of concentration represent the presumably bivariate normal distribution of weight on the two occasions.

Suppose two statisticians analyze these data for differences in weight gain of men versus women. The first statistician analyzes simple gain scores and concludes that "as far as these data are concerned, there is no evidence of any interesting effect of the school diet (or of anything else) on student weight; in particular, there is no evidence of any differential effect on the two sexes, since neither group shows any systematic change."

The second statistician, on the other hand, decides to do an analysis of covariance.

> 'After some necessary preliminaries, he determines that the slope of the regression line of final weight on initial weight is essentially the same for the two sexes. This is fortunate since it makes possible a fruitful comparison of the intercepts of the regression lines . . . . He finds that the difference between the intercepts is statistically highly significant. The second statistician concludes . . . that the [men] showed significantly more gain in weight than the [women] when proper allowance is made for differences in initial weight between the two sexes.'*

As they are stated, the conclusions of the two statisticians are contradictory, and some form of paradox seems implied. On closer inspection, however, it is seen that these alternative methods of analyzing the data are actually directed toward

* From Lord [1967].

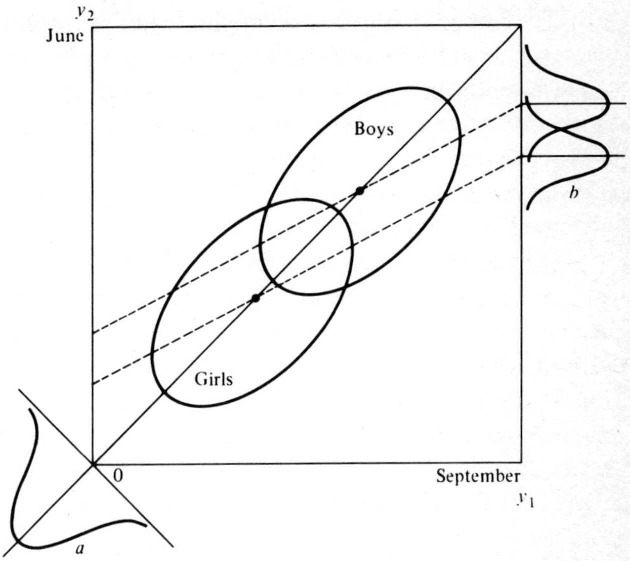

FIGURE 7.3-1
Distribution of gains (a) unconditional and (b) conditional on initial score.

different inferential problems. Moreover, each method provides the correct solution of the problem to which it is relevant.

These inferential problems may be described briefly as *unconditional* and *conditional*, respectively. The first statistician correctly analyzes gain scores to answer the unconditional question, "Is there a difference in the average gain in weight of the populations?" For the data of Fig. 7.3-1, the answer to this question is, "No, there is no difference in average gain represented by the two sexes."

At the same time, the second statistician correctly employs analysis of covariance to answer the conditional question, "Is a man expected to show a greater weight gain than a woman, given that they are initially of the same weight?" For the data in Fig. 7.3-1, the answer to this question is, "Yes, the man will be expected to gain more, for if he is initially of the same weight as the woman, he is either underweight and will be expected to gain, or the woman is overweight and will be expected to lose." Because the regression lines are parallel, this expectation is independent of the given initial weight.

The conditional inference refers only to the distribution of final weight given initial weight, and says nothing about the average weight gain in the populations from which the given subjects are drawn. The paradox in the original statement of the conclusions stems from the ambiguous phrase "when proper allowance is made for the differences in initial weight between the two sexes." The paradox vanishes when the phrase "conditional on initial weight" is substituted with the understanding that conditional statements do not refer to averages in the population as a whole.

These distinctions are brought out clearly in Fig. 7.3-1. The unconditional distribution of normalized gains is obtained by projecting the bivariate distributions on an axis perpendicular to the 45° line to obtain the marginal distribution of gains. Since the marginal distributions of gains in the two groups are identical, there is no difference in average gain.

The conditional distributions of final weight, given initial weight, on the other hand, are the distributions at any given ordinate. On the assumption of bivariate normality, the conditional distributions are similar for all ordinates and take the form shown at the right. These distributions are obviously distinct for the two groups, with the male group having the higher mean at all initial weights.

The conclusion of the conditional inference can be stated in other terms—namely, that relative to weight gains, male and female subjects cannot be regarded as having been drawn from the same population even when all subjects have the same initial weight. Thus, it is essential to take account of sex of subject as well as initial weight when predicting final weight. Analysis of covariance used in this way indicates whether a qualitative independent variable (sex) should be incorporated in a linear statistical model which already contains a quantitative independent variable (initial weight).

7.3.2 Analysis of Gains versus Analysis of Covariance

The method of analysis which is appropriate in a given application depends both upon the sampling procedure and the inferential objective. *Analysis of gains* is appropriate if, and only if:

1 The subjects are drawn randomly (or in a probability sample) from defined populations.

2 The purpose of the study is to compare these populations with respect to average gain, trend, or other intrasubject contrast.

An application where these conditions are largely met is the study of sex differences in rate of vocabulary acquisition which we discussed in Sec. 7.2. The sampling assumption is reasonable because, in a school that includes all children in a stable community, the boys and girls in a given grade at any random time are essentially a random sample of the children produced by that community. Since it is meaningful to compare these populations with respect to average rate of vocabulary growth (which has obvious implications for terminal vocabulary size), an analysis of gains is warranted.

Analysis of covariance of final score given initial score is also justified for samples from specified preexisting populations if the purpose of the study is to determine whether a difference between the group mean final scores can be attributed to a within-

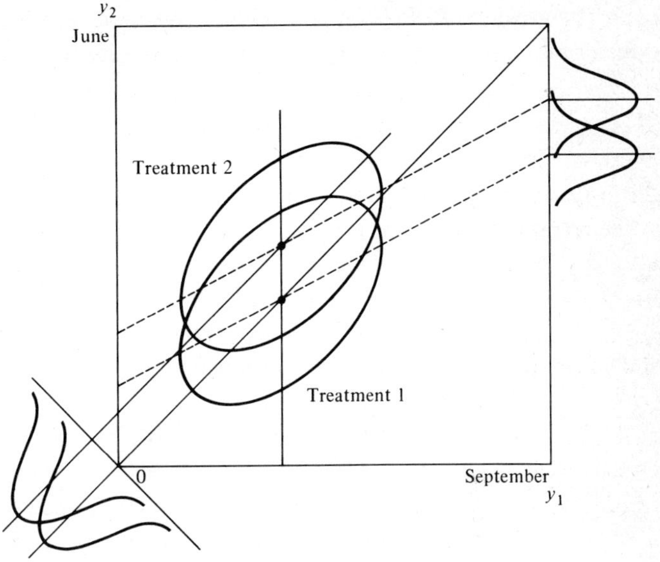

FIGURE 7.3-2
An experiment with random assignment to treatments.

group relationship between initial and final score. This is simply another way of asking whether the qualitative distinction between populations is required in addition to the observed differences in initial score in order to predict final score. As such, it is the legitimate purpose served by analysis of covariance in Lord's example.

Turning now to situations where a conditional analysis is preferable or mandatory, we have:

a Experiments in which subjects are assigned randomly to treatment groups In this case, analysis of gains and analysis of covariance are directed toward the same inferential problem, but analysis of covariance is in general more powerful and should be routinely used. These facts are apparent in Fig. 7.3-2,* which depicts the result of a simple randomized experiment. Because of the random assignment of subjects to treatments, the initial means of the treatment groups are equal. Both marginal distributions of normalized gains and the conditional distributions show that treatment 2 exceeds treatment 1, but the difference in the conditional postscore means relative to conditional variance is greater than the difference of average unconditional gains relative to its variance. Thus, a statistical test of treatment differences is more powerful in the conditional distributions, and analysis of covariance is indicated.

* The score distributions may not actually be bivariate normal in this case, but the interpretation of the regression effects is unchanged.

The greater efficiency of analysis of covariance can be shown formally: Let the transformation to normalized gain scores for treatments 1 and 2 be

$$\begin{bmatrix} v_1 \\ v_2 \end{bmatrix} = \frac{1}{\sqrt{2}}[1, -1]\begin{bmatrix} y_{11} & y_{21} \\ y_{12} & y_{22} \end{bmatrix}$$

and assume that the repeated measures are distributed with means μ, μ_1, and μ, μ_2, in the respective treatment groups, and with common covariance matrix

$$\begin{bmatrix} 1 & \rho \\ \rho & 1 \end{bmatrix}$$

Then the difference in normalized gains is distributed with mean

$$\mathscr{E}(v_1 - v_2) = \frac{1}{\sqrt{2}}[\mu_1 - \mu - (\mu_2 - \mu)] = \frac{1}{\sqrt{2}}(\mu_1 - \mu_2)$$

and variance

$$\mathscr{V}(v_1 - v_2) = \tfrac{1}{2}[2(1 - \rho) + 2(1 - \rho)] = 2(1 - \rho)$$

Now, assume that the regression of postscore on prescore is

$$\mu_2^* = \mu_2 + \rho(y_1 - \mu_1)$$

The conditional difference in postscores given prescore is then distributed with mean

$$\mathscr{E}(y_{22} - y_{12} \mid y_1) = \mu_2 + \rho(y_1 - \mu_1) - [\mu_1 + \rho(y_1 - \mu_1)] = \mu_2 - \mu_1$$

and with variance

$$\mathscr{V}(y_{22} - y_{12} \mid y_1) = (1 - \rho^2) + (1 - \rho^2) = 2(1 - \rho^2)$$

(see Sec. 3.3.5).

Since $1 + \rho$ is less than 2 when $\rho < 1$, the ratio of conditional means to standard deviation

$$\frac{\mu_2 - \mu_1}{\sqrt{2(1 - \rho^2)}} = \frac{\mu_2 - \mu_1}{\sqrt{2(1 + \rho)(1 - \rho)}} \tag{7.3-1}$$

is in general greater than the ratio of unconditional means to standard deviation

$$\frac{1}{\sqrt{2}}\frac{\mu_2 - \mu_1}{\sqrt{2(1 - \rho)}} = \frac{\mu_2 - \mu_1}{\sqrt{4(1 - \rho)}} \tag{7.3-2}$$

Thus, we may express the relative efficiency of unconditional to conditional analysis as the ratio of the expressions under the radical on the right in (7.3-1) and (7.3-2); i.e., as

$$\frac{2(1 + \rho)(1 - \rho)}{4(1 - \rho)} = \frac{1 + \rho}{2} \tag{7.3-3}$$

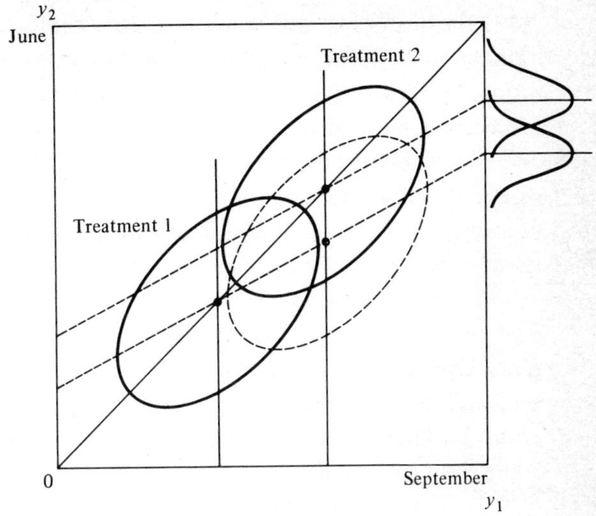

FIGURE 7.3-3
An experiment with biased assignment to treatment 2.

The ratio (7.3-3) shows that, when $\rho = 1$, the analyses are equally efficient (and numerically identical); when $\rho = 0$, the analysis of gains is only half as efficient as analysis of covariance (which is then equivalent to an analysis of postscores only); and when $\rho = -1$, the gains for the two groups have exactly the same mean, and the efficiency of the gains analysis falls to zero. This result illustrates precisely the line of reasoning which led Fisher [1967, page 272 ff] to introduce analysis of covariance (see also Fisher [1966]).

The other case to be considered is

b Experiments in which subjects are assigned to treatment groups with bias relative to the initial score This case is depicted schematically in Fig. 7.3-3. The distribution (which need not actually have the density contour shown) for the biased group is indicated by the dashed ellipse. Note that, because it is drawn from the original population, treatment group 2 necessarily has the same pretreatment regression line and conditional distribution as treatment group 1. If the effect of the treatment is to move the mean upward in group 2, without changing the slope of the regression line or the variance of the conditional distribution, an analysis of covariance with initial score as covariate will lead to the correct inference that response to treatment 2 is greater than that to treatment 1, independent of initial score. Thus, the analysis of covariance of the repeated measures, under the stated assumptions, provides a valid test of the treatment effects even though the assignment of subjects is not random relative to initial score.

In the educational literature especially, this logic has been applied, often indiscriminately, to justify the use of analysis of covariance as a substitute for randomization. Typically, the practice is to introduce an instructional innovation in one or more classrooms and to compare the results with those of control classrooms, possibly in another school. Usually the assignment of classrooms to treatment and control is determined by teacher cooperation or administrative convenience. It is then necessary to allow for initial differences in ability between classrooms, and an analysis of covariance of posttreatment scores is performed with some measure of initial ability, such as IQ, as covariate.

The risk in this use of analysis of covariance is aptly illustrated by Lord's example. Suppose the groups in Fig. 7.3-1 represent two experimental dietary regimens, and, due to failure to randomize, group 2 contains relatively more boys than group 1. Then an analysis of covariance with initial weight as covariate would lead to the erroneous conclusion that treatment 2 produced greater weight gains than treatment 1. The error would be incurred because, in addition to initial weight, the assignment was biased by sex, and, as we have seen, sex is a relevant factor in weight gain among subjects of the same initial weight.

Campbell and Erlebacher [1970] have pointed out that a precisely parallel situation arises in attempts to evaluate gains due to compensatory education in lower-class populations. Because randomization is considered impractical, the investigators seek a control group among children who are not enrolled in the compensatory program. Unfortunately, such children tend to be from somewhat higher social-class populations and have relatively greater educational resources. If a technique such as analysis of covariance, blocking, or matching (on initial ability) is used to compare treatment and control groups, the posttest scores will regress toward their population means and spuriously cause the compensatory program to appear ineffective or even harmful. Such results may be dangerously misleading if they are permitted to influence educational policy.

The lesson to be learned from these examples is clearly that, in behavioral experimentation, there is no substitute for randomization. It is unfortunate that this rule is so often ignored, for if investigators were willing to exert themselves, no substitute would be needed. In the compensatory-education studies, for example, randomized experiments are possible because the programs are usually oversubscribed. This permits random selection of children who will immediately be admitted to the program as opposed to those who will be admitted at a later time when facilities become available. Pretesting of both groups at selection and admission time should provide a basis for a rigorous analysis of the treatment effect in the first-admitted group. That randomized educational experiments are, in fact, possible is amply demonstrated by numerous examples in this text (Example 5.2-1, Exercise 5.3-4) and in the literature (Walberg and Welch [1967]; Welch, Walberg, and Watson [1971]; Busse et al. [1971]).

7.3.3 Step-down Tests of Transformed Repeated Measures

The step-down F tests discussed in Sec. 6.2.3 are equivalent to a series of univariate analyses of covariance in which the dependent variables are successively shifted to the role of independent variables. If the dependent variables remaining at a given stage show no significant departure from the null hypothesis, the variables shifted up to that point are judged sufficient for the linear discriminant functions associated with that hypothesis. It is quite analogous to the use of stepwise regression analysis in deleting independent variables that fail to contribute to prediction.

Employed in this way, step-down tests have special relevance for the multivariate approach to the analysis of repeated measurements. Under case III assumptions, they provide conditional tests of trends and contrasts of the repeated-measures effects. Thus, in an orthogonal polynomial resolution of group differences in trend, the step-down tests aid in determining whether higher-degree terms in the between-groups trend can be attributed to relationships to lower-degree terms in the within-group variation. Similarly, when there is a factorial design on the repeated measures, the tests indicate, for example, whether between-groups differences in interactive effects can be attributed to within-group relationships with main effects or the constant term.

An example of this use of step-down tests appears in a study, conducted by the School Mathematics Study Group, of the effects of textbook content on mathematics achievement [Carry, 1970]. In this study, schools were the sampling unit, and school means (for one or more classrooms) were the primary data. Since in certain areas of mathematics (especially geometry) there is known to be some disparity in performance between boys and girls [Werdelin, 1961], it was thought important to test for interaction between textbook and sex of student. The design adapted was therefore split plots, represented by the boys' and the girls' mean scores within school, and a classification of the whole plots (schools) into textbook groups.

In considering alternative models for this type of data, let us denote respectively by y_{ij1} and y_{ij2} the means for boys and girls in the ith school of the jth textbook group. Then the fixed terms in the possible models are

$$\underset{i}{\mathscr{E}}\,[y_{ij1}, y_{ij2}] = [\mu,\mu] + [\beta_j,\beta_j] + [\gamma_1,\gamma_2] + [(\alpha\beta)_{j1},(\alpha\beta)_{j2}] \tag{7.3-4}$$

$$\underset{i}{\mathscr{E}}\,[y_{ij1}, y_{ij2}] = [\mu,\mu] + [\beta_j,\beta_j] + [\gamma_1,\gamma_2] \tag{7.3-5}$$

$$\underset{i}{\mathscr{E}}\,[y_{ij1}, y_{ij2}] = [\mu,\mu] + [\beta_j,\beta_j] \tag{7.3-6}$$

Model (7.3-4) contains a sex × content interaction $[(\alpha\beta)_{j1},(\alpha\beta)_{j2}]$, (7.3-5) contains only a general sex effect $[\gamma_1,\gamma_2]$, and (7.3-6) contains no sex effects whatsoever. With respect to these models, the transformation of the school means,

$$[y_{ij1}^*, y_{ij2}^*] = \mathbf{y}_{ij}'\mathbf{T}' = \frac{1}{\sqrt{2}}[y_{ij1}, y_{ij2}]\begin{bmatrix} 1 & 1 \\ 1 & -1 \end{bmatrix} \tag{7.3-7}$$

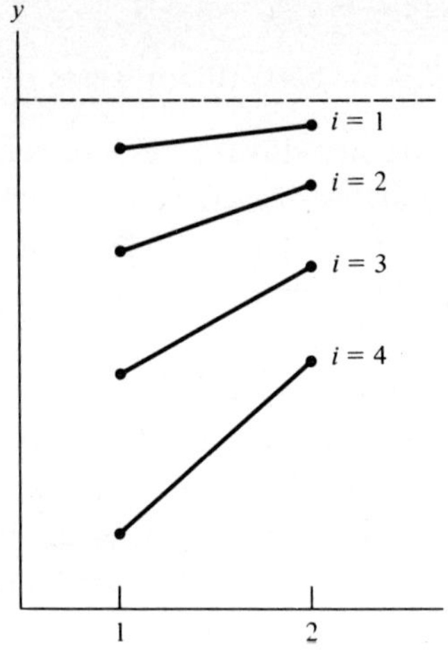

FIGURE 7.3-4
A "ceiling" effect in change scores.

generates an interpretable, ordered set of variables for purposes of the step-down tests. That is,

$$\underset{i}{\mathscr{E}}\,(y^*_{ij1}) = \frac{1}{\sqrt{2}}(\mu + \beta_j) + \frac{1}{\sqrt{2}}[\gamma_1 + \gamma_2 + (\beta\gamma)_{j1} + (\beta\gamma)_{j2}]$$

and
$$\underset{i}{\mathscr{E}}\,(y^*_{ij2}) = \tfrac{1}{2}[\gamma_1 - \gamma_2 + (\beta\gamma)_{j1} - (\beta\gamma)_{j2}]$$

Hence, y^*_{ij2} serves to test

$$H_0 2\colon [(\beta\gamma)_{11} - (\beta\gamma)_{12}] = [(\beta\gamma)_{21} - (\beta\gamma)_{22}] = \cdots = [(\beta\gamma)_{n1} - (\beta\gamma)_{n2}]$$

which is the null hypothesis of no sex $\times$ textbook interaction.

If $H_0 2$ is accepted and the interactive effects assumed null, y^*_{ij1} in turn provides a test of textbook effect ignoring sex, for which the null hypothesis is

$$H_0 1\colon \beta_1 = \beta_2 = \cdots = \beta_n$$

These hypotheses may, of course, be tested unconditionally by means of the corresponding between-group univariate F statistics. In this type of study, however, there may be good reason to test the hypothesis conditionally by means of step-down F statistics in order to suppress artifacts due to poor scaling of the measures. These artifacts may arise from "floor" and "ceiling" effects which induce relationships between the sizes of group differences and the general level of the measure. A ceiling effect is depicted in Fig. 7.3-4.

Figure 7.3-4 represents a condition in which a unit such as $i = 1$, whose average level is high, cannot register a gain as large as units such as $i = 4$, whose average level is low. The ceiling effect can reduce the variance on measure $k = 2$ and so

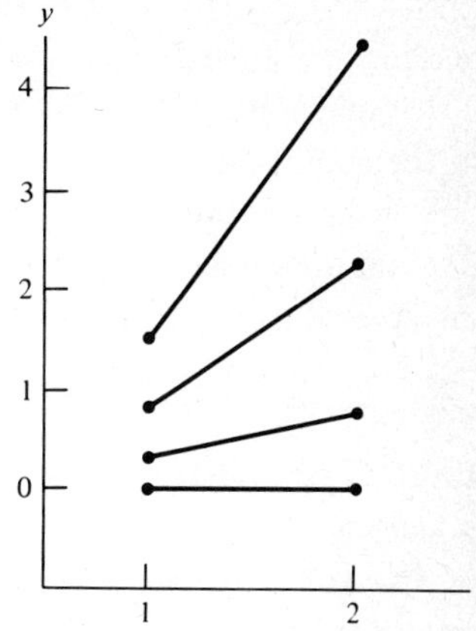

FIGURE 7.3-5
Gain proportional to average level measured from a rational origin.

produce a within-group correlation between the transformed variables y^*_{ij1} and y^*_{ij2}. Thus, if y^*_{ij1} and y^*_{ij2} have the covariance structure

$$\Sigma = \begin{bmatrix} \sigma_1{}^2 & \sigma_{12} \\ \sigma_{12} & \sigma_2{}^2 \end{bmatrix}$$

the covariance structure of the transformed variable is

$$\Sigma^* = \mathbf{T}\Sigma\mathbf{T}' = \begin{bmatrix} \sigma_1{}^2 + 2\sigma_{12} + \sigma_2{}^2 & \sigma_1{}^2 - \sigma_2{}^2 \\ \sigma_1{}^2 - \sigma_2{}^2 & \sigma_1{}^2 - 2\sigma_{12} + \sigma_2{}^2 \end{bmatrix} \tag{7.3-8}$$

The nonzero covariance in (7.3-8) when $\sigma_1{}^2 \neq \sigma_2{}^2$ will presumably also affect the group means if the groups have different average levels. If so, the unconditional analysis will indicate significantly smaller mean differences for groups near the ceiling, and $H_0 2$ will be rejected.

The conditional analysis, on the other hand, will attribute this effect to the regression of y^*_{ij2} on y^*_{ij1} and accept $H_0 2$. The conditional result would imply, in the context of the SMSG study, that the sex × content interactions are artifactual, and further study of them would not be productive. The focus of the study would then shift to testing and estimation of textbook effects for whole classrooms.

With somewhat more stringent qualifications, this line of reasoning can also be carried into the one-sample repeated-measures analysis. If, for example, we are testing the null hypothesis of zero slope in the group mean for data in which individuals are changing as shown in Fig. 7.3-5, the conditional analysis of slope given the mean level may accept the null hypothesis when an unconditional analysis would reject it. The conditional result implies that average slope depends upon average level in such a way that the slope is zero at the origin. If the data have a rational origin, this result may have a bearing on the causal interpretation of the observed slope. For example, when the size of gain in reading speed is proportional to average reading speed for the period of remediation, the gain might be attributed to normal developmental trend rather than to specific treatment effect. Thus, an interpretation of the conditional analysis in the one-group case may clarify the source of effects in certain applications. Where a conditional analysis is not interpretable, the unconditional analysis described in Sec. 7.1 remains applicable and may always be interpreted in a descriptive sense.

EXAMPLE 7.3-1 (*Step-down tests of repeated measures: decisions about upward social mobility*) In a study of factors that influence upward striving in the choice of life goals, Toban [1968] presented subjects with eight stories, each of which described an actor in a goal-conflict situation. Each subject was asked to choose from among various courses the actor might take in this situation. The choice was presented in the form of alternatives, A and B, say, one of which implied upward social striving. The subjects responded categorically on the following five-point bipolar scale: (1) Definitely A; (2) Probably A; (3) Can't say; (4) Probably B; (5) Definitely B.

For purposes of data analysis, Toban scored these categories 0, 1, 2, 3, and 4. If we regard category 3 as a neutral attitude, however, it would be reasonable to adapt the scale -2, -1, 0, 1, 2, which could then be regarded to have a rational origin. This latter scale is especially appropriate to the analysis presented here.

The eight stories were constructed as two replicates of a 2^2 design generated by (1) low- versus middle-class identification of the actor, and (2) internal versus external locus of control (i.e., whether the actor's chance of success depended upon external factors or personal skill). After the subject read each of these stories, he was presented four of the bipolar goal choices described above. The wording of these choices was varied to generate a 2^2 design with dimensions defined by (1) long or short time delay of gratification and (2) large or small chance of success. The crossing of the story classification and goal-choice classification thus generated a 2^4 design on the repeated measures.

For purposes of the present example, we shall collapse over two of the four dimensions and retain only Locus of Control and Delay of Gratification as repeated-measures factors. The primary data then consist in sums of the scaled scores for these factors.

We shall also look at only one of a number of subject background factors investigated by Toban, namely, sex difference in a sample of middle-class adults. The data for this aspect of the study are summarized in Table 7.3-1.

Transforming the data by the solution matrix (7.2-11) for the 2^2 design on the repeated measures, we obtain the multivariate analysis of variance shown in Table 7.3-2. Interpreting Table 7.3-2, we observe first that there is no evidence of sex effect: neither the multivariate F nor any univariate or step-down F approaches significance.

Table 7.3-1 SCALED GOAL CHOICES OF MALE AND FEMALE MIDDLE-CLASS SUBJECTS

	N	Locus: External		Internal	
		Delay: Short	Long	Short	Long
1 Group means					
Male	26	3.7307	−1.4423	3.6923	.9423
Female	34	4.4118	−.6912	4.0294	1.1618
2 Within-group correlations (df = 58)		1.0000			
		.2475	1.0000		
		.4263	.0287	1.0000	
		.0373	.3077	.4257	1.0000
Standard deviations		2.0481	2.3873	2.1623	2.5518

Because there is no sex effect, and because the scale of measurement has an interpretable zero point, the multivariate F for the constant term is meaningful and shows that the hypothesis of a zero mean vector is definitively rejected. The univariate F's indicate that all components of this vector are significantly different from zero, including the Locus × Delay interaction. The significant interaction supports the

Table 7.3-2 MULTIVARIATE ANALYSIS OF TRANSFORMED SCALED GOAL CHOICES

Source	df	SSP (symmetric)				Univariate F	Univariate p	Step-down F	Step-down p
Constant	1	$F_0 = 84.1$	$p = <.0001$						
Constant		972.03				106.8	<.001	106.8	<.001
Locus		−223.39	51.34			10.2	.002	1.2	.28
Delay		959.96	−220.61	948.03		182.3	<.001	73.4	<.001
Locus × delay		279.74	−64.29	276.26	80.51	45.2	<.001	3.4	.07
Sex	1	$F_0 = .59$	$p = .66$						
Constant		14.57				1.6	.21	1.6	.21
Locus		6.41	2.82			.6	.46	.82	.37
Delay		.34	.15	.01		0	.97	.04	.85
Locus × delay		−1.37	−.60	−.03	.12	.1	.79	0	.95
Within Groups	58								
Constant		527.93							
Locus		−51.78	289.83						
Delay		−48.05	3.45	301.61					
Locus × delay		6.17	48.82	14.27	103.31				
Total	60	(Omitted)							

inference that the combinations of Locus and Delay conditions influence in specific ways the subject tendency to choose upward-striving goals. In view of the arbitrary use of equally spaced intervals in the response scale, however, the possibility that this interaction is related to variation in the levels of the Locus and Delay contrasts should be considered. The step-down F for the Locus × Delay interaction suggests this is indeed the case: From a highly significant univariate F for the interaction, the step-down F falls to below the .05 level. The inference is that the interactive effect could be discounted as artifactual, and that the true effect of Locus and Delay on choice is additive. The effect of Delay is clearly much greater than that of Locus. In fact, the Locus effect also appears nonsignificant according to the step-down F, eliminating variation in general level.

This example illustrates the general point that additivity (and hence interaction effects) is not invariant over nonlinear transformations of the scale of measurement. Where the scale metric is arbitrary, the appearance of interactions raises the problem of whether they could be eliminated by a suitable nonlinear transformation. Tukey [1949] has discussed this problem and given a method of determining a polynomial transformation to maximize additivity.

7.3.4 Multiple Repeated-Measurement Variables

Up to this point we have discussed only the case of a single qualitatively distinct repeated-measurements variable. In many behavioral studies, however, a number of qualitatively distinct variables are measured on each of a number of occasions. To facilitate discussion of this latter case, we shall distinguish between *variables* (qualitatively distinct) and *measurements* of each variable (qualitatively similar). In general we shall assume m measures on each of v variables. To simplify matters further, we shall assume that the temporal or treatment structure of the repeated-measures dimension is the same for all variables. On these assumptions, both the mixed-model analysis of Secs. 7.1.1 and 7.2.1 and the multivariate analysis of Secs. 7.1.2 and 7.2.2 are readily generalized to the multiple-variable case.

Mixed-model analysis If a mixed-model analysis is envisioned, it is important that the data record for each subject be organized with variables as the *minor* classification. That is, the format of the data record for subject i in group j should be

$$\begin{matrix} y_{ij1}{}^{(1)} & y_{ij1}{}^{(2)} & \cdots & y_{ij1}{}^{(v)} \\ y_{ij2}{}^{(1)} & y_{ij2}{}^{(2)} & \cdots & y_{ij2}{}^{(v)} \\ \cdots & \cdots & \cdots & \cdots \\ y_{ijm}{}^{(1)} & y_{ijm}{}^{(2)} & \cdots & y_{ijm}{}^{(v)} \end{matrix} \qquad (7.3\text{-}9)$$

With the data in the form of (7.3-9), a mixed-model *multivariate* analysis of variance may be performed on the groups × subjects within groups × occasions design simply by extending the analysis in Sec. 7.1-2 or 7.2-2 to the multivariate case. The extension would involve only changing the designation of the number of occasions from p to m, and working with a partition of sums of squares and products for the v repeated-measures variables. Appropriate multivariate test statistics would then replace the univariate F statistics in these tables.

Multivariate approach If an analysis in the manner of Sec. 7.1.2 or 7.2.2 is in view, there is some advantage in organizing the subject's record with *measures* as the minor classification; i.e.,

$$\begin{array}{cccc} y_{ij1}^{(1)} & y_{ij2}^{(1)} & \cdots & y_{ijm}^{(1)} \\ y_{ij1}^{(2)} & y_{ij2}^{(2)} & \cdots & y_{ijm}^{(2)} \\ \cdots & \cdots & \cdots & \cdots \\ y_{ij1}^{(v)} & y_{ij1}^{(v)} & \cdots & y_{ijm}^{(v)} \end{array} \qquad (7.3\text{-}10)$$

Data in the form of (7.3-10) may be analyzed in an $(m \times v)$-variate multivariate analysis as follows:

Let $\mathbf{P}_m$ be the $m \times m$ solution matrix (orthogonal polynomials, Helmert matrix, Hadamard matrix, etc.) appropriate to the structure of the repeated-measures dimension. Let $\mathbf{I}_v$ be the $v \times v$ identity matrix. Then,

$$\mathbf{P}_{mv} = \mathbf{I}_v \times \mathbf{P}_m$$

is the $mv \times mv$ transformation matrix which, postmultiplying the data matrix, generates the constant term and contrasts among repeated measures for each variable separately. This transformation extends the analysis of Secs. 7.1.2 and 7.2.2 to the case of multiple repeated-measures variables.

The only unresolved problem in the analysis is the choice of transformed variables to be tested jointly and their ordering for purposes of analysis of covariance or step-down tests. An example will make the options clear: In the SMSG study referred to in Sec. 7.3.3, there were a number of achievement variables including, for example, geometry (constructions) and algebra (number properties). A typical observation consisted of the means for boys and girls, respectively, within classroom i and for textbook group j:

$$\mathbf{y}_{ij} = \begin{bmatrix} y_{ij1}^{(1)} \\ y_{ij2}^{(1)} \\ y_{ij1}^{(2)} \\ y_{ij2}^{(2)} \end{bmatrix} \quad \begin{array}{l} \text{Boys, geometry} \\ \text{Girls, geometry} \\ \text{Boys, algebra} \\ \text{Girls, algebra} \end{array}$$

To analyze the data in this form, we may employ the matrix in (7.3-7) to construct

$$\mathbf{T}_4 = \mathbf{I}_2 \times \mathbf{T} = \frac{1}{\sqrt{2}} \begin{bmatrix} 1 & 1 & 0 & 0 \\ 1 & -1 & 0 & 0 \\ 0 & 0 & 1 & 1 \\ 0 & 0 & 1 & -1 \end{bmatrix} \qquad (7.3\text{-}11)$$

We would then transform the vector observations as follows:

$$\mathbf{y}_{ij}^* = \mathbf{T}_4\mathbf{y}_{ij} = \begin{bmatrix} y_{ij1}^{*(1)} \\ y_{ij2}^{*(1)} \\ y_{ij1}^{*(2)} \\ y_{ij2}^{*(2)} \end{bmatrix} \begin{matrix} \text{Boys + Girls, geometry} \\ \text{Boys - Girls, geometry} \\ \text{Boys + Girls, algebra} \\ \text{Boys - Girls, algebra} \end{matrix} \qquad (7.3\text{-}12)$$

If case I or case II assumptions are applied, the analysis of group differences in the transformed observations present no conceptual or interpretational difficulties. Each component in $\mathbf{y}_{ij}^*$ is then independent and thus separately testable. However, if case III assumptions are required and it is proposed to test the sex × textbook interaction conditional on the average level for boys and girls, there may be ambiguity in the ordering of components for the step-down tests. The only guide to choice of order in this case is reference to considerations of substance and parsimony.

In the present example, the parsimonious model is perhaps one in which there is no sex × textbook interaction. Such interactions would be difficult to cope with educationally and, if possible, might better be attributed to within-group relationships. This reasoning would suggest that the order (from top to bottom) of the step-down tests should be one of the following:

Order 1	Order 2
Boys + Girls, geometry	Boys + Girls, geometry
Boys + Girls, algebra	Boys + Girls, algebra
Boys − Girls, geometry	Boys − Girls, algebra
Boys − Girls, algebra	Boys − Girls, geometry

The choice of order for the Boys-Girls contrast is determined by prior expectations about overall sex effects. In this instance, a sex effect in geometry achievement might be expected; hence, order 1 might be the better choice.

We would then have only to justify the elimination of *both* the geometry and algebra sums from the geometry difference. The justification is that achievement and other psychological tests are never pure measures, but often share considerable common variance. In the present instance, the common factor underlying this variance may be influencing the sex effect. If so, variation due to this factor is better controlled when both sums are shifted to the role of independent variables in the step-down tests.

An exception to this entire line of argument would arise, of course, if it were known that geometry (or algebra) actually is subject to sex × textbook interaction.* In that case, we might hope to gain parsimony by eliminating the variable and therefore perform the step-down tests in the order shown originally in (7.3-12).

* No such interaction was observed in the SMSG study (see Carry [1970]).

Finally, of course, there is always the possibility of employing two or more step-down orderings in ambiguous cases. Although the exact Type I error rate of the joint procedure would not be known, this would not be a fatal objection if the substantive background of the problem made clear the plausibility of the results.

All of the considerations in this section generalize in obvious ways to more complex sets of repeated-measurements data.

Exercise 7.3-1 Prove that an analysis of covariance of gain score with prescore as covariate is equivalent to an analysis of covariance of postscore with prescore as covariate.

Exercise 7.3-2 (*Lord's example*) Assume in Fig. 7.3-1:

Mean weight, lb	N	September	June
Men	60	160	160
Women	60	120	120

Within-group covariance matrix:

$$\begin{bmatrix} 100 & \\ 50 & 100 \end{bmatrix}$$

Compare the results of the analysis of gains and the analysis of covariance applied to these data.

Exercise 7.3-3 Generate bivariate normal random numbers with variance 1 and correlation .5 by a suitable linear combination of independent normal deviates from the Rand [1955] table. Sample two groups of 50 numbers from the bivariate population as follows: Draw the first group randomly; draw the second group randomly from among those pairs in which the first number is positive. Test the hypothesis that the two groups were drawn from the same population.

8

MULTIVARIATE ANALYSIS OF QUALITATIVE DATA

Although the metric form of data discussed in earlier chapters encompasses much of the domain of behavioral variables, it does not include data which arise when the subject's responses are classified rather than measured. We refer to such data as *qualitative*, with the understanding that the term applies in this context only to the response variables (i.e., dependent variables). As we have seen in Chaps. 4 and 5, the independent variables in least-squares analysis may be either qualitative or quantitative or both. When the *response* variables are qualitative, however, the statistical analysis changes fundamentally, because the random variable in the statistical model is discrete and must be described by a discrete probability distribution (e.g., the binomial or multinomial). While it is possible in large samples to approximate these discrete distributions by the continuous univariate or multivariate normal distribution and resort to conventional least-squares analysis, the approximations are often inaccurate in practical-sized samples and cannot be recommended in general.

This does not mean, however, that in the presence of qualitative response variables we must abandon altogether the conceptual apparatus we have assembled for the analysis of multivariate normal data. On the contrary, we may retain in full the mathematical part of the statistical models applied in Chaps. 4 through 7. Using the nonlinear statistical methods presented in this chapter, we may examine these models by methods which are closely analogous to the univariate and multivariate analyses in the previous chapters. For the most part, the approach here will follow that of Bock [1970].

To structure the discussion of these methods, we draw a distinction between two major classes of qualitative data, which we call, respectively, *single-response* and *multiple-response* data. If each subject in the sample is assigned, on the basis of his behavioral response, to one of several mutually exclusive categories, the category frequencies thus generated represent *single-response* data. Thus, the classifying of the response is tantamount to the classifying of the subject. The number of subjects in a survey sample who respond "agree," "disagree," or "don't know" to a given attitude item is an example of single-response data.

If each subject in the sample makes a number of responses, and each *response* is assigned to one of several mutually exclusive categories, the resulting frequencies represent *multiple-response* data. Multiple-response data typically occur when the subject is observed in a "free-response" setting—i.e., where the subject is carrying on some relatively unstructured activity and successive units of behavior are classified categorically by an observer. A familiar example is the classification of responses to the Rorschach Inkblot plates according to the system of Beck [1950] or Klopfer et al. [1954]. In general, multiple-response data are more difficult to analyze than single-response data because two stages of sampling are involved—viz., the sampling of subjects and the sampling of responses within subjects. In this chapter, single-response data will be discussed in Sec. 8.1, and multiple-response data in Sec. 8.2.

8.1 SINGLE-RESPONSE DATA

A schematic representation of single-response data is shown in Table 8.1-1. The rows represent groups of subjects assigned randomly to n experimental conditions or drawn in probability samples from n populations. The columns represent m mutually exclusive and exhaustive categories to which each subject is assigned on the basis of

Table 8.1-1 SCHEMATIC REPRESENTATION OF SINGLE-RESPONSE QUALITATIVE DATA

Subject groups	Response categories				Total
	1	2	···	m	
1	r_{11}	r_{12}	···	r_{1m}	N_1
2	r_{21}	r_{22}	···	r_{2m}	N_2
···	······	······	······	······	···
n	r_{n1}	r_{n2}	···	r_{nm}	N_n

his behavioral response. In group j, the number of subjects in category k is denoted by r_{jk}, and the total number of subjects in the group by the marginal sum N_j.

The most elementary statistical question that can be asked of single-response data is whether the n rows could have arisen from random sampling of the same population. This corresponds to the null hypothesis of no differences in the population values of the response probabilities, which can be tested by the familiar chi-square test of association in an $n \times m$ contingency table (see, for example, McNemar [1962]). When the subject groups and/or the response categories have some structure imposed upon them by the logic of the investigation, however, the analysis of this type of data becomes more interesting and complex because the specific effects of the structure may be examined.

With respect to the subject groups, the possible structuring is in every respect identical to that already discussed in Chaps. 4 to 6. Thus, the rows of Table 8.1-1 may represent variously the levels of a quantitative independent variable as in Chap. 4, the randomized block or factorial experimental design (not necessarily complete or orthogonal) of Chap. 5, or the crossed and/or nested design of a comparative study or survey in Chap. 6. This aspect of single-response data will be referred to as the *sample structure*.

Analogously, there may be a *response* structure on the categories that define the *columns* of Table 8.1-1. This structure typically results from a crossed, nested, or graded classification of the response categories. Thus, cross-classifications (e.g., in complex contingency tables) represent cartesian set products of classes of attributes assigned to responses; nested (hierarchical) classifications arise from some type of taxonomical classification of responses; and graded classifications are generated by rating scales that order the responses on a hypothetical continuum. In actual data, these several response structures may appear singly or in combination. The following examples illustrate some of the possibilities.

EXAMPLE 8.1-1 (*A psychophysical experiment*) A classical problem in psychophysics is that of determining the relationship between the discrimination threshold for a stimulus and the level of stimulus intensity at which the discriminations are made. In many cases this relationship conforms to *Weber's law*, which asserts that the discrimination threshold is a constant ratio of the stimulus intensity (Weber's ratio). Table 8.1-2 presents data, obtained by the so-called *method of constant stimuli*, for the test of Weber's law reported by Bock and Jones [1968]. Randomly selected subjects were each presented with one of 16 pairs of sucrose solutions in 1-ounce coded containers. Subjects tasted the contents of each container in a standard manner and reported the code number of the solution that tasted "sweeter."

Table 8.1-2 displays the resulting data in the schema of Table 8.1-1. Rows correspond to the experimental conditions defined by the sucrose concentrations x_A

and x_B of solutions respectively designated A and B. Columns give the number of subjects in each condition who responded "A sweeter than B" ($A > B$) and "B sweeter than A" ($B > A$).

Because only two categories are involved, the response structure in this experiment is unremarkable, while the sample structure, which has been planned so that it has evenly spaced levels in the logarithms of the sucrose concentration, has important implications for the analysis. As we shall see in the continuation of this example in Example 8.1-5, this design exploits the fact that the probability of correct identification of the sweeter stimulus is a function of the log stimulus difference between solution A and solution B in each pair. The concentrations of the A solutions have been selected so that these log differences have the same uniform spacing at each of the four levels of intensity of solution B. Thus the experimental conditions expressed on a log scale represent a 4 × 4 crossed design of four evenly spaced levels of stimulus A and four approximately evenly spaced levels of stimulus B.

Procedures formally identical to the method of constant stimuli used in this experiment are also employed in the assay of biologically active substances (bioassay). In toxicology, for example, groups of organisms are exposed to various concentrations

Table 8.1-2 JUDGMENTS OF THE RELATIVE SWEETNESS OF PAIRED SAMPLES A AND B OF VARIOUS CONCENTRATIONS OF SUCROSE SOLUTION

Sucrose solutions, g/100 ml		Number of subjects responding		
A	B	$A > B$	$B > A$	Total N
1.190	1.500	6	17	23
1.389		6	15	21
1.620		12	9	21
1.890		15	6	21
2.397	3.000	12	12	24
2.778		8	14	22
3.240		17	5	22
4.260		13	4	17
6.344	8.000	5	14	19
7.408		6	15	21
8.640		11	11	22
10.080		18	5	23
15.860	20.000	5	16	21
18.520		14	5	19
21.600		13	6	19
25.200		14	6	20

of a toxic agent, and the number of deaths at each dose level is recorded. The statistical methods of "probit" and "logit" analysis, which have been developed for toxicology and other bioassay [Bliss, 1935; Berkson, 1953], are directly applicable to constant-method data (see Bock and Jones [1968]). In particular, the analysis presented in the continuation in Example 8.1-5 is formally identical to a logit analysis in bioassay by the maximum-likelihood method (see Finney [1952]).

EXAMPLE 8.1-2 (*Contingency data*) In a textbook problem, Maxwell [1961] presents the data shown in Table 8.1-3. Subjects are 95 girls seen in a clinic for maladjusted children and classified by age and "sensitivity." If set out in the form of Table 8.1-1, these data would appear as follows:

*A*1			*A*2			*A*3			
*B*1	*B*2	*B*3	*B*1	*B*2	*B*3	*B*1	*B*2	*B*3	*N*
12	9	5	12	25	3	14	11	4	95

Thus, the data represent one population, have no sample structure, but have a 3 × 3 crossed response structure. The evidence in these data for association between age and sensitivity is examined in the continuation in Example 8.1-6.

EXAMPLE 8.1-3 (*An attitude survey*) An example of sociological data in the form of a complex contingency table appears in Volume I, Chapter 10 of the study by Stouffer et al. [1949] of U.S. soldiers in World War II. These data, which have been analyzed and commented upon by many subsequent authors [Coleman, 1964; Theil, 1970; Goodman, 1972a], are shown in Table 8.1-4 in conformity with the schema of Table 8.1-1.

Table 8.1-3 GIRLS CLASSIFIED BY AGE (*A*) AND SENSITIVITY (*B*)

	B			
A, years	*1* Oversensitive	*2* Normal	*3* Callous	Total
1 5–9	12	9	5	26
2 10–12	12	25	3	40
3 13–15	14	11	4	29
Total	38	45	12	95

The rows of Table 8.1-4 represent the subpopulations of a sample survey of army recruits. Factors of the sampling design are: A, race of respondent (black-white); B, geographical origin of the respondent (north-south); and C, location of the training camp to which the respondent is currently assigned (north-south).

The response categories are generated from the following questionnaire items:

1. If you could go to any Army camp you wanted to, would you rather stay here or would you rather go to some other camp?

   ______ I would rather stay here
   ______ I would rather go to some other camp
   ______ Undecided

2. If you would like to go to some other camp in the United States, which one would you want to go to?

   (Write the name of your choice on this line):

   ____

Responses to the second item were classified as northern camp, southern camp, or no response (undecided).

The sample structure in this study is clearly a 2^3 crossed design, while the response structure is an unbalanced nested arrangement of categories. In the continuation in Example 8.1-7, we examine the interactions between the sampling design and the category structure. This analysis is conditional upon the row totals and conveys no information about the association between the race or origin of the recruit and his training-camp assignment. A separate analysis of the row totals in the manner of Example 8.1-6 would be required for this purpose (see Exercise 8.1-6).

Table 8.1-4 PREFERENCE OF WORLD WAR II RECRUITS FOR LOCATION OF TRAINING CAMP

				Prefer to move to				
Race	Geographical origin	Present camp	Prefer to stay	North	South	Undecided	Undecided	Total
Black	North	North	196	191	36	41	52	516
		South	83	876	167	153	111	1,390
	South	North	261	122	270	113	105	871
		South	924	381	788	353	272	2,718
White	North	North	367	588	162	191	162	1,470
		South	346	874	164	273	164	1,821
	South	North	54	50	176	40	40	360
		South	481	91	389	91	91	1,143

EXAMPLE 8.1-4 (*Behavior ratings*) Certain inbred strains of laboratory mice have been found susceptible to seizures and death when exposed to high-frequency sound. In the C57BL strain, susceptibility to these *audiogenic* seizures is increased if the animal is "primed" by exposure to sublethal sound intensities at a critical period occurring about the twentieth day of life. The severity of seizures in a subsequent exposure can, however, be reduced by the administration of certain psychotropic drugs such as 5-hydroxytryptophan (5-HTP). Data reported by Boggan et al. [1971] and reproduced in Table 8.1-5 appear to indicate that 5-HTP reduces severity if administered $2\frac{1}{2}$ hours before reexposure of primed animals to sound at 28 days of life, but has no effect if administered $2\frac{1}{2}$ hours before priming at 19 or 20 days.

A fatal audiogenic seizure in these mice proceeds through five ordered observable stages, viz., crouching, wild running, clonic seizure (alternating spasm and relaxation), tonic seizure (continuous spasm), and death. Nonfatal seizures may involve stages up to the fourth, and a given animal's response may be classified in terms of the highest stage reached. Thus, the response structure is similar to that of the rating scale in which the categories might represent, for example, severity of symptoms, order of merit, degree of preference, etc. The analysis for this type of data is discussed in Sec. 8.1.6. It has also been studied in connection with bioassay by Aitchison and Silvey [1957], and the method presented in Sec. 8.1.6 is an elaboration of Ashford [1959].

8.1.1 The Response Process

Data such as are illustrated in the foregoing examples are, in biometric and psychometric research, often assumed to be the manifest expression of an unobservable continuous process which is latent within the subject. This process is presumed to be related more directly to the physiological sources of the behavior than is the observed response and, hence, is better suited to explanatory model building. In general, its existence cannot be verified objectively, but may be viewed alternatively as something inferred from regularities evident in the qualitative data or as a hypo-

Table 8.1-5 EFFECT OF 5-HYDROXYTRYPTOPHAN (5-HTP) ON AUDIOGENIC SEIZURES IN C57BL MICE

		Crouching	Wild running	Clonic seizures	Tonic seizures	Death	Total
Priming	Control	1	7	0	2	11	21
	5-HTP	0	6	0	6	10	22
Reexposure	Control	0	2	0	5	11	18
	5-HTP	3	10	2	0	2	17

thetical intervening variable. Whatever its ontological status, the response-process concept is, as we shall see, amply justified by the straightforward account it gives of qualitative behavioral data. This account is based on two alternative but closely related conceptions of the mechanism by which the latent process controls the manifest response:

1 The extremal concept. It is assumed that the underlying process is *vector* valued with one component corresponding to each of the m categories of the response classification. The process is assumed to have a continuous multivariate distribution in the population of subjects. The manifest response of a given subject corresponds to the maximal component of his process, there being no probability that two or more components are equal.

2 The threshold concept. The underlying process is assumed *scalar* valued and distributed continuously in the population of subjects. There are assumed to be certain values on the continuum called *thresholds*, such that the m response categories correspond to the intervals from $-\infty$ to $+\infty$ defined by the $m - 1$ threshold values. The response of a given subject is determined by the interval in which his process value falls, there being no probability that this value will equal a threshold value.

The extremal concept in the case of two categories was introduced into psychophysics by Thurstone [1927]. The extension to three categories was given in the model for choice of one of three objects formulated by Bock [1956], and the general case is discussed in connection with prediction of first choices in Bock and Jones [1968, Chap. 9]. The concept has recently been introduced in the bioassay literature by Ashford and Sowden [1970].

The threshold concept for the two-category case was also implicit in Thurstone's 1927 paper and was introduced independently in bioassay by Bliss [1935] (see Finney [1952]). The m-category extension in the psychological literature is due to Thurstone [Edwards and Thurstone, 1952], and in the bioassay literature to Aitchison and Silvey [1957]. There have been many subsequent applications of the m-category threshold concept, including Ashford [1959], Bock and Jones [1968], Samejima [1969], and Williams and Grizzle [1972].

In the two-category case, the extremal and threshold concepts are formally equivalent and lead to the same method of analysis. By way of introduction to the general problem, we present first the two-category case.

8.1.2 Estimating Binomial Response Relations

The problem of characterizing the relationship between a structured independent variable and a qualitative response variable is easily solved when there are only two response categories. Data in this form are referred to variously as *dichotomous, binary*, or *quantal*. The jth row of Table 8.1-1 specializes in the dichotomous case to

	Category		
	1	2	Total
Group j	r_{j1}	r_{j2}	N_j

We assume that the data for group j arise from a population consisting exclusively of a proportion of subjects P_{j1} who respond in category 1 and a proportion P_{j2} who respond in category 2. Then $P_{j1} + P_{j2} = 1$, and the probability of observing the frequencies r_{1j} and r_{2j}, among N_j subjects randomly sampled from this population, is given by the binomial law

$$P(r_{j1}, r_{j2} \mid N_j) = \frac{N_j!}{r_{j1}!\, r_{j2}!} P_{j1}{}^{r_{j1}} P_{j2}{}^{r_{j2}} \tag{8.1-1}$$

It can be shown that, considering the group-j data separately, the best unbiased estimates of P_{j1} and P_{j2} are, respectively,

$$\begin{aligned} p_{j1} &= \frac{r_{j1}}{N_j} \\ p_{j2} &= \frac{r_{j2}}{N_j} \qquad \text{or} \qquad p_{j2} = 1 - p_{j1} \end{aligned} \tag{8.1-2}$$

[Kendall and Stuart, 1967, vol. 2].

But if there exists a functional relationship between, say, P_{j1} and a vector-valued independent variable $\mathbf{x}_j$, it may be possible to estimate the population proportions more accurately by estimating the parameters of this relationship than by (8.1-2). We consider in this section the problem of specifying and fitting such a *binomial response relation.*

a The response model To fix ideas we shall continue the discussion in the context of sensory comparisons, although the results are of much broader application. We assume two stimuli denoted X_1 and X_2, for which the measured physical intensities are x_1 and x_2, respectively. The extremal concept introduced above enables us to make a plausible assumption about the functional form of the relationship connecting the response probabilities with these stimulus intensities. Following Thurstone [1927] (see Bock and Jones [1968, page 17 ff]), we assume that the two stimuli give rise in the subject to random variables y_1 and y_2, respectively, which are distributed in the population of subjects in the bivariate normal form,

$$\begin{bmatrix} y_1 \\ y_2 \end{bmatrix} \sim N\left(\begin{bmatrix} \mu_1 \\ \mu_2 \end{bmatrix}, \begin{bmatrix} \sigma_1{}^2 & \rho_{12}\sigma_1\sigma_2 \\ \rho_{12}\sigma_1\sigma_2 & \sigma_2{}^2 \end{bmatrix} \right) \tag{8.1-3}$$

We suppose that the subject responds in category 1 when $y_1 > y_2$, and in category 2 otherwise; equivalently, the subject responds in category 1 when the difference $y_{12} = y_1 - y_2$ is positive. The difference y_{12} is distributed in the univariate normal form (Sec. 3.3.7),

$$y_{12} = y_1 - y_2 \sim N[\mu_1 - \mu_2, \sigma_1{}^2 - 2\rho_{12}\sigma_1\sigma_2 + \sigma_2{}^2]$$

or, say,
$$y_{12} \sim N[\mu_{12}, \sigma_{12}{}^2]$$

Thus, the probability of the event ($X_1 > X_2$) ("X_1 preferred to X_2") is

$$P_1 = \text{Prob}(X_1 > X_2) = \frac{1}{\sqrt{2\pi}\,\sigma_{12}} \int_0^\infty e^{-(y-\mu_{12})^2/2\sigma_{12}{}^2}\,dy$$

$$= \frac{1}{\sqrt{2\pi}} \int_{-\mu_{12}/\sigma_{12}}^\infty e^{-t^2/2}\,dt = \Phi\left(\frac{\mu_{12}}{\sigma_{12}}\right)$$

i.e., the normal integral from $-\infty$ to μ_{12}/σ_{12}. If we choose the unit of y_{12} so that $\sigma_{12} = 1$, this becomes

$$P_1 = \Phi(\mu_{12}) \tag{8.1-4}$$

In the present context, we refer to (8.1-4) as a *response function*—specifically, the *normal response function.*

For many sensory stimuli, it is found that μ_{12} has a low-degree (in most cases linear) polynomial relationship with the difference of the *logarithms* of the stimulus intensity; that is,

$$\mu_{12} = \beta_0 + \beta_1(\log x_1 - \log x_2) + \beta_2(\log x_1 - \log x_2)^2 + \cdots + \beta_{r-1}(\log x_1 - \log x_2)^{r-1}$$

$$= \beta_0 + \beta_1 \log\frac{x_1}{x_2} + \beta_2 \log^2\frac{x_1}{x_2} + \cdots + \beta_{r-1}\log^{r-1}\frac{x_1}{x_2}$$

Paralleling our approach to metric data in Chap. 4, we shall test the goodness of fit of this polynomial in a stepwise manner and estimate, with a suitable assessment of precision, the parameters of the polynomial of least degree that exhibits satisfactory fit. In deriving the statistical methods for this purpose, we gain a valuable computational advantage by substituting for (8.1-4) the closely similar logistic distribution function

$$P_1 = \frac{1}{4}\int_{-\mu_{12}}^\infty \text{sech}^2\frac{t}{2}\,dt = \frac{e^{\mu_{12}}}{1 + e^{\mu_{12}}} = \frac{1}{1 + e^{-\mu_{12}}} \tag{8.1-5}$$
$$= \Psi(\mu_{12}), \text{ say}$$

The logistic distribution can be shown to be symmetric with mean 0 and variance $\pi^2/3$ [Gumbel, 1961]. Its density function is unusual in that it can be expressed in terms of the distribution function:

$$\psi(t) = \frac{d\Psi}{dt} = \Psi(1 - \Psi) \qquad (8.1\text{-}6)$$

Note also from (8.1-5) that

$$\mu_{12} = \ln \frac{P_1}{1 - P_1}$$

The approximation of (8.1-5) to a normal distribution function with mean zero and standard deviation $\pi\sqrt{3}$ is excellent; the discrepancy is less than .01 for any deviate. The advantage of using (8.1-5) as a response function in preference to (8.1-4) is apparent in connection with the estimation of the coefficients in the polynomial by the *method of maximum likelihood*, which we now discuss.

b Estimation In the case of discrete data, we define the likelihood function by the probability law for the observations expressed in terms of the given data and the unknown parameters. The maximum-likelihood estimates of the parameters are those values that maximize the likelihood function (see Kendall and Stuart [1967, vol. 2, page 35]).

With binomial data and a logistic response function, the likelihood is

$$L = \prod_{j=1}^{n} \frac{N_j!}{r_{j1}!(N_j - r_{j1})!} P_{j1}{}^{r_{j1}}(1 - P_{j1})^{N_j - r_{j1}}$$

where

$$P_{j1} = \frac{1}{1 + e^{-z_j}}$$

The quantity z_j is called a binomial *logit*. In many behavioral and biological applications, models for the logit similar to those of Chaps. 4 and 5 give a good account of the data. Where there is a single quantitative independent variable, a polynomial model may be suitable:

$$z_j = \beta_0 + \beta_1 x_j + \beta_2 x_j^2 + \cdots + \beta_{r-1} x_j^{r-1}$$

or, in matrix notation,

$$\underset{n\times 1}{\mathbf{z}} = \underset{n\times r}{\mathbf{X}}\ \underset{r\times 1}{\boldsymbol{\beta}} \qquad (8.1\text{-}7)$$

We shall refer to (8.1-7) as the rank-r linear model for the logit. In the sensory-comparisons example, the quantities in the $\mathbf{X}$ matrix are the powers of $x_j = \log(x_{j1}/x_{j2})$.

The parallelism of (8.1-7) with the univariate regression model (4.1-1) is obvious. The vector $\mathbf{z}$ corresponds to the expected values of the observations, the matrix $\mathbf{X}$ contains the known values of the independent variable, and $\boldsymbol{\beta}$ is the vector of coefficients to be estimated.

Proceeding with the ml estimates of $\boldsymbol{\beta}$, we obtain, using the chain rule and (8.1-7), the following necessary condition for the maximum of ln L, and thus of L, with respect to variation in $\boldsymbol{\beta}$:

$$\frac{\partial \ln L}{\partial \boldsymbol{\beta}} = \sum_{j=1}^{n} \left[\frac{r_j \, \partial \ln P_{j1}}{\partial P_{j1}} + \frac{(N_j - r_{j1}) \, \partial \ln (1 - P_{j1})}{\partial P_{j1}} \right] \frac{\partial P_{j1}}{\partial z_j} \frac{\partial z_j}{\partial \boldsymbol{\beta}}$$

$$= \sum_{j=1}^{n} \left(\frac{r_{j1}}{P_{j1}} - \frac{N_j - r_{j1}}{1 - P_{j1}} \right) P_{j1}(1 - P_{j1}) \mathbf{x}_j$$

$$= \sum_{j=1}^{n} (r_{j1} - N_j P_{j1}) \mathbf{x}_j = \mathbf{0} \qquad (8.1\text{-}8)$$

where $\mathbf{x}_j'$ is the jth row of $\mathbf{X}$ in (8.1-7).

In order to determine whether the values of $\boldsymbol{\beta}$ which satisfy this *likelihood equation* correspond to a maximum of L, we obtain the matrix of second derivatives of ln L with respect to $\boldsymbol{\beta}$:

$$\frac{\partial^2 \ln L}{\partial \boldsymbol{\beta} \, \partial \boldsymbol{\beta}'} = -\sum_{j}^{n} N_j P_{j1}(1 - P_{j1}) \mathbf{x}_j \mathbf{x}_j' \qquad (8.1\text{-}9)$$

Because of (8.1-6), this matrix has the remarkable property of being independent of the observations, a condition not typical in most applications of maximum-likelihood estimation. Furthermore, if the vectors $\mathbf{x}_j$ are linearly independent (which implies $r \leq n$), (8.1-9) is positive definite for all finite $\boldsymbol{\beta}$. Thus, the likelihood function under these conditions is convex and has a unique maximum. The system (8.1-8) can therefore readily be solved by an iterative procedure, such as multivariate Newton-Raphson iterations, starting from any trial values. In particular, if $\hat{\boldsymbol{\beta}}_i$ is a trial value for the maximum-likelihood estimate $\hat{\boldsymbol{\beta}}$, a better approximation is given by

$$\hat{\boldsymbol{\beta}}_{i+1} = \hat{\boldsymbol{\beta}}_i - \left[\frac{\partial^2 \ln L}{\partial \boldsymbol{\beta} \, \partial \boldsymbol{\beta}'} \right]_{\boldsymbol{\beta} = \boldsymbol{\beta}_i}^{-1} \left[\frac{\partial \ln L}{\partial \boldsymbol{\beta}} \right]_{\boldsymbol{\beta} = \hat{\boldsymbol{\beta}}_i} \qquad (8.1\text{-}10)$$

Successive iterations of (8.1-10) will converge quadratically to any finite solution. Cases where no finite solution exists sometimes occur when many of the response frequencies are zero. For example, attempts to fit a linear response function to the following data will yield an infinite slope:

j	k: 1	2	N_j
1	5	0	5
2	5	0	5
3	0	5	5

Such cases can usually be avoided by increasing the sample size or adjusting the conditions applied to the experimental groups (see Silverstone [1957] for a discussion of this problem in bioassay).

c Test of fit Once the maximum-likelihood estimates have been obtained, the goodness of fit of the model may be tested by computing the Pearsonian chi-square

$$\chi_P^2 = \sum_{j=1}^{n} \left[\frac{(r_{j1} - N_j\hat{P}_{j1})^2}{N_j\hat{P}_{j1}} + \frac{(r_{j2} - N_j\hat{P}_{j2})^2}{N_j\hat{P}_{j2}} \right] = \sum_{j=1}^{n} \frac{(r_{j1} - N_j\hat{P}_{j1})^2}{N_j\hat{P}_{j1}(1 - \hat{P}_{j1})} \tag{8.1-11}$$

If the model is correctly specified, χ_P^2 is distributed in large samples as a central chi-square variate on $n - r$ degrees of freedom. Significance of this statistic is evidence that discrepancies between observed and expected proportions are too large to be attributed to sampling variation.

Alternatively, the likelihood-ratio chi-square,

$$\chi_L^2 = 2 \sum_{j=1}^{n} \left(r_{j1} \ln \frac{r_{j1}}{N_j\hat{P}_{j1}} + r_{j2} \ln \frac{r_{j2}}{N_j\hat{P}_{j}} \right) \tag{8.1-12}$$

where $r_{jk} \ln r_{jk} = 0$ when $r_{jk} = 0$, is also distributed in large samples as chi-square on $n - r$ degrees of freedom. χ_P^2 and χ_L^2 have the same limiting distribution, but χ_L^2 has been conjectured by Fisher to be slightly more accurate in small samples (see also the discussion in Sec. 8.1.3c).

The theory of maximum-likelihood estimation also indicates that, when the model fits, the large-sample variance-covariance matrix is given by the negative of the inverse of second derivatives of $\ln L$ evaluated at $\hat{\boldsymbol{\beta}}$; that is,

$$\mathscr{V}(\hat{\boldsymbol{\beta}}) = -\left[\frac{\partial^2 \ln L}{\partial \boldsymbol{\beta}\, \partial \boldsymbol{\beta}'}\right]^{-1}_{\boldsymbol{\beta}=\hat{\boldsymbol{\beta}}} \tag{8.1-13}$$

The positive square roots of the diagonal elements of this matrix (i.e., the standard errors of the estimated coefficients) may be used to construct confidence intervals for the population coefficients in the same manner as in Sec. 4.1.12, but with critical values of $\chi^2/(n - r)$ replacing those of F.

EXAMPLE 8.1-5 (*Estimating a binomial response relation*) To illustrate the procedures of Sec. 8.1-1, let us fit the logistic response relation to the data for each level of stimulus B in Table 8.1-2. The first step is the evaluation of the matrix of independent variables $\mathbf{X}$ in terms of difference in log stimulus intensity for each experimental group. Due to the choice of stimulus intensities, the resulting values are the same for each level of B and are equally spaced. For example, the values for

$x_B = 1.5$ g/100 ml are:

$$x_1 = \log_{10} \frac{1.190}{1.500} = -.100$$

$$x_2 = \log_{10} \frac{1.389}{1.500} = -.033$$

$$x_3 = \log_{10} \frac{1.620}{1.500} = .033$$

$$x_4 = \log_{10} \frac{1.890}{1.500} = .100$$

Because of the equal spacing, we may use the orthogonal polynomials of order 4 to represent the polynomial in (8.1-7). In this application there is no advantage in normalizing the terms in the polynomial, so we may freely use the integral values given in Appendix B. Let us assume initially a rank-2 (linear) model for the logits. Then, in (8.1-7), the matrix **X** consists of the leading two columns of the order-4 orthogonal polynomials:

$$\mathbf{X} = \begin{bmatrix} 1 & -3 \\ 1 & -1 \\ 1 & 1 \\ 1 & 3 \end{bmatrix} \qquad (8.1\text{-}14)$$

We may now employ the Newton-Raphson iterations (8.1-10) to solve (8.1-8), with the $\mathbf{x}_j$ given by the rows of (8.1-14), and the r_{j1} and N_j given in Table 8.1-2 at each level of B. In four to six iterations, the first derivatives (8.1-8) are reduced essentially to zero, at which point the chi-squares for the goodness-of-fit tests shown in Table 8.1-6 are obtained.

The fit of the linear logistic function of the log stimulus differences appears reasonably good at all levels of B except level 4 ($x_B = 20.0$ g/100 ml). The response proportions in Table 8.1-2 show that ability to discriminate between the solutions at this level does not increase at high stimulus intensities. Let us therefore test the fit

Table 8.1-6 GOODNESS OF FIT OF THE RANK-2 (LINEAR) LOGISTIC MODEL FOR THE DATA IN TABLE 8.1-2

Level of B, g/100 ml	Residual df	χ_P^2	p	χ_L^2	p
1 (1.5)	2	.89	$.7 > p > .6$	.90	$.7 > p > .6$
2 (3.0)	2	4.71	$.1 > p > .05$	4.77	$.1 > p > .05$
3 (8.0)	2	1.48	$.5 > p > .4$	1.47	$.5 > p > .4$
4 (20.0)	2	6.04	$.05 > p > .025$	6.27	$.05 > p > .025$

of a quadratic function by applying a rank-3 model in which the **X** matrix includes the unnormalized second-degree orthogonal polynomial:

$$\mathbf{X} = \begin{bmatrix} 1 & -3 & 1 \\ 1 & -1 & -1 \\ 1 & 1 & -1 \\ 1 & 3 & 1 \end{bmatrix}$$

With this model the residual chi-square on one degree of freedom gives no reason to reject a quadratic relationship for level 4:

$$\chi_P^2 = 1.54 \quad (.3 > p > .2) \qquad \chi_L^2 = 1.51 \quad (.3 > p > .2)$$

The estimated (unnormalized) orthogonal polynomial coefficients and standard errors for the response relations (linear for the first levels of B, and the quadratic for level 4) are shown in Table 8.1-7. The slopes measured by the linear coefficients are significantly positive at all levels as expected. The quadratic coefficient at level 4 indicates that the function describing the logit is concave down. The transformation of the estimated orthogonal polynomial coefficients into coefficients of the polynomial (8.1-7) is left as an exercise for the reader (see Sec. 5.2.5c).

A further continuation of this example appears in Exercise 8.1-1.

8.1.3 Estimating Multinomial Response Relations

The method of analyzing binomial data presented in the previous section generalizes to multinomial data in a manner closely parallel to the extension of univariate normal analysis to the multivariate case. We assume in the multinomial case that the subject is classified in one, and only one, of m nominal categories. The subject may be required, for example, to choose one of m stimuli which he perceives to be "greatest," "most preferred," "most descriptive," etc., and he is then assigned to the category corresponding to that stimulus.

Table 8.1-7 ESTIMATED UNNORMALIZED ORTHOGONAL POLYNOMIAL COEFFICIENTS AND (SE's) OF THE BINOMIAL LOGISTIC RESPONSE RELATIONS FOR THE DATA OF TABLE 8.1-2

Level of B	Coefficient		
	Constant	Linear	Quadratic
1	−.1899 (.2333)	.3572 (.1086)	
2	.4506 (.2345)	.2595 (.1083)	
3	−.2070 (.2398)	.4027 (.1145)	
4	.3818 (.2490)	.2912 (.1092)	−.5340 (.2494)

a The response model If we assume an extremal mechanism controlling the subject's choice, we suppose that the m stimuli give rise to the vector of continuous latent processes

$$[y_1, y_2, \ldots, y_m]$$

and that the subject chooses the stimulus corresponding to the component with the largest value for him at that moment. Given that the processes have a multivariate distribution $F(\mathbf{y})$ in the population of subjects, this implies that the probability of a randomly selected subject choosing stimulus X_1, say, is

$$\begin{aligned}\text{Prob}(X_1 > X_2 \cup X_3 \cup \cdots \cup X_m) \\ &= \text{Prob}(y_1 > y_1 \cup y_3 \cup \cdots \cup y_m) \\ &= \text{Prob}[(y_1 - y_2) \cap (y_1 - y_3) \cap \cdots \cap (y_1 - y_m) > 0] \\ &= \int_0^\infty \int_0^\infty \cdots \int_0^\infty G(y_1 - y_j)\, d(y_1 - y_j) \qquad j = 2, 3, \ldots, m \qquad (8.1\text{-}15)\end{aligned}$$

where G is the distribution of process differences derived from $F(\mathbf{y})$.

Following Bock [1956] or Ashford and Sowden [1970], we might assume that $F(\mathbf{y})$ is multivariate normal,

$$\mathbf{y} \sim N(\boldsymbol{\mu}, \boldsymbol{\Sigma})$$

in which case $G(y_1 - y_j)$ is multivariate normal

$$\mathbf{Cy} \sim N(\mathbf{C}\boldsymbol{\mu}, \mathbf{C}\boldsymbol{\Sigma}\mathbf{C}')$$

where $\mathbf{C}$ is the matrix of simple contrasts

$$\mathbf{C} = \begin{bmatrix} 1 & 0 & \cdots & 0 & -1 \\ 0 & 1 & \cdots & 0 & -1 \\ \cdots & \cdots & \cdots & \cdots & \cdots \\ 0 & 0 & \cdots & 0 & -1 \end{bmatrix}$$

The assumption of multinormality has, however, the practical difficulty that for $m > 3$, evaluation of the integral (8.1-15) is exceedingly laborious except in special cases (see Bock and Jones [1968, page 249] and Ashford and Sowden [1970] for applications in which $m = 3$). One such special case arises when the variances in $\boldsymbol{\Sigma}$ are equal and the covariances are equal. Then

$$\mathbf{C}\boldsymbol{\Sigma}\mathbf{C}' = \sigma^2 \begin{bmatrix} 1 & \frac{1}{2} & \cdots & \frac{1}{2} \\ \frac{1}{2} & 1 & \cdots & \frac{1}{2} \\ \cdots & \cdots & \cdots & \cdots \\ \frac{1}{2} & \frac{1}{2} & \cdots & 1 \end{bmatrix}$$

that is, the difference processes have constant variance and correlation $\frac{1}{2}$. For this case, certain approximations to (8.1-15) exist (see Gupta [1963]) of which perhaps the simplest may be derived from the multivariate generalization of one of the bivariate logistic distributions introduced by Gumbel [1961]: In our notation,

$$\Psi(t_1, t_2, \ldots, t_p) = \frac{1}{1 + e^{-t_1} + e^{-t_2} + \cdots + e^{-t_p}} \tag{8.1-16}$$

The marginal distributions of (8.1-16) are logistic, each with mean zero and variance $\sigma^2 = \pi^2/3$. The covariance for any pair of variables is $\pi^2/6$, whence the correlation is

$$\rho = \frac{\pi^2}{6}\frac{3}{\pi^2} = \frac{1}{2}$$

For moderate values of t, (8.1-16) approximates reasonably well a multivariate normal distribution with these means, variances, and covariances. For $t_1 = t_2 = -1.0$, for example, the bivariate logistic gives $P = .155$, compared to the bivariate normal $p = .154$.

To use (8.1-16) to approximate (8.1-15), we set $t_1 = \mu_1 - \mu_2$, $t_2 = \mu_1 - \mu_2$, $\ldots$, $t_p = \mu_1 - \mu_m$ with $p = m - 1$. Then,

$$\begin{aligned} \text{Prob}(y_1 > y_2 \cup y_3 \cup \cdots \cup y_m) &= \frac{1}{1 + e^{-(\mu_1-\mu_2)} + e^{-(\mu_1-\mu_3)} + \cdots + e^{-(\mu_1-\mu_m)}} \\ &= \frac{e^{\mu_1}}{e^{\mu_1} + e^{\mu_2} + \cdots + e^{\mu_m}} \end{aligned} \tag{8.1-17}$$

Similar expressions with $e^{\mu_2}, e^{\mu_3}, \ldots, e^{\mu_m}$ in the numerator give the probability that the subject will respond in categories $2, 3, \ldots, m$, respectively.

To apply (8.1-17) to the estimation of multinomial response relations when there are n subject groups and m categories, we define the *multinomial logit* for group j as

$$\underset{m \times 1}{\mathbf{z}_j} = \begin{bmatrix} z_{j1} \\ z_{j2} \\ \cdots \\ z_{jm} \end{bmatrix}$$

Then the category probabilities for group j are

$$\begin{aligned} P_{j1} &= \frac{e^{z_{j1}}}{D_j} \\ P_{j2} &= \frac{e^{z_{j2}}}{D_j} \\ &\cdots\cdots \\ P_{jm} &= \frac{e^{z_{jm}}}{D_j} \end{aligned} \tag{8.1-18}$$

where

$$D_j = e^{z_{j1}} + e^{z_{j2}} + \cdots + e^{z_{jm}}$$

To complete the model we have only to connect the multinomial logit to the independent variables by a function that allows the possibility of a structure among the subject groups and among the response categories. We employ, for this purpose, the multivariate linear model

$$\underset{n\times m}{\mathbf{Z}} = \underset{n\times q}{\mathbf{X}} \cdot \underset{q\times t}{\mathbf{B}} \cdot \underset{t\times m}{\mathbf{A}} \tag{8.1-19}$$

in which the rows of $\mathbf{Z}$ are $\mathbf{z}_j'$ ($j = 1, 2, \ldots, n$), $\mathbf{X}$ is a matrix of the known values of q independent variables associated with each of the subject groups, $\mathbf{B}$ contains unknown parameters, and $\mathbf{A}$ is a matrix incorporating the structure of the m response categories (the matrix is analogous to the matrix of variate transformations in the repeated-measures analysis of Chap. 7).

If the subject groups have a crossed or nested structure, $\mathbf{X}$ will be the model matrix for the design and will in general be of deficient rank $r \leq n$. In that case, it will be necessary to reparameterize the model by setting

$$\mathbf{X} = \underset{n\times r}{\mathbf{K}} \cdot \underset{r\times q}{\mathbf{L}}$$

where $\mathbf{L}$ satisfies the estimability condition

$$\text{rank}\begin{bmatrix}\mathbf{X}\\ \mathbf{L}\end{bmatrix} = \text{rank}[\mathbf{X}] = \text{rank}[\mathbf{L}] = r$$

As in Sec. 5.2, $\mathbf{L}$ may be chosen by the investigator, and $\mathbf{K}$ calculated from

$$\mathbf{K} = \mathbf{XL}'(\mathbf{LL}')^{-1}$$

or generated by means of the algorithms of Secs. 5.3.3 or 6.4.2. We shall refer to $\mathbf{K}$ as the *sample* basis of the model for the multivariate logits.

The matrix $\mathbf{A}$ plays a role similar to $\mathbf{X}$, but with respect to the response categories rather than the subject groups. It too may be of deficient rank s, and may be factored as, say,

$$\underset{t\times m}{\mathbf{A}} = \underset{t\times s}{\mathbf{S}} \cdot \underset{s\times m}{\mathbf{T}}$$

where rank(S) $= s$, and the columns of $\mathbf{S}$ are linearly dependent on those of $\mathbf{A}$. The matrix $\mathbf{T}$ may be obtained from

$$\mathbf{T} = (\mathbf{S}'\mathbf{S})^{-1}\mathbf{S}'\mathbf{A}$$

or generated directly. We shall call $\mathbf{T}$ the *response* basis of the model.

After these reparameterizations, (8.1-18) becomes

$$\mathbf{Z} = \mathbf{K}(\mathbf{LBS})\mathbf{T} = \underset{n\times r}{\mathbf{K}} \cdot \underset{r\times s}{\boldsymbol{\Gamma}} \cdot \underset{s\times m}{\mathbf{T}} \tag{8.1-20}$$

We shall refer to (8.1-20) as the *linear logistic model* (or, briefly, the log-linear model) for the response probabilities corresponding to observed frequencies arrayed as in Table 8.1-1. Note that the form of (8.1-20) is identical to Roy's [1957] formulation of the multivariate linear hypothesis: the matrix $\mathbf{K}$ is the so-called *prefactor*, $\boldsymbol{\Gamma}$ the parameters, and $\mathbf{T}$ the *postfactor*.

b Estimation We now turn to the problem of estimating the elements of $\boldsymbol{\Gamma}$ (which describe the effects of the independent variables upon the multinomial logits and thus upon the response probabilities). We note first that the elements in the rows of (8.1-20) are subject to the restriction $\sum_{k=1}^{m} z_{jk} = 0$, independent of the parameters. This implies that

$$\mathbf{T1}' = \mathbf{0}$$

i.e., that the rows of $\mathbf{T}$ consist entirely of contrasts. No such condition applies to $\mathbf{K}$, which in general will have $\mathbf{1}$ as its first column.

With this restriction on $\mathbf{T}$, we shall show that maximum-likelihood estimates of the effects in the full-rank reparameterization always exist, although in certain degenerate cases the estimates may take on infinite values. Assuming random assignment or sampling of subjects for the n groups, the likelihood function is

$$L = \prod_{j=1}^{n} \frac{N_j!}{r_{j1}!\, r_{j2}! \cdots r_{jm}!} P_{j1}^{\,r_{j1}} P_{j2}^{\,r_{j2}} \cdots P_{jm}^{\,r_{jm}}$$

Let K_{jk} be the j, k element of $\mathbf{K}$, T_{hi} the h, i element of $\mathbf{T}$, and γ_{kh} the k, h element of $\boldsymbol{\Gamma}$. Then the first derivative of the log likelihood with respect to γ_{kh}, $k = 1, 2, \ldots, r$, $h = 1, 2, \ldots, s$, is

$$\frac{\partial \ln L}{\partial \gamma_{kh}} = \sum_{j=1}^{n} \left(\frac{r_{j1}}{P_{j1}} \frac{\partial P_{j1}}{\partial \gamma_{kh}} + \frac{r_{j2}}{P_{j2}} \frac{\partial P_{j2}}{\partial \gamma_{kh}} + \cdots + \frac{r_{jm}}{P_{jm}} \frac{\partial P_{jm}}{\partial \gamma_{kh}} \right)$$

From (8.1-18),

$$\frac{\partial P_{j1}}{\partial \gamma_{kh}} = P_{j1}[T_{h1}(1 - P_{j1}) - T_{h2}P_{j2} - \cdots - T_{hm}P_{jm}]K_{jk}$$

$$\frac{\partial P_{j2}}{\partial \gamma_{kh}} = P_{j2}[-T_{h1}P_{j1} + T_{h2}(1 - P_{j2}) - \cdots - T_{hm}P_{jm}]K_{jk}$$

$$\cdots\cdots\cdots\cdots\cdots\cdots\cdots\cdots\cdots\cdots\cdots\cdots\cdots\cdots$$

$$\frac{\partial P_{jm}}{\partial \gamma_{kh}} = P_{jm}[-T_{h1}P_{j1} - T_{h2}P_{j2} - \cdots + T_{hm}(1 - P_{jm})]K_{jk}$$

Thus, the likelihood equations are, say,

$$g(\gamma_{kh}) = \sum_{j=1}^{n} [T_{h1}(r_{j1} - N_jP_{j1}) + T_{h2}(r_{j2} - N_jP_{j2}) + \cdots + T_{hm}(r_{jm} - N_jP_{jm})]K_{jk} = 0$$

Similarly, the second derivatives of the log likelihood are

$$\begin{aligned} H(\gamma_{kh}, \gamma_{il}) = -\sum_{j=1}^{n} N_j\{&P_{j1}[T_{l1}(1 - P_{j1}) - T_{l2}P_{j2} - \cdots - T_{lm}P_{jm}]T_{h1} \\ &+ P_{j2}[-T_{l1}P_{j1} + T_{l2}(1 - P_{j2}) - \cdots - T_{lm}P_{jm}]T_{h2} + \cdots \\ &+ P_{jm}[-T_{l1}P_{j1} - T_{l2}P_{j2} - \cdots + T_{lm}(1 - P_{jm})]T_{hm}\}K_{jk}K_{ji} \end{aligned}$$

For purposes of a computer solution of the likelihood equations, it is helpful to express these derivatives in matric form. For experimental condition j, define the vectors of response frequencies and response probabilities

$$\mathbf{r}_j = \begin{bmatrix} r_{j1} \\ r_{j2} \\ \cdots \\ r_{jm} \end{bmatrix} \quad \text{and} \quad \mathbf{P}_j = \begin{bmatrix} P_{j1} \\ P_{j2} \\ \cdots \\ P_{jm} \end{bmatrix}$$

The likelihood equations may then be expressed as

$$\underset{rs\times 1}{\mathbf{g}(\boldsymbol{\Gamma})} = \sum_j^n \underset{s\times m}{\mathbf{T}} \underset{m\times 1}{(\mathbf{r}_j - N_j\mathbf{P}_j)} \times \underset{r\times 1}{\mathbf{K}_j} = \mathbf{0} \qquad (8.1\text{-}21)$$

where $\times$ denotes the Kronecker product, and $\mathbf{K}_j$ is the jth row of $\mathbf{K}$ written as a column. Successive elements in this expression represent derivatives taken with respect to γ_{kh} with the second subscript varying first.

Define also the $m \times m$ matrix

$$\mathbf{W}_j = \begin{bmatrix} P_{j1}(1 - P_{j1}) & -P_{j1}P_{j2} & \cdots & -P_{j1}P_{jm} \\ -P_{j2}P_{j1} & P_{j2}(1 - P_{j2}) & \cdots & -P_{j2}P_{jm} \\ \cdots & \cdots & \cdots & \cdots \\ -P_{jm}P_{j1} & -P_{jm}P_{j2} & \cdots & P_{jm}(1 - P_{jm}) \end{bmatrix}$$

The $rs \times rs$ matrix of second derivatives may then be expressed as, say,

$$-\mathbf{H}(\boldsymbol{\Gamma}) = -\sum_j^n N_j \underset{s\times s}{\mathbf{T}\mathbf{W}_j\mathbf{T}'} \times \underset{r\times r}{\mathbf{K}_j\mathbf{K}_j'} \qquad (8.1\text{-}22)$$

For the solution of the likelihood equations to correspond to a maximum of the likelihood, the matrix of second derivatives must be negative definite. Checking on definiteness, we note first that, since $\mathbf{W}_j$ is proportional to the variance-covariance matrix of the multinomial frequencies, it is positive semidefinite with one and only one zero root. The characteristic vector corresponding to the zero root is, say, $\mathbf{1}$, in which each component is unity. The matrix $\mathbf{T}\mathbf{W}_j\mathbf{T}'$ is therefore positive definite provided $s < m$, $\mathbf{T}$ is of full rank, and $\mathbf{T}$ does not contain the vector $\mathbf{1}$ as a row.

The matrix $\mathbf{K}_j\mathbf{K}_j'$ is, of course, positive semidefinite and of rank 1. The Kronecker product of $\mathbf{T}\mathbf{W}_j\mathbf{T}'$ and $\mathbf{K}_j\mathbf{K}_j'$, of which the diagonal matrix of characteristic roots is the Kronecker product of the matrices of roots of the separate matrices [Anderson, 1958, page 348] is positive semidefinite of rank s. Provided $n \geq r$ and $\mathbf{K}$ is of full rank, the sum over j of these Kronecker products will be positive definite. The matrix of second derivatives is therefore the negative of a positive-definite matrix for all finite $\boldsymbol{\Gamma}$. Thus, the likelihood surface is convex with a unique maximum. In principle, a Newton-Raphson solution of the likelihood equations will therefore converge to the maximum-likelihood estimates from any finite initial trial values. It will also do so in practice if the precision of the calculations, especially in the matrix inversion, is sufficient.

The Newton-Raphson solution of the likelihood equations is carried out as follows: Let $\hat{\boldsymbol{\Gamma}}_i$ be the trial value of the estimated parametric functions at the ith iteration of the solution. Then from (8.1-20) the trial logits are

$$[\hat{Z}_{jh}^{(i)}] = \underset{n \times m}{\mathbf{Z}_i} = \mathbf{K}\hat{\boldsymbol{\Gamma}}_i\mathbf{T}$$

and from (8.1-18) the trial probabilities are

$$\underset{n \times m}{\hat{\mathbf{P}}_i} = \underset{n \times n}{\mathbf{D}^{-1}} \underset{n \times m}{[e^{Z_{jh}^{(i)}}]}$$

where $\mathbf{D}_i$ is a diagonal matrix whose elements are the sums of elements in the rows of $[e^{Z_{jh}^{(i)}}]$. The elements in the rows of the matrix $\mathbf{P}_i$ are the components of the vector $\mathbf{P}_j$ required for the calculation of the first and second derivatives using (8.1-21) and (8.1-22). Then the adjustments, say $\delta_{kh}^{(i)}$, to the trial values $\gamma_{kh}^{(i)}$, represented as elements of an $rs \times 1$ vector in which the subscript h varies first, are

$$\boldsymbol{\delta}_i = \mathbf{H}^{-1}(\hat{\boldsymbol{\Gamma}}_i)\mathbf{g}(\hat{\boldsymbol{\Gamma}}_i)$$

where $\mathbf{H}^{-1}(\hat{\boldsymbol{\Gamma}}_i)$ is the negative of the inverse of the matrix of second derivatives evaluated at $\hat{\boldsymbol{\Gamma}}_i$. These corrections are added to the corresponding elements of $\hat{\boldsymbol{\Gamma}}_i$ to obtain improved estimates. The process may be repeated until the corrections vanish. Experience with this solution indicates that the choice of trial values is not critical. The solutions converge rapidly (in five or six iterations) even when all initial trial values are set equal to zero.

We have shown that, if finite, these estimates are unique and correspond to a proper maximum of the likelihood function. The theory of maximum-likelihood estimation establishes that such estimates are consistent, i.e., they converge to the population values as the sample size becomes indefinitely large, and their joint distribution is approximated by the multivariate normal distribution with mean equal to the population value and variance-covariance matrix equal to the negative inverse of the matrix of second derivatives of the likelihood function:

$$\mathscr{V}(\hat{\boldsymbol{\Gamma}}_i) = \mathbf{H}^{-1}(\boldsymbol{\Gamma}) \qquad (8.1\text{-}23)$$

Large-sample standard errors for the estimated parameters of the logistic model are obtained by extracting the diagonal of the matrix of second derivatives in the final iteration of the Newton-Raphson solution. The square roots of the negatives of these elements give the standard errors of the corresponding quantities in $\hat{\boldsymbol{\Gamma}}$.

Because the variances in (8.1-23) may be shown to be the minimum attainment by any unbiased estimator (Cramér-Rao inequality; see Rao [1965]), the maximum-likelihood estimator is said to be *asymptotically efficient*. There is, however, no guarantee or unbiasedness or efficiency in small samples. Fortunately, most behavioral studies giving rise to qualitative data make use of sufficiently large numbers of subjects to justify appeals to large-sample theory.

c Tests of significance Large-sample tests based on the central chi-square distribution are available for testing the fit of any hypothesized model versus an alternative containing additional terms. If the alternative is the full-rank model [rank $n \times (m - 1)$], the estimated cell probabilities are identically equal to the observed cell proportions, and statistics for testing the fit of a hypothesized rank-rs model are given by the Pearsonian chi-square

$$\chi_P^2 = \sum_{j=1}^{n} \sum_{k=1}^{m} \frac{(r_{jk} - N_j \hat{P}_{jk})^2}{N_j P_{jk}} \tag{8.1-24}$$

or the likelihood-ratio chi-square

$$\chi_L^2 = 2 \sum_{j=1}^{n} \sum_{k=1}^{m} r_{jk} \ln \frac{r_{jk}}{N_j P_{jk}} \tag{8.1-25}$$

where, if the hypothesized model obtains, the limiting distribution of each of these statistics is central chi-square on $n(m - 1) - rs$ degrees of freedom.

As a general rule, the probability levels given by the limiting distribution [as read from a chi-square table* or computed by Formula (3.4-3)] may be relied upon if the expected values $N_j P_{jk}$ are 5 or greater. Fisher recommends (8.1-25) in preference to (8.1-24) when the expected values are small. Simulation studies also show that in certain small-sample applications (8.1-25) is more powerful than (8.1-24) when the statistics are referred to the conventional chi-square table [Lassitz, 1972].

Where the alternative model is not of full rank, the difference of chi-squares computed from (8.1-24) or (8.1-25) under the hypothesized and alternative models is also distributed as chi-square with degrees of freedom equal to the difference in degrees of freedom under the two models. This provides the possibility of stepwise testing of a succession of nested models in a prescribed order determined by the same principles as we applied in Chap. 5 to stepwise regression tests of design models. An application of stepwise testing to contingency data appears in Example 8.1-6.

Tests of significance for specified effects in the logistic model are also available. As discussed above, the maximum-likelihood estimates of contrasts $\hat{\boldsymbol{\theta}}$ in the logistic model are distributed asymptotically in a multivariate normal form with mean $\boldsymbol{\theta}$ and variance-covariance matrix given by the inverse of

$$\mathbf{H} = -\frac{\partial^2 \ln L}{\partial \boldsymbol{\theta}\, \partial \boldsymbol{\theta}'} \tag{8.1-26}$$

Thus, the statistic

$$\chi_Q^2 = (\hat{\boldsymbol{\theta}} - \boldsymbol{\theta})'\mathbf{H}(\hat{\boldsymbol{\theta}} - \boldsymbol{\theta}) \tag{8.1-27}$$

is distributed asymptotically as chi-square on rs degrees of freedom. The statistic (8.1-27) may be used to test the hypothesis that elements of $\boldsymbol{\theta}$ have certain prescribed values, usually zero. Where this test is specialized to test the nullity of some subset

* An extensive table of the central chi-square distribution may be found in Hald [1952].

of effects in $\boldsymbol{\theta}$, it corresponds to a stepwise test of these terms *when all other effects are already in the model.* Thus, the tests of fit and the tests of specified effects in the logistic model are exactly parallel logically to the corresponding tests in normal regression analysis.

8.1.4 Applications of Multinomial Response Relations

a Contingency tables Contingency data arise whenever subjects are drawn from a single population and cross-classified, as in Example 8.1-2, according to their attributes or responses. The format is identical to that of the crossed sample-survey design discussed in Sec. 6.4.3b and may be described by the same notation; thus,

$$a \times b \times c$$

designates a three-way contingency table with a categories A, b categories B, and c categories C. The smallest subclasses of the table are customarily referred to as *cells.*

The general model (8.1-19) may be applied to this form of data in order to detect and describe associations among the categories or differences among category frequencies in the population. Except for the method of computation, the resulting analysis is identical to the log-linear treatment of contingency tables presented by Goodman [1968], Bishop [1969], Fienberg [1970], Haberman [1974], Bishop, Fienberg, and Holland [1975], and others. When the Pearsonian chi-square statistic is employed in the test of fit, the results are also numerically identical with those obtained by conventional methods of computing a chi-square for the table after "fixing" various marginal frequencies. The hypotheses tested in the analysis may be expressed alternatively in terms of population proportions or in terms of effects in the logistic model.

Consider, for example, the set of successively less restrictive hypotheses that might be formulated for the $a \times b$ contingency table represented in the sample by

	B				
A	1	2	$\cdots$	b	Total
1	r_{11}	r_{12}	$\cdots$	r_{1b}	$r_{1\cdot}$
2	r_{21}	r_{22}	$\cdots$	r_{2b}	$r_{2\cdot}$
$\cdots$	$\cdots$	$\cdots$	$\cdots$	$\cdots$	$\cdots$
a	r_{a1}	r_{a2}	$\cdots$	r_{ab}	$r_{a\cdot}$
Total	$r_{\cdot 1}$	$r_{\cdot 2}$	$\cdots$	$r_{\cdot b}$	N

Let the corresponding population probabilities be

A	B 1	2	$\cdots$	b	Total
1	P_{11}	P_{12}	$\cdots$	P_{1b}	$P_{1\cdot}$
2	P_{21}	P_{22}	$\cdots$	P_{2b}	$P_{2\cdot}$
$\cdots$	$\cdots$	$\cdots$	$\cdots$	$\cdots$	$\cdots$
a	P_{a1}	P_{a2}	$\cdots$	P_{ab}	$P_{a\cdot}$
Total	$P_{\cdot 1}$	$P_{\cdot 2}$	$\cdots$	$P_{\cdot b}$	1

These hypotheses may be stated equivalently in terms of probabilities or in terms of the linear model for the logits. The rank of the log-linear model is shown at the right.

$H1$: subclass probabilities equal

$$P_{jk} = \frac{1}{ab} \qquad z_{jk} = 0 \quad (\text{rank} = 0)$$

$H2$: A-category probabilities equal

$$P_{jk} = \frac{P_{\cdot k}}{a} \qquad z_{jk} = \beta_k \quad (\text{rank} = a - 1)$$

$H3$: B-category probabilities equal

$$P_{jk} = \frac{P_{j\cdot}}{b} \qquad z_{jk} = \alpha_j \quad (\text{rank} = b - 1)$$

$H4$: Classifications independent [i.e., conditional probability of A given B, or B given A, is equal, respectively, to the unconditional (marginal) probability of A or B]

$$P_{jk} = P_{j\cdot}P_{\cdot k} \qquad z_{jk} = \alpha_j + \beta_k \quad (\text{rank} = a + b - 2)$$

$H5$: Classifications associated (i.e., conditional probability of A given B, or B given A, depends on B or A, respectively)

$$P_{jk} = P_{jk} \qquad z_{jk} = \alpha_j + \beta_k + \gamma_{jk} \quad (\text{rank} = ab - 1)$$

That the two types of models are in one-to-one correspondence is apparent when we take logarithms of the population probabilities:

$$\begin{aligned}
&H1\colon \ln P_{jk} = -\ln ab && \ln P_{jk} = -\ln D \\
&H2\colon \ln P_{jk} = \ln P_{k\cdot} - \ln a && \ln P_{jk} = \beta_k - \ln D \\
&H3\colon \ln P_{jk} = \ln P_{\cdot k} - \ln b && \ln P_{jk} = \alpha_j - \ln D \\
&H4\colon \ln P_{jk} = \ln P_{\cdot k} + \ln P_{j\cdot} && \ln P_{jk} = \alpha_j + \beta_k - \ln D \\
&H5\colon \ln P_{jk} = \ln P_{jk} && \ln P_{jk} = \alpha_j + \beta_k + \gamma_{jk} - \ln D
\end{aligned}$$

In terms of log probabilities, the parametric structure of the two types of models is identical and is, in fact, equivalent to that of the one- and two-way analysis-of-variance models. Thus, the reparameterization required to transform the main-class logistic model to full rank corresponds to an equivalent reparameterization of the probability model. For the 2 × 2 case, for example, we may reparameterize by setting $\theta_0 = (\alpha_1 + \alpha_2)/2 + (\beta_1 + \beta_2)/2 = -\ln D$, $\theta_1 = \alpha_1 - \alpha_2$, and $\theta_2 = \beta_1 - \beta_2$. Then,

$$\begin{aligned}
\ln P_{11} &= \ln P_{\cdot 1} + \ln P_{1\cdot} = \theta_0 + \theta_1 + \theta_2 \\
\ln P_{12} &= \ln P_{1\cdot} + \ln P_{\cdot 2} = \theta_0 + \theta_1 - \theta_2 \\
\ln P_{21} &= \ln P_{2\cdot} + \ln P_{\cdot 1} = \theta_0 - \theta_1 + \theta_2 \\
\ln P_{22} &= \ln P_{\cdot 2} + \ln P_{2\cdot} = \theta_0 - \theta_1 - \theta_2
\end{aligned}$$

Solving for the free parameters θ_1 and θ_2, we have

$$\begin{aligned}
\theta_1 &= \ln P_{1\cdot} - \ln P_{2\cdot} = \ln \frac{P_{1\cdot}}{P_{2\cdot}} \\
\theta_2 &= \ln P_{\cdot 1} - \ln P_{\cdot 2} = \ln \frac{P_{\cdot 1}}{P_{\cdot 2}}
\end{aligned} \tag{8.1-28}$$

The equivalence of these models has an important implication for maximum-likelihood estimation in contingency tables. Because any one-to-one transformations of ml estimates are the ml estimates of the same transformation of the parameters, we have the option of fitting the logistic effects directly by solving (8.1-21), or indirectly by estimating marginal probabilities for the table and taking appropriate log contrasts as in (8.1-28). When the marginal probabilities are completely determined by free parameters in the logistic model (together with the restriction that marginal probabilities must sum to unity), the latter approach is especially simple because the sample marginal proportions are the maximum-likelihood estimates of the marginal probabilities.

This is evident in the form of the likelihood equations given by (8.1-21). In the case of the 2 × 2 main-class model reparameterized in simple contrasts, for example, the matrix in (8.1-20) specializes to

$$\mathbf{T} = \tfrac{1}{2}\begin{bmatrix} 1 & 1 & -1 & -1 \\ 1 & -1 & 1 & -1 \end{bmatrix}$$

Then (8.1-21) (times 2) is

$$\begin{aligned}
r_{11} + r_{12} - r_{21} - r_{22} - N(\hat{P}_{11} + \hat{P}_{12} - \hat{P}_{21} - \hat{P}_{22}) \\
= r_{1\cdot} - r_{2\cdot} - N(\hat{P}_{1\cdot} - \hat{P}_{2\cdot}) = 0
\end{aligned}$$

$$\begin{aligned}
r_{11} - r_{12} + r_{21} - r_{22} - N(\hat{P}_{11} - \hat{P}_{12} + \hat{P}_{21} - \hat{P}_{22}) \\
= r_{\cdot 1} - r_{\cdot 2} - N(\hat{P}_{\cdot 1} - \hat{P}_{\cdot 2}) = 0
\end{aligned}$$

where, with the restrictions, $P_{1\cdot} + P_{2\cdot} = 1$ and $P_{\cdot 1} + P_{\cdot 2} = 1$, we obtain

$$\hat{P}_{1\cdot} = \frac{r_{1\cdot}}{N} \qquad \hat{P}_{2\cdot} = \frac{r_{2\cdot}}{N}$$

and

$$\hat{P}_{\cdot 1} = \frac{r_{\cdot 1}}{N} \qquad \hat{P}_{\cdot 2} = \frac{r_{\cdot 2}}{N}$$

These results generalize to contingency tables of all orders. If the logistic model includes $n - 1$ independent contrasts for a way of classification consisting of n classes, the maximum-likelihood estimates reproduce exactly the corresponding marginal proportions.* We then say that the marginal proportions are "fixed" in the solution. Similarly, the 2-, 3-, . . . , or f-fold marginal proportions are fixed if the model includes the associated main class and 2-, 3-, . . . , or f-factor interactions (see Goodman [1970]).

Interaction terms in the logistic model correspond to association between the interacting classifications, and estimates of these effects serve as a measure of the direction and extent of association. In the 2×2 case, a measure of association independent of the main-class proportions is provided by the contrast of interactive terms,

$$\delta = \gamma_{11} - \gamma_{12} - \gamma_{21} + \gamma_{22}$$

which is estimated by the third term in the response-relations model with the basis

$$\mathbf{T}' = \tfrac{1}{2}\begin{bmatrix} 1 & 1 & 1 \\ 1 & -1 & -1 \\ -1 & 1 & -1 \\ -1 & -1 & 1 \end{bmatrix}$$

A zero value of δ corresponds to no associations; positive values indicate a concentration of probability in the main diagonal of the 2×2 table; and negative values indicate a concentration in the minor diagonal. For a discussion of other measures of association in contingency tables, see Goodman and Kruskal [1954].

EXAMPLE 8.1-6 (*Contingency data*) For purposes of analysis, let us assume that the subjects classified in Table 8.1-3 constitute a random sample from the population served by the clinic. The question of primary interest in these data is whether there is any association between the classification by age and the classification by "sensitivity." In the absence of association, questions of lesser interest, such as the equality of marginal frequencies for age and for sensitivity, may also be examined. To illustrate the general method, let us test hypotheses bearing on each of these issues.

* This assumes that the contingency table is complete. If the table is incomplete, the maximum-likelihood solution estimates the proportion which would be expected if the missing cells were excluded from the population (see Sec. 8.1.5).

In addition, a single-degree-of-freedom portion for the association chi-square will be discussed.

The first step in the calculations is the generation (by the method of Sec. 5.3) of the matrix **T** in (8.1-20), which contains the bases of the logistic models corresponding to each hypothesis. For reasons which will become apparent later, we shall generate this matrix from the Helmert matrix (unnormalized)

$$\mathbf{H}_3 = \begin{bmatrix} 1 & \frac{1}{2} & -\frac{1}{3} \\ 1 & -\frac{1}{2} & -\frac{1}{3} \\ 1 & 0 & \frac{2}{3} \end{bmatrix} \tag{8.1-29}$$
$$\begin{matrix} (0) & (1) & (2) \end{matrix}$$

Taking twofold Kronecker products of the columns of (8.1-29) as designated by the symbolic basis vectors below, we construct the following **T** matrix (transposed):

$$\mathbf{T}' = \begin{bmatrix} \frac{1}{2} & -\frac{1}{3} & \frac{1}{2} & -\frac{1}{3} & \frac{1}{4} & -\frac{1}{6} & -\frac{1}{6} & \frac{1}{9} \\ \frac{1}{2} & -\frac{1}{3} & -\frac{1}{2} & -\frac{1}{3} & -\frac{1}{4} & \frac{1}{6} & -\frac{1}{6} & \frac{1}{9} \\ \frac{1}{2} & -\frac{1}{3} & 0 & \frac{2}{3} & 0 & 0 & \frac{2}{6} & -\frac{2}{9} \\ -\frac{1}{2} & -\frac{1}{3} & \frac{1}{2} & -\frac{1}{3} & -\frac{1}{4} & -\frac{1}{6} & \frac{1}{6} & \frac{1}{9} \\ -\frac{1}{2} & -\frac{1}{3} & -\frac{1}{2} & -\frac{1}{3} & \frac{1}{4} & -\frac{1}{6} & \frac{1}{6} & \frac{1}{9} \\ -\frac{1}{2} & -\frac{1}{3} & 0 & \frac{2}{3} & 0 & 0 & -\frac{2}{6} & -\frac{2}{9} \\ 0 & \frac{2}{3} & \frac{1}{2} & -\frac{1}{3} & 0 & \frac{2}{6} & 0 & -\frac{2}{9} \\ 0 & \frac{2}{3} & -\frac{1}{2} & -\frac{1}{3} & 0 & -\frac{2}{6} & 0 & -\frac{2}{9} \\ 0 & \frac{2}{3} & 0 & \frac{2}{3} & 0 & 0 & 0 & \frac{4}{9} \end{bmatrix} \tag{8.1-30}$$
$$\begin{matrix} (01) & (02) & (10) & (20) & (11) & (12) & (21) & (22) \end{matrix}$$

As required by the constraint on the logits, the (00) column is omitted from (8.1-30).

Other quantities required in the likelihood equations are the sample basis, which in the one-population case is simply $K = 1$, and the vector of observed response frequencies, which appears as a row in Table 8.1-2. For various bases abstracted from (8.1-30), the solution of the likelihood equations may be carried out by the Newton-Raphson method described in Sec. 8.1-3. The estimated cell proportions are then calculated by (8.1-18) and employed in obtaining the residual chi-square under the respective model. The Pearsonian chi-square statistics obtained in this way for models of rank 2, 4, and 8 in this example are shown in Table 8.1-8. The columns of (8.1-30) that make up the **T** matrix for each model are shown in the column labeled SBV.

The residual chi-squares in Table 8.1-8 serve to test the nullity of effects excluded from the model in question. Thus, the chi-square of 6.875 (df = 4) for the model including A and B effects tests hypothesis $H3$ above; i.e., the hypothesis of no association. The probability of this chi-square is greater than .1 and shows no clear indication that the sensitivity classification (B) depends on age (A).

Similarly, the chi-square for the model that includes only B effects shows only a marginal indication ($.1 > p > .05$) that the age and interaction effects jointly may be nonnull. However, the model including A effects only is clearly contradicted ($p < .0005$), indicating that the B effects, measuring differences in sensitivity, cannot be considered null. A more powerful test of this hypothesis is provided by the chi-square for the difference in chi-square between the B-effect model and the rank-0 model; that is,

$$33.937 - 10.844 = 23.093$$

The degrees of freedom of this component of chi-square is obtained by subtracting the corresponding residual df; that is, $6 - 4 = 2$. The p value for this component is even smaller than the already small value for the residual of the A-effect model.

If the rank-2 B-effect model is adopted, the estimated Helmert contrasts and their standard errors are

Contrast	Estimate	SE
$\beta_1 - \beta_2$	$-.1691$	.2203
$\beta_3 - \dfrac{\beta_1 + \beta_2}{2}$	-1.237	.3090

Substituting these estimates in (8.1-18), we obtain the following expected cell proportions, which when compared with the observed proportions show the fixing of the B margin:

EXPECTED

	B			
A	1	2	3	Total
1	.1333	.1579	.0421	.3333
2	.1333	.1579	.0421	.3333
3	.1333	.1579	.0421	.3333
Total	.3999	.4737	.1263	.9999

OBSERVED

	B			
A	1	2	3	Total
1	.1263	.0947	.0526	.2736
2	.1263	.2632	.0316	.4211
3	.1474	.1158	.0421	.3053
Total	.4000	.4737	.1263	1.0000

Table 8.1-8 TESTS OF FIT FOR LOGISTIC MODELS OF THE 3 × 3 CONTINGENCY DATA IN EXAMPLE 8.1-6

Model	Rank of model	SBV	Residual chi-square*	df	p
Constant	0	None	33.937	8	$<.0005$
A	2	(01) (02)	26.644	6	$<.0005$
B	2	(10) (20)	10.844	6	$.1 > p > .05$
A, B	4	(01) (02) (10) (20)	6.875	4	$.25 > p > .1$
A, B, AB	8	All	Null	0	

* Pearsonian.

Had we elected to include A effects as well as B, we would have obtained in addition the following:

Contrast	Estimate	SE
$\alpha_1 - \alpha_2$	−.4308	.2519
$\alpha_3 - \dfrac{\alpha_1 + \alpha_2}{2}$	−.1062	.2244

The expected cell proportions would then fix both margins:

EXPECTED

	B			
A	1	2	3	Total
1	.1095	.1296	.0346	.2737
2	.1684	.1994	.0532	.4210
3	.1221	.1446	.0386	.3053
Total	.4000	.4736	.1264	1.0000

The above test of the rank-4 model is not necessarily the most powerful test of no association in these data. When there is more than one degree of freedom for association, it may be possible to compute single-degree-of-freedom components of chi-square corresponding to effect contrasts that are expected *a priori* to be significant in the data. In the present example the Helmert contrasts have been chosen to define an interaction contrast of the proportions of oversensitive and normal girls at ages 5–9 and 10–12, the expectation being that girls tend to become more confident with the onset of adolescence. To obtain the single-degree-of-freedom components for this and the remaining interaction contrasts, we compute the residual chi-square for the rank 5, 6, and 7 models obtained by adding columns (11), (12), and (21) of (8.1-30) successively to the basis. The difference between the respective residuals then provides the components of chi-squares shown in Table 8.1-9.

Table 8.1-9 COMPONENTS OF THE ASSOCIATION CHI-SQUARE IN TABLE 8.1-8

Model	Rank of model	Residual chi-square*	df	Component chi-square	df	p
A and B	4	6.875	4	4.066	1	$.05 > p > .025$
A, B, A_1B_1	5	2.809	3	1.025	1	$>.3$
A, B, A_1B_1, A_1B_2	6	1.784	2	.757	1	$>.6$
$A, B, A_1B_1, A_1B_2, A_2B_1$	7	.027	1	.027	1	$>.8$
A, B, AB	8	Null	0			

* Pearsonian.

We see in Table 8.1-9 that the chi-square for association is concentrated in the first component to such an extent that the .05 significance level is attained. Provided the corresponding contrast was singled out *a priori*, we have some evidence for association involving the four cells in the upper left corner of the contingency table. The estimate of the corresponding interactive effect is included among the contrast estimates obtained in fitting the rank-5 model:

Contrast	Estimate	SE
$(\gamma_{11} - \gamma_{12}) - (\gamma_{21} - \gamma_{22}) = (\gamma_{11} + \gamma_{22}) - (\gamma_{12} + \gamma_{21})$	1.100	.554

This estimate is positive, indicating a tendency for more girls in the middle age group to be classified "normal."

It is of interest to compare this partition of chi-square for association with the values 3.366, 1.965, 1.493, and 0.051 obtained by Maxwell [1961, page 61] using the Irwin-Lancaster method. The chi-square value of 3.366 for association in cells (11), (12), (21), and (22), which is calculated from an orthogonal contrast among sample proportions rather than a contrast of effects, is less sensitive to association in this part of the table than is the logistic analysis we have performed here.

b Comparative studies The multinomial response-relations model is also useful for comparing response tendencies (or incidence of attributes) in populations defined by demographic or other characteristics. Subjects are assumed to be drawn from each of the populations in a probability sample, but the number of subjects in a given sample may be arbitrary. The subjects in each sample are partitioned among m mutually exclusive response categories, which in general have some prespecified structure.

Of primary interest in data of this type is the possibility of significant interactions between contrasts among populations and contrasts among response categories. If the classification of the populations and the structure of the categories are sufficiently complex, it may be difficult to decide *a priori* which of the many possible interactions might exist and should be tested, or which may be assumed null and omitted from the model. If this is the case, we may wish to adopt the strategy proposed by Goodman [1972], which is to fit a full-rank model (rank n for the populations and $m - 1$ for the categories) and to examine the estimates of the various interactive effects relative to their standard errors. Effects for which the magnitude of the estimates exceeds two to three standard errors would be candidates for retention in the model, and the others would be excluded.

The selection of effects in these models will, of course, be subject to the same logical constraints that we recognized in Chap. 5—namely, that if a factor appears in a higher-order interaction, it must also be represented in the lower-order interactions and main effects. This is a consequence of our having used in the multinomial response-relations model the same reparameterization as we employed in the least-squares analysis of crossed designs.

We illustrate this approach to qualitative data in a continuation of Example 8.1-3, the present analysis of which should be compared with a similar treatment by Goodman [1972], who, however, limits his discussion to the dichotomous case.

EXAMPLE 8.1-7 (*Population comparisons*) Since the populations in this example are classified in a 2^3 factorial design, it is natural to use (8.1-31), a Hadamard matrix of order 8, as the design basis. The columns of (8.1-31) are identified by the symbolic basis vectors in the order ABC, where

$$A = \text{race of respondent}$$
$$B \equiv \text{geographical origin of respondent}$$
$$C \equiv \text{location of present training camp}$$

As a convenience, the normalizing factor $1/2\sqrt{2}$ has been omitted.

$$\mathbf{K} = \begin{bmatrix} 1 & 1 & 1 & 1 & 1 & 1 & 1 & 1 \\ 1 & 1 & 1 & -1 & 1 & -1 & -1 & -1 \\ 1 & 1 & -1 & 1 & -1 & 1 & -1 & -1 \\ 1 & 1 & -1 & -1 & -1 & -1 & 1 & 1 \\ 1 & -1 & 1 & 1 & -1 & -1 & 1 & -1 \\ 1 & -1 & 1 & -1 & -1 & 1 & -1 & 1 \\ 1 & -1 & -1 & 1 & 1 & -1 & -1 & 1 \\ 1 & -1 & -1 & -1 & 1 & 1 & 1 & -1 \end{bmatrix} \qquad (8.1\text{-}31)$$
$$\begin{matrix} (000) & (100) & (010) & (001) & (110) & (101) & (011) & (111) \end{matrix}$$

The response classification, being both crossed and nested, requires a basis such as (8.1-32), which is tailored to this particular structure. Columns in (8.1-32) are numbered consecutively, and the corresponding contrasts are interpreted:

$$\mathbf{T}' = \begin{bmatrix} 1 & 3 & 0 & 0 \\ 1 & -1 & 1 & 1 \\ 1 & -1 & 1 & -1 \\ 1 & -1 & -2 & 0 \\ -4 & 0 & 0 & 0 \end{bmatrix} \qquad (8.1\text{-}32)$$

(1)	(2)	(3)	(4)
Move versus Undecided	Stay versus Move	Names Camp versus Undecided	Northern versus Southern Camp

Since $n = 8$ and $m = 5$, these bases specify a full-rank model which, in one step of the Newton-Raphson solution, reproduces the sample proportions exactly. The estimated effects thus obtained are shown in Table 8.1-10; the standard errors of these estimates, which are the same for all population contrasts, are shown at the bottom of each column.

The results in Table 8.1-10 (in which estimates in excess of 2.5 times their standard errors are set off in boxes) exploit exhaustively the original data. It is clear that the overall Undecided category conveys no useful information about population differences and might be dropped or distributed proportionately over the remaining categories. Each remaining row and column shows at least one significant between-population effect, thus excluding the possibility of simplifying the model by deleting further columns from the sample or response basis. The significant effects may be interpreted concretely by reference to cell or marginal proportions in the original data.

The Stay versus Move contrast, for example, shows significant effects that appear to include a triple interaction. The size and direction of the effects may be seen in the proportion of responses in column 1 of Table 8.1-4 relative to the sum of columns 1, 2, 3, and 4:

Race		Black		White	
Location		N	S	N	S
Origin	N	.236	.065	.281	.209
	S	.341	.378	.168	.457

Table 8.1-10 ESTIMATED EFFECTS IN THE FULL-RANK MODEL FOR THE DATA OF TABLE 8.1-4

SBV	Contrast	*1* Move or stay vs. Undecided	*2* Stay vs. Move	*3* Names camp vs. Undecided	*4* Northern vs. Southern
(000)	Constant	.1238	.0727	.2050	.1285
(100)	Race: B-W	−.0052	−.0063	.0062	.0971
(010)	Origin: N-S	−.0022	−.0587	−.0027	.6575
(001)	Location: N-S	−.0191	.0323	.0042	−.0154
(110)	Race × origin	−.0032	−.0237	.0616	−.0516
(101)	Race × location	.0030	.1033	−.0190	.0083
(011)	Origin × location	.0049	.1321	−.0091	−.0312
(111)	Race × origin × location	−.0008	.0219	−.0114	.0411
SE		.0081	.0083	.0141	.0208

Recruits in camps not in the same region as their home of record tend to prefer to move—a tendency which is especially pronounced for northern Blacks in the South and, to a somewhat lesser extent, southern Whites in the North, thus accounting for the triple interaction. The Origin × Location interaction is substantial in both Blacks and Whites and accounts for a sizable estimate (.1321) of this effect in Table 8.1-10. These effects have obvious interpretations in terms of racial and regional attitudes prevailing at the time the data were collected.

The tendency for the recruits to name a specific camp to which they wish to move versus wanting to move without naming a camp shows little evidence of population differences except for a Race × Origin interaction. The nature of this interaction is seen in the proportion, among those who wish to move, of Blacks and Whites of northern and southern origin who are able to name a camp:

Origin		N	S
Race	B	.868	.769
	W	.794	.888

As the sign of the estimated effect implies, the association is positive. It could perhaps be interpreted to mean that southern Blacks are less well informed about training installations than are northern Blacks, while northern Whites are less well informed than southern Whites.

Finally, among those recruits who name an alternative camp, there is some Race × Origin interaction (−.0516) and an overwhelming Origin effect (.6575). The latter is evident in the proportion of recruits choosing North in preference to South:

Origin		N	S
Race	B	.840	.324
	W	.818	.200

The interactive effect is negative because the tendency of southern Blacks to choose northern camps is relatively greater than that of southern Whites. Much more pronounced, however, is the main effect of Northerners of both races to choose northern camps.

8.1.5 Incomplete Data

It may happen that one or more entries in a table of qualitative data, such as Table 8.1-1, is missing either by accident or because occurrence in any such cell is interdicted physically or logically. On condition that the missing frequencies do not affect the definiteness of the matrix of second derivatives in (8.1-22), the solution of Sec. 8.1-3 remains applicable with only minor modifications. In general, the mathematical model (8.1-20) assumed for the data will define a logit for each cell whether the observations are missing or not. However, the response function (8.1-18) must not be permitted to assign a nonzero probability to that cell. Thus, for example, if cell h of population j corresponds to a missing observation, the response probabilities for that population should be defined as

$$P_{jk} = \frac{e^{z_k}}{\sum_{i \neq h}^{m} e^{z_i}} \qquad k \neq h \qquad (8.1\text{-}33)$$

The corresponding term is then deleted from the likelihood equations by defining for population j the $m \times m$ diagonal matrix $\mathbf{D}_j$, with elements equal to 1 where an observation is present and 0 where it is not, and writing

$$\sum_{j=1}^{n} \mathbf{TD}_j(\mathbf{r}_j - N_j\mathbf{P}_j) \times \mathbf{K}_j = \mathbf{0} \qquad (8.1\text{-}34)$$

Terms are similarly deleted from the matrix of second derivatives:

$$-\mathbf{H}(\Gamma) = -\sum_{j=1}^{n} N_j\mathbf{TD}_j\mathbf{W}_j\mathbf{D}_j\mathbf{T}' \times \mathbf{K}_j\mathbf{K}_j' \qquad (8.1\text{-}35)$$

On condition that the negative of (8.1-35) is positive definite, the Newton-Raphson solution of (8.1-34) in general converges. In actual computation, the effect of the multiplications by $\mathbf{D}_j$ can be obtained merely by setting the corresponding elements of $\mathbf{r}_j$ and $\mathbf{P}_j$ equal to zero.

If $n_0 = \sum \mathbf{1}'\mathbf{D}_j\mathbf{1}$ denotes the number of cells containing observations, the degrees of freedom for the residual chi-square is given by

$$\text{df} = n_0 - rs \qquad (8.1\text{-}36)$$

Other aspects of the solution are the same as in the complete case (see Fienberg [1972] for further details).

EXAMPLE 8.1-8 (*Ethological observations*) Fienberg [1972] makes use of ethological data reported by Ploog [1967] to illustrate an analysis of incomplete data essentially the same as that applied here. The data shown in Table 8.1-11 represent the number of genital displays of paired squirrel monkeys from a colony of six animals. The rows of the table represent the active partner in the display, and columns the passive partner. Since an animal cannot pair with itself, the diagonal cells of this table are undefined. Notice that there are also empirical zero entries in this table, including the marginal frequency for row 3. These values, which do not in general imply zero expected values, are to be distinguished from the *a priori* zero probabilities indicated by dashes in the diagonal of the table.

A question of interest concerning Table 8.1-11 is whether the probability of a display is merely the product of the active and passive animals' probability of participating in a display, that is, whether there are no relationships between specific pairs of animals which influence probability of display. With respect to incomplete contingency tables, this hypothesis has been called *quasi-independence* by Goodman [1968]. Classifications are quasi-independent if the multiplicative relationship holds for that part of the data remaining after *a priori* zeros have been excluded. To test this hypothesis, we fix the marginal proportions by fitting a main-class logistic model and estimate the expected frequencies excluding the *a priori* zeros. The chi-square is computed from these expected values by (8.1-24) or (8.1-25) and referred for the test of hypothesis to the central chi-square distribution with degrees of freedom given by (8.1-36).

To compute this chi-square for the data of Table 8.1-11, it is convenient to regard the active participants as populations, and the passive participants as response categories. Then the row corresponding to animal 3, which is never an active participant, can be eliminated to leave a 5 × 6 table in which the row margins are fixed by the restriction on the multivariate logit. The column margin may then be fixed by choosing the rank-1 design basis

$$\mathbf{K} = \begin{bmatrix} 1 \\ 1 \\ 1 \\ 1 \\ 1 \end{bmatrix}$$

Table 8.1-11 FREQUENCY OF GENITAL DISPLAY BETWEEN EACH PAIR OF ANIMALS IN A COLONY OF SIX SQUIRREL MONKEYS [PLOOG, 1967]

Active participant	Passive participant 1	2	3	4	5	6	Total
1	—	1	5	8	9	0	23
2	29	—	14	46	4	0	93
3	0	0	—	0	0	0	0
4	2	3	1	—	38	2	46
5	0	0	0	0	—	1	1
6	9	25	4	6	13	—	57
Total	40	29	24	60	64	3	

and the rank-5 response basis, say,

$$\mathbf{T}' = \tfrac{1}{2}\begin{bmatrix} 1 & 0 & 0 & 0 & 0 \\ 0 & 1 & 0 & 0 & 0 \\ 0 & 0 & 1 & 0 & 0 \\ 0 & 0 & 0 & 1 & 0 \\ 0 & 0 & 0 & 0 & 1 \\ -1 & -1 & -1 & -1 & -1 \end{bmatrix}$$

The number of residual degrees of freedom is $n(m - 1) - rs$ minus the number of *a priori* zeros, or

$$5 \times 5 - 5 - 5 = 15$$

The figures in the body of Table 8.1-11, far from suggesting independence of the active-passive role, appear to indicate the dominance hierarchy

$$\begin{array}{ccccc} & \nearrow & 1 & \rightarrow & 3 \\ 6 \rightarrow 2 & & & \searrow & \\ & \searrow & 4 & \rightarrow & 5 \end{array}$$

The displays tend to occur most frequently between animals of neighboring rank, and the residual chi-square of 168.05 clearly rejects quasi-independence. If row 5, containing only one occurrence, is deleted, the chi-square drops to 116.69, but it is still highly significant on 10 degrees of freedom.

8.1.6 Ordered Categories

A typical source of ordered categorical data in behavioral studies is the response of subjects or observers to some form of rating scale. The scale defines for the respondent a dimension on which he is required to make a judgment of quantity, intensity, or degree. Usually only a coarsely graded response is expected, as, for example, in the conventional A, B, C, D, F reporting of school grades. It has been shown that the amount of information which subjects are capable of transmitting with such a scale increases as the number of categories are increased to eight or nine. Beyond that, the gain in transmitted information is too small to justify more finely graded responses [Miller, 1963].

Unlike the comparative judgments represented in Fig. 8.1-1, the absolute judgments required in ratings present a semantic problem in defining the intervals of the scale to the respondent. Figure 8.1-2 illustrates various solutions of this problem in rating forms that have become standard in certain areas of psychological research. Item *a* is the so-called *hedonic* scale used in studies of food preference [Jones, Peryam, and Thurstone, 1955]; *b* is the form used in the "semantic differential" technique [Osgood, 1953, page 714]; *c* is a magnitude-estimation scale for similarities used in multidimensional scaling [Wainer, 1973]; and *d* is the so-called *Likert* scale used in attitude studies [Murphy and Likert, 1938, page 14 ff]. Note that in some of these scales each category is defined descriptively, while in others only the end points are described and the intervening points are defined graphically.

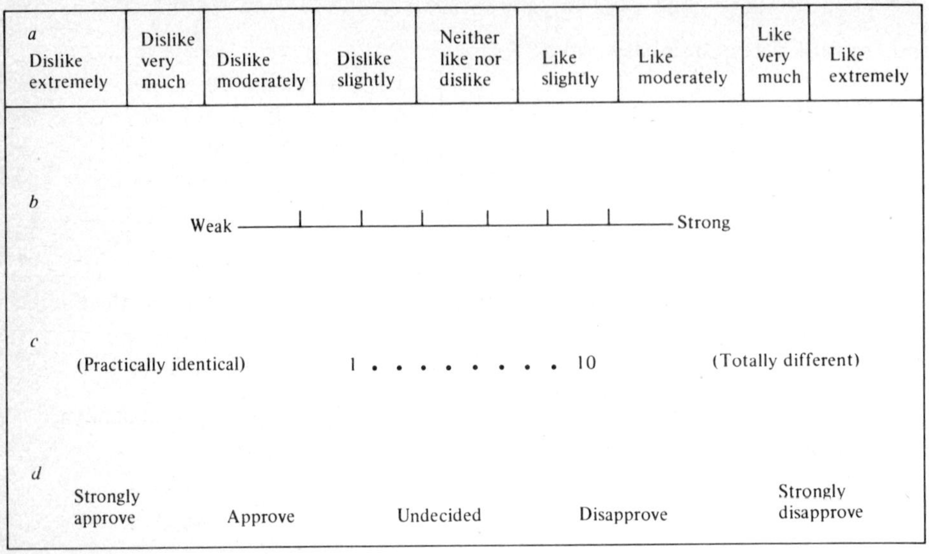

FIGURE 8.1-1
Examples of rating forms with ordered categories.

Regrettably, it is the rule rather than the exception in the literature to find that responses on these forms are quantified merely by assigning integral values 1 through m to the m categories. This practice is justified in that it preserves the ordering of the categories, but not in its assumption of equal intervals between categories.

In the present treatment we avoid this gratuitous assumption by extending the threshold concept of Sec. 8.1.1 to m categories. We suppose that the choice of category is controlled by a response process y distributed $N(\mu_j,\sigma_j)$ in population j. The probability that a subject selected randomly from this population will respond in or below category k is then given by

$$\mathscr{P}_{jk} = \frac{1}{\sqrt{2\pi}\,\sigma_j}\int_{-\infty}^{\tau_k} e^{-(y-\mu_j)^2/2\sigma_j^2}\,dy$$

where τ_k is the threshold value corresponding to the upper boundary of category k. The script letter is used to distinguish this *cumulative* probability from the probabilities for separate categories. Introducing the standard variable $z = (y - \mu_j)/\sigma_j$, we have

$$\mathscr{P}_{jk} = \frac{1}{\sqrt{2\pi}}\int_{-(\tau_k-\mu_j)/\sigma_j}^{\infty} e^{-z^2/2}\,dz = \Phi\left(\frac{\tau_k - \mu_j}{\sigma_j}\right) \qquad (8.1\text{-}37)$$

The response function (8.1-37) is depicted graphically in Fig. 8.1-2. The upper boundary of category m and the lower boundary of category 1 are plus and minus infinity, respectively; the remaining $m - 1$ boundaries correspond to threshold values $\tau_1, \tau_2, \ldots, \tau_{m-1}$, which delimit successive intervals on the latent continuum.

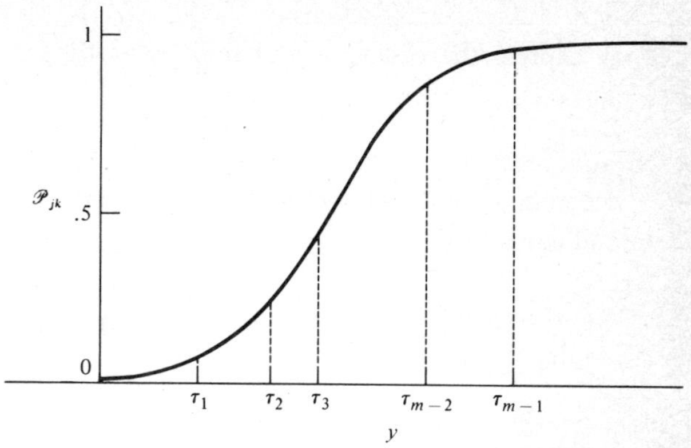

FIGURE 8.1-2
The response function for ordered categories.

To simplify this model further in cases involving several populations (or, as in Table 8.1-5, treatment groups), we assume the homogeneity of the response-process dispersions, that is, $\sigma_j = \sigma$. We may then set $\sigma_j = 1$ by choice of unit, and express (8.1-37) as

$$\mathscr{P}_{jk} = \Phi(\tau_k - \mu_j) \qquad (8.1\text{-}38)$$

Finally, we assume that the vector of population means, $\boldsymbol{\mu}' = [\mu_1, \mu_2, \ldots, \mu_n]$, may be described by the linear model

$$\underset{n\times 1}{\boldsymbol{\mu}} = \underset{n\times m}{\mathbf{A}} \; \underset{m\times 1}{\boldsymbol{\xi}} \qquad (8.1\text{-}39)$$

If $\mathbf{A}$ is of deficient rank $l < m \leq n$, it will be necessary to reparameterize (8.1-39) as

$$\boldsymbol{\mu} = \underset{n\times l}{\mathbf{K}} \; \underset{l\times 1}{\boldsymbol{\theta}} \qquad (8.1\text{-}40)$$

where $|\mathbf{K}'\mathbf{K}| \neq 0$. Note that the constant term in the linear model is absorbed in the threshold values and must not appear in $\boldsymbol{\mu}$. Thus, $\mathbf{K}$ must not include the vector $\mathbf{1}$ as a column.*

Our problem now is to estimate the thresholds τ_h and the effects $\boldsymbol{\theta}$. Again proceeding by the method of maximum likelihood, we have, from the multinomial law, the log-likelihood function

$$\ln L = C + \sum_{j=1}^{n} \sum_{k=1}^{m} r_{jk} \ln P_{jk} \qquad (8.1\text{-}41)$$

where C is a constant independent of the P_{jk}. Defining

$$\mathscr{P}_{j0} = 0 \qquad \text{and} \qquad \mathscr{P}_{jm} = 1$$

* The discussion that follows is adapted from Kolakowski and Bock [1973a].

we may express the category probabilities as differences of successive cumulative probabilities:

$$P_{jk} = \mathscr{P}_{jk} - \mathscr{P}_{j,k-1} \qquad (8.1\text{-}42)$$

Differentiating (8.1-41) with respect to τ_h and $\boldsymbol{\theta}$ and using 8.1-42, we obtain the likelihood equations

$$\frac{\partial \ln L}{\partial \tau_h} = \sum_{j=1}^{n} \left(\frac{r_{jh}}{P_{jh}} - \frac{r_{j,h+1}}{P_{j,h+1}} \right) \frac{\partial P_{jh}}{\partial \tau_h} = 0 \qquad h = 1, 2, \ldots, m-1$$

and

$$\underset{l \times 1}{\frac{\partial \ln L}{\partial \boldsymbol{\theta}}} = \sum_{j=1}^{n} \sum_{k=1}^{m} \frac{r_{jk}}{P_{jk}} \frac{\partial P_{jk}}{\partial \boldsymbol{\theta}} = \mathbf{0}$$

Differentiating again, we obtain the elements of the matrix of second derivatives

$$\frac{\partial^2 \ln L}{\partial \tau_g \, \partial \tau_h} = \begin{cases} \displaystyle\sum_{j=1}^{n} \left[-\left(\frac{r_{jh}}{P_{jh}^2} + \frac{r_{j,h+1}}{P_{j,h+1}^2} \right) \left(\frac{\partial P_{jh}}{\partial \tau_h} \right)^2 + \left(\frac{r_{jh}}{P_{jh}} - \frac{r_{j,h+1}}{P_{j,h+1}} \right) \frac{\partial^2 P_{jk}}{\partial \tau_h^2} \right] & g = h \\ \displaystyle\sum_{j=1}^{n} \frac{r_{j,h+1}}{P_{j,h+1}^2} \frac{\partial P_{j,h+1}}{\partial \tau_{h+1}} & g = h + 1 \\ 0 & |h - g| > 1 \end{cases}$$

$$g = 1, 2, \ldots, m-1$$
$$h = 1, 2, \ldots, m-1$$

$$\underset{l \times 1}{\frac{\partial^2 \ln L}{\partial \tau_h \, \partial \boldsymbol{\theta}}} = \sum_{j=1}^{n} \left[-\left(\frac{r_{jh}}{P_{jh}^2} \frac{\partial P_{jh}}{\partial \boldsymbol{\theta}} - \frac{r_{j,h+1}}{P_{j,h+1}^2} \frac{\partial P_{j,h+1}}{\partial \boldsymbol{\theta}} \right) \frac{\partial P_{jh}}{\partial \tau_h} + \left(\frac{r_{jh}}{P_{jh}} - \frac{r_{j,h+1}}{P_{j,h+1}} \right) \frac{\partial^2 P_{jh}}{\partial \tau_h \, \partial \boldsymbol{\theta}} \right]$$

$$\frac{\partial^2 \ln L}{\partial \boldsymbol{\theta} \, \partial \boldsymbol{\theta}'} = \sum_{j=1}^{n} \sum_{k=1}^{m} \left[-\frac{r_{jk}}{P_{jk}^2} \frac{\partial P_{jk}}{\partial \boldsymbol{\theta}} \frac{\partial P_{jk}}{\partial \boldsymbol{\theta}'} + \frac{r_{jk}}{P_{jk}} \frac{\partial^2 P_{jk}}{\partial \boldsymbol{\theta} \, \partial \boldsymbol{\theta}'} \right]$$

At this point we again shift, for computational convenience, from the normal response function to the logistic function

$$\mathscr{P}_{jk} = \frac{1}{1 + e^{-(\tau_k - \mathbf{K}_j'\boldsymbol{\theta})}} \qquad (8.1\text{-}43)$$

where $\mathbf{K}_j$ is the jth row of $\mathbf{K}$ defined as a column vector. With this choice of response function,

$$P_{jk} = (1 + e^{-(\tau_k - \mathbf{K}_j'\boldsymbol{\theta})})^{-1} - (1 + e^{-(\tau_{k-1} - \mathbf{K}_j'\boldsymbol{\theta})})^{-1} \qquad (8.1\text{-}44)$$

and

$$\frac{\partial P_{jh}}{\partial \tau_h} = \mathscr{P}_{jh}\mathscr{Q}_{jh}$$

$$\frac{\partial P_{j,h+1}}{\partial \tau_h} = -\mathscr{P}_{jh}\mathscr{Q}_{jh}$$

$$\frac{\partial P_{jh}}{\partial \tau_{h-1}} = -\mathscr{P}_{j,h-1}\mathscr{Q}_{j,h-1}$$

and

$$\frac{\partial P_{jk}}{\partial \boldsymbol{\theta}} = -(\mathscr{P}_{jk}\mathscr{Q}_{jk} - \mathscr{P}_{j,k-1}\mathscr{Q}_{j,k-1})\mathbf{K}_j$$

where $\mathscr{Q} = 1 - \mathscr{P}$. Thus,

$$\frac{\partial \ln L}{\partial \tau_h} = \sum_{j=1}^{n} \left(\frac{r_{jh}}{P_{jh}} - \frac{r_{j,h+1}}{P_{j,h+1}} \right) \mathscr{P}_{jh}\mathscr{Q}_{jh} \qquad h = 1, 2, \ldots, m-1 \tag{8.1-45}$$

and

$$\frac{\partial \ln L}{\partial \boldsymbol{\theta}} = -\sum_{j=1}^{n}\sum_{k=1}^{m} \frac{r_{jk}}{P_{jk}} (\mathscr{P}_{jk}\mathscr{Q}_{jk} - \mathscr{P}_{j,k-1}\mathscr{Q}_{j,k-1})\mathbf{K}_j \tag{8.1-46}$$

Unlike the model in Sec. 8.1-3, the second derivatives here are not free of the observations. We may therefore simplify the calculations further by substituting for the matrix of second derivatives the *information matrix*

$$\mathbf{I} = \mathscr{E}\left[-\frac{\partial^2 \ln L}{\partial u \, \partial v} \right] \tag{8.1-47}$$

that is, the expected value of the negative of the second derivatives. The use of the information matrix in the Newton-Raphson solution of the likelihood equations is called Fisher's method of *efficient scores*; it is asymptotically equivalent to a Newton-Raphson solution and in most applications converges almost as quickly. Using (8.1-47) and setting $r_{jk} = N_j P_{jk}$ in the second derivatives above, we obtain

$$\mathscr{E}\left[-\frac{\partial^2 \log L}{\partial \tau_g \, \partial \tau_h} \right] = \begin{cases} \displaystyle\sum_{j=1}^{n} N_j \frac{(\mathscr{P}_{j,h+1} - \mathscr{P}_{j,h-1})\mathscr{P}_{jh}{}^2\mathscr{Q}_{jh}{}^2}{P_{jh}P_{j,h+1}} & g = h \\ \displaystyle -\sum_{j=1}^{n} N_j \frac{\mathscr{P}_{j,h+1}\mathscr{Q}_{j,h+1}\mathscr{P}_{jh}\mathscr{Q}_{jh}}{P_{j,h+1}} & g = h+1 \\ 0 & |h - g| > 1 \end{cases} \tag{8.1-48}$$

$$\underset{l \times 1}{\mathscr{E}\left[-\frac{\partial^2 \log L}{\partial \tau_h \, \partial \boldsymbol{\theta}} \right]} = -\sum_{j=1}^{n} N_j \mathscr{P}_{jh}\mathscr{Q}_{jh} \left(\frac{\mathscr{P}_{jh}\mathscr{Q}_{jh} - \mathscr{P}_{j,h-1}\mathscr{Q}_{j,h-1}}{P_{jh}} - \frac{\mathscr{P}_{j,h+1}\mathscr{Q}_{j,h+1} - \mathscr{P}_{jh}\mathscr{Q}_{jh}}{P_{j,h+1}} \right) \mathbf{K}_j \tag{8.1-49}$$

$$\underset{l \times l}{\mathscr{E}\left[-\frac{\partial^2 \log L}{\partial \boldsymbol{\theta} \, \partial \boldsymbol{\theta}'} \right]} = \sum_{j=1}^{n} N_j \sum_{k=1}^{m} \frac{(\mathscr{P}_{jk}\mathscr{Q}_{jk} - \mathscr{P}_{j,k-1}\mathscr{Q}_{j,k-1})^2}{P_{jk}} \mathbf{K}_j\mathbf{K}_j' \tag{8.1-50}$$

The improved estimates at the ith stage of the Newton-Raphson process are obtained by adding to the estimates from the previous stage the product of the inverse information matrix and the values of the first derivatives at that stage. Also, the asymptotic covariance matrix of the estimator is given by the inverse information matrix.

EXAMPLE 8.1-9 (*Behavior ratings*) In Table 8.1-5, the columns represent five ordered categories, and the rows a 2 × 2 experimental design. A design basis for a full-rank model (excluding the constant term) is, therefore,

$$\mathbf{K} = \begin{bmatrix} 1 & 1 & 1 \\ 1 & -1 & -1 \\ -1 & 1 & -1 \\ -1 & -1 & 1 \end{bmatrix}$$

Fitting successively a rank-2 and rank-3 model by the maximum-likelihood method described above, we obtain the residual χ^2's shown in Table 8.1-12. The main-class model is definitely rejected, but the model including the interaction term is not rejected at the .05 level. Since the rank-3 logistic model is reasonable for these data, the effects of the experiment may be estimated as follows:

Effect	Estimate	SE
θ_1 (Priming − Re-exposure)	.3621	.2295
θ_2 (Control − Drug)	.6945	.2327
θ_3 (Interaction)	−.7400	.2335

A convenient device for illustrating the interactive effect is to compute the estimated cell effects,

$$\hat{\mu} = \mathbf{K}\hat{\theta}$$

and to prepare the conventional interaction plot (see Fig. 5.3-3). In this instance,

$$\hat{\mu}_{11} = .3166 \qquad \hat{\mu}_{12} = .4076$$
$$\hat{\mu}_{21} = 1.0724 \qquad \hat{\mu}_{22} = -1.7966$$

Table 8.1-12

Model	Rank of model	Residual chi-square*	df	p
Main class	2	23.61	10	$<.01$
Main class and interaction	3	15.07	9	$.1 > p > .05$

*Pearsonian

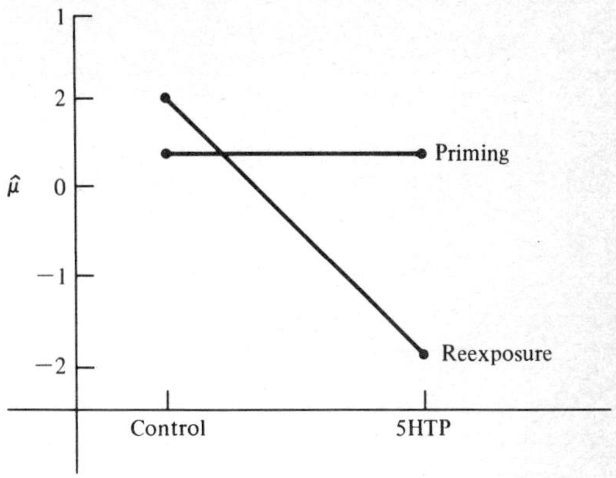

FIGURE 8.1-3
Effect on audiogenic seizures in C57BL mice of 5-hydroxytryptophan administered before priming and before reexposure.

and the plot is as shown in Fig. 8.1-3. The effect of the drug in reducing the severity of seizure during reexposure to auditory stimulation is clearly seen in this figure.

The estimated threshold values for this model are as follows:

Threshold	Estimate	SE
τ_1	−3.3993	.5677
τ_2	−.5138	.2639
τ_3	−.3698	.2601
τ_4	.4756	.2566

Note that the intervals corresponding to the response categories are far from equal and would not justify the assignment of evenly spaced numerical values for purposes of a conventional analysis of variance of these data.

Exercise 8.1-1 (*Constancy of Weber's ratio*) As a test of the constancy of Weber's ratio for sweetness of sugar solutions, examine the homogeneity of regression of the binomial logit on log concentration between *B* levels in Table 8.1-2. A statistical test for homogeneity of regressions may be obtained by incorporating in the logistic model a term for the cross product of the log concentration of solution *A* and the log concentration of solution *B*. Compare this method of testing homogeneity with that in Bock and Jones [1968, Chap. 4].

Exercise 8.1-2 (*Effects of media on health knowledge*) Goodman [1970] illustrates an analysis of interactions in a complex contingency table with data taken from Lombard and Doering [1947], which are shown in Table 8.1-13. The response is knowledge or lack of knowledge of certain facts about cancer. Subjects are classified according to their habitual exposure to newspapers (*A*), radio (*B*), books and magazines (*C*), and lectures (*D*). Level 1 of each factor

Table 8.1-13 KNOWLEDGE OF CANCER SYMPTOMS OF SUBJECTS CLASSIFIED ACCORDING TO EXPOSURE TO VARIOUS MEDIA (SEE TEXT)

Factor *ABCD*	Knowledge Good	Knowledge Poor
1111	84	393
1112	2	10
1121	67	83
1122	3	8
1211	13	50
1212	4	3
1221	16	16
1222	1	3
2111	75	156
2112	7	6
2121	201	177
2122	27	18
2211	35	59
2212	8	4
2221	102	67
2222	23	8

represents no exposure, and level 2 exposure. Examine the effects of the media and their interactions on knowledge of cancer by the method of Sec. 8.1.2. Compare the goodness-of-fit statistics for various models with those given in Goodman's Table 6.

Exercise 8.1-3 (*Attitudes of high-school seniors toward science*) The data in Table 8.1-14 were presented by Solomon [1961] and subsequently reanalyzed by Bock [1970]. The responses of 2,982 New Jersey high-school seniors to four items of a questionnaire entitled "Attitudes toward Science and Scientific Careers" are shown. The items, which were scored 1 for "agree" or 0 for "disagree," were as follows:

1 The development of new ideas is the scientist's greatest source of satisfaction.
2 Scientists and engineers should be eliminated from the military draft.
3 The scientist will make his maximum contribution to society when he has freedom to work on problems which interest him.
4 The monetary compensation of a Nobel Prize winner in physics should be at least equal to that given popular entertainers.

The response classification in Table 8.1-14 represents all possible combinations of response to these four items. The sample design is based on a

Table 8.1-14 ATTITUDE TOWARD SCIENCE OF HIGH-SCHOOL SENIORS WITH HIGH AND LOW VOCABULARY KNOWLEDGE

Response to items 1234	Subject's vocabulary knowledge	
	Low	High
1111	62	122
1110	70	68
1101	31	33
1100	41	25
1011	283	329
1010	253	247
1001	200	172
1000	305	217
0111	14	20
0110	11	10
0101	11	11
0100	14	9
0011	31	56
0010	46	55
0001	37	64
0000	82	53

dichotomization of the subjects into those above and below the median of a brief vocabulary test.

Compare the two vocabulary knowledge groups with respect to their responses on the four questionnaire items. Check the agreement of the results with those of Bock [1970].

Exercise 8.1-4 (*Difference limen for lifted weights*) Guilford [1936, page 187] gives data, reproduced in Table 8.1-15, for judgments of apparent differences in lifted weights obtained by the constant method. The subject, who is blindfolded, lifts two weights successively and states whether the second is "greater" than or "less" than the first. If the subject is in doubt, he reports "doubtful." One of the weights (B) is standard at 200 grams, and the other (A) varies as shown in Table 8.1-15. The sequential position of A and B is balanced and randomized.

Test the hypothesis that the graded response model of Sec. 8.1.6 may be expressed as a linear function of the logarithm of the ratio of the weights of A and B. Discuss the question, raised by Guilford, of how a difference limen should be defined for this type of data.

Table 8.1-15 JUDGMENTS OF LIFTED WEIGHTS

Weight, g		Judgment: A is		
A	B	Greater	Doubtful	Less
185	200	5	4	91
190	200	12	18	70
195	200	15	25	60
200	200	30	42	28
205	200	55	35	10
210	200	70	18	12
215	200	85	9	6

Exercise 8.1-5 (*Food preferences*) Table 8.1-16 contains data given by Bock and Jones [1968, page 244] showing the preference for black olives of Army recruits from different sections of the U. S. The responses were obtained with the nine-category hedonic scale (Fig. 8.1-2), but some of the little-used categories have been combined to simplify the data. Using the method of Sec. 8.1.6, check the goodness of fit of these data to the logistic model for ordered categories, and test the significance of the demographic effects. Compare the maximum-likelihood estimates with the minimum logit chi-square estimates in Bock and Jones and those of Williams and Grizzle [1972].

ANSWER Pearsonian chi-square for the rank-3 main-class model is 22.93; df = 22.

Exercise 8.1-6 (*Survey data*) Analyze and discuss the association between race, geographical origin, and camp assignment of the respondents to the attitude survey discussed in Example 8.1-3.

Table 8.1-16 PREFERENCE RATINGS FOR BLACK OLIVES OF ARMY RECRUITS FROM THE RURAL AND URBAN NORTHEAST (NE), MIDWEST (MW) AND SOUTHEAST (SE)

		Preference categories						
Origin		1	2, 3	4, 5	6	7	8, 9	Total
	NE	23	18	20	18	10	15	104
Rural	MW	30	22	21	17	8	12	110
	SW	11	9	26	19	17	24	106
	NE	18	17	18	18	6	25	102
Urban	MW	20	15	12	17	16	28	108
	SW	12	9	23	21	19	30	114

8.2 MULTIPLE-RESPONSE DATA

The greater part of qualitative multiple-response data in behavioral research comes from studies that attempt to account totally for the production or activity of individual subjects. Some of the types of investigation illustrative of this research strategy are (1) naturalistic observation of the so-called *behavioral ecology* of human or animal subjects (Jay [1968]; Wright [1967]; Stodolsky [1974]); (2) continuous or time-sampled recording of teacher-pupil and pupil-pupil interaction in school classrooms (Medley and Mitzel [1963]); (3) analysis of interpersonal exchanges during small-group decision processes (Bales [1950]; Heyns and Lippitt [1954]); (4) categorizing of units of verbal production, as in the grammatical analysis of normal or aphasic speech (Jones et al. [1963]; Wepman et al. [1956]); (5) the thematic classification of content of stories told in response to standard stimuli (Murray [1938, 1943]; Henry [1856]); and (5) systematic scoring of responses to inkblots or other projective material (Beck [1950]; Klopfer et al. [1954]).

It is customary in these studies to preserve the time dimension in the data collection by seriatum recording of responses and periodic noting of elapsed time. When the initial record is summarized, however, it is common practice to ignore time and sequence and to reduce the data to a simple enumeration of the number of behavioral units from each subject in various predefined response categories.* Schematically, such summary data take the form shown in Table 8.2-1: The quantities

* From the point of view of analysis, a very different form of data results if the time dimension is retained (see Bock [1952] for an example).

Table 8.2-1 FORM OF MULTIPLE-RESPONSE DATA

Group	Subject within group	Categories 1	2	⋯	m	Total
1	1	r_{111}	r_{112}	⋯	r_{11m}	$r_{11.}$
	2	r_{211}	r_{212}	⋯	r_{21m}	$r_{12.}$
	⋯	⋯	⋯	⋯	⋯	⋯
	N_1	r_{N_111}	r_{N_112}	⋯	r_{N_11m}	$r_{N_11.}$
2	1	r_{121}	r_{122}	⋯	r_{12m}	$r_{12.}$
	2	r_{221}	r_{222}	⋯	r_{22m}	$r_{22.}$
	⋯	⋯	⋯	⋯	⋯	⋯
	N_2	r_{N_221}	r_{N_222}	⋯	r_{N_22m}	$r_{N_22.}$
⋯	⋯	⋯	⋯	⋯	⋯	⋯
n	1	r_{1n1}	r_{1n2}	⋯	r_{1nm}	$r_{1n.}$
	2	r_{2n1}	r_{2n2}	⋯	r_{2nm}	$r_{2n.}$
	⋯	⋯	⋯	⋯	⋯	⋯
	N_n	r_{N_nn1}	r_{N_nn2}	⋯	r_{N_nnm}	$r_{N_nn.}$

r_{ijk} are the number of times subject i from group j responds in category k. The total number of responses of subject i is $r_{ij\cdot}$, the number of subjects in group j is N_j, and the number of groups is n. As the overall frequency of use of the categories is generally an artifact of the category definition, primary interest in these data attaches to the differences in response frequency between groups. In this section we consider a statistical procedure for detecting and describing such differences.

8.2.1 A Model for Multiple-Response Data

For purposes of the data analysis, we assume that, during the period of observation, the distribution of responses of the ith subject in group j is in a steady state that may be characterized by the probabilities $P_{ij1}, P_{ij2}, \ldots, P_{ijm}$ of a response in categories 1 through m, respectively. We assume further that, for the given subject, successive responses are independent, so that the frequencies in the i, j row of Table 8.2-1 may be assumed multinomially distributed with parameters given by these probabilities and by the total frequency $r_{ij\cdot}$. These may be called the *person parameters*, because they describe individual subjects. But the subjects are a random way of classification, and the person parameters therefore have a distribution in the population of subjects corresponding to each group. It is the parameters of this latter distribution, i.e., the *population parameters*, which we wish to examine for purposes of comparing the groups. In other words, we are dealing with a problem involving a *compound distribution*, and the question which naturally follows is, "How should this distribution be specified?"

Regrettably, this question has no fully satisfactory answer at present. Mosimann [1962] has proposed a multivariate beta-multinomial model, but it assumes independence of the multinomial probabilities (except for the dependence introduced by the constraint $\sum_{k=1}^{m} P_{ijk} = 1$) and is on that account unsuited to behavioral data. The only workable solution at present appears to be the large-sample approach of using the multivariate normal distribution to approximate the distribution of the person parameters after some suitable variate transformation. This is, of course, just the multivariate extension of techniques for the univariate analysis of variance of enumeration data by means of variance-stabilizing transformations (e.g., the arcsine or square-root transformation [Bartlett, 1947a]). In the multivariate case, however, variance stabilization is not a sufficient criterion for choosing a transformation because covariances are involved as well. Although the choice is not clearcut in this context, perhaps the most defensible is the multivariate logistic transformation defined implicitly by (8.1-17). Since the logits are unbounded, their means in samples of subjects will tend to multivariate normality more quickly than will those of the untransformed response probabilities. Furthermore, the parameters of an assumed full-rank model for the multivariate logit may be readily estimated by maximum likelihood within subjects. This is evident from the following argument.

As in Sec. 8.1.3, we assume that the vector logit for subject i in group j is a linear function of effects associated with the structure of the response classification. That is,

$$\underset{1\times m}{\mathbf{z}'_{ij}} = \underset{1\times l}{\boldsymbol{\beta}'_{ij}} \underset{l\times m}{\mathbf{A}} \tag{8.2-1}$$

Now suppose the model is of full rank; that is, rank(**A**) $= m$. Then (8.2-1) may be reparameterized as

$$\mathbf{z}'_{ij} = \underset{1\times l}{\boldsymbol{\beta}'_{ij}} \underset{l\times m}{\mathbf{S}} \underset{m\times m}{\mathbf{T}} = \underset{1\times m}{\boldsymbol{\gamma}'_{ij}} \underset{m\times m}{\mathbf{T}} \tag{8.2-2}$$

where **T** is a nonsingular square matrix, and **S** is in the row space of **A**.

Assuming the observed frequencies to be multinomially distributed, we may obtain the maximum-likelihood estimates of γ as the solution of

$$\mathbf{T}(\mathbf{r}_{ij} - r_{ij\cdot}\hat{\mathbf{P}}_{ij}) = \mathbf{0}$$

where the elements of $\mathbf{r}_{ij}$ comprise the i, j row in Table 8.2-1, and those of $\mathbf{P}_{ij}$ depend upon $\mathbf{z}_{ij}$ through the response function (8.1-18). Since **T** is nonsingular,

$$\mathbf{r}_{ij} = r_{ij\cdot}\hat{\mathbf{P}}_{ij}$$

and
$$[\ln r_{ijk}] = (\ln r_{ij\cdot})\mathbf{1} + [\ln \hat{P}_{ijk}] = (\ln r_{ij\cdot})\mathbf{1} + [\hat{z}_{ijk}] - (\ln D_{ij})\mathbf{1}$$
$$= \mathbf{T}'\hat{\boldsymbol{\gamma}}_{ij} + c\mathbf{1}$$
$$\hat{\boldsymbol{\gamma}}_{ij} = (\mathbf{T}')^{-1}[\ln r_{ijk}] + c(\mathbf{T}')^{-1}\mathbf{1} \tag{8.2-3}$$

With respect to columns of $\mathbf{T}^{-1}$ which are contrasts, the rightmost term vanishes, and the parameter estimate is given by the corresponding contrast of the natural logarithms of the observed frequencies. In general, it is convenient to choose **T** in the form

$$\mathbf{T} = [\underset{1}{\mathbf{1}}, \underset{m-1}{\mathbf{C}}]$$

where $\mathbf{C}'\mathbf{1} = \mathbf{0}$. The $\hat{\gamma}_{ij0}$ is an arbitrary location constant (which is a function of $\sum \ln r_{ijk}$), and $\gamma_{ij1}, \gamma_{ij2}, \ldots, \gamma_{ij,m-1}$ are the contrasts of logarithms of the observed frequencies. A choice of **T** orthogonal is also convenient because then $(\mathbf{T}')^{-1} = \mathbf{T}$. In practice, it is desirable to add $\frac{1}{2}$ to all frequencies before taking logarithms. This avoids the problem of zero frequencies and reduces bias in the estimates (see Bock and Jones [1968, Chap. 3]).

We now introduce the assumption that parameter estimates obtained in this way are multivariate normal and distributed similarly in each population of subjects. Strictly speaking, this cannot be precisely true, for there will be some variation in the estimates that is due to the sampling of responses within subjects and is a function of the person parameters. However, if the number of responses per subject $r_{ij.}$ is not too small, the variation from this source will not be appreciable relative to the variation in the person parameters, and the assumption of similarly distributed observations will not be much in error. Thus, a practical analysis of group differences in multiple-response data along the following lines can be justified:

1 The observed frequencies in the form of Table 8.2-1 are transformed by

$$z_{ijk} = \ln(r_{ijk} + \tfrac{1}{2})$$

2 The $m \times 1$ vector variates represented by the rows of Table 8.2-1 after the nonlinear transformation (8.2-4) are transformed linearly as

$$\mathbf{y}'_{ij} = \mathbf{z}'_{ij}\mathbf{T}^{-1} \qquad (8.2\text{-}5)$$

where $\mathbf{T}$ is a full-rank $(m \times m)$ basis matrix of the response model for the m categories. In general, $\mathbf{T}$ will take the form $\mathbf{T} = [\mathbf{1},\mathbf{C}]$, where $\mathbf{C}'\mathbf{1} = \mathbf{0}$.

3 An m-variate analysis of variance is carried out on the result of the transformation (8.2-5) for the purpose of detecting and estimating effects of the design on the subject groups.

4 In the absence of group effects, the overall nullity of the contrasts may also be tested.

In essence, this procedure is a repeated-measures analysis of the log-transformed proportions by the multivariate method described in Chap. 7.

EXAMPLE 8.2-1 (*The Rorschach psychogram*) In the Klopfer system, the determinants of responses to the Rorschach inkblots are classified in thirteen major categories as follows [Klopfer et al., 1954]:

Determinant	**Symbol**
1 Movement	
a Human movement	M
b Animal movement	FM
c Minor or inanimate movement	m
2 Diffusion-Vista	
a Shading conveys a three-dimensional expanse projected on the plane	k
b Shading conveys third dimension or depth	K
c Three-dimensional impression combined with definite form	FK
3 Form (response determined only by form)	F
4 Texture and Achromatic Color	
a Object possessing surface or texture qualities has definite form	Fc
b Shading conveys surface or texture	c
c Designation of black, white, or gray without definite form	C′
5 Bright Color	
a Colored objects with definite form	FC
b Colored objects with vague or indefinite form	CF
c Designation of color without reference to form	C

The summary of response determinants in the Rorschach records of Norwegian children studied by Haggard [1973] are shown, together with the age of each subject, in Table 8.2-2. Only the main responses are represented. Note that the Fc response was not scored in these data. The subject groups represent children from isolated farms (Isolates) and urban children (Controls), cross-classified by sex.

Table 8.2-2 RORSCHACH SUMMARIES (DETERMINANTS) OF NORWEGIAN CHILDREN*

Subjects	Age, years	M	FM	m	k	K	FK	F	c	C′	FC	CF	C	Total
		Isolates, male												
1	10	1	3	1	0	0	2	38	2	1	2	4	0	54
2	7	0	1	1	0	0	0	44	1	0	2	2	0	51
3	13	0	1	1	2	0	1	37	2	4	2	1	0	51
4	11	0	2	0	0	0	0	37	2	3	2	1	0	47
5	9	0	1	1	0	0	0	43	0	1	1	0	4	51
6	7	0	0	2	0	0	0	44	0	1	0	5	0	52
7	11	4	8	3	0	1	1	25	3	4	5	3	0	57
8	12	0	7	0	0	0	1	37	5	0	2	1	0	53
9	11	3	2	0	0	0	0	38	0	2	0	3	0	48
10	9	0	0	1	0	3	0	40	1	3	4	2	0	54
11	7	5	2	0	0	1	0	32	2	5	1	4	0	52
12	13	0	3	0	1	0	0	44	0	1	2	0	0	51
13	9	0	0	1	3	0	2	40	1	2	0	3	0	52
14	9	0	0	2	5	0	1	32	9	1	1	2	0	53
15	10	1	4	0	0	0	0	39	0	3	3	0	0	50
16	14	0	3	0	0	0	0	47	0	0	1	1	0	52
17	9	0	0	0	0	0	0	41	3	1	4	3	0	52
18	14	2	0	3	2	0	3	33	2	6	3	5	0	59
19	14	3	9	0	0	0	0	34	1	0	3	2	0	52
Total		19	46	16	13	5	11	725	34	38	38	42	4	991
		Controls, male												
1	7	1	2	5	0	1	2	37	5	2	0	4	0	59
2	9	1	4	2	3	1	1	29	0	2	3	7	0	53
3	12	2	6	2	0	1	2	35	5	1	2	3	0	59
4	14	7	9	1	0	2	1	24	5	2	0	2	0	53
5	12	2	1	0	0	0	0	45	0	0	2	0	0	50
6	14	1	2	2	2	3	3	37	2	1	1	2	0	56
7	13	3	7	4	2	1	1	24	2	4	7	1	0	56
8	9	2	3	0	0	0	0	40	0	3	3	0	0	51
9	10	0	8	1	0	0	0	38	0	3	2	0	0	52
10	10	5	1	5	0	0	2	29	0	4	1	6	0	53
11	11	3	1	1	2	1	0	33	3	6	1	4	4	59
12	7	1	6	2	1	2	0	26	4	7	4	4	0	57
13	8	7	6	4	1	1	1	24	2	6	5	5	0	62
14	12	1	2	2	0	3	1	35	5	1	1	3	0	54
Total		36	58	31	11	16	14	456	33	42	32	41	4	774

* From Haggard [1973].

Table 8.2-2 (continued)

Subjects	Age, years	M	FM	m	k	K	FK	F	c	C′	FC	CF	C	Total
		Isolates, female												
1	11	0	2	1	0	0	0	35	1	5	3	3	0	50
2	7	0	0	0	0	0	0	42	2	2	4	0	0	50
3	7	0	0	0	0	5	0	26	2	7	2	7	1	50
4	7	0	0	1	0	0	0	42	1	3	3	3	0	53
5	10	7	1	0	0	0	1	34	2	2	3	2	0	52
6	9	5	7	2	1	1	0	30	6	1	1	6	0	60
7	12	7	5	4	0	1	3	23	7	2	5	4	0	61
8	14	7	5	4	0	1	3	25	8	4	4	5	0	66
9	13	2	3	0	0	3	0	38	1	5	1	1	0	54
10	12	2	1	0	0	0	0	31	4	3	3	0	0	44
11	7	5	5	2	0	1	0	28	0	1	5	3	0	50
12	13	0	0	0	1	4	0	34	4	7	1	1	0	52
13	13	1	3	0	0	1	0	33	7	1	1	3	0	50
14	11	1	2	2	0	0	0	46	1	0	0	1	0	53
15	10	3	4	2	1	2	2	34	1	2	2	1	0	54
16	13	1	1	0	2	0	1	38	2	3	2	2	0	52
17	8	0	1	1	0	0	0	39	1	1	2	1	5	51
18	7	0	3	2	0	1	2	39	1	1	2	1	0	52
19	12	2	3	0	1	2	0	31	3	3	3	0	0	48
20	10	7	2	1	0	3	0	13	2	4	1	2	0	35
21	9	0	1	5	0	3	4	27	5	3	2	1	0	51
Total		50	49	27	6	28	16	688	61	60	50	47	6	1,088
		Controls, female												
1	13	0	0	0	0	1	0	44	3	0	1	2	0	51
2	13	3	3	1	3	1	0	32	7	5	2	2	0	59
3	12	0	0	0	0	0	0	41	1	3	5	0	0	50
4	9	10	4	0	0	0	0	27	7	3	0	0	0	51
5	8	3	3	1	1	0	0	30	0	1	3	3	2	47
6	12	3	4	1	0	1	1	34	1	5	3	3	0	56
7	9	2	5	0	0	0	0	37	4	1	4	1	0	54
8	7	0	2	0	0	0	0	42	3	1	1	1	0	50
9	10	3	5	2	0	0	0	26	8	4	4	8	0	60
10	14	2	12	0	0	5	5	26	9	2	2	0	0	63
11	10	0	1	1	1	6	0	31	1	6	6	3	0	56
12	7	1	1	2	0	1	0	35	3	4	4	3	0	54
13	7	3	3	1	0	0	3	29	3	3	6	4	0	55
14	8	0	9	0	0	3	1	31	2	3	5	1	0	55
15	14	7	7	2	0	2	6	24	4	3	5	3	0	63
Total		37	59	11	5	20	16	489	56	44	51	34	2	824

* From Haggard [1973].

As can be seen in the column totals for these groups, the C response occurred too infrequently to be used in the data analysis and was therefore incorporated in CF before the log transformation. Thus, the number of categories in the analysis was 11 rather than 12.

The determinant classification does not have a structure which lends itself to the formulation of a response model, but certain ratios of determinant frequencies are recognized as important in interpretation. The log contrasts equivalent to these ratios have been incorporated in the transformation matrix shown in Table 8.2-3. Since there are no specified effects of the response structure to be estimated in this case, it will be perfectly satisfactory to use Table 8.2-3 directly as the transformation matrix $\mathbf{T}^{-1}$. The variates defined by this transformation may then be subjected to a two-way multivariate analysis of covariance with age as the covariate, in order to test the effects of isolation, sex, and the sex × isolation interaction. Note that the subclass numbers are nearly proportional ($\frac{19}{21} \approx \frac{14}{15}$), and the design is essentially orthogonal.

The analysis shows some evidence of a sex effect with the probability level of the generalized F at .06. The effect is concentrated predominantly in the function (FM + m)/(c + C′). Rorschach considered this function to relate to the introversive-extratensive balance of the subject, positive values indicating well-developed imagination and reduced responsiveness to the outer world [Klopfer et al., 1954, page 371]. The rationale is that to see movement in the blots requires a certain exercise of imagination, while being influenced by achromatic shading is a conservative response reflecting conformity to demands of the outer world. As indicated in Table 8.2-4, the

Table 8.2-3 TRANSFORMATION MATRIX USED IN THE ANALYSIS OF THE DATA IN TABLE 8.2-2

Function or ratio	Determinant										
	M	FM	m	k	K	FK	F	c	C′	FC	CF + C
1 R	1	1	1	1	1	1	1	1	1	1	1
2 (M + FM + m)/F	1	1	1	0	0	0	−3	0	0	0	0
3 (FM + m)/(c + C′)	0	1	1	0	0	0	0	−1	−1	0	0
4 Experience Balance	3	0	0	0	0	0	0	0	0	−1	−2
5 Ach/Chr	0	0	0	0	0	0	0	1	1	−1	−1
6 FC/CF	0	0	0	0	0	0	0	0	0	1	−1
7 F/FK	0	0	0	0	0	−1	1	0	0	0	0
8 K/FK	0	0	0	0	1	−1	0	0	0	0	0
9 M/FM	1	−1	0	0	0	0	0	0	0	0	0
10 c/C′	0	0	0	0	0	0	0	1	−1	0	0
11 k/K	0	0	0	−1	1	0	0	0	0	0	0

estimated effect for this function is positive, showing that boys exceed girls in introversive balance, quite as expected for children of this age (mean 10.4 years, SD 2.4 years).

The Experience Balance function, represented in these data by

$$\frac{M}{[FC + 2(CF + C)]}$$

which might be expected to show a similar effect, fails to do so, however. The ratio of achromatic to chromatic response (Ach/Chr) and the ratio of vista to depth responses (k/K) both show some indications of a sex effect when considered separately, but significance is lost in the step-down test, suggesting that their effects are accounted for by other variables. Various other of the functions defined in Table 8.2-3, although interpreted in Klopfer et al. [1954], are not necessarily associated with sex differences and show no evidence of such differences in these data.

Neither the isolation nor the sex × isolation effects show multivariate significance (p = .37 and .19, respectively), although the isolation effects in both R and (M + FM + m)/F have univariate significance levels of .01. The direction of the effects favors the urban group in both cases; i.e., the urban children give more responses and more movement responses. These two functions are fairly highly correlated, however (r = .776), showing that there is a tendency for the subject to shift from definitely formed responses to movement in later responses. As a result, the significance of (M + FM + m)/F fails to appear when R is eliminated in the step-down tests. The only other function which has a suggestion of an isolation effect is Experience Balance (univariate p = .081; step-down p = .152), with the urban children exceeding the rural in introversive balance, as we might expect.

Table 8.2-4 SEX EFFECT IN RORSCHACH RESPONSE DETERMINANTS
$F_0 = 1.74, p = .09$

Variate	Adjusted effects (male-female)	SE	Univariate F	p	Step-down F	p
1 R	−1.017	.905	1.26	.26	1.26	.27
2 (M + FM + m)/F	−.350	.567	.38	.53	.16	.69
3 (FM + m)/(c + C′)	1.016	.387	6.86	.01	9.26	.003
4 Experience Balance	−.753	.728	1.07	.31	.002	.96
5 Ach/Chr	−.658	.338	3.79	.06	.23	.63
6 FC/CF	−.450	.265	2.88	.09	3.29	.07
7 F/FK	.035	.212	.03	.87	.05	.82
8 K/FK	−.461	.239	3.70	.06	2.10	.15
9 M/FM	−.226	.232	.94	.33	.12	.72
10 c/C′	−.326	.254	1.65	.20	2.37	.12
11 k/K	−.636	.238	7.11	.01	1.25	.27

In the complete data analyzed by Haggard [1972], including Location, Content, and the determinant tendencies, clearly significant isolation effects are found for a number of interpretable functions of the category frequencies.

Exercise 8.2-1 (*Pecking preferences of chicks*) Data in Table 8.2-5, from an unpublished paper by Thissen [1972], show the number of times each of 10 socialized and 10 isolated chicks pecked at targets consisting of pinheads of the colors indicated. Each chick was tested in 15-min sessions on the first, second, and fifth day after hatching. Table 8.2-5 shows the totals for these sessions.

Using the method of Sec. 8.2, examine differences in overall rate of pecking and in color preference of the socialized and isolated groups. Where there are no group differences, test overall differences in color preference (see Hess [1956]).

Table 8.2-5 NUMBER OF PECKS OF SOCIALIZED AND ISOLATED CHICKS ON STIMULI (PINHEADS) OF VARIOUS COLORS

	Stimulus color							
Chicks	Blue	Green	Yellow	Orange	Red	Silver	White	Gold
Socialized								
1	27	22	11	20	10	7	26	1
2	4	25	3	6	0	9	9	8
3	3	26	2	4	3	8	5	0
4	13	23	0	3	12	24	11	4
5	6	12	0	2	0	8	11	11
6	2	7	0	14	2	1	6	9
7	20	27	4	2	0	10	30	16
8	10	0	5	13	5	24	5	11
9	7	20	0	6	0	9	10	1
10	4	4	13	18	6	18	17	15
Isolated								
1	4	7	2	10	4	24	0	2
2	2	0	0	14	7	0	0	0
3	15	0	0	21	3	29	8	0
4	0	11	0	0	1	19	1	0
5	5	8	0	0	0	0	0	2
6	8	17	14	14	0	15	7	20
7	15	7	0	20	9	21	5	5
8	8	8	5	14	8	17	13	9
9	2	3	6	6	3	18	2	22
10	21	14	2	29	6	9	11	9

APPENDIX A

A TABLE OF THE GENERALIZED F STATISTIC

$s = 1$ **Upper 5% points**

t \ r:	1	2	4	6	8	10	12	16	22	32
1	161.00	200.00	225.00	234.00	239.00	242.00	244.00	246.00	249.00	250.00
2	18.50	19.00	19.20	19.30	19.40	19.40	19.40	19.40	19.50	19.50
3	10.10	9.55	9.12	8.94	8.85	8.79	8.74	8.69	8.65	8.61
4	7.71	6.94	6.39	6.16	6.04	5.96	5.91	5.84	5.79	5.74
5	6.61	5.79	5.19	4.95	4.82	4.74	4.68	4.60	4.54	4.49
6	5.99	5.14	4.53	4.28	4.15	4.06	4.00	3.92	3.86	3.80
7	5.59	4.74	4.12	3.87	3.73	3.64	3.57	3.49	3.43	3.37
8	5.32	4.46	3.84	3.58	3.44	3.35	3.28	3.20	3.13	3.07
9	5.12	4.26	3.63	3.37	3.23	3.14	3.07	2.99	2.92	2.85
10	4.96	4.10	3.48	3.22	3.07	2.98	2.91	2.83	2.75	2.69
11	4.84	3.98	3.36	3.09	2.95	2.85	2.79	2.70	2.63	2.56
12	4.75	3.89	3.26	3.00	2.85	2.75	2.69	2.60	2.52	2.46
13	4.67	3.81	3.18	2.92	2.77	2.67	2.60	2.51	2.44	2.37
14	4.60	3.74	3.11	2.85	2.70	2.60	2.53	2.44	2.37	2.30
15	4.54	3.68	3.06	2.79	2.64	2.54	2.48	2.38	2.31	2.24
16	4.49	3.63	3.01	2.74	2.59	2.49	2.42	2.33	2.25	2.18
17	4.45	3.59	2.96	2.70	2.55	2.45	2.38	2.29	2.21	2.14
18	4.41	3.55	2.93	2.66	2.51	2.41	2.34	2.25	2.17	2.10
19	4.38	3.52	2.90	2.63	2.48	2.38	2.31	2.21	2.13	2.06
20	4.35	3.49	2.87	2.60	2.45	2.35	2.28	2.18	2.10	2.03
22	4.30	3.44	2.82	2.55	2.40	2.30	2.23	2.13	2.05	1.97
24	4.26	3.40	2.78	2.51	2.36	2.25	2.18	2.09	2.00	1.93
26	4.23	3.37	2.74	2.47	2.32	2.22	2.15	2.05	1.97	1.89
28	4.20	3.34	2.71	2.45	2.29	2.19	2.12	2.02	1.93	1.86
30	4.17	3.32	2.69	2.42	2.27	2.16	2.09	1.99	1.91	1.83
32	4.15	3.29	2.67	2.40	2.24	2.14	2.07	1.97	1.88	1.81
34	4.13	3.28	2.65	2.38	2.23	2.12	2.05	1.95	1.86	1.79
36	4.11	3.26	2.63	2.36	2.21	2.11	2.03	1.93	1.85	1.77
38	4.10	3.24	2.62	2.35	2.19	2.09	2.02	1.92	1.83	1.75
40	4.08	3.23	2.61	2.34	2.18	2.08	2.00	1.90	1.81	1.73
42	4.07	3.22	2.59	2.32	2.17	2.06	1.99	1.89	1.80	1.72
44	4.06	3.21	2.58	2.31	2.16	2.05	1.98	1.88	1.79	1.71
46	4.05	3.20	2.57	2.30	2.15	2.04	1.97	1.87	1.78	1.70
48	4.04	3.19	2.57	2.29	2.14	2.03	1.96	1.86	1.77	1.69
50	4.03	3.18	2.56	2.29	2.13	2.03	1.95	1.85	1.76	1.68
55	4.02	3.16	2.54	2.27	2.11	2.01	1.93	1.83	1.74	1.66
60	4.00	3.15	2.53	2.25	2.10	1.99	1.92	1.82	1.72	1.64
65	3.99	3.14	2.51	2.24	2.08	1.98	1.90	1.80	1.71	1.62
70	3.98	3.13	2.50	2.23	2.07	1.97	1.89	1.79	1.70	1.61
80	3.96	3.11	2.49	2.21	2.06	1.95	1.88	1.77	1.68	1.59
90	3.95	3.10	2.47	2.20	2.04	1.94	1.86	1.76	1.66	1.57
100	3.94	3.09	2.46	2.19	2.03	1.93	1.85	1.75	1.65	1.56
125	3.92	3.07	2.44	2.17	2.01	1.91	1.83	1.72	1.63	1.54
150	3.90	3.06	2.43	2.16	2.00	1.89	1.82	1.71	1.61	1.52
200	3.89	3.04	2.42	2.14	1.98	1.88	1.80	1.69	1.60	1.50
300	3.87	3.03	2.40	2.13	1.97	1.86	1.78	1.68	1.58	1.48
500	3.86	3.01	2.39	2.12	1.96	1.85	1.77	1.66	1.56	1.47
1,000	3.85	3.00	2.38	2.11	1.95	1.84	1.76	1.65	1.55	1.46
2,000	3.84	3.00	2.37	2.10	1.94	1.83	1.75	1.64	1.54	1.44

$s = 1$ **Upper 1% points**

t \ r:	1	2	4	6	8	10	12	16	22	32
1†	405.00	500.00	563.00	586.00	598.00	606.00	611.00	617.00	622.00	627.00
2	98.50	99.00	99.20	99.30	99.40	99.40	99.40	99.40	99.50	99.50
3	34.10	30.80	28.70	27.90	27.50	27.20	27.10	26.80	26.60	26.50
4	21.20	18.00	16.00	15.20	14.80	14.50	14.40	14.20	14.00	13.80
5	16.30	13.30	11.40	10.70	10.30	10.10	9.89	9.68	9.51	9.36
6	13.70	10.90	9.15	8.47	8.10	7.87	7.72	7.52	7.35	7.21
7	12.20	9.55	7.85	7.19	6.84	6.62	6.47	6.27	6.11	5.97
8	11.30	8.65	7.01	6.37	6.03	5.81	5.67	5.48	5.32	5.18
9	10.60	8.02	6.42	5.80	5.47	5.26	5.11	4.92	4.77	4.63
10	10.00	7.56	5.99	5.39	5.06	4.85	4.71	4.52	4.36	4.23
11	9.65	7.21	5.67	5.07	4.74	4.54	4.40	4.21	4.06	3.92
12	9.33	6.93	5.41	4.82	4.50	4.30	4.16	3.97	3.82	3.68
13	9.07	6.70	5.21	4.62	4.30	4.10	3.96	3.78	3.62	3.49
14	8.86	6.51	5.04	4.46	4.14	3.94	3.80	3.62	3.46	3.33
15	8.68	6.36	4.89	4.32	4.00	3.80	3.67	3.49	3.33	3.19
16	8.53	6.23	4.77	4.20	3.89	3.69	3.55	3.37	3.22	3.08
17	8.40	6.11	4.67	4.10	3.79	3.59	3.46	3.27	3.12	2.98
18	8.29	6.01	4.58	4.01	3.71	3.51	3.37	3.19	3.03	2.90
19	8.18	5.93	4.50	3.94	3.63	3.43	3.30	3.12	2.96	2.82
20	8.10	5.85	4.43	3.87	3.56	3.37	3.23	3.05	2.90	2.76
22	7.95	5.72	4.31	3.76	3.45	3.26	3.12	2.94	2.78	2.65
24	7.82	5.61	4.22	3.67	3.36	3.17	3.03	2.85	2.70	2.56
26	7.72	5.53	4.14	3.59	3.29	3.09	2.96	2.78	2.62	2.48
28	7.64	5.45	4.07	3.53	3.23	3.03	2.90	2.72	2.56	2.42
30	7.56	5.39	4.02	3.47	3.17	2.98	2.84	2.66	2.51	2.37
32	7.50	5.34	3.97	3.43	3.13	2.93	2.80	2.62	2.46	2.32
34	7.44	5.29	3.93	3.39	3.09	2.89	2.76	2.58	2.42	2.28
36	7.40	5.25	3.89	3.35	3.05	2.86	2.72	2.54	2.38	2.24
38	7.35	5.21	3.86	3.32	3.02	2.83	2.69	2.51	2.35	2.21
40	7.31	5.18	3.83	3.29	2.99	2.80	2.66	2.48	2.33	2.18
42	7.28	5.15	3.80	3.27	2.97	2.78	2.64	2.46	2.30	2.16
44	7.25	5.12	3.78	3.24	2.95	2.75	2.62	2.44	2.28	2.13
46	7.22	5.10	3.76	3.22	2.93	2.73	2.60	2.42	2.26	2.11
48	7.19	5.08	3.74	3.20	2.91	2.72	2.58	2.40	2.24	2.10
50	7.17	5.06	3.72	3.19	2.89	2.70	2.56	2.38	2.22	2.08
55	7.12	5.01	3.68	3.15	2.85	2.66	2.53	2.34	2.18	2.04
60	7.08	4.98	3.65	3.12	2.82	2.63	2.50	2.31	2.15	2.01
65	7.04	4.95	3.62	3.09	2.80	2.61	2.47	2.29	2.13	1.98
70	7.01	4.92	3.60	3.07	2.78	2.59	2.45	2.27	2.11	1.97
80	6.96	4.88	3.56	3.04	2.74	2.55	2.42	2.23	2.07	1.92
90	6.93	4.85	3.54	3.01	2.72	2.52	2.39	2.21	2.04	1.90
100	6.90	4.82	3.51	2.99	2.69	2.50	2.37	2.19	2.02	1.87
125	6.84	4.78	3.47	2.95	2.66	2.47	2.33	2.15	1.98	1.83
150	6.81	4.75	3.45	2.92	2.63	2.44	2.31	2.12	1.96	1.81
200	6.76	4.71	3.41	2.89	2.60	2.41	2.27	2.09	1.93	1.77
300	6.72	4.68	3.38	2.86	2.57	2.38	2.24	2.06	1.89	1.74
500	6.69	4.65	3.36	2.84	2.55	2.36	2.22	2.04	1.87	1.72
1,000	6.66	4.63	3.34	2.82	2.53	2.34	2.20	2.02	1.85	1.70
2,000	6.63	4.61	3.32	2.80	2.51	2.32	2.18	2.00	1.83	1.68

† Entries in this row should be multiplied by 10.

$s = 2$ **Upper 5% points**

t \ r:	1	2	4	6	8	10	12	16	22	32
12	12.23	7.78	5.59	4.81	4.40	4.15	3.98	3.76	3.58	3.42
14	11.87	7.54	5.39	4.62	4.22	3.98	3.81	3.59	3.41	3.25
16	11.50	7.29	5.19	4.44	4.05	3.80	3.63	3.42	3.24	3.08
18	11.14	7.05	4.99	4.25	3.87	3.62	3.46	3.25	3.07	2.91
20	10.78	6.81	4.79	4.07	3.69	3.45	3.29	3.08	2.90	2.74
25	10.24	6.44	4.49	3.79	3.42	3.19	3.03	2.82	2.64	2.48
30	9.95	6.24	4.33	3.64	3.27	3.04	2.88	2.68	2.50	2.34
35	9.74	6.10	4.22	3.53	3.17	2.94	2.78	2.58	2.40	2.24
40	9.59	6.00	4.14	3.46	3.10	2.87	2.71	2.51	2.33	2.17
45	9.48	5.93	4.07	3.40	3.04	2.81	2.66	2.45	2.27	2.11
50	9.39	5.87	4.03	3.35	3.00	2.77	2.61	2.41	2.23	2.07
60	9.27	5.78	3.95	3.29	2.93	2.71	2.55	2.35	2.17	2.00
70	9.19	5.72	3.91	3.25	2.89	2.67	2.51	2.31	2.13	1.96
80	9.12	5.68	3.87	3.21	2.86	2.63	2.48	2.27	2.09	1.93
90	9.07	5.65	3.84	3.19	2.83	2.61	2.45	2.25	2.07	1.90
100	9.04	5.62	3.83	3.17	2.82	2.59	2.44	2.23	2.05	1.89
150	8.91	5.53	3.75	3.10	2.75	2.53	2.37	2.17	1.98	1.82
200	8.84	5.49	3.72	3.07	2.72	2.50	2.34	2.14	1.95	1.78
300	8.79	5.45	3.69	3.04	2.69	2.47	2.31	2.11	1.92	1.75
500	8.74	5.42	3.66	3.02	2.67	2.45	2.29	2.09	1.90	1.73
1,000	8.71	5.39	3.64	3.00	2.65	2.43	2.27	2.07	1.88	1.71
2,000	8.69	5.38	3.63	2.99	2.64	2.42	2.27	2.06	1.87	1.70

$s = 2$ **Upper 1% points**

t \ r:	1	2	4	6	8	10	12	16	22	32
12	20.36	12.57	8.75	7.40	6.70	6.27	5.98	5.61	5.30	5.03
14	19.50	12.01	8.31	7.01	6.33	5.91	5.63	5.27	4.96	4.70
16	18.63	11.45	7.88	6.61	5.96	5.55	5.28	4.92	4.62	4.37
18	17.77	10.89	7.44	6.22	5.59	5.19	4.92	4.58	4.29	4.04
20	16.90	10.32	7.00	5.83	5.21	4.83	4.57	4.24	3.95	3.71
25	15.64	9.50	6.37	5.26	4.67	4.31	4.06	3.74	3.46	3.23
30	14.98	9.07	6.04	4.96	4.39	4.04	3.79	3.48	3.21	2.97
35	14.52	8.77	5.81	4.75	4.20	3.85	3.61	3.30	3.03	2.80
40	14.20	8.56	5.65	4.61	4.06	3.72	3.48	3.17	2.91	2.68
45	13.96	8.40	5.53	4.50	3.96	3.62	3.39	3.08	2.82	2.59
50	13.77	8.28	5.44	4.42	3.88	3.54	3.31	3.01	2.75	2.51
60	13.50	8.10	5.30	4.30	3.77	3.43	3.20	2.90	2.64	2.41
70	13.33	7.99	5.22	4.22	3.69	3.36	3.13	2.83	2.57	2.34
80	13.17	7.89	5.14	4.15	3.63	3.30	3.07	2.77	2.51	2.28
90	13.08	7.83	5.10	4.11	3.59	3.26	3.04	2.74	2.48	2.25
100	13.01	7.78	5.06	4.08	3.56	3.23	3.01	2.71	2.45	2.22
150	12.74	7.60	4.92	3.96	3.45	3.12	2.90	2.60	2.34	2.11
200	12.61	7.52	4.86	3.90	3.39	3.07	2.85	2.55	2.30	2.06
300	12.49	7.44	4.80	3.85	3.34	3.02	2.80	2.51	2.25	2.01
500	12.40	7.38	4.76	3.81	3.31	2.99	2.76	2.47	2.21	1.98
1,000	12.32	7.33	4.72	3.78	3.27	2.95	2.73	2.44	2.18	1.95
2,000	12.29	7.31	4.70	3.76	3.26	2.94	2.72	2.43	2.17	1.93

$s = 3$ **Upper 5% points**

t \ r:	1	2	4	6	8	10	12	16	22	32
12	20.28	12.12	8.08	6.69	5.98	5.54	5.25	4.88	4.57	4.31
14	19.55	11.66	7.74	6.39	5.70	5.28	4.99	4.63	4.32	4.06
16	18.82	11.20	7.40	6.09	5.42	5.01	4.73	4.37	4.08	3.82
18	18.09	10.74	7.06	5.79	5.14	4.74	4.47	4.12	3.83	3.58
20	17.36	10.29	6.72	5.49	4.86	4.47	4.21	3.87	3.59	3.34
25	16.28	9.60	6.22	5.05	4.44	4.07	3.82	3.49	3.22	2.98
30	15.69	9.23	5.95	4.81	4.22	3.85	3.61	3.29	3.02	2.78
35	15.28	8.97	5.76	4.64	4.06	3.70	3.46	3.14	2.88	2.64
40	14.98	8.78	5.62	4.52	3.95	3.59	3.35	3.04	2.77	2.54
45	14.76	8.64	5.52	4.43	3.86	3.51	3.27	2.96	2.70	2.47
50	14.59	8.53	5.44	4.36	3.80	3.45	3.21	2.90	2.64	2.41
60	14.34	8.37	5.32	4.25	3.70	3.35	3.12	2.81	2.55	2.32
70	14.17	8.27	5.25	4.19	3.64	3.30	3.06	2.76	2.49	2.26
80	14.03	8.18	5.18	4.13	3.58	3.24	3.01	2.70	2.44	2.21
90	13.94	8.12	5.14	4.10	3.55	3.21	2.98	2.67	2.41	2.18
100	13.88	8.08	5.11	4.07	3.52	3.19	2.95	2.65	2.39	2.15
150	13.62	7.92	4.99	3.96	3.42	3.09	2.86	2.56	2.30	2.06
200	13.50	7.84	4.93	3.91	3.38	3.04	2.81	2.51	2.25	2.02
300	13.38	7.77	4.88	3.86	3.33	3.00	2.77	2.47	2.21	1.98
500	13.29	7.71	4.84	3.83	3.30	2.97	2.74	2.44	2.18	1.94
1,000	13.22	7.66	4.80	3.80	3.27	2.94	2.71	2.42	2.15	1.92
2,000	13.19	7.64	4.79	3.78	3.26	2.93	2.70	2.40	2.14	1.90

$s = 3$ **Upper 1% points**

t \ r:	1	2	4	6	8	10	12	16	22	32
12	31.94	18.81	12.30	10.08	8.94	8.25	7.79	7.19	6.70	6.28
14	30.35	17.83	11.61	9.48	8.39	7.73	7.28	6.71	6.24	5.83
16	28.76	16.85	10.92	8.88	7.84	7.21	6.78	6.23	5.77	5.38
18	27.17	15.88	10.22	8.28	7.29	6.68	6.27	5.75	5.31	4.93
20	25.59	14.90	9.53	7.69	6.74	6.16	5.77	5.26	4.84	4.48
25	23.28	13.48	8.53	6.82	5.94	5.40	5.04	4.57	4.17	3.83
30	22.08	12.74	8.01	6.37	5.53	5.01	4.66	4.21	3.83	3.50
35	21.26	12.23	7.65	6.07	5.25	4.75	4.40	3.96	3.59	3.27
40	20.69	11.88	7.41	5.86	5.06	4.56	4.23	3.79	3.42	3.10
45	20.26	11.62	7.22	5.70	4.91	4.42	4.09	3.66	3.30	2.98
50	19.92	11.41	7.08	5.57	4.80	4.32	3.99	3.57	3.20	2.89
60	19.43	11.11	6.87	5.39	4.63	4.16	3.84	3.42	3.06	2.75
70	19.12	10.92	6.74	5.28	4.53	4.06	3.74	3.33	2.98	2.66
80	18.85	10.75	6.62	5.18	4.44	3.98	3.66	3.25	2.90	2.59
90	18.69	10.65	6.55	5.12	4.38	3.92	3.61	3.20	2.85	2.54
100	18.56	10.57	6.49	5.07	4.34	3.88	3.57	3.16	2.81	2.50
150	18.08	10.28	6.29	4.90	4.18	3.73	3.42	3.02	2.67	2.37
200	17.85	10.14	6.19	4.82	4.10	3.66	3.35	2.95	2.61	2.30
300	17.64	10.01	6.10	4.74	4.03	3.59	3.29	2.89	2.55	2.24
500	17.48	9.91	6.03	4.68	3.98	3.54	3.24	2.84	2.50	2.19
1,000	17.34	9.83	5.98	4.63	3.93	3.50	3.20	2.80	2.46	2.16
2,000	17.28	9.79	5.95	4.61	3.91	3.48	3.18	2.78	2.45	2.14

$s = 4$ **Upper 5% points**

t \ r:	1	2	4	6	8	10	12	16	22	32
12	29.37	16.97	10.80	8.70	7.64	7.00	6.57	6.02	5.57	5.19
14	28.15	16.23	10.29	8.27	7.25	6.63	6.21	5.68	5.24	4.87
16	26.94	15.50	9.78	7.84	6.86	6.26	5.85	5.34	4.92	4.56
18	25.72	14.76	9.28	7.41	6.46	5.89	5.50	5.00	4.59	4.24
20	24.51	14.03	8.77	6.98	6.07	5.51	5.14	4.66	4.27	3.93
25	22.70	12.94	8.02	6.34	5.49	4.96	4.61	4.16	3.78	3.46
30	21.72	12.34	7.61	6.00	5.17	4.67	4.32	3.89	3.52	3.20
35	21.04	11.93	7.33	5.76	4.95	4.46	4.12	3.70	3.33	3.02
40	20.56	11.64	7.13	5.59	4.80	4.31	3.98	3.56	3.20	2.90
45	20.19	11.42	6.98	5.46	4.68	4.20	3.87	3.46	3.10	2.80
50	19.90	11.25	6.86	5.36	4.59	4.11	3.79	3.38	3.03	2.72
60	19.49	10.99	6.69	5.21	4.45	3.99	3.67	3.26	2.91	2.61
70	19.22	10.83	6.58	5.12	4.37	3.90	3.59	3.18	2.84	2.54
80	18.98	10.69	6.48	5.03	4.29	3.83	3.52	3.12	2.78	2.47
90	18.84	10.60	6.42	4.98	4.24	3.79	3.48	3.08	2.74	2.44
100	18.73	10.53	6.37	4.94	4.21	3.75	3.44	3.05	2.70	2.40
150	18.31	10.28	6.20	4.79	4.07	3.63	3.32	2.92	2.59	2.29
200	18.10	10.15	6.11	4.72	4.01	3.56	3.26	2.87	2.53	2.23
300	17.92	10.04	6.04	4.66	3.95	3.51	3.20	2.82	2.48	2.18
500	17.77	9.96	5.98	4.61	3.90	3.46	3.16	2.77	2.44	2.14
1,000	17.65	9.88	5.93	4.57	3.86	3.42	3.13	2.74	2.40	2.10
2,000	17.60	9.85	5.91	4.55	3.84	3.41	3.11	2.72	2.39	2.09

$s = 4$ **Upper 1% points**

t \ r:	1	2	4	6	8	10	12	16	22	32
12	44.96	25.74	16.19	12.95	11.32	10.33	9.66	8.82	8.12	7.53
14	42.46	24.26	15.19	12.12	10.57	9.62	8.99	8.19	7.52	6.96
16	39.96	22.77	14.19	11.29	9.82	8.92	8.32	7.56	6.92	6.39
18	37.46	21.28	13.20	10.46	9.07	8.22	7.65	6.93	6.33	5.82
20	34.95	19.80	12.20	9.62	8.31	7.52	6.98	6.30	5.73	5.24
25	31.33	17.65	10.77	8.42	7.23	6.51	6.01	5.39	4.87	4.42
30	29.47	16.54	10.03	7.81	6.68	5.99	5.52	4.93	4.43	4.00
35	28.19	15.79	9.53	7.40	6.31	5.64	5.19	4.61	4.13	3.71
40	27.30	15.26	9.18	7.11	6.05	5.40	4.96	4.39	3.92	3.51
45	26.64	14.87	8.92	6.89	5.85	5.21	4.78	4.23	3.76	3.36
50	26.12	14.56	8.72	6.72	5.70	5.07	4.65	4.10	3.64	3.24
60	25.37	14.12	8.42	6.48	5.48	4.87	4.45	3.92	3.47	3.08
70	24.90	13.84	8.24	6.33	5.34	4.74	4.33	3.80	3.36	2.97
80	24.48	13.59	8.08	6.19	5.22	4.63	4.22	3.70	3.26	2.87
90	24.23	13.45	7.98	6.11	5.15	4.56	4.16	3.64	3.20	2.82
100	24.03	13.33	7.90	6.04	5.09	4.50	4.10	3.59	3.16	2.77
150	23.30	12.89	7.62	5.81	4.88	4.31	3.91	3.41	2.98	2.60
200	22.95	12.69	7.48	5.69	4.78	4.21	3.83	3.33	2.90	2.52
300	22.63	12.50	7.36	5.59	4.68	4.13	3.74	3.25	2.83	2.45
500	22.38	12.35	7.26	5.51	4.61	4.06	3.68	3.19	2.77	2.39
1,000	22.18	12.23	7.18	5.45	4.55	4.00	3.63	3.14	2.72	2.35
2,000	22.08	12.17	7.14	5.42	4.53	3.98	3.60	3.12	2.70	2.33

$s = 5$ **Upper 5% points**

t \ r:	1	2	4	6	8	10	12	16	22	32
12	39.52	22.33	13.76	10.88	9.42	8.54	7.95	7.21	6.59	6.07
14	37.70	21.26	13.06	10.30	8.90	8.06	7.49	6.78	6.18	5.68
16	35.87	20.19	12.36	9.71	8.38	7.57	7.03	6.34	5.77	5.29
18	34.05	19.12	11.65	9.13	7.86	7.08	6.57	5.91	5.36	4.90
20	32.23	18.05	10.95	8.55	7.34	6.60	6.10	5.48	4.96	4.51
25	29.53	16.47	9.91	7.69	6.57	5.88	5.42	4.83	4.35	3.93
30	28.06	15.61	9.35	7.23	6.15	5.49	5.05	4.49	4.02	3.62
35	27.05	15.01	8.96	6.90	5.86	5.22	4.79	4.25	3.79	3.40
40	26.33	14.60	8.68	6.68	5.66	5.03	4.61	4.08	3.63	3.24
45	25.79	14.28	8.47	6.50	5.50	4.89	4.48	3.95	3.50	3.12
50	25.37	14.03	8.31	6.37	5.38	4.78	4.37	3.85	3.41	3.03
60	24.75	13.66	8.07	6.17	5.20	4.61	4.21	3.70	3.27	2.89
70	24.35	13.43	7.92	6.05	5.09	4.51	4.11	3.60	3.18	2.80
80	24.00	13.23	7.79	5.94	4.99	4.42	4.02	3.52	3.10	2.73
90	23.79	13.11	7.71	5.87	4.93	4.36	3.97	3.47	3.05	2.68
100	23.62	13.00	7.64	5.82	4.88	4.31	3.93	3.43	3.01	2.64
150	23.00	12.64	7.40	5.62	4.71	4.15	3.77	3.28	2.86	2.50
200	22.70	12.46	7.29	5.52	4.62	4.07	3.69	3.21	2.80	2.43
300	22.42	12.30	7.18	5.44	4.54	4.00	3.62	3.14	2.73	2.37
500	22.21	12.18	7.10	5.37	4.48	3.94	3.57	3.09	2.68	2.32
1,000	22.03	12.07	7.03	5.31	4.43	3.89	3.52	3.05	2.64	2.28
2,000	21.95	12.03	7.00	5.29	4.41	3.87	3.50	3.03	2.62	2.26

$s = 5$ **Upper 1% points**

t \ r:	1	2	4	6	8	10	12	16	22	32
12	59.47	33.41	20.42	16.05	13.85	12.52	11.63	10.50	9.58	8.80
14	55.86	31.32	19.08	14.96	12.88	11.62	10.78	9.72	8.84	8.10
16	52.26	29.23	17.74	13.86	11.91	10.72	9.93	8.93	8.10	7.40
18	48.66	27.15	16.39	12.77	10.93	9.83	9.08	8.14	7.36	6.70
20	45.05	25.06	15.05	11.67	9.96	8.93	8.23	7.35	6.62	6.01
25	39.86	22.05	13.12	10.10	8.57	7.64	7.02	6.22	5.56	5.00
30	37.20	20.52	12.14	9.30	7.86	6.99	6.40	5.65	5.03	4.50
35	35.38	19.47	11.46	8.76	7.38	6.54	5.98	5.26	4.66	4.15
40	34.12	18.74	11.00	8.38	7.05	6.24	5.69	4.99	4.41	3.91
45	33.18	18.20	10.65	8.10	6.80	6.01	5.47	4.79	4.22	3.73
50	32.45	17.78	10.39	7.88	6.61	5.83	5.31	4.64	4.07	3.59
60	31.39	17.16	10.00	7.57	6.33	5.57	5.06	4.41	3.86	3.39
70	30.72	16.78	9.76	7.37	6.15	5.41	4.91	4.27	3.73	3.26
80	30.14	16.44	9.54	7.19	6.00	5.27	4.78	4.15	3.61	3.15
90	29.79	16.24	9.41	7.09	5.91	5.19	4.70	4.07	3.54	3.08
100	29.50	16.08	9.31	7.01	5.83	5.12	4.63	4.01	3.49	3.03
150	28.47	15.49	8.93	6.70	5.57	4.87	4.40	3.79	3.28	2.83
200	27.98	15.20	8.75	6.56	5.44	4.75	4.29	3.69	3.18	2.74
300	27.53	14.94	8.59	6.43	5.32	4.64	4.18	3.59	3.09	2.65
500	27.18	14.75	8.46	6.32	5.23	4.56	4.11	3.52	3.02	2.58
1,000	26.90	14.58	8.36	6.24	5.16	4.49	4.04	3.46	2.97	2.53
2,000	26.77	14.51	8.31	6.20	5.12	4.46	4.01	3.43	2.94	2.50

$s = 6$ **Upper 5% points**

t \ r:	1	2	4	6	8	10	12	16	22	32
12	50.73	28.22	16.99	13.22	11.32	10.18	9.41	8.45	7.65	6.99
14	48.18	26.76	16.06	12.46	10.66	9.57	8.83	7.91	7.15	6.52
16	45.63	25.29	15.13	11.71	9.99	8.95	8.26	7.38	6.66	6.05
18	43.09	23.83	14.20	10.96	9.33	8.34	7.68	6.85	6.16	5.58
20	40.54	22.37	13.27	10.21	8.67	7.73	7.10	6.31	5.66	5.10
25	36.77	20.20	11.90	9.10	7.69	6.83	6.25	5.53	4.92	4.41
30	34.73	19.04	11.16	8.50	7.16	6.34	5.80	5.10	4.52	4.03
35	33.32	18.23	10.65	8.09	6.79	6.01	5.48	4.81	4.25	3.77
40	32.33	17.66	10.28	7.80	6.54	5.77	5.25	4.60	4.05	3.58
45	31.58	17.23	10.01	7.58	6.34	5.59	5.08	4.44	3.90	3.44
50	30.99	16.89	9.80	7.40	6.19	5.45	4.95	4.32	3.79	3.33
60	30.13	16.40	9.49	7.15	5.97	5.24	4.76	4.14	3.62	3.17
70	29.58	16.08	9.29	6.99	5.82	5.11	4.63	4.02	3.51	3.07
80	29.10	15.81	9.11	6.85	5.70	5.00	4.53	3.92	3.41	2.97
90	28.81	15.64	9.01	6.76	5.62	4.93	4.46	3.86	3.36	2.92
100	28.57	15.50	8.92	6.69	5.56	4.87	4.41	3.81	3.31	2.87
150	27.71	15.01	8.61	6.44	5.34	4.67	4.21	3.63	3.14	2.71
200	27.30	14.77	8.46	6.32	5.23	4.57	4.12	3.54	3.05	2.63
300	26.92	14.56	8.32	6.21	5.14	4.48	4.03	3.46	2.98	2.55
500	26.63	14.39	8.22	6.13	5.06	4.41	3.97	3.40	2.92	2.50
1,000	26.38	14.25	8.13	6.05	5.00	4.35	3.91	3.35	2.87	2.45
2,000	26.27	14.18	8.09	6.02	4.97	4.32	3.89	3.32	2.85	2.43

$s = 6$ **Upper 1% points**

t \ r:	1	2	4	6	8	10	12	16	22	32
12	75.49	41.82	25.02	19.39	16.56	14.85	13.71	12.27	11.08	10.09
14	70.59	39.04	23.29	18.00	15.34	13.74	12.67	11.31	10.20	9.26
16	65.70	36.26	21.55	16.61	14.13	12.63	11.62	10.36	9.31	8.43
18	60.80	33.48	19.81	15.22	12.91	11.52	10.58	9.40	8.43	7.60
20	55.91	30.69	18.08	13.83	11.70	10.40	9.54	8.44	7.54	6.78
25	48.87	26.70	15.58	11.84	9.96	8.81	8.05	7.08	6.27	5.59
30	45.29	24.67	14.33	10.84	9.08	8.01	7.30	6.39	5.64	4.99
35	42.85	23.29	13.47	10.16	8.48	7.47	6.79	5.92	5.20	4.59
40	41.17	22.34	12.88	9.69	8.07	7.09	6.43	5.60	4.90	4.31
45	39.91	21.62	12.43	9.33	7.77	6.81	6.17	5.36	4.68	4.10
50	38.93	21.07	12.09	9.06	7.53	6.60	5.97	5.17	4.50	3.93
60	37.51	20.27	11.60	8.67	7.19	6.28	5.68	4.90	4.25	3.70
70	36.63	19.77	11.29	8.42	6.97	6.09	5.49	4.73	4.10	3.55
80	35.85	19.33	11.01	8.21	6.78	5.92	5.33	4.59	3.96	3.42
90	35.38	19.06	10.85	8.08	6.67	5.81	5.24	4.50	3.88	3.34
100	35.00	18.85	10.72	7.97	6.58	5.73	5.16	4.43	3.81	3.28
150	33.63	18.07	10.24	7.59	6.25	5.43	4.87	4.17	3.57	3.05
200	32.97	17.71	10.02	7.41	6.09	5.29	4.74	4.04	3.45	2.94
300	32.38	17.37	9.81	7.25	5.95	5.16	4.62	3.93	3.35	2.84
500	31.93	17.11	9.65	7.12	5.84	5.06	4.52	3.84	3.27	2.76
1,000	31.55	16.90	9.52	7.02	5.75	4.97	4.44	3.77	3.20	2.70
2,000	31.37	16.80	9.46	6.97	5.71	4.93	4.41	3.74	3.17	2.67

$s = 7$ **Upper 5% points**

t \ *r*:	1	2	4	6	8	10	12	16	22	32
12	62.95	34.62	20.47	15.73	13.35	11.91	10.95	9.75	8.75	7.92
14	59.57	32.71	19.29	14.79	12.53	11.17	10.25	9.11	8.15	7.37
16	56.19	30.80	18.10	13.85	11.71	10.42	9.55	8.47	7.56	6.81
18	52.81	28.89	16.92	12.90	10.89	9.67	8.85	7.83	6.97	6.26
20	49.44	26.98	15.74	11.96	10.06	8.92	8.15	7.18	6.38	5.71
25	44.44	24.15	13.99	10.57	8.85	7.81	7.12	6.24	5.51	4.89
30	41.75	22.63	13.05	9.83	8.20	7.22	6.56	5.73	5.04	4.45
35	39.88	21.58	12.40	9.31	7.75	6.81	6.18	5.38	4.71	4.14
40	38.56	20.83	11.94	8.95	7.44	6.52	5.91	5.13	4.48	3.93
45	37.56	20.27	11.59	8.67	7.20	6.30	5.70	4.94	4.31	3.76
50	36.78	19.83	11.32	8.46	7.01	6.13	5.54	4.79	4.17	3.63
60	35.63	19.19	10.93	8.14	6.74	5.88	5.31	4.58	3.97	3.45
70	34.92	18.79	10.68	7.95	6.57	5.73	5.16	4.44	3.84	3.33
80	34.29	18.43	10.46	7.77	6.41	5.59	5.03	4.32	3.73	3.22
90	33.92	18.22	10.33	7.67	6.32	5.50	4.95	4.25	3.66	3.16
100	33.60	18.04	10.22	7.58	6.25	5.43	4.89	4.19	3.61	3.10
150	32.43	17.40	9.83	7.27	5.97	5.19	4.65	3.98	3.41	2.91
200	31.95	17.10	9.63	7.12	5.84	5.07	4.54	3.87	3.31	2.82
300	31.42	16.81	9.46	6.98	5.72	4.96	4.44	3.78	3.22	2.73
500	31.03	16.59	9.33	6.87	5.63	4.87	4.36	3.70	3.15	2.67
1,000	30.71	16.41	9.21	6.78	5.55	4.80	4.29	3.64	3.09	2.61
2,000	30.58	16.33	9.16	6.74	5.52	4.77	4.26	3.61	3.07	2.59

$s = 7$ **Upper 1% points**

t \ *r*:	1	2	4	6	8	10	12	16	22	32
12	93.02	50.98	30.00	22.97	19.45	17.32	15.90	14.12	12.65	11.42
14	86.65	47.41	27.82	21.26	17.97	15.98	14.65	12.98	11.61	10.46
16	80.28	43.85	25.64	19.55	16.48	14.64	13.40	11.85	10.57	9.49
18	73.90	40.28	23.47	17.83	15.00	13.29	12.15	10.71	9.53	8.53
20	67.53	36.71	21.29	16.12	13.52	11.95	10.90	9.58	8.48	7.56
25	58.39	31.60	18.18	13.67	11.40	10.03	9.11	7.95	7.00	6.18
30	53.78	29.02	16.61	12.44	10.34	9.07	8.22	7.14	6.25	5.50
35	50.63	27.26	15.54	11.61	9.62	8.42	7.61	6.59	5.75	5.03
40	48.46	26.05	14.81	11.03	9.12	7.97	7.19	6.21	5.40	4.70
45	46.84	25.15	14.26	10.60	8.75	7.64	6.88	5.93	5.14	4.46
50	45.58	24.45	13.84	10.27	8.47	7.38	6.64	5.71	4.94	4.28
60	43.76	23.43	13.23	9.79	8.05	7.00	6.29	5.40	4.65	4.01
70	42.63	22.80	12.85	9.49	7.80	6.77	6.08	5.20	4.47	3.84
80	41.63	22.25	12.51	9.23	7.57	6.56	5.89	5.03	4.31	3.69
90	41.04	21.92	12.31	9.07	7.44	6.44	5.77	4.92	4.21	3.60
100	40.55	21.64	12.14	8.94	7.33	6.34	5.68	4.84	4.13	3.53
150	38.80	20.67	11.56	8.48	6.93	5.98	5.35	4.54	3.85	3.27
200	37.96	20.21	11.28	8.27	6.74	5.82	5.19	4.39	3.71	3.14
300	37.21	19.78	11.02	8.07	6.57	5.66	5.05	4.26	3.60	3.03
500	36.63	19.46	10.83	7.92	6.44	5.54	4.93	4.16	3.51	2.94
1,000	36.15	19.19	10.67	7.79	6.33	5.44	4.84	4.08	3.43	2.87
2,000	35.92	19.07	10.59	7.73	6.28	5.40	4.80	4.04	3.40	2.83

$s = 8$ **Upper 5% points**

t \ r:	1	2	4	6	8	10	12	16	22	32
12	76.34	41.58	24.22	18.41	15.51	13.74	12.57	11.10	9.90	8.88
14	71.99	39.16	22.75	17.26	14.51	12.85	11.74	10.34	9.21	8.24
16	67.65	36.73	21.28	16.11	13.52	11.95	10.90	9.59	8.52	7.60
18	63.30	34.31	19.81	14.96	12.53	11.05	10.07	8.83	7.82	6.96
20	58.95	31.88	18.35	13.81	11.53	10.15	9.24	8.08	7.13	6.32
25	52.53	28.31	16.18	12.11	10.07	8.83	8.01	6.97	6.11	5.38
30	49.09	26.39	15.02	11.21	9.29	8.13	7.35	6.37	5.56	4.87
35	46.70	25.06	14.21	10.58	8.75	7.64	6.89	5.96	5.18	4.52
40	45.00	24.12	13.65	10.13	8.36	7.30	6.57	5.67	4.91	4.27
45	43.74	23.42	13.22	9.80	8.08	7.03	6.33	5.45	4.71	4.08
50	42.77	22.86	12.89	9.54	7.85	6.83	6.14	5.28	4.55	3.94
60	41.29	22.60	12.40	9.16	7.52	6.53	5.87	5.02	4.32	3.72
70	40.37	21.55	12.10	8.92	7.32	6.35	5.69	4.87	4.17	3.58
80	39.56	21.10	11.83	8.71	7.13	6.18	5.54	4.72	4.04	3.46
90	39.08	20.83	11.67	8.58	7.02	6.08	5.45	4.64	3.97	3.39
100	38.68	20.61	11.53	8.47	6.93	6.00	5.37	4.57	3.90	3.33
150	37.23	19.80	11.50	8.10	6.61	5.70	5.09	4.32	3.67	3.11
200	36.56	19.42	10.82	7.91	6.45	5.56	4.96	4.20	3.56	3.01
300	35.94	19.06	10.60	7.75	6.31	5.43	4.84	4.09	3.46	2.91
500	35.42	18.79	10.43	7.62	6.19	5.33	4.75	4.00	3.38	2.83
1,000	35.01	18.56	10.30	7.51	6.10	5.25	4.67	3.93	3.31	2.77
2,000	34.84	18.46	10.24	7.46	6.06	5.21	4.63	3.90	3.28	2.74

$s = 8$ **Upper 1% points**

t \ r:	1	2	4	6	8	10	12	16	22	32
12	112.06	60.90	35.34	26.80	22.52	19.94	18.22	16.05	14.28	12.79
14	104.03	56.45	32.68	24.73	20.75	18.35	16.74	14.73	13.07	11.68
16	96.00	52.01	30.02	22.66	18.98	16.75	15.27	13.40	11.87	10.58
18	87.97	47.56	27.36	20.60	17.21	15.16	13.79	12.08	10.66	9.47
20	79.94	43.12	24.70	18.53	15.43	13.57	12.32	10.75	9.46	8.37
25	68.44	36.76	20.90	15.58	12.91	11.30	10.22	8.86	7.74	6.79
30	62.66	33.57	18.99	14.11	11.65	10.17	9.17	7.92	6.88	6.00
35	58.72	31.39	17.70	13.10	10.79	9.40	8.46	7.28	6.30	5.47
40	56.01	29.90	16.81	12.42	10.20	8.87	7.97	6.84	5.90	5.10
45	53.98	28.78	16.14	11.90	9.77	8.47	7.61	6.51	5.60	4.83
50	52.42	27.92	15.63	11.51	9.43	8.17	7.33	6.26	5.37	4.62
60	50.16	26.67	14.89	10.93	8.94	7.73	6.92	5.90	5.04	4.31
70	48.75	25.90	14.43	10.58	8.64	7.46	6.67	5.67	4.83	4.12
80	47.51	25.21	14.02	10.26	8.37	7.22	6.45	5.47	4.65	3.95
90	46.77	24.81	13.78	10.08	8.21	7.08	6.32	5.35	4.55	3.85
100	46.16	24.47	13.58	9.92	8.08	6.96	6.21	5.25	4.46	3.77
150	43.99	23.28	12.88	9.38	7.61	6.54	5.82	4.90	4.14	3.48
200	42.96	22.71	12.54	9.12	7.39	6.34	5.64	4.74	3.99	3.34
300	42.02	22.19	12.24	8.88	7.19	6.16	5.47	4.59	3.85	3.21
500	41.30	21.80	12.00	8.70	7.04	6.02	5.34	4.47	3.74	3.11
1,000	40.70	21.47	11.81	8.55	6.91	5.91	5.24	4.38	3.66	3.03
2,000	40.43	21.32	11.71	8.48	6.85	5.86	5.19	4.33	3.62	2.99

$s = 9$ **Upper 5% points**

t	r: 1	2	4	6	8	10	12	16	22	32
12	90.90	49.05	28.22	21.28	17.78	15.68	14.29	12.52	11.08	9.90
14	85.44	46.05	26.44	19.90	16.60	14.62	13.31	11.65	10.29	9.16
16	79.97	43.06	24.66	18.52	15.42	13.56	12.33	10.77	9.49	8.43
18	74.51	40.07	22.88	17.14	14.25	12.51	11.35	9.89	8.69	7.70
20	69.05	37.07	21.10	15.76	13.07	11.45	10.37	9.01	7.89	6.96
25	61.02	32.67	18.48	13.72	11.34	9.89	8.93	7.72	6.72	5.88
30	56.75	30.31	17.07	12.64	10.41	9.06	8.16	7.03	6.09	5.30
35	53.78	28.67	16.10	11.89	9.77	8.49	7.63	6.55	5.66	4.90
40	51.67	27.53	15.42	11.36	9.32	8.09	7.26	6.22	5.35	4.62
45	50.10	26.66	14.90	10.96	8.98	7.78	6.98	5.96	5.12	4.41
50	48.88	25.98	14.50	10.65	8.71	7.54	6.76	5.77	4.94	4.24
60	47.07	24.99	13.92	10.20	8.33	7.19	6.43	5.47	4.68	4.00
70	45.96	24.37	13.55	9.91	8.08	6.98	6.23	5.29	4.51	3.84
80	44.98	23.82	13.22	9.66	7.87	6.78	6.05	5.13	4.36	3.70
90	44.38	23.49	13.02	9.51	7.74	6.66	5.94	5.03	4.27	3.62
100	43.87	23.21	12.86	9.38	7.63	6.57	5.85	4.95	4.20	3.56
150	42.06	22.23	12.28	8.93	7.24	6.22	5.54	4.67	3.94	3.31
200	41.26	21.77	11.99	8.71	7.06	6.06	5.38	4.53	3.81	3.19
300	40.39	21.32	11.74	8.52	6.89	5.91	5.24	4.40	3.69	3.08
500	39.82	20.99	11.54	8.37	6.76	5.79	5.13	4.30	3.60	3.00
1,000	39.29	20.71	11.38	8.24	6.65	5.69	5.04	4.22	3.53	2.93
2,000	39.09	20.59	11.30	8.18	6.60	5.65	5.00	4.18	3.49	2.89

$s = 9$ **Upper 1% points**

t	r: 1	2	4	6	8	10	12	16	22	32
12	132.59	71.56	41.07	30.88	25.77	22.70	20.65	18.08	15.96	14.22
14	122.72	66.15	37.87	28.43	23.69	20.84	18.94	16.55	14.59	12.96
16	112.85	60.73	34.68	25.98	21.61	18.98	17.23	15.02	13.21	11.70
18	102.98	55.32	31.49	23.52	19.53	17.12	15.51	13.50	11.83	10.45
20	93.12	49.91	28.30	21.07	17.44	15.26	13.80	11.97	10.46	9.19
25	79.01	42.18	23.74	17.58	14.48	12.61	11.36	9.79	8.50	7.41
30	71.94	38.31	21.47	15.84	13.00	11.30	10.15	8.71	7.52	6.52
35	67.13	35.68	19.91	14.65	12.00	10.40	9.33	7.98	6.86	5.92
40	63.83	33.88	18.87	13.84	11.32	9.79	8.77	7.48	6.41	5.51
45	61.36	32.53	18.08	13.24	10.80	9.33	8.35	7.10	6.07	5.20
50	59.45	31.48	17.47	12.77	10.41	8.98	8.02	6.82	5.81	4.96
60	56.70	29.98	16.59	12.10	9.84	8.47	7.56	6.40	5.44	4.62
70	54.99	29.05	16.05	11.68	9.49	8.16	7.27	6.14	5.21	4.41
80	53.48	28.23	15.56	11.32	9.17	7.88	7.01	5.91	5.00	4.22
90	52.59	27.74	15.28	11.10	8.99	7.72	6.86	5.78	4.88	4.11
100	51.85	27.34	15.04	10.92	8.84	7.58	6.74	5.67	4.78	4.02
150	49.21	25.90	14.20	10.28	8.30	7.10	6.29	5.27	4.42	3.69
200	47.97	25.22	13.81	9.97	8.04	6.87	6.08	5.08	4.25	3.53
300	46.83	24.60	13.44	9.70	7.81	6.66	5.89	4.91	4.10	3.39
500	45.96	24.12	13.17	9.49	7.63	6.50	5.75	4.78	3.98	3.28
1,000	45.23	23.73	12.94	9.31	7.48	6.37	5.62	4.67	3.88	3.19
2,000	44.91	23.55	12.83	9.23	7.41	6.31	5.57	4.62	3.83	3.15

$s = 10$ **Upper 5% points**

t \ r:	1	2	4	6	8	10	12	16	22	32
12	106.38	57.09	32.50	24.32	20.21	17.73	16.06	14.01	12.32	11.06
14	99.72	53.46	30.38	22.68	18.83	16.50	14.94	13.01	11.41	10.20
16	93.06	49.84	28.25	21.06	17.45	15.27	13.81	12.00	10.50	9.35
18	86.41	46.21	26.13	19.42	16.07	14.04	12.68	10.99	9.60	8.49
20	79.75	42.58	24.00	17.79	14.68	12.81	11.55	9.98	8.69	7.63
25	69.95	37.25	20.88	15.40	12.65	11.00	9.89	8.50	7.35	6.39
30	64.72	34.40	19.21	14.12	11.57	10.04	9.01	7.71	6.64	5.74
35	61.12	32.43	18.06	13.24	10.83	9.37	8.39	7.16	6.15	5.29
40	58.61	31.05	17.25	12.62	10.30	8.90	7.96	6.78	5.80	4.98
45	56.70	30.01	16.64	12.15	9.90	8.55	7.64	6.49	5.54	4.74
50	55.19	29.19	16.16	11.79	9.59	8.27	7.38	6.26	5.33	4.55
60	53.02	28.00	15.46	11.26	9.15	7.87	7.01	5.93	5.04	4.28
70	51.65	27.25	15.02	10.92	8.86	7.62	6.78	5.73	4.85	4.10
80	50.44	26.59	14.63	10.62	8.61	7.39	6.57	5.54	4.68	3.95
90	49.71	26.19	14.40	10.45	8.46	7.26	6.45	5.43	4.58	3.86
100	49.10	25.86	14.21	10.30	8.33	7.15	6.35	5.34	4.50	3.78
150	46.90	24.68	13.52	9.77	7.89	6.75	5.98	5.01	4.20	3.51
200	45.92	24.11	13.18	9.52	7.67	6.55	5.80	4.85	4.06	3.38
300	44.94	23.59	12.88	9.29	7.48	6.38	5.64	4.71	3.93	3.25
500	44.25	23.20	12.65	9.11	7.33	6.24	5.52	4.60	3.83	3.16
1,000	43.62	22.86	12.45	8.96	7.20	6.13	5.41	4.50	3.74	3.08
2,000	43.32	22.71	12.37	8.89	7.14	6.08	5.37	4.46	3.70	3.04

$s = 10$ **Upper 1% points**

t \ r:	1	2	4	6	8	10	12	16	22	32
12	155.00	82.99	47.17	35.20	29.21	25.61	23.21	20.19	17.73	15.79
14	143.04	76.52	43.40	32.34	26.80	23.46	21.24	18.45	16.17	14.36
16	131.07	70.05	39.63	29.47	24.38	21.32	19.28	16.71	14.61	12.92
18	119.11	63.57	35.86	26.60	21.97	19.17	17.31	14.97	13.05	11.49
20	107.15	57.10	32.09	23.74	19.55	17.03	15.34	13.23	11.49	10.06
25	90.10	47.86	26.72	19.66	16.11	13.98	12.55	10.75	9.28	8.04
30	81.62	43.26	24.05	17.63	14.41	12.46	11.16	9.53	8.18	7.05
35	75.86	40.13	22.24	16.26	13.25	11.44	10.22	8.70	7.44	6.38
40	71.90	37.99	21.00	15.32	12.46	10.74	9.58	8.13	6.93	5.92
45	68.96	36.39	20.07	14.61	11.87	10.21	9.11	7.71	6.55	5.58
50	66.68	35.15	19.36	14.07	11.41	9.81	8.74	7.38	6.26	5.31
60	63.40	33.37	18.33	13.29	10.76	9.23	8.21	6.91	5.84	4.93
70	61.36	32.27	17.69	12.81	10.35	8.87	7.88	6.62	5.58	4.70
80	59.55	31.29	17.13	12.38	9.99	8.55	7.58	6.36	5.35	4.49
90	58.49	30.72	16.79	12.13	9.78	8.37	7.41	6.21	5.22	4.37
100	57.61	30.24	16.52	11.92	9.61	8.21	7.27	6.09	5.10	4.26
150	54.47	28.54	15.54	11.18	8.99	7.66	6.77	5.64	4.70	3.90
200	52.99	27.74	15.08	10.83	8.69	7.40	6.53	5.43	4.51	3.73
300	51.64	27.01	14.66	10.51	8.42	7.16	6.31	5.24	4.34	3.57
500	50.61	26.45	14.33	10.27	8.22	6.98	6.15	5.09	4.21	3.45
1,000	49.75	25.98	14.07	10.07	8.05	6.83	6.01	4.97	4.10	3.35
2,000	49.36	25.77	13.94	9.97	7.97	6.76	5.94	4.91	4.05	3.30

$s = 11$ **Upper 5% points**

t \ r:	1	2	4	6	8	10	12	16	22	32
12	122.70	65.58	37.03	27.50	22.73	19.86	17.95	15.55	13.58	11.94
14	114.77	61.28	34.54	25.60	21.14	18.45	16.65	14.40	12.56	11.02
16	106.84	56.97	32.04	23.71	19.54	17.04	15.36	13.26	11.54	10.10
18	98.92	52.67	29.54	21.82	17.95	15.62	14.07	12.12	10.52	9.18
20	90.99	48.37	27.05	19.93	16.36	14.21	12.78	10.98	9.50	8.26
25	79.32	42.04	23.38	17.15	14.02	12.14	10.88	9.30	8.00	6.90
30	73.10	38.66	21.43	15.66	12.77	11.03	9.87	8.40	7.20	6.18
35	68.79	36.33	20.08	14.64	11.91	10.27	9.17	7.79	6.65	5.68
40	65.76	34.69	19.13	13.92	11.31	9.73	8.68	7.35	6.26	5.33
45	63.48	33.45	18.41	13.38	10.85	9.33	8.31	7.03	5.96	5.07
50	61.70	32.48	17.85	12.96	10.50	9.01	8.02	6.77	5.73	4.86
60	59.12	31.08	17.04	12.34	9.98	8.55	7.60	6.40	5.40	4.56
70	57.49	30.19	16.53	11.95	9.65	8.26	7.33	6.16	5.19	4.37
80	56.02	29.41	16.07	11.61	9.36	8.01	7.10	5.95	5.00	4.19
90	55.15	28.94	15.80	11.40	9.19	7.85	6.96	5.83	4.89	4.09
100	54.43	28.55	15.58	11.23	9.05	7.73	6.84	5.73	4.80	4.01
150	51.86	27.15	14.77	10.62	8.53	7.27	6.42	5.35	4.47	3.70
200	50.63	26.48	14.38	10.33	8.29	7.05	6.23	5.18	4.31	3.56
300	49.49	25.87	14.03	10.06	8.06	6.85	6.04	5.02	4.16	3.42
500	48.62	25.40	13.76	9.85	7.89	6.70	5.90	4.89	4.05	3.32
1,000	47.90	25.00	13.53	9.68	7.74	6.57	5.78	4.78	3.95	3.23
2,000	47.56	24.82	13.42	9.60	7.68	6.51	5.73	4.74	3.91	3.19

$s = 11$ **Upper 1% points**

t \ r:	1	2	4	6	8	10	12	16	22	32
12	178.29	95.18	53.65	39.78	32.84	28.67	25.88	22.40	19.54	17.15
14	164.18	87.55	49.26	36.47	30.07	26.22	23.65	20.43	17.79	15.58
16	150.07	79.93	44.87	33.16	27.29	23.77	21.42	18.47	16.05	14.02
18	135.96	72.30	40.48	29.85	24.52	21.32	19.18	16.50	14.30	12.46
20	121.85	64.67	36.09	26.54	21.75	18.87	16.95	14.54	12.56	10.90
25	101.72	53.81	29.84	21.83	17.81	15.39	13.78	11.75	10.08	8.68
30	91.71	48.41	26.74	19.49	15.86	13.67	12.21	10.37	8.86	7.58
35	84.91	44.74	24.64	17.91	14.54	12.51	11.15	9.44	8.03	6.84
40	80.26	42.23	23.20	16.83	13.63	11.71	10.42	8.80	7.46	6.33
45	76.78	40.36	22.13	16.03	12.96	11.12	9.88	8.33	7.04	5.96
50	74.10	38.92	21.30	15.40	12.44	10.66	9.46	7.96	6.72	5.67
60	70.25	36.84	20.11	14.51	11.70	10.00	8.87	7.43	6.25	5.25
70	67.85	35.55	19.37	13.96	11.24	9.59	8.49	7.11	5.96	4.99
80	65.73	34.41	18.72	13.47	10.83	9.23	8.17	6.82	5.70	4.76
90	64.48	33.74	18.34	13.18	10.59	9.02	7.97	6.65	5.55	4.62
100	63.45	33.18	18.02	12.94	10.39	8.85	7.81	6.51	5.43	4.51
150	59.78	31.21	16.89	12.09	9.68	8.22	7.25	6.01	4.99	4.11
200	58.04	30.27	16.35	11.69	9.35	7.93	6.98	5.78	4.78	3.92
300	56.45	29.42	15.87	11.33	9.04	7.66	6.73	5.56	4.58	3.75
500	55.25	28.77	15.50	11.05	8.81	7.46	6.55	5.40	4.44	3.61
1,000	54.25	28.23	15.19	10.82	8.62	7.29	6.39	5.26	4.31	3.50
2,000	53.77	27.98	15.05	10.71	8.53	7.21	6.32	5.20	4.26	3.44

$s = 12$ **Upper 5% points**

t	r: 1	2	4	6	8	10	12	16	22	32
12	140.51	74.66	41.84	30.88	25.40	22.11	19.91	17.16	14.90	13.01
14	131.11	69.61	38.94	28.70	23.58	20.50	18.45	15.87	13.76	11.99
16	121.72	64.56	36.04	26.53	21.76	18.90	16.98	14.59	12.62	10.97
18	112.32	59.51	33.15	24.35	19.94	17.29	15.52	13.30	11.48	9.95
20	102.93	54.47	30.25	22.17	18.12	15.68	14.05	12.01	10.34	8.93
25	89.13	47.05	26.00	18.97	15.44	13.32	11.90	10.13	8.66	7.44
30	81.80	43.10	23.73	17.26	14.02	12.07	10.76	9.12	7.77	6.64
35	76.73	40.37	22.17	16.09	13.04	11.20	9.97	8.43	7.16	6.08
40	73.17	38.45	21.07	15.26	12.35	10.59	9.42	7.94	6.72	5.70
45	70.48	37.00	20.24	14.64	11.83	10.13	9.00	7.57	6.40	5.40
50	68.39	35.88	19.60	14.15	11.42	9.77	8.67	7.29	6.14	5.17
60	65.34	34.23	18.66	13.45	10.83	9.25	8.20	6.87	5.77	4.84
70	63.42	33.20	18.07	13.00	10.46	8.93	7.90	6.61	5.54	4.63
80	61.71	32.28	17.54	12.61	10.13	8.64	7.63	6.37	5.33	4.44
90	60.69	31.73	17.23	12.37	9.93	8.46	7.48	6.23	5.20	4.33
100	59.85	31.28	16.97	12.18	9.77	8.32	7.34	6.12	5.10	4.24
150	56.83	29.65	16.04	11.48	9.18	7.80	6.87	5.70	4.73	3.90
200	55.38	28.87	15.59	11.14	8.90	7.56	6.65	5.51	4.55	3.74
300	54.05	28.16	15.18	10.83	8.65	7.33	6.44	5.32	4.39	3.59
500	53.03	27.61	14.87	10.60	8.45	7.15	6.28	5.18	4.27	3.48
1,000	52.18	27.15	14.60	10.40	8.29	7.01	6.15	5.06	4.16	3.37
2,000	51.80	26.93	14.48	10.31	8.21	6.94	6.09	5.00	4.10	3.32

$s = 12$ **Upper 1% points**

t	r: 1	2	4	6	8	10	12	16	22	32
12	203.70	108.13	60.51	44.61	36.66	31.88	28.69	24.70	21.42	18.69
14	187.13	99.26	55.45	40.82	33.51	29.10	26.17	22.50	19.48	16.96
16	170.57	90.39	50.39	37.04	30.35	26.33	23.66	20.30	17.54	15.24
18	154.01	81.52	45.33	33.25	27.20	23.56	21.14	18.10	15.60	13.51
20	137.44	72.65	40.27	29.46	24.05	20.79	18.62	15.90	13.66	11.78
25	113.90	60.02	33.08	24.08	19.57	16.86	15.05	12.77	10.90	9.33
30	102.26	53.77	29.52	21.42	17.36	14.92	13.29	11.24	9.55	8.13
35	94.34	49.52	27.11	19.62	15.87	13.60	12.09	10.19	8.63	7.31
40	88.90	46.62	25.46	18.39	14.84	12.71	11.28	9.48	8.00	6.76
45	84.86	44.46	24.23	17.47	14.08	12.04	10.67	8.96	7.54	6.34
50	81.74	42.79	23.29	16.77	13.50	11.53	10.21	8.55	7.18	6.02
60	77.26	40.39	21.93	15.75	12.65	10.79	9.54	7.96	6.66	5.56
70	74.49	38.90	21.09	15.13	12.13	10.33	9.12	7.60	6.34	5.28
80	72.04	37.59	20.34	14.57	11.67	9.92	8.75	7.28	6.06	5.03
90	70.59	36.81	19.90	14.24	11.40	9.69	8.54	7.09	5.90	4.88
100	69.39	36.17	19.54	13.97	11.18	9.49	8.36	6.94	5.76	4.76
150	65.13	33.89	18.25	13.01	10.38	8.79	7.73	6.38	5.27	4.32
200	63.12	32.82	17.64	12.56	10.00	8.46	7.43	6.12	5.04	4.11
300	61.29	31.84	17.09	12.14	9.66	8.16	7.16	5.88	4.83	3.92
500	59.89	31.09	16.66	11.83	9.40	7.93	6.95	5.70	4.67	3.78
1,000	58.73	30.47	16.31	11.57	9.18	7.74	6.77	5.55	4.53	3.65
2,000	58.19	30.18	16.15	11.45	9.08	7.65	6.69	5.48	4.47	3.59

$s = 13$ **Upper 5% points**

t \ r:	1	2	4	6	8	10	12	16	22	32
12	159.15	84.25	46.91	34.44	28.21	24.46	21.96	18.84	16.27	14.13
14	148.21	78.41	43.58	31.96	26.14	22.65	20.32	17.40	15.00	13.00
16	137.28	72.56	40.26	29.47	24.08	20.84	18.67	15.96	13.74	11.88
18	126.34	66.71	36.93	26.99	22.01	19.02	17.02	14.53	12.47	10.75
20	115.41	60.86	33.60	24.50	19.95	17.21	15.38	13.09	11.21	9.63
25	99.36	52.27	28.72	20.86	16.92	14.55	12.96	10.98	9.35	7.98
30	90.83	47.70	26.12	18.92	15.31	13.13	11.68	9.86	8.36	7.10
35	84.94	44.55	24.33	17.58	14.19	12.16	10.79	9.08	7.68	6.49
40	80.81	42.33	23.07	16.64	13.41	11.47	10.17	8.54	7.20	6.07
45	77.69	40.66	22.13	15.93	12.83	10.96	9.71	8.13	6.84	5.75
50	75.26	39.36	21.39	15.38	12.37	10.55	9.34	7.81	6.56	5.49
60	71.71	37.46	20.31	14.58	11.70	9.97	8.81	7.35	6.15	5.13
70	69.49	36.27	19.63	14.07	11.28	9.60	8.47	7.06	5.89	4.90
80	67.52	35.21	19.03	13.62	10.91	9.27	8.18	6.80	5.66	4.69
90	66.34	34.58	18.68	13.36	10.69	9.08	8.00	6.64	5.52	4.57
100	65.36	34.05	18.38	13.14	10.50	8.92	7.85	6.51	5.41	4.47
150	61.84	32.17	17.31	12.34	9.84	8.34	7.33	6.05	5.00	4.10
200	60.17	31.28	16.81	11.96	9.53	8.06	7.07	5.83	4.80	3.92
300	58.64	30.45	16.34	11.61	9.24	7.81	6.84	5.63	4.62	3.76
500	57.45	29.82	15.98	11.35	9.01	7.61	6.67	5.48	4.48	3.64
1,000	56.46	29.29	15.68	11.12	8.83	7.44	6.52	5.34	4.37	3.25
2,000	56.01	29.04	15.54	11.02	8.74	7.37	6.45	5.28	4.32	3.48

$s = 13$ **Upper 1% points**

t \ r:	1	2	4	6	8	10	12	16	22	32
12	230.29	121.82	67.74	49.69	40.66	35.24	31.62	27.09	23.38	20.27
14	211.17	111.62	61.97	45.40	37.10	32.13	28.80	24.64	21.23	18.38
16	192.06	101.41	56.20	41.11	33.55	29.02	25.98	22.19	19.09	16.48
18	172.94	91.21	50.43	36.81	30.00	25.91	23.17	19.75	16.94	14.59
20	153.83	81.01	44.65	32.52	26.44	22.79	20.35	17.30	14.79	12.69
25	126.62	66.50	36.46	26.43	21.40	18.38	16.36	13.83	11.75	10.01
30	113.14	59.33	32.41	23.42	18.92	16.21	14.39	12.13	10.26	8.69
35	104.03	54.46	29.67	21.39	17.23	14.74	13.07	10.97	9.25	7.80
40	97.82	51.14	27.79	20.00	16.09	13.73	12.16	10.18	8.56	7.19
45	93.18	48.67	26.40	18.96	15.23	12.99	11.49	9.60	8.04	6.73
50	89.58	46.76	25.33	18.17	14.58	12.41	10.96	9.15	7.65	6.39
60	84.45	44.02	23.79	17.02	13.63	11.59	10.22	8.50	7.08	5.89
70	81.26	42.32	22.83	16.32	13.05	11.08	9.76	8.10	6.73	5.58
80	78.43	40.82	21.99	15.69	12.53	10.63	9.35	7.75	6.42	5.30
90	76.77	39.93	21.49	15.32	12.23	10.36	9.11	7.54	6.24	5.14
100	75.40	39.20	21.08	15.02	11.98	10.14	8.91	7.37	6.09	5.01
150	70.53	36.61	19.62	13.94	11.08	9.36	8.21	6.76	5.55	4.53
200	68.22	35.38	18.93	13.43	10.66	9.00	7.88	6.47	5.30	4.30
300	66.13	34.26	18.31	12.96	10.28	8.66	7.58	6.21	5.07	4.10
500	64.53	33.41	17.83	12.61	9.99	8.41	7.35	6.01	4.89	3.94
1,000	63.19	32.70	17.43	12.32	9.75	8.19	7.15	5.84	4.75	3.45
2,000	62.59	32.38	17.25	12.18	9.63	8.10	7.07	5.76	4.68	3.75

$s = 14$ **Upper 5% points**

t \ *r*:	1	2	4	6	8	10	12	16	22	32
12	178.72	94.38	52.24	38.18	31.15	26.92	24.11	20.57	17.68	15.27
14	166.15	87.68	48.45	35.37	28.83	24.89	22.27	18.98	16.29	14.04
16	153.59	80.97	44.67	32.56	26.50	22.86	20.43	17.39	14.89	12.81
18	141.03	74.27	40.89	29.75	24.18	20.83	18.59	15.79	13.49	11.57
20	128.47	67.56	37.10	26.94	21.85	18.79	16.75	14.20	12.10	10.34
25	110.03	57.71	31.55	22.82	18.44	15.81	14.06	11.86	10.05	8.53
30	100.24	52.48	28.60	20.63	16.63	14.23	12.63	10.62	8.96	7.57
35	93.47	48.87	26.57	19.12	15.39	13.14	11.64	9.76	8.21	6.91
40	88.72	46.33	25.14	18.06	14.51	12.38	10.95	9.16	7.68	6.44
45	85.14	44.42	24.06	17.26	13.85	11.80	10.43	8.71	7.29	6.09
50	82.33	42.93	23.22	16.64	13.34	11.35	10.02	8.35	6.98	5.82
60	78.25	40.76	22.00	15.73	12.59	10.70	9.43	7.84	6.53	5.42
70	75.69	39.40	21.24	15.16	12.12	10.29	9.06	7.52	6.24	5.17
80	73.42	38.19	20.55	14.66	11.70	9.92	8.73	7.23	5.99	4.94
90	72.07	37.47	20.15	14.36	11.45	9.70	8.53	7.06	5.84	4.81
100	70.95	36.87	19.81	14.11	11.25	9.52	8.37	6.91	5.71	4.70
150	66.92	34.73	18.60	13.21	10.51	8.88	7.78	6.41	5.27	4.30
200	65.00	33.70	18.03	12.79	10.15	8.57	7.50	6.16	5.05	4.11
300	63.24	32.76	17.50	12.39	9.83	8.28	7.25	5.94	4.85	3.93
500	61.88	32.04	17.09	12.09	9.58	8.07	7.05	5.77	4.70	3.79
1,000	60.75	31.43	16.75	11.84	9.37	7.88	6.88	5.62	4.58	3.68
2,000	60.22	31.16	16.60	11.72	9.28	7.80	6.81	5.56	4.52	3.63

$s = 14$ **Upper 1% points**

t \ *r*:	1	2	4	6	8	10	12	16	22	32
12	258.50	136.31	75.35	55.03	44.85	38.75	34.68	29.58	25.39	21.91
14	236.62	124.68	68.82	50.20	40.87	35.28	31.54	26.87	23.03	19.84
16	214.74	113.05	62.29	45.37	36.90	31.81	28.42	24.16	20.68	17.77
18	192.85	101.41	55.76	40.54	32.92	28.34	25.28	21.46	18.32	15.70
20	170.97	89.78	49.23	35.71	28.94	24.87	22.15	18.75	15.96	13.63
25	139.86	73.25	39.96	28.86	23.29	19.95	17.72	14.92	12.62	10.69
30	124.49	65.10	35.40	25.49	20.52	17.53	15.54	13.04	10.98	9.26
35	114.08	59.57	32.31	23.20	18.64	15.90	14.07	11.77	9.88	8.29
40	107.00	55.80	30.20	21.65	17.36	14.79	13.06	10.90	9.12	7.62
45	101.71	53.00	28.63	20.49	16.41	13.96	12.32	10.26	8.56	7.13
50	97.62	50.83	27.42	19.60	15.68	13.32	11.74	9.76	8.13	6.75
60	91.77	47.73	25.69	18.32	14.63	12.40	10.92	9.05	7.51	6.21
70	88.16	45.81	24.61	17.53	13.98	11.84	10.41	8.61	7.13	5.87
80	84.96	44.11	23.66	16.83	13.40	11.34	9.96	8.22	6.79	5.58
90	83.08	43.11	23.10	16.42	13.06	11.04	9.69	7.99	6.59	5.40
100	81.52	42.28	22.64	16.08	12.79	10.80	9.47	7.80	6.42	5.26
150	75.98	39.34	21.00	14.87	11.79	9.94	8.70	7.13	5.84	4.74
200	73.36	37.96	20.23	14.30	11.33	9.53	8.33	6.82	5.56	4.50
300	70.99	36.70	19.53	13.79	10.90	9.16	8.00	6.53	5.31	4.28
500	69.17	35.74	18.99	13.39	10.58	8.88	7.74	6.31	5.12	4.11
1,000	67.66	34.93	18.55	13.06	10.31	8.65	7.53	6.13	4.96	3.97
2,000	66.97	34.57	18.34	12.91	10.18	8.54	7.44	6.04	4.89	3.90

$s = 15$ **Upper 5% points**

t \ r:	1	2	4	6	8	10	12	16	22	32
12	199.51	105.05	57.84	42.10	34.22	29.49	26.33	22.38	19.15	16.45
14	185.18	97.43	53.57	38.95	31.63	27.23	24.29	20.62	17.61	15.10
16	170.85	89.80	49.30	35.79	29.03	24.97	22.25	18.86	16.08	13.76
18	156.53	82.18	45.03	32.64	26.43	22.70	20.22	17.10	14.55	12.42
20	142.20	74.55	40.76	29.48	23.83	20.44	18.18	15.34	13.02	11.07
25	121.15	63.37	34.49	24.85	20.02	17.12	15.19	12.76	10.77	9.10
30	109.95	57.43	31.17	22.40	18.01	15.37	13.60	11.39	9.58	8.05
35	102.23	53.33	28.87	20.70	16.61	14.15	12.51	10.45	8.76	7.33
40	96.83	50.45	27.26	19.52	15.64	13.30	11.74	9.79	8.18	6.83
45	92.75	48.29	26.05	18.62	14.90	12.66	11.17	9.29	7.74	6.44
50	89.56	46.60	25.10	17.93	14.33	12.16	10.72	8.90	7.41	6.15
60	84.94	44.14	23.73	16.91	13.50	11.44	10.06	8.33	6.91	5.71
70	82.03	42.60	22.87	16.28	12.97	10.98	9.65	7.98	6.60	5.44
80	79.44	41.22	22.10	15.71	12.51	10.58	9.29	7.66	6.33	5.19
90	77.90	40.41	21.64	15.37	12.23	10.33	9.07	7.48	6.16	5.05
100	76.62	39.73	21.27	15.10	12.00	10.14	8.89	7.32	6.02	4.93
150	72.05	37.30	19.91	14.10	11.18	9.42	8.24	6.76	5.54	4.50
200	69.87	36.14	19.26	13.62	10.78	9.08	7.93	6.49	5.30	4.29
300	67.87	35.08	18.67	13.18	10.42	8.76	7.65	6.25	5.09	4.10
500	66.32	34.26	18.21	12.84	10.15	8.52	7.43	6.06	4.92	3.95
1,000	65.03	33.58	17.83	12.56	9.91	8.32	7.25	5.90	4.78	3.83
2,000	64.43	33.26	17.65	12.43	9.81	8.23	7.17	5.83	4.72	3.77

$s = 15$ **Upper 1% points**

t \ r:	1	2	4	6	8	10	12	16	22	32
12	288.10	151.52	83.36	60.62	49.24	42.40	37.85	32.14	27.48	23.59
14	263.26	138.37	76.02	55.22	44.82	38.56	34.39	29.17	24.90	21.34
16	238.43	125.22	68.68	49.82	40.39	34.71	30.93	26.20	22.32	19.08
18	213.59	112.07	61.35	44.43	35.96	30.87	27.47	23.22	19.74	16.83
20	188.76	98.92	54.01	39.03	31.53	27.02	24.02	20.25	17.16	14.58
25	153.52	80.26	43.61	31.38	25.25	21.57	19.12	16.04	13.51	11.40
30	136.20	71.07	38.49	27.62	22.17	18.90	16.72	13.98	11.72	9.84
35	124.46	64.85	35.03	25.08	20.09	17.09	15.09	12.58	10.52	8.79
40	116.45	60.60	32.67	23.35	18.67	15.86	13.99	11.63	9.70	8.07
45	110.48	57.44	30.92	22.06	17.62	14.95	13.17	10.93	9.08	7.54
50	105.87	55.01	29.57	21.07	16.81	14.25	12.53	10.38	8.62	7.13
60	99.27	51.52	27.63	19.64	15.64	13.24	11.63	9.61	7.94	6.54
70	95.20	49.36	26.43	18.77	14.92	12.61	11.07	9.13	7.52	6.17
80	91.59	47.45	25.37	17.99	14.29	12.06	10.57	8.70	7.16	5.85
90	89.46	46.33	24.74	17.53	13.91	11.74	10.28	8.45	6.94	5.66
100	87.71	45.40	24.23	17.16	13.61	11.47	10.04	8.24	6.76	5.51
150	81.47	42.11	22.40	15.82	12.51	10.52	9.19	7.51	6.13	4.95
200	78.53	40.55	21.54	15.18	11.99	10.07	8.79	7.17	5.83	4.69
300	75.87	39.14	20.76	14.61	11.53	9.67	8.42	6.85	5.56	4.45
500	73.82	38.06	20.16	14.17	11.17	9.36	8.14	6.61	5.35	4.27
1,000	72.12	37.16	19.66	13.81	10.87	9.10	7.91	6.42	5.17	4.12
2,000	71.34	36.75	19.43	13.64	10.73	8.98	7.81	6.32	5.10	4.05

$s = 16$ **Upper 5% points**

t	r: 1	2	4	6	8	10	12	16	22	32
12	221.49	116.25	63.71	46.19	37.42	32.16	28.65	24.26	20.66	17.65
14	205.24	107.65	58.92	42.67	34.54	29.66	26.40	22.32	18.99	16.20
16	189.00	99.05	54.13	39.15	31.65	27.15	24.15	20.39	17.31	14.74
18	172.75	90.45	49.34	35.63	28.77	24.65	21.90	18.46	15.64	13.28
20	156.51	81.85	44.56	32.12	25.89	22.15	19.65	16.52	13.96	11.82
25	132.67	69.24	37.53	26.96	21.66	18.48	16.35	13.69	11.51	9.68
30	120.01	62.55	33.81	24.22	19.42	16.53	14.61	12.19	10.21	8.55
35	111.28	57.93	31.25	22.34	17.88	15.19	13.40	11.16	9.31	7.76
40	105.17	54.70	29.45	21.02	16.79	14.25	12.56	10.43	8.68	7.22
45	100.57	52.26	28.09	20.02	15.98	13.55	11.92	9.89	8.21	6.80
50	96.97	50.36	27.03	19.25	15.34	13.00	11.43	9.46	7.84	6.48
60	91.76	47.59	25.50	18.12	14.42	12.19	10.71	8.84	7.30	6.01
70	88.48	45.86	24.53	17.41	13.84	11.69	10.26	8.45	6.97	5.71
80	85.56	44.31	23.67	16.78	13.32	11.24	9.85	8.11	6.67	5.45
90	83.83	43.40	23.16	16.41	13.02	10.98	9.61	7.90	6.49	5.29
100	82.39	42.63	22.74	16.10	12.76	10.76	9.42	7.73	6.34	5.16
150	77.23	39.91	21.23	14.98	11.85	9.97	8.71	7.12	5.81	4.70
200	74.76	38.60	20.50	14.45	11.42	9.59	8.37	6.83	5.55	4.47
300	72.51	37.41	19.84	13.97	11.02	9.24	8.06	6.56	5.32	4.27
500	70.77	36.49	19.33	13.59	10.71	8.98	7.82	6.35	5.14	4.11
1,000	69.32	35.72	18.90	13.28	10.46	8.75	7.62	6.18	4.99	3.97
2,000	68.65	35.37	18.71	13.14	10.34	8.65	7.52	6.10	4.92	3.91

$s = 16$ **Upper 1% points**

t	r: 1	2	4	6	8	10	12	16	22	32
12	319.31	167.51	91.73	66.45	53.81	46.21	41.16	34.83	29.64	25.31
14	291.37	152.75	83.54	60.45	48.91	41.97	37.36	31.57	26.83	22.87
16	263.43	137.99	75.36	54.46	44.01	37.73	33.55	28.31	24.02	20.43
18	235.48	123.23	67.17	48.47	39.12	33.49	29.75	25.06	21.21	18.00
20	207.54	108.47	58.99	42.48	34.22	29.25	25.94	21.80	18.40	15.56
25	167.90	87.54	47.38	33.99	27.28	23.25	20.56	17.19	14.43	12.11
30	148.40	77.25	41.69	29.82	23.88	20.31	17.93	14.94	12.49	10.43
35	135.19	70.29	37.84	27.01	21.58	18.32	16.15	13.42	11.17	9.29
40	126.17	65.54	35.21	25.09	20.02	16.97	14.93	12.38	10.28	8.52
45	119.48	62.01	33.26	23.66	18.86	15.96	14.03	11.61	9.62	7.95
50	114.34	59.29	31.76	22.57	17.96	15.19	13.34	11.02	9.11	7.50
60	106.94	55.40	29.61	21.00	16.68	14.08	12.35	10.17	8.38	6.87
70	102.37	52.99	28.28	20.02	15.89	13.40	11.74	9.65	7.93	6.48
80	98.32	50.85	27.10	19.17	15.19	12.80	11.19	9.19	7.53	6.13
90	95.95	49.60	26.41	18.66	14.78	12.44	10.88	8.91	7.30	5.93
100	93.99	48.57	25.84	18.25	14.44	12.15	10.62	8.69	7.10	5.76
150	87.02	44.89	23.81	16.77	13.23	11.11	9.68	7.89	6.42	5.16
200	83.73	43.16	22.86	16.07	12.67	10.62	9.24	7.52	6.09	4.88
300	80.75	41.59	21.99	15.44	12.15	10.17	8.85	7.18	5.80	4.63
500	78.47	40.39	21.33	14.96	11.76	9.83	8.54	6.92	5.57	4.43
1,000	76.58	39.39	20.78	14.55	11.43	9.55	8.29	6.70	5.39	4.27
2,000	75.71	38.94	20.53	14.37	11.28	9.42	8.17	6.60	5.30	4.19

$s = 17$ **Upper 5% points**

t \ r:	1	2	4	6	8	10	12	16	22	32
12	244.40	127.99	69.85	50.46	40.77	34.93	31.05	26.20	22.22	18.90
14	226.15	118.35	64.52	46.56	37.58	32.18	28.58	24.09	20.40	17.32
16	207.90	108.72	59.18	42.66	34.39	29.42	26.11	21.97	18.58	15.74
18	189.65	99.09	53.84	38.75	31.20	26.67	23.64	19.86	16.76	14.16
20	171.41	89.45	48.51	34.85	28.02	23.91	21.17	17.75	14.93	12.58
25	144.64	75.33	40.69	29.13	23.35	19.87	17.55	14.65	12.26	10.27
30	130.45	67.84	36.55	26.10	20.88	17.74	15.64	13.01	10.85	9.05
35	120.66	62.68	33.69	24.02	19.17	16.26	14.32	11.88	9.88	8.20
40	113.80	59.06	31.69	22.55	17.98	15.23	13.39	11.09	9.20	7.61
45	108.64	56.34	30.18	21.45	17.08	14.45	12.70	10.50	8.68	7.17
50	104.60	54.21	29.01	20.60	16.38	13.85	12.15	10.03	8.28	6.82
60	98.74	51.12	27.30	19.35	15.36	12.97	11.37	9.36	7.70	6.31
70	95.06	49.18	26.23	18.56	14.72	12.41	10.87	8.93	7.33	5.99
80	91.78	47.46	25.28	17.87	14.16	11.92	10.43	8.56	7.01	5.71
90	89.84	46.43	24.71	17.45	13.82	11.63	10.17	8.33	6.82	5.54
100	88.23	45.58	24.24	17.11	13.54	11.39	9.95	8.14	6.66	5.40
150	82.46	42.54	22.56	15.88	12.54	10.52	9.17	7.48	6.08	4.90
200	79.71	41.08	21.76	15.30	12.06	10.11	8.80	7.16	5.80	4.66
300	77.18	39.75	21.02	14.76	11.62	9.73	8.46	6.87	5.55	4.43
500	75.24	38.73	20.45	14.34	11.28	9.43	8.20	6.64	5.36	4.26
1,000	73.61	37.87	19.98	14.00	11.00	9.19	7.98	6.46	5.19	4.12
2,000	72.86	37.48	19.76	13.84	10.87	9.08	7.88	6.37	5.12	4.05

$s = 17$ **Upper 1% points**

t \ r:	1	2	4	6	8	10	12	16	22	32
12	351.98	184.23	100.48	72.54	58.57	50.19	44.60	37.59	31.86	27.08
14	320.74	167.78	91.40	65.92	53.18	45.54	40.43	34.04	28.82	24.45
16	289.50	151.32	82.32	59.30	47.79	40.88	36.27	30.50	25.77	21.82
18	258.26	134.87	73.24	52.68	42.40	36.22	32.11	26.95	22.72	19.19
20	227.02	118.41	64.16	46.06	37.00	31.57	27.94	23.40	19.67	16.56
25	182.72	95.09	51.30	36.69	29.37	24.98	22.05	18.38	15.37	12.85
30	160.97	83.64	44.99	32.09	25.64	21.76	19.17	15.93	13.26	11.04
35	146.25	75.90	40.73	28.99	23.12	19.58	17.23	14.27	11.85	9.81
40	136.22	70.62	37.82	26.88	21.40	18.10	15.90	13.15	10.88	8.98
45	128.76	66.70	35.67	25.31	20.12	17.01	14.92	12.31	10.17	8.36
50	123.01	63.68	34.01	24.10	19.14	16.16	14.17	11.67	9.61	7.89
60	114.78	59.36	31.63	22.38	17.74	14.95	13.09	10.75	8.83	7.21
70	109.69	56.68	30.16	21.31	16.87	14.20	12.42	10.18	8.34	6.79
80	105.19	54.32	28.86	20.36	16.10	13.54	11.83	9.68	7.91	6.42
90	102.55	52.93	28.10	19.81	15.65	13.15	11.48	9.38	7.66	6.20
100	100.38	51.79	27.47	19.35	15.28	12.83	11.20	9.14	7.45	6.02
150	92.63	47.71	25.24	17.73	13.96	11.70	10.18	8.28	6.71	5.38
200	88.98	45.79	24.18	16.96	13.34	11.16	9.70	7.87	6.36	5.08
300	85.67	44.05	23.23	16.27	12.78	10.68	9.27	7.50	6.04	4.80
500	83.13	42.72	22.50	15.74	12.35	10.31	8.94	7.22	5.80	4.59
1,000	81.03	41.62	21.89	15.30	11.99	10.00	8.67	6.99	5.60	4.42
2,000	80.06	41.11	21.62	15.10	11.83	9.86	8.54	6.88	5.51	4.34

$s = 18$ **Upper 5% points**

t \ r:	1	2	4	6	8	10	12	16	22	32
12	268.48	140.27	76.26	54.90	44.23	37.82	33.54	28.20	23.83	20.30
14	248.09	129.54	70.35	50.60	40.73	34.80	30.84	25.90	21.85	18.57
16	227.70	118.81	64.44	46.29	37.23	31.78	28.14	23.60	19.88	16.85
18	207.31	108.09	58.53	41.99	33.72	28.76	25.44	21.30	17.91	15.12
20	186.92	97.36	52.61	37.69	30.22	25.74	22.74	19.00	15.93	13.39
25	157.04	81.64	43.95	31.38	25.09	21.31	18.79	15.63	13.04	10.88
30	141.21	73.31	39.37	28.04	22.38	18.97	16.70	13.85	11.51	9.56
35	130.29	67.57	36.21	25.74	20.51	17.36	15.26	12.62	10.46	8.65
40	122.65	63.55	34.00	24.13	19.20	16.23	14.25	11.76	9.72	8.01
45	116.90	60.52	32.33	22.92	18.21	15.38	13.49	11.12	9.17	7.53
50	112.40	58.16	31.03	21.98	17.44	14.72	12.89	10.61	8.74	7.16
60	105.88	54.73	29.14	20.60	16.33	13.75	12.03	9.88	8.11	6.62
70	101.78	52.57	27.96	19.74	15.62	13.15	11.49	9.42	7.71	6.27
80	98.14	50.66	26.91	18.97	15.00	12.61	11.01	9.01	7.36	5.97
90	95.98	49.52	26.28	18.52	14.63	12.29	10.73	8.77	7.15	5.79
100	94.19	48.58	25.76	18.14	14.32	12.03	10.49	8.57	6.98	5.64
150	87.76	45.20	23.90	16.79	13.22	11.08	9.64	7.84	6.35	5.10
200	84.68	43.58	23.02	16.15	12.70	10.63	9.24	7.50	6.06	4.84
300	81.87	42.11	22.20	15.55	12.22	10.21	8.87	7.18	5.79	4.60
500	79.71	40.97	21.58	15.10	11.85	9.89	8.58	6.94	5.58	4.42
1,000	77.90	40.02	21.06	14.72	11.54	9.63	8.35	6.73	5.40	4.27
2,000	77.07	39.58	20.82	14.54	11.40	9.50	8.24	6.64	5.32	4.19

$s = 18$ **Upper 1% points**

t \ r:	1	2	4	6	8	10	12	16	22	32
12	386.24	201.76	109.61	78.91	63.52	54.30	48.14	40.46	34.15	28.99
14	351.51	183.51	99.59	71.62	57.61	49.22	43.60	36.60	30.86	26.14
16	316.77	165.26	89.57	64.34	51.70	44.13	39.07	32.75	27.57	23.30
18	282.03	147.01	79.55	57.06	45.80	39.04	34.53	28.90	24.27	20.45
20	247.29	128.76	69.53	49.78	39.89	33.96	30.00	25.04	20.98	17.61
25	198.08	102.91	55.34	39.47	31.53	26.76	23.58	19.60	16.33	13.60
30	173.94	90.24	48.39	34.43	27.45	23.25	20.45	16.94	14.06	11.65
35	157.62	81.67	43.70	31.03	24.69	20.88	18.33	15.15	12.53	10.34
40	146.51	75.84	40.51	28.72	22.81	19.27	16.90	13.93	11.49	9.45
45	138.25	71.51	38.14	27.00	21.42	18.07	15.83	13.03	10.72	8.79
50	131.90	68.18	36.31	25.68	20.35	17.15	15.01	12.33	10.13	8.28
60	122.78	63.40	33.70	23.78	18.82	15.83	13.84	11.33	9.28	7.55
70	117.15	60.45	32.08	22.61	17.87	15.02	13.11	10.72	8.75	7.10
80	112.17	57.84	30.66	21.58	17.03	14.30	12.47	10.18	8.29	6.70
90	109.25	56.31	29.82	20.97	16.54	13.88	12.10	9.86	8.02	6.47
100	106.85	55.05	29.13	20.47	16.14	13.53	11.79	9.60	7.80	6.28
150	98.29	50.56	26.67	18.70	14.70	12.29	10.68	8.67	7.00	5.59
200	94.26	48.44	25.52	17.86	14.02	11.71	10.17	8.23	6.62	5.27
300	90.59	46.53	24.47	17.10	13.41	11.19	9.70	7.83	6.28	4.98
500	87.80	45.06	23.67	16.53	12.94	10.78	9.34	7.53	6.02	4.75
1,000	85.48	43.85	23.01	16.04	12.55	10.45	9.04	7.27	5.81	4.57
2,000	84.42	43.29	22.70	15.83	12.38	10.30	8.91	7.16	5.71	4.48

$s = 19$ **Upper 5% points**

t \ r:	1	2	4	6	8	10	12	16	22	32
12	293.50	153.07	82.91	59.54	47.83	40.82	36.13	30.27	25.48	21.48
14	270.88	141.19	76.40	54.81	43.99	37.52	33.19	27.77	23.35	19.65
16	248.26	129.31	69.89	50.08	40.16	34.22	30.25	25.28	21.22	17.82
18	225.63	117.44	63.37	45.35	36.33	30.92	27.31	22.79	19.09	16.00
20	203.01	105.56	56.86	40.62	32.50	27.62	24.37	20.29	16.96	14.17
25	169.86	88.16	47.32	33.70	26.88	22.79	20.06	16.64	13.84	11.49
30	152.30	78.95	42.28	30.04	23.92	20.24	17.79	14.71	12.19	10.08
35	140.20	72.59	38.80	27.52	21.87	18.48	16.22	13.38	11.05	9.11
40	131.71	68.15	36.36	25.75	20.44	17.25	15.12	12.45	10.26	8.42
45	125.34	64.81	34.53	24.42	19.37	16.33	14.30	11.75	9.66	7.91
50	120.38	62.20	33.10	23.39	18.52	15.60	13.65	11.21	9.19	7.51
60	113.15	58.41	31.02	21.88	17.31	14.55	12.72	10.41	8.52	6.93
70	108.62	56.03	29.72	20.94	16.54	13.90	12.13	9.91	8.09	6.56
80	104.59	53.91	28.56	20.10	15.86	13.31	11.61	9.47	7.71	6.23
90	102.20	52.66	27.87	19.60	15.46	12.96	11.30	9.21	7.49	6.04
100	100.21	51.61	27.30	19.19	15.12	12.67	11.04	8.99	7.30	5.88
150	93.09	47.88	25.26	17.71	13.92	11.64	10.12	8.21	6.63	5.30
200	89.71	46.10	24.29	17.00	13.35	11.15	9.68	7.83	6.31	5.02
300	86.60	44.47	23.39	16.35	12.82	10.70	9.28	7.49	6.02	4.77
500	84.20	43.22	22.71	15.86	12.42	10.35	8.97	7.23	5.79	4.58
1,000	82.20	42.17	22.13	15.44	12.08	10.06	8.71	7.01	5.60	4.41
2,000	81.28	41.69	21.87	15.25	11.93	9.93	8.59	6.91	5.52	4.34

$s = 19$ **Upper 1% points**

t \ r:	1	2	4	6	8	10	12	16	22	32
12	422.14	220.07	119.15	85.49	68.66	58.56	51.83	43.42	36.51	30.77
14	383.69	199.93	108.14	77.52	62.21	53.03	46.90	39.25	32.96	27.74
16	345.25	179.78	97.12	69.55	55.76	47.49	41.97	35.08	29.42	24.71
18	306.81	159.64	86.11	61.59	49.32	41.96	37.05	30.91	25.87	21.68
20	268.36	139.49	75.10	53.62	42.87	36.42	32.12	26.74	22.32	18.64
25	213.94	110.98	59.52	42.35	33.76	28.60	25.16	20.85	17.32	14.36
30	187.31	97.04	51.90	36.84	29.31	24.78	21.76	17.98	14.88	12.28
35	169.31	87.61	46.76	33.13	26.30	22.20	19.47	16.04	13.23	10.88
40	157.07	81.20	43.26	30.60	24.26	20.45	17.91	14.73	12.12	9.92
45	147.98	76.44	40.66	28.72	22.75	19.16	16.76	13.75	11.29	9.22
50	140.98	72.77	38.66	27.28	21.58	18.16	15.87	13.00	10.65	8.67
60	130.95	67.53	35.80	25.22	19.91	16.73	14.60	11.93	9.74	7.90
70	124.77	64.29	34.04	23.94	18.89	15.85	13.82	11.27	9.18	7.42
80	119.29	61.42	32.48	22.82	17.98	15.07	13.12	10.68	8.68	6.99
90	116.08	59.74	31.56	22.16	17.44	14.61	12.72	10.34	8.39	6.74
100	113.43	58.36	30.81	21.61	17.00	14.23	12.38	10.06	8.15	6.54
150	104.00	53.43	28.13	19.68	15.44	12.90	11.19	9.06	7.29	5.81
200	99.57	51.11	26.86	18.77	14.71	12.27	10.63	8.58	6.89	5.46
300	95.56	49.01	25.72	17.94	14.04	11.70	10.13	8.16	6.53	5.15
500	92.49	47.41	24.85	17.31	13.54	11.26	9.74	7.83	6.25	4.91
1,000	89.93	46.07	24.12	16.79	13.11	10.90	9.42	7.56	6.02	4.72
2,000	88.77	45.46	23.79	16.55	12.92	10.74	9.27	7.43	5.91	4.62

$s = 20$ **Upper 5% points**

t \ r:	1	2	4	6	8	10	12	16	22	32
12	319.69	166.41	89.85	64.33	51.56	43.91	38.79	32.41	27.17	22.97
14	294.70	153.33	82.70	59.17	47.38	40.33	35.60	29.71	24.88	20.99
16	269.71	140.24	75.56	54.00	43.20	36.74	32.42	27.02	22.59	19.00
18	244.71	127.15	68.41	48.83	39.03	33.15	29.23	24.32	20.30	17.01
20	219.72	114.06	61.26	43.66	34.85	29.57	26.04	21.62	18.01	15.02
25	183.11	94.89	50.80	36.09	28.73	24.32	21.37	17.68	14.65	12.13
30	163.75	84.75	45.27	32.09	25.50	21.54	18.90	15.60	12.88	10.61
35	150.40	77.77	41.45	29.34	23.27	19.63	17.20	14.16	11.66	9.57
40	141.07	72.88	38.79	27.41	21.72	18.30	16.01	13.15	10.81	8.84
45	134.05	69.20	36.78	25.96	20.55	17.29	15.12	12.40	10.16	8.29
50	128.56	66.33	35.21	24.83	19.63	16.51	14.42	11.81	9.66	7.86
60	120.59	62.16	32.94	23.19	18.30	15.37	13.41	10.95	8.93	7.24
70	115.60	59.55	31.51	22.16	17.47	14.65	12.77	10.42	8.48	6.85
80	111.15	57.22	30.25	21.24	16.73	14.02	12.21	9.94	8.07	6.50
90	108.52	55.84	29.49	20.70	16.29	13.64	11.87	9.65	7.83	6.29
100	106.33	54.70	28.87	20.25	15.93	13.33	11.60	9.42	7.63	6.12
150	98.49	50.60	26.63	18.63	14.62	12.21	10.60	8.58	6.91	5.51
200	94.76	48.64	25.57	17.86	14.00	11.68	10.13	8.18	6.57	5.21
300	91.34	46.85	24.59	17.16	13.43	11.19	9.69	7.81	6.25	4.94
500	88.70	45.47	23.84	16.61	12.99	10.81	9.36	7.52	6.01	4.73
1,000	86.50	44.32	23.21	16.16	12.63	10.50	9.08	7.29	5.81	4.56
2,000	85.49	43.79	22.92	15.95	12.46	10.35	8.95	7.18	5.72	4.48

$s = 20$ **Upper 1% points**

t \ r:	1	2	4	6	8	10	12	16	22	32
12	459.41	239.10	129.04	92.34	73.99	62.97	55.63	46.45	38.92	32.81
14	417.11	216.98	117.00	83.65	66.98	56.97	50.30	41.96	35.12	29.54
16	374.82	194.86	104.95	74.97	59.97	50.97	44.97	37.46	31.31	26.28
18	332.52	172.74	92.91	66.28	52.96	44.97	39.64	32.97	27.51	23.01
20	290.22	150.62	80.86	57.60	45.96	38.97	34.31	28.48	23.70	19.75
25	230.38	119.33	63.83	45.31	36.05	30.49	26.78	22.13	18.33	15.14
30	201.14	104.05	55.51	39.32	31.22	26.35	23.11	19.04	15.71	12.92
35	181.39	93.72	49.90	35.28	27.96	23.57	20.63	16.96	13.95	11.43
40	167.95	86.70	46.08	32.53	25.75	21.67	18.95	15.55	12.75	10.41
45	157.97	81.49	43.25	30.49	24.10	20.27	17.71	14.50	11.86	9.66
50	150.29	77.48	41.07	28.92	22.84	19.19	16.75	13.69	11.18	9.08
60	139.29	71.74	37.95	26.68	21.03	17.64	15.38	12.54	10.21	8.25
70	132.51	68.20	36.03	25.29	19.92	16.69	14.53	11.83	9.60	7.74
80	126.50	65.06	34.33	24.07	18.93	15.85	13.78	11.20	9.07	7.28
90	122.99	63.22	33.33	23.35	18.36	15.35	13.35	10.83	8.76	7.02
100	120.09	61.71	32.51	22.76	17.88	14.95	12.99	10.53	8.50	6.80
150	109.78	56.33	29.59	20.66	16.19	13.50	11.71	9.45	7.59	6.02
200	104.93	53.80	28.22	19.68	15.40	12.82	11.10	8.94	7.16	5.66
300	100.53	51.51	26.98	18.78	14.68	12.21	10.56	8.49	6.77	5.33
500	97.17	49.75	26.03	18.10	14.13	11.74	10.14	8.13	6.48	5.07
1,000	94.39	48.30	25.24	17.54	13.67	11.35	9.80	7.84	6.23	4.86
2,000	93.11	47.63	24.88	17.28	13.46	11.17	9.64	7.71	6.12	4.77

This table facilitates the use of Roy's largest-root statistic in tests of multivariate hypotheses and in the construction of multivariate confidence bounds. Entries in the table are the .05 and .01 upper percentage points of the statistic

$$F_0 = \frac{t}{r}\lambda_1 \tag{A1}$$

where λ_1 is the largest root of the determinantal equation

$$|\mathbf{S}_h - \lambda \mathbf{S}_e| = 0 \tag{A2}$$

and r and t are defined by (A3) and (A5), or (A6) and (A8).

In (A2), $\mathbf{S}_h$ is a $p \times p$ sum-of-products matrix on n_h degrees of freedom for deviation from the null hypothesis; $\mathbf{S}_e$ is an independent $p \times p$ sum-of-products matrix on n_e degrees of freedom for error.

The percentage points of F_0 appear in a triple-entry table with arguments r, s, and t.

For tests of null hypotheses in a p-variate analysis of variance with n_h degrees of freedom for hypothesis and n_e degrees of freedom for error,

$$r = |n_h - p| + 1 \tag{A3}$$

$$s = \min(n_h,p) \tag{A4}$$

$$t = n_e - p + 1 \tag{A5}$$

For tests of nonassociation in multivariate multiple-regression analysis with p dependent variables, q independent variables, and a sample covariance or correlation matrix on n_e degrees of freedom,

$$r = |p - q| + 1 \tag{A6}$$

$$s = \min(p,q) \tag{A7}$$

$$t = n_e - p - q + 1 \tag{A8}$$

Percentage points for F_0 are tabulated for the following values of the arguments:

r = 1, 2, 4, 6, 8, 10, 12, 16, 22, 32

s = 1(1)10, 12(2)20

t = 12(2)20, 25(5)50, 60(10)100, 150, 200, 300, 500, 1,000, 2,000

The entries for $s = 1$, which are percentage points of the univariate F statistic, include some additional arguments. Entries for $s = 2$ through 20 were obtained from Pillai's [1965, 1966, 1967] tables, using

$$\lambda = \frac{\theta}{1 - \theta}$$

after interpolating for values of Pillai's $m = \frac{1}{2}(|n_h - p| - 1)$ and $n = \frac{1}{2}(n_e - p - 1)$.

Roy's generalized confidence bounds (Secs. 4.2.6 and 5.2.6) may be constructed using the entries of this table as follows:

$$\mathbf{a}'\hat{\boldsymbol{\theta}} - \left[\frac{n_e r}{t} F_{0,\alpha}{}^{(r,s,t)} c_\theta \mathbf{a}'\hat{\boldsymbol{\Sigma}}_{n_e}\mathbf{a}\right]^{1/2} \le \mathbf{a}'\boldsymbol{\theta} \le \mathbf{a}'\hat{\boldsymbol{\theta}} + \left[\frac{n_e r}{t} F_{0,\alpha}{}^{(r,s,t)} c_\theta \mathbf{a}'\hat{\boldsymbol{\Sigma}}_{n_e}\mathbf{a}\right]^{1/2}$$

where $\hat{\boldsymbol{\theta}}$ = estimated effect contrast with $\mathscr{E}(\hat{\boldsymbol{\theta}}) = \boldsymbol{\theta}$

$\mathbf{a}$ = arbitrary variate contrast

c_θ = variance factor for the effect contrast

$\hat{\boldsymbol{\Sigma}}_{n_e}$ = error covariance matrix estimated on n_e degrees of freedom

$F_{0,\alpha}{}^{(r,s,t)}$ = α-percent point of the generalized F statistic with arguments r, s, t

This bound has confidence coefficient *at least* $1 - \alpha$.

For computational convenience, the variate contrast may be introduced by transforming the original variates $\mathbf{y}$ to $z = \mathbf{a}'\mathbf{y}$. Then, $\eta = \mathbf{a}'\theta$ is estimated directly in the fitting of the linear model, and the confidence bound may be expressed in terms of this estimate and its estimated standard error:

$$\hat{\eta} - \left(\frac{n_e r}{t} F_{0,\alpha}{}^{(r,s,t)}\right)^{1/2} \mathrm{SE}(\hat{\eta}) \leq \eta \leq \hat{\eta} + \left(\frac{n_e r}{t} F_{0,\alpha}{}^{(r,s,t)}\right)^{1/2} \mathrm{SE}(\hat{\eta})$$

APPENDIX B

ORTHOGONAL POLYNOMIALS TO $n = 10$

The following table contains the terms of the factorization

$$\mathbf{V}_n^{(0)} = \mathbf{P}_n^{\perp}\mathbf{D}_n^{-1}\mathbf{T}_n'$$

(see Sec. 5.2.5c) in the arrangement

$$[\mathbf{P}_n^{\perp}]$$
$$[\mathbf{D}_n]$$
$$[\mathbf{T}_n]$$

The matrix $\mathbf{P}_n^{\perp}$ assumes a variable coded

$$\frac{2(x_j - \bar{x})}{d} \qquad n \text{ even}$$

and

$$\frac{x_j - \bar{x}}{d} \qquad n \text{ odd}$$

where $\bar{x} = \sum_{j=1}^{n} x_j/n$ and $d = x_j - x_{j-1}$ is the signed constant step size.

The matrix $\mathbf{T}_n$ assumes the coding $2(x_j - \bar{x})/d$ in all cases.

To recover the coefficients $\hat{\boldsymbol{\beta}}$ of the degree-g polynomial, transform the $g + 1$ estimated orthogonal polynomial coefficients

$$\hat{\gamma} = \mathbf{D}_{n(g)}^{-1/2}(\mathbf{P}_{n(g)}^{\perp})'\mathbf{y}.$$

by

$$\hat{\boldsymbol{\beta}} = (\mathbf{D}_{n(g)}^{1/2}\mathbf{T}_{n(g)}^{-1})'\hat{\gamma}$$

where $\mathbf{P}_{n(g)}^{\perp}$ and $\mathbf{D}_{n(g)}$ contain the leading $g + 1$ columns of $\mathbf{P}_n^{\perp}$ and $\mathbf{D}_n$, respectively, and $\mathbf{T}_{n(g)}$ the leading $g + 1$ rows and columns of $\mathbf{T}_n$. (See Example 5.2-6.)

$n = 2$

$$\begin{bmatrix} 1 & 1 \\ 1 & -1 \end{bmatrix}$$

$$[2 \quad 2]$$

$$\begin{bmatrix} 2 & \\ 0 & 2 \end{bmatrix}$$

$n = 3$

$$\begin{bmatrix} 1 & -1 & 1 \\ 1 & 0 & -2 \\ 1 & 1 & 1 \end{bmatrix}$$

$$[3 \quad 2 \quad 6]$$

$$\begin{bmatrix} 3 & & \\ 0 & 4 & \\ 8 & 0 & 8 \end{bmatrix}$$

$n = 4$

$$\begin{bmatrix} 1 & -3 & 1 & -1 \\ 1 & -1 & -1 & 3 \\ 1 & 1 & -1 & -3 \\ 1 & 3 & 1 & 1 \end{bmatrix}$$

$$[4 \quad 20 \quad 4 \quad 20]$$

$$\begin{bmatrix} 4 & & & \\ 0 & 20 & & \\ 20 & 0 & 16 & \\ 0 & 164 & 0 & 48 \end{bmatrix}$$

$n = 5$

$$\begin{bmatrix} 1 & -2 & 2 & -1 & 1 \\ 1 & -1 & -1 & 2 & -4 \\ 1 & 0 & -2 & 0 & 6 \\ 1 & 1 & -1 & -2 & -4 \\ 1 & 2 & 2 & 1 & 1 \end{bmatrix}$$

$$[5 \quad 10 \quad 14 \quad 10 \quad 70]$$

$$\begin{bmatrix} 5 & & & & \\ 0 & 20 & & & \\ 40 & 0 & 56 & & \\ 0 & 272 & 0 & 96 & \\ 544 & 0 & 992 & 0 & 384 \end{bmatrix}$$

$n = 6$

$$\begin{bmatrix} 1 & -5 & 5 & -5 & 1 & -1 \\ 1 & -3 & -1 & 7 & -3 & 5 \\ 1 & -1 & -4 & 4 & 2 & -10 \\ 1 & 1 & -4 & -4 & 2 & 10 \\ 1 & 3 & -1 & -7 & -3 & -5 \\ 1 & 5 & 5 & 5 & 1 & 1 \end{bmatrix}$$

$$[6 \quad 70 \quad 84 \quad 180 \quad 28 \quad 252]$$

$$\begin{bmatrix} 6 & & & & & \\ 0 & 70 & & & & \\ 70 & 0 & 224 & & & \\ 0 & 1{,}414 & 0 & 864 & & \\ 1{,}414 & 0 & 6{,}080 & 0 & 768 & \\ 0 & 32{,}710 & 0 & 27{,}840 & 0 & 3{,}840 \end{bmatrix}$$

$n = 7$

1	−3	5	−1	3	−1	1
1	−2	0	1	−7	4	−6
1	−1	−3	1	1	−5	15
1	0	−4	0	6	0	−20
1	1	−3	−1	1	5	15
1	2	0	−1	−7	−4	−6
1	3	5	1	3	1	1

[7	28	84	6	154	84	924]

7						
0	56					
112	0	336				
0	1,568	0	288			
3,136	0	12,864	0	4,224		
0	50,816	0	13,440	0	7,680	
101,632	0	466,176	0	222,720	0	46,080

$n = 8$

1	−7	7	−7	7	−7	1	−1
1	−5	1	5	−13	23	−5	7
1	−3	−3	7	−3	−17	9	−21
1	−1	−5	3	9	−15	−5	35
1	1	−5	−3	9	15	−5	−35
1	3	−3	−7	−3	17	9	21
1	5	1	−5	−13	−23	−5	−7
1	7	7	7	7	7	1	1

[8	168	168	264	616	2,184	264	3,432]

8							
0	168						
168	0	672					
0	6,216	0	3,168				
6,216	0	34,368	0	16,896			
0	268,008	0	200,640	0	99,840		
268,008	0	1,673,952	0	1,236,480	0	92,160	
0	12,323,976	0	10,717,728	0	8,010,240	0	645,120

$n = 9$

1	−4	28	−14	14	−4	4	−1	1
1	−3	7	7	−21	11	−17	6	−8
1	−2	−8	13	−11	−4	22	−14	28
1	−1	−17	9	9	−9	1	14	−56
1	0	−20	0	18	0	−20	0	70
1	1	−17	−9	9	9	1	−14	−56
1	2	−8	−13	−11	4	22	14	28
1	3	7	−7	−21	−11	−17	−6	−8
1	4	28	14	14	4	4	1	1

[9	60	2,772	990	2,002	468	1,980	858	12,870]

9								
0	120							
240	0	3,696						
0	5,664	0	9,504					
11,328	0	242,880	0	54,912				
0	312,960	0	781,440	0	99,840			
625,920	0	15,265,536	0	5,291,520	0	691,200		
0	18,522,624	0	54,372,864	0	10,752,000	0	1,290,240	
37,045,248	0	961,981,440	0	397,780,992	0	79,994,880	0	10,321,920

$n = 10$

1	−9	6	−42	18	−6	3	−9	1	−1
1	−7	2	14	−22	14	−11	47	−7	9
1	−5	−1	35	−17	−1	10	−86	20	−36
1	−3	−3	31	3	−11	6	42	−28	84
1	−1	−4	12	18	−6	−8	56	14	−126
1	1	−4	−12	18	6	−8	−56	14	126
1	3	−3	−31	3	11	6	−42	−28	−84
1	5	−1	−35	−17	1	10	86	20	36
1	7	2	−14	−22	−14	−11	−47	−7	−9
1	9	6	42	18	6	3	9	1	1

[10	330	132	8,580	2,860	780	660	29,172	2,860	48,620]

10									
0	330								
330	0	1,056							
0	19,338	0	41,184						
19,338	0	86,592	0	109,824					
0	1,330,890	0	4,255,680	0	249,600				
1,330,890	0	6,812,256	0	13,428,480	0	921,600			
0	98,417,418	0	373,105,824	0	34,540,800	0	21,934,080		
98,417,418	0	538,799,232	0	1,282,788,864	0	139,345,920	0	20,643,840	
0	7,558,168,650	0	31,275,480,960	0	3,523,484,160	0	3,514,613,760	0	185,794,560

REFERENCES

ABRAMOWITZ, M., and STEGUN, I. A. (eds.): "Handbook of Mathematical Functions," National Bureau of Standards, Applied Mathematics Series 55 (errata attached), U.S. Government Printing Office, Washington, D.C., 1964.

AITCHISON, J., and BROWN, J. A. C.: "The Lognormal Distribution," Cambridge, New York, 1966.

——— and SILVEY, S. D.: The Generalization of Probit Analysis to the Case of Multiple Responses, *Biometrika*, **44**: 131-140 (1957).

AITKEN, A. C.: Studies in Practical Mathematics II. The Evaluation of the Latent Roots and Latent Vectors of a Matrix, *Proc. R. Soc. Edinburgh*, **57**: 269–304 (1937).

———: "Determinants and Matrices," 9th ed., Interscience, New York, 1956.

ANASTASI, ANNE: "Differential Psychology," 3d ed., Macmillan, New York, 1958.

ANDERSON, R. L., and BANCROFT, T. A.: "Statistical Theory in Research," McGraw-Hill, New York, 1952.

ANDERSON, T. W.: "An Introduction to Multivariate Statistical Analysis," Wiley, New York, 1958.

———: Some Stochastic Process Models for Intelligence Test Scores, pp. 205–220 in K. J. Arrow, S. Karlin, and P. Suppes (eds.), "Mathematical Methods in the Social Sciences," Stanford University Press, Stanford, Calif., 1960.

———: The Choice of the Degree of a Polynomial Regression and a Multiple Decision Problem, *Ann. Math. Stat.*, **33:** 255–265 (1962).

ANTHONY, B. C. M.: The Identification and Measurement of Classroom Environmental Process Variables Related to Academic Achievement, unpublished Ph.D. dissertation, Department of Education, University of Chicago, 1967.

ASHFORD, J. R.: An Approach to the Analysis of Data for Semi-quantal Responses in Biological Assay, *Biometrics*, **15:** 473–581 (1959).

——— and SOWDEN, R. R.: Multivariate Probit Analysis. *Biometrics*, **26:** 535–546 (1970).

AYRES, F.: "Schaum's Outline of Theory and Problems of Matrices," McGraw-Hill, New York, 1962.

BAKAN, D.: The Test of Significance in Psychological Research, *Psychol. Bull.*, **66:** 423–437 (1966).

BALES, R. F.: "Interaction Process Analysis," Addison-Wesley, Reading, Mass., 1950.

BARGMANN, R. E.: "A Study of Independence and Dependence in Multivariate Normal Analysis," Mimeo Series No. 186, Institute of Statistics, University of North Carolina at Chapel Hill, 1957.

———: Matrix Differentiation, pp. 161–165 in R. C. Weast and S. M. Selby (eds.), "Handbook of Tables for Mathematics," 3d ed., Chemical Rubber Co., Cleveland, 1967.

BARTH, W., MORTON, R. S., AND WILKINSON, J. H.: Calculation of the Eigenvalues of a Symmetric Tridiagonal Matrix by the Method of Bisection, *Numer. Math.*, **9:** 386–393 (1967).

BARTLETT, M. S.: Multivariate Analysis, *J. R. Stat. Soc.*, (B) **9:** 176–197 (1947).

———: Use of Transformations, *Biometrics*, **3:** 39–52 (1947a).

———: The General Canonical Correlation Distribution, *Ann. Math. Stat.*, **18:** 1–17 (1947b).

BAUGHMAN, E. E., and DAHLSTROM, W. G.: "Negro and White Children: A Psychological Study in the Rural South," Academic, New York, 1968.

BECK, S. J.: "Rorschach's Test, I: Basic Processes," Grune & Stratton, New York, 1950.

BECKMAN, R. J., and TIETJEN, G. L.: Upper 10% and 25% Points of the Maximum F Ratio, *Biometrika*, **66:** 213–214 (1973).

BEGEL, E. G., and WILSON, J. W.: Evaluation of Mathematics Programs, in E. G. Begel (ed.), "Mathematics Education," Sixty-ninth Yearbook of the National Society for the Study of Education, University of Chicago Press, Chicago, 1970.

BERKSON, J.: A Statistically Precise and Relatively Simple Method of Estimating the Bio-assay with Quantal Response, Based on the Logistic Function, *J. Am. Stat. Assoc.*, **48:** 565–599 (1953).

BILODEAU, E. A.: Prediction of Complex Task Proficiency by Means of Component Responses, *Percept. & Mot. Skills*, **12:** 299:306 (1961).

BIRKOFF, G., and MACLANE, S.: "A Survey of Modern Algebra," 3d ed., Macmillan, New York, 1965.

BIRNBAUM, A.: Estimation of Ability, chap. 20 in F. M. Lord and M. Novick (eds)., "Statistical Theories of Test Scores," Addison-Wesley, Reading, Mass., 1968.

BISHOP, Y. M. M.: Full Contingency Tables, Logits, and Split Contingency Tables, *Biometrics*, **25:** 383–400 (1969).

———, FIENBERG, S. E., and HOLLAND, P. W.: "Discrete Multivariate Analysis: Theory and Practice," M.I.T. Press, Cambridge, Mass., 1975.

BJÖRCK, A.: Solving Linear Least Squares Problems by Gram-Schmidt Orthogonalization, *BIT*, **7:** 1–21 (1967).

BLACKWELL, D., and GIRSHICK, M. A.: "Theory of Games and Statistical Decisions," Wiley, New York, 1954.

BLISS, C. I.: The Calculation of the Dosage Mortality Curve (Appendix by R. A. Fisher), *Ann. Appl. Biol.*, **22:** 134–167 (1935).

BLOCK, J. B.: Hereditary Components in the Performance of Twins on the WAIS, in S. G. Vandenberg(ed.), "Progress in Human Behavior Genetics," Johns Hopkins, Baltimore, 1968.

BOCK, R. D.: A Synthesis of Time-sampling and Sociometric Testing, *Sociometry*, **15:** 263-271 (1952).

———: A Generalization of the Law of Comparative Judgment Applied to a Problem in the Prediction of Choice (abstract), *Am. Psychol.*, **11:** 442 (1956).

———: Computation of Solution Matrices for Orthogonal Factorial Designs, Psychometric Laboratory Research Memorandum No. 4, University of North Carolina, Chapel Hill, 1960.

———: Components of Variance Analysis as a Structural and Discriminal Analysis for Psychological Tests, *Br. J. Stat. Psychol.*, **13:** 151–163 (1960a).

———: Programming Univariate and Multivariate Analysis of Variance, *Technometrics*, **5:** 95–117 (1963).

———: Multivariate Analysis of Variance of Repeated Measurements, pp. 85–103 in C. W. Harris (ed.), "Problems of Measuring Change," University of Wisconsin Press, Madison, 1963a.

———: Contributions of Multivariate Experimental Designs to Educational Research, pp. 820–840 in R. B. Cattell (ed.), "Handbook of Multivariate Experimental Psychology," Rand-McNally, Chicago, 1966.

———: Estimating Multinomial Response Relations, pp. 111–132 in R. C. Bose, et al. (eds.), "Contributions to Statistics and Probability," University of North Carolina Press, Chapel Hill, 1970.

———: Estimating Item Parameters and Latent Ability when Responses Are Scored in Two or More Nominal Categories, *Psychometrika*, **37:** 29–51 (1972).

———: Word and Image: Sources of the Verbal and Spatial Factors in Mental Test Scores, *Psychometrika*, **38:** 437–457 (1974).

——— and BARGMANN, R. E.: Analysis of Covariance Structures, *Psychometrica*, **31:** 507–534 (1966).

———, DICKEN, C., and VAN PELT, J.: Methodological Implications of Content-Acquiescence Correlation in the MMPI, *Psychol. Bull.*, **71:** 127–139 (1969).

——— and HAGGARD, E. A.: The Use of Multivariate Analysis of Variance in Behavioral Research, pp. 100–142 in D. Whitla (ed.), "Handbook of Measurement and Assessment in Behavioral Sciences," Addison-Wesley, Reading, Mass., 1968.

——— and JONES, L. V.: "The Measurement and Prediction of Judgment and Choice," Holden-Day, San Francisco, 1968.

——— and KOLAKOWSKI, D.: Further Evidence of Sex-linked Major-Gene Influence on Human Spatial Visualizing Ability, *Am. J. Hum. Genetics*, **25**: 1-14 (1973).

——— and PETERSEN, A. C.: A Multivariate Correction for Attenuation, *Biometrika*, (1975 in press).

——— and REPP, B. H. (eds.): "MATCAL: Double-Precision Matrix Operations Subroutines for the IBM System/360-370 Computers," National Educational Resources, Chicago, 1974.

——— and VANDENBERG, S. G.: Components of Heritable Variation in Mental Test Scores pp. 233–260 in S. G. Vandenberg (ed.), "Progress in Human Behavior Genetics," Johns Hopkins, Baltimore, 1968.

———, WAINER, H., PETERSEN, A. C., THISSEN, D., MURRAY, J., and ROCHE, A.: A Parameterization for Individual Human Growth Curves, *Hum. Biol.*, **45**: 63–68 (1973).

———and YATES, G.: "MULTIQUAL: Log-Linear Analysis of Nominal or Ordinal Qualitative Data by the Method of Maximum Likelihood," National Educational Resources, Chicago, 1973.

BODEWIG, E.: "Matrix Calculus," 2d ed., Interscience, New York, 1959.

BOGGAN, W. O., FREEDMAN, D. X., LOVELL, R. A., and SCHLESINGER, K.: Studies in Audiogenic Seizure Susceptibility, *Psychopharmocologia*, **20**: 48-56 (1971).

BOSE, R. C.: Lecture Notes, Department of Statistics, University of North Carolina, Chapel Hill, undated.

———, CLATWORTHY, W. H., and SIRKHANDE, S. S.: "Tables of Partially Balanced Designs with Two Associate Classes," Technical Bulletin No. 107, North Carolina Agriculture Experimental Station, Raleigh, 1954.

——— and NAIR, K. R.: Partially Balanced Incomplete Block Designs, *Sankhaya*, **4**: 337–372 (1939).

BOX, G. E. P.: A General Distribution Theory for a Class of Likelihood Criteria, *Biometrika*, **36**: 317–346 (1949).

BRADLEY, J. V.: "Distribution-free Statistical Tests," Prentice-Hall, Englewood Cliffs, N.J., 1969.

BROVERMAN, D. M., and KLAIBER, E. L.: Negative Relationships between Abilities, *Psychometrika*, **34**: 5–20 (1969).

BROWNE, E. T.: "Introduction to the Theory of Determinants and Matrices," University of North Carolina Press, Chapel Hill, 1958.

BUSINGER, P. A.: Algorithm 254 (F-2)—Eigenvalues and Eigenvectors of a Real Symmetric Matrix by the QR Methods, *Comm. Assoc. Comput. Mach.*, **8**: 218–219 (1965).

BUSSE, T. V., ROE, M., GERTRIDE, M., ALEXANDER, T., and POWELL, L. S.: Environmentally Enriched Classrooms and the Cognitive and Perceptual Development of Negro Preschool Children, *J. Educ. Psychol.*, **63**: 15–21 (1972).

CAMPBELL, D. T., and ERLEBACHER, A.: How Regression Artifacts in Quasi-experimental Evaluation can Mistakenly Make Compensatory Education Look Harmful, pp. 185–210 in J. Hellmuth (ed.), "Compensatory Education: A National Debate," vol. III, "Disadvantaged Child," Brunner-Mazel, New York, 1970.

——— and FISKE, D. W.: Convergent and Discriminant Validation by the Multitrait-Multimethod Matrix, *Psychol. Bull.*, **56**: 81–105 (1959).

CARROLL, J. B.: On Sampling from a Lognormal Model of Word-Frequency Distribution, pp. 406–424 in H. Kŭcera and W. N. Francis (eds.), "Computer Analysis of Present-Day English," Brown University Press, Providence, 1967.

CARRY, L. R.: Pattern of Mathematics Achievement in Grades 7 and 8: X-population, NLSMA report No. 11, in H. W. Wilson, et al. (eds.), School Mathematics Study Group, Stanford University, 1970.

CAVALLI-SFORZA, L. L., and BODMER, W. F.: "The Genetics of Human Populations," Freeman, San Francisco, 1971.

CHERNOFF, H., and MOSES, L. E.: "Elementary Decision Theory," Wiley, New York, 1959.

CLYDE, D. J., CRAMER, E. M., and SHERIN, R. J.: "Multivariate Statistical Programs," Biometric Laboratory of the University of Miami, Coral Gables, Fla., 1966.

COCHRAN, W. G.: Observational Studies, in T. A. Bancroft (ed.), "Statistical Papers in Honor of George W. Snedecor," Iowa State University Press, Ames, 1972.

——— and COX, G. M.: "Experimental Designs," 2d ed., Wiley, New York, 1957.

COHEN, J.: "Statistical Power Analysis for the Behavioral Sciences," Academic, New York, 1970.

COLEMAN, J. S.: "Introduction to Mathematical Sociology," Free Press, New York, 1964.

———, CAMPBELL, E. Q., HOBSON, C. J., et al.: "Equality of Educational Opportunity," U.S. Government Printing Office, Washington, 1966.

COOLEY, W. W., and LOHNES, P. R.: "Multivariate Procedures for the Behavioral Sciences," Wiley, New York, 1962.

CORSTEN, L. C. A.: "Vectors, a Tool in Statistical Regression Theory," Institut voor Rassenonderzoek van Landbouwgewassen te Wageningen, Wageningen, Netherlands, 1958.

COURANT, R.: "Differential and Integral Calculus," vol. I, Interscience, New York, 1952.

———: "Differential and Integral Calculus," vol. II, Interscience, New York, 1959.

CRAMÉR, H.: "Mathematical Methods of Statistics," Princeton University Press, Princeton, 1951.

CULLER, E.: Studies in Psychometric Theory, *J. Exp. Psychol.*, **9**: 271–298 (1926).

CUSHNY, A. R., and PEEBLES, A. R.: The Action of Optical Isomers II: Hyoscines, *J. Physiol.*, **32**: 501–510 (1905).

D'AGOSTINO, R. B., and PEARSON, E. S.: Tests for Departure from Normality: Empirical Results for the Distribution of b_2 and $\sqrt{b_1}$, *Biometrika*, **60**: 613-622 (1973.)

——— and TIETJEN, G. L.: Simulation Probability Points of b_2 in Small Samples, *Biometrika*, **58**: 669–672 (1971).

——— and ———: Approaches to the Null Distribution of $\sqrt{b_1}$, *Biometrica*, **60**: 169–173 (1973).

DANIELS, W. J., and MURDOCH, P.: Effectiveness of Learning from a Programmed Text Compared with a Conventional Text Covering the Same Material, *J. Educ. Psychol.*, **56**: 425–431 (1968).

DAS GUPTA, S.: Step-down Multiple Decision Rules, pp. 229–250 in R. C. Bose, et al. (eds.), "Essays in Probability and Statistics," University of North Carolina Press, Chapel Hill, 1970.

———: Theories and Methods of Classification: a Review, pp. 77–137 in T. Cacoullos (ed.), "Discriminant Analysis and Applications," Academic Press, New York, 1973.

——— and PERLMAN, M. D.: On the Power of Wilk's U-Test for MANOVA, *J. Multivariate Anal.*, **3:** 220–225 (1973).

DAVID, H. A.: "The Method of Paired Comparisons," Hafner, New York, 1963.

———, HARTLEY, H. O., and PEARSON, E. S.: The Distribution of the Ratio, in a Single Normal Sample, of Range to Standard Deviation, *Biometrika*, **41:** 482–493 (1954).

DAVIS, F.: Cooperative Achievement Tests, Educational Testing Service, 1950.

DAY, N. E.: Estimating the Components of a Mixture of Normal Distributions, *Biometrika*, **56:** 463–474 (1969).

DELURY, D. B.: "Values and Integrals of the Orthogonal Polynomials up to $n = 26$," University of Toronto Press, Toronto, 1950.

DEMPSTER, A. P.: "Continuous Multivariate Analysis," Addison-Wesley, Reading, Mass., 1969.

DEUTSCH, R.: "Estimation Theory," Prentice-Hall, Englewood Cliffs, N. J., 1965.

DICKMAN, K., and KAISER, H. F.: Program for Inverting a Grammian Matrix, *Educ. & Psychol. Meas.*, **21:** 721-727 (1961).

DOBZHANSKI, T.: On Types, Genotypes and the Genetic Diversity in Populations, pp. 1–18 in J. N. Spuhler (ed.), "Genetic Diversity and Human Behavior," Wenner-Gren Foundation, New York, 1967.

DUNCAN, D. B.: A Bayesian Approach to Multiple Comparisons, *Technometrics*, **7:** 171–222 (1965).

DUNN, O. J.: Multiple Comparisons among Means. *J. Am. Stat. Assoc.*, **56:** 52–64 (1961).

DUNNETT, C. W.: New Tables for Multiple Comparisons with a Control, *Biometrics*, **20:** 482–491 (1964).

DUTT, J. E.: A Representation of Multivariate Probability Integrals by Integral Transforms, *Biometrika*, **60:** 637–645 (1973).

DWYER, P. S.: Some Applications of Matrix Derivatives in Multivariate Analysis, *J. Am. Stat. Assoc.*, **62:** 607–625 (1967).

——— and MACPHAIL, M. S.: Symbolic Matrix Derivatives, *Ann. Math. Stat.*, **19:** 517–534 (1948).

EDWARDS, A. L., and THURSTONE, L. L.: An Internal Consistency Check for the Method of Successive Intervals and the Method of Graded Dichotomies, *Psychometrika*, **17:** 169–180 (1952).

EFROYMSON, M. A.: Multiple Regression Analysis, pp. 191–203 in A. Ralston and H. S. Wilf (eds.), "Mathematical Methods for Digital Computers," Wiley, New York, 1960.

EMERSON, P. L.: Numerical Construction of Orthogonal Polynomials from a General Recurrence Formula, *Biometrics*, **24:** 695–701 (1968).

EZEKIEL, M., and FOX, K. A.: "Methods of Correlation and Regression Analysis," Wiley, New York, 1959.

FEEDEVA, V. N.: "Computational Methods of Linear Algebra, Dover, New York, 1959.

FIENBERG, S. E.: Quasi-independence and Maximum Likelihood Estimation in Incomplete Contingency Tables, *J. Am. Stat. Assoc.*, **65**: 1610–1616 (1970).

———: The Analysis of Incomplete Multi-way Contingency Tables, *Biometrics*, **28**: 177–202 (1972).

FINN, J. D.: "MULTIVARIANCE: Univariance and Multivariance Analysis of Variance, Covariance, and Regression," National Educational Resources, Chicago, 1972.

FINNEY, D. J.: "Probit Analysis: a Statistical Treatment of the Sigmoid Response Curve," 2d ed., Cambridge University Press, London, 1952.

———: "An Introduction to the Theory of Experimental Design," University of Chicago Press, Chicago, 1960.

FISHER, R. A.: On a Distribution Yielding the Error Functions of Several Well-known Statistics, *Proc. Int. Math. Conf., Toronto*, **2**: 805–813 (1924).

———: The Sampling Distribution of Some Statistics Obtained from Non-linear Equations, *Ann. Eugen.*, **9**: 238–249 (1939).

———: "Design of Experiments," 8th ed., Hafner, New York, 1966.

———: "Statistical Methods for Research Workers," 13th ed., Hafner, New York, 1967.

——— and YATES, F.: "Statistical Tables for Biological, Agricultural, and Medical Research," 6th ed., Hafner, New York, 1963.

FISKE, D. W.: The Inherent Variability of Behavior, pp. 326–354 in D. W. Fiske and S. R. Maddi (eds.), "Functions of Varied Experience," Dorsey, Homewood, Ill., 1961.

———: "Measuring the Concepts of Personality," Aldine, Chicago, 1971.

FRANCIS, J. G. F.: The QR Transformation: a Unitary Analogue to the LR Transformation, part 1, *Comput. J.*, **4**: 265–271 (1961).

———: The QR Transformation—Part 2, *Comput. J.*, **4**: 332–345 (1962).

FREEDMAN, D. G.: Constitutional and Environmental Interactions in Rearing of Four Breeds of Dogs, *Science*, **127**: 585–586 (1958).

FULLER, J. L., and THOMPSON, W. R.: "Behavior Genetics," Wiley, New York, 1960.

GAMOW, G.: "Gravity: Classic and Modern Views," Anchor Books, Garden City, N.Y., 1962.

GAUSS, K. F.: "Theory of the Motion of the Heavenly Bodies Moving about the Sun in Conic Sections," reprint, Dover, New York, 1963.

GAYLOR, D. W., and HOPPER, F. N.: Estimating Degrees of Freedom for Linear Combinations of Mean Squares by Satterthwaite's Formula, *Technometrics*, **11**: 691–706 (1969).

GEARY, R. C.: Testing for Normality, *Biometrika*, **34**: 209–242 (1947).

GIVENS, W.: The Characteristic Value-Vector Problem, *J. Assoc. Comput. Mach.*, **4**: 298–307 (1957).

GNEDENKO, B. V., and KOLMOGOROV, A. N.: "Limit Distribution for Sums of Independent Random Variables," Addison-Wesley, Reading, Mass., 1954.

GOLDSTEIN, H.: "Classical Mechanics," Addison-Wesley, Reading, Mass., 1950.

GOLDSTINE, H. H., MURRAY, F. J., and VON NEUMANN, J.: The Jacobi Method for Real Symmetric Matrices, *J. Assoc. Comput. Mach.*, **6**: 59–96 (1959).

GOODMAN, L. A.: The Analysis of Cross-classified Data: Independence, Quasi-independence, and Interaction in Contingency Tables with or without Missing Cells, *J. Am. Stat. Assoc.*, **63**: 1091–1131 (1968).

———: The Multivariate Analysis of Qualitative Data: Interactions Among Multiple Classifications. *J. Am. Stat. Assoc.*, **65:** 226–256 (1970).

———: A General Model for the Analysis of Surveys, *Am. J. Sociol.*, **77:** 1035–1086 (1972).

———: A Modified Multiple Regression Approach to the Analysis of Dichotomous Variables, *Am. Sociol. Rev.*, **37:** 28–46 (1972a).

——— and KRUSKAL, W. H.: Measures of Association for Cross Classifications, part I, *J. Am. Stat. Assoc.*, **49:** 732–764 (1954).

GRAYBILL, F. A.: "An Introduction to Linear Models," McGraw-Hill, New York, 1961.

GRIZZLE, J. E., STARMER, C. F., and KOCH, G. G.: Analysis of Categorical Data by Linear Models, *Biometrics*, **25:** 489–504 (1969).

GUILFORD, J. P.: "Psychometric Methods," 1st ed., McGraw-Hill, New York, 1936.

———: "Psychometric Methods," 2d ed., McGraw-Hill, New York, 1954.

GUMBEL, E. J.: Bivariate Logistic Distributions, *J. Am. Stat. Assoc.*, **56:** 335–349 (1961).

GUPTA, S. S.: Probability Integrals of Multivariate Normal and Multivariate *t*, *Ann. Math. Stat.*, **34:** 792–828 (1963).

HABERMAN, S. J.: "The Analysis of Frequency Data," University of Chicago Press, Chicago, 1974.

HAGGARD, E. A.: "Intraclass Correlation and the Analysis of Variance," Dryden, New York, 1958.

———: On Qualitative Rorschach Scales, unpublished paper, 1972.

———: Some Effects of Geographic and Social Isolation in Natural Settings, pp. 99–143 in J. E. Rasmussen (ed.), "Man in Isolation and Confinement," Aldine, Chicago, 1973.

HALD, A.: "Statistical Tables and Formulas," Wiley, New York, 1952.

HARMAN, H. H.: The Square Root Method and Multiple Group Methods of Factor Analysis, *Psychometrika*, **19:** 39–55 (1954).

———: "Modern Factor Analysis," University of Chicago Press, Chicago, 1960.

HARTLEY, H. O.: Expectations, Variances, and Covariances of ANOVA Mean Squares by "Synthesis," *Biometrics*, **23:** 105–114(errata, 853) (1967).

HASTINGS, C., JR.: "Approximations for Digital Computers," Princeton University Press, Princeton, N.J., 1955.

HECK, D. L.: Charts of Some Upper Percentage Points of the Distribution of the Largest Characteristic Root, *Ann. Math. Stat.*, **31:** 625–642 (1960).

HENDERSON, C. R.: Estimation of Variance and Covariance Components, *Biometrics*, **9:** 226–252 (1953).

———: Design and Analysis of Animal Husbandry Experiments, Chap. 1 in "Techniques and Procedures in Animal Science Research," 2d ed., American Society of Animal Science, 1969.

HENRY, W. E.: "The Analysis of Fantasy: the Thematic Apperception Technique in the Study of Personality," Wiley, New York, 1956.

HESS, E. H.: Natural Preferences of Chicks and Ducklings for Objects of Different Colors, *Psychol. Rep.*, **2:** 477–483 (1956).

HESTON L. L.: The Genetics of Schizophrenic and Schizoid Disease, *Science*, **167:** 249–256 (1970).

HEY, G. B.: A New Method of Experimental Sampling Illustrated on Certain Non-normal Populations, *Biometrika*, **30:** 68–80 (1938).

HEYNS, R. W., and LIPPITT, R.: Systematic Observation Methods, pp. 370–404 in G. Lindzey (ed.), "Handbook of Social Psychology," 1st ed., Addison-Wesley, Reading, Mass., 1954.

HODGES, J. L., and LEHMANN, E. L.: Testing the Approximate Validity of Statistical Hypotheses, *J. R. Stat. Soc.*, (B) **16:** 261–268 (1954).

HOLLAND, J. G., and SKINNER, B. F.: "Analysis of Behavior: A Program for Self Instruction," McGraw-Hill, New York, 1951.

HOLTZMAN, W. H., THORPE, J. S., SWARTZ, J. D., and HERRON, E. W.: "Inkblot Perception and Personality: Holtzman Inkblot Technique," University of Texas Press, Austin, 1961.

HOLZINGER, K. J., and CHURCH, A. E. R.: On the Means of Samples from a U-shaped Population, *Biometrika*, **20A:** 361–388 (1928).

HOTELLING, H.: The Generalization of Student's Ratio, *Ann. Math. Stat.*, **2:** 360–378 (1931).

———: The Most Predictable Criterion, *J. Educ. Psychol.*, **26:** 139–142 (1935).

———: Simplified Calculation of Principal Components, *Psychometrika*, **1:** 27–35 (1936).

———: Relations between Two Sets of Variates, *Biometrika*, **28**: 321–377 (1936a).

———: A Generalized Test and Measure of Multivariate Dispersion, *Proc. Second Berkeley Symp. Math. Stat. & Probab.*, **2:** 23–41 (1951).

HOUSEHOLDER, A. S.: "Principles of Numerical Analysis," McGraw-Hill, New York, 1953.

———: "The Theory of Matrices in Numerical Analysis," Blaisdell, Waltham, Mass., 1964.

HUDSON, W. W.: Autoletic Teaching Experiment with Ancillary Case Work Service, *Am. Educ. Res. J.*, **8:** 467–483 (1971).

HUMMEL, T. J., and SLIGO, J. R.: Empirical Comparison of Univariate and Multivariate Analysis of Variance Procedures, *Psychol. Bull.*, **76:** 49–57 (1971).

IRWIN, S.: Comprehensive Observational Assessment, part Ia: A Systematic, Quantitative Procedure for Assessing the Behavioral and Physiologic State of the Mouse, *Psychopharmocologia*, **13:** 222–257 (1968).

ITO, K., and SCHULL, W. J.: On the Robustness of the T_0^2 Test in Multivariate Analysis of Variance when the Variance-Covariance Matrices are Not Equal, *Biometrika*, **51:** 71–82 (1964).

JAY, P. C.: "Primates: Studies in Adaptation and Variability," Holt, New York, 1968.

JOHN, P. W. M.: "Statistical Design and Analysis of Experiments," Macmillan, New York, 1971.

JONES, L. V.: Analysis of Variance in its Multivariate Developments, pp. 244–266 in R. B. Cattell (ed.), "Handbook of Multivariate Experimental Psychology," Rand-McNally, Chicago, 1966.

———, GOODMAN, M. F., and WEPMAN, J. M.: The Classification of Parts of Speech for the Characterization of Aphasia, *Lang. & Speech*, **6:** 94–107 (1963).

———, PERYAM, D. R., and THURSTONE, L. L.: Development of a Scale for Measuring Soldier's Food Preferences, *Food Res.*, **20:** 512–520 (1955).

JONES, W. S.: Some Correlates of the Authoritarian Personality in a Quasi-therapeutic Situation, unpublished doctoral dissertation, Department of Psychology, University of North Carolina, Chapel Hill, 1961.

JÖRESKOG, K. G.: A General Method of Analysis of Covariance Structures, *Biometrika*, **57:** 239–251 (1970).

KAHANA, E.: The Effects of Age Segregation on Elderly Psychiatric Patients, unpublished Ph.D. dissertation, Committee on Human Development, University of Chicago, 1968.

KAHN, R. L., et al.: Brief Objective Measures of the Determinations of Mental Status in the Aged, *Am. J. Psychiatr.*, **4:** 120–124 (1960).

KAISER, H. F.: Directional Statistical Decisions, *Psychol. Rev.*, **67:** 160–167 (1960).

KEATS, J. A., and LORD, F. M.: A Theoretical Distribution for Mental Test Scores, *Psychometrika*, **27:** 59–72 (1962).

KEESLING, J. W., BOCK, R. D., et al.: The Laboratory School Study of Vocabulary Growth, (in preparation), 1974.

KELLEY, T. C.: "Essential Traits of Mental Life," Harvard University Press, Cambridge, Mass., 1935.

KELLY, E. J., VELDMAN, D. J., and MCGUIRE, C.: Multiple Discriminant Prediction of Delinquency and School Dropouts, *Educ. & Psychol. Meas.*, **24:** 535–544 (1964).

KENDALL, M. G., and STUART, A.: "The Advanced Theory of Statistics," vol. 2, 2d ed., Griffin, London, 1967.

KIRK, R. E.: "Experimental Design Procedures for the Behavioral Sciences," Brooks/Cole, Belmont, Calif., 1968.

KLOPFER, B., AISWORTH, M. D., KLOPFER, W., and HOOT, R. R.: "Rorschach Technique," World, Yonkers-on-Hudson, N.Y., 1954.

KOLAKOWSKI, D., and BOCK, R. D.: "NORMOG: Maximum Likelihood Item Analysis and Test Scoring: Normal Ogive Model," National Educational Resources, Chicago, 1973.

——— and ———: "LOGOG: Maximum Likelihood Item Analysis and Test Scoring: Logistic Model for Multiple Item Responses," National Educational Resources, Chicago, 1973a.

KOLODNY, R. C., MASTERS, W. H., HENDRYX, J., and TORO, G.: Plasma Testosterone and Semen Analysis in Male Homosexuals, *N. Eng. J. Med.*, **285:** 1170–1174 (1971).

KRAMER, K. H.: Tables for Constructing Confidence Limits on the Multiple Correlation Coefficient, *J. Am. Stat. Assoc.*, **58:** 1082–1085 (1963).

KREVISKY, J., and LINFIELD, J. L.: "The Bad Speller's Dictionary," Random House, New York, 1967.

KRISHNAIAH, P. R., and CHANG, T. C.: On the Exact Distribution of the Extreme Roots of the Wishart and MANOVA Matrices, *J. Multivariate Anal.*, **1:** 108–117 (1971).

KRUMBOLTZ, J. D., and YABROFF, W. W.: The Comparative Effects of Inductive and Deductive Sequences in Programmed Instruction, *Am. Educ. Res. J.*, **2:** 223–235 (1965).

KUDER, G. F., and RICHARDSON, M. W.: The Theory of the Estimation of Test Reliability, *Psychometrika*, **2:** 151–160 (1937).

KURKJIAN, B., and ZELEN, M.: A Calculus for Factorial Arrangements, *Ann. Math. Stat.*, **33:** 600–619 (1962).

KURTZ, T. E., LINK, R. F., TUKEY, J. W., and WALLACE, D. L.: Short-Cut Multiple Comparisons for Balanced Single and Double Classifications, part 1: Results, *Technometrics*, **7:** 95–161 (1965).

LACHENBRUCH, P. A.: On Expected Probabilities of Misclassification in Discriminant Analysis, Necessary Sample Sizes, and a Relation with the Multiple Correlation Coefficient, *Biometrics*, **24:** 823–834 (1968).

LASSITZ, R. W.: Comparison of Small Sample Power of the Chi-Square and Likelihood Ratio Tests for Stochastic Models, *J. Am. Stat. Assoc.*, **67:** 574–577 (1972).

LAWLEY, D. N.: On Problems Connected with Item Selection and Test Construction, *Proc. R. Soc. Edinburgh*, **61:** 273–287 (1943).

LEE, Y. S.: Some Results on the Distribution of Wilks Likelihood Ratio Criterion, *Biometrika*, **95:** 649–664 (1972).

LEIBOWITZ, H. W., and GWOZDICKI, J.: The Magnitude of the Poggendorff Illusion as a Function of Age, *Child Dev.*, **38:** 573–580 (1967).

——— and JUDISCH, J. M.: The Relation Between Age and the Magnitude of the Ponzo Illusion, *Am. J. Psychol.*, **80:** 105–109 (1967).

LI, C. C.: "Population Genetics," University of Chicago Press, Chicago, 1955.

LINDQUIST, E. F.: "Design and Analysis of Experiments in Psychology and Education," Houghton-Mifflin, Boston, 1953.

LOMBARD, H. L., and DOERING, C. R.: Treatment of the Four-fold Table by Partial Correlations as it Relates to Public Health Problems, *Biometrics*, **3:** 123–128 (1947).

LORD, F. M.: A Theory of Test Scores, *Psychometric Monogr.*, *No. 7*, 1952.

———: A Paradox in the Interpretation of Group Comparisons, *Psychol. Bull.*, **68:** 304–305 (1967).

——— and NOVICK, M. R.: "Statistical Theories of Mental Test Scores," Addison-Wesley, Reading, Mass., 1968.

MAIR, M.: Evaluation of a New Mathematics Curriculum (abstract), *Am. Psychol.*, **17:** 336 (1962).

MANN, A. B., and WALD. A.: On the Choice of the Number of Intervals in the Application of the Chi-Square Test, *Ann. Math. Stat.*, **13:** 306–317 (1942).

MARGOLESE, M. S.: Homosexuality: a New Endocrine Correlate, *Horm. & Behav.*, **1:** 151–155 (1970).

MAXWELL, A. E.: "Analyzing Qualitative Data," Methuen, London, 1961.

———: The WPPSI: a Marked Discrepancy in the Correlation of the Subtests for Good and Poor Readers, *Br. J. Math. & Stat. Psychol.*, **25:** 283–291 (1972).

MCGEEHEE, W., and GARDNER, J. E.: Music in a Complex Industrial Job, *Pers. Psychol.*, **2:** 405–417 (1949).

MCHUGH, R. B., and MIELKE, P. W.: Negative Variance Estimates and Statistical Dependence in Nested Sampling, *J. Am. Stat. Assoc.*, **63:** 1000–1004 (1968).

MCKEON, J. J.: Measurement Procedures Based on Comparative Judgment, unpublished Ph.D dissertation, Department of Psychology, University of North Carolina at Chapel Hill, 1961.

MCKUSICK, V. A.: "Human Genetics," 2d ed., Prentice-Hall, Englewood Cliffs, N. J., 1969.

MCNEMAR, Q.: "Psychological Statistics," Wiley, New York, 1962.

MEDLEY, D. M., and MITZEL, H. E.: Measuring Classroom Behavior by Systematic Observation, pp. 247–328 in N. C. Gage (ed.), "Handbook of Research on Teaching," Rand-McNally, Chicago, 1963.

MELTON, R. S.: Some Remarks on Failure to Meet Assumptions in Discriminant Analysis, *Psychometrika* **28:** 49–53 (1963).

MENDENHALL, W.: "Introduction to Linear Models and the Design and Analysis of Experiments," Wadsworth, Belmont, Calif., 1968.

MILLER, G. A.: The Magical Number Seven, Plus or Minus Two: Some Limits on our Capacity for Processing Information, pp. 135–151 in Luce, Bush, and Galanter (eds.), "Readings in Mathematical Psychology," Wiley, New York, 1963.

MILLMAN, J., and GLASS, G. V.: Rules of Thumb for Writing the ANOVA Table, *J. Educ. Meas.*, **4:** 41–51 (1967).

MOOD, A. M., and GRAYBILL, F. A.: "Introduction to the Theory of Statistics," 2d ed., McGraw-Hill, New York, 1963.

MOORE, O. K.: "Autotelic Responsive Environments and Exceptional Children," Responsive Environment Foundation, Hamden, Conn., 1963.

MORRISON, D. F.: "Multivariate Analysis," McGraw-Hill, New York, 1967.

MORTER, D. C.: The Effects of Requiring Two Responses Per Card of the Holtzman Inkblot Technique, unpublished Master's thesis, Department of Psychology, University of North Carolina at Chapel Hill, 1963.

MOSIMANN, J. E.: On the Compound Multinomial Distribution, the Multivariate β-Distribution, and Correlations among Proportions, *Biometrika*, **49:** 65–85 (1962).

MOSTELLER, F., ROURKE, R. E., and THOMAS, G. B.: "Probability with Statistical Applications," Addison-Wesley, Reading, Mass., 1961.

MUKHERJEE, B. N.: Derivation of Likelihood-Ratio Tests for Guttman Quasi-simplex Covariance Structures, *Psychometrika*, **31:** 97–123 (1966).

MUMFORD, L.: "The Urban Prospect," Harcourt, Brace & World, New York, 1968.

MURPHY, G., and LIKERT, R.: "Public Opinion and the Individual," Harper, New York, 1938.

MURRAY, H. A., et al. "Explorations in Personality," Oxford University Press, New York, 1938.

———: "Thematic Apperception Test," Harvard University Press, Cambridge, Mass., 1943.

NAMBOODIRI, N. K.: Experimental Designs in Which Each Subject is Used Repeatedly, *Psychol. Bull.*, **77:** 54–64 (1972).

NELDER, J. A.: The Analysis of Randomized Experiments with Orthogonal Block Structure, I and II, *Proc. R. Soc. London*, (A) **283:** 147–162, 163–178 (1965).

NEYMAN, J.: Outline of a Theory of Statistical Estimation Based on the Classical Theory of Probability, *Philos. Trans. R. Soc., London*, (A) **236:** 333–380 (1937).

——— and PEARSON, E. S.: On the Problem of the Most Efficient Tests of Statistical Hypothesis, *Phil. Trans. R. Soc. London*, (A) **231:** 289–337 (1933).

NOBLE, B.: "Applied Linear Algebra," Prentice-Hall, Englewood Cliffs, N. J., 1969.

OLKIN, I., and PRATT, J. W.: Unbiased Estimation of Certain Correlation Coefficients, *Ann. Math. Stat.*, **29:** 201–211 (1958).

ORTEGA, J. M.: On Sturm Sequences for Tridiagonal Matrices, *J. Assoc. Comput. Mach.*, **7:** 260–263 (1960).

——— and KAISER, H. F.: The LL^T and QR Methods for Symmetric Tridiagonal Matrices, *Comput. J.*, **6:** 99–101 (1963).

OSGOOD, C. E.: "Methods and Theory in Experimental Psychology," Oxford University Press, New York, 1953.

OSTROV, E., OFFER, D., MAROHN, R. C., and ROSENWEIN, T.: The "Impulsivity Index": Its Applications to Juvenile Delinquency, *J. Youth & Adolescence*, **1:** 179–196 (1972).

OXNARD, C.: "Form and Pattern in Human Evolution," University of Chicago Press, Chicago, 1973.

PAGE, E. B.: Teacher Comments and Student Performance: a Seventy-four Classroom Experiment in School Motivation, *J. Educ. Psycol.*, **49:** 173–181 (1958).

PALERMO, D. S., and JENKINS, J. J.: "Word Association Norms," University of Minnesota Press, Minneapolis, 1964.

PARRISH, M., LUNDY, R. M., and LEIBOWITZ, H. W.: Hypnotic Age-Regression and Magnitudes of the Ponzo and Poggendorf Illusions, *Science*, **157:** 1375–1376 (1968).

PEARSON, E. S.: On the Variation in Personal Equation and the Correlation of Successive Judgments, *Biometrika*, **14:** 23–102 (1922).

——— and HARTLEY, H. O.: Charts of the Power Function of the Analysis of Variance Tests, Derived from the Non-Central F-Distribution. *Biometrika*, **38:** 112–130 (1951).

——— and ——— (eds.): "Biometrika Tables for Statisticians," vol. 1, 3d ed., Cambridge University Press, New York, 1966.

——— and ———(eds.): "Biometrika Tables for Statisticians," vol. 2, Cambridge University Press, New York, 1972.

PEIZER, D. B.: A Note on Directional Inference, *Psychol. Bull.*, **68:** 448 (1967).

PENROSE, R. A.: A Generalized Inverse for Matrices, *Proc. Cambridge Philos. Soc.*, **51:** 406–413 (1955).

PERLMUTTER, J., and MEYERS, J. L.: A Comparison of Two Procedures for Testing Multiple Contrasts, *Psychol. Bull.*, **79:** 181–184 (1973).

PETERSEN, A. C.: The Relationship of Androgenicity in Males and Females to Spatial Ability and Fluent Production, unpublished Ph.D dissertation, Department of Education, University of Chicago, 1973.

PETRINOVICH, L. F., and HARDYCK, C. D.: Error Rates for Multiple Comparison Methods: Some Evidence Concerning the Frequency of Erroneous Conclusions, *Psychol. Bull.*, **71:** 43–54 (1969).

PILLAI, K. C. S.: Some Results Useful in Multivariate Analysis, *Ann Math. Stat.*, **27:** 1106–1114 (1955).

———: "Statistical Tables for Tests of Multivariate Hypotheses," University of the Philippines Statistical Center, Manila, 1960.

———: On the Non-Central Distributions of the Largest Roots of Two Matrices in Multivariate Analysis, *Mimeograph Series No. 51*, Department of Statistics, Purdue University, 1965.

———: On the Distribution of the Largest Characteristic Root of a Matrix and Percentage Points, *Mimeograph Series No. 76*, Department of Statistics, Purdue University, 1966.

———: Upper Percentage Points of the Largest Root of a Matrix in Multivariate Analysis, *Biometrika*, **54:** 189–194 (1967).

———: On the Exact Distribution of Hotelling's Generalized T_0^2, *J. Multivariate Anal.*, **1:** 90–107 (1971).

——— and GUPTA, A. K.: On the Exact Distribution of Wilks' Criterion, *Biometrika*, **56:** 109–118 (1969).

——— and JAYACHANDRAN, K.: Power Comparisons of Tests of Equality of Two Covariance Matrices Based on Four Criteria, *Biometrika*, **55:** 335–342 (1968).

PLATT, J. R.: Strong Inference, *Science*, **146:** 347–353 (1964).

PLOOG, D. W.: The Behavior of Squirrel Monkeys (Saimiri Sciureus) as Revealed by Sociometry, Bioacoustics, and Brain Stimulation, pp. 149–184 in S. Altman (ed.), "Social Communication among Primates," University of Chicago Press, Chicago, 1967.

POSTMAN, L., and STARK, K.: The Role of Associative Mediation in Retroactive Inhibition and Facilitation, *J. Verbal Learn. & Verbal Behav.*, **8:** 790–798 (1969).

RAND CORPORATION: "A Million Random Digits with 100,000 Normal Deviates," Free Press, New York, 1955.

RAO, C. R.: General Methods of Analysis for Incomplete Block Designs, *J. Am. Stat. Assoc.*, **42:** 541–561 (1947).

———: An Asymptotic Expansion of the Distribution of Wilks' Criterion, *Bull. Int. Stat. Inst.*, **33:** 177–180 (1951).

———: "Advanced Statistical Methods in Biometric Research," Wiley, New York, 1952.

———: "Linear Statistical Inference and Its Applications," Wiley, New York, 1965.

RAO, J. N. K.: On Expectations, Variances and Covariances of ANOVA Mean Squares by "Synthesis," *Biometrics*, **24:** 963–978 (1968).

RASCH, G.: "Probabilistic Models for Some Intelligence and Attainment Tests," Institute of Mathematics and Statistics, University of Copenhagen, 1960.

REINSCH, C., and BAUER, F. C.: Rational QR Transformation with Newton Shift for Symmetric Tridiagonal Matrices, *Numer. Math.*, **11:** 264–272 (1968).

ROBERTS, J. A. F.: The Genetics of Mental Deficiency, *Eugen. Rev.*, **44:** 71–83 (1952).

ROBSON, D. S.: A Simple Method for Constructing Orthogonal Polynomials When the Independent Variable is Unequally Spaced, *Biometrics*, **15:** 187–191 (1959).

ROHDE, C. A., and TALLIS, G. M.: Exact First and Second-Order Moments of Estimates of Components of Covariance, *Biometrika*, **56:** 517–525 (1969).

ROY, J.: Step-down Procedure in Multivariate Analysis, *Ann. Math. Stat.*, **29:** 1177–1187 (1958).

ROY, S. N.: *p*-Statistics or Some Generalizations in Analysis of Variance Appropriate to Multivariate Problems, *Sankhyā*, **4:** 381–396 (1939).

———: The Individual Sampling Distribution of the Maximum, the Minimum and Any Intermediate One of the *p*-Statistics on the Null Hypothesis, *Sankhyā*, **7:** 133–158 (1945).

———: "Some Aspects of Multivariate Analysis," Wiley, New York, 1957.

——— and BARGMANN, R. E.: Tests of Multiple Independence and the Associated Confidence Bounds, *Ann. Math. Stat.*, **29:** 491–503 (1958).

——— and BOSE, R. C.: Simultaneous Confidence Interval Estimation, *Ann. Math. Stat.*, **24:** 513–536 (1953).

RUTISHAUSER, H.: The Jacobi Method for Real Symmetric Matrices, *Numer. Math.*, **9:** 1–10 (1966).

SAMEJIMA, F.: Estimation of Latent Ability Using a Response Pattern of Graded Scores, *Psychometric Monograph No. 17*, 1969.

SATTERTHWAITE, F. E.: An Approximate Distribution of Estimates of Variance Components, *Biom. Bull.*, **2:** 110–114 (1946).

SCHEFFÉ, H.: A Method for Judging All Contrasts in the Analysis of Variance, *Biometrika*, **40:** 87–104 (1953).

SCHENKEL, K. F., LEEDY, H. B., ROSENBERG, N., and MUNDY, J. P.: Evaluation of the Puerto Rican Screening Test (ECFA) Against Success in Training, *Technical Research Report PRB 1097*, Personal Research and Procedures Division, Personnel Research Branch, The Adjutant General's Office, Department of the Army, 1957.

SCHÖNEMANN, P. H.: On the Formal Differentiation of Traces and Determinants, *Research Memorandum No. 27*, The Psychometric Laboratory, University of North Carolina at Chapel Hill, 1965.

SEARLE, S. R.: "Matrix Algebra for the Biological Sciences," Wiley, New York, 1966.

———: "Linear Models," Wiley, New York, 1971.

——— and FAWCETT, R. F.: Expected Mean Squares in Variance Components Models Having Finite Populations, *Biometrics*, **26:** 243–254 (1970).

SHATZOFF, M.: Exact Distribution of Wilks's Likelihood-Ratio Criterion, *Biometrika*, **53:** 347–358 (1966).

SILVERSTONE, H.: Estimating the Logistic Curve, *J. Am. Stat. Assoc.*, **52:** 567–577 (1957).

SKINNER, B. F. "Science and Human Behavior," Macmillan, New York, 1953.

SOLOMON, H.: Classification Procedures Based on Dichotomous Response Vectors, pp. 177–186 in H. Solomon (ed.), "Studies in Item Analysis and Prediction," Stanford University Press, Stanford, 1961.

SPEED, F. M., and HOCKING, R. R.: Computation of Expectations, Variance and Covariance of ANOVA Mean Squares, *Biometrika*, **30:** 157–169 (1974).

STERN, C.: "Principles of Human Genetics," 2d ed., Freeman, San Francisco, 1960.

STODOLSKY, S.: How Children Find Something to Do in Pre-school, *Genet. Psychol. Monogr.*, **90:** 245–303 (1974).

STOLL, R. R.: "Linear Algebra and Matrix Theory," McGraw-Hill, New York, 1952.

STOUFFER, S. A., SUCHMAN, E. A., DEVINNEY, L. C., STAR, S. A., and WILLIAMS, R. M., JR.: "The American Soldier: Adjustment during Army Life: Studies in Social Psychology in Word War II," vol. I, Princeton University Press, Princeton, N. J., 1949.

STUDENT: The Probable Error of the Mean, *Biometrika*, **6:** 1–25 (1908).

———: On Testing Varieties of Cereals, *Biometrika*, **15:** 271–293 (correction, **16:** 411) (1923).

TATSUOKA, M.: "Multivariate Analysis," Wiley, New York, 1971.

THEIL, H. On the Estimation of Relationships Involving Qualitative Variables, *Am. J. Sociol.*, **76:** 103–154 (1970).

THISSEN, D.: Color Preferences in Chicks, unpublished paper (1972).
THURSTONE, L. L.: Psychophysical Analysis, *Am. J. Psychol.*, **38:** 368–389 (1927).
——— and THURSTONE, T. G.: "SRA Primary Mental Abilities," Science Research, Chicago, 1947.
TOBAN, E. V.: Factors Influencing Decisions about Upward Social Mobility, *J. Psychol.*, **70:** 81–91 (1968).
TUKEY, J. W.: Dyadic ANOVA, an Analysis of Variance for Vectors, *Hum. Biol.*, **21:** 65–110 (1949).

U.S. NATIONAL BUREAU OF STANDARDS: "Tables of the Bivariate Normal Distribution Function and Related Functions," *Applied Mathematical Series No. 50*, U.S. Government Printing Office, Washington, D.C., 1959.

WAGENAAR, W. A.: Note on the Construction of Digram-balanced Latin Squares, *Psychol. Bull.*, **72:** 384–386 (1969).
WAINER, H.: Personal communication, 1973.
WALBERG, H. J., and WELCH, W. W.: A New Use of Randomization in Experimental Curriculum Evaluation, *Sch. Rev.*, **75:** 369–377 (1967).
WALD, A.: "Statistical Decision Functions," Wiley, New York, 1950.
WALKER, H. M., and LEV, J.: "Statistical Inference," Holt, New York, 1953.
WALLACE, D. L.: Intersection Region Confidence Procedures with Application to the Location of the Maximum of a Quadratic Regression, *Ann. Math. Stat.*, **29:** 457–475 (1958).
WAMPLER, R. H.: A Report on the Accuracy of Some Widely Used Least Squares Computer Programs, *J. Am. Stat. Assoc.*, **65:** 549–565 (1970).
WELSCH, J. H.: Certification of Algorithm 254(F-2)—Eigenvalues and Eigenvectors of a Real Symmetric Matrix by the QR Methods, *Commun. Assoc. Comput. Mach.*, **10:** 376–377 (1967).
WELCH, W. W., WALBERG, H. J., and WATSON, F.: "Evaluation Strategies, Implementation, and Results: a Case Study of Harvard Project Physics," Educational Technology Press, New York, 1971.
WEPMAN, J. M., BOCK, R. D., JONES, L. V., and VAN PELT, D.: Psycholinguistic Study of Aphasia: a Revision of the Concept of Anomia, *J. Speech & Hear. Disord.*, **21:** 468–477 (1956).
WERDELIN, I.: Geometric Ability and Space Factors, *Lund Stud. Psychol. and Educ.*, University of Lund, Sweden, 1961.
WHANG, J. W.: The Interaction of Short-Term Memory and Instructional Variables on Verbal Ability, unpublished Ph.D. dissertation, Department of Education, University of Chicago, 1971.
WHERRY, R. J.: The Wherry-Doolittle Selection Method, pp. 245–252 in Stead, Shartle, et al. (eds.), "Occupational Counseling Techniques," American Book, New York, 1940.
WILEY, D. E.: Fractional Factorial Designs with Mixed Models, unpublished Ph.D. dissertation, University of Wisconsin, Madison, 1964.
——— and BOCK, R. D.: Quasi-experimentation in Educational Settings: Comment, *Sch. Rev.*, **75:** 353–366 (1967).
WILK, M. B., and KEMPTHORNE, O.: Fixed, Mixed and Random Models, *J. Am. Stat. Assoc.*, **50:** 1144–1167(1955).

WILKINSON, J. H.: Householder's Method for the Solution of the Algebraic Eigenproblem, *Comput. J.*, **3:** 23–27 (1960).

———: Householder's Method for Symmetric Matrices, *Num. Math.*, **4:** 354–361 (1962).

———: "The Algebraic Eigenvalue Problem," Oxford University Press, London, 1965.

WILKS, S. S.: Certain Generalizations in the Analysis of Variance, *Biometrika*, **24:** 471–494 (1932).

WILLIAMS, C. B.: A Note on the Statistical Analysis of Sentence-Length as a Criterion of Literary Style, *Biometrika*, **31:** 356–361 (1940).

WILLIAMS, E. J.: Experimental Designs Balanced for the Estimation of Residual Effects of Treatments, *Aust. J. Sc.. Res.*, (A) **2:** 149–168 (1949).

———: The Analysis of Association among Many Variates, *J. R. Stat. Soc.*, (B) **29:** 199–288 (1967).

WILLIAMS, O. P., and GRIZZLE, J. E.: Contingency Tables Having Ordered Response Categories, *J. Am. Stat. Assoc.*, **67:** 55–63 (1972).

WINER, B. J.: "Statistical Principles in Experimental Design," 2d ed., McGraw-Hill, New York, 1971.

WISHART, J.: The Generalized Product Moment Distribution in Samples from a Normal Multivariate Population, *Biometrika,* **20A:** 32–52 (1928).

WRIGHT, H. F.: "Recording and Analyzing Child Behavior," Harper & Row, New York, 1967.

WRIGHT, S.: The Method of Path Coefficients, *Ann. Math. Stat.*, **5:** 161–215 (1934).

———: "Evolution and the Genetics of Populations," vol. 1, University of Chicago Press, Chicago, 1968.

YATES, F.: Incomplete Randomized Blocks, *Ann. Eugen.*, **1:** 121–140 (1936).

———: The Design and Analysis of Factorial Experiments, *Technical Communication No. 35*, Imperial Bureau of Soil Science, Harpenden, England, 1937

YULE, G. U.: "The Statistical Study of Literary Vocabulary," Cambridge University Press, Cambridge, 1944.

ZULLINGER, H.: "Behn-Rorschach Test," Grune & Stratton, New York, 1956.

NAME INDEX

SUBJECT INDEX